THE OXFORD HANDBOOK OF

STATE AND LOCAL GOVERNMENT

THE
OXFORD
HANDBOOKS
OF
AMERICAN
POLITICS

GENERAL EDITOR: GEORGE C. EDWARDS III

The Oxford Handbooks of American Politics is a set of reference books offering authoritative and engaging critical overviews of the state of scholarship on American politics.

Each volume focuses on a particular aspect of the field. The project is under the General Editorship of George C. Edwards III, and distinguished specialists in their respective fields edit each volume. The *Handbooks* aim not just to report on the discipline, but also to shape it as scholars critically assess the current state of scholarship on a topic and propose directions in which it needs to move. The series is an indispensable reference for anyone working in American politics.

THE OXFORD HANDBOOK OF

STATE AND LOCAL GOVERNMENT

Edited by

DONALD P. HAIDER-MARKEL

OXFORD
UNIVERSITY PRESS

OXFORD
UNIVERSITY PRESS

Great Clarendon Street, Oxford, OX2 6DP,
United Kingdom

Oxford University Press is a department of the University of Oxford.
It furthers the University's objective of excellence in research, scholarship,
and education by publishing worldwide. Oxford is a registered trade mark of
Oxford University Press in the UK and in certain other countries

First Edition published in 2014

Impression: 2

Published in the United States of America by Oxford University Press
198 Madison Avenue, New York, NY 10016, United States of America

British Library Cataloguing in Publication Data
Data available

Library of Congress Control Number: 2013958324

ISBN 978-0-19-957967-9

Printed and bound by
CPI Group (UK) Ltd, Croydon, CR0 4YY

Contents

PART III STATE POLITICAL INSTITUTIONS

PART IV LOCAL POLITICAL INSTITUTIONS

PART V SUB-NATIONAL PUBLIC POLICY PROCESSES

PART VI SUB-NATIONAL PUBLIC POLICIES

PART VII   CONCLUSION

List of Contributors

Robert Agranoff, Indiana University

Jungah Bae, Florida State University

Charles Barrilleaux, Florida State

Brady Baybeck, University of Missouri-St. Louis

Frederick J. Boehmke, University of Iowa

Nicole Bolleyer, University of Exeter

Chris W. Bonneau, University of Pittsburgh

Shaun Bowler, UC Riverside

Brent D. Boyea, University of Texas at Arlington

Paul Brace, Rice University

Regina P. Branton, University of North Texas

Richard A. Brisbin, Jr., University of West Virginia

John Dinan, Wake Forest

Alesha E. Doan, University of Kansas

Todd Donovan, Western Washington University

Richard C. Feiock, Florida State University

Margaret R. Ferguson, Indiana University Purdue University at Indianapolis

Richard C. Fording, University of Alabama

William W. Franko, Auburn University

James C. Garand, Louisiana State University

Donald P. Haider-Markel, University of Kansas

Zoltan L. Hajnal, University of California San Diego

Keith E. Hamm, Rice University

Lisa J. Hammer, Montana State University

Ronald D. Hedlund, Northeastern University

William D. Hicks, University of Florida

Jessica L. Ice, Florida State University

William G. Jacoby, Michigan State University

Bertram Johnson, Middlebury College

Michael D. Jones, Harvard University

Christine Kelleher Palus, Villanova University

John Kincaid, Lafayette College

George A. Krause, University of Pittsburgh

Timothy B. Krebs, University of New Mexico

Suzanne Leland, University of North Carolina-Charlotte

Kelly M. LeRoux, University of Illinois, Chicago

Robert C. Lowry, University of Texas at Dallas

Paul Manna, College of William and Mary

Nancy Martorano Miller, University of Dayton, Ohio

Megan Mullin, Temple University

Anthony J. Nownes, University of Tennessee

Joel W. Paddock, Missouri State University

Garrick L. Percival, San Jose State University

John Poe, University of Kentucky

Colin Provost, University College of London

Mark Carl Rom, Georgetown University

Saundra K. Schneider, Michigan State University

Elizabeth A. Shanahan, Montana State University

Daniel A. Smith, University of Florida

Paul Teske, University of Colorado

Caroline Tolbert, University of Iowa

Justin Ulrich, Louisiana State University

Carol S. Weissert, Florida State University

Holly Whisman,   University of North Carolina-Charlotte

Neal D. Woods,   University of South Carolina

Ping Xu,   Louisiana State University

PART I

INTRODUCTION

CHAPTER 1

··

INTRODUCTION

The Study of State and Local Politics and Policy

··

DONALD P. HAIDER-MARKEL

THE *Oxford Handbook of State and Local Government* is part of the eight-volume *Oxford Handbook of American Politics*. The chapters critically assess both the major contributions to the state and local politics literature and the ways in which the subfield has developed. Each of the chapters represents the author's point of view and outlines an agenda for future research. This means that the authors have chosen to focus on some elements of the literature over others.

This volume can be viewed as a historic undertaking. It contains a wide range of essays that define the important questions in the field, critically evaluates where we are in answering them, and sets the direction and terms of discourse for future work. I believe that the volume will have a substantial influence in defining the field for years to come.

The chapters are organized thematically and cover the main areas of study in sub-national politics by exploring the central contributions to the comparative study of institutions, behavior, and policy in the American context. Each chapter also highlights the gaps in what we know and outlines an agenda for future research.

Despite the fact that the study of state and local politics had long been considered a backwater field of political science, scholars have rediscovered the rich dynamics and theoretical utility of focusing on state and local politics since the mid-1990s. Indeed many would suggest that the field has undergone an incredible rebirth in the past two decades. Of course many questions remain unanswered and in some areas we have barely scratched the surface. But in many areas we have learned a great deal and in the process contributed theoretically and empirically to the general study of politics. My goal in this volume, and the goal of the contributing authors, has been to highlight what we have learned and where we think the most fruitful research agendas still lie.

Those of us who study state and local politics come at the subject from a variety of perspectives. There are those of us who are intense followers of local political conditions, those who are focused on state and local politics as comparative units of analysis, and those who only occasionally dip into the pool of state and local politics because they see the utility for testing broader theories of politics and/or policy. As you will read in these pages, we accept all comers and value the input and contributions. We also invite and encourage those who have yet to see the value of testing their theories of interest in the context of state and local politics to see the value of comparing across governments and policies that are similar but different enough to develop parsimonious models for testing frameworks and theories.

Indeed, what state and local scholars recognize is that this subfield is truly comparative in nature. State and local politics offer researchers the luxury of exploring theoretical questions in the context of political jurisdictions that are similar on manner dimensions but often different on a few, very important, dimensions. By comparison, a social welfare scholar studying policy across nations has incredible variation and finds it difficult to isolate the key variables that might explain why one jurisdiction has less generous social welfare benefits than does another. Or another example: those who try to explain the level of violent crime in different countries find it very difficult to isolate the potential impact of firearm regulations. But when examining these questions within a single country, where sub-national jurisdictions have authority to make policy decisions or policy implementation decisions, the researcher can more easily zero in on variation in a dimension of interest to lend support to a particular hypothesis or possibly dispel some conventional wisdom.

I would be remiss if I did not highlight the fact that scholars such as Bill Berry, Paul Brace, Tom Carsey, Melinda Gann-Hall, Liz Gerber, Virginia Gray, Malcolm Jewell, Ken Meier, Chris Mooney, Peverill Squire, Ron Weber, and Gerry Wright, among many others (see for example Brace and Jewett, 1995; Gray and Lowery, 1996, 2002; Carsey, 1999; Gerber, 1999; Mooney, 2001; Berry and Berry, 2007; Berry et al., 2010), had not preached this perspective for years. But what has really helped the field gain prominence since the 1990s has been Chris Mooney's launch of *State Politics and Policy Quarterly* (*SPPQ*) as well as the inaugural State Politics and Policy Conference in 2000 at Texas A&M. Each year the journal has published some of the best sub-national research in social science, and the conference, sponsored each year in a different city (usually by one or more Universities) has featured the top researchers as well as the brightest graduate students in sub-national politics. Indeed, over the first 10 years of its existence *SPPQ* had several years where it had an impact factor in the top 35 of all political science journals. Both the journal and the annual conference continue to be a major life-blood of the subfield.

OUTLINE OF THE VOLUME

As has been customary in *SPPQ* and at the annual conference, we have tried to explore sub-national politics more broadly in the volume by considering the international arena and other federalist systems in particular chapters. Some chapters are explicit in their titles about this approach, others, such as the regulatory policy chapter, have sections devoted to a comparative perspective.

But as most readers would expect the bulk of the volume focuses on the American federalist system with its particular nuances and frustrations. The volume is organized into several sections beginning with introductory chapters on relations between national, state, and local governments. As these chapters illustrate, the American federalist system of government continues to evolve with the policy jurisdictions and authority of the different levels of government continuing to ebb and flow. Although the 1970s and 1980s clearly introduced a new era of devolution of power and responsibility to state and local governments, and U.S. Supreme Court ruling have largely followed this pattern, the homeland security demands of the 2000s and fiscal crisis of the later portion of the first decade of this century once again made visible so much of the national government power and involvement in virtually every aspect of our lives. Of course the emergencies that made national government authority once again more visible spawned a whole variety of political activity, not the least of which was local and state government attempts to reassert their perceived powers and authority.

The second section of the volume emphasizes political behavior at the sub-national level with chapters devoted to political participation in local and state contests, the role of political parties and interest groups, and the nature of sub-national campaigns and elections. Here we get a clear glimpse of the variation across sub-national jurisdictions, whether it be wide variations in the level of political participation across states or different types of elections, or the variations in the rules that shape everything from participation in elections to reporting of lobbying activities.

Sections 3 and 4 dive into the meat of the utility of sub-national variation in a political system where the overall similarities are greater than the differences. In Section 3 the authors explore the institutional variation at the state level, which chapters on constitutions, legislatures, executives, courts, and bureaucracy, not forgetting the semi-unique aspect of the American system which allows for direct democracy institutions if sub-national jurisdictions choose to allow for. Each chapter highlights the importance of variation for testing social science theory, from the huge size of the New Hampshire lower legislative chamber, to the expansive powers of Wisconsin's governor, to the highly contested state supreme court elections in Texas, to the relative ease at which citizens in California can place policy questions on the ballot.

Likewise in Section 4 the authors examine some of the relatively unique elements of local American political institutions as well as some of their roots in largely European traditions. For example, Mullin explores the explosion of special districts at the sub-national level and their importance for policy and governance, while LeRoux examines the variation in local bureaucratic governance and its importance for policy formation and implementation.

Sections 5 and 6 examine what we know and need to know, about public policy and the policy process at the sub-national level. In Section 5 the authors explain the boundaries of our understanding about the process of policymaking at the sub-national level. Most importantly from my perspective, the chapters in Section 5 delve into elements of the local and state policymaking process that involve economic policymaking the problematic elements of addressing inequality in representation in the process and in policy outcomes.

Section 6 continues this theme but these chapters examine specific issue areas. Admittedly not all possible issue areas are covered and this again reveals the biased guidelines I provided to the authors. My goal was to highlight some of the most relevant issue areas in sub-national politics for the twenty-first century, not every issue sub-national governments address. Here again the focus tends to be on the representation of some issue interests over others and the issues that are likely to be recurrent in sub-national policymaking over the next 50 or so years. As will be noted in the concluding chapter, one gap here is homeland security and emergency management for large scale disasters—the literature here is still in a fairly youthful state at the sub-national level.

The final section of the volume attempts to bring the comparative study of sub-national politics and policy back to its roots in theoretically motivated social science research questions. Although some scholars envy the perceived volumes of data available to sub-national scholars of industrialized countries, especially the U.S., these chapters address ongoing theoretical and methodical issues that confound us and limit our ability to spell out what it is we do understand as well as the so-called dimensions of the known unknowns, as well as potentially point us toward the "unknown unknowns."

It is our hope that this volume will provide an accessible set of works to scholars and students of sub-national politics that provides a foundation for what is most important about what we do know, and, more importantly, what is most important about what we do not yet know. None of the authors here believe that they have had the final word and hope that that the focused presentation of the literature that hey provide will inspire the next generation of scholars to continue in our pursuit of knowledge.

References

Brace, Paul and Aubrey Jewett. 1995. "The State of State Politics Research." *Political Research Quarterly 48* (3): 643–81.

Berry, Frances Stokes and William D. Berry. 2007. "Innovation and Diffusion Models in Policy Research." In Paul A. Sabatier (ed.), *Theories of the Policy Process*. Boulder, CO: Westview Press, pp. 223–60.

Berry, William D., Richard C. Fording, Evan J. Ringquist, Russell L. Hanson, and Carl E. Klarner. 2010. "Measuring Citizen and Government Ideology in the U.S. States: A Re-appraisal." *State Politics and Policy Quarterly 10* (2): 117–35.

Carsey, Thomas M. 1999. *Campaign Dynamics: The Race for Governor*. Ann Arbor, MI: University of Michigan Press.

Gerber, Elisabeth R. 1999. *The Populist Paradox: Interest Group Influence and the Promise of Direct Legislation*. Princeton, NJ: Princeton University Press.

Gray, Virginia and David Lowery. 2002. "State Interest Group Research and the Mixed Legacy of Belle Zeller." *State Politics and Policy Quarterly 2* (4): 388–410.

Gray, Virginia and David Lowery. 1996. *The Population Ecology of Interest Representation*. Ann Arbor, MI: University of Michigan Press.

Mooney, Christopher Z. 2001. "State Politics and Policy Quarterly and the Study of State Politics: The Editor's Introduction." *State Politics and Policy Quarterly 1*: 1–4.

CHAPTER 2

....

RELATIONS BETWEEN STATE AND NATIONAL GOVERNMENTS

....

JOHN DINAN

SCHOLARSHIP regarding relations between state and national governments has been animated by four main concerns. Significant attention has been devoted to chronicling, explaining, and characterizing the shifting balance of power between national and state governments. Scholars have also examined the range of ways that national officials can influence state governments, taking particular note of the changing mix and different effects of the mechanisms by which national officials attain their objectives. Other scholars have examined the range of ways that state officials advance their interests in the national policy process, whether through traditional mechanisms or newfound means of influence. Scholars have also assessed the consequences of expanding national government responsibility for various policy areas versus permitting state governments to retain primary authority or returning some measure of policy responsibility to states.

THE DEVELOPMENT OF AMERICAN FEDERALISM

....

Inquiries into the development of American federalism have been concerned in part with characterizing the trajectory of the shifting balance of power between national and state governments. On one hand, Richard Nathan views national–state relations as developing in a cyclical fashion, with periods of centralization alternating with periods of devolution. In particular, he noted "a tendency for the role of the national government in the domestic public sector to expand in liberal periods and to contract vis-à-vis the states' role in conservative periods" (Nathan, 1990: 250). For the most part, though, scholars have highlighted long-term centralizing trends and emphasized the greater strength and persistence of these tends in comparison with periodic efforts to curb the expansion of federal power. Occasionally, presidents and political parties have proposed to sort out responsibilities of national and state governments with an eye toward devolving authority for various policies or moderating the growth of federal power, as in the late twentieth century under Presidents Dwight Eisenhower, Richard Nixon, and Ronald Reagan and Speaker of the House Newt Gingrich (Conlan, 1998). But few of these movements produced any significant devolution in the sense of actually returning policy authority to state governments, aside from permitting them to resume responsibility for setting highway speed limits and exercise more discretion regarding welfare policy making in the mid-1990s, among other modest steps (Kincaid, 1998).

In offering explanations for the strength and persistence of the long-term trend in favor of centralization, scholars have generally highlighted broad forces and developments. Centralization has often been seen as bound up with and an inevitable byproduct of modernization. In noting that 'In the United States, as in other modernizing societies, the general historical record has spelled centralization,' Samuel Beer argued that "the main reasons for this change are not to be found in the personal, partisan or ideological preferences of office-holders, but in the new forces produced by an advanced modernity" (Beer, 1973: 52). Increasing mobility and economic interdependence, along with the advent of national media outlets have led Americans to view themselves increasingly as members of a national community that looks to the national government rather than state governments to address policy challenges (Nagel, 2001). Moreover, a party system that at one time vested significant power in state and local officials and served as an important decentralizing force (Grodzins, 1966) gave way in the late twentieth century to a system where funding and power were concentrated in national party officials (Milkis and Rhodes, 2007). National government power also increased during each major military conflict and in response to severe economic downturns, in each case on account of the national government's greater resources and capabilities (Kennedy, 1987).

Other scholars have emphasized the choices made in favor of centralization at various points in US history. Martha Derthick has noted that, "As American federalism has steadily grown more centralized, it is tempting to attribute the change to the influence of such (presumably uncontrollable) forces and to overlook the extent to which choices steadily present themselves nonetheless" (Derthick, 2001: 30). At various times, constitutional amendments have contributed to an expansion of national power and curtailment of state authority. None has been more important than the Fourteenth Amendment (1868), which authorized the national government to protect the rights of freedmen and whose equal protection and due process clauses would later serve as the vehicle for the Supreme Court to exercise a general supervisory power over state government acts. The Sixteenth Amendment (1913) authorized the national government to levy a tax on individual income and thereby gain a potent source of revenue for undertaking tasks that were previously the domain of state governments. In the same year, the Seventeenth Amendment brought a formal end to state legislative appointment of US Senators, although this had long ceased to serve as a viable way for states to ensure representation of their interests in the national policy process (Riker, 1955).

Centralization has also been achieved through the passage of congressional statutes that expanded national authority in response to concerns that states were incapable of addressing various problems. In the Progressive Era, congressional statutes authorized federal regulation of railroads and corporate trusts, out of a concern that state governments were unable to regulate these inter-state entities. Congressional statutes during the New Deal created important social insurance programs, some of which were purely federal and others that were joint federal-state programs, on the view that the federal government was better equipped than state governments to fund and manage such programs. Then in the 1960s, along with adopting health insurance statutes as part of the Great Society program, Congress passed major civil rights and voting rights legislation, in response to continued state-sponsored segregation and disenfranchisement of African-Americans and a renewed appreciation for the Madisonian position that minority rights are better secured in a national government than in state governments.

Supreme Court decisions have also played a role in accelerating the centralization of power. For the most part, Supreme Court rulings siding with the federal government have had the effect of legitimating expansion of national power undertaken by Congress and the President. But other Supreme Court rulings have had the independent effect of curtailing state authority and increasing federal supervision over state decision making. Such has been the effect of various rulings in the twentieth and twenty-first centuries applying to state governments almost all of the provisions in the federal bill of rights and limiting state authority over issues such as school attendance policies, redistricting, school prayer, pornography, and abortion.

In assessing the development of state–national relations, scholars have also been concerned with categorizing the various eras in American history and identifying key moments of transformation. Edward Corwin argued in the post-World War II period that an era of "dual federalism" prevailed until the 1930s after which it was superseded by an era of "Cooperative Federalism." This era of dual federalism was distinguished, in Corwin's formulation, by a commitment to the view that "the national government is one of enumerated powers only" and "Within their respective spheres the two centers of government are 'sovereign' and hence 'equal.'" Moreover: "The relation of the two centers with each other is one of tension rather than collaboration' (Corwin, 1950: 4).

Daniel Elazar (1962) and Morton Grodzins (1966), while not denying the importance of the 1930s, nevertheless challenged the view that federal and state governments ever operated in completely separate spheres. Rather than viewing the American federal system as analogous to a layer-cake, as suggested by the theory of dual federalism, Grodzins argued that the system was better compared with a marble-cake. As he argued in the mid-1960s:

> A long, extensive, and continuous cooperative experience is the foundation of the present system of shared functions characteristic of the American federal system. It is a misjudgment of our history and our present situation to believe that a neat separation of governmental functions could exist without drastic alterations in our society and system of government. (Grodzins, 1966: 56–7)

Although cooperative federalism has been the dominant scholarly paradigm in the post-World War II era, John Kincaid (1990) argued that several key features of cooperative federalism were undermined in the 1970s and 1980s, to the point that the system was better characterized as coercive federalism. Among other developments, Kincaid focused especially on changes in the dominant mechanisms by which the federal government sought to achieve its objectives. During this period, he noted, "the federal government reduced its reliance on fiscal tools to stimulate intergovernmental policy cooperation and increased its reliance on regulatory tools to ensure the supremacy of federal policy" (Kincaid, 1990: 139).

Finally, while agreeing that cooperative federalism is no longer an apt description of the contemporary system and acknowledging that the system is more coercive than in the post-World War II era, Timothy Conlan nevertheless contends that "other aspects of contemporary federalism are more seductive, dismissive, or co-optive than openly coercive. Overall, opportunistic federalism seems better able to capture the range and behavioral dynamics of contemporary intergovernmental behavior" (Conlan, 2006: 667). In particular, Conlan highlights that in recent decades officials at all levels "pursue their immediate interests with little regard for the institutional or collective consequences" (Conlan, 2006: 667).

National Government Influence on State Policy Making

Inquiries into national government influence on state policy making have focused on the various mechanisms by which federal officials influence the behavior of state officials. Congress has long relied primarily on grants-in-aid to assist, and later regulate, state governments. Grants-in-aid were originally intended to assist state governments in the pursuit of their own objectives and contained little in the way of federally imposed constraints. At times, grants took the form of land, as when the Morrill Act of 1862 helped states establish universities focused on agricultural and mechanical education. For the most part, though, the federal government provided funding, as when the Federal Aid Highway Act of 1916 supported the construction of state highway systems. Federal funds also supported state agricultural extension programs through the Smith–Lever Act of 1914, vocational education programs through the Smith–Hughes Act of 1917, and maternal health programs through the Sheppard–Towner Act of 1921, to list the leading early-twentieth-century programs that pre-dated a flurry of grant programs adopted in the New Deal, including through various titles of the Social Security Act of 1935 (Johnson, 2007).

By the 1960s Congress was enacting grant programs not so much to help states achieve their own goals but rather to meet federal objectives. During this period, Congress began relying in a significant fashion on cross-cutting requirements—this device made its first appearance in the late 1930s—directing states to abide by anti-discrimination standards as a condition of receiving federal grant funds, as in Title VI of the Civil Rights Act of 1964 and Title VIII of the Civil Rights Act of 1968. Congress also enacted crossover sanctions requiring states to bring their policies in line with federal objectives or else risk losing funds from a separate grant program. This was the approach Congress took in passing the Highway Beautification Act of 1965, which required states to adopt federal requirements regarding highway billboards or lose a portion of their federal highway funding. Congress also relied on crossover sanctions in 1974 when it required states to lower their speed limit to 55 miles per hour and in 1984 when it directed states to raise their drinking age to 21, in both cases on pain of losing some of their highway funds (Advisory Commission on Intergovernmental Relations, 1984).

As the now defunct Advisory Commission on Intergovernmental Relations (1984) noted in a comprehensive and influential report, Congress also began relying, especially after the late 1960s, on a wider range of tools for influencing state policy making aside from grants-in-aid. Congress has long possessed the power to preempt state action, but the frequency of congressional preemptions increased after the late 1960s to the point that Congress enacted more preemptions after 1969 than in all of the years prior to that point. Congress also began relying on partial preemptions, where the federal government permits state governments to administer policy in a certain area, but only as long as each state conforms to federally established standards; in the event that the state is deemed to have fallen short of those standards, then the federal government assumes responsibility for administering the policy. Congress relied on partial preemptions especially when enacting environmental protection statutes, such as in the Water Quality Act of 1965, Clean Air Act of 1970, and Safe Drinking Water Act of 1974 (Zimmerman, 2005).

Congress also began relying to an increasing degree in the 1970s on mandates ordering state officials to take certain actions. Some congressional statutes require states in their capacity as employers to abide by anti-discrimination requirements. Others require states in their capacity as employers to adopt certain minimum wage and overtime provisions that also apply to private employers. After a period from 1976 to 1985 when the US Supreme Court prohibited and eventually permitted application of these mandates to certain categories of state workers, Congress resumed issuance of such orders. A decade later, state officials' concerns led Congress to adopt procedural limits on the imposition of *unfunded* mandates in particular. However, the Unfunded Mandates Reform Act of 1995 has had only modest effects, not only because Congress can overcome the procedural limitations without too much trouble but also because the law leaves existing mandates undisturbed (Posner, 1998).

Members of Congress, along with administrative officials responsible for implementing congressional statutes, are not alone in issuing direct orders to state officials during this period. Beginning in the 1950s with the issuance of various rulings ordering states to cease operating racially segregated schools, and continuing in the 1960s with rulings ordering states and localities to take affirmative steps to integrate public schools, federal judges issued numerous decisions constraining state discretion and requiring state adoption of policies in areas beyond school desegregation. The Supreme

Court constrained state discretion through constitutional decisions requiring states to conform to the one-man/one-vote principle in legislative districting, prohibiting state-sponsored prayer in public schools, preventing states from banning abortions in the first two trimesters of pregnancy, and requiring state officials to abide by certain procedures in their treatment of criminal suspects and defendants (Derthick, 2001). The Supreme Court also interpreted congressional statutes in such a way as to curtail state discretion regarding administration of various social insurance programs (Melnick 1994). The Supreme Court also issued expansive interpretations of Section 1983, a provision of the US Code authorizing individuals to file federal lawsuits against state officials for depriving them of their constitutional or statutory rights (Melnick 2009). Meanwhile, federal district judges ordered states to reform their prisons and mental health institutions (Feeley and Rubin, 1998; Sandler and Schoenbrod, 2003).

One line of research has therefore been devoted to cataloguing the evolving mechanisms by which federal officials influence state policy making, particularly since the 1960s. Toward this end, scholars have also scrutinized the various options available to federal policy makers within these broad categories (grants, preemptions, and mandates) and with particular attention to the different types of grants utilized during this period. Grant programs can be differentiated on various grounds, including by distinguishing between project and formula grants. Presidential initiatives during the Nixon and Reagan administrations to provide states with more discretion in their use of grant funds focused attention on differences among categorical grants, block grants, and revenue sharing. Categorical grants predominated until the late 1960s, when Congress began creating block grants that were broader in scope and intended to give states and localities added discretion regarding use of federal funds. Meanwhile, in 1972 Congress created a revenue sharing program that gave states maximum discretion in their use of federal funds, at least until the discontinuation of the program in the 1980s (Brown, et al. 1984).

Another line of research has been concerned with detailing the effects of these federal mechanisms of influence, whether regarding state governments or intergovernmental relations. In an analysis of public assistance programs in Massachusetts, Derthick (1970) called attention to the ways that federal grants affect the balance of power within states, by reducing local discretion and centralizing power in state officials and increasing the professionalism of state administrative agencies and officials. Derthick's study also highlighted the challenges faced by federal officials in enforcing conditions on grants-in-aid and the way that negotiations between federal and state officials are best understood as a bargaining process. The chief insight is that the main instrument for enforcing conditions accompanying federal grants is to withhold federal funds from state governments that do not comply with federal standards. However, in practice this turns out not to be a viable enforcement mechanism, as is well understood by federal and state officials who are thereby led to engage in negotiations to arrive at a workable arrangement for both parties.

Scholarly concern with the implementation of federal directives has led to some consideration—although this is an area in particular need of further study—of various other instruments available to federal officials for carrying out federal objectives, whether embodied in preemptions, mandates, or conditions on grants-in-aid. Federal officials can file lawsuits against noncompliant states, but outside of school desegregation and voting rights, as R. Shep Melnick (2003) has shown, such lawsuits are rarely brought. As a result, Congress and executive officials have increasingly turned to private lawsuits to enforce state compliance. However, US Supreme Court rulings in recent decades have reduced the availability of this enforcement mechanism, in part by holding that private damages suits cannot be filed against un-consenting states in areas where Congress is powerless to abrogate state sovereign immunity.

Although most research regarding national government influence on state policy making focuses on legal and financial constraints and incentives, another line of scholarship in recent years has examined other ways that federal policy makers can stimulate state policy making, including through their ability to place issues on the state policy agenda. In a study of policy diffusion in the states, Andrew Karch concluded that 'Developments at the national level, such as congressional debates, raise the political profile of specific innovations and foster their widespread consideration' (Karch, 2007: 68). Meanwhile, other scholars have shown that federal officials' consideration and definitive rejection of policy innovations can also increase the likelihood of state legislatures adopting them (Allen et al., 2004).

STATE GOVERNMENT INFLUENCE IN NATIONAL POLICY MAKING

Inquiries into state government influence in national policy making have often been carried out by legal scholars who have primarily been concerned with debating the legitimacy and effectiveness of judicially imposed limits on federal power. The classic text is Herbert Wechsler's 1954 article, in which he contended that "the national political process in the United States—and especially the role of the states in the composition and selection of the central government—is intrinsically well adapted to retarding or restraining new intrusions by the center on the domain of the states" (Wechsler, 1954: 558). Writing in the aftermath of the Supreme Court's effort in the mid-1930s to enforce limits on congressional power and temporarily put a halt to many early New Deal programs, followed by the Justices' retreat from the field by the early 1940s, Wechsler sought to defend judicial deference. He did so in part by highlighting various structural features of the political system that could be counted on to protect state governmental interests, including equal-state representation in the Senate, state responsibility for drawing House districts, and the role of states in the Electoral College.

Other legal scholars (and occasionally judges) have offered additional support for Wechsler's political safeguards thesis in response to various late-twentieth-century efforts on the part of the Supreme Court to return to policing the federal system. Several years after the Court in *National League of Cities v Usery*, 426 U.S. 833 (1976) prevented Congress from applying the Fair Labor Standards Act to states and localities in certain policy areas, Jesse Choper argued that state interests were adequately represented in Congress and did not require judicial protection. He maintained that "the record of experience" provided numerous "examples of congressional hesitancy regarding federal intrusions" as well as various instances when "Presidents have effectively resisted national legislation that they believed would intrude on states' rights" or when Presidents "affirmatively promoted state autonomy" (Choper, 1980: 184, 186). When the Court overturned *Usery* in *Garcia v SAMTA*, 469 U.S. 528 (1985), Justice Harry Blackmun in his majority opinion cited Wechsler and Choper and concluded that "The effectiveness of the federal political process in preserving the States' interests is apparent even today in the course of federal legislation," as illustrated by the proliferation of federal grant-in-aid programs as well as various statutes that explicitly exempted state governments (Banks and Smolla, 2010: 455).

A series of rulings issued from 1992 to 2002 during William Rehnquist's tenure as chief justice provoked another round of scholarly critiques of judicial intervention and generated additional arguments supporting the political safeguards thesis. The Rehnquist Court did not formally overrule *Garcia*. But it rivaled the New Deal Court in the number, though not the importance, of the congressional statutes it invalidated on federalism grounds, whether for exceeding Congress's enumerated powers or improperly commandeering state officials or abrogating state sovereign immunity (Dinan, 2011). In response to these decisions and to several legal scholars who mounted defences of judicial superintendence of the federal system (e.g. Calabresi, 1995; Yoo, 1997), Larry Kramer sought to rehabilitate the political safeguards thesis. Noting that "however convincing Wechsler's reasoning may have been in its original context, subsequent experience and later developments have robbed his analysis of much, if not all, of its force," Kramer argued that the most important political safeguards of federalism were found not in structural features but rather in the party system and especially the non-programmatic and non-centralized aspects of American parties (Kramer, 2000: 218). Kramer acknowledged that parties were much more centralized than in prior years; but he contended nonetheless that "parties continue to play a crucial role in forging links between officials at the state and federal level; the political dependency of state and federal officials on each other remains among the most notable facts of American government" (Kramer, 2000: 282). Moreover, he argued that "while the parties' effectiveness in safeguarding state government may have been compromised to some degree by twentieth-century developments, these same developments have yielded new 'political' safeguards that assure and in some respects even strengthen the states' voice in national politics" (Kramer, 2000: 283).

Whereas legal scholars have been concerned with justifying or critiquing judicial supervision of the federal system, political scientists have been concerned with assessing the specific mechanisms through which state governments advance their interests in national policy making. Their aim has been to assess the effectiveness of these mechanisms and the conditions under which states can wield influence in the national policy process.

Intergovernmental lobbying through the Big Seven organizations (the Council of State Governments, National Governors Association, National Conference of State Legislatures, National League of Cities, US Conference of Mayors, National Association of Counties, and International City/County Management Association) has long been the dominant mechanism for states to assert their interests in the national legislative process (Haider, 1974; Cammisa, 1995; Nugent, 2009). These organizations are most influential when there is bipartisan consensus among state officials, such as on limiting federal mandates, increasing federal funding for federal-state programs, or derailing statutes that encroach on state authority. Intergovernmental groups also stand a good chance of success when they can build coalitions with and are allied with other powerful interests or are capable of mobilizing public opinion in favor of their concerns, as was achieved with the passage of the Unfunded Mandates Reform Act (Dinan, 1997). These groups generally have more success in influencing legislation in the Senate than in the House (Smith, 2008).

State officials also engage in individual lobbying and with some success in recent years in ensuring that Congress is sensitive to state interests when enacting policy reforms. Most governors (and some state legislatures) maintain offices in Washington, DC, that enable them to monitor legislation and at times secure earmarks that benefit their states (Smith, 2008). Governors with expertise in particular policy areas have also worked closely with congressional committees charged with drafting legislation to ensure that the resulting policies benefit from state experience. This expertise-based lobbying was on display during the enactment of welfare reform statutes in 1988, when Arkansas Governor Bill Clinton played a key role crafting the Family Support Act, and then again in 1996, when Michigan Governor John Engler and Wisconsin Governor Tommy Thompson were prominent players in drafting the Personal Responsibility Act (Haskins, 2008).

State officials have also turned increasingly to press their case with executive officials who are tasked with making rules to implement congressional statutes and who are often permitted to issue waivers from federal requirements. It is no surprise, given the numerous ways that the rule making process can moderate or exacerbate the effects of congressionally imposed directives, that state officials have pressed their case with administrative officials and with some notable successes in recent years (Sharkey, 2009). In the mid-1990s, the Department of Health and Human Services (HHS) under President Bill Clinton issued a number of rules regarding implementation of the restructured TANF program pursuant to the Personal Responsibility and Work Opportunity Reconciliation Act of 1996 (PRWORA), and some of these rules were quite favorable to states by giving them more discretion than was originally envisioned during the drafting of the law (Gais and Fossett, 2005). Then, in the mid-2000s, the Department of Homeland Security (DHS) under President George W. Bush was tasked with implementing the REAL ID Act, which required states to change their driver's licences to make them conform to federal standards and to do so within a tight timeframe. After numerous state legislatures made their objections known, DHS officials promulgated a series of rules that went a long way toward accommodating states' interests by giving them nearly a decade longer to fully comply with the law (Regan and Deering, 2009).

Governors and state legislators have also tried to persuade administrative officials to grant relief from federal program requirements through the issuance of waivers, which have been available since 1962 for programs authorized under the Social Security Act and since 1994 for education programs. In the 1980s and 1990s, individual governors were particularly effective in securing waivers from Aid to Families with Dependent Children (AFDC) requirements. As a result, states gained discretion to undertake innovations regarding various elements of their AFDC programs, well before the enactment of federal welfare reform in 1996 (Teles, 1996). Governors have been just as successful in the 1990s and 2000s in securing Medicaid waivers granting states significant leeway regarding the delivery of medical care (Weissert and Weissert, 2008). Governors also enjoyed some success during the second term of the George W. Bush Administration in pressing the Education Department to grant waivers from various requirements of the No Child Left Behind Act of 2001 (NCLB).

State officials have also asserted their interests in the national policy process by declining to participate in federal programs (Gardner, 2005; Bulman-Pozen and Gerken, 2009). As John Nugent has written, "The strongest political safeguards of federalism today involve state officials telling or signaling to their federal counterparts that they will not implement federal laws or policies in their existing form" (Nugent, 2009: 64). These acts of non-acquiescence fall well short of the long-discredited doctrine of nullification asserted by South Carolina in the 1830s regarding the tariff, Wisconsin in the 1850s regarding the Fugitive Slave Act, and various southern states in the 1950s in response to the Supreme Court's school desegregation rulings. Rather, states in the contemporary era have generally declined to participate in federal programs and agreed to accept the consequences of doing so. These consequences generally involve the loss of federal funding, which was the penalty states and localities faced for not abiding by NCLB directives (Shelly, 2008). But federal penalties also take other forms, as when numerous states in the 2000s declared their opposition to the REAL ID Act even though their residents faced the penalty of not being able to use their state driver's licences as acceptable identification for boarding planes or entering federal buildings (Regan and Deering, 2009). State acts resisting NCLB and the REAL ID Act have been credited in both cases with leading administrative officials to relax or grant waivers from federal directives regarding both programs (Dinan, 2008).

State officials have also filed federal lawsuits to try to overturn congressional statutes or administrative regulations seen as encroaching on state prerogatives (Waltenburg and Swinford, 1999). Federal courts have turned back most of these efforts, including California's challenge to the Motor Voter Act of 1993, South Carolina's challenge to the Driver's Privacy Protection Act of 1994, and Connecticut's challenge to NCLB. But these suits have occasionally been successful. The Supreme Court sided with New York in its challenge to a provision in the Low-Level Radioactive Waste Policy Act Amendment of 1985. The Court also sided with state plaintiffs in a series of challenges in the 1990s to congressional statutes abrogating state sovereign immunity regarding intellectual property and age and disability discrimination cases. It is notable in this regard that state officials have taken a lead role in seeking invalidation of the Patient Protection and Affordable Care Act of 2010 by filing federal lawsuits challenging the constitutionality of a provision mandating that individuals carry government-approved health insurance.

State officials influence national policy making in part by securing passage of federal acts or responding to their enactment; they can also respond to federal inaction, whether by filing lawsuits, passing state statutes, or issuing court decisions. State attorneys general have assumed increasing importance since the 1980s in securing regulations that have been unattainable through national legislative or administrative processes (Provost 2003). In the 1990s, attorneys general relied on lawsuits to force the major cigarette companies not only to pay $246.5 billion in damages over a 25 year period, but also to make significant changes in the way they advertise cigarettes and accept limits on their marketing and lobbying practices. In essence, through four individual state settlements and a 46-state Master Settlement Agreement of 1998, state attorneys general were responsible for establishing a national regulatory policy regarding cigarette companies that went far beyond what had been achieved by Congress or the Federal Trade Commission (Derthick, 2005). In the early 2000s, New York Governor Eliot Spitzer relied on lawsuits to force changes in various industries and is most known for brokering a $1.4 billion settlement in 2003 between regulators and financial services companies that required the companies to take significant steps to address conflicts of interest between their research and investment decisions.

State legislatures, meanwhile, often enact statutes intended to fill a perceived void in congressional law making. This longstanding feature of the US federal system has been particularly on display in the 2000s as some state legislatures approved a higher minimum wage, allowed funding for embryonic stem cell research, and imposed restrictions on hiring illegal immigrants, among other initiatives blocked at the national level (Krane, 2007). At a time when congressional and administrative regulation of greenhouse gas emissions was stalled, California was the first of several states to enact their own climate change laws; states in the Northeast, West, and Midwest have also established regional greenhouse gas initiatives that are committed to reducing carbon emissions in these regions (Rabe, 2004).

State processes of direct democracy also serve as a vehicle for citizens to respond to federal inaction or secure policies in excess of what is achieved in Congress or the Supreme Court. In a study of the federalism implications of state-level initiative processes, Kathleen Ferraiolo concluded that "direct democracy is a particularly fruitful institutional venue for policy entrepreneurs who wish to remedy a perceived defect in federal policy at the state level" (Ferraiolo, 2008: 507–8). Several state minimum-wage increases and stem cell research measures in the 2000s were initiated and approved by the people without any participation of state legislators. Meanwhile, affirmative-action opponents and medicinal-marijuana advocates have relied heavily on state initiative processes to secure goals not attainable in the US Supreme Court or through Congress. Moreover, as David Magleby noted, the initiative process has agenda-setting capabilities that often enable policy entrepreneurs to gain much more attention for their cause than would be possible by proceeding through the legislative process, given that "A vote on an issue in a single state can propel an issue onto the national agenda because of the widespread media attention given to some controversial initiatives" (Magleby, 1998: 148).

State judges have also served as "agents of federalism," to use James Gardner's (2005) formulation, by relying on state constitutional provisions to provide heightened protection for individual rights than the US Supreme Court is prepared to guarantee through interpretation of the US Constitution. State courts have long engaged in independent interpretation of state bills of rights; but it was not until the 1970s, when the Burger Court was less aggressive than its predecessor in expanding rights, that state courts began turning to state bills of rights to establish rights that the US Supreme Court was unwilling to recognize. Through such rulings, various state courts have abolished the death penalty, recognized a right to inter-district equity in school spending, legalized same-sex marriage, and secured rights of criminal defendants that have been rejected or gone unrecognized by the US Supreme Court (Williams, 2009).

CONSEQUENCES OF CENTRALIZATION VERSUS DECENTRALIZATION

In addition to chronicling the evolution of national-state relations and the ways that national and state officials influence one another, scholars have also assessed the consequences of permitting states to retain discretion over policy making, as continues to be the case in many areas despite the overall trend toward expansion of national power. At times, scholars have been concerned with identifying the effects of the relatively decentralized nature of the US federal system. At other times, scholars have assessed proposed or enacted measures to return some measure of policy authority to state governments.

Scholars have long investigated whether decentralization of power contributes to the protection of rights, and for much of US history decentralization was associated with the deprivation of rights. Madison in Federalist 10 argued that tyrannical majorities would more easily "concert and execute their plans of oppression" in a smaller society with fewer distinct parties and interests than in a large republic with "a greater variety of parties and interests." For many years, southern states provided a prominent illustration of Madison's argument in the Federalist papers (Hamilton, Madison, and Jay, 1961), due to their maintenance of slavery prior to the Civil War and continued violation of African-Americans' civil and voting rights for a century after the war's end. As William Riker famously argued in the 1960s, "[I]f in the United States one disapproves of racism, one should disapprove of federalism" (Riker, 1964: 155).

Within several decades of this pronouncement, however, after federal power was finally deployed in a sustained and effective fashion to secure African-Americans' civil and voting rights, many scholars were led to revise their automatic association of decentralization with deprivation of rights (though for a notable exception see Feely and

Rubin, 2008: 121–2). Thus, in the 1980s, Riker took note of the "civil rights reforms of the 1960s" that had the effect of "eliminating the protection for local repression" and concluded: "With the racial dimension of judgment thus removed, it became possible, for the first time in American history, to value federalism unambiguously as a deterrent to statism" (Riker, 1987: xiii).

In fact, by the early twenty-first century, various scholars were prepared, on the basis of recent rights-expanding initiatives at the state and local level, to view the decentralization of power as promoting rather than undermining protection of rights. As Kathleen Sullivan noted in the early 2000s: "States' rights have been associated historically with conservative causes, while federal power has been associated with increasing egalitarianism and protection of minorities from Reconstruction through the New Deal and the Civil Rights Acts of the 1960s" (Sullivan, 2006: 800–1). However, the conservative ascendancy at the national level coupled with recent state and local acts protecting minority rights led her to suggest that "champions of liberal causes might need to rethink any reflexive recoil from federalism. Gay weddings in San Francisco and Massachusetts, like popular initiatives authorizing physician-assisted suicide in Oregon and medicinal use of marijuana in California, exemplify recent progressive experimentation at the local level through policies that could not command a national majority" (Sullivan, 2006: 801). In a similar fashion, after noting that "many progressives have decried the devolution of national responsibilities to the states," in part because this is thought to produce "more inequality" and "weaker civil rights," Richard Freeman and Joel Rogers argue that "the progressive disposition against federalism is outmoded," inasmuch as many states in the 1990s and 2000s "have adopted policies that advance individual freedom, protect public goods such as the environment, or strengthen local protection of the interests of workers and the poor" (Freeman and Rogers, 2007: 205).

Another longstanding scholarly concern has been investigating the extent to which decentralization promotes inter-state competition and to what end. Charles Tiebout launched this line of research in the 1950s by applying micro-economic theory to individual decisions regarding where to live and then considering the effects of these decisions on local government policy making. Arguing that the "consumer-voter may be viewed as picking that community which best satisfies his preference pattern for public goods," Tiebout concluded: "The greater the number of communities and the greater the variance among them, the closer the consumer will come to fully realizing his preference position" (Tiebout, 1956: 418). Concluding with an invitation for further research regarding the question of "how do people actually react in choosing a community," he acknowledged that "There has been very little empirical study of the motivations of people in choosing a community" (Tiebout 1956: 423).

Although Tiebout's model focused on the effects of individual decision making, other economists have extended the theory by postulating that both individuals and corporations consider policy variation among states when deciding where to move and that this leads states to compete with one another to attract and retain residents and businesses. As Wallace Oates summarized the implications of these theories: "A decentralized form of government thus possesses the advantage of allowing various levels of output of certain public goods, by means of which resources can be employed more efficiently in satisfying the preferences of consumers" (Oates, 1972: 12).

These economic models have generated a substantial empirical literature examining the degree to which states actually engage in inter-jurisdictional competition. Studies have been conducted regarding the degree of competition in regard to tax rates, government spending, provision of services, corporate regulation, and environmental policy (Kenyon and Kincaid, 1991). Some have been concerned with determining whether state policy makers are in fact influenced by an awareness of comparable policies in other states (Revesz, 1992). Other studies have considered whether inter-state competition can be considered advantageous, in the sense of producing an efficient system whereby policies are suited to state political cultures (Dye, 1990), or problematic, by leading states to engage in a "race to the bottom" that produces sub-optimal levels of corporate regulation, environmental protection, or provision of social services (e.g. Cary, 1974).

Inquiries into the extent and effect of inter-state competition have been particularly prevalent regarding welfare policy making, whether regarding the AFDC program in effect until 1996 or the TANF program implemented in its place. Paul Peterson and various colleagues have long argued that state governments are ill-suited to operate redistributive programs and therefore authority over welfare policy should be exercised at the federal level (Peterson et al., 1986; Peterson, 1995). On their view, permitting states to set welfare benefit levels leads them to reduce benefits in response to competitive pressures from surrounding states, out of a fear of becoming "welfare magnets" (Peterson and Rom, 1990).

This race-to-the-bottom thesis regarding welfare policy has been subjected to extensive scrutiny, particularly through an examination of state behavior before and after passage of the 1996 PRWORA. A number of scholars have taken issue with the assumption that individual migration patterns are influenced by variation in state welfare benefit levels (Schram and Soss, 1998; Allard and Danziger, 2000). Other scholars have not found evidence of states taking advantage of their increased discretion under PRWORA (they already enjoyed a good amount of discretion prior to the law's passage) by reducing benefit levels in response to neighboring state policies in the way that the race-to-the-bottom theory would predict (Berry et al., 2003). A recent study concluded: "At best, empirical evidence for the existence of welfare magnets and a race to the bottom is mixed. More time will have to pass before these dynamics can be clearly assessed with regard to TANF and PRWORA, although state behavior during the 2001 recession is not generally consistent with the two theories" (Johnston, 2008: 136).

Still another line of research focuses on the degree to which decentralization permits states to serve as laboratories of experimentation. Supreme Court Justice Louis Brandeis noted in a dissenting opinion in *New State Ice Co. v Liebmann*, 285 U.S. 262 (1932), that, "It is one of the happy incidents of the federal system that a single courageous state may, if its citizens choose, serve as a laboratory; and try novel social and economic experiments without risk to the rest of the country" (311). Extensive inquiries have been conducted regarding policies or institutional reforms that were initially adopted by one or several states and then borrowed by numerous other states (Osborne, 1988; Nice, 1994;

Karch, 2007). Sometimes these policies were eventually enacted on a national level, as in the case of women's suffrage (pioneered on the state level by Wyoming in the late nineteenth century) and welfare reform (where Michigan and Wisconsin were among the leaders in the late twentieth century). In many other cases, an innovation was eventually adopted by most states but rejected at the federal level, as with balanced-budget rules in 49 states and the line-item veto power in 44 states. In a final set of cases, a single state adopted an innovative policy or institutional device that has been examined but largely or wholly rejected by other states. Such is the case with Nebraska's adoption of a unicameral legislature in the 1930s. Three states experimented with unicameralism in the founding era; but none have opted to follow Nebraska since, though many have considered doing so. Oregon voters' approval of a physician-assisted suicide law in the 1990s also produced an ongoing experiment that has been studied and largely rejected, although Washington became the second state to adopt such a law through a 2008 voter initiative.

There is no denying that decentralization has produced numerous state innovations that have at times led to adoption of a uniform national policy and on other occasions produced inter-state variation; the main scholarly debate concerns whether this experimentation and resulting variation should be deemed beneficial. On one hand, Edward Rubin and Malcolm Feeley maintain that "Very few people argue that normative variation within a polity is inherently desirable"; moreover, arguments to the effect that experimentation is intrinsically valuable in so far as it allows for "norm dispersion" have "the odd effect of consigning some people to bad policies so that others may benefit from good ones" (Rubin and Feeley, 1994: 935). In contrast, Michael Greve has argued that decentralization of policy authority and the resulting opportunity for state policy experimentation might be seen as valuable because "when we do not know what we are doing, it is best not to do it everywhere, all at once." Among the various benefits, he notes that:

> A state-based process facilitates gradualism and, therefore, feedback and institutional learning. Successful state and local experiments with airline deregulation, welfare reform, and school choice taught valuable lessons, built public confidence in innovative policies, and provided a testing ground for social scientists' models and policy recommendations that might well have gone unheeded in a centralized political environment. State-based policy innovation also facilitates adaptation to local needs, circumstances, and preferences. (Greve, 2001: 1)

CONCLUSION

Although future research regarding state–national relations will be driven to a significant degree by unforeseen events and developments that will call for analysis, it is possible to highlight several promising lines of scholarly inquiry that build on and add to existing research. First, in explaining the development of state–national relations, scholars can benefit from comparative studies analyzing the USA in the context of other federal systems. Although the USA is not the most decentralized federal system (Canada, for one, is more decentralized), it is more decentralized than most federations (Watts 2008: 177). Scholars of state–national relations are naturally led to account for why the USA has maintained a relatively decentralized system in comparison with other federal systems where power is more concentrated in the national government. To what extent can the answer be found through analyses of historical circumstances or political identity? And to what extent is decentralization a product of the design of governing institutions and arrangements? In particular, comparative studies can isolate the general effects of institutional features such as the constitutional allocation of powers, the design of the senate, or the structure and power of the federal judiciary, and thereby contribute to a better understanding of the development of state–national relations in the USA and the reasons why the US system, despite powerful long-term trends favoring centralization, has remained relatively decentralized.

Second, in analyzing the ways that state and national officials influence one another, scholars of intergovernmental relations and public law would benefit from a greater engagement with one another's work. The Supreme Court has long played a key role in umpiring state–national relations (Schmidhauser, 1958). However, since the 1950s the federal judiciary has assumed an increasingly important role, whether by issuing orders constraining state policy authority or, on the other hand, insulating state governments from congressional attempts to commandeer state officials or abrogate state sovereign immunity. Legal scholars have undertaken extensive studies of these rulings, but primarily for the purpose of tracking and explaining doctrinal changes. Intergovernmental relations scholars are better positioned to assess the actual consequences of these rulings for national–state relations and some scholars have examined these consequences (Melnick, 2003, 2009). But this area is ripe for further investigation by scholars interested in integrating public-law research into the circumstances when US Supreme Court decisions can be consequential with intergovernmental-relations scholarship regarding the ways these decisions facilitate or obstruct the achievement of federal objectives.

Finally, in assessing the consequences of the relatively decentralized nature of the US federal system, the post-civil rights era presents a fresh opportunity to consider the merits and drawbacks of decentralization of policy authority. The main arguments are by now firmly established; many of them were advanced centuries ago by Madison and De Tocqueville. But there is a continuing need to subject these claims to scrutiny and testing. Scholars have conducted extensive empirical investigations into the existence and effect of inter-jurisdictional competition, particularly regarding welfare policy and to some extent concerning environmental protection. Numerous studies have also been conducted into the extent to which states serve as laboratories of experimentation and enact institutional or policy innovations. However, other propositions are in need of further investigation, such as the purported benefits of increased citizen participation, deliberation, and responsiveness in a decentralized system. Admittedly, some debates about the relative merits of decentralization and centralization are not easily resolved by empirical investigation, given that the contestants assign different weight to goals such as uniformity and diversity of policy outcomes. Nevertheless, there is a value in continuing to investigate the actual effects of decentralization and centralization regarding some of the disputed claims in the literature. And in view of the many choices that are made on an ongoing basis to entrust state or national governments with responsibility for various tasks of governance, continued investigation of this topic can benefit scholars and policy makers alike.

REFERENCES

Advisory Commission on Intergovernmental Relations. 1984. *Regulatory Federalism: Policy, Process, Impact and Reform.* Washington, DC: U.S. Government Printing Office.

Allard, Scott W. and Sheldon Danziger. 2000. "Welfare Magnets: Myth or Reality?" *Journal of Politics* 62 (May): 350–68.

Allen, Mahalley D., Carrie Pettus, and Donald D. Haider-Markel. 2004. "Making the National Local: Specifying the Conditions for National Government Influence on State Policymaking," *State Politics and Policy Quarterly* 4 (Fall): 318–44.

Banks, William C., and Rodney Smolla. 2010. 6th Ed. *Constituional Law: Structure and Rights in Our Federal System.* St Paul, MN: LexisNexis

Beer, Samuel H. 1973. "The Modernization of American Federalism," *Publius: The Journal of Federalism* 3 (Fall): 49–95.

Berry, William D., Richard C. Fording, and Russell L. Hanson. 2003. "Reassessing the 'Race to the Bottom' in State Welfare Policy," *Journal of Politics* 65 (1): 327–49.

Brown, Lawrence D., James W. Fossett, and Kenneth T. Palmer. 1984. *The Changing Politics of Federal Grants.* Washington, DC: The Brookings Institution.

Bulman-Pozen, Jessica and Heather K. Gerken. 2009. "Uncooperative Federalism," *Yale Law Journal* 118: 1256–310.

Calabresi, Steven G. 1995. "A Government of Limited and Enumerated Powers: In Defense of United States v. Lopez." *Michigan Law Review* 94: 752–831.

Cammisa, Anne Marie. 1995. *Governments as Interest Groups: Intergovernmental Lobbying and the Federal System.* Westport, CT: Praeger.

Cary, William L. 1974. "Federalism and Corporate Law: Reflections upon Delaware," *Yale Law Journal* 83 (March): 663–705.

Choper, Jesse H. 1980. *Judicial Review and the National Political Process: A Functional Reconsideration of the Role of the Supreme Court.* Chicago: University of Chicago Press.

Conlan, Timothy J. 1998. *From New Federalism to Devolution: Twenty-five years of Intergovernmental Reform.* Washington, DC: Brookings Institution Press.

Conlan, Timothy J. 2006. "From Cooperative to Opportunistic Federalism: Reflections on the Half-Century Anniversary of the Commission on Intergovernmental Relations," *Public Administration Review* 66 (September/October): 663–76.

Corwin, Edward S. 1950. "The Passing of Dual Federalism," *Virginia Law Review* 36 (1): 1–24.

De Tocqueville, Alexis. [1835] 1969. *Democracy in America,* Translated by George Lawrence and edited by J. P. Mayer. Garden City, NJ: Anchor.

Derthick, Martha. 1970. *The Influence of Federal Grants: Public Assistance in Massachusetts.* Cambridge, MA: Harvard University Press.

Derthick, Martha. 2001. *Keeping the Compound Republic: Essays on American Federalism.* Washington, DC: Brookings Institution Press.

Derthick, Martha. 2005. *Up in Smoke: From Legislation to Litigation in Tobacco Politics.* 2nd edn. Washington, DC: CQ Press.

Dinan, John. 1997. "State Government Influence in the National Policy Process: Lessons from the 104th Congress," *Publius: The Journal of Federalism* 27 (Spring): 129–42.

Dinan, John. 2008. "The State of American Federalism, 2007–2008: Resurgent State Influence in the National Policy Process and Continued State Innovation," *Publius: The Journal of Federalism* 38 (Summer): 381–415.

Dinan, John. 2011. "The Rehnquist Court's Federalism Decisions (review essay)," *Publius: The Journal of Federalism* 41 (Winter): 158–67.

Dye, Thomas R. 1990. *American Federalism: Competition among Governments.* Lexington, MA: Lexington Books.

Elazar, Daniel J. 1962. *The American Partnership: Intergovernmental Cooperation in the Nineteenth Century United States.* Chicago: University of Chicago Press.

Feeley, Malcolm M. and Edward L. Rubin. 1998. *Judicial Policy Making and the Modern State: How the Courts Reformed America's Prisons.* New York: Cambridge University Press.

Feeley, Malcolm M. and Edward L. Rubin. 2008. *Federalism: Political Identity and Tragic Compromise.* Ann Arbor: University of Michigan Press.

Ferraiolo, Kathleen. 2008. "State Policy Innovation and the Federalism Implications of Direct Democracy," *Publius: The Journal of Federalism* 38 (Summer): 488–514.

Freeman, Richard B. and Joel Rogers. 2007. "The Promise of Progressive Federalism". In Joe Soss, Jacob S. Hacker, and Suzanne Mettler (eds), *Remaking America: Democracy and Public Policy in an Age of Inequality.* New York: Russell Sage Foundation: 205–27.

Gais, Thomas and James Fossett. 2005. "Federalism and the Executive Branch". In Joel D. Aberbach and Mark A. Peterson (eds), *The Executive Branch.* New York: Oxford University Press: 486–522.

Gardner, James A. 2005. *Interpreting State Constitutions: A Jurisprudence of Function in a Federal System.* Chicago: University of Chicago Press.

Greve, Michael S. 2001. Laboratories of Democracy: Anatomy of a Metaphor. *AEI Federalist Outlook.* No. 6 (March): 1–8. <http://www.aei.org/outlook/12743>.

Grodzins, Morton. 1966. *The American System: A New View of Government in the United States.* Chicago: Rand McNally.

Haider, Donald H. 1974. *When Governments come to Washington: Governors, Mayors, and Intergovernmental Lobbying.* New York: Free Press.

Hamilton, Alexander, James Madison, and John Jay. 1961. *The Federalist Papers.* New York: Signet.

Haskins, Ron. 2008. "Governors and the Development of American Social Policy". In Ethan G. Sribnick (ed.), *A Legacy of Innovation: Governors and Public Policy.* Philadelphia: University of Pennsylvania Press: 76–106.

Johnson, Kimberley S. 2007. *Governing the American State: Congress and the New Federalism, 1877–1929.* Princeton, NJ: Princeton University Press.

Johnston, Jocelyn M. 2008. "Welfare Reform: A Devolutionary Success?" In Timothy J. Conlan and Paul L. Posner (eds), *Intergovernmental Management for the 21st Century.* Washington, DC: Brookings Institution Press: 124–56.

Karch, Andrew. 2007. *Democratic Laboratories: Policy Diffusion among the American States.* Ann Arbor: University of Michigan Press.

Kennedy, David M. 1987. "Federalism and the Force of History". In Robert A. Goldwin and William A. Schambra (eds), *How Federal is the Constitution?* Washington, DC: American Enterprise Institute for Policy Research: 67–83.

Kenyon, Daphne A. and John Kincaid (eds). 1991. *Competition Among State and Local Governments: Efficiency and Equity in American Federalism.* Washington, DC: Urban Institute Press.

Kincaid, John. 1990. "From Cooperative to Coercive Federalism," *Annals of the American Association of Political and Social Science* 509 (May): 139–52.

Kincaid, John. 1998. "The Devolution Tortoise and the Centralization Hare," *New England Economic Review* (May/June): 13–40.

Kramer, Larry D. 2000. "Putting the Politics Back in the Political Safeguards of Federalism," *Columbia Law Review* 100 (January): 215–93.

Krane, Dale. 2007. "The Middle Tier in American Federalism: State Government Policy Activism During the Bush Presidency," *Publius: The Journal of Federalism* 37 (Summer): 453–77.

Magleby, David B. 1998. "Ballot Initiatives and Intergovernmental Relations in the United States," *Publius: The Journal of Federalism* 28 (Winter): 147–63.

Melnick, R. Shep. 1994. *Between the Lines: Interpreting Welfare Rights.* Washington, DC: The Brookings Institution.

Melnick, R. Shep. 2003. "Deregulating the States: Federalism in the Rehnquist Court". In *Evolving Federalisms: The Intergovernmental Balance of Power in America and Europe.* Syracuse, NY: Campbell Public Affairs Institute: 109–41.

Melnick, R. Shep. 2009. "Taking Remedies Seriously: Can Courts Control Public Schools?" In Joshua M. Dunn and Martin R. West (eds), *From Schoolhouse to Courthouse: The Judiciary's Role in American Education.* Washington, DC: Brookings Institution Press: 17–48.

Milkis, Sidney M. and Jesse H. Rhodes. 2007. "George Bush, the Party System, and American Federalism," *Publius: The Journal of Federalism* 37 (Summer): 478–504.

Nagel, Robert F. 2001. *The Implosion of American Federalism.* New York: Oxford University Press.

Nathan, Richard. 1990. "Federalism: The Great 'Composition.'" In Anthony King (ed.), *The New American Political System.* 2nd ed. Washington, DC: American Enterprise Institute: 231–61.

Nice, David C. 1994. *Policy Innovation in State Governments.* Ames: Iowa State University Press.

Nugent, John D. 2009. *Safeguarding Federalism: How States Protect their Interests in National Policymaking.* Norman: University of Oklahoma Press.

Oates, Wallace E. 1972. *Fiscal Federalism.* New York: Harcourt, Brace, Jovanovich.

Osborne, David. 1998. *Laboratories of Democracy.* Boston, MA: Harvard Business School Press.

Peterson, Paul E. 1995. *The Price of Federalism.* Washington, DC: The Brookings Institution.

Peterson, Paul E., Barry G. Rabe, and Kenneth K. Wong. 1986. *When Federalism Works.* Washington, DC: The Brookings Institution.

Peterson, Paul E. and Mark C. Rom. 1990. *Welfare Magnets: A New Case for a National Standard.* Washington, DC: The Brookings Institution.

Posner, Paul L. 1998. *The Politics of Unfunded Mandates: Whither Federalism?* Washington, DC: Georgetown University Press.

Provost, Colin. 2003. "State Attorneys General, Entrepreneurship, and Consumer Protection in the New Federalism," *Publius: The Journal of Federalism* 33 (1): 37–53.

Rabe, Barry G. 2004. *Statehouse and Greenhouse: The Emerging Politics of American Climate Change Policy.* Washington, DC: Brookings Institution Press.

Regan, Priscilla M. and Christopher J. Deering. 2009. "State Opposition to REAL ID," *Publius: The Journal of Federalism* 39 (Summer): 476–505.

Revesz, Richard. 1992. "Rehabilitating Interstate Competition: Rethinking the "Race to the Bottom" Rationale for Federal Environmental Regulation," *New York University Law Review* 67: 1210–54.

Riker, William H. 1955. "The Senate and American Federalism," *American Political Science Review* 49: 452–69.

Riker, William H. 1964. *Federalism: Origin, Operation, Significance*. Boston: Little, Brown, and Co.

Riker, William H. 1987. *The Development of American Federalism*. Boston, MA: Kluwer Academic Publishers.

Rubin, Edward L. and Malcolm Feeley. 1994. "Federalism: Some Notes on a National Neurosis," *UCLA Law Review* 41 (April): 903–52.

Sandler, Ross and David Schoenbrod. 2003. *Democracy by Decree: What Happens When Courts Run Government*. New Haven, CT: Yale University Press.

Schmidhauser, John R. 1958. *The Supreme Court as Final Arbiter in Federal-State Relations, 1789-1957*. Chapel Hill: University of North Carolina Press.

Schram, Sanford F. and Joe Soss. 1998. "Making Something out of Nothing: Welfare Reform and a New Race to the Bottom," *Publius: The Journal of Federalism* 28 (1): 67–88.

Sharkey, Catherine M. 2009. "Federalism Accountability: 'Agency-forcing' Measures," *Duke Law Journal* 58: 2125–92.

Shelly, Bryan. 2008. "Rebels and their Causes: State Resistance to No Child Left Behind," *Publius: The Journal of Federalism* 38 (Summer): 444–68.

Smith, Troy E. 2008. "Intergovernmental lobbying: How Opportunistic Actors Create a Less Structured and Balanced Federal System". In Timothy J. Conlan and Paul I. Posner (eds), *Intergovernmental Management for the 21st Century*. Washington: Brookings Institution Press: 300–37.

Sullivan, Kathleen. 2006. "From States' Rights Blues to Blue States' Rights: Federalism after the Rehnquist Court," *Fordham Law Review* 75: 799–813.

Teles, Steven M. 1996. *Whose Welfare? AFDC and Elite Politics*. Lawrence: University Press of Kansas.

Tiebout, Charles M. 1956. "A Pure Theory of Local Expenditures," *The Journal of Political Economy* 64 (October): 416–24.

Waltenburg, Eric N. and Bill Swinford. 1999. *Litigating Federalism: The States Before the U.S. Supreme Court*. Westport, CT: Greenwood Press.

Watts, Ronald L. 2008. *Comparing Federal Systems*. 3rd edn. Montreal, Canada: McGill-Queens University Press.

Wechsler, Herbert. 1954. "The Political Safeguards of Federalism: The Role of the States in the Composition and Selection of the National Government," *Columbia Law Review* 54: 543–60.

Weissert, Carol S. and William G. Weissert. 2008. "Medicaid Waivers: License to Shape the Future of Fiscal Federalism". In Timothy J. Conlan and Paul I. Posner (eds), *Intergovernmental Management for the 21st Century*. Washington: Brookings Institution Press: 157–75.

Williams, Robert F. 2009. *The Law of American State Constitutions*. New York: Oxford University Press.

Yoo, John C. 1997. "The Judicial Safeguards of Federalism," *Southern California Law Review* 70 (July): 1311–405.

Zimmerman, Joseph. 2005. *Congressional Preemption: Regulatory Federalism*. Albany: State University of New York Press.

CHAPTER 3

....

RELATIONS BETWEEN LOCAL AND NATIONAL GOVERNMENTS

....

ROBERT AGRANOFF

NATIONAL–LOCAL relationships in the U.S. follow a pattern that is repeated throughout the world, in that virtually every citizen lives and receives basic services within the confines of one or more local units—township, county, municipality, school district, transit district, and so on—but these governments are rarely considered to be central or core players in their country-wide scheme of state building. For over two centuries the basic national debate in the U.S. has been largely over the connections between states and the government in Washington, DC. Local governments are neither constitutionally recognized nor politically powerful. This pattern generally follows in many other countries. In federal Australia, Belgium, Canada, and Germany and in decentralized United Kingdom, Italy, Spain, and South Africa, the constitutional and political focus is also on national–second tier relationships. This intergovernmental focus tends to hold true with regard to the key political issues of the time, on government-to-government connections, and on the research agenda that scholars place on within polity connections. Indeed, to local governments national relationships can be characterized as a form of "junior partnership." In the overall national scheme of multi-jurisdiction, intergovernmental relations (IGR) (Walker, 2000, 21), we do not readily think of local governments as central. For example, during the 1960's the Great Society era of national legislation in the U.S., attempts to build federal-local ties were peripheral and remained a small part of this broad set of intergovernmental policies (Biles, 2011). Local governments in most countries do have a seat at the table, so to speak. It tends to be at the end of the table or around the edge of the room. As a result, one finds local–national IGR to be under-analyzed in government and governing.

Local–federal relations are in fact venerable practices in U.S. history. In the nineteenth century city officials regularly made federal government contacts, to secure commerce routes, freight and passenger services, government installations and buildings,

waterway and harbor dredging, infrastructure assistance and related internal improvements, tariff concessions for local industries, and sought government contracts and subsidies. The first omnibus Rivers and Harbors Act (1826) was ostensibly a federal program
but quickly became cooperative, as projects had to be initiated at the local level, thus it
soon became a federal–local cooperative activity, "because of the exigencies of the federal system" (Elazar, 1962, 266). This form of interaction became notable from the 1840s,
becoming "significant means of improving government services at both levels and of
forging strong, if not informal cooperative lines between Washington and the localities" (Elazar, 1967, 516). It was a time when direct federal–city relations were said to be as
extensive as the urban redevelopment movement of the 1960s (Elazar, 1967, 513).

City government officials and managers in the early twenty-first century, in contrast, like
to say there is less going on with regard to federal–local activity inasmuch as of state-urban
federal grants of the 1960–80s have slowed to a trickle. While federal assistance has diminished in quantity such observers fail to account for the fact that some remain and many
other aspects of the federal presence are real within their jurisdictions (Lawrence, Stoker,
and Wolman, 2010). One arena where a federal–local relation expanded was related to
the 2010 decennial/US census, a federal responsibility, where local governments distributed literature, promoted participation and formed local complete count committees, and
shared their files with the federal government. The local incentive, of course, is to increase
jurisdictions share of the census-based allocations of over $400 billion in federal aid
(Goodman, 2010). Of indirect but less visible continuing impact is the relation between
national economic conditions and local governments fiscal positions. For example, Hoene
and Pagano's (2010) survey of city fiscal officers revealed decreasing property tax revenues due to the collapsed housing market and declining sales tax revenues because of the
economic slowdown. Meanwhile, cities are facing increased costs (e.g., healthcare, pensions, and infrastructure) and declining fiscal aid transfers. More direct examples include
the substantial equal rights federal impact on local government hiring practices and the
regulatory web in such areas as drinking water quality and public access for persons with
disabilities. They impact every local government (Conlan, 1998). Also poorly understood is the local presence of federal programs that operate directly within communities.
Moreover, local officials continue to leverage and broker federal programs and combine
them with state programs that impact their governments (Agranoff and McGuire, 2003;
Agranoff, 2012). These are the type of continuing IGR national–local practices that are
less well understood in research, since federal–local IGR have tended to focus more on
accounting for the rise and fall of federal grants, the regulatory web that impacts local governments, and on how judicial federalism impacts localities.

This essay attempts to redress this imbalance in attention and research by looking
deeper into national–local relations. While primarily focused on the U.S., the issues of
"junior partnership" and universal IGR trends are also identified with regard to other
countries that have relatively developed IGR systems. It begins with an attempt to map
out the entire U.S. national–local terrain, from direct federal services/payments operations to more or less indirect operational practices. Then eight cross-national trends in
local–national relations are identified that will put U.S. relations in a broader context.

Next, a series of distinguishing features of U.S. local–national relations are discussed, from their embeddedness within other governments to the ambivalence between their self-governing role and their state government legal regulation orientation. This is followed by account of the major local–national, national–local interactions, from lobbying to the more recent joint involvement of federal officials in local policy and administrative networks. Finally, a more direct examination of the major research issues in this area is undertaken, raising basic questions about the nature of national–local relations, from impact studies to why local interactions have such low visibility on research agendas.

Mapping the Terrain

National–local relations obviously emanate from a variety of programs and services that not only involve local governments as primary implementers but those that have a notable and substantial federal presence within communities. As Daniel Elazar (1961, 24) once observed, local governments operate within their civil communities, which include units of other governmental bodies, local political parties, and local organizations, among others. It is the units of the federal government within communities that is of primary interest here.

Direct Services to Persons/Programs

Although rarely accounted for in national–local relations federal government direct operations are situated substantially in communities. Every city of notable size (15–30,000+) has offices of the Social Security Administration. Virtually all incorporated towns have a United States Postal Service presence, and the rural areas are reached from the towns. Also in the rural areas the United States Department of Agriculture operates several programs that are housed in most counties, for example the Agricultural and Soil Conservation Service. Other federal offices not in every town would be armed forces recruiting offices, Veteran's Administration offices, and the Federal Bureau of Investigation. Each of these may be relatively small compared to state offices, for example those in state assistance payments or state motor vehicles, but represent a direct federal services/payments presence from the federal government in cities and counties.

Dedicated Federal–Local Programs

Federal funding for urban programs has gone through program eliminations and reductions, and reshaped local priorities (Ross and Levine, 2006, Ch. 14), but some federal programs remain. For cities and surrounding counties over 50,000 and 200,000 respectively in population there is the Community Development Block Grant (CDBG) entitlement portion, which provides aid to jurisdictions for housing, urban renewal, economic development, and public services. Small cities access CDBG funds indirectly, as they now go through their state governments. In very small towns and rural areas there is the counterpart United States Department of Agriculture/Rural Development (USDA/RD) programs, organized by federal offices distributed throughout each state. They are direct federal programs that provide grants and loans for housing, community development, civic infrastructure, and small business development. The U.S. Department of Commerce's Small Business Administration (SBA) and Economic Development Administration (EDA) also have offices and programs within each state, and operate directly with local governments and other clients. Other federal programs may have some nominal state pass-throughs but are essentially federal–local programs, Title I Impact Aid to local school districts, Workforce Investment job training programs, and those early childhood programs through Head Start to community action agencies, school districts, local governments, and nonprofits. Finally, the U.S. Army Corps of Engineers works directly with local governments on its water resource projects.

Federal–State–Local Programs

Other federal programs are local at their end stage or impact but they initially go through state governments. Most remain as the residue, so to speak, of the zeroing out or substantial reduction of programs targeted specifically to cities and other local governments (Judd and Swanstrom, 1998, 246) but touch the states first. They include highways and transportation programs, e.g., Urban Mass Transit or various aspects of highway construction, Small Cities CDBG, housing assistance programs, e.g., Section 8 rental subsidies, historic preservation recognition and assistance, and in some states basic welfare or assistance payments—Temporary Assistance for Needy Families—where the county has a cost-sharing and operational role—in this federal bloc grant. Each of these represent federal programs that are essentially local but some form of intermediary state program role is at work, ranging from nominal support in the case of historic preservation to a complete decision-making role in fund allocation in the Small Cities CDBG program.

National Impact–Local Implementation

The presence of the national government is directly felt in every local government when its standards or regulations apply locally. This is sometimes called government by remote control. In regard to local governments the most important include those regulating land use control and the power of eminent domain for public use, non-discrimination in zoning, a whole range of employment practices, drinking water and waste water quality, air quality, and reuse/redevelopment of "brownfields" or former industrial sites. These standards have come about by a combination of congressional legislation and Supreme Court decisions, largely under the commerce clause of the U.S. Constitution. Regulations come in many ways these days, 1) direct orders under the threat of civil penalties, 2) partial preemptions of state and local powers under the supremacy clause, 3) cross-cutting requirements based on the federal conditional spending power, and 4) crossover sanctions that make the condition of aid based on actions in another arena (ACIR, 1984, 34–44). These forces "make local governments the most federally regulated enterprises of all," a suburban Cleveland, Ohio mayor once related to the author.

Bonds and Loans

Local government revenues are also impacted by federal financial and tax practices. Municipal bonds, such as general obligation and revenue bonds, a $400 billion state and local government activity in 2009, are purchased federal income tax free by investors. In effect, the federal government provides a local government subsidy, in as much as municipalities pay lower interest rates on pay back than do other bond borrowers. While the greatest benefit is obviously to the taxpaying investors, in this way bonding not only allows the federal subsidy to help local governments enter the bond market at lower than competitive interest rates but makes these bonds more attractive to investors. This practice, however, is vulnerable to Congressional tax reform. In 1986, for example, exemptions were limited for industrial revenue bonds and the alternative minimum tax provisions required that interest earned from "tax exempt" municipal bonds be included in persons paying that tax. Moreover, in 1988 the Supreme Court ruled in *South Carolina* vs. *Baker* that there is no constitutional requirement that municipal bonds be tax free, raising the possibility that Congress could sometime eliminate this provision altogether (Ross and Levine, 2006, 474).

Federal loans and loan guarantees for local governments date back as far as colonial days and the federal government continues to loan funds for infrastructure and physical improvements. During the great depression of the 1930s many municipal buildings, county courthouses, public libraries, park pavilions, and new schools were financed by a combination of direct subsidies and loans. The federal government "…sent a message to the towns, Washington is there to help when the town is in trouble, and yet will not intrude on the community to do it" (Shales, 2007, 262). Since then federal loans not only support local government buildings but also housing purchases, urban and rural development projects, water and waste water treatment plants, and disaster recovery. From the late 1960s, federal loan guarantees have grown while direct loans have stabilized in level; by 2000 guarantees exceeded loans by over five times (Stanton, 2002, 388). Guarantees include mortgage insurance, municipal loan credit–buy downs/guarantees, and guarantees of loans for municipal infrastructure and for environmental compliance (e.g., water plants). Such federal loan guarantees facilitate the entry of citizens of local governments to enter housing finance markets and local governments to enter credit markets for various long-term projects.

Federal Presence in Local Areas

A final aspect of the federal landscape within some local governments and nearby areas is federal programs or installations co-located with counties and within cities. This includes national parks and forests and federal land overlapping county governments, military bases overlapping cities and counties, and such other federal programs as Veterans Administration hospitals and clinics located in cities or near cities. Others are singular installations including the National Materials and Information Center in Pueblo, Colorado, the Social Security Administration Headquarters in Baltimore, Maryland, the U.S. Army Payroll Center in Indianapolis, Indiana, and several National Aeronautics and Space Administration facilities in Huntsville, Alabama. Each of these extends the federal presence within some local governments, both contributing to the local economy and also impacting local government services. It also means, of course, that federal officials representing these programs are working with local officials on matters impacting the federal installations and local government, e.g., traffic, land use practices, law enforcement, and other issues. Some local governments also receive modest "impact aid" assessments for added services demand, for example in the case of military bases.

This overview of the U.S. federal government's local presence or footprint extends the scope well beyond the impact of grants. It does not, however, present the complete picture. Since the 1930s with public works projects and then with World War II the federal government has had an important policy imprint on local areas. It began with urban development and housing programs and during the war years as the War Production Board spread industrial sites throughout the country, the Federal Highway Act of 1944 committed 25 percent to city road construction, urban freeways increased to 90 percent federal funding in 1956, tax provisions encouraged house ownership and cooperative apartment conversions, federal grants subsidized new hospital construction and sewage processing facilities, urban renewal and slum clearance programs, and many others. The rise of federal involvement in city development has been well covered in the literature, from Roscoe C. Martin's (1965) *Cities and the Federal System* to Pietro Nivola's (2002) *Tense Commandments, Federal Prescriptions and City Politics*, along with Susan Clarke and Gary Gailie's (1998) work on waves of programming in *The Work of Cities*. Work on small towns and the national government are, while somewhat dated, covered in Galston and Baehler's (1995) *Rural Development in the United States* and Lapping, Daniels and Keller's (1989) *Rural Planning and Development in the United States*.

INTERNATIONALLY NATIONAL–LOCAL IGR

Not all local governments outside the U.S. have the same constitutional standing, that of being legally creatures of their second tier governments. While that indeed is the case with regard to several Western federal systems—Australia, Belgium, Canada, Germany, Switzerland—along with devolved Scotland and Northern Ireland, a more unitary pattern places local governments more directly as constituent units of their central governments, as in the case of the Netherlands, Italy, France, New Zealand, the three Scandinavian countries, and many Latin American countries. A third pattern, characteristic of Latin American federal systems—Argentina, Brazil, Mexico—and federalizing Spain, plus federal India and decentralized South Africa, follow a pattern known in Spain as *bifronte*, where local governments are duly dependent on national and intermediate governments in both a constitutional and legal sense (Allocation of Powers Project, 2010, Ch. VIII). For example, South Africa's constitution contains detailed local government provisions despite the fact they are operated as units of their provinces (Steytler, 2007). In small countries, Steytler (2009, 426) concludes that extensive supervisory powers are present, "… indicating the subordinate position of local governments."

To a certain degree these constitutional concerns help determine the main patterns of IGR within a country, with the historical and primary thrust of local government interactions going to the level that has the greatest influence in legal, political, fiscal, and policy senses over their collective fate. So for federal countries like Australia or Switzerland the focus is on the second level and such unitary countries as Sweden or France on the national level. However, patterns are in practice breaking down as IGR is intensified, for example as France now enhances regionalism and Australia's local governments are increasingly federally financed. In the actual practice of IGR, a much more mixed and often subtle system of interactions occurs. For example, in *bifronte* Spain local governments are constitutionally recognized as possessing autonomy and are entitled to funding for their assigned functions. This has led to basic national legislation regarding local functions and local financing whereas the second tier autonomous communities (ACs) have the broad and basic responsibilities for local government supervision and operation (Agranoff, 2010). In fact, more and more countries are moving to some form of mixed pattern of relationships in and around the legal standing of local governments. In this respect, eight cross-national trends that provide a broad context for understanding U.S. national–local IGR are identified.

Interdependence

The idea of independent and isolated operating governments at any level (once called dual federalism in the U.S.) is no doubt out of date everywhere. Ronald Watts (1999, 38) suggests that when it comes to the boundaries of governments there are no

watertight compartments. "Modern developments in transportation, social communications, technology, and industrial organization have produced pressure at one and the
same time for larger political organizations and smaller ones. . . " (4). Here he is referring
to the expanded scope of national governments while at the same time there is a push for
more self-rule/citizen involvement at the local level.

The prime twentieth-century trigger of interdependency was that of the welfare
state that linked local and central governments in "deep interdependency" (Flora and
Heidenheimer, 1981, 3). Loughlin (2007, 389) explains that the underlying logic of welfare
state subnational policy was the building up of the national polity. Regional and local governments were designed and encouraged to become agents of their central governments.
Most national government social policies (welfare, employment, social services, economic
development) were instituted polity-wide because central governments were suspicious
of local commitment. National programming and financing was coupled with local level
implementation. Central government programs were "parachuted" into local communities by legal requirement and/or financial inducement. In federal countries there were
the obligatory intermediate landings in state/provincial governments (Agranoff, 2007a).
Later in the period came new programs—substance abuse, child and family abuse, mental
disabilities, plus newer programs in economic and community development have brought
in the need for "important intergovernmental adjustments" (Ashford, 1988, 19).

The end result is overwhelming degrees of interdependence. A study of over 90 powers and competencies in 13 federal and unitary countries found that over two-thirds
were indeed mixed by levels. Indeed, the study found mixed patterns of involvement in
a number of areas beyond those of social welfare, employment, public security, tourism
and culture, environmental policy, and immigration (Argullol et al., 2004).

Whereas interdependence within countries was ushered in by growing and expanding social welfare states it is broadly sustained by national fiscal ties. As is the case with
regard to the U.S., spending for the "general welfare" has become a pattern for fostering subnational programs, including local, leading to ties where even constitutions have
divided them. In South Africa, regional and local governments are primarily funded
by the center (Wehner, 2003). Even in Canada, for example, where local governments
are exclusively under provincial powers the spending power involves federal payments
to individuals, institutions, and provincial governments in areas for which the national
parliament does not have the power to legislate (Watts, 1999, 1). It is used to influence
provinces, thus effectuating national purposes throughout the system. It is in this way
that governments at all levels have become increasingly dependent on one another as
exchanges occur over policy design and policy implementation, lubricated by the largely
downward flow of money.

Externalization, Governments, and Governance

Welfare state expansion beyond local governments coupled with international concerns
brought on by globalization has brought on a new era faced by virtually all IGR systems,

that of meeting those governance challenges presented by myriad outside organizations involved in the work of government. National–local programming has expanded to include a host of nongovernmental organizations (NGOs), particularly in the delivery of direct services. The primary vehicle everywhere has been through externalization, particularly through the contract for services. This has brought NGOs into the scheme of government programming at the local level and into the policy stream at the national level as their interests are advanced by national associations (Salamon, 1995). Everywhere nonprofit and for-profit NGOs have become governments for hire (Smith and Lipsky, 1993). In India, for example, federal and state departments concerned with rural development programs (agriculture, health, education, social welfare), are setting up parastatal bodies at the district level. They are registered societies funded and sponsored by and supervised by government agencies as a core element in devolution (Mathew and Hooja, 2009, 194–5). Meanwhile, local and second tier governments are becoming more active on the international scene through a variety of transborder activities, from trade missions and offices in foreign countries to participation as constituent units in cross-national bodies such as the European Union (EU). Involvement in supranational bodies means an entire new set of IGR connections, both within country processes and on the larger scene, for subnational governments (e.g., Closa and Heywood, 2004, 61). For local governments, the EU has also meant new sources of intergovernmental funds, for example EU structural funds for infrastructure, along with a set of supranational regulations (e.g., in urban waste water, landfills, procurement, working hours, environmental impact) that now impact management (Callanan, 2003).

The result is that local governments in most countries are also bound up into systems of governance, a concept captured by Kooiman (2003, 3) as involving public as well as private "governors."

> The essence of the argument is that governance of and in modern societies is a mix of all kinds of governing efforts by all manner of social-political actors, public as well as private; occurring between them at different levels, in different governance modes and orders. These mixes are societal "responses" to persistent and changing governing "demands," set against ever growing societal diversity, dynamics and complexity. Governing issues generally are not just public or private, they are frequently shared, and governing activity at all levels (from local to supra-national) is becoming diffused over various societal actors whose relationships with each other are constantly changing. There has, judged against traditional public governing activities, been an increase in the role of government as facilitator and as co-operating partner. As such it is more appropriate to speak of shifting than of shrinking roles of the state.

The governance phenomenon is one faced by governments in most countries, shifting the effective boundaries outside of the formal confines of local governments, for example with contracts with some agencies for human services delivery, partnerships with business associations for economic development, monitoring of the environment with green organizations, and working with neighborhood associations in planning. Meanwhile, international norms of gender equity, racial nondiscrimination, immigrant settlement, and human rights impact national to local operations. In this sense, IGR have now become considerably more than "governmental."

Municipal Influence

The growth of interdependence and the dynamics of governance has led "impacted" local governments to become more active on their national scenes. The pattern of growth of Washington, DC, representation by U.S. local government associations (Haider, 1974) is well known. In other countries the pattern is much broader and has been set for some time. For example, in much of northern Europe large national interest groups of local authorities are active, through which issues of central–local concerns are advanced and directly negotiated with central governments. In South Africa the nine largest municipalities have joined forces in the South African Cities Network to advocate for more powers and to reduce the influence of provinces over them (deVisser, 2009). These include employee unions and associations of local authorities. In southern Europe a similar pattern of more direct contact of local to central elites (Page and Goldsmith, 1987, 160; see also, Leuprecht and Lazar, 2007). In France, of course, many leading figures in national politics can also be local government leaders—particularly mayors—because more than one mandate can be simultaneously held. In Spain and in Mexico (Agranoff, 2007; Rowland, 2007) multiple channels of political linkage exist, through a national and regional local government associations, political party channels, direct contacts, and by local government representatives holding seats on statutory intergovernmental bodies. The latter pattern is most significant in Australia, where the head of the Australian Local Government Association has a seat at the all-important first ministers body, the Council of Australian Governments. This follows a general pattern in Australia of emphasis on formal mechanisms of IGR that include local input into intergovernmental ministerial councils and joint national-state agency bodies (Brown, 2007, 101). Also of IGR importance are national associations of local officials, mayors, financial officers, city engineers, city health officials, city legal counsel, social services directors, human resource directors, and so on.

The multi-country importance of national representation clearly follows the premise that global forces and national level programming, legal constraints, and funding roles, or some combination, penetrate local governments in degrees that they never have before. Involvement is greater than earlier days when a program "came down" with a program guide and a handful of funding proscriptions. Today in many countries programs are transmitted with detailed rules and regulations, standards and practices that must be followed, administrative orders, performance targets, and audit requirements. This means that local governments are more than funded. Today they are vested in national expectations that programmatically tie them and make them part of the policy machine, so to speak. It is no wonder that local governments seek to work with and to influence national governments.

Mobility

National officials frequently come to their capitals with experiences in local government. France is the champion in this regard, since the accumulation of mandates as stated means that parliamentarians can be cabinet ministers and most often simultaneously local mayors. Brunet-Jailly (2007, 139) refers to the practice of "officials getting elected locally and then protecting this mandate as their political "base camp" before they attempt to gain influence regionally and nationally." With the exception of Austria, which allows for limited double mandates, this is not possible in virtually every other country. Most limit mandates to one at a time. The political career path in Spain, for example, follows a familiar pattern of municipal councilor first, perhaps then mayor, then AC or national parliament, and onto a cabinet or subcabinet post. That means the first two rungs of the office-holding ladder involve local government in some way. Moreover, local councilors and mayors are often also elected to their supra-municipal *diputación* council, where they learn to advocate for their municipality and deal with regional issues. As a local councilor in the majority party or coalition, one administratively heads a department, for example finance, public works, environment, or culture and tourism (Agranoff, 2010, Ch. 4), adding day-to-day intergovernmental management experience. In addition, local government associations attempt to place key local leaders and administrators who are favorable to their interests in national policymaking and administrative positions. All of this builds local government understanding and experience that can be carried to higher levels of governmental involvement, and also that provides potential essential linkage wherever policy and administration affecting local governments is considered. This is a pattern that is true beyond Spain and the U.S., Argentina, Australia, Canada, Belgium, Mexico, Brazil, Ireland, Portugal, and the Netherlands.

National Experience at the Local Level

There is another side to the coin of moving national programs out to local governments. In most countries with interdependent programming local elected officials and administrators develop direct experience in implementing national programs. For example, in Spain policing and traffic control remain national–local administrative concerns. Most countries have national programs for the preservation of historic sites and communities that protect important buildings from indiscriminate demolition or use and offer support for preservation and contemporary use. These programs have numerous rules and procedures attached to them, from initial archaeological surveys to latter stage rules of signage and public use. Virtually every European country has such national programs, rules, procedures, etc. It means that local officials learn how to implement national programs, since few of these programs are ever carried out by some arm of "state administration" (which, incidentally, is not the case with respect to many post-Soviet countries). In carrying out national programs locally, the local government official becomes part agent of the national government while remaining as official and/or employee of the local government. It means that national and local interests must be balanced if there happens to be a conflict. More importantly, it is a binding tie between the levels. The same implementing binding ties occur in many countries with regard to employment, environment, education, housing, and citizen participation programs.

National Regulation

The level of national to local regulations identified earlier with regard to the U.S. is happening virtually everywhere. Most local government regulation in Canada is provincial based, "But when the federal government signs agreements with municipalities, there are arrangements for financial and managerial accountability. These can be quite complex..." (Young, 2009, 119). In the EU there is also the imposition of Europe-wide policies and attending regulations. For example, over a period of years labor market policy in the EU expanded from worker health and safety to working hours and overtime, to labor contract protection, to worker rights, to salary and benefits (Gallego, Gomá y Subirats, 2003, 29). These regulations have been put in each EU country's legal code and now impact a variety of practices that local governments are obliged to follow. Non-EU countries have also adopted similar labor market regulations, along with standards for anticorruption, purchasing, contracting for services, disability access, recycling and reuse, all of which have IGR implications.

Virtually everywhere in the world local governments have become involuntary regulatory agents for their national governments. They are subject to the directives that follow regulations. Local governments and their advocates in most countries are concerned about the erosion of their local autonomy, particularly by assigning of more responsibilities by superior orders, without necessarily additional funding (Steytler, 2009, 433). Additionally, where the second tier government is the constitutionally controlling agent they almost automatically add such regulations to their code. No matter how they come down, local governments normally have to designate a person to be in charge of each set of regulatory/services provisions. They may also have to educate local contractors and employers and the general public about applicable regulatory programs, conduct program audits of compliance, and deal with any potential legal challenges. In the U.S. these practices are called "unfunded mandates." In most other countries they are regarded as orders or directives inasmuch compliance is not a matter of choice but one of national policy. In terms of IGR, however involuntary, it is another form of national–local connection.

Revenue Dependence

One reason why regulations are considered to be simply directives in most countries is because most often they implicitly follow the flow of revenue downward to local governments, whether stipulated or discretionary. To a considerable extent, financial autonomy determines whether a local government can be seen as a distinct order of government and a true partner, concludes Steytler (2009, 419), whereas overreliance on transfers from other levels results in local governments' fiscal dependency and policy subservience. Everywhere local government revenue dependence to a high degree on their centers is the norm, even in more compartmentalized Belgium or Canada. Actually at the extreme is Australia, where local governments are highly own source funded out of local property taxes, but are also dependent on transfers. All transfers in Australia are federal, inasmuch as all income taxes are collected by the Commonwealth. Local governments receive funds from general Financial Assistance Grants, local government bloc grants, and through road grants. In addition, targeted grants from the Commonwealth also flow through the states to municipalities for social services, child care, elderly and disability programs, and native programs (Brown, 2007, 106–7). At the other end of the spectrum is that of Switzerland, where municipalities have income and property tax capacities and just over 80 percent of their revenues are own source, with most transfers coming from the cantons (Bachtinger and Hitz, 2007, 77).

The national fiscal dependency picture for other countries falls somewhere between these extremes; unfortunately, better data are available for federal than for those of unitary countries. Moreover, subnational data tend to be lumped together. Nevertheless the picture is clear. Watts (1999b, 52–3) reports that federal government revenues as a percentage of total revenues range from a low of 48 percent in Canada and Switzerland to a high of 87 percent in Malaysia and Spain. Australia is at 74 percent of revenues and the U.S. is at 65 percent. Subnational governments, both second tier and local governments, receive 72 percent in transfers in Spain (where constitutionally all taxes must be ceded from the center), 40 percent in Australia, 30 percent in the U.S., 20 percent in Canada, and 19 percent in Switzerland.

More detailed local transfer data are available for Spain where second tier ACs are almost exclusively financed by national transfers (except for a few ceded taxes/tax sharings). Among the 17 ACs, the range is considerable from a low of 12.3 percent in Valencia of AC revenues transferred to local governments to a high 74 percent in the Canaries and 52 percent in Navarra (where the provincial and AC governments are merged and a special tax sharing regime exists). The typical region transfers from about 25 percent to 40 percent of its revenues to local governments (Ramos y Cicuéndez, 2005). Likewise in South Africa the tax allocation breakdown in 2003–2004 was 40 percent national, 56.7 percent provincial, and 3.3 percent local (Wehner, 2003, 24) but the local transfer is deceiving because most provincial revenues (80 percent) were dedicated or retransferred to obligated services delivered within local governments for education, health, welfare, and social services (Wehner, 2003, 9).

While the data are clearly not sterling, the picture of vertical fiscal imbalance is clear. Local governments everywhere raise substantial shares of their own revenues but they remain highly dependent on transfers, particularly national transfers to meet their own obligations as well as those imposed by higher levels. German cities, with the exception of the three city-states, account for two-thirds of public investments but are highly controlled. One official of the German Association of Cities compared them to branches of a head office that dictates most spending and provides or regulates most revenue, deciding little themselves (*Economist*, 2011b, 54). Likewise in Canada municipalities lack money and power, "going cap-in-hand to the provincial and federal governments for money for capital projects" (*Economist*, 2011a, 42). One Spanish city councilor of public works put it to the author simply regarding why they contact AC and central governments, "We go for permission and for money." One clear conclusion is that the greater the centralization of tax powers and reliance on transfers the greater degree of control through what has been called "consumption federalism" (Solé-Vilanova, 1990, 351).

Urban Policy Challenges

Local governments everywhere need national partnerships and are facing the challenges of meeting social problems that are manifested within their space but exist due to forces not completely in their control. The highly urban located problems of structural unemployment, substance abuse, the impact of crime, homelessness/substandard housing, immigration integration, and environmental challenges come immediately to mind. This is an arena where the local political influence on the national scene is clearly important. While more focused attention has been paid to these national–local urban concerns in the U.S. (Cleveland, 1969; Baumgartner and Jones, 1993; Wolman, 1999; Kingdon, 2003; Lawrence, Stoker and Wolman, 2010), they are very real in numerous intergovernmental systems. One cross-national assessment of cities' multilevel systems reports that generally national local efforts are better at meeting local basic needs than at attacking such policy challenges (Lazar and Leuprecht, 2007).

Given the "junior partnership" status of most local government systems this is a difficult challenge. Where the locals are more effective in multi-sphere governance, for example Switzerland and France "are the ones where local influence on national policy-making and implementation is most substantial. Specifically, local governments in these two countries appear to have a greater voice in making national policies that affect them than the other studied six do" (Lazar and Leuprecht, 2007, 12). At the more negative end of the spectrum were Mexico and South Africa, both emerging from hegemonic party systems; Mexico demonstrates the reality of government failures, most prominently at the municipal level (Grindle, 2007) in such key issues as poverty reduction, crime control, and environmental protection. In South Africa national municipal policy is reported as over-regulating local government, a complex and burdensome yoke that makes attacking problems near impossible (Steytler, 2007). Somewhere in the middle stands the U.S., where big cities have given way in importance to suburbs and smaller places, and Australia, Germany, and Spain, where city agendas have come and gone depending on the politics of the ruling party and fiscal conditions. In Germany, for example, where local governments have a dual role in self-government and as delivery agents for upper tiers of government, "the leeway granted to local politics in Germany's federal order remains very limited" (Lazar and Leuprecht, 2007, 13).

In a sense this cross-national pattern ends where the assessment began, that of interdependence. Given the "subordinate" constitutional and legal status of local governments in most systems of governing, and their relatively weak political positions vis-à-vis second level governments, along with fiscal dependence, means that breaking through and shaping urban agendas become problematic. Their dependence nevertheless provides few alternatives.

Distinguishing Features of U.S. National and Local Relations

The focus returns to those key features that help define U.S. national–local relations. The analysis ranges from their jurisdictional embeddedness and the legal position of all governments in the U.S. to some of the more political aspects of federal–local IGR.

Nonhierarchical Embeddedness

Local governments in the U.S. are situated with other local governments "horizontally" and with state and federal governments "vertically." A municipality sits within a county government, with few exceptions such as merged city–county Virginia or when combined with a large city like St. Louis, Philadelphia, or San Francisco. Also within the territory are likely to be several special districts, from the most familiar school district to perhaps a mosquito control authority. Stephens and Wikstrom (2007, 25) report that in addition to the national and 56 state, territories, commonwealth and District of Columbia governments there were (at the time of Census) 3,034 counties, 19,424 municipalities, 16,504 township governments, 30,052 special districts, and 13,506 school districts independent of their local governments, plus 1,508 dependent school districts. The distribution and types of special districts, as well as the reasons for their growth, are accounted for in a study by Stephens and Wikstrom (1998). This count would not include other local special arrangements such as business improvement districts, municipal housing authorities, separately incorporated local government run utilities, tax increment financing districts, enterprise zones, and many substate areas created by national and state authorities, for example transportation metropolitan planning organizations (MPOs) or community college districts. It is a complex picture indeed. That is not the issue here. It is that any given local government, for example a municipality, is embedded within a complex of other government arrangements, a special arrangement or more, one to several special districts and federal and state configurations, a county, a state, and the federal government. Moreover, these relationships while clearly influenced and even regulated externally do not exist in a hierarchical fashion. It is more of a "coexistent" nature often requiring coordination or collaboration.

One of the earliest to make this observation of jurisdictional independence was Goodnow (1900), who indicated that unlike the British system, where officials were appointed by and responsible to the crown, the American system of popular control and popular elections removed the hierarchical notion. Here he refers to state–local actions, "The result was to make impossible any state administrative supervision over the main body of officers entrusted with the execution of the law. All of the control which could be exercised in the governmental system in the interest of producing coordination between the functions of expressing and executing the will of the state had to be found in the power of the legislature to regulate in detail the duties of officers entrusted of the law" (101). Short of such compliance the courts were the venue of next resort. From this logic in three editions of *American Federalism, A View from the States*, Elazar (1984) observed that the system is non-centralized, with constitutional diffusion and sharing of powers among many centers. Jurisdictions possess sufficient legal, fiscal, and political independence so that official status notwithstanding, in the case of state–local relations, governments operate or have the potential to operate independently on their own behalf. It leads to what Anderson (1960, 3) identifies as a fundamental IGR issue,

> Underlying the concept of intergovernmental relations is the fact that the nation as a whole, each one of the States, and every county, town, city, village, school district, and other special district or local unit is a territorial and corporate or quasi-corporate entity that has a legal existence, rights, functions, powers, and duties within its territory, distinct from those of every other such unit. This is true even though the similar units are generally embraced geographically within the larger ones. Being all separate legal entities, they are all capable of legal and other relations with each other.

It means that each government jurisdiction is non-hierarchically embedded, adding not only to the tremendous scope and complexity of IGR but putting an added burden on the cooperative aspects of connecting governments.

Constitutional Non-Recognition

It is well known that local governments are not mentioned in the U.S. Constitution. That document was designed to address the countrywide deficiencies of the Articles of Confederation by creating two levels that could both act directly on behalf of the people. Local governments and their charters were assumed to be part of the reserved powers of the states that reach back to the earliest colonial days when counties and municipalities were recognized by the states. For example, the General Laws of New Hampshire in 1680 included the right of the Assembly to confirm "all land, Townships, Town grants, with (sic) all other grants lying with the limits of this Province" (quoted in Lutz, 1998, 16). Special district governments go back to the same time, as colonial governments chartered public and private corporations to provide goods and services beyond municipal capability, for example roads, bridges, canals, and harbors (Foster, 1997). Also, in the late eighteenth century, there was no active concept of IGR, nor were national–local relations of mainline concern. This situation clearly reinforces the junior partnership position of local governments, if for no other reason than they are in a weak political position as local governments are constitutionally recognized as parts of the states.

In terms of the legal system this situation has reinforced the state–local relationship yet has not made federal courts reluctant to enter into the realm of local concerns when federal constitutional issues are at stake. While cities have long attempted to seek Supreme Court protection from state action, in *Hunter* vs. *Pittsburgh* (1907) the court reinforced the legal idea of cities as "political subdivisions of the state created as convenient agencies for exercising such of the governmental powers of the State as may be entrusted to them" (178). This, along with the famous "Dillon's Rule" decision (*City of Clinton* vs. *the Cedar Rapids and Missouri River Railroad*, 1868) that prohibited local implied powers and limited local powers to only those ascribed by states has stood, notwithstanding state grants of home rule, the latter being restricted to specific powers, which in practice states constantly erode.

Despite state protection the U.S. Supreme Court has upheld controls on local governments, usually regarding them within the context of state actions. For example, since the 1970s state and local officials are liable to federal prosecution for bribery, mail fraud, and extortion. Unlike states, cities are subject to federal antitrust laws, have no immunity under the Eleventh Amendment, and are liable for damages under constitutional violations. On the other hand, the Court has upheld the principle of "local control" in several cases involving school financing, desegregation of schools, exclusionary zoning ordinances in cases of non-racial discrimination, local domiciliary arrangements and restrictions, adult movie theater locations (Frug, 2005, 656). The most famous and controversial local control case was *Kelo* vs. *City of New London* (2005), where the highest federal court decided to uphold a city's eminent domain power, taking property for a development. It held that "there is no basis for exempting economic development from our traditionally broad understanding of public purpose" (125 S. Ct. 2655 [2005] p. 2665). Kelo reinforces the idea that local control is to be federally sustained. With the exception of such constitutional issues, local governments remain under the umbrella of the states.

State Subordination

With the exception of federal questions the principle of Dillon's Rule holds in a constitutional and legal sense. There being no inherent right of local self-government in common law, local governments are at the constitutional discretion of their state governments. Early state constitutions recognized but did not define either the structure or powers of local governments, but in the nineteenth century state legislatures expanded their powers in this area as local governments came to be understood as entities whose powers were derived from state legislatures. State constitutions authorized local government codes that prescribed all manners of organization, taxation, and operation. And up to the present only a few state constitutions "have altogether reversed Dillon's Rule, authorizing local governments to tax, regulate, and otherwise deal with matters of local concern, unless specifically prohibited by statute" (Tarr, 1998, 20).

During the twentieth century the states moved from more remote regulation of local governments to the current situation of more detailed operational supervision. In the words of historian Jon Teaford (2002, 6–7),

> As policymakers curbed the authority of local, partisan amateurs and moved responsibility up the governmental ladder to state capitals, they greatly expanded the role of the state. This shift from delegation to control was a notable theme in the history of twentieth-century state government. In the nineteenth century, state legislatures authorized townships, counties, cities, school districts, business corporations, and trustees of educational and charitable institutions to take action and exercised little supervision or control. In the twentieth century, state governments increasingly intervened and often took direct charge. Local road supervisors, township assessors, one-room-school districts, and justices of the peace untutored in the law were no longer thought adequate, and the states transferred the construction and maintenance of highways to professionals in state highway departments, assumed a larger share of the responsibility for levying and collecting taxes, shouldered a growing portion of school expenses while also imposing professional educational standards on local districts, and fixed higher professional standards for local jurists.

Local discretionary authority under home rule and other provisions nonetheless varies considerably from state to state (Zimmerman, 1995, 40–3). Local governments, however, are now less controlled by several means, special constitutional provisions, requests for special legislative action on behalf of groups of local governments, restrictions on forms of local government, and special tax authorizations. The overall trend, argues Zimmerman, is toward states opening up arenas of discretionary authority while increasing financial burdens imposed in the form of mandates and restraints (29).

Representation

Unlike the states, which have the U.S. Senate as a body of equal national representation, local governments do not have any formal means of Congressional delegation. While the U.S. Senate has become much more than a body representing states, as constituent units of the federal system states have formal representation whereas local governments do not. This gives states and their governors considerable advantage over local government interests. Federal allocative programs tend to be channeled through the states. "The federal government deals with the states from the perspective of structure, potential federal influence and leverage, accountability and tradition" (Haider, 1974: 225). As a result, most categorical grant programs, even for localities, have gone through the states.

Representation of cities in the House and Congress as a whole is subject to shifting political influence with populations. Central city voters have steadily declined as a percentage of the electorate. At the peak in 1944 over one quarter of the electorate resided in the core cities of the 32 largest metropolitan areas; by 1992 this figure had declined to 14 percent of the national vote. Cities like New York declined from 51 percent of state voters in 1940 to 31 percent in 1992. Similar figures for the same period include Chicago, which declined from 47 to 21 percent, St. Louis from 22 percent to less than 6 percent, and Philadelphia from 21 to 14 percent. Population has shifted to the suburbs and small towns in metropolitan corridors. In the 1990s Congress shifted as a result, from 98 central city districts to 84 while majority suburban districts grew from 94 in the 1940s to 214. In 1994 when the Republicans captured the House, the proportion of central city leadership positions fell from 30 percent to 10 percent. In fact, the only central cities that gained any population to speak of were coastal cities that experienced a flood of immigration (reported in Judd and Swanstrom, 1998, 248). This means that any sort of urban agenda or decline in focused city programs could well be losing political support. That indeed has been upheld by one study of urban research that found it "politically imprudent to explicitly identify problems as "urban" or "city" problems" (Lawrence, Stoker and Wolman 2010, 427). Also, it has meant that many programs that ultimately are designed for primary implementation in local governments involve a prior state government pass-through and administration, such as the Small Cities CDBG and urban transportation programs mentioned.

Federal Links

If local governments are considered to be instruments of state governments what ties them to the federal government? The role of the federal courts in regard to upholding local control has already been identified. The federal government has additionally been able to reach into several areas of local government by extension of its powers over the states, particularly through six identifiable means. First, is broad use of the Constitution under the commerce power. Second, is through federal implied powers under the "necessary and proper" clause since *McCullough* vs. *Maryland* (17 US 14 Wheat 316 1819). Third, is extension of the Fourteenth Amendment, which forbids states to deny equal protection of the law, to include actions of local governments. Fourth, are other constitutional provisions, such as the requirement of just compensation for expropriation of property by eminent domain. Fifth, are actions of Congress in responding to constituent needs and pressures, ranging from grants and loans to build public infrastructure to drinking water quality standards. Sixth, and finally, is actions of the federal executive branch in linking state and local functions to the federal government, such as the 2001 Bush administration move that changed state and local emergency response powers, in effect "federalizing" emergency management responsibilities. In effect, these forces have led to federal "leapfrogging" of state responsibilities by reaching directly into local action.

Weak Party Ties

Local–national party ties in the U.S. are relatively weak intergovernmental instruments compared to those of other countries. For decades in federal Mexico among the most important, if not the most important, ties were from local (and state) officials who were linked to the president through the ruling Institutional Revolutionary Party (PRI). Today the PRI alternates in power more often with the National Action Party (PAN) but the party links are real through both parties. The situation is similar in France, Germany, and Spain. In the last country the two major state parties, Popular Party (PP) and the Socialist Workers (PSOE), prove to be important vehicles of national–local interaction, through networks of officials who work their way from local to AC to national politics. Local officials tend to weave themselves into higher levels spheres of influence for securing contracts, land use permits, and social benefits, putting in an *enchufe* (literally plug, electric outlet), taking advantage of loyalty and support. Disciplined parties follow a well-known PSOE saying, "*El que se mueva no sale en la photo*" or "Whoever moves will be out of the picture."

These tendencies do not hold as tightly in the U.S. At one time a few big city mayors did hold considerable sway if their party was the same as that of the president and presidential candidates, particularly when state electoral votes were at stake, but the decline of central cities has already been noted. More important in this regard is that political parties are no longer as organizationally disciplined at either state or national levels as they once might have been. The party ties from local to national government may be existent but compared to other linking efforts, for example direct government-to-government contacts, or elite to congressional contacts without regard to party, or through association lobbying, the party channel is not as intergovernmentally significant in the U.S. compared to other countries.

The Local Power of Bargaining/End Stage Implementation

The research literature on grants management offers important insights into the fact that despite legal dependence and lack of political party power local governments have important IGR "weapons" as the "independent operating" end stage of program implementation. This concept emanated from research on grants bargaining. Jeffrey Pressman (1975) initially captured interaction of this type in his study of federal aid to cities. He reminded us that "donor and recipient need each other, but neither has the ability to control fully the actions of the other. Thus, the aid process takes the form of bargaining between partly cooperative, partly antagonistic, and mutually dependent sets of actors" (1975, 106–7). Helen Ingram's (1977) study of environmental grants concluded that programs are not necessarily instruments of federal control but, rather, opportunities to bargain. Similarly, Liebschutz (1991) depicts an intergovernmental fiscal system in New York as one defined by bargaining and negotiation. Whereas federal officials would like to bind state and local program managers to federal policy, subnational governments seek the maximum possible leeway to pursue their own separate goals and objectives with federal help. In social services programs, as Richard Elmore concludes, "this give and take has become a managerial strategy in the implementation process. [The] bargain is a two-way affair, inherently different from hierarchical control. A grant or contract is not an instrument of coercion (1985, 36)." It is a managerial game that, according to Walter Williams" study of manpower and community development, "requires... subtle skill and much knowledge about the roles, the players, and available strategies in the federal–local bargaining situation" (1981, 197).

In recognition of the importance of such local-national give and take, Morton Grodzins concluded that,

> ... the grant-in-aid technique does not tell the whole story; but it tells a good part of it. It is a story of growing expertise; growing professionalization, growing complexities; it is a story most of all, of an ever-increasing measure of contact between officials of the several levels of government within the federal system. Contact points bring some disagreements and produce misunderstanding and some enmity. But most of all, they have produced cooperation, collaboration, and effectiveness in programming and steering the multiple programs of modern government. (1966, 373)

What this means is that local governments are far from mere subordinates when it comes to national programming. Agranoff and McGuire (2003, 70) found some 20 different means of local–federal action that included not only bargaining but information exchanges, regulatory adjustment and negotiation, pursuit of waivers, experimental programming and many others. Clearly, the local government is not powerless with regard to dealing with federal efforts within their midst.

The position of local governments vis-à-vis the federal government is therefore neither non-existent as the Constitution silence might imply nor totally subordinate. Despite increasing constraints associated with legal funding requirements and regulations, locals retain measures of self-rule and are in substantial control over the implementation stages of programs. Local governments have the shared rule capacity to exercise their self-rule position to negotiate and cooperate with federal officials.

Local–National, National–local Interactions

Interaction between local and national governments is not as frequent as they were in the heyday of federal grants to local governments. From the 1930s until the 1980s a plethora of different funding opportunities meant that there was a constant stream of federal government activities, particularly by cities and counties. A number of city governments assigned staff to look for opportunities and orchestrate numerous applications for funding. For example, in the 1960s one small-town mayor attracted more than $16 million in project grants, loans, and credit buy-downs during a 10-year period. His success was said to be related to his regular reading of the *Catalogue of Federal Domestic Assistance*, to his working with a series of local advisory committees, and to his personally filling out applications and working with many federal officials (Hale and Palley, 1981).

Starting in the 1980s many of these programs were reduced, eliminated, or turned over to the states. By the late 1990s, research indicated that city governments turned more to their state governments, for example with regard to economic development (Agranoff and McGuire, 2003, 168). Nevertheless local–federal contact continues through various forms of interaction outlined in this section, interest groups devoted to local government concerns, interactions of national programs in local governments, continued use of grants/contracts and other tools of governance, administrator to administrator contacts, enlistment of the federal government in packaged programs, and through a variety of local collaborative efforts (e.g., MPOs in transportation) that include federal officials (Agranoff, 2012).

Local Lobbying

As important focal points in the federal system local governments work within their communities with citizens and groups and with state and federal officials in an advocacy or lobbying capacity. Daniel Elazar (1961, 24–8) once identified five roles that relate to local lobbying, 1) acquirer of external aid for local needs; 2) adapter of government functions and services to local conditions; 3) experimenter with new functions and services (or new versions of traditional ones); 4) initiator of governmental programs that spread across state and nation; and 5) underlying the others, provider of a means by which a local community can pay the "ante" necessary to "sit in the game," that is, to secure an effective voice in governmental decisions of local impact.

The first of these, aid acquisition, is perhaps the one that comes to mind to most people, but in reality unless local officials are strict compliers virtually all local governments make program adaptations as they carry a program out in their jurisdiction, and/or the attempt to make adjustments to suit local needs by negotiating. Also, some local governments have well worked-out strategies that are then employed to fit federal programs into their plan of action. Research by Agranoff and McGuire (2003, Ch. 3) has identified several of these intergovernmental strategies in their 237 city study, strategic or jurisdiction-based, top-down compliance, donor–recipient bargaining, abstinence, and others.

Local governments, particularly large cities and counties, also have a lobbying presence in Washington, DC, and also before federal offices located around the country. Cincinnati, Ohio, is a very active city with regard to federal activity. It maintains lobbyists in Columbus, Ohio, the state capitol, where many federal field offices are also located, and has a lobbyist on retainer in Washington, DC. At one time it also had a city representation office in Washington that it shared with other city governments, but now places more focus on the state capitol, a one-hour car trip from Cincinnati. It nevertheless is in regular email contact with federal offices, its department heads about once or twice a week, and from the City Manager's office several times daily. All of this is to support an active intergovernmental program based on council-adopted policy and to pursue funding opportunities and to negotiate its regulatory obligations (Agranoff and McGuire, 2003, 10–11). This is not an unusual pattern for large cities in the U.S.

Jurisdictional lobbying may also include more than opening up an office in Washington. It can include contacts with trade and/or professional associations among the large number of functional associations in Washington, establishing federal program coordinators, that is home-based intergovernmental contact/programming offices within the local government, and hiring consultants, public relations specialists, lawyers, or lobbyists to pursue specific interests or programs. All of this is to keep on top of the heavy linkages that develop by groups and federal administrative personnel who work outside of the legislative process. Haider (1974, 88) observes,

> One consequence of increased federal activity has been the delegation of discretionary rule-making authority to federal administrative agencies whose impact upon intergovernmental relations is nearly as great as formal legislative and judicial interpretation. Another consequence, directly related to the first, is the growth of government interest groups, elected, appointed, civil service, union, and professional associations. The latter groups—professional associations—have grown at a tremendous rate, extending into health, education, highways, public works, welfare, urban renewal, housing, and other areas. Close links have emerged between the professional associations, from whose ranks bureaucratic agencies are often staffed and dominant work force is drawn, throughout government levels. These associations often exhibit strong unity formed by training, skills, and professional concepts of status and autonomy. They constitute almost a private form of government the consequences of which are not readily appreciated, with the added importance of setting detailed standards for day-to-day operations of intergovernmental programs.

In this sense traditional lobbying, that is legislative contact, is extended considerably far beyond enactment stages to extensive and involved administrative agency–group interactions.

Interest Associations

Haider's (1974) book on governmental representation in Washington by associations referred to this process as involving vital and vibrant partners in the governmental process. Moreover, he maintains that groups that represent governments have greater legitimacy than other interest groups who represent narrower and special interests. As associations of elected officials Cammissa (1995, 16) concludes, "There exists a level of understanding between members of Congress and the government groups that is not present with other groups. The government groups are lobbyists who themselves have been lobbied, and this gives them special status..."

Five generalist groups stand out in this regard. First, is the United States Conference on Mayors (USCM), which represents large cities. Second, is the National League of Cities (NLC), which focuses more on the medium and small cities. Third, is the National Association of Counties (NACo), which represents rural, suburban, and urban counties. Fourth, is the International City and County Managers' Association (ICMA), which does not formally lobby but takes positions that affect its council-manager members and link up in a number of non-advocacy ways with other local government groups. Fifth, is the less visible National Association of Towns and Townships (NATaT), representing the thousands of small governments, particularly state township associations. Other groups that can be mentioned are the National Civic League (once called the National Municipal League), dating back to the nineteenth century, that promotes citizen involvement in local government, and the National Association of Regional Councils, representing metropolitan areas. Together those groups are called public interest groups (PIGs) because they not only represent generalists in government but their members claim to represent the interests of all of their citizens, adding a "spatial or areal dimension to the national decision-making process" (Cigler, 1995, 138).

These groups, to varying degrees, are involved in what Menzel (1990, 401–3) calls "collecting, conveying and convincing." In other words, their functions include organizing and conducting research on national–local problems and fostering knowledge networks. It also involves preparing numerous reports and written materials to convey to their members, legislators, the media, and to the general public. Indeed, much of group effectiveness, according to Haider (1974, 286), is an outgrowth of their information and feedback functions, as they provide officials with information and research related to operational problems, management concerns and perceived defects in federal programs. Moreover, policy specialization and expertise enables these groups to participate in drafting and amending legislation, pre-legislative clearance, and post-legislative rule making.

Lobbying by USCM, NLC, NACo, and NATaT is based on policy statements that are periodically reviewed and modified, which articulate association policy goals and serve as a guide for their staff and key member representatives before legislative and administrative circles in Washington. The groups then track legislative proposals and monitor federal programs in the executive branch. One study of PIGs in the policymaking process rated the USCM and NLC in second and third place behind the National Governors' Association in overall influence by staff of Congress and association members. NLC and USCM have always had active and visible spokespersons, whereas NACO has not been as visible, perhaps because of the divisions of views among its members and its state associations (Cammisa, 1995, 120).

Functional specialist contacts between local and the federal governments increased from the 1930s to the 1960s and remain highly important today. These include a wide range of groups, for example city engineers and city attorneys, and county planning and county highway administrators. These groups can organize easily around their particular concerns and like the generalist groups provide technical and educational functions as well as lobbying. Beverly Cigler (1995, 140) relates how these groups tap into the system,

> The specialist associations fit well within the functional policy networks at the national level, sharing knowledge and interest with similar professionals at all governmental levels, as well as with nonprofit public interest groups that specialize in particular policy areas. The special associations work through vertical and horizontal ties within the political system, including those with private professional organizations. Because so much of their work is concentrated in large and medium-sized cities, they come in frequent contact with the generalist organizations.

A number of these groups are affiliated with the PIGs, particularly NACo, NLC, and NATaT.

Intergovernmental lobbying is reported by Cammissa's (1995) research to have changed with the decline in federal funding and shift in emphasis on the states beginning in the 1980s. Local groups now face federal deficits and cutbacks in funding, consolidation of some programs, while the Governors Association has been able to ride the tide of emphasis on the states and their experiences as experts in social programs. "The direct federal-city connection is loosened, and the local groups have less clout" (129).

In sum, intergovernmental groups representing local governments nevertheless enjoy recognition and a measure of public legitimacy which underpins their ability to influence policy. In particular, associations representing elected generalists appear legitimate as having the right to speak on behalf of their constituents. However, as claimants before the federal government, concludes Haider (1974, 256), "they have no real formal standing as federal actors." It is, he observes, a "certain political devaluation in transference" (Haider, 1974, 256).

National–State Programs Operating in Communities

In addition to federal programs that are designed for small local governments in community development, rural development, transportation, and housing (identified earlier), there are other programs that are organized state-wide but operate within local governments' jurisdictions. For example, the federal–state Main Street Program, which is actually run by the National Trust for Historic Preservation, assists communities in development and revitalization of downtowns, including technical support in organizational development, marketing activities, commercial business assistance, and historic center design improvements. Other rural programs are leadership development programs, designed to help small town elected officials and community leaders strategically plan and operate programs. These are federally funded through the Cooperative-Extension Services housed at land-grant universities.

Table 3.1   Tools of Governing, Federal–Local

Tool	Description	Hypothetical Example	Core/ Sponsor(s) Jurisdiction	Major Partners	Other Involved Organizations
Direct government service	Good or service by public agency	Jefferson County Public Health Department operates an inoculation program	County government	F/S/L	Schools, home nurses' association, other voluntary organizations
Regulation	Standard setting/ prohibition	Municipal clean drinking water standards	Federal government	F/S/L/NP/FP	Home owners, contractors, school districts, counties, other voluntary organizations
Grant	Award, cash payment	Small Cities Community Development Block Grants	Federal government block grant to states to locals	F/S/L	Business, housing, and local social service organizations
Contracting	Payment for goods or direct service delivered	Columbus, Ohio refuse collection and recycling pickup and disposal	Municipal government	S/L/FP/county waste district programs	Citizens neighborhood organizations, businesses, institutional clients
Direct loan	Cash for a project, normally at lower than market rates	Fillmore City, Nebraska borrows $950,000 to upgrade its water system	Federal government/ state government/ local	F/S/L/private lending institution	Business and homeowners through special assessments
Loan guarantee	Interest buy-down and backup of private loan	Oskaloosa, Iowa builds a new community center	Federal/ SBA/private lending institution	F/L/private lending institution	Business investors, community organizations, chamber of commerce, local economic development corporation
Insurance	Protection against unusual risk/cost	Federal-state-local unemployment insurance	Federal government/ state government/ local government	F/S/L/employers	State chambers of commerce, statewide business associations, local offices of state employment services, local governments

(Continued)

(Continued)

Tool	Description	Hypothetical Example	Core/ Sponsor(s) Jurisdiction	Major Partners	Other Involved Organizations
Tax expenditure	Cash incentives to encourage a project or program outside of government	Chico, California provides 15% of cost of new office complex in core of city using CDBG funds	City government/ state government/ county government/ private developers	F/S/L/private sector	Contractors, building materials companies, labor unions, Downtown Chico, Inc.
Fees, charges	Payment by renters of claimed housing	CDBG	Federal government/ local entitlement government	F/L industry	Local housing authority
Vouchers	Authorization for access to government goods or services	Food distribution	Federal government/ state governments/ local governments	F/S/L/food vendors	Local social welfare organizations, local case managers
Government corporations	Special government entity, normally for one purpose, quasi-public agency	Des Moines, Iowa Transit Authority	Special unit of local government under state government authority	F/S/L	Para-transit contractors, area planning agency, county governments, 13 municipal governments

Key: F=federal government; S=state government; L=local government; NP=non-profit; FP=for profit

Source: Adapted by author, based on Lester M. Salamon, *The Tools of Government* (New York: Oxford University Press, 2002) p. 21.

Every local government is potentially touched by the U.S. Department of Commerce's Small Business Administration (SBA). While it is organized by state offices, its local offices provide technical assistance and arrange for loan guarantees from private lending institutions. The former is provided by SBA-financed Small Business Development Centers (SBDC), often located in community colleges and universities where business plans and loan preparation "dry runs" help inexperienced prospective entrepreneurs. Many applicants seek a small portion of their funding from CDBGs or other governmental sources, which then contract with the SBDCs to make such loans, combining applicant money with technical assistance. Of course, such combined deals can also be brokered by local governments, again working with the SBDC (Fulton, 2010).

The SBA or Main Street stories are not the only federal programs that may fall into local jurisdictions. There are also job training programs, childcare and development programs, substance abuse programs, special needs transportation programs, and programs for the elderly and disabled that tend to be organized as federal–state programs but operate largely within local communities.

The Administrative Tools of Governmental Exchange

In a well-known volume edited by Salamon (2002, 19), he introduces a series of "tools or instruments" through which public purposes are pursued. They range considerably far beyond direct provision of services. As government programs have expanded so have the number of tools that establish interdependencies between public agencies and between governments and third-party actors. The tools and their definitions are identified in the first two columns of Table 3.1,

After each of the tools that Salamon identifies is named and explained in Table 3.1, a hypothetical example of each follows that has federal–local involvement in some way, the core sponsors of the example, the major intergovernmental partners, and other organizations that might possibly be involved. While the examples are hypothetical the programs are real and they cast important light on how administrators work with one another across the lines of government and governing. For example, under "direct loan" cities are eligible to upgrade or reach compliance in their water systems under the U.S. Clean Drinking Water Act. Federal loans are combined with state programs that in turn normally require a match from a local bank or lending institution. These project loans are paid by a combination of increased water fee structures and special local tax assessments, resulting in extensive citizen involvement; business, local lending institutions; local government (or quasi-government) water authority; state and federal governments. This pattern of collaboration and networking around the legal, technical, and financial aspects of projects is true with regard to the other 10 tools illustrated here, with its unique web of participants. These tools establish working interdependencies between government and nongovernment actors, giving rise to a variety of exchanges (Agranoff, 2007, 2012).

Administrative Intergovernmental Management

Earlier the strategies of local governments were identified as they operate in the intergovernmental arena, from non-involvement to extensive adjustment-seeking, on behalf of the local jurisdiction. These strategies, of course, involve specific tactics that local managers and officials use. In the 237 city study Agranoff and McGuire (2003) identified these as "collaborative activities" in as much as not all involve forms of lobbying or bargaining/negotiation, and a number are cooperative in nature. Local officials were asked to identify from a list of 20 the activities that had been undertaken by city staff in the prior two years, for purposes of facilitating local economic development. Table 3.2 lists all 20 from the study. They have been divided between vertical (federal–state) and horizontal (inter-local) and classified as being primarily information or adjustment-oriented for the vertical and policy, resource or project for the horizontal; each of the 20 are explained in detail in the original study (70–1).

The primary concern here is obviously with the vertical activities since they encompass the local–federal administrative connections. The study found that virtually all cities (86 percent) engaged in some form of information-seeking, engaging on average of 3.5 of the 10 tactics while 71 percent engaged in some form of adjustment-seeking, averaging 2.4 of the 10 tactics. Although the highest number of contacts was for general information, around two-thirds of the cities did seek new funding and around half sought regulatory relief or flexibility or some other change in policy (7). Most important for our purposes is that while state government contacts for this study were more prevalent than that of federal, from one-fourth to half of all cities were in some contact with the federal government (108). Interestingly, these contacts ranged over 10 federal agencies (103). Therefore the study indicated that far more than expected local–federal contact existed at the administrative level, and it involves a considerably broader range of tactical approaches than the IGR bargaining and negotiation literature might indicate.

Packaging Local Programs

Local governments often put together efforts that involve multiple jurisdictions and programs. This is particularly true with regard to urban renewal, downtown development, economic development, and rural community development. Normally this involves several local entities, government and nongovernmental, working together and engaging in many of the horizontal-based activities identified in Table 3.2, particularly joint policy and strategy-making, establishing formal partnerships, seeking financial resources, and contracting for planning and implementation. The latter two in particular are most likely to trigger local–federal contacts (Fosler, 1985).

Take the example of a small city wishing to expand its current industrial park. That effort would involve 11 major steps, land acquisition, site preparation, building construction, business attraction tax adjustments, water/infrastructure adjustments, human resource development, road improvements (including a U.S. highway), park operation, business attraction, moderate income housing (for employees), and computer literacy for new hires. There would be some federal involvement in most of these phases. For example, an EDA grant could be sought to help purchase the land, USDA/RD and EPA grants could finance the water/infrastructure improvements, workforce development funds could cover the training, Department of Transportation funds for the road improvements, U.S. SBA loans to start the new businesses or expand existing businesses, U.S. Housing and Urban Development money would cover senior housing, which then would free up other local housing fund commitments, and the literacy could be supported by a U.S. Department of Education grant. The interesting issue is

Table 3.2   Collaborative Management Activities

Vertical Activities	Type*	Horizontal Activities	Type*
Seek general program information	IS	Gain policymaking assistance	PM
Seek new funding of programs and projects	IS	Engage in formal partnerships	PM
Seek interpretation of standards and rules	IS	Engage in joint policymaking and strategy-making	PM
Seek general program guidance	IS	Consolidate policy effort	PM
Seek technical assistance	IS	Seek financial resources	RE
Regulatory relief, flexibility, or waiver	AS	Employ joint financial incentives	RE
Statutory relief or flexibility	AS	Contract for planning and implementation	RE
Request change in official policy	AS	Establish partnership for a project	PB
Seek funding innovation of existing program	AS	Seek technical assistance	PB
Request model program involvement	AS		
Request performance-based discretion	AS		

* IS = information seeking; AS = adjustment seeking; PM = policymaking and strategy-making; RE = resource exchange; PB = project based.

Source: Robert Agranoff and Michael McGuire, *Collaborative Public Management: New Strategies for Local Governments.* Washington, DC: Georgetown University Press, p. 69.

not so much the variety of federal agencies sought out but the number of local entities engaging the federal government—the city government for the land construction, the local economic development corporation for the park development and operation, the county housing authority for the senior construction, the local community college for human resource development and training, and private businesses for the SBA loans. Clearly, a single entity has to orchestrate the entire effort, which normally would be city government or the development corporation, inasmuch as the entire strategy can easily involve over 100 distinct agreements or approvals and funding requests and matching obligations (Agranoff, 2007, 277–8).

To the experienced mayor or manager, this example is no doubt a simplified overview of a real world project effort. Many missing elements, such as local street building, utilities hookups, environmental permitting, relocation costs and projects, workforce recruitment, noise regulation, increased police and fire services, and increased primary and secondary education implications have been overlooked. Each of these involves extensive leveraging after hundreds of consultations and some follow similar approval and funding processes and present other potential means of local–federal linkage. Such placed-based management of programs becomes an increasingly important aspect of federal contact.

Networks and Partnerships

Local and federal officials also connect through various forms of formal networks, partnerships, study groups, task forces, and the like. It has already been mentioned that the transportation MPOs involve federal officials from Department of Transportation sitting on their policy committees as *ex officio* members. In Ohio during the 2010 "bed bug flare-up" local, state, and federal officials formed a task force to deal with safe pesticide uses and prevention strategies. Several studies of networks and partnerships in the environmental arena point to the working involvement of federal officials in researching and solving problems (John 1994; Wondolleck and Yaffee 2000; Imperial 2004). Imperial's work indicates the important role that the U.S. Environmental Protection Agency, USDA Forest Service, the USDA Natural Resource Conservation Service, and the USDA Soil Conservation Service play in making estuary governance work (10–12). In the same way, Agranoff's (2007b) study (16–17) found active federal official involvement in 13 of the 14 networks he investigated in the environment, economic development, rural development, transportation, communication, and human services areas studied. Only in the transportation networks were federal (and state) officials *ex officio*. All of the others involved working partner and leadership roles by federal members, almost all of whom were located in federal offices organized at the state or regional level.

In these fast-paced days of overlapping interests the federal official is challenged to play a more active role than previously when after the fact a grant report review or post-audit was often sufficient. Along with local government officials, the federal (or state) official has important on-the-spot involvement and leadership roles to play, as Wondolleck and Yaffee (2000, 244) conclude,

> ...government agencies and institutions have a unique role and responsibility in these processes. While they should be capitalizing on opportunities to collaborate, they must recognize that they—and only they—are the final decision makers. Some argue that the role of agency participants in collaborative processes is solely as a facilitator of other participants' interactions. However, based on our review of successful

collaborative processes, it is clear that where a group succeeded and was held in high regard by the broader community, the agency did not step back into a purely facilitative role. Rather, it provided essential leadership that guided the group while simultaneously representing its own interests within the process. It ensured that the sideboards provided by existing law and regulation were in place and understood, and that those individuals present recognized that implementation of decisions could occur only through established administrative processes, including procedures for public review and comment. It took on the responsibility of ensuring the accountability of the process while still promoting collaborative interaction among multiple participants.

Although not all government officials as collaborating partners or network members are active in these respects they are increasingly challenged to move to the core of collaboration in this way.

For the local official the opportunity to work in tandem with federal representatives in the field provides another means of access to federal processes. Local government officials who do sit elbow-to-elbow with feds at the table are able to ask questions that are related to their concerns before and after meetings or by telephone or email. They also find that when other local officials find out they have direct access to federal officials through collaboration they try to approach their colleagues who have this direct access. Perhaps most important, it is an opportunity for local–federal give and take, so to speak, as concerns on both sides are exchanged and applied to specific problems. It has become an important vehicle of exchange between local and federal officials at the implementation level (Agranoff, 2012).

Research Issues

The arena of federal–local relations has not been the rich vein that federal-state or even state-local relations has been over the eight or so decades since the era of IGR interdependency brought on federal programming research interest. Federal–state relations studies predominated, for example, with early works by Key, Jr. (1937), Clark (1938), and Benson (1942). The federal–local exception included Gaus and Wolcott's (1940) work on agriculture programs in the field, Anderson's (1960) work on cooperative federalism at the local level, and Grodzin's (1966) work on recreation and other local programs during the 1940s and 1950s. There was also work by Bane (1942) on federal–local connections in cities that were heavily impacted by the World War II production effort and by Durisch (1941) on how the Tennessee Valley Authority interacted with local governments regarding land use, construction projects, and a host of local public service impacts.

The federal–local intergovernmental research connection came on the scene with the advent of "urban policy" during the 1960s and faded as grants and other programs declined by the 1980s, by and large leaving the field to the few urban scholars who focused on the shifts in policies or on the decline. Unfortunately, these areas do not have to be the only research concerns. Other issues might include the following: issues related to rural development, endogenous local–federal relations and their impact, local governments as junior partners, the impact of direct federal programs and local citizens and their governments, the real impact of national regulatory and other national programs on local government services, and the role of local government on "inducing" state action on their behalf before the national government.

Grants and Urban Policy

This was a rich research vein at one time as public housing, model cities, CDBG, UDAG, Empowerment/Enterprise Zones, and Renewal Communities and housing tax credits built on one another. Several studies looked directly at federal urban policy, including those of Cleveland (1969), Baumgartner and Jones (1993), Kantor (1995), Pagano, O'M. Bowman (1997), and Clark and Gailie (1998), and Waste (1998). These works attempt to address the "disparate and amorphous nature" (Lawrence, Stoker, and Wolman, 2010, 414) of city problems and the difficulties of policy development, since "urban problems are a vast and amorphous collection of physical and social conditions in modern society... The plight of America's cities has been a shorthand way of discussing these problems" (Baumgartner and Jones, 1993, 127).

Urban policy interest was supported, as suggested, during its two decades of prominence by a series of federal grants. No one knows exactly how many went directly to local governments because the grant counters normally lumped state and federal aid together. The total count was 591 in 1998 but three or four large grants that go mostly to persons, not governments, take up about 75 percent of the total (Beam and Conlan 2002, 346). Meanwhile, in the 1970s regulation emerged on the federal–local scene in a big way. "Regulation gradually emerged as the key strategy for implementing the new generation of urban aid programs... The creeping growth of new rules... gradually shifted power back to Washington" (Kettl, 1981, 123). Ironically, relates Conlan (1998, 94), revenue sharing and the new bloc grants extended the reach of the federal governments to virtually all local governments regardless of size, "and inducing many hard pressed urban centers to rely more and more on federal aid." Then the decline came, as Pagano and Bowman (1997) explain, as budget cutting hit General Revenue Sharing in 1986, Urban Development Action Grants (UDAG) in 1987, and large cutbacks in CDBG and Economic Development Administration programs. This was accompanied by restrictions on tax-exempt development bonds, increased costs of general obligation bonds, industrial development bond restrictions, and held highway and transit funds, "as the federal government gradually broke its fiscal link with cities" (35).

The decline in urban policy has meant less research interest in either chronicling the grants to cities or in assessing urban policies. The journal *Publius* has an *Annual Review of Federalism*. It puts increasingly less focus on these issues. Journal articles are sparse today. In some urban textbooks this period of grant growth and urban policy is now part of their historical sections. This is unfortunate, inasmuch as the previous discussion has revealed that some federal grants remain, urban financing mechanisms like capital bonds, loans, and other tax programs are still employed as core strategies, and the extensive regulatory web has not been removed. Nevertheless, research on federal contacts, even in policy areas where states are now predominant, for example economic development, continue to show local–federal interaction (Agranoff and McGuire, 2003) and even greater federal–local involvement in the environmental policy arena (Wondolleck and Yaffee, 2000; Thomas, 2003). Whereas federal urban program decline has diminished, intergovernmental interest focus could be redirected to many other aspects of federal–local policy and programming.

Rural Policy

The massive shift to urban areas and the decline of agricultural employment has led to rural economic and community decline, a subject that deserves greater federal–local attention. Rural means any community, incorporated as a municipality or not, that is not located within a metropolitan statistical area, according to state and federal designation. This metro/non-metro distinction then includes all small to medium-sized independent towns of up to 25,000 in population, as well as the majority of towns inhabited by fewer than 10,000 persons (Agranoff and McGuire, 2000, 384). The federal government has important impacts on rural development, not only through such direct programs as farm subsidies, rural telephone/electric cooperatives, and USDA/RD, but in terms of its management of the economy. Galston and Baehler (1995) observe several federal conditions that hindered rural growth, shifts in the 1980s of the national and international economy accompanied by federal currency distortions that impeded rural exports, high interest rates that slowed the rural economy, deregulation in transportation and communication that wiped out implicit rural and cross-subsidies, federal spending in defense tilted toward metropolitan areas, and federal spending emphasizing agriculture (vs. rural development) and current consumption. They call for federal investments in overcoming these obstacles by addressing capital access, human resources, communication infrastructure, and diversification strategies (72–4).

Research on federal–local rural affairs has tended to focus more on federal programming strategies than on how local communities are leveraging federal programs. In addition to the work of Luke et al. (1988), work by Lapping and Keller (1989), Galston and Baehler (1995), Sears and Reid (1995), Radin et al. (1996) all have addressed federal efforts. All of these in some way approach development, which has been defined by rural specialists as "fundamental and sustainable increases in the productivity of individuals and institutions, leading to higher per capita incomes for individuals" (Sears and Reid, 1995, 2). Although the goal of development may be to increase incomes and to improve the quality of life, Ferguson and John (1992) argue that development often destroys old options even as it creates new ones, and it harms interests while it helps others. Therefore, far from being based solely in business development and economic growth, rural development is a broad, community-level process. The importance of geography in the development of rural areas is sometimes framed as a choice between people or places. While obviously interlinked, the most successful efforts in developing rural communities have been place-oriented to the extent that activities are designed to facilitate the ability of communities to plan and implement development programs on their own. These efforts involve not only the development of the local economy, but also improvement of local physical infrastructure, strengthening of local institutions, and enhancement of the social and organizational infrastructures (Bradshaw, 1993: 171). Moreover, providing financial resources does not constitute the totality of federal–local efforts. Programs also emphasize the development of a community's capacity to develop on its own. In this respect research on how local communities access the variety of federal programs and how federal programs affect local communities is in very short supply.

At least five areas of research beyond the federal financing and the farm economy are suggested by Walzer (2003, 14). First, IGR related to investments in the information economy and on providing modern telecommunications infrastructure, inasmuch as low-density rural areas may not be profitable to private investors. The lack of contemporary communications is placing remote rural areas at a decided disadvantage. Second, as mentioned above, how local leaders identify issues and initiate actions, including leveraging other governments, is at the forefront of research. "The time when state and federal governments brought solutions to rural areas has passed." Third, there is a need for a community learning environment that incorporates a broad spectrum of leaders who can vision and take action is important. This includes enlisting business leaders and incorporating technology. Fourth, recognition of the potential of innovative economic development approaches like industrial clusters offer clear advantages. This means partnering and leveraging other governments and educational institutions. Fifth, creative business financing beyond the traditional local bank loan signifies that capital opportunities have changed. This involves leveraging, matching, and packaging from venture capitalists, federal grants and loans, and other sources of non-financial matches. These changes in the rural sector indicate important components of a federal–local research strategy.

Endogenous IGR Effects

The previous research concern related to rural development from within actually applies to IGR in relation to a wide range of local–federal affairs. It basically goes back to the prior identification of managing by jurisdiction and packaging of programs from a local perspective, where local governments are able to take advantage of the opportunities to self-develop by leveraging programs and negotiating regulations to facilitate local aims. It basically flies in the face of the old development idea that "a rising tide lifts all boats," that is, in buoyant economies all communities will automatically improve economically. The problem with this philosophy is twofold. Some communities will improve economically but others will not as the national economy grows. Also, it does nothing to improve the leadership, human resource, and infrastructure core of local governments. Strategically, some governments need to take stock and develop a wide range of resources—social, educational, cultural, economic—to either rise with the tide or to rise in spite of an ebbing tide. This takes effort, including the fostering of an inter-governmental agenda.

Some work has been done on this issue, particularly in the economic and lead-ership development arena (Eisinger, 1988; Foster, 1988; Levy, 1990; Blakely, 1994; McGuire et al., 1994; Walzer, 2003). In the intergovernmental and local capacity area the work of Agranoff and McGuire (2003) in packaging and jurisdictional manage-ment has been mentioned. Also, the work of Luke et al. (1988) fits into this category. On capacity-building the work of Honadle (1981), Mead (1986), and Sokolow (1989) rep-resent early attempts to define this elusive concept. Clearly more needs to be done in this arena. To what extent do local governments that self-develop include critical fed-eral–local interactions to enhance their strategies? What forms of advocacy/adjustment and resource-seeking do they engage? How many local governments mark this effort? Finally, the million dollar question is, does a self-development IGR program make a dif-ference in community/economic improvement?

Junior Partners in Federalism

Currently this point is perhaps more of a studied observation than that of a research conclusion. Those that read the urban affairs tea leaves assume that federal dollars only flowed steadily to local governments from the 1930s to the 1980s, after which declin-ing sums and a shift to the states ensued. Does this make cities and counties junior partners? One has to remember that it is states that authorize, charter, and legally guide local governments in general. Strictly speaking, the federal government com-prises states. At the time that federal aid was first extensively targeted to cities in the 1930s many state governments were not "trusted" to help cities. State capacities have improved in many ways (Walker, 2000; Stenberg, 2010) and today many programs that end up assisting local governments flow through the states. Today's federal regula-tory regime also touches both state and local governments. So the seat at the federal table is there in some capacity. But since the early IGR work of Haider (1974), with the exception of Biles (2011) not a lot is known about this changing role. It is known at the state-local level that city officials' self-perceptions reveal that local governments have experienced an erosion of authority at the hands of their state governments (Bowman and Kearney, 2012). Despite the presence of many voices in Washington and in state capitols are local governments really junior partners? If they are, why are they? If not, in what ways do groups and individual cities and counties overcome the state level orien-tation of intergovernmental affairs in Washington?

Local Impact of Federal Programs for People and Places

Earlier in this essay the federal presence within local governments through such programs as Medicare/Medicaid, Social Security, Department of Agriculture programs, CDBG, and Title I Education impact aid, along with federal installations in local jurisdictions were all mentioned. In addition, industrial development bonds, tax-exempt development bonds and general obligation bonds are impacted by federal tax laws. There are programs targeted at people, for example food stamps, and programs targeted at places, for example USDA/RD community development grants. Research in these arenas of federal impact, if at all, tend to be "top-down" rather than "bottom-up," that is, they focus on the overall count of federal funds, their rise and decline (e.g., Beam and Conlan, 2002) or on the decline of federal aid to local governments (e.g., Ross and Levine, 2006). Research is needed on the federal impact at the bottom. What is the overall impact of municipal bonding rule changes on local governments? How are cities coping with reduced federal assistance? To some extent the national public interest groups have looked at these issues, for example Hoene and Pagano (2010).

In the same way that Nathan and Doolittle (1983) and Wallin (1998) have examined the consequences of the loss of revenue sharing, virtually absent from the analysis of federal–local relations is the individual impact of federal programs within local governments. That is, what is the impact on a particular local government of programs for people? How do Social Security, food stamps, Medicare, and so on, alleviate poverty and thus allow people to pay for and reduce the fiscal impact on city services? What does an EDA grant or other grants for job creation mean to a city? What is the net impact of federal transportation/highway funds (through the state and direct) on a county government? While these are issues that have not really been addressed in a direct way they would appear to be part of the understanding of federal–local relations.

National Impacts on Local Governments

Clearly more than anecdotal knowledge needs to be known about how national programs impact local governments. The typical example is as follows, "Adjusting for inflation, local expenditures to build and run treatment plants up to federal standards ballooned from about $7.5 billion a year in 1978 to more than $2.3 billion a year in 1998." Likewise New York City in 2001 estimated it would have to finance at least $8 billion in mandatory capital expenditures for water quality projects in the next 10 years (Nivola, 2002, 4–5, 6). The mandate madness issue, decrying forced local spending and loss of budget discretion, with regard to national–local programs (Conlan, 1998) tends to overlook several important issues. First, is that only costs and not benefits are pointed out. Is it not also true that higher water quality standards, or safe and professional childcare, or quality roads also accrue from federal standards? Second, it is not clear that federal standards often supplement or replace state–local standards, which had their baseline costs, which are rarely considered in cost estimates. The real issue would appear to be the marginal costs of federal versus prior standards. Third, one cannot assume that there is no local constituency for federal mandates/regulations. They are adopted by officials through national political processes and some of this political support includes local citizens. One cannot assume that there is a total absence of support for water or daycare or road quality standards. Fourth, federal standards have professionalized many areas of public service, generating competence in programming that might not otherwise be there. It could be that local government works better because of federal standards. As a result, today's public works directors run better programs and are able to be conversant up the line and exchange technical issues according to agreed-upon standards, a principle that is hard to oppose despite attendant costs. Indeed, the federal government rarely gets the proper "credit" for any such local impacts. The point is, however, that more needs to be known about the relevant interactions, processes, and impact of nationally induced programs on local governments, particularly on those potential benefits beyond concerns for extant costs. As Young (2009, 24) concludes with regard to Canada, "Indeed, beyond the big intergovernmental initiatives exists a largely unexplored world of municipal-federal contacts... New principles of public management have increased officials" discretion at all levels of government and transgovernmental coalitions can assemble to undertake particular projects.'

State-Induced Action

An interesting corollary of federal–local relations would appear to be an almost unknown issue, the extent to which local governments or local governments through their state associations or municipal leagues or counties' associations work with their states to take national action. To some extent, school districts often lobby and link with state education agencies to approach the federal government over key issues. This has been particularly true with regard to special education requirements and with the No Child Left Behind legislation. Recently, federal voting mandates have led counties to work through their states. It is a subject rarely covered in IGR work, although Berman (2003, 24) does analyze the rise of increased local governments' willingness to fend off costly federal mandates and protect from further funding federal cuts by fighting these challenges at the state level. It would appear to be a hidden issue of federal–local affairs that could be ripe for further research. One question is, what issues or policies generate local mobilization for state action? Another is, how do local governments or their groups foster national action through their states? Finally, at the program implementation level, what intergovernmental tactics do local governments use to influence national issues through their states?

CONCLUSION

A local–national IGR research agenda could go far beyond the identified concerns. Because local governments are constitutionally bound to the states, national–local and local-national interactions are less well understood, however dynamic and real they have become since the founding period. Research has been caught up in tracing the ebbs and flows of funding streams, court cases, and presidential policies while thousands of local governments routinely impact and are impacted by the federal government. This legal political–managerial dynamic could well be part of the next wave of knowledge-seeking.

Local governments are less visible and less powerful actors than states within the U.S. federal system but very real actors indeed. Like their counterparts in many other countries they are legally constituent to states but jurisdictionally independent entities that exist in political, fiscal, and programmatic interdependence with other governments. Since the advent of the growing welfare state they have become the operational venues for expanded government services, adding to their basic local social and physical life amenities and community services responsibilities.

In the U.S. this led to growing federal concern for the plight of disadvantaged populations and places, from the 1930s to the 1980s, linking local and federal governments. While a number of these programs have been eliminated or reduced, local–federal relations are real, through aid to persons, targeted programs for persons living in disadvantaged places, many programs that are channeled through states to localities, and through contracted services that operate within communities. Meanwhile, as populations have shifted from inner cities to suburbs and smaller towns, local governments are challenged with the need to promote their economies, foster socially attractive amenities, provide infrastructure and services, and otherwise promote livable communities. These challenges cannot be met by local governments going it alone. They must take up the intergovernmental challenge of linking with inter-local NGO and government partners, access the legal and fiscal opportunities their states afford, and continue to forge linkages with the federal government in Washington and in their federal field offices.

ACKNOWLEDGEMENT

The author would like to thank Timothy Conlan for his guidance and suggestions.

REFERENCES

ACIR. 1984. *Regulatory Federalism*. Washington, DC: Advisory Commission on Intergovernmental Relations.

Agranoff, Robert. 2012. *Collaborating to Manage: A Primer for the Public Sector*. Washington, DC: Georgetown University Press.

Agranoff, Robert. 2010. *Local Governments and Their Intergovernmental Networks in Federalizing Spain*. Montreal: McGill-Queen's University Press.

Agranoff, Robert. 2007. "Local Governments in Spain's Multilevel Arrangements." In Harvey Lazar and Christian Leuprecht (eds), *Spheres of Governance, Comparative Studies of Cities in Multilevel Governance Systems*. Montreal: McGill-Queen's University Press.

Agranoff, Robert. 2007a. "Intergovernmental Policy Management, Cooperative Practices in Federal Systems." In Michael A. Pagano and Robert Leonard (eds), *The Dynamics of Federalism in National and Supranational Political Systems*. Houndmills: Palgrave Macmillan, 248–84.

Agranoff, Robert. 2007b. *Managing Within Networks, Adding Value to Public Organizations*. Washington, DC: Georgetown University Press.

Agranoff, Robert and Michael McGuire. 2003. *Collaborative Public Management, New Strategies for Local Governments*. Washington, DC: Georgetown University Press.

Agranoff, Robert and Michael McGuire. 2000. "Administration of State Government Rural Development Policy." In John J. Gargan (ed.), *Handbook of State Government Administration*. New York: Marcel Dekker, 385–420.

Allocation of Powers Project. 2010. *The Allocation of Powers in Politically Decentralized Countries, A Comparative Study*. Barcelona: University Pompeu Fabra, Observatory of Institutions.

Anderson, William. 1960. *Intergovernmental Relations in Review*. Minneapolis: University of Minnesota Press.

Argullol, Enric, et al. 2004. *Federalismo y Autonomía*. Barcelona: Ariel.

Ashford, Douglas E. 1988. "Decentralizing Welfare States, Social Policies and Intergovernmental Politics." In Bruno Dente and Francesco Kjellborg (eds), *The Dynamics of Institutional Change, Local Government Reorganization in Western Democracies*. London: Sage, 19–38.

Bächtiger, André and Anina Hitz. 2007. "The Matrix Extended, Federal-Municipal Relations in Switzerland." In Harvey Lazar and Christian Leuprecht (eds), *Spheres of Governance, Comparative Studies of Cities in Multilevel Governance Systems*. Montreal: McGill-Queen's University Press, 71–96.

Bane, Frank. 1942. "Cooperative Government in Wartime." *Public Administration Review* 45 (March/April): 95–103.

Baumgartner, Frank and Bryan Jones. 1993. *Agendas and Instability in American Politics*. Chicago: University of Chicago Press.

Beam, David R. and Timothy Conlan. 2002. "Grants." In Lester M. Salamon (ed.), *The Tools of Government*. New York, Oxford, 340–80.

Benson, George S. 1942. *The New Centralization*. New York: Rinehart.

Berman, David R. 2003. *Local Government and the States*. Armonk, NY: M. E. Sharpe.

Biles, Roger. 2011. *The Fate of Cities: Urban America and the Federal Government*. Lawrence, KS: University of Kansas Press.

Blakely, E. J. 1994. *Planning Local Economic Development*, 2nd ed. Newbury Park, CA: Sage Publications.

Bowman, Ann O'M. and Richard C. Kearney. 2012. "Are U.S. Cities Losing Power and Authority? Perceptions of Local Government Actors" *Urban Affairs Review* 48 (4): 528–46.

Bradshaw, T. K. 1993. "Multicommunity Networks, A Rural Transition." *Annals of the American Academy of Political and Social Science* 529: 164–175.

Brown, Douglas M. 2007. "Federal-Municipal Relations in Australia." In Harvey Lazar and Christian Leuprecht (eds), *Spheres of Governance, Comparative Studies of Cities in Multilevel Governance Systems*. Montreal: McGill-Queen's University Press, 97–124.

Brunet-Jailly, Emmanuel. 2007. "Municipal-Central Relations in France, Between Decen-
    tralization and Multilevel Governance." In Harvey Lazar and Christian Leuprecht (eds),
    Spheres of Governance, Comparative Studies of Cities in Multilevel Governance Systems.
    Montreal: McGill-Queen's University Press, 125–62.
Callanan, Mark. 2003. "Local Government and the European Union." In Mark Callanan
    and Justin Keogan (eds), *Local Government in Ireland*. Dublin: Institute of Public
    Administration, 3–13.
Cammissa, Anne Marie. 1995. *Governments as Interest Groups, Intergovernmental Lobbying and
    the Federal System*. Westport, CT: Praeger.
Cigler, Beverly A. 1995. "Not Just Another Special Interest, Intergovernmental Representation."
    In *Interest Group Politics*, 4th ed. Washington, DC: Congressional Quarterly Press.
Clark, Jane Perry. 1938. *The Rise of a New Federalism*. New York: Columbia University Press.
Clarke, Susan E. and Gary L. Gaile. 1998. *The Work of Cities*. Minneapolis: University of
    Minnesota Press.
Cleveland, Frederick. 1969. *Congress and Urban Problems*. Washington, DC: Brookings.
Closa, Carlos and Paul M. Heywood. 2004. *Spain and the European Union*. New York: Palgrave
    Macmillan.
Conlan, Timothy J. 1998. *From New Federalism to Devolution, Twenty-Five Years of
    Intergovernmental Reform*. Washington, DC: Brookings.
Durisch, Lawrence L. 1941. "Local Government and the T.V.A. Program." *Public Administration
    Review* 1 (July/August): 326–34.
Economist. 2011a. "Canada's Cities, Poor Relations," 11 June, p. 42.
Economist. 2011b. "Germany's Local Finances," 23 April, p. 54.
Eisinger, Peter K. 1988. *The Rise of the Entrepreneurial State, State and Local Economic
    Development Policy in the United States*. Madison, WI: University of Wisconsin Press.
Elazar, Daniel J. 1961. *Illinois Local Government*. Urbana, IL: University of Illinois Press.
Elazar, Daniel J. 1962. *The American Partnership*. Chicago: University of Chicago Press.
Elazar, Daniel J. 1984. *American Federalism, A View from the States*, 3rd ed. New York: Harper
    and Row.
Elazar, Daniel J. 1994. *The American Mosaic*. Boulder, CO: Westview Press.
Elazar, Daniel J. 1963. "Urban Problems and the Federal Government, A Historical Inquiry."
    Political Science Quarterly 82 (December): 511–23.
Elmore, Richard F. 1985. "Forward and Backward Mapping, Reversible Logic in the Analysis
    of Public Policy." In Kenneth Hanf and Theo A. J. Toonen (eds), *Policy Implementation in
    Federal and Unitary Systems*. Dordrecht, the Netherlands: Martinus Nijhoff Publishers, 33–70.
Ferguson, R. F. and DeWitt John. 1992. *Making the Right Distinctions, Basic Ideas for the Rural
    Development Movement at the State Level*, unpublished manuscript.
Flora, Peter and Arnold Heidenheimer. 1981. *The Development of Welfare States in Europe and
    America*. New Brunswick, NJ, Transaction Books.
Fosler, R. S. 1988. *The New Economic Role of States*. New York: Oxford University Press.
Foster, Kathryn A. 1997. *The Political Economy of Special Purpose Government*. Washington,
    DC: Georgetown University Press.
Frug, Gerald E. 2005. "Municipal Corporations." In Kermit L. Hall (ed.), *Oxford Companion to
    the Supreme Court of the United States*, 2nd ed. New York: Oxford, 655–7.
Fulton, William. 2010. "Lending a Small Hand, A Revived Small Business Administration Is
    Good News for Local Government." *Governing* 23 (May): 18–19.
Gallego, Raquel, Ricard Gomà and Joan Subirats. 2003. "Las Políticas Sociales de la Union
    Europea." In Taquel Gallego, Ricard Gomà and Joan Subirats (eds), *Estado de Bienestar y
    Comunidades Autónomas*. Madrid: Technos.

Galston, William A. and Karen T. Baehler. 1995. *Rural Development in the United States*. Washington, DC: Island Press.

Gaus, John M. and Leon O. Wolcott. 1940. *Public Administration and the United States Department of Agriculture*. Chicago: Public Administration Service.

Goodman, Josh. 2010. "Counting Conundrum." *Governing* 23 (6): 38–41.

Goodnow, Frank J. 1900. *Politics and Administration*. New York: The Macmillan Company.

Grindle, Merilee S. 2007. *Going Local, Decentralization, Democratization, and the Promise of Good Governance*. Princeton, NJ: Princeton University Press.

Grodzins, Morton. 1966. *The American System*. Chicago, IL: Rand McNally.

Haider, Donald. 1974. *When Governments Come to Washington*. New York, NY: Free Press.

Hale, George E. and Marian L. Palley. 1981. *The Politics of Federal Grants*. Washington, DC: Congressional Quarterly Press.

Hoene, Christopher W. and Michael A. Pagano. 2010. "City Fiscal Conditions in 2010." Washington, DC: National League of Cities, Research Brief, October.

Honadle, B. W. 1981. "A Capacity-Building Framework, A Search for Concept and Purpose." *Public Administration Review* 41: 575–80.

Imperial, Mark. 2004. *Collaboration and Performance Management in Network Settings*. Washington, DC: IBM Center for the Business of Government.

Ingram, Helen. 1977. "Policy Implementation Through Bargaining, The Case of Federal Grants-in-Aid." *Public Policy* 25 (4): 499–526.

John, DeWitt. 1994. *Civic Environmentalism, Alternatives to Regulation in States and Communities*. Washington, DC: Congressional Quarterly Press.

Judd, Dennis R. and Todd Swanstrom. 1998. *City Politics, Private Power and Public Policy*. New York, NY: Longman.

Kantor, Paul. 1998. *The Dependent City Revisited*. Boulder, CO: Westview.

Kettl, Donald F. 1981. "Regulating the Cities." *Publius* 11 (Spring): 115–131.

Key, Jr., V. O. 1937. *The Administration of Federal Grants to States*. Chicago, Public Administration Service.

Kingdon, John. 2003. *Agendas, Alternatives, and Public Policies*. 2nd ed. New York, NY: Longman.

Kooiman, Jan. 2003. *Governing as Governance*. London: Sage.

Lapping, Mark B., Thomas Daniels, and J. Keller. 1989. *Rural Planning and Development in the United States*. New York, NY: Guilford Press.

Lawrence, Eric, Robert Stoker, and Harold Wolman. 2010. "Crafting Urban Policy, The Conditions of Public Support for Urban Policy Initiatives." *Urban Affairs Review* 45 (January): 412–430.

Leuprecht, Christian and Harvey Lazar. 2007. "From Multilevel to 'Multi-Order' Governance." In Harvey Lazar and Christian Leuprecht (eds), *Spheres of Governance, Comparative Studies of Cities in Multilevel Governance Systems*. Montreal: McGill-Queen's University Press, 1–22.

Levy, John. 1990. "What Economic Developers Actually Do, Location Quotients Versus Press Releases." *Journal of the American Planning Association* 56: 153–160.

Liebschutz, Sarah F. 1991. *Bargaining Under Federalism, Contemporary New York*. Albany, NY: State University of New York Press.

Loughlin, John. 2007. "Reconfiguring the State, Trends in Territorial Governance in European States." *Regional and Federal Studies* 17 (Winter): 385–404.

Luke, Jeffrey S., Cutrtis Ventriss, B. J. Reed, and Christine Reed. 1988. *Managing Economic Development, A Guide to State and Local Leadership Strategies*. San Francisco, CA: Jossey-Bass.

Lutz, Donald S. 1998. "General Laws and Liberties of New Hampshire." In *Colonial Origins of the American Constitution*. Indianapolis, IN: Liberty Fund, 5–30.

Martin, Roscoe C. 1965. *The Cities and the Federal System.* New York, NY: Atherton.

Mathew, George and Rakesh Hooja. 2009. "Republic of India." In Nico Steytler (ed.), *Local Governments and Metropolitan Regions in Federal Systems.* Montreal: McGill-Queens University Press, 166–99.

McGuire, Michael, Rubin, Barry, Agranoff, Robert, and Richards Craig. 1994. "Building Development Capacity in Nonmetropolitan Communities." *Public Administration Review* 54: 433.

Mead, Timothy D. 1986. "Issues in Defining Local Management Capacity." In Beth Walter Honadle and Arnold M. Howitt (eds), *Perspectives on Management Capacity Building.* Albany, NY: State University of New York Press, 24–46.

Menzel, Donald. 1990. "Collecting, Conveying, and Convincing, The Three C's of Local Government Interest Groups." *Public Administration Review* 50 (May/June): 401 5.

Nathan, Richard P. and Fred C. Doolittle. 1983. *The Consequences of Cuts, The Effects of the Reagan Domestic Program on State and Local Governments.* Princeton, NJ: Princeton Urban and Regional Research Center.

Nivola, Pietro S. 2002. *Tense Commandments, Federal Prescriptions and City Problems.* Washington, DC: Brookings.

Pagano, Michael A. and Ann O'M. Bowman. 1997. *Cityscapes and Capital, The Politics of Urban Development.* Baltimore, MD: Johns Hopkins University Press.

Page, Edward C. and Michael J. Goldsmith. 1987. "Centre and Locality, Explaining Cross-National Variation." In Edward C. Page and Michael J. Goldsmith (eds), *Central and Local Government Relations, A Comparative Analysis of West European States.* London: Sage, 1–11.

Pressman, Jeffrey L. 1975. *Federal Programs and City Politics, The Dynamics of the Aid Process in Oakland.* Berkeley, CA: University of California Press.

Radin, Beryl A., Robert Agranoff, Ann O'M. Bowman, Gregory C. Buntz, Steven J. Ott, Barbara S. Romzek, and Robert H. Wilson. 1996. *New Governance for Rural America, Creating Intergovernmental Partnership.* Lawrence, KS, University of Kansas Press.

Ramos, Juan A. and Ruth Cicuéndez. 2005. "La Dimensión Institucional de las Relaciones Autonómico-Locales en el Contexto de Gobierno Multinivel." Ponencia presentada al Congreso de Ciencias Políticas Española, Madrid, 3–6 April.

Ross, Bernard and Myron Levine. 2006. *Urban Politics, Power in Metropolitan America,* 7th ed. Belmont, CA, Thomson Wadsworth.

Rowland, Allison. 2007. "The Interaction of Municipal and Federal Governments in Mexico, Trends, Issues and Problems." In Harvey Lazar and Christian Leuprecht (eds), *Spheres of Governance, Comparative Studies of Cities in Multilevel Governance Systems.* Montreal: McGill-Queen's University Press, 201–28.

Salamon, Lester M. 2002. *The Tools of Government.* New York, NY: Oxford University Press.

Salamon, Lester M. 1995. *Partners in Public Service.* Baltimore, MD: Johns Hopkins University Press.

Sears, David W. and J. Norman Reid. 1995. "Successfully Matching Development Strategies and Tactics with Rural Communities, Two Approaches." In David W. Sears and J. Norman Reid (eds), *Rural Development Strategies.* Chicago, IL: Nelson-Hall Press, 282–96.

Shales, Amity. 2007. *The Forgotten Man, A New History of the Great Depression.* New York, NY: Harper.

Smith, Stephen Rathgeb and Michael Lipsky. 1993. *Nonprofits for Hire, The Welfare State in the Age of Contracting.* Cambridge, MA: Harvard University Press.

Sokolow, A. D. 1989. "Small Local Governments as Community Builders." *National Civic Review* 78: 362–70.

Solé-Vilanova, Joaquim. 1990. "Regional and Local Government Finance in Spain, Is Fiscal Responsibility the Missing Element?" In Robert J. Bennett (ed.), *Decentralization, Local Government, and Markets*. Oxford: Clarendon, 331–54.

Stanton, Thomas H. 2002. "Loans and Loan Guarantees." In Lester M. Salamon (ed.), *The Tools of Government*. New York, NY: Oxford, 381–409.

Stenberg, Carl W. 2010. "Intergovernmental Management at 50, An ACIR Perspective on Institutional Developments." Paper prepared for IGR in 2020 Symposium, San Jose, CA, April 9.

Stephens, G. Ross and Nelson Wikstrom. 2007. *American Intergovernmental Relations*. New York, NY: Oxford University Press.

Stephens, G. Ross and Nelson Wikstrom. 1998. "Trends in Special Districts." *State and Local Government Review* 30 (Spring): 129–38.

Steytler, Nico. 2009. "Comparative Conclusions." In Nico Steytler (ed.), *Local Government and Metropolitan Regions in Federal Systems*. Montreal: McGill-Queen's University Press, 393–436.

Steytler, Nico. 2007. "National, Provincial and Local Relations (in South Africa)." In Harvey Lazar and Christian Leuprecht (eds), *Spheres of Governance, Comparative Studies of Cities in Multilevel Governance Systems*. Montreal: McGill-Queen's University Press, 229–256.

Tarr, G. Alan. 1998. *Understanding State Constitutions*. Princeton, NJ: Princeton University Press.

Teaford, Jon C. 2002. *The Rise of the States, Evolution of American State Government*. Baltimore, MD: Johns Hopkins University Press.

Thomas, Craig. 2003. *Bureaucratic Landscapes*. Cambridge, MA: MIT Press.

deVisser, Jaap. 2009. "Republic of South Africa." In Nico Steytler (ed.), *Local Government and Metropolitan Regions in Federal Systems*. Montreal: McGill-Queen's University Press, 267–97.

Walker, David B. 2000. *The Rebirth of Federalism, Slouching Toward Washington*. New York, NY: Chatham House.

Wallin, Bruce A. 1998. *From Revenue Sharing to Deficit Sharing, General Revenue Sharing and Cities*. Washington, DC: Georgetown University Press.

Walzer, Norman. 2003. *The American Midwest, Managing Change in Rural Transition*. Armonk, NY: M. E. Sharpe.

Waste, Robert J. 1998. *Independent Cities, Rethinking U.S. Urban Policy*. New York, NY: Oxford University Press.

Watts, Ronald L. 1999a. *Comparing Federal Systems in the 1990s*, 3rd ed. Kingston, Ontario, Institute of Intergovernmental Relations.

Watts, Ronald L. 1999b. *The Spending Power in Federal Systems, A Comparative Study*. Kingston, Ontario: Institute of Intergovernmental Relations.

Wehner, Joachim. 2003. "The Institutional Politics of Revenue Sharing in South Africa." *Regional and Federal Studies* 13 (Spring): 1–30.

Williams, Walter W. 1981. *Government by Agency, Administering Grants-in-Aid Programs*. New York, NY: Academic Press.

Wolman, Harold. 1999. "Urban Policy Processes at the National Level, The Hidden World of Urban Politics." In Stuart Nagel (ed.), *The Policy Process*. Hauppauge, NY: Nova Science, 25–46.

Wondolleck, Julia and Steve L. Yaffee. 2000. *Making Collaboration Work, Lessons from Innovation in Natural Resource Management*. Washington, DC: Island Press.

Young, Robert. 2009. "Canada." In Nico Steytler (ed.), *Local Government and Metropolitan Regions in Federal Systems*. Montreal: McGill-Queen's University Press, 106–35.

Zimmerman, Joseph F. 1995. *State-Local Relations, A Partnership Approach*. New York, Praeger.

CHAPTER 4

RELATIONS BETWEEN STATE AND LOCAL GOVERNMENTS

The Home Court (Dis)Advantage

CAROL S. WEISSERT AND JESSICA L. ICE

STATE and local governmental relationships are multi-faceted, variable, and dynamic. Although there is a considerable amount of research on state and local government by political scientists, economists, attorneys, and public administration and urban scholars, there remain many gaps in our understanding of these relationships. This essay will highlight the strengths and weaknesses of the theoretical and empirical research in the area across various disciplines and will outline an agenda for future research. In short, the research is not comprehensive and many questions remain.

Intergovernmental relations (IGR), the everyday workings of federal, state, and local governments, were once described by Senator Edmund Muskie in 1962 as the "hidden dimension of government" (Wright, 1978). State–local relationships—the least salient component of the rather non-salient IGR system—must therefore be nearly invisible. While there have been several excellent textbooks and edited volumes describing state and local governments and their interactions (Wright, 1978; Zimmerman, 1995; Weber and Brace, 1999; Berman, 2003; Stephens and Wikstrom, 2007), there has been considerably less interest in answering long-standing questions that have persisted at least since Sen. Muskie's pithy description. Clearly there are "lodes" where research has been well-mined—particularly in fiscal federalism and intergovernmental grants. Far less research has been undertaken to answer questions of effectiveness and innovation, implementation and politics. And questions raised by early intergovernmental scholars remain unanswered.

State–local relationships in the USA are the "stepchild" of three subfields (State Politics, Urban Politics, Economics/Fiscal Federalism). Typically, research conducted in those subfields stays in those subfields with other researchers unaware of the work. There has been recent interest in the cross-nation comparative federalism literature on state–local relationships and decentralization (Bolleyer, 2006; Freitag and Vatter, 2008; Gonzales, 2008; Steytler, 2009; Bakvis and Brown, 2010; Falleti, 2010), but that work is similarly not generally cited by US scholars. Although the paucity of theory is a fairly common complaint in urban and, to a lesser extent, federalism literature, this criticism also applies to state–local relationships.

This chapter highlights the research that has been undertaken to understand state–local relationships, to examine different types of local governmental units and their relationship to the state, to chart the trends toward—and impact of—decentralization and local autonomy, and evaluate state oversight and funding. Political realities and implementation are areas where the paucity of research is a bit surprising given the widespread recognition of the importance of these issues by scholars and practitioners. Finally, in the conclusion, we summarize the strengths and weaknesses of research on state–local relationships and offer some suggestions for future research questions.

Understanding State–Local Relationships

State–local relationships occur within the American federal system—which provides an additional level for financial and resource assistance and as well as governance oversight. Local governments are creatures of their states (and their state constitutions). The system was fairly simple until the 1960s when federal grants were targeted first to central cities, then to counties—sometimes bypassing states and at other times going through state budgets and agencies. The popularity of federal grants to localities has waned over time, except for a few block grants, but waxed again with the passage of the 2009 federal stimulus package. Despite the federal government's varying presence in local finances and programs, there is little scholarship spanning the three governmental levels or assessing the federal role in state–local relationships. Some recent research on the federal system offering "venue" shopping for advocates and interest groups is an excellent example of what can be done to trace the impact of various governments on public policy choice (see for example Miller, 2008)

Federalism scholars often ignore local governments—preferring to deal with the constitutional federal–state relationships. One of the few exceptions is fiscal federalism scholarship which sees local government as a way to improve resource allocation within the public sector (Oates, 1972). Others note that localism reflects the values of liberty, promotes democratic values and practices and allows experimentation (Connolly et al., 2010).

Apart from the structure of federalism, state and local relationships are shaped by a number of possible factors including competition, functional assignment, and incentives through grants, cooperation, multi-level governance and principal–agent relationships.

Competition

Probably the most influential theory that links efficiency (economics) and democratic values (political science) is Tiebout's (1956) model of local governmental markets where residents can move to communities that best meet their service and taxation preferences. While most often applied to local governments, Peterson and Rom (1989) and others have applied the possible mobility of residents to states in what they dub 'the race to the bottom', where states attempt to repel high-maintenance residents by limiting their benefits.

Tiebout's mobility scenario relies on the notion of competition—local governments compete for citizens by devising packages of services that will attract residents. Ostrom et al. (1988), among others, promote the desirability of having many governments independent of each other. Competition can keep taxes low, can assure that services are the ones citizens desire and, according to Qian and Weingast (1997: 88), force governments "to represent citizen interests and preserve markets." While the logic of competition would lead local governments to provide differing services depending on their own citizens' needs, Stein (1987) found that most cities offer the same set of functions but with differences in quality (which is hard to quantify). Stein also found that race was the only variable accounting for differentiation among community services packages.

Finally, competition can help "tame" the governmental "Leviathan." As monopolies, local governments might maximize revenue (rather than profits) which provides them with resources to satisfy rent-seeking and bureaucratic slack—thus leading to the Leviathan hypothesis (Brennan and Buchanan, 1980). But the extent to which localities can do this varies depending on the number and types of competing jurisdictions (Craw, 2008). State laws allowing or constraining revenues, annexation, and zoning, and mandating services also define the context in which localities can compete.

Competition—not cooperation–seems to best characterize state–local relationships as governments compete for funding while they simultaneously attempt to take the credit for keeping taxes low and maintaining desired services. States can take the credit for keeping local taxes low (through restrictions on local property taxes and revenue constraints) *and* lay the blame on local governments when resulting services are cut. In turn, localities compete with each other and do their own blame casting at the state.

Functional Assignment

Normative theory posits what levels of government should be providing what services. Musgrave (1959) differentiated the functions of government with the federal government providing macro-economic stabilization and income redistribution while states and localities provide allocative functions or services desired by their constituents. Peterson (1981) applied Tiebout's and Musgrave's contributions to cities. Because cities cannot control the flow of capital across their borders, they pursue economic policies that maximize their economic well-being (allocative or distributive services) while avoiding those that threaten the community with loss of capital or labor (redistributive services). Stein (1987) and Craw (2006, 2008) found that cities do pursue redistributive policies, contrary to the Peterson thesis. Functional assignment is important for state–local relationships since it is the state that defines what localities can and should do.

Incentives/Intergovernmental Grants

Probably the best developed theoretical economic explanation relating to state–local relations is that relating to intergovernmental grants under federalism. In a federation, one level of government may potentially not provide a function itself but will instead transfer money to another level to implement the desired policy. While much of the work here is on the national–state relationship, the rationale applies to national–state–local (second-order devolution) or state–local relationships as well (Bowman and Kearney, 2011). Intergovernmental grants can improve the allocation of resources when the good or service provided has positive externalities, and they can offset differences in fiscal capacities across jurisdictions (Mueller, 2003). But grants can also be reduced when states face tough economic times, leaving localities in the fiscal lurch.

Second-order devolution is less a theory and more of a descriptive term that is applied to cases where the national government has delegated responsibility to the states which in turn grant authority to local governments or community organizations. It is most often used in connection with the Temporary Assistance to Needy Families (TANF) block grant. Nathan and Gais (1999), Gainsborough (2003), and Fording et al. (2007) are examples of research that traces the federal–state–local delegation of responsibility and implementation. Watson and Gold (1997) dated second-order devolution back to the mid-1980s—calling it a "de facto devolution because most of the changes occurred implicitly, as states assigned a low priority to helping local governments because of state budget pressures and became more willing to allow localities to handle their own problems without state interference."

Cooperation/Networks

Although competition is the driving force behind the Tiebout and Peterson research, some scholars, particularly those in public administration, have focused on cooperation and coordination. One often-used theoretical undergirding of this work is transaction costs theory, whereby local governmental officials will choose cooperation as the best course to limit transaction costs associated with duplication and competition (Feiock et al., 2003; Feiock, 2007). Network theory has also been used to understand local governmental decisions regarding other governments (as well as the private and non-profit sector). Feiock and Scholz (2010) have proposed a promising approach to coordinate policies that spans horizontal and vertical governmental jurisdictions and mitigates resulting collective action dilemmas. They dub their contribution as an institutional collective action (ICA) framework that recognizes the importance of self-organization actions by affected authorities and stakeholders. Their work has developed and applied the framework in several metropolitan area services.

Krueger and Bernick (2010) look at the likelihood of cities' cooperation with other jurisdictions and conclude that state constraints play an important role in this cooperation. In this study, when the state limits local revenue raising, the ability to annex, and the creation of special districts, its municipalities are more likely to cooperate rather than provide the service alone. Carr et al. (2007) looked at horizontal and vertical cooperation in Michigan local governments. They found that general fiscal capacity was not a predictor of vertical cooperation or horizontal cooperation. Better predictors were the type of service: horizontal cooperation occurs most frequently for services that require significant capital investments; vertical cooperation occurs more often for services that require significant expertise or training.

Multi-level Governance and Principal–Agent Models

Multi-level governance (MLG), designed initially for application to the European Union, is now used to examine other federal relationships. With the development of MLG, Hooghe and Marks (2003) recognize that in addition to the rather stable set of relationships that lead to policy outcomes, there are the more complex, temporary, and fluid relationships among governmental and non-governmental units that differ by issue and situation. Studlar (2010) and other political scientists are beginning to apply MLG to intergovernmental relationships in specific policy areas and find the approach helpful in understanding policy formation and implementation. Economists are apparently not as impressed. As Berry (2009: 17) noted: "Surprisingly, although the essence of federalism is multi-level government, the fiscal federalism literature has devoted relatively little attention to vertical fiscal externalities apart from the issue of intergovernmental grants."

Interestingly, while principal–agent models have been used to theorize about national and state relationships, they are less common in the study of state–local relationships where seemingly they would seem to be a better fit. Much of the work at the national–state level has asked and answered the question of why does the national government delegate to the states (some work has also addressed the interesting question of why and how do states respond). The principal–agent model is always a bit of a stretch at the national–state level, since in a federation states are independent sovereign governments (with some key limitations of course) and not precisely agents. For localities, however, the relationship with their "higher order" governments—the states—is more like the principal–agent model, particularly for counties, which are in fact agents of the states. Even the most "autonomous" local governments—home rule municipalities—are essentially and eventually "creatures of the states" thus much closer to agents than the US states could ever be to the US national government.

In summary, competition has been most frequently used to describe inter-local and to a lesser degree state–local relationships. The role of intergovernmental grants as incentives for sub-national action and a way to offset differences in fiscal capacity has been examined, but the effect of federal grants on state–local relationships and state grants on local competition and cooperation are largely unexplored. The principal–agent model has not been applied to the extent it might be to state–local issues and questions remain that might be answered by stronger theory and improved empirics. Potential applications of network theory and multi-level governance to state–local relationships may also be appropriate in future research.

A LOOK AT THE INTERGOVERNMENTAL LANDSCAPE

Three types of local governments are prevalent across the United States: counties, municipalities or cities, and special districts (especially school districts). While all are local governments, they differ substantially in their structures, functions, and relationships with the state. Not surprisingly, researchers often consider only one of the governmental choices in their work.

Counties

County–state relationships are important because counties are the closest local government to "agents" since they serve as the administrative arms for state government in health, welfare, courts, corrections, roads, tax administration, vital statistics, and elections. However, they also provide municipal services (in unincorporated areas) and serve as provider/coordinator/regulator/negotiator of city services that cross municipal boundaries such as pollution control, emergency medical services, public communications, drug enforcement, and mass transit. Indeed, Benton (2002: 5) calls counties "front-liners" in public service provision. Much of the current research on counties is largely descriptive or uses counties as a convenient unit of analysis.

State law defines how and what counties do. Schneider and Park (1989) looked at spending and found that government structure has a significant, independent influence on the role of county government as a service provider. County governments with reformed structures spend more and provide more services (Schneider and Park, 1989; Benton, 2002). County governance also made a difference in the impact of developmental interests and the adoption of development policies (Feiock et al., 2003; Lubell et al., 2005).

Among local governments, counties are relatively poorly studied and have been so for decades. In 1969 John Bollens criticized county research, arguing that there were few behavioral studies, little analysis, and less theorizing. Over two decades later Berman and Salant (1996: 23) continued the criticism, noting that "current knowledge of the specifics of how counties seek to exert influence on the federal and state activities and the extent to which they are able to do so is very limited." They also noted that researchers failed to analyze and predict the differences of counties and municipalities in response to state direction. This remains an item for future study.

Cities

While better studied than counties—especially in urban politics—the research is often confined to city boundaries, not vertical relationships. Peterson (1981) addressed what he called the "logic of federalism" that constrains cities to minimize their social service expenditures: "If businesses do not find existing city policies agreeable, not only can they leave, but they can also create their own cities or special districts with their own boundaries and their own definitions of citizenship" ' (Peterson, 1981: 114). One might add—when the state allows it to do so.

Key issues of urban politics are taxes and tax bases, eminent domain, infrastructure provision and land improvement, zoning, services, and race (Peterson, 1981: 115)—all of which are defined, in part, by state law. But by far the most studied component of state participation in municipal choices relates to intergovernmental aid. From fiscal federalism tenets, we would expect state aid to stimulate local spending and it does (Morgan and Kickham, 1999; Pagano and Johnston, 2000; Craw, 2006, 2008). Eger and Marlowe (2006) found that state aid was a significant determinant in whether the municipality would initiate urban transit.

Schneider (1989) examined spending in municipalities within standard metropolitan areas (SMSAs) at two points in time. He looked at exogenous demand (community income, home ownership, racial effects, population size and growth rate, economic composition, tax base, functional responsibility), demographic factors, and state aid. He found that exogenous factors were strongest, especially SMSA location and state aid.

Special Districts and School Districts

While most of the local governmental research has focused on general purpose government, by far the largest number of units of governance are special districts. Comparative scholars studying multi-level governments and networks have recently included special districts in their research, recognizing that they play an important role in local governance. Hooghe and Marks (2003) recognize special districts as what they call Type II governments—which are functional, overlapping, and competing jurisdictions. Proponents of these jurisdictions argue that they are efficient, lower barriers to exit and can dissolve when their purpose is met. But as Berry (2009) notes, these characteristics of the ideal type do not fit well with the US experience of special districts.

One problem with the study of special districts in the United States is that they are defined at the state level in ways that are far from consistent. National and state data on these districts are not always trustworthy. Even at the local level, such districts often fly "below the radar screen" with citizens unaware of what they are and what they do. (School districts, a special type of special district, are the exception.)

Special districts are often governed by appointed officials who are only indirectly accountable to the public but are given the ability to tax that very public. Berry (2009) finds that special district services were inferior to those of general purpose governments and were more costly. Further, he finds that they are more likely to be responsive to interest groups than their general purpose counterparts. Clearly state laws that define special districts are important in how those districts operate in the state, what services they perform, and what revenues they enjoy. Less known is the accountability argument raised by Berry and others. Are there ways to ensure more accountability and what impact do those provisions have on services provided and taxation? How might the accountability–competition tradeoff be better understood and defined?

Unlike other special districts, school districts are highly visible and politically salient. They rely heavily on the state (and increasingly the national government) for funding *and* substance (curriculum, book selection, graduation and reporting requirements, and, importantly, performance measures). Since local schools are funded in substantial measure by the local property tax, tax effort and the use of the property tax to fund education is a major topic of research (Berkman and Plutzer, 2005). Property tax in and of itself is not an unconstitutional way to fund schools (Odden and Picus, 2004), but inequities are politically unpalatable. States began to take over a large part of school funding through distribution rather than redistribution. There remains a great variation in of the extent to which school districts rely on local revenues—from below 20 per cent to 100 per cent—as well as which states are most likely to engage in redistribution. Other concerns with funding have arisen from time to time including per-pupil and instructional spending (Kozol, 1991; Wong, 1991; Burtless, 1996; Fischel, 2001; Weimer and Wolkoff, 2001; Odden and Picus, 2004).

In recent years, the focus of school district research has been on performance—how well are the schools serving their students (and how is this measured to control for obvious differences in students' backgrounds and expectations)? Also studied is the governance of school districts—whether they are dependent or independent school districts (Morone, 1998; Bryan, 2004), whether the superintendent is elected or appointed by the board, and the role of citizen input, initiative, and referendum (Howards, 1967; Magleby, 1984; Cronin, 1989; Eule, 1990; Wirt and Kirst, 1997). The states play key roles in funding local schools and setting curricula. How school districts respond to these directions has only recently been studied by Berkman and Pluzer (2011)

The types of local governments share some similarities and many differences. All are subject to state direction and largess, but the state is only one of many factors in local governmental choices and ways of responding to local preferences. Special districts are the least responsive to the citizenry (and to the state); counties are generally more responsive than other entities but can also engage in activities and have their own funding in ways that make generalizations difficult.

In summary, all three types of governments (counties, municipalities, and special districts) are not only understudied in their own right but most notably they are not studied within a system of interacting governments, vertical or horizontal. A better understanding of how state governments view local governments and how they treat the heterogeneous types of local governments differently is a potential avenue of exploration. Additionally, intergovernmental relations research could benefit from a more theoretical understanding of how—and perhaps when—each local government works with its respective state government in a bottom-up approach and with other local governments horizontally.

Decentralization and Local Autonomy

Decentralization has been studied at the federal–state, state–local, and comparative nation level. Decentralization has considerable theoretical appeal given that decentralization allows governments to meet local tastes and circumstances without waste (Oates, 1993; Weingast, 1995). Measures of state–local decentralization go back to 1981 when the US Advisory Commission on Intergovernmental Relations (ACIR) identified four measures of state discretion to their local governments (Zimmerman, 1981). Stephens (1974) developed centralization measures that were recently updated by Bowman and Kearney (2011). While comparative work emphasizes the effect of decentralization on economic development, the US work tends to be descriptive (but see Xie et al., 1999, and Stansel, 2005, for more rigorous studies of the impact on decentralization on economic growth).

There is less agreement over local autonomy and whether in fact there is such a thing. Local government scholars of course, say that there is. Wolman et al. (2010: 4) define local autonomy as "a system of local governments in which local governments (1) have an important impact on their larger economy and intergovernmental system (2) have the discretion to engage in fiscal, functional and organization activities without restraints from higher levels of government (3) have the capacity or means to achieve their policy and governance preferences" (Wolman et al., 2010: 4).

Others are more sceptical or think there is no such thing as local autonomy (Frug and Barron, 2008; Weissert, 2010). Frug and Barron (2008) point out that the current legal structure does not grant autonomy to any local governments; rather it grants them some substantive powers while denying them others. The key feature of the current legal system is that it directs the substantive ways in which local power is exercised through a complex mix of grants and limits that it establishes. Frug and Barron say there is surprisingly little support among legal scholars for increasing the legal powers of local government.

On the other hand Briffault (1990) argues that it is no longer true that cities are creatures of the state and that direct state efforts to overturn local governmental decisions are relatively rare. He thinks that suburbs have benefited relative to central cities in controlling growth and preserving the status quo and that local autonomy has helped them in this quest. He argues that the principal constraint on local power is often not legal but economic. The argument concerning local autonomy is largely waged in law school journals and a full recounting is beyond this essay. However, the point is that while local scholars assume autonomy, their counterparts across disciplinary lines are not necessarily in agreement.

One aspect of local autonomy is home rule which is granted by the state (either in statute or constitution) giving local governments the right to select their own form of governmental organization (Krane et al., 2001). There remain large differences in the scope of home rule and in its "take-up" by localities. According to Stephens and Wikstrom (2007) only 28 states provide municipalities with broad functional authority under home rule. And only about 10 per cent of counties eligible to adopt a home rule charter have done so (Berman, 2003). Further, even for local home rule local governments, the states retain the authority to enact legislation in an area of paramount and substantial state concern—essentially overruling home rule (Zimmerman, 2004).

The institutional components of local governments matter and many are set by the state. Apart from intergovernmental aid, states directly or indirectly determine policies concerning the annexation and creation of special districts, zoning, designation of local officials (specifically constitutional officers in counties), borrowing and spending policies, choice of governance, and involvement of the public through recall and initiative. Scholars including Portz, Stein, and Jones (1999), Clingermayer and Feiock (2001), and Benton (2002) have called for more attention to institutions in urban scholarship. When institutional variables are included in analysis they are often additive, not interactive, which is more likely the case in the real world (Clingermayer and Feiock, 2001).

The degree of decentralization and local autonomy—and what difference they make—relates to institutional issues of local governments—home rule, reformed institutions, and the extent of funding independence from the state. Institutions are important—but how and when are still fertile areas for future research.

THE STATE GIVES AND IT TAKES AWAY

We know that state aid (and federal aid) plays a major role in understanding local spending. For example, Craw (2010) found that municipal redistributive spending is largely a function of intergovernmental revenues, and Morgan and Kickham (1999) found that intergovernmental aid stimulated spending for both reformed and non-reformed counties. However, Pagano and Johnston (2000) found that intergovernmental aid did not mitigate revenue burdens on city and county residents.

State revenue sharing, categorical grants, shared revenue, and block grants are all common means that states use to provide financial assistance to their localities. Most studied are the long-term trends in the relative share of governmental spending by states and localities. These trends clearly show a move toward state centralization and now state financial assistance provides nearly one-third of all local revenues (Stephens and Wikstrom, 2007). States typically share revenue with localities to take advantage of the economies and efficiencies of the centralized collection of revenue at the state level, to compensate local governments for taxes that have been moved to the state level, to equalize local revenues on some basis other than the point of collection, or to compensate local jurisdictions for the spillover effects of services they provide that benefit larger regions or the state as a whole (Taylor and Weissert, 2002).

A number of researchers have examined the impact of state revenue sharing—particularly which local governments tend to benefit. Chernick and Reschovsky (2001) in a study of New York, California, and Wisconsin found that state revenue sharing in those states tended to favor faster-growing suburban communities rather than central cities. A study of Michigan (Taylor and Weissert, 2002) found similar results. In that state, fast-growing suburban townships fared better than rural or urban ones. The authors note that since these growing suburban communities usually lose productive farmland as residential areas are developed, it might be argued that Michigan's state revenue sharing supports land use policies that encourage sprawl.

Unfunded Mandates

State-imposed mandates and restrictions on local revenues have been studied empirically but without strong underlying theory. Since the 1980s, political scientists have documented the growth of mandates and the impact of tax and expenditure limitations on local government. However, questions remain about the conditions that are most likely to lead to states imposing mandates and restricting revenues.

Further, mandates are not equally intrusive or unwanted. But efforts to parcel out the types of mandates and their differing effects have been limited, perhaps in part because there is no recognized, comprehensive typology. Early mandate scholars Lovell and Tobin (1981) developed a typology highlighting requirements and constraints. Brown and Cousineau (1984) examined programmatic and procedural mandates. Jenks (1994) developed a typology based on level of concern for the mandating party's own outcomes and for the mandated party's outcomes. May and Burby (1996) identified coercive and cooperative policies. Apart from the differing conceptualizations, the findings from these studies differ in which of the expected determinants, including local governmental receptivity and resources and state oversight and use of sanctions, are significant.

ACIR (1990) noted that in the absence of sufficient funds—whether by legislative choice or economic constraint—there is a strong temptation to satisfy policy demands by mandating that the functions be performed by other governments. During times of economic stress, it is particularly tempting for the state to authorize new programs, modify existing programs, or increase implementation requirements on localities without providing the state dollars to do so (Berman and Salant, 1996). This way state officials get to "take the credit" for the services without having to pay for them directly. Obviously local governments dislike unfunded state mandates and often consider them unfair.

As some protection against unfunded mandates, localities have successfully spearheaded the adoption in many states of provisions requiring pending legislation to estimate the fiscal impact on local governments and prohibiting states from adopting unfunded mandates (usually with a relatively high financial threshold). The outcomes of this genre of legislation are mixed at best. While there was a flurry of studies in this area in the 1980s, the research interest has waned, and there remain few empirical studies of their impact. However, there is at least some view that unfunded mandates may be viewed more as a political, rather than an economic, problem. For example, Berman and Salant (1996: 21) conclude that, "County officials have fewer complaints over the goals of mandated programs than with the fact that they are not adequately involved in shaping the programs and are often stuck with the bills." There is, however, a real concern about the cumulative nature of the state requirements for new programs, uniformity in procedures, changes in existing programs, and accountability and reporting requirements—to name just five. As Berman (2002: 49) described it, "Although some of the shifts cost relatively little money, their aggregate effects can be staggering."

Tax and Spending Limitations

States can constrain the revenues and spending of local governments through limiting their revenue base, their revenue rate, or their expenditures. A common means of such constraint is through statewide tax and expenditure limitations (TELs). The literature on the consequences of TELs is extensive and contradictory. In part this results from differing questions relating to definitions of both the dependent and independent variables. Dependent variables include tax growth, state and local spending growth, aggregate and per capita spending, government size, revenue source reliance, state (or local) revenue shares, state (or local) expenditure shares, and the ratio of state taxes collected to personal income. Some work also uses TELs as the dependent variable (Brennan and Buchannan, 1979; Cox and Lowery, 1990). Recent research has revisited this topic, challenging the common perception that historical tax revolts lead to the adoption of TELs (Baker, 2003).

Most research, both older and current, tends to find that TELs are ineffective at stopping various levels of government from spending (Bails, 1990; Joyce and Mullins, 1991; Mullins and Joyce, 1996; Hoene, 2004). However, there is research showing that TELs has had moderate success (Bails, 1990; Poulson and Kaplan, 1994; Dye and McGuire, 1997). Still others contend that the degree of success is dependent on other factors within a state such as high income growth (Shadbegian, 1996). Nelson (1986) finds that state-mandated municipal debt limits reduce local spending while property tax limits do not. He also finds that as the state share of total state and local revenue decreases, local spending increases.

Governments have responded to TELS in a variety of ways, both directly and indirectly, for example by: creating new local governments (Bowler and Donovan, 2004); raising fees (Johnston et al., 2000; Hoene, 2004; Kousser et al., 2008); debt financing and other rules (Clingermayer and Wood, 1995; Poterba and Rueben, 2001); and reducing local responsiveness (Mullins and Joyce, 1996). While differing impacts of constitutional and statutory TELs remains an open question, there has been little work here beyond the ranking of state TELs (Brennan and Buchanan, 1979; Abrams and Dougan, 1986).

Although states provide funding for local government and encourage efficiencies and uniformities that might be useful, there are also the not-so-positive components including mandates and restrictions on taxing and spending. These have long been identified but uniform taxonomies have not been adopted and findings frequently vary.

Political Realities

Perhaps most surprising is the lack of empirical work on the political relationships between states and their local government. Obviously state actions are important for localities and thus they need to make their preferences known to state officials. As a former National Association of Counties official told David Berman (2003), "County governments live and die at the state legislature. What Congress does to us is irrelevant in many ways."

One way localities find a voice is through their statewide associations. Another potential mechanism is through members of the state legislature who once served in local government. One empirical study—Lovich and Newman (2004)—found that members who had served in city and county government did have improved knowledge of local government issues over those members who had no such experience. They also found that the longer a legislator had served as a local official, the more likely he/she was to make local government issues a priority. They conclude (based on a national and Washington state survey) that "legislators who lack concrete, sustained experience in city or county government are not as inclined to be attentive to the needs and interests of local governments as those who possess this background" (Lovich and Newman, 2004: 75).

But the temptation to shift assignments to local governments can outweigh these experiences. Berman (2003) notes, "The underlying problem may be as a former League of California Cities lobbyists remarked not long ago, that 'Legislators find out very quickly they can stiff cities with impunity... There are no political consequences...'"

Indeed, many city and county officials feel that legislators regard them as special interests seeking special favors, rather than partners in the governing system. DeSoto (1995) in a survey of state and municipal officials found that state officials were more likely to perceive local municipalities as special interests rather than valued government partners. He found that the governor's office was somewhat more responsive than the state legislature. Several association directors interviewed in one study felt that legislators treat counties "no differently than from a tavern association or a tobacco lobby" (Berman, 2003: 41). Berman noted that local governments are in some sense rival institutions. And thus local governments and their associations often work defensively to try to ward off threats to their authority.

Tipton put it this way,

> Over the past couple of years, I've noticed an increase in the number of Home Rule attacks across Florida....I recognize the unfunded mandates and other legislative measures as Home Rule attacks, but what I see happening now is more than just legislation. It is an attitude among policy-makers that deeply concerns me. What has made counties and municipalities the enemy of the state?...I don't understand where the anger against counties and municipalities comes from. (Tipton, 2008: 2)

Further study of these relationships, particularly given legislative term limits in many state legislatures, would be a worthwhile endeavor and help to put a more analytical framework on these fascinating perceptions.

The Dog that didn't Bark, or Areas Where There is Little or no Research

Probably one of the greatest gaps in state–local research is in the implementation of state mandates and directions. How do localities respond to mandates? Do some levels and local governments with certain characteristics respond differently from others? Of course, implementation in federal–state relationships is also poorly studied, and state–local activities are even much harder to quantify. However, the responsiveness of local governments to states has both theoretical and empirical promise. Two recent articles in the area of education illustrate this promise. Berkman and Plutzer (2011) find that state curricular and testing standards affect the behavior of public school teachers but that local community sentiment also plays a role in teachers' response. Marschall et al. (2011) examine state English-only laws and find that the content of the laws are key in their implementation. But even where the state laws are explicit and detailed, not all targeted local activities are eliminated and when theses laws are vague, the preference of local actors tend to prevail.

While innovation is an argument for local policy making, there have been few careful examinations of the validity of the argument. Benton (2005) notes that we know very little about counties (or cities for that matter) as laboratories of democracy; in some highly publicized areas such as gay rights and gun control, we know some cities do take strong positions—often ahead of the state and national governments. But do states learn from and emulate cities? One study that answered in the affirmative was by Shipan and Volden (2006), who looked at the upward diffusion of anti-smoking policies from US cities to states. They found that policies do "bubble up" but a key variable is the professionalism of the state legislature and strength of health advocates rather than characteristics of the cities.

Another area that is largely understudied is the impact of state law on local elections. Elections and the subjects concerning elections have typically explored local and state levels in a parallel manner. Research on institutions, incumbency, vote share, turnout, mobilization, race, gender, for example, has been conducted for state elections and for local elections but rarely have the two levels met in election research. Areas that could potentially be explored include examining turnout differences based on election timing, the effects of the interactions between state and local level party organizations on elections, and the impact of election laws on local governmental turnout, selection of candidates, and responsiveness to citizens' preferences.

Interest groups and how they operate at state and local levels is another area that is largely understudied. Berkman and Plutzer's (2005) work on school districts and teachers' unions illustrate the importance of this topic. They find that unions attempt to influence policy at both local and state levels—often going to the state when the local school districts do not satisfactorily meet their demands. In general, unions attempt to increase spending on the education budgets at the state level while simultaneously negotiating specific (and generous) teacher benefits at the local level.

CONCLUSION

Research on state–local relationships is broad but often not deep. It is sometimes theoretical but usually more descriptive. And the research questions tend to be narrow and limited in scope. In short, research on state–local relationships needs to go beyond city limits, encompass more than federal and state grants, and answer ambitious questions posed by shared governance and concurrent responsibilities. Finally, political factors undermining governmental actions and reactions need to be more fully explored and explained.

The variety and dynamic nature of state–local relationships make their study difficult—but not daunting. When do states provide more autonomy and when do they take it back? How do localities use this autonomy when it is provided? What is the impact of state election laws on local elections and how are state laws implemented at the local level? Do the same "push-back" and "talling" techniques used by the states occur at the local levels? Do states treat cities and counties differently and how does this matter? How strong are local governmental interest groups in state capitals?

Are states facilitators or obstructionists of local governance? The answer, in short, is that they are both. The question that remains to be answered is how and when.

REFERENCES

Abrams, Burton A., and William R. Dougan. 1986. "The Effects of Constitutional Restraints on Governmental Spending," *Public Choice* 49 (2): 101–16.

Advisory Commission on Intergovernmental Relations. 1990. *Mandates: Cases in State–Local Relations*. Washington, DC: Government Printing Office.

Bails, Dale. 1990. "The Effectiveness of Tax-Expenditure Limitations: A Re-Evaluation," *Social Science Quarterly* 49 (2): 223–38.

Bakvis, Herman and Douglas Brown. 2010. "Policy Coordination in Federal Systems: Comparing Intergovernmental Processes and Outcomes in Canada and the US," *Publius: The Journal of Federalism* 40 (3): 484–507.

Baker, Samuel H. 2003. "The Tax Revolt and Electoral Competition," *Public Choice* 115: 333–45.

Benton, J. Edwin. 2002. "County Service Delivery: Does Government Structure Matter?" *Public Administration Review* 62 (4): 471–9.

Benton, J. Edwin. 2005. "An Assessment of Research on American Counties," *Public Administration Review* 65 (4): 462–74.

Berkman, Michael B. and Eric Plutzer. 2005. *Ten Thousand Democracies*. Washington, DC: Georgetown University Press.

Berkman, Michael B. and Eric Plutzer. 2011. "Local Autonomy vs. State Constraints: Balancing Evolution and Creationism in U.S. High Schools," *Publius: The Journal of Federalism* 41 (4): 610–35.

Berman, David R. 1992. "State–Local Relations: Mandates, Money, Partnerships." In *Municipal Yearbook* 51–57. Washington DC: International City Management Association.

Berman, David R. 2002. "State–Local Relations: Authority, Finances, Cooperation." In *Municipal Year Book 2002*. Washington, DC: International City Management Association.

Berman, David R. 2003. *Local Government and the States*. Armonk, NY: ME Sharpe.

Berman, David R. and Tanis J. Salant. 1996. "The Changing Role of Counties in the Intergovernmental System." In Donald C. Menzel (ed.), *The American County: Frontiers of Knowledge*. Tuscaloosa: University of Alabama Press, 19–33.

Berry, Christopher. 2009. *Imperfect Union: Representation and Taxation in Multilevel Governments*. New York: Cambridge University Press.

Bollens, John C. 1969. *American County Governments*. Beverly Hills, CA: Sage Publications.

Bolleyer, Nicole. 2006. "Federal Dynamics in Canada, the United States, and Switzerland. How Substates' Internal Organization Affects Intergovernmental Relations," *Publius: The Journal of Federalism* 36 (4): 471–502.

Bowler, Shaun and Todd Donovan. 2004. "Evolution in State Governance Structures: Unintended Consequences of State Tax and Expenditures Limitations," *Political Research Quarterly* 59 (2): 189–96.

Bowman, Ann and Richard Kearney. 2011. "Second Order Devolution: Data and Doubt," *Publius: The Journal of Federalism* 41 (4): 563–85.

Brennan, Geoffrey, and James M. Buchanan. 1979. "The Logic of Tax Limits: Alternative Constitutional Constraints on the Power to Tax," *National Tax Journal* 32(2):11–22.

Brennan, Geoffrey, and James M. Buchanan. 1980. *The Power to Tax: Analytical Foundations of a Fiscal Constitution*. Cambridge: Cambridge University Press.

Brown, E. Richard and Michael R. Cousineau. 1984. "The Effectiveness of State Mandates to Maintain Local Government Health Services for the Poor," *Journal of Health Politics, Policy and Law* 9 (2): 223–36.

Briffault, Richard. 1990. "Our Localism: Part I—the Structure of Local Government Law," *Columbia Law Review* 90: 1–115.

Bryan, Frank M. 2004. *Real Democracy: The New England Town Meeting and How It Works*. Chicago: University of Chicago Press.

Burtless, Gary (ed.) 1996. *Does Money Matter? The Effects of School Resources on Student Achievement and Adult Success*. Washington, DC: Brookings Institution Press.

Carr, Jered, Elisabeth Gerber, and Eric Lupher. 2007. *Explaining Horizontal and Vertical Cooperation on Public Services in Michigan: The Role of Local Fiscal Capacity*. Wayne State University Working Group on Interlocal Services Cooperation.

Chernick, Howard and Andrew Reschovsky. 2001. *Lost in the Balance: How State Policies Affect the Fiscal Health of Cities*. Washington, DC: The Brookings Institution.

Clingermayer, James and Richard C. Feiock 2001. *Institutional Constraints and Local Policy Choices: An Exploration of Local Governance*. Albany: State University of New York Press.

Clingermayer, James and B. Dan Wood. 1995. "Disentangling Patterns of State Debt Financing," *American Political Science Review* 89 (1): 108–20.

Connolly, Katrina, David Brunori, and Michael Bell. 2010. "Are State and Local Finances Become More or Less Centralized and Should We Care?" In Michael E. Bell, David Brunori, and Joan Youngman (eds), *The Property Tax and Local Autonomy*. Cambridge, MA: Lincoln Institute of Land Policy.

Cox, James and David Lowery. 1990. "The Impact of the Tax Revolt Era State Fiscal Caps," *Social Science Quarterly* 71(3): 492–509.

Craw, Michael. 2006. "Overcoming City Limits: Vertical and Horizontal Models of Local Redistributive Policymaking," *Social Science Quarterly* 87 (2): 361–79.

Craw, Michael. 2008. "Taming the Local Leviathan: Institutional and Economic Constraints on Municipal Budgets," *Urban Affairs Review* 43 (5): 663–90.

Craw, Michael. 2010. "Deciding to Provide: Local Decisions on Providing Social Welfare," *American Journal of Political Science* 54 (4): 906–20.

Cronin, Thomas E. 1989. *Direct Democracy: The Politics of Initiative, Referendum, and Recall*. Cambridge, MA: Harvard University Press.

DeSoto, William. 1995. "Cities in State Politics: Views of Mayors and Managers," *State and Local Government Review* 27 (Fall): 188–94.

Dye, Richard F. and Therese J. McGuire. 1997. "The Effect of Property Tax Limitation measures on Local Government Fiscal Behavior," *Journal of Public Economics* 66: 469–87.

Eger, Robert J. and Justin Marlowe. 2006. "Hofferbert in Transit: A Dynamic Stages Model of the Urban Policy Process," *Review of Policy Research* 23 (2): 413–32.

Eule, J. 1990. "Judicial-Review of Direct Democracy," *Yale Law Journal* 99 (7): 1503–90.

Falleti, Tulia G. 2010. *Decentralization and Subnational Politics in Latin America*. New York: Cambridge University Press.

Feiock, Richard C. 2007. "Rational Choice and Governance," *Journal of Urban Affairs* 29 (1): 47–63.

Feiock, Richard C. and John T. Scholz. 2010. "Self-Organizing Governance of Institutional Collective Action Dilemmas: An Overview." In Richard C. Feiock and John T. Scholz (eds), *Self-Organizing Federalism*. New York: Cambridge University Press, 3–32.

Feiock, Richard C., M. Jeong, and J. Kim. 2003. "Credible Commitment and Council-manager Government: Implications For Policy Instrument Choices," *Public Administration Review* 63 (5): 616–25.

Fischel, William A. 2001. *The Homevoter Hypothesis*. Cambridge, MA: Harvard University Press.

Fording, Richard C., Joe Soss, and Sanford Schram. 2007. "Devolution, Discretion and the Effect of Local Political Values on TANF Sanctioning," *Social Service Review* 81 (2): 285–316.

Freitag, Markus and Adrian Vatter. 2008. "Decentralization and Fiscal Discipline in Subnational Governments: Evidence from the Swiss Federal System," *Publius: The Journal of Federalism* 38 (2): 272–94.

Frug, Gerald E. and David J. Barron. 2008. *City Bound: How States Stifle Urban Innovation*. Ithaca: Cornell University Press.

Gainsborough, Juliet F. 2003. "To Devolve or not to Devolve? Welfare Reform in the States," *Policy Studies Journal* 31 (4): 603–23.

Gonzalez, Lucas. 2008. "Political Power, Fiscal Crises and Decentralization in Latin America," *Publius: The Journal of Federalism* 38 (2): 211–47.

Hoene, Christopher. 2004. "Fiscal Structure and the Post-Proposition 13 Fiscal Regime in California's cities," *Public Budgeting and Finance* 24 (4): 51–72.

Hooghe, Liesbet and Gary Marks. 2003. "Unraveling the Central State but How? Types of Multi-level Governance," *American Political Science Review* 97: 233–43.

Howards, Irving. 1967. "Property-Tax Rate Limits: A View of Local Government." In Richard W. Lindholm (ed.), *Property Taxation: USA*. Madison: University of Wisconsin Press.

Jenks, Stephen. 1994. "County Compliance with North Carolina's Solid-Waste Mandate: A Conflict-Based Model," *Publius: The Journal of Federalism* 24 (2): 17–36.

Johnston, Jocelyn M., Michael Pagano, and Phillip Russo. 2000. "State Limits and State Aid: An Exploratory Analysis of County Revenue Structure," *State and Local Government Review* 32 (2): 86–97.

Joyce, Philip and Daniel R. Mullins. 1991. "The Changing Fiscal Structure of the State and Local Public Sector: The Impact of Tax and Expenditure Limitations," *Public Administration Review* 51 (3): 240–53.

Kousser, Thad, Mathew D. McCubbins, and Ellen Moule. 2008. "For Whom the TEL Tolls: Can State and Expenditure Limitations Effectively Reduce Spending?" *State Politics and Policy Quarterly* 8 (4): 331–61.

Kozol, Jonathan. 1991. *Savage Inequalities*. New York: Crown.

Krane, Dale, Platon Rigos, and Melvin Hill. 2001. *Home Rule in America: A Fifty-State Handbook*. Washington, DC: CQ Press.

Krane, Dale, Carol Ebdon, and John Bartle. 2004. "Devolution, Fiscal Federalism and Changing Patterns of Municipal Revenues: The Mismatch Between Theory and Reality," *Journal of Public Administration Research and Theory* 14 (4): 513–33.

Krueger, Skip and Ethan Bernick. 2010. "State Rules and Local Governance Choices," *Publius: The Journal of Federalism* 40 (4): 697–718.

Lovell, Catherine and Charles Tobin. 1981. "The Mandate Issue," *Public Administration Review* 41 (3): 318–31.

Lovich, Nicholas P. and Meredith A. Newman. 2004. "The Hearing of Local Government Interests in State Legislatures: The Effects of Prior Service in City or County Government," *State and Local Government Review* 36 (1): 67–77.

Lubell, Mark, Rick Feiock, and Edgar Ramirez. 2005. "Political Institutions and Conservation by Local Governments," *Urban Affairs Review* 40 (6): 706–29.

Magleby, David B. 1984. *Direct Legislation: Voting on Ballot Propositions in the United States*. Baltimore: Johns Hopkins University Press.

Marschall, Melissa, Elizabeth Rigby, and Jasmine Jenkins. 2011. "Do State Politics Constrain Local Actors? The Impact of English Only Laws on Language Instruction in Public Schools," *Publius: the Journal of Federalism* 41 (4): 586–609.

May, Peter J. and Raymond J. Burby. 1996. "Coercive versus Cooperative Policies: Comparing Intergovernmental Mandate Performance," *Journal of Policy Analysis and Management* 15 (2): 171–201.

Miller, Lisa L. 2008. *The Perils of Federalism: Race, Poverty and the Politics of Crime Control*. New York: Oxford University Press.

Morgan, David and Kenneth Kickham. 1999. "Changing the Form of County Government: Effects on Revenue and Expenditure Policy," *Public Administration Review* 59 (4): 315–24.

Morone, James A. 1998. *The Democratic Wish: Popular Participation and the Limits of American Government*. New Haven, CT: Yale University Press.

Mueller, Dennis C. 2003. *Public Choice III*. New York: Cambridge University Press.

Mullins, Daniel R, and Philip G Joyce. 1996. "Tax and Expenditure Limitations and State and Local Fiscal Structure: An Empirical Assessment," *Public Budgeting and Finance* 16 (1): 75–101.

Musgrave, Richard. A. 1959. *The Theory of Public Finance*. New York: McGraw-Hill.

Nathan, Richard and Thomas Gais. 1999. "Early Findings about the Newest New Federalism for Welfare," *Publius: The Journal of Federalism* 28 (3): 95–103.

Nelson, Michael A. 1986. "An Empirical Analysis of State and Local Tax Structure in the Context of the Leviathan Model of Government," *Public Choice* 49 (3): 283–94.

Oates, Wallace. 1972. *Fiscal Federalism*. New York: Harcourt Brace Javanovich.

Oates, Wallace. 1993. "Fiscal Decentralization and Economic Development," *National Tax Journal* 46: 237–43.

Odden, Allan R. and Lawrence O. Picus. 2004. *School Finance: A Policy Perspective*, 3rd edn. New York: McGraw-Hill.

Ostrom, Vincent, Robert Bish, and Elinor Ostrom. 1988. *Local Government in the United States*. Richmond, CA: Institute for Contemporary Studies Press.

Pagano, Michael A. and Jocelyn M. Johnston. 2000. "Life at the Bottom of the Fiscal Food Chain: Examining City and County Revenue Decisions," *Publius: The Journal of Federalism* 30 (1): 159–70.

Peterson, Paul. 1981. *City Limits*. Chicago: University of Chicago Press.

Peterson, Paul and Mark Rom. 1989. "American Federalism, Welfare Policy and Residential Choices," *American Political Science Review* 83 (3): 711–28.

Portz, John, Lana Stein, and Robin R. Jones. 1999. *City Schools and City Politics: Institutions and Leadership in Pittsburgh, Boston, and St. Louis*. Lawrence: University Press of Kansas

Poterba, James M. and Kim S Rueben. 2001. "Fiscal News, State Budget Rules, and Tax-Exempt Bond Yields,", *Journal of Urban Economics* 50: 537–62.

Poulson, Barry W. and Jay Kaplan. 1994. "A Rent-Seeking Model of TELs," *Public Choice* 79: 117–34.

Qian, Yingyi and Barry R. Weingast. 1997. "Federalism as a Commitment to Preserving Market Incentives," *The Journal of Economic Perspectives* 11 (4): 83–92.

Schneider, Mark. 1989. *The Competitive City: The Political Economy of Suburbia*. Pittsburgh: University of Pittsburgh Press.

Schneider, Mark and Kee Ok Park. 1989. "Metropolitan Counties as Service Delivery Agents: the Still Forgotten Government," *Public Administration Review* 49 (July/August): 345–52.

Shadbegian, Ronald J. 1996. "Do Tax and Expenditure Limitations Affect the Size and Growth of State Government?" *Contemporary Economic Policy* 14 (1): 22–35.

Shipan, Charles R. and Craig Volden. 2006. "Bottom-Up Federalism: The Diffusion of Antismoking Policies from U.S. Cities to States," ' *American Journal of Political Science* 50 (4): 825–43.

Stansel, Dean. 2005. 'Local Decentralization and Local Economic Growth: A Cross-Sectional Examination of US Metropolitan Areas," *Journal of Urban Economics* 57: 55–72.

Stein, Robert. 1987. "Tiebout's Sorting Hypothesis," *Urban Affairs Review* 23 (1): 140–60.

Stephens, G. Ross. 1974. "State Centralization and the Erosion of Local Autonomy," *Journal of Politics* 36 (1): 44–76.

Stephens, G. Ross and Nelson Wikstrom. 2007. *American Intergovernmental Relations: A Fragmented Federal Polity*. New York: Oxford University Press.

Steytler, Nico. 2009. *Local Government and Metropolitan Regions in Federal Systems*. Kingston: McGill-Queen's University Press.

Studlar, Donley. 2010. "What Explains the Paradox of Tobacco Control Pricing Under Federalism in the U.S. and Canada? Comparative Federalism Theory Versus Multi-Level Governance," *Publius: the Journal of Federalism* 40 (3): 389–411.

Taylor, Gary D. and Carol S. Weissert. 2002. "Are We Supporting Sprawl Through Aid to High-Growth Communities: Revisiting the 1998 State Revenue Sharing Formula Changes." In Dozier W. Thornton and Carol S. Weissert (eds), *Urban Policy Choices for Michigan Leaders*. East Lansing: Michigan State University Press, 161–73.

Tiebout, Charles. 1956. "A Pure Theory of Local Expenditures," *Journal of Political Economy* 64: 416–24.

Tipton, Lynn. 2008. "More on the 'Pendulum Swing' of Governance," *The Manager* 30 (4). <http://www.fccma.org>. April newsletter.

Watson, Keith and Steven Gold. 1997. *The Other Side of Devolution: Shifting Relationships between State and Local Governments*. Washington, DC: The Urban Institute.

Weber, Ronald and Paul Brace. 1999. *American State and Local Politics: Directions for the 21st Century*. New York: Chatham House.

Weimer David L. and Michael J. Wolkoff. 2001. "School Performance and Housing Values: Using Non-Contiguous District and Incorporation Boundaries to Identify School Effects," *National Tax Journal* 54 (3): 231–53.

Weingast, Barry. 1995. "The Economic Role of Political Institutions: Market-Preserving Federalism and Economic Development," *Journal of Law, Economics and Organization* 11 (1): 1–31.

Weissert, Carol S. 2010. "Commentary." In Michael E. Bell, David Brunori, and Joan Youngman (eds), *The Property Tax and Local Autonomy*. Cambridge, MA: Lincoln Institute of Land Policy, 115–19.

Weissert, Carol S. 2011. "Beyond Marble Cakes and Picket Fences: What U.S. Federalism Scholarship Can Learn from Comparative Research," *Journal of Politics* 73 (4): 966–79.

Wirt, Frederick M. and Michael W. Kirst. 1997. *The Political Dynamics of American Education*. Berkeley, CA: McCutchan.

Wolman, Hal, Robert McManmon, Michael E. Bell, and David Brunori. 2010. "Comparing Local Government Autonomy Across States." In Michael E. Bell, David Brunori, and Joan

Youngman (eds), *The Property Tax and Local Autonomy*. Cambridge, MA: Lincoln Institute of Land Policy, 69–114.

Wong, Kenneth. 1991. "State Reform in Education Finance: Territorial and Social Strategies," *Publius: The Journal of Federalism* 21 (3): 125–42.

Wright, Deil S. 1978. *Understanding Intergovernmental Relations*. Belmont, CA: Brooks Cole.

Xie, Danyang, Heng-fu Zou, and Hamid Davoodi. 1999. "Fiscal Decentralization and Economic Growth in the United States," *Journal of Urban Economics* 45 (1): 228–39.

Zimmerman, Joseph. 1981. *Measuring Local Government Authority*. M-131. Washington, DC: Government Printing Office.

Zimmerman, Joseph. 1995. *State–Local Relations: A Partnership Approach*. 2nd edn. Westport, CN: Praeger.

Zimmerman, Joseph F. 2004. Trends in State–Local Relations. In *The Book of the States 2004*. Vol 36. Lexington, KY: The Council of State Governments, 28–33.

PART II

POLITICAL BEHAVIOR IN THE STATES AND LOCALITIES

CHAPTER 5

···

LOCAL POLITICAL PARTICIPATION

···

BRADY BAYBECK

PHILOSOPHERS and observers from the early days of the American republic have applauded, even romanticized, citizen participation in local self governance. Thomas Jefferson's ideal of democracy required the participation of the yeoman farmer in local affairs. Although Jefferson did not use the term, localism is an apt descriptor for his belief that small government, close to the people, would promote citizenship and virtue among the population (Syed, 1966). Alexis de Tocqueville suggested that the participatory nature of town and township government in the early- to mid-18th century United States was one of the young republic's defining characteristics, and that the high degree of participation in local affairs by citizens was important to the success of the U.S. as a vibrant democracy (Tocqueville, 1990).

Even in the nationalized media environment of the 21st century, local participation is still held in high regard. In the 2008 presidential campaign, Sarah Palin emerged on the national scene as Senator John McCain's vice presidential running mate. At the time, much was made of her start in politics as a city council member of the small Anchorage suburb of Wasilla, Alaska. The narrative was that local issues engaged her and started her on her journey to national prominence. Although her case is obviously not the norm, local political participation is seen as both a steppingstone in and as a cornerstone of American political culture, as the "proving ground of a democratic citizenry" (Oliver, 2001: 15).

Philosophers, pundits, and scholars alike hold local participation in high regard, at least in the abstract sense. However, in many ways local political participation is like family farming—romanticized in the political culture but practiced by relatively few. For example, most city council meetings are lightly attended affairs at best, turnout in local elections can be abysmal when compared with national voting rates, and the average citizen would likely have difficulty naming her mayor, let alone county commissioner. It is fair to say that the philosophical promise of local political participation far exceeds the actual outcomes.

A similar point could be made about scholarly examinations of local participation. Theoretically, the strong tradition of local participation and the large number of relatively autonomous local political entities could provide a rich set of possibilities for research. But it is fair to say that the study of local political participation lags behind this potential. Why is this? With a few exceptions, local political participation is not considered a separate form of participation, different from participation at the state or national levels. What logically follows, perhaps, is that the concept thus does not require its own set of models to explain outcomes; scholars interested in local political participation need not reinvent the wheel. However, the present essay argues otherwise: Local political participation does have some unique and substantively interesting characteristics that deserve more exploration and analysis than they have been receiving.

This essay explores local political participation and how it differs from "other" forms of political engagement. The first question to answer is, "Is there a theory of local political participation?" Surprisingly, as described in the next section, this question does not have an easy answer. The second question is "What is local political participation?" Scholars do not always make a clear distinction between local and other forms of participation, so a discussion is warranted. Finally, the essay will conclude with a discussion of some of the unanswered and conceivably important issues in local political participation.

THE SUBFIELD OF LOCAL POLITICAL PARTICIPATION?

Most review essays about urban and/or local politics begin with a lament that the subfield in question is woefully understudied (e.g., Marschall, 2010), and in most cases this type of claim is justified. At first glance it would appear that local political participation is no exception. Other than perhaps the area of local turnout and voting (see Hajnal and Lewis, 2003; Kelleher and Lowery, 2004), there have been relatively few studies that focus exclusively on local political participation narrowly defined and as a distinct behavior. Rather, local political participation is usually considered as a category—a measurement—of political participation more generally.

The most important studies of American political participation in the last 50 years include measures of participation that could be considered local. Indeed, *most* of the behaviors in these studies are connected to the local political environment. In other words, local political participation has been extensively, if not explicitly, studied under the more general category of political participation. Because the act of political participation is almost always inherently local ("all politics is local"!) the vast field of political participation contains studies that touch upon local political participation through questions asked or behaviors studied.

This presents an interesting conundrum. It is inaccurate to say that local political participation has been ignored—it is present as a quantity of interest or dependent variable in a significant proportion of participation studies. Yet there are very few theories that focus exclusively on the local aspect of participation, and perhaps more important, the determinants of them. In other words, there is no grand theory of local political participation—outside of some theories specific to distinct contexts (e.g. Oliver, 2001, focuses on the suburbs), there is no theory of local participation.

What does this mean? In most subfields, this would present a problem—it would indicate a distinct lack of understanding about some important aspect of the political world. This is not so clear in the case of local participation. It may be that most of what needs to be known is "taken care of" by the more general theories of political participation, or that there is no local component worth examining. Thinking in these terms gives rise to questions: Is local participation different? Why? Does it matter? The answers to these questions are not as easy to answer as one might think—the concept of local has many different meanings and it is not always easy to classify the behavior.

THE CHARACTERISTICS OF LOCAL PARTICIPATION

The United States has a long tradition of a strong civil society that presents many opportunities for citizens to become engaged and involved with the political process. Many of these opportunities arise at the local level, as there is also a tradition of local autonomy and there are many entities of local government. This surfeit of opportunity is also a challenge as it increases the complexity of the system in which individuals choose to— or choose not to—participate. This section describes the complexity of the participatory process at the local level in the United States and how this complexity makes difficult a single theoretical orientation of local political participation.

What is Local Political Participation?

In Verba et al.'s classic formulation, political participation refers to activities individuals engage in with the intent of influencing government outcomes. This action needs to be voluntary and active rather than passive (Verba et al., 1995: 38). These activities range from the relatively lowcost activities of voting to the more costly and engaging acts of lobbying government officials and participating in political protest. Almost without exception, each act of participation can occur at any level of government, in local, state, or national politics—there is a direct analogue. For example, voting occurs in municipal elections as well as in national ones; one can contact a city council person as well as a member of congress; and one can lobby an official to change his or her vote on an act of legislation. The costs may be different, as well as the titles, but at all levels there are more similarities than differences—participation is participation is participation.

Local political participation, then, should be easy to define as those acts that individuals engage in with the intent of influencing local government activity, where "local government" means those entities defined by the United States Bureau of the Census (2007): General purpose governments, like counties, cities, towns, and townships, and special purpose districts like school districts and single function districts. While this seems intuitive to the point of banality, it is important to note that it is not always clear what the terms "local" or "participatory" mean. First, every participatory act, regardless of level, has some local angle to it because of the highly geographic nature of American politics. In Tip O'Neill's famous formulation, all politics is local. Contacting a member of congress, for example, is in many ways a local act; the member of congress, after all, does represent the locality in which a constituent lives. Even that most national of acts, voting for president, has some localness to it, at least if one has to go to the precinct polling place to cast a ballot.

Second, the line between community participation and political participation can be fuzzy. Neighborhood associations, for example, are local and political, and being involved in one can influence the lives of those who live within the neighborhoods' boundaries (Putnam, 2000). Yet neighborhood associations are not governmental in the traditional public administration sense of the term, with public authority granted by constitution or statute. In other words, formal boundaries may unduly limit how participation is defined. This is similar to the difficulties scholars have had in distinguishing between civic engagement and political participation where voluntary problem-solving community activity can be considered the former rather than the latter (Zukin et al., 2006: 7). Yet studies of political participation usually consider informal community activity to be a form of participation (Verba et al., 1995: 42).

Finally, it is not always so easy to classify participation at the local level because local governments are, in most cases, direct service providers—or are at least responsible for the provision of the service. Citizens can be considered consumers of a local good or a bundle of local goods provided by the locality (Tiebout, 1956). This creates an interesting dynamic for participation, in that sometimes the contact with government is akin to calling the cable company to complain about a service disruption. Is calling a city's citizen service bureau (e.g. 311 in New York City) a participatory act? Does a complaint logged on a city website about a pothole mean that a citizen has fulfilled his Jeffersonian duty in the arena of self-governance and reliance? The line between what is participation and what is merely interaction, can be pretty difficult to determine.

Most surveys of participation contain a question about whether a respondent has contacted a government official, but it is not clear if this is the type of contact that pollsters have in mind. The act of contacting an elected official certainly requires a certain amount of engagement even if the purpose is to solve a specific problem, i.e., constituent service, although calling a city department to complain about a burned-out streetlight certainly seems less political and perhaps less participatory. In any event, this is an area where perhaps clearer distinctions need to be made.

The more general literature on political participation has in the main not worried about these nuances. Much, but not all, of the literature on political participation is not concerned with the local aspect of the action and makes very little distinction between the levels at which individuals participate. For many, the very act of participation—voting, contacting, protesting, etc.—is more interesting than the level of government at which the act is targeted. For example, in their classic study *Who Votes?*, Wolfinger and Rosenstone (1980) focus on the act of voting in the general, without regard to context, and the factors that lead to compel individuals to engage in the act of voting (or not). Although substantively speaking they focus on national elections, in some sense the actual election is irrelevant—why someone votes is a function of individual socioeconomic status and this relationship holds true whether the vote is being cast for the president of the United States, for the governor of a state, or the county drain commissioner. With some notable exceptions, this lack of focus on context is common in the literature on political participation.

In a similar vein, some scholars use local acts of participation as variables to be explained, but the "localness" of participation can be seen as merely incidental to political participation. Thus, while many surveys ask questions about local political participation they are seen more as one of many aspects of participating and not as independent, theoretically distinct activities. For example, the Citizen Participation Study used by Verba et al. (1995) asked questions specific to local participation but they were more or less treated as measures of *participation* rather than measures of *local* participation. At the same time, they are certainly not excluding local participation, either; the civic voluntarism model they outline transcends the boundaries between national, state, and local participation.

The above caveats aside, scholars studying local political participation have focused on a relatively few sets of common types of participation and they are essentially defined as participatory acts at governmental levels other than the state or the federal. If you vote in a local election you have participated in local politics. If you attend a meeting or contact a local official, even for very specific service questions, you have participated locally. And obviously those scholars believe that the differences merit attention.

What Sets Local Political Participation Apart?

If local political participation is merely a subset of the field of political participation, why study it? As will be described in this section, there are two aspects that distinguish local political participation from its more general counterpart—the large number of participatory opportunities and the relative accessibility of those opportunities. These aspects really give local political participation a distinct character worthy of its own classification.

The first aspect that sets local political participation apart is the wealth of opportunities. The tradition of localism and the high degree of autonomy afforded local governments in the United States means that there are many potential points where citizens can get involved and engaged. The term "potential points" refers to governmental institutions and individuals with which citizens can interact in a participatory fashion. There are tens of thousands, perhaps hundreds of thousands, of these potential points. The actual number of opportunities to participate is impossible to quantify exactly, but a decent proxy is the number of local governments provided in Table 5.1.

Each one of the 89,476 governments provides a set of participatory opportunities. The county and sub-county governments are classified by the Census Bureau as "general purpose" governments as they tend to provide more than one service. The services provided, however, vary from state to state and even vary within states. For example, in many states counties provide all the services most associate with a municipality—police, fire, public health, etc. In other states, primarily in the northeast, counties exist more or less in name only. "Special purpose" governments provide a single service. To provide a few examples, school districts educate the children, sewer districts collect and treat the wastewater, and parks districts provide recreational opportunities to the citizens of a specific geographic area. The U.S. Census Bureau provides an exhaustive list and is very careful with its definitions—both general and special purpose governments need to exist as organized entities, have governmental character, and substantial autonomy (U.S. Bureau of the Census, 2007).

Some of the entities are more participatory than others, primarily due to their institutional structure. Many of the entities have elected governing boards, which means

Table 5.1 Governments in the United States, 2007

Type	Sub-Type	Totals
Federal		1
States		50
Counties		3,033
	Municipal	19,492
	Town or Township	16,519
Subcounty		36,011
	Special Districts	37,381
	Public School Systems	13,051
Special Purpose		50,432
Total		89,527

Developed by the author based on data from United States Bureau of the Census (2007).
Source: United States Census of Governments (2007).

that citizens are needed to run for office and citizens are needed to vote in elections that select from those running for office. Each of the entities also represents a point of access for citizens who want to advocate (lobby) on a specific issue or set of issues. Finally, these many entities provide many public hearings and board meetings that provide chances for public input—a form of public participation. This public input could range from speaking during the public comments session to staging a noisy protest during a local council meeting.

Table 5.1 provides a good sense of the participatory opportunities but it both under- and overestimates the number of possible participation access points. Because certain types of school districts ("dependent school districts") are excluded from this table, the number of participatory opportunities is likely higher. Dependent school districts are those that are under control of the state or local governments, for example, "interme- diate" school districts in Michigan or the state-appointed board in the City of Louis, Missouri. Not all would have elected school boards (although some do) but they likely have a nonprofessional representational structure of some sort and would thus provide opportunities to participate. At the same time, Table 5.1 likely overstates the number of possible opportunities for participation, as many of the special districts are single function districts that have appointed boards, very little visibility, and that operate like a business or a nonprofit. For example, many water districts have "customers" and seem more like a regulated utility than like a government entity that encourages political participation.

As noted above, there is a great deal of institutional variation both within and across the categories of local government, providing a rich yet asymmetric environ- ment for individual participation. There is variation in representative structure. For example, some counties have a commission form of government while others have a county council and executive; some cities have a strong mayor form while others have a council-manager form; and special districts greatly vary in the level of independence they have from other jurisdictions. Certainly the varied types of structures offer citizens different opportunities for participation.

But yet there is more variation of the representative structures. Some local gov- ernments elect their executives and their governing bodies, while in others they are appointed by some other authority. In many, but not all, cases, the "other" appoint- ing authority is the state or the elected board. The literature in this area is scant, but the elected versus appointed distinction not only changes the politics (see Huber and Gordon, 2004 for a study of judicial appointment) it also changes the incentive struc- tures for an individual to participate. And yet there is still more variation. For those structures that have elections, the mechanisms used to select the officials differ. Some entities have nonpartisan elections while others are partisan; there are local govern- ments represented by At-large, district, and mixed representative bodies; and some hold elections in conjunction with state and national elections while others explicitly hold them at different times of the year.

It should be clear by now that there is significant variation in institutional structure. An exhaustive classification of the variation across the types would be exhausting and not particularly helpful to the task of this essay. But it is important to keep in mind that this variation provides a useful laboratory to assess the effects of institutional structure on participation, and, as will be discussed later, scholars have taken advantage of these opportunities.

The second aspect that sets local participation apart is accessibility. Although there is very little (if any) research in this area, it seems reasonable to assume that local government is more accessible than state government and certainly the federal government. Given the high degree of fragmentation, it is likely that a citizen knows someone in local government personally, or at least knows someone who knows someone. By extension, the probability of obtaining a desired outcome through personal networks should be higher. Although this concept of accessibility is more of a theoretical Jeffersonian ideal—there is very little research in this area—there is some evidence to suggest that citizens know their local officials personally in small town and small suburban contexts (Oliver, 2001: 39).

Rates of Participation

Local political participation also differs from other levels in the rates at which individuals engage in the activity. Interestingly, the differences are context dependent and are somewhat contradictory; there seems to be an inverse relationship between the cost of the act and the likelihood of an individual doing it. When the participation is relatively costless to the individual, participation is lower at the local when compared to the state and national levels; when the cost is relatively high, there is a distinct local advantage.

The relatively costless form of participation is, of course, voting. Study after study has shown that turnout in local elections is abysmal, even when compared with the already low rates in state or non-presidential national elections. Hajnal and Lewis (2003) cite a number of studies (Alford and Lee, 1968; Morlan, 1984; Bridges, 1997) to argue that local turnout is so low as to be a threat to democracy. Although there is significant variation across cities (Trounstine, 2010: 410), most local elections are low turnout affairs. The best estimate is that turnout in municipal elections is approximately half that of national elections (Hajnal and Lewis, 2003: 645–6). Caren (2007: 31) cites examples of single digit percentage turnout in (relatively) major cities like Fort Worth, Texas, and Oklahoma City, Oklahoma. Berry (2009: 64–5) convincingly draws upon logic and case studies to argue that turnout in special elections is probably even worse than general purpose government elections. That is, citizens are far less likely to vote for drain commissioner than they are for mayor, and they are less likely to vote for mayor than they are for president. The reasons for this are complex (and discussed later in this essay), but this is one of the few consistent findings in local political participation—turnout in local elections occupies last place in an already low division.

But of course participation is not just about voting, there are other aspects that are perhaps more important and perhaps more effective for the engaged citizen. Contacting an official directly with one's concerns, for example, is a much more precise and proactive way to offer feedback than is voting against an incumbent who may not understand the message one is trying to convey. To continue the example, if one is not happy with the response from the official through direct contact, then running for city council against that official is certainly an even more direct way to strive for, and perhaps achieve, one's political and policy goals. Voting is neither direct nor proactive.

The findings on other forms of local political participation are not so clear in terms of the differences between the local, state, and national levels. It is first important to make a simple logical point based upon elementary algebra. Because there are by definition more local elected officials—in fact, many more—there are more opportunities for individuals to participate by running for office. The most recent estimate, made by the Census Bureau in 1992, was that there are 493,830 local elected officials in the United States (U.S. Bureau of the Census, 1995, 1). This exceeds by a factor of nearly 1000 the number of elected officials at the national level and by 26 the number at the state level. Whether this fulfills the Jeffersonian ideal of small democracy is beyond the scope of this essay, but it is clear that, by definition, rates of running for office are higher at the local than at the state or national levels.

Even though the number of local elected officials is high in absolute terms, it is probably too much to assume that more than a very small percentage of the population will ever run for office. Other forms of participation beyond turnout and running for office are worth examining. As with turnout, there are few studies that focus on obtaining a national portrait of other forms of participation. However, some of the fundamental works on political participation over the past few decades have measured the extent of non-turnout participation. In lamenting the decline of community in the United States, Putnam (2000, Ch. 2) argues that participation in local political activities has, without exception and across multiple dimensions, dropped over the 25 year period from 1970–95. Using Roper data, Putnam does not compare the trends across the levels of government, but it is clear he is arguing that local political participation is becoming an exceedingly rare if not extinct part of American political life.

One could come to a more sanguine perspective on local political participation after reading Verba et al.'s (1995, Ch. 3) definitive description of participation from their Citizen Participation Study (CPS) data. Local political participation is not the focus of Verba and his colleagues but their CPS did ask questions specific to the activity. As with Putnam's data, involvement with local politics beyond voting is a relatively rare act. For example, only 17 percent of the respondents in their study participate in an informal community activity, which is quite a low threshold for participation, and this was the highest percentage of the questions asked specific to local participation. Yet when they compared specific acts of local participation with the state and the national levels, there were some intriguing and consistent differences. For example, of those who worked on a political campaign, 50 percent of respondents worked on a *local* campaign, twice the levels in state or national campaigns. Contact with public officials had similar if not so dramatic differences. The only act in which local did not exceed the others was in the area of campaign contributions, which suggests that, at least for local political participation, time is more important than money. This seems reasonable as the relatively micro nature of local politics means that campaigning is more than just buying ads in the metropolitan television market.

As the discussion has hopefully made clear, local political participation does have some factors that distinguish it from its other colleagues. It still is not clear though if these differences amount to a variable to be factored into a model of political participation more generally, or if the differences mean that local political participation warrants its own set of theories. The next section assesses the explanations of political participation in light of the intriguing differences presented above.

EXPLAINING LOCAL POLITICAL PARTICIPATION

What sets explanations of local participation apart from national and/or state participation, or political participation more generally? In local political participation there is a focus on the contexts, institutional and social, in which individuals reside and their effects on participation. Arguably, the *American Voter* (Campbell et al., 1960) model of behavior, with its reliance on a national sample, ignores the possible effects of location and context when it comes to explaining political participation; the focus instead is on individual factors. Scholars of local political participation differ from this perspective by arguing that the characteristics of where individuals live have explanatory power on whether they participate and in what fashion. In other words, geographic context plays a role in an individual's participatory calculus.

The focus on context does not mean that individual factors are dismissed or completely ignored. In fact, the individual reasons for participating are always included in models that explain political participation. There are no theories arguing, for instance, that local political participation is disconnected from socioeconomic status (SES), or that Verba et al.'s (1995) Civic Voluntarism Model of resources, engagement, and recruitment does not explain at least some aspect of an individual's decision to participate in some facet of local political life. No one argues that mobilization does not play a key role in the calculus (Leighley, 1995). An individual with a grade school education is not more likely to contact his city council member than a college-educated fellow citizen. Every model, then, contains individual-level measures along the lines of education, income, and other "usual suspect" demographics.

The focus on context is the primary additional factor that gives local participation an orientation distinct from other participation subfields. There is a rich, albeit relatively recent, tradition of scholarship that emphasizes the importance of geographic context. Huckfeldt's (1983) work was certainly not the first study of context (see Durkheim, 1951; or Berelson et al., 1954), but it was among the first to make a direct theoretical and empirical link between the local geographic context and local political participation. The basic theoretical link, if you will, is that the characteristics of context act upon an individual in ways different from her individual traits.

Political science more generally has engaged in a lively debate about context and its effects (see Books and Prysby, 1991; Agnew, 1996; King, 1996), and the debate has yet to be settled. This is because direct evidence—evidence that is more than correlational—is difficult if not impossible to come by; most findings are like Oliver and Ha (2007), which concludes that community characteristics are statistically significant after controlling for individual factors. These types of findings will always encourage skepticism among those who do not believe that context is worth measuring (King, 1996). Most scholars interested in local political participation argue however that local context is theoretically a strong idea and that the statistical correlations are applicable evidence. To argue otherwise would suggest that local political participation is dependent only on individual factors, which would mean that the local participation would be no different from participation at any other level.

Assuming, then, that the context matters, which is the appropriate geographic context to use when assessing local political participation? There are two broad categories; institutional and social. Institutional refers to the political, usually formal and legal, environment in which individuals are located. The general and special purpose governments described above are the institutional contexts of interest in local political participation: Counties, cities, school districts, and special districts. Social contexts are those entities whose boundaries are not necessarily proscribed in law, primarily neighborhoods and social networks (Huckfeldt, 1986). The choice of which level is driven by careful theorizing and there may be multiple levels at work on a single individual (Baybeck, 2006). Although they are substantively different, the institutional and social contexts work in similar ways on the individual; they factor into an individual's decision calculus on whether to participate, and they do so (but not necessarily in the same way) for every person in the same context.

The vast majority of studies on institutional context focus on one variable, turnout in local elections. A significant majority of these focus specifically on turnout in municipal elections. Very little work, if any, has been done on explaining the turnout in elections for county, school district, and special district governing boards (but see Berry, 2009, for special districts), and few focus on cities outside of major metropolitan areas. Work that has been done on municipal elections focuses on the various mechanisms of election described above and their effects on turnout. Other recent review articles have covered these differences in detail (see Marschall, 2010; Trounstine, 2010), but it is useful to briefly note some key findings and to discuss their effects on participation.

Studies of turnout in municipal elections suggest that the so-called "progressive" reforms depress turnout. These include the council-manager form of government, where a professional city manager performs the administrative function, nonpartisan elections, At-large elections, and elections not held concurrently with state and national elections. All of these institutional structures lead to lower turnout in municipal elections (Alford and Lee, 1968; Welch and Bledsoe, 1988; Hajnal and Lewis, 2003; Caren, 2007) and there is a distinct effect of depoliticizing municipal government—the more administrative the city, the lower the turnout (Wood, 2002).

Another strain of the literature dealing with institutional effects on participation has been a focus on the size of the locality (almost always the city), where size is defined not by geographic area but by population. Kelleher and Lowery (2004: 721) nicely encapsulate the primary debate as one between "small is beautiful" and "large is lively." In the small is beautiful camp, the theoretical argument suggests that local political participation is higher in small, homogeneous communities, as the population shares a significant number of interests and thus feels more efficacious (Oliver, 2001). This idea is consistent with a long line of literature that examines the effects of suburbanization on politics and participation (e.g. Gainsborough, 2001). The larger is lively camp argues that larger cities, particularly ones that span metropolitan areas, are more likely to contain heterogeneous populations. When there is heterogeneity, there is conflict, and when there is conflict there is incentive to participate. Thus citizens in large, metropolitan areas are more engaged and more likely to participate (Dahl, 1967; Kelleher and Lowery, 2004: 726).

Like any good academic debate, the end result has been somewhat conflicting findings when the theoretical abstractions are translated into specific tests of hypotheses using empirical data. Oliver's (2001) exhaustive study examines many aspects of local participation and finds that participation decreases as city size increases, while Kelleher and Lowery's (2004) analysis finds that large, concentrated metropolitan governments lead to increased voting turnout in local elections. Both use somewhat indirect methods of testing—finding significant relationships after controlling for demographic factors—and neither has conclusively established causality. Since they each use different data, the former at the level of the individual and the latter at the aggregated metropolitan area level, they do not exactly contradict, either. Quite clearly, more research needs to be done in this area.

Social context provides the other geographic frame by which to examine local political participation. In this context, the theoretical link is not about how the environment impacts incentives, as it does with the institutional context. Rather, it focuses on how an individual's surroundings control, constrain, or filter the flow of information to the individual. Depending on the composition of the context, these flows either encourage or discourage the individual to participate in local politics (Huckfeldt, 1986).

The primary unit, at least in research on local political participation, has been on the neighborhood, and the findings have been relatively consistent—the more challenging the conditions, the lower the level of participation. That is, residence in low-income, minority-dominated, and/or poverty-concentrated neighborhoods diminishes the likelihood of participation, all else equal. These findings have been confirmed across a variety of local acts of participation, including voting (although in national and not necessarily local elections (Alex-Assensoh, 1997) and community group participation (Huckfeldt, 1979). Being a member of a minority group in a poor neighborhood further reduces the likelihood of local political participation (Cohen and Dawson, 1993). Neighborhood is not the only unit used—some have used counties to find similar results (Giles and Dantico, 1982; Matsubayashi, 2010). The sum of these findings strongly suggests that social context matters.

The above two contextual environments—institutional and social—have dominated the research that attempts to explain local political participation. This research has clearly demonstrated that there are factors other than someone's individual characteristics that influence her decision to participate. However, it would be quite myopic to assume that these two factors, no matter how expansively examined, cover the universe of possible effects. To some extent, the domination by the contextual approaches has nearly, but not completely, drowned out other possible causal factors. For example, an intriguing area of research focuses on the role that nonprofit groups play in participation through community organizing. Nonprofit groups can be neighborhood associations, social-service agencies, and churches. In political science, at least, this is a relatively novel direction, but the initial findings are at best mixed. Much of the research focuses on urban areas and finds that nonprofits do have a positive impact on the political incorporation of minorities into the political process (Hula and Jackson-Elmore 2001). At the same time, however, evidence is somewhat preliminary and has focused on the outputs of community organizations rather than the actual effect on individual participation (LeRoux, 2007: 414). Studies that have focused on the effects of participatory institutions such as neighborhood associations echo Berry et al. (1993) and suggest that the correlation between the existence of these entities and the participation rates at the local level is very complex and subtle.

FUTURE RESEARCH DIRECTIONS

As should be clear by now, much of the research on local political participation has focused on the geographic aspects of the behavior—how the spatial environment influences the likelihood of participation. This is reasonable, considering that local political life is inherently rooted in (relatively) small spaces that we call communities, cities, counties, or neighborhoods, to name a few. In order to move forward, however, scholars need to have a clearer understanding of the implications that modern life has for local political participation. That is, telecommunications and transportation technology have made it easier for individuals to transcend neighborhood and city boundaries and to build and maintain regional, national, or even international networks of friends, family, and/or like-minded colleagues (Cairncross, 1997; Wuthnow, 1998; Baybeck and Huckfeldt, 2002). Gone are the days, if they ever truly existed, of the relatively isolated but highly participatory community. In other words, the meaning of geography has changed.

Scholars of local political participation need to do a better job of understanding this relatively new geographic reality. Will place-based measures remain as important predictors of local participation? Have they declined? Are less geographically-constrained social environments and networks (Huckfeldt and Sprague, 1995; Huckfeldt et al., 2004) better predictors of local political participation? For example, is a national friendship network a better explanatory variable than one's community? At the very least, research on local participation should pay attention to the emerging literature on social networks and non-local political participation (e.g. McClurg, 2006), which has done a good job of making the causal connections between the aggregate and the individual behavior.

Technology also brings about a second set of questions regarding the media environment and its effect on local political participation. The decimation of the daily newspaper—or at least the local content in it—and the emergence of social media have changed the means by which citizens get their political information and these changes have had impacts, usually negative, on political participation (Prior, 2007; Hindman, 2009). This shift has accelerated in recent years and it is difficult to project what things will look like in two, five, or ten years, but it is reasonable to assume that rapid change will continue and that the metropolitan daily as traditionally understood will be an anachronism. This new environment presents both obstacles and opportunities for participation. On the one hand, local news stories are no longer covered in depth by the major news outlets of the locality, which may mean that citizens are unaware of an issue that might motivate them to participate. On the other hand, an issue may go viral and reach citizens through social networking sites, motivating them to get involved. How does the new media environment influence participation? Are the mechanisms different at the local, as opposed to the state and national levels?

The third set of questions deals with the normative aspects of participation. Most view participation and citizen engagement as positive for a democracy and to be encouraged. A logical corollary of this is that a society should maximize opportunities for its citizens to participate—and with its smorgasbord of local governments, the United States certainly does provide these opportunities. However, as noted in this essay, the complex arrangements may actually confuse citizens and depress local participation by increasing the information costs (Baybeck, 2006; Berry, 2009). So it is important to ask, can there be too much of a good thing? Is a complicated institutional structure, with overlapping authority and accountability, good for a democratic and participatory society? These questions are not so easily answered, but they get at the heart of what the American ideal of localism is all about—that decentralization, fragmentation, and autonomy of local government leads to more democratic, participatory, and representative government.

Finally, we know comparatively little about non-electoral forms of local political participation. The relatively well-developed literature on local voting should continue to move forward, of course, but other aspects of participation—contacting, attending meetings, just getting involved—are as important. What are the effects of institutional and geographic context, for example, on the likelihood of a citizen attending a school board meeting? Why would anyone attend a public comment session? Why do people run for unpaid local government offices that usually mean constant hassle and complaints from your neighbors? Oliver's (2001) work on the broader aspects in the suburbs represents a good first step, but there is room for analysis that includes other, very different, contexts, and there is also room for work on the multiple layers of local politics.

CONCLUSION

What would the early boosters of localism make of the environment of local political participation today? It is of course difficult to say—the institutional arrangements and technology are far more complicated today than in Jefferson and de Tocqueville's day. It is clear, however, that localism survives through the immense number of participatory opportunities that exist at the local level in American society. Today there are more opportunities to participate than there were 200 years ago. But it is also clear that most citizens are not taking advantage of the opportunities. Perhaps citizens are easily overwhelmed by the possibilities—there are many different types of local governments, functions and authority overlap and are contradictory, and there are likely too many of them. Should we want to increase local participation—and most agree this is a good idea—we need to better understand the causal factors behind it.

As this essay has noted, it is these environmental characteristics—variation, complexity, abundance—that set local political participation apart from its state and federal colleagues. Substantively speaking, the rich number of opportunities means that by definition participation is higher at the local level, atleast when looking beyond the relatively simple and relatively costless act of voting. Because more citizens participate locally than at any other level (again, independent of voting), understanding its determinants is important. Theoretically speaking, localism has been and remains an important philosophy in American politics. Because of this, measuring and explaining localism through local political participation is also crucial. In other words, local political participation deserves more attention than it gets from political science, and hopefully the next few years will take us there.

REFERENCES

Agnew, John. 1996. "Mapping Politics: How Context Counts in Electoral Geography." *Political Geography* 15: 129–146.

Alex-Assensoh, Yvette. 1997. "Race, Concentrated Poverty, Social Isolation, and Political Behavior." *Urban Affairs Review* 33: 209–27.

Alford, Robert R., and Eugene C. Lee. 1968. "Voting Turnout in American Cities." *American Political Science Review* 62: 796–813.

Baybeck, Brady. 2006. "Sorting Out the Competing Effects of Racial Context." *The Journal of Politics* 68: 386–96.

Baybeck, Brady, and Robert Huckfeldt. 2002. "Urban Contexts, Spatially Dispersed Networks, and the Diffusion of Political Information." *Political Geography* 21: 195–220.

Berelson, Bernard R., Paul F. Lazarsfeld, and William N. McPhee. 1954. *Voting: A Study in Opinion Formation in a Presidential Campaign* (Chicago, IL: University of Chicago Press).

Berry, Christopher R. 2009. *Imperfect Union: Representation and Taxation in Multilevel Governments* (New York, NY: Cambridge University Press).

Berry, Jeffrey M., Kent. E. Portney, and Ken Thompson. 1993. *The Rebirth of Urban Democracy* (Washington, DC: Brookings Institution Press).

Books, John, and Charles L. Prysby. 1991. *Political Behavior and the Local Context* (New York, NY: Praeger Publishers).

Bridges, Amy. 1997. *Morning Glories: Municipal Reform in the United States* (Princeton, NJ: Princeton University Press).

Cairncross, Frances. 1997. *The Death of Distance* (Cambridge, MA: Harvard Business School Press).

Campbell, Angus, Philip E. Converse, Warren E. Miller, and Donald E. Stokes. 1960. *The American Voter* (Chicago: University of Chicago Press, originally published by John A. Wiley and Sons, Inc.).

Caren, Neal. 2007. "Big City, Big Turnout? Electoral Participation in American Cities." *Journal of Urban Affairs* 29: 31–46.

Cohen, Cathy J., and Michael C. Dawson. 1993. "Neighborhood Poverty and African American Politics." *American Political Science Review* 87: 286–302.

Dahl, Robert A. 1967. "The City in the Future of Democracy." *American Political Science Review* 61: 953–70.

de Tocqueville, Alexis. 1990. *Democracy in America*, Volume I (New York: Vintage Classics).

Durkheim, Emile. 1951. *Suicide. Translated by John Spaulding*, originally published in 1897 (New York: Free Press).

Gainsborough, Juliet F. 2001. *Fenced Off: The Suburbanization of American Politics* (Washington, DC: Georgetown University Press).

Giles, Michael W., and Marilyn Dantico. 1982. "Political Participation and Neighborhood Social Context Revisited." *American Journal of Political Science* 26: 144–50.

Hajnal, Zoltan L., and Paul G. Lewis. 2003. "Municipal Institutions and Voter Turnout in Local Elections." *Urban Affairs Review* 38: 645–68.

Hindman, Matthew. 2009. *The Myth of Digital Democracy* (Princeton, NJ: Princeton University Press).

Huber, Gregory A., and Sanford C. Gordon. 2004. "Accountability and Coercion: Is Justice Blind When It Runs for Office?" *American Journal of Political Science* 48: 247–63.

Huckfeldt, Robert. 1983. "Political Participation and the Neighborhood Social Context." *American Journal of Political Science* 23: 579–92.

Huckfeldt, Robert. 1986. *Politics in Context: Assimilation and Conflict in Urban Neighborhoods* (New York, NY: Agathon Press).

Huckfeldt, Robert, Paul E. Johnson, and John Sprague. 2004. *Political Disagreement: The Survival of Diverse Opinions within Communication Networks* (New York, NY: Cambridge University Press).

Huckfeldt, Robert, and John Sprague. 1995. *Citizens, Politics, and Social Communication* (New York: Cambridge University Press).

Hula, Richard C., and Cynthia Jackson-Elmore. 2001. "Nonprofit Organizations as Political Actors: Avenues for Minority Political Incorporation." *Policy Studies Review* 18: 27–47.

Kelleher, Christine, and David Lowery. 2004. "Political Participation and Metropolitan Institutional Contexts." *Urban Affairs Review* 39: 720–57.

King, Gary. 1996. "Why Context Should Not Count." *Political Geography* 15: 159–64.

LeRoux, Kelly. 2007. "Nonprofits as Civic Intermediaries: The Role of Community-Based Organizations in Promoting Political Participation." *Urban Affairs Review* 42: 410–22.

Leighley, Jan E. 1995. "Attitudes, Opportunities and Incentives: A Field Essay on Political Participation." *Political Research Quarterly* 48: 181–209.

Marschall, Melissa J. 2010. "The Study of Local Elections in American Politics," in *The Oxford Handbook of American Elections and Political Behavior* (New York: Oxford University Press), pp. 471–492.

Matsubayashi, Tetsuya. 2010. "Racial Environment and Political Participation." *American Politics Research* 38: 471–501.

McClurg, Scott. 2006. "Political Disagreement in Context: The Conditional Effect of Neighborhood Context, Disagreement and Political Talk on Electoral Participation." *Political behavior* 28: 349–66.

Morlan, Robert L. 1984. "Municipal Versus National Election Voter Turnout: Europe and the United States." *Political Science Quarterly* 99: 457–70.

Oliver, J. Eric. 2001. *Democracy in Suburbia* (Princeton, NJ: Princeton University Press).

Oliver, J. Eric, and Shang E. Ha. 2007. "Vote Choice in Suburban Elections." *American Political Science Review* 101: 393–408.

Prior, Markus. 2007. *Post-Broadcast Democracy: How Media Choice Increases Inequality in Political Involvement and Polarizes Elections* (New York, NY: Cambridge University Press).

Putnam, Robert D. 2000. *Bowling Alone: The Collapse and Revival of American Community* (New York: Simon & Schuster).

Syed, Anwar Hussain. 1966. *The Political Theory of Local Government* (New York: Random House).

Tiebout, Charles M. 1956. "A Pure Theory of Local Expenditures." *The Journal of Political Economy* 64: 416–24.

Trounstine, Jessica. 2010. "Representation and Accountability in Cities." *Annual Review of Political Science* 13: 407–23.

United States Bureau of the Census. 1995. *1992 Census of Governments*, Volume 1, Number 2 (Washington, DC: Government Printing Office).

United States Bureau of the Census. 2007. *2007 Census of Governments*. Retrieved from <http://www.census.gov/govs/cog/>. June 10, 2013.

Verba, Sidney, Kay Lehman Schlozman, and Henry E. Brady. 1995. *Voice and Inequality: Civic Voluntarism in American Politics* (Cambridge, MA: Harvard University Press).

Welch, Susan, and Timothy Bledsoe. 1988. *Urban Reform and Its Consequences: A Study in Representation* (Chicago, IL: University of Chicago Press).

Wolfinger, Raymond E., and Steven J. Rosenstone. 1980. *Who Votes?* (New Haven, CT: Yale University Press).

Wood, Curtis. 2002. "Voter Turnout in City Elections." *Urban Affairs Review* 38: 209–31.

Wuthnow, Robert. 1998. *Loose Connections: Joining Together in America's Fragmented Communities* (Cambridge, MA: Harvard University Press).

Zukin, Cliff, Scott Keeter, Molly Andolina, Krista Jenkins, and Michael X. DelliCarpini. 2006. *A New Engagement? Political Participation, Civic Life, and the Changing American Citizen* (New York: Oxford University Press).

CHAPTER 6

STATE POLITICAL PARTICIPATION

Election Law, Electoral Competition, and Inequality

CAROLINE TOLBERT AND WILLIAM W. FRANKO

A large body of theory and research has improved our understanding of demographic and attitudinal characteristics that distinguish voters from nonvoters in the U.S. (for reviews, see Campbell et al., 1960; Wolfinger and Rosenstone, 1980; Leighley and Nagler, 1992; Rosenstone and Hansen, 2003; Lewis-Beck et al., 2008). It is widely understood that individuals with higher socioeconomic status, age, white ethnicity, and strong partisanship are associated with an increased probability of voting and other forms of political participation, such as contributing money to campaigns or parties. Or to highlight the other face of the coin, a long tradition of research shows nonvoters are disproportionally poor, uneducated, non-white, and young (Piven and Cloward, 1988). But in traditional voting behavior models, such as the *American Voter* (Campbell et al., 1960), the environment or state context in which individuals live is largely overlooked. The 50 American states vary in a multitude of ways in terms of politics, policies, institutions, and reform (Donovan, Mooney, and Smith 2011) and these contextual factors can have a profound impact in shaping turnout and other forms of participation. We argue the American states are where the real action in studying political participation over the past two decades can be found, and the robust scholarship in this area is proof of its importance. This essay is divided into three sections, focusing on the impact of political institutions (election laws), political environments (electoral competition), and inequality in participation rates, or class bias, across the states. We highlight a few, emphasis on a few, of the myriad ways that the American states matter for participation in our democracy.

The States and Participation Historically

The states have played a central role in citizen participation since the colonial era. Although not commonly discussed in contemporary American politics textbooks, one of the most contentious debates at the Constitutional Convention of 1878 among the Founding Fathers was voting qualifications in national elections. Those that wanted to expand suffrage framed the debate in terms of rights, while those that desired to restrict voting framed the debate in terms of privilege (Keyssar, 2000). Unable to agree, the compromise they drafted gave "congressional authority over regulation of congressional elections to the state legislatures, a decision that would have profound consequences for voting rights and turnout rates in subsequent years" (McDonald, 2010: 126). Until the early 1900s, state legislatures elected U.S. senators and there were no direct elections for members of the Electoral College, so congressional elections were the mechanism for citizen participation in government. This compromise gave virtually exclusive power over representation in the federal government to the states, as well as regulating participation by the masses in politics.

Over the past two centuries of American history, a dominant trend has been federal constitutional amendments designed to override state voting barriers, expanding suffrage to non-land owning classes, African Americans, women, citizens 18 and older and more (Donovan and Bowler, 2004, Ch. 1). As McDonald notes (2010, 126) countervailing this trend are periods when the states acted aggressively to restrict suffrage, including poll taxes, and literacy tests used first as a means to curtail the immigrant base of the urban Northern political machines, and later imported to the Southern states to disfranchise Africans Americans and uneducated white people during the Jim Crow era following Reconstruction (Kousser, 1999). It would take over 100 years for these voting restrictions to be lifted by the 1965 Voting Rights Act. Today voting rights are granted to all American citizens age 18 and older, some states revoke this right from those who have committed a felony or are mentally incompetent. Voter identification laws in the states, however, disproportionately affect minority citizens and the less affluent (Barreto, Nuño, and Sanchez, 2009). Despite the amendments, the decentralized system of elections established by the Founding Fathers remains intact, with the states retaining control of voter registration and regulating voting. This decentralized system creates tremendous variation in the laws governing elections and voting, and participation in politics (Cain, Donovan, and Tolbert, 1998).

Overview: What Influences Participation?

A common starting point for scholars examining the causes of participation is the idea that individuals face a number of costs and benefits related to their decision to become involved in the political process (Downs, 1957; Riker and Ordeshook, 1968). The general belief is that if the benefits of an individual participating—for example, voting in an election—outweigh the costs for a particular person, that individual is likely to participate and vice versa. One benefit associated with voting, for instance, may include obtaining policy benefits as a result of having one's preferred candidate or party in office, which is balanced by the likelihood of an individual's vote influencing the outcome of the election. Another benefit of voting is the sense of pride gained from fulfilling an individual's perceived notion of civic duty. The costs related to voting can include the time and resources needed to cast a ballot, or one's ability to obtain and process political information.

This rational choice approach to understanding political participation has led to the identification of several factors found to affect whether an individual decides to cast a ballot on Election Day. These factors can be grouped into three general categories: a person's socioeconomic characteristics and attitudes about politics, the institutions that shape the political process, and the political environment in which elections take place. We focus on the last two in this essay. While these elements of voter turnout do not necessarily operate independently from one another, it is conceptually useful to think about the causes of participation as components of these three broader groupings. The combination of these factors creates varying degrees of inequality in turnout rates across the states, discussed in the third section of this essay.

In order to overcome the costs of participating in an election, individuals typically need some degree of political resources and skills. Evidence of this is provided by the many studies showing those most likely to vote are upper-class citizens (e.g., Wolfinger and Rosenstone, 1980; Rosenstone and Hansen, 1993; Verba, Schlozman, and Brady, 1995). More affluent individuals have the money, time, education, and capacity to effectively participate in the political system. These characteristics are also related to attitudes toward politics, which can influence whether one turns out to vote. Higher levels of political interest, psychological involvement in politics, and political efficacy are associated with individuals higher on the socioeconomic scale (Verba and Nie, 1972).

Although studying the personal attributes related to voter turnout has certainly advanced our understanding of participation, our knowledge of political engagement is incomplete when only considering individual-level factors. Paralleling the nature versus nurture debate about human behavior generally, state election environments are the "nurture" in terms of influencing participation, where as individual-level factors are the "nature." Our incomplete understanding based on individual-level factors is demonstrated by the apparent paradox related to voter participation from a cross-national perspective. If more political resources lead to a greater likelihood of voting, why does the U.S., one of the most prosperous countries in the world, have such a dismal history of participation? The effects of political environments and political institutions on participation have often been the focus of research looking to answer this question. Studies comparing the electoral contexts of various countries have found that political context may be the most important influence on voter turnout (Powell, 1986; Franklin, 1996).

The American states vary in terms of political environments and political institutions. Political institutions are typically thought of as the rules and laws governing the political process, specifically elections. This may include procedures for electing candidates to office, how and when individuals cast their ballots, or who can vote. Again, certain rules are believed to lower the costs of voting while others may increase costs or diminish benefits by way of making the vote seem meaningless. For instance, having lenient registration requirements may decrease the costs of voting, while electing representatives under proportional representation can make an individual's vote more worthwhile. A number of factors associated with political environments—closeness of the election, campaign spending, and elite mobilization efforts, to name a few—have been identified as playing an important role in turnout rates. Political environments can be measured by competition between parties and political candidates to win an election. Electoral competition is thought to lower the costs of voting by making an individual's vote more likely to matter and easing the costs of obtaining information.

Studying these contextual political influences has placed a greater emphasis on the value of the American states as units of analysis. The 50 states provide researchers with variation in levels of voter turnout and other forms of engagement in politics, as well as differences in political environments and institutions. This state-level diversity allows scholars to expand our knowledge of participation by testing the ways in which political context influences voter turnout within the U.S. (Caldeira and Patterson, 1982; Patterson and Caldeira, 1983; Cox and Munger, 1989; Hill and Leighley, 1993; Cain, Donovan, and Tolbert, 1998; Brown, Jackson, and Wright, 1999).

Scholars have used broad brush-strokes to explore American state political environments and participation. Daniel Elazar (1966) argued Northern states settled by immigrants from Scandinavian and German countries developed a moralistic political culture that valued, and in fact expected, high participation from its citizenry; today these states have some of the highest turnout rates in the country. In contrast, mid-Atlantic and eastern states developed an individualist political culture where business entrepreneurship was prioritized over citizen participation. Southern states, driven by an economy dependent on slavery, developed a traditionalistic political culture where only elites and members of the upper class were expected to participate in politics, excluding African Americans and poor whites. Putnam (2000) has shown states with high social capital or community networks have significantly higher participation rates over time, as well as engagement in politics and trust. Others have argued both state political culture and levels of social capital are in large part driven by variation in the racial and ethnic diversity of the American states (Hero and Tolbert, 1996; Hero, 1998, 2007). Ethnically homogeneous (white) states may encourage high participation via lenient voter registration laws, while states with large minority populations are more likely to adopt laws to restrict registration and reduce participation (Hill and Leighley 1999) allowing the white majority to retain power (Key, 1949). From history, demography, community, and political values develop political norms and laws across the states that can directly influence how average citizens are informed by and participate in politics. In this essay we focus on state political institutions and political environments, demonstrating how the states have been used to better understand political participation.

We focus on several areas of participation research where the American states have been central to the development of the literature. By necessity, however, we omit as much as we discuss given the scope of this article. We do not discuss state variation in legislative redistricting practices (McDonald, 2004), for example, which can affect levels of electoral competition or party competition (Holbrook and Van Dunk, 1993), both important topics on their own. We provide only passing discussion of direct democracy (state ballot initiatives) that have been found to increase turnout and other forms of participation in the states over time (Smith, 2001; Tolbert, Grummel, and Smith, 2001; Smith and Tolbert, 2004), including the diversity and size of interest groups (Boehmke, 2002). We discuss but a small slice of variation in state election reforms in the states.

Institutional Environments

State Voter Registration

Voter registration laws are state political institutions that can influence turnout. Given the two-step process of voting (registration followed by voting), the 50 American states and their registration and voting laws have dramatically affected political participation over the past century (e.g., Squire, Wolfinger, and Glass, 1987; Highton and Wolfinger, 1998). As Brown argues: "the impact of registration on voter turnout is robust, occurring across electoral contests and providing a systematic impediment to voting over time" (2010: 66). This is one of the rare areas in political science where there is virtual consensus.

There is significant state-level variation in terms of in-person registration closing dates to register to vote. Some states require registration to vote 30 days before an election, and some, such as North Dakota, have no voter registration at all. The longest registration deadlines prior to the election is 30 days and exists in Alaska, Arkansas, Hawaii, Louisiana, Michigan, Mississippi, Montana, Ohio, Pennsylvania, Rhode Island, South Carolina, Tennessee, Texas, and Washington. The remaining states have shorter registration windows. As of 2010, eight states allow for registration on election day (election day registration (EDR)) including Idaho, Iowa, Maine, Minnesota, North Carolina, New Hampshire, Wisconsin, and Wyoming, and North Dakota does not require registration. By requiring citizens to be aware of registration deadlines and to register up to 30 days prior to the election, where you live, and hence state election laws can provide a substantial barrier to participation. Thus, where you live can influence the likelihood of voting as much as socioeconomic characteristics, such as education level.

How much do voter registration laws matter? Wolfinger and Rosenston (1980) find state registration deadlines significantly decreased voter turnout by a 9 percent decline, on average (see also Teixeira, 1992). Rather than a two-step process, most Western democracies use automatic voter registration (or even compulsory voting). Powell (1986) found U.S. registration laws reduced turnout by up to 14 percent compared to other countries, controlling for other differences among nations. The finding that removing lengthy pre-election registration laws would increase turnout is also supported by the careful empirical work of numerous scholars (Erikson, 1981; Patterson and Caleira, 1983; Piven and Cloward, 1988; Nagler, 1991; Rosenstone and Hansen, 1993; Mitchell and Wlezien, 1995; Jackson, Brown, and Wright, 1998; Brians and Grofman, 1999).

Squire, Wolfinger, and Glass (1987) show the impact of registering on reducing turnout is exacerbated by residential mobility; the reduced turnout effect from registering is most severe for those people who had recently moved, and that a change in residence itself represents an important barrier to voting. Since the poor and young tend to be more mobile, this work suggests registration requirements may shape the composition of state electorates, as well as overall turnout rates. Portable or mobile voter registration used in some states may eventually eliminate or lessen these registration barriers (McDonald, 2008) as some states move towards universal voter registration. Hawaii is the first state to adopt universal high school student registration (see <http://www.fairvote.org>).

State election laws, particularly voter registration, can also impact the composition of state electorates, or the degree to which certain segments of the population are differentially affected by registration deadlines (Wolfinger and Rosenstone, 1980; Piven and Cloward, 1988; Nagler, 1991; Rosenstone and Hansen, 1993; Mitchell and Wlezien, 1995; Jackson, Brown, and Wright, 1998; Rigby and Springer, 2010). Rosenstone and Hansen (1993) find that over the past century when more people vote, the electorates are more representative of the population in terms of both education and income levels. Jackson, Brown, and Wright (1998) and Brown, Jackson, and Wright (1999) reveal that registration laws have a significant effect on the social composition of the electorate in terms of education, income, and age representativeness (but see Hill and Leighley 1994, 1996 for null findings).

A representative electorate, where the characteristics of voters match the population, is important for normative reasons discussed at length in the concluding section. The class bias of state electorates has can affect public policy in the states (Hill and Leighley, 1992). New research shows that elected officials respond more to the preferences of voters than nonvoters, confirming long-held fears that socioeconomic and race biases of the electorate holds consequences for public policy (Lijphart, 1997; Griffin and Kean, 2005), including tax policy (Bartels, 2008). If elected officials have incentives to respond to the preferences of the electorate, the composition of the electorate matters, as does the act of voting.

State Election Laws

Building on the research on voter registration, election reform efforts in the U.S. over the past quarter of a century have focused attention on changing rules to ease voter registration and make voting more convenient, with the explicit goal of increasing turnout (Highton, 1997; Cain, Donovan, and Tolbert, 2008; Hamner, 2009). Focusing on the natural innovation and variation in the 50 American states, scholars have studied the effects of election reforms, such as early voting, voting by mail, EDR, absentee voting laws, among others (Cain, Donovan, and Tolbert, 2008). Studies have ranged from those that examine single reforms such as EDR (Fenster, 1994; Highghton, 1997; Brians and Grofman, 1999; Knack, 2001; Francia and Herrnson, 2004; Gronke, 2008; Hamner, 2009) to those that study many voting laws together (Fitzgerald, 2005; Tolbert et al., 2008; Mitchell and Wlezien, 1995; Teixeira, 1992).

One of the most important reforms is EDR in that it combines the two-step process of voting into one, removing a significant barrier to voting. The logic behind EDR is straightforward to the degree that registration presents significant costs to participation (Highton, 2004). Early studies found EDR to significantly increase turnout (Highton, 1997; Knack and White, 2000; Brians and Grofman, 2001), while later studies found more modest effects (Fitzgerald, 2005; Tolbert et al., 2008; Hamner, 2009). Fenster (1994), Fitzgerald (2005), and Tolbert et al. (2008) find EDR, on average, increases turnout by 5 percent, with all other factors held constant, while Rhine (1996) finds a 10–14 percent increase and Highton and Wolfinger (1998) report approximately a 10 percent increase. One of the most sophisticated recent studies evaluating the effects of relaxing voter registration laws on turnout is by Michael Hamner (2009), who introduces a quasi-experimental design (difference in difference method) where he measures the change in turnout over time using pre- and post test (surveys), before and after adoption of EDR in a state. He then compared the change in turnout rates in similar states with and without EDR (treatment and control cases). This allows scholars to grapple with endogeneity concerns that states that adopt reforms to ease registration and voting may have higher turnout rates in the first place, and a political culture that supports citizen participation. The results indicate EDR does increase turnout, but the effects are quite modest compared with the published literature. However, the largest effects of EDR are in the composition of the electorate (consistent with Jackson, Brown and Wright, 1998, and Brown, Jackson, and Wright, 1999, a decade earlier regarding the impact of registration laws on the composition of the electorate). Turnout among the young, low educated, and the poor is significantly higher in the dozen states allowing citizens to register to vote on the same day as the election than in states with longer registration windows (Knack and White, 2000; Hamner, 2009). Thus the real effect of state election reforms may be in who turns out, rather than in overall turnout rates.

Oregon deserves special attention, as it was an innovator by passing a citizen-initiated ballot measure to create all-mail elections in 1988 eliminating polling places. Washington followed suit and the majority of Californians and citizens of Western states now cast votes using permanent absentee ballots (mail ballots) (Cain, Donovan, and Tolbert, 2008, Ch. 1). Early research found a significant increase in participation in Oregon from voting by mail (Karp and Banducci, 2000; Southwell and Burchett, 2000; Berinsky, Burns and Traugott, 2001), up to a 10 percent boost in turnout. However, others argues early voting—over one-third of Americans voted early in the 2008 presidential election—may not significantly increase turnout (Gronke et al., 2008; Tolbert et al., 2008; Fitzgerald, 2005). There is agreement among scholars that early voting tends to advantage those citizens most likely to vote any-way—those who are older, educated, and have higher incomes (Karp and Banducci, 2000), potentially altering the composition of the electorate in opposite ways to EDR. Scholars have thus begun to study how these laws effect participation when combined (Burden et al., 2010). The ripple effects of these institutional changes can alter more than turnout rates. Casting ballots any time the month before the election has been found to modify candidate campaigns and candidate spending (Burden et al., 2010).

More obscure state election laws also affect participation. Post-registration laws, which vary tremendously across the states, such as mailing voting guides, have been shown to increase turnout, especially for the young (Wolfinger, Highton, and Mullin, 2005). Substantial attention has been paid to how states laws regulate felon voting laws and their effects in disenfranchising African Americans (Behrens, Uggen, and Manza, 2003; Manza, Brooks, and Uggen, 2004). Studies suggest felon disenfranchisement laws significantly reduce turnout over time, all other factors held constant (Fitzgerald, 2005; Tolbert et al., 2008). Cumulative voting and proportional representation in local elections has been found to increase turnout by roughly 5 percent (Bowler, Donovan, and Brockington, 2003). Given the decentralized system of administrating elections in the U.S. (Donovan and Bowler, 2004), the potential variation in how states administer elections—from purging voter rolls to electronic voting machines—is significant, and requires further research by scholars, especially the interaction of many co-existing laws (Burden et al., 2010).

As mentioned above, some suggests election reforms making voting easier or more convenient, such as early voting or mail voting, may fail to significantly increase turn-out or alter the demographic composition of an electorate (Karp and Banducci, 2000; Berinsky, 2005; Fitzgerald, 2005; Cain et al., 2008; Hanmer, 2009). Why? Beyond individual-level factors, or electoral rules, what contextual factors affect voter turnout? Individuals must have a motivation to vote and be interested and engaged in the election and knowledgeable of the candidates (Verba, Schlozman, and Brady, 1995). How might electoral context shape political participation, as well as the composition of the electorate by mobilizing some more than others? The idea that whatever spurs electoral turnout should have stronger effects on categories of individuals with otherwise partic-ularly low turnout has received less attention in the American case (Gimpel et al., 2007; Donovan and Tolbert, 2009).

Political Environments

State Electoral Competition

An important contextual factor that is often overlooked in analyses of turnout and election reform is competitive elections (McDonald and Samples, 2006). As Donovan (2007) writes in "A Goal for Reform: Make Elections Worth Stealing":

Electoral competition—the mobilization of candidates and campaign recourses in an environment where election outcomes are relatively uncertain—is also a force that can mobilize people to participate in politics.... The argument about electoral reforms here may be understood in terms of a baseball analogy. Administrative reforms are analogous to perfecting how balls, strikes, and base-running are called in a baseball game. Accurate calls are critical, but they are not likely to fill the stands with fans. People watch a game to see their team win, or because of interest in an important game. Perfect scoring is meaningless if only one team takes the field, and attendance will suffer if two teams are playing that no one can cheer for.

When candidate and political elites spend more effort and resources to contest elections, more information becomes available to voters. The resource-laden environment associated with electoral competition may reduce information costs of voting for individuals, leading to higher turnout. Conversely, if elections are uncompetitive or uncontested, they generate little political information. Absent active campaigns, individuals may have fewer opportunities to become interested in a contest, and may have less incentive to vote (Donovan, 2007). A lack of interest in politics may be a significant barrier to voting on its own (Gimpel, Kaufmann, and Pearson-Merkowtiz, 2007; Donovan and Tolbert, 2009).

Every two years the American states vary dramatically in the competition between the two major presidential candidates (battleground vs. non-battleground states discussed below), congressional elections, gubernatorial elections, and salient ballot measures (Cain, Donovan and Tolbert, 2008, Ch. 1). Some U.S. House districts are so uncompetitive that they are uncontested; up to one-third of congressional races are uncontested in some election years (Donovan and Bowler, 2004, Ch. 3; McDonald and Samples, 2006; Jacobson, 2008). With only one name appearing on the election ballot, there is little incentive for a rational citizen to vote.

A number of studies have identified the effects of electoral competition, campaign spending, and up-ticket contests on turnout (e.g., Copeland, 1983; Patterson and Caldeira, 1983; Caldeira et al., 1985; Cox and Munger, 1989; Hill and Leighley, 1993; Jackson, 1996, 1997, 2002; Rosenstone and Hansen, 2003; Holbrook and McClurg, 2005). Cross-nationally Blais (2000, 60) reports electoral competition is consistently associated with voter turnout across nations (see also Blais and Dobrzynska, 1998; Franklin, 2004; Blais, 2006). Scholars often measure electoral competition using aggregate measures such as vote margins between the two major parties (Barzel and Silberberg, 1973; Cox and Munger, 1989; Leighley and Nagler, 1992; Blais and Dobrzynska, 1998; Brown et al., 1999; Franklin, 2004) or campaign expenditures (Tolliver and Willett, 1973; Settle and Abrams, 1976; Copeland, 1983; Jackson, 1996a; Kahn and Kenny, 1999; Holbrook and McClurg, 2005; Tolbert, Bowen, and Donovan, 2009) to predict voter turnout in the aggregate or at the individual level using multi-level models.

An assumption of previous work is that campaign activity increases turnout, not citizen interest and motivations. Cox and Munger (1989) examine the link between victory margin, expenditures and turnout in House elections and find elites decide to expend more money in close elections (Tolliver et al., 1975). They find both campaign spending and electoral competition increase voter turnout. When House incumbents face opposition, campaign expenditures have a positive influence on aggregate turnout rates (Jackson, 1996a). Although presidential contests may have the greatest effects on mobilization, close congressional races may also stimulate turnout (Cox and Munger, 1989). Other state and local campaigns may also have mobilizing effects (Burden and Wichowsky 2010). Gubernatorial and U.S. Senate races have larger effects on turnout in midterms than presidential years (Jackson, 2002, 1996b; also see Patterson and Caldeira, 1983; Caldeira et al., 1985). Jackson finds that while individual characteristics are the principal determinants of voter registration status, campaign factors are the most important in explaining the turnout of those individuals who are registered to vote (1996b, 2002). Kahn and Kenny (1999) show that spending in U.S. Senate races increases awareness and knowledge of Senate candidates. Copeland (1983) argues that most research has been conducted on district-level data, so we do not know how campaigns influence individual voters. Copeland finds that at least part of the effect of campaigns is due to the increased likelihood of people voting when campaigns are more intense; thus engaging citizens and motivation are important ingredients in how the states shape participation in politics.

Increased spending in ballot measure and candidate races has been linked with higher turnout over time, with the greatest boost of salient ballot measures for the low educated (Tolbert, Bowen, and Donovan, 2009). More initiatives on state ballot or salient ballot measures have also been found to increase voter turnout (Smith 2001; Tolbert, Grummel, and Smith, 2001; Smith and Tolbert, 2004; Tolbert and Smith, 2005). These studies all point to campaigns providing the motivation to engage citizens to participate in politics, beyond reducing barriers to voter registration or voting.

Surprisingly, many voting studies either omit measures of the competitiveness of elections or campaign activity (e.g., Highton and Wolfinger, 1998; Brians and Grofman, 1999; Highton and Burris, 2002; Highton, 2004) or include a single variable as a control for state-level electoral context (e.g., Nagler, 1991; Oliver, 1996; Brians and Grofman, 2001). Other studies focus exclusively on turnout in presidential elections and thus don't measure state elections (Leighley and Nagler, 1992). Studies that do account for state-level electoral competition typically find significant effects even when relying on single-item measures or competitiveness indices as controls (e.g., Nagler, 1991; Leighley and Nagler, 1992; Oliver, 1996; Brians and Grofman, 2001).

Few studies of turnout have combined measures of electoral competition and election laws together (see Francia and Herrnson, 2004, for an exception). Tolbert et al. (2008) find that closely contested gubernatorial elections and EDR may interact, increasing turnout in midterm elections. A general tendency to rely either on aggregate or individual-level data means few studies of turnout include rich measures of variation in state or congressional district electoral competition merged with data identifying characteristics of individual citizens and use appropriate methods for modeling the multilevel data (see Primo et al., 2007; Tolbert, Bowen, and Donovan, 2009).

Jackson (1996, 1997, 2002) provides some of the most detailed evidence establishing that state-level campaign activity affects turnout in presidential and midterm elections. As with state election laws, competitive elections may affect overall turnout rates, but more importantly influence the composition of electorate as discussed below.

Electoral College: Battleground versus Non-Battleground States

An important source of state variation in electoral competition is America's unique structure for presidential elections (Karp and Tolbert, 2010). Some citizens reside in battleground states, while most live in non-battleground states, including large population states such as New York, Texas, and Florida. No other country uses an Electoral College to mediate between a national or direct/popular vote for presidential candidates and the winner. And few democracies in the world elect a president that does not win a majority of the popular vote. To win, a U.S. presidential candidate must receive a majority of the votes in the Electoral College, which are awarded to states based on the size of their congressional delegation (Shaw, 2006). Each state is awarded electors equal to the number of U.S. Senators and number of U.S. House of Representatives. In doing so, the system protects the interests of small population states, especially those that are competitive, as well as large battleground states such as Florida, Ohio, and Pennsylvania to the detriment of other states. The result is repeated calls for reform (Bowler and Donovan, 2007; Karp, 2007; Karp and Tolbert, 2010).

The Electoral College system forces presidential campaigns to allocate resources disproportionately to competitive states. Shaw (2006) argues that presidential campaigns "see the world in terms of amassing 270 electoral votes, which requires identifying, persuading, and/or mobilizing a requisite number of voters in battleground states" (4). Campaigns do not seek to talk to voters in all states, and avoid wasting effort (Patterson, 2002). In presidential races, residents of battleground states get smothered with attention from candidates and media, while citizens in states that vote later in the process barely get noticed (Panagopoulos, 2009). Building on Shaw, Panagopoulos argues, "...lopsided communications that relegate voters in uncompetitive states to bystander status in presidential campaigns are potentially significant and merit greater scrutiny." His analysis of the 2000 National Annenberg Election Survey finds that the preferences of voters in battleground states are more variable but are more stable over time than their counterparts in non-battleground states.

It is reasonable to expect that campaigns mobilize voters and that this might increase political participation and even affect the composition of the electorate. Key (1949) proposes that close elections may increase the incentives that parties have to appeal to society's "have nots"; this suggests that electoral competition may mobilize less affluent voters. In terms of political participation, scholars have also found turnout is higher and less biased in terms of participation by the poor and young in battleground states (Gimpel, Kaufmann, Pearson-Merkowtiz, 2007; Pacheco, 2008; Lipsitz, 2009). But the mechanisms may not be elite mobilization but increased citizen engagement. Political interest has also been found to be higher in battleground states (Gimpel, Kaufmann, Pearson-Merkowtiz, 2007), leading to higher participation in the election. Competition in battleground states is so intense it can even moderate class bias. The Electoral College thus makes battleground states winners and non-battleground states losers in terms of campaign communication, mobilization by elites, and participation.

In a working paper Donovan and Tolbert (2009) take this argument one step further and argue multiple forms of electoral competition may increase turnout, and that competition can have stronger mobilizing effects on a distinct set of citizens. By stimulating interest among people who are less engaged with politics, electoral competition has a greater propensity to mobilize the young, those with less formal education, and non-partisans. Drawing on survey data merged with measures of a state's electoral environment, the authors demonstrate the differential mobilizing effects of exposure to presidential, congressional and ballot issue elections, and suggest limited exposure to competitive elections may be one reason for lower levels of turnout recorded since the 1960s. Competitive elections may be a process that affects the existing bias in who votes in America (see also Tolbert, Bowen, and Donovan, 2009).

Other research outside of presidential elections, suggests active campaigns encourage seldom voters to participate. Parry et al. (2008) look at which citizens are contacted, how, and with what effect using data from a telephone survey conducted in a pair of highly competitive 2002 U.S. Senate races. The authors find that even in high-dollar Senate races there are positive effects of campaign communication among "seldom" voters, defined as registered but rarely active participants. Whether one is most interested in overall turnout, or who votes, the literature provides able evidence that campaigns matter for participation (Holbrook, 1996).

Nominating Presidential Candidates:
Early versus Late Voting States

Even the structure for nominating presidential candidates in the U.S. has implications for participation in government. Presidential elections under the Electoral College system are simultaneous elections, fiercely fought in large battleground or swing states. In contrast, presidential nominations involve a sequential voting process fought in a handful of small population states voting early in the process, such as Iowa and New Hampshire (Karp and Tolbert, 2010). The privileged position of Iowa and New Hampshire, the nation's first caucus and primary, respectively, are increasingly called into question (Squire, 1989; Winebrenner, 1998; Mayer and Busch, 2004; Hull, 2007; Kamarck, 2009; Smith and Springer, 2009; Redlawsk, Tolbert, and Donovan, 2011). Frequently the nomination contest is over almost before it starts, leaving many citizens (sometimes the majority of Americans) with no role in selecting their party's nominee—turnout in these later states naturally plummets (Tolbert, Keller, and Donovan, 2010). In 2008, the Republican nomination was decided soon after Super Tuesday held in early February, leaving Republicans voting in later states with no meaningful choice, while the choice for Democrats was limited to either Barack Obama or Hillary Clinton. In contrast, studies have shown that citizens residing in early voting states, such as Iowa, New Hampshire, or a Super Tuesday state, are more likely to vote and be engaged and interested in the election (Redlawsk, Tolbert, and Donovan, 2011). Redlawsk et al. find turnout in early-voting states, such as the Iowa caucuses, tends to be less biased in terms of income and education than primaries and caucuses in later voting states. In myriad ways, then, participation in politics and who votes is structured by state political institutions (election laws) and political environments, including the intensity of candidate campaigns.

Political Inequality

Who Are the Nonvoters? Biases in Political Participation

A theme of this essay has not only been relatively low levels of participation in America, but researchers have addressed the composition of voters and nonvoters in relation to the overall citizenry. Not only are turnout rates relatively low but a sizable class bias also exists among those who do decide to participate in elections. That is, the politically engaged tend to be wealthier and better educated than the politically apathetic (Leighley and Nagler, 1992). Many have suggested the two phenomena—low turnout and electoral class bias—are likely linked. For example, Schattschneider (1960) viewed low political participation as one of the primary failures of American politics because he believed it would produce a bias between the general population and those who are represented. A number of studies testing these expectations have supported the claim that greater turnout makes for a more representative electorate (Teixeira, 1992; Rosenstone and Hansen, 1993).

As scholars have become more aware of the contextual influences on overall participation they have also asked whether these same influences can increase or decrease class bias. Much attention has been given to the potential for electoral reforms to improve the representativeness of the electorate (Piven and Cloward, 1988). Findings showing the generally positive relationship between more lenient voting regulations and higher turnout (as discussed above) suggested these reforms were also promoting greater participation among the less well off. Direct evidence of the connection between electoral reforms and voter class bias, however, has proven to be quite complicated. In fact, some studies have shown less restrictive voting laws may increase class bias in the electorate.

Karp and Banducci (2000), for instance, use data from six special elections in Oregon to find that voting by mail increased voter turnout, but only among those groups already predisposed to vote. Berinsky, Burns, and Traugott (2001) find results similar to those of Karp and Banducci (2000), concluding that voting by mail reinforces the stratification of higher turnout among the upper class, and nonvoting among the lower class. Berinsky (2005) provides an explanation for these seemingly contradictory findings by suggesting voting convenience reforms (e.g., voting by mail, early voting, and absentee voting) simply reinforce the behavior of those most likely to vote. These reforms do not lower the costs of voting enough to engage those with few political resources, but instead lower the costs enough for the upper class to vote more consistently.

Berinsky (2005) also argues registration reforms (e.g., motor vehicle registration and EDR) pose problems similar to those related to voting reforms. That is, removing barriers to registration will not lower the costs of voting to the extent necessary to increase the participation of those with fewer political resources. This claim, however, has been challenged by several studies suggesting reforms aimed at lowering the restrictiveness of registration laws can create a more representative electorate. Registration reforms differ from voting convenience reforms in that it focuses on the first stage of the voting process (becoming eligible to vote) instead of the last stage (casting a ballot). Jackson, Brown, and Wright (1998) explicitly model the stages concept into their analysis of participation. The authors show registration closing dates closer to the election produce an indirect, positive effect on the representativeness of a state's electorate. More lenient registration laws lead to higher rates of registration, which increases overall levels of turnout and decreases voter biases based on income, education, and age.

In a comprehensive analysis of state participation bias and election reform, Rigby and Springer (2010) provide evidence suggesting a conditional influence of reform on electoral representation does exist. The study uses both presidential and midterm election data spanning from 1978 to 2008, and examines the influence of both registration and voting convenience-based reforms on the composition or class bias of electorates in all 50 states. The results of the analysis are consistent with the idea that reducing barriers to registration can increase the likelihood of voting for those not already a part of the electoral system (consistent with Jackson, Brown and Wright 1998), and more convenient voting mainly helps those most likely to vote (see Berinsky, 2005). Motor voter registration has a small but significant effect on reducing electoral biases, while EDR (which essentially removes the registration step of the voting process) has a relatively strong influence on turning out lower income voters (see Hamner, 2009). Conversely, in-person early voting, a convenience voting reform, led to greater biases in turnout. Additionally, these results are dependent on the levels of voter bias prior to the adoption of the reforms. That is, registration reforms are most influential in states that had high electoral bias when the reform was adopted.

Research examining the causes of participation bias outside the realm of election reform is sparse. One notable study is Hill and Leighley's (1994) analysis of variations in class bias across the states in the 1986 midterm election. While the authors do consider the restrictiveness of voter registration laws, their primary concern is uncovering a broader understanding of class bias in the electorate. The study also considers the influence of party competition, party ideology, and aggregate measures of state socioeconomic characteristics on differences in turnout based on income. The findings show state per capita income and ethnic heterogeneity to have greater effects on class bias than the observed effects of the elite mobilization variables. The results challenge the assumption that factors influencing overall turnout will have similar consequences for the biases found in participation rates.

Understanding the Composition of State Electorates

Explaining variation in participation biases has proven to be difficult, although we currently know more about the influences of election reforms on class representation. The possibility that simply increasing turnout rates would reduce the gap between upper and lower class voters has been disputed by a number of studies. Hill and Leighley's (1994) work suggests greater mobilization efforts by political elites may not create a more equally representative electorate, but state socioeconomic conditions drive political inequality. But the research leaves many unanswered questions. For instance, if class bias varies by state does it also vary over time? If it does, how can relatively stable socioeconomic variables explain changes in the composition of state electorates over time? Moreover, most of the research on electoral class bias discussed above focuses mainly on differences between the turnout rates of the rich and poor (for an exception see Jackson, Brown, and Wright, 1998). Do other biases exist in the electorate, based on age, or education or race, and, if so, can these disparities be explained by the same factors?

The complexity of participation bias is evident when exploring some of its basic features. Figure 6.1 displays a measure of income based participation bias for each of the 50 states over time, similar to the one used by many scholars studying class bias in the electorate (e.g., Hill and Leighley, 1992, 1994; Rosenstone and Hansen, 1993; Jackson, Brown, and Wright, 1998; Rigby and Springer, 2010). The measure is somewhat different from previous measures in that participation inequality in each state is quantified using individuals from all income groups in the calculation (rather than simply comparing the rich and the poor) and the measure of inequality is based on an income distribution that is relative to the wealth of each state (see Wichowsky, 2012; Franko, 2013).[1] The participation bias measure ranges from -1 to 1, with negative values indicating low-income individuals are more likely to vote than the rich, 0 meaning the rich and poor have an equal probability of voting, and positive values meaning the rich vote at a higher rate than the poor. A value of 0.3, for example, indicates the rich are 30 percent more likely to vote than the poor.

Figure 6.1 illustrates turnout bias based on income for each of the 50 states over a period of more than 35 years. What can be seen from examination of Figure 6.1 is the variation in class bias of the electorate across the states and over time. Some states have relatively high levels of inequality (bar is higher) than others (bar is lower), and some states exhibit more variance over the decades. For instance, states such as Idaho and Kentucky have relatively consistent increasing trends in participation bias based on income levels, while South Carolina and Virginia appear to be trending downward. California, Illinois, Maine, and Nebraska have more constant levels of income bias, and Alaska and New Hampshire have more non-monotonic patterns of voter income bias. We can also see the relative magnitude of income bias in the electorate in Figure 6.1, with large population states (CA, MA, MI, IL, PA) having lower levels of participation inequality based on income groups over time. In general Southern states with lower overall turnout tend to have higher levels of class bias in their electorates.

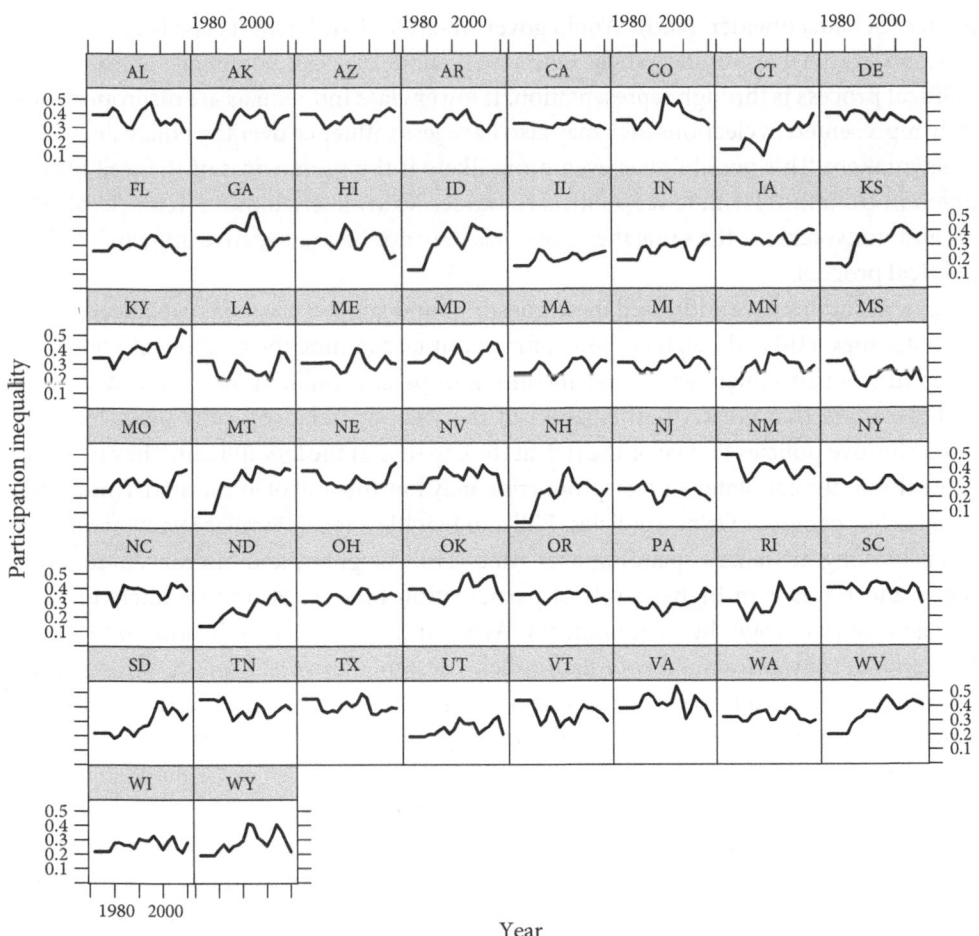

FIGURE 6.1 Income based turnout bias in the states over time (1972–2008)

Note: All estimates were developed by the authors using Current Population Survey (CPS) Voter Supplements. Larger participation inequality values indicate a larger participation gap between the rich and poor.

This descriptive look at income bias in the electorate should give some insight into the challenges associated with more fully understanding electoral representation. Examining other forms of participation bias (e.g., those based on education, age, or race) will likely add to these complexities (for an initial consideration, see Franko and Tolbert, 2010). In any case, much more can still be learned about the causes of biases in the electorate.

The Consequences of Electoral Bias

As the class bias in state electorates, or participation inequality, can be measured and more fully understood, scholars must also address the question of whether these biases matter (Schattschneider, 1960). Would government look different if class bias was non-existent? If so, what would change? One way turnout bias can potentially affect on the political process is through representation. If lower class individuals are disproportionately represented in elections they may also have less influence over the policy decisions of lawmakers. This possibility is even more likely if the preferences of the well off are different from those with fewer political resources. Conversely, if the preferences of voters and nonvoters are the same then class bias may not have a negative influence on the political process.

Several studies have addressed these questions and suggest class bias can affect political outcomes. Hill and Leighley (1992), for example, examine the relationship between voter turnout of upper- and lower-income groups and public policy outcomes. The authors argue that greater participation of the wealthy, relative to the poor, leads to redistributive policies that favor the rich at the expense of the less affluent. They demonstrate the American states with disproportionately low turnout of lower-status individuals have less generous welfare policies (Hill and Leighley, 1992). Similar results are found when looking at welfare spending over time (Hill, Leighley, and Hinton-Andersson, 1995), and states with higher levels of participation bias are also more likely to have stringent welfare eligibility requirements (Avery and Peffley, 2005). In addition to cash aid welfare programs, a number of state policies designed to assist the disadvantaged are also affected by unequal participation rates. Franko (2013) shows that participation bias leads to housing, health care, and minimum wage policy outcomes that are less beneficial to poor.

Other scholars have attempted to provide a direct link between subgroup preferences and the actions of politicians. Gilens (2005, 2009), for instance, shows those with higher incomes are more likely to have their policy preferences represented by policy outcomes. Similarly, Griffin and Newman (2007) offer support for the claim that politicians are more likely to represent whites than Latinos when comparing the issue priorities of each group's to roll-call votes. This evidence indicates not only that the policy preferences of certain groups are different, but also that elected officials are more responsive to the interests of whites and the rich.

An important study by Griffin and Newman (2005) provides evidence supporting the assumption that voters are better represented than nonvoters, justifying our focus on composition of state electorates. Comparing the ideologies of voters and nonvoters to the roll-call votes of state senators, the authors demonstrate elected officials are responsive to voters but not nonvoters. They also test a number of hypotheses that link participation to representation, resulting in findings that indicate voters are better represented because "voters select like-minded Senators, voters are more likely to communicate their desires to their Senators, and only voters can reelect Senators" (Griffin and Newman, 2005, 1207). Finally, Griffin and Newman show voters and nonvoters differ in their ideological orientation, which has important implications for the bias of political outcomes (see also Griffin and Newman, 2006, 2007, and 2008). This is apparent when considering the historical record of low participation rates of individuals with low-income, education, the young, and minority groups (Wolfinger and Rosenstone,

1980; Leighley and Nagler, 1992; Verba, Schlozman, and Brady, 1995; Rosenstone and Hansen, 2003).

Although this research suggests reducing electoral class bias would create a more representative political process, one study shows equal participation may not be enough. In a study of U.S. inequality, Bartels (2008) finds even when participating in the political process, the poor (defined by the bottom third of the income distribution America) may still not have equal influence over government. He finds that Senators, both Republican and Democratic, are less likely to respond to the opinion of low-income constituents compared to the high-income portion of the electorate. That is, Senate roll-call votes on various issues such as minimum wage, civil rights, and abortion are more likely to reflect the opinion of the upper-income constituency. Most importantly, these results hold when accounting for participation rates and degrees of political knowledge; that is, among those who vote and those with high levels of political knowledge, Senators are still more responsive to the rich (Bartels, 2008; also see Bartels et al., 2005).

Conclusion: Participation in the States and Representation

Elections are fundamental to any form of democracy. In a representative democracy, elections give citizens some amount of control over political processes, an action that serves as a way for the public to reveal its political preferences. In an ideal system, citizens can shape government action (policy) by way of their power to elect politicians deemed worthy of serving the citizenry and reject those not living up to the public's standards. The importance of electoral participation is demonstrated by Key's suggestion that "The marking of the ballot, an act by which a citizen can participate in the choice of his rulers, epitomizes and symbolizes the entire democratic process" (1949, 508). With such great importance placed on participation in democratic societies, research seeking to understand the factors that lead to citizen participation is ubiquitous among those studying politics.

Another reason for emphasis on political engagement, especially among observers of American politics, is the U.S.'s notoriously relatively low levels of electoral participation compared to other advanced democracies (Powell, 1986; Franklin, 1996). While voting is not the only form of political participation, many scholars have focused on this particular form of engagement in response to the American public's seemingly apathetic view of elections. As discussed above, the American states have proved to be fundamental in understanding political participation. Political participation requires motivation, capacity, and mobilization, according to Verba, Schlozman, and Brady (1995, 3), and state election contexts influence each of these factors. Future research should continue to explore the three major avenues we have highlighted here, including how political institutions and political environments shape participation overall, and inequality in participation. We encourage more research on the conditional or interactive effects of state laws and political factors in shaping turnout, and especially turnout of subgroups of the population, such as the young, poor, low-educated, non-partisans, or racial and ethnic minorities (see Griffin and Newman, 2008). Focusing on the dynamics of elections, representation and policy—what we might call ERP—is a fruitful avenue for future scholarship.

As the world of politics moves online to a digital democracy (Mossberger and Tolbert, 2010; Tolbert and McNeal, 2001), some traditional voting barriers may be reduced and new inequalities, such as the digital divide (Mossberger, Tolbert, and McNeal, 2008) have emerged. We encourage scholars to continue thinking "outside the box" to challenge traditional assumptions and seek new answers for encouraging full participation in a continued effort to strengthen American democracy. Drawing on the 50 American states—true laboratories of democracy—will provide the theoretical leverage and robust empirical tests to meet the challenges of the future.

NOTE

1. Consistent with previous studies, the data used to create the measures in Figure 6.1 comes from Current Population Survey (CPS) Voter Supplements. The CPS has several properties that are, for the most part, unmatched by other sources. First, the survey asks questions about voting behavior and turnout and includes very large samples of Americans (over 100,000 respondents). Second, the CPS interviews thousands of individuals in every state allowing for representative estimation of turnout rates in each state, even in small population states. Finally, questions about voting have been consistently asked for each presidential and midterm election for several decades.

   The participation inequality variable is created by first assigning all CPS respondents to a cumulative proportion distribution based on their family income when compared to the family incomes of all other respondents in their state. This income scale is then used as a determinant of voter turnout in the following OLS regression model:

$$\text{vote} = b_0 + b_1(\text{income}) + e$$

   where *vote* is coded as 1 if the individual reported voting and 0 if the person did not vote, and *income* indicates each individual's position on their state's cumulative income distribution. A unique regression modeled is specified for each state and each election year under analysis. Since both variables (*vote* and *income*) are bounded between 0 and 1, the resulting coefficient (b_1) on the cumulative income scale is interpreted as the absolute difference in the probability of voting for the poorest and richest income group in each state.

REFERENCES

Avery, James M. and Mark Peffley. 2005. "Voter Registration Requirements, Voter Turnout, and Welfare Eligibility Policy: Class Bias Matters." *State Politics and Policy Quarterly* 5 (1): 47–67.

Barreto, Matt A., Stephen A. Nuno, and Gabriel R. Sanchez. 2009. "The Disproportionate Impact of Voter-ID Requirements on the Electorate–New Evidence from Indiana." *PS: Political Science and Politics* 42 (1): 111–16.

Bartels, Larry M. 2008. *Unequal Democracy: The Political Economy of the New Gilded Age.* Princeton, NJ: Princeton University Press.

Bartels, Larry M., Hugh Heclo, Rodney E. Hero, and Lawrence R. Jacobs. 2005. Inequality and American Governance. In Lawrence R. Jacobs and Theda Skocpol (eds), *Inequality and American Democracy: What We Know and What We Need to Learn.* New York, NY: Russell Sage Foundation, pp. 88–155.

Barzel, Yoram and Eugene Silberberg. 1973. "Is the Act of Voting Rational?" *Public Choice* 16 (1): 51–8.

Behrens, Angela, Christopher Uggen, and Jeff Manza. 2003. "Ballot Manipulation and the 'Menace of Negro Domination': Racial Threat and Felon Disenfranchisement in the United States, 1850–2002." *American Journal of Sociology* 109 (3): 559–605.

Berinsky, Adam J. 2005. "The Perverse Consequences of Electoral Reform in the United States." *American Politics Research* 33 (4): 471–91.

Berinsky, Nancy Burns and Michael W. Traugott 2001. "Who Votes by Mail? A Dynamic Model of the Individual-Level Consequences of Voting-by-Mail Systems." *Public Opinion Quarterly* 65 (2): 178–97.

Blais, Andre. 2000. *To Vote Or Not To Vote? The Merits and Limits of Rational Choice.* Pittsburgh, PA: University of Pittsburgh Press.

Blais, Andre. 2006. "What Affects Voter Turnout?" *Annual Review of Political Science* 9: 111–25.

Blais, Andre and Agnieszka Dobrzynska. 2003. "Turnout in Electoral Democracies." *European Journal of Political Research* 33 (2): 239–61.

Boehmke, Frederick J. 2002. "The Effect of Direct Democracy on the Size and Diversity of State Interest Group Populations." *Journal of Politics* 64 (3): 827–44.

Bowler, Shaun, Todd Donovan, and David Brockington. 2003. *Electoral Reform and Minority Representation: Local Experiments With Alternative Elections.* Columbus, OH: Ohio State University Press.

Bowler, Sean and Craig Donovan. 2007. "Reasoning About Institutional Change: Winners, Losers and Support for Electoral Reforms." *British Journal of Political Science* 37 (3): 455–76.

Brians, Craig Leonard and Bernard Grofman. 1999. "When Registration Barriers Fall, Who Votes? An Empirical Test of a Rational Choice Model." *Public Choice* 99: 161–76.

Brown, Robert D. 2010. "Voter Registration: Turnout, Representation, and Reform." In *The Oxford Handbook of American Elections and Political Behavior*, ed. Jan E. Leighley. New York, NY: Oxford University Press, pp. 162–81.

Brown, Robert D., Robert A. Jackson, and Gerald C. Wright. 1999. "Registration, Turnout, and State Party Systems." *Political Research Quarterly* 52 (3): 463–79.

Burden, Barry C. and Amber Wichowsky. 2010. "Local and National Forces in Congressional Elections." In *The Oxford Handbook of American Elections and Political Behavior*, ed. Jan E. Leighley. New York, NY: Oxford University Press.

Burden, Barry, David Canon, William Mayer, and Moynihan. 2010. "Election Laws, Mobilization, and Turnout: The Unanticipated Consequences of Election Reform." Paper presented at the Chicago Area Political Behavior Conference, Northwestern, IL. May 7, 2010.

Cain, Bruce E., Todd Donovan, and Caroline J. Tolbert. 2008. *Democracy in the States: Experiments in Election Reform.* Washington, DC: Brookings Institution Press.

Caldeira, Gregory A. and Samuel C. Patterson. 1982. "Contextual Influences on Participation in U.S. State Legislative Elections." *Legislative Studies Quarterly* 7 (3): 359–81.

Campbell, Angus, Philip E. Converse, Warren E. Miller, and Donald E. Stokes. 1960. *The American Voter*. New York, NY: Wiley.

Copeland, Gary W. 1983. "Activating Voters in Congressional Elections." *Political Behavior* 5 (4): 391–401.

Cox, Gary W. and Michael C. Munger. 1989. "Closeness, Expenditures, and Turnout in the 1982 U.S. House Elections." *American Political Science Review* 83 (1): 217–31.

Donovan, Todd. 2007. "A Goal for Reform: Make Elections Worth Stealing." *PS: Political Science and Politics* 40 (4): 681–6.

Donovan, Todd and Shaun Bowler. 2004. *Reforming the Republic: Democratic Institutions for the New America*. Upper Saddle River, NJ: Pearson Education.

Donovan, Todd, Christopher Mooney and Daniel A. Smith. 2001. *State and Local Politics and Policy: Institutions and Reform*, 2nd Ed. Boston, MA: Wadsworth Press.

Donovan, Todd and Caroline Tolbert. 2009. "Competitive Elections, Voter Participation and Electoral Bias." Presented at the Annual Meeting of the American Political Science Association, Toronto, Canada. September 3–9.

Downs, Anthony. 1957. *An Economic Theory of Democracy*. New York, NY: Harper and Row.

Elazar, Daniel J. 1966. *American Federalism: A View from the States*. New York, NY: Crowell.

Erikson, Robert S. 1981. "Why Do People Vote? Because They Are Registered." *American Politics Research* 9 (3): 259–76.

Fenster, Mark J. 1994. "The Impact of Allowing Day of Registration Voting On Turnout in U.S. Elections From 1960 To 1992." *American Politics Research* 22 (1): 74–87.

Fitzgerald, Mary. 2005. "Greater Convenience But Not Greater Turnout: The Impact of Alternative Voting Methods on Electoral Participation in the United States." *American Politics Research* 33 (6): 842–67.

Francia, Peter L. and Paul S. Herrnson. 2004. "The Synergistic Effect of Campaign Effort and Election Reform on Voter Turnout in State Legislative Elections." *State Politics and Policy Quarterly* 4 (1): 74–93.

Franklin, Mark N. 1996. Electoral Participation. In Lawrence LeDuc, Richard G. Niemi, and Pippa Norris (eds), *Comparing Democracies: Elections and Voting in Global Perspective*. Thousand Oaks, CA: Sage, pp. 216–235.

Franklin, Mark N. 2004. *Voter Turnout and the Dynamics of Electoral Competition in Established Democracies since 1945*. New York, NY: Cambridge University Press.

Franko, William W. 2013. "Political Inequality and State Policy Adoption: Predatory Lending, Children's Health Care, and Minimum Wage." *Poverty & Public Policy* 5 (1): 88–114.

Franko, William and Caroline Tolbert. 2010. "Reexamining Political Inequality: Voter Turnout Bias and the Composition of State Electorates." Presented at the Annual Meeting of the American Political Science Association, Washington, DC. September 2–5.

Gimpel, James G., Karen M. Kaufmann and Shanna Pearson-Merkowitz. 2007. "Battleground States versus Blackout States: The Behavioral Implications of Modern Presidential Campaigns." *Journal of Politics* 69 (3): 786–97.

Griffin, John D. and Michael Keane. 2005. "Are Voters Better Represented?" *Journal of Politics* 67 (4): 1206–27.

Griffin, John D. and Michael Keane. 2006. "Descriptive Representation and the Composition of African American Turnout." *American Journal of Political Science* 50 (4): 998–1012.

Griffin, John D. and Michael Keane. 2007. "The Unequal Representation of Latinos and Whites." *Journal of Politics* 69 (4): 1032–46.

Griffin, John D. and Brian Newman. 2008. *Minority Report: Evaluating Political Equality in America*. Chicago: University of Chicago Press.

Gronke, Paul, Eva Galances-Rosenbaum, and Peter A. Miller. 2008. Early voting and voter turnout. In Bruce E. Cain.Todd Donovan, and Caroline J. Tobert (eds), Democracy in the states: experiments in election reform. Washington, DC: Brookings Institution Press, pp. 68–82.

Hanmer, Michael J. 2009. *Discount Voting: Voter Registration Reforms and their Effects*. New York, NY: Cambridge University Press.

Hero, Rodney E. and Caroline J. Tolbert. 1996. "A Racial/Ethnic Interpretation of Politics and Policy in the States of the U.S." *American Journal of Political Science* 40: 851–71.

Hero, Rodney E. 1998. *Face of Inequality: Social Diversity in American Politics*. Oxford University Press.

Hero, Rodney E. 2007. *Racial Diversity and Social Capital: Equality and Community in America*. New York, NY: Cambridge University Press.

Highton, Benjamin. 1997. Easy Registration and Voter Turnout. *Journal of Politics* 59: 565–75

Highton, Benjamin. 2004. "Voter Registration and Turnout in the United States." *Perspectives on Politics* 2 (3): 507–15.

Highton, Benjamin and Arthur L. Burris. 2002. "New Perspectives on Latino Voter Turnout in the United States." *American Politics Research* 30 (3): 285–306.

Highton, Benjamin and Raymond E. Wolfinger. 1998. "Estimating the Effects of the National Voter Registration Act of 1993." *Political Behavior* 20 (2): 79–104.

Hill, Kim Quaile and Jan E. Leighley. 1992. "The Policy Consequences of Class Bias in State Electorates." *American Journal of Political Science* 36 (2): 351–65.

Hill, Kim Quaile and Jan E. Leighley. 1993. "Party Ideology, Organization, and Competitiveness as Mobilizing Forces in Gubernatorial Elections." *American Journal of Political Science* 37 (4): 1158–78.

Hill, Kim Quaile and Jan E. Leighley. 1994. "Mobilizing Institutions and Class Representation in U.S. State Electorates." *Political Research Quarterly* 47 (1): 137–50.

Hill, Kim Quaile and Jan E. Leighley. 1999. "Racial Diversity, Voter Turnout, and Mobilizing Institutions in the United States." *American Politics Research* 27 (3): 275–95.

Hill, Kim Quaile, Jan E. Leighley and Angela Hinton-Andersson. 1995. "Lower-Class Mobilization and Policy Linkage in the U.S. States." *American Journal of Political Science* 39 (1): 75–86.

Holbrook, Thomas M. 1996. *Do Campaigns Matter?* Thousand Oaks, CA: Sage.

Holbrook, Thomas M. and Emily Van Dunk. 1993. "Electoral Competition in the American States." *American Political Science Review* 87 (4): 955–62.

Holbrook, Thomas M. and Scott D. McClurg. 2005. "The Mobilization of Core Supporters: Campaigns, Turnout, and Electoral Composition in United States Presidential Elections." *American Journal of Political Science* 49 (4): 689–703.

Hull, Christopher C. 2007. *Grassroots Rules: How the Iowa Caucus Helps Elect American Presidents*. Stanford, CA: Stanford University Press.

Jackson, Robert A. 1996a. "The Mobilization of Congressional Electorates." *Legislative Studies Quarterly* 21 (3): 425–45.

Jackson, Robert A. 1996b. "A Reassessment of Voter Mobilization." *Political Research Quarterly* 49 (2): 331–49.

Jackson, Robert A. 1997. "The Mobilization of U.S. State Electorates in the 1988 and 1990 Elections." *Journal of Politics* 59 (2):520–37.

Jackson, Robert A. 2002. "Gubernatorial and Senatorial Campaign Mobilization of Voters." *Political Research Quarterly* 55 (4): 825–44.

Jackson, Robert A., Robert D. Brown and Gerald C. Wright. 1998. "Registration, Turnout, and the Electoral Representativeness of U.S. State Electorates." *American Politics Quarterly* 26 (3): 259–87.

Jacobson, Gary. 2008. *The Politics of Congressional Elections,* 7th edn. New York: Longman.

Kahn, Kim Fridkin and Patrick J. Kenney. 1999. *The Spectacle of U.S. Senate Campaigns.* Princeton, NJ: Princeton University Press.

Kamarck, Elaine C. 2009. *Primary Politics: How Presidential Candidates have Shaped the Modern Nominating System.* Washington, DC: Brookings Institution Press.

Karp, Jeffrey A. and Caroline J. Tolbert. 2010. "Support for Nationalizing Presidential Elections." *Presidential Studies Quarterly* 40 (4): 771–93.

Karp, Jeffrey A. and Susan A. Banducci. 2000. "Going Postal: How All-Mail Elections Influence Turnout." *Political Behavior* 22 (3): 223–39.

Karp, Jeffrey A. 2007. "Reforming the Electoral College and Support for Proportional Outcomes." *Representation* 43 (4): 239–50.

Key, V. O. 1949. *Southern Politics in State and Nation.* New York, NY: Alfred A. Knopf.

Keyssar, Alexander. 2000. *The Right to Vote: The Contested History of Democracy in the United States.* New York, NY: Basic Books.

Knack, Stephen. 2001. "Election-Day Registration: The Second Wave." *American Politics Research* 29 (1): 65–78.

Knack, Stephen and James White. 2000. "Election-Day Registration and Turnout Inequality." *Political Behavior* 22 (1): 29–44.

Kousser, J. Morgan. 1999. *Colorblind Injustice: Minority Voting Rights and the Undoing of the Second Reconstruction.* Chapel Hill, NC: University of North Carolina Press.

Leighley, Jan E. and Jonathan Nagler. 1992. "Socioeconomic Class Bias in Turnout, 1964–1988: The Voters Remain the Same." *American Political Science Review* 86 (3): 725–36.

Leighley, Jan E. and Jonathan Nagler. 2007. "Unions, Voter Turnout, and Class Bias in the U.S. Electorate, 1964–2004." *Journal of Politics* 69 (2): 430–41.

Lewis-Beck, Michael S., William G. Jacoby, Helmut Norpoth, and Herbert F. Weisberg. 2008. *The American Voter Revisited.* Ann Arbor, MI: University of Michigan Press.

Lijphart, Arend. 1997. "Unequal Participation: Democracy's Unresolved Dilemma." *American Political Science Review* 91 (1): 1–14.

Lipsitz, Keena. 2009. "The Consequences of Battleground and 'Spectator' State Residency for Political Participation." *Political Behavior* 31 (2): 187–209.

Manza, Jeff, Clem Brooks and Christopher Uggen. 2004. "Public Attitudes Toward Felon Disenfranchisement in the United States." *Public Opinion Quarterly* 68 (2): 275–86.

Mayer, William G. and Andrew E. Busch, 2003. *The Front-Loading Problem in Presidential Nominations.* Washington, DC: Brookings Institution Press.

McDonald, Michael P. 2004. "A Comparative Analysis of Redistricting Institutions in the United States, 2001–02." *State Politics and Policy Quarterly* 4 (4): 371–95.

McDonald, Michael P. 2008. "Portable Voter Registration." *Political Behavior* 30 (4): 491–501.

McDonald, Michael P. 2010. "American Voter Turnout in Historical Perspective." In Jan E. Leighley (ed.), *The Oxford Handbook of American Elections and Political Behavior.* New York, NY: Oxford University Press, pp. 125–43.

McDonald, Michael P. and John Samples, eds. 2006. *The Marketplace of Democracy: Electoral Competition and American Politics.* Washington, DC: Brookings Institution Press.

Mitchell, Glenn E. and Christopher Wlezien. 1995. "The Impact of Legal Constraints on Voter Registration, Turnout, and the Composition of the American Electorate." *Political Behavior* 17 (2): 179–202.

Mossberger, Karen and Caroline J. Tolbert. 2010. "Digital Democracy: How Politics Online is Changing Electoral Participation." In Jan E. Leighley (ed.), *The Oxford Handbook of American Elections and Political Behavior*. New York, NY: Oxford University Press, pp. 200–218.

Mossberger, Karen, Caroline J. Tolbert, and Ramona McNeal. 2008. *Digital Citizenship: The Internet, Society and Participation*. Cambridge, MA: MIT Press.

Nagler, Jonathan. 1991. "The Effect of Registration Laws and Education on U.S. Voter Turnout." *American Political Science Review* 85 (4): 1393–405.

Oliver, J. Eric. 1996. "The Effects of Eligibility Restrictions and Party Activity on Absentee Voting and Overall Turnout." *American Journal of Political Science* 40 (2): 498–513.

Pacheco, Julianna Sandell. 2008. "Political Socialization in Context: The Effect of Political Competition on Youth Voter Turnout." *Political Behavior* 30 (4):415–36.

Panagopoulos, Costas. 2009. "Campaign Dynamics in Battleground and Nonbattleground States." *Public Opinion Quarterly* 73 (1): 119–29.

Parry, Janine, Jay Barth, Martha Kropf, and E. Terrence Jones. 2008. "Mobilizing the Seldom Voter: Campaign Contact and Effects in High-Profile Elections." *Political Behavior* 30 (1): 97–113.

Patterson, Samuel C. and Gregory A. Caldeira. 1983. "Getting Out the Vote: Participation in Gubernatorial Elections." *American Political Science Review* 77 (3): 675–89.

Patterson, Thomas E. 2002. *The Vanishing Voter: Public Involvement in the Age of Uncertainty*. New York: Vintage.

Piven, Frances Fox and Richard A. Cloward. 1988. *Why Americans Don't Vote*. New York, NY: Pantheon.

Piven, Frances Fox and Richard A. Cloward. 2000. *Why Americans Still Don't Vote: And Why Politicians Want It That Way*. Boston, MA: Beacon Press.

Powell, G. Bingham. 1986. "American Voter Turnout in Comparative Perspective." *American Political Science Review* 80 (1): 17–43.

Putnam, Robert. 2000. *Bowling Alone: The Collapse and Revival of American Community*. New York, NY: Simon and Schuster.

Primo, David M., Matthew L. Jacobsmeier, and Jeffrey Milyo. 2007. "Estimating the Impact of State Policies and Institutions with Mixed-Level Data," *State Politics and Policy Quarterly* 7: 446–59.

Redlawsk, David P., Caroline J. Tolbert and Todd Donovan. 2010. *Why Iowa? How Caucuses and Sequential Elections Improve the Presidential Nominating Process*. Chicago, IL: University of Chicago Press.

Rhine, Staci L. 1996. "An Analysis of the Impact of Registration Factors on Turnout in 1992." *Political Behavior* 18 (2): 171–85.

Rigby, Elizabeth and Melanie J. Springer. 2010. "Does Electoral Reform Increase (or Decrease) Political Equality?" *Political Research Quarterly* 64 (2): 1–15.

Riker, William H. and Peter C. Ordeshook. 1968. "A Theory of the Calculus of Voting." *American Political Science Review* 62 (1): 25–42.

Rosenstone, Steven J. and John Mark Hansen. 1993. *Mobilization, Participation, and Democracy in America*. New York, NY: Macmillan.

Settle, Russell and Buron A. Abrams. 1976. "The Determinants of Voter Participation: A More General Model." *Public Choice* 27 (1): 81–9.

Schattschneider, E. E. 1960. *The Semi-sovereign People*. New York: Harcourt Brace.

Shaw, Daron R. 2006. *The Race to 270: The Electoral College and the Campaign Strategies of 2000 and 2004*. Chicago, IL: University of Chicago Press.

Smith, Daniel A. and Caroline J. Tolbert. 2004. *Educated by Initiative: The Effects of Direct Democracy on Citizens and Political Organizations in the American States*. Ann Arbor, MI: University of Michigan Press.

Smith, Mark A. 2001. "The Contingent Effects of Ballot Initiatives and Candidate Races on Turnout." *American Journal of Political Science* 45 (3): 700–6.

Smith, Steven S. and Melanie J. Springer, eds. 2009. *Reforming the Presidential Nomination Process*. Washington, DC: Brookings Institution Press.

Southwell, Priscilla L. and Justin I. Burchett. 2000. "The Effect of All-Mail Elections on Voter Turnout." *American Politics Research* 28 (1): 72–9.

Squire, Peverill, ed. 1989. *The Iowa Caucuses and the Presidential Nominating Process*. Boulder, CO: Westview Press.

Squire, Peverill, Raymond E. Wolfinger, and David P. Glass. 1987. "Residential Mobility and Voter Turnout." *American Political Science Review* 81 (1): 45–66.

Teixeira, Ruy A. 1992. *The Disappearing American Voter*. Washington, DC: Brookings Institution Press.

Tolbert, Caroline J. and Daniel A. Smith. 2005. "The Educative Effects of Ballot Initiatives on Voter Turnout." *American Politics Research* 33 (2): 283–309.

Tolbert, Caroline J., Daniel C. Bowen, and Todd Donovan. 2009. "Initiative Campaigns: Direct Democracy and Voter Mobilization." *American Politics Research* 37 (1): 155–92.

Tolbert, Caroline J., John A. Grummel and Daniel A. Smith. 2001. "The Effects of Ballot Initiatives on Voter Turnout in the American States." *American Politics Research* 29 (6): 625–48.

Tolbert, Caroline J. and Ramona McNeal. 2003. "Unraveling the Effects of the Internet on Political Participation." *Political Research Quarterly* 56 (2): 175–85.

Tolbert, Caroline J., Todd Donovan, Bridgett King, and Shaun Bowler. 2008. Election Day Registration, Competition, and Voter Turnout. In Bruce E. Cain, Todd Donovan, and Caroline J. Tolbert (eds), *Democracy in the States: Experiments in Election Reform*. Washington, DC: Brookings Institution Press, pp. 83–98.

Tolbert, Caroline J., Amanda Keller, and Todd Donovan. 2010. "A Modified National Primary: State Losers and Support for Changing the Presidential Nominating Process." *Political Science Quarterly* 125 (3): 393–424.

Verba, Sidney, Kay Lehman Schlozman and Henry E. Brady. 1995. *Voice and Equality: Civic Voluntarism in American Politics*. Cambridge, MA: Harvard University Press.

Verba, Sidney and Norman H. Nie. 1972. *Participation in America: Political Democracy and Social Equality*. New York, NY: Harper and Row.

Wichowsky, Amber. 2012. "Competition, Party Dollars, and Income Bias in Voter Turnout, 1980–2008." *Journal of Politics* 74 (02): 446–59.

Winebrenner, Hugh. 1998. *The Iowa Precinct Caucuses: The Making of a Media Event*. Ames, IA: Iowa State University Press.

Wolfinger, Raymond E., Benjamin Highton and Megan Mullin. 2005. "How Postregistration Laws Affect the Turnout of Citizens Registered to Vote." *State Politics and Policy Quarterly* 5 (1): 1–23.

Wolfinger, Raymond E. and Steven J. Rosenstone. 1980. *Who Votes?* New Haven, CT: Yale University Press.

CHAPTER 7

....

LOCAL AND STATE INTEREST GROUP ORGANIZATIONS

....

ANTHONY J. NOWNES

INTEREST groups are older than the republic itself. As James Yoho (1999: 1) points out, "the movement for American independence from Great Britain significantly stimulated organizational activity," as the Society for Encouraging Trade and Commerce, local Sons of Liberty groups, Anti-Tea Leagues, and hundreds of other groups formed to agitate against various trade policies. Interest groups have virtually always been a part of our politics, and their numbers have grown steadily since the founding.

Not surprisingly given their prominence in American politics, interest groups have received a great deal of scholarly attention. Indeed, some of the most important and influential works in all of political science, including Bentley's (1908) *The Process of Government*, Truman's (1951) *The Governmental Process*, and Olson's (1965) *The Logic of Collective Action*, are about interest groups. Scholarly attention to interest groups peaked in the 1950s and early 1960s, as groups were "at the center of political science" (Baumgartner and Leech, 1998: 46). The study of groups declined in the late 1960s and 1970s, as "the group approach to politics" was discredited and political scientists turned their attention to other subjects (especially voting). The scholarly study of interest groups roared back, however, in the 1980s, and groups have received a steady dose of research attention ever since. But something important happened when interest groups made their comeback—scholarly focus tilted decidedly toward national politics and away from state and local politics. Prominent among the studies published during the "golden age" of interest group research were several studies of sub-national politics, including Hunter's (1953) *Community Power Structure*, Zeller's *American State Legislatures* (American Political Science Association and Zeller, 1954), and Dahl's (1961) *Who Governs?* Studies like these are conspicuous by their absence in the more recent interest group research canon. The study of group politics has become decidedly Washington-centric. Indeed, almost all of the most influential and prominent interest group studies of the last 30 years are studies of Washington politics—Hansen's (1991)

Gaining Access, Walker's (1991) *Mobilizing Interest Groups in America*, Heinz et al.'s (1993) *The Hollow Core*, and Baumgartner et al.'s (2009) *Lobbying and Policy Change* come to mind.

This is not to say that the new wave of studies has ignored state and local politics altogether. Some editions of the Cigler and Loomis edited volumes (Cigler and Loomis, 1983, 1986, 1991, 1995, 1998, 2002, 2007) contain (limited) coverage of interest groups in state politics, and two pairs of scholars—Ronald Hrebenar and Clive Thomas, and Virginia Gray and David Lowery (each of which I will discuss in some detail later in the chapter)—have worked tirelessly over the last three decades to enhance our understanding of interest group politics in the United States. In addition, many scholars of local politics posit a large role for private interests in local government decision making (see, for example, Stone, 1989; Logan and Rabrenovic, 1990; Ferman, 1996; Austin and McCaffrey, 2002; Smith and Harris, 2005; Adams, 2007). All of these efforts notwithstanding, with few exceptions the most prominent studies of interest group politics conducted in the past 30 years are studies of Washington interest group politics.

In the end, this means that there are huge gaps in our understanding of local and state interest group politics. One of my primary goals in this chapter is to identify these gaps. But my focus is not entirely negative. I will also identify areas in which our knowledge of local and state interest groups is extensive. In fact, this is where I will start. I will ask: What have we learned about state and local interest group politics? From here, I will examine where we have failed. That is, I will explore what we do not know. In the course of this discussion I will offer a number of suggestions about what we should be doing to improve our understanding of state and local interest group politics.

WHAT HAVE WE LEARNED?

While the Washington-centric nature of interest group research has inhibited our knowledge of many aspects of interest group politics in America, there are some topics about which scholars of sub-national interest groups have learned a great deal. We have learned a great deal about the following aspects of state and local interest group politics: (1) the composition of the state interest group universe; (2) the determinants of state interest group community density and diversity; (3) the activities of state-level interest groups and their lobbyists; (4) the behavior of state-level interest groups in state initiative campaigns and the effects of direct democracy on interest group communities; and (5) how participation in local interest groups affects individual participants.

The State Interest Group Universe

What types of interest groups are active in the United States, and in what numbers? Is the group universe relatively representative of the views of the American people? Are some interests better represented than others? These are important questions because they speak to the very nature of American democracy. Starting in the 1970s, interest group scholars began to address these questions in earnest. Their findings were remarkably uniform. First, they found that the number of interest groups active in America rose substantially after World War II, especially after 1960 (Walker, 1983, 1991; Schlozman and Tierney, 1986; but see Tichenor and Harris, 2005). Second, they found that the variety of interest groups active in America is quite broad, as individual business firms (Vogel, 1978; Wilson, 1981; Ryan et al., 1987), charities and churches (Liebman et al., 1983; Berry and Arons, 2003; Djupe et al., 2005), citizen groups (McFarland, 1976; Berry, 1977, 1999; Walker, 1983; Bosso, 2005), colleges and universities (Cook, 1998), think tanks (Ricci, 1993; Rich, 2004; Stone and Denham, 2004; McGann, 2007), and other types of groups compete for power alongside traditional interest group stalwarts such as labor unions, professional associations, and trade associations. Finally, the group universe shows an unmistakable bias—one toward institutions (i.e. non-membership organizations). The most prominent types of institutions active in American politics are individual business firms (Baumgartner and Leech, 2001; see also, Salisbury, 1984; Schlozman and Tierney, 1986).

In sum, as interest group studies proliferated in the 1970s and 1980s, we learned a great deal about the composition of the interest group universe. Most of the research on this subject, however, spoke only about the nature of the *Washington* interest group universe. Fortunately, the nature of the contemporary interest group universe was a topic to which some scholars of state politics also paid attention. Specifically, multi-state and multi-year studies conducted by Virginia Gray and David Lowery, and Ronald Hrebenar and Clive Thomas have told us a great deal about what the 50 state interest group communities look like. First, the painstaking substantive research of Gray and Lowery has shown us that the American states, like Washington, have experienced an advocacy explosion of sorts since the 1970s. In the vast majority of states Gray and Lowery report there were many more interest groups active in the late 1990s than there were in the late 1970s (Gray and Lowery, 2001a, 2001b; for a summary, see Lowery and Brasher, 2004: 76–7). Second, Gray and Lowery show that state interest group communities are, like the Washington interest group community, quite diverse (Gray and Lowery, 2001b), with large numbers of charities, citizen groups, government entities, religious organizations, and other types of groups lobbying alongside business firms, labor unions, professional associations, and trade associations. The empirically rich case studies found in the Hrebenar and Thomas (1987, 1992, 1993a, 1993b) volumes confirm that state interest group communities are quite diverse, though some are more diverse than others. Third, Gray and Lowery demonstrate that the well-known bias toward institutional representation exists in states just as it does in Washington (Lowery and Gray, 1998; Gray and Lowery, 2001b). Further, they show that prominent among institutions are individual businesses.

In sum, the literature shows that in their broad contours interest group communities in the states bear some resemblance to each other (though there are, of course, differences, which I will discuss later), as well as to the community of interest groups in Washington. The 50 case studies published in the Hrebenar and Thomas volumes, together with the work of Gray and Lowery, have given us a solid idea of what types of interest groups are active in the American states and in what numbers.

What Explains Differences in Density and Diversity Across States

Seizing upon the research opportunities presented by the existence of 50 unique and discrete bounded areas (the states), Virginia Gray and David Lowery (various, but see especially Gray and Lowery, 1993, 1995, 1996a, 1996b, 1996c, 1998a, 1998b; Lowery and Gray, 1993, 1994, 1995) worked throughout the 1980s and 1990s (and continue to work) to improve our understanding of interest group communities. Not content simply to describe interest group communities in the states, Gray and Lowery compared state interest group communities and then attempted to explain the differences between them.

Gray and Lowery began their theory-building exercise by arguing that the dominant scholarly focus on internal group processes (see especially Olson, 1965; Salisbury, 1969; Walker, 1983) could not help us explain differences in interest group politics across states. To explain these differences, they argued, we must step back and examine the characteristics of interest group populations. Gray and Lowery pay particular attention to two attributes of interest group populations—*density* and *diversity*. At the most basic level, density refers simply to the size of an interest group population. As for diversity, it refers to the "extent to which a variety of economic and noneconomic interests are articulated by organized groups" (Gray and Lowery, 1993: 83). Density is important for several reasons, the most important of which is that it affects formation and survival processes. Specifically, there is evidence that at relatively high levels of density—that is, in crowded interest group communities—group death is more likely and group mobilization is relatively difficult (Gray and Lowery 2001a). There is also evidence that density affects lobbying behavior. For example, it appears that interest groups are more likely to engage in "alliance activity" with other interest groups in crowded interest group communities (Gray and Lowery, 1998b). As for diversity, it too is important. Most important, it speaks to the very nature of interest group representation. Most scholars agree that more diversity is better than less, as it suggests a more inclusive and representative interest group community.

In short, density and diversity are important attributes of interest group communities. Both, according to Gray and Lowery, vary widely across states. But what explains differences in density across states? And what explains differences in diversity? Let us turn first to density. Gray and Lowery, borrowing from organizational ecology models, explain variations in density across states using an ESA, or energy–stability–area, model. Energy and area, they maintain, are the crucial determinants of density. Gray and Lowery find that energy and density are positively associated. For interest groups, there are two primary sources of energy. First, there are issues. Simply, more issues mean more interest groups. Issues, Gray and Lowery argue, are what interest groups "exploit in securing members" (Lowery and Brasher, 2004: 84). Thus, "as new issues arise or old issues are aggravated, the environment should provide a more congenial, richer setting for founding interest organizations" (Lowery and Brasher, 2004: 84). Second, there is party competition. Party competition is important because it is indicative of the likelihood of policy change. Issues are important, but "(n)o matter how salient an issue is to potential members or sponsors, few will support an interest organization if there is no chance that the political system will address it" (Lowery and Brasher, 2004: 84). "If the out-party has a good chance of becoming the in-party at the next election, then old policies may be overturned and new policies actively considered" (Lowery and Brasher, 2004: 86). In short, more party competition means more interest groups. As for the area term in the ESA model, it is essentially the number of members and other supporters available to interest groups for mobilization. For example, a state with no farmers is unlikely to have many farm groups, while a state with hundreds of thousands of farmers is likely to have many farm groups and many types of farm groups. In sum, more members and supporters means more interest groups. The relationship between area and density, however, is not linear. Even in states with lots of members and supporters— that is, in states with large area terms—there is a limit on density. In other words, at some point growth rates level off.

Gray and Lowery also attempt to explain variations in levels of diversity across states. Again, they begin with the simple premise, supported by their empirical research, that some states have more diverse interest group communities than others. From here, Gray and Lowery make several arguments about the determinants of diversity. First, state interest group community diversity is positively associated with state economic size. Second, state interest group community diversity is positively related to state economic diversity. Third, state interest group diversity is negatively related to state interest group community density. Gray and Lowery go much further than this, arguing that diversity varies across states in complex ways because "interest guilds respond differently to the availability of potential members depending on their unique economies of scale of organization and the homogeneity of their members' interests" (Lowery and Brasher, 2004: 98). Suffice to say that Gray and Lowery have developed a sophisticated and elegant theory to explain interest group diversity.

The work of Gray and Lowery has taught us a great deal about what state interest group communities look like, how they differ, and why. Their ESA model of interest group density, together with their related model of interest group diversity, has given us powerful tools to understand how and why interest group communities look different over time and across space. In short, one of the things we have learned is what explains differences in density and diversity across states.

What State-level Interest Groups and Their Lobbyists Do

Another area where we have learned a great deal about sub-national interest group politics is what state-level interest groups and their lobbyists do. Following the lead of Zeller (American Political Science Association and Zeller, 1954) and Morehouse (1981), who showed us that states were hotbeds of interest group activity, a number of scholars have demonstrated empirically precisely what state-level interest groups do (see, for example, Hrebenar and Thomas, 1987, 1992, 1993a, 1993b; King and Robin, 1994, 1995; Nownes and Freeman, 1998a, 1998b; Gerber, 1999; Rosenthal, 2001; Alexander, 2002; Nownes and DeAlejandro, 2009). This research suggests several general conclusions about what state interest groups and their lobbyists do, including the following: (1) state lobbyists are active across all three branches of state government; (2) state lobbyists utilize some tactics (e.g. testifying before legislative committees, meeting personally with state legislators, meeting personally with state legislative aides) more than others (e.g. filing suit or otherwise litigating, engaging in protests and demonstrations); (3) while direct lobbying (that is, lobbying aimed at government officials) remains predominant, state lobbyists are big users of grassroots techniques (e.g. inspiring letter-writing or email campaigns to state legislators, issuing press releases, running advertisements in media), and direct democratic techniques (e.g. campaigning for or against a ballot initiative, seeking to put a measure on the state ballot as an initiative); (4) despite the ongoing professionalization of state politics in general and lobbying in particular, more state lobbyists than not utilize informal lobbying techniques (e.g. engaging in informal contacts with legislators, doing favors for officials who need assistance); (5) many state-level interest groups engage in electoral lobbying (e.g. forming PACs [where this is necessary] and contributing money to candidates, endorsing candidates); (6) state lobbyists regularly enter into coalitions; and (7) many state lobbyists spend a large portion of their time on non-lobbying activities (including monitoring government and monitoring other interest groups).

In all, empirical research conducted over the past 20 years has provided us with a rather thorough understanding of the activities of state-level interest groups and their lobbyists. This research demonstrates that lobbying in the states is now very much like lobbying in Washington.

Interest Groups and Direct Democracy in the States

There is no direct democracy at the national level. The states, however, are a different story, as many present interest groups a variety of opportunities to take part directly in proposing and making policy. Scholars of state politics have learned a great deal about the role of interest groups in direct democracy. First, they have learned that large numbers of interest groups participate in direct democratic processes. For example, one recent survey showed that more than half of all responding state lobbyists reported "campaigning for or against a state initiative or referendum" (Nownes and DeAlejandro, 2009). Numerous other studies confirm the centrality of interest groups in many direct democratic campaigns (Cronin, 1984; Gerber, 1999; Alexander, 2002). Second, we have learned a great deal about what types of interests win in direct democratic campaigns. Early studies argued that well-financed business interests (i.e. business firms and trade groups, as opposed to citizen groups and labor unions) dominated direct democratic campaigns (Cronin, 1984; Magleby, 1984). Gerber (1998, 1999), however, has shown that the relationship between spending on direct democracy and winning is not straight-forward. She shows, in fact, that there is a negative relationship between how much "dominant" economic interest groups—business firms, trade groups, and professional groups—spend in support of an initiative and the probability that the initiative will succeed. This said, these groups tend to have more success when they are playing defense—that is, when they are spending to defeat an initiative supported by citizen or labor groups (Gerber, 1998). In short, it appears that spending by business firms, professional associations, and trade groups, which generally outstrips spending by citizen groups and labor unions, is capable of defeating initiatives, but not necessarily passing them.

We have also learned that the mere presence of direct democracy affects interest group communities. Specifically, Boehmke (2005) has shown that states with the initiative have more diverse interest group communities than states without the initiative. This suggests that the mere opportunity directly to propose legislation enhances opportunities for all sorts of groups to mobilize.

How Participation in Local Organizations Affects Individuals

How does participation in interest groups affect individuals? Scholars of national and state interest groups have paid surprisingly little attention to this question (and should pay more). Scholars of local groups, however, have addressed this question extensively, and their findings have contributed to the ongoing scholarly debate about the determinants and benefits of social capital. Overall, studies show that participation in local organizations can enhance individual civic skills. Berry et al. (1993), for example, find that participation in neighborhood associations can enhance individuals' sense of community, and can increase trust in government and political efficacy. All of this is good for democratic governance. Other studies find a variety of positive effects of group participation (Adams, 2007, Ch. 10; Hays and Kogl, 2007; Ohmer, 2007) including increased knowledge of public affairs, enhanced leadership and organizational skills, and an increased sense of empowerment. In short, there is a small but important body of research which shows that participation in local organizations is good for individuals and good for social capital.

A Few Loose Ends

Before moving on to what I consider our most glaring gaps, I want to make mention of a few other things that we have learned. First, we have learned that interest groups are much more powerful in some states than others (Thomas and Hrebenar, 1996, 1999, 2004). In general, groups are more powerful in states with weak party systems, and in states with "traditionalistic" political cultures. Second and similarly, we have learned that interest groups are more powerful in some localities than others (Schumaker, 1991). Unfortunately, we do not know enough about what explains the differences across localities. Third, studies of local politics show that neighborhood associations are singularly important group actors in some cities, and they are capable of profoundly affecting local government decisions (Thomas, 1986; Berry et al. 1993). I will have more to say about neighborhood associations later. Fourth, we have learned that Alinsky-type direct action organizations are not uncommon in American cities. The Industrial Areas Foundation (IAF) and its local affiliates, as well as the Association of Community Organizations for Reform Now (ACORN) have received some research attention. This work shows that groups like these are anything but powerless in local politics (Berry et al., 1993; Warren, 2001; Wood, 2002). Fifth, we have learned a great deal about the role of interest groups in state elections, especially about the strategies of state political action committees (Thompson and Cassie, 1992; Thompson et al., 1994; Malbin and Gais, 1998; for a summary, see Ramsden, 2002). This work is especially notable because it has largely confirmed notions gleaned from studies of Washington interest groups, and thus represents a triumph of theory testing.

Summary

In sum, we have learned a considerable amount about state and local interest groups in the past 50 years. We know a great deal, for example, about the contours of state interest group communities, and what explains the differences between these communities. We also know a lot about what state lobbyists do. We know a little bit about several other topics, including how participation in local organizations affects citizens, and how direct democracy affects interest groups in the states and interest groups in the states affect direct democracy. Yet in the end, anyone who studies local or state politics knows that there is a great deal about sub-national interest group politics in America that we do not know. In short, there are many gaps in our understanding of state and local interest group politics. It is to these gaps I now turn.

WHAT WE NEED TO LEARN MORE ABOUT

Although there are gaps in our understanding of both state and local interest group politics, I believe that we are especially deficient in our understanding of local interest group politics. I say this because despite the existence of a vibrant literature on neighborhood associations and a flexible theoretical framework (regime theory) for understanding public–private relations in cities, there are several aspects of local interest group politics about which we know virtually nothing. In my opinion, we are particularly deficient in our knowledge of the following: (1) the makeup of county and special district interest group communities; (2) the activities of local lobbyists; and (3) the electioneering activities of interest groups in local elections. I will begin my discussion of research gaps with these three topics. From here, I will examine a few other aspects of sub-national interest group politics about which we need to learn more, including the role of interest groups in land-use politics and procurement politics, intergovernmental lobbying that does not involve Washington, and interest group electioneering in state elections. Finally, I will highlight a major fault with the literature on sub-national interest groups—its failure to engage dominant theories of interest group politics.

What do Local Interest Group Communities Look Like?

One topic about which we know surprisingly little is the composition of the local interest group universe. What types of interest groups lobby local governments and in what numbers? We do not know the answer to this question. Some of what we do know comes from case studies of specific cities. For example, from case studies of Atlanta (Stone, 1989), Boston (O'Connor, 1993), New York (Sites, 1997), and Philadelphia (McGovern, 2009), we know that business firms (and their leaders)—both individually and through participation in formal (see Austin and McCaffrey, 2002) and informal coalitions (Stone, 1989)—are power players in many municipalities. Other studies confirm the power and activity of business (Abney and Lauth, 1985; Logan and Molotch, 1987). We have also learned about what types of businesses are most active in local politics. Specifically, studies show that because a great deal of local politics is about land use, "the most active of all business interests in city and county politics are those related to land and development...," including architectural firms, builders, developers, and real estate companies (Logan and Molotch, 1987; Christensen and Hogen-Esch, 2006: 239; Nownes, 2006). From other sources, we learn that neighborhood organizations also are active in many municipalities (Dilger, 1992; Berry et al., 1993; Elkins, 1995; Cooper et al., 2005; Berry et al., 2006; Adams, 2007), as are faith-based organizations and churches (Button et al., 1997; Sharp, 1999; Smith and Harris, 2005), "public interest" groups (Sharp, 1999), labor unions (Regalado, 1991; DeLeon, 1992), and ethnic and racial minority groups (Browning et al., 1997).

In short, we have a reasonably good idea of what types of interest groups are active in local politics. Nonetheless, there are a number of conspicuous gaps in our knowledge of local interest group communities. First, we know little or nothing about *county* interest group communities. What types of interest groups are active in American counties and in what numbers? We do not have even the most rudimentary answers to these questions, as studies of county interest group politics are virtually non-existent. Second, we know very little about interest group communities in small cities, towns, and villages. Most studies of local politics that concern themselves at all with interest groups are studies of cities (and large ones at that). Third, we know very little about (what I call) special district interest group communities—that is, about the types of groups that lobby special districts. There are tens of thousands of special districts in the United States, and as Mullin (2009) shows, special district officials are rational political actors just like other public officials and are thus open to persuasion. Studies of special district lobbying (that is, lobbying aimed at special districts, not conducted by special districts) are non-existent. In short, we need to learn much more about what local interest group communities look like.

What Local Lobbyists Do

Over the years several large-scale surveys of lobbyists have been conducted (see, for example, Milbrath, 1963; Berry, 1977; Walker, 1983; Schlozman and Tierney, 1983, 1986; Knoke, 1990; Heinz et al., 1993; Kollman, 1998; Nownes and Freeman, 1998a, 1998b; Nownes and DeAlejandro, 2009). Moreover, there are excellent empirical studies of lobbying based on actual observation of lobbyists at work (Rosenthal, 2001; Kersh, 2002, 2007). As Baumgartner and Leech (1998, 162) point out, these studies have done an excellent job of "enumerating various tactics of lobbying" used at the national and state level. Unfortunately, no comparable surveys of local lobbyists have been conducted, and thus no one has enumerated the various tactics of *local* lobbying. Though some studies of local politics give us vague ideas about what local interest groups do to influence policy (see, for example, Stone, 1989; Berry et al., 1993; Austin and McCaffrey, 2002; Krebs, 2005a, 2005b), there are simply no large scale studies of local lobbying (like those conducted in the states) that enumerate the range of tactics that local lobbyists use. As such, we do not have much of an understanding of the tactics that local lobbyists use.

What Land-use and Procurement Lobbying Look Like

In my opinion, we need to do much more to understand two types of lobbying that have received very little attention from state and local interest group scholars (or national interest group scholars for that matter)—procurement lobbying, and land-use lobbying. In my own research (Nownes, 2006), I have found that many state and local lobbyists (and Washington lobbyists) care very little about public policy if by this we mean government decisions (i.e. laws, rules, regulations, or court decisions) about important societal issues such as abortion, education, gay rights, health care, immigration, and the like.

So what *do* state and local lobbyists care about if not public policy? First, they care about government decisions concerning purchasing and contracting. Data show that state and local governments spend even more money on goods and services each year than does the federal government (Cooper, 2003). And while several studies note that interest groups play some role in state and local contracting and purchasing decisions (see, for example, DeHoog, 1984; O'Looney, 1998; Lavery, 1999; LeRoux and Harney, 2007; Curry, 2009), we have very little knowledge about what this role is. To what extent do local and state interest groups want to influence these sorts of decisions? What proportion of local and state lobbying is aimed at receiving private goods such as contracts rather than public goods? What do interest groups and their lobbyists do to affect contracting and purchasing decisions? How much influence do interest groups wield over these decisions? We do not have answers to these questions, and we will not fully understand state and local interest group politics until we address them. Second, many state and local lobbyists (especially local) care about government decisions concerning land use; unfortunately, we know very little about the role of interest

groups in land-use politics. Land use, of course, is of paramount interest to local government (see Feiock, 2004; Christensen and Hogen-Esch, 2006; Bowman and Kearney,
2008). In my own work, I have found that a great deal of (if not most) local lobbying
concerns land use rather than public policy as we usually define it. A summary perusal
of city lobbyist registration lists indicates that the majority of registered lobbyists in cities represent development interests such as contractors, home builders, and real estate
developers. How do interest groups attempt to influence land-use decisions? How do
the activities of land-use lobbyists differ from those of other types of lobbyists? How
successful are land-use lobbyists at getting what they want from local government? To
be sure, these questions have received some attention. Fleischmann and Pierannunzi
(1990), for example, examine how the presence of lobbyists affects land-use decisions,
while in my own work I have examined the activities of land-use lobbyists (Nownes,
2006). Moreover, neighborhood groups, which are often powerful players in land-use
battles, have attracted a great deal of scholarly attention, as dozens of studies have analyzed what they do and to what effect (see, for example, Thomas, 1986; Hutcheson and
Prather, 1988; Logan and Rabrenovic, 1990; Green and Schreuder, 1991; Swindell, 2000).
So-called "NIMBY" groups have also received scholarly attention (see, for example,
Kraft and Clary, 1991; Munton, 1996; McAvoy, 1999; Matejczyk, 2001). Much of this literature finds that neighborhood associations and other organized groups of citizens are
indeed capable to stopping unpopular development projects, especially if they are active
and voluble.

Nonetheless, our knowledge of interest group and lobbyist activity surrounding
land-use issues remains limited. Surprisingly, we probably know less about the land-use
lobbying behavior of purported dominant political interests—that is, partners in the
"growth machines" that many scholars say dominate local politics—than we do about
neighborhood organizations and other citizen groups. Regime theory (which I will say
more about later) and growth machine theories of local politics posit a central role for
business interests in local (that is, land use) politics, but tell us very little about the specific actions they take to affect government decisions.

In sum, we have a great deal to learn about one type of lobbying that takes place virtually exclusively at the local level, land-use lobbying, and another that takes place at all
three levels of government but is unquestionably very important at the state and local
level, procurement lobbying.

Intergovernmental Lobbying in the States

The study of intergovernmental lobbying is decidedly Washington-centric and focuses
primarily upon how and why sub-national governmental institutions lobby the national
government (see, for example, Haider, 1974; Hays, 1991; Berch, 1992; Cammisa, 1995;
Marbach and Leckrone, 2002). Fortunately, there is a small literature that has taught us a
few things about sub-national intergovernmental lobbying. For example, we learn from
Thomas and Hrebenar (1996, 1999, 2004) that "general local government organizations"

are consistently among the top 10 most powerful types of interest groups in state politics, while specific cities and towns consistently make the top 40. From Cigler (1994) we learn that state associations of counties bring their concerns to state governments quite regularly, and from De Soto (1995) we learn that municipal officials spend considerable time communicating their concerns to state policy makers. Finally, from Abney (1988), we have learned that state agency lobbyists have unusually high levels of access to state decision makers, and from the Thomas and Hrebenar studies we learn that state agencies are consistently ranked among the top 25 most powerful types of interest groups in the states.

Yet while we have learned that sub-national intergovernmental lobbying takes place and that state agencies and local governments are powerful players in state politics, we have learned little else. Do state agency lobbyists have unusually high levels of access in all states (Abney's 1988 study is limited to Georgia)? How successful are state agency lobbyists when they lobby the legislature? How do local officials and their associations attempt to influence state policy? How successful are they? And do state government lobbyists ever lobby local government officials? If so, how and why? These are just a few of the many questions about sub-national intergovernmental lobbying that we do not know the answers to. Given the large number of sub-national intergovernmental lobbyists and their purported power (at least in state politics), it is imperative that we pay them more attention.

The Electoral Activities of Local Interest Groups

The electoral activities of interest groups have received substantial research attention in the past 25 years. Most of this attention has been focused on Washington interest groups (see, for example, Sabato, 1985; Wright, 1985; Hall and Wayman, 1990; Gais, 1996; Wawro, 2001; Rozell and Wilcox, 2006), though some has focused on state groups (see, for example, Arceneaux and Kolodny, 2009). We know very little about interest group activity in local elections. One thing we do know is that interest groups are indeed active in local elections. In their influential empirical study of elections in Atlanta and St Louis, Fleischmann and Stein (1998) show that interest groups are large contributors to local candidates. Business firms are especially large contributors, though other types of groups also give. Other studies confirm that interest groups of all kinds contribute to candidates for local office (Hogan and Simpson, 2001; Krebs and Pelissero, 2001; Krebs, 2005a, 2005b; Adams, 2008). These studies are quite literally trailblazers, as they illuminate political phenomena that traditionally have received minimal research attention.

But these studies are only a beginning. There is still a great deal we do not know about interest group activity in local elections. We know little, for example, about non-contributory electoral behavior. How common are other forms of electoral activity such as endorsing candidates, making in-kind contributions to candidates, recruiting candidates, running issue advertisements, and spending independently? We do not know.

And how and why does interest group electoral activity vary across localities? We do not know. Do business firms and other types of groups with primarily economic concerns engage in different types of activities than non-business interest groups such as labor unions? Again, we do not know. Finally, we have little or no idea of how interest group giving or helping affects either election outcomes or the behavior of elected officials who receive interest group help. In sum, we have a lot to learn about the electoral activities.

How Well Our Dominant Theories Explain State and Local Interest Group Politics

By now it should be clear that we lack even the most basic descriptive information on many aspects of sub-national (especially local) interest group politics. This is why my discussion in this section has so far focused primarily upon our empirical research needs. There is no question, however, that one of the most urgent research needs facing people who study sub-national interest groups is, as Gray and Lowery (2002: 405) recently put it, the "need to engage fully in the theoretical debates motivating the larger interest organization literature." Gray and Lowery go on to note that at least at the state level, there is more data than theory. I am not sure I am willing to go that far, especially in light of Gray and Lowery's own theoretical work, the body of work generally referred to as "regime theory" (I will say more about this in the next subsection), and the lack of even the most rudimentary substantive information on many aspects of local interest group politics. But Gray and Lowery's basic point is well-taken. Clearly scholars of state and local interest group politics have done less than we should to engage theories of interest group politics developed by scholars of national politics.

Group influence in states and localities: Nowhere is the need to engage broader theoretical issues more clear than in the study of interest group influence. Scholars of state and local interest groups have been slow to test notions gleaned from studies of Washington-based interest group influence. Neither state nor local interest group scholars, for example, have tested Browne's (1990) elegant and appealing "niche theory" of interest group influence to any serious degree. Moreover, scholars of sub-national interest groups have paid little attention to theoretical ideas derived from arguably the largest study of interest group influence ever conducted—Heinz et al.'s (1993) *The Hollow Core*, a neopluralist manifesto. The lack of engagement with neopluralist notions of group influence is particularly surprising given neopluralism's emphasis on contextual factors affecting groups' ability to exercise influence. States and localities are natural laboratories that provide us with seemingly endless opportunities to test notions gleaned from neopluralist theories of influence.

Testing neopluralist notions of influence in the state context should be relatively easy. I say this because there is no state-specific theoretical perspective on interest group influence. The literature on influence is there, to be sure, and it has taught us some things about the influence of interest groups in state politics. Wiggins et al. (1992), for example, show us that interest groups in the states do indeed wield influence, but that their influence can be blunted by elected officials. For her part, Gerber (1999) demonstrates the contingent nature of interest group influence, while Ambrosius and Welch (1988) reach a more conventional conclusion about the power of business. Bowling and Ferguson (2001) approach interest group power indirectly, assessing whether or not interest group density and diversity affect bill passage rates. But the fact is that there is no state-specific body of theory that seeks to explain the influence of interest groups in state politics. However, there *is* a body of theory on interest group (or at least extra-governmental) influence that could be termed local government specific. That large and diverse body of theory is generally called *regime theory*. This body of theory has been "a dominant paradigm in the field of urban politics and policy" since the 1980s (Mossberger and Stoker, 2001, 810). I cannot do justice to regime theory in such a short space, but a few summative words are in order. At the core of regime theory is the idea that cities are governed by public–private partnerships—partnerships between public officials and land interests (read: developers). "Public officials," the argument goes, "feel obliged to consult land interests" when they make important decisions (Elkin, 1987, 46, in Elkins, 1995, 586). Indeed, landed interests are part and parcel of the governing coalitions that run cities, as they work with public officials to promote the growth that politicians and businesspeople alike believe is crucial to economic and political success. There is much more to regime theory than this, of course, but even my summary words should make it clear that regime theory holds that interest groups—especially individual business firms and coalitions of businesses—are enormously influential in local (especially city) policy making (Stone, 1989, 1993; Mossberger and Stoker, 2001; Austin and McCaffrey, 2002). Many scholars working in the basic regime theory tradition have argued that other types of interest groups including citizen and neighborhood groups (Stone, 1989; Ferman, 1996; Cooper et al., 2005; Berry et al., 2006) also are often part of urban regimes, and some urban scholars go so far as to say that an urban regime need not have much business participation at all (Imbroscio, 1997, 1998).

However, regime theorists seldom if ever use the term "interest groups" in their work. Neither do they normally use the words "lobbyist" or "lobbying." Their work, in other words, is almost entirely disconnected from the work of interest group scholars in general and scholars of group influence specifically. Perhaps it is too much to ask, but I think it is time that interest group scholars begin to look closely at the work of regime theorists (and closely related "growth machine" perspectives). We need to attend more to their empirical observations about the role of non-governmental organizations and individuals in local politics, and we need to take their theoretical contributions more seriously. After all, regime theorists and urban affairs scholars have spent much more time studying non-governmental actors in local politics than interest group scholars have. Most important, we need to determine if local interest group politics truly is unique and thus worthy of an entirely different theoretical lens than state or national interest group politics. Only after we address this issue can we make theoretical progress. At the same time, perhaps scholars of local politics can take a closer look at some of the theoretical work conducted by scholars of national politics.

Group mobilization and maintenance in the states: In 1982, R. Douglas Arnold characterized the interest group field of study as "theory rich and data poor" (Arnold, 1982, 97). He reached this conclusion partially because during the 1960s and 1970s there was substantial theoretical activity concerning collective action and the formation and maintenance of interest groups (see especially Olson, 1965; Salisbury, 1969; Frohlich and Oppenheimer, 1970). In the 1970s and 1980s, this theoretical work was complimented by high quality empirical studies that spoke to theoretical questions (for example, Berry, 1977; Marwell and Ames, 1979, 1980; Moe, 1980; Godwin and Mitchell, 1982; Walker, 1983; Hansen, 1985). Theoretical progress continued in the 1980s and beyond (Hardin, 1982; Axelrod, 1984; Ostrom, 1990; Chong, 1991; Sandler, 1992; Lichbach, 1995; Medina Sierra, 2007), and empirical studies continue to address the collective action dilemma (Jordan and Maloney, 1997; Lowry, 1997, 1998; Shaiko, 1999; Ainsworth, 2000; Miller and Krosnick, 2004; Bosso, 2005; Lubell et al., 2006, 2007).

In short, the literature on collective action and interest group mobilization and survival is massive. Most of the literature, both theoretical and empirical, focuses on individual-level explanations for, and determinants of, group formation and maintenance. In other words, the bulk of the literature adopts Olson's rational actor assumption and proceeds from there. Interestingly, most studies of state interest group mobilization and survival explicitly shun individual-level analysis and focus upon the group itself as the unit of analysis. The work of Gray and Lowery (cited above), for example, avoids individual-level questions almost completely, focusing instead on the contextual determinants of group activity. Other studies of state-level groups do the same (Lowry, 2005; Baumgartner et al., 2009). In the end, this means that the literature on state interest groups does not have much to say about precisely how state-level interest groups overcome the substantial barriers to formation and survival. In other words, the state-level literature fails to utilize the dominant theoretical lens through which interest group scholars examine group mobilization and maintenance. I think it should. Of course, focusing on the group instead of the individual as the unit of analysis has led Gray and Lowery to reach many important conclusions about interest group politics (for example, that interest group systems have carrying capacities, and that like groups are often engaged in competition for scarce resources and thus must adapt to survive), and their theories have been so influential that their group-level focus increasingly is being adopted by scholars of national politics (see, for example, Nownes, 2004; Nownes and Lipinski, 2005).

One of the reasons I believe that engaging the collective action literature is necessary is that many state interest groups—especially membership groups—are fundamentally different than national interest groups. They are different in that they are affiliates or chapters of larger national organizations. As such, it is quite possible that they face collective action dilemmas far different from the ones faced by national-level only organizations or the national "headquarters" organizations of federated groups (see, for example, Johnson, 2001). As Skocpol (2003) points out, sub-national group affiliates vary in the extent to which they receive formation and maintenance assistance and encouragement from national-level leaders. Many of the most active citizen groups, labor unions, professional associations, and trade associations in the states are parts of larger federated organizations, and we simply need to learn more about the way these groups overcome collective action dilemmas.

An additional point about our lack of knowledge of intra-group relations in federated organizations: first, our lack of research in this area means that we know very little about the way business firms (whom everyone believes are very important actors in state politics) that operate in numerous places make decisions about political action. Many business firms, of course, are active in many states. Some, in fact, are active in dozens of states. How much contact does Altria's lobbying operation in California have with its lobbying operation in Washington, DC, or West Virginia? Is what Altria does in California dictated by Altria's central office in Virginia? Or are state public affairs personnel left to their own devices to determine when, how, and to what extent they engage politically? These are not formation and maintenance questions per se, but they speak to the question of when and how established business firms choose to engage in political activity. We have learned a lot about corporate lobbying in the last decade, but we have learned very little about questions such as these.

Group mobilization and maintenance in localities: There has been much more attention given to collective action in general and group mobilization and maintenance in particular by scholars of local politics. This is the case primarily because many scholars of local politics have studied neighborhood organizations and other types of community groups. Many of these studies have adopted the individual-level focus utilized by scholars of national politics. This literature is large, and most of it comes from outside of political science. Community psychologists, for example, have even come up with their own theory—empowerment theory—to explain local group (and individual) participation (see, for example, Zimmerman and Rappaport 1988; Perkins et al. 1990; Prestby et al. 1990; Peterson and Reid 2003; Kirst-Ashman 2008). Work in this vein explores the determinants of individual participation in community-based organizations. Some of this work focuses on "psychological empowerment" (which is similar to the concept of efficacy), while some focuses on contextual factors (e.g. macro-economic changes, governmental interventions) that affect participation. Similarly, there is a large sociological literature on membership of neighborhood associations, much of which proceeds from an Olsonian perspective (see, for example, O'Brien, 1975; Nachmias and Palen, 1982; Rich, 1988; Olsen et al., 1989; Oropesa, 1996). There are even communications scholars who study local group participation (see, for example, Jeffres et al., 2002), focusing on how it is affected by patterns of media use and interpersonal communication. There is insufficient space here to go over the findings of these diverse studies. If we are to build a solid political science literature on local group mobilization and participation, it will be necessary for us to attend to this work.

As for non-membership groups, again, the regime theory literature assumes that business firms and other institutions with an interest in local economic development will mobilize and become politically active to pursue this interest. But studies of actual mobilization are scarce. It seems obvious that a company or a hospital or a university with a direct interest in a specific land-use decision will mobilize to affect that decision.

Indeed, as I note in my book *Total Lobbying* (Nownes, 2006), an organization that wishes to utilize land it owns or purchases virtually *must* mobilize politically to get permission to act. But why and when do institutions get involved in policy (i.e. non land-use) battles? And who within institutions makes the decision to get involved? Why do some business firms lobby while others do not? And why do some business firms decide to sell to government while others do not? We do not have answers to any of these questions.

A Few Loose Ends

There are several other aspects of local and state interest group politics about which we need to learn more. First, we need to discover more about the role of interest groups in local direct democratic campaigns. While direct democracy in the states has been studied extensively, direct democracy in localities has received very little attention from political scientists in general and interest group scholars in particular. Second, we need to learn more about the internal operations of organizations. Work on the "iron law of oligarchy" notwithstanding, there is a lot we do not know about how state and local interest groups are governed and maintained. Third, we know next to nothing about the tactical and strategic choices that local and state interest groups make. What factors affect the kinds of arguments groups make and the kind of tactics they use? We do not know the answer to this question as it pertains to national interest groups, and we certainly do not know the answer as it pertains to state and local interest groups. Fourth, we know very little about variations in density and diversity across local interest group communities and what explains them. As far as I can tell, there are no comparative studies of local interest groups that explain or even describe differences in density and diversity. This is particularly unfortunate for two reasons. First, unbeknownst to many interest group scholars, many local governments make lobbyists and interest groups register with local government and then make lobbyist registration data available on-line. Second, as I note above, Gray and Lowery have given us the theoretical tools necessary to understand and explain differences in density and diversity. But until we describe and detail these differences we are certainly not in position to explain them. Sixth, we know very little about local lobbying regulations and their effects. Thomas (1998) wrote over a decade ago that local regulation of lobbying was not extensive. This is no longer the case. My own admittedly unscientific search of city, town, and county websites indicates that more local governments than ever regulate lobbying. What do these regulations look like? Why were they enacted? What effects do they have on the behavior of local lobbyists? We do not have the answers to any of these questions.

CONCLUSION

Interest groups are important players in American politics. They are just as important in state and local politics as they are in Washington politics. They may be more important.

This point has not been lost on scholars of either interest groups or state and local politics. As this chapter suggests, we know a lot about state and local interest organizations. And there is no question that we know a lot more today than we knew 20 or 30 years ago. We have made huge strides in understanding several aspects of state and local interest group politics, including the makeup and dynamics of state interest group communities, what state-level interest groups and their lobbyists do, how participation in local groups affects individuals, and how interest groups engage direct democratic processes in the states. Nonetheless, we lack even the most rudimentary understanding of many aspects of state and local interest group politics. For example, we lack descriptive studies of local interest group communities, and thus not surprisingly we know little about what types of groups are active in localities across the country, what they want, and how they try to get what they want. In my opinion, this is where our need is the strongest. We must do more foundational work on local interest groups and their activities. We have a lot of other things to learn as well. We know little, for example, about intergovernmental lobbying aimed at states, and about the electoral activities of local interest groups. Finally, scholars of state and local interest groups have done a poor job of engaging dominant theories of interest group politics—theories devised primarily by scholars of Washington interest groups.

In closing, I will offer a few suggestions—suggestions that I think may help us begin to fill the gaps in our understanding of state and local interest group politics. First, I have a suggestion for graduate students—study state or local interest group politics. The field of interest groups is, in my opinion, still "undertilled." While voting and a few other fields of study in American politics continue to get disproportionate attention, few graduate students study interest groups. This is a shame, as data are available now more than ever before. It is also a shame because studying interest groups makes a scholar versatile and capable of contributing to the literature of political science, public administration, sociology, and even psychology and urban affairs. Second, I suggest that scholars who study state or local interest groups spend more time trolling the Internet looking for data. A couple of years ago I discovered that many American cities and counties force lobbyists to register, and many make lobbyist registration reports available to the public. We have done a poor job thus far of tapping these data sources. Finally, I suggest that scholars who study state or local interest groups broaden their attention and read more work by psychologists, sociologists, and other scholars who study interest groups. In the course of writing this chapter I learned that scholars from other disciplines have done a great deal of work on questions related to state (and especially) local interest groups. We have a lot to learn from other disciplines.

REFERENCES

Abney, G. 1988. "Lobbying by the Insiders: Parallels of State Agencies and Interest Groups." *Public Administration Review* 48: 911–17.

Abney, G. and Lauth, T. P. 1985. "Interest Group Influence in City Policy-making: The Views of Administrators." *Western Political Quarterly* 38: 148–61.

Adams, B. E. 2007. *Citizen Lobbyists: Local Efforts to Influence Public Policy*. Philadelphia: Temple University Press.

Adams, B. 2008. "Fund-raising Coalitions in School Board Elections." *Education and Urban Society* 40: 411–27.

Ainsworth, S. H. 2000. "Modeling Political Efficacy and Interest Group Membership." *Political Behavior* 22: 89–108.

Alexander, R. M. 2002. *Rolling the Dice with State Initiatives: Interest Group Involvement in Ballot Campaigns*. Westport, CT: Praeger.

Ambrosius, M. M. and Welch, S. 1988. "State Legislators' Perceptions of Business and Labor Interests." *Legislative Studies Quarterly* 13: 199–209.

American Political Science Association, Committee on American Legislatures, and Zeller, B. 1954. *American State Legislatures: Report*. New York: Crowell.

Arceneaux, K. and Kolodny, R. 2009. "Educating the Least Informed: Group Endorsements in a Grassroots Campaign." *American Journal of Political Science* 53: 755–70.

Arnold, R. D. 1982. "Overtilled and Undertilled Fields in American Politics." *Political Science Quarterly* 97: 91–103.

Austin, J. and McCaffrey, A. 2002. "Business Leadership Coalitions and Public–Private Partnerships in American Cities: A Business Perspective on Regime Theory." *Journal of Urban Affairs* 24: 35–54.

Axelrod, R. M. 1984. *The Evolution of Cooperation*. New York: Basic Books.

Baumgartner, F. R. and Leech, B. L. 1998. *Basic Interests: The Importance of Groups in Politics and in Political Science*. Princeton, NJ: Princeton University Press.

Baumgartner, F. R. and Leech, B. L. 2001. "Interest Niches and Policy Bandwagons: Patterns of Interest Group Involvement in National Politics." *Journal of Politics* 63: 1191–213.

Baumgartner, F. R., Berry, J. M., Hojnacki, M., Kimball, D. C., and Leech, B. L. 2009. *Lobbying and Policy Change: Who Wins, Who Loses, and Why*. Chicago: The University of Chicago Press.

Bentley, A. F. 1908. *The Process of Government: A Study of Social Pressures*. Chicago: The University of Chicago Press.

Berch, N. 1992. "Why do some States Play the Federal Aid Game better than Others?" *American Politics Quarterly* 20: 366–77.

Berry, J. M. 1977. *Lobbying for the People: The Political Behavior of Public Interest Groups*. Princeton, NJ: Princeton University Press.

Berry, J. M. 1999. *The New Liberalism: The Rising Power of Citizen Groups*. Washington, DC: Brookings Institution Press.

Berry, J. M. and Arons, D. F. 2003. *A Voice for Nonprofits*. Washington, DC: Brookings Institution Press.

Berry, J. M., Portney, K. E., and Thomson, K. 1993. *The Rebirth of Urban Democracy*. Washington, DC: Brookings Institution.

Berry, J. M., Portney, K. E., Liss, R., Simoncelli, J., and Berger, L. 2006. *Power and Interest Groups in City Politics*. Boston: Rappaport Institute for Greater Boston. Available on-line at <http://ase.tufts.edu/polsci/faculty/berry/CityPolitics.pdf>.

Boehmke, F. J. 2005. *The Indirect Effect of Direct Legislation: How Institutions Shape Interest Group Systems*. Columbus: The Ohio State University Press.

Bosso, C. J. 2005. *Environment, Inc: From Grassroots to Beltway*. Lawrence: University Press of Kansas.

Bowling, C. J. and Ferguson, M. R. 2001. "Divided Government, Interest Representation, and Policy Differences: Competing Explanations of Gridlock in the Fifty States." *Journal of Politics* 63: 182–206.

Bowman, A. O. M. and Kearney, R. C. 2008. *State and Local Government*. 7th edn. Boston: Houghton Mifflin.

Browne, W. P. 1990. "Organized Interests and their Issue Niches: A Search for Pluralism in a Policy Domain." *Journal of Politics* 52: 477–509.

Browning, R. P., Marshall, D. R., and Tabb, D. H. 1997. *Racial Politics in American Cities*. 2nd edn. New York: Longman.

Button, J. W., Rienzo, B. A., and Wald, K. D. 1997. *Private Lives, Public Conflicts: Battles over Gay Rights in American Communities*. Washington, DC: CQ Press.

Cammisa, A. M. 1995. *Governments as Interest Groups: Intergovernmental Lobbying and the Federal System*. Westport, CT: Praeger.

Chong, D. 1991. *Collective Action and the Civil Rights Movement*. Chicago: The University of Chicago Press.

Christensen, T. and Hogen-Esch, T. 2006. *Local Politics: A Practical Guide to Governing at the Grassroots*. 2nd edn. Armonk, NY: M.E. Sharpe.

Cigler, B. A. 1994. The County–State Connection: A National Study of Associations of Counties. *Public Administration Review* 54: 3–11.

Cigler, A. J. and Loomis, B. A. 1983. *Interest Group Politics*. Washington, DC: CQ Press.

Cigler, A. J. and Loomis, B. A. 1986. *Interest Group Politics*. 2nd edn. Washington, DC: CQ Press.

Cigler, A. J. and Loomis, B. A. 1991. *Interest Group Politics*. 3rd edn. Washington, DC: CQ Press.

Cigler, A. J. and Loomis, B. A. 1995. *Interest Group Politics*. 4th edn. Washington, DC: CQ Press.

Cigler, A. J. and Loomis, B. A. 1998. *Interest Group Politics*. 5th edn. Washington, DC: CQ Press.

Cigler, A. J. and Loomis, B. A. 2002. *Interest Group Politics*. 6th edn. Washington, DC: CQ Press.

Cigler, A. J. and Loomis, B. A. 2007. *Interest Group Politics*. 7th edn. Washington, DC: CQ Press.

Cook, C. E. 1998. *Lobbying for Higher Education: How Colleges and Universities Influence Federal Policy*. 1st edn. Nashville: Vanderbilt University Press.

Cooper, C. A., Nownes, A. J., and Roberts, S. 2005. "Perceptions of Power: Interest Groups in Local Politics." *State and Local Government Review* 37: 206–16.

Cooper, P. J. 2003. *Governing by Contract: Challenges and Opportunities for Public Managers*. Washington, DC: CQ Press.

Cronin, T. E. 1984. *Direct Democracy: The Politics of Initiative, Referendum, and Recall*. Cambridge, MA: Harvard University Press.

Curry, W. S. 2009. *Contracting for Services in State and Local Government Agencies*. Boca Raton, FL: CRC Press.

Dahl, R. A. 1961. *Who Governs? Democracy and Power in an American City*. New Haven, CT: Yale University Press.

De Soto, W. 1995. "Cities in State Politics: Views of Mayors and Managers," *State and Local Government Review* 27: 188–94.

DeHoog, R. H. 1984. *Contracting out for Human Services: Economic, Political, and Organizational Perspectives*. Albany, NY: State University of New York Press.

DeLeon, R. E. 1992. *Left Coast City: Progressive Politics in San Francisco, 1975–1991*. Lawrence, KS: University Press of Kansas.

Dilger, R. J. 1992. *Neighborhood Politics: Residential Community Associations in American Governance*. New York: New York University Press.

Djupe, P. A., Olson, L. R., and Gilbert, C. P. 2005. "Sources of Clergy Support for Denominational Lobbying in Washington." *Review of Religious Research* 47: 86–99.

Elkin, S. L. 1987. *City and Regime in the American Republic*. Chicago: The University of Chicago Press.

Elkins, D. R. 1995. "The Structure and Context of the Urban Growth Coalition: The View from the Chamber of Commerce." *Policy Studies Journal* 23: 583–600.

Feiock, R. C. 2004. "Politics, Institutions and Local Land-use Regulation." *Urban Studies* 41: 363–75.

Ferman, B. 1996. *Challenging the Growth Machine: Neighborhood Politics in Chicago and Pittsburgh*. Lawrence, KS: University Press of Kansas.

Fleischmann, A. and Pierannunzi, C. A. 1990. "Citizens, Development Interests, and Local Land-use Regulation." *Journal of Politics* 52: 838–53.

Fleischmann, A. and Stein, L. 1998. "Campaign Contributions in Local Elections. *Political Research Quarterly* 51: 673–89.

Frohlich, N. and Oppenheimer, J. A. 1970. "I Get By with a Little Help from my Friends." *World Politics* 23: 104–20.

Gais, T. 1996. *Improper Influence: Campaign Finance Law, Political Interest Groups, and the Problem of Equality*. Ann Arbor, MI: University of Michigan Press.

Gerber, E. R. 1998. *Interest Group Influence in the California Initiative Process*. San Francisco: Public Policy Institute of California.

Gerber, E. R. 1999. *The Populist Paradox: Interest Group Influence and the Promise of Direct Legislation*. Princeton, NJ: Princeton University Press.

Godwin, K. and Mitchell, R. C. 1982. "Rational Models, Collective Goods and Nonelectoral Political Behavior." *Western Political Quarterly* 35: 161–81.

Gray, V. and Lowery, D. 1993. "The Diversity of State Interest Group Systems." *Political Research Quarterly* 46: 81–97.

Gray, V. and Lowery, D. 1995. "The Demography of Interest Organization Communities: Institutions, Associations, and Membership Groups." *American Politics Quarterly* 23: 3–32.

Gray, V. and Lowery, D. 1996a. *The Population Ecology of Interest Representation: Lobbying Communities in the American States*. Ann Arbor, MI: The University of Michigan Press.

Gray, V. and Lowery, D. 1996b. "Environmental Limits on the Diversity of State Interest Organization Systems: A Population Ecology Interpretation." *Political Research Quarterly* 49: 103–18.

Gray, V. and Lowery, D. 1996c. "A Niche Theory of Interest Representation." *Journal of Politics* 58: 91–111.

Gray, V. and Lowery, D. 1998a. "The Density of State Interest-Communities: Do Regional Variables Matter? *Publius–the Journal of Federalism* 28: 61–79.

Gray, V. and Lowery, D. 1998b. "To Lobby Alone or in a Flock: Foraging Behavior among Organized Interests." *American Politics Quarterly* 26: 5–34.

Gray, V. and Lowery, D. 2001a. "The Expression of Density Dependence in State Communities of Organized Interests." *American Politics Research* 29: 374–91.

Gray, V. and Lowery, D. 2001b. "The Institutionalization of State Communities of Organized Interests." *Political Research Quarterly* 54: 265–84.

Gray, V. and Lowery, D. 2002. "State Interest Group Research and the Mixed Legacy of Belle Zeller." *State Politics and Policy Quarterly* 2: 388–410.

Green, B. M. and Schreuder, Y. 1991. "Growth, Zoning, and Neighborhood Organizations: Land Use Conflict in Wilmington, Delaware." *Journal of Urban Affairs* 13: 97–110.

Haider, D. H. 1974. *When Governments Come to Washington: Governors, Mayors, and Intergovernmental Lobbying*. New York: Free Press.

Hall, R. L. and Wayman, F. W. 1990. "Buying Time: Moneyed Interests and the Mobilization of Bias in Congressional Committees." *American Political Science Review* 84: 797–820.

Hansen, J. M. 1985. "The Political Economy of Group Membership." *American Political Science Review* 79: 79–96.

Hansen, J. M. 1991. *Gaining Access: Congress and the Farm Lobby, 1919–1981.* Chicago: The University of Chicago Press.

Hardin, R. 1982. *Collective Action.* Baltimore: The Johns Hopkins University Press.

Hays, R. A. 1991. "Intergovernmental Lobbying: Toward an Understanding of Issue Priorities." *Western Political Quarterly* 44: 1081–98.

Hays, R. A. and Kogl, A. M. 2007. "Neighborhood Attachment, Social Capital Building, and Political Participation: A Case Study of Low- and Moderate-income Residents of Waterloo, Iowa." *Journal of Urban Affairs* 29: 181–205.

Heinz, J. P., Laumann, E. O., Nelson, R. L., and Salisbury, R. H. 1993. *The Hollow Core: Private Interests in National Policy Making.* Cambridge, MA: Harvard University Press.

Hogan, S. and Simpson, D. 2001. "Campaign Contributions and Mayoral/Aldermanic Relationships: Building on Krebs and Pelissero." *Urban Affairs Review* 37: 85–95.

Hrebenar, R. J. and Thomas, C. S. 1987. *Interest Group Politics in the American West.* Salt Lake City, UT: University of Utah Press.

Hrebenar, R. J. and Thomas, C. S. 1992. *Interest Group Politics in the Southern States.* Tuscaloosa, AL: University of Alabama Press.

Hrebenar, R. J. and Thomas, C. S. 1993a. *Interest Group Politics in the Northeastern States.* University Park, PA: Pennsylvania State University Press.

Hrebenar, R. J. and Thomas, C. S. 1993b. *Interest Group Politics in the Midwestern States.* 1st edn. Ames, IA: Iowa State University Press.

Hunter, F. 1953. *Community Power Structure: A Study of Decision Makers.* Chapel Hill, NC: University of North Carolina Press.

Hutcheson, J. D. and Prather, J. E. 1988. "Community Mobilization and Participation in the Zoning Process." *Urban Affairs Review* 23: 346–68.

Imbroscio, D. L. 1997. *Reconstructing City Politics: Alternative Economic Development and Urban Regimes.* Thousand Oaks, CA: Sage Publications.

Imbroscio, D. L. 1998. "Reformulating Urban Regime Theory: The Division of Labor between State And Market Reconsidered." *Journal of Urban Affairs* 20: 233–48.

Jeffres, L. W., Atkin, D., and Neuendorf, K. A. 2002. "A Model Linking Community Activity and Communication with Political Attitudes and Involvement in Neighborhoods." *Political Communicatio,* 19: 387–421.

Johnson, B. L. 2001. "Micropolitical Dynamics of Education Interests: A View from Within." *Educational Policy* 15: 115–34.

Jordan, A. G. and Maloney, W. A. 1997. *The Protest Business: Mobilizing Campaign Groups.* New York: Manchester University Press.

Kersh, R. 2002. "Corporate Lobbyists as Political Actors: A View from the Field." In A. J. Cigler, and B. L. Loomis (eds), *Interest Group Politics.* 6th edn. Washington, DC: CQ Press, 225–48.

Kersh, R. 2007. "The Well-informed Lobbyist: Information and Interest-group Lobbying." In A. J. Cigler and B. L. Loomis (eds), *Interest Group Politics.* 7th edn. Washington, DC: CQ Press, 389–411.

King, James D. and Helenan S. Robin. 1994. "Party Committees, Nonconnected PACs, and Affiliated PACs in State Elections: Same Species or Different Political Animals?" *Southeastern Political Review* 22: 559–72.

King, James D. and Helenan S. Robin. 1995. "Political Action Committees in State Elections." *American Review of Politics* 16: 61–77.

Kirst-Ashman, K. K. 2008. *Human Behavior, Communities, Organizations, and Groups in the Macro Social Environment.* 2nd edn. Belmont, CA: Thomson/Brooks/Cole.

Knoke, D. 1990. *Organizing for Collective Action: The Political Economies of Associations.* New York: A. de Gruyter.

Kollman, K. 1998. *Outside Lobbying: Public Opinion and Interest Group Strategies.* Princeton, NJ: Princeton University Press.

Kraft, M. E. and Clary, B. B. 1991. "Citizen Participation and the NIMBY Syndrome: Public Response to Radioactive Waste Disposal." *Western Political Quarterly* 44: 299–328.

Krebs, T. B. 2005a. "Urban Interests and Campaign Contributions: Evidence from Los Angeles." *Journal of Urban Affairs* 27: 165–75.

Krebs, T. B. 2005b. "Money and Machine Politics: An Analysis of Corporate and Labor Contributions in Chicago City Council Elections." *Urban Affairs Review* 41: 47–64.

Krebs, T. B. and Pelissero, J. P. 2001. "Fund-raising Coalitions in Mayoral Campaigns." *Urban Affairs Review* 37: 67–84.

Lavery, K. 1999. *Smart Contracting for Local Government Services: Processes and Experience.* Westport, CT: Praeger.

LeRoux, K. and Harney, D. F. 2007. *Service Contracting: A Local Government Guide.* 2nd edn. Washington, DC: ICMA Press.

Lichbach, M. I. 1995. *The Rebel's Dilemma.* Ann Arbor, MI: University of Michigan Press.

Liebman, R. C., Wuthnow, R., and Guth, J. L. 1983. *The New Christian Right: Mobilization and Legitimation.* Hawthorne, NY: Aldine Pub. Co.

Logan, J. R. and Molotch, H. L. 1987. *Urban Fortunes: The Political Economy of Place.* Berkeley, CA: University of California Press.

Logan, J. R. and Rabrenovic, G. 1990. "Neighborhood Associations: Their Issues, their Allies, and their Opponents." *Urban Affairs Review* 26: 68–94.

Lowery, D. and Brasher, H. 2004. *Organized Interests and American Government.* New York: McGraw-Hill.

Lowery, D. and Gray, V. 1993. "The Density of State Interest Group Systems." *Journal of Politics* 55: 191–206.

Lowery, D. and Gray, V. 1994. "The Nationalization of State Interest Group System Density and Diversity." *Social Science Quarterly* 75: 368–77.

Lowery, D. and Gray, V. 1995. "The Population Ecology of Gucci Gulch, or the Natural Regulation of Interest Group Numbers in the American States." *American Journal of Political Science* 39: 1–29.

Lowery, D. and Gray, V. 1998. "The Dominance of Institutions in Interest Representation: A Test of Seven Explanations." *American Journal of Political Science* 42: 231–55.

Lowry, R. C. 1997. "The Private Production of Public Goods: Organizational Maintenance, Managers' Objectives, and Collective Goals." *American Political Science Review* 91: 308–23.

Lowry, R. C. 1998. "Religion and the Demand for Membership in Environmental Citizen Groups." *Public Choice* 94: 223–40.

Lowry, R. C. 2005. "Explaining the Variation in Organized Civil Society across States and Time." *Journal of Politics* 67: 574–94.

Lubell, M., Vedlitz, A., Zahran, S., and Alston, L. T. 2006. "Collective Action, Environmental Activism, and Air Quality Policy." *Political Research Quarterly* 59: 149–60.

Lubell, M., Zahran, S., and Vedlitz, A. 2007. "Collective Action and Citizen Responses to Global Warming." *Political Behavior* 29: 391–413.

McAvoy, G. E. 1999. *Controlling Technocracy: Citizen Rationality and the Nimby Syndrome.* Washington, DC: Georgetown University Press.

McFarland, A. S. 1976. *Public Interest Lobbies: Decision-making on Energy.* Washington, DC: American Enterprise Institute for Public Policy Research.

McGann, J. G. 2007. *Think Tanks and Policy Advice in the US: Academics, Advisors and Advocates.* New York, NY: Routledge.

McGovern, S. J. 2009. "Mobilization on the Waterfront: The Ideological/Cultural Roots of Potential Regime Change in Philadelphia." *Urban Affairs Review* 44: 663–94.

Magleby, D. B. 1984. *Direct Legislation: Voting on Ballot Propositions in the United States.* Baltimore, MD: Johns Hopkins University Press.

Malbin, M. J. and Gais, T. 1998. *The Day after Reform: Sobering Campaign Finance Lessons from the American States.* 1st edn. Washington, DC: Rockefeller Institute Press.

Marbach, J. R. and Leckrone, J. W. 2002. "Intergovernmental Lobbying for the Passage of TEA-21." *Publius—the Journal of Federalism* 32: 45–64.

Marwell, G. and Ames, R. E. 1979. "Experiments on the Provision of Public Goods. I. Resources, Interest, Group Size, and the Free-rider Problem." *American Journal of Sociology* 84: 1335–60.

Marwell, G. and Ames, R. E. 1980. "Experiments on the Provision of Public Goods. II. Provision Points, Stakes, Experience, and the Free-rider Problem." *American Journal of Sociology* 85: 926–37.

Matejczyk, A. P. 2001. "Why not NIMBY? Reputation, Neighbourhood Organisations and Zoning Boards in a US Midwestern City." *Urban Studies* 38: 507–18.

Medina Sierra, L. F. 2007. *A Unified Theory of Collective Action and Social Change.* Ann Arbor, MI: University of Michigan Press.

Milbrath, L. W. 1963. *The Washington Lobbyists.* Chicago: Rand McNally.

Miller, J. M. and Krosnick, J. A. 2004. "Threat as a Motivator of Political Activism: A Field Experiment." *Political Psychology* 25: 507–23.

Moe, T. M. 1980. *The Organization of Interests: Incentives and the Internal Dynamics of Political Interest Groups.* Chicago: The University of Chicago Press.

Morehouse, S. M. 1981. *State Politics, Parties, and Policy.* New York: Holt, Rinehart|Winston and Holt, Rinehart|Winston.

Mossberger, K. and Stoker, G. 2001. "The Evolution of Urban Regime Theory: The Challenge of Conceptualization." *Urban Affairs Review* 36: 810–35.

Mullin, M. 2009. *Governing the Tap: Special District Governance and the New Local Politics of Water.* Cambridge, MA: MIT Press.

Munton, D. 1996. *Siting by Choice: Waste Facilities, NIMBY, and Volunteer Communities.* Washington, DC: Georgetown University Press.

Nachmias, C. and Palen, J. J. 1982. "Membership in Voluntary Neighborhood Associations and Urban Revitalization." *Policy Sciences* 14: 179–93.

Nownes, A. J. 2004. "The Population Ecology of Interest Group Formation: Mobilizing for Gay and Lesbian Rights in the United States, 1950–98." *British Journal of Political Science* 34: 49–67.

Nownes, A. J. 2006. *Total Lobbying: What Lobbyists Want (and How They Try to Get It).* New York: Cambridge University Press.

Nownes, A. J. and DeAlejandro, K. W. 2009. "Lobbying in the New Millennium: Evidence of Continuity and Change in Three States." *State Politics & Policy Quarterly* 9: 429–55.

Nownes, A. J. and Freeman, P. 1998a. "Interest Group Activity in the States." *Journal of Politics* 60: 86–112.

Nownes, A. J. and Freeman, P. K. 1998b. "Female Lobbyists: Women in the World of 'Good Ol' Boys." *Journal of Politics* 60: 1181–201.

Nownes, A. J. and Lipinski, D. 2005. "The Population Ecology of Interest Group Death: Gay and Lesbian Rights Interest Groups in the United States, 1945–98." *British Journal of Political Science* 35: 303–19.

O'Brien, D. J. 1975. *Neighborhood Organization and Interest-Group Processes.* Princeton, NJ: Princeton University Press.

O'Connor, T. H. 1993. *Building a New Boston: Politics and Urban Renewal, 1950–1970.* Boston: Northeastern University Press.

Ohmer, M. L. 2007. "Citizen Participation in Neighborhood Organizations and its Relationship to Volunteers' Self- and Collective Efficacy and Sense of Community." *Social Work Research* 31: 109–20.

O'Looney, J. 1998. *Outsourcing State and Local Government Services: Decision-making Strategies and Management Methods.* Westport, CT: Quorum.

Olsen, M., Perlstadt, H., Fonseca, V., and Hogan, J. 1989. "Participation in Neighborhood Associations." *Sociological Focus* 22: 1–17.

Olson, M. 1965. *The Logic of Collective Action: Public Goods and the Theory of Groups.* Cambridge, MA: Harvard University Press.

Oropesa, S. R. 1995. "The Ironies of Human Resource Mobilization by Neighborhood Associations." *Nonprofit and Voluntary Sector Quarterly* 24: 235–52.

Ostrom, E. 1990. *Governing the Commons: The Evolution of Institutions for Collective Action.* New York: Cambridge University Press.

Perkins, D. D., Florin, P., Rich, R. C., Wandersman, A., and Chavis, D. M. 1990. "Participation and the Social and Physical Environment of Residential Blocks: Crime and Community Context." *American Journal of Community Psychology* 18: 83–115.

Peterson, N. A. and Reid, R. J. 2003. "Paths to Psychological Empowerment in an Urban Community: Sense of Community and Citizen Participation in Substance Abuse Prevention Activities." *Journal of Community Psychology* 31: 25–38.

Prestby, J. E., Wandersman, A., Florin, P., Rich, R., and Chavis, D. 1990. "Benefits, Costs, Incentive Management and Participation in Voluntary Organizations: A Means to Understanding and Promoting Empowerment." *American Journal of Community Psychology* 18: 117–49.

Ramsden, Graham P. 2002. "State Legislative Campaign Finance Research: A Review Essay." *State Politics and Policy Quarterly* 2: 176–98.

Regalado, J. A. 1991. "Organized Labor and Los Angeles City Politics: An Assessment in the Bradley Years, 1973–1989." *Urban Affairs Review* 27: 87–108.

Ricci, D. M. 1993. *The Transformation of American Politics: The New Washington and the Rise of Think Tanks.* New Haven, CT: Yale University Press.

Rich, A. 2004. *Think Tanks, Public Policy, and the Politics of Expertise.* New York: Cambridge University Press.

Rich, R. C. 1988. "A Cooperative Approach to the Logic of Collective Action: Voluntary Organizations and the Prisoners' Dilemma." *Journal of Voluntary Action Research* 17: 5–18.

Rosenthal, A. 2001. *The Third House: Lobbyists and Lobbying in the States.* 2nd edn Washington, DC: CQ Press.

Rozell, M. J., Wilcox, C., and Madland, D. 2006. *Interest Groups in American Campaigns.* 2nd edn. Washington, DC: CQ Press.

Ryan, M. H., Swanson, C. L., and Buchholz, R. A. 1987. *Corporate Strategy, Public Policy, and the Fortune 500: How America's Major Corporations Influence Government*. New York: Blackwell.

Sabato, L. 1985. *PAC Power: Inside the World of Political Action Committees*. New York: Norton.

Salisbury, R. H. 1969. "An Exchange Theory of Interest Groups." *Midwest Journal of Political Science* 13: 1–32.

Salisbury, R. H. 1984. "Interest Representation: The Dominance of Institutions." *American Political Science Review* 78: 64–76.

Sandler, T. 1992. *Collective Action: Theory and Applications*. Ann Arbor, MI: University of Michigan Press.

Schlozman, K. L. and Tierney, J. T. 1983. "More of the Same: Washington Pressure Group Activity in a Decade of Change." *The Journal of Politics* 45 (2): 351–77.

Schlozman, K. L. and Tierney, J. T. 1986. *Organized Interests and American Democracy*. New York: Harper & Row.

Schumaker, P. 1991. *Critical Pluralism, Democratic Performance, and Community Power*. Lawrence, KS: University Press of Kansas.

Shaiko, R. G. 1999. *Voices and Echoes for the Environment: Public Interest Representation in the 1990s and Beyond*. New York: Columbia University Press.

Sharp, E. B. 1999. *Culture Wars and Local Politics*. Lawrence, KS: University Press of Kansas.

Sites, W. 1997. "The Limits of Urban Regime Theory: New York City under Koch, Dinkins, and Giuliani." *Urban Affairs Review* 32: 536–57.

Skocpol, T. 2003. *Diminished Democracy: From Membership to Management in American Civic Life*. Norman, OK: University of Oklahoma Press.

Smith, R. D. and Harris, F. C. 2005. *Black Churches and Local Politics: Clergy Influence, Organizational Partnerships, and Civic Empowerment*. Lanham, MD: Rowman and Littlefield Publishers.

Stone, C. N. 1989. *Regime Politics: Governing Atlanta, 1946–1988*. Lawrence, KS: University Press of Kansas.

Stone, C. N. 1993. "Urban Regimes and the Capacity to Govern: A Political Economy Approach." *Journal of Urban Affairs* 15: 1–28.

Stone, D. and Denham, A. 2004. *Think Tank Traditions: Policy Research and the Politics of Ideas*. New York: Manchester University Press.

Swindell, D. 2000. "Issue Representation in Neighborhood Organizations: Questing for Democracy at the Grassroots." *Journal of Urban Affairs* 22: 123–37.

Thomas, C. S. 1998. "Interest Group Regulation across the United States: Rationale, Development and Consequences." *Parliamentary Affairs* 51: 500–15.

Thomas, C. S. and Hrebenar, R. J. 1996. "Interest Groups in the States." In V. Gray, and H. Jacob (eds), *Politics in the American States: A Comparative Analysis*. 6th edn. Washington, DC: CQ Press, 125–58.

Thomas, C. S. and Hrebenar, R. J. 1999. "Interest Groups in the States." In V. Gray, R. Hanson, and H. Jacob (eds), *Politics in the American States: A Comparative Analysis*. 7th edn. Washington, DC: CQ Press, 113–43.

Thomas, C. S. and Hrebenar, R. J. 2004. "Interest Groups in the States." In V. Gray and R. Hanson (eds), *Politics in the American States: A Comparative Analysis*. 8th edn. Washington, DC: CQ Press, 100–28.

Thomas, J. C. 1986. *Between Citizen and City: Neighborhood Organizations and Urban Politics in Cincinnati*. Lawrence, KS: University Press of Kansas.

Thompson, J. A. and Cassie, W. 1992. "Party and PAC Contributions to North Carolina Legislative Candidates." *Legislative Studies Quarterly* 17: 409–16.

Thompson, J. A., Cassie, W., and Jewell, M. E. 1994. "A Sacred Cow or just a Lot of Bull: Party and PAC Money in State Legislative Elections." *Political Research Quarterly* 47: 223–37.

Tichenor, D. J. and Harris, R. A. 2005. "The Development of Interest Group Politics in America: Beyond the Conceits of Modern Times." *Annual Review of Political Science* 8: 251–70.

Toma, E. F., Berhane, I., and Curl, C. 2006. "Political Action Committees at the State Level: Contributions to Education." *Public Choice* 126: 465–84.

Truman, D. B. 1951. *The Governmental Process: Political Interests and Public Opinion.* 1st edn. New York: Knopf.

Vogel, D. 1978. *Lobbying the Corporation: Citizen Challenges to Business Authority.* New York: Basic Books.

Walker, J. L. 1983. "The Origins and Maintenance of Interest Groups in America." *American Political Science Review* 77: 390–406.

Walker, J. L. 1991. *Mobilizing Interest Groups in America: Patrons, Professions, and Social Movements.* Ann Arbor, MI: University of Michigan Press.

Warren, M. R. 2001. *Dry Bones Rattling: Community Building to Revitalize American Democracy.* Princeton, NJ: Princeton University Press.

Wawro, G. 2001. "A Panel Probit Analysis of Campaign Contributions and Roll-call Votes." *American Journal of Political Science* 45: 563–79.

Wiggins, C. W., Hamm, K. E., and Bell, C. G. 1992. "Interest-Group and Party Influence Agents in the Legislative Process: A Comparative State Analysis." *Journal of Politics* 54: 82–100.

Wilson, G. K. 1981. *Interest Groups in the United States.* New York: Clarendon Press.

Wood, R. L. 2002. *Faith in Action: Religion, Race, and Democratic Organizing in America.* Chicago: The University of Chicago Press.

Wright, J. R. 1985. "PACs, Contributions, and Roll Calls: An Organizational Perspective." *American Political Science Review* 79: 400–14.

Yoho, James. "Interest Groups in America, 1498–1861." Dissertation at the University of Virginia. Ann Arbor, Michigan: UMI, 1999.

Zimmerman, M. A. and Rappaport, J. 1988. "Citizen Participation, Perceived Control, and Psychological Empowerment." *American Journal of Community Psychology* 16: 725–50.

CHAPTER 8

LOCAL AND STATE POLITICAL PARTIES

JOEL W. PADDOCK

IN the mid-twentieth century, scholars described the two major political parties in the United States as diffuse collections of state and local organizations that came together every four years to select a presidential nominee. These state and local parties were portrayed in the literature as lacking ideological cohesion, and primarily concerned with fashioning the pragmatic compromises necessary to win the material spoils of electoral victory within their particular state or locality. Eldersveld (1964) used the term "stratarchy" to describe the generally autonomous nature of the component parts of American political parties. Key (1952) described party structure in the United States as more confederative than federal in nature, and Schattschneider (1942: 131–2) wrote that "decentralization constitutes the most important single fact concerning the American parties." "He who understands this fact, and knows nothing else," wrote Schattschneider, "knows more about American parties than he who knows everything except this fact." (Schattschneider, 1942: 131–2).

Scholars such as Schattschneider, however, were frustrated by the implications of such a party structure for the democratic process in the United States. Decentralized parties lacking in ideological cohesion, they thought, undermined electoral accountability. The anti-majoritarian components of the American constitutional system combined with a decentralized party system, these scholars argued, contributed to an environment in which the interests of average citizens were not being adequately represented in the political system. A 1950 Committee on Political Parties of the American Political Science Association (1950: v) was critical of the "two loose associations of state and local organizations, with very little national machinery and very little national cohesion." They contended that the Democrats and Republicans were not well equipped to formulate broad national platforms and organize their party- in- government to implement broad national policies responsive to an electoral majority. "This," the committee concluded, "is a very serious matter, for it affects the very heartbeat of American democracy" (Committee on Political Parties, 1950: v).

The party system described by Schattschneider and the American Political Science Association (APSA) committee at mid-century, however, was undergoing fundamental changes. Traditional patronage-based party organizations, which had controlled nominations and had been major players in voter mobilization activities in many states since the nineteenth century, were in decline. After the eventual collapse of traditional party organizations, it was initially thought that state and local parties had lost their relevance in a candidate-centered era of electoral politics. Scholars in the 1960s and 1970s talked about the decline, and even the demise, of party organizations in the United States. However, by the 1980s and 1990s scholars spoke of party "adaptation" and "resurgence," and the rise of the "service-vendor party," which provided money and campaign-related services to candidates in a more candidate-centered and capital-intensive electoral environment. These service vendor parties were much more dependent on their national organizations for financial resources than the more autonomous traditional party organizations had been. In this more integrated party system state and local party organizations have become what appear to be rather small cogs in a "party network" that includes the national party committees, congressional campaign committees, allied interest groups, state legislative campaign committees, political consultants, and candidate-centered campaign organizations. The "two loose associations of state and local organizations," that the APSA committee had described at mid-century, have been replaced by more ideologically distinct and organizationally integrated parties. Some scholars now talk about at least the potential for responsible party government in the United States (Pomper, 2003).

This chapter analyzes the current state of political science literature on state and local parties. The chapter is organized around three broad themes in the literature. The first theme relates to the adaptation of state and local parties to the more candidate-centered politics of the telecommunications age. In an apparently more integrated party system, are state and local party organizations still relevant in mobilizing and integrating mass interests at the grassroots level? Or have they become merely conduits of money and services from their national organizations and allied groups in a complicated process of funneling campaign resources to the most competitive national races within the confines of existing federal and state campaign-finance laws? Related to this issue is the very definition of a state and local party organization. Are state and local parties simply the legally defined state, county, and precinct committees that have been regulated by state law since the Progressive era? Or should a modern conceptualization of state and local parties include other party-like actors (e.g. state legislative campaign committees, allied groups at the state and local levels, candidate organizations, etc.)? And if parties are conceptualized as a broader network, what is the relationship between the various actors within that network? What is the relationship, for example, between state and local parties and interest groups? Do the specific policy goals of interest groups interfere with the broader coalitional goals of the parties?

The second theme relates to the issue of ideological polarization in the party system. A number of scholars have noted a fundamental change in the nature of American party activism over the past several decades. A growing number of state and local party activists are motivated less by the material spoils of victory than the purposive incentives of promoting a cause or an ideology. This has contributed to growing ideological differences, some say ideological polarization, between the Democratic and Republican Parties. What is not clear is how uniform this polarization has been across the states. Are some state parties more ideologically polarized than others? What factors might account for interstate differences in ideological polarization? Does the polarization of party elites (i.e. organizational activists and elected officials) contribute to mass polarization? Or are party elites responding to a more ideologically polarized electorate in their states? If polarization has indeed occurred, what are the policy and political implications of these growing interparty ideological differences? Does polarization contribute to a more responsive party system, as the advocates of the responsible party model school contended? Or does the polarization of party elites suppress voter turnout among a more moderate electorate who see the parties as out of touch with their policy concerns?

Finally, the third theme relates to the issue of regionalism in American politics. Despite the apparent organizational integration and nationalization of American parties, the United States is still a culturally, economically, and politically diverse nation. State and local parties are competing in political environments that differ significantly by region. The California Democratic Party, for example, is competing in a political environment which is very different to the one experienced by the Mississippi Democratic Party. Likewise, the Nassau County, New York (Long Island) Republican Party has significantly different coalitional and organizational concerns than the Jim Hogg County, Texas (rural south Texas) Republican Party. In a more organizationally integrated party system, does regionalism still matter? Does the sharing of campaign-related resources among national, state, and local organizations necessarily contribute to an environment in which those organizations will be more likely to agree on national policies and priorities? Do the coalitional bases of the state parties significantly differ? Are state-level elections operating on a different set of dynamics than national-level elections? In short, do state and local parties still constitute what Schattschneider called a decentralized party system, or are they part of more nationalized and ideologically coherent party system capable of delivering responsible party government?

These three themes are important not only to our understanding of the role of state and local parties in the political process, but also to our understanding of the broader democratic process in the United States. If indeed state and local parties have been integrated into a more nationalized and ideologically coherent party system, one might argue that at least a form of responsible party government is possible in the United States. This would challenge the conventional wisdom about the decentralized nature of American parties, as well as the anti-majoritarian nature of the Madisonian model of the US Constitution. However, if this intra-party integration is nothing more than an effort to legally funnel money from the most economically privileged segments of society to candidates for public office, then the democratizing elements of party nationalization would be called into serious question.

ORGANIZATIONAL ADAPTATION
AND INTEGRATION

If we accept Epstein's (1967: 9) definition of a political party as "any group, however loosely organized, seeking to elect government officeholders under a given label," state and local party organizations in the United States can come in a wide variety of forms. A considerable amount of scholarship on state and local party adaptation focuses on the formal party organizations (i.e. the state, county, town, and precinct committees). And even among these formal party structures, there is considerable variation in the nature and strength of the various organizations (Cotter et al., 1989). However, other scholars contend that we need to more broadly conceptualize parties to include networks of party committees, allied interest groups, campaign contributors, political consultants, and media outlets (Schlesinger, 1984; Schwartz, 1990; Aldrich, 1995; Koger et al., 2009). One of the central challenges for scholars of state and local party organizations is to more precisely define what constitutes a party organization.

From the 1830s to the 1950s, a common form of party organization, at least in some states and localities, was what Mayhew (1986) calls the "traditional party organization." Such organizations, had "substantial autonomy" from other organizations, controlled the nomination of candidates for a variety of offices, relied on material incentives (i.e. patronage) to motivate people to work for the party, and were most common in the predominantly individualistic subcultures of the middle Atlantic region and the industrial Midwest (Mayhew 1986: 19–20). However, a combination of anti-party reforms passed during the Progressive era, the emergence of television and candidate-centered campaigns, changes in both the class structure and the nature of political party activism, and the nationalization of American politics after the New Deal and World War II contributed to the demise of traditional party organizations. By the 1960s and after, state and local parties neither controlled the nominating process, nor the process of mobilizing voters at the grassroots. In this more candidate-centered campaign environment, Aldrich (1995: 282) argues, "the party can still provide useful services, but the politician's choice to accept those services is, more regularly than before, voluntary."

Much of the literature on party adaptation to politics in the telecommunications age focuses on the geographical sub-units of parties traditionally regulated by state law— the state, county, and precinct-level committees. Since the Progressive era, states have treated parties like public utilities. In exchange for granting the two major parties a virtual duopoly to ballot access, the states have heavily regulated the parties in such areas as creating direct primary elections, regulating the size and methods of selection for state and local party committees, and prohibiting pre-primary endorsements (Epstein, 1986). These state and local committees (usually county and precinct, but in some states town or state legislative district) are the focus of a considerable amount of research revolving around the broad theme of "party adaptation" and the rise of "service-vendor party" (Cotter et al., 1989; Appleton and Ward, 1997; Aldrich, 2000). This literature emphasizes

that the collapse of traditional party organizations and rise of candidate-centered campaigns did not lead to the total collapse of state and local party organizations. To the
contrary, many state parties have established permanent headquarters with full-time
staff, have substantial budgets, and are involved in such activities as polling, developing
campaign issues, opposition research, voter registration, phone banks, direct mail, and
conducting seminars on campaign techniques. There tends to be greater variation in
the strength of county-level organizations. In some areas they have permanent headquarters and are quite active in providing campaign resources; in other areas they are
weak or even non-existent (Cotter et al., 1989; Frendreis et al., 1996). And the strength
of these organizations can ebb and flow due to a variety of factors, including changes in
party leadership, the relative strength of allied groups, and even changes in federal campaign finance laws (Blumberg et al., 1999, 2003, 2007). However, the general theme of
this literature is that, despite the collapse of traditional party organizations and the rise
of candidate-centered politics, state and local parties have reinvented themselves and
become relevant political actors in a candidate-centered and capital-intensive electoral
process.

The adaptation, and some say revitalization, of state and local parties in the 1980s
and 1990s was in large part related to the strengthening of national party organizations
(Epstein, 1982; Wekkin, 1984; Appleton and Ward, 1997). The Republican National
Committee led the way in this process. Utilizing electronic databases, direct mail fundraising, and loopholes in federal campaign finance laws that allowed the parties to
raise unlimited campaign contributions for "party-building activities," the national
Republican Party raised large sums of money and invested that money in developing a
sophisticated national party bureaucracy. This bureaucracy played a big role in developing a national communications strategy, recruiting and training candidates for state
and national offices, and providing those candidates with financial assistance and technical services (Price, 1984: 40–1). As part of this process, the national Republican Party
invested heavily in their state and local organizations. The Democrats were slower to
develop a national fundraising capacity, but by the 1980s both parties had developed a
system in which the national parties had become much bigger players than they had
been in the traditionally decentralized party structure. So while some state and local
parties have acquired important resources to establish permanent headquarters and
to provide campaign-related services to their candidates, they have also become more
like sub-units of the national party organization rather than the autonomous actors
they tended to be in a an earlier era. "To a much greater extent than earlier," write
Huckshorn et al. (1986: 990), "the state parties are constituent units of a national party,
influenced by national party performance norms, and capable of coordinated effort
to influence the party's electoral standing both in targeted areas of the country and at
specific office levels."

Because the process of party integration involves the relationship between the
national parties, 50 separate Democratic and Republican state organizations, and literally thousands of local party organizations, we do not have a comprehensive understanding of how this process took place. One of the best historical overviews of the

process of party adaptation and integration is Appleton and Ward's (1997) compilation of 50 separate state party profiles. Appleton and Ward commissioned scholars from each of the 50 states to examine the theme of party adaptation at the state level. Many of these scholars used state party archives, a still under-utilized data source for understanding the process of state party adaptation and integration. A common theme in these individual state studies was that the rise of the service-vendor party at the state level coincided with these organizations developing closer relationships with individual candidate organizations, political action committees, legislative campaign committees, and, perhaps most importantly, their national organizations. The enhanced capacity of the national party organizations to raise large sums of money (due, in part, to the emergence of electronic databases, direct mail, and loopholes in the federal campaign finance laws) allowed them to "transmit knowledge and resources down to the state level" (Appleton and Ward, 1997: xxi). "That many (state) parties have adapted in the same way," Appleton and Ward (1997: xxii) write, "that is, toward a service-vendor type of organization, is attributable to the fact that the most compelling environmental shock for a majority of (state) parties has been nationalization."

The state parties, however, that receive the greatest assistance from their national organizations are those with the most competitive elections for national office (i.e. presidential and congressional elections). In a complex process of maximizing party expenditures under federal campaign finance laws, the national parties would transfer soft money to their state organizations to run issue advertisements written and produced by the national party in the most competitive states and districts (Bibby, 1999: 73). If the national parties needed more hard money to be spent directly on national races, they would sometimes "trade" soft money to their state and local parties in exchange for hard money raised by the state parties in compliance with federal and state campaign finance laws. The state parties would often get a "commission" on this exchange (i.e. they would get a greater amount of soft money for party building activities than they were exchanging in hard money) (Bibby, 1999: 74; Dwyre and Kolodny, 2002). There has been some debate in the literature about whether this Rube Goldberg-type campaign finance process actually benefitted the state and local parties. A number of scholars argue that despite the fact that the national parties were financing campaigns for primarily federal candidates, state and local organizations in these states indirectly benefitted "from better-financed and better-staffed state parties and from the state parties' mobilization and campaign efforts carried out on behalf of all candidates" (Gierzynski 2002: 204). La Raja (2003: 147) found that "parties that spend additional increments of soft money (funneled to them by their national party) recruit and train candidates more regularly, provide services more frequently, and have larger budgets and staff size in the off season than lower spending parties."

In 2002 Congress passed the Bipartisan Campaign Reform Act (BCRA), which, among other things, banned unlimited soft money contributions to the national parties, and limited individual contributions to the national parties at $25,000 per year, and to state and local parties at $10,000 per year. It was initially thought that this legislation could fundamentally alter the relationship between local, state, and national party organizations. Because the national parties could no longer raise money in unlimited increments, the state and local parties would need to find alternative sources of money. If they were unsuccessful, their ability to adapt and even survive might be in question. If they were successful, they might become less dependent on their national organizations for money and campaign-related services. The BCRA had the potential to reverse the trend toward intra-party integration.

Although it is still too early to fully measure the impact of the BCRA on the finances of state and local parties, the current evidence suggests that these organizations have successfully adapted to the new legal environment. In the elections immediately after the passage of the BCRA, political spending on national elections became more concentrated at the national level as the national organizations paid for advertisements with hard money rather than funneling soft money through their state parties for such purposes (Appollonio and La Raja, 2006). However, there is little evidence that this has significantly affected the capacity of state and local organizations. While the Democrats were somewhat more vulnerable to the changes brought about by the BCRA (i.e. they had invested less than the Republicans in their state organizations prior to BCRA and they were generally more dependent on allied 527 groups to campaign on behalf of their candidates), most of the evidence suggests that the BCRA did not seriously weaken the party organizations and that a significant number of state organizations continue to be very adept at raising "a very high proportion" of their own funds to conduct "ground war" operations in state legislative and gubernatorial elections (Morehouse and Jewell, 2003: 165; Corrado, 2006). La Raja et al. (2007) contend that the impact of BCRA is largely contingent on the campaign finance regulations of a particular state, and whether or not that state has competitive national elections in a particular year. State parties with competitive federal races generally have had little trouble raising large amounts of hard money contributions to offset the loss of soft money. Both parties, but particularly the Republicans, have continued to transfer money (now hard money) to their state affiliates with the most competitive federal elections. The Democrats have relied more on the independent spending of various "527 organizations." It is less clear, however, how parties in states without competitive federal elections will fare in the long term after BCRA. Future research will need to track the transfer of money from national parties to their state and local affiliates, the ability of state and local organizations to raise hard money under both federal and state campaign finance laws, and the long-term health of state and local organizations in the aftermath of BCRA.

If we take a broader view of what constitutes a political party, party adaptation goes beyond merely the reinvigoration of formal state and local organizations. Aldrich (1995: 20) contends that the key elements of the new "parties-in- service" are "ambitious office seekers and holders" and "those who hold, or have access to, critical resources that office seekers need to realize their ambition." Defining those who control such resources poses conceptual challenges for scholars of state and local parties. Interest groups, political consultants, state legislative campaign committees, and individual contributors (to name a few) provide resources both for candidates and the statutorily-defined state, county, and precinct committees. Should networks of such actors be part of a formal definition of state and local parties? Do such actors actually constitute a formal network? Future research on party adaptation at the state and local levels should focus on the interaction not only between the formal national and state organizations (though this, too, should be a continued focus of research) but also the interaction between the various actors who provide these resources.

The conceptualization of parties as broader networks rather than simply formal organizations is nothing new. Schwartz's (1990) study of the Illinois Republican Party, for example, reveals a broader "party network" of not only state and local committees, but also candidates, elected officials, legislative campaign committees, financial contributors, political action committees, and interest groups. Other scholars have focused on the rise of state legislative campaign committees, often linked with party leaders in state legislatures, which provide resources such as money, survey research, candidate seminars, media production, and electronic databases to state legislative candidates in the most competitive districts (Gierzynski, 1992; Shea, 1995). State legislative campaign committees tend to be most common in states with professional, full-time legislatures, relatively weak state party organizations, and relatively high levels of electoral competition (Bibby and Holbrook, 1996). Still other scholars describe the emergence of "party-like" organizations associated with individual candidates, and the personal political apparatus of incumbents and leaders in state legislatures (Lunch, 1987; Monroe, 2001; Masket, 2002).

Our understanding of the interaction between the various actors in party networks, and even who constitutes the party network is limited. One of the under-researched areas involving state and local parties is their relationship with allied interest groups. Scholars have long noted a symbiotic relationship between party organizations and interest groups (Cigler, 1993; Rozell et al., 2006; Berry and Wilcox, 2007). Interest groups provide political parties with important resources in electoral campaigns, while parties mobilize support for policies favored by groups and help groups develop access to elected officials. Yet, as Berry and Wilcox (2007: 59) note, distinct groups of scholars study parties and interest groups, and the two "subfields share little in terms of their theoretical perspectives." There is considerable evidence that interest groups have expanded their activities at the state and local levels in recent decades and that many of these groups have attempted to develop a formal presence in the party organizations (Thomas and Hrebenar, 1996; Rozell et al., 2006). However, we know little about how these organizations interact with each other. For example, do the narrow goals of an allied interest group interfere with a state party's goal to build a more broad-based electoral coalition? What is the extent of overlap between interest group activists and party activists? What role do policy entrepreneurs play in linking interest groups with state and national party organizations? Is the creation of a party network a bottom-up process driven by political entrepreneurs at the grassroots, or a top-down process driven by the national parties and their allied groups?

A promising direction for future research on party adaptation involves going beyond looking at state and local parties as distinct entities, and focusing on where they fit in a broader informal party network. What are the links, if any, between organizational activists in state and local parties and various 527 groups (Skinner, 2005)? How might theoretical approaches such as social network theory help us to identify patterns of informal links between political contributors, interest groups, liberal and conservative publications and websites, 527 groups, and the formal party organizations (Koger et al., 2009)? How do differences in state campaign finance laws affect the relationship between political contributors and these informal networks of national, state, and local activists?

In addition to the empirical questions about party adaptation discussed above, we must also address the more fundamental question of the ability of state and local parties to represent mass interests. Skeptics of the party adaptation argument such as Lawson (1992: 14) contend that modern service vendor parties are nothing more than fund raising electoral machines, "elite organizations that work only for themselves and fellow elites." Rather than serving as responsible intermediaries between citizens and policy makers, she argues, parties are becoming increasingly beholden to the narrow interests that fund their organizations and candidates. Service-vendor parties act as intermediaries between candidates and contributors in a convoluted attempt to maximize campaign resources for competitive national, state, and local races within the context of national and state campaign finance laws. Rather than mobilizing voters at the grassroots with broad party appeals, modern parties are more likely to target and activate narrow segments of the electorate that normally support their candidates (Schier, 2000, 2003). "Historically," Shea (2003: 298) writes, "party units first cultivated voter loyalty and then transmitted this base into a resource for candidates." Service-vendor parties, however, provide campaign resources for ambitious office seekers, without any apparent long-term cultivation of voters (Shea, 2003). Schattschneider (1948: 22) contended that "the most legitimate question to be asked in a democracy is: how can people get control of the government." Any serious consideration of the role of state and local parties in the American democratic process must address these reservations about the ability of service vendor parties to expand the scope of political conflict, and thereby enhance the power of average citizens.

Ideological Polarization

According to advocates of the responsible party model, political parties play a crucial role in the democratic process by providing voters "a proper range of choice between alternatives of action" (Committee on Political Parties, 1950: 15). "The party, in one sense," writes Eldersveld (1964: 180–1), "is what it believes—its attitudes and perspectives at all echelons.... And what the party leaders believe may certainly determine in large part the image it communicates to the public, and the success with which it mobilizes public support." The advocates of the responsible party model at mid-century, were frustrated by what they perceived to be ideologically indistinct and decentralized parties. While the lack of ideological conflict in the American party system of the mid-twentieth century can be overstated (see Gerring, 1998, there is a considerable amount of scholarship that contends that traditional party organizations were largely non-ideological. Activists in traditional party organizations were primarily motivated by material incentives (Mayhew, 1986). State and local parties, whose primary interest was to win the material spoils of electoral victory, attempted to build broad-based coalitions through compromise and policy ambiguity (Herring, 1940; Key, 1952; Duverger, 1959; Rossiter, 1960).

The demise of traditional patronage-based party organizations coincided with changes in the nature of party activism. By the 1960s and 1970s scholars noted the emergence of a new type of party activist—upper-middle class, professional, and motivated more by the desire to express a cause or ideology than by winning the material spoils of electoral victory (Wilson, 1962; Wildavsky, 1965). Wilson's (1962: 358) seminal work on "issue-oriented" activists in club politics in New York, Chicago, and Los Angeles described the emergence of a new breed of party activist who was "insulated from traditional channels of party recruitment," and who had "the need to employ issues as incentives and to distinguish one's party from the opposition along policy lines." The result, Wilson contended, is that "political conflict will be exaggerated, party leaders will tend to be men skilled in the rhetorical arts, and the party's ability to produce agreement by trading issue-free resources will be reduced" (Wilson, 1962: 358). Over the next several decades, issue-oriented activists would become more common in state and local party organizations (Abramowitz et al., 1986; Moreland, 1990; Hadley and Bowman, 1998). This would contribute to growing ideological differences between the parties, and challenge the assumptions made by scholars in the mid-twentieth century that American political parties were essentially non-ideological.

One of the more comprehensive attempts to measure the attitudes of state and local party activists is the Southern Grassroots Party Activists Project, a series of surveys of precinct-level party activists in 11 southern states (Hadley and Bowman, 1995, 1998; Steed et al., 1998). Overall, the data compiled from these surveys demonstrate the increased presence in both major parties of issue-oriented and ideologically distinct grassroots activists. "Southern grassroots activists," write Bowman et al. (1998: 219), "cannot be accused of Tweedledee and Tweedledum politics." This has contributed to a programmatic style of party politics that challenges the pragmatic model of party activism. "In the South," write Shaffer and Breaux (1998: 45), "both the Democratic and Republican county party organizations risk being torn apart by their more ideologically pure younger element, elected party leaders who appear to value 'principles' and being 'right' more than winning in November." This type of issue-oriented party activism is not limited to the southern states. Other studies, which employ surveys of national convention delegates, surveys of state and county-level party activists, and the content analysis of state party platforms, indicate issue-oriented activism and party polarization in other regions of the country as well (Erikson et al., 1993; Paddock, 1997, 1998; Coffey, 2007; Jackson et al., 2007).

While it is well established in the literature that state and local party activists exhibit clear inter-party ideological differences, we know much less about how states differ in the nature of party activism. Are some state parties more ideologically polarized than others? If so, what factors (e.g. political culture, degree of party competition) might account for such inter-state differences? For example, would we expect states with a pre-dominantly moralistic political subculture, where, according to Elazar (1972), parties are more likely to put forth competing visions of the common good, to have more ideologi-cally polarized parties? Likewise, would we expect states with a predominantly individ-ualistic political subculture, where politics is conceived as a marketplace (Elazar, 1972), to have more coalitional (and presumably less ideologically polarized) parties intent on appealing to the median voter? Are more polarized state parties associated with higher or lower levels of party competition? The small body of literature is mixed on these ques-tions. Studies utilizing content analysis of state party platforms and surveys of state party committee members and national party convention delegates have demonstrated the theoretically expected relationship between higher levels of pragmatic party activ-ism and lower levels of inter-party ideological differences on one hand, and state politi-cal environments characterized by party professionalism, traditions of traditional party organizational activity, and the individualistic subculture on the other hand (Paddock, 1997, 1998; Carsey et al., 2006; Coffey, 2007). However, studies of state party platforms find higher levels of polarization associated with higher levels of state party competi-tion (Paddock, 1998; Coffey, 2007), while a study of national party convention delegates associates higher levels of pragmatic activism with higher levels of state party competi-tion (Carsey et al., 2006). More systematic empirical research needs to be carried out on the nature of inter-state differences in the degree of party polarization.

The link between the polarization of party activists and the nature of state public opinion is still a matter of considerable debate in the academic literature. Some have argued that party polarization is largely an elite phenomenon; party activists and elected officials are generally more polarized than a more ideologically moderate electorate (Dimaggio et al., 1996; Fiorina et al., 2006; Fiorina and Levendusky, 2006; Hetherington, 2009). While mass attitudes are now more clearly sorted by party, this line of argument goes, the electorate is not polarized. Voters must choose between polarized alterna-tives put forth by partisan elites. Others argue that in recent decades partisanship in the American electorate has become based more on ideological differences between vot-ers, and that there are real and growing ideological differences between Democrats and Republicans in the mass public (Jacobson , 2004; Abramowitz et al., 2006, 2008). Part of this debate revolves around which part of the American electorate one is examining. The most engaged and informed segment of the electorate tends to be the most partisan and the most ideologically polarized. Those who are less engaged in politics are less partisan and ideologically polarized, and more "inclined to withdraw from the political fray as the major parties become more polarized" (Beck, 2003: 51).

One of the problems with measuring mass polarization at the state level is the lack of consistent and empirically reliable mass survey data from the states. Almost 30 years ago Jewell (1982) noted that most state-level surveys were conducted by non-academic entities (e.g. interest groups, candidate organizations, and the media). Many times the results of these surveys are not made available to scholars or the public, and even when they are, the surveys may not have questions that are of theoretical significance to political scientists. Although progress has been made in the development of various state-wide academic polls, and there have been several collaborative efforts to share the results of state-level surveys, there is still much work to be done before political scientists will have access to consistent and theoretically significant state-level survey data (Parry et al., 2008). As Jewell (1982: 648) noted almost three decades ago, there is a need not only for more regular statewide surveys of citizen attitudes, but also for the organizations who conduct the surveys to "cooperate in preparing questions of common interest that would be used in as many of these polls as possible, and to cooperate in the collection and analysis of the data from these questions."

Because of the lack of reliable state-level survey data, scholars have been forced to develop alternative mechanisms to measure state public opinion. Erickson et al. (1993), in their seminal work on the relationship between state public opinion and public policy, develop an index of mass polarization based on CBS-*New York Times* surveys of Democratic and Republican identifiers for the period 1976–88. The least polarized states are in the South, where Democratic identifiers tend to be much more conservative than Democrats in other states. Of course, these data are drawn from the 1970s and 1980s, a time when Democratic identifiers in the South were probably more conservative than today. Erikson et al. (1993) found that in every state, Democratic identifiers were more liberal than Republican identifiers. And, crucial to the theoretical question addressed earlier in this essay, they found that the ideology of state party elites is correlated with the ideology of the mass public. Democratic activists are more liberal than Democratic identifiers, and Republican activists are more conservative than Republican identifiers. But "the ideologies represented by the state party elites are a reflection of state opinion" (Erikson et al., 1993: 119).

There is still considerable debate about the best method for measuring state-level public opinion. Brace et al. (2002), for example, disaggregate survey data to the state-level data from the General Social Survey between 1974 and 1998. Berry et al. (1998) estimate state-level measures of mass ideology based on interest group ratings of members of Congress, the estimated ideology score for a challenger, and electoral results from congressional districts. The citizen ideology score for each district forms the basis for calculating a state ideology score. These varying methods of measuring mass attitudes at the state level have led to debates about both the empirical validity of the different measures, but also about the question of whether state public opinion is stable over time (Berry et al., 2007; Brace et al., 2007). Until reliable state-level public opinion surveys are more widely available, such debates about alternative methods of measuring state opinion will likely continue.

If public opinion has indeed become more polarized, and there is some evidence to suggest it has (Fleisher and Bond, 2001; Jacobson, 2004; Abramowitz and Saunders, 2008), has it resulted from or contributed to the polarization of state party activists? Are party elites more polarized in response to growing polarization in their state's electorate? Or has the ideological polarization of party elites contributed to an environment in which citizens more clearly detect ideological distinctions between the parties and vote on the basis of those ideological differences? There is considerable evidence that elite (party activists and elected officials) polarization has contributed to higher levels of party-line voting in both state and national elections (Brown and Wright, 1992; Hetherington, 2001; Layman and Carsey, 2002). However, this does not necessarily lead to mass polarization. Party-line voting and mass polarization are not the same thing. Fiorina et al. (2006) contend that elite polarization has polarized the choices, but not the positions, of most voters. There is greater partisan sorting in the electorate, and therefore higher levels of party-line voting, but not necessarily ideological polarization between large numbers of voters. Others, however, contend that partisan sorting in the electorate goes hand-in-hand with increased ideological polarization (Abramowitz and Saunders, 2008). Polarization, argues Abramowitz (2006), is not simply a function of ideological conflict in a society, but is also dependent on how the political parties organize that conflict. "Partisan polarization," he writes, "makes it much more likely that ideological and cultural conflicts in society will be expressed politically" (Abramowitz, 2006: 80).

While it is difficult to measure the causal relationship between elite and mass polarization, it is even more difficult to measure the relationship between the polarization of state and local party activists and the polarization of state and local electorates. Because state and local party activists are part of broader party network that include a variety of other actors, and because these actors are operating in different political and cultural milieus in the states, it is a challenge to isolate their direct influence on mass polarization in their state. Fleisher and Bond (2001: 74) suggest that there has been a "simultaneous influence of mass and elite polarization in which each actor's more partisan attitudes reinforced the other." Clearly, more empirical work needs to be done not only on measuring elite and mass polarization at the state level, but also on explaining interstate differences in the degree of mass polarization, and clarifying the relationship between the polarization of state party activists and citizen attitudes at the state level.

Another empirical question that deserves further scholarly inquiry is the relationship between party polarization at the state level and voter turnout. Some argue that polarized partisan activists depress voter turnout. According to this view, ideologically polarized party activists and elected officials draft platforms, recruit candidates, and pass policies that are out of touch with a generally more moderate electorate (Fiorina et al., 2006). Others argue that a large part of the electorate, particularly those who are most politically active and informed, are increasingly polarized on ideological grounds, and that elite polarization stimulates greater electoral participation (Abramowitz and Saunders, 2008). One study of voter turnout at the state level found a relationship between liberal party elites and higher levels of voter turnout. "Party elites," write Brown et al. (1999: 476), "convey issue positions and ideologies that opinion leaders, the media, and eventually citizens recognize as part of the ongoing fabric of state politics.... A liberal political context facilitates registration across the electorate, but especially among the poor." Because of interstate differences in the polarization of party elites, states are excellent laboratories to examine the relationship between party polarization and voter turnout. Further scholarship needs to more systematically develop this relationship.

The growth of more ideologically distinct parties has fostered scholarly discussion on the possibility of responsible party government in the United States (Pomper, 2003). The proponents of the responsible party model in the mid-twentieth century were frustrated by the loose collection of state and local organizations which largely lacked ideological coherence. In the early twenty-first century, those same state and local parties are part of a more integrated and nationalized network of party and interest group activists, campaign contributors, political consultants, and other actors who comprise more ideologically distinct, and ideologically coherent, coalitions. The conventional wisdom of the traditional party government school is that this should contribute to greater democratic accountability.

Several studies linking party polarization to legislatures, legislative outcomes, and democratic accountability focus on the theory of conditional party government. According to this theory, conditions exogenous to the legislature (e.g. the polarization of party activists, partisan sorting in the electorate) contribute to an environment within the legislature in which legislative party leaders enhance party control through committee assignments, a whip system, shaping the legislative agenda, and attempts to influence other aspects of the legislative institution. The polarization of political parties enhances the ability of majority party leaders to structure the legislative institution in such a way as to favor the passage of their legislative agenda (Aldrich and Battista, 2002; Bianco and Sened, 2005). Much of the conditional party government literature focuses on Congress (Aldrich and Rohde, 2000). However, a small, but growing, body of literature addresses conditional party government in state legislatures.

Given the importance of variables exogenous to the legislature to the theory of conditional party government, surprisingly little research has examined the impact of state party activists on state legislatures. Masket (2007) examines the impact of state party and interest group activists on the California legislature between 1849 and 2006. Masket's fundamental question revolves around why elected officials are "single minded seekers of reelection" in some eras, and "fierce ideological warriors" in other eras. Masket uses California's 1914–51 experiment with cross-filing, a Progressive reform which effectively cut party activists out of the party nominations process, to measure the effects of outside activists on the behavior of California legislators. During the period of cross-filing, legislative polarization and party discipline were minimal. After 1952, when labor unions and liberal activists from the club movement successfully pushed for ending cross-filing, polarization and party discipline slowly returned to the California Assembly. Legislative polarization and party discipline, Masket concludes, are largely a function of activists outside of the legislature who control the nomination of candidates. In contrast to Aldrich's (1995) argument that parties are created by ambitious politicians to serve their electoral interests, Masket contends that "those who control the party nominations rule the party" (Masket, 2007: 495).

Because of the variation between states, state legislative parties provide an excellent opportunity "to build and test more generalized theories" about conditional party government (Aldrich and Battista, 2002: 169). Aldrich and Battista (2002) utilize Poole and Rosenthal's (1997) approach to analyzing roll call votes in Congress to develop unidimensional NOMINATE scores estimating legislator preferences in 11 states from the late 1990s. They conclude that there is considerable variation between states in the extent of party polarization. Parties in the 11 states were either very polarized or not polarized. Legislative polarization is related to electoral competition (measured by the number of effective parties in the state), and these two factors are linked to more representative legislative committees. Wright and Shaffner (2002) compare the partisan Kansas Senate with the constitutionally non-partisan Nebraska Legislature, and find less polarized parties in Nebraska than in Kansas. In the more partisan environment in Kansas, pressures from party activists, primary elections, and campaign contributors contribute to more polarized legislative parties. Citing the responsible party model school's emphasis on the importance of integrated and coherent parties to democratic accountability, Wright and Shaffner (2002: 377) write that the constitutionally-mandated non-partisan elections in Nebraska "effectively break the policy linkage between citizens and their elected representatives in the statehouse." The Kansas Senate's more ideologically coherent parties, they argue, promote greater democratic accountability.

Jenkins (2008) analyzes roll call votes in state legislatures in Colorado, Florida, Illinois, Missouri, and Wisconsin during three legislative sessions during the 1990s. Her findings provide mixed support for the model of conditional party government. "On the one hand," Jenkins writes, "neither ideological heterogeneity nor polarization impact party support after controlling for the ideology of individual caucus members, majority party leader powers, and majority party status" (Jenkins, 2008: 255). However, her data also show that greater ideological homogeneity could enhance the powers granted to party leaders in the legislature. Party leaders are therefore in a better position to provide important resources to members of their caucus, giving members an additional incentive to cast a party vote.

Clucas (2009) measures the relationship between polarization and the influence of majority party leadership by utilizing a 1995 nationwide survey of state legislators and determining whether state Republican parties adopted their own Contract with the American People. It is assumed that adoption of such a state-level contract is a reliable measure of the conditions necessary for conditional party government: intra-party homogeneity and inter-party polarization (Little, 1997). Clucas constructs a regression model in which the dependent variable is based on a survey item asking about the "relative influence" of the "majority party leadership." He finds that "in the states in which intraparty policy preferences were the most homogenous and the interparty preferences were the most polarized, the leadership was perceived as being the most powerful" (Clucas, 2009: 326).

Empirical analyses of the policy consequences of party polarization also focus on specific policy outcomes. For example, party polarization has occurred at the same time that the national government and many states have pursued more conservative social welfare policies. This has prompted some scholars to test whether there is a relationship between the two trends. McCarty et al. (2006) examine this relationship at the national level and conclude that polarization in Congress and in public opinion has directly contributed to the weakening of policies that redistribute resources to the poor. This conclusion runs

contrary to the conventional wisdom of the responsible party model school that ideologically distinct and competitive parties empower average citizens by expanding the
scope of political conflict (Schattschneider, 1942). Very little empirical research examines the relationship between state party polarization and policy outcomes at the state
level. Because states differ in the extent of ideological polarization among citizens, party
activists, and elected officials, they could serve as excellent test cases to examine the
effects of party polarization on public policy (Rigby and Wright, 2008).

REGIONALISM AND THE AMERICAN PARTY SYSTEM

While state and local parties are less organizationally autonomous than they were a
generation ago, they still compete in vastly different political environments. The United
States is a geographically diverse nation, despite various nationalizing trends in the
nation's politics and culture. County Democratic and Republican parties contesting
elections in the Mississippi Delta region, for example, face significantly different organizational and coalitional challenges than town organizations in western Massachusetts,
or precinct organizations in Chicago. Such parties are increasingly part of a more nationalized and integrated party network, but they must also recruit candidates, fashion policy alternatives, and devise voter mobilization strategies that work in their cultural and
political setting. In a party system moving in the direction of greater integration, one
might expect regional differences to wane, as the parties adopt similar voter mobilization strategies and ideological orientations, and appeal to similar coalitions of voters.
However, American federalism, where all elections are contested at the state and local
levels, continues to foster an essentially decentralized party system. "Decentralization,"
Pomper (1992: 90) contends, "is the rational party team's response to American conditions.... It allows politicians to pursue their presumed self interest in winning office
while adjusting to the local conditions of the political market."

One of the seminal works on regionalism and American parties was Key's (1949)
extensive study of southern politics. Key directed a large-scale study of southern politics
funded by a Rockefeller Foundation grant through the Bureau of Public Administration
at the University of Alabama. The grant allowed Key and his assistants to conduct over
500 interviews of southern political actors. The study also included extensive data analysis of county-level voting patterns in the region. The result was 11 case studies of state
party politics in the South, as well as various thematic chapters on the politics of the
region. Key concluded that the South has parties and electoral politics systems that differ substantially from other parts of the country. And even within the South, the upland
regions of western North Carolina and Virginia, eastern Tennessee and Kentucky,
northern Georgia and Alabama, and northwestern Arkansas differ substantially from
the lowland areas of the South.

Some of the scholarship on regionalism and state parties has focused on organizational differences between parties in different states and local areas. Some of this literature focuses on the impact of political subcultures on state and local party organizations. Pragmatic, job-oriented traditional party organizations, it is argued, were more common in the more urbanized states of the middle Atlantic region and the industrial Midwest than in either the South or northern tier of states (Fenton, 1966; Mayhew, 1986). These states were located in areas where the individualistic subculture predominated (Elazar, 1972). Issue-oriented party organizations were more closely associated with the moralistic subculture of New England, the upper Midwest, and the Pacific Northwest (Fenton, 1966; Elazar, 1972; Mayhew, 1986). The weakest party organizations, at least historically, were associated with the traditionalistic subculture of the South (Key 1949). Many of these findings come from the era of traditional party organizations. We know less about regional variation in party strength in the era of the service-vendor party.

Cotter et al.'s (1989) extensive study of state and local party organizations reinforced some of the earlier findings about local parties. Local organizations in both parties were strongest in the Middle Atlantic region and weakest in the South. Local party organizational strength, they contend, is largely a function of regional variation. However, among state party organizations, their findings were less consistent with previous scholarship. In fact, some of the strongest Republican state organizations were in the South, a function, they speculate, of the effort by the Republican National Committee to invest money in party building programs in a region where Republicans were gaining in electoral strength. State party strength in the era of the service-vendor party, they argue, is less related to regional variation than to the parties committing resources to the process of developing bureaucratic organizations. State party organizations are less labor-intensive than local parties and therefore better able to overcome regional obstacles to party development (Cotter et al., 1989: 50). Regional variation in the strength of state and local party organization is an area that deserves greater academic inquiry. In the era of capital-intensive service-vendor parties, are regional differences as important as they once were in accounting for the strength of state and local organizations?

Other literature examines the relationship between the distribution of Democratic and Republican constituencies within states and the nature of party organizations within those states. For example, in many states the Democrats traditionally have had more geographically concentrated constituencies in major metropolitan areas. This has contributed to more labor-intensive local Democratic machines. Republicans, with typically more dispersed constituencies, have had to depend more upon capital-intensive voter mobilization strategies (Key, 1956; Gimpel and Schuknecht, 2002). In addition, larger states with more dispersed party constituencies have been associated with greater party factionalism and more contentious primary elections. "When pockets of party support are scattered across multiple, large, geographic bases, write Pearson-Merkowitz and McTague (2008: 23), state party organizations and candidates face greater difficulty achieving unity in their primaries."

Scholars have also noted substantial interstate differences in the coalitional bases of the parties (Brown, 1995; Gimpel, 1996; Gimpel and Schuknecht, 2004). In a decentralized party system, the electoral coalitions parties put together at the national level for their presidential candidates may differ from the coalitions put together by parties at the state and local levels. Some state parties put together similar coalitions of voters for their candidates in gubernatorial and state legislative elections that the national parties put together for their presidential candidate. In other states, however, state and local coalitions look very different from the national coalitions. Gimpel (1996) explores the concept of "autonomous state party systems" in his comparison of state electoral systems in the West with those in the Northeast and Midwest. He argues that Arizona, New Mexico, California, Oregon, Washington, and Idaho, which all have relatively weak party organizational structures, have had party systems that tend to be independent of national party conflicts. His examination of county-level voting patterns showed these western states' frequent incongruities between presidential and state-level elections. In contrast, New York, New Jersey, Pennsylvania, and Ohio, all with traditions of stronger party organizational structures, exhibited coalitional patterns that were established during the New Deal realignment. State-level candidates put together similar coalitions in these states as their party's candidate for president.

A problem with conducting state-level research on party coalitions is the previously-mentioned lack of reliable survey data. Scholars have had to rely on county-level voting returns and census data. From these data, they have made estimates about the voting patterns of various demographic groups (Gimpel, 1996; Gimpel and Schuknecht, 2004). Such analysis, as these scholars readily acknowledge, is subject to the ecological inference problem. In addition, scholars of state-level voting behavior must account for longitudinal change in state public opinion. Gimpel and Schuknecht (2004), for example, emphasize population mobility, generational change, party conversion, and the mobilization of new voters as factors contributing to changes in a state's partisan divisions. This returns us to the debate about the stability of state-level public opinion, and reemphasizes the need for reliable and comprehensive state-level survey data.

The concept of autonomous party systems is addressed by scholars of state legislative and gubernatorial elections. Do parties play the same role in structuring the vote at the national level that they do in state-level elections? As campaigns have become more candidate-centered in the telecommunications age, parties have played a declining role in structuring the vote at both levels. This, coupled with the fact that many states hold their gubernatorial elections in non-presidential election years, has contributed to a de-coupling of state-level elections from national elections. Scholarly comparisons of gubernatorial and US senate elections, for example, have demonstrated that different dynamics are at work in these contests (Carsey and Wright, 1998; Brown and Jacobson, 2008). "State economic evaluations are relevant in gubernatorial contests," write Carsey and Wright (1998: 1001–2), "while national economic performance matters in voting for senator." However, they also note that presidential approval ratings affect both gubernatorial and US Senate races in a major way.

Candidate-centered elections have also contributed to increased levels of divided government at the state level (Jewell and Morehouse, 2001). While parties play a role in structuring the vote in gubernatorial and state legislative elections, factors such as incumbency, voter ideology, campaign spending, and local economic and budgetary conditions can also shape voter preferences (Partin, 1995; Svoboda, 1995; Jewell and Morehouse, 2001; Brown and Jacobson, 2008; Carsey et al., 2008). These factors may lead to increased incidences of divided government at the state level. The most obvious regional trend in party control of state government in the modern era was in the South after the civil rights revolution of the 1950s and 1960s. From the Reconstruction period to the mid-1960s, many southern states had unified Democratic governments. However, as the national Democratic Party became increasingly associated with progressive positions on civil rights and some of the other cultural issues emerging in the 1960s, Democratic dominance in the South began to erode. "By the mid-1980s," note Jewell and Morehouse (2001: 223), southern states "still had Democratic legislatures, but most of them had elected a Republican governor at least once, and thus divided government had begun to appear in the South." While the major changes in southern politics over the past several decades have received considerable scholarly attention, we lack a systematic understanding of the factors that may account for regional variation in incidences of divided government. A more developed understanding of regional differences in the incidences of divided government at the state level may also provide important insights into the debate about the significance of divided government to policy outcomes. Does unified party government promote greater democratic accountability, as proponents of the responsible party model suggest (Leyden and Borrelli 1995)? Do increasing incidences of divided government at the state level counter the other trends discussed in this chapter (intra-party integration and ideological polarization) that seem to be contributing to more responsible parties?

Conclusion

One of the recurring dilemmas in American politics is the apparent contradiction between representing mass interests and avoiding the tyranny of the majority. Political parties are in the business of representing mass interests by mobilizing voters on behalf of their candidates. However, the traditionally decentralized nature of the American party system contributed to an environment in which the parties seemed incapable of the kind of internal cohesion necessary to make public policies responsive to an electoral majority. Some of the anti-majoritarian aspects of the American constitutional system (e.g. federalism) contributed to a party system composed of largely autonomous state and local parties. James Madison famously wrote in Federalist 10 that in a large and diverse republic, "the influence of factious leaders may kindle a flame within their particular States, but will be unable to spread a general conflagration through the other States" (Hamilton et al., 1961: 83–4). Such a system frustrated democratic theorists of a more majoritarian persuasion, who argued that mass interests could not be adequately represented in a decentralized party system (Schattschneider, 1942; Committee on Political Parties APSA, 1950).

Two major trends in the American party system discussed in this chapter—organizational integration and ideological polarization—have contributed to the possibility of responsible party government in the United States. Despite the continuation of significant regional differences in a large and diverse republic like the United States, state and local parties have become part of a broader national network of actors that present voters with clear policy alternatives. This national network potentially has the internal cohesion necessary to make public policy responsive to their electoral coalitions. However, there are a lot of obstacles to responsible party government in the United States. The separation of powers, federalism, and a large and diverse American republic limit the impact of these majoritarian trends in the party system. In addition, the capital-intensive nature of the modern electoral system makes the parties increasingly dependent on large infusions of cash from some of the most economically privileged segments of society, polarized party elites may be out of touch with the policy views of a large segment of the electorate, and candidate-centered campaigns have contributed to increasing incidences of divided government at the state level. These trends clearly run counter to the potentially majoritarian aspects of more organizationally integrated and ideologically distinct parties.

Since all elections in the United States are conducted at the state and local levels, state and local parties will continue to be important institutional actors in the American democratic process. While their role has been somewhat diminished by the nationalizing trends in the party system, understanding their changing role is crucial to our understanding of the broader political process, and how responsive that process is to the American electorate.

REFERENCES

Abramowitz, A. I. 2006. "Disconnected or Joined at the Hip?" In P. S. Nivola and D. W. Brady (eds), *Red and Blue Nation: Characteristic and Causes of America's Polarized Politics*. Washington, DC: Brookings Institution Press, 72–85.

Abramowitz, A. I. and Saunders, K. L. 2006. "Exploring the Bases of Partisanship in the American Electorate: Social Identity vs. Ideology." *Political Research Quarterly* 59 (2): 175–87.

Abramowitz, A. I. and Saunders, K. L. 2008. "Is Polarization a Myth?" *Journal of Politics* 70 (2): 542–55.

Abramowitz, A. I., McGlennon, J., and Rapoport, R. B. 1986. "An Analysis of State Party Activists." In R. B. Rapoport, A. I. Abramowitz, and J. McGlennon (eds), *The Life of the Parties: Activists in Presidential Politics*. Lexington, KY: University Press of Kentucky, 44–58.

Aldrich, J. H. 1995. *Why Parties? The Origin and Transformation of Parties in America*. Chicago: University of Chicago Press

Aldrich, J. H. 2000. Southern Parties in State and Nation. *Journal of Politics* 62: 643–70.

Aldrich, J. H., and Battista, J. S. 2002. "Conditional Party Government in the States." *American Journal of Political Science* 46: 164–72.

Aldrich, J. H. and Rohde, D. W. 2000. "The Republican Revolution and the House Appropriation Committee." *Journal of Politics* 62: 1–33.

Appleton, A. M. and Ward, D. S. (eds) 1997. *State Party Profiles: A Fifty-State Guide to Development, Organization, and Resources.* Washington, DC: Congressional Quarterly Press.

Appollonio, D. E., and Raymond J. La Raja. 2006. "Term Limits, Campaign Contributions, and the Distribution of Power in State Legislatures." *Legislative Studies Quarterly* 31 (2): 259–81.

Beck, P. A. 2003. "A Tale of Two Electorates: The Changing American Party Coalitions, 1952–2000." In J. C. Green and R. Farmer (eds), *The State of the Parties.* Lanham, MD: Rowman & Littlefield, 38–53.

Berry, J. M. and Wilcox, C. 2007. *The Interest Group Society.* 4th edn. New York: Person, Longman.

Berry, W. D., Ringquist, E. J., Fording, R. C., and Hanson, R. L. 1998. "Measuring Citizen and Government Ideology in the American States, 1960–93." *American Journal of Political Science* 42 (1): 327–48.

Berry, W. D., Ringquist, E. J., Fording, R. C., and Hanson, R. L. 2007. "The Measurement and Stability of State Citizen Ideology." *State Politics and Policy Quarterly* 7 (2): 111–32.

Bianco, W. T. and Sened, I. 2005. "Uncovering Evidence of Conditional Party Government: Reassessing Majority Party Influence in Congress and State Legislatures." *American Political Science Review* 99 (3): 361–71.

Bibby, J. F. 1999. "Party Networks: National-State Integration, Allied Groups, and Issue Activists." In J. C. Green and D. M. Shea (eds), *The State of the Parties.* Lanham, MD: Rowman and Littlefield, 69–85.

Bibby, J. F. and Holbrook, T. M. 1996. "Parties and Elections." In V. Gray and H. Jacob (eds), *Politics in the American States: A Comparative Analysis.* Washington, DC: Congressional Quarterly Press, 78–121.

Blumberg, M. J., Binning, W. C., Green, J. C. 1999. "Do the Grassroots Matter? The Coordinated Campaign in a Battleground State." In J. C. Green and D. M. Shea (eds), *The State of the Parties.* Lanham, MD: Rowman and Littlefield, 154–67.

Blumberg, M. J., Binning, W. C., and Green, J. C. 2003. "No Mo(mentum) in Ohio: Local Parties and the 2000 Presidential Campaign." In J. C. Green and R. Farmer (eds), *The State of the Parties.* Lanham, MD: Rowman & Littlefield, 203–13.

Blumberg, M. J., Binning, W. C., and Green, J. C. 2007. "The (Un)Coordinated Campaign: The Battle for Mahoning County, Ohio." In J. C. Green and D. J. Coffey (eds), *The State of the Parties.* Lanham, MD: Rowman & Littlefield, 187–97.

Bowman, L., Clark, J. A., and Steed, R. P. 1998. "Summing Up: Organization and Activism at the Grassroots Level in the 1990s." In R. P. Steed, J. A. Clark, L. Bowman, and C. D. Hadley (eds), *Party Organization and Activism in the American South.* Tuscaloosa, AL: University of Alabama Press, 218–27.

Brace, P., Sims-Butler, K., Arceneaux, K., and Johnson, M. 2002. "Public Opinion in the American States: New Perspectives Using National Survey Data." *American Journal of Political Science* 46 (January): 173–89.

Brace, P., Arceneaux, K., Johnson, M., and Ulbig, S.G. 2007. "Reply to 'The Measurement and Stability of State Citizen Ideology.'" *State Politics and Policy Quarterly* 7 (2): 133–40.

Brown, A. R. and Jacobson, G. C. 2008. "Party, Performance, and Strategic Politicians: The Dynamics of Elections for Senator and Governor in 2006." *State Politics and Policy Quarterly* 8 (4): 384–409.

Brown, R. D. 1995. "Party Cleavages and Welfare Effort in the American States." *American Political Science Review* 89 (March): 23–33.

Brown, R. D. and Wright, G. C. 1992. "Elections and State Party Polarization." *American Politics Quarterly* 20 (October): 411–26.

Brown, R. D., Jackson, R. A., and Wright, G. C. 1999. "Registration, Turnout, and State Party Systems." *Political Research Quarterly* 52 (September): 463–79.

Carsey, T. M. and Wright, G. C. 1998. "State and National Factors in Gubernatorial and Senatorial Elections." *American Journal of Political Science* 42 (3): 994–1002.

Carsey, T. M., Green, J. C., Herrera, R., and Layman, G. C. 2006. "State Party Context and Norms Among Delegates to the 2000 National Party Convention." *State Politics and Policy Quarterly* 6 (3l): 247–71.

Carsey, T. M., Niemi, R. G., Berry, W. D., Powell, L. W., and Snyder, J. M. 2008. "State Legislative Elections, 1967–2003: Announcing the Completion of a Cleaned and Updated Dataset." *State Politics and Policy Quarterly* 8 (4): 430–43.

Cigler, A. J. 1993. "Political Parties and Interest Groups: Competitors, Collaborators, and Uneasy Allies." In E. Uslaner (ed.), *American Political Parties*. Itaca, IL: F.E. Peacock, 407–33.

Clucas, R. A. 2009. "The Contract With America and Conditional Party Government in State Legislatures." *Political Research Quarterly* 62 (2): 317–28.

Coffey, D. J. 2007. "State Party Activists and State Party Polarization." In J. C. Green and D. J. Coffey (eds), *The State of the Parties*. Lanham, MD: Rowman & Littlefield, 75–91.

Committee on Political Parties, American Political Science Association. 1950. "Toward a More Responsible Two-Party System." *American Political Science Review* 44: Supplement.

Corrado, A. 2006. "Party Finance in the Wake of BCRA: An Overview." In M. J. Malbin (ed.), *The Election After Reform: Money, Politics, and the Bipartisan Campaign Reform Act*, Lanham, MD: Rowman and Littlefield, 19–37.

Cotter, C. P., Gibson, J. L., Bibby, J. F., and Huckshorn, R. J. 1989. *Party Organizations in American Politics*. Pittsburgh, PA: University of Pittsburgh Press.

Dimaggio, P., Evans, J., and Bryson, B. 1996. "Have Americans' Social Attitudes Become More Polarized?" *American Journal of Sociology* 102 (3): 690–755.

Duverger, M. 1959. *Political Parties*. New York: Wiley.

Dwyre, D. and Kolodny, R. 2002. "Throwing Out the Rule Book: Party Financing of the 2000 Elections." In D. B. Magleby (ed.), *Financing the 2000 Election*. Washington, DC: Brookings Institution Press.

Elazar, D. J. 1972. *American Federalism: A View from the States*. New York: Crowell.

Eldersveld, S. 1964. *Political Parties*. Chicago: Rand McNally.

Epstein, L. D. 1967. *Political Parties in Western Democracies*. New York: Praeger.

Epstein, L. D. 1982. "Confederations and Party Nationalization." *Publius* 12: 67–102.

Epstein, L. D. 1986. *Political Parties in the American Mold.* Madison, WI: University of Wisconsin Press.

Erikson, R. S., Wright, G. C. and McIver, J. P. 1993. *Statehouse Democracy: Public Opinion and Policy in the American States*. Cambridge, UK: Cambridge University Press.

Fenton, J. H. 1966. *Midwest Politics*. New York: Holt, Rinehart, and Winston.

Fiorina, M., Abrams, S. J., and Pope, J. C. 2006. *Culture War? The Myth of a Polarized America*. New York: Pearson.

Fleisher, R. and Bond, J. R. 2001. "Evidence of Increasing Polarization Among Ordinary Citizens." In J. E. Cohen, R. Fleisher, and P. Kantor (eds), *American Political Parties: Decline or Resurgence?* Washington, DC: Congressional Quarterly Press, 55–77.

Fiorina, Morris P., and Matthew Levendusky. 2006. "Disconnected: The Political Class versus the People—Rejoinder." In *Red and Blue Nation?* Volume I: *Characteristics and Causes of*

America's Polarized Politics, ed. P.S. Nivola and D.W. Brady. Washington, DC: Brookings Institution Press and Stanford: Hoover Institution Press, 95–110.

Frendreis, J., Gitelson, A. R., Flemming, G., and Layzell, A. 1996. "Local Political Parties and Legislative Races in 1992 and 1994." In J. C. Green and D. M. Shea (eds), *The State of the Parties*. Lanham, MD: Rowman and Littlefield, 149–62.

Gerring, J. 1998. *Party Ideologies in America, 1828–1996*. New York: Cambridge University Press.

Gierzynski, A. 1992. *Legislative Campaign Committees in the American States*. Lexington, KY: University Press of Kentucky.

Gierzynski, A. 2002. "Financing Gubernatorial and State Legislative Elections." In D. B. Magleby (ed.), *Financing the 2000 Election*. Washington, DC: Brookings Institution Press.

Gimpel, J. 1996. *National Elections and the Autonomy of American State Party Systems*. Pittsburgh, PA: University of Pittsburgh Press.

Gimpel, J. and Schuknecht, J. E. 2002. "Reconsidering Political Regionalism in the American States." *State Politics and Policy Quarterly* 2 (40): 325–52.

Gimpel, J. and Schuknecht, J. E. 2004. *Patchwork Nation: Sectionalism and Political Change in American Politics*. Ann Arbor, MI: University of Michigan Press.

Hadley, C. D. and Bowman, L. (eds) 1995. *Southern State Party Organizations and Activists*. Westport, CT: Praeger.

Hadley, C. D. and Bowman, L. (eds) 1998. *Party Activists in Southern Politics: Mirrors and Makers of Change*. Knoxville, TN: University of Tennessee Press.

Hamilton, A., Madison, J., and Jay, J. 1961. *The Federalist Papers*. New York: Mentor.

Herring, P. 1940. *The Politics of Democracy: American Parties in Action*. New York: Norton.

Hetherington, M. J. 2001. "Resurgent Mass Partisanship: The Role of Elite Polarization." *American Political Science Review* 95 (3): 619–31.

Hetherington, M. J. 2009. "Putting Polarization in Perspective." *British Journal of Political Science* 39 (2): 413–48.

Huckshorn, R. J., Gibson, J. L., Cotter, C. P., and Bibby, J. F. 1986. "Party Integration and Party Organizational Strength." *The Journal of Politics* 48: 976–91.

Jackson, J. S., Bigelow, N. S., and Green, J. C. 2007. "The State of the Party Elites: National Convention Delegates, 1992–2004." In J. C. Green and D. J. Coffey (eds), *The State of the Parties*. Lanham, MD: Rowman & Littlefield, 51–74.

Jacobson, G. C. 2004. "Partisan and Ideological Polarization in the California Electorate." *State Politics and Policy Quarterly* 4 (2): 113–39.

Jenkins, S. 2008. "Party Influence on Roll Call Voting: A View from the U.S. States." *State Politics and Policy Quarterly* 8 (3): 239–62.

Jewell, M. E. 1982. "The Neglected World of State Politics." *Journal of Politics* 44 (3): 638–57.

Jewell, M. E. and Morehouse, S. M. 2001. *Political Parties and Elections in the American States*. Washington, DC: CQ Press.

Key, V. O. 1949. *Southern Politics in State and Nation*. New York: Knopf.

Key, V. O. 1952. *Politics, Parties, and Pressure Groups*. New York: Crowell.

Key, V. O. 1956. *American State Politics: An Introduction*. New York: Alfred A. Knopf,

Koger, G., Masket, S., and Noel, H. 2009. "Partisan Webs: Information Exchange and Party Networks." *British Journal of Political Science* 39: 633–53.

La Raja, R. J. 2003. "State Parties and Soft Money: How Much Party Building." In J. C. Green and R. Farmer (eds), *The State of the Parties*. Lanham, MD: Rowman & Littlefield, 132–50.

La Raja, R. J., Orr, S. E., and Smith, D. A. 2007. "Surviving BCRA: State Party Finance in 2004." In J. C. Green and D. J. Coffey (eds), *The State of the Parties*. Lanham, MD: Rowman & Littlefield, 113–34.

Lawson, K. 1992. "Why We Still Need Real Political Parties." In J. M. Burns, W. Crotty, L. L. Duke, and L. D. Longley (eds), *The Democrats Must Lead: The Case for a Progressive Democratic Party*. Boulder, CO: Westview Press, 13–27.

Layman, G. C. and Carsey, T. M. 2002. "Party Polarization and 'Conflict Extension' in the American Electorate." *American Journal of Political Science* 46 (October): 786–802.

Leyden, K. M. and Borrelli, S. A. 1995. "The Effect of State Economic Conditions on Gubernatorial Elections: Does Unified Government Make a Difference?" *Political Research Quarterly* 48 (2): 275–90.

Little, T. H. 1997. "An Experiment in Responsible Party Government: National Agenda Setting and State Replicas of the Contract with America." *The American Review of Politics* 18: 1–23.

Lunch, W. M. 1987. *The Nationalization of American Politics*. Berkeley, CA: University of California Press.

McCarty, N., Poole, K. T., and Rosenthal, H. 2006. *Polarized America: The Dance of Ideology and Unequal Riches*. Cambridge, MA: The MIT Press.

Masket, S. 2002. "The Emergence of Unofficial Party Organizations in California." *Spectrum: The Journal of State Government* Fall: 29–33.

Masket, S. 2007. "It Takes an Outsider: Extralegislative Oraganization and Partisanship in the California Assembly, 1849–2006." *American Journal of Political Science* 51 (3): 482–97.

Mayhew, D. 1986. *Placing Parties in American Politics*. Princeton, NJ: Princeton University Press.

Monroe, J. P. 2001. *The Political Party Matrix: The Persistence of Organization*. Albany, NY: State University of New York Press.

Morehouse, S. M. and Jewell, M. E. 2003. "State Parties: Independent Partners in the Money Relationship." In J. C. Green and R. Farmer (eds), *The State of the Parties*, Lanham, MD: Rowman & Littlefield, 151–68.

Moreland, L. W. 1990. "The Ideological and Issue Bases of Southern Parties." In T. A. Baker, C. D. Hadley, R. P. Steed, and L. W. Moreland (eds), *Political Parties in the Southern States: Party Activists in Partisan Coalitions*. New York: Praeger, 123–34.

Paddock, J. 1997. "Political Culture and the Partisan Style of Party Activists." *Publius* 27: 127–32.

Paddock, J. 1998. "Explaining State Variation in Interparty Ideological Differences." *Political Research Quarterly* 51: 765–80.

Parry, J. A., Kisida, B., and Langeley, R. E. 2008. "The State of State Polls: Old Challenges, New Opportunities." *State Politics and Policy Quarterly* 8 (2): 198–216.

Partin, R. W. 1995. "Economic Conditions and Gubernatorial Elections." *American Politics Quarterly* 23: 81–95.

Pearson-Merkowitz, S. and McTague, J. M. 2008. "Partisan Mountains and Molehills: The Geography of U.S. State Intraparty Factionalism." *State Politics and Policy Quarterly* 8 (1): 7–31.

Pomper, G. 1992. *Passions and Interests: Political Party Concepts of American Democracy*. Lawrence, KS: University Press of Kansas.

Pomper, G. 2003. "Parliamentary Government in the United States: A New Regime for a New Century?" In J. C. Green and R. Farmer (eds), *The State of the Parties*. Lanham, MD: Rowman & Littlefield, 267–86.

Pomper, G. and Weiner, M. D. 2002. "Toward a More Responsible Two Party Voter." In J. C. Green and P. S. Herrnson (eds), *Responsible Partisanship: The Evolution of American Political Parties Since 1950*. Lawrence, KS: The University Press of Kansas, 181–200.

Poole, K. and Rosenthal, H. 1997. *Congress: A Political-Economic History of Roll-Call Voting*. New York: Oxford University Press.

Price, D. 1984. *Bringing Back the Parties*. Washington, DC: Congressional Quarterly Press.

Ranney, A. 1965. Parties in State Politics. In H. Jacob and K. N. Vines (eds), *Politics in the American States*. Boston: Little Brown, 61–99.

Rigby, E. and Wright, G. C. 2008. "Does Party Polarization Impede Redistribution? Evidence from the American States." Presented at the Annual Meeting of the American Political Science Association, August 28, Boston, MA.

Rossiter, C. 1960. *Parties and Politics in America*. Ithaca, NY: Cornell University Press.

Rozell, M. J., Wilcox, C., and Madland, D. 2006. *Interest Groups in American Campaigns: The New Face of Electioneering*. Washington, DC: Congressional Quarterly Press.

Schattschneider, E. E. 1942. *Party Government*. New York: Farrar and Rinehart.

Schattschneider, E. E. 1948. *The Struggle for Party Government*. College Park, MD: University of Maryland Press.

Schier, S. E. 2000. *By Invitation Only: The Rise of Exclusive Politics in the United States*. Pittsburgh, PA: University of Pittsburgh Press.

Schier, S. E. 2003. *You Call This an Election? America's Peculiar Democracy*. Washington, DC: Georgetown University Press.

Schlesinger, J. A. 1984. "On the Theory of Party Organization." *Journal of Politics* 46: 369–400.

Schwartz, M. A. 1990. *The Party Network: The Robust Organization of Illinois Republicans*. Madison, WI: University of Wisconsin Press.

Shaffer, S. D. and Breaux, D. A. 1998. "Clashing Generations: Youthful Purists Challenge Pragmatic Professionals." In C. D. Hadley and L. Bowman (eds), *Party Activists in Southern Politics: Mirrors and Makers of Change*. Knoxville, TN: University of Tennessee Press, 37–57.

Shea, D. M. 1995. *Transforming Democracy: Legislative Campaign Committees and Political Parties*. Albany, NY: State University of New York Press.

Shea, D. M. 2003. "Schattschneider's Dismay: Strong Parties and Alienated Voters." In J. C. Green and R. Farmer (eds), *The State of the Parties*. Lanham, MD: Rowman & Littlefield, 287–99.

Skinner, R. M. 2005. "Do 527's Add Up To a Party? Thinking About the 'Shadows' of Politics." *The Forum* 3 (3): 1–19.

Steed, R. P., Clark, J. A., Bowman, L., and Hadley, C. D. (eds) 1998. *Party Organization and Activism in the American South*. Tuscaloosa AL: University of Alabama Press.

Svoboda, C. J. 1995. "Retrospective Voting in Gubernatorial Elections." *Political Research Quarterly* 48: 135–50.

Thomas, C. S. and Hrebenar, R. J. 1996. "Interest Groups in the States." In V. Gray and H. Jacob (eds), *Politics in the American States*. Washington, DC: Congressional Quarterly Press, 122–58.

Wekkin, G. D. 1984. "National-State Party Relations: The Democrats' New Federal Structure." *Political Science Quarterly* 99: 45–72.

Wildavsky, A. 1965. "The Goldwater Phenomenon: Purists, Politicians, and the Two-Party System." *Review of Politics* 27: 386–413.

Wilson, J. Q. 1962. *The Amateur Democrat: Club Politics in Three Cities*. Chicago: University of Chicago Press.

Wright, G. C. and Shaffner, B. F. 2002. "The Influence of Party: Evidence from the State Legislatures." *American Political Science Review* 96 (2): 367–79.

CHAPTER 9

··

LOCAL CAMPAIGNS AND ELECTIONS

··

TIMOTHY B. KREBS

IN the first paragraph of Howard D. Hamilton's 1971 *American Political Science Review* article on voting in Toledo, Ohio, he writes:

> An anomalous deficiency in the voluminous voting behavior literature is its almost exclusive preoccupation with national presidential elections although the bulk of voting in the United States, if not in Europe, occurs in local elections. Curiously, this neglect has occurred even though the granddaddy of voting research—Merriam and Gosnell's herculean investigation of the causes of nonvoting—was a study of the Chicago city election of 1923. (1135)

Writing in 1990, Charles Bullock, in a study of turnout in six U.S. cities, commented: "Municipal turnout has continued to generate little scholarly interest even in the face of growing academic curiosity in the correlates of participation in other contexts (539) Amazingly, these statements remain largely true today. Furthermore, one can argue that other aspects of local elections—such as candidate recruitment, money in politics, voter choice, campaign strategy, and the role of media—have been ignored as well.

Although the study of urban elections and campaigns remains in its infancy there are very promising signs of growth in this field. During the past 15 years there have been at least 11 works published in peer-reviewed outlets that explicitly examine the role and influence of money in urban campaigns, and that prior to 1998 there were no empirically systematic studies on this question. By contrast, the study of money in electoral politics has consumed the attention of congressional and campaigns and election scholars alike (Gierzynski, 2000; Jacobson, 2009), and an entire volume has been devoted to the study of money in state politics (Thompson and Moncrief, 1998). Likewise, since 1990 there have been approximately 20 studies of voter turnout in city elections, employing a variety of methodological approaches, but importantly a very serious effort at large-N, multivariate analysis.

Lack of attention to local elections reflects data constraints. Unlike national elections, there are no central repositories of election and campaign data for local contests. Thus, despite the fact that there are tens of thousands of local governments in the U.S., and hundreds of thousands of local elections (Berry and Howell, 2007: 857), we remain relatively in the dark about the election contests that determine the leadership of them, and the candidates who participate in them.

I begin this article by discussing the context of local elections before discussing trends in municipal voter turnout and models of local voting behavior. I then discuss the connection between local representation systems and descriptive representation on American city councils, a critical topic especially in the wake of the Civil Rights Era and substantial growth in the number of minority elected officials. I then focus on individual level factors that influence election outcomes in cities, including explanations of vote choice, the incumbent advantage, and characteristics of successful non-incumbents. After discussing the theory of deracialization and the role of campaign finance in local elections research, in the penultimate section I discuss school board candidates and elections. I conclude by offering a number of new directions I think scholars of urban campaigns and elections should take in the future.

CITY ELECTIONS

City elections differ from state and federal elections in many key respects. First are the rules that structure city elections and the nature of political representation. While all city councils are elected by the people, only 76 percent of cities directly elect their mayors. Approximately 77 percent of U.S. cities employ nonpartisan ballots in the selection of local officials (MacManus and Bullock, 2003: 15). By contrast, nonpartisan elections are nonexistent at the national level and only one state—Nebraska—employs nonpartisan ballots in the selection of state officials. Nonpartisan ballots mean that most cities use nonpartisan primaries and runoffs in the selection of local officials.

Some 17 percent of cities elect city councilors on the basis of single member districts, while 66 percent elect councilors At-large or via multi-member districts. Seventeen percent of cities employ a combination of districts and At-large seats in what are commonly referred to as mixed systems. Whereas state and national general elections typically occur at the same time, elections to local office are more often than not held in years in which state and national contests are not on the ballot. There are no bicameral city councils, and the typical council has only six members (Moulder, 2008: 33). Term limits is a more recent institutional adaptation, but its reach is fairly limited with only nine percent of cities using them (MacManus and Bullock, 2003). Whether city council terms are staggered or coterminous and the timing of local elections also varies across cities. Most cities employ staggered city council terms in order to maintain a sense of continuity in policymaking, and to minimize the disruption that would likely result from the removal—in one fell swoop—of all incumbent councilors. See Table 9.1.

The second important difference from state and national elections is the nature of local populations, and, importantly, local electorates. Elections and campaigns in large

Table 9.1 Descriptive Data on Election Structures by Institution

City Councils		Mayors	
Average Size	6	Directly Elected	76%
District Representation	17%	Directly Elected (Mayor Council)	96%
At-large Representation	66%	Directly Elected (Council Manager)	67%
Mixed Representation	17%	1 year terms	14%
2 year terms	22%	2 year terms	35%
4 year terms	59%	3 year terms	6%
Staggered Terms	85%	4 year terms	45%

Note: Data for cell entries are from MacManus and Bullock (2003) and Moulder (2008).

U.S. cities—and increasingly in smaller suburban jurisdictions—are directly affected by the intense population diversity that exists in these places. This diversity affects all aspects of the electoral process, from voter turnout to candidate emergence to election outcomes. This is especially true in elections for citywide office where multi-ethnic and multi-racial candidate pools are commonplace, and where racial voting is a big part of the campaign storyline. Consequently, urban scholars have devoted considerable attention to the role of race and ethnicity in local elections.

Voter Turnout

There is no central database that allows scholars to gauge urban voter turnout in the U.S. What we know about urban voter turnout comes from the efforts of individuals or teams of scholars collecting data on samples of cities. One thing is certain, however—cities have witnessed a decline in participation in local elections over the last several decades. According to Caren's (2007) study of large U.S. cities (peak population of 500,000), average turnout between 1978 and 2003 was 27 percent of eligible voters. Moreover, average turnout had declined 20 percent during this time frame. It is apparent then that broader trends in voting seen in American politics apply locally as well (but see McDonald and Popkin, 2001), despite the fact that local elections take place in relatively smaller jurisdictions, where the value of each vote cast is, theoretically, higher.

Like voting in state and national elections, those who vote in local elections tend to be better educated and have higher incomes—potentially biasing the local electoral and policy process. Other factors may exacerbate or alleviate the upward socioeconomic bias in turnout. For example, there is a good deal of evidence that institutional arrangements such as council manager government, nonpartisan ballots, and the timing of local elections (Karnig and Walter, 1983; Schaffner, Streb, and Wright, 2001; Wood, 2002; Hajnal and Lewis, 2003; Caren, 2007) influence local voter turnout. Reformed cities and cities that hold their elections in years in which state and national partisan elections are not being held usually see lower turnout. Cities that are economically diverse may stimulate greater interest in local political affairs thus increasing turnout (Oliver, 1999). Some evidence indicates that turnout is greater in areas where there is less neighborhood poverty and more social connectedness (Alex-Assensoh, 1997).

A significant question concerns the effect of city size on turnout in municipal elections, and bears directly on the debate concerning the structure of metropolitan regions and the effects of fragmentation versus consolidation on democratic citizenship. Residents of large cities are less likely to know, much less be mobilized by, neighbors to participate in city elections, consequently, they are less likely to be interested in local politics, another factor that causes residents of these locales to withdraw from civic activities (Oliver, 2000). Kelleher and Lowery (2004), however, argue that city size has little effect on voter turnout in city council elections. Their study of aggregate voter turnout in 332 municipalities in 12 urban areas suggests that city size is unimportant to voter participation and that greater concentration of local governments within metropolitan areas is likely to produce greater turnout. At the core of their argument, in contrast to Oliver, is the notion that in highly concentrated areas the scale and magnitude of local political issues generates substantial discourse and interest, key variables in stimulating greater voter turnout. According to this argument, political fragmentation within metro areas is a key cause of the decline in turnout seen in municipal elections.

Although their primary interest was in determining the influence of institutional factors in voter turnout, Hajnal and Lewis (2003) found that city size has a significant and negative effect on aggregate turnout in California municipalities. Caren (2007), however, found an insignificant relationship between city size and turnout in his over time study of large U.S. cities. Thus there is a great deal of disagreement in the literature about the independent effect of city size on voter turnout. Two of the four studies discussed here, one individual level survey (Oliver, 2000) and one aggregate analysis (Hajnal and Lewis, 2003) suggest a significant and negative effect for city size indicating that closer community ties and greater mobilization opportunities found in smaller places stimulate turnout. But, in two aggregate studies (Kelleher and Lowery, 2004; Caren, 2007), city size is not a significant variable. Instead, as Kelleher and Lowery suggest, turnout is lower in areas that are highly fragmented due to the overall lack of salience and scale of politics required to stimulate enthusiasm and interest about local issues and candidates.

Turnout may also be a function of campaign-related variables. For example, turnout is greater in places where there is aggressive door-to-door canvassing (Green, Gerber, and Nickerson, 2003) and strong electoral competition (Trounstine, 2008). Minority voter turnout is greater when a candidate of the same race or ethnicity is on the ballot (Kleppner, 1985; Barreto, Villareal, and Woods, 2006). Depending on the electoral context, party organizations may work to stimulate or suppress turnout (Bledsoe and Welch, 1987; Erie, 1988; Pelissero, Krebs, and Jenkins, 2000). Erie's (1988) classic study of machine politics shows clearly how party organizations attempt to manipulate turnout for their own ends. Niven (2006), in the only study ever produced on the topic, shows that negative campaign advertising may have positive effects on voter turnout in city elections. In sum, although we tend to think of voter turnout as a class biased activity, a number of other factors—institutional, contextual, and electoral—work to reinforce (or diminish) the bias.

REPRESENTATION SYSTEMS AND DESCRIPTIVE REPRESENTATION

In order to isolate the effects of the election system (district, At-large, mixed) on the descriptive representation of particular population subgroups, numerous factors have to be controlled. In particular scholars have focused on minority population size, minority education, income, and voting age population, mobilization and leadership, and the presence of willing political coalition partners, such as white liberal voters (Engstrom and McDonald , 1981, 1982; Zax, 1990; Browning, Marshall, and Tabb, 2003). All of these factors influence the ability of minorities to be elected to city councils.

The number of seats on the city council—a structural characteristic of local government in the U.S. that varies from place to place—has been linked to the presence of minority councilors (Alozie and Manganaro, 1993: 281). The presence of a minority councilor is a watershed event that positively affects the future electoral prospects of other minority candidates. More generally, At-large elections harm the chances of minorities to be adequately represented on city councils (Engstrom and McDonald, 1981, 1982; Welch, 1990; Zax, 1990; Trounstine and Valdini, 2008) although owing to lower levels of residential concentration, At-large systems harm Latinos less than they harm African Americans (Sass, 2000). By contrast, women generally do better under At-large arrangements (Alozie and Manganaro, 1993; MacManus and Bullock, 1993; Trounstine and Valdini, 2008), in larger cities (Bullock and MacManus, 1991: 185), and in cities with larger councils (Alozie and Manganaro, 1993: 395). District elections also appear to benefit gay and lesbian candidates (Button, Wald, and Rienzo, 1999).

Because African American voters tend to be residentially concentrated, district systems produce more adequate descriptive representation for this group than for Latinos, who are less residentially concentrated. In short, districts matter less for groups that are either not concentrated or are so large that At-large systems are more beneficial to a group's electoral prospects, for example, women (Bullock and MacManus 1991; Trounstine and Valdini, 2008). However, because of changes in the law that have expanded black political opportunities, greater acceptability of black political involvement, and changes in the campaigns of black candidates, the negative effect of at-large systems for African Americans appears to have diminished over time (Sass and Mehay, 1995; Hajnal, 2007).

By turning to individual election outcomes at the mayoral level, two recent studies add to the important discussion of descriptive representation in cities. Hajnal and Trounstine's (2005) research on simulated election turnout and mayoral election outcomes in 10 large U.S. cities indicates that had whites and minorities voted at the same rate, election outcomes would have been different in three of the ten cases they examined. Although this is not particularly impressive, their simulation indicates that Latino voters would have gained the most with even turnout. In each of the three cases where even turnout by racial group would have changed the outcome of the election, the candidate favored by Latinos would have won. They also found, based on a sample of nearly 1700 cities, that higher actual turnout is linked to significantly greater levels of city council representation of Latinos and Asian Americans, holding constant the institutional and social/demographic variables identified as important to descriptive representation on U.S. city councils.

Descriptive representation on city councils may also enhance the ability of minorities to win in mayoral elections. Marschalland Ruhil (2009) show that the election of an African American is a function in part of the degree to which blacks are represented on city councils. Although it is not clear why these relationships hold, one might speculate that minority presence on the council not only provides a kind of farm system for mayoral candidates, but as a base of official support in mayoral election campaigns as well. They also argue that African American mayors are more likely to be elected in unreformed systems (i.e., those that employ a council manager form of government as opposed to the more politicized mayor council form) because of the lack of strong parties or established organizations that may limit the advancement of "outsider" candidates. Studies of the effects of voter turnout on descriptive representation and possible connections among elected officials, political organizations, and the election of minority mayors offer new insights and new questions for scholars of urban elections and institutional effects.

VOTE CHOICE IN URBAN ELECTIONS

The race or ethnicity of candidates plays a considerable role in determining election outcomes in local politics because it can signal to voters that candidates are in some way either like them or unlike them in terms of goals, values, and experiences. The finding that candidates' race or ethnicity provides voters with useful information can have powerful influence on elections. As Lieske (1989: 169) concluded in his study of Cincinnati: "In sum, there is nothing…to alter our ethnocultural interpretation of urban electoral politics. If anything, the results of this research provide support to a growing body of thought that is reinterpreting American electoral politics within a framework of racial, ethnic, and cultural conflict." Because voters often choose candidates on the basis of racial or ethnic reasons, it is important to consider this variable in models of election outcomes.

Because urban electorates tend to be more racially and ethnically diverse than state and national electorates, a central issue is under what circumstances will voters of one race crossover to support candidates of another race. Some argue that crossover voting is a function of context, and that voters who reside in diverse neighborhoods are more likely to support candidates of a different race (Carsey, 1995). Others suggest that racial competition within voting precincts is likely to produce more racially polarized voting, and that crossover voting is more likely when one group is dominant at the neighborhood or precinct level (Liu and Vanderleeuw, 2007). In other words, racial polarized voting is more likely as groups compete at the local level but diminishes when one group dominates.

Racial factors may only dominate urban elections when race explicitly enters the campaign or issue environment (for example, in the event of a high profile racial incident), and that under normal conditions party and ideology matter more in local voters' decisions (Kaufmann, 2004; but see Abrajano, Nagler, and Alvarez, 2005). Others point to the role of performance in reducing the effect of race in voters' decisions. Stein, Ulbig, and Post's (2005 study of multiethnic Houston found that race mattered in minority candidates' first bid for office, but that after winning, white and African American voters (but not Hispanics) evaluated incumbents on the basis of their performance. Hajnal (2007) examined 52 black challenger and black incumbent elections involving white opponents. He found that white candidate quality, and newspaper and party endorsements were more important considerations for white voters when black candidates were running as incumbents. Race alone, however, was a far more significant predictor of white support for black challengers. Because the shift in white support cannot be statistically attributable to indicators of job performance (crime rates, per capita income, and housing values), Hajnal argues that information generally, in particular experience under black leadership, explains whites' greater willingness to support black incumbents. One's race then (rather than qualifications or experience) would appear to be more important to white voters when black candidates make their first bid for an office, and less when they run as incumbents.

URBAN ELECTION OUTCOMES: THE INCUMBENT ADVANTAGE

A much smaller literature examines city council elections from the standpoint of individual candidates, and in this regard resembles work on state legislative and congressional elections (Hamm and Moncrief, 2008; Jacobson, 2009). Like legislative elections generally, local incumbents—especially in nonpartisan cities—have an electoral advantage (Schaffner, Streb, and Wright, 2001). Survey data from 1986 to 2001 indicate that approximately 86 percent of council incumbents who seek re-election win (Trounstine 2010). Studies of individual cities like Chicago demonstrate that city council incumbents enjoy a roughly 20 point advantage over challengers, with other variables held constant (Krebs, 1998; Gierzynski, Kleppner, and Lewis, 1998).

The sources of the advantage are not clear. Greater name recognition, campaign money and endorsements have been noted as possible sources of the incumbent advantage (Krebs, 1998, 2001). Larger constituencies may provide local incumbents with a buffer from electoral competition vis-à-vis smaller constituencies (Lascher, 2005). The ability to deliver favors and benefits to constituents would also appear to be a critical resource for incumbents (Clingermayer and Feiock, 1995). Examples abound of incumbent mayors, city councilors and school board members using their positions to provide policy benefits to specific constituency groups, be they minority groups (Fraga, Meier, and England, 1986; Meier, Stewart, and England, 1991; Kerr and Mladenka, 1994; Leal, Martinez-Ebers, and Meier, 2004), women (Saltzstein, 1986) or gays and lesbians (Haider-Markel, Joslyn, and Kniss, 2000). Benefits may go beyond material ones. Black city residents report greater satisfaction with their neighborhoods, public schools and police services, when represented by an African American in city government and on school boards (Marschall and Ruhil, 2007). There is also evidence that whites' attitudes about black leadership and race relations generally improve after the election of black mayors (Hajnal, 2007).

Oliver and Ha (2007) focused on suburban jurisdictions to understand if and how incumbents are advantaged. Their survey of voters suggested that the decision of suburban voters to vote for challengers is a function of candidate traits (such as whether they are personally likeable), issue agreement, shared partisan affiliation, and perceptions of local government performance. Context matters as well for whether a voter chooses to vote for an incumbent or challenger in a city council election. In smaller and more diverse suburbs, voters are significantly more likely to be interested in and aware of local political affairs and are therefore more likely to know something about challengers, a contextual effect that produces greater support for challengers. This research suggests that the incumbent advantage in city council elections may be limited to big cities, and that models of voting in legislative elections developed with data on state and national candidates may not apply to American suburbs.

The larger implication of electoral competition is democratic accountability. After all, if we cannot hold elected officials accountable at the ballot box, elections may be irrelevant. Unfortunately, despite Oliver and Ha's (2007) finding that incumbent councillors enjoy less of a personal advantage in suburban elections, they still tend to be re-elected, especially in larger cities (Krebs, 1998). If the key to accountability is electoral competition that draws voters into the political process (Schattschneider 1960), what factor might work to undermine the incumbent advantage? There have been only a few studies that examine council election outcomes in a multivariate context at the level of individual candidates. In large cities especially, strong challengers need money to translate their experience and qualifications into votes. This, however, is hard to come by given the strategic behavior of donors who hedge their bets and protect their interests by giving disproportionately to incumbents and candidates for open seats (Fleischmann and Stein, 1998; Krebs, 2001; Adams, 2007). Challengers with some name recognition, familiarity, and legitimacy among voters do better than challengers with fewer of these political resources (Lieske, 1989; Krebs, 1998). Newspaper endorsements—a key source of information for voters—have been shown to be important predictors of election outcomes (Stein and Fleischmann, 1987). Candidates with high status occupations (e.g. attorneys) and experience in nonpartisan and civic organizations often perform better in city council elections than candidates who lack these experiences (Lieske, 1989).

In addition to personal attributes, party and/or group support is often a prerequisite for political success. Nonpartisanship has clearly weakened local political parties but by no means has it removed partisan activity in cities with such ballot forms (Bledsoe and Welch, 1987). This is clearly the case in Chicago where the Democratic Party remains one of the most powerful institutions in local politics. Similarly, the Democratic and Charter parties play important roles in Cincinnati politics, influencing the outcomes of city council elections there (Lieske, 1989). In cities without strong party organizations, nonpartisan slating groups may play a key role in election outcomes. Endorsements from nonpartisan slating organizations, for example, have been significantly linked to local election outcomes in Texas cities (Fraga, 1988). Both party and nonparty endorsements confer legitimacy on candidates, and more importantly offer up a source of financial support and foot soldiers key to victory in these local contests.

Even if all of these factors are in place, voters ultimately have to decide to part with the familiar, namely the incumbent. Moreover, it is unlikely that challengers with these qualifications and advantages are likely to emerge against strong incumbents. Instead they will wait for an open seat opportunity and take their chances against other strong non-incumbents (Krebs, 1999).

Urban Campaigns

The Role of Deracialization

Political candidates use campaigns to court voters and generate support. For minority candidates competing in white dominant contexts an important strategic consideration is whether or not to deracialize their appeals in an effort to attract white crossover support. In a deracialized campaign racial issues are deemphasized and issues with broader appeal are stressed (Hajnal, 2007). The political downside of deracialized campaigning is that it may trigger a backlash among one's core supporters whose support on Election Day is only lukewarm (Longoria, 1999; Austin Wright and Middleton, 2004). Considerable research has considered the implications of deracialized campaigns.

According to McCormick and Jones (1993: 77) a deracialized campaign is one that seeks to "deemphasize those issues that may be viewed in explicitly racial terms, for example, minority set-asides, affirmative action, or the plight of the black underclass, while emphasizing those issues that appear to transcend the racial question," such as government management, public safety and economic growth (McCormick and Jones,

1993; Metz and Tate, 1995; Underwood, 1997; Liu, 2003; Austin Wright and Middleton, 2004). A deracialized campaign is in contrast to an insurgent campaign designed to mobilize minority group members and liberal white supporters by stressing progressive themes on social issues like economic justice, discrimination, and civil rights. An insurgent campaign is one bent on challenging the existing political order (Persons, 1993: 45).

Focusing on black candidates, Perry (1991: 184–6) highlights three types of successful electoral activity. The first most closely reflects insurgent campaigns in which black candidates running in majority white districts stick primarily to issues of concern to blacks, with only token appeal to issues of more general concern. The second involves black candidates running against each other in black majority districts. Given the likelihood of a split in the black electorate, small shifts in the preferences of white voters decide the election. Thus, candidates quietly seek support from whites, fearing a black voter backlash if candidates court white voters too aggressively. A third type of successful black electoral activity is when blacks running against whites in majority white districts make strong appeals for white votes. This third type of campaign strategy is the prototypical deracialized campaign. Although most research on deracialization has focused on African-American candidates (Liu, 2003; Vanderleeuw, Liu, and Marsh, 2004), a deracialized strategy may apply equally to Latino candidates (Hero, 1987; Juenke and Sampaio, 2008).

Attracting crossover votes is one strategic issue for minority candidates. A second is maintaining minority group unity in the face of internal threats. Internally, blacks may splinter on socioeconomic, religious, and issue lines, causing a failure to successfully unify behind black candidates (Jackson, 1987). There also may be generational factors that divide older from younger minority voters (Jackson, Gerber and Cain, 1994). In Memphis, disagreements among blacks and a majority vote rule conspired to keep an African American from the mayoralty long after demographic conditions suggested it was possible. Only in 1991 with a direct appeal to black interests and a change in the rules allowing a plurality vote winner did Memphis elect its first black mayor (Vanderleeuw, Liu, and Marsh, 2004). Machine-style politics in cities such as New York, Chicago, and Baltimore, often splits minority group leaders aligned with white ethnic machine officials from more progressive minority leaders, creating a barrier to successful minority political action (Mollenkopf, 2003; Orr, 2003; Pinderhughes, 2003). While the nature of black and Latino group cohesion is potentially problematic under the best of circumstances, recent immigration patterns that diversify these groups in terms of nationality, further complicate the picture (Rogers, 2006).

Campaign Finance

While racial politics in cities has received the lion's share of attention from urban scholars, scant attention has been given to the topic of campaign finance in city contests, despite the fact that Michael Bloomberg spent approximately $70 million of his own funds to win the mayoralty of New York City in 2001. A significant research complication is that there is no one place to go to gather fundraising and spending data on municipal candidates. Moreover, the laws are different across states and cities complicating comparisons. The availability of information electronically has lessened the data collection problem considerably, but any number remain of issues regarding the quality of campaign finance reports.

Existing work has focused entirely on a handful of big cities. In general, donors to local campaigns are by and large strategic. Money tends to flow to the most important executive offices and to incumbents and candidates in open seat races (Fleischmann and Stein, 1998). Given the state of our knowledge concerning local campaign finance it is important to discuss who or what types of interests participate by giving to candidates and campaigns. According to Fleischmann and Stein's (1998) study of contributions to local candidates in St. Louis and Atlanta, business and the legal community were the primary donors in these contests followed by donations from the development community (e.g. commercial/residential developers, property management, real estate, title firms, construction and contracting, planning, architecture, and engineering interests). Krebs (2005) found that corporate interests dominate campaign contributions in Los Angeles city elections, but not all corporate interests are equally active. Within the corporate community, professional and development interests are most active, followed by several different corporate interests (entertainment, financial, retail/services, miscellaneous business), and manufacturing and transportation/public works concerns. Among non-corporate donors, homeowner, environmental and social advocacy interests were key players. Both studies indicate that development interests are not as dominant in city politics as might be expected given the prominence of land use matters on local policy agendas, and in theoretical models of city politics (Peterson 1981).

Candidates' fund-raising coalitions, or the mix of groups and individuals they get to back them financially, may depend on the ideological and issue positions candidates represent. For example, Chicago mayor Harold Washington's political coalition was based in neighborhood organizations and progressive activists. Consequently, he raised more money from political sources, public employee unions, and neighborhood interests and less from downtown corporate, real estate and financial interests. By contrast, Richard M. Daley, a more centrist and probusiness mayor, raised more money from downtown corporate, real estate and financial interests. As incumbents, however, both mayors' fundraising coalitions became more inclusive as one would expect given the power of incumbency (Krebs and Pelissero, 2001). In open seat mayoral elections, competitive candidates draw funds from a remarkably similar coalition of donors, mainly from those in the business community, including real estate, legal, and financial sources, as well as smaller amounts from labor organizations (Adams, 2007).

Although certain candidate attributes like incumbency and political experience advantage some over others (Krebs, 2001), the flow of contributions within local races is a dynamic process prone to change as candidates move up or down in the polls or are subject to positive and negative information about their campaigns. Fuchs, Adler, and Mitchell (2000) found that candidates in New York City mayoral elections benefited from polls showing the race narrowing as Election Day neared. Using a measure of momentum based on positive and negative news coverage, Krebs and Holian (2007 found that candidates' weekly contributions largely tracked positive and negative news coverage in the 2001 Los Angeles mayoral elections. Both studies found that contributing behavior is a function of candidate ideology. Viable, but ideologically more extreme candidates benefitted from defensive contributing—the tendency of committed followers to rally to their favored candidate—in the face of negative information.

School Board Elections

Minority Representation

A second area of local elections research—not as large the city elections research, but one in which there is currently a great deal of research activity—is that of school boards. In many ways school board elections resemble other types of urban elections. School board members are typically elected in nonpartisan elections, and are selected in At-large elections. The size of most school boards is relatively small, between 5 and 9 members, who are typically elected in off cycle contests. As in municipal elections, the institutional foundations of school board elections were constructed during the progressive era when education reformers sought to rid public education of partisan politics and machine dominance, and to inject professionalism into school administration. Indeed, the school board and superintendent model of school administrations mirrors the council-manager form of government advocated by urban government reformers, and found in approximately 50 percent of U.S. cities. The major difference of course between school boards and city governments is that school boards deal only with education, while cities are general purpose governments.

Given these similarities it is not surprising then that research on school board elections has largely followed the trajectory of research on city elections. In the wake of the Civil Rights Era, scholars turned their attention to the efforts of black and Latino communities to achieve representation on local school boards, asking the same question posed by city government scholars (indeed, many of the principal players in this literature were and are the same people); namely, what is the effect of different representation schemes on the election of minorities to school boards? Before turning to this question, however, it is important to point out that political resources, in particular the size of the minority population within a school district, is key to understanding variation in minority representation on school boards (Fraga, Meier, and England, 1986; Meier, Stewart, and England 1991; Marschall, 2005; Rocha, 2007). Research also indicates some regional differences with blacks underrepresented on school boards in southern states (Arrington and Watts, 1991; Meier, Stewart, and England, 1991), and Latinos overrepresented in the American Southwest (Marschall, 2005: 194) and underrepresented in the Midwest and Northeast (Rocha, 2007).

Minority population within a district works in concert with structural characteristics to advance minority representation. Leal, Martinez-Ebers, and Meier (2004), for example, demonstrate that the presence of district elections positively affects Latino representation on school boards (but see Rocha, 2007). There is an interaction effect, however, between the size of the minority population and the type of representation scheme in place. Latinos are underrepresented regardless of whether At-large or district systems are in place, but when Latinos are a minority of the population, the negative effect of At-large arrangements makes this situation worse. More specifically, the relationship between population size and election structure is nonlinear; when Latinos are in the minority they are underrepresented regardless of the election system in place, but the size of the underrepresentation is greater when Latinos are in the minority and when At-large is the selection method used (Leal et al., 2004: 1235; see also Meier and Juenke, 2005). As is the case with city elections, school board elections held under districts are more beneficial to black representation than to Latinos (Stewart, England, and Meier, 1989; Marschall 2005).

Voting

Systematic data on turnout in school board elections is difficult to come by. Studies of voter turnout in school districts note that average voter turnout in school board elections is often less than a quarter of eligible voters (Michelson, 2003). Some refer to turnout being "notoriously low" (Moe, 2005: 286). Berry and Howell's (2007) otherwise terrific piece on retrospective voting references no data on voter turnout. Suffice it to say the school board elections are low turnout, low salience affairs that involve minimal campaigning and voters who possess minimal information.

Marschall (2001) studied a number of different forms of political participation among parents of school age children in New York City, one of which was voting in school board elections. Different variables predict voting by Whites, African Americans, and Latinos in a model of turnout in school board elections. For Whites and Latinos, the number of social ties a voter has the more likely he or she is to vote in school board elections. The depth of one's involvement in the community is linked to voting for both Latinos and African-Americans, while the degree that one is politically integrated is a significant predictor of Anglo-White voters' participation in school board elections. Thus, a combination of one's psychological orientation, social context and political resources is thought to predict local political involvement, although the nature of the sample in this study limits generalizability. Both Michelson (2003), and Green, Gerber, and Nickerson (2003), report that participation in school board elections increases as a result of direct mobilization efforts, i.e., door-to-door voter contacts.

Others have examined minority coalition-building in school elections. Marschall (2005) examined black and Latino representation on school boards in 196 districts contained in four U.S. metro areas (Los Angeles, Atlanta, Boston, and Detroit). Although her study was primarily concerned with the link between selection method—districts or At-large—and the number of blacks and Latinos serving on school boards, she did find that the percentage of Latinos living in the district was positively related to the number of both Latinos and blacks serving on local school boards. Interestingly she found that the percentage of blacks, although significantly linked to the number of black school board representatives, was negatively related to the number of Latino school board representatives.

A possible explanation for this somewhat curious finding regarding the link between blacks in the population and Latino school board representatives is offered by Rocha (2007). Analyzing black and Latino school board representation in over 1,300 school districts, Rocha finds that interminority voter coalitions in school board elections are not only difficult to fashion, but influenced by the presence of Latino noncitizens and partisan election ballots. For example, both blacks and Latinos are better represented in places with larger Latino populations, but Latinos are worse off in places with larger black populations, whereas blacks are better off. The benefit that blacks gain from larger Latino populations stems predominantly from the presence of Latino noncitizens who are counted in the overall population but, because they cannot vote, do not play a role in multi-racial coalition building. This suggests black and Anglo voters coalesce to elect black in places with large Latino noncitizen populations. The challenge of interminority coalition building is perhaps lessened under partisan ballot arrangements, as, presumably, party affiliation and loyalty smooth over interethnic tensions. In places with partisan ballots, the size of the African American population has a negative but not significant effect on Latino representation, whereas the Latino population is significantly related to the representation of both blacks and Latinos. Importantly, the tendency of blacks to be better represented in places with larger Latino populations does not appear to be a function of the presence of Latino noncitizens. Indeed, as the percentage of Latino citizens in a district increases, so too does the likelihood of black representation. The actual role of local party organizations in bridging these divides, however, is not examined.

School board incumbents who seek re-election are very likely to be returned to office. But, as Berry and Howell (2007) point out under the right conditions voters may reward and punish incumbents based on the performance of local public schools. Changes in test scores from one year to the next decreased support for school board incumbents while increases in school funding improved incumbent vote shares. Furthermore, incumbents are more likely to strategically retire, and to face competition when made vulnerable by declining test scores. It is important that these results held in only one of three election cycles examined by Berry and Howell, and that the one in which these findings held was accompanied by substantially more media attention. When school board elections decreased in salience, so too did evidence of retrospective voting.

School Board Campaigns

In general, school board campaigns are generally low salience affairs with candidates spending very little money and with interest groups not being a major factor (Deckman, 2004: 168). Spending and interest group involvement tends to be greater in larger school districts given the relative attractiveness of those seats compared to seats on smaller school boards (Hess and Leal, 2005). School board candidates are, at root, community volunteers.

One point of debate in school board elections research is the role of interest groups. Conventional wisdom suggests that teachingunions, parent organizations, racial and ethnic groups, religious organizations, and the business community are the dominant actors in helping to shape outcomes in ways favorable to their interests. However, according to Hess and Leal's (2005) national survey of school boards, teachers' unions and business contribute very little in the way of campaign contributions, and "neither religious organizations nor race-based groups were thought by board members to wield much influence on board decisions or on elections" (249). Interestingly, teachers' unions were thought to be influential despite their limited role in funding local political campaigns, suggesting that their power stems from non-monetary activities such as recruiting campaign volunteers, and working for favored candidates (see also Adams, 2008).

Moe's (2005) survey of school board candidates in California suggests that teachingunions play a powerful role in elections, one that is nevertheless conditioned by local circumstances and political strategy. In larger school districts, unions have greater capacity and are far more active than they are in smaller districts. In smaller districts, however, because there are fewer interest group competitors, teacher unions are actually more successful in getting favored candidates elected. There is also a partisan component to this: the power of unions is less in Republican than in Democratic districts in part because unions endorse candidates whose views are more moderate with respect to union concerns. Not so in Democratic districts where unions who, behaving strategically, endorse candidates more closely aligned with union interests. Union strength appears at its height in the case of the endorsements they make in open seat elections. In these contests union-backed candidates are far more aggressive in their commitment to and advocacy of union issues. In incumbent races, unions endorse less sympathetic incumbents knowing that incumbents are likely to win re-election. In summary, union power comes through endorsements and non-monetary campaign activities, and is constrained by practical politics and the strategic needs of union political interests.

Others have studied candidate emergence patterns in school board contests. Using a national sample of school board candidates, stratified by school district size, Deckman (2004, 2007a, 2007b) focused on a number of issues pertinent to our understanding of candidate emergence and campaigns for school board offices. Most school board candidates, like candidates for other offices, are better educated and have higher incomes than the average person, and most are encouraged to run by friends and family, community and school board leaders, rather than political elites or political parties (Deckman, 2004: 168). Men are more likely than women to say they decided to run for school board to influence education policy, and to apply their religious or moral beliefs to school policy. Very few candidates are motivated to serve on a school board by a desire to gain political experience, but of those who are, most are politically active and were encouraged to run by a party or politician (Deckman, 2007a: 552). In contrast to what we know of women candidates for other offices, more female school board candidates are Republican than Democrat and more are moderate-to-conservative as opposed to liberal in their ideological leanings. Women candidates, though, take less extreme positions on hot button school issues—teaching evolution, multiculturalism, prayer in school—than men candidates, and women tend to have more mainstream policy views than do men (Deckman, 2007b). Interestingly and contra conventional wisdom, candidates aligned with the Christian Right—a group that became very active in school board politics during the 1990s—are no more successful than candidates who are not aligned (Deckman, 2004).

Areas of Future Inquiry

Serious study of local elections and campaigns is becoming a real possibility as more information about local candidates, election outcomes, and campaign finance become available in electronic format. Systematic, large-N studies will remain difficult to execute, but moving beyond case studies and therefore toward greater generalizability is clearly now a do-able option. Not only is the future bright when it comes to assembling data to investigate local campaigns and elections, the field is wide open in terms of possible topic areas. As noted at the outset, institutional and demographic variety across local governments makes these units particularly inviting venues to test our most significant theories of politics.

How representation systems affect the composition of city councils and school boards is fairly well settled. Districts help groups that are geographically concentrated. Importantly, district election systems may not always be called upon to increase minority representation. As the nation continues to diversify it may be that white residents in many areas will be turning to districts to ensure representation on local governing bodies. Others areas of inquiry have received a large amount of coverage (voter turnout, racial voting patterns), but by no means are the issues settled as we see in the case of the institutions-representation studies.

One area that requires significant attention is candidate emergence. Although this was a critical component of the Bay Area Studies research agenda of the early 1970s, it has gone largely forgotten in the intervening years (see Black, 1972; Krebs, 1999; Deckman, 2007a). Interestingly, that agenda produced the insight that local politicians were largely volunteers unconcerned with re-election, and remains a standard way to think about how these actors approach their roles (Prewitt, 1970). The striking aspect of this work related to the fact that local officeholders lacked ambition and therefore an incentive to adequately represent the public's views in policy-making. Of course, much has changed since that time, especially with regard to the role played by the local business communities in recruiting candidates. Local candidates in the same Bay Area communities studied by Prewitt and others are far more likely to bring with them a policy-driven ideological agenda in direct contrast to the status quo oriented candidates of the past (Ehrenhalt, 1992). With close to 90,000 local governments in the United States, the question of what motivates citizens to enter the political realm as candidates and the process of candidate recruitment is a critical one because of connection to democratic accountability and the policies produced by these governing bodies.

Along these lines research into urban elections has largely ignored candidates' campaigns, especially at the city council level. By contrast mayoral campaigns have received a great deal of attention, although the case study orientation of this work has limited its impact. What are the major issues of these campaigns? How are the issues framed? Oliver and Ha's (2007) recent work on suburban elections tells us a great deal about the role of issues, challengers, and incumbents on the decisions of suburban voters, but the role of candidates in presenting issues and arguments for their continuation in office or repudiation of incumbent officeholders is missing. How does official nonpartisanship influence the kinds of issues candidates focus on? How does it affect the voters' choices? Schaffner, Streb, and Wright (2001) provide some sense of this, but their analysis is limited to three cities, making generalizations difficult.

Campaign finance has been and continues to be a major topic in state and federal elections research, but we know relatively little about the role of campaign finance in local elections. Because most city council and school board elections do not require much in the way of campaign spending, one can reasonably argue that extensive inquiry is not needed or is irrelevant. In large cities where incumbency return rates are higher, political positions are more important, and public scrutiny is more intense, campaign finance issues are not only more prominent but more pertinent to the health of local political systems. Like we find at the state level (see Thompson and Moncrief, 1998), there is great variation across cities in terms of how cities regulate campaign finance. Portland and Albuquerque, for example, have an option for candidates to have their campaigns entirely publicly financed. New York City and Los Angeles have a matching funds program. Chicago, by contrast, has very few limits on campaign finance. How do these different systems influence election outcomes, peoples' trust in the political process, and public policy outputs? Fundraising networks or coalitions and fundraising dynamics also deserve greater attention.

Urban scholars have been at the forefront of minority candidates' rhetorical strategies, especially deracialization. Empirically, though, the case study orientation of the research, although necessary and often the only route to studying the issue, limits efforts to test the theory. In most cases the campaigns of candidates in a particular city in a particular election are compared to each other with a focus on the nature of issues discussed by the minority candidate(s). If a minority candidate downplays racial issues, to what standard might this be compared? Often the evidence here is mostly anecdotal with researchers making a case that a particular candidate ran a deracialized campaign based on news coverage or some other indicators of the campaign, followed by an empirical treatment of the effects, in particular votes won by minority candidates from different racial and ethnic groups. What is needed is a more systematic treatment of the campaigns run by both minorities and non-minorities in both multiracial and single race contexts. In this way we can determine how the presence of a minority candidate influences the content of issue discussion. As Collet (2008) notes, the campaigns of minority candidates are highly subtle and different issues are interpreted differently by different constituencies. The degree to which campaigns are geared to particular segments of the voting population is therefore a key issue.

The link between incumbents' policy and constituency activities and electoral margins has not been studied. One area therefore for future research then is to explore the nature of the local electoral connection. Another area ripe for additional study is the influence of partisanship and ideology in vote choice. Although Browning, Marshall and Tabb (2003) have long noted the significance of ideology in urban voter coalitions, only Kaufmann (2004) explicitly models partisanship and ideology as central to voters' decisions in cities. And while roughly threequarters of all cities employ nonpartisan ballots, the issue of voters' partisan preferences and how they influence who wins and, more generally, the dynamics of campaigns, is never far from the surface. A very promising sign of research in this vein has to do with retrospective voting. Berry and Howell (2007) make a compelling case that studying voting in elections to single function positions (like school boards, sheriff, controller) is a useful way to test the theory of retrospective voting since voters have only one functional responsibility to consider. There has, however, been very little effort to examine systematically the evidence for retrospective voting in mayoral and council elections. How do crime rates, housing starts, local unemployment influence the re-election prospects of local incumbents? Do voters reward and punish on the basis of performance? Some evidence suggests that performance matters. More evidence and analysis is required to test this.

The study of local elections has made numerous contributions to our understanding of politics in America. While great strides have been made in the last 20 years (after a fallow period following the outpouring of research on the structure-descriptive representation question), there is nevertheless much work to de done in virtually all aspects of the urban campaigns and elections field. Certainly the lack of progress on many questions reflects the costs of data acquisition on cities and other local governments, but it also reflects the interests of urban scholars, who have largely downplayed the notion that electoral politics is at all important to city governance. Now that many have debunked this notion, and because national demographic trends suggest that America will look more like its major cities by mid-century, it is time for urbanists to once again put politics, elections and campaigns at the center of urban scholarship.

References

Abrajano, Marisa A., Jonathan Nagler, and R. Michael Alvarez. 2005. "A Natural Experiment of Race-Based and Issue Voting: The 2001 City of Los Angeles Elections." *Political Research Quarterly* 58: 203–18.

Adams, Brian. 2008. "Fund-Raising Coalitions in School Board Elections." *Education and Urban Society* 40: 411–27.

Adams, Brian E. 2007. "Fundraising Coalitions in Open Seat Mayoral Elections." *Journal of Urban Affairs* 29: 481–99.

Alex-Assensoh, Y. 1997. "Race, Concentrated Poverty, Social Isolation, and Political Behavior." *Urban Affairs Review* 33: 209–27.

Alozie, Nicholas O. and Lynne L. Manganaro. 1993. "Black and Hispanic Council Representation: Does Council Size Matter?" *Urban Affairs Quarterly* 29: 276–98.

Arrington, Theodore S., and Thomas Gill Watts. 1991. "The Election of Blacks to School Boards in North Carolina." *Western Political Quarterly* 44: 1099–105.

Austin Wright, Sharon D., and Richard T. Middleton, IV. 2004. "The Limitations of the Deracialization Concept in the 2001 Los Angeles Mayoral Election." *Political Research Quarterly* 57: 283–93.

Barreto, M. A., Villarreal, M. and Woods, N. D. 2005. "Metropolitan Latino Political Behavior: Voter Turnout and Candidate Preference in Los Angeles." *Journal of Urban Affairs* 27: 71–91.

Berry, Christopher R. and William G. Howell. 2007. "Accountability and Local Elections: Rethinking Retrospective Voting." *Journal of Politics* 69: 844–58.

Black, Gordon S. 1972. "A Theory of Political Ambition: Career Choices and the Role of Structural Incentives." *American Political Science Review* 66: 144–59.

Bledsoe, Timothy, and Susan Welch. 1987. "Patterns of Political Party Activity Among U.S. Cities." *Urban Affairs Quarterly* 23: 249–69.

Browning, Rufus P., Dale Rogers Marshall, and David H. Tabb, eds. 2003. *Racial Politics in American Cities.*" 3rd ed. New York: Longman.

Bullock, Charles S. 1990. "Turnout in Muncipal Elections." *Policy Studies Review* 9: 539–49.

Bullock, III, Charles S. and Susan A. MacManus. 1991. "Municipal Electoral Structure and the Election of Councilwomen." *Journal of Politics* 53: 75–89.

Button, James W., Kenneth D. Wald, and Barbara A. Rienzo. 1999. "The Election of Openly Gay Public Officials in American Communities." *Urban Affairs Review* 35: 188–209.

Caren, Neal. 2007. "Big City, Big Turnout? Electoral Participation in American Cities." *Journal of Urban Affairs* 29: 31–46.

Carsey, Thomas M. 1995. "The Contextual Effects of Race on White Voter Behavior: The 1989 New York City Mayoral Election." *Journal of Politics* 57: 221–8.

Clingermayer, James C. and Richard C. Feiock. 1995. "Council Views Toward Targeting of Development Policy Benefits." *Journal of Politics* 57: 508–20.

Collet, Christian. 2008. "Minority Candidates, Alternative Media, and Multi-Ethnic America: Deracialization or Toggling?" *Perspectives on Politics* 6: 707–28.

Deckman, Melissa M. 2004. *School Board Battles: The Christian Right in Local Politics.* Washington, DC: Georgetown University Press.

Deckman, Melissa 2007a. "Gender Differences in the Decision to Run for School Board." *American Politics Research* 35: 541–63.

Deckman, Melissa M. 2007b. "School Board Candidates and Gender: Ideology, Party, and Policy Concerns." *Journal of Women, Politics & Policy.* 28: 87–117.

Ehrenhalt, Alan. 1992. *United States of Ambition: Politicians, Power, and the Pursuit of Office.* New York: Times Books.

Engstrom, Richard and Michael McDonald. 1981. "The Election of Blacks to City Councils: Clarifying the Impact of Electoral Arrangements on the Seats/Population Relationship." *American Political Science Review* 75: 344–54.

Engstrom, Richard and Michael McDonald. 1982. "The Underrepresentation of Blacks on City Councils: Comparing the Structural and Socioeconomic Explanations for South/Non-South Differences." *Journal of Politics* 44: 1088–99.

Erie, Steven P. 1988. *Rainbow's End: Irish-Americans and the Dilemmas of Urban Machine Politics, 1840–1985*. Berkeley: University of California Press.

Fleischmann, Arnold, and Lana Stein. 1998. "Campaign Contributions in Local Elections." *Political Research Quarterly* 51: 673–89.

Fraga, Luis Ricardo. 1988. "Domination Through Democratic Means: Nonpartisan Slating Groups in City Electoral Politics." *Urban Affairs Quarterly* 23: 528–55.

Fraga, Luis R., Kenneth J. Meier, and Robert E. England. 1986. "Hispanic Americans and Educational Policy: Limits to Equal Access." *Journal of Politics* 48: 850–76.

Fuchs, Ester R., E. Scott Adler, and Lincoln A. Mitchell. 2000. "Win, Place, Show: Public Opinion Polls and Campaign Contributions in a New York City Election." *Urban Affairs Review* 35: 479–501.

Gierzynski, Anthony. 2000. *Money Rules: Financing Elections in America*. Boulder, CO: Westview Press.

Gierzynski, Anthony, Paul Kleppner and James Lewis. 1998. "Money or the Machine: Money and Votes in Chicago Aldermanic Elections." *American Politics Research* 26: 160–73.

Green, Donald P., Alan S. Gerber, and David W. Nickerson. 2003. "Getting Out the Vote in Local Elections: Results from Six Door-to-Door Canvassing Experiments." *Journal of Politics* 65: 1083–96.

Haider-Markel, Donald P., Mark R. Joslyn, and Chad J. Kniss. 2000. "Minority Group Interests and Political Representation: Gay Elected Officials in the Policy Process." *Journal of Politics* 62: 568–77.

Hajnal, Zoltan L. 2007. *Changing White Attitudes toward Black Political Leadership*. Cambridge: Cambridge University Press.

Hajnal, Zoltan L. and Paul G. Lewis. 2003. "Municipal Institutions and Voter Turnout in Local Elections." *Urban Affairs Review* 38: 645–68.

Hajnal, Zoltan, and Jessica Trounstine. 2005. "Where Turnout Matters: The Consequences of Uneven Turnout in City Politics." *Journal of Politics* 67: 515–35.

Hamilton, Howard D. 1971. "The Municipal Voter: Voting and Nonvoting in City Elections." *American Political Science Review* 65: 1135–40.

Hamm, Keith and Gary Moncrief. 2008. "Legislative Politics in the States." In *Politics in the American States: A Comparative Analysis, 9th ed.*, eds. Virginia Gray and Russell L. Hanson, Washington DC: CQ Press, 154–91.

Hero, Rodney. 1987. "The Election of Hispanics in City Government: An Examination of the Election of Federico Pena as Mayor of Denver." *Western Political Quarterly* 40: 93–105.

Hess, Frederick M. and David L. Leal. 2005. "School House Politics: Expenditures, Interests, and Competition in School Board Elections." In *Besieged: School Boards and the Future of Education Politics*, ed. William G. Howell. Washington, DC: Brookings Institution Press, 228–53.

Jackson, Byran O. 1987. "The Effect of Racial Group Consciousness on Political Mobilization in American Cities." *Western Political Quarterly* 40: 631–46.

Jackson, Byran O., Elisabeth R. Gerber, and Bruce E. Cain. 1994. "Coalitional Prospects in a Multi-Racial Society: African American Attitudes toward Other Minority Groups." *Political Research Quarterly* 47: 277–94.

Jacobson, Gary C. 2009. *The Politics of Congressional Elections*. 7th ed. New York: Longman.

Juenke, Eric Gonzales, and Anna Christina Sampaio. 2008. "Deracialization and Latino Politics: The Case of the Salazar Brothers in Colorado." *Political Research Quarterly* 61: 1–12.

Karnig, Albert K., and Walter, Oliver. 1983. "Decline in Municipal Voter Turnout." *American Politics Quarterly* 11 (October): 491–506.

Kaufmann, Karen. 2004. *The Urban Voter: Group Conflict and Mayoral Voting Behavior in American Cities*. Ann Arbor, MI: University of Michigan Press.

Kelleher, Christine and David Lowery. 2004. "Political Participation and Metropolitan Institutional Contexts." *Urban Affairs Review* 39: 720–57.

Kerr, Brinck and Kenneth Mladenka 1994. "Does Politics Matter? A Time Series Analysis of Minority Employment Patterns". *American Journal of Political Science* 38: 918–43.

Kleppner, Paul. 1985. *Chicago Divided: The Making of a Black Mayor*. DeKalb, IL: Northern Illinois University Press.

Krebs, Timothy B. 1998. "The Determinants of Candidates' Vote Share and the Advantages of Incumbency in City Council Elections." *American Journal of Political Science* 42: 921–35.

Krebs, Timothy B. 1999. "The Political and Demographic Predictors of Candidate Emergence in City Council Elections." *Urban Affairs Review* 35: 278–99.

Krebs, Timothy B. 2001. "Political Experience and Fundraising in City Council Elections." *Social Science Quarterly* 82: 537–51.

Krebs, Timothy B. 2005. "Urban Interests and Campaign Contributions: Evidence from Los Angeles." *Journal of Urban Affairs* 27: 165–75.

Krebs, Timothy B., and David B. Holian. 2007. "Competitive Positioning, Deracialization, and Attack Speech: A Study of Negative Campaigning in the 2001 Los Angeles Mayoral Election." *American Politics Research* 35: 123–49.

Krebs, Timothy B., and John P. Pelissero. 2001. "Fund-Raising Coalitions in Mayoral Campaigns." *Urban Affairs Review* 37: 67–84.

Lascher, Edward L. 2005. "Constituency Size and Incumbent Safety: A Reexamination." *Political Research Quarterly* 58: 269–78.

Leal, David L., Martinez-Ebers, Valerie, and Kenneth J. Meier. 2004. "The Politics of Latino Elections: The Biases of At-Large Elections." *Journal of Politics* 66: 1224–44.

Lieske, Joel. 1989. "The Political Dynamics of Urban Voting Behavior." *American Journal of Political Science* 33: 150–74.

Liu, Boadong. 2003. "Deracialization and Urban Racial Contexts." *Urban Affairs Review* 38: 572–91.

Liu, Boadong and James Vanderleeuw. 2007. *Race Rules: Electoral Politics in New Orleans, 1965–2006*. Lanham, MD: Lexington Books.

Longoria, Tomas. 1999. "The Impact of Office on Cross-Racial Voting: Evidence from the 1996 Milwaukee Mayoral Election." *Urban Affairs Review* 34: 596–603.

MacManus, Susan A., and Charles S. Bullock III. 1993. "Women and Racial/Ethnic Minorities in Mayoral and Council Positions." In *The Municipal Year Book 1993*. Washington, DC: International City/County Management Association, 70–84.

MacManus, Susan A. and Charles S. Bullock III. 2003. "The Form, Structure, and Composition of America's Municipalities in the New Millennium." In *The Municipal Year Book 2003*. Washington, DC: International City/County Management Association, 3–18.

Marschall, Melissa J. 2001. "Does The Shoe Fit? Testing Models of Participation for African-American and Latino Involvement in Local Politics." *Urban Affairs Review* 37: 227–48.

Marschall, Melissa J. 2005. "Minority Incorporation and Local School Boards." In *Besieged: School Boards and the Future of Education Politics*, ed. William G. Howell. Washington, DC: Brookings Institution Press, 173–98.

Marschall, Melissa J., and RuhilAnirudh V. S. Ruhil. 2006. "The Pomp of Power: Black Mayoralties in Urban America" *Social Science Quarterly* 87: 828–50.

Marschall, Melissa J., and Anirudh V. S. Ruhil. 2007. "Substantive Symbols: The Attitudinal Dimension of Black Political Incorporation in Local Government." *American Journal of Political Science* 51: 17–33.

McCormick, II, Joseph P., and Charles E. Jones. 1993. "The Conceptualization of Deracialization." In *Dilemmas of Black Politics: Issues of Leadership and Strategy*, ed., Georgia A. Persons. New York: HarperCollins College Publishers, 66–84.

McDonald, Michael P. and Samuel L. Popkin. 2001. "The Myth of the Vanishing Voter." *American Political Science Review* 95: 963–74.

Meier, Kenneth J., and Eric Gonzalez Juenke. 2005. "Electoral Structure and the Quality of Representation on School Boards." In *Besieged: School Boards and the Future of Education Politics*, ed. William G. Howell. Washington, DC: Brookings Institution Press, 199–227.

Meier, Kenneth J., Joseph Stewart, and Robert E. England. 1991. "The Politics of Bureaucratic Discretion: Education Access as an Urban Service." *American Journal of Political Science* 35: 155–77.

Metz, David Haywood, and Katherine Tate. 1995. "The Color of Urban Campaigns." In *Classifying By Race*, ed. Paul E. Peterson. Princeton, N.J.: Princeton University Press, 262–77.

Michelson, Melissa R. 2003. "Getting Out the Latino Vote: How Door-to-Door Canvassing Influences Voter Turnout in Rural Central California." *Political Behavior* 25: 247–63.

Moe, Terry M. 2005. "Teacher Unions and School Board Elections." In *Besieged: School Boards and the Future of Education Politics*, ed. William G. Howell. Washington, DC: Brookings Institution Press, 254–87.

Mollenkopf, John. 2003. "New York: Still the Great Anomaly." In *Racial Politics in American Cities.* 3rd edn, ed. Rufus P. Browning, Dale Rogers Marshall, and David H. Tabb. New York: Longman, 115–42.

Moulder, Evelina R. 2008. "Municipal Form of Government: Trends in Structure, Responsibility and Composition." In *The Municipal Year Book 2008*. Washington, DC: International City/County Management Association, 27–33.

Niven, David. 2006. "A Field Experiment on the Negative Effects of Campaign Mail on Voter Turnout in a Municipal Election." *Political Research Quarterly* 59: 203–10.

Oliver, J. Eric. 1999. "The Effects of Metropolitan Economic Segregation on Local Civic Participation." *American Journal of Political Science* 43: 186–212.

Oliver, J. Eric. 2000. "City Size and Civic Involvement in Metropolitan America." *American Political Science Review* 94: 361–73.

Oliver, J. Eric, and Shang E. Ha. 2007. "Vote Choice in Suburban Elections." *American Political Science Review* 101: 393–408.

Orr, Marion. 2003. "The Struggle For Black Empowerment in Baltimore." In *Racial Politics in American Cities.* 3rd edn, ed. Rufus P. Browning, Dale Rogers Marshall, and David H. Tabb. New York: Longman, 255–74.

Pelissero, John P., Timothy B. Krebs, and Shannon Jenkins. 2000. "Asian Americans, Political Organizations, and Participation in Chicago Electoral Precincts." *Urban Affairs Review* 35: 750–69.

Perry, Huey L. 1991. "Deracialization as an Analtyical Construct in American Urban Politics." *Urban Affairs Quarterly* 27: 181–91.

Persons, Georgia, ed. 1993. *Dilemmas of Black Politics*. New York: HarperCollins.

Peterson, Paul. 1981. *City Limits*. Chicago: University of Chicago.

Pinderhughes, Dianne M. 2003. "Chicago Politics: Political Incorporation and Restoration." In *Racial Politics in American Cities*. 3rd edn, ed. Rufus P. Browning, Dale Rogers Marshall, and David H. Tabb. New York: Longman, 143–66.

Prewitt, Kenneth. 1970. *The Recruitment of Political Leaders: A Study of Citizen-Politicians*. New York: The Bobbs-Merrill Company, Inc.

Rene, R. Rocha. 2007. "Black-Brown Coalitions in Local School Board Elections." *Political Research Quarterly* 60: 315–27

Rogers, Reuel R. 2006. *Afro-Caribbean Immigrants and the Politics of Incorporation: Ethnicity, Exception, or Exit*. New York: Cambridge University Press.

Saltzstein, Grace Hall. 1986. "Female Mayors and Women in Municipal Jobs." *American Journal of Political Science* 30: 140–64.

Sass, Tim R. 2000. "The Determinants of Hispanic Representation in Municipal Government." *Southern Economic Journal* 66: 609–30.

Sass, Tim R., and Stephen L. Mehay. 1995. "The Voting Rights Act, District Elections, and the Success of Black Candidates in Municipal Elections." *Journal of Law and Economics* 38: 367–92.

Schaffner, Brian F., Matthew Streb, and Gerald Wright. 2001. "Teams Without Uniforms: The Nonpartisan Ballot in State and Local Elections." *Political Research Quarterly* 54: 7–30.

Schattschneider, E. E. 1960. *The Semi-Sovereign People: A Realist's View of Democracy in America*. Hinsdale, IL: Dryden Press.

Stein, Robert M., Stacey Ulbig, and Stephanie Post. 2005. "Voting for Minority Candidates in Multi-Racial/Ethnic Communities." *Urban Affairs Review* 41: 157–81.

Stein, Lana, and Arnold Fleischmann. 1987. "Newspaper and Business Endorsements in Municipal Elections: A Test of Conventional Wisdom." *Journal of Urban Affairs* 9: 325–36.

Stewart, Jr., Joseph, Robert E. England, and Kenneth J. Meier. 1989. "Black Representation in Urban School Districts: From School Board to Office to Classroom." *Western Political Quarterly* 42: 287–305.

Thompson, Joel A. and Gary F. Moncrief, eds. 1998. *Campaign Finance in State Legislative Elections*. Washington, DC: Congressional Quarterly Press.

Trounstine, J. 2008. *Political Monopolies in American Cities: The Rise and Fall of Bosses and Reformers*. Chicago: University of Chicago Press.

Trounstine, Jessica. 2010. "Incumbency and Responsiveness in Local Elections." Working Paper.

Trounstine, Jessica and Melody E. Valdini. 2008. "The Context Matters: The Effects of Single-Member versus At-Large Districts on City Council Diversity." *American Journal of Political Science* 52: 554–69.

Vanderleeuw, James, Baodong Liu, and Gregory Marsh. 2004. "Applying Black Threat Theory, Urban Regime Theory and Deracialization: The Memphis Mayoral Elections of 1991, 1995 and 1999." *Journal of Urban Affairs* 26: 505–19.

Underwood, Katherine. 1997. "Ethnicity Is Not Enough: Latino-Led Multiracial Coalitions in Los Angeles." *Urban Affairs Review* 33 (1): 3–27.

Welch, Susan. 1990. "The Impact of At-Large Elections on the Representation of Blacks and Hispanics." *Journal of Politics* 52: 1050–76.

Wood, Curtis. 2002. "Voter Turnout in City Elections." *Urban Affairs Review* 38: 209–31.

Zax, Jeffrey S. 1990. "Election Methods and Black and Hispanic City Council Membership." *Social Science Quarterly* 71: 338–55.

CHAPTER 10

STATE CAMPAIGNS AND ELECTIONS

WILLIAM D. HICKS AND DANIEL A. SMITH

THE study of campaigns and elections in the American states has a decidedly institutional flavor, as well it should. Capitalizing on the variation existing across what are otherwise similar sub-national units of government, scholars of sub-national politics in the United States have examined how an array of political institutions may lead to different campaign environments and electoral outcomes. The range of political institutions affecting political campaigns and elections across the 50 states is dynamic, as the states are continually experimenting with their methods of voter registration, convenience voting (no-excuse absentee, early, and mail), legislative redistricting, campaign finance regulations, political party ballot access, and other institutional rules and procedures. Given the tremendous variation across the states, it only makes sense to take into consideration how political institutions may facilitate—but also may constrain—political participation, as they create incentive structures for candidates, political parties, special interests, and of course, voters. Thus, when it comes to campaigns and elections in the American states, the electoral process is heavily contingent on political institutions.

Arguably, the rise in the scholarly interest of campaigns and elections in the American states is tied to the institutional variation afforded by the 50 states. To be sure, for decades the study of elections and voting has been one of the "mainstays of state politics subfield" (Brace and Jewett, 1995: 648), in large part because the institutional variation across the states has allowed scholars to highlight the contingency of the electoral behavior. There is a distinct methodological advantage in comparing phenomena across similar units with different institutional constraints, as scholars are able to hold constant cultural, economic, and political factors in order to isolate the impact of institutions. As such, campaigns and elections in the American states remain a fruitful topic of study for scholars, as they offer a wealth of research design opportunities, in large part due to the impressive amount of individual- and aggregate-level data across the 50 states.

Of course, as it is with most social science applications, there are limitations to and inherent biases in examinations of state politics. The most commonly leveled criticism of empirical explorations of the effects of institutions on state politics and policy is endogeneity. While institutions affect state politics, "their form and their functioning depend on the conditions under which they emerge and endure" (Przeworski, 2004: 527). Put simply, institutions not only affect political and policy outcomes, but are also the product of political arrangements and conditions. Despite the tendency to acknowledge and theorize about the importance of institutional arrangements, the consequence of endogeneity is that estimating the marginal impact of any single institution becomes exponentially more difficult as underlying conditions vary. Measuring the effects of institutions on political outcomes not only requires comparability across contexts in underlying conditions, but also variation in institutional arrangements and outcomes over time. Meeting these criteria, nevertheless, is probably more likely to occur when examining political participation and policy outcomes across the 50 states, where underlying socioeconomic and political demographics tend to be somewhat similar, than in cross-national studies. While findings regarding institutional effects at the sub-national level may be inherently limited and even biased, instead of providing an incentive for scholars to abandon examinations of state politics, they should inspire scholars of American politics to explore in greater depth the relationships between variables with increasingly sophisticated techniques.

Because of the tremendous analytic advantage of studying the 50 states across space and over time, several studies focusing on campaigns and elections in the American states have rightly become part of the broader American voting and elections scholarly canon. Using comparative state data, scholars have controlled for state-level, socioeconomic conditioning effects—such as education, race and ethnicity, gender, age, and income—in order to isolate potential mobilizing influences—such as electoral and registration laws as well as the use of direct democracy—on political participation, specifically voter turnout (Wolfinger and Rosenstone, 1980; Patterson and Caldeira, 1983; Chubb, 1988; Leighley and Nagler, 1992; Tolbert and Smith, 2005). Our effort here is to assess some important studies that have recently shed light on how state-level political institutions may affect campaigns and electoral competition in the American states.

Throughout our essay, we focus on a central question that frequently animates the study of campaigns and elections in the American states: do political institutions enhance or stymie voter turnout and electoral competition? We begin by considering studies that examine how electoral laws in general may affect voter turnout, electoral competition, and party and candidate strategies. Then we assess whether more stringent campaign contribution limits and clean election laws might provide a greater incentive for potential candidates to challenge incumbents. We then assess, in turn, how primary systems, redistricting, term limits, and direct democracy may affect competition and turnout in the American states. We conclude with a discussion about lingering concerns over endogeneity when it comes to measuring the effect of political institutions on electoral competition and outcomes.

The Impact of Electoral Laws on Turnout, Competition, and Party and Candidate Strategies

What are the effects of electoral laws on voter turnout and electoral competition in the American states? It has become common wisdom that voter turnout fluctuates between presidential and midterm election years. Theories explaining a drop in turnout in midterm years vary, but most assume that information about candidates in midterm elections is costlier for the average voter. High-visibility elections, particularly presidential elections, are argued to stimulate participation by making information more accessible to citizens, whereas low-visibility elections often require citizens to educate themselves about the candidates and thereby reduce the incentives to participate. Contests for state legislature and statewide offices are often described as low-information contests, which raise a host of normative questions concerning democratic accountability, as Matson and Fine (2006) show with their study of local elections.

Might the institutional variation across the states help to explain voter turnout? Jackson (2002) carves out an innovative baseline from which to observe fluctuations in turnout conditional on individual level and contextual factors. He begins by analyzing turnout in midterm years and uses as explanatory variables an interaction term denoting high-visibility elections (Senatorial and/or gubernatorial contest) and the amount of campaign expenditures spent on such elections, controlling for individual characteristics of survey respondents. In midterm election years, high-visibility elections, like an election for governor or U.S. Senate, produce notably higher turnout rates and this effect becomes more pronounced the more money that is spent on these contests. In fact, high-spending, high-visibility contests stimulate nearly as much turnout in midterm years as is expected to occur in presidential years. By showing that elections for governor and Senate have the potential to produce turnout rates as high in midterm election years as they are in presidential years, Jackson's (2002) contribution is a new baseline from which campaign effects on turnout can be more appropriately assessed. Subsequent research, including work by Rigby and Springer (2011) examining electoral reforms—such as the adoption of motor voter and election-day registration laws—have found mixed support in election laws reducing inequality in the electoral process. Even so, these studies are unable to ascertain whether citizens who turn out to vote do so down ballot; that is to say, we know little about voter roll-off.

For their part, Francia and Herrnson (2004) analyze voter turnout in state legislative elections. Basing their analysis on the theoretical bedrock of incentives and barriers, they are primarily concerned with the effect of campaign efforts (incentives), the effect of campaign laws (barriers), and the interaction between the two on voter turnout. The outcome they model is the percentage of the voting-age population that casts votes for state legislative candidates in the 1998 electoral cycle. The data for their independent variables was collected from a hodgepodge of sources, including a survey among

state legislative candidates for information on campaign activity and several referen-
tial sources for demographic and legal characteristics of legislative districts. Their most
important finding is the conditional (they call the synergistic) effect of a three-way
interaction effect of campaign spending, party GOTV efforts, and election-day registration on voter turnout. The multiplicative term is used as an attempt to demonstrate
the effect of incentives, conditional on barriers, on voter turnout. Francia and Herrnson
find that districts with election-day registration and high levels of campaign spending
and party GOTV efforts, are estimated to have 11 percentage points higher turnout than
states without election-day registration and with low levels of campaign spending and
party GOTV efforts. Francia and Herrnson (2004) provide a strong analysis of voter
turnout by controlling for political (for example, the presence of an initiative, statewide
election, and partisan characteristics of the district) and demographic characteristics
(such as aggregate levels of education, age, and ethnicity), while exploring the possible
non-additive effects of incentives and barriers. Even so, as they acknowledge, one major
limitation of this analysis is that it is temporally limited. What is left to be determined is
whether or not the findings can be generalized to other state legislative elections in different years. In other words, the findings may be limited to the 1998 election.

Schaffner, Streb, and Wright (2001) assess the extent to which ballot information
can affect voter behavior. Their creative analysis is framed as a debate between progressive reformers in the early 20th century and more recent political science research.
Progressives, they argue, believed that nonpartisan elections would inspire citizens to
seek out information about candidates independent of party identification, yielding a
more informed electorate and a less corrupt government. Political scientists, however,
have long touted the potential benefits of partisan elections in terms of low cost cues
which funnel reliable information to voters, without which voters will likely abstain or
turn to less reliable information. Based on this discussion, they develop three hypotheses with respect to partisan elections versus nonpartisan elections: (1) turnout is likely
to be lower in nonpartisan races, (2) voters are less likely to vote based on party identification in nonpartisan elections, and (3) given less information, voters in nonpartisan elections are more likely to vote based off the cue of incumbency relative to the
party identification of the office-seekers. Their analysis, more or less, confirms this with
a number of paired tests including an examination of precinct data from Champaign
versus Urbana mayoral races and state Senatorial elections in Nebraska versus Kansas.
Schaffner, Streb, and Wright (2001), no doubt, provide a creative test of the effects of partisan versus nonpartisan elections. One problem, which they acknowledge, with their
analysis is that it relies on precinct- and district-level data. The common worry with
such data is ecological fallacy, inferring individual-level effects based on aggregate data.
Their analysis on voter turnout seems more accurate in the sense that aggregate turnout
tends to be lower in precincts and districts with nonpartisan elections. However, the
effects of incumbency and partisanship as cues seem to be more open to fallacy. It cannot be ascertained the extent to which individuals in nonpartisan districts or precincts
tend to rely on incumbency or partisanship in generating their vote choices. A second
dilemma is that because their data are aggregate, they have insufficient cases to develop

empirical models that control for potential confounding factors. Nevertheless, their analysis is innovative and makes good use of available data.

There is also a growing body of literature suggesting that political institutions can have a major impact on political party and candidate strategies. When it comes to campaigns and elections in the American states, scholars have utilized a variety of research designs to assess how political institutions affect the strategies of candidates and political parties. Ordinarily candidate and party strategies are argued to be a function of incumbent vulnerability, national moods, and campaign spending, in addition to socio-economic and political conditions of the environment. However, it is also conceivable that candidate and party strategies might be related to certain institutions. For example, candidate and political party strategies might be conditioned by electoral laws, as well as the visibility of the offices which candidates seek. How might the variation in political institutions across the states leverage explanatory power for why parties are more engaged in some campaigns than others? In an effort to explain state political party campaign activities, some scholars have undertaken considerable effort to conduct original surveys of political elites so as to isolate the effect of institutional factors on candidate decisions and party campaign activities across the states. While much of the research is concerned with the effect of incumbency and national moods on challenger emergence (Van Dunk, 1997; Kang, Niemi, and Powell, 2003), recent scholarship suggests that electoral laws may have significant effects on the candidate pool.

A good example of this line of research is that of Hogan (2002), who surveyed legislative candidates in seven states following the 1994 elections. Using Likert scale questions with respect to various party activities (broadly categorized as "Grassroots Activities," "Building the Campaign," and "Running the Campaign"), Hogan creates "helpfulness scores" intended to gauge the extent to which candidates perceive party activities as helpful to their campaign efforts. His analysis focuses on both district-level (the competitiveness of the election in terms of campaign spending and electoral margins) and candidate-level (the incumbency status of the candidate and his or her political party) factors. Hogan's most notable finding is the effect of campaign spending on candidates' perceptions of party helpfulness: as campaign spending nears parity between two candidates, they tend to receive more favorable party assistance. The findings, that is, suggest that candidates turn to their respective parties, and parties tend to be more helpful, as elections become more competitive. Although his analysis provides evidence about candidate perceptions of party organizations when it comes to legislative campaigns, it is nonetheless limited in a number of ways. In addition to its cross-sectional (only seven states) and temporal (only 1994) limitations, Hogan overlooks many other state-level institutional or electoral-level effects, such as election-specific effects like the type of primary system and whether or not initiatives were on the ballot. Although Hogan uses fixed-effects for the seven states included in his sample, thereby controlling for such observable and unobservable factors, questions remain about the effects that certain unobserved institutional factors may have on party–candidate relations.

Leveraging the comparative advantage of studying campaigns governed by different political institutions across the 50 states can also help in identifying why some challengers are able to emerge in state legislative elections. Drawing on an original survey of elites conducted in the late 1990s, Abbe and Herrnson (2003) probe alternative explanations for campaign professionalism among state legislative candidates. In order to measure campaign professionalism, they use a count variable derived from survey responses of certain campaign activities in 1997–8, including campaign management, media advertising, issue or opposition research, press relations, and fundraising. In keeping with Carey, Niemi, and Powell's (2000) finding that professional legislatures are more likely to attract career-minded candidates, they argue states with more professional legislative chambers provide candidates with greater incentives to gain and retain office. As such, they expect candidates in these states to be more likely to rely on professional campaigns. Controlling for other factors, including campaign spending and the population of the legislative district, they find mixed results for their legislative professionalism hypothesis, as it tends to be associated with more professional activities among challengers, but not incumbents. They find that district population size tends to have a small and insubstantial effect on campaign professionalism, and that campaign spending is a reliable and substantive predictor of campaign professionalism. In addition, they test the extent to which campaign professionalism (now as an independent variable) affects candidates' vote-share. All else equal, they find campaign professionalism increases vote-share margins for challengers, but not substantially for open-seat candidates or incumbents.

The most apparent challenge to Abbe and Herrnson (2003) is conceptual in origin. First, part of their theoretical framework, especially with respect to legislative professionalism, is based on the notion that campaigns in state legislative elections have become more professional since the 1960s. Hence, campaign professionalism is argued to be a function of growing legislative professionalism over time. This may very well be a true assumption, but the hypothesis is conceptually distinct from the strictly cross-sectional survey research they perform. That is, their empirical tests are not falsifiable in the sense that they do not speak to whether or not campaign professionalism has changed over time. Second, the most notable and substantive finding, that campaign professionalism is a function of campaign spending, although perhaps distinct in measurement, conceptually suffers from endogenous simultaneity. That is to say, despite the fact that these two factors appear to be statistically related, that relationship is potentially biased if campaign spending is simultaneously determined along with campaign professionalism. Insofar as that is true, it is likely that the estimation of the relationship is biased as the error term in the model is statistically related to campaign spending.

It is not news that incumbent state lawmakers tend to have a high likelihood of winning reelection. Although compared to Congress there are a relatively high number of uncontested legislative races (Squire, 2000), reelection rates do vary across the states. Berry, Berkman, and Schneiderman (2000) find that in the 1970s and 1980s, the probability of incumbent victory increased as legislative professionalism increased. In other words, incumbents who serve in professional legislatures are more insulated from spillover effects and national moods (external shocks) relative to incumbents who serve in less professional legislatures, and are thus more likely to win reelection campaigns. Their analysis suggests that professionalism leads to institutionalization, conceived of as an organization's differentiation from the environment. In addition, and notably, they find that district electoral rules affect incumbent success (incumbents in single-member districts are more likely to win relative to incumbents in post-election and multi-member districts). Incumbents, furthermore, benefit from redistricting when the legislature has control over the redistricting process and his or her party has unified control of the government.

Comparing legislative campaigns across the states, Hogan (2001) challenges scholars to reexamine strategic candidate entry at the sub-national level. Specifically, he is interested in whether or not an incumbent state legislator draws a challenger. Compiling data from eight states for two election cycles (midterm and presidential), Hogan assesses the extent to which incumbent war chests (the amount of money they have for campaign purposes prior to the period of challenger entry) affect challenger emergence. He finds that the larger the war chest of an incumbent, the lower the probability of challenger entry. In addition, he finds that the effect of war chests on challenger entry is conditional on legislative professionalism: the negative impact of an incumbent's war chest is most pronounced in states with less professional legislatures, where the seats are presumably less attractive. Hogan's analysis is innovative in the sense that it attempts to provide empirical evidence of the impact of money in state legislative races, as well as to gain some purchase on an integral part of the incumbent advantage. Even so, estimation of challenger emergence is a tricky endeavor. As discussed more below, candidate emergence is not only associated with the amount of money an incumbent raises, but also the expected vote for an incumbent. That is to say, it might be the case that an incumbent has a small war chest, but has a high enough expected vote to dissuade a challenger from entering the race. Bias in estimating the effect of campaign spending on vote shares is consistent with the notion of endogenous simultaneity (Wooldridge, 2002), as campaign spending is determined simultaneously along with the expected vote.

Taking advantage of a unique *Survey USA* poll from May 2005 to 2006, Brown and Jacobson (2008) further prod speculations regarding strategic candidate decision making. Among other things, the strategic candidate thesis generally proposes that the quality of challengers to incumbents is a function of the vulnerability of the incumbent and national moods. The survey they use provides useful information to analyze closer the effect of moods and incumbent vulnerability, given that in 2006 there was a strong anti-Republican national mood associated with the war in Iraq. They prod their survey data in numerous ways with the overall outcome of support for strategic candidate entry: lower levels of support for incumbents in 2005 tend to predict higher spending for challengers in 2006. This, furthermore, tends to be conditional on the party of the incumbent in the sense that Republicans in this time period were relatively more vulnerable and, thus, strategic candidate entry effects were more pronounced for them. What is most notable, though, is that they find differential effects for strategic candidate entry between U.S. Senators and state governors. In Senatorial races, strategic candidate entry was much more apparent than in gubernatorial races.

Speculating as to why they find such a divergence between the offices, Brown and Jacobson argue that Senators, given their lower level of public visibility, tend to be especially prone to blame for national political affairs, while governors tend to be relatively more insulated. They also notably find, in contrast to the strategic candidate thesis, that when incumbent governors spend more money, they generally increase their approval ratings. This effect is usually not observed in congressional elections, in the sense that dollars buy few votes in addition to the incumbency advantage. Although they provide a number of useful tests with respect to strategic candidate entry, their analysis is far from a perfect test. They mostly test simple models which control for very little. Although their tests are certainly suggestive, specification issues remain open to question.

Rather than analyzing the quality of the challengers in gubernatorial elections or the fractionalization of vote margins, Dowling and Lem (2009) provide a cross-sectional analysis of the number of major-party candidates and third-party candidates running for governor over time. Building on their earlier work (Lem and Dowling 2006), they use a count model to predict the number of major-party and third-party gubernatorial candidates running from 1980 to 2005. Additionally, instead of only looking at election-specific factors, such as incumbency and the strength of the incumbent, they use as explanatory variables a number of election-law factors (the percentage of signatures required for candidate entry, the cost of a filling fee for entering, and if pre-primary party endorsements are allowed), as well as the social and political climate of the state (ideological heterogeneity between the two parties, the level of two-party competition, and the social-capital index). Not surprisingly, as Bardwell (2002) showed, their count models show that election laws and the social and political climate of a state have significant effects on the number of major-party and third-party candidates entering a race. They also find that the election-specific effect of incumbency is contingent on the strength of the incumbent, with incumbency having a larger impact the weaker the incumbent becomes. Dowling and Lem's (2009) study is important in that it provides an innovative way—a count of candidates—to conceptualize and analyze the "democraticness" of the electoral processes. In contrast to Lacy and Monson (2002), who use polling data to analyze the determinants of voting for a third-party candidate (Jesse Ventura, the Minnesota Reform Party gubernatorial candidate in 1998), it is important to note that count models are aggregations, meaning that many important individual-level factors (such as candidate quality) are omitted from the analysis.

THE IMPACT OF CAMPAIGN FINANCE REGULATIONS ON ELECTORAL COMPETITION

Money is like mother's milk, former Speaker of the California State Assembly, Jesse "Big Daddy" Unruh liked to say. There is little question that campaign expenditures affect the outcomes of statewide and state legislative races (Caldeira and Patterson 1982; Giles and

Pritchard, 1985; Tucker and Weber 1987; Gierzynski and Breaux, 1991, 1993). Candidates who spend more money than their opponents generally win. But how might differing political institutions across the states affect the money chase, and more importantly, electoral outcomes?

Research on elections is often concerned with the effect of certain legal institutions on electoral outcomes. One of the most important legal institutions is contribution limits. Contribution limits have been argued to, among other things, reduce corruption, promote more democratic contests, and reduce escalating campaign spending. However, theoretical and empirical research has suggested that contribution limits may have consequences unforeseen by reformers. In keeping with the literature on U.S. House races, challengers in statewide and statehouse races—who are generally less known than incumbents—are particularly in need of raising contributions to be competitive.

One of the most apparent unforeseen consequences is that contribution limits may inadvertently benefit incumbents, increasing the incumbency advantage. One logic of this argument is based on the assumption that particularistic donors (those most interested in influencing policy outcomes) are likely to distribute money to candidates who are most likely to win: incumbents. Donation of funds for incumbents, so it is thought, is likely to be exacerbated in the face of a ceiling provided by contribution limits. Eom and Gross (2006) use time-series cross-sectional data on gubernatorial elections to assess whether or not contribution limits affect the ratio of funds received by incumbents relative to challengers or the absolute difference of funds received between the two most competitive office-seekers. They find that, in contrast to speculations about the potential of contribution limits to increase the incumbency bias, contribution limits actually reduce the ratio of funds between incumbent and challenger, all else equal. Unfortunately, Eom and Gross offer little in the way of theory when trying to explain why contribution limits might fail to benefit incumbents, specifically, why contribution limits should level the playing field for challengers. Although they speculate a few reasons why contribution limits reduce the disparity between funds for incumbents and challengers, ultimately they lack a theoretical rationale to shed light on the empirical evidence.

While it is certainly important to assess the potential effects of contribution limits on the disparity between incumbent and challenger campaign funds, additional concern revolves around the potential effects of contribution limits on whether or not incumbents will be challenged at all. Hamm and Hogan (2008) seek to add some theoretical and empirical insight into the effect of contribution limits on challenger emergence with a large time-series cross-sectional dataset comprising lower-house elections in 25 state legislatures between 1994 and 1998. Using an additive variable for contribution limits (consisting of limits on donations from labor unions, PACs, corporations, individuals, and political parties), they find that challengers are more likely to emerge as contribution limits become more stringent. The rationale for this finding is that challengers take note of campaign finance law and choose to run when they have the greatest potential to match the funding prowess of incumbents, which of course appears to be more likely if incumbents are limited. Additionally they find that harsh filing requirements lower the probability of challenger emergence, all else equal. One notable caveat to Hamm and Hogan's article is that they also examine if these effects are consistent with the emergence of independent or minor-party challengers. They find, similarly, that stringent contribution limits tend to increase the probability of independent or minor-party challenges to incumbents and harsh filing requirements have the opposite effect. Hamm and Hogan's (2008) article advances the literature in terms of examining the effect of legal institutions on the electoral process. One limitation to their study, which is a function of the data they use, is that they do not control for important variables regarding individual characteristics of incumbents. That is to say, besides controlling for past electoral competitiveness of the district, they do not include information specific to the incumbent which might dissuade major-or minor-party challengers. This is important particularly when bearing in mind findings about strategic candidate entry.

In estimating the effects of campaign spending on gubernatorial election results, Bardwell (2003) advances the literature by attempting to account for the problem of simultaneity. Regressing vote-share on campaign spending is generally considered biased because spending not only affects the vote but is, itself, affected by the *expected vote*. That is to say, incumbents tend to only spend more when they face credible challengers. Challengers are limited, similarly, in campaign spending by the vulnerability of the office-holders they challenge. Bardwell uses instrumental variables regression in order to reduce the bias in estimating the effect of campaign spending on vote-shares. As instruments for campaign spending he uses a number of factors (population size, length of the campaign, size of the geographic area, campaign finance limits) that are statistically related to campaign spending but conceptually unrelated to vote-shares. Bardwell's findings are consistent with findings for other offices, namely congressional elections, in that spending by challengers reduces incumbents' vote-share, but incumbent spending tends to be unrelated to incumbent vote-shares. Theoretically this is justified by the proposition that governors' name recognition and office-holding perks are so large that spending tends to buy few additional votes. Additionally, he finds that challenger quality tends to reduce incumbent vote-shares while incumbent popularity tends to increase incumbent vote-shares.

Partin (2002) also examines the effect of campaign spending on gubernatorial election outcomes with an instrumental variable regression to account for the problem of simultaneity. Although in many ways his analysis mirrors, theoretically and analytically, that of Bardwell, he differs in one important respect. While Bardwell finds that incumbent spending tends to be unrelated to their received vote-shares, Partin finds that both incumbent spending and challenger spending tend to affect vote-shares. The caveat, however, is that it is less certain in Partin's analysis if incumbent spending is genuinely related to vote-shares, as instead of coding the variables as incumbent campaign expenditures, he codes the variable as out-party candidate expenditures. Therefore, this variable includes both incumbents and non-incumbents of the same party as the outgoing governor. Bardwell (2005) additionally criticizes the instruments used by Partin, as they have little explanatory power for campaign spending, and provides additional evidence that while challenger spending increases their share of the two-party vote, incumbent spending tends to buy few additional votes.

Although Bardwell (2003) adds some empirical sophistication to the estimation of incumbent vote-shares in gubernatorial contests, his analysis is not without methodological issues. First, little effort is made to substantiate the claim that the instruments used for campaign spending are strictly exogenous from incumbent vote-shares. To the extent that they are not, then despite the sophistication, the parameter estimates remain biased. Second, Bardwell's data is time-series cross-sectional, gubernatorial primary races from 1980 to 2000, and yet little effort is made to account for the biases that tend to afflict such data. Bardwell does allude in a footnote that he used panel-corrected standard errors in an alternative model, and the results did not substantially differ. Even so, panel-corrected standard errors should be used, in addition to controlling for unobserved heterogeneity across the states and through time (Beck and Katz, 1995, 1996). It is uncertain, however, the extent to which a model that accounted for the time-series cross-sectional structure of the data would provide different, if not reduced, parameter estimates for the effect of campaign spending on incumbent vote-shares.

Accounting for the political context of state legislative elections, Seabrook (2010) examines legislative campaigns in the upper and lower houses in nine states in the 2002 election. Building on the work of Gierzynski and Breaux (1996), who find significant evidence that district-level factors can condition the influence of money in legislative elections, Seabrook theorizes that the effectiveness of campaign spending is conditional on whether or not there are voters in a district who can potentially be targeted and thereby influenced by the expenditures. He operationalizes his study by examining the conditional impact of candidate spending on the Democratic vote-share of legislative races. Controlling for several factors, he finds that positive effectiveness of campaign spending is conditional on the percentage of registered independents in a district, as well as the level of legislative professionalism and whether a district has multiple members. However, he finds that campaign spending is less effective in those states with legislative term limits.

Recently, scholars have begun to examine more closely the effects of "clean election" reforms on political competition in the American states. Reformers tout how public financing of electoral contests is able to simultaneously reduce the potential for corruption and increase the competitiveness of electoral contests. Malhotra (2008) provides an empirical assessment of the latter by focusing on state Senate election outcomes in Arizona (1992–2000) and Maine (1994–2002). In both states, clean election programs were implemented via referenda. Accordingly, Malhotra takes advantage of within-state variation in the competitiveness of Senate elections pre and post implementation of clean election programs. He analyzes two separate dependent variables: the inverse of the Herfindahl-Hirschman Index (intended to reflect the number of *effective* candidates in an electoral contest) and the margin of victory. His findings show that clean election programs alone have little effect of the competitiveness of electoral outcomes. However, competitiveness of electoral outcomes increased if the challenger participated in the program. Furthermore, this effect is exacerbated by the presence of an incumbent in the election. His findings, thus, demonstrate that the effect of clean election programs on electoral competitiveness is conditional on both whether or not the challenger participated in the program and whether or not an incumbent was present.

Malhotra's (2008) analysis is certainly substantively intriguing. Although reform-minded arguments have often proposed that public financing will reduce corruption and increase competitiveness, little empirical evidence has been marshaled in favor of the latter hypothesis. Taking advantage of the laboratories of state politics provides Malhotra with two unique cases to verify any expectations regarding public financing. Even so, the time periods analyzed for both states are short; while his findings are substantively interesting, they may be subject to change. Additionally, he only analyzes the effect of public financing in states pre and post reform. While his approach is useful, failing to provide comparisons of states that have not implemented the same laws means that it is difficult to determine the possible effect of confounding factors omitted from the analysis.

The Impact of Primaries on Electoral Competition

For much of the 20th century, electoral competition in gubernatorial primaries, to say nothing of legislative contests, was lacking. In their survey of the literature, Jewell and Olson (1988) found that roughly three-quarters of gubernatorial primaries were contested between 1960 and 1986, but that most of the competition was due to open seats. They also found more primary competition in southern and western states, as well as those that were Democratic-leaning or with two-party competition. Of course, the political and partisan landscape has changed dramatically since their study. As Norrander (2010) discusses in her comprehensive review of the literature on state legislative primaries in the American states, state primary elections still provide several distinct methodological advantages for scholars interested in electoral dynamics, especially when using cross-sectional time-series analyses.

For instance, might the type of primary system in a state affect electoral competition? Despite conventional wisdom, the scholarly evidence for such a causal relationship is thin. By stockpiling campaign contributions, incumbent lawmakers are often able to thwart intra-party challenges (Hogan, 2001; Goodliffe, 2007), although others have found that cash-on-hand may only be an effective deterrent if the incumbent is able to maintain his or her popularity (Bardwell, 2002; Kang, Niemi, and Powell, 2003). Scholars have conducted little empirical work, though, on whether run-off primaries—which were once synonymous with southern politics—disadvantage certain candidates more or less than others. Today, eight southern states continue to require run-offs in primary elections if the winning candidate fails to top 50 percent of the vote total. Scholars have begun to investigate whether candidates who face inter-party competition in a primary are weaker or stronger candidates when facing off in a general election. Hogan (2005) finds that when it comes to the general election—especially in open seats—candidates who face stiff primary challenges might fare better than their opponents who go unchallenged. Examining electoral results across nine states in the 1990s, he posits that his counterintuitive findings may be the result of party leaders working harder to recruit better candidates and build up their campaign war chests. Besides the narrow time frame and limited number of states in his dataset, Hogan's study is further limited by the fact that he fails to account for the interstate institutional differences, including the type of primary system (open or closed) in operation.

Though Hogan's study is likely not the last word as to whether polarizing primaries actually drive down turnout in the general election, it does raise a host of questions that have not been adequately addressed by scholars interested in campaigns and elections in the American states. Do states with open primaries have more competitive primary elections than those with closed primaries? Certainly, from a resource mobilization perspective, open primaries should give candidates the opportunity to mobilize a wider spectrum of voters during the campaign. Are incumbents more likely to face intra-party challenges in a closed primary, as opposed to an open or blanket primary?

Pearson-Merkowitz and McTague (2008) use geographic size and distance to explain variations in the competitiveness (or as they term it, factionalism) of primary elections for gubernatorial and Senatorial elections between 1993 and 2004. It is their contention that geography potentially has an effect on the competitiveness of elections in that the concentration of voters may affect potential candidate pools and competitiveness between candidates of the same party. They operationalize geography as size, the proportion of counties in a state that make up 70 percent of a party's electoral base, and distance, the distance between the counties that make up the parties' electoral base. Their analysis and theory demonstrate conditional effects of size and distance on factionalism: large, scattered electoral bases are associated with more factionalism or competition in primary elections and small, concentrated electoral bases are associated with less factionalism and competition.

Progressive reformers thought that the adoption of direct primaries might reduce partisan identification as a consideration and enhance competition (Ansolabehere et al., 2010). With respect to legislative elections, though, scholars have found little competition in party primaries. Grau (1981), in what is now a dated study examining competition in the 1970s, found that less than one in five Republican primaries for state legislative office had at least two candidates contesting the office. Democratic primaries were considerably more competitive during the period, with nearly 50 percent of primaries having two or more candidates. The heavy hands of state and local political parties have limited the amount of competition in state legislative races.

Some scholars have taken advantage of natural experiments to test the relative impact of primary systems on vote choice and partisanship. In California, for a short period beginning in the late 1990s, a blanket primary was put to use. Alvarez and Nagler (2002) examine whether or not voters were more likely to engage in crossover voting in the 1998 state primary and whether they were more strategic when offered the chance to vote for the candidate of their choice, regardless of party, in the primary. They find that most voters do not cross party lines when given the chance, and that those who do largely do so because they sincerely like a candidate from the other major party, and were not doing so for strategic reasons. Masket (2007) also uses a natural experiment to look cross-sectionally at the effects of primary rules on the political ideology of California legislators. When cross-filing of state lawmakers was introduced in 1914, Masket argues that the power of partisan elites—activists, interest groups, and, of course, party bosses—became diminished. As a result, when it came to the selection process of state lawmakers, partisan divisions in the halls of Sacramento were less pronounced. Theoretically, he reasons, party cross-listing by legislative candidates encourages them to move ideologically to the center in the quest for the median voter, rather than catering to partisan elites who have more power over the nomination process in a closed primary system.

Might state primary electoral rules also shape voters' partisanship? Might polarization within the electorate—a hot topic in the broader discipline of American politics—be exacerbated in states that require voters to register with a political party if they want to participate in a primary election? After all, registration reforms in some states have not necessarily reduced the costs to vote (Brown, Jackson, and Wright 1999). Taking advantage of the variation in party registration laws across the states to probe partisan attachments in the electorate, Burden and Greene (2000) challenge the Michigan School model of individual partisan identification as being a function largely of psychological and sociological attachments. Using the NES Senate Election Study, 1988–92, they investigate whether in some circumstances the relationship might be the opposite. Specifically, they explore the issue of party registration, making the claim that the act of partisan voter registration might, in fact, cause individuals to have stronger attachments to the party to which they are registered. Party registration laws, of course, vary considerably by state. They theorize that states that have closed primary systems, which induce voters to register in order to participate, are likely to have more strong partisans relative to states with open primary systems. Assuming, then, that behavior can affect attitudes, Burden and Greene show that a state's legal environment may have an effect on party identification. They show that the probability of being an independent voter is significantly higher in states with no party registration than in states with party registration.

THE IMPACT OF REDISTRICTING ON ELECTORAL COMPETITION

There is good reason to suspect that racial or partisan gerrymandering of electoral districts makes legislative races less competitive, thereby depressing electoral competition, and perhaps even voter turnout (though see Barreto, Segura, and Woods, 2004). Studies have shown that in gubernatorial and state legislative races, voter turnout is considerably higher when the vote differential between the winning and losing candidate is narrower, in large part because the likelihood of a register voter not casting a ballot becomes more consequential. From a Downsian perspective (Downs, 1957), closeness of elections impels political parties and outside groups to mobilize potential voters.

Interest in the effect of legal institutions on electoral competitiveness has focused on the impact of redistricting. Forgette, Garner, and Winkle (2009) show that since 1968 the number of uncontested state legislative races has increased and the percentage of marginal electoral contests has reduced. It is often claimed that evidence of reduced electoral competitiveness is a consequence of redistricting and partisan gerrymandering. Forgette, Garner, and Winkle attempt to assess the extent to which redistricting is to blame by testing models which predict the probability of an uncontested race and the absolute margin of victory in competitive races following the 1990 and 2000 redistricting cycles. Their analysis suggests that certain redistricting principles have substantial effects on electoral competitiveness. The particular redistricting principles of interest are: population-based principles (the extent to which political subdivisions, cores of prior districts, and communities of interest are maintained), the prohibition of incumbency protection, if redistricting is carried out by an independent board, and if there are court-imposed plans. Their analysis shows that, after controlling for certain district characteristics, population-based principles reduce the probability of an uncontested race and incumbency protection increases the probability of an uncontested race, as well as the margin of victory.

Forgette, Garner, and Winkle (2009) provide empirical evidence in support of the claim that redistricting principles affect electoral competitiveness. This finding has broad import for legal institutions governing statewide electoral processes. Even so, their article is limited in the sense that it only focuses on immediate electoral contests following two specific redistricting cycles. It is not altogether apparent if the observed effects will continue for the next decade, reduce, or even become more pronounced. Furthermore, it is still open to debate the impact of redistricting principles after an incumbent is defeated, term-limited out, or retires. That is, should we expect the effect to be maintained for a new legislator? Even so, their study helps to validate the potential biases imbedded in the redistricting process.

THE IMPACT OF TERM LIMITS ON ELECTORAL COMPETITION

During the 1990s, citizens in 21 states adopted term limits on state lawmakers, though several of the laws were subsequently overturned. Of the remaining 15 states with term limits, are there any discernable effects on turnout and legislative competition? Engstrom and Monroe (2006) provide an analysis of strategic candidate decision making in state legislative elections. To do so, they test a resource-based hypothesis against a strategic-candidate hypothesis, consistent with much of the research on congressional elections. The resource-based hypothesis posits that incumbents tend to benefit from office-holding perks and, as such, they tend to receive larger amounts of the two-party vote-share. This hypothesis suggests that if an incumbent voluntarily leaves office then vote-shares received by the same party as the incumbent should precipitously drop. This makes sense insofar as the resource hypothesis argues that such office-holding perks benefit sitting incumbents independent of his or her party identification. The challenge by the strategic-candidate hypothesis is that incumbents tend to be self-selective: if they perceive their electoral prospects to be dim, they choose not to run. This self-selection results in an overestimation of the resource-based effect. Engstrom and Monroe cleverly use a natural experiment, the introduction of term limits in California, to test the hypotheses against each other. In brief, Engstrom and Monroe regress incumbent-party vote-shares on a variable denoting whether or not the seat was voluntarily open and another denoting whether or not the seat was involuntarily open (term-limited out). The strategic-candidate hypothesis suggests that the incumbent party's vote-share should drop more in voluntarily open seats, reflecting the incumbent's dim perception of his or her chances, relative to involuntarily open seats. Their analysis confirms this expectation, with voluntarily open seats having a more robust effect on incumbent-party vote-shares.

Two issues are raised by the Engstrom and Monroe (2003) article. First, the two hypotheses do not directly oppose each other. Vote-shares for the incumbent-party candidate are negatively affected by both voluntary and involuntary open seat contests. This suggests that while one explanation may be more robust than another, it does not rule out that both play a vital role. Second, although incumbents may strategically choose to run or not run, that decision is conditional on certain factors, such as partisan mood swings in the electorate. Engstrom and Monroe control for partisan mood swings, which have a robust effect on vote-shares. Although strategy may play a role, Engstrom and Monroe may be conceptually and empirically undervaluing contextual factors.

Lazarus (2006) examines the effects of term limits on legislator behavior. Expanding beyond the traditional, and generally accepted hypothesis, that term-limited legislators are more likely to seek election to other offices than non-term-limited legislators, Lazarus examines a number of additional hypotheses. Grounding his theory in the "rational entry model," he argues that the presence of term limits simultaneously reduces the benefits of seeking offices and reduces the costs associated with seeking other offices. Based on these assumptions, Lazarus shows that state lawmakers eligible for reelection in term-limit states are less likely to run for reelection than their peers in non-term-limit states, and that those who are term-limited legislators are more likely to be career movers by seeking election to other offices. He also finds that when seeking other political offices, term-limited lawmakers perform worse relative to non-term-limited legislators; specifically, those who are term-limited tend to seek less prestigious offices relative to non-term-limited legislators. A major limitation of Lazarus' study, though, is that his large cross-sectional dataset with 20 states is limited temporally (spanning only

2000–2). The temporal dimension of the dataset limits claims that can be made about legislative behavior through time, while allowing for clear comparisons to be made across legislators. That is, cross-sectional variance is used to infer individual behavioral variation over time.

In another use of a natural experiment, Schraufnagel and Halperin (2006) take advantage of the Florida experience with term limits to test two general hypotheses: (1) that the presence of term limits should lead to more electoral competition, and (2) that the presence of term limits should lead to more descriptive representation in the legislature. Both hypotheses are predicated on the notion that term limits serve as a tool to disrupt entrenched incumbency that simultaneously reduces electoral competition and remains stable despite demographic changes to legislators' districts. They find very limited support, however, for these expectations. Using a dataset that consists of electoral margins for Florida House and Senate elections from 1988 to 2004, they find null effects for electoral competition (operationalized as the difference between the two top candidates in votes received) and descriptive representation (as women and minorities elected to serve in the chamber). Using a time-series cross-sectional design, their data fail to confirm existing expectations about the consequences of term limits. The major limitation of Schraufnagel and Halperin's article is that it is always risky to base an argument on null findings. Typical hypothesis tests assume a population model, namely a normal distribution with a mean of 0, and examine whether the data are atypical "enough" to warrant that population model unlikely. Because the data analyzed by Schraufnagel and Halperin are not atypical "enough" does not suggest that the assumed population model is correct, only that it cannot definitively be rejected. This limitation is more notable when one considers that their findings and data are limited to only the term-limit experience in the Florida legislature and not similar experiences in different states.

Powell (2008) examines two related and oft-discussed hypotheses with respect to the implementation of term limits. It has been hypothesized that term limits have the effect of benefiting minority-party candidates, by reducing, if not eliminating, the incumbency advantage. In doing so, it was also hypothesized that overall composition of state legislative chambers would become more Republican in states where term limits were implemented. This follows from the speculation that state legislative chambers tend to be more heavily Democratic in composition and if term limits benefit the minority party, they ought to benefit the Republican Party. Using fixed-effects, dynamic, time-series cross-sectional models, Powell investigates these hypotheses and finds very limited support. In all cases he is interested in the aggregate compositions of state legislative chambers, first as the split between Democratic seats and Republican seats, and second as the percentage of seats held by the minority party. In all of the models he presents null effects for the presence of term limits and in one a negative effect, suggesting that the majority party actually benefited from term limits. Powell argues that this is likely the case because there is something specific about the states that did enact term limits (they tend to be Democratic). Powell's (2008) article has two problems. First, as usual with articles of this sort, arguing the null does not prove the null to be true. Second, his analysis is concerned with aggregate compositional characteristics of state legislative chambers. This means that he is not able to speak to whether or not the propensity of Democratic incumbents to lose was more likely after the implementation of term limits. To do so would require data on individuals, which he does not present. Additional research would benefit from doing so, understanding the difficult data-collection limitations that would be associated with doing so.

DIRECT DEMOCRACY

Over the past decade, direct democracy scholars have weighed in on the impact of ballot measures on voter turnout and electoral competition (for an extensive review of the literature, see Smith and Tolbert 2007). In general, scholars have found that states with the initiative have higher voter participation than states without the initiative process. On average, Tolbert and Smith (2005) find, each statewide initiative on the ballot between 1980 and 2004 increased a state's turnout by almost 1 percent in presidential elections and almost 2 percent in midterm elections, holding constant other state demographic (high school graduation rates, region, racial diversity), economic (income), and political (voter registration laws, U.S. Senate and gubernatorial races) factors. Although the robustness of the turnout effect of ballot measures in presidential elections has been recently challenged (Childress and Binder, 2011), longitudinal, cross-sectional, aggregate-level studies reaffirm the finding that ballot measures can mobilize citizens to the polls (Abramowitz, 2004; Burden, 2004; Campbell and Monson, 2008). At the individual level, national and state survey data confirm that citizens living in states with ballot issue campaigns are more likely to turn out to vote. Holding all other factors constant, national survey data show that statewide ballot initiatives increase the likelihood of an individual voting in midterm elections, and that low-propensity voters are more likely to turn out when the issue on the ballot is salient (Donovan, Tolbert, and Smith, 2009). Finally, direct democracy scholars have demonstrated that ballot measures can frame elections by elevating certain issues, such as gay marriage or the minimum wage, weaken party government (Phillips, 2008), and, perhaps most importantly, prime candidate vote choice in statewide races (Nicholson, 2005; Donovan, Tolbert, and Smith, 2008; Smith and Tolbert, 2010).

For example, Grummel (2008) analyzes this proposition with the exception that he is primarily interested in the effect of certain moral initiatives and referenda on voter turnout: defense of marriage, gay rights, abortion, stem-cell research, and physician-assisted suicide. To do so, he estimates models which predict voter age turnout (VAT) and voter eligible turnout (VET) for all states between 1980 and 2006. With separate models for presidential election years and midterm election years, Grummel finds that the presence of a moral initiative or referenda on the ballot is associated with higher levels of turnout in midterm elections, but not presidential elections. As an explanation for the divergence between presidential and midterm election years, he speculates that because midterm election years are generally lower-information and lower-interest relative to presidential election years, moral initiatives and referenda may inspire more interest and information. Grummel's (2008) research further confirms earlier studies on the educative effects of direct democracy. It is notable in the sense that it may suggest certain conditional effects of direct democracy on voter turnout: (1) that the effects may be more pronounced in midterm years relative to presidential years, and (2) that the effect may be conditional on the type of referenda and initiative (moral policies). However, in order to test the second possibility, Grummel would have needed to create an interaction term between the presence of the initiative and referenda and the presence of a moral initiative and referenda. This would have allowed him to make claims about the differential effects of a state which has an initiative without any moral implications, and one that does not.

LINGERING QUESTIONS OF ENDOGENEITY

For some scholars, it is not enough to explain how institutions may affect campaigns and elections in the American states. The more important question is why do states adopt particular institutions that affect campaigns and elections, and how do they evolve over time? For example, Witko (2007) analyzes institutional variation with regard to campaign finance regulations across the states and over time. Most analyses of campaign finance regulation begin with the assumption that elected officials in general, and legislators in particular, resist stringent regulatory changes. Direct tests of the self-interest hypothesis are difficult because (1) self-interest is, theoretically, a constant, and (2) measuring elected officials' level of self-interest, if it is not a constant, is problematic. Witko proposes, however, to test the effect of self-interest on stringent changes to campaign finance regulation indirectly. First, if self-interest prohibits politicians from enacting stringent changes to campaign finance, then states with the initiative should have more stringent laws as direct democracy either allows citizens to enact changes directly or the presence of the initiative may spur legislative action indirectly. Second, stringent changes to campaign finance should be more likely in states with term limits, as legislators are less career-oriented. Third, politicians who represent more populous and costly (in terms of campaigns) legislative districts should be less likely to implement stringent changes which might disadvantage them with respect to challengers. Additionally, Witko examines what he terms a "normal politics" model which alleges that changes to campaign finance regulatory law may reflect states' ideology, culture, and interest-group climate. Liberal, moralistic states with influential citizen groups should be more likely to adopt stringent changes to campaign finance.

To analyze these claims, Witko uses pooled time-series cross-sectional models where the dependent variable reflects whether or not a state adopted a stringent change to campaign finance in time t. He uses time-series cross-sectional probit models, and opts not to use fixed effects, because of the time-invariant independent variables. Due to multicollinearity, time-invariant independent variables are unable to be estimated with fixed unit effects; failing to do so may result in biased parameters for the time-variant independent variables that he does have. Nevertheless, this is an issue that plagues most research on state politics: what to do with time-invariant covariates? His results suggest that changes to campaign finance are more likely in states with the initiative and less likely as population size increases. His analysis of the normal politics model is more mixed. Although ideology is related to the propensity for a state to adopt stringent changes to campaign finance law, culture does not have a substantive effect. However, he finds support that a scandal in the previous biennium is associated with changes to campaign finance regulation in the current biennium, in concert with the findings of Rosenson (2005) on the adoption of legislative ethics reforms.

Similarly, analyzing an institution as a dependent variable, Malhotra (2006) seeks to explain why legislative professionalism varies across the states. Arguing a different point of view from previous work on the subject, he posits that increasing professionalism is a function of legislators' rational goal of reelection. A means to achieve the goal of reelection is serving as ombudsman. Increasing social service spending by state governments has provided a need and, more importantly, an incentive for legislators to act as intermediaries between the bureaucracy and citizens. Acting as ombudsman, efficiently, requires developing more professional (spending more time in session, increasing staff, and increasing legislator pay) organizations. He shows that increasing state social-service spending (which is mostly a function of state revenue from the federal government) has led to increasing professionalism within states, over time. The underlying premise, of course, follows from the assumption of self-interest in that elected officials have benefited under the status quo and are thus resistant to changes, as Smith and Fridkin (2008) and others have shown.

CONCLUSION

Elections are the central mechanism through which representatives are bound to citizen preferences. The nature and quality of electoral practices raise both normative and empirical questions, which are unquestionably of interest to political scientists. Research on American elections and campaign finance is often conducted at the federal level. Elections for state office, however, provide tremendous leverage for scholars in assessing more expansive empirical and normative implications of electoral practices. More importantly, they provide a valuable means to examine the potential effects institutional arrangements might have on a broad range of electoral phenomena. In this review we surveyed recent articles with this goal in mind. Outcomes of interest vary across the articles, but most concern themselves with some notion of electoral competition or voter turnout. How, and with what significance, might political institutions across the states affect voter turnout and electoral competition? Throughout this essay, we have discussed numerous studies that have shown how political institutions can have significant effects on political participation by voters as well as elite actors. In short, electoral rules and laws matter.

To be sure, there are numerous limitations with the findings in the scholarly literature on campaigns and elections in the American states. Our criticisms noting some of the limitations and biases in the scholarly studies should be taken as constructive. Recent examinations of electoral reforms and state elections clearly have benefited from the new availability of data at the individual and aggregate levels. But scholars must grapple with the many difficulties associated with the time-series and cross-sectional nature of the data. It is somewhat ironic, then, that these new data sources offer a new means to test causal models more rigorously because scholars can evaluate variation both within cases over time or between cases, but that perhaps the most common criticism of state politics research, especially that with an institutionalist theoretical bent, is the possibility of endogeneity. That institutions both affect and are affected by the underlying conditions of politics presents theoretical and empirical difficulties. However, managing the problem of endogeneity may inspire technical and theoretical innovations in the study of politics more generally.

While technical innovations will undoubtedly lead to less biased examinations of the effects of institutions on turnout and competition, theoretical explorations of the nature and sources of institutions are becoming increasingly necessary. Much less work has focused on explanations for particular institutional arrangements and even less has prodded the extent to which institutions can be conceived of as intermediaries, both product and producer of political conditions. Gaining theoretical insight into the sources and role of institutions vis-à-vis political behavior may provide an avenue through which the dynamic field of state elections can achieve a sense of coherence; in fact, it may advance an understanding of elections far beyond those only for state offices. In this vein, studying American elections at the state level provides an opportunity to test more general theories, both normative and empirical, about the nature of democratic elections. In sum, explaining state politics across the American states should not be undervalued, as comparative studies of campaigns and elections can help us understand more broadly the political process and the key role of institutions.

References

Abbe, Owen G. and Paul S. Herrnson. 2003. "Campaign Professionalism in State Legislative. Elections." *State Politics and Policy Quarterly* 3 (3): 223–245.

Abramowitz, Alan. 2004. "Terrorism, Gay Marriage, and Incumbency: Explaining the Republican Victory in the 2004 Presidential Election." *The Forum* 2 (4): Article 3. Available at: <http://www.bepress.com/forum/vol2/iss4/art3>.

Alvarez, Michael R. and Jonathan Nagler. 2002. "Should I Stay or Should I Go? Sincere and Strategic Crossover Voting in California Assembly Races." In Bruce Cain and Elisabeth Gerber (eds), *Voting at the Political Fault Line: California's Experiment with the Blanket Primary*. Berkeley: University of California Press, 107–23.

Ansolabehere, Stephen, John M. Hansen, Shigeo Hirano, and James M. Snyder Jr. 2010. "More Democracy: The Direct Primary and Competition in U.S. Elections?" *Studies in American Political Development* 24: 190–205.

Bardwell, Kedron. 2002. "Money and Challenger Emergence in Gubernatorial Primaries." *Political Research Quarterly* 55 (3): 653–67.

Bardwell, Kedron. 2003. "Campaign Finance Laws and the Competition for Spending in Gubernatorial Elections." *Social Science Quarterly* 84 (4): 811–25.

Bardwell, Kedron. 2005. "Reevaluating Spending in Gubernatorial Races: Job Approval as a Baseline for Spending Effects." *Political Research Quarterly* 58 (1): 97–105.

Barreto, Matt A., Gary M. Segura, and Nathan D. Woods. 2004. "The Mobilizing Effect of Majority-Minority Districts on Latino Turnout." *American Political Science Review* 98 (1): 65–75.

Beck, Nathaniel and Jonathan N. Katz. 1995. "What to Do (and not to Do) with Time-Series Cross-Section Data." *American Political Science Review* 89 (3): 634–47.

Beck, Nathaniel and Jonathan N. Katz. 1996. "Taking Time Seriously: Time-Series-Cross-Section Analysis with a Binary Dependent Variable." *American Journal of Political Science* 42 (4): 1260–88.

Berry, William D., Michael B. Berkman, and Stuart Schneiderman. 2000. "Legislative Professionalism and Incumbent Reelection: The Development of Institutional Boundaries." *American Political Science Review* 94 (4): 859–74.

Brace, Paul and Aubrey Jewett. 1995. "The State of State Politics Research." *Political Research Quarterly* 48: 643–81.

Brown, Adam R. and Gary C. Jacobson. 2008. "Party, Performance, and Strategic Politicians: The Dynamics of Elections for Senator and Governor in 2006." *State Politics and Policy Quarterly* 8 (4): 384–409.

Brown, Robert, Robert Jackson, and Gerald Wright. 1999. "Registration, Turnout, and State Party Systems." *Political Research Quarterly* 52 (3): 463–79.

Burden, Barry. 2004. "An Alternative Account of the 2004 Presidential Election." *The Forum* 2 (4): Article 2. Available at: <http://www.bepress.com/forum/vol2/iss4/art2>.

Burden, Barry C. and Steven Greene. 2000. "Party Attachments and State Election Laws." *Political Research Quarterly* 53 (1): 63–76.

Caldeira, Gregory. A. and Samuel C. Patterson. 1982. "Bringing Home the Votes: Electoral Outcomes in State Legislative Races." *Political Behavior* 4: 33–67.

Campbell, David and Quinn Monson. 2008. "The Religion Card: Gay Marriage and the 2004 Presidential Election." *Public Opinion Quarterly* 72: 399–419.

Carey, John. M., Richard. G. Niemi, and Linda W. Powell. 2000. "Incumbency and the Probability of Reelection in State Legislative Elections." *Journal of Politics* 62: 671–700.

Childress, Matthew A. and Mike Binder. 2011. "Engaged by the Initiative? How the Use of Citizen Initiatives Increases Voter Turnout." *Political Research Quarterly* 65 (1): 93–103.

Chubb, John. E. 1988. "Institutions, the Economy, and the Dynamics of State Elections." *American Political Science Review* 82: 133–54.

Donovan, Todd, Caroline J. Tolbert, and Daniel A. Smith. 2008. "Priming Presidential Votes by Direct Democracy." *Journal of Politics* 70: 1217–31.

Donovan, Todd, Caroline J. Tolbert, and Daniel A. Smith. 2009. "Political Engagement, Mobilization, and Direct Democracy." *Public Opinion Quarterly* 73: 98–118.

Dowling, Conor M. and Steven B. Lem. 2009. "Explaining Major and Third Party Candidate Entry in U.S. Gubernatorial Elections, 1980–2005." *State Politics and Policy Quarterly* 9 (1): 1–23.

Downs, Anthony. 1957. *An Economic Theory of Democracy*. New York: Harper and Row.

Engstrom, Erik J. and Nathan W. Monroe. 2006. "Testing the Basis of Incumbency Advantage: Strategic Candidates and Term Limits in the California Legislature." *State Politics and Policy Quarterly* 6 (1): 1–20.

Eom, Kihong and Donald A. Gross. 2006. "Contribution Limits and Disparity in Contributions between Gubernatorial Candidates." *Political Research Quarterly* 59 (1): 99–110.

Forgette, Richard, Andrew Garner, and John Winkle. 2009. "Do Redistricting Principles Affect State Legislative Electoral Competition?" *State Politics and Policy Quarterly* 9 (2): 151–75.

Francia, Peter L. and Paul S. Herrnson. 2004. "The Synergistic Effect of Campaign Effort and Election Reform on Voter Turnout in State Legislative Elections." *State Politics and Policy Quarterly* 4 (1): 74–93.

Gierzynski, A. and D. Breaux. 1991. "Money and Votes in State Legislative Elections." *Legislative Studies Quarterly* 16: 203–17.

Gierzynski, A. and D. Breaux. 1993. "Money and the Party Vote in State House Elections." *Legislative Studies Quarterly* 18: 515–33.

Gierzynski, A. and D. Breaux. 1996. "Legislative Elections and the Importance of Money." *Legislative Studies Quarterly* 21: 337–57.

Giles, Michael W. and Anita Pritchard. 1985. "Campaign Expenditures and Legislative Elections in Florida." *Legislative Studies Quarterly* 10 (1): 71–88.

Goodliffe, Jay. 2007. "Campaign War Chests and Challenger Quality in Senate Elections." *Legislative Studies Quarterly* 32 (1): 135–56.

Grau, Craig H. 1981. "Competition in State Legislative Primaries." *Legislative Studies Quarterly* 6 (1): 35–54.

Grummel, John A. 2008. "Morality Politics, Direct Democracy, and Turnout." *State Politics and Policy Quarterly* 8 (3): 282–92.

Hamm, Keith E. and Robert E. Hogan. 2008. "Campaign Finance Laws and Candidacy Decisions in State Legislative Elections." *Political Research Quarterly* 61 (3): 458–67.

Hogan, Robert E. 1997. "Voter Contact Techniques in State Legislative Elections: The Prevalence of Mass Media Advertising." *Legislative Studies Quarterly* 22: 551–71.

Hogan, Robert E. 2001. "Campaign War Chests and Challenger Emergence in State Legislative Elections." *Political Research Quarterly* 54: 815–30.

Hogan, Robert E. 2002. "Candidate Perceptions of Political Party Campaign Activity in State Legislative Elections." *State Politics and Policy Quarterly* 2 (1): 66–85.

Hogan, Robert E. 2005. "Gubernatorial Coattail Effects in State Legislative Elections." *Political Research Quarterly* 58: 587–97.

Jackson, Robert A. 2002. "Gubernatorial and Senatorial Campaign Mobilization of Voters." *Political Research Quarterly* 55 (4): 825–44.

Jewell, Malcolm E. and David M. Olson. 1988. *Political Parties and Elections in American States.* Chicago: Dorsey Press.

Kang, Insun, Richard G. Niemi, and Lynda W. Powell. 2003. "Strategic Candidate Decision-making and Competition in Gubernatorial Nonincumbent-Party Primaries." *State Politics and Policy Quarterly* 3 (4): 353–66.

Lacy, Dean and Quin Monson. 2002. "The Origin and Impact of Votes for Third-Party Candidates: A Case Study of the 1998 Minnesota Gubernatorial Election." *Political Research Quarterly* 55 (2): 409–37.

Lazarus, Jeffrey. 2006. "Term Limits' Multiple Effects on State Legislators' Career Decisions." *State Politics and Policy Quarterly* 6 (4): 357–83.

Leighley, Jan E. and Jonathan Nagler. 1992. "Individual and Systematic Influences on Turnout: Who Votes? 1984." *The Journal of Politics* 54: 718–40.

Lem, S. and C. Dowling. 2006. "Picking Their Spots: Minor Party Candidates in Gubernatorial Elections." *Political Research Quarterly* 59 (3): 471–80.

Malhotra, Neil. 2006. "Government Growth and Professionalism in U.S. State Legislatures." *Legislative Studies Quarterly* 31 (4): 563–84.

Malhotra, Neil. 2008. "The Impact of Public Financing on Electoral Competition: Evidence from Arizona and Maine." *State Politics and Policy Quarterly* 8 (3): 263–81.

Masket, Seth E. 2007. "It Takes an Outsider: Legislative Organization and Partisanship in the California Assembly, 1849–2006." *American Journal of Political Science* 51 (3): 482–97.

Matson, Marsha and Terri Susan Fine. 2006. "Gender, Ethnicity, and Ballot Information: Ballot Cues in Low-Information Elections." *State Politics and Policy Quarterly* 6 (1): 49–72.

Nicholson, Stephen. 2005. *Voting the Agenda: Candidates, Elections and Ballot Propositions*. Princeton, NJ: Princeton University Press.

Norrander, Barbara. 2010. "Primary Elections." In Jan E. Leighley (ed.), *Oxford Handbook of American Elections and Political Behavior*. New York: Oxford University Press, 514–30.

Partin, Randall W. 2002. "Assessing the Impact of Campaign Spending in Governors' Races." *Political Research Quarterly* 55 (1): 213–33.

Patterson, Samuel C. and Gregory Caldeira. 1983. "Getting out the Voter: Participation in Gubernatorial Elections." *American Political Science Review* 77: 675–89.

Pearson-Merkowitz, Shanna and John M. McTague. 2008. "Partisan Mountains and Molehills: The Geography of U.S. State Intraparty Factionalism." *State Politics and Policy Quarterly* 8 (1): 7–31.

Phillips, Justin H. 2008. "Does the Citizen Initiative Weaken Party Government in the U.S. States?" *State Politics and Policy Quarterly* 8 (2): 127–49.

Powell, Richard J. 2008. "Minority Party Gains Under State Legislative Term Limits." *State Politics and Policy Quarterly* 8 (1): 32–47.

Przeworski, Adam. 2004. "Institutions Matter?" *Government and Opposition* 39 (4): 527–40.

Rigby, Elizabeth and Melanie J. Springer. 2011. "Does Electoral Reform Increase (or Decrease) Political Equality?" *Political Research Quarterly* 64 (2): 420–34.

Rosenson, Beth A. 2005. *The Shadowlands of Conduct: Ethics and State Politics*. Washington, DC: Georgetown University Press.

Schaffner, Brian F., Matthew Streb, and Gerald Wright. 2001. "Teams Without Uniforms: The Nonpartisan Ballot in State and Local Elections." *Political Research Quarterly* 54 (1): 7–30.

Schraufnagel, Scot and Karen Halperin. 2006. "Term Limits, Electoral Competition, and Representational Diversity: The Case of Florida." *State Politics and Policy Quarterly* 6 (4): 448–62.

Seabrook, Nicholas. 2010. "Money and State Legislative Elections: The Conditional Impact of Political Context." *American Politics Research* 38 (3): 399–424.

Smith, Daniel A. and Dustin Fridkin. 2008. "Delegating Direct Democracy: Interparty Legislative Competition and the Adoption of the Initiative in the American States." *American Political Science Review* 102 (3): 333–50.

Smith, Daniel A. and Caroline J. Tolbert. 2004. *Educated by Initiative: The Effects of Direct Democracy on Citizens and Political Organizations in the American States*. Ann Arbor: University of Michigan Press.

Smith, Daniel A. and Caroline Tolbert. 2007. "The Instrumental and Educative Effects of Ballot Measures: Research on Direct Democracy in the American States." *State Politics and Policy Quarterly* 7 (4): 417–46.

Smith, Daniel A. and Caroline J. Tolbert. 2010. "Direct Democracy, Public Opinion, and Candidate Choice." *Public Opinion Quarterly* 74: 85–108.

Squire, Peverill. 2000. "Uncontested Seats in State Legislative Elections." *Legislative Studies Quarterly* 25: 131–46.

Tolbert, Caroline J. and Daniel A. Smith. 2005. "The Educative Effects of Ballot Initiatives on Voter Turnout." *American Politics Research* 33: 283–309.

Tucker, H. J. and R. E. Weber. 1987. "State Legislative Election Outcomes: Contextual Effects and Legislative Performance Effects." *Legislative Studies Quarterly* 12: 537–53.

Van Dunk, Emily. 1997. "Challenger Quality in State Legislative Elections." *Political Research Quarterly* 50: 793–807.

Witko, Christopher. 2007. "Explaining Increases in the Stringency of Campaign Finance Regulation, 1993–2002." *State Politics and Policy Quarterly* 7 (4): 369–93.

Wolfinger, Raymond E. and Stephen J. Rosenstone. 1980. *Who Votes?* New Haven: Yale University Press.

Wooldridge, Jeffrey M. 2002. *Econometric Analysis of Cross Section and Panel Data.* Cambridge, MA: The MIT Press, Ch. 4.

PART III

STATE POLITICAL INSTITUTIONS

CHAPTER 11

....

EARLY STATE HISTORY AND CONSTITUTIONS

....

JOHN KINCAID

THE most significant academic and judicial state-constitutional developments in recent decades have been rising interests in teaching state constitutional law comparatively (U.S. Advisory Commission on Intergovernmental Relations, 1988; Williams, 2009) and in using state constitutions to reform state governance (Tarr and Williams, 2006), achieve objectives not attainable in the national arena (U.S. Advisory Commission on Intergovernmental Relations, 1989; Shaman, 2008), and influence federal policy-making (Gardner, 2005). These developments partly reflect liberal responses to conservative federal trends, especially a more conservative Supreme Court and Republican control of the presidency for 20 of the last 32 years. These trends also reflect reactions to the increasing nationalization of public policy, which has led both liberals and conservatives to employ state constitutional tools to protect state prerogatives from federal intrusions and project state values onto the national scene. Voters have been especially active in approving amendments that express their values and restrain state and federal power. Nationalization also has prompted originalists to examine the first state constitutions for insights into the meaning of the federal Constitution as a constraint on federal power (e.g., Rakove, 1990).

A state constitution is a state's highest law, except when the U.S. Constitution, federal statutes, or treaties are applicable. State constitutions also are dynamic because they are substantially democratic. Unlike the U.S. Constitution, they are, except in Delaware, revised and amended only with voter consent. This democratic foundation, coupled with the need for state constitutions to address numerous matters, such as education, corporations, and local government, also makes them bellwethers of socioeconomic and cultural change. Every era of state constitutional development has involved struggles over the nature of democracy and government, the socioeconomic structure of society, and the culture of the polity. Indeed, state constitutional histories have been defined by recurring struggles to reform, and usually restrain, governments believed to have been captured by interests hostile to the public's interest.

BACKGROUND

Many Americans do not know that their state has its own constitution. In a 1988 national poll, only 44 percent of the respondents knew their state has its own constitution. Five percent volunteered that it has its own constitution and also relies on the U.S. Constitution. Nineteen percent believed that their state relies on the U.S. Constitution only, and 32 percent did not know or answer the question. Another question was whether their constitution has "a bill of rights or some other provisions that protect individual rights." The results were slightly better: 56 percent said "yes"; only 6 percent said "no." However, 38 percent did not know or answer the question (U.S. Advisory Commission on Intergovernmental Relations, 1988, 6).

One reason for low visibility may be that even when state political developments involve the constitution, it is often invisible to the public. In 2011, for instance, Wisconsin captured headlines when its Democratic senators fled to Illinois for several weeks so as to prevent a Senate vote on a Republican-sponsored bill repealing most collective-bargaining rights for most public employees. The media hardly explained that Wisconsin's Constitution (Art. VIII, Sec. 8) requires a quorum of three-fifths of the Senate's thirty-three members in order to vote on a fiscal-affairs bill. Republicans held 19 seats, one short of the 20 needed for the quorum. The 14 Democratic senators fled Wisconsin because the constitution allows the legislature to compel its members' attendance. After negotiations failed to bring the Democrats back, the Republican Senate majority removed the collective-bargaining provisions from the fiscal-affairs bill and, by an 18–1 vote, enacted the provisions separately. This required, under the constitution, only a simple-majority (17 senators) quorum. These events unfolded, moreover, while thousands of people protested at the state capitol, exercising the free-speech and assembly rights guaranteed by Sections 3 and 4 of the Wisconsin Constitution's declaration of rights.

Political scientists are well aware of state constitutions, but those documents are like the dark side of the moon. Research has illuminated most other facets of state and local government more extensively. The dearth of research may be due to the challenge of studying 50 documents that have 7,227 amendments and vary in length from New Hampshire's 9,200 words to Alabama's 365,000 words (*The Book of the States*, 2010: 11). Moreover, the states have operated under 147 constitutions since 1775. Historical documents are scattered across the states and many have beenlost over time, making systematic comparative research difficult. Although there are general similarities—such as the separation of legislative, executive, and judicial powers—across all 50 constitutions, there is a daunting diversity of specifics. For example, 49 states have a balanced budget requirement, but that rule is constitutionally mandated in only thirty-two states, and even those requirements vary as to their definition of a balanced budget, exemptions, and other details (Snell, 2010: 3).

More attention is given to state constitutions by the law profession, in part because lawyers and law professors must stay abreast of constitutional developments in their state. The constitution is subject to frequent amendment in some states, and in all states the highest court engages in constitutional interpretation and judicial review. Another important reason for legal attention has been a concerted effort since the 1970s to elevate the importance of state constitutional interpretation as a countervailing power to the conservative trend in constitutional interpretation emanating from the U.S. Supreme Court since the appointment of Chief Justice Warren Burger by Republican President Richard M. Nixon in 1969. The most notable manifestation of this development is the so-called new judicial federalism, triggered largely by U.S. Associate Justice William J. Brennan (1977). The new judicial federalism refers to state courts, legislatures, and voters providing more rights under state constitutions than the U.S. Supreme Court provides under the U.S. Constitution (Friedelbaum, 1988; Kincaid, 1988). More recently this has spawned an effort to dethrone the U.S. Supreme Court as the monopolistic interpreter of constitutional norms. As two advocates of this view assert: "Successive generations of scholars and jurists have lurched violently from a dismissive view of state constitutions as documents of purely parochial import . . . to an aggressively ambitious approach that understands state constitutions as fundamentally freestanding sources of fully developed, independent legal norms" (Gardner and Rossi, 2010: 3).

Although the general public lacks awareness of state constitutions, public officials and advocacy groups recognize their importance. Consequently there is considerable constitutional activity. One measure is the 112 state constitutional amendments adopted in 2004–5, 158 in 2006–7, and 84 in 2008–9 (Dinan, 2010: 5).

Recent controversies over gay marriage illustrate the importance of state constitutions to advocacy groups. When it seemed that Hawaii's supreme court might legalize same-sex marriage in 1995, opponents campaigned to enact state laws banning it. As illustrated in Figure 11.1, a spate of such enactments occurred in 1996–2000.

Only three constitutional bans were adopted then. But after the high court of Massachusetts ruled (*Goodridge*, 2003) that the Bay State's constitution compels legal recognition of gay marriage, opponents campaigned for constitutional bans rather than statutory bans on same-sex marriage. Iowa's supreme court ruled unanimously (*Varnum*, 2009) that its state statutory prohibition of same-sex marriage violated the state constitution's equal protection clause. Opponents have failed to overturn this ruling with a constitutional amendment, but they exercised another constitutional right by unseating the three justices, including the chief justice, during their retention elections in 2010.

State constitutions, therefore, play central roles in state and local governance (Tarr, 1996, 1998). Insofar as states are laboratories of democracy, they are important for national policy debates (Kincaid, 1988).

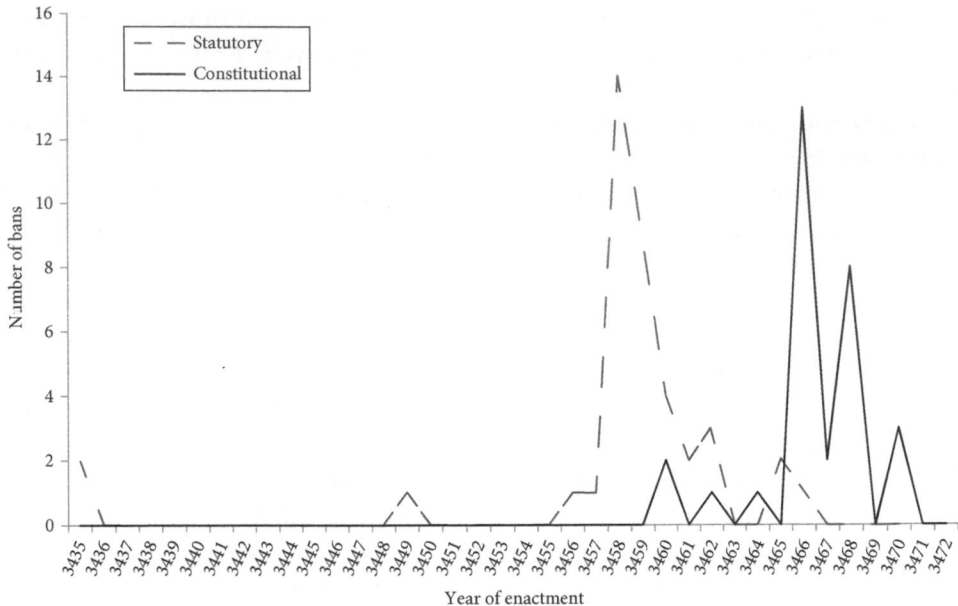

FIGURE 11.1 Enactments of state same-sex marriage bans

Sources: <http://en.wikipedia.org/wiki/Same-sex_marriage_status_in_the_United_States_by_state> and <http://www.lambdalegal.org/states-regions/>.

FUNDAMENTAL DIFFERENCES BETWEEN STATE CONSTITUTIONS AND THE U.S. CONSTITUTION

The fundamental difference between the federal and state constitutions is that the peoples of the American states delegate powers to the federal government through the U.S. Constitution, while they limit government powers through their state constitution. Except for what the U.S. Supreme Court declared to be inherent "powers of external sovereignty" (*United States* 1936), the U.S. Constitution consists of limited, delegated powers; the U.S. government can do only what it is permitted to do by the Constitution. All non-delegated powers are reserved to the states or the people, as affirmed in the Tenth Amendment.

A common misunderstanding is that the U.S. Constitution also grants powers to the states. It does not. It imposes some limits on state powers (especially Art. I, Sec. 10) and a few requirements on the states (especially Art. IV, Secs. 1–2). Otherwise, it reserves to the states certain key powers needed for the federal government's operation, such as holding elections for Congress and the presidency and ratifying amendments. The U.S. Constitution is, therefore, "incomplete" (Lutz, 1988). It does not vest plenary power in the federal government, and it relies on the states for much of its execution: "The states are mentioned explicitly or by direct implication 50 times in 42 separate sections of the U.S. Constitution" (Lutz, 1988: 24–5).

State constitutions limit rather than delegate powers because the states possess inherent powers. Their governments can do whatever they are not prohibited from doing by the federal or state constitution. This conception stems from the liberal social-compact theory that underlies American constitutionalism. Under this theory, the people consent to a body politic that possesses all conceivable government powers. The operation of this polity, however, is subject to majority rule and abuses of power. State constitutions, therefore, limit the inherent plenary powers of the state by imposing certain prohibitions (e.g. a declaration of rights found in all state constitutions), certain structural requirements (e.g. the separation of powers), certain procedural rules on the exercise of power (e.g. size of legislative quorums), and certain mandates (e.g. a requirement that the state provide free, public elementary and secondary education). Occasionally, citizens authorize the legislature to exercise a particular power, such as levying a specific tax; however, the legislature could exercise that power without such authorization.

Another important federal-state difference is that state constitutions delegate powers to local governments: counties, municipalities, townships, school districts, and special districts. Such power conferrals imply limits on state authority to intervene in local matters; however, because it is impossible to demarcate the boundaries between state and local authority precisely, the boundaries are fluid and often contested.

State Constitutional History

Modern written constitutions were invented by the states based on their colonial charter (Hsueh, 2010) and indigenous covenantal experiences (Lutz, 1980a). Eighteen state constitutions were adopted prior to ratification of the U.S. Constitution in 1788. The Massachusetts Constitution of 1780 (Peters, 1978), written mostly by John Adams, is the world's oldest written constitution still in effect. The states were seedbeds of constitutional debate during 1776–89 (Hoffman and Albert, 1981; Kruman, 1997) and produced constitutional designs that were both models and warnings for the framers of the U.S. Constitution (Adams, 1980).

Revolutionary Era: Democratic Experimentation and Political Identity Formation, 1776–88

An enduring state constitutional theme is the importance of public consent and control of government. Notions of democracy embedded in many early state constitutions stemmed from the assumption in Whig political theory of the existence of "a homogeneous people" (Lutz, 1980b: 11) who share a community of interest that is rooted in civic virtue and ascertainable through public deliberation. A constitution was not merely a frame of government but also a vision of the polity and definition of the people who constitute it. By contrast, Federalist theory emphasized self-interest as the proper basis of constitutionalism and sought means "of curing the mischiefs of faction," as James Madison put it in *Federalist* 10. Whigs encouraged factional consensus while Federalists welcomed factional contests.

This Whig orientation toward a common public interest also was rooted in the police power, which is possessed by state governments but not the federal government and which necessitates state legislation governing public health, safety, welfare, and morals—all of which originally fell beyond federal purview. Although, in reality, matters subject to the police power are contested by various interests, Whig theory emphasized deliberative consensus and cultural homogeneity. For example, while Whig theory tolerated religious diversity, at least among Protestants, it sought deliberative consensus on key moral principles common across sects. However, as the nation's population became more diversified from Jewish and Roman Catholic immigration, Whig theory experienced strains. Additionally, many police-power matters, such as prohibitions of abortion, alcoholic beverages, same-sex marriage, and Sunday shopping, entail zero-sum outcomes not amenable to consensual compromise. Exercise of the police power, therefore, has generated some sort of *kulturkampf* in every era of state constitutional development.

The Continental Congress advised the colonial legislatures in 1775 to draft constitutions. During 1776–88, 12 states drafted their first constitution. Connecticut relied on two slightly modified colonial charters; Rhode Island also adapted its colonial charter; and three states revised their constitution by replacing their first one with a new one. Massachusetts and New Hampshire pioneered election of a special convention to draft a constitution and citizen approval of a constitution. Today, these are widely accepted international standards of democratic constitutional adoption.

The early state constitutions established various styles of democratic government, with the Pennsylvania Constitution of 1776 being regarded as the most radically democratic (Selsam, 1971). For example, it created a unicameral legislature with no gubernatorial veto. (It was replaced by a less democratic constitution in 1790.)

Eight of the early constitutions contained a distinct declaration of rights. The Virginia Declaration of Rights, written mostly by George Mason in 1776, became the model of modern bills of rights. In accord with Whig theory's emphasis on public control of government, the early constitutions emphasized frequent rotation through short terms of office (1–3 years). All of the constitutions instituted a separation of powers, usually with an explicit statement, such as that in Article XXX of the Massachusetts Declaration of Rights of 1780; however, the legislature, as the people's principal representative, was made dominant (Williams, 1988), and also bicameral in 12 states, while most governors were weakened by short tenure, restricted re-eligibility, and few veto, appointment, or budget powers. In Maryland, the governor was selected by the legislature for a one-year term. New York established a council of revision headed by the governor to exercise veto powers. It was abolished in 1821, but such a council was included in the Virginia Plan for the proposed federal constitution and debated extensively by the Constitutional Convention before being rejected (Anderson, 2006). State high courts, however, began exercising judicial review in 1780, even though this power was not explicitly included in any constitution.

Most state constitutions also imposed property qualifications for holding public office as well as property or taxpaying requirements for voting (usually white males only), although the franchise was then broader than anywhere else in the world (Lutz 1980b). Some also set forth pay details. For example, Tennessee's 1796 Constitution limited, until 1804, legislators' per diems to $1.75, the governor's salary to $750 per year, and judges' salaries to $600 (about $10,200 in 2011).

Antebellum Era: Expanding Democracy and Restraining Entrepreneurial States, 1789–1865: This era was the most fecund. Twenty-two states entered the union with new constitutions, and 42 revised their constitution (i.e. replaced an old constitution with a new one). The revision number is high in part because southern states adopted one or more constitutions after secession.

This era was marked by expansions of public consent and control, most notably, the abolition of property and taxpaying qualifications for voting and office-holding and the movement to universal white-male suffrage during the Jacksonian era (1824–40). In a major departure from federal constitutional practice, state constitutions also established elections of judges, beginning with Mississippi in 1832 and New York in 1845. By 1865, most states held judicial elections.

From 1789 to about 1842, states were the major actors in the federal system. They financed infrastructure, development, and government operations from asset income derived from canal tolls, bank-stock dividends, and land sales, as well as indirect business taxes. By 1841, state debt stood at $193 million compared to $25 million for local governments and $5 million for the federal government (Wallis, 2000: 67). This aggressive economic policy-making produced excessive debt, economic dislocations, corruption, and other problems that motivated citizens to impose further constitutional limits on state powers.

The era was characterized, therefore, by substantive and procedural limitations on state legislatures, such as debt and tax limits, prohibitions on lending the state's credit to private entities and on subsidizing economic development, limits on banks, prohibitions on special legislation for private interests and for specific localities, and provisions for general laws governing private business incorporations. Legislatures were reined-in by making representation more equitable, reducing legislative membership, limiting the duration of legislative sessions, and creating semi-independent boards and commissions to oversee various functions. Executive power was enhanced by subjecting all governors to popular election, increasing tenure to four years, and improving veto, appointment, and pardon powers. At the same time, the Jacksonian impulse for popular control begat many independently elected executive officials, such as lieutenant governor, attorney general, secretary of state, treasurer, and comptroller, as well as popular election of judges having limited tenure.

Provisions also were made to amend and revise constitutions with more popular participation, especially the submission of amendments to the people for ratification. Overall, the era solidified three elements of popular sovereignty.

> First, the people, through their elected delegates, "represent" their sovereignty in a convention called to constitute a government. Second, the constitution thus framed is ratified by the people and given effect by their majority. Third, the people retain the right to revise, and presumably to abolish, the constitution by the ongoing exercise of their sovereignty. (Peterson, 1966: xiv)

Constitutional changes also expanded the role of government as citizens sought to regulate corporations and the emerging railroad industry. Most constitutions also established free public schools, and 15 state universities were created by 1850 (Richards, 1955: 47), even while the southern states maintained slavery.

It was this era of state constitutionalism that was observed by Alexis de Tocqueville. He did not like what he saw. The federal Constitution, he argued, is vastly superior to the state constitutions because the latter are too democratic. They are vulnerable to the "two main dangers" that "threaten the existence of democracies"; "complete subjection of the legislative power to the will of the" people and "concentration of all the other powers of government in the" legislature (de Tocqueville, 1969: 155).

Urban-Industrial Immigrant Era: Racism, Equality, and Assimilation, 1866–1899: This era was marked by extensive constitutional change in the South as those states adopted Reconstruction constitutions in 1866–9 and then dismantled those documents, especially during 1890–1908, to write new charters that rejected federally imposed values of Reconstruction and restored white supremacy, excluding blacks from elections, politics, and government, segregating races in public places, and banning interracial marriage. For the most part, the U.S. Supreme Court upheld these constitutions (e.g. *Williams,* 1898).

The era saw thirty-one constitutional revisions and nine new constitutions produced by states entering the union, making it the second most fertile period for constitutional change. Together, this and the antebellum era account for 76 percent of all state constitutional revisions in U.S. history and 65 percent of all first state constitutions.

The post-war era—which was marked by considerable interstate borrowing of constitutional ideas as well as the rise of Populism and Progressivism—continued the democratization, government limitations, and government expansions of the previous era. With the rise of giant corporations and big cities, constitutional change also focused on regulating business and the economy, protecting agriculture, recognizing labor unions, altering state-local relations, providing social services, and initiating natural-resource conservation. The 1870 Illinois Constitution regulated warehouses and grain elevators. Colorado (1876) and Idaho (1889) outlawed child labor in mines (Friedman, 1988), and New York (1894) mandated that a preserve "be forever kept as wild forest lands."

With the rise of strong political parties, Cook County, Illinois, introduced nonpartisan judicial elections, but by the end of the era, only several states had amended their constitutions to adopt this innovation. Today, only 14 states use nonpartisan elections to select appellate court judges for a full term; 18 employ nonpartisan elections to choose some or all trial-court judges.

Constitution-makers continued to adhere to the Whiggish idea of a common good, but this good was defined less by what it was than by what it was not, namely, rule by or on behalf of a segment of society. Nineteenth-century constitution-makers believed that powerful minorities, rather than tyrannical majorities, posed the most serious threat to liberty, and so they included numerous provisions designed to protect the many against the special privileges and advantages of the wealthy or well-connected few (Tarr, 1998, 100). Such provisions included numerous subject-matter restrictions imposed on legislatures and rules requiring equal and uniform taxation (Binney, 1894).

Voters also insisted that bills deal with single subjects and have clear titles, be read several times in open chamber before floor votes, and be enacted quite often by a majority of the members of the legislature, with some types of bills needing super-majority support. By 1900, legislatures had lost their once exalted position as "thirty-three state constitutions limited the length of legislative sessions, and only six state legislatures met annually" (Tarr, 1998: 121). Boards and commissions continued to proliferate as did elective executive offices, both state and local, even while some governors were given the item veto and more were offered re-election opportunities.

This era also marked the flowering of local governments as the nation's workhorse governments. From 1842 to the mid-1930s, local governments were the major fiscal actors, relying heavily on property taxes. By 1902, property taxes accounted for 42 percent of all federal, state, and local revenues (Wallis, 2000: 70). Even by 1932, local governments accounted for more than half of all government revenue. Cities borrowed heavily after the Civil War "to build schools, improve streets, establish water supplies, and erect public buildings," but the 1873–79 depression "brought many cities to the brink of bankruptcy, resulting in new constitutional provisions limiting the extent and character of local borrowing" (Sturm, 1982: 67). In the face of heightened state-local tensions, produced also by conflict between growing urban Catholic and Jewish immigrant populations and rural-dominated Protestant legislatures, a significant innovation was the introduction of home rule for cities in the Missouri Constitution of 1875 (now contained in about three-fourths of state constitutions).

The principal source of intrastate cultural conflict was immigration, which brought many Catholic and Jewish immigrants from southern and eastern Europe, and Asian immigrants as well, into an historically northern European Protestant country. Struggles emerged over voter qualifications, mechanisms to control state and local government institutions, and cultural issues such as alcoholic beverages and religion. Many states adopted Blaine amendments that prohibit appropriations of public funds for "sectarian" schools such as those established by Catholic and Jewish immigrants. U.S. House Speaker James G. Blaine proposed such an amendment to the U.S. Constitution in 1875, but it was narrowly defeated in the Senate. Such a provision, found in thirty-seven state constitutions today, is more restrictive than the U.S. Constitution's establishment clause.

Era of Progressive Reaction: Professional Efficiency and Public Efficacy, 1900–1945: This era was marked by almost schizophrenic constitutional reform. Progressives advocated not only professional, elitist, and nonpartisan expertise and efficiency in government but also popular control of government through such mechanisms as the initiative, referendum, recall, and primary elections. The era continued the democratization, government limitations, and government expansions of the previous eras, but Progressives mounted a trenchant critique of the constitutionalism of the previous eras. They attacked such core principles as the separation of powers (seen as obstructing efficient and equitable policy-making), bicameralism (seen as obstructive, especially senates), representative government (seen as too easily captured by special interests), and limited constitutionalism (seen as too restrictive of political reform). Overall, contended Progressives, "an increase in popular participation would actually invigorate the spirit of these principles" (Dinan, 1999: 985 and 2009). The principal Progressive innovation was direct democracy, first adopted in Oregon in 1902. By the mid-1920s, 19 states had adopted the statutory initiative, 14, the constitutional initiative, 21, the referendum, and ten, the recall (Sturm, 1982: 69).

Although the National Municipal League (1963), a Progressive group, issued a widely consulted Model State Constitution in 1924 that emphasized efficient, streamlined constitutionalism, Progressive successes were limited and mostly blunted in the South and Northeast. Only Nebraska adopted a unicameral legislature in 1934. However, the Missouri Plan (or merit plan) for selecting and retaining judges was first adopted in 1940 and is now used by 23 states. At the same time, southern states consolidated white supremacy.

Seven constitutional revisions occurred during this era, and Arizona, New Mexico, and Oklahoma entered the union with their first constitutions, making this era the fifth most fecund in U.S. history. However, the era witnessed the biggest expansion and diversification of state taxation in U.S. history. Forty-nine states adopted a gasoline tax; thirty-two states enacted an individual and/or corporate income tax; 33 levied a cigarette tax; 29 introduced taxes on distilled spirits; and 24 adopted a general sales tax. Although most of these innovations required no constitutional authorization, they laid the foundation for later legislative rate increases that triggered constitutional revolts against taxes.

Meanwhile, departments, agencies, boards, and commissions proliferated to address expanded economic and social policy-making. Attempting to improve efficiency, Progressive governors such as Robert M. LaFollette of Wisconsin (1901–6) Charles Evans Hughes of New York (1907–10), and Woodrow Wilson of New Jersey (1911–13) pressed for executive reorganization and consolidation. By 1938, 26 states had instituted some reorganization (Sturm, 1982: 69).

The federal Immigration Act of 1924 substantially reduced immigration. However, cultural struggles from the previous era continued as white ethnic political machines in northern and Midwestern states battled native Protestant and rural interests to control local and state governments. The enactment of national Prohibition in 1919 and its repeal in 1933, for example, made state constitutions fields of combat again over alcoholic beverages. Otherwise, the northern white ethnic political machines and southern white party organizations that sustained President Franklin D. Roosevelt's New Deal coalition did not champion Progressive constitutional reform.

Post-War Professional Reform Era: Modernizing States and Complementing Federal Power, 1945–1977: This era also emphasized professionalism and efficiency, with the New Jersey Constitution of 1947 and Alaska Constitution of 1956 epitomizing the ideals. Alaska's constitution followed many tenets of the Model State Constitution. The New Jersey document created the nation's most powerful governor and abolished all other elected executive offices, including lieutenant governor (re-established in 2005). By allowing the governor to appoint all executive officials, most with Senate consent, the constitution reflected the value of managerial efficiency that drove many of this era's reformers. Another "major goal was to reform New Jersey's creaky and archaic court system. The guiding impulse was not a change in substantive law or in the balance of power; the impulse was strictly technocratic" (Friedman, 1988: 39).

Also illustrative of professionalism were the decline of popularly elected constitutional conventions and rise of constitutional commissions consisting of appointed experts. It became more common for "political elites and professional reformers" to campaign "for constitutional revision, with the populace reduced to rejecting convention calls and proposed constitutions" in order "to register its distrust of a process it no longer" felt under its control (Tarr, 1998: 170).

This era also opened new fields by embedding rights to a clean or healthful environment in the constitutions of Illinois and Pennsylvania in 1970, Massachusetts in 1971, Montana in 1972, and Hawaii in 1978 and providing for environmental protection in some constitutions. Fourteen states (e.g. Illinois in 1971 and Connecticut in 1974) also adopted amendments guaranteeing equal rights for women (i.e. "little ERAs") from 1971 through 1974. A movement to constitutionalize a right to privacy began with Illinois in 1970 and spread to South Carolina (1971) and Alaska and Montana (1972).

This era was the fourth most fecund. Eleven constitutional revisions occurred during 1946–77, with the Georgia Constitution of 1976 being the last. In addition, Alaska and Hawaii entered the union with their first, and still only, constitutions. Emphasis was placed on professionalizing legislatures, increasing legislator salaries and benefits, instituting longer sessions and annual sessions, increasing office, equipment, and staff resources, and providing research and bill-drafting services. In 1947, only six legislatures met annually; by the end of this era, 36 did so (45 by 2010). Efforts also were made to streamline the executive branch, especially by reducing independently elected executive officials and increasing gubernatorial tenure. In 1947, only 26 governors served a four-year term; at the start of 1978, 45 did so (48 by 2010). Reformers eliminated many elected offices, but voters insisted on retaining elections of the attorney general in 43 states, the treasurer in 36 states, and the secretary of state in 35 states. Attempts were made, as well, to reorganize, rationalize, and professionalize state court systems and to improve equity, efficiency, and ethics in their operation.

This era also completed the previous era's precedent of tax adoptions. Seventeen more states adopted cigarette taxes; 16 introduced a general sales tax; 13 more enacted a corporate income tax; 12 more adopted an individual income tax; three more levied distilled spirits taxes; and one added a gasoline tax. State adoptions of such major taxes stopped in 1976 when New Jersey enacted an individual income tax in the face of a state supreme-court mandate. However, a constitutional amendment stipulated that all income-tax revenue be dedicated to property-tax relief (Salmore and Salmore 1998: 247).

Overall, what characterized this era was elite-driven change intended to modernize states' constitutions. Many reformers echoed de Tocqueville's criticism of state constitutions and embraced the more elitist federal document as their model.

Another facet of elite reform was a turn toward federal intervention to improve state and local governments. Federal intervention increased exponentially during this era, beginning with efforts to end racial desegregation. These interventions triggered needs to adjust state constitutions to federal programs and requirements and to ignore provisions overridden by federal laws (Kincaid, 1993), producing a bump-up in constitutional revision compared to the previous and following eras. The U.S. Supreme Court played a major role in altering state constitutional norms by, among other things, leading state high courts to interpret state constitutions in ways similar to federal constitutional interpretation, ordering "one person, one vote" legislative redistricting (*Reynolds*, 1964, striking down provisions of the Alabama Constitution), which destroyed historic community bases of representation, and voiding state prohibitions on abortion (*Roe*, 1973), which sparked a continuing nationalized *kulturkampf* having numerous state ramifications.

Another theme of the era was that modernization would enhance states' capacities for modern governance sufficiently to complement federal intervention by enabling states to manage burgeoning federal programs and also fend off needs for more intervention. Reformers argued that archaic constitutions presiding over horse-and-buggy governments invited federal intervention and that by modernizing state constitutions and waving goodbye to the good-time Charlies who occupied many governors' mansions (Sabato, 1983), states would be better able to counterbalance and complement federal power. One prominent reformer endorsed both federal intervention and state constitutional reform when he opined that many states "need to modernize their constitutions in order to bring them up to the requirements of the twentieth century" (Anderson, 1955: 213) while also contending that state and local governments "do their work much better" when they are "under firm and forward-looking national leadership" (Anderson, 1955: 243).

Reformers also sought to destroy traditional party organizations. The corruption associated with those "machine" organizations was seen as requiring root-and-branch reform. This era also saw the rise of public employee unions and organized interests in state capitals such that by 1980, "there were 15,064 organizations registered to lobby in the states" (Gray and Lowery, 2003: 257). Many states instituted collective bargaining rights for public employees, though only a few (e.g. Florida and Hawaii) constitutionalized the right. Although this era produced tremendous benefits, such as greater racial and gender equality and social welfare, it left a legacy that became a target of revolt.

CURRENT ERA: PUBLIC REVOLT AND MODERNIZING RESTRAINT, 1978-PRESENT

Voter approval of California's Proposition 13 in 1978 can be said to mark the onset of the current state constitutional era, which has seen a reassertion of public control. The Jarvis-Gann citizen initiative amended California's constitution by shifting property-tax valuation from current market values to acquisition values. It limited tax increases to 2 percent per year (unless a property is sold) and required two-thirds majorities to approve state statutes and local referenda increasing other taxes. Many observers argued that Proposition 13 triggered a nationwide tax revolt (e.g. Massachusetts' statutory Proposition 2½ in 1980) and helped usher Ronald Reagan (California's 1967–75 governor) into the White House in 1981, although evidence for these claims is weak. Nevertheless, Proposition 13 acquired iconic status and marked the start of a popular revolt against the modernization and professionalization of government of the previous era, as reflected in efforts since 1978 to impose term limits on state legislators and tax-and-expenditure limits on state and local governments.

An outstanding characteristic of this era is that no state has adopted an individual or corporate income tax, general sales tax, or distilled spirits tax since New Jersey adopted its income tax in 1976 (although in 1991 Connecticut expanded its tax from capital gains and dividends to earned income as well). Since 1978, moreover, Californians have added more property tax limits and also rejected a 2004 proposition to lower from two-thirds to 55 percent the legislative vote needed to pass a budget and enact new budget-related taxes.

Dearth of Constitutional Revision: Another remarkable characteristic of this era is the paucity of constitutional revision. This is the most infertile era of state constitutional history (see Figure 11.2). Only two states have adopted revised constitutions: Georgia (1982) and Rhode Island (1986), although the latter was merely a rewrite involving eight amendments.

Calls to revise constitutions have failed, even though 14 constitutions require a call for a constitutional convention to be placed before voters periodically (e.g. every ten or 20 years). This idea originated in New York in 1846, but eight of the 14 states did not adopt it until the 1945–77 era, perhaps because it was included in the Model State Constitution (Benjamin, 2002). The provision is intended to facilitate modernization and prevent constitutions from being captured by special interests.

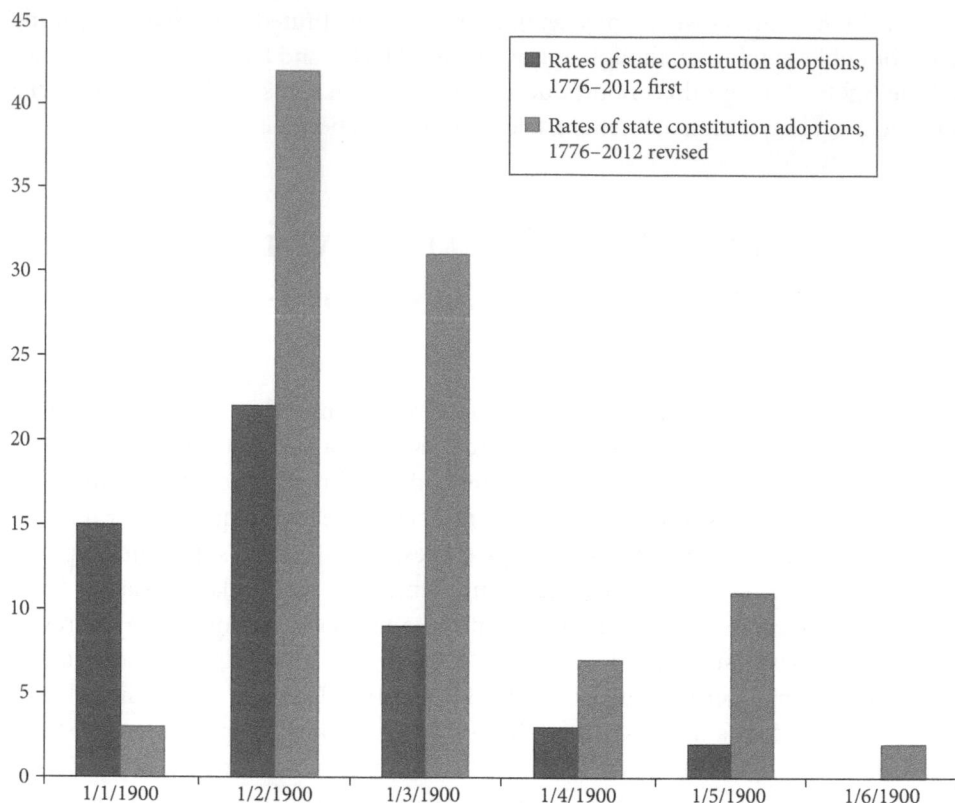

FIGURE 11.2 State constitutional adoptions

Yet, during 1978–2010, voters in these 14 states rejected 29 of 32 convention calls, and courts rejected one of the three approvals (Hawaii in 1996) because the "yes" vote did not reach a majority of those who voted in the election. Missouri, for instance, has a 20-year call cycle, but voters have not approved a call since 1942 (which produced the current 1945 constitution). Iowans rejected calls in 1980, 1990, 2000, and 2010, and, despite severe socioeconomic decline, Michiganders rejected convention calls in 1978, 1994, and 2010. New Yorkers, whose constitution is 118 years old, overwhelmingly rejected such a call in 1997. Oklahoma has a 20-year call cycle, but the legislature has not placed a call on the ballot since 1970.

In 2002, anticipating a convention, Alabamians mandated that any convention-proposed constitution be ratified by a majority of the state's qualified electors voting on the question. However, Alabama, which has no periodic calls, failed to convene a convention, and, in 2003, voters rejected a gubernatorially initiated package of constitutional tax reforms (Thomson, 2006). Vermonters rejected a convention in 1982; in Florida, which also lacks periodic calls, voters rejected a constitutional revision in 1978. In 2002, Floridians required all citizen-initiated amendments to be accompanied by an economic impact statement (an idea also adopted in North Dakota in

2004); in 2006, they required constitutional amendments or revisions to be approved by 60 percent of the electors voting on the measure.

The only document-wide revisions commonly approved by voters during this era have been calls, such as that in Texas in 1999, "to eliminate duplicative, executed, obsolete, archaic, and ineffective provisions" and to convert to gender- and race-neutral language. However, Nebraskans rejected a 2000 proposal to gender-neutralize their constitution.

Absent research on the dearth of contemporary constitutional revision, one can only speculate on the reasons. One possibility is the absence of a broadly accepted vision of state constitutionalism, such as Whig theory, Progressivism, or the Model State Constitution. These conceptions still influence debates, but no new rationale has surfaced to motivate revision. A recent call for "constitutional reform" by a project supported by the Ford Foundation, reiterated the previous era's rationale that reform is needed "to make state governments more effective, equitable, and responsive, and to equip them to deal with the challenges of the twenty-first century" (Tarr 2006: 4). This rationale hardly stirs citizens' souls. Instead, it is what many Americans distrust because they believe that Progressive-type reforms will increase state governments' ability to tax and regulate them.

Another revision obstacle may be the decline of public trust in all governments since Watergate. Furthermore, on various confidence measures, state government often ranks below local and the federal government (Cole and Kincaid, 2006). Voters may doubt the ability of any legislature, commission, or convention to produce an acceptable new constitution.

Increased intrastate party competition since the 1930s may also inhibit revision. Rising party competition was especially evident during the previous era (1945–77) when reliably one-party states disappeared, especially as Republicans gained ground in the South. There was a further increase in competitive states after 1977 (Jewell and Morehouse, 2001). Polarization among party elites and activists during the current era (McCarty et al., 2008; Abramowitz, 2010) has likely further weakened possibilities for reaching bipartisan compromises on constitutional revision. The parties espouse different views on the nature of government. The composition of a constitutional convention, moreover, could be similar to that of presidential nominating conventions in which the activists who capture delegate seats hold more extreme views than those of the median voter.

The rise of the religious right since the early 1970s has added another impediment to revision. A constitutional convention would attract ardent proponents and opponents of abortion, affirmative action, gay marriage, and other divisive cultural issues. Such activists could easily derail a convention.

Another possible obstacle is that the tremendous increase in the number of interest groups operating in state capitals since the 1960s, coupled with the diversification of state economies and state populations, has reduced the ability of reformers and state leaders to generate a common will and rationale for constitutional revision. The heightened organizational consciousness of racial and ethnic minorities in the current era adds more voices to revision politics. Revision, moreover, affects powerful private and public interests. Hence, centrifugal forces may predominate over the centripetal forces of compromise needed for revision. The multiplicity of entrenched interests may also make groups risk averse. Why open a Pandora's Box with constitutional revision when many interests can achieve objectives through statutes and amendments?

The vastly increased scope and depth of state government since the 1960s has created considerable complexity and interdependence that can be difficult for citizens to sort out in a convention. Governance could be unsettled and complicated, even inadvertently, by constitutional revision. State high courts have become more activist as well, promulgating major policies through constitutional interpretations that could be altered or reversed by constitutional revision. Prominent examples are the New Jersey Supreme Court's 1982 *Mount Laurel II* decision, which ordered all municipalities to permit construction of specified numbers of low-income homes, and *Abbott* decisions, beginning in 1985, that require redistribution of state funds to poor school districts. Recent political developments have led the court to weaken these controversial policies such that neither proponents nor opponents would probably want to risk combat in a constitutional revision process. Likewise, in California, citizen constitutional and statutory initiatives have cluttered government with so many rules and policies favorable to diverse interests that a call for an overall revision of the 1879 constitution to streamline and rationalize state and local government could encounter a buzz saw of resistance (cf. Cain, 2006).

Another possible reason for the dearth of revision is the massive increase of federal involvement in state and local governments since the late 1960s. State and local governance is so infused with federal funds and regulations that disentangling purely state functions for purposes of constitutional revision could be difficult. This massive federal presence also narrows the scope of state constitutional discretion. During the current era, Medicaid alone has become the second largest category of state spending. Medicaid and other federally funded programs, along with numerous federal restrictions on state tax powers, narrow the scope of fiscal reform available to state constitution reformers.

Another recent example is the U.S. Supreme Court's *McDonald* (2010) decision, which incorporated the Second Amendment to the federal Constitution into the Fourteenth Amendment, thereby recognizing a federal individual right to bear arms. The last time the Court incorporated a provision of the U.S. Bill of Rights was in 1969 (*Benton*). Fifty-five percent of all incorporations occurred during the 1960s, and all narrowed the space available for state constitutional action. *McDonald* will constrain state constitutional and statutory regulation of guns.

The dearth of revision is reflected even in Florida, the only state having a constitutional requirement for the three branches of government to appoint a constitution revision commission every twenty years. Voters rejected all of the first commission's (1977–8) proposals, but approved eight of nine proposals proffered by the second commission (1997–8). However, except for an equal-rights-for-women amendment, the 1998 proposals involved modest technical matters and government reorganization, not significant constitutional change. To achieve success, the commission avoided volatile issues such as abortion, homosexuality, and medical marijuana (Salokar 2006).

Consequently, Florida's initiative process has produced more significant constitutional changes than its revision process. Floridians have used constitutional initiatives to, for example, prohibit indoor smoking, animal cruelty, and gay marriage; impose tax and revenue limits, term limits on legislators, medical practice, malpractice, and tort reforms; and mandate government transparency, English as the official state language, universal access to pre-Kindergarten, reduced K-12 class sizes, and establishment of an Everglades Trust Fund.

Amendment Proliferation: Although many characteristics of the contemporary era appear to hinder constitutional revision, these factors do not impede piecemeal amendments. Amendomania (Comment, 1949) is flourishing. Amendment rather than revision may be more successful because single amendments affect fewer powerful interests than revision. Revision packages of constitutional changes easily become a "can of worms" rejected because of one or two controversial provisions or because different interests reject different provisions of a package. A revision also can be rejected if voters object to an unrelated proposition on the ballot, as happened with Florida's 1978 revision proposals, which suffered a backlash from voters opposed to an initiated amendment to establish casino gambling. Piecemeal amendments originated by legislatures have already surmounted major interest-group hurdles, such as super-majority legislative votes, before they reach the citizens. In 1996, New Mexicans even allowed amendments to be proposed by an independent commission established by the legislature for that purpose. In addition, amendments initiated by citizens circumvent the legislative interest-group process and appeal directly to voters, thus requiring interest groups to organize differently and behave more diffusely than when they lobby legislators or constitutional conventions and commissions. Failed amendments, moreover, can be proposed again more easily than can rejected revision packages.

It might be argued that change through a convention or commission is superior because those bodies can manage change logically and coherently. Piecemeal amendments can produce a hodgepodge of incoherent provisions. However, few conventions or commissions produce logical, coherent documents because their processes are subject to political forces during deliberations and their products are subject to electoral forces during ratification. Prospective concerns about electoral forces shape convention or commission deliberations. Furthermore, after voters approve a new constitution, it experiences later amendment.

Amendment may also trump revision because another characteristic of this era is that use of the initiative (constitutional and statutory) has reached historic highs. The average number of initiatives "doubled from 31 a year in the 1970s to 62 a year in the 2000s" (Bowser, 2009: 18). Constitutional amendment by initiative is available in 18 states: Arizona, Arkansas, California, Colorado, Florida, Illinois, Massachusetts, Michigan, Mississippi, Missouri, Montana, Nebraska, Nevada, North Dakota, Ohio, Oklahoma, Oregon, and South Dakota. Successful initiatives encourage legislators and interest groups in other states to propose similar policies.

In summary, the current era has been defined by voter enthusiasm for piecemeal amendments that restrain government, and voter aversion to overall revision.

Tax and Expenditure Limits: Amendment support has been driven partly by public desires for tax and expenditure limits (TELs). TELs reflect a backlash against the Progressively driven modernization movements of the previous two eras, which fostered income and sales tax adoptions, especially during the Great Depression when widespread revolts targeted the mainstay of state and local finance—the property tax. Revolts became so severe in Chicago that Mayor Anton Cermak urged Congress to send "money now or militia later" (Beito, 2009: 78), and Illinois enacted a sales tax in 1933. Numerous constitutional limits were placed on property taxes, a pattern revived by California's Proposition 13.

In 2003, Texans approved an amendment, labeled Proposition 13, permitting counties, cities, towns, and junior-college districts to freeze property taxes on the residence homesteads of the disabled and elderly. Arkansans approved a new property tax limit in 2000, and Indianans approved a tax cap in 2010. Many amendments grant exemptions for specific taxpayers such as widows and widowers (e.g. Florida 1988), disabled veterans (e.g. New Mexico 1998), and individuals age 65 or more (e.g. Tennessee 2006) and for specific property such as motor vehicles owned by former prisoners of war (Georgia 1998) and home additions constructed to house elderly parents, grandparents, or a spouse (Florida 2002). In 2004, Oregonians authorized owners whose property values are reduced by environmental or land-use regulations to claim compensation. If government fails to compensate within two years, the claimant can use the property under regulations in place when the property was purchased. Voters weakened this provision, however, by a 2007 amendment.

TELs broader than Proposition 13 also arrived in 1978 when Michiganders approved the Headlee Amendment, which limits the state's own-source revenue collection to no more than 9.49 percent of state personal income. If revenue exceeds the limit by more than one percent, the excess must be remitted to taxpayers. If the excess falls below one percent, it can be deposited in the state's budget stabilization ("rainy day") fund. The amendment also curbs backdoor tax increases by prohibiting the state from reducing its funding of existing state mandates on local governments. The state also cannot deny reimbursement to local governments for new mandates or reduce the proportion of state funds awarded all local governments below the level of fiscal year 1979. In 1979, Washingtonians limited the growth of state revenue to the growth of total state personal income. Missouri's Hancock Amendment (1980) limits total state revenues and expenses to a percentage of state personal income, requires the state to fund mandates on local governments, and requires new local taxes, licenses, and fees to be approved by local voters. In 1982, Mainers required the state's income tax to be adjusted for inflation, and Floridians limited state revenue growth in 1994. Such amendments gained traction in part because revenue growth in most states during recent decades has exceeded personal-income growth.

After rejecting a TEL in 1986, Coloradans approved a new device in 1992—a Taxpayer Bill of Rights (TABOR). This amendment received considerable national publicity, but was later weakened and did not spread to other states. In fact, Nebraskans rejected a TABOR cap on their state budget in 2006. Utahans rejected a TEL in 1988, and Oregonians rejected major TELs in 2000 and 2006.

Other approaches to tax limits include, for example, a 1993 Texas amendment prohibiting the legislature from imposing a personal income tax without voter approval, a 1994 Florida amendment allowing initiated amendments to cover multiple subjects, a 1996 Florida requirement that new taxes to be enacted by constitutional amendment be approved by two-thirds of the voters, 1996 Nevada and South Dakota rules for a two-thirds legislative vote to enact a new tax or tax increase, and a 1998 Montana amendment requiring an election and voter approval of any new or increased tax enacted by state or local governments, school districts, and other taxing districts. In 2010, Nevadans rejected an amendment to allow the legislature to make certain tax changes without voter approval. Maine finally repealed its poll tax in 1978, and, in 1981, Washington repealed its inheritance and gift taxes and limited the state's death tax to the allowable federal estate-tax credit. In 2000, South Dakotans repealed the inheritance tax and prohibited the legislature from enacting a new one.

Voters have not embraced all anti-tax amendments. In 1983, Ohioans rejected the need for a three-fifths legislative vote to raise taxes; in 1999, Iowans rejected a proposal to require a 60 percent legislative vote to increase taxes. A few small tax increases have been adopted, such as a 2008 Minnesota vote increasing the sales tax by three-eights of one percent. In 2010, Arizonans approved a temporary (three-year) sales tax increase. However, even when taxes are maintained, there have been numerous amendments dedicating specific tax revenues to specific purposes, such as a 1988 California vote requiring a minimum of 40 percent of the state's budget to be spent on education and a 2006 Minnesota vote dedicating 40 percent of vehicle sales tax revenues to public transportation. Voters also have approved many specific trust funds (e.g. the Alabama Capital Improvement Trust Fund and County and Municipal Government Capital Improvement Trust Fund in 2000).

Limits on state borrowing proliferated during the 1840s, and limits on local borrowing spread after the Panic of 1873, thus reducing the need for contemporary restraints. In 1988, Missourians even loosened a restraint by mandating a four-sevenths majority of those voting to approve bond issues for constructing and improving schools, roads, bridges, and job development projects on municipal, primary, and general election days, while keeping a two-thirds majority rule for other election days. In 2010, Arkansans made it easier for their state to issue bonds to attract industry, and Arizonans authorized more higher education bonds in 2006. In 2008, though, New Jersey voters expanded the categories of bonds needing their approval.

A marked characteristic of this era also has been adoption of a rainy day fund by 47 states. Prior to this era, only New York (1945), Florida (1959), and Tennessee (1972) had such a fund. Most recently, Missourians created a budget reserve fund in 2000 for use by the governor with approval of two-thirds of the legislature during a disaster or revenue shortfall. In 2007, Washingtonians approved transferring 1 percent of general state revenues to a rainy day fund every year. However, Alabamans rejected a fund in 2002.

Term Limits: Although term limits date back to Pennsylvania's 1776 constitution, the federal Constitution, much to Anti-Federalists' objections, did not follow the precedent of the Articles of Confederation by term limiting members of Congress. However, rotation in office and popular support for it during the nineteenth century obviated the need to constitutionalize term limits, but when the Progressives' push to professionalize state government contributed to rising incumbent reelections after World War II, a term-limits movement emerged during the late 1980s and succeeded in limiting legislators in twenty-one states during 1990–6. The movement lost steam by 1997, although Nebraskans constitutionalized legislator term limits in 2000 because their 1992 and 1994 approvals were voided by their supreme court.

Thus far, the only other constitutional term limits vacated by a state supreme court occurred in Oregon in 2002. The court held that the ballot measure violated the constitution's single-subject rule. Fourteen states now have standing constitutional limits. By contrast, of the six states that adopted statutory term limits, only Maine's law remains intact. Term-limit laws were struck down by the high courts of Massachusetts (1997), Washington (1998), and Wyoming (2004) and repealed by the legislatures of Idaho (2002) and Utah (2003). Thus, while the term-limits movement has made little progress since 1996, voters have not repealed any term limits. In 2006, South Dakotans rejected a package of legislatively proposed constitutional changes because it included a term-limits repeal. They refused to repeal term limits again in 2008. Only Mississippians have rejected constitutional limits on legislators (1999). In 2006, Coloradans rejected limits on appellate court judges. However, voters in Arkansas (2004), Montana (2004), and Maine (2007) rejected proposals to increase the number of terms served by limited legislators. In 1992, Ohioans imposed term limits on their lieutenant governor (governor was already term limited), attorney general, secretary of state, treasurer, and auditor; in 2010, Oklahomans approved term limits for the same officers as well as the state labor commissioner, schools superintendent, and insurance commissioner. In 2008, Louisiana voters imposed term limits on members of boards and commissions.

Additionally, Minnesotans adopted recall of state officials in 1996; New Mexicans approved recall of county officials in 1996; and, in 2010, Illinoisans adopted recall of their governor in response to scandals that precipitated Governor Rod Blagojevich's impeachment and removal from office in January 2009.

Government Organization, Structure, and Powers: Government organization continues to be subject to constitutional adjustment. In 1996, for example, North Carolinians finally gave their governor a veto power; in 1995, Mainers gave their governor an item veto. In 2002, Wyoming voters rejected an amendment to limit the governor's item veto only to appropriations bills. In 1990 and 2008, though, Wisconsinites deprived their governor of the item-veto power to create new words in bills or veto words and numbers in appropriations bills.

In 1995, Texans removed the office of treasurer from their constitution, as did Minnesotans in 1998, while voters in North Dakota (2000) and Nebraska (2010) rejected such a measure. Texans (1991) and Utahans (2010) amended their constitutions to establish an ethics commission. In 1988, Floridians created a Department of Veterans Affairs and a Department of Elder Affairs.

During this era, several more states authorized annual legislative sessions (e.g., Washington in 1979, Kentucky in 2000, Arkansas in 2008, and Oregon in 2010), although the legislature is limited every other year in Arkansas to a 30-day budget session and to a 35-day session in Oregon. In 1998, Nevadans reined in their legislature to 120 days every two years. Coloradans did the same for their annual legislative sessions. In 1980, Illinoisans reduced their house of representatives from 177 to 118 members, and, in 1994, they moved adjournment from June 30 to May 31. In 2010, Alaskans rejected adding seats to their legislature. In 2004, Nebraskans mandated that their legislature achieve a two-thirds rather than simple-majority vote to amend, repeal, modify, or impair an initiated statute enacted by the people.

Judicial selection has become contested in recent years, and the Missouri Plan—a product of the previous two eras—has not fared well against direct election. In 1987, Ohioans rejected a proposal to abolish direct election of their supreme court and appeals court judges. In 2000, Arkansans approved nonpartisan judicial elections, and Floridians declined to end elections of circuit and county court judges. In South Dakota, where the Missouri Plan covers appellate judges, voters in 2004 rejected merit selection for circuit court judges. In a highly publicized and externally financed 2010 vote in which former U.S. Supreme Court Justice Sandra Day O'Connor urged Nevadans to adopt the Missouri Plan, voters rejected the plan by 57.7 percent. Otherwise, in Hawaii, where judges are appointed by the governor with legislative consent, voters refused to repeal judges' mandatory 70-year-old retirement age. Reflecting public concern about high-court activism, moreover, Oklahomans in 2010 forbad their state courts from using international law or Sharia in their rulings

In 2002, Rhode Islanders answered the following ballot question affirmatively: "Should the Rhode Island Constitution be changed to eliminate Article 6, Section 10, which preserves to the General Assembly today broad powers granted to it by King Charles II of England in 1663 and also be changed to expressly provide that the legislative, executive, and judicial branches of Rhode Island government are to be separate and co-equal consistent with the American system of government?" An amendment was approved in 2004.

Transparency has been a public concern as well. In 2004, for example, Californians enhanced public access to government information. In 2007, Texans required a recorded vote to be taken by their house of representatives on final passage of any bill or resolution proposing or approving a constitutional amendment, or any other non-ceremonial resolution, and to provide public access to those votes on the internet for two years.

A few state constitutions (e.g., Utah in 1990, Indiana in 2004, and Colorado 2010) have been amended to provide for relocation of the state capital and continuity of government in the event of a major disaster.

Local Government and State-Local Relations: Given that local governments are constitutional creatures of the states, they figure prominently in state constitutions. The principal trend during the current era has been to try to restrict state imposition of unfunded mandates on local governments (e.g., the 1978 Headlee Amendment in Michigan, Florida in 1990, Maine in 1992, Oregon in 1996 and 2000, and Louisiana in

2006). In 2004, Californians provided that local property and sales tax revenues stay with local governments rather than being sent to the state treasury, except if the governor declares an emergency and two-thirds of the legislature concurs. In 2006, Virginians allowed local governments to create tax increment finance (TIF) districts, but in 1986, Coloradans required any franchise to be granted by a home-rule municipality to be subject to initiative and referendum. In 2002, Floridians required free pre-kindergarten education to be offered to all 4-year-olds.

Several states (e.g. Colorado in 1980, Nebraska in 1996 and 1998, and Alabama in 2008) imposed requirements for voter approval of local government mergers. In 2000, South Dakotans authorized local voters to initiate ballot measures to merge, eliminate, or jointly finance local offices, functions, or governments so long as any measure is approved by a majority vote in each affected government unit. In 1998, Californians authorized municipalities to enter sales-tax revenue-sharing agreements with other local governments. In New Hampshire in 2000, however, voters rejected municipal home-rule by a narrow margin. Otherwise, in Texas (2001), voters approved municipal donations of outdated and surplus firefighting equipment to less-developed countries; in 2003, they approved such donations to the Texas Forest Service.

Campaigns, Elections, and Voting: In this post-Watergate era, election reform has been on state agendas, but reforms have been managed more through statutes than constitutional change. The Florida Sunshine Amendment of 1976, which was the first successful constitutional initiative in Florida's history, imposed certain disclosure requirements on state and local candidates and election officials. A sweeping 1998 amendment authorized public financing of campaigns for statewide candidates who consent to campaign spending limits, mandated that ballot-access requirements for independent and minor-party candidates not exceed those for majority-party candidates, permitted all electors to vote in any party's primary if the winner will have no general-election opposition, and made school-board elections nonpartisan.

In 1996, Nevadans approved campaign contribution limits, and Coloradans approved an amendment that included caps on individual and PAC contributions to candidates, a ban on direct corporate and union contributions, stricter disclosure rules for campaign contributions, and voluntary spending limits. Coloradans strengthened contribution and spending limits in 2002 and also authorized citizens to organize small-donor committees. In 1984, Coloradans had approved a voting integrity measure and also authorized motor-voter registration. In 2002, Arkansans repealed a constitutional election-purity rule that ballots be traceable back to individual voters through a tracking number.

Constitutional changes in California have included, for example, disqualification for federal, state, and local office of a candidate adjudged to have libeled an opponent (1984); prohibition of party endorsements of candidates for nonpartisan offices (1986); extension to 180 days the time available to hold a recall election (1994); a requirement to count every vote legally cast (2002), which was a reaction to the 2000 recount controversy in Florida; approval of a nonpartisan Citizens Redistricting Commission (2008); and establishment of a single primary open to all voters, with the top two winners competing in the general election (2010). In 2002, though, Californians rejected election-day voter registration. In 1998, Arizonans approved open primaries.

In 2010, Floridians mandated that legislative and congressional districts be drawn so as to create "fairness," be "as equal in population as feasible," and utilize "city, county and geographical boundaries." In 2010, Oklahomans approved a redistricting commission consisting of three Democrats and three Republicans. In 2006, they authorized package stores to sell alcoholic beverages on election days. Oregonians in 2002 prohibited circulators of initiative petitions from being paid on a per-signature basis, and Alaskans in 2004 required initiative petitions to have signatures from more voting districts.

In 1977, Ohioans ensured the voting eligibility of persons registered for at least 30 days; in 2008, Marylanders approved early voting; and in 2010, Vermont voters allowed 17-year-olds to vote in primaries if they will be 18 by the general election. A number of states, like New Jersey in 2007, removed such words as "idiot" and "insane person" from the voter qualifications section of their constitution and substituted language such as "person[s] who have been adjudicated by a court of competent jurisdiction to lack the capacity to understand the act of voting."

Civil Rights: The proliferation of "little ERAs" in the early 1970s did not extend into the current era. Vermont rejected an ERA in 1986. Only Florida and Iowa adopted such amendments, both in 1998. Florida's amendment also bans discrimination based on national origin and physical disability. Eighteen constitutions (including California from 1879 and Wyoming from 1890) have such a provision now. Similarly, a movement to constitutionalize a right to privacy, which began with Illinois in 1970, did not accelerate in the current era. Only Hawaii (1978) and Florida (1980) added an explicit right to privacy to their bills of rights.

Most prevalent has been voter approval of victims' bills of rights in about twenty states, starting with California in 1982 (and supplemented in 2008). A movement also has developed to make the right to bear arms more constitutionally explicit (e.g. North Dakota in 1984, Maine in 1987, Wisconsin in 1998, and Kansas in 2010). Idiosyncratically, Californians adopted a reporter shield right in 1980; in 2004, they constitutionalized a right to engage in stem-cell research. In 1998, Nebraskans added an equal-protection-of-the-laws clause to their constitution, while South Carolina repealed its miscegenation clause, as did Alabama in 2000. In 2009, Texans elevated a statutory right of access to public beaches to a constitutional right. Washingtonians prohibited student busing for racial integration in 1978, and New Mexicans rejected a legal holiday honoring Cesar Chavez in 2002, but Wyoming constitutionally strengthened equalization of school funding in 2006. A number of states, such as Missouri (1998), Alabama (2000), California (2000), and Arkansas (2006) have constitutionalized a right of religious organizations and other nonprofits to conduct bingo games, raffles, and sweepstakes.

This era has not, however, been friendly to others. In 2006, Arizonans denied publicly funded services to illegal aliens (California's 1994 Proposition 187 was a statute that was quickly blocked by federal courts). In 1998, Tennessee voters repealed their constitution's requirement that prisons be "comfortable." Montanans amended their constitution to specify that criminal law and punishment are based on principles not only of prevention and reformation but also public safety and restitution. Massachusetts limited the voting rights of incarcerated felons in 2000, and Rhode Island denied such rights in 2006 (but with post-prison restoration). New Jersey voters in 2000 authorized their legislature to disclose publicly information such as the identity and location of sex offenders. In 2010, North Carolinians prohibited convicted felons from running for sheriff; several other states prohibited convicted felons from serving in the legislature and other offices. In 2002, though, Virginians authorized their supreme court to consider DNA evidence that might exonerate a convicted felon. In 2009, New Yorkers permitted prisoners to perform volunteer work for nonprofit organizations.

Abortion, Assisted Suicide, and Stem-Cell Research: The U.S. Supreme Court nationalized legal abortion in 1973 but left assisted suicide to the states in 1996. Despite controversies over these issues, there has been less state constitutional than statutory action. In 1984, Coloradans banned public funding for abortions while Washingtonians rejected such a ban. In 2004, Floridians amended their constitution to allow the legislature to enact a parental notification law; in 2008, Californians rejected such notification. In 2008 and 2010, Coloradans rejected amendments applying the word "person" to any fertilized egg, embryo, or fetus.

Interestingly, voters have declined to treat assisted suicide as a constitutional right. Voters approved assisted suicide statutes in Oregon (1997) and Washington (2008); voters in California (1992), Michigan (1998), and Maine (2000) rejected such statutes. In 2009, Montana's supreme court ruled that state statutes protect physicians from prosecution for aiding the deaths of terminally ill patients but declined to declare assisted suicide a state constitutional right.

Stem-cell research became controversial when President George W. Bush curtailed federal support in 2001. This produced reactions in a number of states, with voters in California (2004) and Michigan (2008) constitutionally approving it. Missouri voters also approved it, but with some limits.

Affirmative Action: During this era, affirmative action has been subject to constitutional challenges. In 1996, California became the first state to ban affirmative action by public institutions. Subsequently, voters approved bans in Nebraska (2008), Michigan (2006), and Arizona (2010). Coloradans defeated a proposed ban in 2008. By contrast, in 1997, New Yorkers approved preferential treatment of veterans in civil service, and, in 2004, Louisianans approved preference points for veterans in the civil service and state police service.

English as Official State Language

Responding to a rising Latino population, a movement emerged during the current era to make English the official language of states. Constitutional amendments accomplishing this were approved in California (1986), Colorado and Florida (1988), Alabama (1990), Arizona (2006), Missouri (2008), and Oklahoma (2010). Earlier constitutional adoptions of English occurred in Louisiana (1812) as a precondition of admission to the union, Nebraska (1920), Massachusetts (1975), and Hawaii (1978).

Eminent Domain: The U.S. Supreme Court's 2005 *Kelo* decision upholding the authority of local governments to take private property and transfer it to another private party for economic development triggered a counter movement in the states. Nevadans approved a Property Owners Bill of Rights in 2006 and adopted it in 2008. Voters also approved eminent domain restrictions in Florida, Georgia, Louisiana, Michigan, New Hampshire, North Dakota, and South Carolina in 2006, followed by California in 2008. In 2007, Texans approved an amendment providing that if the purpose of a taking is not implemented, the original owner can repurchase the land for the price paid by the government to acquire it. Voters in a few states (e.g. California and Idaho in 2006) rejected eminent domain restrictions.

Environmental Protection, Animal Rights, and Hunting: Although more than 21 state constitutions have environmental protection provisions and six guarantee some environmental rights (Wilson 2004), the environmental rights movement begun in the previous era did not continue in the current era. Instead, voters have approved numerous amendments for specific purposes such as forest preservation in Georgia (2008), a Michigan Natural Resources Trust Fund (1984), and a Clean Water Trust Fund in New Mexico (2006). In 1993, Maine voters mandated a two-thirds legislative vote to reduce the size or change the purpose of any state park or recreation land.

By contrast, animal rights emerged as an issue in the current era. In 1988, for example, South Dakotans banned corporate hog farms. In 2002, Floridians protected pregnant pigs, Oklahomans banned cockfighting, and Georgians provided for sterilization of dogs and cats. Californians prohibited narrow confinement of farm animals in 2008, and Ohioans created a Livestock Care Standards Board in 2010, while Missourians imposed constitutional rules on dog breeders. Alabamans, though, approved amendments to promote production and marketing of sheep and goats (2002) and shrimp and seafood (2004).

Rights to hunt and fish first appeared in the Vermont Constitution of 1777. Rights to fish were included in the constitutions of Rhode Island in 1844 and California in 1910. In response to animal-rights and environmental advocates, voters have recently approved a spate of amendments guaranteeing rights to hunt and fish in Alabama (1996), Arkansas (2010), Georgia (2006), Louisiana (2004), Minnesota (1998), Montana (2004), North Dakota (2000), Oklahoma (2008), South Carolina (2010), Tennessee (2010), Virginia (2000), and Wisconsin (2003), although Arizonans rejected such a right in 2010. In 1998, Utah voters imposed a two-thirds vote requirement in order to enact an initiated state law that would allow, limit, or prohibit the taking of wildlife or the season for or method of taking wildlife. In 2004, Alaskans rejected an amendment to prohibit baiting or feeding bears in order to hunt, photograph, or view them. In 2008, they rejected an amendment to prohibit the shooting of wolves, wolverines, or grizzly bears on the day they are spotted from aircraft. In 2010, North Dakotans rejected a ban on fenced hunting on game preserves.

Gambling and Lotteries: The contemporary era has witnessed widespread adoptions of state lotteries (43 at present) as state officials have searched for new revenue sources in the face of public resistance to taxes. However, only a few have been established by constitutional amendment, such as Colorado (1980), California (1984), Florida (1986), Wisconsin (1987 and 1993), Texas (1991), South Carolina (2000), and Arkansas (2008). In 1986, North Dakotans rejected a lottery, but in 2002, they approved a statutory initiative for North Dakota to join a multi-state lottery. The paucity of constitutional action might be due to fears by proponents that constitutional measures might fail on the ballot. Voters in a number of states, such as Colorado (1984), Florida (1994), and Oklahoma (1998) have rejected constitutional proposals to establish casino gambling, though more recently, voters may have become more receptive, as in Ohio's 2009 constitutional vote approving casinos in the state's four major cities. However, in 2004, Michiganders made any new forms of gambling subject to voter approval.

Health Issues and Tort Reform: Medical marijuana has achieved legality in 15 states since first being legalized by statute in California (1996), but only Nevada in 1998 and 2000 and Colorado in 2000 have enshrined it in their constitutions, presumably making it less vulnerable to repeal than the statutes in the other 13 states. Meanwhile, a few states have constitutionalized prohibitions on tobacco smoking in enclosed workplaces (e.g., Florida in 2002) or all indoor places. By contrast, Oregon voters in 2007 rejected an 84.5-cent cigarette-tax increase to fund a Healthy Kids Program, and Californians rejected a similar amendment in 2006. A few states (e.g., Oklahoma in 2000) established some type of tobacco-settlement trust fund.

In 2003, Texans approved a constitutional limit on medical malpractice awards. In 2004, Floridians prohibited the licensing of physicians adjudged to have had three malpractice incidents. They also imposed limits on amounts of attorneys' contingency fees.

Most dramatic, and in direct contradiction of the federal Affordable Care Act of 2010, were constitutional amendments approved in Arizona and Oklahoma in 2010 prohibiting the enactment of laws or rules requiring any person, employer, or health-care provider to participate in any health-care program.

Labor and Unions: Minimum-wage increases require constitutional action in some states. Increases were approved, for example, by voters in Florida and Nevada in 2004 and Ohio in 2006, but not by voters in Missouri in 1996.

Michiganders granted constitutional collective bargaining and binding arbitration rights to state troopers and sergeants in 1978, but, in 2002, they rejected collective bargaining rights for all state employees. Missourians rejected collective bargaining for firefighters and ambulance personnel in 2002. In 2008, however, Californians rejected a ban on automatic deductions of union dues from public employee paychecks.

In 2001, Oklahomans banned new employment contracts that require joining, remaining, quitting, or paying dues to a labor organization to get or keep a job, or paying a labor union or obtaining labor union approval to get or keep a job. Employees must approve deductions from wages paid to unions.

In 2010, Save Our Secret Ballot pushed four states—Arizona, South Carolina, South Dakota, and Utah—to pass constitutional amendments to ban card check for union organizing. The South Dakota amendment was phrased as a right to secret ballots in federal, state, and union representation elections. The National Labor Relations Board has challenged these amendments, arguing they are preempted by federal laws.

Other Issues: Ohioans rejected a 1982 amendment to allow the Ohio Rail Transportation Authority to levy a 1 percent sales tax to construct high-speed rail. In 2004, Floridians repealed an earlier amendment to their constitution that required the state to build and operate high-speed ground transport. In 2011, Florida, Ohio, and Wisconsin rejected federal grants for high-speed rail, and President Barack Obama sharply reduced his high-speed rail initiative in a budget compromise with Congress. In a seemingly ill-timed move in 2006, South Carolinians authorized "prudent investing in all stocks as a means of seeking higher profits" for the state's retirement systems.

RESURGENCE OR DEATH OF STATE CONSTITUTIONALISM?

In certain respects, state constitutions have resurged in recent decades, as reflected in the large numbers of amendments on diverse subjects approved by voters. Also, since the 1980s, originalists have promoted the relevance of the first state constitutions by combing them for clues about the original meanings of the federal Constitution, although there is debate over the appropriate scope of this comparison (Nitz, 2011). Originalists have turned to contemporary state constitutions, too, in efforts by some to expand state high-court activism and by others to deter state high courts from interpreting the state documents as "living" constitutions.

The most prominent manifestation of state constitutional resurgence has been the so-called new judicial federalism whereby state high courts, legislatures, and voters grant more rights protections than the U.S. Supreme Court affords under the U.S. Constitution. States also recognize rights not available under the federal Constitution. The movement's paradigmatic cases involved shopping malls. In 1972, the U.S. Supreme Court held that protestors had no First Amendment right to distribute leaflets in a privately owned shopping mall (*Lloyd*, 1972). In 1979, California's supreme court ruled that protestors do have such a right under California's declaration of rights (*Robins*, 1979). In 1980, the U.S. Supreme Court declined to reverse the California court, acknowledging instead the state court's authority to employ its constitution to protect rights not recognized by the U.S. Supreme Court. Subsequently, in 1983, the U.S. Supreme Court clarified state authority by holding that when a state court makes a "plain statement" basing a rights ruling solely on "independent and adequate" state constitutional grounds, the ruling is immune from U.S. Supreme Court review (*Michigan*, 1983).

State high courts have since issued hundreds of such rulings, and a huge and mostly supportive literature has developed around the new judicial federalism. For example, while the U.S. Supreme Court since Earl Warren's era (1953–69) has constrained the exclusionary rule and restrained criminal defendants' rights, many state courts have retained and expanded Warren-era precedents under their constitutions. The New Jersey Supreme Court has been especially active, ruling, for example, in contradiction of the U.S. Supreme Court (*California*, 1988) that under the New Jersey Constitution's search-and-seizure provision, police need a warrant to search a person's curbside trash (*State*, 1990). A few other high courts (e.g. New Hampshire in 2003) have ruled similarly. Consequently, in these states, federal agents do not need a warrant to search curbside trash, but state and local police do. In 2008, Vermont's Supreme Court departed from federal precedents by ruling that a warrantless helicopter survey of a person's yard in order to discover marijuana violated the defendant's state constitutional rights of privacy (*State* 2008). Another example is a Tennessee Supreme Court ruling (*Planned Parenthood* 2000) that the state constitution's privacy provisions make abortion a "fundamental right" and that any law related to abortion is subject to strict judicial scrutiny—a greater abortion protection than required by the U.S. Constitution.

Some advocates urge state high courts to uncouple themselves from canons of federal constitutional interpretation so as to forge independent state constitutional rules of interpretation. Others argue a much more assertive role whereby state courts would interpret state constitutions oppositionally "with the deliberate purpose of undermining acts of the national government that the state court believes threaten liberty" (Gardner, 2005: 19). Others argue that state constitutional interpretation should perform an important instructive function for the federal courts.

However, efforts by the bench and the bar to capture state constitutions via interpretation are encountering opposition. In 1990, for example, Californians amended their constitution to stipulate that criminal defendants have no greater constitutional rights than those available under the federal Constitution. In 1982, Floridians mandated that their constitution's search-and-seizure provisions be interpreted in lockstep with the U.S. Supreme Court's interpretation of the Fourth Amendment to the U.S. Constitution. In 2000, they approved an amendment preserving capital punishment and requiring the state constitution's cruel-or-unusual-punishment provision to conform to the U.S. Supreme Court's interpretation of the U.S. Eighth Amendment. After the Florida Supreme Court voided this amendment, voters in 2002 changed their constitution's "cruel or unusual punishment" provision to "cruel and unusual punishment" in conformity with the Eighth Amendment and again mandated that their constitution be conformed to the U.S. Supreme Court's Eighth Amendment jurisprudence.

Opposition also is expressed by voters unseating judges whose state constitutional interpretations violate prevailing norms and by voters rejecting proposals to abolish judicial elections that have been forwarded by such prominent groups as Justice O'Connor's Judicial Selection Initiative, Justice at Stake, the Brennan Center for Justice, American Judicature Society, League of Women Voters, Open Society Institute, National Center for State Courts, and *New York Times*. The political, economic, and cultural stakes now involved in state constitutional interpretation are reflected in dramatically increased spending on judicial elections, as seen in the sudden infusion of large sums of money into an April 2011 nonpartisan Wisconsin judicial election that pitted a conservative incumbent against a liberal challenger whom public employee unions believed would vote to nullify the state's new Republican-supported anti-collective bargaining statute. The high-court activism characteristic of the current era appears to be provoking voter desires for restraints. Historically, state high courts have been, to borrow Alexander Hamilton's phrase, "the least dangerous branch" of state government, but many voters no longer believe this.

Both high-court interpretation and voter amendment of constitutions reflect the demise of state constitutionalism as a grand vision of the body politic. Whereas constitutional development and revision in previous centuries often involved efforts to define or redefine a state's polity, the dearth of constitutional revision since the 1970s appears to reflect an inability to forward any compelling vision or definition of state political life. Instead, state constitutions are mainly arenas for interest-group contests. A key contest is between advocates of interpretation and advocates of amendment. Most advocates of interpretation seek expansions of state powers; many, perhaps most, advocates of amendment seek restraints. However, given that voters can initiate amendments in 18 states and must approve amendments in 49 states, the historically most fundamental feature of state constitutionalism seems to be enduring, namely, the constitution as the people's limit on state power.

References

Abramowitz, Alan I. 2010. *The Disappearing Center: Engaged Citizens, Polarization, and American Democracy*. New Haven: Yale University Press.

Adams, Willi Paul. 1980. *The First American Constitutions: Republican Ideology and the Making of the State Constitutions in the Revolutionary Era*. Chapel Hill: University of North Carolina Press.

Anderson, Jeffrey H. 2006. "Learning from the Great Council of Revision Debate." *Review of Politics* 68: 79–100.

Anderson, William 1955. *The Nation and the States, Rivals or Partners?* Minneapolis: University of Minnesota Press.

Beito, David. 2009. *Taxpayers in Revolt: Tax Resistance During the Great Depression*. Auburn, AL: Ludwig von Mises Institute.

Benjamin, Gerald. 2002. "The Mandatory Constitutional Convention Question Referendum: The New York Experience in National Context." *Albany Law Review* 65: 1017–50.

Benton v. Maryland, 395 U.S. 784 (1969).

Binney, Charles C. 1894. *Restrictions upon Local and Special Legislation in State Constitutions*. Philadelphia: Kay and Brother.

Bowser, Jennie Drage. 2009. "Battle for the Ballot." *State Legislatures* 35 (January): 18–19.

Brennan, William J., Jr. 1977. "State Constitutions and the Protection of Individual Rights." *Harvard Law Review* 90: 489–504.

Cain, Bruce E. 2006. "Constitutional Revision in California: The Triumph of Amendment over Revision." In *State Constitutions for the Twenty-first Century: The Politics of State Constitutional Reform*, eds. G. Alan Tarr and Robert F. Williams, 59–71. Albany: SUNY Press.

California v. Greenwood, 486 U.S. 35 (1988).

Cole, Richard L. and John Kincaid. 2006. "Public Opinion on U.S. Federal and Intergovern-mental Issues in 2006: Continuity and Change." *Publius: The Journal of Federalism* 36 (Summer): 443–59.

Comment. 1949. California's Constitutional Amendomania." *Stanford Law Review* 1 (January): 279–88.

Dinan, John. 1999. "Framing a 'People's Government': State Constitution-Making in the Progressive Era." *Rutgers Law Journal* 30: 933–85.

Dinan, John. 2009. *The American State Constitutional Tradition.* Lawrence: University Press of Kansas.

Dinan, John. 2010. "State Constitutional Developments in 2009." In *The Book of the States*, 3–10. Lexington, KY: Council of State Governments.

Friedelbaum, Stanley H. ed. 1988. *Human Rights in the States: New Directions in Constitutional Policymaking.* New York: Greenwood Press.

Friedman, Lawrence W. 1988. "State Constitutions in Historical Perspective." *Annals of the American Academy of Political and Social Science* 496 (March): 33–42.

Gardner, James A. 2005. *Interpreting State Constitutions: A Jurisprudence of Function in a Federal System.* Chicago: University of Chicago Press.

Gardner, James A. and Jim Rossi. 2010. "Dual Enforcement of Constitutional Norms." In *New Frontiers of State Constitutional Law: Dual Enforcement of Norms*, ed. James A. Gardner and Jim Rossi, 1–14. New York: Oxford University Press.

Goodridge v. Dept. of Public Health, 798 N.E.2d 941 (Mass. 2003).

Gray, Virginia and David Lowery. 2003. "Trends in Lobbying in the States." In *The Book of the States*, 257–62. Lexington, KY: Council of State Governments.

Hoffman, Ronald and Peter J. Albert, eds. 1981. *Sovereign States in an Age of Uncertainty.* Charlottesville: University Press of Virginia.

Hsueh, Vicki. 2010. *Hybrid Constitutions.* Durham: Duke University Press.

Jewell, Malcolm E. and Sarah M. Morehouse. 2001. *Political Parties and Elections in American States*, 257–62. 4th ed. Washington, DC: CQ Press.

Kelo v. City of New London, 545 U.S. 469 (2005).

Kincaid, John. 1988. "State Constitutions in the Federal System." *Annals of the American Academy of Political and Social Science* 496 (March): 12–22.

Kincaid, John. 1993. "From Cooperation to Coercion in American Federalism: Housing, Fragmentation, and Preemption, 1780–1992." *Journal of Law and Politics* 9 (Winter): 333–433.

Kruman, Marc W. 1997. *Between Authority and Liberty: State Constitution Making in Revolutionary America.* Chapel Hill: University of North Carolina Press.

Lutz, Donald S. 1980. "From Covenant to Constitution in American Political Thought." *Publius: The Journal of Federalism* 10 (Fall): 101–33.

Lutz, Donald S. 1980b. *Popular Consent and Popular Control: Whig Political Theory in the Early State Constitutions.* Baton Rouge: Louisiana State University Press.

Lutz, Donald S. 1988. "The United States Constitution as an Incomplete Text." *Annals of the American Academy of Political and Social Science* 496 (March): 23–32.

Lloyd Corp. v. Tanner, 407 U.S. 551 (1972).

McCarty, Nolan, Keith T. Poole, and Howard Rosenthal. 2008. *Polarized America: The Dance of Ideology and Unequal Riches.* Cambridge: MIT Press.

McDonald v. City of Chicago. 561 U.S. ___, 130 S.Ct. 3020 (2010).

Michigan v. Long, 463 U.S. 1032 (1983).

National Municipal League. 1963. *Model State Constitution*. 6th edn. New York: National Municipal League, rev. 1968.

Nitz, Eric R. 2011. "Comparing Apples to Apples: A Federalism-Based Theory for the Use of Founding-Era State Constitutions to Interpret the Constitution." *Georgetown Law Journal* 100 (November): 296–329.

Peters, Ronald M., Jr. 1978. *The Massachusetts Constitution of 1780: A Social Compact*. Amherst: University of Massachusetts Press.

Peterson, Merrill D. 1966. *Democracy, Liberty, and Property: The State Constitutional Conventions of the 1820's*. Indianapolis: Bobbs-Merrill.

Planned Parenthood of Middle Tennessee v. Sundquist, 38 S.W. 3d 1 (Tenn 2000).

Rakove. Jack N. ed. 1990. *Interpreting the Constitution: The Debate Over Original Intent*. Boston: Northeastern University Press.

Reynolds v. Sims, 377 U.S. 533 (1964).

Richards, Allan R. 1955. "The Traditions of Government in the States." In *The American Assembly, The Forty-Eight States: Their Tasks as Policy Makers and Administrators*, ed. James W. Fesler, 40–64. New York: Graduate School of Business, Columbia University.

Robins v. PruneYard Shopping Center, 592 P.2d 341 (Cal. 1979).

Roe v. Wade, 410 U.S. 113 (1973).

Sabato, Larry. 1983. *Goodbye to Good-Time Charlie: The American Governorship Transformed*. 2nd edn. Washington, DC: CQ Press.

Salokar, Rebecca Mae. 2006. "Constitutional Revision in Florida: Planning, Politics, Policy, and Publicity." In *State Constitutions for the Twenty-first Century: The Politics of State Constitutional Reform*, eds. G. Alan Tarr and Robert F. Williams, 19–57. Albany: SUNY Press.

Salmore, Barbara G. and Stephen A Salmore. 1998. *New Jersey Politics and Government*. Lincoln: University of Nebraska Press.

Selsam, J. Paul. 1971 [c1936]. *The Pennsylvania Constitution of 1776: A Study in Evolutionary Democracy*. New York: Da Capo.

Shaman, Jeffrey M. 2008. *Equality and Liberty in the Golden Age of State Constitutional Law*. New York: Oxford University Press.

Snell, Ronald. 2010. *NCSL Fiscal Brief: State Balanced Budget Provisions*. Denver: National Conference of State Legislatures, October.

State v. Bryant, 183 Vt. 355, 950 A.2d 467 (2008).

State v. Hempele, 120 N.J. 182, 576 A.2d 793 (1990).

Sturm, Albert L. 1982. "The Development of American State Constitutions." *Publius: The Journal of Federalism* 12 (Winter): 57–98.

Tarr, G. Alan. 2006. "Introduction." In *State Constitutions for the Twenty-first Century: The Agenda of State Constitutional Reform*, eds. G. Alan Tarr and Robert F. Williams, 1–6. Albany: SUNY Press.

Tarr, G. Alan. 1998. *Understanding State Constitutions*. Princeton: Princeton University Press.

Tarr, G. Alan, ed. 1996. *Constitutional Politics in the States: Contemporary Controversies and Historical Patterns*. Westport, CT: Greenwood.

Tarr, G. Alan and Robert F. Williams, eds. 2006. *State Constitutions for the Twenty-first Century: The Agenda of State Constitutional Reform*. Albany: SUNY Press.

The Book of the States. 2010. Lexington, KY: Council of State Governments.

Thomson, H. Bailey. 2005. "Constitutional Reform in Alabama: A Long Time in Coming." In *State Constitutions for the Twenty-first Century: The Politics of State Constitutional Reform*, Pt. II eds. G. Alan Tarr and Robert F. Williams, 113–43. Albany: SUNY Press.

Tocqueville, Alexis de. 1969. *Democracy in America*, trans. George Lawrence, ed. J. P. Mayer. Garden City: Doubleday Anchor Books.

U.S. Advisory Commission on Intergovernmental Relations. 1988. *Changing Public Attitudes on Governments and Taxes, 1988*. Washington, DC: U.S. ACIR.

U.S. Advisory Commission on Intergovernmental Relations. 1988. *State Constitutional Law: Cases and Materials*. Washington, DC: U.S. ACIR.

U.S. Advisory Commission on Intergovernmental Relations. 1989. *State Constitutions in the Federal System: Selected Issues and Opportunities for State Initiatives*. Washington, DC: U.S. ACIR.

United States v. Curtiss-Wright Export Corp., 299 U.S. 304 (1936).

Varnum v. Brien, 763 N.W.2d 862 (Iowa 2009).

Wallis, John Joseph. 2000. "American Government Finance in the Long Run: 1790 to 1990." *Journal of Economic Perspectives* 14 (1) (Winter): 61–82.

Williams v. Mississippi, 170 U.S. 213 (1898).

Williams, Robert F. 1988. "Evolving State Legislative and Executive Power in the Founding Decade." *Annals of the American Academy of Political and Social Science* 496 (March): 43–53.

Williams, Robert F. 2009. *The Law of American State Constitutions*. New York: Oxford University Press.

Wilson, Bryan T. 2004. "Comment: State Constitutional Environmental Rights and Judicial Activism: Is The Big Sky Falling?" *Emory Law Journal* 53 (Spring): 627–655.

CHAPTER 12

STATE DIRECT DEMOCRACY

SHAUN BOWLER AND TODD DONOVAN

DEMOCRATIC theory must deal with questions about how responsive policy should be to majority opinion. Studies of direct democracy provide us with vehicles to examine empirically how much mass opinion affects what governments do. This essay assesses the relationships between opinion, public policy, and state-level direct democracy. We suggest that despite assumptions about the dramatic effects of direct democracy on state policy, evidence on the matter is mixed and we know relatively little about how popular initiatives translate public opinion into policies. In the first section we place the citizen initiative process in the context of the broader study of cross-state variation in policy. We then consider how initiatives might make policy more responsive to public opinion, and examine evidence related to this question. In the second section we evaluate the two-way relationship between state initiatives and national politics, and then focus on how federal courts may constrain the initiative's ability to shape policy. We conclude with a discussion of ideas for further research.[1]

STATE INSTITUTIONS, OPINIONS AND POLICY

One of the more enduring questions in the study of American state politics has been, "how much do differences in political institutions affect policy and politics?" Early scholarship placed a greater emphasis on economic rather than institutional forces as determinants of cross-state differences in public policy (e.g. Dawson and Robinson, 1963; Dye, 1966; Hofferbert, 1966; Sharkansky, 1968). Some of these studies concluded that core political features, such as party competition, voter turnout, legislative apportionment, and differences in how state legislatures functioned, had little if any relationship with state policy (measured in terms of government spending). From these studies the major and somewhat disturbing implication for normative democratic theory was that popular control of government and the structure of democratic politics have little effect on what government does. Variation in state spending was explained by levels of "industrialization" and "affluence." Put differently, there was little evidence that governmental policies were responsive to citizen preferences.

These "politics doesn't matter much" studies stimulated additional research that subsequently determined that democratic politics does, in fact, affect what states do in terms of public policy. One problem with the 1960s vintage research was that it lacked adequate measures of state partisanship and of the policy preferences of each state's electorate. Cross-state comparative research using robust measures of public opinion has since established that states with more liberal electorates have more liberal public policy (Erickson, Wright, and McIver, 1993; Wright, Erickson, and McIver, 1985, 1987). Policy specific opinions may be an even stronger, direct predictor of state policy than general measures of mass and elite opinion liberalism (Lax and Phillips, 2009a).[2] Other studies demonstrate links between class differences in voter turnout and liberal policy outcomes (Hill and Leighley, 1992; Hill, Leighley, and Hinton-Anderson, 1998), and that the timing of elections affects fiscal policy innovations (Berry and Berry, 1990, 1992). The important question for state politics research is no longer, "is there a linkage between state politics and policy?", but, "how is state opinion translated into state policy?"

Erickson, Wright, and McIver (1993: 130) offer a model of state policy that echoes themes from Miller and Stokes (1963). In this model, state opinion liberalism and mass party identification are eventually translated into public policy by affecting how liberal (or conservative) a state's political elites are, and then, by affecting the liberalism (or conservativism) of the state legislature. Berry and Berry (1992) offer a related model where fiscal policy adoption is structured by political constraints and opportunities that affect elites. Strategic politicians are shown to adopt new taxes when they are least likely to pay an electoral cost for doing so. Although these models clearly emphasize political over economic forces, both place little emphasis on the effects of cross-state variation in political institutions. They are, to an extent, more behavioral than overtly institutional models. Cross-state variation in direct democracy, party systems, primary election rules, legislative arrangements, executive/legislative relationships, and the structure of state courts need no place in such models.

Of course, models are meant to be simplifications of complex realities. There may, however, be a larger reason for the pre-eminence of the electoral forces over political institutions in political models of state policy. As much as the American states do provide an excellent setting for conducting empirical comparative political analysis, the 50 states share many basic political institutions. Cross-state variation in key political institutions is much more limited than what exists when comparisons are made about major political institutions across nations. Within a range, all states have roughly similar two party systems. All use nearly identical winner-take-all election rules. All 50 have similar systems of separating executive, legislative, and judicial powers. All but one has bicameralism. Rather than comparing, say, unitary to federal systems, parliamentary to presidential systems, or comparing multi-party to two-party systems, we are left with shades of grey—variation in legislative professionalism; inter-party competition within a two-party structure; courts appointed with retention elections versus elected courts, etc. This truncated variation in major political institutions across the states may limit our ability to detect systematic effects of political institutions on politics and policy. One recent detailed study of the link between mass opinion for specific policies and state policy outputs concluded that only legislative professionalism[3] had a consistent relationship with policy responsiveness to mass opinion (Lax and Phillips, 2009a).

Direct Democracy: A Unique Institution

Direct democracy is one political institution that clearly varies from state to state. Twenty-four states allow legislation to be proposed without a legislative process, and twenty-five states have provisions for popular repeal of legislative acts (Magleby, 1984). With a few exceptions, initiative and referendum states are the same places. When only the initiative is considered, institutional variation can be seen as dichotomous. States either allow the process, or they do not. Several thousands of proposals for popular initiatives have been filed in direct democracy states since states began adopting the process in 1898. Over two-thousand of these initiative proposals have qualified for popular vote in these states, with hundreds of the measures being approved by voters. Depending on the state, there are few limits on the subjects of initiative and referendums. Seventeen states allow proposals for voters to amend their state's constitution independent of the legislature. Where the process is used in America, it remains widely popular with voters, although it enjoys less unflinching support among state legislators (Bowler et al., 2001).

Compared to institutional variation that we observe cross-nationally, the presence (or absence) of direct democracy across the American states is striking. Apart from Switzerland, there is nowhere else where direct democracy is a regular institutional feature. This means we cannot get leverage with cross-national research on questions about how direct democracy affects the way mass opinion is translated into policy. We must compare across the American states (or Swiss cantons) for this.

What Consequences on Policy?

Given the amount of critical attention given to direct democracy—particularly the initiative process—we might expect profound consequences of initiatives on public policy. Observers have argued that direct democracy will make state judges more deferential to popular majorities when deciding cases (Eule, 1993). Others note that it increases the power of narrow, economic interests (Smith, 1998; Broder, 2000; Ellis, 2002; but see Gerber, 1999), and that it weakens the influence of racial, ethnic, and sexual orientation minorities (Gamble, 1997). Nobel laureate James Buchanan and his coauthor (Buchanan and Wagner, 1977) proposed that direct voting on policy could produce more conservative policy, since legislatures have incentives to spend more than the public might actually tolerate. Still others observe that direct democracy as practiced in the American states is something fundamentally different from the representative government that Madison and the founders proposed (Haskell 2001) and that "the impact of state ballot initiatives on state policy is beyond question" (Sabato, et al., 2001: x). In short, direct democracy is expected to affect state policy in some fundamental way by somehow altering how public opinion is translated into specific policies.

Despite these claims and assumptions about notable and unambiguous consequences of state direct democracy on policy, as of 2010 we know relatively little about how direct democracy affects what state governments do. Part of the muddle can be seen in the claims above. They are somewhat logically contradictory. Depending on which authors we read, initiatives may empower the majority at the expense of a minority while simultaneously empowering some economic minorities.

DIRECT AND INDIRECT EFFECTS

There are also theoretical issues involved with the way initiative and referendum process may be used in America that present difficulties for those attempting to specify how initiatives might affect state policy. At the level of theory, initiatives may have direct and (or) indirect effects on policy and policymaking. Direct effects assume that initiative propagates policies in some manner that would not be possible absent the initiative process. That is, the initiative somehow produces policies that differ in kind from what the legislature would produce. Indirect effects assume that the main force of the initiative process operates via the legislature. In terms of Erickson, Wright, and McIver's model, the initiative process indirectly affects policy by affecting how mass preferences for policy operate on the legislature. From this perspective, policy differences across initiative and non-initiative states, then, are not so much a matter of kind, as much as a matter of degree. An example of a direct effect would be where initiatives produce outcomes legislatures would never adopt, such as legislative term limits (Tolbert, 1998). An example of an indirect effect might be variation in state taxing and spending that is conditioned by how initiatives send signals to legislators about public preferences (Matsusaka, 2004; see also Gerber, 1996).

LINKING OPINION, INITIATIVES AND POLICY: MEASUREMENT ISSUES

In addition to the question of whether initiatives translate popular opinion into policy directly or indirectly, studies of the effects of initiatives on state policy must deal with the fact that direct democracy states vary in how the initiative process can be used. All state initiative processes were not created alike. Ballot access is much less of a barrier in some direct democracy states than it is in others.[4] As a result, over 60 percent of all popular initiatives have appeared in just six states (Oregon, California, Colorado, North Dakota, Arizona, and Washington). The six initiative states with the fewest initiatives per election cycle have produced only four percent of all initiatives appearing on state ballots (Illinois, Mississippi, Wyoming, Utah, Idaho, and Maine). States also differ markedly in terms of how much the legislature is bound by measures if voters approve them (Bowler and Donovan, 2004). Theories and tests of how direct democracy conditions the effect of opinions on policy must disentangle the fact that not only is California not Utah on a host of demographic and institutional measures, but the initiative process in California is something much more robust than that in Utah.

In short, initiatives are much more common and more binding in some states than in others where initiatives exist. If we expect that initiatives mainly have a direct effect on policy, this would suggest that analysis of the opinion -> policy linkage should include some kind of measures of the volume of (and types) of initiatives that voters approve. In other words, if initiatives affect policy by allowing voter opinion to be expressed directly in policies that voters approve, then we would likely need to know what policies have been approved in each state. Correspondingly, given that ballot qualification (and, subsequently, voter approval) of initiatives is quite rare in many initiative states, this would suggest that nearly all effects of direct democracy on the opinion -> policy linkage could be limited to a handful of states.

However, Gerber (1996, 1999) and Matsusaka and McCarty (2001) propose models of indirect effects, where the general threat of the initiative process is the main causal force affecting how public opinion affects policy. With this perspective, the number of initiatives and referendums that appear on a state's ballot, and the number that voters might approve, are less relevant than when we are considering the direct effects of initiatives. Indirectly, initiatives may operate on policy a number of ways—by signaling legislators about what voters think, but mainly by giving interest groups a device to cajole legislators into moving policy away from the legislature's status quo. The causal force operating on policy need not be actually qualifying something for the ballot and convincing voters to approve it. Rather, by having the capacity to do so, groups external to the legislature can threaten to use initiatives and referendums and, in doing so, have leverage on moving legislative outcomes closer to where the median voter might be. Thus, we need not measure the number of initiatives used. The influence of the initiative process operating via the threat of its use can be represented by a dichotomous measure of its presence or absence in a state.

This approach assumes, however, first that absent direct democracy, legislative outcomes would be out of synch with the median voter (in other words, that there is an agency problem); second that legislators will respond to the credible threat of an initiative; and third that the threat potential of the initiative is the same across states that have the process.

Matsusaka (2001, see also Achen, 1978) presents another problem related to assessing the question of how direct democracy might condition the link between public opinion and policy. Measures of opinions and of policies are generally imprecise, and in different units. Models that estimate the slope of the relationship between the two may find a positive relationship, but it is difficult to judge from the magnitude of the estimated slope how responsive policy is to opinion. Without knowing, a priori, how units of "liberalism" are supposed to translate into some units of a specific policy, we cannot really know if policy is over- or under-responsive to mass preferences (Lax and Phillips, 2009a: 5).[5]

EVIDENCE THAT DIRECT DEMOCRACY AFFECTS STATE POLICY

Most influential studies of state policy diffusion, and of the link between public opinion and state policies, do not consider if the initiative process affects policy adoption or if it makes policy more responsive to opinion (e.g. Dye, 1966, Hofferbert and Sharkansky, 1969; Walker, 1969; Weber and Shaffer, 1972; Berry and Berry, 1990; Erickson, Wright, and McIver, 1993; Hill and Hinton-Anderson, 1995). This may reflect, in large part, that initiatives were rarely used in the 1960s, and that initiative use remained relatively rare through the 1970s. Compared to the 1960s, there were twice as many initiatives on state ballots in the 1970, and four times as many by the 1990s.[6] Several more recent studies have modeled the relationship between opinion and policy as being affected by direct democracy, with a number of these studies searching for an indirect effect of initiatives on policy. Studies vary in the methods and measures used, and have not produced unambiguous evidence that direct democracy indirectly causes state policy to be more responsive to state opinions.

Lasher, Hagen and Rochlin (1996) and Camobreco (1998) examined the interaction between opinion liberalism and various state fiscal policies (measured as continuous variables), and concluded there was no relationship.[7] Matsusaka (2004) estimates the effect of direct democracy on fiscal policy by estimating policy outcomes with a simple intercept difference that distinguishes between initiative and non-initiative states. He concludes that initiative states spend about ten percent less than non-initiative states, other things being equal. Matsusaka attributes the lower spending in initiative states (in the later part of the twentieth century) to the initiative process solving the agency problem and pushing fiscal policy closer to the median voter's position.

Gerber (1996) concluded that the interaction between the existence of the initiative and public attitudes about parental consent requirements for abortion made state consent rules more reflective of a state's median voters' preferences. Gerber (1999) reported a similar pattern with state death penalty laws. However, Gerber models the relationship between opinion and policy as an interaction, but does not follow standard practice (see Brambor et al., 2006) of including all constitutive terms of the interaction in her estimations. Burden's replication (2005) of Gerber demonstrates that there are no significant effects of the initiative on abortion notification or death penalty responsiveness to opinion when the interactions are properly specified.

Gerber's results for abortion policy, with some modifications to how policy and direct democracy were measured, have been replicated (Arceneaux, 2002; Bowler and Donovan, 2004). Policy responsiveness to opinion is more apparent when modeled as the interaction between opinion and the frequent use of initiative, rather than when modeled as opinion interacting with the existence of the initiative process (Bowler and Donovan, 2004). This suggests that direct democracy may affect the link between opinion and policy via actual initiatives that appear on state ballots, rather than simply via threats of initiative use. We should note, however, that few of these studies can point to public votes on specific abortion policy initiatives or death penalty measures that may have shaped state policy. One study of policy responsiveness to opinions across 39 policies (including parental consent for abortion) dismissed the idea that the threat of initiatives affects policy indirectly. Lax and Phillips (2009a: 25) concluded that the initiative is "insufficient as a 'gun behind the door'; only high levels of use are correlated with increased responsiveness and congruence."

The evidence for direct effects of initiatives on policy—that is, opinion being translated into policy as a result of what reaches the ballot—appears more convincing. Matsusaka (2007) estimates policy congruence as instances where a state adopts a policy that matches the preferences of a majority of the state's voters. Across nine policy areas, he finds that policy is congruent in non initiative states in about 52 percent of cases.[8] This compares to 60 percent of cases being congruent in initiative states and 55 percent congruence for national government policy and public opinion (Monroe, 1998). However, where initiatives on the specific policy appeared on a state's ballot and were approved by voters, 78 percent of policies were congruent with majority opinion.[9] Bowler and Donovan (2009) also find state spending across several policy areas to be more representative of state opinion as the number of fiscal initiatives on a state's ballot increases, and as more fiscal initiatives are approved by voters. Tolbert (1998) demonstrates that initiative states are more likely to adopt term limits and tax and expenditure measures than non-initiative states, and that such policies are the clear results of specific ballot measures (rather than the threat of potential measures).

This evidence of direct effects and mixed evidence of indirect effects of initiatives on policy, should be considered in light of where and when initiatives are used. As noted above, 60 percent of all initiatives appear in just six states. Although the initiatives' direct effects on causing some policies to be more reflective of voter preferences may be substantial, these effects may be limited to a handful of states.

DIRECT DEMOCRACY AS CONDITIONING POLITICAL INSTITUTIONS

As we note above, one of the most dramatic examples of the direct effect of citizens' initiatives on state policy can be found with term limits. Nearly every state adopting term limits—particularly restrictive limits—adopted via popular initiatives. This has led us to suggest elsewhere that one of the major direct effects of citizens' initiatives on policy may be the initiative's ability to reshape state political institutions, including the environment that political parties operate in. As Matsusaka (2005: 195) notes, initiative states "keep their governments on a shorter rein," with legislative term limits, executive term limits, and tax and expenditure limitations (TELs). More restrictive TELs appear to be generated by popular initiative in places like Oregon and Colorado (New, 200x). High use initiative states have more restrictions on political parties, and less autonomous party organizations (Bowler and Donovan, 2006).

Yet, here again, we have a situation where direct democracy may have less dramatic transformative effects than many expect of it. Persily and Anderson (2005) examine the history of several reforms to electoral institutions, including term limits, campaign finance, redistricting, women's suffrage, adoption of direct primaries. They conclude that, other than term limits and perhaps redistricting and campaign finance, laws were mostly adopted through legislatures that look similar in initiative and non-initiative states. They conclude that where initiatives have effects, these are largely indirect, with legislators passing something in response to the threat of an initiative. Pippen et al. (2002) also conclude that rapid adoption of more restrictive campaign finance rules corresponded with initiative use. Ellis (2002: 240) dismisses the idea that the initiative device had any influence as an indirect, "gun behind the door" factor (per Banaszak, 1996: 184) in the diffusion of women's suffrage. Lawrence et al. (2009) conclude that between 1900 and 1915 direct democracy states adopted the direct primary earlier than non direct democracy states, but that only few had actually adopted in the initiative process prior to direct primaries. Indeed, direct democracy may as much reflect larger political pressures for electoral reforms during the Progressive Era, than it was a causal force used directly to change electoral laws.

DIRECT DEMOCRACY, MINORITIES, AND POLICY

State initiatives target minority rights on a regular basis (Gamble, 1997), however court intervention often mutes the implementation of many anti-minority measures (Donovan, Wenzel, and Bowler 2000). There are clearly policy consequences: notable voter approved rights-constraining initiatives are affirmed by courts (e.g. anti-affirmative action measures) or may linger for years before higher courts nullify them (e.g. anti-gay marriage and anti-gay adoption measures).[10]

Yet as much as initiatives highlight conflicts over rights it is not clear that initiative states translate mass opinion into policies that are more restrictive of minority rights than policies in non-initiative states. There are studies that find no relationship between direct democracy and state policy in an area, gay civil rights, where many (see Gamble,

1997) might expect the initiative to amplify how majority opinion is expressed in state policy. Lax and Phillips (2009b) model state policy responsiveness to public opinion across eight gay rights issues and find that policy is highly responsive to opinions about gay rights. However, they conclude that "direct democracy does not significantly affect the adoption of gay rights policies one way or the other" (2009b: 383).[11] Bowler and Donovan (2001) also found that state adoption of Defense of Marriage Amendments (DOMAs) from 1993 to 2000 occurred independently of the initiative process. Haider-Markel et al. (2007: 307) do find that direct democracy produces fewer pro-gay outcomes than the legislative process, but the difference was small. Thirty-nine percent of outcomes from direct democracy were pro-gay, compared to 44 percent from the legislative process. This preponderance of anti-gay outcomes under both institutional settings matches up with Lax and Phillips' assessment that "representative institutions do a poor job protecting minority rights even when the public *supports* the pro-minority position" (2009b: 383).

This begs the question, then, of why these studies fail to detect a substantial role for direct democracy. One possibility is that elected representatives may be more sensitive to popular opinion about policies affecting minority rights than they are to opinions about other topics. If this is the case, initiatives may not be needed to make policies about minority rights responsive to opinion.[12] Again, the evidence is mixed. Monroe (1998) found that general opinion/policy congruence was relatively low on civil rights issues (compared to other issues). Matsusaka (2007) found that initiatives tend to move state social policy toward more conservative outcomes, and toward outcomes that are more congruent with mass opinion. Initiative states were highly likely (over 90 percent) to have a same sex marriage policy that was congruent with state opinion. However, over 80 percent of non-initiative states also had marriage policies that matched majority opinions in the state, and initiative states appeared much *less* likely to have laws protecting homosexuals from job discrimination that were congruent with majority opinion (Matsusaka, 2007).

FEDERALISM, POLICY DIFFUSION AND THE LIMITS TO DIRECT DEMOCRACY

The previous section has highlighted substantial ambiguity about the magnitude of the citizens' initiatives effects on state policy. This is not to say that there are no effects. There are measurement issues that constrain our ability to quantify how initiatives make policy more responsive to popular opinion. Many of the effects of direct democracy, while critical, may be too subtle to capture with econometric analysis. Matsusaka's body of work demonstrates that a state with the initiative appears more likely to have policies in line with opinion majorities in the state. However, our discussion of gay rights illustrates the ambiguity about quantifying how initiatives translate majority opinion into rights.

One important point here is that initiatives do affect how, and also reflect when, questions of rights become prominent.

In this section, we take up the relationship between direct democracy, federalism, and the federal courts. We examine the implications of direct democracy for the workings of federalism and the way in which the federal courts may impose limits on how state initiatives can affect policy. The American states are guaranteed a degree of independence in the constitutional order. But even though the states may be insulated from each other they are not isolated from each other and can influence each other in a variety of ways. As an extensive body of research shows, policy agendas may diffuse from one state to another or, even, shape federal policy in a bottom-up process in a variety of ways (see e.g. Haider-Markel, 2001; Boehmke and Witmer, 2004; Shipan and Volden, 2006, 2008; Karch, 2007).

In principle, direct democracy may contribute to both these processes of diffusion (Magleby, 1998; Boehmke, 2005; Ferraiolo, 2008; Moule and Weller, n.d.). The process of diffusion across states is a common one that has long been identified in the literature on state politics, and we seem to see examples of this in direct democracy when we see rashes of similar policy proposals on the ballot in different states. In 2006, for example, eminent domain measures were on the ballot in 12 states; tobacco and smoking issues were the focus of 10 measures (Ballotwatch, 2006; see also Magleby, 1998: and Ferraiolo, 2008). A notable issue that falls into this category of proposals that diffuse is that of gay marriage which was on the ballot 33 times from 1998 to 2008. At various times clusters of term limit, nuclear freeze, and anti-affirmative action initiatives appeared on ballots across many states. All these examples suggest that ballot measure politics are not easily confined or limited to being within one state.

That said, labeling this process diffusion—and noting that it is a way in which the policy effects of direct democracy may not be containing neatly within state borders—is the beginning rather than the end of the task. There are difficulties in trying to establish just how issues and measures spread. Take, for example, the spread of proposals relating to gay marriage. The spread of proposals across time and across states can plausibly be seen to be categorized as "diffusion" (see Table 12.1). But the process of diffusion is a complex one (Boehmke and Witmer, 2004; Shipan and Volden, 2008) and even the simple example of Table 12.1 illustrates several points in the literature to date. First, to the extent that this is an example of diffusion then it points up the problems of seeing state policy innovation by initiative to be confined within state borders. Arguably, models of policy innovation may be under-specified by not taking into account the influence of the initiative process— even for non-initiative states. Second, and relatedly, even a quick glance at Table 12.1 shows that some proposals come from the "bottom up" (i.e. were proposed by voters via an initiative process) but others came from the legislature via the referendum in non-initiative states suggesting that the initiative process can—as Magleby suggests—be a source of diffusion that occurs from initiative states to non-initiative states (Magleby, 1998; Boehmke, 2005) and so is an important factor to include more generally in models of policy innovation.

Table 12.1 Gay Marriage Measures on the Ballot by State and Year

State	Year	Measure	Vote	Source
Alaska	1998	Ballot Measure 2	68-32	Legislature
Hawaii	1998	Amendment 2	69-31	Legislature
California	2000	Prop 22	61-39	Initiative
Nebraska	2000	Measure 416	70-30	Initiative
Nevada	2000	Question 2	70-30	Initiative
Nevada	2002	Question 2	67-33	Initiative
Arkansas	2004	Amendment 3	75-25	Initiative
Georgia	2004	Amendment 1	77-23	Legislature
Kentucky	2004	Amendment 1	75-25	Legislature
Louisiana	2004	Amendment 1	78-22	Legislature
Michigan	2004	Proposal 04-2	59-41	Initiative
Mississippi	2004	Amendment 1	86-14	Legislature
Missouri	2004	Amendment 2	71-29	Legislature
Montana	2004	CI-96	67-33	Initiative
N. Dakota	2004	Amendment 1	68-32	Initiative
Ohio	2004	Issue 1	62-38	Initiative
Oklahoma	2004	Question 711	76-24	Legislature
Oregon	2004	Measure 36	57-43	Initiative
Utah	2004	Amendment 3	66-34	Legislature
Kansas	2005	Amendment	70-30	Legislature
Texas	2005	Prop 2	76-24	Legislature
Alabama	2006	Amendment	81-19	Legislature
Arizona	2006	Prop 107	48-52	Initiative
Colorado	2006	Amendment 43	55-45	Initiative
Idaho	2006	HJR 2	63-37	Legislature
S. Carolina	2006	Amendment 1	78-22	Legislature
S. Dakota	2006	Amendment C	52-48	Legislature
Tennessee	2006	Amendment 1	81-19	Legislature
Virginia	2006	Ballot Question 1	57-43	Legislature
Wisconsin	2006	NA	59-41	Legislature
Arizona	2008	Prop 102	56-44	Legislature
California	2008	Prop 8	52-48	Initiative
Florida	2008	Amendment 2	62-38	Initiative

Source: Initiative and Referendum Institute, election reports.

Third, what we see in Table 12.1 illustrates the uneasy relationship between states and federal politics in a number of ways. One is that it helps identify specific agents of policy diffusion. Often, discussions of diffusion seem to suggest a general process of information and signaling without always a clear sense of who is sending or receiving the signals (Karch, 2007). For the issues displayed in Table 12.1 several of these proposals may be associated with the George Bush re-election campaign in 2004. To the extent that national and regional GOP officials played a role in promoting these measures then, in addition to grass-roots/bottom-up diffusion to the federal level we see an astro-turf/top-down kind of diffusion and a specific set of agents that promoted diffusion.

In many ways even this simple discussion shows that there are questions for which we do not yet know the answers. We do not, for example, know whether some policies are more likely to diffuse than others because of the initiative process. Proposals that limit the actions of politicians—tax and expenditure limits or term limits—are common to initiative states and not likely to be ones adopted by politicians themselves but it is not clear just how (or if) they are spread from initiative to non-imitative states. It is not clear, for example, whether there are networks of reformers that work across state lines or whether the effect is simply informational. It does, however, seem quite likely that of the proposals that may spread, those aimed at constraining state-level politicians are ones likely to be spread by the initiative as opposed to other kinds of channels and political action. The diffusion of some proposals that constrain politicians, then, may be limited to other initiative states.

It may also be the case that proposals that have been established as very popular with voters via initiative proposals may be more likely to spread, and ones that have been proposed but defeated less likely to spread (Moule and Weller, n.d.). Moule and Weller's argument is especially interesting in distinguishing between policy innovation and policy adoption and pointing out that although diffusion is generally thought of as promoting policy adoption the signal from failed initiatives may lead other states to conclude there is no need to adopt a policy.

Diffusion need not simply be a "horizontal" process; that is, issues need not simply spread from state to state. It can also be a process that has "vertical" implications for state-federal relations. Several discussions of diffusion by initiative note that issues arising via the initiative process are subsequently given greater attention on the national political stage. The anti-tax measures of the late 1970s seemed to tap into broader public sentiment and then were transmitted both across state lines and into federal politics (Magleby, 1998). Nationalization of the gay marriage issue followed a similar path, albeit prodded by state court decisions and initiatives.[13]

One interpretation of this process is that it helps bring federal policy in line with popular opinions at the state level and so direct democracy can be seen as a way to foster congruence between policy outputs and popular preferences. But as Ferraiolo notes, congruence is not the only possible outcome when we consider the effects of innovations in state policy via direct democracy, nor does it come without conflict (Ferraiolo, 2008). Direct democracy allows voters to challenge federal policy in a number of ways. They can challenge what they see as federal inaction—as in the example of immigration policy and gay rights. In the cases of stem cell research and marijuana laws, voters can challenge federal action by setting up state exceptions to federal policy.

Although it is intuitively appealing to discuss policy innovations via the initiative in terms of congruence between state public opinion and state policy outputs, the work of Magleby, Ferraiolo and others suggests that state voters may be reacting to federal policy output. Putting these kinds of possibilities together, Ferraiolo notes:

> When ballot measures seeking to fill a policy void lead to federal action, they promote intergovernmental policy consensus and narrow the distance between public opinion and federal policy; if the federal government fails to address the issue at stake, additional state innovation will result and voter preferences and federal policy outcomes will move farther apart. Meanwhile, initiatives that challenge federal law create conflict and polarization between states and the federal government and widen the distance between public opinion and federal policy. (Ferraiolo, 2008: 488)

All these examples suggest that discussions of state policy innovation via the initiative should give some consideration to factors beyond the borders of the state. Direct democracy can be seen to provide examples of policy innovation and policy adoption at the state level (Moule and Weller, n.d.). What we might note, however, is that the federal dimension to state politics muddies the waters a little because the innovation at the state level may be influenced not simply by state level factors such as state opinion, interest group density, or ideological position, but by events in other states and, also, at the federal level. Direct democracy thus has the potential to increase conflict between states and the federal government. This suggests that there is a direct democracy component both to state-federal relations and to the process of policy diffusion.

The Federal Courts and Direct Democracy at the State Level

One consequence of conflicts between state and federal law is that the courts are left to adjudicate state-federal boundaries thrown up by state policies pushed by voters themselves. As David Magleby notes: "The willingness of federal courts to overturn state initiatives on U.S. Constitutional grounds is an important manifestation of federalism" (Magleby, 1998: 152).

Generally speaking what this willingness means is that limitations on direct democracy are imposed via the federal judicial process. A count of Supreme Court cases that arose in relation to the initiative process between 1970–2010 shows roughly 20 cases that went to the Supreme Court. At the time of writing it seems likely that *Perry v Schwarzenegger*—the California court case arising from Proposition 8—will provide an additional example. But this pattern of Supreme Court involvement only tells part of the story since this accounting will not consider cases settled at lower Federal courts or ones that the Court refused to hear. Looking at cases that were addressed by US District Courts in the same period shows over 190 cases.[14] The number of cases by year first heard in federal courts is displayed in Figure 12.1.

This figure allows us to make several points. First, David Magleby is correct in suggesting that the federal courts are one way in which we clearly see a federal dimension to, and involvement in, direct democracy. Furthermore, this trend has increased markedly over the past ten years or so. The courts are an important mechanism in this federalization of initiative politics and possibly the most commonly seen one.

Second, these are cases in which the court adjudicates on the expression of democratic popular opinions at the state level, not simply elite dissent between state and federal levels. In effect, courts are ruling on the results of democratic elections. Courts, as Eule noted, have tended to treat laws as laws regardless of whether they derive from a legislative or initiative process (Eule, 1990: 1505). As Eule went on to note, this does present some problems because, if the people are indeed sovereign, it seems reasonable to suppose that initiated proposals should be treated with more respect than legislative ones (Eule, 1990: 1505) but he goes on to conclude that courts—and in particular federal courts that can make authoritative pronouncements on the Bill of Rights—are, and should be, the ultimate "line of defence against majoritarian tyranny" (Eule, 1990: 1584). Generally speaking it is the courts, and in particular the federal courts with

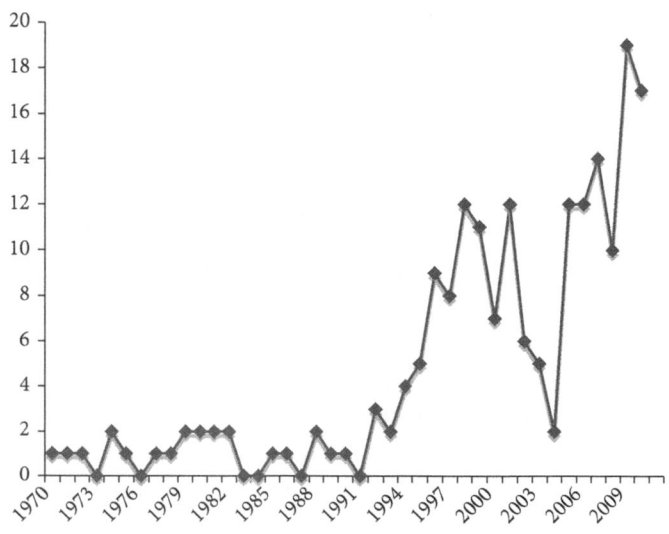

FIGURE 12.1 Cases relating to voter initiatives in federal district courts, 1970–2010

Source: Lexis-Nexis.

their authority to rule on questions of rights, that are the institutions that can and do veto proposals made via direct democracy (Sirico, 1980; Eule, 1990; Linde, 1993). The main consequence of this judicialization of initiative politics is to provide a federally imposed constraint on policies proposed and passed by initiative. This likely constrains how much the state initiative might make policy congruent with majority opinion in a state.

This federal judicialization of initiative politics places courts in both a responsible and highly visible position and this may have consequences for popular support of the judiciary. The legitimacy of the judiciary means that voters support its decisions even when they disagree with the judges. If courts repeatedly overturn initiated proposals—not only highly popular ones but ones that have been authorized by majorities in free and fair elections—then the popular legitimacy of courts may be affected. As Eule notes:

> There is no denying that protecting republicanism is a high-stakes proposition. The very volatility of transient passions both warrants stricter review of direct democracy and renders execution of this task by the federal judiciary a treacherous venture.
>
> (Eule, 1990: 1586)

This veto power of the federal courts can shape how proposals are crafted—and which proposals are crafted. The initiative is often discussed in terms of the agenda-setting ability of state voters and in terms of the initiative's capacity to make state policy more responsive to public opinion. The veto power of other players is rarely mentioned because, at least at the state level, state legislatures and state executives may have only limited capacity to amend or veto proposals passed by initiative (see however, Gerber et al. 2001 on the autonomy that elected officials have implementing initiatives). As federal court intervention becomes more familiar it seems likely that more initiative proposals will be made anticipating the reaction of federal courts. In anticipating these vetoes, initiative proponents could, eventually, learn strategic moderation of proposals that impact the rights of others (Christmann, 2000; Donovan, Wenzel, and Bowler, 2000). All of this veto playing and anticipated reaction gives a distinctly federal dimension to state direct democracy politics. It also gives a very different meaning to the phrase "the gun behind the door" often used in discussions of initiative politics. Rather than the only gun being one hidden behind the voter's door to threaten legislators, there may also be a gun hidden under judicial robes that helps keep initiative proponents from being too extreme when it comes to minority rights.

But there are limits to the degree to which courts are willing to intervene in the workings of the process. To date, courts have been reluctant to rule on the constitutionality of the process itself. In *Pacific States Telephone and Telegraph Company v. Oregon* (1912) the US Supreme Court decided on the conformity of the initiative process with republican form of government and, hence, its constitutionality. The Court essentially dodged the question by deferring to Congress:

...the issues presented, in their very essence, are, and have long since by this court been, definitely determined to be political and governmental, and embraced within the scope of the powers conferred upon Congress, and not therefore within the reach of judicial power, it follows that the case presented is not within our jurisdiction....

(*Pacific States Telephone and Telegraph Company v. Oregon*. 1912 US Supreme Court)

This ruling does leave open the door for Congress to impose limits on the practice of direct democracy at the state level, although in practical terms it seems unlikely that Congress would act to limit the popular voice in such a way.

DISCUSSION: FUTURE RESEARCH ON DIRECT DEMOCRACY, WHAT DON'T WE KNOW?

Direct democracy—as a process—has generated interest among political scientists in large part because it has been a source of questions, many of which have implications for the wider study of politics. The workings of direct democracy in American states have, for example, energized debates over whether voters are up to the demands of voting and have generated questions over the impact of political institutions. As with many areas of state politics, data availability places limits on how far these studies can progress. For example, while many extensive surveys exist on popular attitudes to federal politics there are far fewer surveys on state politics. There is less polling data still on direct democracy and many of those that do exist come from the "outlier" states like California. There is, plainly, value in a more sustained effort to generate more data on direct democracy in order to be able to assess—for example—changes in opinion during the course of campaigns and/or variation in opinion formation in high- and low-use states. One likely path for direct democracy studies goes in the direction of data collection and is likely to lead to revision of earlier conclusions (including our own) that were based on limited available data. Questions remain, but their answers depend on the development of data sources that take the state level seriously, especially in terms of public opinion.

Still, in some ways, many of the more accessible questions relating to direct democracy have at least been raised using available data from surveys, election results, and spending totals. To the extent that other aspects of the process are to be explored they would seem to require a change of tack and a different kind of data collection effort. What direct democracy has the potential to do is ask a series of questions both about federalism and about the policy-making process. It also raises the issue of rights versus majority rule in a very pointed way as scholars such as Christmann and Gamble have noted. All that said, it is far easier to identify a federal dimension to initiative politics than to come to terms with it analytically within a political science, as opposed, say, to a constitutional law perspective.

Some questions do seem related to innovation and diffusion. How do initiatives spread across state lines? Are there identifiable networks of interest groups or citizen action groups? Other questions seem to relate to the nature of federalism itself. Some initiatives—on immigration, drugs and, possibly, on support for stem cell research—do not simply differ from federal policy but challenge it. Other questions will relate to the impact of courts as veto players and the more conscious "venue shopping" of actors (Boehmke). What determines whether cases go to court and why are they heard in federal as opposed to state court?

These questions on federalism may be interesting ones but they are difficult to address and to do so we need to develop different kinds of data than have been the case to date, data which expressly looks for links across state lines and data that begins to code more fully court cases and their resolution.

But the good thing about direct democracy—and perhaps the quality that makes it among the more interesting areas to study in political science—is that it has the ability to surprise us all. Pronouncements on what to study are likely to come unstuck pretty fast. After all, the agenda for the initiative process is set by the voters themselves. Who knows what they will come up with next?

Notes

1. Our 2010 essay in *The Oxford Handbook of American Elections and Political Behavior* (ed. Jan Leighley) addresses the electoral dimension of direct democracy in America.

2. Several additional studies, using various measures of state opinion, also find a relationship between specific state opinion (preferences for policy) and specific state policy outputs. See Hill and Hinton-Anderson (1995); Norrander (2001); Brace et al. (2002).

3. Burden (2005) and Lax and Phillips (2009) both shows effect for legislative professionalism. Both studies provide no controls for state economic conditions (such as affluence) that may determine legislative professionalism.

4. Primary barriers are the proportion of voter signatures required to qualify, and the presence of geographic distribution requirements for collecting signatures.

5. Following Page and Shapiro (1983), Lax and Phillips (2009), Lupia et al. (2010), and Matsusaka (2006) gain leverage on this problem by assessing if dichotomous policy outcomes are congruent with majority opinion.

6. Magleby (1994) attributes the diffusion of imitative use to its discovery by a growing number of interest groups since the 1970s. Boehmke (2002) demonstrates that the presence of the initiative process also stimulates interest group mobilization and group activity—particularly (non economic) citizens' groups.

7. Camobreco focuses on the sign of the initiative opinion interaction in his models, and does not interpret the substantive meaning of the conditional estimates of the effects of opinion and the initiative that his interaction model specifies (see Brambor, Clark and Golder, 2006). Lasher et al. (1996) also ignore the substantive meaning of their conditional estimates.

8. In other words, congruence with mass opinion is rather random. Monroe (1998) found a similar rate (55 percent) of congruence in US government policy from 1980–93, down

from 63 percent during 1960–79. Page and Shapiro (1982) report policy changes were congruent with changes in mass opinion 66 percent of the time between 1935 and 1979.

9. Matsusaka (2007) also finds that elected judges also have a substantial effect on increasing policy congruence.

10. At the time of this writing (late 2010) Arkansas voter approved anti-gay adoption measure and California's voter approved anti-gay marriage measure were working their ways through the court system. Lower courts had rejected Arkansas' and Florida's anti-adoption laws.

11. Lupia et al. (2010) suggest that this might miss a critical point. All states that have constitutional restrictions on same sex marriage adopted restrictions via a popular vote. Moreover, states with constitutional initiatives have constitutions that are more easily changed in response to changes in public opinion.

12. Indeed, Alan Rosenthal (1998) laments that polling and other forces including initiatives are moving all state legislatures toward a more directly democratic process.

13. Three anti-gay marriage initiatives appeared prior to 2004. Attention to gay marriage at the national level was heightened by state court decisions that prompted President G. W. Bush to propose a constitutional amendment banning same sex marriage early in 2004. Almost all state constitutional marriage measures appeared on ballots after that.

14. This is a very loose accounting. A search in Lexis-Nexis for cases that included the terms "initiative" AND "passed" AND "voters" showed a total of 464 cases. These cases were read and hand coded for content. If a case dealt with a law created by direct democracy—at local or state level—or sought to regulate the direct democracy process it was coded as concerning direct democracy. While likely coding errors lead us to be cautious about the precision in these figures the general pattern is so striking as to be robust to anything but coding errors of massive proportions. A full list of the cases is available on request.

References

Achen, Christopher. 1978. "Measuring Representation." *American Journal of Political Science* 22 (3): 475–510.

Arceneaux, Kevin. 2002. "Direct Democracy and the Link Between Public Opinion and State Abortion Policy." *State Politics and Policy Quarterly* 2 (4): 372–87.

Ballotwatch. 2006. *Ballotwatch: Election Results 2006.* Los Angeles: Initiative and Referendum Institute.   <http://www.iandrinstitute.org/BW%202006-5%20%28Election%20results-update%29.pdf>.

Banaszak, Lee Ann. 1996. *Why Movements Succeed or Fail: Opportunity, Culture, and the Struggle for Woman Suffrage.* Princeton University Press.

Berry, Frances Stokes and William D. Berry. 1990. "State Lottery Adoptions as Policy Innovations: An Event History Analysis." *American Political Science Review* 84 (2): 395–415.

Berry, Frances Stokes and William D. Berry. 1992. "Tax Innovation in the States: Capitalizing on Political Opportunity." *American Journal of Political Science* 36 (3): 715–42.

Boehmke, Frederick J. 2002. "The Effect of Direct Democracy on the Size and Diversity of State Interest Groups." *Journal of Politics* 64 (3): 827–44.

Boehmke, Frederick J. 2005. *The Indirect Effect of Direct Legislation: How Institutions Shape Interest Group Systems.* Columbus, OH: Ohio State University Press.

Boehmke, Frederick J., and Richard Witmer. 2004. "Disentangling Diffusion: The Effects of Social Learning and Economic Competition on State Policy Innovation and Expansion." *Political Research Quarterly* 57 (1): 39–51.

Bowler, Shaun and Todd Donovan. 2001. "The Rush to Defend Marriage: State Institutions, Opinion and the Adoption of Same Sex Marriage Bans." New York: Western Political Science Association.

Bowler, Shaun and Todd Donovan. 2004. "Measuring the Effects of Direct Democracy on State Policy: Not all Initiatives are Created Equal." *State Politics and Policy Quarterly* 4 (3): 345–63.

Bowler, Shaun and Todd Donovan. 2006. "Direct Democracy and Political Parties in America." *Party Politics* 12 (5): 649–69.

Bowler, Shaun and Todd Donovan. 2009. "Public Opinion, Direct Democracy and Fiscal Policy." Midwest Political Science Association. Chicago, IL.

Bowler, Shaun, Todd Donovan, Max Neiman and Johnny Peel. 2001. "Institutional Threat and Partisan Outcomes: Legislative Candidates' Attitudes toward Direct Democracy." *State Politics and Policy Quarterly* 1 (4): 364–79.

Brace, Paul, Kellie Sims-Butler, Kevin Arceneaux and Martin Johnson. 2002. "Public Opinion in the American States: New Perspectives Using National Survey Data." *American Journal of Political Science* 46 (1): 173–89.

Broder, David. 2000. *Democracy Derailed: Initiative Campaigns and the Power of Money.* New York: Harcourt.

Buchanan, James and Richard E. Wagner. 1977. *Democracy in Deficit: The Political Legacy of Lord Keynes.* Academic Press.

Burden, Barry. 2005. "Institutions and Policy Representation in the States." *State Politics and Policy Quarterly* 5 (4): 373–93.

Brambor, Thomas, William R. Clark and Matt Golder. 2006. "Understanding Interaction Models." *Political Analysis* 14: 63–82.

Camobreco, John. 1998. "Preferences, Fiscal Policies and the Initiative Process." *Journal of Politics* 60 (3): 819–29.

Christmann, P. 2000. "Effects of 'Best Practices' of Environmental Management on Cost Advantage: The Role of Complementary Assets." *Academy of Management Journal* 43: 663–80.

Dawson, Richard E. and James A. Robinson. 1963. "Interparty Competition, Economic Variables and Welfare Policies in the American States." *Journal of Politics* 25: 265–89.

Donovan, Todd, Jim Wenzel and Shaun Bowler. 2000. "Direct Democracy and Gay Rights After Romer." In C. Rimmerman, K. Wald and C. Wilcox (eds.) *The Politics of Gay Rights.* University of Chicago Press, 161–92.

Dye, Thomas R. 1966. *Politics, Economics, and the Public: Policy Outcomes in the American States.* Chicago: Rand McNally.

Ellis, Richard J. 2002. *Democratic Delusions: The Initiative Process in America.* Lawrence: University Press of Kansas.

Erickson, Robert, Gerald Wright and John McIver. 1993. *Statehouse Democracy: Public Opinion and Policy in the American States.* Cambridge University Press.

Eule, Julian N. 1993. Crocodiles in the Bathtub: State Courts, Voter Initiatives and the Threat of Electoral Reprisal. *University of Colorado Law Review* 65: 733.

Eule, Julian N. 1990 "Judicial Review of Direct Democracy." *Yale Law Journal.* 99: 1503.

Ferraiolo, Kathleen. 2008. "State Policy Innovation and the Federalism Implications of Direct Democracy." *Publius: The Journal of Federalism* 38 (3): 488–514.

Gamble, Barbara S. 1997. "Putting Civil Rights to a Vote." *American Journal of Political Science* 41 (1): 245–69.

Gerber, Elisabeth. 1996. "Legislative Response to the Threat of Popular Initiatives." *American Journal of Political Science* 40 (1): 99–128.

Gerber, Elisabeth. 1999. *The Populist Paradox: Interest Group Influence and the Promise of Direct Legislation*. Princeton University Press.

Gerber, Elisabeth, Arthur Lupia, Mathew D. McCubbins and D. Roderick Kiewiet. 2001. *Stealing the Imitative: How State Government Responds to Direct Democracy*. Prentice Hall.

Haider-Markel, Donald P. 2001. "Policy Diffusion as a Geographical Expansion of the Scope of Political Conflict." *State Politics and Policy Quarterly* 1 (1): 5–26.

Haider-Markel, Donald P., Alana Querze and Kara Lindman. 2007. "Lose, Win or Draw? A Re-examination of Direct Democracy and Minority Rights." *Political Research Quarterly* 60 (2): 304–14.

Haskell, John. 2001. *Direct Democracy or Representative Government? Dispelling the Populist Myth*. Westview Press.

Hill, Kim Quaile. and Angela Hinton-Anderson. 1995. "Pathways of Representation: A Causal Analysis of Public Opinion-Policy Linkages." *American Journal of Political Science* 39 (4): 924–35.

Hill, Kim Quaile and Jan E. Leighley. 1992. "The Policy Consequences of Class Bias in State Electorates." *American Journal of Political Science* 36 (2): 531–65.

Hill, Kim Qualie, Jan Leighley and Angela Hinton-Anderson. 1998. "Lower Class Mobilization and Policy Linkages in the U.S. States." *American Journal of Political Science* 39 (1): 75–86.

Hofferbert, Richard I. 1966. "The Relation Between Public Policy and Some Structural and Environmental Variables in the American States." *American Political Science Review* 60: 73–82.

Hofferbert, Richard I. and Ira Sharkansy. 1969. "Dimensions of State Politics, Economics and Public Policy." *American Political Science Review* 63 (3): 867–79.

Karch, Andrew. 2007. *Democratic Laboratories: Policy Diffusion Among the American States*. Ann Arbor: University of Michigan Press.

Lascher, Edward L., Michael G. Hagen, and Steven A. Rochlin. 1996. "Gun Behind the Door? Ballot Initiatives, State Policies and Public Opinion." *Journal of Politics* 58 (3): 760–75.

Lawrence, Eric D., Todd Donovan and Shaun Bowler. 2009. "Adopting Direct Democracy: Tests of Competing Explanations of Institutional Change." *American Politics Research* 37 (6): 1024–47.

Lax, Jeffrey R. and Justin H. Phillips. 2009a. "*Institutions and Representation: Policy Responsiveness in the U.S. States.*" State Politics and Policy Conference, Chapel Hill, NC.

Lax, Jeffrey R. and Justin H. Phillips. 2009b. "Gay Rights in the States: Public Opinion and Policy Responsiveness." *American Political Science Review* 103 (3): 367–86.

Linde, Hans A. 1993. "When Initiative Lawmaking Is Not 'Republican Government': The Campaign Against Homosexuality." *Oregon Law Review* 72: 19.

Lupia, Arthur, Yanna Krupnikov, Adam Seth Levine, Spencer Piston, Alexander Von Hagen-Jamar. 2010. "Why State Constitutions Differ in their Treatment of Same-Sex Marriage." *Journal of Politics* 72 (4): 1222–35.

Matsusaka, John G. 2001. "Problems with a Methodology Used to Evaluate the Voter Initiative." *Journal of Politics* 63 (4): 1250–6.

Matsusaka, John G. 2004. *The Initiative, Public Policy and American Democracy*. Chicago: Chicago University Press.

Matsusaka, John G. 2005. "Direct Democracy Works." *Journal of Economic Perspectives* 19 (2): 185–206.

Matsusaka, John G. 2007. "Direct Democracy and Social Issues." University of Southern California Marshall School of Business, Los Angeles, CA 90089 (unpublished manuscript) <http://www-bcf.usc.edu/~matsusak/Papers/Matsusaka_DD_and_Social_Issues_2007.pdf>.

Matsusaka, John G. and Nolan McCarty. 2001. "Political Resource Allocation: Benefits and Costs of Voter Initiatives." *Journal of Law, Economics, and Organizations* 17: 413–48.

Magleby, David B. 1984. *Direct Legislation: Voting on Ballot Propositions in the American States.* Johns Hopkins University Press.

Magleby, David B. 1994. "Direct Legislation in the American States." In D. Butler and A. Ranney (eds.) *Referendums Around the World.* Washington DC: AEI Press, 218–57.

Magleby, David B. 1998. "Ballot Initiatives and Intergovernmental Relations in the United States." *Publius: The Journal of Federalism* 28 (1): 147–63.

Miller, Warren E. and Donald E. Stokes. 1963. "Constituency Influence in Congress." *American Political Science Review* 57 (1): 45–56.

Monroe, Alan. 1998. "Public Opinion and Public Policy, 1980-1993." *Public Opinion Quarterly* 62 (1): 6–28.

Moule, Ellen, and Nicholas Weller. n.d. "Learning in Laboratories of Democracy: The Diffusion of Political Information via Direct Democracy in the U.S. States." University of California San Diego, Political Science, accessed February 22, 2011. <college.usc.edu/labs/weller/documents/MW_Diffusion.pdf>.

New, Michael. 2001. Limiting Government through Direct Democracy: The Case of State Tax and Expenditure Limitations. Washington, DC: CATO Institute. <http://www.cato.org/sites/cato.org/files/pubs/pdf/pa420.pdf>.

Norrander, Barbara. 2001. "Measuring State Public Opinion with the Senate National Election Study." *State Politics and Policy Quarterly* 1 (1): 111–25.

Page, Benjamin I. and Robert Y. Shapiro. 1983. "Effects of Opinion on Policy." *American Political Science Review* 77 (1): 175–90.

Persily, Nathaniel and Melissa Cully Anderson. 2005. "Regulating Democracy Through Democracy: The Use Direct Legislation in Election Reform." *Southern California Law Review* 78 (4): 997–1034.

Pippen, John, Shaun Bowler, and Todd Donovan. 2002. "Election Reform and Direct Democracy: Campaign Finance Reform Regulation in the American States." *American Politics Research* 30 (4): 559–82.

Rosenthal, Alan. 1998. *The Decline of Representative Democracy.* Washington, DC: CQ Press.

Sabato, Larry J., Bruce A. Larsonand Howard R. Ernst. 2001. *Dangerous Democracy? The Battle over Ballot Initiatives in America.* Rowman and Littlefield.

Sharkansky, Ira. 1968. *Spending in the American States.* Chicago: Rand McNally.

Shipan, Charles R. and Craig Volden. 2006. "Bottom-Up Federalism: The Diffusion of Antismoking Policies from U.S. Cities to States." *American Journal of Political Science* 50 (4): 825–43.

Shipan, Charles R. and Craig Volden. 2008. "The Mechanisms of Policy Diffusion Issue" *American Journal of Political Science* 52 (4): 840–57.

Sirico, Louis J. 1980. "The Constitutionality of the Initiative and Referendum" *Iowa Law Review* 65: 637–41.

Smith, Daniel A. 1998. *Tax Crusaders and the Politics of Direct Democracy.* New York: Routledge.

Tolbert, Caroline. 1998. "Changing Rules for State Legislatures: Direct Democracy and Governance Policies." In Donovan, T., S. Bowler and C. Tolbert (eds.) *Citizens as Legislators: Direct Democracy in the American States*. Columbus, OH: Ohio State University Press, 171–90.

Walker, Jack. 1969. "The Diffusion of Innovations Among the American States." *American Political Science Review* 63 (3): 880–99.

Weber, Ronald E. and William, R. 1972. "Public Opinion and American State Policy-making." *Midwest Journal of Political Science* 16 (4): 683–99.

Wright, Gerald, Robert Erickson and John McIver. 1985. "Measuring State Partisanship and Ideology with Survey Data." *Journal of Politics* 47 (2): 469–89.

Wright, Gerald, Robert Erickson and John McIver. 1987. " Public Opinion and Policy Liberalism in the American States." *American Journal of Political Science* 31 (4): 980–1001.

CHAPTER 13

....

STATE LEGISLATURES

....

KEITH E. HAMM, RONALD D. HEDLUND, AND NANCY MARTORANO MILLER

SEVERAL essays have charted the growth and sophistication of the state legislative literature (Jewell, 1976, 1981, 1983, 1997; Moncrief, Thompson, and Cassie, 1996; Clucas, 2003; Mooney 2009). Our intent in this chapter is not to provide an update to these excellent reviews, but instead to highlight the major approaches to studying state legislatures, illustrate how they have changed over time and provide a modest agenda for future research efforts. To accomplish this task, we establish four time periods for analysis: pre-1980 (from Jewell, 1981); 1981–95 (from Moncrief, Thompson, and Cassie, 1996); 1996–2000 (from Hamm, 2001); and 2006–10 (from our calculations). [1] Using these four time periods we will demonstrate that state legislative research has attained a high level of scholarly visibility, in part due to the greater number of research outlets (e.g., *Legislative Studies Quarterly, State Politics and Policy Quarterly*), but also due to the increased sophistication of the research.

TRENDS IN THE STATE LEGISLATIVE LITERATURE

The Early Years

In his 1976 essay, Malcolm Jewell provided a negative assessment of state legislative research. Basic descriptive analysis was missing in a good many states. Few comparative undertakings had been pursued and there was a failure to utilize hypotheses developed and tested at the congressional level. Finally, theoretical development that accounted for major institutional variation across state legislatures was lacking.

When Jewell wrote his second essay in 1981, less than one-third of his citations involved peer-reviewed journal articles. The largest category were books or book chapters, most of which dealt with a single state; important examples of research that utilized data from just one legislature include those by Bell and Price (1975) and Harder and Davis (1979). This emphasis on single-state studies is confirmed by Goehlert and Musto's (1985) encyclopedic bibliographic study of all state legislative articles (published or unpublished) from 1945–84. Almost 60 percent of the entries dealt with just one state. Comparative research, while infrequent, was utilized in a few notable book-length research projects, including such key topics as roles and norms (Wahlke et al., 1962), legislative issues (Francis, 1967), legislative support (Patterson, Hedlund, and Boynton, 1975), committees and legislative performance (Rosenthal, 1974), lobbying (Zeigler and Baer, 1969) and patterns of decision making (Uslaner and Weber 1977).

More surprisingly, fully 20 percent of Jewell's citations were of dissertations or unpublished work. While Congressional research was proceeding at a rapid pace, only a smattering of state legislative research was being added to the collective wisdom via major political science journals. In fact in his 1981 essay, Jewell cites only 19 articles that were published in referred journals from 1965 to 1975, or less than two articles per year. The situation hardly improved over the next five years since he mentions only about three relevant articles per year that were published.[2]

Establishing a Presence (1981–2000)

Over the next 20 years, state legislative research overcame some of the shortcomings, although some significant problems remained. On the positive side, state legislative research was now frequently published in the mainstream journals, comparative cross-state studies were becoming more common, and theoretical development improved in terms of differentiating key components across legislatures. On the negative side, good descriptive studies of single states were still rare, the bridge between congressional theories and state legislative research was tenuous, and major theoretical advances using the rich variation in internal operations across legislatures was lacking.

Research Visibility: The situation changed dramatically in terms of visibility in respected political science journals by the time Moncrief et al. published their review essay in 1996. Only 1 percent of their citations referred to unpublished material or dissertations. Greater than 80 percent of the new citations were for articles in peer reviewed journals. This works out to roughly 10 new state legislative articles per year over the 15-year period. A major reason for the uptick in journal publication was the arrival of *Legislative Studies Quarterly (LSQ)* in the mid-1970s. By our count, over 70 articles appeared in *LSQ* from 1981 to 1995 dealing with state legislatures. Analysis of articles appearing in nine top journals from 1996–2000 confirms the important role that state legislative research played, with roughly 13 articles per year appearing during this time period (Hamm, 2001).

Several important books were also published during this 20-year period. Single state studies were less frequent, but important contributions were made by such scholars as Loomis (1994), Loftus (1994), and Clucas (1995). The real advance, however, was in the comparative cross-state research. Important examples include Jewell's *Representation in State Legislatures* (1982), Erikson, Wright and McIver's *Statehouse Democracy* (1993) and Carey, Niemi and Powells' *Term Limits in State Legislatures* (2000). A very thoughtful treatment on the role of state legislatures in a democracy was provided by Alan Rosenthal in *The Decline of Representative Democracy* (1998). Edited volumes were also a major outlet including Moncrief and Thompson's *Changing Patterns in State Legislative Careers (1992)*. Finally, collaborative research by a large group of scholars resulted in an edited volume on campaign finance entitled *Campaign Finance in State Legislative Elections* (Thompson and Moncrief, 1998).

Single State or Comparative Studies: During this period, state legislative scholars began a gradual migration away from a focus on legislative behavior in a single setting. This is not to say that the single-state study was no longer adopted. Roughly 36 percent of the articles cited in the Moncrief, Thompson and Cassie (1996) review from 1981 to 1995 involved just one legislature. This figure dropped to only 16 percent of the research studies published in nine leading journals during 1996–2000. In many of these single-state studies, the state of interest was chosen for its theoretical attributes, rather than its proximity or familiarity to the researcher. Examples include contrasting legislative institutionalization and professionalization in California (Squire, 1992b), describing campaign contributions in the unregulated environment of California (Box-Steffenmeiser and Dow, 1992), describing a party role in the no-party Texas legislature (Harmel and Hamm, 1986), tracing committee assignments over time in Wisconsin (Hedlund, 1989), and evaluating the impact of public financing on electoral competition in Wisconsin (Mayer and Wood, 1995).

During this period we also see the rise in the limited case studies. For example, roughly one in five journal citations from Moncrief, Thompson and Cassie involved a limited analysis using two to seven legislatures. Some of these studies were excellent examples of the value of limited case selection. We single out Squire's (1998a, 1988b) three state research of the relationship between career opportunities and the internal organization of state legislatures as the exemplar of what scholars can accomplish with limited cases when they have a clear theoretical focus.

The big change during this period was that a large number of studies utilized data from a large number of state legislatures (>45).[3] Four types of studies dominated. The first sought to differentiate state legislatures in terms of such characteristics as important decision-making centers (Francis, 1989) and level of professionalization (Squire, 1992a). These studies constituted a key development in the evolution of state legislative research and served as the template for future work on institutional differences among state legislatures. Second, the advent of large data collection projects (e.g. Jewell, 1991) unleashed a flurry of studies focusing on elections (see the next section for further comments). Third, survey research permitted scholars to study a sample of legislators in all 50 states (e.g., Moncrief, Thompson, and Kurtz, 1996; Carey, Niemi, and Powell, 1998). Finally, aggregate studies of the legislative process permitted comparisons across all 50 states. Examples include influences on state legislative professionalism (Mooney, 1995; King, 2000) and factors affecting bill introduction and enactments (Gray and Lowery, 1995).

State Legislative Research in the Twenty-first Century

Progress in state legislative research has accelerated in the last decade. On average, 20 articles per year were published in ten major political science journals. We now have more systematic comparative and historical knowledge about state legislatures (e.g., Squire and Hamm, 2005; Hamm, Hedlund and Martorano, 2006; Squire and Moncrief, 2010). While we agree with Clucas (2003) that greater attention needs to be devoted to building theory, sometimes the sophistication of the theoretical undertakings match those for the U.S. Congress (e.g. Kousser, 2005; Chen, 2010). Research designs are more imaginative (e.g. Wright and Schaffner, 2002; Kousser, Lewis, and Masket, 2007), and data collection efforts are more extensive (e.g., Wright, 2007) and cover a larger period of history (e.g., Masket, 2007). New methodological techniques also permit researchers to answer questions that have stymied them to date (e.g. Shor et al.'s bridging technique, 2010). We document the most promising areas in the following section.

Large N Comparative Studies: By our count, fully four in ten studies published during this period included most or all state legislatures (i.e., >45). We differentiate two types of studies at this level: systemic and individual level.

As expected, the studies which concentrate on explaining system level factors focus almost exclusively on the entire set of state legislatures. Sometimes the goal is to show how the institutions have changed over time as in Squire's work tracing professionalism across time (2007). Other studies disentangle the relationship between level of professionalism and government spending (Malhotra, 2008); explain the impact of courts on legislative introductions and enactments in a specific policy area (Wilheim, 2007); and clarify the factors that affect the number of committee outliers in a chamber (Richman, 2008).

Another set of studies focuses on the individual legislator or actor across the totality of state legislatures. In years past, this type of study was most difficult to undertake because of the costs of data collection. Our assessment is that the growth in this area has been significantly aided by the availability of large datasets. Comparative state election data became available many years ago (Jewell, 1991) and led to a rapid proliferation of publications in this area. Recently, through various collaborative efforts, the earlier data (1968–89) have been cleaned and a major update has occurred so that the subfield now has a continuous set of election data from 1968–2003 (Carsey et al., 2008). We already see the impact of the release of this data with the recent publication on the impact of redistricting principles (Forgette, Garner, and Winkle, 2009).

Surveys and interviews of legislators have proven to be significant contributors to the storehouse of knowledge about state legislatures (e.g., Wahlke et al., 1962; Francis,

1989). This technique has continued into the present (e.g., Carey et al., 2006; Kurtz et al., 2006; Herrnson et al., 2007). Over time, data collected for one purpose (e.g., term limits study by Carey, Niemi, and Powell, 1995) have been used in an innovative manner to address other research concerns such as change in lobbying regulations on perception of interest group influence (Ozymy, 2010) or the impact of the Contract with America on perceived influence of majority party leadership (Clucas, 2009). Systematic surveys of citizens, while a goal of the subfield, have been sporadic. Recent research questions have also addressed confidence in government (Kelleher and Wolak, 2007).

Roll-call data can be seen as the bread and butter of legislative scholars. However, large comparative studies using roll-calls have been hindered by the lack of a systematic collection of the necessary data. Thankfully, this situation has changed due to the large data collection efforts of Wright and his colleagues (e.g. Wright, 2007; Hays et al., 2009). These efforts have permitted tests of the impact of term limits on voting behavior and polarization (Wright, 2007) as well as permitting tests of major theories derived from congressional work on legislative organization (Battista, 2009; Richman, 2008). Additionally, the data are now being analyzed using ideal point estimation via NOMINATE scores (Poole and Rosenthal, 1991). A limitation of this method has been the inability to compare the ideal point estimates across state legislatures. This problem appears to have been overcome by the use of bridging techniques that permit the development of a common ideological scale (Shor, Berry, and McCarty, 2010). Using bridge actors, those who have served in both state legislatures and in Congress, Shor et al. were able to estimate the ideal points for state legislators using congressional common space. This breakthrough offers numerous research applications, including an insightful analysis of differences in partisan polarization in 11 states (Shor, Berry, and McCarty, 2010). The full effect of this contribution will be seen as more extensive data collection is undertaken.

A Large Sample of State Legislatures: Another set of studies have in common their focus on a relatively large sample of state legislatures. A common approach in this area is to suggest that a sample of state legislatures (e.g. 15) is fairly representative of all 99 chambers. Some scholars justify their choice of states by demonstrating that there are no statistically significant differences between the sample of states utilized in the study and the remaining states (e.g. Hogan, 2008). Sometimes due to the nature of the data collection activity, all 50 states are not included, but this disadvantage is offset by examining the evolution of legislatures over time. Examples include the establishment of the formal powers of committees across the house and senates in 33 states chambers over a hundred-year period (Hamm, Hedlund, and Martorano, 2006), and factors affecting committee system autonomy in 24 chambers over a 40-year period (Martorano, 2006).

Small N Studies: The modest surprise in our survey of journals is that more than 22 percent of the articles focus on just one state legislature while another 13 percent include fewer than seven states. If data availability is not as large an issue as in years past, what accounts for the emphasis on just one or a few legislatures? We believe there are five contributing factors.

First, several studies have taken advantage of a natural or quasi-experimental design to evaluate the impact of a specific variable. This research approach was largely absent from earlier studies but came to the fore with the adoption and scholarly study of the impact of term limits. As Mooney noted in the title of his recent article, it was a "boon to legislative scholarship"(2009: 204). While several of the studies involved a large number of states, some addressed key research questions by focusing on one or just a few states (e.g. Engstrom and Monroe, 2006; Sarbaugh-Thompson et al., 2004, 2006). Aside from term limits, we see a host of questions being addressed using a quasi-experimental approach. These studies include, but are not limited to, the impact of cross-filing on partisanship in California (Masket, 2007); the impact of a recall election for governor on legislators' voting behavior (Kousser, Lewis, and Masket, 2007); and the ability of the majority party to control the legislative agenda in California and Colorado (Cox, Kousser, and McCubbins, 2010).

Another creative approach is to use the power of field experiments. Although this approach is widely used to examine the impact of different techniques to turn out the vote, rarely is it applied to state legislative elections. One exception is Arceneaux and Kolodny's (2009) recent work. They examine the impact of group endorsements on voting preferences in two competitive state legislative districts in Pennsylvania. Another field experiment demonstrates the potential benefit of focusing on a state with key factors that provide significant explanatory leverage. Bergan's recent study (2009) of the impact of outside lobbying on legislative behavior using the multi-member nature of the New Hampshire lower chamber is a case in point. Given that the constituency of the legislators in the treatment and control groups are the same due to the multimember nature of the districts means that the impact of the grass roots lobbying contacts can be ascertained with significant precision.

A third approach is to use a paired comparison of a few legislatures in which the main difference between them is a key explanatory factor. While true matching of legislatures is impossible, under certain conditions it is possible to construct a critical test involving just a few legislatures. Wright and Schaffner's (2002) extremely creative work on the influence of party in the Kansas Senate (with parties) and Nebraska Unicameral (without parties) is an exemplar of this approach.

Fourth, while formal models serve as the basis for a number of studies of the U.S. Congress, their appearance using state legislative data is a recent phenomenon. For example, Chen (2010) extends Mayhew's credit-claiming theory to account for bicameralism. The theory is then applied to see the effects on pork-barreling in the New York Senate. Using a natural experiment that expanded the number of Senate districts, the author examines the effect of district fragmentation on pork earmarks across the senate districts.

Fifth, a few studies take advantage of a unique dataset that exists only in one state. For example, Miquel and Snyder (2006) use data collected by the North Carolina Center for Public Policy Research to evaluate the determinants of legislative effectiveness and the consequential effect on legislative careers. What makes this dataset unique is that the

Center has asked state legislators, lobbyists, and capital news correspondents to grade the effectiveness of each legislator at the end of every legislative session since 1977.

Congress and State Legislatures: In the early years, studies of Congress and state legislatures appeared to proceed without an awareness of each other. Over time, however, state legislative scholars adopted hypotheses from the congressional literature in their own research. Then, as positive political theory took hold and theories were modeled on the U.S. Congress, voices were raised that the better test of these models would be found in the various internal legislative configurations at the state level. A case in point: why legislatures create committee systems. Over time, a significant literature developed around this question. The distributive, informational, and some variant of political party theory were originally tested using only the U.S. Congress. Greater leverage, however, in assessing these theories occurred when they were applied to state legislatures. In fact, we now have a robust set of findings regarding the relevant generalizability of these theories using comparative data from the states (e.g., Overby, Kazee, and Prince, 2004; Prince and Overby, 2005; Battista, 2006; Martorano, 2006; Richman, 2008; Battista, 2009). This development is one way to overcome Clucas's well-founded concern (2003) regarding the lack of theoretical coherence in the literature.

A more ambitious research strategy would involve including Congress along with the state legislative chambers in analyses (see Squire and Hamm, 2005). This type of research is relatively rare at this time. One advantage of this approach is that it helps to situate the U.S. Congress in a larger context. Four recent examples suggest the utility of this approach. First, Casellas (2009) tests the probability of a Latino being elected in seven houses—six state legislative chambers and the U.S. House. The interesting point is that the U.S. House is treated simply as one of seven chambers; no exclusive discussion is given to its unique aspects. Second, Lublin et al. (2009) test models of Black and Latino representation. The impressive feature of this article is that they test three models using state houses, state senates and the U.S House. Third, Battista (2009) goes to the next level. He tests a model of committee informativeness using state legislatures. Utilizing the results from the state analysis, he then calculates the scores for the U.S. Congress, without treating it as a unique body in terms of institutional structure, or constitutional powers. Finally, most legislative theories assume that legislators are able to change the rules under which they operate without many legal constraints. On this key assumption, Martorano, Hedlund, and Hamm (2010) demonstrate tremendous variation exists across American legislatures. They find that in comparing the U.S. Constitution to the state constitutions, it is quite clear that the U.S. Congress is a legislature where the constitution has left quite a bit of flexibility regarding legislative structure and procedure. Of the 75 items they examine, only 11are included in the U.S. Constitution. Only two state constitutions (Rhode Island and New Hampshire) say less about the legislative branch. This insight permits us to propose the first aspect of a research agenda.

Proposed Research Agenda 1

State Legislative Development: How Constitutions and Statutes "Tie the Hands" of Present and Future Legislators

Before it will be possible to understand the development and evolution of American state legislatures, we must first understand how the past impacts the ability of these institutions to operate. The ability of legislators to alter legislative structures and procedures is limited through state constitutions and statutes. If a particular aspect of the legislative process is codified in the state constitution, it is significantly harder to alter as extraordinary majorities and public approval is often required. Existing law (e.g. statutes) is also more challenging to alter than chamber rules of procedures, precedents, or norms because alterations require the adoption of a new/revised law. The costs of altering constitutional and statutory arrangements is high, and thus the longer they remain unchanged, the more entrenched they become as legislators adopt other institutions to complement or sometimes circumvent these provisions. It is often the case that these complimentary or circumventing institutions further complicate rather than simplify the legislative process.

What Do We Know About Legislative Development?

Very little is known about the development of state legislative institutions. Many of the studies of state legislative evolution and development that do exist were conducted long ago and typically focus on the development of a legislative institution in a single state. More modern explorations of state legislatures have focused on explaining institutional differences across state legislatures at a single point in time. One exception is *101 Chambers: Congress, State Legislatures and the Future of Legislative Studies*, where Peverill Squire and Keith Hamm (2005) outline how American state legislatures have come to differ from one another as well as Congress over time. Squire and Hamm then challenged scholars to explain the causes or evolution of the differences they outlined. Very few scholars have accepted this challenge.

Stresses, Strains, and Bounded Rationality

One avenue for explaining the evolution of state legislative institutions is through the lens of organization theory. Several scholars focusing their studies on the state legislatures have championed the ability of organizational theory to be adapted to the study of the legislative process (Hedlund, 1984a, 1984b). This research applying organizational theory to the study of state legislatures asserts that in order to survive, a legislative body must change its practices and procedures in reaction to changes, or stresses and strains, in the legislature's external and internal environments (Froman, 1968; Davidson and Oleszek, 1976; Thompson and Moncrief, 1992). State legislative scholars have used this perspective to successfully study the existence of short-term changes in legislative institutions (Hedlund and Hamm, 1976; Hedlund, 1978; Harder and Davis, 1979; Hedlund and Freeman, 1981).

The organization theory perspective, however, applies only to part of the institutional development story—the portion that identifies when an institution needs to change. It provides little insight as to what the change would or should be or how members decide what changes to make. Rather, the institutional development of a state legislative chamber is likely to be greatly influenced by past events and past decisions since institutionalization and change rarely occur in a vacuum. Where an institution starts greatly influences where it can go. That is to say, the ability to adopt new institutional structures and procedures or alter existing ones is highly dependent upon earlier choices regarding institutional development. Scholars who have addressed institutional adoption and change seem to acknowledge this limitation.

Scholars outside of the state legislative arena have asserted that political processes are by their nature path dependent and that any attempt to account for phenomenon associated with these processes must take this path dependency into account (Pierson, 2000a, 2000b; Jervis, 2000; Thelen, 2000; Bridges, 2000). Paul Pierson has been the most vocal advocate for correctly including temporality or path dependence into explanations of political processes, and he asserts small, contingent events are just as likely as large events to result in large changes. This criticism of political science's focus on large causes is aimed in part at rational choice scholars whose theories assume that individuals alter institutions in ways that suit their needs without any regard to limitations because of past decisions.

For example, in the congressional literature three schools of thought exist regarding the purpose of committees in the legislative process. Each school treats members as rational actors with a specific purpose for the committee system. The distributive school asserts that the committee system exists as a venue for individual members to secure reelection by securing benefits for their constituents (Shepsle, 1986; Weingast and Marshall, 1988); the informational school asserts that the purpose of the committee system is to reduce information costs for members (Krehbiel, 1991); and the partisan school suggests that the purpose of the committee system is to secure the power and future success of the majority political party through agenda control (Cox and McCubbins, 1993). Common to these three perspectives on committee systems is the notion that the past simply does not matter—what is important are the objectives sought by the relevant actors for the institution. In fact, most studies that address institutional structure and procedure through a rational choice perspective assume that structures and procedures will change if those who have control over them discover that a different configuration of structures and procedures will allow them to attain their goals more efficiently. Very little consideration is given to the notion that change in certain directions may not be possible or that options for change may be tied to decisions made long ago. When considering the development of state legislative institutions it is our contention that decisions made by actors in the past greatly influence the ability of current and future actors to shape those institutions.

The Limiting Effects of Constitutions and Statutes

If a particular aspect of the legislative process is codified in the constitution or statutory law, it is significantly harder to alter. The U.S. Congress and every state legislature derive its basic form constitutionally. The U.S. Constitution and each state constitution clearly outline the basic legislative structures that will exist. Virtually all constitutions in the United States lay out the bicameral system,[4] the number of members in each chamber, the form of representation (i.e., districts vs. states), requirements for office, etc. in the section outlining the legislative branch. Beyond these basic characteristics, the items describing the legislative process in American constitutions vary considerably. Some state constitutions are similar to the U.S. Constitution and provide only the basic structures and service requirements for the state's legislative body. Others provide quite a bit of detail regarding legislative structure and practice. A similar instance exists when exploring state statutory law. In some states there are virtually no laws on the books regarding legislative structure and procedure, and in others there are quite a few.

Table 13.1 categorizes 48 of the 50 states concerning the extent to which the state constitution and state statutes determine state legislative structure and procedure.[5] In about half the states there is a moderate level of detail in both the state constitution and statutes. In Arkansas and California, there are a number of detailed directives on legislative structure and procedure. In no state is it the case that there is a low amount of detail in both the constitution and statutes. In four states (Massachusetts, New Hampshire, North Carolina, and Rhode Island) little detail on state legislative institutions can be found in constitutions and only moderate directives are included in statutory law.[6]

State constitutions, as well as statutory law are important components to any evaluation of the development and evolution of state legislative structures and procedures. While there is great variation in the extent to which the state constitutions and statutes

Table 13.1 Level of Detail in State Constitution and State Statutes for State Legislative Structure and Procedure

STATUTES	Constitutions		
	Low	Moderate	High
Low		HI, KY, MI, NE, ND, VT, WA, MI	PA
Moderate	MA, NH, NC, RI	AZ, CO, DE, FL, GA, ID, IN, KS, ME, MD, MN, NV, NJ, NM, NY, OH, OR, SC, SD, TN, UT, VA, WV, WY	AL, LA, MS, MO, TX
High	CT, WI	AK, IL, MT	AR, CA

Source: Table developed by the authors based on data collected from state constitutions and statutes.

provide for legislative structure and procedure, it is clear that in some states they provide distinct structures and procedures for their law-making bodies. Some relatively common provisions that are likely to have the largest impact on the development and evolution of state legislatures over time are those that limit session length, limit member terms and salary, place restrictions on the timing of introduction and passage of legislation, limit the agenda of special sessions, and those that impact the structure and processes of the standing committee system.

The discovery that many states have imbedded legislative structure and procedures into their constitutional and statutory documents also has important implications for the study of state legislatures. Many scholars have simply applied the theories developed by congressional scholars to the state legislatures. Given the findings of this review, this may be somewhat problematic. These congressional theories (e.g. distributive, informational and partisan theories of committees, theories concerning structures and member goals, etc.) rely on the assumption that members during any given legislative session have full power and authority to adopt or alter any structure or procedure they choose. Research (see Martorano, Hedlund, and Hamm, 2009 and 2010) clearly shows that while this generally holds true for the U.S. Congress, it does not hold true in most of the states. In most states, members may be severely restrained by what previous members have passed via statutory law or what has been imposed constitutionally. Thus, a major assumption of this congressional work is violated at the state-level, which means any application of congressional theories to the state legislatures must be very conscious of this potential limitation and modify the theories and expectations accordingly.

Case 1: Professionalization and Professionalism

One potent feature for understanding state legislatures in the last 50 years is the legislative organization—its structure, configuration and processes. Research has repeatedly affirmed the impact of the organization on legislative effectiveness, on outcomes, and on policies formulated. This area of state legislative research has also proven to be especially beneficial for testing and refining Congress-based, rational choice theories regarding the organization and its performance. Advances for these theories are due primarily to the great variety of structural, design and procedural characteristics found across the 50 states, which offers a fertile research environment for using truly "comparative" research designs.

By far, the most significant research related to the legislative organization at the state level has been done in the area of *legislative professionalization* and *legislator professionalism*. One scholar, Peverill Squire, is largely responsible for initiating and nurturing much of the current work on legislative professionalization (Squire, 1992a, 1992b), while Alan Rosenthal, Gary Moncrief and Joel Thompson have played a similar role regarding legislator professionalism—*ital* "careerism" (Moncrief and Thompson, 1992; Thompson and Moncrief, 1992; Moncrief, Thompson, and Cassie, 1996; Rosenthal, 1996, 1998; Kurtz et al., 2006). These scholars presented theoretical as well as operational understanding of these important concepts and also provided the measurement indicators that dozens of political scientists studying state legislatures now use with substantial explanatory success.

Legislative Professionalization: Building on the works of S. N. Eisenstadt regarding general social organizations (1964), of Huntington regarding organizations and political development (1965) and Polsby's classic historical tracing of the emergence of institutionalization in the U. S. House of Representatives (1968), Squire argued that what was taking place in state legislatures—professionalization—was related to institutionalism, but was different. He noted that while professionalization and institutionalization are connected, professionalization is likely to precede and help produce institutionalization (Squire, 1992b: 1027).

A professionalized legislature is characterized by higher compensation levels, staff and facilities availability, and adequate time for legislative activities as well as expectations for services. "Essentially, such a body offers potential and current members incentives sufficient to consider service as a career" (Squire, 1992b: 1028). Squire also offered a measurement framework that includes indicators of professionalization (legislative staff or expenditures, session length and legislator compensation) and their assessment based on comparisons between states and Congress. This measurement approach fostered and facilitated systematic and across-time research regarding the professionalization levels of various state legislatures. As state legislatures professionalize, the members re-shape the organization structurally and procedurally and with regard to relationships with other governmental components, thereby becoming more independent, assertive, powerful and decisive in policy making. Squire has developed his indicator for the professionalization level in all 50 state legislatures and extended the range of years from 1909 through 2003 (Squire, 2007).

Mooney (1994) has noted that a variety of other terms have been used in the last 50 years to describe and measure the enhanced nature of a state legislature's capacity to perform its role (1994). However, the core of all these definitions has been very congruous, suggesting that all these definitions/measurements actually indicated impressive stability and continuity regarding the understanding of the professionalization concept, but Squire's definition and operationalization dominates current research.

In addition to the roles played by constitutions and statutes in the development of professionalization in state legislatures, existing research identifies several possible contributing factors. For example studies have identified various social and demographic factors associated with the nature of the state (population size and wealth); rising citizen expectations; inter-branch differences (at times rising to clashes between governors and legislators regarding their role in decision-making); partisan control and interparty competition; and a history regarding spending (Fiorina, 1994, 1999; Mooney, 1995; Squire, 1997; King, 2000; Malhotra, 2006). Recent research (Bowen and Greene, 2011) suggests that the explanation for professionalization is much more complex and nuanced and benefits from a separate analysis of the three common components comprising professionalization.

Regarding the potential impact of professionalized legislatures, Squire and Hamm offered that "professionalization has been found to impact an extensive web of relationships involving legislators and the organizations in which they serve" (2005: 95). Examples of the varying impact of professionalization across states are:

- *Legislative institutions,* including legislative efficiency—bills passed as well as bill passage per day, the "quality" of legislative output and legislatures positioning vis-à-vis the executive.
- *Electoral consequences,* including who runs for legislative seats, levels of contestation, incumbency effects, divided government, and election campaigns.
- *Legislative careers and ambition* specifically providing disincentives for existing members to leave the profession thereby reducing member turnover while also increasing job satisfaction, fostering a trend for legislators to vacate their seat and seek another office, increasing legislative attention and responsiveness to constituents, and affecting voting and voting cues.
- *Partisan makeup of legislatures,* specifically a Democratic bias in state legislatures.
- *Legislative leaders,* including their formal powers, the path to leadership; and leadership style itself.
- *Committees,* specifically the restructuring of committee systems in order to improve activity structuring, reinforcing the committee role at the forefront of policy development as well as diffusion, and increasing committee representativeness as well as committee "informativeness."
- *Political representation,* especially the prominence of constituent interests and preferences, and the type of representation and policy outcomes that result.
- *The role of other political organizations,* including interest group responsiveness, gubernatorial effectiveness, e-government implementation, and public opinion of state legislatures.

The conclusion is that professionalization of state legislatures provides legislators with the capacity, resources and facilities to not only deal with expanded public policy responsibility, but also to improve the representation of their constituents. This impressive list regarding the impact of professionalization suggests that it will continue being used as an explanatory factor in future research.

Constraints on Professionalization: When evaluating research on and understanding of professionalization, it is critical to note that state legislatures vary in their ability and ease in becoming more professionalized. As noted above, state legislatures are constrained in what they can do organizationally and structurally by their governing constitutions and statutes. Adopting new institutional structures and procedures or even altering existing ones takes place within the context of "constrained choices"— restrictions created by the setting within which a state legislature exists and the path taken to arrive there profoundly affects how it can change. Hence, to truly understand professionalization, one needs to comprehend what might restrict the adoption of its various facets. One major element is the degree to which basic documents affecting and constricting state legislatures—constitutions and statutes—restrain the development of professionalization. Three traits of professionalization are often found in these documents—compensation, time in session, and staff expenditure levels.

An examination of state constitutions and statutes as well as the national constitution shows that legislator compensation is covered in 90.2 percent of the constitutions; however, there are profound differences across states. In most (58.8 percent) of the constitutions it is ordered that legislative salary be determined by law, usually with the caveat that any increase will take effect following the current legislative session. In 15.7 percent of the constitutions, a compensation committee composed of individuals outside of the legislature determines pay and in 9.8 percent (5 constitutions) a specific dollar amount is specified for legislator salaries. Hence, the task of raising legislator salaries to attract a full-time commitment is virtually impossible in these five states because amending a constitution is a long process and requires citizen approval. In addition, 90 percent of the states have adopted one or more laws regarding compensation. Typically these laws cover the salary of members and officers, per diems, expense allowances, mileage and travel reimbursement and legislative retirement benefits. A legislature's ability to alter its own compensation, thereby attracting persons able to make a stronger time commitment, varies substantially across the states.

A second set of restrictions frequently constraining legislative professionalization by "compressing" the amount of effort/attention that can be given to decision making are limits placed on the time a legislature can be in session. Over 56 percent of the constitutions place a limit on the length of a session while five states place limits on the length of special sessions. These limits create a restriction that is difficult to change in the effort to evolve into a professional, full-time legislature.

Regarding legislative staffing, over half the states have passed statutes regarding the employment of staff, thus limiting that aspect of professionalization. Included here are specifications about the types of positions to be provided, organizations to provide various services and even salary/budget information. Unfortunately there is not much political science research regarding staffing and this is an area for future research.

A highly regarded observer of state legislatures—Alan Rosenthal—has suggested that legislative professionalization must be differentiated between the *legislature* as an organization and the *legislator* as an individual (Rosenthal, 1996; see also Squire, 2007; Squire and Moncrief, 2010). He posited that "institutional professionalism" is separate and distinct from what is taking place at the individual level—legislator professionalism. Organizational characteristics like full-time legislative scheduling, size and nature of staffs, the availability of information, and legislative facilities create the *institutional* setting within which legislators operate and should be kept analytically differentiated. Similarly, *legislators* themselves can become more "professional" in how they go about their activity within the organization—amount of time spent on legislative tasks, self-identity with a legislative/public servant occupation, reliance on non-legislative employment, and future political ambitions—somewhat independent of what is transpiring at the chamber level. While professionalization and professionalism are obviously related, they are not the same and need to be treated separately in research, an important task for the future.

Another feature observed by many state scholars was the creation of a "new breed" of legislator—careerists—who were not only spending less time with their constituents (e.g. district business and constituent services), but were focusing a majority of their time and energy initiating new policy, specifically in areas that were more "general," rather than parochial, to appease a larger constituency in their attempt to "move up" to a higher political office (Copeland and Rausch, 1991; Carey, Niemi, and Powell, 2000). A key question is what role is identified for careerists in future research?

Related to this is a long-standing concern regarding the nature of service as a state legislator. Throughout U.S. history there has been a belief among many that legislators should be citizens who, temporarily and on a part-time basis, serve in the legislature only to return to private life (Thompson and Moncrief, 1992; Rosenthal, 1996; Wills, 1999; Kurtz et al., 2006). The legislative reform movement of the 1960s and 1970s advocated the transition of state legislators from amateurs to professionals as well as altering the nature of legislative bodies. The assumption was that the emergence of full-time, careerist legislators would foster legislative body professionalization and expertise development thereby transforming the nature of legislatures at the state level. Recent analysis of a sample of state legislators showed that the relationship is much more complex; amateur, part-time legislators exist in very professional legislatures and within legislative bodies there often is a wide range of time commitments to legislative activities (Kurtz et al., 2006). These findings raise questions for future research about the interaction between member orientations to service and the nature of the legislative organization.

Further adding to the complexity of professionalization/professionalism research is citizen reaction to these trends and the effort to eliminate "careerist" or ambitious politicians. One approach has been to impose term limits on state legislators.

Case 2: Term Limits in the American States

The widespread adoption of term limits in the early to mid 1990s represents one of the most important institutional changes impacting state legislatures. The members of one-third of the state legislatures in the United States are limited in the number of terms they may serve. Scholars have only just begun to study the impacts of term limits as in many states the limits did not take effect until the early 2000s. Regardless of the specific impact of term limits on the states, we are certain that they are a significant force with regards to the institutional development and evolution of state legislatures. Further, the adoption of term limits has provided us with a unique situation with regards to research design. It is very rare that we are able to utilize quasi-experimental designs that can test both pre and post event behaviors as well as compare those behaviors in cases that experienced the event versus those that did not.

Given the challenges of data collection, the earliest examinations of the actual impact of term limits were single state studies that explored specifically how term limits changed explicit aspects of the legislatures. The most significant single state research has been carried out by a group of scholars at Wayne State University in their study of the impact of term limits on legislative life and politics in Michigan (Sarbaugh-Thompson et al., 2004, 2006, 2010). They found that term limits have not lived up to expectations. For example, supporters urged Michigan voters to approve term limits, arguing that they would lead to better oversight of state agencies. The Wayne State University research team has found that state legislators actually spend less time monitoring state agencies than before term limits. They have also found that the ties between legislators and lobbyists/interest groups has been strengthened rather than weakened by the adoption of term limits.

The earliest multi-state studies explored the impact of term limits on the characteristics of members and found that in most cases, term limits did not significantly alter the diversity of state legislative chambers (Thompson and Moncrief, 1993; Carey, Niemi, and Powell, 2000; Carroll and Jenkins, 2001). Another set of studies has focused on using elite surveys to determine how term limits have impacted the way legislators approach their duties. The first of these projects is a massive survey of state legislators by John Carey, Richard Niemi, and Lynda Powell. Their research culminated in the book *Term Limits in the State Legislatures* (2000). Key findings from this study include: term limits having no effect on the demographic composition of legislatures; a tendency of term-limited legislators to behave more individualistically, but also pursue less pork and favor more statewide issues; a shifting of power in term limited states away from committee chairs and political party leaders and towards the executive and legislative staff; and evidence that term limits may make elections more competitive in term limited states. The Joint Project on Term Limits, a separate project, was undertaken jointly by the National Conference on State Legislatures, Council of State Governments, the State Legislative Leaders Foundation and a group of legislative scholars, and investigates the impact of term limits on aspects of legislative life such as capacity for policy making, types of legislators elected, the legislative process, and relationships amongst branches of government in the states. The research by this collaborative group is presented in *The Case of Term Limits* (Kurtz, Cain, and Niemi, 2007). This massive 99 chamber study found generally the impact of term limits varies with the nature of the term limit (e.g. short vs. long; lifetime ban vs. consecutive limit, etc.). It also finds that term limits have had more of an impact in some states (California) than in others (Louisiana). Like Carey, Niemi and Powell, the study found that term limits did not significantly alter the composition of state legislative chambers, and term-limited members were less inclined to pursue pork for their districts. Other findings include the notion that legislators in term limited states are more reliant for information on lobbyists, interest groups, and staff, and that the legislative branch has been institutionally weakened relative to other branches in term limited states.

Thad Kousser has also explored the impact of term limits on state legislatures. In a study of 11 states impacted by term limits, his overall conclusion is that "whatever a higher level of professionalism produces more of, term limits has reduced (Kousser, 2005: 204)." He finds that, on average, the type of legislator elected may have changed and the flood of new members and quick turnover rates seems to have impacted how chambers function. For example, it appears that the reign of legislative leaders has been cut short, and many only serve as a chamber leader for a single term. However, he also finds that the effects of term limits can be very different from state to state. In some states bill introductions increased, but in others they have decreased. Kousser's findings illustrate that the path of legislative development is highly variable and influenced greatly by past forces both internal and external to the chambers.

PROPOSED RESEARCH AGENDA 2

The Case for Reinvigorating the Study of Political Support

The concern with support for political institutions has a long tradition in political science, derived from a far-reaching range of research efforts. Jewell, in his 1981 review of the literature, called for more detailed studies at the state legislative level of public support. Thirty years later little progress has been made. We believe that a significant research effort should be undertaken to examine the impact of support on political institutions and processes in the post 2010 era since the levels of confidence and support from the citizenry for state legislatures as well as government itself, appear to be at all-time lows, perhaps so low that diminished support will affect government operations.

What is Political Support?

Mishler and Rose, in describing the relationship of political support to the emergence of new national democracies, note:

> A defining feature of democratic regimes is that they depend for their survival and effective functioning on the public's willing acquiescence and support... Given the importance that democratic theory ascribes to political support, it is not surprising that the current democratic wave has revived scholarly interest in the concept and its measurement. (Mishler and Rose 2001: 303)

Hence, political support is considered essential for decision making and committing state resources in a democracy without reliance on coercion. Studies of political support typically differentiate among varying political "objects" (i.e. community, regime, and authorities) for that support and between types of support, diffuse (reservoir of goodwill/attachment) versus specific support (based on policy fulfillment) (Easton, 1965, 1975; Wahlke, 1971; Patterson, Wahlke, and Boynton, 1973; Anderson and Guillory, 1997; Mishler and Rose, 2007).

Various terms have been used in the political science literature to embody this concept as well as its measurement—satisfaction, confidence, trust, legitimacy, popularity and approval. While each of these concepts has subtle but real differences in meaning and connotation, they have been used largely interchangeably since they each capture some component of support (Mishler and Rose, 1997, 2001).

Causes and Consequences of Support

An impressive amount of work on the nature and consequences of support in a variety of non-U.S. settings provides a fruitful foundation. Collectively, this research has affirmed the impact of support on regime legitimacy, including obeying laws and support for incumbents (Loewenberg and Patterson, 1979, and Mezey, 1985); the nature of support as countries transition to democracy (Mishler and Rose, 1994); the relationship between legislative and regime support including "antisystem" behavior (Mishler and Rose, 1994, 1997, and Muller, Jukam, and Seligson, 1982); the speed with which countries have developed support for democracy after regime change (Weil, 1989); and, the impact of citizen fears and hopes on support (Mishler and Rose, 1994). All this work reinforces the perspective that, in a dynamic context of changing citizen perspectives on and perceptions of political institutions and their role in governing, a focus on the support for governmental structures and personnel may become a critical topic for study. If this evolves, researchers will have to deal with how to measure support and the validity of using public opinion questions as surrogates for indicators of support as conceptualized in the discipline.

Regarding state legislatures, research indicates that factors such as a state's economic health, social-cultural factors (levels of crime, joblessness and poverty), perceived representation of citizen interests (policy outcomes representing citizen preferences), governmental performance (level of legislative professionalization) and even the nature of the political process itself (the quality of government management, and divided government), all affect levels of support (Squire, 1993a, 1993b; Chanley, Rudolph, and Rahn, 2000; Kelleher and Wolak, 2007; Squire and Moncrief, 2010).

Proposed Research Agenda

The literature on support and its measurement is replete with examples of multiple indicator approaches—a tactic widely advocated in measurement theory (Boynton, Patterson, and Hedlund, 1968; Muller and Jukam, 1977; Iyengar, 1980; Muller, Jukam, and Seligson, 1982; Mishler and Rose, 2001; Inglehart, 2003). We have precious few examples of a multiple indicator approach in the study of state legislatures. The reason for such an outcome rests squarely on the costs for doing such research at the state level and the need to adopt compromises—the use of data collected for other purposes to provide generalizations of relevance to political science.

At the state legislative level, one academic research effort provided a much more complex, nuanced and multifaceted measure of support. This research provided important insights regarding the operationalization of support (a compliance and commitment dimension), the nature of support, factors affecting support and levels of support among different political elites—legislators, lobbyists, local party leaders and attentive constituents as well as citizens (Boynton, Patterson, and Hedlund, 1968, 1969a 1969b; Patterson, Wahlke, and Boynton, 1973; and Patterson, Hedlund, and Boynton, 1975). This work demonstrated that a more focused, distinctive and tailored set of indicators for support is possible and may actually elicit a more accurate representation of support for a legislative institution. Given the emerging importance of citizen support and its likely target for research, developing a valid and accurate set of indicators is a critical first step if we are to understand the complicated nature of support, its importance and its impact.

CONCLUSION

This essay has sought to outline the evolution of research regarding state legislatures for the past 50 years and has found an increased use of state legislatures as the venue for study, enhanced complexity in research methods and data, and an amplified appearance of theory-based research and analysis. This development poses a challenge for future research to identify germane research questions, gather appropriate data, and utilize ever-evolving research methodologies. This challenge is derived largely from some of the most important aspects of state legislative research:

- We have multiple cases for study with 99 legislative chambers;
- A wide variety of characteristics are associated with these chambers;
- A different set of constraints in terms of constitutions and statutes are associated with these states within which one works;
- A quite different history and setting is associated with the states although they are part of a single national context.

These traits pose enormous challenges for data collection since there is no single source of information, except what is available through the National Conference of State Legislatures and various web sites (e.g. Vote Smart, National Institute on Money in State Politics). Hence, state legislative researchers must become their own data collection initiators and repositories. Yet, in light of these challenges, there is, as noted, increasing effort for state legislative study as a means for understanding the legislative process.

This essay has also discussed three over-arching thrusts for future state legislative research—Legislative Development, Stresses Strains and Bounded Rationality, and the Limiting Effects of State Constitutions—two cases for future research—Term Limits and, Professionalization, and a reinvigorated study of Legislative Support. In each we have summarized the nature of research and at times even suggested possible questions for future research in order to encourage future efforts for understanding better the legislative process in general as well as sub-national politics and political institutions in the United States.

NOTES

1. One of the authors of this article (Hamm 2001) conducted a survey of legislative articles published in 9 journals from 1996 to 2000. The journals examined included *American Political Science Review, American Journal of Political Science, Journal of Politics, Legislative Studies Quarterly, Political Research Quarterly (formerly Western Political Quarterly),*

    Social Science Quarterly, Polity, and *American Politics Research (formerly American Politics Quarterly).* We updated the analysis for 2006–10 and added *State Politics and Policy Quarterly.*

2. Of course, one should be cautious in treating these numbers as constituting the population of published material since Jewell only focused on seven research areas—legislative recruitment and elections, career patterns, legislative organization and structure, roles and norms, representing the constituency, legislative decision making, and legislative budgeting and oversight. Moncrief et al. utilized the same seven topics in their review piece.

3. Using the Moncrief et al. bibliography for the 1981–95 period, we calculate that roughly 29 percent of the journal articles included 45 or more legislatures. Using Hamm's bibliography (2001), we calculate that this figure is 40.5 percent during 1996–2000.

4. An exception is Nebraska, which is the only state to have a unicameral legislature. Thus, its constitution provides for a legislature with a single chamber.

5. Iowa and Oklahoma are excluded due to missing information on statutes.

6. For additional detail regarding the directives on legislative structure and procedure found in state constitutions and statutory law see Martorano, Hedlund and Hamm (2009 and 2010).

References

Anderson, Christopher J. and Christine A. Guillory. 1997. "Political Institutions and Satisfaction with Democracy: A Cross-National Analysis of Consensus and Majoritarian Systems." *American Political Science Review* 91: 66–81.

Arceneaux, Kevin and Robin Kolodny. 2009. "Educating the Least Informed: Group Endorsements in a Grassroots Campaign." *American Journal of Political Science* 53: 755–70.

Battista, James Coleman. 2006. "Jurisdiction, Institutional Structure, and Committee Representativeness." *Political Research Quarterly* 59: 47–56.

Battista, James Coleman. 2009. "Why Information? Choosing Committee Informativeness in U.S. State Legislatures." *Legislative Studies Quarterly* 34: 375–97.

Bell, Charles G. and Charles M. Price. 1975. *The First Term.* Beverly Hills, CA: Sage Publications.

Bergan, Daniel E. 2009. "Does Grassroots Lobbying Work? A Field Experiment Measuring the Effects of an e-Mail Lobbying Campaign on Legislative Behavior." *American Politics Research* 37: 327–52.

Bowen, Daniel and Zachary Greene. 2011. "Legislating Professionalism: Disentangling the Conditional Effects of Workload and Partisanship." Paper presented at the 11th Annual State Politics and Policy Conference, Dartmouth College, June 2–4.

Boynton, G. R., Samuel C. Patterson and Ronald D. Hedlund. 1969a. "Perceptions and Expectations of the Legislature and Support for it." *American Journal of Sociology* 75: 62–76.

Boynton, G. R., Samuel C. Patterson and Ronald D. Hedlund. 1969b. "The Missing Links in Legislative Politics." *Journal of Politics* 31: 720–1.

Boynton, Samuel C. Patterson and Ronald D. Hedlund. 1968. "The Structure of Public Support for Legislative Institutions." *Midwest Journal of Political Science* 12: 163–80.

Box-Steffensmeier, Janet, and J. K. Dow. 1992. "The Allocation of Political Resources in an Unregulated Setting: The 1984 and 1986 California Assembly Elections." *Western Political Quarterly* 45: 609–28.

Bridges, Amy. 2000. "Path Dependence, Sequence, History, Theory." *Studies in American Political Development* 14: 109–12.

Carey, John, Richard Niemi and Lynda Powell. 1995. "State Legislative Survey and Contextual Data, 1995 (United States) (Computer file) ICPSR Version." Columbus, OH: Kathleen Carr, Ohio State University Polimetrics Lab (producer), 1995. Ann Arbor, MI: ICPSR (distributor) 2000.

Carey, John, Richard Niemi and Lynda Powell. 1998. "The Effects of Term Limits on State Legislatures." *Legislative Studies Quarterly* 23: 271–300.

Carey, John, Richard Niemi and Lynda Powell. 2000a. *Term Limits in State Legislatures.* Ann Arbor: University of Michigan Press.

Carey, John, Richard Niemi, Lynda Powell and Gary Moncrief. 2006. "The Effects of Term Limits on State Legislatures: A New Survey of the 50 States." *Legislative Studies Quarterly* 31: 105–34.

Carroll, Susan J. and Krista Jenkins. 2001. "Do Term Limits Help Get Women Elected?" *Social Science Quarterly* 82: 197–201.

Carsey, Thomas M., Richard G. Niemi, William D. Berry, Lynda W. Powell, and James M. Snyder. 2008. "State Legislative Elections, 1967–2003: Announcing the Completion of a Cleaned and Updated Dataset." *State Politics and Policy Quarterly* 8: 430–43.

Casellas, Jason P. 2009. "The Institutional and Demographic Determinants of Latino Representation." *Legislative Studies Quarterly* 34: 399–26.

Chanley, Virginia Thomas J. Rudolph and Wendy M. Rahn. 2000. "The Origins and Consequences of Public Trust in Government: A Time Series Analysis." *Public Opinion Quarterly* 64: 239–56.

Chen, Jowei. 2010. "The Effects of Electoral Geography on Pork Barreling in Bicameral Legislatures." *American Journal of Political Science* 54: 301–22.

Clucas, Richard A. 1995. *The Speaker's Electoral Connection: Willie Brown and the California Assembly.* Berkeley: University of California Institute of Governmental Studies Press.

Clucas, Richard A. 2003. "Improving the Harvest of State Legislative Research." *State Politics and Policy Quarterly.* 3: 387–419.

Clucas, Richard A. 2009. "The Contract with America and Conditional Party Government in State Legislatures." *Political Research Quarterly* 62: 317–28.

Copeland, Gary W., and John David Rausch Jr. 1991. The End of Professionalism: The Dynamics of Term Limitations. Paper delivered at the Annual Meeting of the Southwestern Political Science Association, San Antonio, Texas, March 27–30.

Cox, Gary W., Thad Koussser, and Matthew D. McCubbins. 2010. "Party Power or Preferences? Quasi-Experimental Evidence from American State Legislatures." *The Journal of Politics* 72: 799–811.

Cox, Gary W. and Mathew D. McCubbins. 1993. *Legislative Leviathan: Party Government in the House.* Berkeley, CA: University of California Press.

Davidson, Roger H. and Walter J. Oleszek. 1976. "Adaptation and Consolidation: Structural Innovation in the U.S. House of Representatives." *Legislative Studies Quarterly* 1: 37–65.

Easton, David. 1965. *A Systems analysis of Political Life.* New York: Wiley.

Easton, David. 1975, "A Reassessment of Concept of Political Support." *British Journal of Political Science* 5: 435–57

Eisenstadt, S. N. (1964). "Institutionalization and Change." *American Sociological Review* 29: 235–47.

Engstrom, Erik J. and Nathan W. Monroe. 2006. "Testing the Basis of Incumbency Advantage: Strategic Candidates and Term Limits in the California Legislature." *State Politics and Policy Quarterly* 6: 1–20.

Erikson, Robert, Gerald Wright and John McIver, 1993. *Statehouse Democracy: Public Opinion and Policy in the American States.* Cambridge, MA: Cambridge University Press.

Fiorina, Morris. 1994. "Divided Government in the American States: A By Product of Legislative Professionalism." *American Political Science Review* 88: 304–16.

Fiorina, Morris, 1999. "Further Evidence of the Partisan Consequences of Legislative Professionalism." *American Journal of Political Science* 43: 974–77.

Forgette, Richard, Andrew Gardner, and John Winkle. 2009. "Do Redistricting Principles and Practices Affect U.S. State Legislative Electoral Competition." *State Politics and Policy Quarterly* 9: 151–75.

Francis, Wayne L. 1967. *Legislative Issues in the Fifty States.* Chicago: Rand McNally.

Francis, Wayne L. 1989. *The Legislative Committee Game: A Comparative Analysis of Fifty States.* Columbus, Ohio: The Ohio State University Press.

Froman, Lewis. 1968. "Organization Theory and the Explanation of Important Characteristics of Congress." *American Political Science Review* 62: 518–26.

Goehlert, Robert U. and Frederick W. Musto. 1985. *State Legislatures: A Bibliography.* Santa Barbara, CA: ABC-Clio Information Services.

Gray, Virginaand David Lowery. 1995. "Interest Representation and Democratic Gridlock." *Legislative Studies Quarterly* 20: 531–52.

Hamm, Keith E. 2001 "Comparative Legislative Research: An Observer's Perspective." Conference on the Comparative Study of Deputy "Hill Style" in Latin American Legislatures. (February 2001). Texas A&M University.

Hamm, Keith E., Ronald D. Hedlund, and Nancy Martorano. 2006. "Measuring State Legislative Committee Power: Change and Chamber Differences in the 20th Century." *State Politics and Policy Quarterly* 6: 88–111.

Harder, Marvin A. and Raymond G. Davis. 1979. *The Legislatures as an Organization: A Study of the Kansas Legislature.* Lawrence, KS: Regents Press of Kansas.

Harmel, Robert, and Keith Hamm. 1986. "Development of a Party Role in a No-Party Legislature." *Western Political Quarterly* 39: 79–92.

Hays, Jennifer, Tracy Osborn, Jonathan Winburn, and Gerald C. Wright. 2009. "Representation in U.S. State Legislatures: The Acquisition and Analysis of U.S. State Legislative Roll-Call Data." *State Politics and Policy Quarterly* 9: 356–70.

Hedlund, R. D. 1984a. "Organizational Attributes of Legislatures: Structure, Rules, Norms, Resources." *Legislative Studies Quarterly* 9: 51–121.

Hedlund, Ronald. 1989. "Entering the Committee System: State Government Assignments." *Western Political Quarterly* 42: 597–625.

Hedlund, Ronald D. 1978. "A Path-Goal Approach to Explaining Leadership's Impact on Legislator Perceptions." *Social Science Quarterly* 59: 178–91.

Hedlund, Ronald D. 1984b. "Organizational Attributes of Legislative Institutions: Structure, Rules, Norms, Resources." In *Handbook of Legislative Research*, ed. Gerhard Loewenberg, Samuel C. Patterson and Malcolm E. Jewell. Cambridge, MA: Harvard University Press, 321–91.

Hedlund, Ronald D. and Patricia Freeman. 1981. "A Strategy for Measuring the Performance of Legislatures in Processing Decisions." *Legislative Studies Quarterly* 6: 87–113.

Hedlund, Ronald D. and Keith Hamm. 1976. "Conflict and Perceived Group Benefits from Legislative Rules Changes." *Legislative Studies Quarterly* 1: 181–99.

Herrnson, Paul S., Atiya Kai Stokes-Brown, Matthew Hindman. 2007. "Campaign Politics and the Digital Divide: Constituency Characteristics, Strategic Considerations, and Candidate Internet Use in State Legislative Elections." *Political Research Quarterly* 60: 31–42.

Hogan, Robert E. 2008. "Policy Responsiveness and Incumbent Re-election in State Legislatures." *American Journal of Political Science* 52: 858–73.

Huntington, Sameul. P. 1965. "Political Development and Political Decay." *World Politics* 17: 386–430.

Inglehart, Ronald. 2003. "How Solid Is Mass Support for Democracy: And How Can We Measure It?" *PS: Political Science and Politics* 36: 51–7.

Iyengar, Shanto. 1980. "Subjective Political Efficacy as a Measure of Diffuse Support." *Public Opinion Quarterly* 44: 249–56.

Jervis, Robert. 2000. "Timing and Interaction in Politics: A Comment on Pierson." *Studies in American Political Development* 14: 93–100

Jewell, Malcolm E. 1976. "Editor's Introduction." *Legislative Studies Quarterly* 1: 1–9.

Jewell, Malcolm E. 1981. "Editor's Introduction: The State of U.S. State Legislative Research." *Legislative Studies Quarterly* 6: 1–25.

Jewell, Malcolm E. 1983. "Legislator-Constituency Relations and the Representative Process." *Legislative Studies Quarterly* 8: 303–37.

Jewell, Malcolm E. 1991. "State Election Returns in the United States Dataset." Inter-University Consortium for Political and Social Research (Study # 8907).

Jewell, Malcolm E. 1997. "Trends in Research on U.S. State Legislatures: A Review Article." *Legislative Studies Quarterly* 22: 265–74.

Kelleher, Christine A. and Jenifer Wolak. 2007. "Public Confidence in the Branches of State Government." *Political Research Quarterly* 60: 707–21

King, James D. 2000. "Changes in Professionalism in U.S. State Legislatures." *Legislative Studies Quarterly* 25: 327–43.

Kousser, Thad, Jeffrey B. Lewis and Seth E. Masket. 2007. "Ideological Adaptation? The Survival Instinct of Threatened Legislators." *The Journal of Politics* 69: 828–43.

Kousser, Thad. 2005. *Term Limits and the Dismantling of State Legislative Professionalism.* Cambridge, UK: Cambridge University Press.

Krehbiel, Keith. 1991. *Information and Legislative Organization.* Ann Arbor, MI: University of Michigan Press.

Kurtz, Karl T., Bruce Cain and Richard Niemi. 2007. *Institutional Change in American Politics: The Case of Term Limits.* Ann Arbor, MI: University of Michigan Press.

Kurtz, Karl T. Gary Moncrief, Richard G. Niemi and Linda W. Powell. 2006. "Full-Time, Part-Time, and Real Time: Explaining State Legislator Perceptions of Time on the Job." *State Politics and Policy Quarterly* 6: 322–38.

Loftus, Tom. 1994. *The Art of Legislative Politics.* Washington, DC: CQ Press.

Loewenberg, Gerhard and Samuel C. Patterson. 1979. *Comparing Legislatures.* Boston: Little Brown.

Loomis, Burdett A. 1994. *Time, Politics, and Policies: A Legislative Year.* Lawrence: University of Kansas.

Lublin, David, Thomas L. Brunell, Bernard Grofman and Lisa Handley. 2009. "Has the Voting Rights Act Outlived Its Usefulness: In a Word 'No'." *Legislative Studies Quarterly* 34: 525–53.

Malhotra, Neil. 2006. "Government Growth and Professionalism in U.S. State Legislatures." *Legislative Studies Quarterly* 31: 563–84.

Malhotra, Neil. 2008. "Disentangling the Relationship between Legislative Professionalism and Government Spending." *Legislative Studies Quarterly* 33: 387–414.

Martorano, Nancy. 2006. "Balancing Power: Committee System Autonomy and Legislative Organization." *Legislative Studies Quarterly* 31: 204–34.

Martorano, Nancy, Ronald D. Hedlund and Keith E. Hamm. 2009. "Paths, Events and Strategic Choices: The Evolution of American State Legislatures." Paper presented at the annual meeting of the American Political Science Association, Toronto, Ontario, Canada.

Martorano, Nancy, Ronald D. Hedlund and Keith E. Hamm. 2010. "State Legislative Evolution: Path Dependency, Organization Theory and Bounded Rational Choice." Paper delivered at the 2010 State Politics and Policy Conference. Springfield, IL.

Masket, Seth. 2007. "It Takes an Outsider: Extralegislative Organization and Partisanship in the California Assembly, 1849–2006." *American Journal of Political Science* 51: 482–97.

Mayer, Kenneth P., and John Wood. 1995. "The Impact of Public Financing on Electoral Competitiveness: Evidence From Wisconsin, 1964–1990." *Legislative Studies Quarterly* 20: 69–87.

Mezey, Michael L. 1985. "The Functions of Legislatures in the Third World." In *Handbook of Legislative Research*, ed, Gerhard Loewenberg, Samuel C. Patterson and Malcolm E. Jewell. Cambridge: Harvard University Press, 733–72.

Miquel, Gerard Padró I and James M. Snyder, Jr. 2006. "Legislative Effectiveness and Legislative Careers." *Legislative Studies Quarterly* 31: 347–81.

Mishler, William and Richard Rose. 1994. "Support for Parliaments and Regimes in Transition Toward Democracy in Eastern Europe" *Legislative Studies Quarterly* 19: 5–32.

Mishler, William and Richard Rose. 1997, "Trust, Distrust and Skepticism: Popular Evaluations of Civil and Political Institutions in Post-Communist Societies." *The Journal of Politics* 59: 418–51.

Mishler, William and Richard Rose. 2001, "Political Support for Incomplete Democracies: Realist vs. Idealist Theories and Measures." *International Political Science Review* 22: 303–20.

Mishler, William and Richard Rose. 2007, "Generation Age and Time: The Dynamics of Political Learning During Russia's Transformation" *American Journal of Political Science* 51: 822–34.

Moncrief, Gary and Joel A. Thompson, Eds. 1992. *Changing Patterns in State Legislative Careers*. Ann Arbor, MI: University of Michigan Press.

Moncrief, Gary, Joel A. Thompson, and William Cassie. 1996. "Revisiting the State of U.S. State Legislative Research." *Legislative studies Quarterly* 21: 301–35.

Moncrief, Gary Joel A. Thompson, and Karl T. Kurtz. 1996. "The Old Statehouse, It Ain't What It Used to Be." *Legislative Studies Quarterly* 21: 57–72.

Mooney, Christopher. 1994. "Measuring U.S. State Legislative Professionalism: An Evaluation of Five Indices." *State and Local Government Review* 26: 70–8.

Mooney, Christopher. 1995. "Citizens, Structures, and Sister States: Influences on State Legislative Professionalism." *Legislative Studies Quarterly* 20: 47–67.

Mooney, Christopher. 2009. "Term Limits as a Boon to Legislative Scholarship: A Review." *State Politics and Policy Quarterly* 9: 204–28.

Muller, Edward M. and Thomas O. Jukam 1977 "On the Meaning of Political Support." *American Political Science Review* 71: 1561–95.

Muller, Edward M., Thomas O. Jukam and Mitchell A. Seligson 1982 "Diffuse Political Support and Antisystem Political Behavior: A Comparative Analysis." *American Journal of Political Science* 26: 240–64.

Overby, L. Marvin, Thomas A. Kazee, and David W. Prince. 2004. Committee Outliers in State Legislatures. *Legislative Studies Quarterly* 29: 81–107.

Ozymy, Joshua. 2010. "Assessing the Impact of Legislative Lobbying Regulations on Interest Group Influence in U.S. State Legislatures." *State Politics and Policy Quarterly* 10: 397–420.

Patterson, Samuel C., Ronald D. Hedlund and G. R. Boynton. 1975. *Representatives and Represented*. New York: Wiley.

Patterson, Samuel C., John C. Wahlke and G. R. Boynton 1973; "Dimensions of Support in Legislative Systems" in Alan Kornberg (ed), *Legislatures in Comparative Perspective*. New York: McKay, 282–313.

Pierson, Paul. 2000a. "Increasing Returns, Path Dependence, and the Study of Politics." *American Political Science Review* 94: 251–67.

Pierson, Paul. 2000b. "Not Just What, but When: Timing and Sequence in Political Processes." *Studies in American Political Development* 14: 72–92.

Polsby, Nelson S. 1968. "The Institutionalization of the U.S. House of Representatives." *American Political Science Review* 62: 144–68.

Poole, Keith T. and Howard Rosenthal. 1991. "Patterns of Congressional Voting." *American Journal of Political Science* 35: 228–78.

Prince, David W. and L. Marvin Overby. 2005. "Legislative Organization Theory and Committee Preferences Outliers in State Senates." *State Politics and Policy Quarterly* 5: 68–87.

Richman, Jesse. 2008. "Uncertainty and the Prevalence of Committee Outliers." *Legislative Studies Quarterly* 33: 323–47.

Rosenthal, Alan. 1974. *Legislative Performance in the States*. New York, NY: Harper and Row Publishers.

Rosenthal, Alan. 1996. "State Legislative Development: Observations from Three Perspectives." *Legislative Studies Quarterly* 21: 169–98.

Rosenthal, Alan. 1998. *The Decline of Representative Democracy: Process, Participation, and Power in State Legislatures*. Washington, DC: CQ Press.

Sarbaugh-Thompson, Marjorie, John Strate, Kelly Leroux, Richard C. Elling, LykeThompson and Charles D. Elder. 2010. "Legislators and Administrators: Complex Relationships Complicated by Term Limits." *Legislative Studies Quarterly* 35: 57–89.

Sarbaugh-Thompson, Marjorie, LykeThompson, Charles D. Elder, Meg Comins, Richard C. Elling, and John Strate. 2006. "Democracy among Strangers: Term Limits' Effects on Relationship between State Legislators in Michigan." *State Politics and Policy Quarterly* 6: 384–409.

Sarbaugh-Thompson, Marjorie, LykeThompson, Charles D. Elder, John Strateand Richard C. Elling. 2004. *Political and Institutional Effects of Term Limits*. New York: Palgrave Macmillan.

Shepsle, Kenneth A. 1986. "Institutional Equilibrium and Equilibrium Institutions." In *Political Science: The Science of Politics*, ed. Herbert Weisberg. New York, NY: Agathon, 51–82.

Shor, Boris, Christopher Berry and Nolan McCarty. 2010. "A Bridge to Somewhere: Mapping State and Congressional Ideology on a Cross-Institutional Common Space." *Legislative Studies Quarterly* 35: 417–48.

Squire, Peverill. 1988a. "Career Opportunities and Membership Stability in Legislatures." *Legislative Studies Quarterly* 13: 65–82.

Squire, Peverill. 1988b. "Member Career Opportunities and the Internal Organization of Legislatures." *Journal of Politics* 50: 726–44.

Squire, Peverill. 1992a. "Legislative Professionalization and Membership Diversity in State Legislatures." *Legislative Studies Quarterly* 17: 69–79.

Squire, Peverill. 1992b. "The Theory of Legislative Institutionalization and the California Assembly." *The Journal of Politics* 54: 1026–54.

Squire, Peverill. 1993a. "Professionalization and Public Opinion." *The Journal of Politics* 55: 479–91.

Squire, Peverill. 1993b. "Divided Government and Public Opinion in the States." *State and Local Government Review* 25: 150–4.

Squire, Peverill. 1997. "Another Look at Legislative Professionalization and Divided Government in the States." *Legislative Studies Quarterly* 22: 417–32.

Squire, Peverill. 2007. "Measuring State Legislative Professionalism: The Squire Index Revisited." *State Politics and Policy Quarterly* 7: 211–27.

Squire, Peverill and Keith E. Hamm. 2005. *101 Chambers: Congress, State Legislatures and the Future of Legislative Studies.* Columbus, OH: The Ohio State University Press.

Squire, Peverill and Gary Moncrief 2010 *State Legislatures Today: Politics Under the Dome.* Boston: Pearson Education, Inc.

Thelen, Kathleen. 2000. "Timing and Temporality in the Analysis of Institutional Evolution and Change." *Studies in American Political Development* 14: 101–8.

Thompson, Joel A. and Gary Moncrief. 1992. "The Evolution of the State Legislature: Institutional Change and Legislative Careers." In *Changing Patterns in State Legislative Careers.* Gary Moncrief and Joel A. Thompson (eds). Ann Arbor, MI, University of Michigan Press, 195–206.

Thompson, Joel A. and Gary Moncrief. 1993. "The Implications of Term Limits for Women and Minorities: Some Evidence from the States." *Social Science Quarterly* 74: 300–9.

Thompson, Joel A. and Gary Moncrief. 1998. *Campaign Finance in State Legislative Elections.* Washington, DC: CQ Press.

Uslaner, Eric S. and Ronald J. Weber. 1977. *Patterns of Decision Making in State Legislatures.* New York: Praeger.

Wahlke, John C. 1971. "Policy Demands and System Support: The Role of the Represented." *British Journal of Political Science* 1: 271–90.

Wahlke, John C., Heinz Eulau, William Buchanan, and Leroy C. Ferguson. 1962. *The Legislative System.* New York: John Wiley.

Weil, Frederick. 1989. "The Sources and Structure of Legitimation in Western Democracies: A Consolidated Model Tested with Time Series Data in Six Countries since World War II." *American Sociological Review* 54: 652–706.

Weingast, Barry R. and William Marshall. 1988. "The Industrial Organization of Congress." *Journal of Political Economy* 96: 132–63.

Wilheim, Teena. 2007. "The Policymaking Role of State Supreme Courts in Education Policy." *Legislative Studies Quarterly* 32: 309–33.

Wills, Garry. 1999. *A Necessary Evil: A History of American Distrust in Government.* New York: Simon and Schuster.

Wright, Gerald C. 2007. "Do Term Limits Affect Legislative Roll Call Voting? Representation, Polarization and Participation." *State Politics and Policy Quarterly* 7: 256–80.

Wright, Gerald C. and Brian F. Schaffner. 2002. "The Influence of Party: Evidence from State Legislatures." *American Political Science Review* 96: 367–79.

Zeigler, L. Harmon and Michael A. Baer. 1969. *Lobbying: Interaction and Influence in American State Legislatures.* Belmont, CA: Wadsworth.

CHAPTER 14

....

STATE EXECUTIVES

....

MARGARET R. FERGUSON

THE American states are headed by executive officials. Though the governor is the most important of state executive actors, the vast majority of governors, unlike the US President, are obligated to work with (and perhaps contend with) other elected executive officials. In fact, most states elect a variety of other executive actors including, most commonly, lieutenant governors, secretaries of state, attorneys general, treasurers, and education department heads. Even lieutenant governors are not necessarily allies of the governor. Although in some states, governors and lieutenant governors are elected as a ticket, in others they run as separate candidates. Governors and their lieutenants may not even share party affiliation. Given this "plural executive" sometimes other executive actors serve as competing power centers to the governors. Other times, they are partners with governors, counted upon to carry outthe governor's agenda.

For a variety of reasons, some of which will be examined in this chapter, scholarship on state executive actors lags behind the very well developed body of work on state legislatures. In their reflection on the state of state politics research, Brace and Jewett (1995), for example, devote a single paragraph on the scholarship on the governor. Scholarship on executive actors other than governors is almost nonexistent.

Though there are noteworthy holes in the literature, there are elements about which we know a lot. Much is known, for example, about the electoral fortunes of gubernatorial incumbents and the factors that work against them. The role of the governor as party leader has been well examined, likewise the role of governor in the budgetary arena. A large body of work on the formal powers of the governors attests to the fact that governors have obtained the tools that should make them equal or even dominant players in the state policymaking arena. Yet research that empirically measures the role of the governor in policymaking has been slow to develop. While there was, for many years, a great deal of scholarship which asserted that governors played very significant roles in the states and indeed in the nation, there was very little empirical work that actually tested these hypotheses. I refer to Jewell (1982) for a partial explanation. We lacked data.

It was not readily available or it was too difficult to bring together from the multiple sources.

Meanwhile, various widely read empirical models of state policymaking have essentially ignored the governor (Barrilleaux and Berkman, 2003). So, depending upon the scholar one consulted, governors were the "change masters"(Durning, Education Reform in Arkansas: The Governor's Role in Policymaking, 1991), "chief legislators" (Ransone, 1985); (Bernick and Wiggins, Executive-Legislative Relations: The Governor's Role as Chief Legislator, 1991) and "the embodiment of the states"(Sanford, 1967) or they were one of many players with only a peripheral influence upon what goes on in the states—they were largely irrelevant (Erikson, Wright, and McIver, 1993). This second interpretation is gleaned more from what is left unsaid than from what is said. Scholars of state legislative processes have paid very little attention to governors, focusing instead upon the powers, characteristics and behaviors of members of the legislative branch (Barrilleaux and Berkman, 2003). Yet gubernatorial scholars christen the governor "chief legislator." How can this be? This irony is the basis of the challenge that faces those who work to study American governors.

In this chapter I will examine the extant scholarship on state executives (principally governors), speculate on the reasons for the relative paucity of research on these important institutions and point to some potential avenues for future study. I make no claim that I have captured all of the work that has been done on governors in the last twenty years. However, this summary and the research examined is, I believe, representative of the scholarship that has been completed over the last two decades.

GUBERNATORIAL ELECTIONS AND PUBLIC OPINION

First, I turn to an arena that has received a lot of scholarly attention. Electoral politics is a large and vibrant field of study in state politics. Not surprisingly, scholars of elections often turn to statewide elections such as those for the governorship to test their theories of vote choice and voting dynamics. As other chapters in this volume examine voting, elections and public opinion, I will make only brief mention of this topic here. Research on gubernatorial elections often compares gubernatorial campaigns to other statewide races such as the U.S. Senate since they share electoral constituencies. From this work we know that, for example, compared to senators, gubernatorial incumbents are somewhat more vulnerable as they attract more widely recognized challengers (Squire and Fastnow, 1994). There are other differences as well. Atkeson and Partin find that senators' electoral fortunes are linked to presidential popularity while gubernatorial elections are more affected by the state economy (1995). This last point is the subject of some controversy in the literature. Various scholars have attempted to assess whether voters hold governors accountable for the state of the economy, either the national or that of

the state. Most voting studies say "yes", though findings vary as to the relative importance of the state of the economy on assessments of gubernatorial performance (see for
example, Kenney, 1983; Peltzman, 1987; Chubb, 1988; Svoboda, 1995; Niemi, Stanley, and
Vogel, 1995; Carsey and Wright, 1998; Stein, 1990; King, 2001). Retrospective voting, this
backwards looking assessment by which governors are held accountable for prior performance, is particularly strong under conditions of unified government as the responsible party model would predict (Leyden and Borelli, 1995). Additionally, some research
finds a linkage between presidential popularity and gubernatorial elections (Carsey and
Wright, 1998).

Other election scholars point to the importance of other factors such as campaign
spending (especially for out-party challengers, Partin, 2002; Bardwell, 2005) or specific
salient issues such as abortion (Cook, Jelen, and Wilcox, 1994). In sum, races for governor are high profile, expensive, and fit some of the patterns of presidential elections,
including being candidate-centered. The outcomes are influenced by the performance
of the incumbents, some assessment of the state of the economy and (perhaps surprisingly) the performance of the president (especially when the governor and president are
of the same party).

Public approval of governors is of course related to elections since positive assessments of gubernatorial performance often predict success at the ballot box. However,
these are in fact separate phenomena as the research findings presented below illustrate.
MacDonald and Sigelman (1999) warn against extrapolating our understanding of public approval of governors generally from the findings on gubernatorial elections. Since
electoral results represent necessarily a single point in time, this might not be predictive
of public assessments of gubernatorial performance more generally. Indeed, they find
that only in election years do voters hold governors accountable for having presided
over tax increases.

Much of the scholarship on gubernatorial popularity revolves around economic
effects, and the absence or presence thereof. Although research has very clearly shown
that the public holds presidents accountable for the performance of the national economy, scholars have found competing evidence on whether governors are similarly held
accountable. Echoing the title of her article "Life is not Fair" Hansen (1999) finds that
gubernatorial popularity suffers under high state unemployment. Governors do not,
however, experience a commensurate boost in popularity from low unemployment.
MacDonald and Sigelman (1999) find no significant effect for the state of the economy on gubernatorial popularity. The authors speculate that including some indicator
accounting for the individual incumbent (were that possible) might help. Orth (2001)
finds no evidence of the "presidency centered" model which says that due to the president's high level of visibility, people hold all members of the president's party responsible for economic conditions. Instead, she finds that gubernatorial performance ratings
reflect an "incumbency centered" model where governors are held responsible for state
but not national economic performance. This finding indicates that people distinguish
among the responsibilities of different government actors when assessing responsibility
and giving credit or laying blame. However, Crew and Weiher (1996) found that state

economic conditions had little influence over the popularity of governors in California, Minnesota and Iowa but national economic factors were predictive. This is clearly an unsettled controversy in the literature. Adams and Squire (2001) turn their attention to explaining these divergent findings on the effect of the local economy on gubernatorial popularity. Using time series data from ten states, they find that unemployment rates affect some governors while leaving others unscathed. They conclude that gubernatorial approval is highly idiosyncratic and the unique features of individual incumbents and constituent expectations are at least as important as the economic variables that are typically the source of study.

Crew et al. (2002) also find that public approval of governors appears largely idiosyncratic. They tested for the effect of significant political events such as threats to the health of the governor or his/her family, policy accomplishments, new policy initiatives and scandals upon public assessments of gubernatorial performance and found no impact for these. They did, however, find evidence for the importance of the state economy. Other scholars have come to different conclusions. Cohen and King (2004) assert that the cause for disparate findings is that citizens are more sophisticated in their assessments of gubernatorial performance. People recognize that governors have limited influence over the state economy. As a result, they judge their governors on the state unemployment situation relative to levels in the national economy. Irrespective of the level of unemployment in a state, governors are rewarded when state unemployment is less than the national average and punished when it is higher. Similarly, Howell and Vanderleew (1990) employed survey data to find strong state economic effects on approval of gubernatorial performance while indicators of national economic performance were largely insignificant.

Beyond economic conditions, Alt, Lassen and Skilling (2002) find that more transparent fiscal institutions result in higher levels of approval for governors. Kelleher and Wolak (2007) examine public confidence in state institutions (as opposed to support for particular incumbents). They find that surveys indicate people have fairly high levels of confidence in the office of the governor, with support for the particular incumbent contributing to confidence in the office. However, confidence in the governors erodes when states experience corruption. Low taxes and low unemployment contribute to public confidence in governors while high crime rates detract from it.

Gubernatorial approval also differs from presidential approval in some distinctive ways. Jacobson (2006) compares public assessments by Democratic and Republican respondents of President George Bush to assessments of US senators and governors. He finds that partisan divergence is much smaller for governors and senators than for the president. That is, there is a larger divide between the parties in approval of the president than of governors and senators. Governors with high national visibility or a background of participation in national politics are more polarizing than Governors with a parochial focus. Further, Jacobson finds that Democratic governors in "red" states and Republican governors in "blue" states are actually more popular than their counterparts in states dominated by their own parties. Finally, governors in less populous states are more popular than those in larger (and often more heterogeneous) states, even though gubernatorial popularity suffers in states with high unemployment (Jacobson, 2006).

Finally, those who assert that gubernatorial approval is idiosyncratic in regards to economic conditions often point to the importance of the individuals who hold the office. For example, Barth and Ferguson (2002a) attempt to measure the effect of personality features of governors upon their popularity. They find evidence that gubernatorial personality does impact upon popularity in predictable ways (albeit not precisely in the way that they originally predicted).

GUBERNATORIAL LEADERSHIP

Gubernatorial ratings may in fact be shaped by what governors actually do once gaining the office. One could label this research broadly as studies of gubernatorial leadership, and this research has two strains: the individual model, which focuses upon the individual people who have occupied the office and their personalities, skills and experiences, and the other, the institutional model, which emphasizes the nature of the office itself and particularly the changing characteristics of the office relative to the past and to other states. Some research, of course, straddles both traditions. Most research nods to the importance of the other perspective, but typically only embraces one. It is also the case that scholars in the two traditions tend to employ different methods. Those most interested in examining the importance of the particular incumbent are more likely to employ qualitative methods. Scholars in the institutional tradition are likely to use quantitative methods.

Unfortunately, many gubernatorial scholars in both traditions have examined the governor as a stand-alone actor, as thoughthe office functioned alone, without legislatures or courts. This is, I believe, the source of the dichotomy one observes in the treatment of the role of the governor in state policymaking. When one fails to place the governor into the context in which she really governs, it is impossible to accurately assess her leadership. Similarly, a failure to recognize the informal role of factors such as personality and charisma can often mean that our understanding will fall short.

The Individual Model: In the first tradition, scholars emphasize features of the incumbents who hold the office. Some examine the personal characteristics of the governor such as age and education, others point to political skill, personality or orientation to politics—the love of the game. Each of these personal factors is examined (implicitly or explicitly) because it is thought to impact upon the ability of governors to exert leadership. Scholars in this tradition typically treat the governor's environment as control variables. They do not specify theoretical expectations as to the effects of the environment, but simply account for these influences as they arise.

The individual model has a long and rich tradition in gubernatorial research. Sabato (1983) argues that the people who hold the governor's offices in the various states have changed. No longer "good time Charlies," they are now highly educated, articulate, and ambitious. They are ready and willing to lead the way for the heightened importance of the states in the national arena. Other research more directly points to the importance of the skill of the incumbent. Success or failure is often attributed to gubernatorial skill (or the lack thereof). Governors are expected to understand the legislative process and be willing to work within the system. Those who have served as governor before, or who previously served in the state's legislature are expected to be ahead of the game (Rosenthal, 1990; Bernick and Wiggins, 1991).

Due to the nature of studying such individualistic features, many of these analyses are case studies of particular governors. Kaplan and O'Brien's (1991) examination of eight governors coping with and perhaps benefitting from President Reagan's "New Federalism" is a good example of research which emphasizes the importance of the incumbent in shaping gubernatorial leadership success. The authors examine the experiences of each of these governors, given their immediate contexts, their personal goals and characteristics. They conclude by drawing comparisons, where possible, based upon the experiences of this diverse set of governors in states across the country attempting to lead at a single point in time. The governor herself is clearly the subject and the unit of analysis. Data are drawn primarily from the individual governors who participated in an oral-history colloquium. Although the importance of the context is understood and recognized, its impact is not specified in systematic hypotheses.

Behn (1991) represents a different method, compiling essays on serving written by governors. Again, the value of this study lies primarily in the notion that it focuses on the people who actually held the office. Who knows better than the governor what the job is like? This work emphasizes the goals, characteristics and skills of the individuals holding the office (presented through their own analyses, in their own words). It treats features of the state in which the governors lead as "forces that constrain how governors govern" and the "essential context for governing." But the primary emphasis is upon how governors behave given the context." Behn (1991: vii) summarizes the importance of this method in this way "Understanding how governors view their roles and how they define leadership and management can help predict and explain their actions. The ways governors meet the challenges of their office and play their roles are best illustrated through case studies." There is also a wealth of biographies and autobiographies of governors which help illuminate their individual drives and experiences (Beyle and Muchmore, 1983; Beyle and Williams, 1972).

Sribnick examines the leadership of governors across a variety of policy areas including civil rights, the environment, education, welfare and economic development over the last hundred years. He argues that the changing politics in the federal system and the constant struggle between administrative expertise and democracy has been reflected in the changing roles of governors. "Yet bridging the gap between lab-like innovation, factory-like production and democratic participation has been the governors' most distinctive contribution to public policy"(2008: 1).

Empirical work on the personal features of governors most commonly incorporates some notion of political skill. Such studies typically measure skill as prior experience in elective office. However, findings as to the significance of such experience are mixed

(Ferguson, 2003). More commonly, scholars have asserted the importance of the personal characteristics of governors in their models of leadership, while concluding they cannot be accurately measured (Scher, 1997; Van Assendelft, 1997). The personality of chief executives is usually taken as a given rather than measured explicitly.

Barber's (1972) work on presidential personality is a notable exception to this rule. His work has been influential and controversial, particularly criticized for being largely impressionistic (for example, see criticisms of Barber in Nelson (2006). Another exception in the executive literature has been the work of Winter and Stewart (1977) and Winter (1987) who developed a method of measuring elements of personality employing written text. Barth and Ferguson (2002b) applied Winter's coding scheme to governors and examined the influence of three distinct motives upon gubernatorial success. They found that the ambition drive does significantly influence gubernatorial success, and that there are different motives between female and male governors (see also Ferguson and Barth, 2002).

However, most of the research in the individual tradition does not empirically control for the various contextual factors—the opportunity structure available for governors in terms of ability to lead. Rather the choice of the case usually attempts to account for the context. These studies offer important and useful examinations of gubernatorial leadership. They are interesting because they are about politics. They offer examples of real governors grappling with the challenges facing them. They also tend to have an underlying assumption that who is governor has an effect upon what happens—it influences what issues they attempt to lead on, how they go about pursuing their goals, and whether and to what degree they are successful. This recognition is also intuitively appealing; it assigns human agency that is generally lacking in the institutional literature.

A concern with the individual perspective is of course the reality that institutional and political context impacts successful leadership—whatever the characteristics of the individual governor. These studies offer insight into how these factors impacted upon the individual under study but the question of generalizability remains. Typically, the influence of the context upon the governor's role is not specified theoretically. It is treated as a series of events that, in some ad hoc manner, are seen to influence the governor and her success at governing. Another overriding difficulty in performing work in this tradition is the difficulty in measuring the personal characteristics of the governors. Some scholars have developed creative solutions to this problem, as noted earlier, and these efforts, including attempts to study the strategic goals of governors in their broader context along with their individual characteristics, may allow for the possibility of generalizing across governors along predictable dimensions.

The Institutional Model

The second strand of scholarship on state executives emphasizes the institutional factors which characterize the office. In this vein, I would place the large body of research surrounding the formal powers of the governor both in the development of indices of formal powers and attempts at specifying how these powers are employed by governors and to what degree of success. Empirical examinations of the actual application of formal powers to gubernatorial leadership have largely centered upon the use of the veto and the gubernatorial role in the budgetary arena, but the index has been very widely employed in a variety of studies.

From this line of research it becomes clear that the governorship has been transformed. Once barely powerful enough to "sign the receipt for his salary" in Lipson's phrase (1939) the modern governor cannot be said to suffer from such institutional impotence. Formal powers have been strengthened across the states and across the board. The governorship in all the states is more "powerful" than it used to be—by the definition of the formal powers index first developed by Schlesinger and modified and updated by various authors, most recently by Beyle and Ferguson (2008) and Kousser and Phillips (2012). These include, tenure potential, the veto, appointment power, and budget making power, and each dimension has largely been enhanced in the past 40 years (Schlesinger, 1965; Dometrius, 1979, 1987; Beyle, 1983, 1990; Beyle and Muchmore, 1983; Mueller, 1985; Ransone, 1985).

The institution of today is clearly different from that at the turn of the last century and even from that a few decades ago. The variation among governorships has also diminished (Beyle, 1999). Whereas some governors possessed quite a few formal powers in 1965, nearly ALL governors did so by 1995. In that sense, the institutions themselves are more alike than ever before. A glance at the most recent formulation of the index finds the governorships essentially maintaining their levels of power, though notable deficiencies remain. Most governors, for example, still must work with multiple other statewide elected officials (Ferguson, 2006; Beyle and Ferguson, 2008) despite the fact that advocates of executive power have long argued for a shortening of the "long ballot."

A substantial body of literature has employed the formal powers index as a proxy for institutional power. Those who employ the index do so generally in the context of examining the relative importance of social, economic, and political variables on state policy outputs (Dometrius, 1979). These studies examine a variety of issues of significance to policy making in the states. They range from examinations of gubernatorial support of agency budget requests (Sharkansky, 1968) to the effect of formal powers upon administrative oversight (Hebert, Brudney, and Wright, 1983; Brudney and Hebert, 1987), to studies of gubernatorial effectiveness in the legislative arena (Dilger, Krause, and Moffett, 1995), and success of gubernatorial proposals (Ferguson, 2003).[1] Other scholars assert that individual elements of the index should be broken out and, most importantly, used to predict success in the appropriate context (Dometrius, 1979; Gross, 1991; Barrilleaux and Berkman, 2003; Ferguson, 2003).

Some scholars point to additional political elements such as party control of the legislature that should be included in the index (Beyle, 1990; Beyle and Ferguson, 2008). Others remind us that formal powers are merely potential power. They must be skillfully mobilized by the governor if they are to be of any use (Sigelman and Dometrius, 1988). Finally, many scholars have asserted that formal powers are necessary but not sufficient tools for governors attempting to lead—in whatever arena (Bernick, 1979; Sigelman and Dometrius, 1988; Durning, 1991; Dilger, Krause, and Moffett, 1995; Ferguson, 2003).

Given the governor's advancement in institutional resources during the 20th Century the dominant assessment of the governor's role in the legislative arena is that the governors are the major policy actors, the major policy initiators. They are the "change masters" and "chief legislators"(Ransone, 1985; Durning, 1987; Bernick and Wiggins, 1991). The media view the governor as holding this important position, as do state legislators (Rosenthal, 1990). Far from seeing this role as an intrusion of the governor in the legislative domain, to the extent there is concern on the part of the legislators about the policy role of the governor, it is often that the governor is *not active enough* (Bernick and Wiggins, 1991). The formal powers to which the governor has access assure that the governor is a legitimate player in the legislative arena. Indeed, the constitutional system of separation of powers means that legislatures depend upon the governor to serve as a partner in the formulation of public policy.

Another factor which seems to facilitate the governor's role in the legislative domain relates to the governor's political party. A large body of research has addressed this role of the governor. Governors are connected to decision-makers in the legislative branch by virtue of their position as "chief of party"(Morehouse, 1981). Research points to the importance of the role of the governor in the state party organization—not just the Governor's party control of legislative seats (Morehouse, 1981). In states with strong party organizations, party line voting for the governor is much higher than in states with weak party organization (Morehouse, 1996). Parties marked by factions, even where large numbers might appear to be on the governor's side by virtue of party attachment, may not serve to support the governor's leadership role (Gross, 1991; Hall, 2002).

However, the making of public policy is a long and complicated process. Thus, the legislative leadership role of the governor encompasses at least two of the "phases" of the policy process. Governors must employ their resources to raise concerns for consideration by the legislature (agenda setting) and then to influence the types of solutions adopted to address these problems (policy formulation). During the agenda setting phase, problems requiring governmental action are identified. Unresolved conflicts that bear upon the lives of large numbers of people tend to be the issues that make it to the public agenda (Gleiber and Shull, 1992). At this phase, the chief executive can make a large contribution (Rosenthal, 1990; Bernick and Wiggins, 1991; Gross, 1991; Herzik, 1991). The governor's role as agenda setter arises from several sources, most notably the responsibility to prepare the budget, to present state of the state addresses and to call special sessions (Jewell, 1969; Francis and Weber, 1980; Ransone, 1985; Bernick and Wiggins, 1991). The visibility of the office also offers governors access to the media and the public and the opportunity to credit claim which encourages gubernatorial agenda setting (Beyle and Muchmore, 1983; Rosenthal, 1990; Bernick and Wiggins, 1991).

What is less clearly understood is the governor's role in the next phase of the policy process. As Neustadt (1960) points out, executives must be able to bargain to achieve their goals in policy formulation. It seems obvious from the literature that governors do possess a variety of tools that ought to empower them in this regard (Rosenthal, 1990;

Bernick and Wiggins, 1991; Beyle, 1999). Governors might use each of these resources as they bargain with legislators to achieve their goals. However, scholarship on state policy-making does not tend to incorporate governors to any great degree. As noted earlier, one of the most thorough and influential studies of state policy making (Erikson, Wright, and McIver, 1993) essentially sets the governor aside. Barrilleaux (1999) adds governors to the model created by Erickson, Wright and McIver and finds that formal powers asso-ciated with the office of the governorship do enable governors to play a significant role in state policymaking. Barrilleaux (1999) concludes with a call to other scholars to be more mindful of the role of governors in policy making:

> If the sole purpose of constructing models is to explain variation, ignoring the politi-cal and institutional influences of the executive comes at a relatively small cost. But if the purpose is to develop theories of politics and policy, ignoring the executive presents a greater problem. Given that the focus of comparative policy output studies has been to explain how governments work, it is important to incorporate models of policymaking that capture as closely as possible the factors that drive state actions.

Nevertheless, a brief review of scholarship on state policymaking suggests that some authors do account for the role of governors. For example, in an examination of state tax policy, Berch (1995) found that Democratic governors are associated with greater tax progressivity, though this is not the primary focus of the study. Burke and Ferguson (2010) examine the role of governors in leadership on greenhouse gas emissions. Daley, Haider-Markel, and Whitford (2007) consider the role of formal powers of the governor in the costs of regulatory compliance and find little effect.

Likewise, McNeal, Tolbert, Mossberger and Dotterweich (2003) report anecdotal evidence that support by the governor is a central factor in determining the success of e-government initiatives, but this is not the primary focus of the findings. Most telling, though they characterize e-government initiatives as an administrative reform, they focus on professionalization of the legislature as a key predictor while the governor is essentially absent from their empirical work.

But many studies of state policymaking leave the governor out of the equation. To take a few recent examples, studies of the welfare state (Howard, 1999; Lieberman and Shaw, 2000), education policy (Smith and Rademacker, 1999), and regulatory policy (Gerber and Teske, 2000) essentially make no reference to governors.

Scholarship on budgeting has given the governor greater attention. In most states, the budget has historically been a primary domain of the governor (Sharkansky, 1968; Gross, 1980; Moncrief and Thompson, 1980; Abney and Lauth, 1985; Gosling, 1985, 1986). However, state legislatures have not necessarily been content merely to follow the lead of the governor in this pivotal decision area. State legislatures certainly vary as to the tendency to actually use the power they have available but some scholarship asserts that the trend is toward greater legislative branch budget activity and the end of executive dominance of the budgetary process (Gosling, 1985; Abney and Lauth, 1986; Thompson, 1987; Clynch and Lauth, 1991; Rosenthal, 1990). Others characterize the budgetary pro-cess today as more balanced, dominated by neither the legislature nor the executive, with each playing a key role (Goodman, 2007). Dometrius and Wright (2009) find that governors remain key actors in the budgetary arena while governors and legislatures compete in a non-zero-sum game for influence over varying elements of the budgetary process. Barrilleaux and Berkman (2003) found that both governors and legislatures influence budgetary policymaking and they point to the importance of formal powers in empowering the governor in this arena. Breunig and Koski (2009), in their study of punctuated budgets, find that institutionally strong governors can dominate budgetary agendas and also block legislative alternatives, though both of these actions cause governors to accrue a variety of costs.

But much of the scholarship on budgeting draws data from surveys of state agency heads (in the case of Dometrius and Wright, 2009) or budget analysts (in the case of Abney, Lauth and Goodman). Scholarship employing addition types of data might help to clarify this disagreement in the literature.

A significant body of work has arisen around the effects of political party and divided government upon the budgeting process. Employing "setter models," this work asserts that governors have weak bargaining positions. It typically captures the role of the governor by the proxy of their political party and predicted partisan preferences (Alt and Lowry, 1994, 2000; Kousser, 2002).

But Kousser and Phillips (2009) present a different approach. They employ a "staring match" framework to compare gubernatorial budget proposals from 1989–2004 to the ultimate legislative enactments. They find evidence of high levels of gubernatorial influence over final state budgets. The influence of the legislature (in contrast) is dependent upon the level of professionalism. Legislatures that meet in long sessions are better able to bargain with the governor and hold out for their preferences.

Another field of inquiry regarding governors in the legislative arena has been veto use and its efficacy. Wiggins (1980) found that over 94 percent of gubernatorial vetoes were sustained. This near guarantee that the governor will have the "final word" on legislation does indicate a certain amount of policy leverage. On the other hand, various scholars note that the use of the veto might be interpreted as evidence of weakness rather than strength. It might indicate failure to achieve the governor's goals at some previous stage (Beyle, 1990; Rosenthal, 1990).

Hedge (1998) uses number of vetoes and percent of vetoes sustained as measures of "gubernatorial assertiveness" and "extent of legislative-executive conflict." He found that both institutional powers and informal powers affected the likelihood that governors would use the veto and the likelihood that the veto would be sustained. Meanwhile, Klarner and Karch (2008) consider variables specific to the individual incumbents and their institutional settings to predict the use of vetoes. Although they find little evidence of influence of individualistic gubernatorial variables (such as having previously served in the legislature) their work attributes substantial influence to institutional features of both the governorship and the legislature.

To put it simply, governors with greater formal powers actually issue more vetoes. Where states set a higher bar for overriding vetoes, governors make greater use of them. Governors issue more vetoes under divided government and when they are term-limited. Indeed, rather than being idiosyncratic, when it comes to the use of the veto, governors in similar institutional situations behave in predictably similar ways.

Additionally, Wilkins and Young (2002) examine the governors' ability to influence veto overrides. Drawing on Keith Krehbiel's pivotal politics model, Williams and Young examine gubernatorial influence on veto override votes by two governors in Missouri. They find that governors are able to influence legislators toward their preferred positions—especially when they share a party attachment.

Another consideration is veto type. The amendatory and item vetoes which most governors have at least some ability to employ, presumably offer them more flexibility in influencing legislation once it reaches their desks. The item veto grants the governor the opportunity to strike out certain elements of a bill, particularly unwanted spending. Dearden and Husted (1993) find that governors can make use of the line item veto to obtain their desired budgets. Though not much research has been conducted on the use of these vetoes, there is some evidence that these are useful tools for governors attempting to influence the actions of the legislature (Bernick and Wiggins, 1991). There is also some evidence that governors might (occasionally) use this veto to unilaterally make policy, bypassing legislative intent altogether (see Beyle, 1990, on Tommy Thompson of Wisconsin).

It seems clear that the subfield would benefit from more attention to systematic studies of veto use, particularly given that override rules vary from state to state. In Indiana, for example, a mere majority is required for a veto override, yet overrides rarely occur. In other states, where a supermajority is required, legislative overrides are more common. What explains this seemingly unlikely pattern? Nevertheless, it should be clear that although veto studies are enlightening on a certain aspect of gubernatorial/legislative relations, they are almost by definitionatypical. They may represent situations of high conflict involving governors and legislatures and they occur in relatively rare instances across most states.

Perhaps most important for understanding gubernatorial and legislative relations are studies on budgetary politics, even though they might not be generalizable to the broader understanding of governors in the policy process (Kousser and Phillips, 2012) To fully understand the larger role of the governor in this domain, research that links specific gubernatorial proposals to specific legislative enactments is necessary. Though this is not an easy task (Bernick and Wiggins, 1991; Gross, 1991; Ferguson, 2003) some scholars have examined this issue. Morehouse (1996) points to the prime importance of support from the governor's party in the legislature for achieving gubernatorial agenda items. She finds specifically that the type of party organization a state employs is predictive of party support for the governor. Scholars who followed her continued to find a key importance for party support for the governor. In a study examining all governors in 1993 and 1994, Ferguson (2003) found that both factors related to the governor him- or herself (such as prior experience or involvement in a major scandal) and factors related to the political, economic and institutional environment predict the success of gubernatorial proposals. Examining Georgia governors between 1991 and 1994, Hall (2002) finds that support for gubernatorial initiatives varies significantly by political party and time as well as by the specific proposals the governor puts forward. Gubernatorial partisans are more supportive and opposing party members are less supportive in election years.

The institutional line of gubernatorial research has clearly resulted in a great deal of knowledge about the changing character of the governor's office. The ascent of the governorship to its position of equality (if not dominance) in the states calls out for more systematic analyses of the governor within his/her various arenas of leadership. A full understanding of the ability of governors to lead requires that particular governors with their various personal characteristics and political and strategic motivations be placed within the changing context that the institutional line of research has explicated in such detail.

CHIEF EXECUTIVE

In addition to serving as legislative leaders, governors today are in name and in practice the chief executives of the states, though this was not always true. Early work by Wright (1967) found that state agency heads perceived the legislature to exert greater influence over them than did the governor. By the 1990s, however, at least half of agency heads reported that governors exerted greater control while less than a third said the legislature was more influential (Bowling and Wright, 1998). This is true despite the fact that research indicates the governors spend less time on this role than others such as legislative leadership. It is a challenging job and the benefits are not always clear (Elling, 1992). Further, control of the bureaucracy is a constant struggle as governors must sometimes compete with legislatures, bureaucrats, and other elected executives (i.e. attorneysgeneral) for control (Abney and Lauth, 1986, 1998; Rosenthal, 1990; Elling, 2004). Much like the scholarship on gubernatorial leadership in the legislative arena, studies of gubernatorial influence over the bureaucracy tend to focus upon the formal powers of the governorship (Dometrius, 2002; Elling, 2004; Woods, 2004). Although not all research finds a significant relationship between formal powers (taken together) and executive influence over the bureaucracy (Potoski and Woods, 2001), scholarship universally emphasizes the significance of the governor's appointment power (Abney and Lauth, 1983; Hebert, Brudney, and Wright, 1983; Brudney and Hebert, 1987; Bowling and Wright, 1998a, 1998b). Some governors do have the power to appoint a great number of executive branch officials. And while many top level actors remain outside gubernatorial appointment, states have taken steps to "shorten the ballot" and thereby give governors greater control (Elling, 2004).

The ability to reorganize the state bureaucracy is another potentially important tool for gubernatorial control of the bureaucracy (Rosenthal, 1990; Beyle, 1995; Elling, 2004; Gormley, 2006). Bowman, Woods and Stark (2010) examine the development of the gubernatorial office. They find that the growth of state government and the related growing workload as well as rivalry with the legislature all contribute to the institutionalization of governors' offices, a change which presumably empowers governors seeking to oversee the bureaucracy.

Recent scholarship has moved beyond traditional understandings of the tools available to governors as they attempt to influence the bureaucracy. Administrative rule review, or the ability to modify or strike down administrative rules promulgated by state agencies, is one of these important tools for governors though it has received very little scholarly attention. Gubernatorial power in this regard varies greatly across the states. In some states governors have review authority over only proposed rules while in other states, governors may also review existing rules. Some states require gubernatorial approval before proposed rules can take effect while others do not. In some cases this power is provided for in statute; in other cases governors use executive orders to carry out this power (Grady and Simon, 2002). Woods (2004) finds that more formalized means of rule review lead to greater influence upon agency rule making.

Likewise, executive orders are another potentially important tool for governors in the executive arena, but they have received scant attention in the literature. In one example, Ferguson and Bowling (2008) find significant variation across states in the use and purposes of executive orders. While some of these orders are symbolic in nature, most are employed to exert significant influence over the bureaucracy. Some carry significance beyond the executive arena.

Finally, other gubernatorial resources might play an important role in directing the bureaucracy but they have not received much attention from social scientists. For example, Woods and Baranowski (2007) demonstrate the importance of newer resources such as economic analysis (cost-benefit analysis, economic impact analysis or regulatory analysis), program evaluation and administrative rule review as potential sources of gubernatorial influence over the bureaucracy. They find little support for the importance of traditional means of control such as the power to reorganize the bureaucracy and the personal features of the governor. Meanwhile, Dometrius (2002) finds that governors with higher approval ratings exhibit greater control over the bureaucracy, but this is the only study of its kind.

OTHER EXECUTIVE OFFICERS

In most states there are other executive branch officials besides the governor that can shape state policymaking. Probably the most significant of these are Lieutenant Governors, Secretaries of State, and Attorneys General, many of whom are elected separately from the governor. This means they may not share policy preferences or party affiliation with the governor and they often aspire to the governorship. Despite their obvious importance, very little scholarship has addressed the roles of these actors. An exception is the state Attorneys General. A small but significant body of scholarship has arisen examining their place in the states and the federal system. Various scholars have examined the joint litigation activities of the Attorneys General. AGs routinely prosecute cases against large corporations jointly, coordinating with one another, sharing legal theories, costs and even staff. Although some observers argue the AGs are acting unconstitutionally by joining forces in this way, they have been very effective at forcing changes in business practices by major corporations that would not have been possible without multi-state lawsuits. This has, in turn, carved out a place for AGs as important national political actors (Clayton, 1994; Lynch, 2001).

In one such study of AGs, Zimmerman (1998) examines the agreement among 40 AGs with the five major tobacco companies. Drawing upon surveys of Attorneys General, he tests five competing explanations for AGs joining together in pursuit of shared policy goals. Though his findings are limited by incomplete survey responses, one clear observation is the importance of the National Association of Attorneys General in fostering cooperation among the states. In many states, the Attorney General issues advisory opinions at the request of the governor or legislature as to the constitutionality of questions. These opinions and the growing public advocacy activities of attorneys general also point to their importance as key state actors (Morris, 1987).

Scholarship on other statewide officials is even sparser. This is probably because the roles and activities of these actors vary significantly across the states. The lieutenant governor, for example, exerts a great deal of legislative leadership in some states while serving largely a symbolic role in others (Ferguson, 2006). Secretaries of State present another potential avenue of study. They often oversee large sections of state government activity such as elections and motor vehicle registration. These activities are of great importance to the citizenry of the states and therefore deserve greater attention than they have received thus far. The great variation across the functioning of these offices in the states should mean that they provide fertile ground for testing a variety of theories about executives.

Governors: Where Do we Go from Here?

Clearly, scholars of state politics have gained a great deal of knowledge about governors (if not other executive officials). However, as noted at the beginning of this chapter, the study of governors still lags behind work on the presidency (which was itself slow to develop) and state legislatures. Data availability, once a nearly overwhelming problem, has improved significantly as states have moved toward greater use of digital media and the internet. The growing research on the presidency offers a host of theories that would benefit from testing at the state level. What is needed at this time is a more unified framework for the study of governors. Scholars of state politics and those of public administration and public policy appear to know very little about one another's work (Meier, 2007). Studies of governors as legislative leaders stand separate from those of governors as executive actors which ultimately means that we have an incomplete picture of the role of governors in the American policymaking process. Political scientists and public administration scholars have much to learn from one another.

The idea of leadership might serve as a useful framework for building a more integrated analysis of governors since, at base, the study of governors is the study of leadership. Whether in the legislative, executive or some other arena, governors have tools at their disposal with which they might exert leadership. Some of these tools are attached to the office (what we might call formal or quasi-formal powers) while others attach to the governor himself/herself. Governors, as leaders, must make strategic choices as to what combination of tools to employ in pursuit of their goals. Further, different times call for more ambitious or more restrained leadership from the governor's office. In particular, times of stalemate or inactivity on the part of the national government might open the door for more ambitions assertions of gubernatorial leadership. Times of divided government in the state might call for more restrained attempts at leadership. Governors must recognize, understand and adapt to the environment in which they function. This means that we as scholars have to take account of the complex context in which governors attempt to lead. It also means we as scholars of state executives need to rethink the idea of executive power. While the formal powers index has been a useful means of comparing the relative institutional arrangements across the states, a broader notion of power is necessary to really understand how governors go about exercising leadership.

The process of gubernatorial leadership can be understood as a multi-stage game. Governors come to office with a particular set of goals and various skills and political knowledge. These goals and orientations, as well as the governor's assessment of the political environment, structure the governor's decision-making. Having formed a policy goal, governors must decide how best to pursue that goal. Should they offer a proposal to the legislature? Or take some executive action? Is a law necessary for achieving the goal? If not, is it advisable for some other reason?

If the governor chooses the legislative course, he/she makes an assessment of the characteristics of the legislature (the degree of professionalization, for example) and its likely response. In this first round, governors may stand pat on their proposals (and win or lose), they may negotiate by offering support for other initiatives or by offering strategic changes to their proposals. They might use a harder bargain such as a threat of veto. They might take advantage of their access to the media to go public in pursuit of legislative support. Given the iterative process of lawmaking, governors will have to make this decision multiple times.

This first experience in the legislative arena structures future interactions. The legislative response is largely predictable—governors should draw upon their staffs (a quasi-formal power) and their own knowledge of politics in the state (skill, in informal power), to generate a short list of key actors surrounding any legislative proposal. As such, governors ought to be able to vet their proposals (assuming the desire and willingness to do so) or at the very least they should be able to predict the legislative response given the positions of these identified actors and perhaps previous legislative behavior. Governors might have to adapt their goals given the response of legislative foes and friends. And this makes gubernatorial leadership a dynamic process. Experiences in the first leadership attempt (in one legislative session) influence the governor's behavior in the second (in the same session) by influencing the governor's goals and/or expectations as to future likely legislative behavior. Particularly in the first term, there is a potentially steep learning curve. More importantly, attempts at gubernatorial leadership the next time around—in the next session or the next legislative year—will be impacted by previous experiences (strategic choices and successes or failures). Behaviors and motivations of particular key legislators will also change and adapt given the experience of previous interaction with the governor. Further, the behavior and makeup of the legislature itself may change due to intervening legislative elections, or changing legislative rules. As a result, governors who wish to lead in the legislative arena must understand that it is a dynamic environment and they must adapt their behaviors accordingly.

All of that having been said, the legislative response is clearly not perfectly predictable; this is particularly the case since legislators' responses are partially structured by gubernatorial behavior which is then partially structured by the legislative response. This argues for caution (on the part of governors) in pursuing the legislative option when it isn't absolutely necessary. And it argues for a solid understanding of the ins and outs of legislative politics when studying gubernatorial leadership attempts here.

If the governor, having identified a policy goal, decides that a new law is not absolutely necessary (for either legal/constitutional reasons) or strongly advisable (for political reasons) he/she may choose to pursue the goal through executive means. Unlike the legislative arena, where tens or hundreds of other officials can hinder or help the governor's goals, the executive arena is more (though not entirely) under the control of the governor. At this juncture, governors have a variety of tools at their disposal as well. The governor might decide to issue an executive order or he/she might instead pursue some other type of executive action. Executive orders are a more public and formal tool. These carry the force of law and presumably survive beyond the current incumbent's term. They are often accompanied by photo opportunities and public ceremony. Certain gubernatorial goals will best be pursued by this mechanism. When preferring to pursue a policy with less fanfare (and one can think of a variety of reasons why this might be so) the governor might choose executive action. Executive action is a less public (and usually less permanent) option and the list of potential executive actions is nearly limitless. Some of these actions grow from personal features of the governor, some from formal powers of the office and some informal tools depend upon formal powers to make them stick. For example, governors might contact an agency head and direct him/her to take some action in pursuit of a policy goal. This contact might be informal; a phone call, email or other personal communication. The governor might employ more concrete tools such as issuing a policy memorandum directing some or all agencies to pursue a particular policy. In each case, agency actors who are appointed by the governor (and could therefore be fired by the governor) are likely to respond to the governor's requests affirmatively and follow through on them. The potential list of actions that the governor directs the agency to take is likewise vast and depends in large part on the goal. It might involve changes in hiring and firing decisions. It might involve changing the way the agency does business (contracting out versus doing in house for example). Given that the governor is the putative head of the bureaucracy, other executive branch actors are very likely to obey gubernatorial commands or requests, even when they are not appointed by the governor. When they are appointed by the governor the impulse should be even stronger.

The governor might instead employ the rule making process to pursue policy goals. The governor's influence in rulemaking varies from final approval or veto power in some states to an executive order undoing proposed or extant rules in others. Influence here might be informal as well in that agencies might take the governor's preferences into account when promulgating rules even if the governor lacks a formal hand in the process. The governor could make use of his/her influence over state money to pursue a policy goal. States vary significantly in how much autonomy governors have in moving money among various purposes once it has been authorized by the legislature. They also vary in how much control governors have over whether money is actually spent. Generally speaking, while legislatures authorize and appropriate money, it is up to the governor to spend it. If he/she chooses not to do so, or chooses to spend less than the legislature prefers, then he/she has left a mark on public policy. A governor could also pursue a policy goal by NOT exercising some power. For example, a governor who would like to minimize the importance of boards and commissions might simply refuse to appoint new members when seats open.

Governors clearly have alternatives available in the pursuit of policy change. Not all policy goals could be achieved through each of the potential powers delineated here (and this is by no means an exhaustive list) but most goals could be at least partially addressed through some combination of these potential administrative actions. Further, we should leave open the possibility that governors might choose to pursue some combination of legislative/executive means of achieving their goals. Governors might lay the groundwork for a policy change by issuing an executive order or pursuing some executive action but they might then pursue legislation to expand upon or consolidate the change. Alternatively, when a governor believes legislation is necessary to achieve a policy goal but is unlikely to be well received by the legislature, he or she might use some executive means to take the first step. Going first by taking some administrative action might change the status quo in some way that affects the likely legislative response.

Such a complicated leadership environment, of course, makes studying the actual role of the governor a challenging endeavor. However, such a framework embraces the politics which structures the relationship and this is what makes the study of political science both interesting and unique. If the study of governors is to move beyond the disjointed collection of different and often unrelated theories examined above, a more unified theoretical framework similar to the one presented here should be a step in the right direction.

NOTE

1. Dometrius (Dometrius, Measuring Gubernatorial Power 1979) provides an extensive list of studies incorporating the formal powers index.

References

Abney, Glenn, and Thomas P. Lauth. 1983. "The Governor as Chief Administrator." *Public Administration Review* 40–9.

Abney, Glenn, and Thomas P. Lauth. 1985. "The Line Item Veto in the States." *Public Administration Review* 372–7.

Abney, Glenn, and Thomas P. Lauth. 1986. *The Politics of State and City Administration.* Albany: State University of New York Press.

Abney, Glenn, and Thomas P. Lauth. "The End of Executive Dominance in State Appropriations." *Public Administration Review* 388–95.

Adams, Greg D., and Peverill Squire. 2001. "A Note on the Dynamics and Idiosyncrasies of Gubernatorial Popularity." *State Politics and Policy Quarterly* 380–93.

Alt, James E., David Dreyer Lassen, and David Skilling. 2002. "Fiscal transparency, Gubernatorial Approval, and the Scale of Government: Evidence from the States." *State Politics and Policy Quarterly* 230–50.

Alt, James E., and Robert C. Lowry. 1994. "Divided Government, Fiscal Institutions, and Budget Deficits: Evidence from the States." *American Political Science Review* 811–28.

Alt, James E., and Robert C. Lowry. 2000. "A Dynamic Model of State Budget Outcomes under Divided Partisan Government." *Journal of Politics* 1035–69.

Atkeson, Lonna Rae, and Randall W. Partin. 1995. "Economic and Referendum Voting: A Comparison of Gubernatorial and Senatorial Elections." *American Political Science Review* 99–107.

Barber, James David. 1972. *The Presidential Character: Predicting Performance in the White House.* Englewood Cliffs: Prentice Hall.

Bardwell, Kedron. 2005. "Reevaluating Spending in Gubernatorial Races: Job Approval as a Baseline for Spending Effects." *Political Research Quarterly* 97–105.

Barrilleaux, Charles. 1999. "Governors, Bureaus, and State Policymaking." *State & Local Government Review* 53–9.

Barrilleaux, Charles, and Michael Berkman. 2003. "Do Governors Matter? Budgeting Rules and the Politics of State Policymaking." *Political Research Quarterly* 409–17.

Barth, Jay, and Margaret R. Ferguson. 2002a. "American Governors and Their Constituents: The Relationship between Gubernatorial Personality and Public Approval." *State Politics and Policy Quarterly* 268–82.

Barth, Jay, and Margaret R. Ferguson. 2002b. "Gender and Gubernatorial Personality." *Women & Politics* 63–82.

Behn, Robert. 1991. *Governors on Governing.* Washington, DC: National Governor's Association.

Berch, Neil. 1995. "Explaining Changes in Tax Incidence in the States." *Political Research Quarterly* 629–41.

Bernick, E. Lee. 1979. "Gubernatorial Tools: Formal vs. Informal." *Journal of Politics* 656–64.

Bernick, E. Lee, and Charles W. Wiggins. 1991. "Executive-Legislative Relations: The Governor's Role as Chief Legislator." In *Gubernatorial Leadership and State Policy*, by Eric Herzik and Brent Brown. New York: Greenwood Press.

Beyle, Thad, and J. Oliver Williams. 1972. *The American Governor in Behavioral Perspective.* New York: Harper and Row, Publishers.

Beyle, Thad. 1983. "Governors." In *Politics in the American States 4th ed*, by Virginia Gray, Herbert Jacob and R. B. Albritton Boston: Little Brown.

Beyle, Thad. 1990. "Governors." In *Politics in the American States 5th ed*, by Virginia Gray, Herbert Jacob and R Albritton, 568–573 Boston: Little Brown.

Beyle, Thad. 1995. "Enhancing Executive Leadership in the States." *State and Local Government Review* 18–35.

Beyle, Thad. 1999. "The Governors." In *Politics in the American States 7th ed*, by Virginia Gray, Russell L Hanson and Herbert Jacob, 191–231. Washington DC: CQ Press.

Beyle, Thad, and Margaret Ferguson. 2008. "Governors and the Executive Branch." In *Politics in the American States 9th ed*, by Virginia Gray and Russell L. Hansen, 192–228. Washington, DC: CQ Press.

Beyle, Thad, and Lynn Muchmore. 1983. *Being Governor: The View from the Office*. Durham, NC: Duke Policy Studies Press.

Bowling, Cynthia J., and Deil S. Wright. 1998a. "Change and Continuity in State Administration: Administrative Leadership Across Four Decades." *Public Administration Review* 429–44.

Bowling, Cynthia J., and Deil S. Wright. 1998b. "Public Administration in the United States: A Half-Century Administrative Revolution." *State and Local Government Review* 52–64.

Bowman, Ann O'M., Neal D. Woods, and Milton R. Stark II. 2010. "Separation of Powers and the Institutionalization of the American Governorship." *Political Research Quarterly* 304–15.

Brace, Paul, and Aubrey Jewett. 1995. "The State of State Politics Research." *Political Research Quarterly* 643–81.

Breunig, Christian, and Chris Koski. 2009. "Punctuated Budgets and Governors' Institutional Powers." *American Politics Review* 1116–38.

Brudney, Jeffrey L., and F. Ted Hebert. 1987. "State Agencies and their Environments: Examining the Influence of Important External Actors." *Journal of Politics* 186–206.

Burke, Brendan, and Margaret Ferguson. 2010. "Going Alone or Moving Together: Canadian and American Middle Tier Strategies on Climate Change." *Publius* 436–59.

Carsey, Thomas M., and Gerald C. Wright. 1998. "State and National Factors in Gubernatorial and Senatorial Elections." *American Journal of Political Science* 994–1002.

Chubb, John E. 1988. "Institutions, the Economy, and the Dynamics of State Elections." *American Political Science Review* 133–54.

Clayton, Cornel W. 1994. "Law, Politics and the New Federalism: State Attorneys General as National Policymakers." *Review of Politics* 525–53.

Clynch, Edward J., and Thomas P. Lauth. 1991. "Conclusion: Budgeting in the American States— Conflict and Diversity." *In Governors, Legislatures and Budgets, ed*, by Edward J. Clynch and Thomas P. Lauth, 149–55. New York: Greenwood Press.

Cohen, Jeffrey E., and James D. King. 2004. "Relative Unemployment and Gubernatorial Popularity." *Journal of Politics* 1267–82.

Cook, Elizabeth A., Ted G. Jelen, and Clyde Wilcox. 1994. "Issue Voting in Gubernatorial Elections: Abortion and Post-Webster Politics." *Political Research Quarterly* 187–99.

Crew Jr., Robert E., David Branham, Gregory Weiher, and Ethan Bernick. 2002. "Political Events in a Model of Gubernatorial Approval." *State Politics and Policy Quarterly* 283–97.

Crew Jr., Robert E., and Gregory Weiher. 1996. "Gubernatorial Popularity in Three States: A Preliminary Model." *Social Science Quarterly* 39–55.

Daley, Dorothy M., Donald P. Haider-Markel, and Andrew B. Whitford. 2007. "Checks, Balances, and the Costs of Regulation: Evidence from the American States." *Political Research Quarterly* 696–706.

Dearden, James A., and Thomas A. Husted. 1993. "Do Governors Get What They Want?An Alternative Examination of the Line-Item Veto." *Public Choice* 707–23.

Dilger, Robert J., George A. Krause, and Randolph R. Moffett. 1995. "State Legislative Professionalism and Gubernatorial Effectiveness, 1978–1991." *Legislative Studies Quarterly* 553–71.

Dometrius, Nelson C. 1979. "Measuring Gubernatorial Power."*Journal of Politics* 589–610.

Dometrius, Nelson C. 1987. "Changing Gubernatorial Power: The Measure vs. Reality." *Western Political Quarterly* 319–33.

Dometrius, Nelson C. 2002. "Gubernatorial Approval and Administrative Influence."*State Politics and Policy Quarterly* 251–67.

Dometrius, Nelson C., and Deil S. Wright. 2009. "Governors, Legislatures and State Budgets Across Time." *Political Research Quarterly* 63: 783–95.

Durning, Dan. 1987. "Change Masters for the States." *State Government* 145–49.

Durning, Dan. 1991. "Education Reform in Arkansas: The Governor's Role in Policymaking." In *Gubernatorial Leadership and State Policy*, by Eric Herzikand Brent Brown New York: Greenwood Press.

Elling, Richard C. 1992. *Public Management in the States: A Comparative Study of Administrative Performance and Politics.* Westport, Conn: Praeger.

Elling, Richard C. 2004. "Administering State Programs: Performance and Politics." In *Politics in the American States: A Comparative Analysis*, by Virginia Gray and Russell L. Hanson, 261–89 Washington DC: Congressional Quarterly Press.

Erikson, Robert S., Gerald Wright, and John McIver. 1993. *Statehouse Democracy.* New York: Cambridge University Press.

Ferguson, Margaret R. 2003. "Chief Executive Success in the Legislative Arena." *State Politics and Policy Quarterly* 158–82.

Ferguson, Margaret R. 2006. *The Executive Branch of State Government: People, Process and Politics.* Santa Barbara, CA: ABC-CLIO.

Ferguson, Margaret R., and Jay Barth. 2002. "Governors in the Legislative Arena: the Importance of Personality in Shaping Success." *Political Psychology* 787–808.

Ferguson, Margaret R., and Cynthia J. Bowling. 2008. "Executive Orders and Administrative Control." *Public Administration Review* S20–S28.

Francis, Wayne, and Ronald Weber. 1980. "Legislative Issues in the 50 States." *Legislative Studies Quarterly* 407–21.

Gerber, Brian J., and Paul Teske. 2000. "Regulatory Policymaking in the American States: A Review of Theories and Evidence." *Political Research Quarterly* 849–86.

Gleiber, Dennis, and Steven A. Shull. 1992. "Presidential Influence in the Policymaking Process." *Western Politics Quarterly* 442–68.

Goodman, Doug. 2007. "Determinants of Perceived Gubernatorial Budgetary Influence among State Executive Budget Analysts and Legislative Fiscal Analysts." *Political Research Quarterly* 43–54.

Gormley, William T. 2006. "Accountability Battles in State Administration." In *The State of the States: 4th ed*, by Carl E. Van Horn, 101–19 Washington DC: CQ Press.

Gosling, James. 1985. "Patterns of Influence and Choice in the Wisconsin Budgetary Process." *Legislative Studies Quarterly* 457–82.

Gosling, James. 1986. "Wisconsin Item Veto Lessons." *Public Administration Review* 292–300.

Grady, Dennis O., and Kathleen M. Simon. 2002. "Political Restraints and Bureaucratic Discretion: The Case of State Government Rule Making." *Politics and Policy* 646–77.

Gross, Donald. 1980. "House Senate Conference Committees: A Comparative State Perspective." *American Journal of Political Science* 769–78.

Gross, Donald. 1991. "The Policy Role of Governors." In *Gubernatorial Leadership and State Policy*, by Eric Herzik and Brent Brown. New York: Greenwood Press.

Hall, Thad E. 2002. "Changes in Legislative Support for the Governor's Program Over Time." *Legislative Studies Quarterly* 107–22.

Hansen, Susan. 1999. "Life is Not Fair: Governors' Job Performance Ratings and State Economies." *Political Research Quarterly* 167–88.

Hebert, F. Ted, Jeffrey Brudney, and Deil S. Wright. 1983. "Gubernatorial Influence and State Bureaucracy." *American Politics Quarterly* 243–63.

Hedge, David M. 1998. *Governance and the Changing American States*. Boulder: Westview Press.

Herzik, Eric. 1991. "Policy Agendas and Gubernatorial Leadership." *In Gubernatorial Leadership and State Policy*, by Eric Herzik and Brent Brown. New York: Greenwood Press.

Howard, Christopher. 1999. "The American Welfare State, or States." *Political Research Quarterly* 421–42.

Howell, Susan E., and James M. Vanderleew. 1990. "Economic Effects On State Governors." *American Politics Research* 158–68.

Jacobson, Gary C. 2006. "'The Polls': Polarized Opinion in the States: Partisan Differences in Approval Ratings of Governors, Senators and George W. Bush." *Presidential Studies Quarterly* 732–57.

Jewell, Malcolm. 1969. *The State Legislature: Politics and Practices 2nd ed.* New York: Random House.

Jewel, Malcolm E. 1982. "The Neglected World of State Politics." *Journal of Politics* 638–57.

Kaplan, Marshall, and Sue O'Brien. 1991. *The Governors and the New Federalism*. Boulder, CO: Westview Press.

Kelleher, Christine A., and Jennifer Wolak. 2007. "Explaining Public Confidence in the Branches of State Government." *Political Research Quarterly* 707–21.

Kenney, Patrick. 1983. "The Effect of State Economic Conditions on the Vote for Governor." *Social Science Quarterly* 154–62.

King, James D. 2001. "Incumbent Popularity and Vote Choice in Gubernatorial Elections." *Journal of Politics* 585–97.

Klarner, Karl E. and Andrew Karch. 2008. "Why Do Governors Issue Vetoes? The Impact of Individual and Institutional Influences." *Political Research Quarterly* 574–94.

Kousser, Thad. 2002. "The Politics of Discretionary Medicaid Spending 1980–1993." *Journal of Health Politics, Policy & Law* 639–71.

Kousser, Thad, and Justin H. Phillips. 2009. "Who Blinks First? Legislative Patience and Bargaining with Governors." *Legislative Studies Quarterly* 55–86.

Kousser, Thad, and Justin H. Phillips. 2012. *The Power of American Governors: Winning on Budgets and Losing on Policy*. Cambridge University Press.

Leyden, Kevin M., and Stephen A. Borelli. 1995. "The Effect of State Economic Conditions on Gubernatorial Elections: Does Unified Government Make a Difference?" *Political Research Quarterly* 275–90.

Lieberman, Robert C., and Greg M. Shaw. 2000. "Looking Inward, Looking Outward: The Politics of Welfare Innovation under Devolution." *Political Research Quarterly* 215–40.

Lipson, Leslie. 1939. *The American Governor from Figurehead to Leader*. Chicago: University of Chicago Press.

Lynch, Jason. 2001. "Federalism, Separation of Powers, and the Role of State Attorneys General in Multistate Litigation." *Columbia Law Review* 1998–2032.

MacDonald, Jason A., and Lee Sigelman. 1999. "Public Assessments of Gubernatorial Performance: A Comparative State Assessment." *American Politics Research* 201–15.

McNeal, Ramona S., Caroline J. Tolbert, Karen Mossberger, and Lisa J. Dotterweich. 2003. "Innovating in Digital Government in the American States." *Social Science Quarterly* 52–70.

Meier, Kenneth J. 2007. "The Public Administration of Politics, or What Political Science Could Learn from Public Administration." *PS: Political Science and Politics* 3–9.

Moncrief, Gary F., and Joel A. Thompson. 1980. "Partisanship and Purse Strings: A Research Note on Sharkansky." *Western Political Quarterly* 336–40.

Morehouse, Sarah McCally. 1981. *State Politics, Parties and Policy.* New York: Holt, Rinehart and Winston.

Morehouse, Sarah McCally. 1996. "Legislative Party Voting for the Governor's Program." *Legislative Studies Quarterly* 359–81.

Morris, Thomas R. 1987. "State Attorneys General as Interpreters of State Constitutions." *Publius* 133–52.

Mueller, Keith J. 1985. "Explaining Variation and Change in Gubernatorial Powers, 1960–1982." *Western Political Quarterly* 424–30.

Nelson, Michael. 2006. "The Psychological Presidency." In *The Presidency in the Political System*, by Michael Nelson, 170–94. Washington, DC: CQ Press.

Neustadt, Richard E. 1960. *Presidential Power: The Politics of Leadership.* New York: Wiley.

Niemi, Richard G., Harold W. Stanley, and Arnold J. Vogel. 1995. "State Economies and State Taxes: Do Voters Hold Governors Accountable?" *American Journal of Political Science* 936–57.

Orth, Deborah A. 2001. "Accountability in a Federal System: The Governor, the President, and Economic Expectations." *State Politics and Policy Quarterly* 412–32.

Partin, Randall W. 2002. "Assessing the Impact of Campaign Spending in Governors' Races." *Political Research Quarterly* 213–33.

Peltzman, Sam. 1987. "Economic Conditions and Gubernatorial Elections." *American Economic Review* 293–7.

Potoski, M., and Neal D. Woods. 2001. "Designing State Clean Air Agencies: Administrative Procedures and Bureaucracy Autonomy." *Journal of Public Administration Research and Theory* 203–21.

Ransone, Coleman. 1985. *The American Governorship.* Westport: CT: Greenwood Press.

Rosenthal, Alan. 1990. *Governors and Legislatures: Contending Powers.* Washington DC: CQ Press.

Sabato, Larry. 1983. *Goodbye to Good Time Charlie.* 2nd ed. Washington DC: CQ Press.

Sanford, Terry. 1967. *Storm Over the States.* New York: McGraw Hill Book Company.

Scher, Richard K. 1997. *Politics in the New South: Republicanism, Race and Leadership in the Twentieth Century 2nd ed.* Armonk, NY: M.E. Sharpe.

Schlesinger, Joseph A. 1965. "The Politics of the Executive." In *Politics in the American States*, by Henry Jacob and Kenneth N. Vines Boston: Little Brown.

Sharkansky, Ira. 1968. "Agency Requests, Gubernatorial Support and Budget Success in State Legislatures." *The American Political Science Review* 1220–31.

Sigelman, Lee, and Nelson C. Dometrius. 1988. "Governors as Chief Administrators: The Linkage Between Formal Powers and Informal Influence." *American Politics Quarterly* 157–70.

Smith, Kevin B., and J. Scott Rademacker. 1999. "Expensive Lessons: Education and the Political Economy of the American State." *Political Research Quarterly* 709–27.

Squire, Peverill, and Christina Fastnow. 1994. "Comparing Gubernatorial and Senatorial Elections." *Political Research Quarterly* 705–20.

Sribnick, Ethan G. 2008. *A Legacy of Innovation: Governors and Public Policy.* Philadelphia: University of Pennsylvania Press.

Stein, Robert M. 1990. "Economic Voting for Governor and US Senator: The Electoral Consequences of Federalism." *Journal of Politics* 29–53.

Svoboda, Craig J. 1995. "Retrospective Voting in Gubernatorial Elections: 1982 and 1986." *Political Research Quarterly* 135–50.

Thompson, Joel A. 1987. "Agency Requests, Gubernatorial Support, and Budget Success in State Legislatures Revisited." *The Journal of Politics* 757–79.

van Assendelft, Laura A. 1997. *Governors, Agenda Setting and Divided Government.* Lanham, MD: University Press of America.

Wiggins, Charles W. 1980. "Executive Vetoes and Legislative Overrides in the American States." *The Journal of Politics* 1110–17.

Wilkins, Vicky M., and Garry Young. 2002. "The Influence of Governors on Veto Override Attempts: A Test of Pivotal Politics." *Legislative Studies Quarterly* 557–75.

Winter, David G. 1987. "Leader Appeal, Leader Performance, and the Motive Profile of Leaders and Followers: A Study of American Presidents and Elections." *Journal of Personality and Social Psychology* 196–202.

Winter, David G., and A. J. Stewart. 1977. "Content Analysis as a Method of Studying Political Leaders." In *A Psychological Examination of Political Leaders*, by Margaret G. Hermann. New York: Free Press.

Woods, Neal D. 2004. "Political Influence on Agency Rule Making: Examining the Effects of Legislative and Gubernatorial Rule Review Powers." *State and Local Government Review* 174–85.

Woods, Neal D., and Michael Baranowski. 2007. "Governors and the Bureaucracy: Executive Resources as Sources of Administrative Influence." *International Journal of Public Administration* 1219–30.

Wright, Deil S. 1967. "Executive Leadership in State Administration: Interplay of Gubernatorial, Legislative and Administrative power." *Midwest Journal of Political Science* 1–26.

Zimmerman, Joseph F. 1998. "Interstate cooperation: the roles of the State Attorneys General." *Publius* 71–89.

CHAPTER 15

....

STATE COURTS

Past, Present, and Future

....

CHRIS W. BONNEAU AND BRENT D. BOYEA

As a singular area of research, studies of state courts represent a growing area of scholarship. With varying features connected to the institutional, social, and political environments in which state judges operate, the comparative advantage of state courts differs from studies of the U.S. federal courts which tend to operate within standardized settings. Debates within studies of state supreme courts, however, emerge from the distinct attributes of state court systems including the controversial methods by which states select and then retain their judges. As opposed to federal judgeships which require nominations by the U.S. president with the advice and consent of the U.S. Senate, state methods of judicial selection vary with some states utilizing judicial elections, other states using appointments, and still others using a hybrid form involving a combination of appointments and elections. With distinct state approaches toward the design of state court systems, studies of state courts are well positioned to both uncover the effects of political institutions and to provide normative commentary on the particular value of judicial structures (see Bonneau and Hall's (2009) commentary on the positive effects of judicial elections for selecting judges).

The importance of state courts extends beyond state methods of selection, however, to a diverse range of topics that include the policymaking role of state courts and public perceptions of state courts and their functions. As a result of using state courts to assess judicial decision making through an increasingly sophisticated comparative lens, state courts scholarship now presents a well-developed and methodologically advanced body of research. Further, contrary to Brace, Hall, and Langer's (2001) caution about the deficiencies of state courts research, studies of state courts have made powerful advances in relation to data and methodology. As problems associated with data collection have subsided owing largely to increased online data access and data contributions by Paul Brace, Melinda Gann Hall, and Laura Langer, among others, 50-state studies of state courts are now frequent.

Although systematic studies of state supreme courts have grown, studies of one state or small samples of states have made important contributions to the understanding of state courts. These studies have devoted attention to judicial elections and methods of judicial selection (Dubois, 1980; Baum, 1987; Sheldon and Maule, 1997; Klein and Baum, 2001), money spent in judicial elections (Cheek and Champagne, 2000), the legitimacy of state supreme courts (Gibson, 2008a, 2008b), the voting behavior of state supreme court judges (Glick and Vines, 1969; Hall, 1987, 1992, 1995; Hall and Brace, 1992; Brace and Hall, 1993, 1995, 1997; Traut and Emmert, 1998; Sheldon, 1999; Steffensmeier and Britt, 2001), the effects of money on judicial votes (Cann, 2007), and the policymaking characteristics of state supreme courts (Tarr and Porter, 1988). These studies provide information about judicial elections and the actions of judges using highly specific information about limited venues. Further, the advances of each study form insight about not only the state investigated, but the character of courts and their judges at the state level.

Studies of single institutions have certainly taught us much, but deficiencies sometimes occur due to the absence of varying institutional, political, or social environments that permit comparisons. For example, Bonneau and Hall's (2009) multiple-state examination of judicial elections illustrates that opponents of judicial elections sometimes make sweeping and erroneous statements based on empirically incorrect assumptions or anecdotes formed from experiences within a single state. Their findings show that rather than suppressing judicial accountability as anecdotal evidence sometimes suggests, judicial elections create a democratic connection between voters and judges caused by increasingly competitive elections. In addition to empirical advances about the utility of judicial elections, instructive conclusions derived from systematic investigations have led to changing notions about the effects of judicial selection on judicial behavior, the coalitional effects of the internal structures of courts, and understanding about the role of professional judicial environments.

Multiple-state or systematic studies of state supreme courts have produced an array of essential studies focusing on professionalism and prestige (Brace and Hall, 2001; Caldeira, 1983; Squire, 2008), judicial legitimacy (Cann and Yates, 2008; Gibson, 2009), the composition of courts (Canon, 1972; Glick and Emmert, 1987; Bonneau, 2001; Hurwitz and Lanier, 2001, 2003; Bratton and Spill, 2002; Langer and Wilhelm, 2005), the ideological preferences of state supreme court justices (Brace, Langer, and Hall, 2000), the effect of campaign spending on election results (Bonneau, 2005a, 2007), the performance of incumbent judges in elections (Hall, 2001; Bonneau, 2005b; Hall and Bonneau, 2006), the participation of voters in judicial elections (Hall, 2007; Hall and Bonneau, 2008), state supreme court policy agendas (Atkins and Glick, 1976; Brace and Hall, 2001, 2005; Kritzer et al., 2007; Brace and Boyea, 2010), judicial dissent and agreement (Glick and Pruet, 1986; Hall and Brace, 1989; Brace and Hall, 1990; Boyea, 2007, 2010), the ideological characteristics of judicial voting (Brace and Boyea, 2008), the substantive impact of representation in particular forms of cases (Songer and Tabrizi, 1999; Songer and Crews-Meyer, 2000), and the exercise of judicial review (Langer, 2002). These studies demonstrate that states and their judicial institutions can be explored effectively using a comparative form of analysis. As such, empirical findings derived from studies of two or more state courts form a compelling story about the utility for comparative research and the complex understandings that emerge where comparing the institutional and contextual attributes of states.

Jurisdiction and Design of State Supreme Courts

Much like the U.S. Supreme Court, all state supreme courts have both original and appellate jurisdiction, and their original jurisdiction is limited to well-specified types of cases. Besides this, though, there are several factors on which these courts vary:

Method of Selection: Judges in state supreme courts are selected and retained in five different ways: partisan elections, nonpartisan elections, "merit" selection/retention, gubernatorial appointment, and legislative appointment. The selection and retention of judges is one of the most controversial topics in judicial politics, and we will have much more to say about it in the next section.

Jurisdiction: State supreme courts are the final arbiters of their state laws and constitution in both criminal and civil matters (unless a violation of the federal constitution is alleged). Two states (Texas and Oklahoma) have separate courts of last resort for each type of case: the supreme court in each state deals exclusively with civil matters, while the Court of Criminal Appeals has jurisdiction over criminal cases. In the other states, the supreme court handles all types of cases.

In the majority of states, the supreme court has discretionary jurisdiction over most types of cases. This means that the court gets to choose which cases it hears (and decides) and which cases to let the lower court's decision stand. (Even in states where there is mostly discretionary jurisdiction—like California—the court must hear certain types of cases, like those involving capital punishment and attorney/judicial discipline.) According to the Bureau of Justice Statistics (2006), in 11 states (Arizona, Maine, Mississippi, Montana, Nevada, North Dakota, Rhode Island, South Dakota, Utah, Virginia, West Virginia, and Wyoming), the court has to make decisions on all appeals that come before it or only has discretionary jurisdiction in a very limited number of issues. That is, the court essentially has mandatory jurisdiction.

Types of Cases: There is a lot of variation in the types of cases heard by state supreme courts. Using data on all state supreme court decisions from 1995 and 1996, Brace and Butler (2001) examine the variation in the dockets of these courts. For example, "in Alaska, less than 5 percent of the cases heard by that state's high court are criminal, with over 95 percent of the cases being civil. At the other extreme, over 70 percent of the cases in North Carolina were criminal…" (Brace and Butler, 2001: 250). This same variation exists with tort cases: in Alabama, tort cases comprise almost 60 percent of its total docket, while tort cases are just over 10 percent of the docket in Georgia (Brace and

Butler 2001). Clearly, the type of work being done on these courts varies widely among the states.

Lower Appellate Courts: In 39 states, there is an intermediate appellate court that functions similarly to the U.S. Courts of Appeals. These courts have mandatory jurisdiction and must render a decision on all cases appealed from the trial court. Generally speaking, states with a higher number of court filings have intermediate appellate courts.

The Functioning of State Supreme Courts: There is quite a bit of variation in how state supreme courts operate. In some states (like Louisiana), the justices have their own building and meet in one centralized location. Litigants before the court have to travel to the court in order to have their case heard. This is similar to the U.S. Supreme Court. In other states, like Tennessee, the justices travel around the state and meet in several different locations. This minimizes travel for the litigants at the same time it turns the court into a bit of a traveling show. It also means that the justices live in different parts of the state and likely see each other only when the court hears arguments.

In some states, like Michigan, the members of the court decide cases en banc (all the judges sit together and decide the case), while in other states, like Connecticut, the judges decide cases in panels that change composition periodically (in Connecticut, the panel changes daily). This allows the court to decide more cases in less time. In states with panels, they can decide to hear cases en banc if they feel that the case is sufficiently important.

Professionalism: It should not be surprising that, much like state legislatures, state supreme courts vary widely on measures of professionalism. "Professionalism" is an index that takes into account such things as salary, workload, docket control, staff, etc. The more professionalized a court, the more desirable a seat on that court. Based on different ways of calculating salary and docket control, Squire (2008) develops four measures of state supreme court professionalism (all of which are highly correlated with each other). California emerges as the most "professionalized" supreme court, even scoring higher than the U.S. Supreme Court! Other states that are highly professionalized are Michigan, Pennsylvania, and West Virginia. At the bottom end of professionalization are Vermont, South Dakota, Utah, and North Dakota. Interestingly, Squire (2008: 231) finds that "state courts of last resort are much more like the U.S. Supreme Court than state legislatures are like the U.S. Congress." This indicates that courts at the state level might be career destinations in their own right, as opposed to stepping-stones to federal courts as state legislatures are stepping-stones to the U.S. Congress. (For additional information about career movement to the federal courts, see Bratton and Spill, 2004). This is an interesting avenue for future research to pursue.

ATTRIBUTES OF JUDGES

The composition of state supreme court benches has changed pretty dramatically over the past couple of decades. While these benches used to be dominated by white males who were born and received their law degrees in-state, the picture is quite different now (Bonneau 2001 documents these changes over time).

Race: Perhaps not surprisingly, the number of racial minorities serving on state courts has increased significantly over time. Hurwitz and Lanier (2001, 2008) examine the percentage of racial minorities on state appellate courts (courts of last resort and intermediate appellate courts). In 1985, only 6.5 percent of these judges were from racial minorities; in 1999, it had increased to 7.3 percent; in 2005, 11.7 percent of state appellate judges were from racial minorities. So, in the course of 20 years, the percentage of state appellate court judges who come from racial minorities has almost doubled. Moreover, Hurwitz and Lanier (2003, 2008) find that judicial diversity is not associated with the method by which judges are selected. That is, no method of selection better promotes judicial diversity on the bench.

Gender: The results for gender diversity on state appellate courts are similar. In 1985, only 6.8 percent of state appellate judges were female; in 1999, this number jumped to 21.1 percent; in 2005, it was 26.2 percent. Over 20 years, the percentage of female judges quadrupled. Additionally, women have held a majority of seats on several state supreme courts, starting with Minnesota in 1991. According to the National Center for State Courts, eight other states have also been majority female at some point: Michigan, Massachusetts, New Jersey, New York, Ohio, Tennessee, Washington, and Wisconsin. Of these states, consistent with the findings of Hurwitz and Lanier (2008), five states select judges via elections (Minnesota, Michigan, Ohio, Washington, and Wisconsin), three use gubernatorial appointments (Massachusetts, New Jersey, and New York), and one uses a variation of the "merit" system (Tennessee).

Tenure: Another way in which judges vary is the length of time they are on the bench. A recent paper by Curry and Hurwitz (2010) examined average length of tenure in state supreme courts from 1980–2005. They found that the average lengths of tenure in states that elect their judges are, on average, shorter than those who appoint their judges. In states with partisan elections, the average length of tenure is 8.3 years and it is 8.6 years for states that utilize nonpartisan elections. In contrast, states that appoint their judges have an average tenure of 9.3 years and those that use "merit" selection (in which judges are initially appointed), it is 11.3 years, a full 3 years longer than states that utilize partisan elections. The consequences of this differential tenure on judicial outcomes, the collegiality of courts (rates of consensus), and judicial efficiency are all topics for future research.

CONTROVERSIES OVER STATE METHODS OF JUDICIAL SELECTION

As mentioned above, states choose (and keep) their judges using a variety of methods, including standard elections (partisan and nonpartisan), retention elections, and appointments. Moreover, some states select their judges using one method and retain them using another, and methods of selection can vary within a state as well, with judges at some levels of courts being elected (for example) and judges at other levels of courts being appointed. Over the past two decades, research on state judicial selection has exploded, with scholars examining everything from the conduct of judicial elections to whether or not elections affect the behavior of judges once on the bench. The vast major- ity of this work has been conducted on state supreme court elections and decisions (but see Streb, Frederick, and LaFrance, 2007, 2009; Frederick and Streb, 2008a, 2008b; Streb and Frederick, 2009). Extending this research to lower courts is an area ripe for exami- nation. Given the differences between, say, trial courts and state supreme courts, further developing the research on state judicial selection is of utmost importance for scholars and policymakers alike.

Methods of Appointment and Election: There are five different methods by which states select and retain their judges. States that use *partisan elections* have elections where the partisan affiliation of judges appears next to their name on the ballot. These elections are just like elections for any other office; voters know which candidate is endorsed by which political party. In states that utilize *nonpartisan elections*, candidates still run in compet- itive elections, but there is no indication of their political party. Indeed, there could be two democrats (or two republicans) running against each other for a seat on the bench. Some states utilize *"merit"/retention elections*. While the exact process varies slightly across states, generally a judicial selection commission presents the governor with a list of names (usually 3–5) and the governor is forced to appoint someone from this list to the bench. (In some states the governor can add names to this list, while in other states the governor can choose to reject the entire slate and instruct the commission to give her new names.) After a period of time (usually 1–2 years), the newly appointed judge faces the electorate, which is simply asked "Should Judge X be retained?" If the judge receives more "yes" than "no" votes, she keeps her job (Illinois requires judges to attain 60 per- cent of "yes" votes; New Mexico requires candidates to have 57 percent). The judge then serves a full term (anywhere from 6 to 10 years) before facing the electorate again; if the judge is defeated, the process of selection begins anew. A few states have kept *gubernato- rial appointments*, usually requiring the advice and consent of the Senate for success- ful nominations. The distinguishing feature of these schemes compared to the "merit" system is that even if a judicial nominating commission is involved, these judges never face the electorate. They either serve for life (rarely), until a mandatory retirement age, if one is legislated, or require a reappointment by the executive to remain on the bench. Finally, and most rare, two states appoint their judges using *legislative appointment*. Here, the state legislature is in charge of the appointment and retention of judges.

Debates about methods of selection and judicial elections: Much of what we know about the different methods of selection revolves around the debate over whether judges should be elected or appointed. Empirically, the bulk of the evidence is on elections and their consequences for judges (e.g., Brace and Boyea, 2008; Gibson, 2008a, 2008b, 2009; Bonneau and Hall, 2009). Studies of appointment are quite rare, possibly owing to the fact that judges in appointed states are almost always reappointed (if they desire additional service) and that judges who do not face any sort of election are quite rare (only 12 states, with 11 of them being states—or part of states, like Maine—that were part of the original 13 states admitted into the Union). Clearly, much more should be investigated about how insulating state judges affects their behavior on the bench.

In terms of electing judges, there are several interest groups (such as the American Bar Association and the American Judicature Society) who are actively lobbying states to eradicate elections. Although this movement had considerable success in the 1960s and 1970s, it has stalled, and no state has ended competitive elections for their state high court bench since the early 1990s. Moreover, there is a movement in some states (like Tennessee and Missouri) to change from retention elections back to partisan elections.

The debate over electing judges comes down to where one falls on the judicial independence spectrum. At one extreme are those who believe judges should be completely independent and accountable to no one (either other branches of government or the electorate). At the other extreme are those who believe the judges should be held accountable for their decisions by the electorate (or other branches of government) and judges should be removed if they make decisions that are displeasing to the electorate. (Note that whether a decision is displeasing is independent of whether the judge is following the law/constitution when making his/her decision.) No system perfectly provides for independence (even the federal system, where the U.S. Supreme Court is not completely independent from Congress) or accountability. But, some systems better provide for independence or accountability.

The argument for judicial independence is quite simple (and familiar to most, since it is taught in civics classes across the country). The job of judges is to make decisions consistent with the constitution and the law and this often means they have to make decisions that are unpopular with the masses. Since the legislature relies on the public to keep their jobs, they are prone to pass laws that might trample on the rights of politically unpopular minorities. The judiciary is therefore a check on the legislature and the protector of civil rights and liberties. Without an independent judiciary, the harmful effects of majority opinion would run rampant. Consequently, the protection of individual rights would result from the actions of the majority to extend protections rather than judicial decisions based on the U.S. and state constitutions.

The argument for judicial elections is a bit more complicated, and, in the eyes of some, disturbing. Proponents of judicial elections are in favor of judges as neutral, impartial arbiters who simply apply the constitution and the law in a fair manner. However, this naïve notion has been disproven by political scientists for decades (e.g. Segal and Spaeth, 2002). Simply put, it is just not possible for judges to behave this way in many types of cases. Many issues that state supreme court judges decide are complex and the "correct" outcome is far from obvious. Particularly in highly salient and divisive disputes, like the death penalty and gay marriage, judges must draw upon their personal beliefs, values, and experiences in making decisions because the law is simply not a sufficient guide. Given that this is an empirical fact, why should judges not be elected or held accountable for their decisions? Indeed, the evidence that U.S. Supreme Court judges make decisions based on their personal policy preferences is clear (Segal and Spaeth, 2002), and these judges are as structurally "independent" as one can get. Proponents of elections argue that it is far better for justice to draw upon public perceptions and the prevailing state political climate when resolving difficult disputes rather than engaging in unfettered pursuit of their own personal preferences. Judicial independence does not exclusively mean that judges are independent from other branches of government or the electorate; it also means that judges are independent from the law or the constitution. Thus, holding judges accountable for their decisions can actually *increase* their faithfulness to the law.

Evidence on Judicial Elections: Of course, one can agree that judicial accountability (and judicial elections) are great ideas but still doubt the ability of elections to hold judges accountable. Recently, Bonneau and Hall (2009) undertook a systematic, comprehensive look at state supreme court elections from 1990–2004 to see if these elections were, in fact, able to hold judges accountable. Their major findings are highlighted below.

- Voters participate in state supreme court races in significant numbers. Moreover, surveys of voters indicate that they are interested in these races and want to keep voting in them. Voter participation is higher in races where the partisan identification of the voters is on the ballot because this provides an important informational cue to the voters. Finally, voter participation is higher when there is more campaign spending in the race since higher amounts of spending lead to more advertisements being run and more information being provided to voters. Obviously, for elections to promote accountability, voters must first be interested in these races and participate in them by voting. This necessary condition is met. Of course, if voters do not participate meaningfully (that is, if their choices are random), then this would erode the argument that elections can promote accountability.
- Voters are able to make meaningful choices in these elections. The evidence indicates that challengers to incumbents with prior judicial experience perform better than those without such experience. Thus, voters are seemingly able to distinguish between "qualified" candidate alternatives to an incumbent and "not qualified" alternatives. Candidates who serve (or previously served) as a lower court judge perform in judicial elections.
- Without a doubt, state supreme court elections are becoming increasingly expensive, though high-cost campaigns have not occurred in all states, or even in all races within a state in the same election cycle. One of the conditions necessary for elections to be efficacious is that they be competitive. We have already mentioned how voters participate in these elections and participate meaningfully. Campaign spending helps voters to participate meaningfully by providing information about the candidates. Consistent with the congressional literature, campaign spending helps challengers reduce the advantage of incumbency and makes elections more competitive. Thus, far from being problematic, campaign spending (at least for the challenger) can be a positive attribute for these races as it helps to make the election more competitive and provides information to help the voter make her choice.

A final objection to electing judges comes from those who think the process of judges soliciting contributions from parties and attorneys who are likely to appear before them creates an appearance of impropriety. It is certainly true that the public feels that there is an appearance of impropriety, as this has been documented in several surveys. However, Gibson (2009) found that this perception is not limited to courts: the public feels the same way about state legislatures. This suggests that the public is uncomfortable with campaign contributions in general and not campaign contributions *to judges*. This is an important distinction because it indicates that the public supports systematic reform on the funding of elections, thus, judicial elections are not unique. More importantly, Gibson (2009) has found that elections do not lead to decreased legitimacy for state courts. This is contrary to rhetoric from the opponents of judicial elections who allege that the perception of impropriety that accompanies elections leads to an erosion of legitimacy. There is simply no empirical evidence that this is the case. Finally, it is worth noting that an *appearance* of impropriety is far different than *actual* impropriety. To date, scholars have found a correlation between campaign contributors and judicial decisions (e.g. McCall, 2003; Cann, 2007; but see Cann, 2002). However, we must be very careful not to infer causation from this relationship. If contributors are rational, we would expect to see a correlation: conservative individuals and groups should contribute to conservative candidates to help them get elected and liberal individuals and groups should do the same for liberal candidates. But this does not imply that the recipients of these contributions are influenced by these contributions. Rather, it is far more likely that the candidate has well-formed views on the issues and that contributors that agree with the candidate's views will assist with her re-election contest. This is much the same process as happens in legislatures: do pro-life groups contribute to pro-life candidates or do they convince candidates to become pro-life because of their contributions? The former is far more plausible than the latter.

PROCESS AND PROCEDURE: CRIMINAL AND CIVIL LITIGATION

As noted throughout this chapter, state courts play a critical role in the stable functioning of state governments. In total, state courts adjudicate a large volume of cases, contributing to approximately 99 percent of the nation's caseload (Hall, 2007). At the highest level of state courts, state supreme courts process much of the nation's appellate litigation settling more than 84,000 filings in 2008, while state appellate courts in general received in excess of 270,000 filings (National Center for State Courts, 2010). As such, state courts play an essential role in settling disputes among litigants. As the court of last resort for each state, decisions by state supreme courts decide salient legal and political disputes about most legal policies, causing state appellate courts to become the final appellate arbiter for many legal disputes.

Role of state supreme courts in dispute resolution: With the responsibility of concluding large sums of legal disputes, state courts of last resort directly and indirectly affect the lives of millions of state residents. Yet, this effect receives relatively little attention within the popular press or the academic literature, which is generally devoted to the U.S. Supreme Court. The causes for inattention are understandable due to the consequences of decisions rendered by the U.S. Supreme Court in relation to legal policy within the United States. For states, however, the legal and constitutional authority vested in state supreme courts gives those judicial systems extraordinary authority to shape public policy within each state (see Langer, 2002; Roch and Howard, 2008). Failure to understand the role of state supreme courts undervalues their influence for both the state and nation.

Important for the well-being of the political arena of each state, state courts address issues affecting societal and economic questions that are often too controversial for elected officials to handle effectively (Brace and Hall, 2005). In turn, the decisions of state courts clarify state policies and provide guidance to those inside and outside of a state's judiciary, including the executive or legislative branch of each state. Roch and Howard's (2008) examination of education policy illustrates the manner by which state courts may deter legislative action. Where politically insulated and judicially active, state courts insert their view into the public policy forum thereby channeling the preferences of the court into debates about policy. Because popular impulses compel political parties to appease their partisan supporters either directly or indirectly (Aldrich, 1995), the actions of courts permit divided political systems to avoid failures caused by extreme factionalism. With the actions of state courts affecting many state policies, such as the structure and content of state elections (Langer, 2002) and the application and use of the death penalty (Brace and Hall, 1997; Traut and Emmert, 1998), state courts remain popular institutions in relation to their trustworthiness and fairness (Cann and Yates, 2008). Support among state citizens illustrates that state courts enjoy a high degree of public support regardless of their different structural designs (Gibson, 2008a, 2008b, 2009; Cann and Yates, 2008).

Process of Law, Civil Litigation: State courts display varying levels of attention to distinct areas of policies. While some state courts specialize in criminal litigation, others focus on civil matters which include disputes related to contested elections, taxation, family law, and torts. The process of appeal for lower court civil decisions resembles the litigation process found in the federal courts: cases originate in trial courts and thereafter appeals are generally brought to intermediate appellate courts (where present) and then to state supreme courts as the final venue for state review. Civil litigants, therefore, calculate their certainty about an appeal's outcome and the costs of litigation before deciding to appeal cases to both a state's intermediate appellate court and state supreme court. Calculations about litigation are influenced by the preferences of judges and organizational features of state high courts including state methods of judicial retention (Brace and Hall, 1997), length of tenure (Hanssen, 1999), and discretionary authority to

accept or reject appeals (Brace, Yates, and Boyea, 2006). Related to discretionary jurisdiction, many state supreme courts enjoy considerable authority over the volume and
characteristics of civil litigation, while other supreme courts have less control. From
mandatory civil litigation in the Alabama Supreme Court to discretionary jurisdiction
in the Connecticut Supreme Court, state supreme courts possess varying degrees of latitude to structure their agendas. Thus, where courts have discretion in the case selection
process, litigants experience uncertainty about whether their case will be selected for
review prior to calculating the case's expected outcome.

Process of Law: Criminal Litigation. The characteristics of criminal litigation largely
follow the process of appeal for civil litigation. Like civil cases, criminal cases maneuver
through the different tiers of state courts with the final venue being the state supreme
courts. Further, many criminal defendants engage in plea bargains prior to trial thereby
reducing the volume of trial cases (Meador, 2002). While most state supreme courts are
aligned with civil litigation following the tort revolution of the 1970s (Kagan et al., 1977;
Kritzer et al., 2007), state supreme courts now allocate larger shares of their agendas to
criminal litigation. High volume criminal agendas can be found in the high courts of
North Carolina, Florida, Arizona, and Indiana, where each court allocates more attention to criminal conflicts than civil matters (Brace and Hall, 2005). Among the dispute
areas tied to criminal litigation, including rape and sexual assault, drug trafficking, and
white collar crimes, no criminal litigation policy surpasses the attention directed to capital convictions. For courts like the Texas Court of Criminal Appeals and the Florida
Supreme Court, where capital crimes are a frequent and critical concern given mandatory review of lower court capital convictions, commitment to the area of criminal and
capital crime litigation drives the behavior and activities of those courts.

Trends in State Supreme Court Policy: An established tradition has mapped the pattern
of appeals within state supreme courts. Kagan et al. (1977) identified the period before
1970 as a time of significant change for state courts. Reacting to changes within society, ideological transition within the U.S. Supreme Court, and the devolution of federal
authority to state governments, state supreme courts now oversee a larger role within
the settlement of legal disputes. Legal changes connected to the emergence of the internet, growth of crime, and higher divorce rates throughout the later 20th century led to
courts with larger and more varied agendas. Further, the areas of criminal and tort litigation experienced dramatic upward shifts as courts adjudicated larger quantities of disputes between criminal defendants and state governments and between civil plaintiffs
and civil defendants. At present, according to Kritzer et al. (2007), criminal litigation
remains the most recurrent area of litigation, followed by tort and public law litigation.
Thus, while debt and property claims once dominated the attention of state supreme
courts, state high courts now rarely focus on either area. Leading to the evolution of state
supreme court policymaking, states reformed their judicial systems to counter severe
caseload problems during the 1960s. As such, state governments increased the agenda
authority of several state supreme courts, freeing state high courts to select more contentious and important issues. Conversely, state supreme courts reduced the quantity
of straightforward disputes such as those involving debt and real property conflicts. To

permit smaller caseloads, states increased the discretion of state supreme courts over their dockets (Flango and Rottman, 1998) and increased the quantity of state intermediate appellate courts (Kagan et al., 1977; Hall, 1999). Relating to the emergence of intermediate appellate courts, states both formed circuits to extant intermediate appellate court systems and introduced intermediate appellate courts to two-tier judicial systems. For state high courts, like those in California, Texas, and New York, intermediate lower appellate courts handle and settle the bulk of appeals thereby reducing the volume of appeals present at the highest state court level. At present, there are 39 states with lower appellate courts, contributing to state supreme courts with discretionary control over their agendas.

Judicial Outcomes

Because state supreme courts are diverse and vary in terms of their structure, studying them offers unique advantages over alternative judicial institutions due to differences that exist from state to state. Particular attention has been devoted to the impact of judicial selection on judicial decisions and the divergent effects of judicial appointments and elections. In particular, research on outcomes in state supreme courts has been focused on whether judges in appointive or elective courts are more or less accountable to their constituency. Using both single-state studies and systematic investigations where courts are compared to one another, research has focused on the coalitional and ideological behavior of judges, as well as the exercise of judicial review.

Issue Composition of State Supreme Courts. Systematic studies of state supreme courts have uncovered important characteristics of civil dockets. While Brace and Hall (2005) note that most state supreme courts devote more of their attention to civil rather than criminal or miscellaneous litigation, torts as a form of civil policy are an active area of litigation before most state supreme courts. At one extreme are state supreme courts in Tennessee, Minnesota, Illinois, or Alabama, which apply about half of their civil litigation attention to tort litigation. At the other extreme are institutions like the Georgia Supreme Court which allocates less than 15 percent of its civil court docket to torts. Within tort cases, there is additional variation related to support for original plaintiffs, which is identified as the party seeking remedy or correction. In both Nevada and Arizona, success rates for original plaintiffs approach 60 percent making those courts active in the redistribution of money. Alternatively, the Minnesota and Wyoming supreme courts support the counterclaims of tort defendants in about four of five tort cases.

Similar observations can be made for state supreme courts relating to criminal cases, including serious matters like murder. Indeed, Brace and Hall (2005) report that seven states devote a majority of their criminal docket to murder and death penalty decisions. Among those courts is the North Carolina Supreme Court, where approximately 90 percent of the criminal cases feature convictions for murder, with about half of those cases featuring questions about the death penalty. Connected to appeals of the death penalty, states like Florida, Virginia, Ohio, and Arizona specialize in capital decisions, making the death penalty very relevant to a judge's activities in those courts. Related to the outcome of death penalty cases, Oregon and New Mexico stand out as the least hospitable venues for convicted criminals seeking reversal, while Maryland and Arkansas favor criminal defendants in nearly half of their capital appeal decisions.

Explanations of systematic trends relating to the composition of issues faced by state supreme courts suggests that court agendas are responsive to the institutional structures (Kagan et al., 1977; Glick and Pruet, 1986; Brace and Hall, 2001), state political (Atkins and Glick, 1976) and social environments (Atkins and Glick, 1976), and the laws and legal provisions of each state (Brace and Boyea 2010). Among institutional factors affecting the volume of cases are the designs of state constitutions, structure of appellate court systems, professionalism of courts, and methods of judicial selection. Civil cases, for example, are preferred to criminal cases where state constitutions serve not only as the provisions of government but also as a fundamental source of civil rights and public policies (Brace and Boyea, 2010). The presence of intermediate appellate courts also affects the disposition of courts toward higher civil case volumes. Where states utilize lower appellate courts, fewer civil cases are found within a court's overall agenda leaving greater space for criminal disputes (Brace and Boyea, 2010). Where courts are highly professionalized, as observed where salaries are higher, staffs are larger, and agenda discretion is greater, those courts are inclined to give attention to civil tort cases as opposed to alternative civil or criminal matters (Brace and Hall, 2001). Professionalized courts serve as agents of social redistribution where possessed with more significant resources. Additionally, elective courts, with their need to appear responsive to public concerns, encourage the placement of civil and tort disputes on state supreme court agendas at the expense of criminal disputes (Brace and Hall, 2001). Atkins and Glick (1976) demonstrate the issue composition of state supreme court dockets is further linked to the social and economic environments of states. Their empirical findings suggest that private litigation is more likely where states are wealthier and rural, while criminal litigation is weakly connected to poorer, more industrialized state environments.

Judicial Behavior, Decision Consensus: Judicial decision making has been conceptualized as responses to the institutional features that constrain or liberate judges, the personal preferences of judges, the environments in which judges serve, and the facts of each case. Recent studies (Brace and Hall, 1990, 1993, 1997; Traut and Emmert, 1998; Langer, 2002) have evaluated how varying institutional arrangements modify the behavior of judges. Dissent behavior, both at the individual and court level, has been connected to a variety of institutional arrangements including those related to judicial elections (Hall, 1987; Brace and Hall, 1993), size of courts (Glick and Pruet, 1986), internal discussion rules (Brace and Hall, 1993), methods of opinion assignment (Hall and Brace, 1989; Brace and Hall, 1990), and the presence of intermediate appellate courts (Glick and Pruet, 1986; Brace and Hall, 1990; Sheldon, 1999). Further, studies of state supreme courts suggest that the ideological cohesion of courts (Brace and Hall, 1993; Boyea, 2007), the seniority of judges (Boyea, 2010), the ideological and political environments of states

(Glick and Pruet, 1986; Brace and Hall, 1993), a judge's electoral security (Hall, 1992), and the features of cases (Brace and Hall, 1993) each affect decisions by judges to join a majority opinion.

Judicial Behavior, Judicial Votes: Studies of state supreme courts portray judges as actors connected to their environments in terms of how they vote. With states providing an opportunity to explore the varying aspects of states in terms of their structural and contextual environments, research has explored the ideological decisions of judges. Within studies of state courts, judicial decisions appear to be influenced by state methods of judicial selection and retention, as well as by the characteristics of judges, the environments of states, and characteristics of cases. Commentary on the role of judicial selection and retention shows that judges and courts make popular choices where elected and confronted with salient cases involving capital crimes (Hall, 1987; Brace and Hall, 1997; Traut and Emmert, 1998; Brace and Boyea, 2008), abortion (Caldarone, Canes-Wrone, and Clark, 2009), and torts (Brace and Hall, 2001). Hall's (1987) investigation of the Louisiana Supreme Court, illustrates how judges modify their votes in death penalty decisions when their preferences do not align with their constituent's views or the general views of the court. To retain their positions on courts, judges avoid alienating voters by standing alone against the preferences of their state or district. Studies also find that the electoral connection between elected state judges and their constituents influences the representational style of judges (Hall, 1992), encourages less support for criminal defendants (Brace and Hall, 1997; Traut and Emmert, 1998; Brace and Boyea, 2008), disrupts the policy consonance between state courts and U.S. Supreme Court decisions (Hoekstra, 2005), and contributes to the more assertive use of judicial review (Langer, 2002). Of the institutional effects on behavior, the independence of judges within salient decisions is reduced where judges must seek re-election to remain in office. Comparatively much less has been written about the constraints faced by judges who rely on the other branches of government to keep their jobs. Also, studies of the constraints faced by trial court judges are relatively rare (but see Huber and Gordon, 2004; Gordon and Huber, 2007). These are two areas where much more study is needed.

Additionally, commentary on alternative influences finds that judicial characteristics ranging from gender and racial background (Steffensmeier and Britt, 2001; Bonneau and Rice, 2009) to judicial attitudes (Brace and Hall, 1997; Benesh and Martinek, 2002; Brace and Boyea, 2008) affect the decisions of judges serving in state supreme courts. Relating to the role of ideology, which has received significant scrutiny within studies of the federal courts (Segal and Spaeth, 2002), Brace and Boyea (2008) demonstrate that liberal ideology among judges contributes to the reversal of lower court death penalty verdicts. Such evidence supports the longstanding view within the larger study of American courts that judges are guided by their personal preferences.

Judicial Policymaking and Judicial Review: Two avenues of judicial policymaking emerge from research on the interaction between the branches of state government: the effect of state courts on state lawmaking and the impact of state courts on the review and invalidation of state laws. Related to state courts as policymakers, Tarr and Porter's (1988) description of the high courts in Alabama, New Jersey, and Ohio depicts branches of state government that are sometimes responsive to one another. Within their investigation, Tarr and Porter describe state supreme courts with increasing yet varied authority during the post-World War II period. In each of the three states examined, public policies were influenced by the preferences of their supreme court through decisions to invalidate legislation or by the assertive stances used by courts to promote social and legal change. Such actions not only affected the character of state policy, they both strengthened and weakened relationships between state high courts and state governments. More recently, Langer and Brace (2005), Roch and Howard (2008) and Wilhelm (2009) have described the responsiveness of state legislatures to the preferences of state courts. Within these studies, state legislatures are depicted as uncertain institutions where the threat of judicial review looms over legislation. For example, Roch and Howard (2008) establish that courts are unwilling to make activist reform decisions in education policy unless positive conditions exist to encourage activity, such as where judges are elected, constitutional provisions protect the status of a state's education system, and where judges are ideologically liberal. For the non-judicial branches of state government, the policy reach of state courts influences their decisions about the initiation and passage of state legislation.

Furthermore, like the U.S. Supreme Court, state supreme courts use their authority to review (and veto) enacted state policy. The exercise of judicial review is exercised primarily where conditions are ripe for independence. Langer (2002) finds that both the placement of cases on a court's docket and decisions to invalidate policy occur where judges are elected and insulated from the other branches of state government. Moreover, judicial review and policy invalidation are both subject to institutional and environmental influences. Langer identifies that where states allow constitutional change through the public initiative process, review and policy invalidation by state supreme courts are more frequent events. Like research on the separation of powers between the U.S. Supreme Court and the U.S. Congress (Eskridge, 1991), where ideological distance between state supreme courts and state legislatures is greater, courts are more willing to exercise their authority.

Conclusion

In this chapter, we provide support for the theoretical importance of state supreme courts. At the broadest level, the work and activities of state supreme courts are extremely important for the settlement of disputes and the continuation of a stable legal and political order. Research summarized throughout this chapter underscores this importance through the expanding scope of studies on both the selection of state supreme court justices and their behavior in office. This growing interest using both single-state studies and more systematic inquiry acknowledges the opportunities that exist when scholars look beyond the federal courts to courts with diverse institutional structures. As such, state supreme courts with widely varying structures allow researchers to make theoretical assumptions about the impact of structural design and political and social context as they relate to courts.

This review also demonstrates the methodological and theoretical advancements made within studies of state supreme courts. Through testing hypotheses about the impact of structural design on the selection and decision processes of judges, research devoted to state high courts has expanded our understanding of not only the role of elections and appointments for selecting judges, but also the function of judges on courts. Due to studies of judicial selection at the state level, for example, we know much about the role of money, voter comprehension, and political competition by directing attention to courts staffed by elections. Likewise, studies of state supreme courts depict an active group of courts that manage a multitude of policies with diverse forms of legal and political pressures.

Where studies of state supreme courts are placed in the broader context of state politics research, the performance of this research sits very well and makes powerful suggestions about the role of state courts for both the states and nation. While these institutions were once overlooked, the growth of this research area has produced unique and methodologically advanced studies that contribute strongly to the field of political science and the subfield of state politics.

In terms of future research, we have suggested several areas where more study is needed. First, much of our knowledge is limited to state supreme courts. While these courts are undoubtedly important, the fact remains that the vast majority of cases do not make it this far up the judicial hierarchy: the workhorses of the state judicial system (just as for the federal system) are the trial courts and trial court judges. While gathering data on these courts and judges is incredibly time-consuming, understanding more about these courts and the judges on them is essential to our understanding of state judicial systems. Second, more research is needed on the constraints faced by judges who do not face the electorate. While much ink has been spilled on the empirical examination of the different methods of judicial selection, judges who face reappointment by either the governor or the legislature have largely been ignored. Third, and finally, it is important for scholars to continue to examine the link between campaign contributions and judicial decision-making. Again, data limitations here are severe. However, given the importance of the topic to perceptions of judicial fairness and legitimacy, this topic is one that scholars simply cannot afford to ignore.

References

Aldrich, John H. 1995. *Why Parties? The Origin and Transformation of Political Parties.* Chicago: The University of Chicago Press.

Atkins, Burton M. and Henry R. Glick. 1976. "Environmental and Structural Variables as Determinants of Issues in State Courts of Last Resort." *American Journal of Political Science* 20 (1): 97–115.

Baum, Lawrence. 1987. "Explaining the Vote in Judicial Elections: The 1984 Ohio Supreme Court Elections." *Western Political Quarterly* 40 (2): 361–371.

Benesh, Sara C. and Wendy L. Martinek. 2002. "State Supreme Court Decision Making in Confession Cases." *Justice System Journal* 23 (1): 109–133.

Bonneau, Chris W. 2001. "The Composition of State Supreme Courts, 2000." *Judicature* 85 (1): 25–31.

Bonneau, Chris W. 2005a. "What Price Justice(s)? Campaign Spending in State Supreme Court Elections." *State Politics and Policy Quarterly* 5 (2): 107–125.

Bonneau, Chris W. 2005b. "Electoral Verdicts: Incumbent Defeats in State Supreme Court Elections." *American Politics Research* 33 (6): 818–841.

Bonneau, Chris W. 2007. "The Effects of Campaign Spending in State Supreme Court Elections." *Political Research Quarterly* 60 (3): 489–499.

Bonneau, Chris W. and Melinda Gann Hall. 2009. *In Defense of Judicial Elections*. New York: Routledge.

Bonneau, Chris W. and Heather Marie Rice. 2009. "Impartial Judges? Race, Institutional Context, and U.S. State Supreme Courts." *State Politics and Policy Quarterly* 9 (4): 381–403.

Boyea, Brent D. 2007. "Linking Judicial Selection to Consensus: An Analysis of Ideological Diversity." *American Politics Research* 35 (5): 643–670.

Boyea, Brent D. 2010. "Does Seniority Matter? The Conditional Influence of State Methods of Judicial Retention." *Social Science Quarterly* 91 (1): 208–226.

Brace, Paul and Brent D. Boyea. 2008. "State Public Opinion, the Death Penalty, and the Practice of Electing Judges." *American Journal of Political Science* 52 (2): 360–372.

Brace, Paul and Brent D. Boyea. 2010. "State Supreme Courts, State Constitutions, and Civil Litigation." *Albany Law Review* 73 (4): 1441–1458.

Brace, Paul and Kellie Sims Butler. 2001. "New Perspectives for the Comparative Study of the Judiciary: The State Supreme Court Project." *Justice System Journal* 22 (3): 243–262.

Brace, Paul and Melinda Gann Hall. 1990. "Neo-Institutionalism and Dissent in State Supreme Courts." *Journal of Politics* 52 (1): 54–70.

Brace, Paul and Melinda Gann Hall. 1993. "Integrated Models of Judicial Dissent." *Journal of Politics* 55 (4): 914–935.

Brace, Paul and Melinda Gann Hall. 1995. "Studying Courts Comparatively: The View from the American States." *Political Research Quarterly* 48 (1): 5–29.

Brace, Paul and Melinda Gann Hall. 1997. "The Interplay of Preferences, Case Facts, Context, and Rules in the Politics of Judicial Choice." *Journal of Politics* 59 (4): 1206–1231.

Brace, Paul and Melinda Gann Hall. 2001. "'Haves' Versus 'Have Nots' in State Supreme Courts: Allocating Docket Space and Wins in Power Asymmetric Cases." *Law and Society Review* 35 (2): 393–417.

Brace, Paul and Melinda Gann Hall. 2005. "Is Judicial Federalism Essential to Democracy? State Courts in the Federal System." In Kermit L. Hall and Kevin T. McGuire, eds., *Institutions of American Democracy: The Judicial Branch*, 174–99. New York: Oxford University Press.

Brace, Paul, Melinda Gann Hall, and Laura Langer. 2001. "Placing State Supreme Courts in State Politics." *State Politics and Policy Quarterly* 1 (1): 81–108.

Brace, Paul, Laura Langer, and Melinda Gann Hall. 2000. "Measuring the Preferences of State Supreme Court Judges." *Journal of Politics* 62(2): 387–413.

Brace, Paul, Jeff Yates, and Brent D. Boyea. 2006. "The Conditional Effects of Ideology and Institutional Structure on Judicial Voting in State Supreme Courts." Paper Presented at the Annual Meeting of the American Political Science Association, August 31–September 3, Philadelphia, PA.

Bratton, Kathleen A. and Rorie L. Spill. 2002. "Existing Diversity and Judicial Selection: The Role of the Appointment Method in Establishing Gender Diversity in State Supreme Courts." *Social Science Quarterly 83* (2): 504–518.

Bratton, Kathleen A. and Rorie L. Spill. 2004. "Moving Up the Judicial Ladder: The Nomination of State Supreme Court Justices to the Federal Courts." *American Politics Research 32* (2): 198–218.

Bureau of Justice Statistics. 2006. *State Court Organization 2004.* Washington, DC: U.S. Department of Justice.

Caldarone, Richard P., Brandice Canes-Wrone, and Tom S. Clark. 2009. "Partisan Labels and Democratic Accountability: An Analysis of State Supreme Court Abortion Decisions." *Journal of Politics 71* (2): 560–573.

Caldeira, Gregory A. 1983. "On the Reputation of State Supreme Courts." *Political Behavior 5* (1):83–108.

Cann, Damon M. 2002. "Campaign Contributions and Judicial Behavior." *American Review of Politics 23* (Fall): 261–274.

Cann, Damon M. 2007. "Justice for Sale? Campaign Contributions and Judicial Decisionmaking." *State Politics and Policy Quarterly 7* (3): 281–297.

Cann, Damon M. and Jeff Yates. 2008. "Homegrown Institutional Legitimacy: Assessing Citizens' Diffuse Support for State Courts." *American Politics Research 36* (2): 297–329.

Canon, Bradley C. 1972. "The Impact of Formal Selection Processes on the Characteristics of Judges—Reconsidered." *Law & Society Review 6* (4): 579–594.

Cheek, Kyle and Anthony Champagne. 2000. "Money in Texas Supreme Court Elections: 1980–1998." *Judicature 84* (1): 20–25.

Curry, Todd A. and Mark Hurwitz. 2010. "Does Accountability Vary: Examining the Tenure of State Supreme Court Justices." Paper Presented at the Annual Meeting of the American Political Science Association, September 2–5, 2010, Washington, DC.

Dubois, Philip L. 1980. *From Ballot to Bench: Judicial Elections and the Quest for Accountability.* Austin: University of Texas Press.

Eskridge, William N, Jr. 1991. "Overriding Supreme Court Statutory Interpretation Decisions." *Yale Law Journal 101* (2):825–841.

Flango, Carol R. and David B. Rottman. 1998. *Appellate Court Procedures.* Williamsburg, VA: National Center for State Courts.

Frederick, Brian and Matthew J. Streb. 2008a. "Women Running for Judge: The Impact of Candidate Sex in State Intermediate Appellate Court Elections." *Social Science Quarterly 89* (4): 937–954.

Frederick, Brian and Matthew J. Streb. 2008b. "Paying the Price for a Seat on the Bench: Campaign Spending in Contested Elections for State Intermediate Courts of Appeals." *State Politics and Policy Quarterly 8* (4): 410–429.

Gibson, James L. 2008a. "Challenges to the Impartiality of State Supreme Courts: Legitimacy Theory and 'New Style' Judicial Campaigns." *American Political Science Review 102* (1): 59–75.

Gibson, James L. 2008b. "Campaigning for the Bench: The Corrosive Effects of Campaign Speech?" *Law & Society Review 42*(4): 899–928.

Gibson, James L. 2009. "'New-Style' Judicial Campaigns and the Legitimacy of State High Courts." *Journal of Politics 71* (4): 1285–1304.

Glick, Henry R. and Craig F. Emmert. 1987. "Selection Systems and Judicial Characteristics: The Recruitment of State Supreme Court Judges." *Judicature 70* (4): 228–235.

Glick, Henry R., and George W. Pruet, Jr. 1986. "Dissent in State Supreme Courts: Patterns and Correlates of Conflict." In Sheldon Goldman and Charles M. Lamb, eds., *Judicial Conflict and Consensus: Behavioral Studies of American Appellate Courts*, 199–214. Lexington, KY: University of Kentucky Press.

Glick, Henry R. and Kenneth N. Vines. 1969. "Law-Making in the State Judiciary: A Comparative Study of the Judicial Role in Four States." *Polity* 2 (2): 142–159.

Gordon, Sanford C. and Gregory A. Huber. 2007. "The Effect of Electoral Competitiveness on Incumbent Behavior." *Quarterly Journal of Political Science* 2 (2): 107–138.

Hall, Melinda Gann. 1987. "Constituent Influence in State Supreme Courts: Conceptual Notes and a Case Study." *Journal of Politics* 49 (4): 1117–1124.

Hall, Melinda Gann. 1992. "Electoral Politics and Strategic Voting in State Supreme Courts." *Journal of Politics* 54 (2): 427–446.

Hall, Melinda Gann. 1995. "Justices as Representatives: Elections and Judicial Politics in the American States." *American Politics Quarterly* 23 (4): 485–503.

Hall, Melinda Gann. 1999. "State Judicial Politics: Rules, Structures, and the Political Game." In Ronald E. Weber and Paul Brace, eds., *American State and Local Politics: Directions for the 21st Century*, 114–38. New York: Chatham House Publishers.

Hall, Melinda Gann. 2001. "State Supreme Courts in American Democracy: Probing the Myths of Judicial Reform." *American Political Science Review* 95 (2): 315–330.

Hall, Melinda Gann. 2007. "Voting in State Supreme Court Elections: Competition and Context as Democratic Incentives." *Journal of Politics* 69 (4): 1147–1159.

Hall, Melinda Gann and Chris W. Bonneau. 2006. "Does Quality Matter? Challengers in State Supreme Court Elections." *American Journal of Political Science* 50 (1): 20–33.

Hall, Melinda Gann and Chris W. Bonneau. 2008. "Mobilizing Interest: The Effects of Money on Citizen Participation in State Supreme Court Elections." *American Journal of Political Science* 52 (3): 457–470.

Hall, Melinda Gann and Paul Brace. 1989. "Order in the Courts: A Neo-Institutional Approach to Judicial Consensus." *Western Political Quarterly* 42 (3): 391–407.

Hall, Melinda Gann and Paul Brace. 1992. "Toward an Integrated Model of Judicial Voting Behavior." *American Politics Quarterly* 20 (2): 147–168.

Hanssen, F. Andrew. 1999. "The Effect of Judicial Institutions on Uncertainty and the Rate of Litigation: The Election versus Appointment of State Judges." *Journal of Legal Studies* 28 (1): 205–232.

Hoekstra, Valerie. 2005. "Competing Constraints: State Court Responses to Supreme Court Decisions and Legislation on Wages and Hours." *Political Research Quarterly* 58 (2): 317–328.

Huber, Gregory A. and Sanford C. Gordon. 2004. "Accountability and Coercion: Is Justice Blind When It Runs For Office?" *American Journal of Political Science* 48 (2): 247–263.

Hurwitz, Mark A. and Drew Noble Lanier. 2001. "Women and Minorities on State and Federal Appellate Benches, 1985 and 1999." *Judicature* 85 (2): 84–92.

Hurwitz, Mark A. and Drew Noble Lanier. 2003. "Explaining Judicial Diversity: The Differential Ability of Women and Minorities to Attain Seats on State Supreme and Appellate Courts." *State Politics and Policy Quarterly* 3 (4): 329–352.

Hurwitz, Mark A. and Drew Noble Lanier. 2008. "Diversity in State and Federal Appellate Courts: Change and Continuity across 20 Years." *Justice System Journal* 29 (1): 47–70.

Kagan, Robert A., Bliss Cartwright, Lawrence M. Friedman, and Stanton Wheeler. 1977. "The Business of State Supreme Courts, 1870–1970." *Stanford Law Review* 30 (1): 121–156.

Klein, David and Lawrence A. Baum. 2001. "Ballot Information and Voting Decisions in Judicial Elections." *Political Research Quarterly* 54 (4): 709–728.

Kritzer, Herbert M., Paul Brace, Melinda Gann Hall and Brent D. Boyea. 2007. "The Business of State Supreme Courts, Revisited." *Journal of Empirical Legal Studies* 4(2): 427–439.

Langer, Laura. 2002. *Judicial Review in State Supreme Courts: A Comparative Study.* Albany: State University of New York Press.

Langer, Laura, and Paul Brace. 2005. "The Preemptive Power of State Supreme Courts: Adoption of Abortion and Death Penalty Legislation." *The Policy Studies Journal* 33 (3): 317–340.

Langer, Laura and Teena Wilhelm. 2005. "The Ideology of State Supreme Court Chief Justices." *Judicature* 89 (2): 78–86.

McCall, Madhavi. 2003. "The Politics of Judicial Elections: The Influence of Campaign Contributions on the Voting Patterns of Texas Supreme Court Justices, 1994–1997." *Politics & Policy* 31 (2): 314–343.

Meador, Daniel John. 2002. *American Courts.* 2nd ed. St. Paul, MN: West Group.

National Center for State Courts. 2010. *Examining the Work of State Courts: An Analysis of 2008 State Court Caseloads.* Williamsburg, VA: National Center of State Courts.

Roch, Christine H. and Robert M. Howard. 2008. "State Policy Innovation in Perspective: Courts, Legislatures, and Education Finance Reform." *Political Research Quarterly* 61 (2): 333–344.

Segal, Jeffrey A. and Harold J. Spaeth. 2002. *The Supreme Court and the Attitudinal Model Revisited.* New York: Cambridge University Press.

Sheldon, Charles H. 1999. "The Incidence and Structure of Dissensus on a State Supreme Court." In Cornell W. Clayton and Howard Gillman, eds., *Supreme Court Decision-Making: New Institutionalist Approaches*, 115–34. Chicago: The University of Chicago Press.

Sheldon, Charles H. and Linda S. Maule. 1997. *Choosing Justice: The Recruitment of State and Federal Judges.* Pullman, WA: Washington State University Press.

Songer, Donald R. and Kelley A. Crews-Meyer. 2000. "Does Judge Gender Matter? Decision Making in State Supreme Courts." *Social Science Quarterly* 81 (3): 750–762.

Songer, Donald R. and Susan J. Tabrizi. 1999. "The Religious Right in Court: The Decision Making of Christian Evangelicals in State Supreme Courts." *Journal of Politics* 61 (2): 507–526.

Squire, Peverill. 2008. "Measuring the Professionalization of U.S. State Courts of Last Resort." *State Politics and Policy Quarterly* 8 (3): 223–238.

Steffensmeier, Darrell and Chester L. Britt. 2001. "Judges' Race and Judicial Decision Making: Do Black Judges Sentence Differently?" *Social Science Quarterly* 82 (4): 749–764.

Streb, Matthew J. and Brian Frederick. 2009. "Conditions for Competition in Low-Information Judicial Elections: The Case of Intermediate Appellate Court Elections." *Political Research Quarterly* 62 (3): 523–537.

Streb, Matthew J., Brian Frederick, and Casey LaFrance. 2007. "Contestation, Competition, and the Potential for Accountability in Intermediate Appellate Court Elections." *Judicature* 91 (2): 70–78.

Streb, Matthew J., Brian Frederick, and Casey LaFrance. 2009. "Voter Roll-Off in a Low Information Context: Evidence from Intermediate Appellate Court Elections." *American Politics Research* 37 (4): 644–669.

Tarr, G. Alan and Mary Cornelia Aldis Porter. 1988. *State Supreme Courts in State and Nation.* New Haven, CT: Yale University Press.

Traut, Carol Ann and Craig F. Emmert. 1998. "Expanding the Integrated Model of Judicial Decision Making: The California Justices and Capital Punishment." *Journal of Politics* 60 (4): 1166–1180.

Wilhelm, Teena. 2009. "Strange Bedfellows: The Policy Consequences of Legislative Judicial Relations in the American States." *American Politics Research* 37 (1): 3–29.

CHAPTER 16

STATE BUREAUCRACY

Policy Delegation, Comparative Institutional Capacity, and Administrative Politics in the American States

GEORGE A. KRAUSE AND NEAL D. WOODS

BUREAUCRATIC agencies play a vital role in the governance of the American states. For many citizens these agencies are the "face of government" due to their role in providing public services such as unemployment benefits, environmental conservation, college education, and police protection. Less obviously, perhaps, they often also play a significant role a role in determining the content of public policy, both through the discretion afforded them in interpreting their legislative mandates and through the part they play, both formally and informally, in determining important features of these mandates to begin with.

State agencies reflect what state governments do (Dresang and Gosling, 1989). Thus, the importance of state agencies in the U.S. system of government is proportional to the policy activism of state governments. While state governments have probably never been the lethargic backwaters that some have portrayed them as (Teaford, 2002), their importance as policymakers has increased dramatically over the latter half of the 20th century. During this period a "silent revolution" took place in the states, as large numbers of state governments simultaneously adopted reforms that increased policymaking capacity in all three branches of government and took on expanded roles in domestic public policymaking (Walker, 1995). This increased policy activism is reflected in a significant growth in the overall size of state governments. A common measure of the size of government is total state expenditure as a share of total state personal income. By this indicator, the average size of the states' public sectors, which was just over four percent of state personal income at the end of World War II, had more than tripled to over 14 percent by 2000 (Garand and Baudoin, 2004).

This expansion in the policy roles of state governments has necessitated the creation of new agencies to fulfill new functions. The earliest agencies had responsibilities related to general, well recognized state needs—in areas such as agriculture, education,and highways. As new problems or needs were recognized, succeeding generations of agencies emerged to address issues such as civil rights, occupational safety, environmental protection, and drug and alcohol abuse (Jenks and Wright, 1993).

Besides serving the needs of their constituents, public agencies in the American states play a critical role as an institutional fulcrum in American federalism, coordinating policy implementation efforts between U.S. national and local governments. This intermediary function has grown through time as federal governments have devolved policymaking authority to state governments, as well as the resources necessary to undertake such increased policy responsibilities. The national government has undertaken a variety of federalism initiatives over the postwar period, ranging from the Creative Federalism of Lyndon Johnson to the New Federalism initiatives of Richard Nixon and Ronald Reagan, during which program responsibilities were pushed to the states (Walker, 1995; Conlan, 1998). Cutting across these initiatives has been an increased state reliance on federal grants-in-aid; the number of federal aid programs increased from 40 in 1946 to over 600 in 2008 and the amounts allocated rose from $7 billion to $454 billion over the same period (Milakovich and Gordon, 2010). The combination of joint responsibility for implementing programs under the mantle of cooperative federalism and joint funding under the burgeoning number of federal grant programs has created an expansive network of connections between state agencies and their national counterparts, and highlights the role of state agencies as intermediaries in the U.S. federal system (Bowling and Wright, 1998).

Current research on bureaucratic politics in the American states has made great strides in understanding how state government agencies administer policies (Brudney and Hebert, 1987; Elling, 1999), as well as how they function within the American federal system (Chubb, 1985; Gormley, 1992; Wood, 1992; Hedge and Schicchitano, 1994; Keiser, 2001; Cho et al., 2004; Nicholson-Crotty, 2004; Collins and Gerber, 2006; Cline, 2010). This body of research has focused predominantly on applying theories of U.S. national politics to understanding bureaucratic policymaking in the American states (Potoski, 1999; Teske, 2004; Kim and Gerber, 2005; Poggione and Reenock, 2009). We thus know a good deal about the effect of partisan control of electoral institutions, partisan gridlock, budgetary resources, public opinion, and institutional pressures from other governmental levels on bureaucratic policymaking.

However, this focus largely ignores the capacity of governmental institutions, which is often critical for understanding political outcomes in the American states. In their path-breaking work on comparative legislative delegation, John Huber and Charles Shipan (2002: 79) aptly note that "In the United States, for example, there is a great deal of difference in legislative capacity across state legislatures, with some legislatures having very low levels and others having very high levels of capacity." This claim of varying institutional capacity also contains merit for both governors and public bureaucracies. After all, governors' capacity to influence the bureaucracy depends upon the formal and informal powers of the office (e.g. Abney and Lauth, 1983; Hebert, Brudney, and Wright, 1983; Sigelman and Dometrius, 1988; Dometrius, 2002; Beyle, 2004; Woods and Baranowski, 2007). Moreover, state bureaucracies' influence in the policymaking process systematically varies across states (Elling, 1992; Barrilleaux, 1999).

In this essay, we propose a comparative-institutional theoretical framework for analyzing policy delegation in the American states. The novel aspect of this theoretical framework is centered on a comparative analysis of the institutional capacities possessed by the legislature, chief executive (governor), and bureaucracy. This theoretical framework is undergirded by an assumption that institutions seek to maximize administrative policy control, subject to their relative endowments of institutional capacity. That is, although both partisan and ideological preferences are critical for determining policy outcomes, they are either constrained or empowered by institutions' capacity for policymaking.

Bureaucratic politics research focused at the U.S. national level has generally assumed that institutional capacity is exogenously fixed by either constitutional arrangements or legislative statutes. However, in the American states, institutional capacity varies in systematic ways both between and within states. Our approach encourages students of state bureaucracy to place greater emphasis on fully exploiting the leverage provided by comparative analysis of the American states. Research in cross-national comparative politics, we argue, remains an under-utilized resource that can provide a useful reservoir of theory that may be applied to better understand how state institutions affect policy outcomes.

The outline of this essay is as follows. The next section presents a discussion of what is known from the current literature on policy delegation and political control of the bureaucracy. The third section explains why a focus on comparative institutional capacity is critical for understanding policy outcomes, and proceeds to define legislative capacity, gubernatorial capacity, and bureaucratic capacity over policy administration. A comparative institutional capacity theoretical framework for understanding policy delegation in the American states is advanced in the fourth section. This theoretical framework is centered on "state capacity" in terms of absolute levels across all institutions, as well as (im)balances that occur in relative terms. The essay concludes with some prescriptions for how this nascent theoretical framework can be applied to the study of comparative state bureaucracy research in other areas beyond policy delegation.

DOES THE DELEGATION LOGIC OF U.S. NATIONAL INSTITUTIONS DIRECTLY APPLY TO THE AMERICAN STATES?

The empirical literature on public bureaucracy in the American states is a rather large, heterogeneous, mass of studies. This literature grows out of separate research traditions

in political science, public administration, and to a lesser extent sociology and economics. Within political science, research tends to focus on broad questions about the role
of the bureaucracy in the larger political system (*bureaucratic politics*). In general, the
bureaucratic politics literature can be characterized as emphasizing three core problems
confronting the administrative state in democratic settings. First, *delegation* research
focuses on the conditions under which politicians delegate policymaking authority to
state governmental agencies. Second, *bureaucratic compliance* research analyzes the
conditions that produce greater agency responsiveness to the preferences of elected officials or the mass public. Finally, *federalism* research examines state bureaucracies' role
in the federal system, especially the effect of intergovernmental policy implementation
on issues of bureaucratic responsiveness. These studies generally provide empirical tests
of theoretical propositions derived from the literature on bureaucratic politics at the
U.S. national level and, to a lesser extent, formal models of bureaucratic behavior developed with the U.S. national context in mind. In this essay, our attention is restricted to
the extant literature on policy delegation. Yet the logic and insights advanced in this
essay can be easily extended and modified to address other areas of administrative politics, including issues of bureaucratic compliance and federalism.

The Logic of Delegation in U.S. National and State Politics

The delegation of policymaking authority to government agencies is a defining feature
of modern industrial societies. This fact has sparked concern in some quarters over
whether government agencies lie outside the realm of democratic accountability (e.g.
Lowi, 1979). In delegating this authority, however, political officials do not necessarily
abdicate all control over the direction of public policy. Nonetheless, political officials
retain several mechanisms which may be employed ex post to direct agency behavior,
such as budgets, personnel appointments, administrative reorganizations, and oversight
hearings (Wood and Waterman, 1994). Moreover, there may be ways in which political
officials can affect the substance of agency policymaking ex ante, through the design of
agency structure and process (McCubbins et al., 1987, 1989; Moe, 1989, 1990).

The political science literature on national bureaucracy, both theoretical and empirical, has focused on the relationship of bureaucracy to external political actors in general
and the effectiveness of mechanisms of ex post and ex ante political control specifically.
Research on public bureaucracy in the American states has in many ways paralleled this
national level literature. On a conceptual level, this literature generally views Congress
as the principal, that is, the "supplier" of policy authority, and the executive branch as the
agent, the "recipient" of this authority (but see Wilson, 1989; Carpenter, 2001; Krause,
2003, for important exceptions).

By delegating authority to the executive branch through vague legislation, legislatures may gain technical expertise but give up some policy control in the process
(Bawn, 1995). From the legislature's perspective, this loss of control is more problematic
under circumstances where the governor has preferences that diverge from those of the

legislative branch. Thus, policy delegation may be greater when the policy preferences of the executive and legislative branches' converge. In an empirical test of this relationship, Huber and Shipan (2002) find that the amount of policy authority delegated to state agencies for designing Medicaid managed care reforms largely depends in predictable ways on the amount of preference divergence between the governor and the legislature. This relationship is mediated, however, by institutional context: highly institutionalized legislatures are less likely to delegate policy authority than their less institutionalized brethren. The costs of not exploiting bureaucratic expertise for low capacity legislatures may outweigh any benefits of maintaining statutory control, even in situations where the governor's policy preferences are substantially different from those of the legislature. This research illustrates the value of using states as laboratories for institutional comparison, since it is difficult to test propositions regarding differential legislative capacity at the national level, where legislative capacity is effectively fixed.

Because there is little variation in institutional capacity, delegation research applied to U.S. national policymaking institutions instead focuses on the temporal dynamics associated with the delegation dilemma. Policies designed today may be overturned by future political coalitions whose policy preferences differ from the current political coalition, a process sometimes termed coalitional drift. One potential solution to the threat of coalitional drift lies in insulating the implementing agency from external political interference, thus protecting policy decisions from potential political opponents, a form of ex ante political control.

Although developed with reference to specific national level bureaucracies, a relatively large portion of the empirical literature on ex ante political control has focused on the state level. Most of this research looks at the question of whether greater political uncertainty leads to greater bureaucratic insulation from external political interference. Some state-level studies have shown that political uncertainty leads legislators to insulate the bureaucracy from external influence by elected officials, in order to guard their policies from future political interference. This may be achieved through political insulation granted to agency heads (Volden, 2002a), or the adoption of state administrative procedure acts (De Figueiredo and Vanden Bergh, 2004). Yet, the possibility of ex ante political control through agency design remains controversial. The theoretical underpinnings of these arguments have been challenged (Spence, 1997, 1999; Pierson, 2000), and empirical evidence for the existence of such control is mixed (e.g. Potoski, 1999). Using data from a survey of state legislators, Reenock and Poggione (2004) find little support for the notion that legislators use agency design as a tactic of ongoing legislative influence over the bureaucracy. Thus, scholarly opinion remains split on the possibility of legislators making effective use of ex ante mechanisms of political control.

In delegating policy tasks to agencies, elected political officials lose some control over policy direction. As a consequence, agency policy choices may not reflect the preferences of their politician supervisors, a situation commonly referred to as *bureaucratic drift*. Political officials are thus faced with another tradeoff: in taking steps to reduce the possibility of coalitional drift by delegating tasks to agencies, they increase the threat of bureaucratic drift (Horn and Shepsle, 1989). Legislators may reduce the probability of bureaucratic drift by delegating less policy authority to agencies. This strategy requires the expenditure of time and effort; thus a rational political principal is likely to use it only when considering also the availability of effective ex post mechanisms of control. Research into the possible substitution between ex ante and ex post mechanisms of political control is in its infancy. Empirical evidence suggests that legislators' preferences for direct intervention in bureaucracies and their preferences for statutory intervention are not substitutes (Poggione and Reenock, 2009). Rather, members who are concerned about bureaucratic drift prefer direct intervention for more permeable agencies, but this effect diminishes as agencies become more insulated. The level of permeability has no effect on legislators' preferences for statutory intervention. A recent analytical model predicts that statutory control should be greater only when the legislature's preferences are sufficiently distinct from the executive's and when non-statutory controls in that state are neither too high nor too low (McGrath, 2010). Further state-level research holds great promise for investigating issues such as these due to the significant variation in powers of ex post political control across the states.

The question of exactly what effects institutional design features have on agency performance remains an open one. A significant structural design issue facing legislators is whether to delegate policy to either an executive branch agency or an independent commission. Several state-level studies indicate that this choice is a consequential one: the choice of commission, the mechanisms by which commissioners are selected, and their professionalism and resources all appear to influence regulatory decisions in a variety of policy areas (Berry, 1979; Teske, 1991, 2004). Moreover, the results of Craig Volden's (2002b) analytical model suggest that this element of agency structure affects the amount of discretion afforded administrators, with executive agencies being delegated greater discretionary authority under conditions of unified government, while independent agencies are afforded more discretion under divided government. In addition to agency structure, another potentially important design feature is the imposition of procedural requirements on agency decision makers. Studies have found that policy analysis procedures may limit agency discretion (Potoski, 2002) as well as increase the amount of influence the legislature is reported as having on agency activities (Potoski and Woods, 2001), and that the amount of discretion that street-level administrators possess affects the nature of interest group involvement and influence (Reenock and Gerber, 2008).

The Advantages and Disadvantages of the Federal-Based Approach

Applying and testing theories of bureaucracy developed in the U.S. national context to state bureaucracies has undoubtedly contributed to our knowledge of bureaucracy. This is for the same reason that states are such a fertile ground for theory testing generally: there is generally significant variation in theoretically important variables across states, such as gubernatorial powers, legislative capacity, statutory and constitutional provisions, and agency insulation. This institutional variation across states can yield greater analytical leverage in testing theory than is often available at the national level.

Numerous studies have been used this variation to their advantage, leading to substantial advances in our understanding of bureaucratic dynamics.

But the approach of simply taking theories developed at the national level and empirically testing them using the states has inherent limitations. Such an approach precludes investigation into institutional features that predominate at the state level, but not the national. In areas beyond public bureaucracy, the empirical literature on the American states has provided a much richer, more complete understanding of political and policy dynamics. No mechanisms for direct democracy exist at the national level in the U.S. for instance, but there is a rich literature that explores the impact of direct democracy in the states (for an overview consult Lupia and Matsusaka, 2004). Research on the mass public's influence over public bureaucracy lags behind in this respect (but see Spence 2003, Gerber, Lupia, and McCubbins, 2004, for notable exceptions), which has precluded the development of an organic theory of bureaucratic politics in the American states.

Taking key differences in institutional features into account promises advances in our understanding of legislative delegation; consider, for instance, the legislative veto, which has been ruled unconstitutional for the national government (*INS v. Chadha*) but exists in many states. This mechanism has been found to interact in important ways with aspects of policy delegation. Huber and Shipan (2002) find that the availability of the legislative veto as a mechanism of ex post control increases the amount of statutory discretion that policymakers are willing to delegate to state administrative agencies. More recently, Poggione and Reenock (2009) similarly find that the availability of a legislative veto changes legislators' strategies of bureaucratic control.

More generally, there is substantial variation across state bureaucratic and gubernatorial institutions, in addition to legislatures, in the tools that they have to effectively engage in policy administration. The extant literature's focus on testing theory developed at the national level has largely precluded assessing how this variation may impact the conclusions drawn from national-level studies. Moreover, state politics scholars have largely ignored an important source of theory about bureaucracy from the cross-national comparative literature (Weissert, 2011). In the next section, we urge scholars to redirect their focus away from U.S. national politics towards a truly comparative institutional focus by assessing how relative capacity differences among the legislature, governor, and bureaucracy, can shape how policy preferences are translated into administrative policymaking in the American states.

INSTITUTIONAL CAPACITY AND THE STUDY OF PUBLIC BUREAUCRACY IN THE AMERICAN STATES

Somewhat interestingly, the extant literature examining bureaucratic politics in the American states rarely draws upon the rich variation in the institutions of governance. With few exceptions (e.g., Huber, Shipan, and Pfahler, 2001; Huber and Shipan, 2002), research on comparative bureaucracy in the American states has relied on applying the logic of U.S. federal governance to the subnational level. This is hardly surprising; given that the American states are constituent units in the U.S. federal system. Moreover, adapting theories that were initially formulated to explain politics at the national level makes considerable sense given the many institutional features shared by U.S. federal and state governments—separation of powers, a unitary elected chief executive, bicameralism [save Nebraska], two major political parties resulting from single member districts, and so on. It is thus understandable that the American states are often treated as versions of the national government in miniature. While advantages exist for drawing upon theories of U.S. national politics to enhance our understanding of bureaucratic politics in the American states, the logic emanating from the approach largely confines scholarship to puzzles of a "temporal" dimension—e.g. partisan control, divided party government, the effect of particular rules applied in a given state, the sequence of politically appointed agency heads, and budgetary change through time.

Theories of bureaucratic politics emanating from the U.S. national government, however, often fail to consider important differences in structural features that are relatively fixed at the national level. In contrast, comparative, cross-national research on public bureaucracies highlights the considerable heterogeneity in administrative systems that exist across nations. For example, southern European nations such as Italy, Greece, Portugal, and Spain possess highly politicized civil service systems that create a special class of patronage that hinders the development of bureaucratic expertise and reputations for competent administration (Sotiropoulos, 2004). Further, the lack of a professionalized public bureaucracy has tangible implications ranging from stifling economic growth (Evans and Rauch, 1999) to increasing political corruption (Golden, 2003).

More generally, the cross-national comparative politics literature highlights the importance of differences involving institutional capacity. Institutional capacity is defined here as the potential capabilities of legislative, executive, and bureaucratic institutions to make and implement policy, net of partisan and ideological policy preferences. Put another way, institutional capacity can be thought of as the amount of authority ascribed to institutions via constitutional, statutory, and external means. Therefore, institutional capacity provides the parameters by which governmental institutions can convey their policy preferences into actual policymaking and administration. Analyzing the comparative institutional capacity of legislatures, governors, and public bureaucracy in the American states is especially salient given the considerable variations involving constitutional powers, institutional powers, and "state" powers centered on the role of bureaucracy in the governmental system.

This article advances a theoretical framework for analyzing bureaucratic politics in the American states by focusing on comparative institutional capacity. Viewed in this manner, preferences (either of a partisan or ideological nature) become factors that are governed by the underlying relationship between institutional capacity and bureaucratic policymaking in the American states. In this way, the approach advocated here has considerably more in common with bureaucratic politics in cross-national political contexts than it does with the U.S. federal government. This is because the institutional capacities of governmental institutions systematically vary in cross-national settings.

One aspect of institutional capacity is grounded in the role of constitutions, which serve to define both the potential and limits of institutional authority—i.e., "the parameters of governance." For instance, political economists have highlighted the mechanisms contained in constitutions that are important for studying the allocation of formal powers across governmental institutions (Persson and Tabellini, 2003; Berkowitz and Clay, 2012). Another aspect of institutional capacity is affected by legal-statutory variations that are critical for assessing the role bureaucracies play in policymaking (e.g., McNollGast, 1987, 1989; Epstein and O'Halloran, 1999; Huber and Shipan, 2002). If policymaking is merely the product of the intersection between "*preferences*" and "*institutions*" (Plott, 1991), then it naturally follows that the interaction between institutional capacities' and actors' policy preferences will produce variable bureaucratic policy outputs and resulting outcomes. A final component of institutional capacity rests with the extent to which structural limitations constrain institutions from exercising their authority. One should anticipate that these capacities will not merely vary across agencies by policy tasks (Rourke, 1984), agency structure (Seidman and Gilmour, 1986), or clientele support (Carpenter, 2001) as is commonly ascribed at the U.S. federal government level. Rather, the performance of public agencies executing the same policy tasks, for example, may systematically vary across states simply due to variations in bureaucratic capacity.

States provide advantages for developing and testing a comparative institutional capacity theory of bureaucratic politics relative to nations, due to the fact that the macro-structural features of the American states are effectively fixed. In contrast to cross-national research, which often must make comparisons across widely different constitutional systems, electoral institutions, and federalism structures, all of the American states operate under the same general constitutional framework (separation of powers system), electoral institutions (single-member districts, majority rule), and national sovereignty (all states are members of the U.S. federal system). Studying the American state governments thus enables scholars to more clearly isolate differences arising from institutional capacity independent of these broader macro-structural differences that may confound causal inferences. Thus, applying theories of institutional capacity can have great predictive import for understanding not only which institution controls the bureaucracy, but also address normative issues associated with both professionalism and governance quality in the American states.

Legislative Capacity

According to Huber and Shipan (2002: 79), legislative capacity can be defined as "the costs to politicians of *drafting* detailed legislation." We broaden this definition to include the legislature's capacity to engage in both formal and latent oversight activities as well. Thus, legislative capacity is inversely related to *both* the costliness of drafting detailed legislation and performing oversight-based monitoring. Ceteris paribus, legislatures possessing high levels of institutional capacity will be less inclined to delegate policymaking authority to the executive branch since they have sufficient expertise and resources to write specific legislative statutes that explain what they want done and how it should be executed. Moreover, high capacity legislatures are also better equipped to perform effective monitoring of government agencies through their oversight activities. As a consequence of both these factors, states possessing high capacity legislatures are in a better position to influence the content of bureaucratic policymaking if they so desire.

Legislative capacity is closely related to the concept of legislative professionalism, "the capacity of legislatures to generate and digest information in the policy process" (Squire, 2007: 211). Empirically, legislative professionalism indices generally include measures of legislative session length, staff resources, and legislator compensation (Mooney, 1994; Squire, 2007), although in some empirical studies these are reduced to a single measure of compensation (e.g. Huber, Shipan, and Pfahler, 2001; Huber and Shipan, 2002; Shipan and Volden, 2006). While compensation captures increased incentives for attracting qualified individuals for legislative careers (e.g. Maestas, 2000; Squire, 2007), it is the institutional resources that allow legislators to engage in activities that influence bureaucratic behavior that are of greater analytic utility.[1] These resources include legislative staff, which is primarily responsible for the labor effort in conducting legislative oversight activities (e.g. Grossback and Peterson, 2004), and session length, which allows the legislature to serve as a full time counterweight to the executive branch (Woods and Baranowski, 2006). Some state legislatures also have resources that more specifically allow them to direct bureaucratic behavior, including rule review powers (Ethridge, 1981; Woods, 2004; Gerber, Maestas, and Dometrius, 2005; Poggione and Reenock, 2009), sunset laws (Clingemayer, 1991; Clingemayer and West, 1992), and legislative program evaluation offices (Boerner, 2002; Woods and Baranowski, 2007).

In addition to the resources that legislators have at their disposal to engage in bureaucratic oversight, other factors may affect its capacity to influence bureaucratic behavior. High legislative turnover can undermine legislative capacity; a "revolving door" among its members may reduce the institutional stability, memory, and experience necessary to effectively draft detailed legislation and subsequently monitor agency performance. Legislatures with high degrees of party competition are more likely to experience greater member turnover than those which are dominated by one party (such as the Republican party in South Carolina or the Democratic party in Massachusetts). Legislative term limits may also inhibit institutional continuity by forcing skilled legislators to exit office thus reducing a critical source of institutional memory and legislative expertise in dealing with the bureaucracy.[2] Term limits, for instance, have been found to substantially increase the number of legislators who say that administrative reports are too confusing or that they do not know where to get the information they need (LeRoux et al., 2002), a trend suggesting a decline in legislator expertise in dealing with the bureaucracy in term limited legislatures.

Executive (Gubernatorial) Capacity

Executive (Gubernatorial) capacity refers to how the application of governors' formal powers affects their ability to shape policy administration. Typically, more powerful governors are viewed as being more effective for implementing their policy agenda (e.g. Sigelman and Dometrius, 1988; Ferguson, 2003). Executive capacity in the realm of bureaucratic politics can be defined as containing five components. First, *organizational powers* constitute a governor's capacity to organize the bureaucracy. This may include the extent to which governors have unbridled unitary executive authority powers, how many agencies they are responsible for (i.e. span of control), and their ability to reorganize state government agencies with as little interference as possible from other state-level institutions (Beyle, 2004; Beyle and Ferguson, 2008). Powerful governors exhibit certain common characteristics: they share executive authority with few other elected executives, possess a manageable administrative terrain with a small number of agencies and commissions/boards, and possess authority to reorganize executive branch agencies without legislative approval.

Second, *budget powers* represent the ability of governors to control the provision of bureaucratic resources. These resources can be used for either accentuating or undermining an agency's mission based on the governors' policy preferences, as well as for targeting specific policy and administrative priorities within state agencies. Beyle's (2004) definition of gubernatorial budget powers relies on the extent to which governors can both formulate and adopt budget proposals with as little legislative interference as possible. Another important element of executive budgetary influence pertains to the governor's authority to control the allotment of funds to agencies after they have been appropriated by the legislature (Woods, 2003).

Third, *appointment* powers provide the governor with a formal mechanism for staffing the top-levels of state executive agencies. The importance of appointment powers in directing bureaucratic behavior has been extensively documented in past studies (Dometrius, 1979; Abney and Lauth, 1983; Elling, 1992; Dometrius, 2002). Governors with fewer potential veto players in the appointment process possess the greatest control over staffing bureaucratic leaders (Beyle, 2004; Beyle and Ferguson, 2009).

Fourth, *tenure potential* represents governors' duration in office without facing re-election (i.e. term length) and doing so in a repeated manner (i.e. the absence of term limits) (see Beyle, 2004, 2009). In turn, governors with strong tenure potential can more effectively resolve credible commitment problems with other institutions since they are not easily deposed from office. More specifically, governors that are able to serve lengthier terms are more likely to deal effectively with the bureaucracy since they have more time to learn on the job. Similarly, a governor who is eligible to seek re-election an unlimited number of times will be a more formidable political actor than one who must exit office due to term limit restrictions.

Finally, a set of specific *oversight tools are* designed to give the governor greater control of the bureaucracy. Some of these tools are designed to provide governors with institutionalized access to information and evaluation of bureaucratic performance in the form of policy analysis studies, financial and compliance audits, and sunset reviews (Boerner, 2002). Similar to the increasing role of the Office of Management and Budget in evaluating proposed federal agency rules (Cooper and West, 1988), executive review of agency regulations, which is typically housed in the state budget office, may be conducted using a variety of economic analysis techniques, including cost-benefit analysis, economic impact analysis, or regulatory analysis (Hahn, 2000). Moreover, many states have created program evaluation offices to provide ongoing analysis and oversight of government functions. In conjunction with these reviews governors in many states been granted the authority to modify, or even strike down administrative rules before they go into effect (Grady and Simon, 2002). Both the information provided through program evaluation and policy analysis offices and gubernatorial rule review authority have been found to provide governors with increased influence on agency rulemaking (Woods, 2004; Woods and Baranowski, 2007).

Bureaucratic Capacity

Bureaucratic capacity affords public administrators the ability to effectively administer governments' public policies. Assessing bureaucratic capacity requires one to ask "To what extent does the bureaucracy have the requisite resources, skill, and autonomy to effectively administer public policies?" Bureaucracies that exhibit high capacity tend to adapt and learn at a faster rate than those that exhibit low capacity (Downs, 1967; Simon, 1976; Stinchcombe, 1990). Conversely, low levels of bureaucratic capacity contain a dual reinforcing effect for muting the exercise of bureaucratic authority. Low bureaucratic capacity makes it easier for politicians to control policy administration since agencies do not have sufficient autonomy to establish an independent source of power through either clientele support (e.g., Rourke, 1984; Wilson, 1989; Carpenter, 2001) or by establishing a favorable organizational reputation (e.g., Krause and Douglas, 2006; Krause and Corder, 2007; Carpenter, 2010; Carpenter and Krause, 2012). Further, politicians will also be less willing to vest discretionary policymaking authority to "low capacity" public agencies possessing similar preferences since politicians' desire for competent policy administration (and obtaining proper electoral credit for policies) outweighs their desire to delegate to an "easy to control" bureaucracy (Huber and McCarty, 2004). Therefore, high levels of bureaucratic capacity are not only necessary for administrative institutions having an independent voice in governance, but is also requisite for the effective exercise of discretionary authority granted to them by political institutions.

Bureaucratic capacity can be defined on two distinct dimensions: Resources and Structure-Process. *Bureaucratic Resources* provide public agencies with the requisite budgetary, clientele, and reputational resources to be equipped to effectively perform administrative tasks. According to resource dependence theory, budgetary resources are critical since they provide the lifeblood to ensure that agencies are adequately funded to perform administrative tasks (Pfeffer and Salancik, 1978). Clientele support from either organized interests or relevant professional associations also serves as a vital institutional resource by affording public agencies with an external buffer from politicians who seek to limit the policy influence of bureaucrats (Rourke, 1984; Wilson, 1989). In turn, clientele support not only serves to insulate bureaucratic agencies from political control, but it can also empower them as an independent institution within governmental systems. Professional associations and networks also play a vital role in cultivating bureaucratic autonomy by externally reinforcing the policy expertise displayed by government agencies (Carpenter, 2001). This is because public agencies possess strong incentives to cultivate an organizational reputation for performing in a competent and professional manner in order to attain greater autonomy on their own accord, as well as obtaining greater policy discretion from their political principals.

Bureaucratic Structures-Processes provide public agencies with the formal organizational context in which they perform their policy and administrative functions. Along this particular dimension, bureaucratic capacity is enhanced in three distinct ways. First, structures which devolve executive power from a unitary elected chief executive to multiple elected executives heading individual departments diffuse authority across several independently elected executive officials (Bowman, Woods, and Stark, 2010). Second, states with the strongest personnel systems that advocate merit-based recruitment and promotion (via civil service procedures), as well as good pay (relative to comparable private sector compensation), will reflect stronger bureaucratic capacity. This is because public agencies that select, reward, and retain members based on their policy expertise will enhance the administrative capacity of the American states. For example, over the past few decades American states have experienced a sharp trend towards "deregulating" their civil service systems (e.g., Coggburn, 2001). This pattern has reflected a general trend toward decentralizing state personnel functions by declassifying state agency personnel, placing restrictions on state employees' rights during the grievance process, and fortifying executive control over personnel selection systems for purposes of recruiting, rewarding, and retaining loyalists to the governor (Hays and Sowa, 2006).

Finally, states that adopt appropriate organizational routines and procedures will be most capable of managing the government programs they are charged with administering. For example, the Government Performance Project (GPP) initiated at Syracuse University (Barrett and Greene, 2001) and currently housed at the Pew Center for the States, seeks to measure the management capacity of state governments based largely upon measuring the "best practices" of state governments that relate to criteria involving human resources, financial [fiscal], capital, information technology, and results-based management (see Ingraham and Kneedler, 2000, for an application using these GPP scores). The utility of these organizational routines and procedures are not limited to the internal functioning of public agencies, but rather have policy implications for the "reach" of public bureaucracies in the American states. For example, Coggburn and Schneider (2003) find that states with high levels of management capacity (i.e. desirable organizational routines and procedures) are inclined to tackle more challenging policies of a collectivist nature, whereas lower levels of management capacity are preoccupied with distributive/particularistic policies which are easier to manage in both scope and conflict. Similarly, Jennings and Woods (2007) find that higher levels of management capacity result in the development of stronger environmental programs (as well as the more effective implementation of existing policies). This pattern makes intuitive sense and is consistent with bounded rationality theories of the firm (March and Simon, 1958; Cyert and March, 1963). Put simply, states with better organizational routines and procedures will be able to administer more ambitious policies than those that fall in short in this dimension which must "satisfice" by simplifying their task environment.

In the next section of the essay we develop a theoretical framework that attempts to provide a coherent logic expressing how variations in each institutional actor's relative capacities interact with the actor's preferences to influence policy delegation in the American states. Our aim is to provide a theoretical framework that can serve as the basis for further theoretical development and empirical testing in the realm of American state bureaucratic politics.

RECONSIDERING POLICY DELEGATION IN THE AMERICAN STATES: THE LOGIC OF COMPARATIVE INSTITUTIONAL CAPACITY

As discussed in the previous section, high levels of institutional capacity afford institutions both expertise and policy control benefits. However, the depiction of institutional capacity alone does not explain outcomes involving policy administration among multiple institutions. This requires that a predictive theory be advanced to specify the conditions under which specific institution(s) possess a comparative advantage in policy administration. In this section we propose a theoretical framework for this purpose.

Our theoretical framework is motivated by the simple notion that institutions seek to maximize administrative policy control in order to achieve their policy preferences, subject to their relative endowments of institutional capacity. This theory is thus in the tradition of New Institutionalism in that it adheres to Charles Plott's (1991) "fundamental equation of policymaking" which posits that *Preferences* × *Institutions* = *Policy* (see also, Hinich and Munger, 1997). In the context of the framework advanced here, administrative control is determined by two factors: (1) the extent to which institutions' policy preferences converge (or diverge), and (2) the relative institutional capacity of each institution. Applied to comparative delegation choices, this means that the legislature will discount preference divergence at varying rates based upon the relative institutional capacities among relevant policy actors. A comparative assessment of institutional capacity among the legislature, governor, and bureaucracy (agency) can thus be thought of as setting the parameters by which policy preferences are transmitted into policy administration.

Specifically, we consider three classes of comparative legislative delegation problems that are distinguished by the relative comparative institutional capacity among the legislature, governor, and agency. *Absence of Institutional Dominance* occurs when all three institutions possess uniform levels of institutional capacity, *Singular Institutional Dominance* exists when only a single institution is classified as a *High* capacity type and the remaining two are *Low* capacity types, and *Shared Institutional Dominance* exists when a pair of institutions are classified as a *High* capacity types and the lone remaining institutions possesses *Low* capacity.

Next, we offer a preliminary logic and resulting set of comparative statics based on the aforementioned assumptions regarding maximizing policy control that is subject to the constraint of the legislature's relative level of institutional capacity. The stylized model that we propose in this section only considers two capacity types (*High* vs. *Low*), and does not distinguish between binary (delegate or do not delegate?) and continuous (what amount to delegate?) delegation choices. We also assume that institutional capacity is identical within a capacity type. Moreover, institutional capacity not only determines which actors' preferences the legislature takes into account involving the implementation of public policy, but also affects the rate at which they discount preference divergence among key policy actors. Because our focus is centered on policy administration, the stylized theoretical logic advanced here further assumes that the politics underlying policy adoption is exogenously determined. Finally, we maintain the common simplifying assumptions that actors possess symmetric, risk-neutral ideological policy preferences. Obviously, a more general (and satisfying) model would relax these assumptions, while also offering additional institutional details. We leave this for scholars to take up in future research on this topic.

Absence of Institutional Dominance (Uniform Institutional Capacity)

For this particular class of comparative delegation problems, all three institutions (legislature, governor, and agency) exhibit uniform institutional capacities—i.e. each actor possesses an identical amount of institutional capacity. Therefore, the legislature's calculus will produce the same comparative-static predictions. In the first instance of uniform institutional capacity, the legislature, governor, and bureaucracy are each defined as being "Low" capacity types (*Low State Capacity*).[3] Because all three institutions possess low institutional capacity in the first scenario, we can infer that (aggregate) state capacity is low. Alternatively, uniform institutional capacity may also result when aggregate institutional capacity is maximized by all three institutions possessing high capacity (*High State Capacity*). Under such a scenario, this competitive balance reflects three robust institutions which can not only check the power of one another, but have sufficient capacity to make them capable of effective governance.

Comparative delegation outcomes are illustrated in Figure 16.1.

In **panel 1a**, the legislature's (*L*) ideal point is an endpoint on this conservative-liberal ideological policy space, while the agency is on the other endpoint (*A*), and governor's ideal point (*G*) lies between *L* and *A*. In this instance, *L*'s willingness to delegate

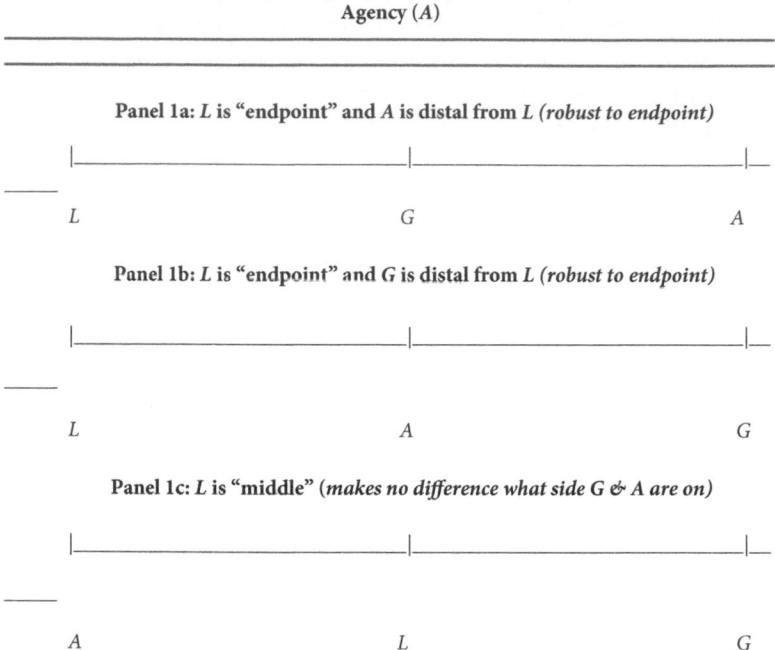

FIGURE 16.1 Simple ideological policy configurations: legislature (*L*), governor (*G*), and agency (*A*)

Notes: Panel 1a: L is "endpoint" and A is distal from *L (robust to endpoint)* Panel 1b: L is "endpoint" and G is distal from *L (robust to endpoint)* Panel 1c: L is "middle" *(makes no difference what side G & A are on)*. The ideological continuum moves from liberal (left) to conservative (right).

policymaking authority to equal capacity institutions (*G* and *A*) is decreasing in ideological divergence between itself and the distal actor, subject to the constraint of a formidable "centrist" actor that has the capacity to check the distal actor. Because the legislature has no comparative institutional capacity advantage vis-à-vis the governor or agency in either the *Low State Capacity* or *High State Capacity* cases, the rate at which preference divergence is discounted is fixed at $\alpha = 1$. This is the implied assumption of federal-based delegation models, which do not account for variable levels of institutional capacity. Under the assumption of risk-neutrality, these models focus solely on the absolute distance between actors' ideal points.

More precisely, our model predicts that legislative delegation will be decreasing in the distance between the legislator's ideal point (L) and the midpoint between the governor

(*G*) and Agency (*A*)—i.e., $\left| L - \dfrac{A+G}{2} \right|$ under both the **panel 1a** and **panel 1b** scenarios.[4]

In the final scenario characterized by **panel 1c**, the legislature (*L*) will lie between the agency (A) on the left (liberal) and governor on the right (conservative) (G). In this particular situation, the key ideological chasm depends upon L's relative position to G vis-à-vis A. When the legislature is closer to the governor (G) than the agency (i.e.,

$$L > \frac{G-A}{2}$$), the legislature's proclivity for delegation will be decreasing in $|L\text{-}A|$. This is

because A is the most distal actor and can effectively check G since they possess the same level of institutional capacity. Conversely, when the legislature is closer to the agency (A)

than compared to the governor (i.e. $L < \frac{G-A}{2}$), then the legislature's proclivity for del-

egation will be decreasing in $|L\text{-}G|$. In the special case when the legislature's ideal point

bisects that of the governor and agency—i.e. $L = \frac{G-A}{2}$ —the legislature's willingness to

delegate will be at its (relative) apex for these uniform capacity cases since it will be unaffected by changes in $|G\text{-}A|$ because the balance of institutional capacity between G and A means that resulting policy will fall at L.

Although the comparative static predictions in the realm of legislative delegation are observationally equivalent in the *Low State Capacity* and *High State* Capacity scenarios, the normative implications are vastly different. In the *Low State Capacity* case, administrative governance will be problematic on two levels. First, all institutions will lack sufficient capacity to make and administer policy in an effective manner. Second, because they each possess similar levels of institutional capacity, severe policy gridlock will arise when the critical institutional preferences diverge. This will result in low caliber policy administration that produces inadequate action when institutional preferences are aligned with each other, and inaction when they are not. As a result, policy stalemate under *Low State Capacity* may actually be desirable under certain circumstances if governmental inaction is deemed superior to incompetent policy action. Yet, when institutional preferences diverge under *High State Capacity*, policy stalemate is an acute problem. Unlike the *Low State Capacity* case where governmental inaction due to conflicting preferences is preferable to incompetent action, such policy gridlock in the *High State Capacity* case is undesirable since it prohibits institutions from effectively exercising their robust institutional capacity to undertake policy administration.

Singular Institutional Dominance

While the two previous cases presume a balance of powers attributable to all institutions possessing the same caliber of institutional capacity, the distribution of authority in the American states is uneven due to both varying constitutional and statutory provisions. As discussed in the previous section, this variation includes (but is not limited to) differences in institutional resources provided to state legislatures (Hahn, 2000; Grossback and Peterson, 2004; Gerber, Maestas and Dometrius, 2005; Squire, 2007), and governors (Dometrius, 1987; Grady and Simon, 2002; Beyle, 2004; Ferguson, 2006), as well as the structural and procedural resources afforded bureaucratic agencies (Barrilleaux, Feiock, and Crew, 1992; Barrilleaux, 1999; Ingraham and Kneedler, 2002). A second set of cases cover those instances where an imbalance of institutional capacity exists among policy actors. Although this imbalance imposes costs by reducing competition among governmental institutions—thereby stifling innovation—it also contains benefits for quick and decisive action (i.e., it lowers the transaction costs of policy administration) in a democratic system of governance.

Under *singular institutional dominance*, a single institution serves as the dominant policy actor in state-level administrative governance. *Legislative Dominance* occurs when the legislature is endowed with strong formal powers and a strong level of professionalism, but the governor and agency are not. In these instances, the legislature has the means to direct policymaking activities, but the executive branch is not fully capable of implementing the legislature's policy plans. Referring again to Figure 16.1, in the two scenarios when L is an endpoint on the ideological policy space (**panels 1a and 1b**) and both A & G possess the same (low) level of institutional capacity, the legislature's willingness to delegate is decreasing in $\alpha \mid L - \dfrac{A+G}{2} \mid$, where $\alpha > 1$ That is, the legislature is not only less willing to delegate authority to either a governor or agency with divergent preferences, but this willingness is also declining in α—the extent to which the legislature enjoys an institutional capacity advantage over an equally weak governor and agency. When the legislature (L) lies between the agency (A) on the left (liberal) and governor on the right (conservative) (G), one should observe policy outcomes consistent with those observed under the assumption of uniform capacity noted under **panel 1c**[5], except that preference divergence will be discounted at a high rate due to the fact that the legislature enjoys relatively greater institutional capacity than either executive branch policy actor. Therefore, when $L > \dfrac{G-A}{2}$, the legislature's proclivity for delegation will be decreasing in $\alpha \mid L-A \mid$, where $\alpha > 1$. When $L < \dfrac{G-A}{2}$, the legislature's proclivity for delegation will be decreasing in $\alpha \mid L-G \mid$, where $\alpha > 1$. The institutional capacity discount parameter is trivial in the special case of $L = \dfrac{G-A}{2}$ since the legislature's policy preferences will be implemented (at L) if delegated to either G or A, irrespective of how distant they are from one another, because the latter pair possess equal levels of institutional capacity.

Put simply, L is less willing to delegate to authority to G as preferences diverge, and this rate of unwillingness increases in L's institutional capacity advantage over G. If α

is sufficiently high, then the legislature may choose not to delegate to agencies responsible for policy administration even when they possess very similar policy preferences (Huber and McCarty, 2004). Under *Legislative Dominance*, policymaking will most closely mirror popular will that is embodied by elected assemblies. Forgoing any professional and technical expertise that is housed within public agencies, any advantages associated with unilateral action by governors is not problematic for the legislature since the executive branch is ill equipped to use what little powers they possess—that is, the governor suffers from low institutional capacity.

However, when the legislature is a low capacity type, its willingness to delegate is solely a decreasing function of its own preferences vis-à-vis those of the high capacity institution, but at a declining rate since the legislature incurs an institutional capacity deficit. This is because the dominant executive branch actor will dictate the terms of policymaking. Therefore, if the governor (G) is the dominant institution (*Gubernatorial Dominance*), then the legislature's willingness to delegate policymaking authority is decreasing in $\alpha |L-G|$, where $0 < \alpha < 1$. For such strong governor/weak legislature states, executive influence over bureaucratic activities is quite easy to attain. Under this particular configuration of powers, the bureaucracy is not sufficiently insulated from the governor's reach, nor can it fully exploit any common agency problems confronting both governors and legislatures as a pair of political principals seeking to obtain control over bureaucratic policymaking (e.g. Bertelli and Lynn, 2004; Gailmard, 2009). Moreover, the legislature may possess rational incentives to delegate to the executive branch under these circumstances, thus abdicating additional institutional authority to governors. Although governors represent broad state constituencies, this is potentially problematic for making sound policies since unfettered unilateral executive action can produce undesirable policy outcomes resulting from the fact that governors' short-run electoral impulses cannot be sufficiently checked by other democratic institutions (Krause and Melusky, 2012).

Similarly, if the agency (A) is the dominant institution (*Bureaucratic Dominance*), then the legislature's willingness to delegate policymaking authority is decreasing in $\alpha |L-A|$, where $0 < \alpha < 1$. In this particular situation, the bureaucracy is highly professional, well-resourced, and has either ample discretion (Hammond and Knott, 1996) or autonomy (Carpenter, 2001) from political institutions, where each political institution possesses low levels of institutional capacity. In this particular case, the bureaucracy plays the preeminent role in policymaking since it is afforded both the requisite autonomy and discretion to undertake administrative tasks with little effective interference from either political branch. Bureaucratic dominance leads to policy administration that may deviate from democratic preferences in the direction of bureaucratic preferences (*bureaucratic drift*). A "strong" agency's ability to control policy administration will increase as its preferences diverge from both a "weak" legislature and governor. This logic suggests that political institutions will have limited means to effectively check the exercise of bureaucratic authority if the bureaucracy chooses to flex its considerable muscles. While this may lead to greater technical expertise in policymaking, it also poses normative concerns for democratic governance due to a lack of policy responsiveness to popular will, as reflected in the policy preferences of elected officials.

Shared Institutional Dominance

This final class of comparative delegation problems is characterized by a pair of institutions that coexist as the dominant (i.e., high capacity) policy actors in state-level administrative governance. In general, under shared institutional dominance, the extent to which dominant institutions are successful coordinating to obtain their policy objectives determines their effectiveness for shaping policy administration. In each case, these institutions will be able to exercise greater shared control over policy administration as their preferences converge toward one another.

The first two scenarios treat the legislature as one of the dominant institutions in this arrangement. *Legislative-Bureaucratic Shared Dominance* means that the governor is essentially on the sidelines of policymaking and the real action lies with a highly professionalized legislature possessing ample formal powers and a bureaucracy that has the attributes of a dominant bureaucracy, except that it may lack discretion and autonomy from the legislature when their preferences diverge. Specifically, the legislature and agency can effectively counterbalance one another since they are each high capacity types. Therefore, the legislature's willingness to delegate is decreasing in $\frac{|L-A|}{2}$.[6]

Political Shared Dominance is the flip side of *Bureaucratic Dominance* insofar as both the governor and legislature each possesses abundant institutional capacity in relation to a weak bureaucracy. Under these conditions, the bureaucracy is, at best, capable of merely executing the will of elected officials—especially when the legislature and governor share similar policy preferences. In terms of the comparative delegation logic proposed here, the legislature's propensity for delegation is decreasing in $\frac{|L-G|}{2}$ since the legislature and governor can effectively check one another so policy outcomes will be the bisection between their ideal points.[7] Thus, political shared dominance leads to outcomes that approximate the normative ideal for many democratic theorists: policy that reflects the preferences of two coequal elected political institutions. The downside of such an arrangement generally is that policymakers neglect to take into account the specialized knowledge and expertise that resides in the bureaucracy. Under conditions of political shared dominance, however, this concern is mitigated by the fact that bureaucratic capacity is low relative to the institutional capacity that resides in the elected branches of government.

The final scenario, *Executive Shared Dominance*, is less straightforward since both the governor and bureaucracy each possess high levels of institutional capacity, and the legislature does not. Because the legislature realizes that it is the sole low capacity institution, the battle for policy control within the executive branch between the governor and bureaucracy will be determinative. Yet, the comparative-static predictions are less straightforward than in the previous two cases of shared institutional dominance. The simplest case is when the legislature's preferences (L) lie between those of the governor

(G) and agency (A) as characterized in **panel 1c**. Specifically, when the legislature is closer to the governor (G) than the agency (i.e. $L > \dfrac{G-A}{2}$), then the legislature's proclivity for delegation will be decreasing (at a slower rate) in $\alpha \, |L\text{-}A|$, where $0 < \alpha < 1$. Conversely, when the legislature is closer to the agency (A) than the governor (i.e. $L < \dfrac{G-A}{2}$), then the legislature's proclivity for delegation will also be decreasing (at a slower rate) in $\alpha \, |L\text{-}G|$ where $0 < \alpha < 1$. Finally, when the legislature's ideal point bisects that of the governor and agency—i.e. $L = \dfrac{G-A}{2}$—the legislature's willingness to delegate policymaking authority will be high because the "balance" of institutional capacity between G and A means that resulting policy will fall at L. The final two cases are variants of the uniform institutional capacity scenarios illustrated in **panels 1a** and **1b**, where L is at an endpoint of the ideological spectrum. Specifically, legislative delegation will be decreasing in the policy distance between L and the midpoint between A and G—i.e. $|L - \dfrac{A+G}{2}|$ (where $0 < \alpha < 1$) irrespective whether A or G is distal from L. However, because the legislature is comparatively weaker vis-à-vis either executive branch institutions ($0 < \alpha < 1$), they will discount this observed level of ideological preference divergence.

A summary of these comparative statics for all cases in each given scenario type is listed in **Table 16.1**. On the whole, greater (aggregate) institutional capacity in the cases of shared dominance provides the potential for more effective policy administration than in the cases of *Low State Capacity* and singular dominance. Yet fully realizing the benefits of greater aggregate institutional capacity often requires goal congruence among the high capacity institutions. In the cases of legislative-bureaucratic shared dominance and political shared dominance, especially, a high capacity legislature will rationally forgo some of the benefits of coordinating with other high capacity institutions so as to retain greater policy control as their policy preferences diverge.

Discussion

In this essay, our central purpose has been to claim that bureaucratic politics in the American states is fundamentally different from its counterpart in U.S. national politics. This is because institutional capacity varies across state governments in both absolute and relative terms. As a result, we argue that future research on bureaucratic politics in the American states should possess a truly comparative politics focus that emphasizes

Table 16.1 Summary of Legislature's Decision Rule for Policy Delegation—The Role of Ideological Policy Preferences and Comparative Institutional Capacity

Institutional Capacity Regime	Location of L	Delegatee Endpoint(s)	L's Relative Capacity	Legislative Delegation Decision Rule
Absence of Institutional Dominance (Low & *High State Capacity*)	Endpoint	A	$\alpha = 1$	$\left\| L - \dfrac{A+G}{2} \right\|$
	Endpoint	G	$\alpha = 1$	$\left\| L - \dfrac{A+G}{2} \right\|$
	Center	A & G	$\alpha = 1$	$if\ L > \dfrac{G-A}{2}: \left\| L-A \right\|$ $if\ L < \dfrac{G-A}{2}: \left\| L-A \right\|$ $if\ L = \dfrac{G-A}{2}: L$
Singular Institutional Dominance				$\left\| L - \dfrac{A+G}{2} \right\|$
Legislative Dominance	Endpoint	A	$\alpha > 1$	$\alpha \left\| L - \dfrac{A+G}{2} \right\|$
	Endpoint	G	$\alpha > 1$	α
	Center	A & G	$\alpha > 1$	$if\ L > \dfrac{G-A}{2}: \alpha \left\| L-A \right\|$ $if\ L < \dfrac{G-A}{2}: \alpha \left\| L-G \right\|$ $if\ L = \dfrac{G-A}{2}: L$
Gubernatorial Dominance	_____	_____	$0 < \alpha < 1$	$\alpha \left\| L\text{-}G \right\|$
Bureaucratic Dominance	_____	_____	$0 < \alpha < 1$	$\alpha \left\| L\text{-}A \right\|$
Shared Institutional Dominance				
Legislative-Bureaucratic Shared Dominance	_____	_____	$\alpha = 1$	$\dfrac{\left\| L-A \right\|}{2}$
Political Shared Dominance	_____	_____	$\alpha = 1$	$\dfrac{\left\| L-G \right\|}{2}$
Executive Shared Dominance	Endpoint	A	$0 < \alpha < 1$	$\alpha \left\| L - \dfrac{A+G}{2} \right\|$
	Endpoint	G	$0 < \alpha < 1$	$\alpha \left\| L - \dfrac{A+G}{2} \right\|$
	Center	A & G	$0 < \alpha < 1$	$if\ L > \dfrac{G-A}{2}: \alpha \left\| L-A \right\|$ $if\ L < \dfrac{G-A}{2}: \alpha \left\| L-G \right\|$ $if\ L = \dfrac{G-A}{2}: L$

cross-state differences in the design, powers, and external support for legislatures, governors, and public agencies. Although current theoretical research in bureaucratic politics has made critical strides in focusing on the capacity of a single institution, in the form of the legislature (Huber and Shipan, 2002) or bureaucracy (Huber and McCarty, 2004), what is needed is for a comparative assessment of institutional capacity and its implications for control over policy administration.[8]

This essay has made an initial attempt to address this puzzle by sketching out a simple spatial theoretical model of legislative delegation that is motivated by comparative institutional capacity among the legislature, governor, and public agencies. Specifically, the legislature seeks to maximize policy control in accordance with preference divergence between itself and executive branch institution(s), subject to the constraint of the legislature's relative level of institutional capacity. The spatial model offers an interesting set of comparative-static predictions regarding how the legislature makes delegation decisions under varying institutional capacity scenarios and ideological preference configurations. Institutional capacity affects the legislature's choice involving delegation decisions. Specifically, we posit that the rate at which preference divergence between the legislature and executive branch institution(s) is discounted will be an increasing function of the legislature's capacity deficit.

Research analyzing the implications of comparative institutional capacity on bureaucratic politics can be extended beyond the case of delegation in the American states. For instance, although federalism is exogenous to our comparative institutional capacity framework, the logic advanced in this essay can be extended to incorporate the delegation issues involved in intergovernmental policy administration. Two tiered principal-agent models have already been applied to the intergovernmental system (Chubb, 1985; Hedge, Scicchitano, and Metz, 1991; Wood, 1992). More recently, preference congruence between the federal and state levels of government has been incorporated into our understanding of American federalism (Nicholson-Crotty, 2004; Krause and Bowman, 2005; Clouser McCann, 2010). Our theoretical perspective suggests that the next step is to extend this research program to incorporate variations involving institutional capacity. For instance, partial preemption regulatory agencies, such as EPA and OSHA, oversee state implementation of federal regulatory laws. Although the states have lead implementation and enforcement authority, the federal agency retains a residual capacity to conduct monitoring inspections and enforcement actions within those states. Our theory suggests that these agencies will expend more effort thus monitoring state agencies when preferences diverge between the federal agency and strong capacity institutions in the state. For instance, a state with legislative dominance and a conservative Republican legislature may face stronger EPA oversight than another legislatively dominant state with a more pro-environment Democratic legislature. Phrased somewhat differently, the federal agency is more likely to delegate implementation discretion to states where the strong institutions have preferences that converge with the federal agency's preferences.[9]

This essay has served as an initial foray into thinking more seriously about evaluating institutional capacity of the legislature, governor, and bureaucracy in furthering our understanding of policy administration in a democratic system. Clearly, the ideas and logic represent an initial, preliminary attempt to address these issues, and should be interpreted accordingly. Building upon the seminal work of Huber and Shipan (2002), our hope is that future scholarship in bureaucratic politics in the American states develops organic theories that take the best from U.S. national politics, while augmenting them with insights that reflect the truly comparative nature of administration among this class of policy laboratories.

Notes

1. Indeed, Woods and Baranowski (2006) argue that greater political careerism (most notably, progressive ambition and salary compensation) dampens the incentives for legislatures to allocate scarce time and effort to influence public agencies. This is because legislative efforts at directing administrative behavior do not yield the same career benefits as constituent casework and bill sponsorship (see also, Rosenthal, 1981).

2. Squire (2007: 215) notes that the link between professionalized and career legislatures is a somewhat tenuous one; part of this rationale is attributed to state legislative careers being far less prestigious and lucrative compared to serving in the U.S. Congress. Moreover, term limits disproportionately affect the lower chamber (House/Assembly) since the upper chamber (Senate) becomes a base for former lower chamber members who are term limited out of office (Moncrief, Niemi, and Powell, 2004: 369–370).

3. We treat *state capacity* in the context of our theoretical framework as being the aggregate institutional capacity derived from the legislature, governor, and bureaucracy. In the comparative politics literature, this concept is often conceptualized as the ratio of total governmental revenues to GDP (e.g. Steinmo, 1993; Cheibub, 1998), robust property rights (e.g. North, 1991; Weingast, 1995), and low levels of political corruption (Nye, 1967).

4. Because $\alpha = 1$ for the *Absence of Institutional Dominance* class of problems, this discounting parameter is dropped under uniform institutional capacity scenarios for notational ease.

5. These comparative-static predictions would be reversed if the agency (A) was the most conservative actor and governor (G) was the most liberal actor.

6. Please recall that $\alpha = 1$ since the legislature (L) and agency (A) possess identical institutional capacities.

7. Please recall that $\alpha = 1$ since the legislature (L) and governor (G) possess identical institutional capacities.

8. Huber and Shipan's (2002) theoretical logic is currently the "gold standard" for students of bureaucratic politics analyzing the American states. Yet, Huber and Shipan's theory (and empirical tests) treats both governors and bureaucracies' institutional capacities as being exogenously fixed—i.e., only legislative capacity plays a role in conditioning how policy preferences get translated into outcomes pertaining to delegated policymaking authority.

9. For simplicity's sake we are assuming that the federal agency's preferences are fixed. If it is responsive to the preferences of national political principals, then it is congruence between these preferences and those of the strong subnational institution(s) that would matter.

REFERENCES

Abney, Glenn and Thomas P. Lauth. 1983. "The Governor as Chief Administrator." *Public Administration Review* 43(January/February): 40–49.

Barrett, K., and Greene, R. 2001. *Powering up: How public managers can take control of information technology*. Washington, DC: CQ Press.

Barrilleaux, Charles. 1999. "Statehouse Bureaucracy: Institutional Consistency in a Changing Environment." In *American State and Local Politics: Directions for the 21st Century*, Ronald E. Weber and Paul Brace, eds. New York: Chatham House.

Barrilleaux, Charles, Richard Feiock, and Robert E. Crew, Jr. 1992. "Measuring and Comparing American States' Administrative Characteristics." *State and Local Government Review* 24(Winter): 12–18.

Bawn, Kathleen. 1995. "Political Control versus Expertise: Congressional Choices about Administrative Procedures." *American Political Science Review* 89(March): 62–73.

Berkowitz, Daniel B., and Karen Clay. 2012. *The Evolution of a Nation: How Geography and Law Shaped the American States*. Princeton, NJ: Princeton University Press.

Berry, William. 1979. "Utility Regulation in the States: The Policy Effects of Professionalism and Salience to the Consumer." *American Journal of Political Science* 23 (May): 263–277.

Bertelli, Anthony M., and Laurence E. Lynn, Jr. 2004. "Policymaking in the Parallelogram of Forces: Common Agency and Human Service Provision." *Policy Studies Review* 32(August): 167–185.

Beyle, Thad. 2004. "The Governors." In *Politics in the American States*, Virginia Gray, Russell L. Hanson, and Herbert Jacob, eds., 7th ed, 194–231. Washington, DC: CQ Press.

Beyle, Thad, and Margaret Ferguson. 2008. "Governors and the Executive Branch." In *Politics In the American states: A Comparative Analysis*. Virginia. Gray and Russell L. Hanson, eds., 8th ed, 192–228. Washington, DC: CQ Press

Boerner, Robert D. 2002. "Program Evaluation in the States." *Legisbrief* 10:24. Denver, CO: National Conference of State Legislatures.

Bowling, Cynthia J. and Deil S. Wright. 1998. "Change and Continuity in State Administration: Administrative Leadership across Four Decades." *Public Administration Review* 58(September/October): 429–444.

Bowman, Ann O'M., Neal D. Woods, and Milton R. Stark II. 2010. "Governors Turn Pro: Separation of Powers and the Institutionalization of the American Governorship." *Political Research Quarterly* 63(June): 304–315.

Brudney, Jeffrey L. and F. Ted Hebert. 1987. "State Agencies and Their Environments: Examining the Influence of Important External Actors." *Journal of Politics* 49(February): 186–206.

Carpenter, Daniel P. 2001. *The Forging of Bureaucratic Autonomy: Reputations, Networks, and Policy Innovation in Executive Agencies, 1862–1928*. Princeton, NJ: Princeton University Press.

Carpenter, Daniel P. 2010. *Reputation and Power: Organizational Image and Pharmaceutical Regulation at the FDA*. Princeton, NJ: Princeton University Press.

Carpenter, Daniel P., and George A. Krause. 2012. "Reputation and Public Administration." *Public Administration Review* 72(January/February): 26–32.

Cheibub, Jose Antonio. 1998. "Political Regimes and the Extractive Capacity of Governments: Taxation in Democracies and Dictatorships." *World Politics* 50(April): 349–376.

Cho, Chung-Lae and Deil S. Wright. 2004. "The Devolution Revolution and Intergovernmental Relations in the 1990s: Changes in the Cooperative and Coercive State-National Relations as Perceived by State Administrators." *Journal of Public Administration Research and Theory* 14(October): 447–468.

Chubb, John E. 1985. "The Political Economy of Federalism." *American Political Science Review* 79 (December): 994–1015.

Cline, Kurt D. 2010. "Working Relationships in the National Superfund Program: The State Administrators Perspective." *Journal of Public Administration Research and Theory* 20 (January): 117–135.

Clingemayer, James C. 1991. "Administrative Innovations as Instruments of State Legislative Control." *Western Political Quarterly* 44(June): 389–403.

Clingemaycr, James C. and William F. West. 1992. "Imposing Procedural Constraints on State Administrative Agencies: An Empirical Investigation of Competing Explanations." *Review of Policy Research* 11(June): 37–56.

Clouser McCann, Pamela. 2010. "Policy in Disguise: Congressional Delegation of Policy Authority in a Federal Context." Paper presented at the 2011 Midwest Political Science Association Meetings. Chicago, IL. April.

Coggburn, Jerrell D. 2001. "Personnel Deregulation: Exploring Differences in the American States." *Journal of Public Administration Research and Theory* 11(April): 223–244.

Coggburn, Jerrell D. and Saundra K. Schneider. 2003. The Quality of Management and Government Performance: An Empirical Analysis of the American States. *Public Administration Review* 63(March): 206–213.

Collins, Brian K. and Brian J. Gerber. 2006. "Redistributive Policy and Devolution: Is State Administration a Road Block (Grant) to Equitable Access to Federal Funds." *Journal of Public Administration Research and Theory* 16(October): 613–632.

Conlan, Timothy. 1998. *From New Federalism to Devolution: Twenty Five Years of Intergovernmental Reform*. Washington, DC: Brookings.

Cooper, Joseph and William West. 1988. "Presidential Power and Republican Government: The Theory and Practice of OMB Review of Agency Rules." *Journal of Politics* 50(November): 864–895.

Cyert, Richard M., and James G. March. 1963. *A Behavioral Theory of the Firm*. New York: Wiley.

De Figueiredo, Rui J. P., Jr. and Richard Vanden Bergh. 2004. "The Political Economy of State-Level Administrative Procedure Acts." *Journal of Law and Economics* 47(October): 569–588.

Dometrius, Nelson C. 1979. "Measuring Gubernatorial Power." *Journal of Politics* 41(May): 589–610.

Dometrius, Nelson C. 1987. "Changing Gubernatorial Power: The Measure vs. Reality." *Western Political Quarterly* 40(June): 319–328.

Dometrius, Nelson C. 2002. "Gubernatorial Popularity and Administrative Influence." *State Politics and Policy Quarterly* 2(Fall): 251–267.

Downs, Anthony, 1967. *Inside bureaucracy*. Boston: Little, Brown.

Dresang, Dennis L. and James J. Gosling. 1989. *Politics, Policy, and Management in the American States*. New York: Longman.

Elling, Richard C. 1992. *Public Management in the States: A Comparative Study of Administrative Performance and Politics*. Westport, CT: Praeger.

Elling, Richard C. 1999. "Administering State Programs: Performance and Politics." In *Politics in the American States*, Virginia Gray, Russell L. Hanson, and Herbert Jacob, eds., 7th ed, 267–303. Washington, DC: CQ Press.

Epstein, David and Sharyn O'Halloran. 1999. *Delegating Powers: A Transaction Cost Politics Model of Policy Making under Separate Powers*. Cambridge: Cambridge University Press.

Ethridge, Marcus E. 1981. "Legislative-Administrative Interactions as 'Intrusive Access': An Empirical Analysis." *Journal of Politics 43*(May): 473–492.

Evans, Peter, and James E. Rauch. 1999. "Bureaucracy and Growth: A Cross-National Analysis of the Effects of Weberian State Structures on Economic Growth." *American Sociological Review 64*(October): 748–765.

Ferguson, Margaret. 2006. *The Executive Branch of State Government; People, Processes, and Politics.* Santa Barbara, CA: ABC-CLIO.

Ferguson, Margaret R. 2003. "Chief Executive Success in the Legislative Arena." *State Politics and Policy Quarterly 3* (Summer): 158–182.

Gailmard, Sean. 2009. "Multiple Principals and Oversight of Bureaucratic Policymaking." *Journal of Theoretical Politics 21*(April): 161–186.

Garand, James C. and Kyle Baudoin. 2004. "Fiscal Policy in the American States." In *Politics in the American States; A Comparative Analysis, 8th ed.* Virginia Gray and Russell Hanson, eds., 290–317. Washington, DC: CQ Press.

Gerber, Brian J., Cherie D. Maestas, and Nelson C. Dometrius. 2005. "State Legislative Influence over Agency Rulemaking: The Utility of Ex Ante Review." *State Politics and Policy Quarterly 5* (Spring): 24–46.

Gerber, Eilsabeth R., Arthur Lupia, and Mathew D. McCubbins. 2004. "When Does Government Limit the Impact of Voter Initiatives? The Politics of Implementation and Enforcement" *Journal of Politics 66*(1): 43–68.

Golden, Miriam. 2003. "Electoral Connections: The Effects of the Personal Vote on Political Patronage, Bureaucracy and Legislation in Postwar Italy." *British Journal of Political Science 33*(April): 189–212.

Gormley, William T. 1992. "Food Fights: Regulatory Enforcement in a Federal System." *Public Administration Review 52*(May/June): 271–280.

Grady, Dennis O. and Kathleen M. Simon. 2002. "Political Restraints and Bureaucratic Discretion: The Case of State Government Rule Making." *Politics & Policy 30*(December): 646–679.

Grossback, Laurence J. and David A. M. Peterson. 2004. "Understanding Institutional Change: Legislative Staff Development and the State Policymaking Environment." *American Politics Research 32*(January): 26–51.

Hahn, Robert W. 2000. "State and Federal Regulatory Reform: A Comparative Analysis." *Journal of Legal Studies 29*(June): 873–912.

Hammond, Thomas H. and Jack H. Knott. 1996. "Who Controls the Bureaucracy? Presidential Power, Congressional Dominance, Legal Constraints, and Bureaucratic Autonomy in a Model of Multi-Institutional Policy-Making." *Journal of Law, Economics and Organization 12*(April): 121–168.

Hays, Steven W. and Jessica E. Sowa. 2006. "A Broader Look at the Accountability Movement: Some Grim Realities in State Civil Service Systems." *Review of Public Personnel Administration 26*(June): 102–117

Hebert, F. Ted, Jeffrey L. Brudney, and Deil S. Wright. 1983. "Gubernatorial Influence and State Bureaucracy." *American Politics Quarterly 11*(April): 243–264.

Hedge, David M. and Michael J. Schicchitano. 1994. "Regulating in Space and Time: The Case of Regulatory Federalism" *Journal of Politics 56*(February): 134–153.

Hedge, David M., Michael J. Scicchitano, and Patricia Metz. 1991. "The Principal-Agent Model and Regulatory Federalism." *Western Political Quarterly 44*(December): 1055–1080.

Hinich, Melvin J., and Michael C. Munger. 1997. *Analytical Politics*. Cambridge: Cambridge University Press.

Horn, Murray J. and Kenneth Shepsle. 1989. Commentary on "Administrative Arrangements and the Political Control of Agencies: Administrative Process and Organizational Form as Legislative Responses to Agency Costs." *Virginia Law Review 75*(March): 499–508.

Huber, John D., and Nolan McCarty. 2004. "Bureaucratic Capacity, Delegation, and Political Reform." *American Political Science Review 98*(August): 481–494.

Huber, John D. and Charles R. Shipan. 2002. *Deliberate Discretion? The Institutional Foundations of Bureaucratic Autonomy*. New York: Cambridge University Press.

Huber, John D., Charles R. Shipan, and Madelaine Pfahler. 2001. "Legislatures and Statutory Control of the Bureaucracy." *American Journal of Political Science 45*(April): 330–345.

Ingraham, Patricia and Amy Kneedler Donahue. 2000. "Dissecting the Black Box Revisited: Characterizing Government Management Capacity." In *Governance and Performance: New Perspectives*. Carolyn J. Heinrich and Laurence E. Lynn, Jr., eds., 292–319. Washington, DC: Georgetown University Press.

Jenks, Stephen S. and Deil S. Wright. 1993. An Agency-Level Approach to Change in the Administrative Functions of American State Governments. *State and Local Government Review 25*(Spring): 78–86.

Jennings, Edward, and Neal D. Woods. 2007. "Does Management Really Matter? Management Quality and State Environmental Performance." Presented at the 2007 Biannual Meeting of the Public Management Research Association.

Keiser, Lael R. 2001. "Street-Level Bureaucrats, Administrative Power and the Manipulation of Federal Social Security Disability Programs." *State Politics and Policy Quarterly*. *1*(June): 144–164.

Kim, Junseok and Brian J. Gerber. 2005. "Bureaucratic Leverage over Policy Choice: Explaining the Dynamics of State-Level Reforms in Telecommunications Regulation." *Policy Studies Journal 33*(November): 613–634.

Krause, George A. 2003. "Agency Risk Propensities Involving the Demand for Bureaucratic Discretion." In *Politics, Policy, and Organizations: Frontiers in the Scientific Study of Bureaucracy*. George A. Krause and Kenneth J. Meier, eds., 41–72. Ann Arbor, MI: University of Michigan Press.

Krause, George A., and Ann O'M. Bowman. 2005. "Adverse Selection, Political Parties, and Policy Delegation in the American Federal System." *Journal of Law, Economics, and Organization 21*(October): 359–387.

Krause, George A., and J. Kevin Corder. 2007. "Explaining Bureaucratic Optimism: Theory and Evidence from U.S. Executive Agency Macroeconomic Forecasts." *American Political Science Review 101*(February): 129–142.

Krause, George A., and James W. Douglas. 2006. "Does Agency Competition Improve the Quality of Policy Analysis: Evidence from OMB and CBO Fiscal Projections." *Journal of Policy Analysis and Management 25*(Winter): 53–74.

Krause, George A., and Benjamin F. Melusky. 2012. "Concentrated Powers: Unilateral Executive Authority and Fiscal Policymaking in the American States." *Journal of Politics 74*(January): 98–112.

LeRoux, Kelly, John M. Strate, Richard C. Elling, Marjorie Sarbough-Thompson, and Lyke Thompson. 2002. "Bureaucrats and Legislators in Michigan: A Complex Relationship Complicated by Term Limits." Paper presented at the annual meeting of the American Political Science Association, Philadelphia, PA.

Lowi, Theodore J. 1979. *The End of Liberalism, 2nd ed.* New York: W.W. Norton.

Lupia, Arthur and John J. Matsusaka. 2004. Direct Democracy: New Approaches to Old Questions. *Annual Review of Political Science 7*: 463–482.

Maestas, Cherie. 2000. "Professional Legislatures and Ambitious Politicians: Policy Responsiveness of State Institutions." *Legislative Studies Quarterly 25*(November): 663–690.

March, James G., and Herbert A. Simon. 1958. *Organizations.* New York: Wiley.

McCubbins, Matthew, Roger G. Noll and Barry R. Weingast. 1987. "Administrative Procedures as Instruments of Political Control." *Journal of Law, Economics and Organization* 3(April): 243–277.

McCubbins, Matthew, Roger G. Noll, and Barry R. Weingast. 1989. "Structure and Process as Solutions to the Politician's Principal-Agency Problem." *Virginia Law Review* 75(March): 431–482.

McGrath, Robert J. 2010. "Explaining Statutory Discretion Across the U.S. States." University of Iowa. *Typescript.*

Mooney, Christopher Z. 1994. "Measuring U.S. State Legislative Professionalism: An Evaluation of Five Indices" *State and Local Government Review 26*(Spring): 70–78.

Milakovich, Michael E. and George J. Gordon. 2010. *Public Administration in America*, 11th ed. New York: Wadsworth/Cengage.

Moe, Terry M. 1989. "The Politics of Bureaucratic Structure." In *Can the Government Govern?* John E. Chubb and Paul E. Peterson, eds. Washington, DC: Brookings.

Moe, Terry M. 1990. "Political Institutions: The Neglected Side of the Story." *Journal of Law, Economics, and Organization 6*(April): 213–253.

Moncrief, Gary, Richard Niemi and Lynda Powell. 2004. "Time, Term Limits and Turnover: Trends in Membership Turnover in U.S. State Legislatures." *Legislative Studies Quarterly 29*(August): 357–382.

Nicholson-Crotty, Sean. 2004. "Goal Conflict and Fund Diversion in Federal Grants to the States." *American Journal of Political Science 48*(January): 109–121.

North, Douglass C. 1991. "Institutions." *Journal of Economic Perspectives 5*(Winter): 97–112.

Nye, Joseph. 1967. "Corruption and Political Development: A Cost-Benefit Analysis." *American Political Science Review 61*(June): 417–427.

Persson, Torsten, and Guido Tabellini. 2003. *The Economic Effects of Constitutions.* Cambridge, MA: MIT Press.

Pfeffer, Jeffrey A., and Gerald R. Salancik. 1978. *The External Control of Organizations: A Resource Dependence Perspective.* New York: Harper and Row.

Pierson, Paul. 2000. "The Limits of Design: Explaining Institutional Origins and Change." *Governance 13*(October): 475–499.

Plott, Charles R. 1991. "Will Economics Become an Experimental Science?" *Southern Economic Journal 57*(April): 901–919.

Poggione, Sarah and Christopher Reenock. 2009. "Political Insulation and Legislative Interventions: The Impact of Rule Review." *State Politics and Policy Quarterly 9* (December): 456–485.

Potoski, Matthew. 1999. "Managing Uncertainty through Bureaucratic Design: Administrative Procedures and State Air Pollution Control Agencies." *Journal of Public Administration Research and Theory 9*(October): 623–639.

Potoski, Matthew. 2002. "Designing Bureaucratic Responsiveness: Administrative Procedures and Policy Choice in State Environmental Policy." *State Politics and Policy Quarterly 2* (March): 1–23.

Potoski, Matthew and Neal D. Woods. 2001. "Designing State Clean Air Agencies: Administrative Procedures and Bureaucratic Autonomy." *Journal of Public Administration Research and Theory* 11(April): 203–221.

Reenock, Christopher and Sarah Poggione. 2004. "Bureaucratic Control by Design: Explaining State Legislators Willingness to Use Ex Ante Tactics in Air Pollution Control." *Legislative Studies Quarterly* 29(August): 393–406.

Reenock, Christopher M. and Brian J. Gerber. 2008. "Political Insulation, Information Exchange, and Interest Group Access to the Bureaucracy." *Journal of Public Administration Research and Theory* 18(July): 415–440.

Rourke, Francis E. 1984. *Bureaucracy, Politics, and Public Policy.* Third Edition. Boston, MA: Little, Brown.

Rosenthal, Alan 1981. "Legislative Behavior and Legislative Oversight." *Legislative Studies Quarterly* 6(February): 115–131.

Seidman, Harold, and Robert S. Gilmour. 1986. *Politics, Position, and Power: From the Positive to the Regulatory State.* Fourth Edition. New York: Oxford University Press.

Shipan, Charles R., Craig Volden. 2006. "Bottom-Up Federalism: The Diffusion of Antismoking Policies from U.S. Cities to States." *American Journal of Political Science* 50(4):825–843.

Sigelman, Lee and Nelson C. Dometrius. 1988. "Governors as Chief Administrators: The Linkage Between Formal Powers and Informal Influence." *American Politics Quarterly* (April): 157–170.

Simon, Herbert A. 1976. *Administrative Behavior.* 3rd edn. New York: Free Press.

Sotiropoulos, Dmitri A. 2004. "Southern European Public Bureaucracies in Comparative Perspective." *West European Politics* 27 (May): 405–422.

Spence, David B. 1997. "Administrative Law and Agency Policymaking: Rethinking the Positive Theory of Political Control." *Yale Journal of Regulation* 14: 406–450.

Spence, David B. 1999. "Agency Discretion and the Dynamics of Procedural Reform." *Public Administration Review* 59 (September/October): 425–458.

Spence, David B. 2003. "The Benefits of Agency Policymaking: Perspectives from Positive Political Theory." In *Politics, Policy, and Organizations: Frontiers in the Scientific Study of Bureaucracy.* George A. Krause and Kenneth J. Meier, eds., 104–132. Ann Arbor, MI: University of Michigan Press.

Stinchcombe, Arthur L. 1990. *Information and Organizations.* Vol. 19. Univ of California Press.

Squire, Peverill. 2007. "Measuring State Legislative Professionalism: The Squire Index Revisited." *State Politics and Policy Quarterly* 7(June): 211–227.

Steinmo, Sven H. 1993. *Taxation and Democracy: British, Swedish, and American Approaches to Financing the Modern State.* New Haven, CT: Yale University Press.

Teaford, Jon C. 2002. *The Rise of the States: Evolution of American State Government.* Baltimore: The Johns Hopkins University Press.

Teske, Paul. 1991. "Interests and Institutions in State Regulation." *American Journal of Political Science* 35(February): 139–154.

Teske, Paul. 2004. *Regulation in the States.* Washington, DC: Brookings Institution.

Volden, Craig. 2002a. "Delegating Power to Bureaucracy: Evidence from the States." *Journal of Law, Economics, and Organization* 18(April): 187–220.

Volden, Craig. 2002b. "A Formal Model of the Politics of Delegation in a Separation of Powers System." *American Journal of Political Science* 46(February): 111–133.

Walker, David B. 1995. *The Rebirth of Federalism: Slouching Toward Washington.* Chatham, NJ: Chatham House.

Weingast, Barry R. 1995. "The Economic Role of Political Institutions: Market-Preserving Federalism and Economic Development." *Journal of Law, Economics, and Organization* *11*(April): 1–31.

Weissert, Carol S. 2011. "Beyond Marble Cakes and Picket Fences: What U.S. Federalism Scholars Can Learn From Comparative Politics." *Journal of Politics 73*(October): 965–979.

Wilson, James Q. 1989. *Bureaucracy: What Government Agencies Do and Why They Do It*. NewYork: Basic Books.

Wood, B. Dan. 1992. "Modeling Federal Implementation as a System: The Clean Air Case." *American Journal of Political Science 36*(February): 40–67.

Wood, B. Dan, and Richard Waterman. 1994. *Bureaucratic Dynamics: The Role of a Bureaucracy in a Democracy*. Boulder, CO: Westview Press.

Woods, Neal D. 2004. "Political Influence on Agency Rule Making: Examining the Effects of Legislative and Gubernatorial Rule Review Powers." *State and Local Government Review 36* (Autumn): 174–185.

Woods, Neal D. 2003. "Rethinking Regulation: Institutions and Interests in State Regulatory Enforcement." University of Kentucky: Unpublished PhD dissertation.

Woods, Neal D. and Michael Baranowski. 2006. "Legislative Professionalism and Influence on State Agencies: The Effects of Resources and Careerism." *Legislative Studies Quarterly 31*(November): 585–609.

Woods, Neal D. and Michael Baranowski. 2007. "Governors and the Bureaucracy: Executive Resources as Sources of Administrative Influence." *International Journal of Public Administration 11*(September): 1219–1230.

PART IV

LOCAL POLITICAL INSTITUTIONS

CHAPTER 17

....

LOCAL BOUNDARIES

....

MEGAN MULLIN

A map of local government boundaries in the United States reveals a governing structure that is fragmented and multi-layered. Over 87,000 independent local governments divide responsibility for providing public education, police and fire protection, land use regulation, parks and libraries, infrastructure, social services, and various other public goods and services. Local government boundaries overlap and intersect, and they move with some regularity as governments form, disintegrate, and expand or contract their geographic territories. One outcome of this fragmentation is confusion for citizens; people typically know their city of residence but may not be familiar with the special districts that have power to tax them and influence their quality of life. In densely populated metropolitan areas, political boundaries can seem arbitrary, poorly matched to current population distributions. Yet the boundaries have important consequences for people's tax obligations and access to services.

Although fragmentation reigns, the degree of fragmentation varies considerably, even between metropolitan areas within the same state. In 2002, 273 local governments existed in Allegheny County, Pennsylvania, providing services to the county's 1.3 million residents. Across the state in Philadelphia, just 17 local governments served 1.5 million residents. In addition to Pittsburgh, 127 other municipalities carve up the territory contained within Allegheny County's borders; more than a dozen of these cities and boroughs are home to fewer than 1000 residents. Governments pile on top of each other as well, with 145 school districts and special districts layered on top of general-purpose cities and counties, dividing up functional responsibilities. The result is a mosaic of intersecting jurisdictional boundaries that define both the geographic and the functional reach of a local government's authority. In contrast, the Philadelphia boundary map is much sparser: the city and county are consolidated into a single government, and the county's school district and several of its special districts have boundaries that are coterminous with the city and county. Boundary lines outside the city are more complex, however, with nearly 900 independent governments coexisting in the Philadelphia metropolitan region.

The complexity of local boundaries, and the political fragmentation that produces that complexity, have long attracted the attention of those who study local politics. This essay reviews the literature investigating the functions, determinants, and effects of local government boundaries. The emphasis is on the state of research on local boundaries, but I close with some recommendations for future research.

FUNCTIONS OF BOUNDARIES

Boundaries demarcate a jurisdiction's territory, differentiating land that falls under a local government's authority from land that falls outside it. Local boundaries are highly porous to the movement of people and goods; a daily commute to work or even a short trip to the store can require one to traverse any number of jurisdictional borders. At the same time, boundaries create clear lines of division that determine the extent of a government's responsibilities and obligations. Boundary lines may seem arbitrary and irrelevant in a densely populated metropolitan area, but they serve four important functions. Their location defines citizens' rights, obligations, and access to services, and they help shape the patterns of interaction within a community.

By determining who is counted as a resident of a jurisdiction, boundaries define fundamental rights. By and large, only those who live within a jurisdiction's boundaries can vote for its governing officials, even as those officials make decisions that have consequences for non-residents. Local policy choices about growth, infrastructure, and the provision of social services have effects that spill over into neighboring communities. Residents on both sides of a political boundary may equally experience congested traffic as a result of new development, but the boundary dictates who can participate in selecting the officials who grant the development permits. Even where local governments directly provide services such as drinking water or fire protection outside of jurisdictional boundaries, only those inside the boundaries have an opportunity to vote. Since the extension of the one-person, one-vote requirement to local governments in *Avery v. Midland County*,[1] residence in a jurisdiction has carried the promise of equal representation in the jurisdiction's government. An exception to this rule lies in the case of landowner-voter special districts, which confer voting rights based on property ownership. The U.S. Supreme Court has upheld franchise limitations for special districts if a district has a "special limited purpose" and its activities have "disproportionate effect" on landowners as a group, on the logic that restricting the franchise only to landowners is justified by landowners' economic stakes in district decisions (Briffault, 1993).[2] Land owners typically do not need to reside in the district to vote, and some districts even apportion voting power based on the amount or value of land held. Although this type of voting rule is relatively uncommon among special districts, it constitutes an important departure from the norms of democratic representation and reduces the significance of boundaries in establishing citizenship within a jurisdiction.[3]

Boundaries also define the extent and nature of individuals' property rights. Through their control over land use and zoning, local governments dictate how people can use and modify their land and homes. Local governments affect property rights most directly when they exercise eminent domain to seize property for public use or for transfer to another private owner in the interest of economic development. A government may take property by eminent domain only within its own boundaries, of course, and may further be limited by the boundaries of established redevelopment zones. Even without direct appropriation, governments may impinge on the value of property and its intended use with regulations restricting subdivisions, requiring that land be dedicated to specific uses, and controlling the size and style of building structures. Boundary lines determine the rights associated with otherwise identical properties, affecting individuals' relationships with their land and shaping where and how a community will grow. The fact that local governments exercise such strong control over property values gives homeowners a large stake in local politics. Because homeowners tend to have significant investments in their homes, they take more interest in the activities of local government in order to protect and enhance their home values (Fischel, 2001). Courts have recognized that this functional role of local government in determining property use and value affects residents differentially, and it is an important justification for the exceptions described above to one-person, one-vote representation (Briffault, 1993).

In addition to defining residents' representational and property rights, boundaries determine access to public goods and services. In a foundational article titled "A Pure Theory of Local Public Expenditures," Charles Tiebout (1956) depicted local governance as a marketplace in which jurisdictions compete for residents by offering rival packages of public goods. Some jurisdictions offer high levels of public services and impose high taxes, while others offer fewer services and have lower taxes. By choosing their place of residence, individuals opt into the bundle of public goods that best matches their preferences. It is this competition between localities, Tiebout argued, that creates an incentive for local governments to provide public goods efficiently. The configuration of local boundaries dictates the package of services available in a given location from the city, county, school district, and special districts that have jurisdiction over the location. Crosscutting boundaries create bundles of services that can vary by neighborhood or even by household. Moreover, because each local government must rely on its own tax base or other revenue stream to fund its activities, boundaries establish inequalities in service delivery. Differences in service bundles are a product not only of current preferences and capacity but also a legacy of earlier policy decisions: older cities provide more services, and spend more on services (Stein, 1990; Burns, 1994). Overall, one's access to public goods depends heavily on one's location.

The flip side of defining residents' access to services is to define their obligations. In the Tiebout model, individuals choosing where to live are weighing the benefits of access to a community's public services against the cost of the tax liability in that community. The dominant source of local taxation is the property tax; it accounts for 45 percent of the general revenue that localities collect from their own sources.[4] Part of what makes the property tax an attractive revenue source for local governments is the immobility of the tax's target. A high sales tax can drive sales transactions outside of a jurisdiction's boundaries; in contrast, property improvements such as building structures, and especially the land beneath them, are relatively immobile, allowing a jurisdiction to protect and easily identify its tax base. The rates for property taxes as well as other local taxes and fees can vary widely across communities within a state or a metropolitan region, and the ability of some school districts and special districts to levy their own taxes and fees add to the disparities that may exist across boundary lines. Boundaries define not only current tax obligations but also the level of indebtedness that a resident shares with others in her community. Because local governments often finance growth by taking on debt, residents may bear the burden of paying for policy decisions enacted before they moved to the community.

Finally, through their role in delimiting formal differences between jurisdictions in rights, services, and obligations, local boundaries have the additional function of shaping community. Boundaries create the opportunity to include and exclude. As a consequence, they demarcate and solidify socioeconomic inequalities, promoting homogeneity within communities (Altshuler et al., 1999; Drier, Mollenkopf, and Swanstrom, 2001). First, local governments' power in establishing property rights affects potential residents' access to a community. Although cities and towns cannot adopt explicitly discriminatory policies, they can use their control over land use and zoning to attract certain types of residents (Danielson, 1976; Downs, 1994). Because middle- and upper-class residents tend to want to live near those with the same means, they will use regulations that slow the pace of development, set minimum lot sizes, and dictate the mix of housing stock to discourage those with fewer resources from settling in the community. Control over services also contributes to homogeneity because of shared preferences. Through Tiebout sorting, individuals can choose to reside in jurisdictions that provide the kind of services they prefer, so a community with a set distribution of investments will tend to attract residents with similar preferences. Finally, apart from individuals' preferences about the identity of their neighbors, residents of high-income communities have an economic interest in protecting homogeneity in order to maintain a high tax base and low demand for redistributive social services, which will help keep tax obligations low (Peterson, 1981; Schneider, 1989). In sum, boundaries create both motivation and opportunity for localities to differentiate themselves. Less formally, boundaries serve as a device to provide potential residents with information about the character of the community, reinforcing the tendency toward homogeneity. As Weiher (1991: 194) explains, "political boundaries support the recruitment that is the complement to exclusion in urban sorting." They also can influence the organization of civic and political engagement, strengthening the ties among residents within a jurisdiction and encouraging individuals to self-identify as residents of a specific locality.

EFFECTS OF BOUNDARY ORGANIZATION

The largest and most developed literature related to boundary organization addresses fragmentation, or the density of independent governments within a given area. A local governance system may be fragmented horizontally, with many small general-purpose governments densely packed next to one another, or the fragmentation may be vertical, with independent special districts layered on top of cities and towns, dividing responsibility for the provision of local goods and services. In the most fragmented regions such as the area surrounding Pittsburgh, fragmentation occurs along both horizontal and vertical lines.

An enduring debate in the literature addresses the costs and benefits of fragmented governance. On one side of the debate are those who argue, following Tiebout, that competition among governments in a fragmented local political economy promotes efficiency and responsiveness in the provision of public goods and services. On the other side, many contend that fragmentation leads to wasteful duplication of effort and reduces public officials' accountability to their constituents.

In his classic article, Tiebout was responding to recent work in the economics literature arguing that market mechanisms could not provide public goods efficiently because of the free-rider problem that creates an incentive for individuals to understate their preferences. Tiebout made the case that governments could provide goods and services efficiently at the local level if enough jurisdictions exist and the bundles of public goods they provide differ from one another. In that case, fully mobile "consumer-voters" effectively reveal their preferences by "voting with their feet" and moving to the jurisdictions whose bundles of services most closely match their preferences. Competition for residents promotes market efficiency because individuals sort into communities where everyone has similar taste. In later work with Vincent Ostrom and Robert Warren, Tiebout introduced the concept of metropolitan governance as a "polycentric political system" with many independent centers of decision making (Ostrom, Tiebout, and Warren, 1961). Polycentrism further promotes efficiency by allowing appropriate scaling of public goods, decoupling of the production and provision of services, and flexible contracting arrangements among local governments. More recent work shows that efficient outcomes require not just competition between jurisdictions but also flexible boundaries to accommodate increases or decreases in demand for a bundle of public goods (Epple and Zelenitz, 1981; Epple and Romer, 1989).

Tiebout's original model emphasized the efficiency effects of fragmented governance, but he and other scholars additionally argued that dividing public authority among numerous independent governments increases responsiveness to public preferences. He and his colleagues warned about the absence of responsiveness in gargantua, a metropolitan political system with a single dominant center of decision making:

> [Gargantua] is apt to become a victim of the complexity of its own hierarchical or
> bureaucratic structure . . . Some decision-makers will be more successful in pursuing

their interests than others. The lack of effective organization for these others may result in policies with highly predictable biases. Bureaucratic unresponsiveness in gargantua may produce frustration and cynicism on the part of the local citizen who finds no point of access for remedying local problems of a public character.

(Ostrom, Tiebout, and Warren, 1961: 837)

They reasoned that because a large jurisdiction is composed of smaller publics whose composition might vary across issues, responsive governance therefore may require different organizational forms for different services. Robert Bish (1971) elaborated on polycentrism's benefits for responsiveness, arguing that it allows for more congruence between citizens' preferences and those of their public officials. Vertical fragmentation in particular reduces the scope of responsibilities that any one politician oversees, so voters casting ballots for these more narrowly defined public offices are more likely to find candidates whose positions coincide with their own. If residents are unsatisfied with the service they receive from government, a vertically fragmented system offers multiple venues where they can express their complaints and demands. In a less fragmented system where a single unit of government controls a large territory and a diverse set of functions, it is easier for a small group to gain dominance and to bias outcomes away from what a majority would prefer (Ostrom, Bish, and Ostrom, 1988).

Another stream of literature challenges these optimistic assessments of fragmentation and instead calls for consolidation of governing structures across geographic and functional boundaries. A group of scholars writing in the mid-twentieth century argued that fragmentation promotes redundancy and wasteful spending and increases the influence of special interests over policy outcomes. In his 1942 book *Metropolitan Government*, Victor Jones highlighted the mismatch between the metropolitan-wide scale of problems such as transportation, sewage treatment, and drinking water protection and the fragmentation of governing authorities responsible for addressing these problems. He and others who advocated government reform contended that the transaction costs, duplication of service, and failure to take advantage of economies of scale all contributed to higher service costs (Jones, 1942; Gulick, 1957; Wood, 1958, 1961; Advisory Commission on Intergovernmental Relations, 1964; Committee for Economic Development, 1966, 1970). Moreover, they argued that fragmentation reduced democratic accountability. Citizens are less able to express preferences and grievances to the many public officials who represent them, and they lack the information they need to cast informed ballots for the many county, city, school district, and special district offices. As Jones (1942) described, "Unnecessary impediments to popular control of local government arise when the electors of metropolitan areas find it necessary to express their preferences by marking a long "jungle ballot," when they must watch intelligently and simultaneously the activities of many units of government, and when the issues, because they have not proceeded from a consideration of the needs and resources of the entire metropolitan area, are often petty and unrelated to the large needs of the community" (335). Metropolitan reformers were particularly skeptical about special districts, whose low public profile and complex governing structures created additional obstacles to accountability (Bollens, 1957).

Empirical evidence on how fragmentation affects efficiency and responsiveness is mixed. With respect to horizontal fragmentation, the evidence accumulated from extensive empirical investigations suggests that fragmentation of general-purpose governments generally is associated with lower levels of expenditure. As Ostrom, Tiebout, and Warren (1961) predicted, optimal size of a jurisdiction may vary based on the nature of the public good: fragmentation seems to have the biggest payoffs for labor-intensive services, while capital-intensive goods may be provided more efficiently by large jurisdictions.[5] Horizontal fragmentation also appears to offer benefits in terms of government performance and citizen satisfaction (Ostrom, Parks, and Whitaker, 1978; Parks and Oakerson, 1993; Ostrom and Parks, 1999; Hoxby, 2000 but see Lowery and Lyons, 1989; Lyons and Lowery, 1989). The efficiency gains from interjurisdictional competition do not apply when governments are layered on top of one another, however. County-level analyses by both Foster (1997) and Berry (2008) show that vertical fragmentation, measured as reliance on special districts to provide public services, is associated with higher levels of public spending. Berry (2008) attributes this result to overtapping of a fiscal common pool, arguing that governments that share a tax base each internalize only part of the costs of taxation and therefore have a tendency to spend more than they would if they had a territorial monopoly. Nonetheless, vertical fragmentation may promote responsiveness; Mullin (2008) finds that on issues that have low public salience, special districts make policy decisions that are more congruent with public preferences than decisions made by general-purpose governments.

Although horizontal fragmentation can be applauded for promoting efficient, responsive policy making, these outcomes can have negative consequences for the broader population. Responsiveness to constituents' demands for lower taxes, higher property values, and more homogeneous communities has contributed to racial segregation and economic inequality across jurisdictions.[6] By Tiebout's logic, localities are able to provide public goods efficiently because individuals have sorted among communities according to their preferences.

In his stylized model, all individuals are perfectly mobile; in reality, individuals' ability to move is highly correlated with income, so it is high- and middle-income households that are most able to seek out communities that have desirable bundles of services. A city will be able to provide more services at a lower tax rate if its tax base is high and it does not have to invest in redistribution. Those with the resources to move thus have an incentive to sort into communities with high-income populations and then to use control over land use to exclude low-income and minority residents. This sorting leaves some communities—especially central cities and inner-core suburbs—with a disproportionate share of needy populations and a tax base inadequate to support them.

Moreover, the fragmentation of governments, both horizontally and vertically, creates significant coordination challenges. Many of the public goods and services that local governments provide have effects that spill over into neighboring communities. These effects may be positive, as when a city builds a park that residents of neighboring communities can enjoy, but very often they are negative. A city's failure to provide adequate police protection leads to crime that spills over city boundaries; development on the periphery of a jurisdiction causes traffic in an adjoining community; inadequate sewage treatment contaminates a river that serves as a regional recreational and drinking water resource. Externalities can cause problems in a vertically fragmented system as well, as when a city authorizes housing development that the local water district does not have the capacity to serve, jeopardizing water quality and reliability systemwide. Other problems that arise in a fragmented governance system include the failure to take advantage of economies of scale and the overuse of some common pool resource such as a shared aquifer. This type of problem often stems from a mismatch between existing political boundaries and the boundaries that would be most appropriate for providing some public good or managing a public resource. Collective action among governments often can help reduce inefficiencies or arrange compensation for externalities, but strategic local actors may have an incentive to cause hold-up problems or engage in venue shopping (Mullin, 2009). Feiock and Scholz have launched a stream of research dedicated to understanding the nature of institutional collective action problems and the variety of cooperative mechanisms that can help to mitigate them (Feiock, 2004, 2009; Scholz, Berardo, and Kyle, 2008; Feiock, Steinacker, and Park, 2009; Feiock and Scholz, 2010). They argue that self-organization among local governments, both formally through the creation of special districts and regional authorities and informally through the development of contracting agreements and policy networks, helps regions address large-scale problems and adapt to changing conditions (Feiock and Scholz, 2010).

A final set of consequences from boundary organization relates to political participation. How does the organization of local boundaries define community and influence people's engagement with politics? Eric Oliver has investigated the effect of city size on civic participation, finding that residents of small municipalities are more likely to have knowledge of and interest in local affairs and to engage in civic activities than those who live in larger cities (Oliver, 2001; Oliver and Ha, 2007). Racial and economic homogeneity suppress participation, however, perhaps by reducing the variation in policy preferences and therefore the amount of conflict in a community (Oliver, 2001). Oliver works only with city-level data, assuming that the city defines the local political community. However, it is possible that county, school district, and other jurisdictional boundaries also help to shape political communities. We have little understanding of patterns of political interaction at the local level, and how party and interest group organization and informal political networks correspond to the boundaries of local governments. In most U.S. metropolitan areas, local government organization resembles what Hooghe and Marks (2003) call Type II governance, in which jurisdictions are often functionally specific rather than general-purpose, have flexible designs, and operate at varying territorial scales (see also Frey and Eichenberger, 1999). The alternative Type I system is characterized by general-purpose governments with more permanent designs that operate at a limited number of jurisdictional levels. Hooghe and Marks (2003) argue that the two systems entail contrasting models of community. Type I governance is based on encompassing communities, where citizens are oriented toward voice rather than exit and multifunction governments must prioritize among numerous competing priorities. In a Type II system, intersecting membership and functional specialization produce more pragmatic political communities in which individuals have the option of avoiding political conflict by voting with their feet or establishing a new government to manage a public good. Special districts have multiplied in recent decades, creating more complex boundary maps that divide authority both geographically and by function. We know little about the effects of this transformation for the development and maintenance of common interest in a community and the promotion of civic participation.

DETERMINANTS OF BOUNDARY ORGANIZATION

Establishing boundaries is an essential part of forming a new local government, and the location of a jurisdiction's boundaries is the product of purposeful decision making by actors involved in government formation. Formations may result from any of three different mechanisms: incorporation of previously unincorporated territory; secession of territory from an existing municipality or special district; or the layering of a special district on top of existing governments either to provide a new service or to take over a service from a general-purpose government. Because formations typically require consent from a majority of those who would reside within the new jurisdiction, the specific location of boundaries is a strategic decision dictated by local political context and constrained by the configuration of existing boundaries. On the more general question about why actors form new local governments, however, research has identified several important factors.

The overriding reason for establishment of a new local government is to provide access to services. Leading the effort may be citizens seeking a higher level of service delivery than what is available under existing governing arrangements, or developers with an interest in extending infrastructure to the properties they hold while avoiding financial risk. By carving out a new municipality from previously unincorporated territory or laying a new special district on top of existing jurisdictions, local actors are able to create a bundle of services (and corresponding tax or fee obligations) that more closely matches local preferences. However, because only those with a concentrated stake in local governing structure are likely to invest effort in altering local boundaries, developers and other business interests dominate the politics of city and special district formation (Burns, 1994). Developers are particularly attracted to the bonding powers of special districts, which provide access to capital for major infrastructure projects while avoiding the public visibility of general-purpose cities and counties (Foster, 1997).[7]

Another reason that development interests might lead an effort for government formation is to gain control over land use (Miller, 1981; Teaford, 1997; Fischel, 2001). Zoning decisions have direct impact on where and how property owners may develop their land. Authority over these decisions is a power firmly held by cities and towns, and a developer with extensive holdings of unincorporated land may have an incentive to pursue municipal incorporation as a means to secure a favorable regulatory climate. Of course, homeowners also have a stake in land use decisions because of the effect these decisions can have on property values. In his analysis of municipal incorporations in King County, Washington, Fischel (2001) highlights residents' dissatisfaction with the county's predevelopment stance in explaining local support for creating ten new cities.

A third motivation for government formation is financial. Local actors may seek to incorporate or create a new special district in order to lower the cost of service delivery or capture external revenue collected through a sales tax (Miller, 1981; Tkacheva, 2008). During the 1950s, dozens of incorporations occurred in Los Angeles County under the Lakewood Plan, creating cities that contracted with the county for basic services and offered few services on their own. In his study of the Lakewood Plan cities, Miller (1981) argued that residents' support for formation of these minimal cities was attributable to preferences about redistribution: taxpayers sought to avoid the financial burden of redistributive programs that would benefit few who lived in the newly incorporated cities. Local residents behaving rationally produced in the aggregate a "revolt of the rich against the poor" (9), as middle- and upper-class residents were able to create jurisdictions that excluded service-demanding populations.

More generally, an important factor driving new government formations is residents' preferences to shape the racial and income composition of their community (Weiher, 1991; Burns, 1994; Downs, 1994). In a study of U.S. local governments over time, Alesina, Baqir, and Hoxby (2004) found that county-level racial heterogeneity (and, to a lesser extent, income heterogeneity) has a positive effect on the number of municipalities and school districts in a county. Local residents respond to heterogeneity by forming new governments or, more likely in the case of school districts, refusing to consolidate existing districts. The growth of special districts over time is not related to heterogeneity, however, perhaps because special districts involve lower levels of interaction among residents.

The Alesina, Baqir, and Hoxby study highlights important differences between government types. Cities seem to define citizenship and community in a way that special districts do not; school districts are likely to fall somewhere in between (Danielson, 1972). The degree to which cities are viewed as coherent and united political communities can be seen in the controversy that arises over secession proposals, such as those that have arisen in New York City's Staten Island and the San Fernando Valley in Los Angeles (Briffault, 1992; Hogen-Esch, 2001; Frug, 2002; Sonenshein, 2004). Secession proposals bring into even sharper relief the significance of boundaries in delineating residents' rights and responsibilities, and in defining residents either into or outside of local citizenship. They also facilitate the process of sorting into distinctly rich and distinctly poor communities (Penn, 2004).

The barriers to municipal incorporation are high: there must be some supply of unincorporated land, otherwise creating a new city requires residents to secede from their existing community. A similar barrier exists for school districts, whose jurisdictions typically may not overlap. Special districts, on the other hand, can layer on top of one another. Although a special district usually has a monopoly on the specific service it provides within its jurisdiction, another district may be formed to provide additional service of a similar type—for example, a transit district providing rail service may overlap one that operates buses. The consequence of these lower barriers to formation is a proliferation of special districts: while the number of cities and towns increased by 6 percent during the period 1952–2002, the number of independent special districts nearly tripled.[8]

Much more common than the formation of a new local government is boundary reorganization among existing governments. Thousands of municipal annexations occur each year, in which the boundaries of a city or town expand to include nearby, unincorporated territory.[9] The U.S. Census tracks annexation activity with its annual Boundary and Annexation Survey; special districts also regularly expand their jurisdictions through annexation, but these changes are not well monitored. A city's ability to annex territory has consequences for how it adapts to changes in its population and its economic circumstances. Annexation is an important tool for capturing tax revenue and taking advantage of economies of scale. Rusk (1993) classifies cities based on their elasticity, or whether they have expanded to encompass a large portion of the metropolitan area population. Rusk argues that elastic cities, most of which are located in the Sun Belt, are better able to guide and accommodate growth. Factors contributing to municipal annexation are similar to those driving incorporation. A key motivation seems to be expansion of the tax base to support services for existing residents (MacManus and Thomas, 1979; Liner and McGregor, 1996). Cities also may seek to enlarge their service territory in order to close service gaps or capture economies of scale (Carr and Feiock, 2001). Finally, local actors may treat annexation as a means to change the racial balance of the city (Austin, 1999).

In addition to incorporation and annexation, a third form of boundary change is the consolidation or merger of existing governments. A nationwide effort to consolidate rural school districts during the mid-twentieth century dramatically reconfigured local school district boundaries and the organization of public education. In contrast, consolidation of general-purpose governments is uncommon. Regionalists have long argued for consolidation of fragmented local governments within a metropolitan area, arguing that it would reduce wasteful duplication of effort and promote broader perspectives on metropolitan problem-solving (Jones, 1942; Gulick, 1957; Rusk, 1993). Yet numerous efforts to merge city and suburban governments, especially through city-county consolidation, have failed to win local support. Seven consolidations have occurred since 2000, increasing the total number of consolidated city-county governments to 40, but these represent just a small fraction of the number of serious consolidation efforts. Consolidation typically requires a referendum of citizens who will be affected by the reform, and over 80 percent of merger referenda fail (Leland and Thurmaier, 2004). Research on consolidation efforts have attributed successful campaigns to a crisis climate, effective arguments about consolidation's benefits for economic development, and the pursuit of selective benefits by local political actors (Rosenbaum and Kammerer, 1974; Feiock and Carr, 2001; Leland and Thurmaier, 2004; Feiock, Carr, and Johnson, 2006). More generally, Calabrese, Cassidy, and Epple (2002) show analytically that although consolidation can have positive aggregate effects on social welfare, high-income residents are adversely affected and therefore will likely vote against consolidation efforts.

A recurring theme in the literature on boundary organization is the importance of state policy in creating opportunities for government formation and boundary change. State law has both direct effects by setting the rules for different types of institutional reform and indirect effects by shaping the larger institutional context that makes a specific reform more or less attractive to local actors. States influence local government organization most directly by enabling the formation of local governments. The most powerful and consistent factor contributing to special district formation is the number and breadth of state enabling laws (Burns, 1994; Foster, 1997; Carr, 2006); the more types of districts available, the more likely that local actors will opt for special district formation as a mechanism to satisfy unmet demand for services. Among general-purpose governments, state rules requiring a special act of the legislature for municipal incorporation have a more modest effect in discouraging city formations.

Once a government has been established, its likelihood of expanding through annexation may also depend on the procedural requirements contained in state law. Findings are mixed with respect to how state rules governing the boundary change process affect local annexation activity (Dye, 1964; MacManus and Thomas, 1979; Galloway and Landis, 1986; Liner, 1990; Liner and McGregor, 1996; Carr and Feiock, 2001). Scholars have obtained varying results depending on how they measure annexation laws (whether the emphasis is on the locus of authority or specific procedural hurdles) and annexation activity (whether the emphasis is on scope or frequency of annexations). In a recent study, Carr and Feiock (2001) reported that more restrictive annexation rules actually increase the frequency of municipal annexation, perhaps because restrictive rules create an incentive for annexation supporters to pursue smaller proposals that then encounter less public resistance. Federal law can affect government formation and boundary change as well. After 1965, counties covered by Section 5 of the Voting Rights Act needed to obtain preclearance from the U.S. Department of Justice before making any changes to their voting practices, which has been ruled to include government formation and annexation. Burns (1994) has shown that from the 1960s onward, the Voting Rights Act slowed special district formation in counties that require federal preclearance.

In addition to its direct effects, state law can contribute to boundary organization indirectly by shaping the institutional environment in which local actors make decisions. Government formation and boundary reorganization are tools to solve some problem, and decision makers will weigh the costs and benefits of potential solutions against one another. Scholars have made some attempt to understand the relationship among different institutional solutions but have not reached firm conclusions. Although many have suspected that tax and expenditure limitations on general-purpose governments promote the formation of special districts as a means to finance local infrastructure, the evidence for this relationship is mixed (MacManus, 1981; Burns, 1994; Foster, 1997; Carr, 2006). Austin (1998) treats annexation and special district formation as potential substitutes and develops a model in which cities will oppose district formation to provide services in an adjacent territory if the city has state authority to annex and would experience a positive net gain from annexation. This line of inquiry about the relationship among various institutional solutions is worthy of further investigation. Decisions about institutional design rarely are dichotomous choices, at least in the early stages; local actors have a variety of mechanisms they can use to satisfy unmet demand or to achieve cost savings. They are likely to consider the costs of other strategies that might allow them to achieve the same policy goals. It is important to consider the strategic environment when examining institutional choices.

A RESEARCH AGENDA

The literature on local boundaries long has focused on testing and responding to Tiebout's model of public good provision; this is not surprising given the model's broad implications for competition, residential sorting, and government formation and dissolution. This research has revealed important insights about the causes and consequences of boundary organization, particularly about the policy effects of horizontal and vertical fragmentation. Recently, many scholars and practitioners have turned their attention from questions about efficiency and started to focus on the consequences of boundary organization for socioeconomic equity, economic development, and environmental protection. This is a welcome development, especially where the research acknowledges how institutions channel potentially competing demands from individuals' rational self-interest and pursuit of these larger collective goals.

As we begin paying attention to the broader implications of boundary organization, one set of questions that merits consideration relates to the appropriateness of existing jurisdictional boundaries given the distribution of populations and the nature of the underlying problems that governments aim to address. Efficient provision of public goods requires internalizing externalities by matching jurisdictional boundaries to populations with demand for the good (Oates, 1999). Optimal size of boundaries will vary across goods, so that the smaller the number of functions overseen by a jurisdiction, the more likely it should be that boundaries will be optimal (Ostrom, Tiebout, and Warren, 1961; Dahl and Tufte, 1973). These expectations have received little empirical testing because of the difficulty in defining the boundaries of a problem or the geographic distribution of demand. It is difficult enough to find the best scale for a park or a fire protection system; the task becomes even more complicated when addressing complex problems such as environmental justice or nonpoint source pollution. Those who study watershed management have grappled with this question (Ostrom, 1953; Ostrom, 1990; Blomquist, 1992; Blomquist, Schlager, and Heikkila, 2004; Scholz and Stiftel, 2005), but little conversation exists between scholars of urban politics and those who study alternative institutional forms in natural resources management. This is unfortunate, because the intersection of these fields through scholars such as Vincent Ostrom in the mid-twentieth century produced work that remains influential to this day.

Another area ripe for further inquiry is the effect of local boundaries on political community. We have little understanding about how boundaries help shape civic capacity and engagement. Since Tiebout, scholars have emphasized the exit option in local politics, and how boundaries and the possibility of boundary change may facilitate that option. The exercise of voice within existing communities has received less attention. Through their influence on the organization of local interest groups and social networks, we should expect political boundaries to affect the opportunity structure for political participation, and potentially the formation of individuals' policy preferences. Much remains unknown about whether and how these relationships operate, however. To what degree, and through what mechanisms, does sharing rights, services, and obligations create a community of interest? Does informal political community generally follow municipal boundary lines, or do the boundaries of school and special districts also influence how people interact and engage with politics? Is informal political organization more likely to follow municipal boundaries where the city population is more homogeneous or where the city is older and performs more functions? How do internal political boundaries such as city council districts and business improvement districts contribute to the organization of civic life? Finally, scholars and practitioners promoting a "new regionalism" have advocated making political boundaries more porous through mechanisms such as tax base sharing or the establishment of regional governments that coordinate local decision making (Downs, 1994; Orfield, 1997; Katz, 2000; Dreier, Mollenkopf, and Swanstrom, 2001). How might more porous boundaries change political community? Would it make interest group organization easier across jurisdictional lines, for example?

Both of these tasks present significant data challenges. Understanding the appropriateness of boundaries requires research with detailed, textured focus on the nature of specific public goods and policy problems. Examining the development of political communities calls for fine-grained data on group organization and political engagement at the neighborhood level. The hurdles to this type of data collection are substantial, and carrying out this research may require studies of small numbers of jurisdictions. Scholars have made good use of revenue, expenditure, and annexation data collected by the U.S. Census Bureau, but advancing our knowledge about the nature of local boundaries will require a broader view of local communities and the problems they face.

NOTES

1. 390 U.S. 474 (1968).
2. *Salyer Land Company v. Tulare Lake Basin Water Storage District* (410 U.S. 719, 1973).
3. More common are land ownership requirements for voting to approve certain types of bonds and fees, a rule that applies in many cities as well as special districts.
4. Data from the 2008 Annual Survey of State and Local Government Finance conducted by the U.S. Census Bureau. The largest overall source of local revenue is intergovernmental transfers, mostly from state governments.
5. For reviews of the empirical literature, see Dowding, John, and Biggs (1994) and Altshuler et al. (1999).
6. The empirical literature offers strong support for a relationship between fragmentation and racial segregation and mixed evidence for fragmentation's effect on segregation by income. For a review, see Altshuler et al. (1999).

7. The influence of developers on special district formation is a finding that emerges more strongly in case studies than in quantitative analyses of district formation, perhaps due to measurement problems in accounting for developer presence (Burns 1994; Foster 1997).

8. Calculated from Census of Governments data (U.S. Census Bureau 2002). The number of school districts declined by 80 percent during that period as a result of widespread district consolidations.

9. Secession combined with detachment occurs only rarely: of the 62,382 boundary changes during the 1970s, over 98 percent were annexations of previously unincorporated land rather than land that had been incorporated within another jurisdiction (Epple and Romer 1989).

REFERENCES

Advisory Commission on Intergovernmental Relations. 1964. *The Problem of Special Districts in American Government*. Washington, DC: ACIR.

Alesina, Alberto, Reza Baqir, and Caroline Hoxby. 2004. Political Jurisdictions in Heterogeneous Communities. *Journal of Political Economy 112*: 348–396.

Altshuler, Alan, William Morrill, Harold Wolman, and Faith Mitchell, eds. 1999. *Governance and Opportunity in Metropolitan America*. Washington, DC: National Academies Press.

Austin, D. Andrew. 1998. A Positive Model of Special District Formation. *Regional Science and Urban Economics 28*: 103–122.

Austin, D. Andrew. 1999. Politics vs. Economics: Evidence from Municipal Annexation. Journal of Urban Economics 45: 501–532.

Berry, Christopher R. 2008. Piling On: Multilevel Government and the Fiscal Common Pool. *American Journal of Political Science 52*: 802–820.

Bish, Robert L. 1971. *The Public Economy of Metropolitan Areas*. Chicago: Markham.

Blomquist, William. 1992. *Dividing the Waters: Governing Groundwater in Southern California*. San Francisco: ICS Press.

Blomquist, William, Edella Schlager, and Tanya Heikkila. 2004. *Common Waters, Diverging Streams: Linking Institutions and Water Management in Arizona, California, and Colorado*. Washington, DC: Resources for the Future.

Bollens, John C. 1957. *Special District Governments in the United States*. Berkeley: University of California Press.

Briffault, Richard. 1992. Voting Rights, Home Rule, and Metropolitan Governance: The Secession of Staten Island as a Case Study in the Dilemmas of Local Self-determination. *Columbia Law Review 92*: 775–850.

Briffault, Richard. 1993. Who Rules at Home? One Person/One Vote and Local Governments. *University of Chicago Law Review 60*: 339–424.

Burns, Nancy. 1994. *The Formation of American Local Governments: Private Values in Public Institutions*. New York: Oxford University Press.

Calabrese, Stephen, Glenn Cassidy, and Dennis N. Epple. 2002. Local Government Fiscal Structure and Metropolitan Consolidation. *Brookings-Wharton Papers on Urban Affairs 1–43*.

Carr, Jered B. 2006. Local Government Autonomy and State Reliance on Special District Governments: A Reassessment. *Political Research Quarterly 59*: 481–492.

Carr, Jered B., and Richard C. Feiock. 2001. State Annexation"Constraints" and the Frequency of Municipal Annexation. *Political Research Quarterly* 54: 459–470.

Committee for Economic Development. 1966. *Modernizing Local Government to Secure a Balanced Federalism*. New York: Committee for Economic Development.

Committee for Economic Development. 1970. *Reshaping Government in Metropolitan Areas*. New York: Committee for Economic Development.

Dahl, Robert A and Edward R. Tufte. 1973. *Size and Democracy*. Stanford, CA: Stanford University Press.

Danielson, Michael N. 1976. *The Politics of Exclusion*. New York: Columbia University Press.

Dowding, Keith, Peter John, and Stephen Biggs. 1994. Tiebout: A Survey of the Empirical Literature. *Urban Studies* 31: 767–797.

Downs, Anthony. 1994. *New Visions for Metropolitan America*. Washington, DC: Brookings Institution and Cambridge, MA: Lincoln Institute of Land Policy.

Drier, Peter, John Mollenkopf, and Todd Swanstrom. 2001. *Place Matters: Metropolitics for the Twenty-first Century*. Lawrence: University Press of Kansas.

Dye, Thomas. 1964. Urban Political Integration: Conditions Associated with Annexation in American Cities. *Midwest Journal of Political Science* 8: 430–466.

Epple, Dennis, and Thomas Romer. 1989. On the Flexibility of Municipal Boundaries. *Journal of Urban Economics* 26: 307–319.

Epple, Dennis, and Allan Zelenitz. 1981. The Implications of Competition among Jurisdictions: Does Tiebout Need Politics? *Journal of Political Economy* 89: 1197–1217.

Feiock, Richard C., ed. 2004. *Metropolitan Governance: Conflict, Competition, and Cooperation*. Washington, DC: Georgetown University Press.

Feiock, Richard C. 2009. Metropolitan Governance and Institutional Collective Action. *Urban Affairs Review* 44: 356–377.

Feiock, Richard C. and Jered B. Carr. 2001. Incentives, Entrepreneurs, and Boundary Change: A Collective Action Framework. *Urban Affairs Review* 36: 382–405.

Feiock, Richard C., Jered B. Carr, and Linda S. Johnson. 2006. Structuring the Debate on Consolidation: A Response to Leland and Thurmaier. *Public Administration Review* 66: 274–278.

Feiock, Richard C. and John T. Scholz, eds. 2010. *Self-Organizing Federalism: Collaborative Mechanisms to Mitigate Institutional Collective Action Problems*. New York: Cambridge University Press.

Feiock, Richard C., Annette Steinacker, and Hyung Jun Park. 2009. Institutional Collective Action and Economic Development Joint Ventures. *Public Administration Review* 69: 256–270

Fischel, William A. 2001. *The Homevoter Hypothesis: How Home Values Influence Local Government Taxation, School Finance, and Land-Use Politics*. Cambridge, MA: Harvard University Press.

Foster, Kathryn A. 1997. *The Political Economy of Special Purpose Government*. Washington, DC: Georgetown University Press.

Frey, Bruno S. and Reiner Eichenberger. 1999. *The New Democratic Federalism for Europe: Functional, Overlapping and Competing Jurisdictions*. Northampton, MA: Edward Elgar.

Frug, Gerald E. 2002. Is Secession from the City of Los Angeles a Good Idea? *UCLA Law Review* 49: 1783–1798.

Galloway, Thomas D. and John Landis. 1986. How Cities Expand: Does State Law Make a Difference? *Growth and Change* 17: 25–45.

Gulick, Luther. 1957. Metropolitan Organization. *Annals of the American Academy of Political and Social Science 314*: 57–65.

Hogen-Esch, Tom. 2001. Urban Secession and the Politics of Growth: The Case of Los Angeles. *Urban Affairs Review 36*: 783–809.

Hooghe, Liesbet and Gary Marks. 2003. Unraveling the Central State, but How? Types of Multi-Level Governance. *American Political Science Review 97*: 233–243.

Hoxby, Caroline M. 2000. Does Competition among Taxpayers Benefit Students and Taxpayers? *American Economic Review 90*: 1209–1238.

Jones, Victor. 1942. *Metropolitan Government*. Chicago: University of Chicago Press.

Katz, Bruce, ed. 2000. *Reflections on Regionalism*. Washington, DC: Brookings Institution.

Leland, Suzanne, and Kurt Thurmaier, eds. 2004. *Case Studies of City-county Consolidation: Reshaping the Local Government Landscape*. Armonk, NY: M.E. Sharpe.

Liner, Gaines H. 1990. Annexation Rates and Institutional Constraints. *Growth and Change 21*: 80–94.

Liner, Gaines H., and Rob Roy McGregor. 1996. Institutions and the Market for Annexable Land. *Growth and Change 27*: 55–74.

Lowery, David, and William E. Lyons. 1989. The Impact of Jurisdictional Boundaries: An Individual-level Test of the Tiebout Model. *Journal of Politics 51*: 73–97.

Lyons, William E., and David Lowery. 1989. Governmental Fragmentation versus Consolidation: Five Public Choice Myths about How to Create Informed, Involved, and Happy Citizens. *Public Administration Review 49*: 533–543.

MacManus, Susan A. 1981. Special District Governments: A Note on their Use as Property Tax Relief Mechanisms in the 1970s. *Journal of Politics 43*: 1206–1214.

MacManus, Susan and Robert Thomas. 1979. Expanding the Tax Base: Does Annexation Make a Difference? *The Urban Interest 1*: 15–28.

Miller, Gary J. 1981. *Cities by Contract: The Politics of Municipal Incorporation*. Cambridge, MA: MIT Press.

Mullin, Megan. 2008. The Conditional Effect of Specialized Governance on Public Policy. *American Journal of Political Science 52*: 124–140.

Mullin, Megan. 2009. *Governing the Tap: Special District Governance and the New Local Politics of Water*. Cambridge, MA: MIT Press.

Oates, Wallace E. 1999. An Essay on Fiscal Federalism. *Journal of Economic Literature 37*: 1120–1139.

Oliver, J. Eric. 2001. *Democracy in Suburbia*. Princeton, NJ: Princeton University Press.

Oliver, J. Eric, and Shang E. Ha. 2007. Vote Choice in Suburban Elections. *American Political Science Review 101*: 393–408.

Orfield, Myron. 1997. *Metropolitics: A Regional Agenda for Community and Stability*. Washington, DC: Brookings Institution and Cambridge, MA: Lincoln Institute of Land Policy.

Ostrom, Elinor. 1990. *Governing the Commons*. New York: Cambridge University Press.

Ostrom, Elinor, and Roger B. Parks. 1999. Neither Gargantua nor the Land of Lilliputs: Conjectures on Mixed Systems of Metropolitan Organization. In Michael McGinnis, ed., *Polycentricity and Local Public Economies: Readings from the Workshop in Political Theory and Policy Analysis*. Ann Arbor: University of Michigan Press, 284–305.

Ostrom, Elinor, Roger B. Parks, and Gordon P. Whitaker. 1978. *Patterns of Metropolitan Policing*. Cambridge, MA: Ballinger.

Ostrom, Vincent. 1953. *Water and Politics: A Study of Water Policies and Administration in the Development of Los Angeles*. Los Angeles: Haynes Foundation.

Ostrom, Vincent, Robert Bish, and Elinor Ostrom. 1988. *Local Government in the United States*. San Francisco: ICS Press.

Ostrom, Vincent, Charles M. Tiebout, and Robert Warren. 1961. The Organization of Government in Metropolitan Areas: A Theoretical Inquiry. *American Political Science Review 55*: 831–842.

Parks, Roger B., and Ronald J. Oakerson. 1993. Comparative Metropolitan Organization: Service Production and Governance Structures in St. Louis (MO) and Allegheny County (PA). *Publius 23*: 19–39.

Penn, Elizabeth Maggie. 2004. Institutions and Sorting in a Model of Metropolitan Fragmentation. *Complexity 9*: 62–70.

Peterson, Paul E. 1981. *City Limits*. Chicago: University of Chicago Press.

Rosenbaum, Walter A., and Gladys M. Kammerer. 1974. *Against Long Odds: The Theory and Practice of Successful Governmental Consolidation*. Beverly Hills, CA: Sage.

Rusk, David. 1993. *Cities Without Suburbs*. Washington, DC: Woodrow Wilson Center Press.

Schneider, Mark. 1989. *The Competitive City: The Political Economy of Suburbia*. Pittsburgh: University of Pittsburgh Press.

Scholz, John T. and Bruce Stiftel, eds. 2005. *Adaptive Governance and Water Conflict: New Institutions for Collaborative Planning*. Washington, DC: Resources for the Future.

Scholz, John T., Ramiro Berardo, and Brad Kyle. 2008. Do Networks Solve Collective Action Problems? Credibility, Search, and Collaboration. *Journal of Politics 70*: 393–406.

Sonenshein, Raphael J. 2004. *The City at Stake: Secession, Reform, and the Battle for Los Angeles*. Princeton, NJ: Princeton University Press.

Stein, Robert M. 1990. *Urban Alternatives: Public and Private Markets in the Provision of Local Services*. Pittsburgh, PA: University of Pittsburgh Press.

Teaford, Jon C. 1997. *Post-Suburbia: Government and Politics in the Edge Cities*. Baltimore, MD: Johns Hopkins University Press.

Tiebout, Charles M. 1956. A Pure Theory of Local Expenditures. *Journal of Political Economy 64*: 416–424.

Tkacheva, Olesya. 2008. New Cities, Local Officials, and Municipal Incorporation Laws: Supply-Side Model of City Formation. *Journal of Urban Affairs 30*: 155–174

U.S. Census Bureau. 2002. *20002 Census of Governments*. Volume 1, *Government Organization*. Washington, DC: Department of Commerce.

Weiher, Gregory. 1991. *The Fractured Metropolis: Political Fragmentation and Metropolitan Segregation*. Albany: State University of New York Press.

Wood, Robert C. 1958. The New Metropolis: Green Belts, Grass Roots, or Gargantua. *American Political Science Review 52*: 108–122.

Wood, Robert C. 1961. *1400 Governments: The Political Economy of the New York Region*. Cambridge, MA: Harvard University Press.

CHAPTER 18

LOCAL LEGISLATURES

SUZANNE LELAND AND HOLLY WHISMAN

LOCAL legislatures, an important component of municipal governance, are not as easily defined as they are at the federal and state level. While they comprise a significant portion of policymaking authority, they remain absent from the United States Constitution. Local legislatures—city councils, city commissions, county commissions, special districts boards, school boards, etc.—instead derive their power from state constitutions and statues. Power is not shared between state and local governments as it is shared between federal and state governments; instead the intergovernmental relationship is hierarchical or unitary in nature. Therefore, local legislative power is entirely dependent upon what authority a particular state grants. For example, in the case of cities, specific powers derived from state government are laid out in a city charter and are roughly similar to a state or the federal constitution. Typically states rely on a general act or classified charter that places cities into different categories based on population and/or the local tax base. More power is typically given to larger cities than smaller towns or villages.

The 89,000 plus local government legislative bodies are characterized by their diversity of structure, largely shaped by the history of political machines and the subsequent reform movements. While some mirror a similar system of checks and balances analogous with Congress and the President, others mix executive and legislative functions. In many cases, cities and counties have delegated power to special districts, the fastest growing and most popular form of government in the United States (See Table 18.1). As boundary lines become more obscure as a result of urbanization and decentralization, communities continually tinker with the structure of local government (Swartz, 2010). The following chapter will detail the formal and informal powers and the state of the research on local legislative bodies including cities, counties, special districts, and school boards. We start by discussing the legislative functions and the literature on city councils and commissions, then county legislatures, special districts, and school boards and assess prospects for future research.

Table 18.1   Census of Local Governments

Local Governments as of 2007	
Total	89,476
General Purpose	
County	3,033
Municipal	19,492
Town or Township	16,519
Total General Purpose	39,044
Special Purpose	
Special Districts	37,381
School Districts	13,051
Total Special Purpose	50,432

Note: developed by the authors based on U.S. Census Bureau (2007) data, <http://www.census.gov/govs/cog/GovOrgTab03ss.html>.

THE LEGISLATIVE FUNCTIONS OF CITY COUNCILS

City structure does not mirror the federal or state separation of powers and ranges from a fulltime legislative body with both administrative and political authority to a part-time legislative body with limited political authority. Therefore defining the formal rules and structure of city government is at times difficult, but nevertheless important because it not only helps us understand what local governments do but also dictates who gets what from government in the local arena.

The Role of State Government and Home Rule

As mentioned in the introduction, state constitutions and laws essentially determine the different structures of local government. Home rule refers to the powers of self-government afforded to municipalities by a given state. Dillon's rule provides the legal precedent for determining the level of autonomy local governments possess. Unless a power is expressly granted, it rests with the state rather than the municipality. Home rule can be provided by a state's constitution or can be statutory.

Defining the difference between home rule and Dillon's rule is not necessarily a simple distinction, as each state provides for some level of autonomy for local government while retaining other powers (Richardson et al., 2003). Even in states governed by

Dillon's rule, state legislatures have the ability to grant specific powers to local governments, and may do so based on the size of a municipality or other criteria.

As home rule pertains to local legislatures, city councils tend to have greater constraints, and less power than legislatures at higher levels of government (Krebs and Pelissero, 2003), particularly related to the ability to raise revenue through taxation. The issue of home rule can be confusing, even to local government officials. Some argue for greater autonomy in order to address issues currently facing cities. On the other hand, some have argued that home rule actually limits the ability of cities and suburbs to respond to current challenges, particularly those that are regional in nature (Barron, 2003). Development issues provide an example of this. Cities experiencing growth may be concerned with designing and implementing growth management policies. However, those types of policies are not likely to be carried out by a single jurisdiction, but are regional in scope. In such a case, home rule may work against the adoption of region-wide growth management strategies, as individual jurisdictions perceive their priorities as contrary to or in competition with those of neighboring jurisdictions (Richardson et al., 2003). Likewise, cities in declining regions may seek regional responses to diminishing population and tax base and the associated challenges. A high level of local autonomy may work to hamper regional cooperation in either example. The next section addresses the structure and functions of city councils in more detail.

Types of City Structure

In most cities across the US, elected legislative officials are part-time and hold meetings only once or twice a month. Only large cities with over a half-million people are likely to hold weekly meetings or have fulltime council members. When compared to Congress, city councils are not organized along partisan lines and they have fewer members and committees. Most attempt no great oversight of the executive branch. Turnover is considerably higher than in Congress, and staff members are few. There are three "types" of city governments: the mayor-council plan, the commission plan, and council-manager plan.

The mayor council plan (popular in larger cities) has two varieties, the weak-mayor and the strong-mayor form. The primary difference in the structure is the administrative power given to the mayor, and therefore it can directly impact the city council's power. As the name implies, in the weak-mayor system, the mayor has less formal power. The council is involved in the appointment and dismissal of administrative personnel. It is important to note that legislative power does not necessarily have to flow more freely in the weak-mayor model. Legislative power (and the power of the mayor) is typically weakened in this form if there are several independently elected officials or independent boards. This means that the council could potentially have more power because of the safeguards preventing the mayor from acting too powerfully—such as no veto power—but such gains may be eroded by the level of fragmentation of power. For this reason, this form of government is often criticized for inaction. In strong-mayor systems councils may still have the power to confirm mayoral appointments, control of appropriations to restrict purchasing authority, and the power to investigate the executive department activities (Ross and Levine, 2001).

In the council-manager form of government, the city manager has the day-to-day administrative power and the council (even in the absence of the mayor) is involved in legislative policy making. The council retains the authority to dismiss or replace its appointed manager. The mayor's role is minor and ceremonial in nature. He or she can even be selected from among the council as opposed to being directly elected by the public. In the case of Charlotte, the mayor does not vote on most issues but retains veto power. The legislative branch is typically smaller than in the other forms of government and they are non-partisan and selected at-large or a mix of both at-large and by districts. This reflects the reform movement's model city charter and is frequently found in mid-sized cities.

The least common form of municipal government is commission government where the legislative body is typically made up of five to seven fulltime elected officials who act as administrative department heads. Like the council-manager form, the legislative body is elected at-large and on a nonpartisan ballot. But unlike the council-manager and mayor-council form, both day-to-day administrative and policymaking power is concentrated in the legislative body (Ross and Levine, 2001).

THE ROLE OF CITY COUNCILS AND COMMISSIONS

The foremost role of city councils and similar bodies (commissions) is representing the interests of the public through local legislation and policy adoption. Council members are the primary policymakers of a municipality; however the mayor or manager may also have a role in making policy. The relationship of the council to the executive is likely to vary, depending on whether the form of government is mayor-council or council-manager, and perhaps upon the personality of the mayor as a public figure (Krebs and Pelissero, 2003).

Representation

The representativeness of municipal legislatures has been a topic of reformers for many years, in what is frequently a contentious and controversial process (Welch and Bledsoe, 1988). Since many cities are still racially segregated by neighborhood, the structure of elections (that is, at-large, by district, or a combination) can influence the likelihood of minority representation on council. A long-standing concern regarding the representation of African Americans in municipal legislatures is the notion that at-large systems—advocated by urban reformers a century ago—have the potential to block African

American candidates from office, resulting in numerous court cases. Welch (1990) found that the negative effect of at-large council elections on African American representation has dwindled in recent years but still persists. Her research also revealed an impact on Hispanic representation that seemed to vary by region. This is a potentially fruitful area of research, as in some parts of the country the Hispanic population is rapidly expanding.

The structure of elections for local legislator can also influence the political attitudes of residents. Welch and Bledsoe (1988) found significant differences in the political attitudes of residents whose local representatives were elected by district or at-large, based on the race of the respondent. African Americans living in at-large cities were substantially less likely than their white counterparts to report having political efficacy. The sense of efficacy is related to political participation, and therefore might be just as concerning as descriptive representation in terms of who participates in local politics. Such an attitude could even persist long after the actual gap in representation has disappeared, having lingering consequences for traditionally disadvantaged groups.

Hajnal (2010) considered the impact of institutional structure on representation at the local level. For both election timing and district type, the impact of reform appears to be significant. When a city switches from at-large to district elections the number of black representatives on the city council increases by a little over 3 percent, holding everything else equal. Similarly, altering the dates of local elections to coincide with when national elections are held increases black representation in a city by 3 percentage points. Combined, these two types of election reforms could have a substantial impact. According to his model, reform on both measures increases the proportion of blacks on a city council by a little over 6 percentage points, again all else equal. Given that blacks average 9 points below parity this represents a significant improvement in black representation (Hajnal, 2010: 91).

Downs characterizes the importance of representation by stating, "Everyone who is significantly affected by some public policy has a right to have a voice in determining that policy. This does not mean exercising sole power over the policy. But it does mean being included within the community whose welfare is explicitly considered in the formation and adoption of policies (Downs, 1994: 58). Descriptive representation, however, does not necessarily indicate that the issues of concern to minorities are being addressed by council. Austin (2002) raised a concern that racial polarization can have implications for council members with high proportions of minority constituents, with those councilors more likely to be on the losing side of council votes, once in office. For all the work that researchers have conducted on descriptive representation, many questions remain unanswered about whether decisions made by city councils represent the interests of minority or disadvantaged residents.

The Changing Roles of Municipal Legislatures

The roles and expectations citizens place on city councils vary as much as the cities they represent. Different regions tend to place different responsibilities upon their city councils, and as taxing authority varies by state, so does the ability of a council to raise revenue (MacManus, 1999). Further, as MacManus (1999) points out, "The average city official today serves in an antigovernment, antitax environment" (181). This sentiment, if anything, has grown stronger in the past decade.

Though prior public office or political service is not a prerequisite for individuals wishing to run for council, in larger cities inexperienced politicians are unlikely to be elected (Krebs and Pelissero, 2003). Even suburban councils have become more professionalized and now must address more pressing issues than in the past, such as growth management (Schneider et al., 1995), infrastructure and environmental concerns. Those emerging issues tend to be regional in nature and require the cooperation of multiple municipalities, raising questions of inter-local governance and constituencies.

As the challenges facing cities evolve, the historic jurisdictional boundaries are not always ideally structured for responding to issues that involve multiple localities. Councils of governments (COGs) represent one manner of addressing multi-jurisdictional concerns; however the level of contentiousness of a particular issue may limit the usefulness of these bodies. Gunlicks (1981) asserted COGs are unlikely to take place in issues such as "poverty, unemployment, housing or busing" (Gunlicks, 1981: 22). While this statement still pertains, the past several decades have brought new issues of contention between municipalities attempting to work together to address metropolitan concerns related to environment, transportation, and regional competitiveness in a global marketplace.

The boundaries that fragment regions into municipal jurisdictions are perceived by some as outdated, and approaches to addressing regional issues range from structural, such as city-county consolidations and the formation of special districts, to purely functional, such as interlocal cooperative agreements (ILAs). The roles of local legislators are evolving as the issues facing them change, along with the approaches to addressing those issues. Thurmaier and Wood (2002) explored ILAs through the lens of social network theory in the context of public management, paving the way for researchers to explore questions of cooperation and networking and the roles of local legislators, as well as their executive counterparts, in brokering ILAs. Issues of accountability also provide an agenda for future research, as "there is no central repository of ILA information" (Thurmaier and Wood, 2002: 595). Additionally, Vogel and Nezelkewicz (2002) examined the role of the federal government in promoting metropolitan governance through metropolitan planning organizations (MPOs), and found disappointing results in terms of integrated planning. Their findings imply the need for "strong intergovernmental managers able to operate in such a complex network" (129). The role of local legislatures in metropolitan governance structures, though not clearly prescribed, will be essential and will yield important research opportunities.

Most studies of regional governance efforts are case studies, as the contextual specificity of each metropolitan area warrants. Data regarding ILAs tend to be difficult, if not impossible, to collect, which prevents researchers from broad comparative analysis.

County Legislatures

The significance to researchers of the study of counties has grown over time despite numerous complications of making comparisons across the different structures and functions of the more than 3000 county and county-like[1] jurisdictions that operate across the United States. Many important questions regarding county governance—and the roles of legislative bodies in particular—remain unanswered, however the differences among county governing structures across the country make the study of counties exceedingly complex (Menzel et al., 1992; Cigler, 1995).[2] Just like in the case of cities, state statutes play an important role in the structure and function of county governments—including the structure of the legislative branch—which were organized as administrative extensions of each state. As state constitutions were drafted, each approached the structure of counties in its own manner. The state-level variations resulting from the freedom to structure counties independently complicate cross-state comparisons. For example, county legislatures are known by 17 different names (Sokolow, 1993). The two most common are county commissions and boards of supervisors. Even the number of counties operating in the United States is debated (Cigler, 1995). For example, there is controversy over considering counties in Virginia as analogous units to counties in other states because cities are separate and their boundaries do not overlap. Therefore counties in Virginia only serve areas that are unincorporated unless they are consolidated like Virginia Beach and Princess Anne County. This is further complicated by Virginia's complex annexation law, which states that once a county has become "urban" the city sues the county for that portion of landmass and a three-judge panel in annexation court makes the determination. It is important to note that what we consider a "county" is typically a local government entity set-up to create and perform state functions locally, including the collection of taxes and administrative, judicial and legislative functions.

In an introduction to the topic of county government research, Lewis and Taylor (1994b) admitted that only within recent years had researchers begun to study "the growing importance of counties as providers of local governmental services and as valuable partners in the intergovernmental relations arena" (803). Changing citizen expectations regarding services, and geographic, land use, and population dynamics contribute to the evolution of county governance (Menzel et al., 1992; Sokolow, 1993; Cigler, 1995). The increasing urban and suburban population and the urban reform movement also influenced changes in the services provided by counties over the past century as well as structural changes in the legislative bodies of counties in some cases (Salant, 1991).

Additionally, the roles of counties have changed as a trend has emerged in recent decades for states to shift functional responsibilities to counties (Marando and Reeves, 1991). As they have taken on greater service provision responsibilities for states, counties have become an increasingly important topic of scholarship (Menzel et al., 1992; Sokolow, 1993; Cigler, 1995). At the same time, the goals of local government reformers, though directed at counties as well as municipalities, have not been realized as broadly among counties as in city government (Sokolow, 1993; Cigler, 1995).

Despite the importance of counties in the study of local governing structures, "county board behavior is not studied systematically nor on a broadly generalized basis" (Sokolow, 1993: 37). Cigler (1995) concurs, "We know little about the governing boards of counties or the 17,000 individuals who serve on them" (57). The scarcity of knowledge about who governs counties continues to be an important component of the ongoing research agenda regarding local government and governance.

HISTORICAL COUNTY CORRUPTION

Svens (2005) defines corruption as, "the misuse of public office for private gain" (20). Prior to the Progressive Era, county government officials had earned a reputation for corruption, in part through the compensation structure that was known as the fee system. Particularly in the largest counties in the U.S., the abuse of this system resulted in officials pocketing large sums from the collection of fines, penalties and other fees from citizens (Martin, 1993).[3] Cook County, Illinois, is often cited as a hotbed for this and other types of local government corruption, though it was by no means the only example. Though the fee system fell out of favor, the perception of corruption in county government has persisted (Waugh and Streib, 1993; Berman, 1993). Further, the push toward greater levels of professionalism in county legislatures has been hampered by political partisanship and the very structure of counties with commissions or multiple executives (Svara, 1996).

Most current research on corruption deals not with U.S. counties, but with developing countries. This does not indicate, however, that corruption among county officials has been eliminated. Karahan, Razzolini and Shughart (2006)[4] found that corruption in county government is more likely to occur in rural counties and in counties with a relatively more educated electorate. They also found evidence that counties in which supervisors or commissioners receive higher compensation were also more likely to experience corruption. This finding runs counter to what we might expect—that higher paid elected officials would be less likely to engage in corrupt practices.

Structures of County Legislatures

County legislative structures are generally categorized in three forms: commission form, council-executive form or commission-administrator form (Salant, 1991; Cigler, 1995). Additionally, city-county consolidations employ legislatures such as city-county councils (in Indiana and Kentucky).

The most common county governing structure is still the traditional three to five member commission form, which holds both legislative and executive powers. The commission is alternately referred to as a board of supervisors (as in Virginia, Iowa, California, Mississippi, and Wisconsin), and a freeholder board (as in New Jersey). While most county commissions are comprised of six or fewer commissioners, some have as many as 50. In some counties commissioners are elected by districts while in others they are elected at-large, depending in part on state law and the history of each county.

The commission-administrator form of county government, also known as commission-manager form, employs elected officials as legislators who work with an appointed, professionally-trained manager or administrator (Salant, 1991). It is the county analog of the council-manager (or administrative) structure of municipal government and is intended to enhance the separation of powers. This commission-manager form is now utilized by roughly 800 counties in the United States (NACo, 2009).

The council-executive form employs a manager who is elected directly by the public rather than being appointed by the commission or board. The form is mandated by three states—Arkansas, Kentucky and Tennessee—and is also employed in some others. It is the county-level equivalent of the strong mayor (or political) form of municipal government. Councils under this form of county government are alternately referred to as a county delegation (as in New Hampshire) and a quorum court (as in Arkansas).

County legislative bodies are commonly compared to city councils as a point of reference (Sokolow, 1993; Cigler, 1995). However Marando and Thomas (1977) point out the cities and counties are quite distinct from one another. Counties are both sub-units of states and operate as local governments; they have less freedom than cities when it comes to taxation and finances. As mentioned, counties have been the subject of reform, much as cities, though the objectives of urban reform seem to have had less impact on counties than municipalities (Sokolow, 1993; Cigler, 1995). County legislators are more likely than city council members to be elected by district, with nearly 75 percent of county legislators representing districts, while only approximately 20 percent of all city council members are elected by district (Sokolow, 1993: 31). County legislators are more likely than their municipal counterparts to be selected through partisan elections and the presiding officers on county boards are more likely to be appointed by the board rather than independently elected by the voters (Cigler, 1995). Further, the majority of county boards still do not have a professional manager as recognized by ICMA (Sokolow, 1993). Benton (2005) notes, however, that scholars still do not have a solid understanding of whether structural reform within county legislatures results in more efficiency, accountability, responsiveness or effectiveness (Benton, 2005: 464). MacManus (1996) similarly notes that increases in representation through female and minority county legislators have not yet engendered much research on those same outcomes. The structure of county legislatures, as it relates to these outcomes, represents a substantial opportunity for research.

The Roles of County Legislatures

In counties employing the commission form of government, elected officials hold both legislative and administrative responsibilities. Though the policy agendas of county governments have expanded greatly since the middle of the 20th century, county board members have maintained their administrative involvement in specific tasks, dating back to a more rural time, despite the gradual addition of professional administrators (Sokolow, 1993). This is consistent with the description by Marando and Reeves (1991: 50) of the "dual role" of counties... "Along with their activities as administrative units of the state, counties have assumed a growing role as local governments." The "... emphasis on administration is also rooted in some long-standing ideas about the obligations of elected officeholders in county government that obscure the distinction between policy and administration" (Sokolow, 1993: 32). Case studies of four rural counties revealed between 56 and 93 percent of boards' time was spent on administrative tasks (Sokolow, 1993).

The focus on policy is more pronounced for county legislators in urbanizing and suburban regions. Even while advocating for reformed county government structures, Streib (1996) acknowledges, "Elected leaders must strive to understand the complexities of county governance, and appointed administrators must become more involved in policy making" (144). This represents another kind of "dual role"—that of county legislators. At the county level, legislation and administration have traditionally been part of the same job. Even as reformed structures transform county governments and legislators are accompanied by professional administrators and managers, Streib's argument implies that the two tasks are not mutually exclusive at the county level. In fact, Lewis and Taylor (1994a) confirmed that whether elected or appointed, administrators and managers play important roles in policymaking. This issue represents an important avenue for research regarding the separation of powers in local governments.

Counties and Home Rule

DeSantis and Renner (1993) assert that states are gradually recognizing that, in order to meet the public's changing preferences for service provision, counties require greater latitude in terms of structure, elections and authority. As of 1965, only 18 states afforded any type of home rule for counties; now only 12 states still do not allow home rule or charter authorities to their counties (Berman and Salant, 1996). However, Cigler (1995) notes even counties that have home rule often do not utilize it.

Dillon's rule and its role in limiting the discretion of county governments can have an impact on the ability of county leaders to innovate and respond to changing circumstances. Parks (1991: 32) argues that "States that hold strictly to Dillon's rule may dampen local public entrepreneurship and interlocal self-governance to such an extent that important intergovernmental opportunities cannot be pursued." Today's counties are important intermediaries between the state and municipalities, as well as between the various cities within a county's boundaries (Streib, 1996). Interlocal cooperation is an important problem-solving mechanism utilized by counties but home rule is not necessarily essential to cooperation; as Berman and Salant (1996: 28) point out, "many states are simply giving all counties greater authority regardless of home-rule status."

As counties mature, so do research agendas

When Bollens (1969) laid out an ambitious research agenda for the study of county governments, he placed particular emphasis on relationships and network linkages, including intergovernmental relations and interlocal arrangements, as well as accountability; encouraging researchers to move away from descriptive analysis toward empirical work. Menzel et al. (1992) and ten other prominent scholars of counties and local governance worked together to update the research agenda for counties in the 1990s. In agreement with Bollens (1969), Menzel et al. (1992) stated that county government research "has suffered from a lack of concern about relationships," as well as too much reliance on description of structure as opposed to empirical analysis (175). More recently, Benton (2005) and Streib et al. (2007) have further updated the research agenda for counties. Well as scholars understand what should be researched, we have only begun to brush the surface of knowledge about how counties function. Data concerns and the complexity of making comparisons across counties still plague researchers. However, we must find ways to do so, utilizing innovative methodologies that allow both practitioners and academic researchers to respond knowledgably to the ever-changing expectations placed on counties. For the purposes of this chapter, we will focus on the portion of the research agenda that directly relates to the legislative branch of county government.

Intergovernmental and Interlocal Relations

Bollens (1969) recognized the important role county leaders would take on in terms of intergovernmental and interlocal cooperation. Indeed, this is perhaps the most frequently discussed role of county leadership in recent literature. Streib et al. (2007) discuss the continuing prominence of relationships in county research, particularly in light of "the emergence of many county governments as significant service providers and political entities in their own right" (972). Additionally, researchers recognize that these relationships form at multiple levels—between counties and the federal and state governments, local governments, private and nonprofit and tribal entities. In terms of interlocal arrangements, Parks and Oakerson (2000) emphasize the importance of provision units that are scaled according to the collective goods they provide. Counties are uniquely suited to provide public goods and services that are broader in scale than individual municipalities, as well as for cooperating with other counties to form regional provision units (Streib et al., 2007).[5]

In recent years, county legislatures have increasingly taken on this role of conducting intergovernmental relations (Sokolow, 1993). As Parks (1991) asserts, counties are ideally situated for negotiating intergovernmental agreements between central cities and suburbs, state and federal entities, NGOs and private firms. Each of these has an interest in service provision to address particular public goods, and counties are increasingly at the center of arranging interlocal cooperative agreements. In an era of expanded governance, public-private partnerships and the like, relationships will continue to present important questions for researchers.

The structure of metropolitan governance is a frequent topic of debate within the literature on counties, as well as for municipalities as discussed earlier in this chapter. Cigler (1995: 59) writes, "The fragmentation of units involved in providing county services means that county officials routinely must deal with highly complex interlocal relations that cut across economic, social, geographic, and political boundaries." She argues the fragmented structure of organization in counties "makes comprehensive, regional policy perspectives difficult to promote, however, and works against the development of the strong, effective, integrated service delivery systems needed to deal with intertwined problems" (Cigler, 1995: 58).

One potential alternative to a fragmented structure is one that is consolidated. Though approximately 40 city-county consolidated governments exist in the United States, that structure is not always ideal (Rosentraub and al-Habil, 2009) or even feasible (Leland and Thurmaier, 2005). Rosentraub and al-Habil (2009, 41) argue that "Consolidation is not the only route to achieving higher levels of regional cooperation." Since scale is an important issue to consider in service provision, cooperation rather than consolidation allows for provision of each good or service at the appropriate level. It is this flexibility of arrangements that will allow policymakers to respond to changing needs and evolving citizen preferences (Rosentraub and al-Habil, 2009).

Meanwhile, the issue of intergovernmental relationships endures as an important topic of study. Streib, et al. (2007) outline numerous research questions along these lines, including the changing relationships between counties and private and nonprofit producers; the types of networking that counties use as they interact with other local governments, state and federal government; how regional governance is shaped by the various types of consolidated, fragmented, formal and informal cooperative arrangements in use. Additionally, we would add that the changing circumstances facing counties will provide new avenues for cooperation and collaboration, and these will yield new avenues of research.

Changing Structure in American Counties

The urban reform movement that began in the early 20th Century influenced counties as well as cities. Reform as it applied to counties called for a county executive, smaller boards, financial reforms, functional consolidation and in some cases consolidation of urban city-county structures as well as rural county consolidation (Menzel et al., 1992).

Marando and Thomas (1977) contended that it was time to move away from reform rhetoric that was not necessarily based on empirical evidence, toward a better understanding of the way counties' governing bodies were responding to changing circumstances. Certain questions still remain unanswered.

As mentioned, Benton (2005) writes that scholars have not concluded whether reform has achieved its goals. Reformed county governments tend to spend more than "unreformed" counties but the results of such studies are mixed (DeSantis and Renner, 1993; Park, 1996). The relationship between reform structures and spending seems to be more closely related with growth and urbanization (Benton, 2005). Counties that become more urban are faced with more demand for service provision. They are also more likely to adopt legislative structures that are complemented by a professional manager or administrator. Those "reformed" structures are more likely to spend more, however this seems to be a recursive relationship, rather than a direct correlation between structure and spending.

Still, structure remains important in terms of the manner in which counties respond to changing circumstances. Parks (1991) emphasizes public entrepreneurship and suggests that greater numbers of public officials yield greater potential for those individuals to innovate and take initiative. This observation suggests that centralizing county legislative (and row office) authority among fewer officials would decrease the latitude of county-level leaders in responding to public problems. Klinger (1991) agreed that innovation was essential to county leaders attempting to respond to change. Regardless of the structure adopted, policymakers need the ability to solve problems in new ways.

Perhaps the impact of reform overall has been contextually specific and dependent on the personalities of the influential figures of each county. As we move forward, a focus on the leadership traits of county commissioners/council members is needed to illuminate the interactions between structure and leadership. "Strong executive leadership depends heavily on coalition-building for policymaking...It may be, however, that coalition-building skills and/or negotiation and bargaining skills are less a factor of the structural form of government than are the attributes of individuals. Or it may be that structure matters in a different way. For example, the county commission form which works through the building of consensus among equal commissioners may actually help build necessary governance skills" (Cigler, 1995: 60). Among the questions Menzel et al. (1992) raised was whether structure is more important, or is the quality of leadership more closely related to the county performance?

Leadership and Accountability

Leadership and accountability, as well the public perception of accountability, are central to the legitimacy of county government. Bollens (1969: 25) argued for better understanding of issues related to the accountability of county legislators. Twenty-five years later, Cigler (1995: 58) asserted, "Questions about accountability abound due to structural fragmentation and also because of the highly politicized nature of some offices."

Public perceptions of corruption can lead to structural changes[6] although as we have mentioned, structure alone does not determine outcomes.

Placing more emphasis on the potential for conflict than on accountability, Benton (2005) discusses the challenges faced by county leaders and indicates that, while Menzel et al. (1992) encouraged research in this area, scholarship regarding county leadership has been somewhat limited. Improving county leadership and management skills is an important goal (Streib, 1996), and introducing management tools and best practices into county government is essential, regardless of the legislative structure. Svara (1996) characterizes county governments as sitting on the "sidelines" of the professionalism debate, while municipal governments have taken center stage.

Streib et al. (2007: 972) write, "The state of county government administration has a come a great distance since the days of corruption, favoritism, nepotism, and gross incompetence." Although this may be true in general, corruption is still endemic in some counties. The current research agenda should continue to address the manner in which professionalism is being advanced in county legislative and administrative structures. Streib et al. (2007: 973) provide researchers with some important questions regarding professional leadership that have yet to be adequately addressed. Those include the influence of elected row officers on "the effective delivery of critical public services and on the representativeness and accountability of county government"; the difference between counties with professional managers and those without; the interactions between professional managers and row officers, which is a situation unique to county governments; and even the basics of "what do we know about ethics and accountability among elected public officials and public managers at the county level?"

Additional Questions on County Legislatures: Representation, Security, Data

Menzel et al. (1992: 178) ask if counties, as "laboratories of democracy," function in a democratic manner. Issues related to decision-making and representation will continue to be important, particularly as demographics change. Additionally, concerns over how county legislators are elected, who is elected to serve, and how policy decisions are made remain an important part of the research agenda.

Streib et al. (2007) bring up the importance of security, as "terrorism has changed national priorities in fundamental ways and county priorities in direct and indirect ways" (975). The county's role in emergency preparedness has expanded to include homeland security and counterterrorism efforts. These responsibilities will generate new questions for researchers and practitioners as counties grapple with how to manage and finance security related operations.

Changes in information technology continue to provide new questions in the quest to understand how counties and their leaders function (Streib et al., 2007). E-government, privacy protection, and efficient operation of county government provide ample research opportunities. Additionally, Wallace (2007) asserts that younger generations will provide new and different leadership as they rise through the ranks into policymaking positions in county government, and "will be much more open to working in groups and using technology in a much different manner" (985). Wallace argues that these changes will require a change in the research agenda as well as in the manner that research is conducted and its findings are communicated.

Advancing Scholarship on County Legislatures

We have outlined the common structures of county legislatures and examined the changing environment of research on counties and their unique blend of legislative and administrative roles. With each update of the county research agenda, scholars have acknowledged the limitations placed on researchers by the difficulty of making comparisons across diverse structures and circumstances. Streib et al. (2007) heralded an ambitious call for county databases that are properly structured to allow for comparative analysis. The conflict between the need for a "more rigorous, comparative approach that is set within a systematic framework" (Benton, 2005: 463), and the difficulty of making comparisons across such disparate units, substantiates the call for adequate databases for conducting rigorous research at the county level.

Although case studies of individual counties or counties within a particular state may not offer generalizable knowledge regarding the legislative functions of all counties, they can provide us with an understanding of how particular circumstances shape the roles of county legislatures. Scholars such as Bollens (1969) recommend both greater use of statistical methods and case studies in order to make valid comparisons. One example is of a promising technique is propensity score matching. The basic concept is to identify a large group of nonparticipants that are similar to the participant in all relevant characteristics to act as a control group in a non-experimental design (Caliendo and Kopeinig, 2008). The need for a database as Streib et al. (2007) suggest is felt heavily as researchers and practitioners muddle through the conventional wisdom in search of solid, research-based responses.

SPECIAL PURPOSE GOVERNMENTS' LEGISLATIVE BODIES

Over the last 50 years, the number of special purpose governments has tripled while general purpose governments (cities and counties) have only grown by about five percent. The proliferation of special purpose governments means that they now make up over one-third of local governments (See table 18.1.). Several scholars such as Bollens (1986), Sbragia (1996), Foster (1997), and Eger (2002) examined the growth of special purpose government and found that their popularity can be attributed to the fact that they are singularly focused, have flexible geographic boundaries and may have the ability to circumvent state limitations on the issuance of bond and nonguaranteed debt. Smirnova, Leland and Johnson (2008) also find that in the case of transit agencies, special purpose governments have proliferated because of their ability to secure federal transit funding.

Like cities and counties, special purpose governments are largely shaped by state law (Bollens, 1986; Burns, 1994; Foster, 1997). State laws and provisions dictate exactly what formal powers are allotted to them. General purpose governments have little say in whether a special purpose government will be formed in their area. However, state involvement or the "parent" government's relationship is usually "hands off." They are independent because they are governed by elected or appointed boards other than the legislative body that created them. They carry out their duties without the parent government's approval (McCabe, 2000). Special purpose governments are narrow units of local government that provide a single service or a related set of services such as fire protection, drainage and flood control, transportation, housing, or economic development. Though their legislative bodies vary, they are all involved in setting policy, their own budgets and tax rates (Foster, 1997). Special purpose governments typically have a governing structure akin to the council-manager form of government. Therefore, their legislative power lies with their board, whether elected or appointed. The following section will discuss what we know about the different types of special purpose governments and their board characteristics.

Types of Special Purpose Governments

There is no uniform agreement on what constitutes the different existing types of special purpose governments. The matter is further complicated when organizations, such as the Council of State Governments, use such terms as *public authority* and sometimes *special district* generically to apply to classes of entities with similar characteristics, regardless of particular names given to these entities in enabling legislation. The generic use of such terms results in confusion when a state uses the term "special district" for an entity labeled a "public authority" by a social scientist. For example Gerwig (1956), Walsh (1980), Doig (1983), and the Council of State Governments all exclude, by definition, from their studies of public authorities the quasi-government organizations that have taxing power. Yet by 1982, 23 states allowed some types of entities formally identified in state statutes as authorities to levy taxes (U.S. Department of Commerce, 1983). The argument is often made that districts and authorities can be distinguished from one another on the basis of financing methods, that districts levy taxes (and sometimes issue general obligation bonds) and authorities issue revenue bonds and are prohibited from levying taxes. Gerwig claims that the power to issue revenue bonds is a "major distinguishing characteristic" of public authorities (1956: 390). Walsh (DATE) maintains that most special districts do not borrow heavily. This generic use of terminology is awkward because it means that a majority of states have somehow applied the name *special district* to entities that are in reality *public authorities*.

Special Districts and their Governing Boards

The distinguishing feature of special districts is that they have the ability to tax, whereas public authorities raise their revenues and they are more likely to have elected legislative bodies. However, they still have a similar degree of independence because citizens are typically unaware of who represents them on the legislative body. Special district elections have even lower voter turnout than other local elections and many incumbents run unopposed (Burns, 1994). Terms are often staggered to insulate members from further manipulation by other elected officials (McCabe, 2000).

Public Authorities' Governing Boards

The progressive movement inspired the use of public authorities in the United States as a way to depoliticize administrative operations for the management of bridges, parks, housing, transportation and other infrastructure. They were constructed to separate politics from administration, just like the city manager form of government, and advocated over traditional governments because their structure incorporated business practices and expertise and their roots are in the managerial approach to public administration (Rosenbloom and Kravchuk, 2002). Neutral competence is valued as opposed to responsiveness to the electorate. The typical public authority, therefore, has a part-time appointed board of directors with a fulltime appointed administrator who runs the day-to-day operations. Board member terms are typically staggered as an additional obstacle to the ability of elected politicians to influence board members, whether that be from the parent government (the state) or an overlapping general purpose government (such as a municipality) (Doig and Mitchell, 1992). Public authority boards are often involved in adopting their own corporate name, making by-laws. They have the right to sue and be sued, possess the power of eminent domain, exercise the discretion to establish rates and charges, are exempt from property tax, enter into agreements with other public and private organizations, and have the ability to utilize private money markets (Leland and Johnson, 2004). And as previously mentioned, they are typically distinguished from special districts because they do not have the power to tax.

Public authority boards have become influential in the United States, operating at the national, state and local level and performing and influencing the delivery of local government services. They borrow more in the tax-exempt bond market than state or local governments. They have the ability to bypass debt and taxation limits to which state and local governments are often subjected (Mitchell, 1990). They are powerful economic and political institutions that control trade, shipping, waste disposal and transportation in most major cities. Increasingly, authorities are utilized as conduits for intergovernmental grants and aids. They have been justified as a mechanism to rescue ailing industries, promote regional economic development and subsidize private industry (Axelrod, 1992). But some argue that public authorities are undemocratic institutions too insulated from the electorate. Others criticize them as being heavy borrowers created to provide better access to capital markets (Frant, 1997).

Although little research has been conducted on public authorities, and their boards and legislative powers in particular, by their sheer numbers and budgets they occupy an integral role in the policy process in the United States. They are powerful quasi-governmental institutions that influence the implementation of economic and social policy. Public authorities affect how millions of Americans receive services such as mass transit, housing, and provide power. In the future we can expect public authorities to continue to expand in numbers, increase the amount of money they borrow and expand into new policy areas such as the justice and welfare systems. Still, systematic study of their boards is needed.

School Boards

A vital part of a community's prestige and desirability as a place to live is the reputation of the school district. School board members are much better known than city council or county commissioners in many areas (Usdan, 1994). School boards are also one of the largest groups of special purpose governments and therefore worth mentioning separately. Early in the 20th century as public education expanded, some fundamental decisions about school governance were made that have impacted the role and function of school boards as legislative bodies. Reformers spearheaded the idea of creating separate governance structures for schools in most jurisdictions and schools were deemed to be of singular importance in socializing and shaping the lives of citizens, in particular the growing number of immigrants. They were so important they were institutionally separated from general purpose governments so their legislators would be insulated from patronage politics. The idea of "separatism" has prevailed and the primary responsibilities of school boards are decision-making in general and policy decisions in particular (Usdan, 1994). School board "legislative" bodies provide a way to assert local preferences and control into education policymaking. School board members are part-time, generally non-partisan officials, and can be elected at-large, by district or a combination. Although they are usually non-partisan, education politics surrounds school boards in a politically charged environment. Board members are expected to confront the community's economic and social problems reflected in the classroom. Due to the controversial nature of school board policymaking, the National School Boards Association formed a task force to develop a clear definition of the governance responsibilities of school boards. This definition is premised on the assumption that certain core decision-making functions must be left to a locally elected government body. The decision-making functions are: a longer term vision for the school district, the establishment and maintenance of the organization structure including the hiring and firing of the superintendent, the adoption of an annual budget and governance politics, the establishment of systems of accountability for the community, including fiscal accountability, accountability for programs and student outcomes, teacher and staff accountability (including collective bargaining where applicable), and advocacy of the education of children (Campbell and Greene, 1994: 392).There appears to be even less research on school boards as legislating bodies than on any other type of government in terms of representation and accountability. But because school boards are so environmentally diverse but institutionally similar, they provide an opportunity to test the effects of context of public policy decisions.

CONCLUSION

In this chapter we reviewed the current research on local legislative bodies. The staggering number of local governments and the vast diversity of their structures and functions have contributed to a body of research that is limited in terms of comparative analysis and large-N studies, and tends toward methodologies that focus on contextual specificity. Whether examining municipalities, counties, school boards or special districts, data availability frequently prevents rigorous quantitative studies across multiple jurisdictions. This is a complication that is likely to continue to influence the ability of researchers to answer important questions about decision-making, accountability, cooperation and other important questions.

Among the research agenda items we have discussed throughout this chapter, the approach local legislatures employ to address issues that span across jurisdictional boundaries warrants continued attention. Additionally, the influence of interest groups on local policymaking is an important topic that has not yet received much attention. The role of private interests in particular, and the formation of public-private partnerships in addressing public issues calls for research that examines the role of local legislators in brokering such arrangements as well as the implications on the democratic process at the local level. Smaller communities' legislatures and rural policymaking bodies are frequently overlooked when compared to larger communities or those located in urban areas. More attention needs to be paid to such governing bodies. Finally, in the wake of a far-reaching recession that has shaken the financial stability of local governments everywhere, the responses of local legislatures to financial pressures will undoubtedly be an important topic of research.

NOTES

1. Including Alaska's boroughs and Louisiana's parishes
2. For example, the U.S. Census of Governments lists 3,033 county governments (as of 2007) while NACo lists 3028 county governments, plus 40 city-county consolidated governments (as of 2009; NACO, 2010).

3. Gilbertson's 1917 book was instrumental in exposing corruption and advocating reform. The title *The County: The "Dark Continent" of American Politics* expressed the frustration of reformers with what appeared to be intractable corruption.
4. Based on data from Mississippi, where an FBI operation in the mid-1980s led to the conviction of one-eighth of Mississippi's county supervisors on corruption charges.
5. For example, Streib et al. (2007: 974) argue that the increasing importance of environmental issues will largely be addressed by counties, which "possess the coordinating and linking mechanisms needed for this type of activity."
6. For example, in 2009, Cuyahoga County, Ohio, voters elected to revamp the structure of the county legislature. The traditional 3-member commission was replaced with an elected executive and a county council elected by districts. Two competing referenda in the November, 2009 election followed a string of indictments of county leaders (including the elected sheriff and auditor and one of the three commissioners) on a variety of charges.

References

Austin, R.A. (2002). Seats that may not Matter: Testing for Racial Polarization in U.S. City Councils. *Legislative Studies Quarterly*, 27(3): 481–508.

Axelrod, D. (1992). *Shadow Government*. New York: John Wiley and Sons, Inc.

Barron, D.J. (2003). Reclaiming Home Rule. *Harvard Law Review*, 116(8): 2255–2386.

Benton, J.E. (2005). An Assessment of Research on American Counties. *Public Administration Review*, 65(4): 462–474.

Berman, D.R. (1993). Counties, Other Governments and the Future. In *County Governments in an Era of Change*. Edited by Berman, D.R., 135–42. Westport, CN: Greenwood Press.

Berman, D.R., and Salant, T.J. (1996). The Changing Role of Counties in the Intergovernmental System. In *The American County: Frontiers of Knowledge*. D.C. Tuscaloosa Menzel, ed. 19–33. AL: The University of Alabama Press.

Bollens, Scott A. 1986. "Examining the Link between State Policy and the Creation of Local Special Districts." *State & Local Government Review*, 18(3): 117–124

Bollens, J.C. (1969). *American County Government with an Annotated Bibliography*. Beverly Hills, CA: Sage Publications.

Burns, N. (1994). *The Formation of American Local Governments: Private Values in Public Institutions*. New York: Oxford University Press.

Caliendo, M. and Kopeinig, S. (2008). Some Practical Guidance For The Implementation Of Propensity Score Matching. *Journal of Economic Surveys*, 22(1): 31–72.

Campbell, D.W. and D. Greene (1994). Defining the Leadership Role of School Boards in the 21st Century. *Phi Delta Kappa International*. 75(5): 391–395.

Cigler, B.A. (1995). County Governance in the 1990s. *State and Local Government Review*, 27(1): 55–70.

DeSantis, V.S., and Renner, T. (1993). Governing the County: Authority, Structure, and Election. In *County Governments in an Era of Change*. D.R. Berman, ed., 55–84. Westport, CN: Greenwood Press.

Doig, J. W. (1983). If I See a Murderous Fellow Sharpening a Knife Cleverly ... The Wilsonian Dichotomy and the Public Authority Tradition. *Public Administration Review*, 43: 292–304.

Doig, Jameson W., and Jerry Mitchell. 1992. Expertise, Democracy, and the Public Authority Model: Groping Toward Accommodation. In *Public Authorities and Public Policy*. Jerry Mitchell, ed., 17–30. New York: Greenwood Press.

Downs, A. (1994). *New Visions for Metropolitan America*. Washington, DC: Brookings Institution.

Eger, Robert J. 2002. "Casting Light on Shadow Government: An Exploratory Analysis of Public Authorities in the Southern States." Paper presented at the Association for Budgeting and Financial Management at Washington, DC, January 17–19.

Foster, Kathryn A. 1997. *The Political Economy of Special-Purpose Government*. Washington, DC: Georgetown University Press.

Frant, Howard. (1997). Reconsidering the Determinants' of Public Authority Use. *Journal of Public Administration Research and Theory*, 7: 571–590

Gerwig, Robert. 1956. Public Authorities: Legislative Panacea? *Journal of Public Law*, 5 (fall): 387–407.

Gunlicks, A.B. (1981). "Problems, Politics, and Prospects of Local Government Reorganization in the United States," in *Local Government Reform and Reorganization: An International Perspective*. A.B. Gunlicks, ed., 7–25. Port Washington, NY: Kennikat Press.

Hajnal, Z.L. (2010). *America's Uneven Democracy: Race, Turnout, and Representation in City Politics*. New York, NY: Cambridge University Press.

Karahan, G.R., Razzolini, L., and Shughart, W.F. (2006). No Pretense to Honesty: County Government Corruption in Mississippi. *Economics of Governance*, 7: 211–227.

Klinger, A. (1991). County Leadership and Models for Change. *Intergovernmental Perspective*, 17(1): 45–48.

Leland, S., and G. Johnson. 2004. Consolidation as a Local Government Reform, In *City-County Consolidation and Its Alternatives: Reshaping the Local Government Lanndscape*, J. B. Carr and R.C. Feiock, eds, 25–38. Armonk, NY: M.E. Sharpe.

Leland, S., and K. Thurmaier. (2005). When Efficiency is Unbelievable: Normative Lessons from 30 Years of City-County Consolidations. *Public Administration Review*, 65(4): 475–489.

Lewis, E.B. and Taylor, G.A. (1994a). County Government Administration. *International Journal of Public Administration*, 17(5): 803–809.

Lewis, E.B. and Taylor, G.A. (1994b). Policy Making/Implementing Activities of Elected County Executives and Appointed County Administrators: Does Form of Government Make a Difference? *International Journal of Public Administration*, 17(5): 935–953.

MacManus, S.A. (1996). County Boards, Partisanship and Elections. In *The American County: Frontiers of Knowledge*. D.C. Menzel, ed. 53–79. Tuscaloosa, AL: The University of Alabama Press.

MacManus, S.A. (1999). The Resurgent City Councils. In *American State and Local Politics: Directions for the 21st Century*, Ronald E. Weber and Paul Brace, eds, 167–193. New York, NY: Chatham House.

Marando, V.L., and Reeves, M.M. (1991). Counties as Local Governments: Research Issues and Questions. *Journal of Urban Affairs*, 13(1): 45–53.

Marando, V.L., and Thomas, R.D. (1977). *The Forgotten Governments: County Commissioners as Policy Makers*. Gainesville, FL: The University Presses of Florida.

Martin, L.L. (1993). American County Government: An Historical Perspective. In *County Governments in an Era of Change*. D.R. Berman, ed., 1–13. Westport, CN: Greenwood Press.

McCabe, Barbara. (2000). Special-District Formation among the States. *State and Local Government Review*, 32(2): 121–131

Menzel, D.C. (1996). *The American County: Frontiers of Knowledge*. Tuscaloosa, AL: The University of Alabama Press.

Menzel, D.C., Marando, V.L., Parks, R.B., Waugh, W.L. Jr., Cigler, B.A., Svara, J.H., Reeves, M.M., Benton, J.E., Thomas, R.D., Strieb, G., and Schneider, M. (1992). Setting a Research Agenda for the Study of the American County. *Public Administration Review*, 52(2): 173–182.

Mitchell, J. (Date) The Policy Activities of Public Authorities. *Policy Studies Journal*, 18, (4): 928–42.

NACo (National Association of Counties). (2009). *The Commission-Manager Form of Government*. NACo Research Brief. <http://www.naco.org/newsroom/pubs/Documents/County%20Management%20and%20Structure/Commission-Manager%20Form%20of%20Governmnet.pdf>.

NACo (National Association of Counties). (2010). *County Government Overview*. <http://www.naco.org/newsroom/pubs/Documents/County%20Management%20and%20Structure/County%20Government%20Overview%20June2010.pdf>.

Park, K.O. (1996). Determinants of County Government Growth. In *The American County: Frontiers of Knowledge*. D.C. Menzel, ed., 34–50. Tuscaloosa, AL: The University of Alabama Press.

Parks R.B. (1991). Counties in the Federal System: The Interlocal Connection. *Intergovernmental Perspective*, 17(1): 29–32.

Parks, R.B., and Oakerson, R.J. (2000). Regionalism, Localism, and Metropolitan Governance: Suggestions from the Research Program on Local Public Economies. *State and Local Government Review*, 32(3): 169–179.

Pelissero, J.P. (2003). *Cities, Politics and Policy: A Comparative Analysis*. Washington, DC: CQ Press.

Richardson, J.J., Gough, M.Z., and Puentes, R. (2003). Is Home Rule the Answer? Clarifying the Influence of Dillon's Rule on Growth Management. Washington, DC: Brookings Institution. <http://www.brookings.edu/research/reports/2003/01/01metropolitanpolicy-richardson>.

Rosenbloom, David H. and Kravchuk, Robert. 2002. *Public Administration: Understanding Management, Politics and Law in the Public Sector*. 5th edn. New York, New York: McGraw Hill.

Rosentraub, M.S., and al-Habil, W. (2009). Why Metropolitan Governance is Growing, as is the Need for Elastic Governments. In *Governing Metropolitan Regions in the 21st Century*. Don Phares, ed., 39–53. Armonk, NY: M.E. Sharpe.

Ross B.R. and Levine. M.A. (2001). *Urban Politics: Power in Metropolitan Areas*. 6th edn. Belmont CA: Wadsworth.

Salant, T.J. (1991). County Governments: An Overview. *Intergovernmental Perspective*, 17(1): 5–9.

Sbragia, Alberta M. (1996). *Debt Wish: Entrepreneurial Cities, U.S. Federalism and Economic Development*. University of Pittsburgh Press.

Schneider, Mark, Paul Teske, and Michael Mintrom. (1995). *Public Entrepreneurs*. Princeton, NJ: Princeton University Press.

Smirnova, Olga, Suzanne Leland, and Gary Johnson. (2008). Popular, but More Influential? A Test of Whether Special Purpose Governments Affect Federal Transit Financing. *Municipal Finance Journal*, 28: 43–61.

Smith, R.G. (1990). The Web of Actors in Authority Policy Implementation. *Policy Studies Journal*, 18(4): 986–98.

Sokolow, A.D. (1993). Legislatures and Legislating in County Government, In *County Governments in an Era of Change*. D.R. Berman, ed., 29–42. Westport, CN: Greenwood Press.

Streib, G. (1996). Strengthening County Management. In *The American County: Frontiers of Knowledge*. D. C. Menzel, ed., 128–48. Tuscaloosa, AL: The University of Alabama Press.

Streib, G., Svara, J.H., Waugh, W.L. Jr., Klase, K.A., Menzel, D.C., Salant, T.J., Benton, J.E., Byers, J., and Cigler, B.A. (2007). Conducting Research on Counties in the 21st Century: A New Agenda and Database Considerations. *Public Administration Review, 67*(6): 968–983.

Svara, J.H. (1996). Leadership and Professionalism in County Government. In *The American County: Frontiers of Knowledge*. D.C. Menzel, ed., 109–27. Tuscaloosa, AL: The University of Alabama Press.

Svens, J. (2005). Eight Questions about Corruption. *The Journal of Economic Perspectives, 19*(3): 19–42.

Swartz, N.J. (2010). Does Consolidation Make a Difference? A Comparative Analysis of Richmond and Virginia Beach, Virginia. In *City-County Consolidation: Promises Made, Promises Kept?* S. Leland and K. Thurmaier, ed., 57–82. Washington, DC: Georgetown University Press.

Thurmaier, K., and Wood, C. 2002. Interlocal Agreements as Overlapping Social Networks: Picket-Fence Regionalism in Metropolitan Kansas City. *Public Administration Review, 62*(5): 585–598.

US Bureau of the Census. 1983. *Census of Governments*. Volume 1: *Government Organization*. Washington, DC: US Department of Commerce.

US Bureau of the Census. 2007. *Census of Governments*. Volume 1: *Government Organization*. Washington, DC: US Department of Commerce.

Usdan, M. 1994. The Relationship Between School Boards and General Purpose Government. *Phi Delta Kappa, 75*(5): 374–377.

Vogel, Ronald K., and Norman Nezelkewicz. 2002. "Metropolitan Planning Organizations And The New Regionalism: The Case of Louisville." *Publius* 32: 107–129.

Wallace, C.B. (2007). Conducting Research on Counties: Commentary from County Government Practitioners. *Public Administration Review, 67*(6): 984–990.

Walsh, A. (1980). *The Public's business: The politics and practices of government corporations*. Cambridge, MA: MIT Press.

Waugh, W.L., Jr., and Streib, G. (1993). County Capacity and Intergovernmental Relations. In *County Governments in an Era of Change*. Edited by Berman, D.R., 43–52. Westport, CN: Greenwood Press.

Welch, S. (1990). The impact of at-large elections on the representation of Blacks and Hispanics. *The Journal of Politics, 52*(4): 1050–1076.

Welch, Susan, and Timothy Bledsoe. 1988. *Urban Reform and its Consequences*. Chicago: University of Chicago Press.

CHAPTER 19

···

LOCAL EXECUTIVES

···

RICHARD C. FEIOCK AND JUNGAH BAE

HALF a century ago Robert Dahl (1961) investigated "who governs" in cities and found evidence supporting democratic pluralism rather than elitism. Yet, it was the role and leadership of local executives that was central to the pluralist city. In the decades since, there has been sustained interest in the role of local executives and how they shape the governance of communities. Executive office at the local level is vastly different than at the state or national level.

There are a variety of perspectives on the roles public executives play in local government. We may inform the historical overview in light of political science understandings of the limits of local power and the role of institutions, and private interests in shaping power in urban regimes (Peterson, 1981; Stone, 1989; Clingermayer and Feiock, 2001).

Historical perspectives have provided a foundation for understanding local executives' roles. Thus, we start with a historical overview of the executive in local governance as the roles of the modern mayor and city manager are the historical products of developments in local government theory and practice over the last century. There is tremendous variation in executive roles because of the different types of contextual factors and the different types of institutional incentives and constraints among local governments.

Theories of urban politics may account for contemporary trends of the role of local executives, however we draw from an institutional approach for a more comprehensive explanation of the variations across time and place. Based on this, we separately examine the unique history of cities, counties and special districts in the U.S. We then ask what difference local executives make for policy and collaborative governance and then explore what factors affect turnover among local government executives. We conclude with a discussion of the role of mayors and managers in the future of local governance.

HISTORICAL ROOTS OF LOCAL EXECUTIVE ROLES

In this chapter we suggest that the roles of the modern mayors and managers are essentially the institutional products of developments in local government theory and practice over the last hundred years. Institutions matter because they shape the diverse policy and management roles that local executives play in local government (Clingermayer and Feiock, 2001). Beginning with the progressive era in the early twentieth century, there has been a desire to separate policymaking and administration, i.e., the so-called politics-administration dichotomy. The intent was to strengthen executive office and recruit highly qualified officers to these positions. Institutional arrangements such as the council manager form of government and civil service reform formalized the separated roles of local executives from politics.

Next, in the post progressive era that followed, executive policy leadership was emphasized to a great extent. This reflected the reality of a leadership vacuum in local politics at the time. In the absence of political power, local government executives often faced substantial obstacles in trying to implement their management priorities or the policy goals of the elected body. The goal conflict between politician and administrators put them into the situation of managerial dilemma. Over time, the need for both political and managerial leadership have shaped contemporary expectation regarding the role of local government executives. The modern role of local executives blends a management (administrative activities), and a political role (community leadership) (Ammons and Newell, 1989: 68–69). Svara (1990) also suggests that the contemporary role of local executives mingles four dimensions of the governmental process: mission, policy, administration, and management.

Progressive Era

It is meaningful that the starting point of the discussion for the role of local executives is the progressive era because professionally trained local executives were introduced and institutionalized at that time. At the federal level this era was marked by the civil service movement. At the local level by efforts to professionalize bureaucracy and to reduce the dominance of elected legislatures in local policy and administration. Local government in this era was characterized by the absence of an executive office or weak mayors with limited formal powers. This meant that in order for executives to exercise authority they had to rely on the resource of the political machine. Using the lens of urban regime theory, local leaders sought to mobilize groups and resources for solving immediate urban problems.

Reformers in the Progressive Era sought to remove the corrupt and inefficient partisan political machines that controlled patronage and service delivery in many large American cities. To address those problems, local government reformers first advocated strengthening the formal powers of the mayor. When this proved inadequate, they focused on creation of a city manager position and promoted the hiring of a professional non-partisan manager to act as a CAO for local government.

In this historical context, the role of local executives evolved into more of a professional management position responsible for implementing policy and operating organizations and carrying out policy goals and programs neutrally. Rapidly growing and diverse populations increased service demands on government creating a need for more professional management of urban public services to address the diverse needs of residents. The reform movement to the council-manager plan defined the professionalized managerial role of local executives in the Progressive Era.

Administrative State Era

The reformers in the Progressive Era created the opportunity to institutionalize the role of professional managers separated from local politics and insulated from the political machine and party bosses. The Administrative State Era was the culmination of a sustained reform movement over the previous half century. Institutional arrangements of the Administrative State Era were distinguished by reform charters that integrated the politics-administration dichotomy, at-large elections, merit system, and council-manager plan. By adopting civil service systems and other business-like or technical processes, political corruption became rarer and institutionalized professionalism resulted in "efficient, better-managed, and less corrupt local government" (Frederickson, 2004: 49–51).

Anti-Orthodoxy Era

The Administrative State defined executive institutions and roles dichotomously based on a separation of policy and administration. The Anti-Orthodoxy period pushed back against this dichotomous classification of the role of local executives and municipal structure and focused attention on its limitations. Conventional notions of local executives were demonstrated to be at odds with the practice (Adrian, 1987).

The anti-orthodoxy was a dose of political realism arguing the separation of politics from administration was both impossible and undesirable. However it is difficult to say that institutionalized dichotomy no longer operates to differentiate between professional and political executives and structures among local governments. In some sense, the perceptions of professional managers were more differentiated from those of political executives with regard to their roles over time. Wright compared and captured this in his 1965 and 1985 surveys. Only 5.8 percent of professional managers responded that the political role is most important in his 1985 survey while 33 percent of city managers had accorded it to be most important in his 1965 survey.

Nevertheless, the distinction between policy and politics is sometimes obscured in these discussions. Svara (1990) suggests the political role includes setting mission and policy adoption. If we follow Svara's dimension then the perception of managers of their political roles could be interpreted differently because 55.8 percent of the 1985 city managers regarded the policy role as most important.

New Public Management Era

One of the key features of the New Public Management Era of the 1990s was to significantly modify civil service systems and the governing role of local executives beyond the public sector. Local executives such as city managers, CAOs and department heads were allowed greater latitude in selecting or firing their immediate subordinates (Osborn and Gaebler, 1992).

Unlike the spoil system in pre-Progressive Era, the movement for reinventing government gives professional executives autonomy to manage and to demote or fire subordinates who are not effective. However elected city officials do not intervene in matters of civil service appointments or promotions. The New Public Management movement originated for the resolution of managerial dilemmas and inefficient bureaucracy related to the civil service system. Public servants were to be evaluated through well-designed merit systems and citizens' satisfaction with their performance. The governing role of local executives also emerged as one of most important roles. Executives were expected to play a more proactive role as innovators and policy and management entrepreneurs (Schneider Teske and Mintrom, 1995). Mayors and managers in the role of public entrepreneur advance their careers by pursuing efficiency, innovation, resources and development.

Contracting-out with private firms and nonprofits was one of the key entrepreneurial solutions to break through bureaucracy in the New Public Management Era. According to Svara (1990) the governance role of local executives includes setting missions, adopting and implementing policy. Moreover the governing role in reinventing government goes beyond the internal bureaucracy. Local executives have a brokerage role to link other jurisdictions, citizen volunteers, private or non-profit organizations for better and more efficient provision of local services.

Special districts have particular geographic flexibility and they perform only a few functions such as water service, garbage pick-up, or bus services, while general purpose cities or counties provide a broader range of services. Special districts tend to be formed by small groups of businesses so developers' and manufacturers' preferences are much more institutionalized than in the other forms of government. Thus, the power and position of local executives will be decided within the incentive structures influenced by those selective interests groups.

Governance and Globalization Era

Metropolitan regions have emerged as the dominant economic units in global society, and it is regional resources that are most important to large-scale investment decisions (Feiock, Moon, and Park, 2008). Yet in most instances no single jurisdiction has the scale, resources, or authority to act regionally. Does this make local government executives irrelevant? On the contrary, we believe that global governance provides new opportunities for executive leadership, but it also requires skills in network management and collaboration to accompany political and administrative skills.

How is local executive leadership shaped in contemporary local governance? Urban policy problems constantly spill over city boundaries. In addition the increased involvement of state and national government and the increased interactions with neighborhood groups have become too complex to be dealt with effectively by a sole jurisdiction. Thus networks and collaborative management are essential for local executive leadership and governance. Governance is generally defined as steering the changing processes of policy decisions and actions across the boundaries of the private, public and civic sectors rather than rowing by governments themselves (O'Leary, Gerard, and Bingham, 2006). The concept of governance has been widely employed in local government policy areas such as service delivery, emergency management, education and environment (Biermann et al., 2009).

Local leadership matters tremendously to the achievement of a governing role to solve contemporary wicked problems. Individual leaders respond differently based on their different capacities and resources. One reason why the formal and informal differences in executive powers and roles matter is that elected and appointed executives operate under different institutional constraints in pursuing their public agendas.

EXECUTIVE ROLES IN CITIES, COUNTIES AND SPECIAL DISTRICTS

In much of the literature local governments are treated monolithically, as a single institutional type. In reality there are numerous entities each with their own institutions and governance arrangements. The three most common are cities, counties, and special districts. The power and position of local executives can differ dramatically among cities, counties, and districts. As Burns (1994) observed, over the course of the past 350 years Americans have created almost 50,000 new local governments. The history described above shaped the role and power of local executives, more so in municipal governments than counties or districts. Thus the role of local executives is often distinct within each of these local governments.

Executives in Municipal Government

Most U.S. cities have two executive leaders—an elected mayor and an appointed professional manager. The balance of power and authority of these two offices is a function of the form of municipal government. The two dominant forms of government, mayor-council and council-manager, are based on competing principles and values. Mayor-council form places a premium on the political process and democracy, whereas the council-manager form is based more on values of professionalism and efficiency (Nalbandian, 1990; Hansell, 1998, 1999; Kearney et al., 2000; Frederickson and Johnson, 2001; Hassett and Watson, 2002; Svara, 2003).

Mayor-council forms were purposely designed to emphasize a separation between legislative and executive powers supported through a series of legally-based checks and balances intended to limit the authority of both the council and the mayor (as the elected executive) (Frederickson and Johnson, 2001). In comparison, council-manager forms of government are intended to support efficient implementation of policy. It assumes policies are made by the city council and that these policies are then implemented by a city manager, who is appointed by the council. This approach allows the council to focus on reaching consensus in the policy development process, and leaves the implementation and management of these policies to a professional city administrator.

A strong mayor can be a powerful chief executive who exercises a central role responsible for budget formulation and having extensive appointment and removal powers, and veto power over council-enacted ordinances (Bowman and Kearney, 2006). A strong mayor is elected by the voters rather than selected by the council, and he or she serves a four-year term of office with no limitation on re-election while a weak-mayor usually serves as a part-time job and the council structures substantial policy such as budgetary formation and personnel issues.

Mayoral power varies as a function of how much control the mayor has over city policy decisions: full-time status, the authority to formulate and administer budgets, appoint key administrators with council approval, and veto statutes approved by council. Strong mayors have incentives to pursue short term political gain in their development choices (Frant, 1993, 1996) and constrain the role of council and professional administrators in informing public decisions (Sharp, 2002; Feiock, Jeong and Kim, 2003).

Mayors who can exercise strong executive power may be responsive to proposed changes advanced by any political interest in the community. Schneider et al. (1995) found the presence of strong mayors predicted emergence of both pro-growth and anti-growth entrepreneurs. A popularly elected executive officer provides greater access to decision-making because this form of government attracts politically ambitious leaders with different orientations and career interests to weak mayors. Clingermayer and Feiock (2001) contend that directly elected executives are more likely to be full time politicians attuned to political credit-claiming opportunities and thus having incentives to become entrepreneurs on both sides of development issues. So if a mayor is motivated by interests that match with citizens' policy priorities, then a strong, rather than a weak mayor may be dominant in local politics. Even if a strong mayor attempts to reflect minority welfare, well mobilized groups could try to change the government structure from a strong to weak mayor system or could adopt a council-manager form of government to lessen the political leadership of local executives.

It is not uncommon to have a CAO in a mayor-council government system. The technical role and skills are similar but the political and policy role is subordinated to the elected executive. In fact, in most cases the CAO is appointed by the mayor, often without council approval being needed. Urban regime theories see local executives in mayor-council governments as proactive in mobilizing selective interests and their resources for resolving various urban problems (Stone, 2005). Some regimes call for strong political leadership to solve a given immediate problem effectively, others need a professional city manager having more long-term perspectives to preserve given administrative functions and a status quo. The position of the chief administrative officer (CAO) may be located between political and professional leaderships with a professionally modified mayoral form of government. From the perspective of the regime those struggling with urgent issues are apparently more challenging and demand a strong political executive.

The executive role of managers in council manager systems can be dramatically different. Strong managerial power does not necessarily come at the cost of mayoral power. Reformed city governments are often criticized for weak political leadership because the mayors lack clearly-established institutional authority for policy leadership (Adrian and Press, 1977; Morgan and Watson, 1992; Morgan, England and Pelissero, 2007). Appointed executives can fill this vacuum. Previous studies depict city managers as compelled by necessity to play an active policy role when the mayor lacks substantial formal authority or has difficulty exercising policy leadership (Adrian and Press, 1977; Morgan and Watson, 1992).

What explains the strength of managers as executives? In some cases managerial leadership is a product of administrative entrepreneurism. Empirical research finds that entrepreneurial city managers are less likely to emerge when there is an elected mayor position in the community (Teske and Schneider, 1994). The professional technocratic training and socialization of city managers make them responsive to efficiency and the economic interests of the city.

Council-manager government provides a potential for mangers to play a more active policy role than in mayor-council governments, but even with an entrepreneurial manager executive leadership requires delegation by the governing body. Why do elected officials share policy power with the manager and even defer to the manager's policy leadership in local government? One proposition is that managers take a substantial policy-making role because the elected officials exert weak political leadership and the professional managers possess significant policy expertise (Protasel, 1988; Nalbandian, 1991; Hasett and Watson, 2002; Feiock, Jeong, and Kim, 2003). Strangely, very few studies have explored this phenomenon. Consequently we are still largely unaware of whether other factors systematically shape a manager's policy role. Councils may be more inclined to assign policy-making power to managers who identify with their political perspectives. The work of Zhang and Feiock (2009) begins to explore these questions, but most remain unanswered. Much of the scholarship written on different forms of government reflects an attempt to explore and frame the balance struck between democratic representation and managerial professionalism. In "adapted" hybrid forms of government, executive leadership is even more complex.

Adapted Cities

As discussed above, city governments are generally classified as either mayor-council or council-manager, based on how their institutional structures distribute political and administrative power among appointed and elected executives. Mayor-council cities are characterized by a separation of powers and elected chief executives; council-manager governments by unification of powers structure and appointed professional executives. This dichotomous classification of municipal structure has significant limitations. These conventional categories are inconsistent with practice (Svara, 1990; Renner and DeSantis, 1994). In recent years new approaches have been proposed to describe differences in government structures in cities within the two traditional categories. A major contribution to this literature is the adapted cities framework developed by George Frederickson and his associates (Frederickson and Johnson 2001; Frederickson, Johnson and Wood, 2004; Carr and Karuppusamy, 2008, 2009).

The adapted cities framework focuses on specific charter provisions that define relationships among elected and appointed officials in city government and arrays them on a political-administrative structural dimension. According to the adapted cities framework, after the 1970s, changing values and disappointment with the status quo would change both political and administrative cities just as the reform movement had driven earlier change. New s-curves of innovation would change city structures in the coming decades. The era of adapted cities was under way (Frederickson, 2004, 51).

As adaptive or mixed forms of government have become increasingly popular (Frederickson, Johnson, and Wood, 2004; Carr and Karuppusamy, 2008), the position of mayor in a council-manager government can be strengthened by direct election of the mayor (Clingermayer and Feiock, 2001). Since by this institutional arrangement the mayor possesses greater authority, the manager may feel less compelled to lead in policy-making.

Executives in Counties

The Progressive reform movement changed the structure of city government and, at the municipal level, instituted city managers. Counties, however, were largely left behind by the reformers. Counties are characterized by unique legal distinctions not applicable to many other local governments. Following the British precedent, American counties were created as administrative arms of the state to provide local residents with judicial, electoral, and other services as a convenient way for the state government to exercise power over a large territory. Home rule authority extends only as far as state constitutions and statutes allow. Among the 48 states with county governments, 37 permit some type of home rule authority.

Most counties have not taken advantage of opportunities to adopt home rule charters, but there has been more willingness to centralize executive authority. Counties generally follow one of three forms of government: commission, commission/

administrator, and commission-executive. The commission form is the traditional "unreformed" county government in which an elected commission exercises both legislative and executive authority. The commission usually selects a member to be the presiding officer. Members of the governing body divide responsibilities to serve as department heads, or oversee specific departments. Elected county commissioners are more heavily involved in operations than are city council members; only in counties does the governing body directly manage specific agencies. The persistence of the commission form in county government is a visible reminder that the Progressive reform movement largely bypassed county government. Few cities today use the commission form, but the majority of U.S. counties retain the commission as their organizational design.

About a third of counties operate under a commission/executive system that grants legislative authority to a commission or council, but also employs an appointed county manager or administrator who manages the county day-to-day affairs. Thus, while a majority of counties still operate under the commission form, substantial numbers have shifted to the commission/administrator (manager) form. The International City and County Management Association (ICMA) recognizes over 300 counties that generally meet the requirements of the single executive, with over 60 percent of those located in the South

The elected executive is uncommon in U.S. counties. In fact, the elected executive plan is employed only in about 60 of the larger county governments. Generally, larger urban counties adopt this structure. Unlike the other forms, the elected executive form retains separation of powers. Elected county executives have the authority to veto ordinances enacted by the board or commission, and the governing board does not have overriding power with a majority vote. Strong executives formulate and administer budgets, appoint key administrators with council approval, and provide executive-style political leadership. The elected executive form mirrors the strong mayoral system which was the object of attack by the progressive reform movement.

The office of elected county executive attracts leaders with different orientations, values, and career interests than those serving under other forms of government. Like their city counterparts, elected county executives are expected to be attuned to political credit- claiming opportunities and have incentives for entrepreneurism (Schneider, Teske, and Mintrom, 1995). Elaine Sharp (2005) argues that the more politicized character of elected executives translates into outcomes that are responsive to interest group activism and mass political pressures as well as being more favorable toward entrepreneurial action and its associated credit-claiming opportunities.

Executives in Special Districts

The powers and positions of local executives are different among cities, counties, and special districts. Burns (1994) observed that over the course of the past 350 years

Americans created almost 50,000 new cities and special districts. Special districts have geographic flexibility and they perform only a few functions such as water service, garbage pick-up, or bus services, while general purpose cities or counties have more fixed boundaries and provide a broader range of services.

Special district governments are unique compared to other public agencies due to their ability to exploit complex financial markets with the public purse, free from the political influences so often seen in government agencies (Smith, 1974; Walsh, 1978; Doig, 1983; Mitchell, 1991). They are corporate in structure and established or chartered by the state, county or municipal government. They possess characteristics that are similar to both governments and private corporations as seen in their governing boards, and executive offices. Many districts governments have the power to raise funds from private money markets (Smith, 1974; Walsh, 1978; Doig, 1983; Mitchell, 1991). The benefit to the enabling government occurs as district government isolates financial risk, reduces the cost of financing, and removes debt or services from either the income statement or the balance sheet of the enabling government. These actions provide the enabling government with the ability to meet financial ratios, service expenditure goals, or address loan covenants.

The extant literature on the governing bodies of special districts is quite modest and the literature on executives of special districts almost non-existent. It is difficult to generalize about executive powers and responsibilities because each district type is created by its own enabling legislation and thus has its own unique structure. Nevertheless, districts are the fastest growing form of local government and the increasing complexity of their functions require strong executive leadership. In contrast, the power and position of counties' executives are less various because their responsibilities are more defined by state and federal mandates for public services than those in cities or special districts. (Cigler and Joslyn, 2002).

THE POLICY CONSEQUENCES OF EXECUTIVE LEADERSHIP

One of the fundamental questions in the study of public administration is what influence does executive position, role or power have on the policy choices that governments make? What differences do local executives make? What is the evidence from practice? Despite the importance of these questions, the answers remain incomplete. Moreover, it is unclear whether or not strong executive leadership pulls local government toward one specific policy path. As much previous literature shows, the institutional efforts to reform local government for efficiency or responsiveness informed the distinction between administrative and political governments (Frederickson, Johnson and Wood, 2004; Carr and Karuppusamy, 2008, 2009a). It was rooted in the politic-administration dichotomy of the Progressive Era (Svara, 1990; Mouritzen and Svara, 2002). Mouritzen and Svara's (2002) study of local government focuses on "how political power is obtained, maintained, exercised and shared" based on the empirical analysis of structural impacts. They classified the structure and culture of local government into four categories (2002: 260):

- Strong-mayor form with an elected official who is the primary political leader of the governing board and possesses considerable executive authority
- Committee-leader form with a quasi-parliamentary form with standing committees, an executive (or finance) committee, and a mayor, or majority leader in the case of Britain, drawn from the dominant party or party coalition in the city council
- Collective leadership form with a cabinet leadership structure in which an executive committee of the council exercises executive officer primarily responsible to the executive committee
- Council-manager form with a governing board headed by a nonexecutive leader and an appointed chief executive officer

Their analysis suggests two explanations are possible. In rational choice institutionalism, local executives attempt to maximize their goals which include constructive as well as self-serving ends, while in normative institutionalism, they tend to have "logic of appropriateness to promote public interests rather than their own". The blending of the two perspectives is better for understanding the variation of local policy outcomes. At some point, regardless of institutional arrangements with different incentives, local leaders with appropriate norms make innovative policy and produce better outcomes.

Based on a mixed perspective, Mouritzen and Svara (2002) propose a complementary framework as an alternative to the politic-administration dichotomy model. In other words the best policy consequences could be possible when political incentives lead to administrative competence and executive leaderships are committed to normative values,. In this case partnerships among elected officials and administrators can reflect the normative values and make the appropriate contribution to the democratic process.

The relative efficiency effect of elected versus appointed officials is a long-standing and contentious issue for scholars in economics, political science, and public administration. Some work identifies systematic differences in performance under different executive institutions, but others find no supporting evidence (Booms, 1966; Morgan and Pelissero, 1980; Deno and Mehay, 1987; Duffy-Deno and Dalenberg, 1990; Hayes and Chang, 1990; Stumm and Corrigan, 1998; Campbell and Turnbull, 2003). The results are inconclusive at best. Most recently Folz and Abdelrazek's (2009) investigation of the effect of local government executives on qualitative public service levels finds that cities with professional managers produce higher levels of service than cities run by elected mayors.

LOCAL EXECUTIVES AND NETWORK GOVERNANCE

Contemporary scholarship has focused on executives as network managers. Uncertainties about the actions and strategies of other organizations make collaboration risky. In addition, attitudes toward uncertainty and ways of addressing risks differ among local executives. Theory and empirical evidence indicate that elected officials are more risk averse and have shorter time horizons than appointed officials (Steinacker, 2004). Both politicians and administrators may be somewhat risk averse but are exposed to different risks depending on their distinct incentives.

The efficiency orientation of appointed executives leads them to seek connections with "popular" actors central to networks to reduce the transaction costs in obtaining information (Feiock, Lee, Park and Lee, 2010). Confronted with many potential partners, choosing who would be best to partner with requires substantial search time and resources. In addition, actors cannot perfectly foresee exchange risks. In this situation, network actors are expected to consult with actors who are believed to possess abundant information and resources. In doing so, managers reduce the potential transaction cost for information seeking and pursue administrative efficiency. Here, their professional attachment plays an important role in forming a particular network structure to seek valuable and reliable information (Feiock et al., 2010).

Professional associations that nurture professional identity may inform and screen who would be the best partners. Professional identity creates an environment in which appointed officials connect with others. In other words, complexity and uncertainty around cooperation and coordination are expected to create the network structure where appointed officials make linkages with the local governments that already maintain ties with many other actors. This implies that appointed officials' networking activities are not jurisdictionally bounded (Zhang and Feiock, 2009; Lee, Feiock, and Lee, 2011).

Local elected executives, like mayors or elected county executives, on the other hand, present a different networking style in seeking policy coordination and cooperation. Local elected officials tend to care more about community and neighborhood interests than professional associations because their most important political assets derive from their standing with electoral constituencies. Therefore, their network activities are expected to be more independent in that they do not necessarily count on information from only a single source. Rather, they invest time and build relationships with diverse network actors that can verify the information they receive. Creating these redundant relations takes a substantial amount of time and resources but offers them little new information. Nevertheless, maintaining multiple information sources is critical because the political consequences of being misled by wrong information are substantial, and, typically, elected executives do not regularly interact with each other through professional associations or affiliations.

Steinacker (2002) also argues that elected officials are politically more risk-averse and so their networking activities are constrained by their jurisdictional boundary. This suggests that elected officials will not necessarily seek to connect with popular actors. Their access to other actors may be limited to geographically neighboring governments. Therefore their network is maintained in a more ego-centered way. Reliance on globally or locally popular actors is not a strategy that politicians pursue in a situation where they can create ties with other actors. Based on this discussion, we develop general network hypotheses regarding coordination and cooperation. Empirical support for these relationships comes from a recent study of economic development collaboration in the Orlando metropolitan area. Analysis of the networks in which mayors and managers are embedded suggests that local executives, whether elected or appointed, forge tightly-clustered network structures to reduce the political and economic risks they perceive in collaboration (Lee and Feiock, 2008).

EXECUTIVE TURNOVER: CAUSES AND CONSEQUENCES

Understanding executive turnover is important for both theory and practice. The average tenure of an appointed local government manager is typically less than five years. The tenure of elected mayors is shorter than other elected officers and depends on mayoral political ambition and electoral success. While the factors that influence local election outcomes are much studied in political science, the factors that influence the tenure of professional managers is less well known. Turnover in elected office may signal some sort of electoral controversy. Community conflict has also been linked to manager turnover. In heterogeneous areas, cleavages based on wealth, race, or other social conditions can result in conflicts that spill over to local government (Clingermayer and Feiock, 2001).

What accounts for the tenure of local appointed executives? Over the past two decades several studies have attempted to explain why some city managers leave their positions while others stay. Prior studies of local government manager turnover explain the phenomenon as a product of "push" and "pull" factors (DeHoog and Whitaker, 1990; Whitaker and DeHoog, 1991). Push factors are roughly defined as those which contribute to conflict between managers and their elected overseers. The nature and intensity of these conflicts may ultimately result in a manager exiting his or her position either voluntarily, by force, or by threat of force. The existing literature on city manager turnover and tenure indicates that managers leave for a variety of reasons. Many city managers are fired or are forced to leave due to electoral changes that alter the composition of city councils. They may leave after disagreements with the city council that create a situation where the manager cannot stay. Managers may decide to leave voluntarily because they perceive political turmoil on the horizon such as an upcoming change of council membership or a new policy direction. The types of electoral controversy that influence re-election of mayors can also put politicians and administrators at odds. Several studies conclude that electoral changes in council can dramatically alter the tenure of managers.

Pull factors, on the other hand, are most routinely associated with managers' professional aspirations, or other personal objectives. These factors have the effect of drawing a manager away from his or her current position. The literature points to managers who leave voluntarily because they decide to pursue new career opportunities or seek positions of higher status, responsibility, or compensation. The traditional career path of a city manager often involves several jurisdictions, usually from smaller to larger communities. Recent work has linked managers' professional success in fiscal policy and economic development to opportunities for career advancement by moving to another government (McCabe et al., 2008).

Though popular practitioner and academic interest in explaining manager turnover is great, to date the empirical findings about what affects manager turnover have yet to yield a consistent story. This may be due to several limitations of this work. First, much of the literature is descriptive and does not seek to test causal explanations. Second, some studies have focused primarily on community social and economic factors, while others have focused almost exclusively on managers' backgrounds, experience and career paths. Third, some studies measure key concepts such as role conflict based on the perceptions of managers themselves (Kammerer et al., 1962; DeHoog and Whitaker, 1990; Whitaker and DeHoog, 1991), while others rely on objective measures of managers' work situations. Fourth, most of this work neglects the importance of political institutions in shaping the individual incentives of managers (though see Feiock and Stream, 1998). Because institutions shape the environment in which they operate we should expect executive and legislative structures to influence managerial tenure.

Managers who serve under a form of government with a directly elected mayor are viewed as more likely to experience short tenure because the presence of another full-time city executive with substantive formal authority increases potential for conflict and creates an environment that is less conducive to long-term policy management. Several studies report that the presence of a popularly elected mayor is negatively associated with city manager tenure.

City manager tenure in communities that rely on district representation may be shorter because the chances for greater political conflict and strong expression of parochial interests are greater in district than in at-large elections. In addition, district representation, which presumably promotes geographically specific interests rather than the interests of the whole community, may lead to divergence between the program goals of administrations and those of elected representatives.

What Difference Does Executive Turnover Make?

Executive turnover creates political uncertainty which alters the transaction costs of policy decisions and the time horizons of local leaders. A central assumption of the literature described above that seeks to identify factors that account for turnover among mayor and city managers, is that turnover of executives matters for government. Surprisingly, this proposition has been subjected to little scrutiny or empirical test.

One way that turnover might influence policy is by altering the time horizons in which policy choices are made. Time horizons and transaction costs are of critical concern with governments making decisions on programs involving long-term, credible commitments (Clingermayer and Feiock, 2001). When local officials are faced with electoral threats and political uncertainty their time horizons shorten considerably. Such a situation could exist when the city experiences high turnover among managers, mayors, and elected officers.

Clingermayer and Feiock (2001) elaborate on this idea by examining how the uncertainty caused by executive turnover affects the transaction costs in privatizing or utilizing alternative delivery mechanism for the provision of local services. Empirical analysis of the native delivery survey reveals that turnover in the city manager or appointed chief administrative officer position discourages contracting.

Turnover has been linked to a variety of inconsistent organizational outcomes (Finkelstein and Hambrick, 1990; Feiock and Stream, 1998). Clinger et al. (2008) identify significant impacts of leadership turnover on municipal borrowing patterns. In addition, some commentators argue that turnover erodes institutional integrity and neutral competence of executive institutions (Heclo, 1977; Haas and Wright, 1989; Lewis, 1991; Wilson, 1994).

Given the salience of local executives in the policy process, it is important to understand the tenure of managers. It is not enough simply to know how turnover can influence policy; it is also important to know what factors within and around cities can explain city manager tenure in the first place.

Conclusion: The Future of Local Executives

The Future of Executive Practice

Leadership beyond the local governing body and the boundaries of the jurisdiction are critical to executive governance in contemporary local governments. In an era of global governance defined by metropolitan regions, local executives matter more than ever (Feiock Moon and Park, 2008). The new role that executives must take on is that of coordinator. If individual governments lack the scale, resources, or authority to act regionally, local government must coordinate and collaborate. These new opportunities for executive leadership also require new skills in network management. Collaborative management is increasing recognized as essential for local executive leadership (Agranoff and McGuire, 2003).

Coordination among local governments is inherently challenging, but theoretical and empirical work demonstrates that local governments can overcome transaction cost barriers to promote regional cooperation (Feiock, 2004, 2007; Feiock, Park, and Steinacker, 2007). Executive leadership plays a critical role in that success by establishing positive reputations, pursuing repeating interactions, and making credible commitments (Feiock Park, and Steinacker, 2007).

Who will fill the role of local government executives in the 21st century? Recruitment of talented individuals to these positions has become a critical concern. It is generally recognized that recruitment of citizens to run for public office has become increasingly difficult in the last decade. This is an issue at all levels of government but especially at that of local government. What is less recognized is the aging of the city and county management profession and the ongoing problems of recruiting managers for local governments. ICMA reports that fewer than 10 percent of managers are under age 45. In addition, fewer than 15 percent are women. Retention is the complement to recruitment. We need to better understand the causes of executive turnover, especially those forces that push or pull an executive from public service.

The Future of Executive Research

This chapter also highlights important gaps in our understanding of the local executives. Although we identify counties and special districts as pervasive and increasingly important governments, the theory and empirical work drawn upon to discuss key issues such and policy outcomes, network governance and turnover is almost entirely based on the study of municipal governments. Investigation and comparison across different government types promises to enhance our understanding of executive roles in local government and local governance.

This chapter investigated the roles of elected and appointed executives in the context of the forms of government in which they operate and other institutional factors. In part this reflects the difficulty of isolating the office holder from the authority and responsibilities defined by the office he or she holds. In addition and related, it reflects the interaction of individuals and institutions in defining the executive role in local government. This highlights what is perhaps the most significant lacuna in the empirical study of local executives, the lack of integration of social, personal, and institutional factors to explain executive roles, behavior and performance.

Few commentators would disagree that an executive's background and personal characteristics, the demands placed on her by citizens, and the institutional constraints she operates under are each important. This is generally confirmed in case studies. What is lacking are theoretical models that can provide precise predictions based on interactions among these factors, and non-additive empirical tests that combine these elements. Pursuing this agenda promises to enrich our understanding of local government and governance and more generally contribute to political science, public administration and urban affairs.

References

Adrian, Charles R. (1987). *A History of American City Government, 1920–1945*. Lanham, Md.: University Press of America.

Adrian, Charles R. and Charles Press. (1977). *Governing Urban America*, 5th ed. New York: McGraw-Hill.

Agranoff, R., and McGuire, M. (2003). *Collaborative Public Management: New Strategies for Local Governments*. Washington, DC: Georgetown University Press.

Ammons, D. N., and Newell, C. (1989). *City Executives: Leadership Roles, Work Characteristics, and Time Management*. Albany: State University of New York Press.

Biermann, F., Biermann, F., and Siebenhüner, B. (2009). *Managers of Global Change: The Influence of International Environmental Bureaucracies*. Cambridge, Mass.: MIT Press.

Booms, B. H. (1966). City Governmental Form and Public Expenditure Levels. *National Tax Journal*, 19(2): 187–99.

Bowman, Ann O'M and Kearney, Richard C. (2006). *State and Local Government: The Essentials*. NY: Charles Hartford.

Burns, N. (1994). *The Formation of American Local Governments: Private Values in Public Institutions*. New York: Oxford University Press.

Campbell, R. J., and G. K. Turnbull. (2003). "On Local Government Structure and Spending Behavior: The Effects of Separation of Powers and Management Form." *Urban Studies*, 40: 23–34.

Carr, J. B., and S. Karuppusamy. (2009). Beyond Ideal Types of Municipal Structure. *American Review of Public Administration*, 39(3): 304–21.

Carr, J. B., and S. Karuppusamy. (2008). The Adapted Cities Framework. *Urban Affairs Review*, 43(6): 875.

Cigler, A., and M. Joslyn (2002). The Extensiveness of Group Membership and Social Capital: The Impact on Political Tolerance Attitudes. *Political Research Quarterly*, 55(1): 7–25.

Clinger, J.C., R.C. Feiock, B. C. McCabe, and H. J. Park. (2008). Turnover, Transaction Costs, and Time Horizons: An Examination of Municipal Debt Financing. *The American Review of Public Administration* 38(June): 167–179.

Clingermayer, James C., and Feiock, Richard C. (2001). *Institutional Constraints and Policy Choice: An Exploration of Local Governance*. Albany: State University of New York Press.

Dahl, R. A. (1961). *Who Governs? Democracy and Power in an American City*. New Haven: Yale University Press.

DeHoog, R., & Whitaker G. (1990). Political Conflict or Professional Advancement. *Journal of Urban Affairs*, 12(4): 361–77.

Deno, Kevin T. and Stephen L. Mehay (1987). "Municipal Management Structure and Fiscal Performance: Do City Managers Make a Difference?" *53 Southern Economic Journal*, 627–642.

Doig, J. W. (1983). "If I See a Murderous Fellow Sharpening a Knife Cleverly...": The Wilsonian Dichotomy and the Public Authority Tradition. *Public Administration Review*, 43(4): 292–304.

Duffy-Deno, K. T. and Dalenberg (1990). Do Institutions Matter? An Empirical Note. *National Tax Journal*, 43(2): 207–15.

Feiock, R. C. (2004). Politics, Institutions and Local Land-use Regulation. *Urban Studies*, 41(2): 363–75.

Feiock, R. C. (2007). Rational Choice and Regional Governance. *Journal of Urban Affairs*, 29(1): 47–63.

Feiock, R. C. and Christopher Stream. (1998). Explaining the Tenure of Local Government Managers. *Journal of Public Administration Research and Theory, 8*(1): 117–30.

Feiock, R. C., In Won Lee, Hyung Jun Park, and Kyong-Hyung Lee (2010). Collaboration Networks Among Local Elected Officials: Information, Commitment, and Risk Aversion. *Urban Affairs Review, 46*(2): 241–62.

Feiock, R. C., M. J. Moon, and H.J. Park. (2008). Is the World "Flat" or "Spiky"? Rethinking the Governance Implications of Globalization for Economic Development. *Public Administration Review, 68*(1): 24–35.

Feiock, Richard C., Hyung Jun Park, and Annette Steinacker. (2007). Institutional Collective Action and Economic Development Joint Ventures. Working paper, Devoe Moore Center Program in Local Governance. <http://www.fsu.edu/~localgov>.

Feiock, Richard C., Moon-Gi Jeong and Jaehoon Kim. (2003). Credible Commitment and Council-Manager Government: Implications for Policy Instrument Choices. *Public Administration Review, 63*(5): 616–625.

Finkelstein, S., and Hambrick, D. C. (1990). Top-management-team Tenure and Organizational Outcomes The Moderating Role of Managerial Discretion. *Administrative Science Quarterly, 35*(3): 484–503.

Folz, D. H. and R. Abdelrazek. (2009). Professional Management and Service Levels in Small US Communities. *American Review of Public Administration, 39*(5): 553–69.

Frant, H. (1993). Rules and Governance in the Public Sector: The Case of Civil Service. *American Journal of Political Science, 37*(4): 990–1007.

Frant, H. (1996). High-powered and Low-powered Incentives in the Public Sector. *Journal of Public Administration Research and Theory, 6*(3): 365–381.

Frederickson, H. G., and G. A. Johnson. (2001). The Adapted American City: A Study of Institutional Dynamics. *Urban Affairs Review, 36*: 872–84.

Frederickson, H. G. (2004). The Changing Structure of American Cities: A Study of the Diffusion of Innovation. *Public Administration Review, 64*(3): 320–30.

Frederickson, H. G., Johnson, G. A., and Wood, C. H. (2004). *The Adapted City: Institutional Dynamics and Structural Change.* Armonk, N.Y.: M.E. Sharpe.

Haas, P. J., and D. S. Wright. (1989). Administrative Turnover in State Government. *Administration Society, 21*(2): 265–77.

Hansell, Bill. 1998. Is it Time to "Reform" the Reform? Changes in the Council-Manager Form of Government. *Public Management, 80*(12): 15–16.

Hansell, B. (1999). Reforming the Reform: Variations on Mayor-council Form of Government, part 2. *Public Management, 81*(1): 28.

Hassett, Wendy L., and Douglas Watson. (2002). Long-Serving City Managers: Practical Application of the Academic Literature. *Public Administration Review, 62*(5): 622–629.

Hayes, Kathy, and Semoon Chang. (1990). The Relative Efficiency of City Manager and Mayor-Council Forms of Government. *Southern Economic Journal, 57* (1): 167–177.

Heclo, H., & Brookings Institution. (1977). *A Government of Strangers: Executive Politics in Washington.* Washington: Brookings Institution.

Kammerer, G. M., Farris, C. D., DeGrove, J. M., and Clubok, A. B. (1962) *City Managers in Politics: Analysis of Manager Tenure and Termination.* Gainesville: University of Florida Press.

Kearney, R., B. M. Feldman, and C. P. F. Scavo. (2000). Reinventing Government: City Manager Attitudes and Actions. *Public Administration Review, 60*(6): 535–548.

Lee, In Won, Richard C. Feiock, and Youngmi Lee. (2012). Competitors and Cooperators: A Micro-Level Analysis of Regional Economic Development Collaboration Networks, *Public Administration Review, 72*(2).

Lewis, Gregory B. (1991). "Turnover and the Quiet Crises in the Federal Service." *Public Administration Review, 51*: 328–343.

McCabe, Barbara, Richard Feiock, James Clingermayer, and Christopher Stream (2008). Turnover among City Managers: The Role of Political and Economic Change. *Public Administration Review, 68*(2): 380–86.

Morgan, David R., Robert E. England, and John P. Pelissero, 2007. *Managing Urban America*. 6th ed. Washington, DC: CQ Press.

Mitchell, J. (1991). Education and Skills for Public Authority Management. *Public Administration Review, 51*: 429–437.

Morgan, David R. and John P. Pelissero (1980). "Urban Policy: Does Political Structure Matter?" *American Political Science Review, 74*: 999–1006.

Morgan, David R., and Sheilah S. Watson, 1992. Policy Leadership in Council-Manager Cities: Comparing Mayor and Manager. *Public Administration Review 52*(5): 438–446.

Mouritzen, P. E., and Svara, J. H. (2002). *Leadership at the Apex: Politicians and Administrators in Western Local Governments*. Pittsburgh: University of Pittsburgh Press.

Nalbandian, J. (1991). *Professionalism in Local Government: Transformations in the Roles, Responsibilities, and Values of City Managers*. 1st edn. San Francisco: Jossey-Bass Publishers.

Nalbandian, John. (1990). Tenets of Contemporary Professionalism in Local Government. *Public Administration Review, 50*(6): 654–662.

O'Leary, Rosemary, Catherine Gerard and Lisa Blomgren Bingham. (2006). Introduction to the Symposium on Collaborative Public Management. Special Issue. *Public Administration Review, 66*: 6–9.

Osborne, D., and Ted Gaebler. (1992). *Reinventing Government: How the Entrepreneurial Spirit is Transforming the Public Sector Reinventing Government*: Reading, MA: Addison-Wesley Publishing, 405.

Peterson, P. E. (1981). *City Limits*. Chicago: University of Chicago Press.

Protasel, G. J. (1988). Abandonments of the Council-manager Plan: A New Institutionalist Perspective. *Public Administration Review, 48*(4): 807–12.

Renner, T., and DeSantis, V. S. (1994). City Manager Turnover: The Impact of Formal Authority and Electoral Change. *State & Local Government Review, 26*(2): 104–111.

Schneider, Mark, Paul Teske, and Michael Mintrom. 1995. *Public Entrepreneurs: Agents for Change in American Government*. Princeton, NJ: Princeton University Press.

Sharp, E. B. (1999). *The Sometime Connection: Public Opinion and Social Policy*. Albany, NY: State University of New York Press.

Sharp, Elaine B. (2002). Culture, Institutions, and Urban Officials' Responses to Morality Issues. *Political Research Quarterly, 55*: 861–84.

Sharp, Elaine. B. (2005). *Morality Issues and City Politics*. Lawrence, KS: University Press of Kansas.

Smith, Robert G. (1974). *Ad Hoc Governments*. London: Sage Publications.

Steinacker, A. (2004). Game Theoretic Models of Metropolitan Cooperation. In Richard C. Feiock ed., *Metropolitan Governance: Conflict, Competition and Cooperation*, 46–66. Washington DC: Georgetown University Press.

Stone, C. (2005). Looking Back to Look Forward: Reflections on Urban Regime Analysis. *Urban Affairs Review, 40*(3): 309–341.

Stone, C. N. (1989). *Regime Politics: Governing Atlanta, 1946–1988*. Lawrence, KS: University Press of Kansas

Stumm, T., and M. T. Corrigan (1998). City Managers: Do They Promote Fiscal Efficiency? *Journal of Urban Affairs*, 20(3): 343–351.

Svara, J. H. (1990). *Official Leadership in the City: Patterns of Conflict and Cooperation*. New York: Oxford University Press.

Svara, J. H. (2003). Effective Mayoral Leadership in Council-manager Cities: Reassessing the Facilitative Model. *National Civic Review*. 92(2): 157–72.

Teske, Paul, and Mark Schneider. (1994). The Bureaucratic Entrepreneur: The Case of City Managers. *Public Administration Review*, 54: 331–340.

Walsh, Anna H. (1978). *The Public's Business: The Politics and Practices of Government Corporations*. Cambridge, MA: MIT Press.

Watson, D., and Watson, D. (2004). Career Paths of City Managers in America's Largest Council-manager Cities. *Public Administration Review*, 64(2): 192–199.

Whitaker, Gordon and Ruth Hoogland DeHoog, 1991. City Managers under Fire: How Conflict Leads to Turnover. *Public Administration Review*, 51 (2): 156–165.

Wilson, Patricia A. (1994) Power Politics and Other Reasons Why Senior Executives Leave the Federal Government. *Public Administration Review*, 54: 12–19.

CHAPTER 20

··

LOCAL COURTS

··

RICHARD A. BRISBIN, JR.

THE task of resolving the vast majority of private social and economic conflicts and public crimes falls within the jurisdiction of state courts in the United States. In contrast to the courts discussed in the chapter on State Courts in this volume, this chapter examines the politics of courts that possess "local" or regional, county, or municipal jurisdiction and that address disputes that arise under state law and local ordinances. As utilized in this chapter, "local court" means not just a physical space or a judge and her employees but a matrix of relatively autonomous institutions. This matrix of institutions engages in a "triadic conflict resolution process;" two disputants refer to a third party to assist in resolving their conflict (Shapiro, 1981, 1–2). Local courts therefore include judges or other "third parties" and a community or "legal complex" of attorneys, prosecutors, public defenders, and other personnel who represent disputants. In efforts to penalize crime and resolve other disputes the three participant persons or organizations rely on a complex assemblage of norms, standard operating procedures, state statutes, local ordinances, and previous judicial decisions to guide their actions (Rose and Valverde, 1998). In the conduct of their activity, judges and the legal complex employ law and their discretion in ways that can affect the authority of other political institutions, create law and policy, impose norms of social and economic control, and define the rights and liberties of individuals (Shapiro, 1981, 2–64).

In particular, American local courts include state courts of general jurisdiction or "trial" courts with various official names whose personnel address civil disputes with larger monetary claims and more serious or felony criminal cases. Local courts of limited jurisdiction or "inferior" or "lower" courts with a variety of names consider local civil monetary disputes of less than a few thousand dollars, minor crimes and misdemeanors, and sometimes specific crimes such as those involving drugs. In addition courts of limited jurisdiction conduct the preliminary stages of criminal prosecutions, including notification of defendant's rights, notice of charges, and possible pretrial release. There are also local courts of specialized jurisdiction that consider divorce, family, and probate matters, juvenile delinquency, traffic citations, and housing code violations. To evaluate what is known about the politics of local courts and legal complex, the chapter first assesses the general state of research about them. Then it describes the political dimensions of local court activity, and closes with a detailed appraisal of information about the political functions of these courts.

THE POLITICS OF LOCAL COURTS: AN OVERVIEW OF THE STATE OF RESEARCH

The study of the politics of local courts is not at the top of the agenda of judicial scholarship. Political scientists who research law and courts have traditionally centered their work on the Supreme Court of the United States and other appellate courts. Few political science graduate programs educate scholars with an interest in empirical research into the politics of local courts (Provine, 2007). Instead, scholars from other academic disciplines have contributed much of what is known about local courts. For example, during recent decades an explosion in the number of academic departments of criminal justice has resulted in numerous case studies of the administration of local criminal courts. Attention to civil justice has come from scholars associated with the Law and Society Association. A multidisciplinary group that includes a small number of political scientists, Law and Society scholars have used both ethnographic and critical quantitative case study methodologies in focused studies that explore the origins of conflicts, settlement of disputes outside of courts, administrative legal institutions, the nature and implications of judicial procedures, lawyers, and the outcomes and effects of legal activity (Munger, 1998; Provine, 1998). The law professorate traditionally has written prescriptive critiques of substantive law and court procedures and has only infrequently published empirical studies of local courts. The disciplinary background of these scholars has often meant that their publications accord implicit rather than explicit attention to the political function of local courts.

Regardless of their discipline, researchers who examine the political significance of local courts confront a difficult data collection problem. There are more than 2100 state courts of general jurisdiction that operate within counties or districts of a state and more than 11,800 courts state and local courts of limited geographic or subject-matter jurisdiction (computed from National Center for State Courts, 2013b). Since 1975 the National Center for State Courts Court Statistics Project has collected comparative statistical information on the business of state courts (LaFountain et al., 2009; National Center for State Courts, 2013a). Although a valuable resource, the quality of data by the CSP is limited by the collection practices of state and local court personnel. The Bureau of Justice Statistics (BJS) of the United States Department of Justice (2013) collects statistical data on arrests and criminal cases. It has published quantitative studies that analyze specific aspects of the criminal and civil judicial process. Other units of the Department of Justice fund projects to improve the operation of criminal and juvenile courts that generate comparative quantitative data on court operations. Since the path-breaking Civil Litigation Research Project of the early 1980s (Trubek et al., 1983) empirical comparative studies of state and local civil litigation have remained rare. However, law and society scholars have published case studies that provide thicker descriptions of the political functions of local courts and their personnel. What then is known—and not known—about the politics of local courts?

Politics and Local Courts

State and local politics is never far away from local courts. Because the federal Constitution restricts the authority of federal courts, local courts consider about 90 percent of the cases filed in the nation. Local courts and the adjunct legal complex are institutions constructed by state constitutional conventions and state legislatures. They address conflicts and crimes that arise under laws largely drafted by state or local legislators and operate under procedures established by legislators and the judiciary of federal and state appellate courts. They are staffed by locally elected, politically appointed, or civil service personnel. Since they depend on the discretionary decisions of other institutions such as police, government regulators, or private individuals for their business, local courts cannot address all conflicts. When they make decisions, they rely on the influence of the ideology of the rule of law to induce compliance with the decision by private parties or other governmental institutions.

Although other institutions define the authority of local courts, as described by Mather (1991, 1995, 1998) conversely local courts can define the legitimate range of policies and influence the behavior of other state and local political institutions, private persons, and corporations in several ways. First, whether the dispute is civil and between private parties or involves government, or is criminal, local courts are *agenda-setting forums*. Local courts define civil problems in legal terms and afford a place for parties to engage in the orderly expression of arguments for alternative outcomes. They provide a site for the determination of whether behavior is criminal and deserving of correction or penalization.

Local courts are sites for *problem definition*. The procedures of the courts force individuals and their lawyers to construct a causal story about disputes and crimes. In so doing the lawyers frame norms of social, economic, and political justice, and they communicate these views in a public forum where they can influence community views and executive and legislative politicians. The local court therefore provides an opportunity for *issue-framing and political mobilization*. The existence of law and the actions of its judges and lawyers can make people aware of social, economic, or political problems, influence mass opinion about local crime, housing, and government regulations and taxes, shape media portrayals of the law, and indirectly encourage political participation or group mobilization. In this sense, courts act as a catalyst for political action (Handler, 1978, 214–22; McCann, 1994, 48–91). On the other hand, symbolic appeals to judicial independence and the relative autonomy of court personnel from media and public oversight means that local courts can frame and address political issues, such as crime control, without popular awareness of their definition of the characterization of the problem (Scheingold, 1991).

Local court personnel can *define or create local legal norms*. Judges can enforce the literal meaning of the law or interpret statutes or the common law in light of case-specific factual aspects of the case to offer new legal interpretations of statutory language or adaptations of case law. Through the application of evidentiary and procedural rules judges can also narrow or expand the meaning of legal texts when framing or resolving a civil conflict or defining and determining criminal guilt (Jacob, 1992; Mather, 1995, 176–8). Alternatively, judges and attorneys develop norms and standard operating procedures to govern the negotiated settlement of civil case settlements. Prosecutors, judges, and defense counsel can construct norms for plea bargains, bail, and sentencing in criminal cases.

Finally, through their decisions, the personnel of the local court *convey messages* about responsible economic and political behavior and the seriousness of criminal offenses. They can generally educate the public about the requirements of the law, the legitimacy of its disputes, and the proper use of governmental power. Their decisions can create a sense of empowerment among a group of disadvantaged persons and encourage other persons to act legally in similar contexts. Their decisions can induce individuals and firms to adopt prophylactic measures such as insurance and security devices to protect against civil litigation or criminal victimization, encourage legislators to pass new laws to address public or corporate misbehavior or anomalies in existing laws, or afford symbolic recognition and psychological satisfaction of the interests of litigants. From court decisions, interest groups or corporations can also gain knowledge of how to use the law to leverage political changes beneficial to their interests (Handler, 1978, 212–14; Galanter, 1983; McCann, 1994, 138–310; Epp, 2009). The remainder of this chapter addresses the state of research on these aspects of local court politics and policymaking.

The Conflicts before Local Courts

An independent or nonpolitical judiciary is an ideal rather than reality (Cross, 2008). External political institutions create a limited agenda of conflicts for local court consideration, and the rules of local courts define which conflicts appear as cases they can consider. In particular, state politics shapes the role of a local court as an institution, including its jurisdiction and administrative independence as a forum for conflict disposition and the legal matters on its docket. Nonetheless, local courts still possess considerable discretion in the composition and management of their caseload.

Jurisdiction: The jurisdiction, or geographic area of responsibility and range of conflicts assigned to a local court, depends on state constitutions and legislation. Despite campaigns by interest groups to have states devise a "unified" court structure with one set of general jurisdiction courts and a single set of limited jurisdiction courts to serve a locality (e.g. California, Florida, Iowa, Virginia, Wisconsin), many states have more than one type of general jurisdiction court (or separately for civil and criminal cases) (e.g. New York, Tennessee, Texas). The majority of states have several courts of limited or specialized jurisdiction such as municipal, magistrate, justice of the peace, family, drug, traffic, juvenile, tax, claims against government, and probate or orphan's courts (National Center for State Courts, 2013b). The effect of the jurisdictional arrangement of courts on case dispositions and the ways in which politics figures in the designation of the duties of court personnel have received limited scholarly attention (Ryan et al., 1980, 47–79; Flango, 1994). It is known that judicial and bar associations or groups of local lawyers and legislative judiciary committees are the key participants in the political decisions that determine the business, finances, and facilities of local courts and the institutional authority of their personnel (Cook, 1969–70; Baar, 1980; Scheb and Matheny, 1988; Wice, 1995; Winkle and Oswald, 2008). Related to jurisdictional arrangements, court fees and institutional rules such as the legal requirements for standing to sue also can effect the use of courts for civil conflicts. The exact effects of these rules on the business of local courts are unknown.

Oversight and the Political Independence of Local Courts: As discussed in the chapter on State Courts in this volume, most states have placed their local courts under the administrative oversight of the state's court of last resort, a state court administration office, and judicial and attorney ethics offices or commissions. Descriptions of the administrative oversight of local courts exist, but there is little information on whether any interest group or bureaucratic political activity has shaped the state's administrative management of local courts and, consequently, the conflicts they consider. Additionally, since local governments fund and staff some court offices and operations, the political behavior of county commissions and other local officials in court funding and personnel matters needs much more scholarly attention (Hartley and Douglas, 2003).

Despite central court administration, a number of studies have found that local courts exhibit a unique "culture" and rely on distinctive local procedures to manage conflicts. The consequence is that a set of informal norms guides the administration of business in a court. For example, informal norms affect the negotiation of civil cases, such as divorces (Mather, McEwen, and Maiman, 2001, 110–32) and bail setting, plea-bargaining, and sentencing in criminal cases (Eisenstein, Flemming, and Nardulli, 1988; Nardulli, Eisenstein, and Flemming, 1988, 85–162; Spohn, 2009, 122–5). Important descriptive and analytical studies of variations in court culture have established the existence of distinctive styles of court and case management, judicial leadership of a court, judicial-staff relations, and social interactions among participants. Research links these variations to the management of court business (Eisenstein, Flemming, and Nardulli, 1988; Nardulli, Eisenstein, and Flemming, 1988, 163–97; Ostrom et al., 2007). However, more comparative research is needed on why shared local norms emerge, how they are maintained, and what affect they have on the agenda of cases before local courts.

Problem Definition, Framing, and the Mobilization of Legal Action

The legal resolution of problems depends on public choices to mobilize the authority of courts. Some problems, including debt relief and divorce, require at least minimal local court action. However, several institutions and practices provide means of dispute resolution that reduce the caseload of local courts or place the judge in the position of ratifying out-of-court agreements. The evidence also is that people frequently choose not to use the civil courts to resolve their problems and do not report crime.

Civil Problems: Studies of civil disputes reveal that the availability of institutional options affects public use of the courts (Sagy, 2011). Indeed, the considerable research on legal mobilization also indicates that many persons do not recognize their civil grievances are amenable to judicial resolution. They can "lump" their problem or resort to local norms governing face-to-face negotiation, confrontation, or violence to settle it (Ellickson, 1991; Merry, 1990). If they recognize their grievances have a legal aspect and choose to act, they often need information if they decide to assert a claim against another party and then, possibly, enter into an adversarial dispute with them (Felstiner, Abel, and Sarat, 1980–81; Miller and Sarat, 1980–81; Conley and O'Barr, 2005, 78–94). They might lack knowledge of rights, or confront corporations, governmental institutions, or lawyers who impede their recognition of legal subjection (Sarat, 1990). Other reasons associated with the failure to recognize a situation of injustice and pursue a dispute include self-identity, race, gender, experiences with legality, expectations about what courts can do, fear of retribution, shame, and other social and psychological attributes of self-identification (Zemans, 1982; Bumiller, 1988, 98–108; Conley and O'Barr, 1990, 58–81, 126–49; Merry, 1990; McCann, 1994, 92–137; Engel and Munger, 2003; Marshall, 2003; Albiston, 2005; McCann, 2006). The relative significance of these reasons for a failure to litigate appears to be rooted in a mix of historical experience, personal identity, and cultural and other normative beliefs in varying and often unique situations (Greenhouse, 1986; Merry, 1990; Sarat, 1990; Ewick and Silbey, 1998, 108–64; Silbey, 2005, 351–5; McCann, 2008, 524–5, 528–32). Additionally, corporate recognition of legal problems and corporate decisions to mobilize the law and file civil complaints have received little study.

The demand for court services also depends on knowledge of opportunities to access alternative public and private dispute resolution services. In a classic study Macauley (1966; updated in Kenworthy, Macauley, and Rogers, 1996) first described formal law and litigation as supporting the alternative ways of defining and managing disputes. Numerous case studies illustrate how private firms devise practices to resolve conflicts with consumers and employees (Ross and Littlefield, 1978; Nader, 1980; Best, 1981; Edelman, 1990; Edelman, Erlanger, and, Lande, 1993). State laws requiring auto insurance have resulted in practices for the settlement of disputes to avoid the use of courts (Ross, 1980). A wide range of government agencies and community mediation services have employed personnel who mediate complaints about consumer purchase, utility bills, insurance company practices, debts, and other individual-business disputes

(Serber, 1980; Silbey, 1980–81; Brisbin and Hunter, 1990b; Merry and Milner, 1993). Commonly used in credit card billing disputes, businesses and individuals can agree to employ arbitrators or private judges to settle disagreements (Issacharoff and Delaney, 2006; Eisenberg, Miller, and Sherwin, 2008). Judges have encouraged or required the mediation or arbitration of some conflicts, notably in divorce cases (Boersema, Hanson, and Keilitz, 1991; Burns, 2000; Steegh, 2008). Despite the many alternatives for out-of-court settlement of disputes, the political aspects and outcomes of the decision-making of mediation and arbitration, including possible institutional processes and ideological, gender, or racial biases in the process and their effect on local court business, have received limited study (but see Talesh, 2012). However, the alternatives might cause some rights-claims and moral issues to be devalued rather than receive attention from a local court (Kritzer and Anderson, 1983; Harrington, 1985; Harrington and Merry, 1988; Silbey and Sarat, 1989; Cobb, 1997; Burns, 2000; Conley and O'Barr, 2005, 39–59). Regardless, the rate and outcome of settlements of local court filings remains in need of quantitative examination. All that can be said is that the civil cases that survive out-of-court settlement efforts appear to be a small and atypical portion of the universe of civil conflicts.

Problems and Administrative Agencies: Administrative agencies, boards, and commissions complement the institutions that engage in the mediation and arbitration of civil cases. Originally created to provide an informal process for settling disputes about the enforcement of government regulations and disputes about transfer payments, over time these agencies became more like specialized courts as the states adopted administrative procedure acts, the agencies adopted evidentiary rules, participation of counsel expanded, and the states created an administrative judiciary (Nonet, 1969; Kritzer, 1998, 6–14). Today agencies and boards enact, enforce and adjudicate state and local public health, safety, housing, zoning, environmental, insurance, banking, and public utility regulations. They also can adjudicate disputes about workers' compensation and unemployment benefits. However, agency personnel commonly settle many regulatory disputes through negotiation. When settling cases they often rely on informal norms with political ramifications (Brisbin and Hunter, 1990a; Lempert, 1989; Gilboy, 1992; Ross, 1995; Brisbin, Hunter, and Leyden, 2010). Little comprehensive information exists on the sources and numbers of disputes addressed by these agencies, the public's mobilization of these agencies to address its problems, variations in the norms of regulatory enforcers, the attitudes and behavior of administrative law judges and other agency personnel in settling disputes, and the role of lawyers and their clients in the agency process (but see Kagan, 1989 and the case studies by Kritzer, 1998; Lens, 2007; Ramji-Nogales, Schoenholtz, and Schrag, 2007).

Criminal Problems: Since victims, police, and prosecutors define away problems, potential criminal litigation also disappears and the legal process is not mobilized. BJS data shows that persons report only about half of all criminal victimizations (U.S. Dept. of Justice, BJS, 2013, Table 33.3 [2008]). When victimization is not reported or a suspect is not identified by victims or witnesses, arrest is uncommon. Police make relatively few arrests based on their own investigations or observations of the occurrence of a crime.

They devise their own standards for when to make an arrest. Whether emanating from department supervisors, the street-level norms and practices of officers, or external political demands, case studies find that these policies introduce additional selectivity into decisions and, ultimately, potential activity for local courts (for summaries of studies on this topic, see Walker and Katz, 2011, 344–69; for examples, see Grattet and Jenness, 2005; Moskos, 2008, 38–157). There is a lack of comparison across jurisdictions of the nature and effect of victim, witness, and police decisions on the business of courts.

Mobilization Assessed: The presence of gate-keeping practices and institutions that diminish the caseloads of local courts calls into question claims of a litigation explosion raised by some authors and interest groups (Lieberman, 1981; Olson, 1991, 2003) or assertions that the U.S. is an intensely adversarial culture in which courts generate extensive social and economic costs and displace the functions of other political institutions (Kagan, 2001; Burke, 2002). Indeed, empirical studies have disclosed a *decline* in the number of trials in state courts during the past quarter century (Ostrom, Strickland, and Hannaford-Agor, 2004; Moog, 2009). Although local courts dispose of more disputes today than in the past, negotiation between lawyers, alternative dispute resolution, and plea-bargaining has made the courtroom trial less frequent (Kagan 1984; Stipanowich 2004; Yeazell 2004). The reasons for and political implications of the decline in the use of local courts for trials is need of considerably more attention, but it is possible to hypothesize that the local court trials are less a public institution to be used to resolve disputes and assess criminality than a threat employed to leverage civil settlements and criminal plea bargains.

LAW, PROCEDURAL RULES, AND NORMS

In public institutions that enforce or make law and policy, substantive law and procedural rules and norms matter. Largely established by legislatures and appellate courts or found in constitutions, the law and procedures governing local courts regulate institutional discretion and protect the rights and interests of the parties to a dispute. Yet, when people pursue court action, local judges and other officials possess the political power to employ their discretion or local norms to transform the definition of the conflict and shape its disposition. Incremental modification or adjustment of external law and procedural rules thus mark how local courts handle conflicts and convey the meaning of law and policy.

Popular misconceptions about the law often mask the transformation process. The first misconception is that local judges simply apply statutes written by legislatures to specific case facts and the second is that local judges are bound by interpretive precedents set in previous cases, most commonly by courts of last resort. Formal law and litigation remain as a boundary on dispute management by judges; however, judges have discretion to modify the meaning of statutes and precedents and to devise civil remedies and criminal sentences in the cases that go to trial. Scholars have described how judges incrementally adjust the texts of the law during the process of local court decision-making (Levi, 1948; Shapiro, 1965; 1972; 1981, 28–49; Macintyre, 1985). Also, when the conflict is about a new problem or technology, it can end up in local court trials and often in new interpretations of legal texts.

The third misconception is that that the judge alone controls the meaning of the law. Although the judiciary possesses discretion in the interpretation and application of the substantive law, local court culture usually means that a mix of procedural legal requirements and local routines guides the disposition of cases. Court culture and profession-focused studies have noted that judges and lawyers often develop shared norms and practices for the disposition of cases. The identification of shared norms and practices in the processing of criminal cases have led scholars to identify "courtroom workgroups" or "communities" comprised of prosecutors, public defenders, and judges interacting in local courts (Eisenstein and Jacob, 1977, 19–171; Eisenstein, Flemming and Nardulli, 1988, 22–56, 202–28; Nardulli, Eisenstein, and Flemming, 1988, 123–62). Often in areas of specialized civil practice, such as family law, routines and expectations develop that promote "normal" case dispositions (Mather, McEwen, and Maiman, 2001, 87–109). Other personnel who can be included in the court's norms are clerks, probation and parole officers, and employees or volunteers with social service agencies (Feeley, 1979, 111–20). Research indicates that these local operating procedures and norms affect policy outcomes and the social, economic, and political interests of litigants, but more jurisdiction to jurisdiction comparisons could provide greater insight into the policy effects.

Limited and Special Jurisdiction Courts

Examinations of limited jurisdiction criminal courts have found that local norms often mean that these courts normally operate more as case processors than as an adversarial forum rigidly governed by formal law and procedural rules. The process is often rapid, and many defendants choose not to have an attorney. With the more than 56 million traffic cases each year (LaFountain et al., 2009, 36), the routines of the process often neglect the unique circumstances of each case in order to dispose of them based on norms that define the "worth" of the case. Norms of behavior and rules of thumb encouraging cooperation buttress the willingness of judges, prosecutors, and defense counsel to support rapid criminal case disposition by plea bargain or what critics call "assembly line justice." Rapid case processing and the use of normal criminal sentences, especially probation, usually transpire regardless of the caseload of the court (Feeley, 1979, 123–98). Many of these courts employ non-lawyer judges who are often criticized for being neglectful of adversary procedures and biased toward police and prosecutorial interests. For defendants, however, the cost of possible pretrial detention, lawyer fees, and time away from work or awaiting case processing often seem greater than the sentences that these courts impose (Feeley, 1979, 199–243). This finding has generated continuing scholarly debate about the extent and significance of case processing (Earl, 2008).

The judges of limited jurisdiction courts usually must bind over more serious crimes to the judges of the trial court of general jurisdiction. Unless pretrial release is gained by a lesser court judge's decision to release a defendant on his own recognizance or the defendant posts bail that he will forfeit to a bondman if he does not show up for trial, he might be detained in jail during this period. Although dated, the important studies suggest that both bondsman and judicial decisions about pretrial release on the defendant's own recognizance or money bail rely on politically influenced local norms and discretionary assessments of the risk of nonappearance, prior criminal record, and the seriousness of the crime. Available jail space and the economic interests of the insurance firms that back bail bondsmen's decisions to pledge money also affect pretrial release on money bail (Dill, 1975; Feeley, 1979, 96–108; Flemming, 1982).

Courts of limited jurisdiction often exist or have the authority to consider civil small claims cases such as consumer complaints as well as neighborhood nuisance, landlord-tenant, debt collection, and minor personal liability cases, and cases that might result in possible civil penalties for local regulatory ordinance violations. Studies have found that the parties often resolve many of the cases filed with these courts through negotiation or mediation ordered or conducted by the judge (Vidmar, 1984; Wissler, 1995). One study has shown that the mediation service offered by these courts is more effective than trial in securing a resolution of the dispute with which the parties will comply (McEwen and Maiman, 1984). When disputes reach these courts, non-lawyer judges often hear them and apply a mix of law and local norms about moral order to dispose of them (Yngvesson, 1993). Often the parties misunderstand the need to bear the burden of proof and provide evidence of their claim and they overestimate the power of the court to resolve their claim (O'Barr and Conley, 1988). Unfortunately, more recent comprehensive studies of the political importance of the rules and norms of small claims court operations do not exist.

Other local courts specialize in specific conflicts (see Baum, 2011, 105–31, 191–94). Juvenile courts or juvenile divisions of trial courts have the largest caseload, more than 2.1 million cases per year (LaFountain et al., 2009, 30). First appearing during the Progressive era of the early twentieth century, proponents of these courts sought to remove young criminal offenders and children who created "trouble" or "status offenses" from trial courts, employ a less adversarial and more informal procedure to assess the youth's delinquency based on what would be in the best interests of the child, and then require the delinquent youth or youth's parents to correct the sources of delinquency or, in some instances, assign the youth to a training or reform school (Platt, 1970). Today these courts are replacing therapy for youths with a more punitive approach in cases that consider the delinquency of a disproportionate number of poor and minority youths (Feld, 1999, 189–244; Harris, 2007). The federal Office of Juvenile Justice and Delinquency Prevention has stimulated continuing study of the operations of these courts (U.S. Dept. of Justice, OJJDP 2010). But despite these and many other studies that focus on the criminology, law, and remedial aspects of juvenile justice (see Zimring, 2005), few have concentrated on the political importance of the informal norms and institutional practices of the judges, prosecutors, lawyers, police, social service agencies, and parents in the disposition of juvenile cases (but see Emerson, 1969; Feld, 1999, 109–88; Kupchik, 2006).

Other specialized local courts also employ a therapeutic or problem-solving approach rather than an adversarial procedure (Rottman and Casey, 1999; Berman and Feinblatt, 2001; Higgins and Mackinem, 2009; Nolan, 2009, 7–23). As a response to large numbers of drug possession cases, many states have established drug courts. As with juvenile courts, these institutions deemphasized adversarial procedures and opted for a therapeutic approach that requires nonviolent offenders to enter addiction treatment programs. Employing a similar therapeutic approach to problems, some communities have created courts to address "community" or neighborhood disputes, ordinance violations, and minor crimes (Malkin, 2004), domestic violence courts (Tsai, 2000), and mental health courts (Goldkamp and Irons-Guynn, 2000; Schneider 2008). The political factors contributing to the establishment of these courts and the norms employed by therapeutic court personnel in assessing individuals and the effectiveness of these courts in coping with the use of illegal drugs, crime, violence, and mental illness remains unclear. A number of studies suggest that they might be more of a symbolic response to a social problem than a solution because of the limited financial resources available for treatment programs, (Nolan, 2001, 2002).

Although courts have long existed with jurisdiction limited to problems associated with the family such as the probate of the estate of a deceased family member, the loosening of legal restrictions on divorce greatly increased litigation about divorce, child custody, and the implementation of post-divorce economic agreements. Some states have created family courts or family divisions of trial courts to manage these cases without jury trial. As a consequence, attorneys today negotiate settlements of divorce following learned norms about child custody and the law on the allocation of child support payments (Mather, McEwen, and Maiman, 2001). The task of the family court judge is simply to double-check the legality and approve the divorce settlement. More difficult matters for the judge arise in disputes about the fulfillment of the divorce settlement. Despite the extensive use of divorce, more study could be undertaken of the procedures and norms of family law courts. The considerable influence that these local courts might have on policies that affect the lives of women and children also needs more attention. Finally, the states have established a variety of mental health, homeless, domestic violence, business, housing, and environmental courts to adjudicate specific conflicts that arise at the local level (Baum, 2011, 122–31, 191–94). Few of these courts have received extensive scholarly attention.

Overall, law, procedural rules, and the norms and operating procedures developed by limited and specialized jurisdiction courts personnel serve a politically important objective. They allow judges and other public officials to keep the peace and manage common problems, often without the costs of adversary trial. The result is the reinforcement of court-developed public policies for treating crimes, public order and traffic violations, juvenile misbehavior, and family disputes that might have different implications for diverse socioeconomic and racial groups.

Courts of General Jurisdiction

Various procedural rules governing case preparation and trials delimit the activity of courts of general jurisdiction. In civil cases the rules permit attorneys to offer motions related to the pleadings, such as requests for the judge to amend or reject the plaintiff's complaint. In criminal cases, defense counsel can make motions to dismiss or amend charges against a client. In both civil and criminal cases the parties can raise discovery issues, such as motions about the collection of evidence or motions filed by parties to collect and admit or exclude witness testimony and other evidence in their hands or in the hands of their opponent. In response to motions by an attorney, the judge can issue subpoenas and orders to produce evidence so there are no surprises at trial and the parties can focus on key points of conflict. At the same time the attorneys will prepare their arguments and evidence for their client's case, and they can continue to negotiate or plea-bargain a settlement in the case. To facilitate preparation for trial, judges will hold pretrial conferences. Very few social scientific studies have examined the frequency of these various activities and how they affect the outcomes of disputes.

Additionally, few social scientific studies also have inquired into how trial procedures, including judicial rulings on the admission of evidence, the presentation of expert testimony, judicial instructions and charge to jurors, and the variables that influence trial judge decisions on these procedural matters, affect case outcomes (Champagne, Shuman, and Whitaker, 1992; English and Sales, 2005). Research on the questioning of witnesses, however, indicates that patterns of lawyer examination of victims and witnesses can result in the disempowerment and victimization of some of these individuals, especially women (Matoesian, 1993; Conley and O'Barr, 2005, 15–38, 60–77). Procedures thus might establish professional dominance and the neglect or abuse of the interests of some participants in local court processes.

The jury is another distinctive procedural aspect of the general jurisdiction. In civil cases that escape settlement, about two-thirds the litigants opt for a jury trial, including about 90 percent of personal liability litigants (Langton and Cohen, 2008, 2). A much studied institution, scholars have found that most jurors try to follow judicial instructions and decide on the merits of the case rather than upon biases and prejudices (the literature on juries is ably assessed in Vidmar and Hans, 2007; Devine 2012). In most cases they tend to rely on common sense criteria and personal experiences in assessing evidence. They will change their minds during trial, and they are influenced by one another during deliberations (Feigenson, 2000; Waters and Hans, 2009). Compared to judges they are less likely to convict in criminal cases and less supportive of the claims of corporations in civil cases. Yet, despite numerous jury studies, few examinations exist of judicial post-verdict rejection or amendment of civil jury findings of liability and award of remedies and of criminal convictions.

Finally, the decisions of local courts can be challenged by appeal or through other procedures used to remove the case to another court. Courts of limited jurisdiction might have to assign or "bind over" some cases to trial courts for jurisdictional reasons, but the decisions of their judges rarely result in appeal. Appeal to an appellate is far more common with the decisions of trial courts of general jurisdiction. There are, however, few studies of the reasons for and outcomes of appeal or the removal of state court and agency decisions into state trial and appellate courts, and the political meaning of appeal (but see Barclay, 1999).

Court Personnel and the Definition of Norms

Formal law and procedures and local norms interact to affect the disposition of conflicts by local courts, but it is important to note how the norms arise. As an intersection of several relatively autonomous groups of personnel and organizations, the norms and operating procedures developed in a local court emerge from the underlying differences in the institutional commitments, selection processes, and the political goals of judges, lawyers, prosecutors, public defenders, and other participants. Research suggests that the development of norms and operating procedures in part depends on the discretionary power these officials exploit in the course of pursuing their official duties. However, the discretion they possess has limits imposed by law and interactions with other court officers. What then is known about the discretion of local court officers and the norms that guide their exercise of that discretion?

The Judiciary

The chapter on State Courts in this volume describes the politics of the selection of the local judiciary. Other studies have described the socialization and training of both attorney and non-lawyer local judges (Alpert, Atkins, and Ziller, 1979; Ryan et al., 1980, 121–45; Provine, 1986, 82–121; Wice, 1991, 202–13). However, what is most important in the selection is the creation of a locally-oriented judiciary. Whether the judge is an attorney or a non-lawyer, he or she often resides within the jurisdiction and acquires a familiarity with its social and political values. The judge also often has previous experience with the norms of local court culture. Relatively few studies have examined how local social relations among judges in a multi-judge court, personal values, and legal experiences shape the behavior of the local judiciary or the extent to which attorney judges differ in their values and behavior from non-lawyer judges (Ryan et al., 1980, 196–234; Flemming, Nardulli, and Eisenstein, 1992, 79–104). Additionally there are few recent comparative studies of how trial and lesser court judges allocate their time and when and how they interact with counsel and litigants (Ryan et al., 1980, 17–46; Provine, 1986; Conley and O'Barr, 1990, 82–125; Wice, 1991, 251–78).

Among the activities of judges, perhaps the most important are decisions affecting the admissibility of evidence and the imposition of remedies. For example, judges possess the discretion to assess the admissibility of witness and expert testimony and whether there was probable cause to conduct a search for evidence of a crime both prior to and during trial. In civil cases judges possess the discretion to modify or reject jury decisions on remedies. There are no comprehensive comparative studies of these uses of discretion. In some jurisdictions judges can participate in civil negotiation and criminal plea bargaining (Heumann, 1978, 127–52; Ryan et al., 1980, 173–95; Nardulli, Eisenstein, and Flemming, 1988, 331–51; Wice, 1991, 258–72; Flemming, Nardulli, and Eisenstein, 1992, 105–32). In criminal cases judges can apply local norms and set bail bond amounts in ways that result in the incarceration of poor defendants (Flemming, 1982). More importantly, local court judges have considerable discretion in criminal sentencing. Although affected by state legislation on mandatory sentences and the funding of prisons and alternatives to incarceration, the judicial use of discretionary powers can incrementally generate normal ways of resolving cases—a local policy for penalizing convicted criminals that can result in disparate outcomes for different gender, racial, and ethnic groups (Bushway and Piehl, 2001; Spohn, 2009, 33–224 offer able summaries of the extensive studies of sentencing).

Attorneys and Civil Litigation

Although largely unexamined, most civil actions involving state and local governments are the responsibility of a State Attorney General's office or local government counsel. However, the vast majority of attorneys who engage in civil litigation are "officers of the court" in private practice. Although their ethical duties, *pro bono* representation requirements, and other public obligations are often regulated by a quasi-public state bar association, they operate a profit-seeking business. Scholars have subjected the ethics, organization of practice, race and gender, and social stratification of the legal profession to a multitude of intensive studies (for summaries see Macfarlane, 2008; Seron, 2007). Studies also have examined how clients find attorneys and the economics of lawyer-client relationships (Trubek et al., 1983, S-29–52, II-1–239; Kritzer, Felstiner, Sarat, and Trubek, 1985; Kritzer, 1990, 55–67; Bowen, 1995; Kritzer, 2004, 47–76). Receiving less attention is the politics of the bar, including the influence of individual lawyers and bar associations on state and local legislative activity, local court operations and management, and administrative legality.

Most lawyers will screen clients and review their claim before taking on a case (Kritzer, 1990, 56–59; Mather, McEwen, and Maiman, 2001, 92–96; Kritzer, 2004, 76–95). The effect of screening on court business has received only limited attention. In interaction with clients there is evidence that lawyers can transform the client's demands and attempt to fit the dispute into the norms of local court practice (Sarat and Felstiner, 1995; Conley and O'Barr, 2005, 78–98). However, the study of the nature and quality of the representation or service provided by attorneys in civil cases has to confront the barrier of the confidentiality of lawyer-client relations. Studies of divorce actions depict the efforts of lawyers to gain control of a client's emotions and expectations, inform them what is legally possible, and guide them to a negotiated settlement (Sarat and Felstiner,

1995; Mather, McEwen, and Maiman, 2001, 87–109). Other studies have found that some lawyers who deal with "one-shot" clients in a high volume practice leave their clients feeling rushed and their problems unheard (Van Hoy, 1997, 72–75). Interactions between corporate clients and their lawyer employees and corporations and private law firms have also received limited attention (Slovak, 1979; Spangler, 1986, 28–106; Nelson and Nielsen, 2000). Finally, some poor clients can avail themselves of publicly funded civil legal services. Political opposition to the provision of lawyers for the poor and instances of public lawyers winning cases that created costs for corporations and governments has limited their funding and restricted the range of services they provide (Kilwein, 1999). Again more study could be undertaken of the interaction of these lawyers with clients and the norms they employ in managing disputes.

All attorneys interact with other lawyers, witnesses, government employees, and judges. In these relationships they often devise norms as they act as broker between the interests of a client and opposing parties or government (Kritzer, 1990, 68–76) and help define the business of local courts. Usually lawyers will try to negotiate settlements to disputes. Lawyers recognize that through negotiations they can protect a client's interests without the costs of trial preparation and courtroom time and the uncertainties or marginal gains associated with trial. Consequently they adopt a pattern of negotiation that usually follows local norms. Because they will work with some opposing attorneys in the future, they want to protect their reputation as "reasonable" and as a cooperative, efficient, and honest negotiator rather than an advocate who seeks trials (Kritzer, 1990, 79–134; 1991, 30–98, 112–29; 2004, 139–79, 219–52; Mather, McEwen, and Maiman, 2001, 48–56). Given the frequency of negotiated settlements, local courts infrequently address disputes with an overt political aspect. Indirectly, however, lawyers' arguments in seemingly mundane auto accident and family cases help the public's judges and juries construct a set of normal expectations about social and economic duties. If conveyed in series of decisions over time, they impart a local policy about proper behavior (Harrington, 1994).

Not only do lawyers affect the civil business of local courts, they represent clients before state and local executive branch agencies. In disputes before these agencies the private lawyer often faces a government lawyer. Most of these attorneys are civil servants who are selected for their job on the basis of their credentials but the attorneys who manage public agencies and who supervise the work of lawyer civil servants often are political appointees of the president, a governor, or a mayor. They can experience political pressures from the executive and legislative branches of government and governmentally-regulated enterprises. Few studies of the role of attorneys in administrative disputes exist and there is limited information on their norms and the policy ramifications of their activities (but see Spangler, 1986, 107–43; Kritzer, 1998).

Prosecutors and Crime

In most states the prosecutor is an elected county officer who represents the government in criminal cases. To cope with the caseload, in most jurisdictions the prosecutor hires lawyers as assistant prosecutors. In large cities or populous counties there can often be hundreds of assistant prosecutors, with many of them specializing in the prosecution of specific crimes. Also prosecutors in some states will deal too with some civil cases in which municipal or county governments are a party. Only limited studies of the politics of the administration of these prosecutorial bureaucracies exist (Flemming, Nardulli, and Eisenstein, 1992, 23–79).

The prosecutors or assistant prosecutors make a series of decisions about the case that effectively define local policies for regulating crime and criminals and that result in a considerable attrition of cases (Flemming 1990; Boland, Mahanna, and Sones, 1992). Many of these decisions indicate that the prosecutor desires to avoid cases in which a guilty plea or verdict is uncertain (Albonetti, 1987). The first decision is to take the case. Normally this involves either a meeting with police or a review of police reports and an assessment of the evidence against a suspect or arrested individual. Then prosecutors determine if there is enough evidence to win the case. If not, unless the law requires mandatory prosecution (required in some states for domestic violence cases), they can dismiss the case. Alternatively, they might divert some defendants for treatment of mental illness or drug or alcohol dependency (Albonetti, 1992). If a prosecutor decides to proceed with the case, state and local laws require different kinds of charging procedures. In some states the prosecutor files a document called "information" with the court. The trial judge, usually at the request of the defendant, then holds a preliminary hearing to determine if there is probable cause that the defendant committed the crime. If there is probable cause, the case is set for trial. Case studies rather than larger scale comparative studies have provided information on the process of norms creation and application in all of these events. In other states the prosecutor must go or can opt to go before a grand jury, present evidence about the crime, and ask the grand jury to indict the defendant. Since studies find that most grand juries defer to the prosecutor, the prosecutor effectively has the power to establish policies about when the criminal process is invoked and the charge facing the defendant, discretionary decisions that have an important effect on the subsequent disposition of the case (Greenwood and Wildhorn, 1976; Eisenstein and Jacob, 1977, 190–226; Nardulli, Eisenstein, and Flemming, 1988, 261–75; Davis, 2007, 19–41; Sarat and Clarke, 2008).

The defendant is notified of these charges and given the opportunity to plead to them at an arraignment. Meanwhile, the prosecutor and defense counsel have often initiated plea- bargaining. Today plea-bargaining results in the defendant's decision to plead guilty in 95 percent of state felony criminal cases (U.S. Dept. of Justice, BJS 2013, Table 5.46 [2006]). Plea-bargaining usually involves the prosecutor granting some mix of sentence reduction, reduction of the severity of charges, or reduction of number of crimes or counts. Numerous case studies have found that the bargaining operates according to widely known standards or a "going rate" for certain crimes. However, local variations exist about the aspects of the crime that define the going rate, what mix of sentences and charges are bargained, how it is conducted, and when it occurs. Often there is limited exchange between the two sides to reach a plea. The judge then normally follows the plea bargain at sentencing. Studies tend to argue that plea-bargaining provides benefits and reduces the costs of managing crime. Through this process a prosecutor avoids the costs of trials that tax government budgets, and appeases public demands for the punishment of criminals. The defendant can receive less harsh treatment, and his lawyer saves the time and costs of trial preparation, costs often borne by taxpayers (Eisenstein and Jacob, 1977, 244–59; Heumann, 1978, 92–126; Eisenstein, Flemming and Nardulli, 1988, 232–37; Nardulli, Eisenstein, and Flemming, 1988, 230–59, 305–62; Emmelman, 1996; Spohn, 2009, 65–67). Plea-bargaining illustrates the power of prosecutor's norms. If prosecutors agree to bargain and if they arrange an acceptable offer with the defense, they have ultimate control over who is penalized for crime and how they are penalized, which in effect is a policy choice. However, these policies can inadvertently reflect prosecutorial stereotyping of defendants, crimes, and the location where the crime occurred (Frohmann, 1997). Such stereotyping deserves further comparative inquiry.

Public Defenders, Other Criminal Defense Counsel, and their Clients

Defense counsel can be hired by criminal defendants, but defendant indigence makes this choice available to less than 30 percent of defendants in most local court jurisdictions. Since indigent defendants can request a publicly-funded attorney, the local judge or her staff can assign counsel for the indigent. Lawyers can register for the assignment or the judge can randomly or deliberately select them. A few jurisdictions contract with law firms to provide counsel to indigents. Much more commonly, the government has established a state or local public agency, a public defender's office, to represent criminal defendants. Salaried lawyers from the office—assistant public defenders—will defend indigents. The amount of criminal business in cities or states means that public defender's offices, as with prosecutor's offices, are often large, bureaucratically organized agencies with assistant public defenders assigned to specific kinds of crimes. Because of the frequent contact of public defenders with the prosecutor's office, public defenders often develop norms to guide the disposition of cases. The effect of the variations in the provision of counsel on case outcomes, particularly for minorities, remains in need of comprehensive comparative examination.

Defense counsel frequently face situations when the case against their client is strong or "dead bang" and the clients are gang members, career criminals, or simply vicious (Flemming, Nardulli, and Eisenstein, 1992, 135–62; Wice, 2005, 95–143). In such circumstances counsel can try to use procedural rules to assess the strength of the prosecution's case. To address the prosecution's case, defense counsel can file motions to exclude evidence as the fruit of unlawful searches or interrogations or to discover errors by the police that might free the client. Additionally, by raising issues about the discriminatory behavior or effectiveness of other criminal justice agencies, such as corrections and juvenile facilities, the practices of police departments, and biases in legal norms and the law in local courts, the defense counsel can also publicize and place issues on the policy agenda (Bohne, 1978). These problems can mobilize affected individuals to file or threaten civil suits, and the fear of liability can generate policy change in public criminal justice agencies (Feeley and Rubin, 1998; Epp, 2009).

Although often serving a guilty client, the frequent contact between public defenders and prosecutors provides them with valuable information about prosecutorial plea-bargaining norms such as "how much a case is worth," and what would be a typical and satisfactory plea bargain for a particular crime (Heumann, 1978, 47–91; Flemming, Nardulli, and Eisenstein, 1992, 163–94; Wice, 2005, 96–120). The prosecutor's office often learns that pushing its discretion in plea-bargaining to the maximum can induce defense counsel to go to trial and increase the uncertainty of a politically valuable conviction. Through the threat of trial, defense counsel thus exerts significant influence on local criminal sentencing policies.

Because most defendants are indigent, less educated, unemployed males, they tend to defer to defense counsel decisions about the disposition of their case (Casper, 1972). Overall the limited studies of litigants and defendants indicate that defendants have limited influence over the decisions that can affect their economic condition, social status, or political liberty. Whether defendant influence over problem definition varies because of wealth, race, gender, or other social characteristics remains in need of more exploration.

Local Courts and the Politics of Law and Norms: A Summary

The intersection of formal law, procedural rules, norms, and operating procedures of the various officers who serve local court contributes to distinctive and relatively independent decision- making practices among local courts. This situation introduces a variability and sometimes localism into the meaning and application of state legislation and the decisions of state and federal appellate courts. Although criticism of local variability in court practices and outcomes sometimes surfaces in campaigns by business interests to change tort law (see Haltom and McCann, 2004), more scholarly exploration of the extent to which it occurs and its implications for the power of economic organizations, governments, women, minorities, and the poor is needed.

DISPUTE OUTCOMES AND POLICY MESSAGES FROM LOCAL COURTS

Scholars have assessed the outcome of local court activity along three dimensions: distributive justice or the fairness of the outcome—as win or loss—achieved by negotiation or ordered by the judge, procedural justice or the fairness of the process by which the outcome is achieved, and messages to the public about policies that distribute social, political, and economic power in the regime. Research about distributive justice often addresses the hypothesis that the "haves come out ahead" first proposed by Marc Galanter (1974). Limited evidence indicates that the government usually "wins" and defendants "lose" in criminal cases, whether by pleading guilty or conviction at trial (U.S. Dept. of Justice, BJS 2013, Tables 5.57, 5.58 [2006]), pretrial detention, the cost of bond, or, even when not convicted, harm to reputation, loss of job, or disorder in family life.

Although much more extensive data needs to be collected, evidence about civil litigation suggests the process produces more winners among plaintiffs, including creditors such as banks and finance companies, governments (in tax collection and regulatory enforcement cases), landlords, and other firms which have ready access to legal services, familiarity with the legal process, and, often, influence over the legislators who draft the laws. Individual plaintiffs won most frequently in vehicle accident and animal attack cases. Also, a study of housing cases discloses that tenants, especially poor tenants, frequently do not respond to suits by landlords. Subsequently the landlord secures a default judgment (Larson, 2006). Studies conducted by the U.S. Department of Justice have found that over 60 percent of plaintiff winners were granted final awards of $50,000 or less with a median of $28,000, and punitive damages were awarded to 5 percent of plaintiff winners in general civil trials (Langton and Cohen, 2008, 4–6; Cohen, 2009). However, research suggests that it is difficult for victors to collect the full amount of money damage judgments (Hyman et al., 2007). The results of civil litigation are even more mixed in family law, especially because a divorce can either provide relief to the parties or stimulate ongoing litigation about child custody and support payments. However, because they negotiate settlements in most cases, even attorneys who work for a contingency fee (which means compensation except for a loss at trial) usually come out financially ahead in civil suits (Kritzer, 1991, 99–111; 2004, 180–218).

Procedural justice studies have disclosed that a learned obligation to obey the law and respect court actions is strongest when individuals have felt that the process was fair. For both civil litigants and criminal defendants fairness has two dimensions. It means the decision-making process is perceived to exhibit opportunity for representation and some control over the decision-making process, honesty and ethicality, and a clear and reasonable decision. Also, fairness means perceived attentive or personalized treatment by court personnel. Many studies find that a majority of criminal and civil litigants perceive a sense fair treatment by local courts. However, a person's feeling that he or she has experienced unfair procedures or treatment and lacks trust in the honesty of the institutions of the legal complex can reduce the political legitimacy of local courts as civil and criminal dispute resolution forums, of plea bargains in criminal cases, and of local judicial decisions (Howard et al., 2000; Casper, Tyler, and Fisher, 1988; Tyler, 1988; 1990).

Although partially dependent on litigant demands, local court decisions can send forceful messages that affect public policy. Local courts can modify state and local legislation and the political meaning of their interpretative powers. If published, their decisions can radiate and affect legislators in other localities. Although a haphazard process, other courts can cite the decision of a local court as a precedent and allow it to guide their decisions (Canon and Baum, 1981; Bird and Smythe, 2008). Decisions also convey messages that educate the public about the law, how to use the law to leverage political changes beneficial to their interests, the proper use of governmental power and, as a source of empowerment, the need for prophylactic measures to protect against civil litigation or criminal victimization, and the necessity of new laws and funding to enforce existing laws (Handler, 1978, 212–14; Galanter, 1983; McCann, 1994, 138–310; 2008; Albiston, 2003; Epp, 2008, 2009).

However, communicators can transform the policy message sent by a local court. News coverage, reality shows, and televised fiction about local courts largely focus on dramatic crimes and unusual criminal trials (Haltom, 1998, 157–243; Rapping, 2003). Interest groups also contribute to the overall public perception of local courts. For example, business and professional interest groups have engaged in publicity campaigns to depict the judiciary as the source of a "crisis" in personal liability law that threatens jobs, the availability of physicians, and business growth while rewarding deadbeats. In making their claims, these groups often neglect or skew the scholarly research on local courts (Garber and Bower, 1999; Kritzer, 2001; Haltom and McCann, 2004, 2009). There is also probably considerable popular misconception of the role of politics in the work of these courts. More studies need to be conducted to measure and assess the consequences of media messages about local courts on the willingness of the public to report crime, use the civil justice process, trust the decisions of judges and juries, and support the adoption or revision of laws.

Finally, any message about a discrete dispute or a public policy sent by a local court might expand a personal or political conflict. Although difficult to measure, the "success" of litigation for policy change in local courts can be an immediate victory that is offset by longer term actions by governments, corporations, or the general public that limit the scale of the success or that do not produce a remedy (Handler, 1978, 34–41, 192–209; Feeley and Rubin, 1998, 362–88; Barnes and Burke, 2012; Nielsen and Parker, 2012). The result can be further litigation or legislation as various interests attempt to cope with a court's decisions (McIntosh, 1990). Additionally, when local courts apply, make, or influence the meaning of policy, their "success" can be tempered by resistance to their rulings. Although there is a need for more examination of the psychological and social origins of resistance, it can take many forms. Individuals and groups can complain, appeal, file related claims, apply political pressure on courts, and encourage other political institutions to oppose court rulings or change the law. They can engage in subversion, civil disobedience, law-breaking, and violence to avoid or challenge either individual decisions or patterns of behavior by judges and legal personnel. Studies of these actions expose how the political legitimacy of local court decisions and policies is always unstable (Ewick and Silbey, 1998, 165–220; Gilliom, 2001; Brisbin, 2002, 2009, 2010; Kelly, 2010).

DIRECTIONS FOR THE STUDY OF THE POLITICS OF LOCAL COURTS

As indicated in this chapter, many aspects of the political world of local courts still need extensive study by social scientists. More attention needs to be paid to the subtle ways in which legality and bureaucratic politics influence the mobilization of the powers of local courts and their administration and procedures. More attention needs to be paid to the reasons for the development of norms that supplement or replace the formal law. In particular, the effect on women and minorities of the local norms about disposition of disputes needs further analysis. More attention also should be paid to the legitimacy of local courts as they redistribute wealth, regulate personal conduct, and reinforce or reconstruct the local social order. Richer comparative information on all of these topics would do much to advance the understanding of the place of local courts and court personnel in American state and local governance. Whether these issues are addressed, however, depends on the education of political scientists eager to study local courts and on financial support for their research.

REFERENCES

Albiston, C. 2003. The Rule of Law and the Litigation Process: The Paradox of Winning by Losing. In *In Litigation: Do the "Haves" Still Come Out Ahead?* ed. H.M. Kritzer and S.S. Silbey. Stanford: Stanford University Press, 168–209

——. 2005. Bargaining in the Shadow of Social Institutions: Competing Discourses and Social Change in Workplace Mobilization of Civil Rights. *Law and Society Review, 39*: 11–49.

Albonetti, C. A. 1987. Prosecutorial Discretion: The Effects of Uncertainty. *Law and Society Review, 21*: 281–313.

——. 1992. Charge Reduction: An Analysis of Prosecutorial Discretion in Burglary and Robbery Cases. *Journal of Quantitative Criminology, 8*: 317–333.

Alpert, L., Atkins, B. M., and Ziller, R. C. 1979. Becoming a Judge: The Transition from Advocate to Arbiter. *Judicature, 62*: 325–335.

Baar, C. 1980. The Scope and Limits of Court Reform. *Justice System Journal, 5*: 274–290.

Barclay, S. 1999. *An Appealing Act: Why People Appeal in Civil Cases.* Evanston, IL: Northwestern University Press, The American Bar Foundation.

Barnes, J. and Burke, T. E. 2012. Making Way: Legal Mobilization, Organizational Response, and Wheelchair Access. *Law and Society Review, 46*: 167–198.

Baum, L. 2011. *Specializing the Courts.* Chicago: University of Chicago Press.

Berman, G. and Feinblatt, J. 2001. Problem-Solving Courts: A Brief Primer. *Law and Policy, 23*: 125–140.

Best, A. 1981. *When Consumers Complain.* New York: Columbia University Press.

Bird, R. and Smythe, D. 2008. The Structure of American Legal Institutions and the Diffusion of Wrongful Discharge Laws. *Law and Society Review, 42*: 833–863.

Boersema, C., Hanson, R., and Keilitz, S. 1991. State Court-annexed Arbitration: What Do Attorneys Think?. *Judicature*, 75: 28–33.

Bohne, B. H. 1978. The Public Defender as Policy-maker. *Judicature*, 62: 176–184.

Boland, B., Mahanna, P. and Sones, R. 1992. *The Prosecution of Felony Arrests, 1988*. Washington, DC: U.S. Department of Justice.

Bowen, L. 1995. Advertising and the Legal Profession. *Justice System Journal*, 18: 43–54.

Brisbin, R.A., Jr. 2002. *A Strike Like No Other Strike: Law and Resistance during the Pittston Coal Strike of 1989-1990*. Baltimore: The Johns Hopkins University Press.

—— 2009. Resistance to the Judiciary: The Boundaries of Judicial Power. In *Exploring Judicial Politics*, ed. M. C. Miller. New York: Oxford University Press, 213–230.

—— 2010. Resistance to Legality. *Annual Review of Law and Social Science*, 6: 25–44.

—— and Hunter, S. 1990a. Disputing and Regulatory Policy: The Example of a State Utility Regulatory Agency. *Policy Studies Review*, 10: 41–61.

—— and Hunter, S. 1990b. Alternative Dispute Resolution and the Serial Adoption of Policy: A Study of a State Consumer Protection Agency. *Policy Studies Journal*, 19: 22–39.

——, Hunter, S., and Leyden, K. M. 2010. The Limits of *Kelo*: Bureaucratic Legality and Adversarial Conflict in Land Use Regulation. In *Property Rights and Neo-liberalism: Cultural Demands and Legal Actions*, ed. W. V. McIntosh and L. J. Hatcher. Burlington, VT: Ashgate, 141–160.

Bumiller, K. 1988. *The Civil Rights Society: The Social Construction of Victims*. Baltimore: The Johns Hopkins University Press.

Burke, T. F. 2002. *Lawyers, Lawsuits, and Legal Rights: The Battle Over Litigation in American Society*. Berkeley: University of California Press.

Burns, S. L. 2000. *Making Settlement Work: An Examination of the Work of Judicial Mediators*. Burlington, VT: Ashgate.

Bushway, S. D. and Piehl, A. M. 2001. Judging Judicial Discretion: Legal Factors and Racial Discrimination in Sentencing. *Law and Society Review*, 35: 733–764.

Canon, B. C. and Baum, L. 1981. Patterns of Adoption of Tort Law Innovations: An Application of Diffusion Theory to Judicial Doctrines. *American Political Science Review*, 75: 975–987.

Casper, J. D. 1972. *American Criminal Justice: The Defendant's Perspective*. Englewood Cliffs, NJ: Prentice-Hall.

——, Tyler, T., and Fisher, B. 1988. Procedural Justice in Felony Cases. *Law and Society Review*, 22: 483–507.

Champagne, A., Shuman, D., and Whitaker, E. 1992. Expert Witnesses in the Court: An Empirical Examination. *Judicature*, 76: 5–10.

Cobb, S. 1997. The Domestication of Violence in Mediation. *Law and Society Review*, 31: 397–440.

Cohen, T. H. 2009. *Tort Bench and Jury Trials in State Courts, 2005*. Washington, DC: Department of Justice. <http://bjs.ojp.usdoj.gov/content/pub/pdf/tbjtsc05.pdf> (June 26, 2013).

Conley, J. M. and O'Barr, W. M. 1990. *Rules versus Relationships: The Ethnography of Legal Discourse*. Chicago: University of Chicago Press.

—— 2005. *Just Words: Law, Language, and Power*, 2nd ed. Chicago: University of Chicago Press.

Cook, B. B. 1969-1970. The Politics of Piecemeal Reform of Kansas Courts. *Judicature*, 53: 274–281.

Cross, F. 2008. Judicial Independence. In *The Oxford Handbook of Law and Politics*, eds. K.E. Whittington, R. D. Kelemen, and G. A. Caldeira. New York: Oxford University Press, 557–575.

Davis, A. J. 2007. *Arbitrary Justice: The Power of the American Prosecutor*. New York: Oxford University Press.

Devine, D. J. 2012. *Jury Decision Making.* New York: New York University Press.

Dill, F. 1975. Discretion, Exchange, and Social Control: Bail Bondsmen in Criminal Courts. *Law and Society Review,* 9: 639–674.

Earl, Jennifer. 2008. The Process is the Punishment: Thirty Years Later. *Law and Social Inquiry,* 33: 737–778.

Edelman, L. 1990. Legal Environments and Organizational Governance: The Expansion of Due Process in the American Workplace. *American Journal of Sociology,* 95: 1401–1440.

——, Erlanger, H. and Lande, J. 1993. Internal Dispute Resolution: The Transformation of Civil Rights in the Workplace. *Law and Society Review,* 27: 497–534.

Eisenberg, T., Miller, G.P., and Sherwin, E. 2008. Mandatory Arbitration for Customers but not for Peers: A Study of Arbitration Clauses in Consumer and Non-Consumer Contracts. *Judicature,* 92: 118–124.

Eisenstein, J., Flemming, R. B. and Nardulli, P. 1988. *The Contours of Justice: Communities and their Courts.* Boston: Little, Brown.

Eisenstein, J. and Jacob, H. 1977. *Felony Justice: An Organizational Analysis of Criminal Courts.* Boston: Little, Brown.

Ellickson, R. C. 1991. *Order without Law: How Neighbors Settle Disputes.* Cambridge: Harvard University Press.

Emerson, R. M. 1969. *Judging Delinquents: Context and Process in the Juvenile Court.* Chicago: Aldine.

Emmelman, D. S. 1996. Trial by Plea Bargain: Case Settlement as a Product of Recursive Decisionmaking. *Law and Society Review,* 30: 335–360.

Engel, D. M. and Munger, F. W. 2003. *Rights of Inclusion: Law and Identity in the Life Stories of Americans with Disabilities.* Chicago: University of Chicago Press.

English, P. W. and Sales, B. D. 2005. *More than Law: Behavioral and Social Facts in Legal Decision Making.* Washington, DC: American Psychological Association.

Epp, C. R. 2008. Law as an Instrument of Social Reform. In *The Oxford Handbook of Law and Politics,* eds K. E. Whittington, R. D. Kelemen, and G. A. Caldeira. New York: Oxford University Press, 595–613.

——. 2009. *Making Rights Real: Activists, Bureaucrats, and the Creation of the Legalistic State.* Chicago: University of Chicago Press.

Ewick, P. and Silbey, S.S. 1998. *The Common Place of the Law: Stories from Everyday Life.* Chicago: University of Chicago Press.

Feeley, M. M. 1979. *The Process is the Punishment: Handling Cases in a Lower Criminal Court.* New York: Russell Sage Foundation.

—— and Rubin, E. L. 1998. *Judicial Policymaking and the Modern State: How the Courts Reformed America's Prisons.* Cambridge: Cambridge University Press.

Feigenson, N. 2000. *Legal Blame: How Jurors Think and Talk about Accidents.* Washington, DC: American Psychological Association.

Feld, B. C. 1999. *Bad Kids: Race and the Transformation of the Juvenile Court.* New York: Oxford University Press.

Felstiner, W. L. F., Abel, R. L. and Sarat, A. 1980–81. The Emergence and Transformation of Disputes: Naming, Blaming, Claiming.... *Law and Society Review,* 15: 631–654.

Flango, V. E. 1994. Court Unification and the Quality of States Courts. *Justice System Journal,* 6(3): 33–56.

Flemming, R. B. 1982. *Punishment Before Trial: An Organizational Perspective of Felony Bail Processes.* New York: Longman.

———. 1990. Political Styles and Organizational Strategies of American Prosecutors: Examples from Nine Courthouse Communities. *Law and Policy*, 12: 25–50.

———, Nardulli, P. F., and Eisenstein, J. 1992. *The Craft of Justice: Politics and Work in Criminal Court Communities*. Philadelphia: University of Pennsylvania Press.

Frohmann, L. 1997. Convictability and Discordant Locales: Reproducing Race, Class, and Gender Ideologies in Prosecutorial Decisionmaking. *Law and Society Review*, 31: 531–556.

Galanter, M. 1974. Why the "Haves" Come out Ahead: Speculations on the Limits of Legal Change. *Law and Society Review*, 9: 95–160.

——— 1983. The Radiating Effects of Courts. In *Empirical Theories about Courts*, eds. K.O. Boyum and L. Mather. New York: Longman, 177–142

Garber, S. and Bower, A. 1999. Newspaper Coverage of Automotive Product Liability Verdicts. *Law and Society Review*, 33: 93–122.

Gilboy, J. A. 1992. Penetrability of Administrative Systems: Political "Casework" and Immigration Inspections. *Law and Society Review*, 26: 273–314.

Gilliom, J. 2001. *Overseers of the Poor: Surveillance, Resistance, and the Limits of Privacy*. Chicago: University of Chicago Press.

Goldkamp, J. D. and Irons-Guynn, C. 2000. *Emerging Judicial Strategies for the Mentally Ill in the Criminal Caseload: Mental Health Courts in Fort Lauderdale, Seattle, San Bernardino, and Anchorage*. Washington, DC: U.S. Department of Justice.

Grattet, R. and Jenness, V. 2005. The Reconstitution of Law in Local Settings: Agency Discretion, Ambiguity, and a Surplus of Law in the Policing of Hate Crime. *Law and Society Review*, 39: 893–941.

Greenhouse, C. J. 1986. *Praying for Justice: Faith, Order, and Community in an American Town*. Ithaca: Cornell University Press.

Greenwood, P. W. and Wildhorn, S. 1976. *Prosecution of Adult Felony Defendants in Los Angeles County-A Policy Perspective*. Washington, DC: Government Printing Office.

Haltom, W. 1998. *Reporting on the Courts: How the Mass Media Cover Judicial Actions*. Chicago: Nelson-Hall.

——— and McCann, M. W. 2004. *Distorting the Law: Politics Media, and the Litigation Crisis*. Chicago: University of Chicago Press.

———. 2009. Framing Fast-Food Litigation: Tort Claims, Mass Media, and the Politics of Responsibility in the United States. In *Fault Lines: Tort Law as a Cultural Practice*, ed. D. M. Engel and M. McCann. Stanford: Stanford University Press, 97–118.

Handler, J. F. 1978. *Social Movements and the Legal System: A Theory of Law Reform and Change*. New York: Academic Press.

Harrington, C. B. 1985. *Shadow Justice: The Ideology and Institutionalization of Alternatives to Court*. Westport, CT: Greenwood Press.

———. 1994. Outlining a Theory of Legal Practice. In *Lawyers in a Postmodern World: Translation and Transgression*, eds. M. Cain and C .B. Harrington. New York: New York University Press, 49–69.

Harrington, C. B. and Merry, S. E. 1988. Ideological production: the making of community mediation. *Law and Society Review*, 22: 709–735.

Harris, A. 2007. Diverting and Abdicating Judicial Discretion: Cultural, Political, and Procedural Dynamics in California Juvenile Justice. *Law and Society Review*, 41: 387–428.

Hartley, R. E. and Douglas, J. W. 2003. Budgeting for State Courts: The Perceptions of Key Officials Regarding the Determinants of Budget Success, *Justice System Journal* 24, 251–262.

Heumann, M. 1978. *Plea Bargaining: The Experiences of Prosecutors, Judges, and Defense Attorneys*. Chicago: University of Chicago Press.

Higgins, P. and Mackinem, M. B., eds. 2009. *Problem-solving Courts: Justice for the Twenty-first Century?* Santa Barbara: ABC-CLIO.

Howard, R. M., Chard, R. E., Kaji, J. T., Davis, J. 2000. Pre-Trial Bargaining and Litigation: The Search for Fairness and Efficiency. *Law and Society Review, 34*: 431–456.

Hyman, D. A., Black, B., Zeiler, K., Silver, C., and Sage, W. M. 2007. Do Defendants Pay What Juries Award? Post-Verdict Haircuts in Texas Medical Malpractice Cases, 1988–2003. *Journal of Empirical Legal Studies, 4*: 3–68.

Issacharoff, S. and Delaney, E. 2006. Homo Economicus, Homo Myopicus, and the Law and Economics of Consumer Choice: Credit Card Accountability. *University of Chicago Law Review, 73*: 157–182.

Jacob, H. 1992. The Elusive Shadow of the Law. *Law and Society Review, 26*: 565–590.

Kagan, R. A. 1984. The Routinization of Debt Collection: An Essay on Social Change and Conflict in the Courts. *Law and Society Review, 18*: 322–372.

——. 1989. Understanding Regulatory Enforcement. *Law and Policy, 11*: 89–119.

——. 2001. *Adversarial Legalism: The American Way of Law*. Cambridge: Harvard University Press.

Kelly, E. L. 2010. Failure to update: An institutional perspective on noncompliance with the Family and Medical Leave Act. *Law and Society Review, 44*: 33–66

Kenworthy, L., Macauley, S. and Rogers, J. 1996. "The More Things Change…": Business Litigation and Governance in the American Automobile Industry. *Law and Social Inquiry, 21*: 631–678.

Kilwein, J. 1999. The Decline of the Legal Services Corporation: "It's Ideological, Stupid!" In *The Transformation of Legal Aid: Comparative and Historical Studies*, ed. F. Regan, A. Paterson, T. Goriely, and D. Fleming. New York: Oxford University Press, 41–64.

Kritzer, H. M. 1990. *The Justice Broker: Lawyers and Ordinary Litigation*. New York: Oxford University Press.

——. 1991. *Let's Make a Deal: Understanding the Negotiation Process in Ordinary Litigation*. Madison: University of Wisconsin Press.

——. 1998. *Legal Advocacy: Lawyers and Nonlawyers at Work*. Ann Arbor: University of Michigan Press. (1998).

——. 2001. Public Perceptions of Civil Jury Verdicts. *Judicature, 85*: 78–82.

——. 2004. *Risks, Reputations, and Rewards: Contingency Fee Legal Practice in the United States*. Stanford: Stanford University Press.

—— and Anderson, J. K. 1983. The Arbitration Alternative: A Comparative Analysis of Case Processing Time, Disposition Mode, and Cost in American Arbitration Association and the Courts. *Justice System Journal, 8*: 6–19.

——, Felstiner, W. L. F., Sarat, A., and Trubek, D. M. 1985. The Impact of Fee Arrangement on Lawyer Effort. *Law and Society Review, 19*: 251–278.

Kupchik, A. 2006. *Judging Juveniles: Prosecuting Adolescents in Adult and Juvenile Courts*. New York: New York University Press.

LaFountain, R., Schauffler, R., Strickland, S., and Holt, K. 2012.. *Examining the Work of State Courts: An Analysis of 2010 State Court Caseloads.*. Williamsburg, VA: National Center for State Courts. <http://www.courtstatistics.org/Other-Pages/~/media/Microsites/Files/CSP/DATA%20PDF/CSP_DEC.ashx> (June 26, 2013).

Langton, L. and Cohen, T. H. 2008. *Civil Bench and Jury Trials in State Courts, 2005*. Washington, DC: Department of Justice. <http://www.ojp.usdoj.gov/bjs/abstract/cbjtsco5.htm> (June 26, 2013).

Larson, E. 2006. Case Characteristics and Defendant Tenant Default in a Housing Court. *Journal of Empirical Legal Studies*, 3: 121–144.

Lempert, R. 1989. The Dynamics of Informal Procedure: The Case of a Public Housing Eviction Board. *Law and Society Review*, 23: 347–398.

Lens, V. 2007. In the Fair Hearing Room: Resistance and Confrontation in the Welfare Bureaucracy. *Law and Social Inquiry*, 32: 309–332.

Levi, E. H. 1948. *An Introduction to Legal Reasoning*. Chicago: University of Chicago Press.

Lieberman, J. K. 1981. *The Litigious Society*. New York: Basic Books.

Macauley, S. 1966. *Law and the Balance of Power: The Automobile Manufacturers and their Dealers*. New York: Russell Sage Foundation.

Macfarlane, J. 2008. *The New Lawyer: How Settlement is Transforming the Practice of Law*. Vancouver: UBC Press.

Macintyre, A. 1985. A Court Quietly Rewrote the Federal Pesticide Statute: How Prevalent is Judicial Statutory Revision? *Law and Policy*, 7: 249–279.

Malkin, V. 2004. Community Courts and the Process of Accountability: Consensus and Conflict at the Red Hook Community Justice Center. *American Criminal Law Review 40*: 1573–1593.

Marshall, A. 2003. Injustice Frames, Legality, and the Everyday Construction of Sexual Harassment. *Law and Social Inquiry*, 28: 659–689.

Mather, L. 1991. Policy Making in State Trial Courts. In *The American Courts: A Critical Assessment*, eds. J. B. Gates and C. A. Johnson. Washington, DC: CQ Press, 119–157.

——. 1995. The Fired Football Coach (or, How Trial Courts Make Policy). In *Contemplating Courts*, ed. L. Epstein. Washington, D.C: CQ Press, 170–205.

——. 1998. Theorizing about Trial Courts: Lawyers, Policymaking, and Tobacco Litigation. *Law and Social Inquiry*, 23: 897–940.

——, McEwen, C. A. and Maiman, R. J. 2001. *Divorce Lawyers at Work: Varieties of Professionalism in Practice*. New York: Oxford University Press.

Matoesian, G. M. 1993. *Reproducing Rape: Domination through talk in the courtroom*. Chicago: University of Chicago Press.

McCann, M. W. 1994. *Rights at Work: Pay Equity Reform and the Politics of Legal Mobilization*. Chicago: University of Chicago Press.

——. 2006. On Legal Rights Consciousness: A Challenging Analytical Tradition. In *The New Civil Rights Research: A Constitutive Approach*, ed. B. Fleury-Steiner and L. B. Nielsen. Burlington, VT: Ashgate, ix–xxx

——. 2008. Litigation and Legal Mobilization. In *The Oxford Handbook of Law and Politics*, ed. K.E. Whittington, R. D. Kelemen, and G. A. Caldeira. New York: Oxford University Press, 522–540.

McEwen, C. A. and Maiman, R. J. 1984. Mediation in a Small Claims Court. *Law and Society Review*, 18: 11–50.

McIntosh, W. V. 1990. *The Appeal of Civil Law: A Political-Economic Analysis of Litigation*. Urbana: University of Illinois Press.

Merry, S. E. 1990. *Getting Justice and Getting Even: Legal Consciousness among Working Class Americans*. Chicago: University of Chicago Press.

—— and Milner, N. eds. 1993. *The Possibility of Popular Justice: A Case Study of Community Mediation in the United States*. Ann Arbor: University of Michigan Press.

Miller, R. E. and Sarat, A. 1980–1. Grievances, Claims, and Disputes: Assessing the Adversary Culture. *Law and Society Review*, 15: 525–566.

Moog, R. 2009. Piercing the Veil of Statewide Data: The Case of Vanishing Trials in North Carolina. *Journal of Empirical Legal Studies*, 6: 147–176.

Moskos, P. 2008. *Cop in the Hood: My Year Policing Baltimore's Eastern District*. Princeton: Princeton University Press.

Munger, F. 1998. Mapping Law and Society. In *Crossing Boundaries: Traditions and Transformations in Law and Society Research*, ed. A. Sarat, D. Engel, V. Hans, and S. Lawrence. Evanston, IL: Northwestern University Press, 21–80.

Nader, L., ed. 1980. *No Access to Law: Alternatives to the American Judicial System*. New York: Academic Press.

National Center for State Courts. 2013a. "State Court Caseload Statistics," <http://www.courtstatistics.org/Other-Pages/StateCourtCaseloadStatistics.aspx> (June 26, 2013).

National Center for State Courts. 2013b. "State Court Structure Charts." <http://www.courtstatistics.org/Other-Pages/State_Court_Structure_Charts.aspx> (June 26, 2013).

Nardulli, P. F., Eisenstein, J., and Flemming, R. B. 1988. *The Tenor of Justice: Criminal Courts and the Guilty Plea Process*. Urbana: University of Illinois Press.

Nelson, R. L. and Nielsen, L. B. 2000. Cops, Counsel, and Entrepreneurs: Constructing the Role of Inside Counsel in Large Corporations. *Law and Society Review*, 34: 457–497.

Nielsen, V. L and Parker, C. 2012. Mixed Motives: Economic, Social and Normative Motivations in Business Compliance. *Law and Policy*, 34: 428–462.

Nolan, J. L., Jr. 2001. *Reinventing Justice: The American Drug Court Movement*. Princeton: Princeton University Press.

——ed. 2002. *Drug Courts in Theory and in Practice*. New York: Aldine de Gruyter.

——. 2009. *Legal Accents, Legal Borrowing: The International Problem-Solving Court Movement*. Princeton: Princeton University Press.

Nonet, P. 1969. *Administrative Justice: Advocacy and Change in a Government Agency*. New York: Russell Sage Foundation.

O'Barr, W. and Conley, J. M. 1988. Lay Expectations of the Civil Justice System. *Law and Society Review*, 22: 137–162.

Olson, W. K. 1991. *The Litigation Explosion: What Happened When America Unleashed the Lawsuit*. New York: Truman Talley Books-Dutton.

——2003. *The Rule of Lawyers: How the New Litigation Elite Threatens America's Rule of Law*. New York: St. Martin's Press.

Ostrom, B. J., Ostrom, C. W., Jr., Hanson, R. A. and Kleiman, M. 2007. *Trial Courts as Organizations*. Philadelphia: Temple University Press.

Ostrom, B. J., Strickland, S. M., Hannaford-Agor, P. L. 2004. Examining Trial Trends in State Courts, 1976–2002. *Journal of Empirical Legal Studies*, 1: 755–782.

Platt, A. M. 1970. *The Child Savers: The Invention of Delinquency*. Chicago: University of Chicago Press.

Provine, D. M. 1986. *Judging Credentials: Nonlawyer Judges and the Politics of Professionalism*. Chicago: University of Chicago Press.

——. 1998. Courts in Law and Society Research. In *Crossing Boundaries: Traditions and Transformations in Law and Society Research*, ed. A. Sarat, D. Engel, V. Hans, and S. Lawrence. Evanston, IL: Northwestern University Press, 296–316.

——. 2007. Law and Society and Political Science: On Separate Paths. *Law and Courts*, 17 (1): 6–8.

Ramji-Nogales, J. Schoenholtz, A. I., Schrag, P. G. 2007. Refugee Roulette: Disparities in Asylum Adjudication. *Stanford Law Review, 60*: 295–411.

Rapping, E. 2003. *Law and Justice as Seen on TV*. New York: New York University Press.

Rose, N. and Valverde, M. 1998. Governed by Law? *Social and Legal Studies, 7*: 541–551.

Ross, H. L. 1980. *Settled Out of Court: The Social Process of Insurance Claims Adjustment, rev.* 2nd ed. New York: Aldine Publishing Co.

——. 1995. Housing Code Enforcement as Law in Action. *Law and Policy, 17*: 133–160.

—— and Littlefield, N. O. 1978. Complaint as a Problem Solving Mechanism. *Law and Society Review, 12*: 199–216.

Rottman, D. and Casey, P. 1999. Therapeutic Jurisprudence and the Emergence of Problem-Solving Courts. *National Institute of Justice Journal, 240*: 12–18.

Ryan, J. P., Ashman, A., Sales, B. D., and Shane-DuBow, S. 1980. *American Trial Judges*. New York: The Free Press.

Sagy, T. 2011. What's So Private about Public Ordering? *Law and Society Review, 25*: 923–954.

Sarat, A. 1990. "...The law is all Over": Power, Resistance and the Legal Consciousness of the Welfare Poor. *Yale Journal of Law and the Humanities, 2*: 343–379.

—— and Clarke, C. 2008. Beyond Discretion: Prosecution, the Logic of Sovereignty, and the Limits of Law. *Law and Social Inquiry*, 387–416.

—— and Felstiner, W. L. F. 1995. *Divorce Lawyers and their Clients*. New York: Oxford University Press.

Scheb, J. and Matheny, A. 1988. Judicial Reform and Rationalization: The Diffusion of Court Reforms Among the American States. *Law and Policy, 10*: 25–42.

Scheingold, S. A. 1991. *The Politics of Street Crime: Criminal Process and Cultural Obsession*. Philadelphia: Temple University Press.

Schneider, R. D. 2008. Mental Health Courts. *Current Opinion in Psychiatry, 21*: 510–513.

Serber, D. 1980. Resolution or Rhetoric: Managing Complaints in the California Department of Insurance. In *No Access to Law: Alternatives to the American Judicial System*, ed. L. Nader. New York: Academic Press, 317–343.

Seron, C. 2007. The Status of Legal Professionalism at the Close of the Twentieth Century: Chicago Lawyers and Urban Lawyers, Law and Social Inquiry 32: 581–607.

Shapiro, M. 1965, Stability and Change in Judicial Decision-Making: Incrementalism or Stare Decisis? *Law in Transition Quarterly, 2*: 134–157.

——. 1972. Toward a Theory of Stare Decisis. *Journal of Legal Studies, 1*: 125–134.

——. 1981. *Courts: A Comparative and Political Analysis*. Chicago: University of Chicago Press.

Silbey, S. S. 1980–81. Case Processing: Consumer Protection in an Attorney General's Office. *Law and Society Review, 15*: 849–910.

——. 2005. After legal consciousness. *Annual Review of Law and Social Science, 1*: 323–368.

—— and Sarat, A. 1989. Dispute Processing in Law and Legal Scholarship: From Institutional Critique to Reconstruction of the Juridical Subject. *Denver University Law Review, 66*: 437–498.

Slovak, J. S. 1979. Working for Corporate Actors: Social Change and Elite Attorneys in Chicago. *American Bar Foundation Research Journal, 4*: 465–500.

Spangler, E. 1986. *Lawyers for Hire: Salaried Professionals at Work*. New Haven: Yale University Press.

Spohn, C. 2009. *How Do Judges Decide? The Search for Fairness and Justice in Punishment*, 2nd ed. Los Angeles: Sage.

Steegh, N. V. 2008. Family Court Reform and ADR: Shifting Values and Expectations Transform the Divorce Process. *Family Law Quarterly, 42:* 659–671.

Stipanowich, T. J. 2004. ADR and the "Vanishing Trial": The Growth and Impact of "Alternative Dispute Resolution." *Journal of Empirical Legal Studies, 1:* 843–912.

Talesh, S. A. 2012. How Dispute Resolution System Design Matters: An Organizational Analysis of Dispute Resolution Structures and Consumer Lemon Laws. *Law and Society Review, 46:* 463–496.

Trubek, D.M., Grossman, J.B., Felstiner, W. L. F., Kritzer, H. M. and Sarat, A. 1983. *Civil Litigation Research Project: Final Report,* 3 vol. Madison: Institute for Legal Studies, University of Wisconsin.

Tsai, B. 2000. Trend toward Specialized Domestic Violence Courts: Improvements on an Effective Innovation. *Fordham Law Review, 68:* 1285–1327.

Tyler, T.R. 1988. What is Procedural Justice? Criteria Used By Citizens to Assess the Fairness of Legal Procedures. *Law and Society Review, 22:* 103–135.

———. 1990. *Why People Obey the Law.* New Haven: Yale University Press.

United States Department of Justice, Bureau of Justice Statistics. 2013. *Sourcebook of Criminal Justice Statistics.* <http://www.albany.edu/sourcebook/index.html> (June 26, 2013).

United States Department of Justice, Office of Juvenile Justice and Delinquency Prevention. 2010. Publications. <http://www.ojjdp.ncjrs.gov/publications/index.html> (June 26, 2013).

Van Hoy, J. 1997. *Franchise Law Firms and the Transformation of Personal Legal Services.* Westport, CT: Quorum Books.

Vidmar, N. 1984. The Small Claims Court: A Reconceptualization of Disputes and an Empirical Investigation. *Law and Society Review, 18:* 515–550.

———and Hans, V. P. 2007. *American Juries: The Verdict.* Amherst, NY: Prometheus Books.

Walker, Samuel and Charles M. Katz. 2011. *Police in America: An Introduction,* 7th ed. Boston: McGraw-Hill.

Waters, N. L., Hans, V. P. 2009. A Jury of One: Opinion Formation, Conformity, and Dissent on Juries. *Journal of Empirical Legal Studies, 6:* 513–540.

Wice, P. B, 1991. *Judges and Lawyers: The Human Side of Justice.* New York: HarperCollins.

———. 1995. *Court Reform and Judicial Leadership.* Westport, CT: Praeger.

———. 2005. *Public Defenders and the American Justice System.* Westport, CT: Praeger.

Winkle, J. W. III and Oswald, R. H. 2008. The Role of Trial Judges in State Court Reform: The Case of Mississippi. *Judicature, 91:* 288–297.

Wissler, R. L. 1995. Mediation and Adjudication in Small Claims Court: The Effects of Process and Case Characteristics. *Law and Society Review, 29:* 323–358.

Yeazell, S. 2004. Getting What We Asked For, Getting What We Paid For, and Not Liking What We Got: The Vanishing Civil Trial. *Journal of Empirical Legal Studies, 1:* 943–971.

Yngvesson, B.1993. *Virtuous Citizens, Disruptive Subjects: Order and Complaint in a New England Court.* New York: Routledge.

Zimring, F. E. 2005. *American Juvenile Justice.* New York: Oxford University Press.

Zemans, F. 1982. Framework for the Analysis of Legal Mobilization. *American Bar Foundation Research Journal, 7:* 911–1071.

CHAPTER 21

....

LOCAL BUREAUCRACY

....

KELLY M. LEROUX

LOCAL bureaucracy is the administrative apparatus of local political jurisdictions—mainly cities and counties—that exist for the primary purposes of carrying out state and federal policy objectives, and for planning and providing local public services. While the term bureaucracy often evokes images of rigid and unresponsive organizations, local bureaucracies have proven to be quite flexible political institutions, adapting in significant ways to the changing economic and political contexts in which they operate. As discretionary federal aid to cities has declined with each successive decade, local bureaucracies have grown increasingly entrepreneurial and attentive to citizen feedback in an effort to advance their competitive position in the market for commercial and residential taxpayers. Moreover, local bureaucracies have steadily evolved from autonomous and exclusive producers of local public services to *managers* of local service delivery, outsourcing at least some of their responsibility for service provision to external providers—for-profit, nonprofit, and other local governments—and in the process, shifting at least some of the local bureaucracy's power to these outside actors.

These shifts toward increased entrepreneurship and reliance on third party actors have been inspired by three trends, each of which stand to guide local bureaucratic decision-making for the foreseeable future. First, management reforms such Reinventing Government and the New Public Management that diffused throughout local bureaucracies in the early 1990s demanded improved government performance, increased responsiveness to citizens, and a shift toward more market-based governance. Adherence to these reform tenets is very much alive and well in local bureaucracy today, placing efficiency and responsiveness at the forefront of decision-making in local governments. Second, local bureaucracies operate under conditions of increasing fiscal austerity, as federal mandates to local governments have increased without commensurate increases in intergovernmental revenue, ushering in an era that local bureaucracy scholars have described as "fend for yourself federalism" and "limited local capacity and increased demands" (Morgan, England, and Pelissero, 2007). Finally, there appears to be a growing recognition among local government officials that local policy choices have consequences beyond their own borders, and an increased political willingness to manage local services accordingly (Downs, 1994; Frederickson, 1999). Crime, pollution, and the economy are quintessential examples of local issues that transcend jurisdictional boundaries, and if not effectively managed through coordinated inter-jurisdictional action, may accumulate into state-level, national, or perhaps even global problems.

Reinventing Government and New Public Management reforms emphasizing cost savings, improved performance, and better "customer" service represent a natural alignment in many ways with traditional values of efficiency, effectiveness, and responsiveness that are at the core of professional public management. The pursuit of these goals has in fact been an enduring characteristic of local bureaucracy. However, the pursuit of these goals today is made more complicated and challenging by the growing reality of operating in a networked environment. Moreover, the increased jurisdictional and sectoral fragmentation characterizing local bureaucracies today creates starker tradeoffs among these objectives, as local bureaucratic actors must prioritize these goals while taking into consideration other public interests such as equity and accountability in any given policy-making scenario. This chapter examines evidence and debates related to three key themes in the literature on local bureaucracy: efficiency, responsiveness, and effectiveness. In summarizing key debates within each of these three themes, this chapter also highlights a number of unanswered questions and promising theoretical developments that might serve as guides for future research on local bureaucracy and local public service delivery.

Theories and Research on Local Bureaucratic Efficiency

The changing composition of the local electorate has given rise to increasingly complex demands for local services. At the same time, the median voter has a limited tolerance for taxation and is thought to be especially averse to tax increases at the local level (Peterson, 1981). Faced with demands for new and expanded services, and a lack of commensurate increases in revenue, local bureaucracies engage in a perpetual quest for greater efficiency in the design and delivery of local services. Public administration theories have led to the consideration, and in many cases implementation, of proposals for efficiency enhancements. Alternatives for achieving the objective of increased efficiency in local bureaucracy have spanned the gamut from political consolidation to functional consolidation—contracting with private providers on a service-specific basis. Although the prospect of increased efficiency provides the theoretical rationale as well as the political rhetoric employed in the pursuit of these alternatives, the robust literature developed around each of these alternatives suggests that other public management considerations may arise from these choices, including compromised accountability and less attention to equity concerns.

Consolidated Local Bureaucracy

One central and enduring debate among local government scholars has revolved around the question of whether local bureaucracy is more efficient when one large local government serves residents of multiple communities within a region, or whether local bureaucracy operates with greater economy when it has many competitors. The centralized approach to local bureaucracy has been advocated by progressive reformers who argue that consolidating city and county governments will lead to greater efficiency by eliminating service duplication, capturing economies of scale, encouraging business growth, and reducing the cost of government per capita (Hawkins, Ward, and Becker, 1991). By contrast, public choice theorists have argued that the existence of multiple local bureaucracies within a given region will lead to greater efficiency, as it enables a competitive market of local public goods and forces jurisdictions to compete for citizen-consumers through lower tax rates (Tiebout, 1956). The question that arises from these two opposing theoretical views is whether a centralized or decentralized system of local government is more efficient.

Although it is difficult to generalize from what amounts to a series of case studies—40 city-county consolidations in a population of some 3,034 counties and more than 19,000 cities—there is a distinct lack of evidence to support the claim that consolidation results in cost-savings. Indeed, the evidence available, although somewhat limited, has shown that consolidation leads to *higher* taxes and expenditures (Benton and Gamble, 1984), and increased personnel costs (Condrey, 1994). Public choice scholars on the other hand, have brought a robust body of evidence to bear on the claim that fragmentation of local government units leads to more efficient local bureaucracy (Schneider, 1989; Teske et al., 1993). Schneider has demonstrated that local government administration generally costs less in areas where bureaucracy is more decentralized (Schneider, 1989), and other evidence has confirmed that local governments are in fact strategic in their choice of tax rates, establishing rates that will enable them to compete with neighboring communities (Brueckner and Saavedra, 2001). Some neo-progressive scholars have attempted to discredit this evidence based on the fact that Tiebout assumptions about citizen-consumers being fully informed with regard to tax-service bundles largely do not hold up (Lowery and Lyons, 1989). However, third generation Tiebout scholars have thus far had the last word on this subject. These scholars have produced a compelling body of research suggesting that it is not necessary for all citizens in a local public goods market to be knowledgeable about tax rates and service bundles. Rather, a limited subset of informed citizen-consumers can drive the local public goods market toward competitive outcomes that benefit all (Bickers and Stein, 1998; Schneider et al., 1998 Schneider et al., 1999). Thus, while decentralization creates more efficient local government, it has clear consequences for equity. Service qualities and quantities will vary throughout a region and these disparities are particularly apparent among central cities and suburbs.

Despite the failures of consolidation to deliver on its promise of greater efficiency, it represents an "issue that won't die" (Leland and Johnson, 2004), and thus the question for local bureaucracy scholars is why this issue continues to resurface on the local agenda. The question of how consolidation attempts succeed has been largely answered through in-depth, longitudinal studies by Leland and Thurmaier (2004, 2010). What are much less clear are the motivations of various interests and local bureaucratic actors that continue to push for this structural reform. Why do many city managers align themselves with business interests and other "pro-consolidation" interests to put this issue on the local political agenda? Perhaps it is a desire to increase equity by standardizing services throughout the region, but recent work on regional cooperation for services suggests that the pursuit of equity is an unlikely motive LeRoux and Pandey (2011). Feiock, Carr, and Johnson (2006) have offered an interesting theory, arguing that consolidation is motivated by a desire to seize power from those interests advantaged by the status quo. Feiock and Carr (2001) have elsewhere argued that the prospect of selective rather than collective benefits, may be the driving force behind city managers' and other interests' attempts to push for consolidation. For example, the achievement of consolidation may provide career incentives for city managers with ladder-climbing ambitions. These authors provide an interesting line of theoretical reasoning that through empirical testing may enhance our understanding of why local bureaucratic actors and other interests continue to pursue consolidation.

Interjurisdictional Cooperation

Given that the prospect of achieving consolidation is relatively rare, local bureaucracy scholars have increasingly turned their attention in recent years to other alternatives for maximizing the efficiency of local government. Intergovernmental agreements represent one such key alternative, commonly negotiated between two or more local jurisdictions in the form of a formal contract or informal memoranda of understanding dictating service delivery responsibilities of each party to the agreement. Interjurisdictional service agreements have become increasingly popular among local bureaucratic actors, functioning as a means to reduce service costs, coordinate action to minimize spillover effects, manage boundary-spanning infrastructure, and leverage increased federal funding for regional initiatives. Interlocal service agreements are a preferred means to the pursuit of cost-savings among both local elected officials as well as local bureaucrats, as they are far easier to reverse than political consolidation or special district formation, providing local government actors with the flexibility to renegotiate terms or end the agreement when circumstances dictate a change in the direction of service delivery.

Research related to interlocal service agreements has burgeoned in the last few years, although most this work has set out to explain why these agreements form, rather than the outcomes they produce. Recent studies of interlocal service agreements have been largely pursued through the lens of cooperation theories, seeking to explain the formation of interjurisdictional agreements through theories of institutional collective action (Feiock, 2004), administration conjunction (Frederickson, 1999; Frederickson and Smith, 2003), and social network theory (Thurmaier and Wood, 2002). A large body of empirical evidence by Feiock and associates has linked municipal use of inter-local agreements to the council-manager form of government, city manager tenure, geographic proximity, permissive state legislation, population homogeneity, and the presence of both strong and weak tie networks that minimize the transaction costs of cooperation (Feiock, 2004; 2007). Other evidence has shown that social networks of local bureaucratic actors (city managers and department heads) encourage the forma-tion of interlocal service agreements, and help to sustain them over time (Thurmaier and Wood, 2002; LeRoux, and Pandey, 2009; LeRoux and Carr, 2010).

Although the determinants of interlocal agreement formation have thus been well studied, the lack of research speaking to the consequences of these agreements repre-sents a glaring omission in the literature. Do interlocal service agreements produce effi-ciency gains? Only one study to date has attempted to address this question, and the evidence is limited to a small number of municipalities in a single metro area. Wood (2006) interviewed forty local government managers about their experiences with interlocal agreements and while the majority cited cost-savings as an outcome, other work has shown that fiscal stress does not explain municipal choices for interlocal service contracting (Morgan and Hirlinger, 1991; Thurmaier and Wood, 2002). Given that efficiency is the most commonly used rationale for entering into interlocal service agreements (Ferris and Graddy, 1986), this is an important question that remains to be answered. Questions related to other types of outcomes are important as well. Do inter-local agreements eliminate negative externalities as many have suggested, or are they simply shifted beyond the boundaries of the two or three cooperating governments? How are opportunities for citizen participation affected by these interjurisdictional arrangements, when at least some of the bureaucracy's control over services is lost to the other parties?

Privatization and Contracting

Another policy increasingly adopted by local bureaucracies in the name of efficiency is that of contracting with private suppliers (both for-profit and nonprofit) for local public goods and services. The logic of contracting with private firms is guided by public choice assumptions that competitive markets will yield lower prices and higher service qual-ity than monopolistic local bureaucracies. Even though the assumptions of competi-tion among private providers are often unmet (Boyne, 1998), contracting with private firms has in fact been shown to lower production costs for local bureaucracies (Berenyi and Stevens, 1988; Kiewiet, 1991; Savas, 2005). Critics of privatization have long argued that any cost-savings achieved through lowered production costs are offset by increased transaction costs, which are costs associated with bargaining, negotiating, and ex-post monitoring (Williamson, 1981). However, newer evidence suggests this may not be the case; local bureaucracies monitor internal performance at levels that are comparable to monitoring the performance for-profit firms, revealing that transaction costs *within* local bureaucracies are nearly equal to costs of monitoring outside firms (Marvel and Marvel, 2007). Moreover, this work has shown that local bureaucracies monitor their own internal performance much more intensively than nonprofit or other government providers, suggesting that transaction costs of contracting for some types of services are actually lower than internal monitoring costs.

The rationale for local bureaucracies to closely monitor contracted firms is provided by principal-agent theory which assumes that contractors will act opportunistically and exploit information asymmetries to their own advantage. Implicit within this theory is the notion that principals (local bureaucracies) and agents (their contractors) have incongruous goals (Miller, 1992). While this may be true to a greater extent when the contractor is a for-profit firm, local bureaucracies also contract extensively with non-profits and other local governments whose goals are relatively consistent with that of the principal. Thus, some public management scholars have begun to emphasize stewardship theories over principal-agent theories in explaining contract monitoring decisions (Van Slyke, 2007). Through this theoretical lens contractors are viewed as stewards and as such, trust functions as a substitute for monitoring. While the results of Marvel and Marvel's (2007) study provide some indirect support for the stewardship theory, particularly for explaining contracting decisions related to nonprofits and governmental providers, it has yet to be subjected to an explicit test. Indeed, evidence on "reverse privatization" reveals that principal-agent problems account for at least some of the decision of local bureaucratic actors to contract services back in, including services previously contracted out to nonprofits (Hefetz and Warner, 2004). To what extent do public managers design contract monitoring programs based on their level of trust in providers? Clearly other factors besides trust account for the design of contract monitoring, including management capacity, along with political and institutional considerations. However, the big question for accountability relates to the trust variable. Although the choice to limit or avoid monitoring the performance of certain types of providers may yield efficiency gains, the consequences of this decision for accountability and service effectiveness are unclear.

Brown and Potoski (2003a, 2003b, 2003c, 2004a, 2004b) have offered some of the most important contributions to date in the local government contracting literature by demonstrating how specific characteristics of public goods and services shape governments' choices about which sector to contract with for different types of services. By using a theoretical approach that blends rational choice explanations with institutional explanations, these authors have provided a comprehensive framework for predicting local bureaucracies outsourcing decisions. This body of work has demonstrated that sector choice for any given service in an outsourcing decision is a function of a transaction cost calculus on the part of local bureaucratic actors, professional norms and values, fiscal considerations, as well as the characteristics of the good or service itself. While Brown and Potoski's work thus offers a fairly comprehensive explanation for local bureaucracies' choice of production mode for various services at a given point in time, longitudinal research by Hefetz and Warner (2004) has shown that service delivery choices are dynamic and change over time. How do changes in local economic, political, or other circumstances shape local government decisions to switch production modes? How do past experiences and knowledge acquired by managers shape these decisions? While Warner and Hefetz have provided a start, further longitudinal research is needed to answer these questions. Privatization and contracting research should also expand to include studies of mixed public-private delivery, as this appears to be one way local public managers can balance goals of efficiency with citizen satisfaction (Warner and Hefetz, 2008).

BUREAUCRATIC RESPONSIVENESS

Responsiveness is the goal of local public bureaucracies to ensure that services meet citizens' needs and expectations. While responsiveness has long been a shared value among professionally trained local government managers, (Nalbandian and Edwards, 1983), municipal efforts to align services with citizen expectations have accelerated in recent years. Driven by Reinvention principles of "customer-driven government" and "competitive government," (Osborne and Gaebler, 1993), local bureaucracies behave to some extent like private firms, competing for citizens and businesses who become consumers of municipalities' goods and services. Local governments engage in a wide variety of activities as well as maintain a number of institutions and rules designed to promote responsive service delivery, but the key question is whether these efforts translate into services or policies that attempt to satisfy citizen preferences. Three common mechanisms employed by local bureaucracies to promote responsive local governance are creating a representative workforce, citizen satisfaction surveys, and citizen participation forums.

Bureaucratic Representation

Maintaining a representative workforce is a principal means through which local bureaucracies might achieve responsive service delivery. An abundant literature has empirically established the link between passive representation and active representation whereby public organizations that are demographically representative of their clientele become more inclined to implement policies and deliver services in ways that are consistent with the interests of those clients (Meier, 1993; Keiser et al., 2002; Sowa and Selden, 2003; Meier and Nicholson-Crotty, 2006; Wilkins and Keiser, 2006). Research investigating the passive-active representation link at the local level of the bureaucracy has largely focused upon the service domains of local public education and local law enforcement, and studies within each of these contexts have produced affirmative evidence that active representation occurs on the basis of both race and gender. Within the domain of local public education, Meier and Stewart (1992) and Meier (1993) found that greater representation of minority teachers leads to higher educational achievement by minority students. Demonstrating a similar link for gender, Keiser et al. (2002) found that girls performed better at math in school districts that had a greater presence of women math teachers. In the context of local law enforcement, Meier and Nicholson-Crotty (2006) found that sexual assault reports and arrests increase as the percentage of female officers in the local law enforcement workforce increases, and Wilkins and Keiser (2006) similarly demonstrated a passive-active link for women in child support enforcement.

Conventional wisdoms held by scholars in this area have included the notions that active representation is premised upon the bureaucracy employing a "critical mass" of administrators representing the target group (Meier, 1993) and representatives having sufficient discretion to make decisions that will benefit the represented (Meier and Bohte, 2001). Yet, as others have recently argued, much of the active representation research fails to explicitly test whether bureaucratic partiality is truly the causal factor influencing client outcomes (Lim, 2006; Theobald and Haider-Markel, 2009). Lim (2006) has argued that passive representation creates important symbolic effects that may lead to changes in the attitudes or perceptions of under-represented groups, and has criticized previous research on the basis that it assumes passive representation equates to discretionary actions, and for failing to consider the possibility that symbolic representation alone leads to substantive change for target groups. Indeed, there is some evidence that symbolic representation has substantive effects. Examining citizen perceptions of police legitimacy, Theobald and Haider-Markel (2009) demonstrated that African American citizens were more likely to view being stopped by the police as a legitimate action when the officer was black, than when white. Their conclusion that substantive effects can occur simply based on the race, rather than any direct action of the officer, points to the need to parse the effects of passive representation from bureaucratic partiality in future studies of active representation. In order to isolate bureaucratic partiality as the cause of active representation, more explicit tests of such are needed.

Although Bradbury and Kellough (2008) do not examine active representation, they conducted a detailed study of local bureaucrats' adoption of the minority representation role, which is an assumed prerequisite for active representation. In a survey of several hundred managers and administrators, as well as citizens in the unified government of Athens-Clarke County, these authors found that Black administrators exhibited attitudes that were highly congruent with Black citizens with regard to local issues that affected the African American community, such as access to public transportation, fair treatment by police, and equitable access to affordable quality housing and day care. Moreover, the Bradbury and Kellough (2008) study showed that substantial differences exist between African American and white administrators with regard to the appropriate role of local government in affirmative action, ensuring equitable access to and distribution of local public services, and enactment of local policies that promote economic opportunities for African Americans. While minority bureaucratic representation was the outcome variable in Bradbury and Kellough's study, and race the key predictor of it, future studies of active representation would benefit from using their index of minority bureaucratic representation as a predictor of active representation or outcomes that benefit the target group.

Looking ahead, the rapidly changing demographic characteristics of American cities underscore the need for racially representative local bureaucracies and suggest this will become an increasingly important area for public administration research in the future. Immigration is driving U.S. population growth, and conservative estimates by the U.S. Census Bureau suggest that approximately one million new immigrants come to permanently reside in the U.S. each year, the majority from Latin America (Frey et al., 2009). Based on a projection of one million new immigrants per year, the U.S. is expected to become "majority- minority" with whites comprising roughly 45 percent of the population by 2042 (Frey et al., 2009). This signals an urgent need for minority leadership in higher-level administrative ranks of local bureaucracies, yet racial minorities are dramatically under-represented in these capacities with African Americans comprising only three percent of all U.S. city managers and Latino/a comprising one percent (Morgan, England and Pelissero, 2007). Will these demographic changes in the electorate be enough for city councils to place a greater premium on hiring minority managers? If this racial mismatch between the electorate and administrative leadership persists, how will local bureaucratic responsiveness be affected? Another key question relates to the treatment of Latino/a citizens through the discretionary decisions of local law enforcement. As state and local governments adopt formal and informal policies that are hostile toward immigrants, particularly Latinos, it is unclear whether representation in the police force and/or the administrative ranks of the local bureaucracy will cause this group to fare better in discretionary law enforcement decisions.

Citizen Satisfaction

One of the most common and straightforward methods of promoting responsive local governance is the use of citizen surveys. More than 60 percent of U.S. cities and counties collect citizen feedback via surveys in any given year (Miller and Miller Kobayashi, 2000). Soliciting feedback from citizens on a regular basis is important for local bureaucratic accountability, because the vast majority of citizens do not contact city government about service delivery (Morgan, England, Pelissero, 2007). While citizen satisfaction with local services might be considered on some level a measure of local bureaucracies' effectiveness, in theory local governments collect citizen feedback in order to adjust the quality and level of service supply to better match service demands and preferences.

Extant research suggests that, on the whole, citizens tend to be satisfied with the services provided by their local government (Miller and Miller Kobayashi, 2000), and citizen ratings of services on average are much higher than local government administrators anticipate (Melkers and Thomas, 1998). Yet, citizen satisfaction with local services is not uniformly distributed. Most notably, research has shown that satisfaction levels vary by race. Earlier work on the subject of local government service distribution concluded that although inequalities in service delivery existed among neighborhoods, they were "unpatterned" and therefore not amenable to correction through bureaucratic response (Lineberry, 1977; Mladenka, 1981). More recent work has demonstrated however, that distinct patterns exist in the service preferences and satisfaction levels of minority citizens versus white citizens. Kelly and Swindell (2002) examined 96 neighborhoods across 12 cities and counties and found significant variation in the distribution of service satisfaction outcomes. In their analysis, satisfaction levels with routine city services such as police, fire, trash collection, street repair, and parks and recreation, were substantially lower in neighborhoods with higher concentrations of racial minorities. Similarly, Bradbury and Kellough (2008) found dramatic variation in responses from African American and white citizens in consolidated Athens-Clarke County, with African Americans reporting much lower levels of fair treatment by police and lower levels of general satisfaction with county government than white citizens.

Although these race-based variations in satisfaction with services underscore the importance of paring this information down to the neighborhood level, citizen satisfaction data are ultimately subjective and research has shown that they do not necessarily correlate with more objective measures of performance (Kelly, 2003). Are variations in service quality more matters of perception, or are there observable inequities in the quality or quantities of services delivered to various neighborhoods? If inequities in the distribution of local services exist, local administrators may respond by targeting additional resources to underserved neighborhoods. However, a major dilemma for bureaucratic responsiveness arises from the alternative scenario. How do administrators respond to neighborhood-level differences in service satisfaction, when such differences appear to be based mainly on citizen perceptions? In either case, it is unclear from existing literature how administrators respond to these variations in service satisfaction outcomes. While much of the decision-making related to local public service delivery is conditioned by bureaucratic decision rules, technical considerations, and professional standards, local administrative leaders also wield considerable discretion in service delivery decisions. Research examining how administrators respond to variations in service satisfaction outcomes would contribute to a more complete understanding of administrative responsiveness in local bureaucracy.

Since most citizens would prefer to have more services and lower taxes, Morgan, England, and Pelissero (2007) argue that citizen surveys must force respondents to confront trade-offs between services and taxes if they are to be of any value. While local governments historically have not presented citizens with such choices, doing so provides the benefit of civic education and thus such an exercise may help to mediate dissatisfaction with services. Citizen perceptions of poor service quality and/or inequities in service distributions may also be mitigated through increased participation in local government.

The "New" Citizen Participation

Local bureaucracies have a long history of seeking input from their citizens through public hearings and providing opportunities for participation through citizen advisory boards, commissions, steering committees, task forces, and similar forums. These "old" forms of citizen participation were designed with the goal of enhancing administrative accountability and responsiveness to citizen preferences. While these original forms of citizen participation remain a fixture among America's 87,000 plus local governments, these jurisdictions function as laboratories of democracy by experimenting with a variety of newer and more innovative forms of participation. What distinguishes the "new" citizen participation from the old? Whereas older forms of participation are largely pro forma and only occasionally provoke changes in bureaucratic decisions, newer citizen participation forms place a premium on civic education, co-production, and deliberative democracy in effort to foster authentic participation. Old citizen participation is a one-way mode of communication in which citizens are the senders of messages and local bureaucratic actors are the (often uninterested) receivers. By contrast, "new" citizen participation relies more on *collaboration* with the public.

New citizen participation promises a more authentic role for citizens in local bureaucratic decision-making. As the need for local bureaucracies to make decisions within a networked context becomes increasingly the norm, situations requiring traditional hierarchical organizational decision-making are becoming less frequent. Blomgren-Bingham, Nabatchi, and O'Leary (2005) identified several collaborative forms of citizen participation, distinguishing between quasi-legislative and quasi-judicial mechanisms for citizen participation in today's networked environment of public management. According to these authors, quasi-legislative forms of citizen participation include deliberative democracy, e-democracy, public conversations, participatory budgeting, citizen juries, study circles, collaborative policy making, while quasi-judicial forms of citizen participation include alternative dispute resolution processes such as mediation, facilitation, early neutral assessment, and arbitration (Blomgren-Bingham, Nabatchi, and O'Leary, 2005, 547).

Blomgren-Bingham, Nabatchi, and O'Leary's (2005) articulation of these processes is useful for assigning labels to many of the practices used informally by local governments in an effort to achieve more authentic participation. Moreover, these authors describe the legal frameworks enabling these forms of participation such as the model State Administrative Procedures Act, and suggest that local governments are adopting their own ordinances and procedures to support these new forms of citizen participation. While anecdotal evidence suggests these new forms of citizen participation are diffusing rapidly, they have not been studied in any systematic way. The adoption and use of these "new" forms of citizen participation represents an important issue and a new terrain that is wide open for study by local bureaucracy scholars.

Social media often provides the technology through which many of these new forms of citizen participation are implemented. The emergence of social networking utilities and other online interactive tools has created new opportunities for local governments to expand citizen participation opportunities. Yet the rapid diffusion of these technologies has outpaced academic research, and, as such, it remains unclear how extensively these tools have been adopted and are being used by local governments to increase citizen participation. While there is evidence that social media is playing an increasingly important role in electoral campaigns and citizen participation in the activities of political parties (Carty, 2011), it remains unclear as yet how these new technologies will transform citizen participation in local administrative decision-making. The interactivity enabled by Web 2.0 tools has created new prospects for participatory governance within local bureaucracies and for programs, services, and activities to become more responsive to the citizens' needs and interests. These technologies hold tremendous potential for expanding the scope and quality of citizen participation, and may be particularly useful for engaging younger citizens (Bimber, 2003), a demographic whose voice is highly under-represented in local government decision-making. On the other hand, the use of these technologies for citizen participation at the local level also has the potential to reinforce the existing participation gap between the wealthy and poor. Although internet access in homes and through smartphones is becoming more widespread in America, a "digital divide" continues to exist, in which poorer citizens are more likely to lack consistent access to the internet (Mossberger, Tolbert, and McNeal, 2008).

In sum, there is an urgent need for research that systematically examines the adoption and implementation of "new" citizen participation modes. In what ways does the use of these new methods change local policy-making and administrative decision-making? Do local bureaucratic actors view these new processes as being beneficial for local governance, or do they perceive these activities to be a resource drain and distraction? When these new forms of citizen participation are implemented using social media or other online technologies, how is the quality of participation affected? What kinds of rules are made by local bureaucracies regarding online content to be posted by citizens? Who among the local electorate participates in these activities? In what observable ways does online citizen interaction with local government translate into greater responsiveness? These are simply a few of the questions that are important to our understanding of newer citizen participation methods and especially those that occur through social media and online technologies.

BUREAUCRATIC EFFECTIVENESS AND ISSUES OF PERFORMANCE

Although local government effectiveness has been a core value of professional public managers ever since the urban reform movement of the 1930s, political and institutional pressures for improved government performance have increased substantially in recent years. Results-oriented management philosophies such as Reinventing Government and the New Public Management emerged with widespread popularity in the early 1990s and led to the passage of the Government Performance and Results Act (GPRA) of 1993, which required all federal agencies to establish a strategic plan outlining goals and objectives to be measured and reported each year in the annual budget process. Soon after the passage of GPRA many state bureaucracies passed similar legislation and performance measurement programs diffused throughout local governments (Moon and DeLeon, 2001).

The renewed emphasis on effective local governance and widespread institutionalization of performance measurement systems has raised a number of new challenges for local governments as they grow more interdependent with and on organizations and actors in their external environment. First among these challenges is the problem of measuring performance and managing for results when the local bureaucracy must carry out its work through a network or through a contractual arrangement with a third party. Second is the challenge of motivating public employees for high performance in an atmosphere in which hiring freezes, wage freezes, and outsourcing of public jobs are an increasingly frequent means of balancing the budget. Third is the challenge of working within the structure of bureaucratic rules and regulations that constrain decision-making and hamper organizational effectiveness. This public management literature related to each of these issues is examined briefly in this section.

Performance Management

Instituting performance measurement programs into organizations assumes that managers will use the information generated by these systems to make decisions that enhance organizational effectiveness in some way (Wholey, 1999; Moynihan, 2005). In other words, performance measurement is assumed to lead to performance *management*. Much of the recent academic work on public sector performance measurement within the public sector has aimed to identify the factors leading to the purposeful use of performance data by public managers. Scholars have demonstrated that the use of performance information by managers is neither universal nor automatic (Moynihan and Ingraham, 2004). Bureaucratic actors may respond passively to performance measurement directives, doing the minimum required to comply by collecting data and disseminating information without actually using the information to make programmatic changes. Empirical studies have shown that the quality and availability of performance data are linked to increased use by managers for decision-making (de Lancer Julnes and Holzer, 2001; Moynihan and Ingraham, 2004; Bourdeaux and Chikoto, 2008; Moynihan and Landuyt, 2009). There is also evidence that public managers are more likely to use performance data for decision-making when their organization has a goal-oriented culture (de Lancer Julnes and Holzer, 2001; Moynihan and Landuyt, 2009), and supportive leadership (Moynihan and Ingraham, 2004; Melkers and Willoughby, 2005; Askim et al., 2008). Still other factors are likely to affect performance information use, including individual traits such as experience, organizational commitment, perception of the value of performance measurement, as well as job characteristics. However, these explanations have not been well tested in the performance management literature (Moynihan et al., 2011).

Although in theory performance measurement should enhance the accountability and effectiveness of public bureaucracies, it also presents a very real danger of diminishing accountability for programs that have complicated or long-term objectives. Given the reality that public programs often have vague and ambiguous goals, a "performance paradox" (Van Thiel and Leeuw, 2002) may occur when public managers establish precise performance expectations for their programs. The paradox arises from the unintended consequence of employees performing in ways that meet the measure, while displacing the underlying or unmeasured goals of a program. For example, performance-based contracting for welfare-to-work programs has led to such a paradox, whereby government contractors are rewarded for meeting performance expectations aimed at short-term outcomes which conflict with activities necessary for the long-term goal of helping clients to become self-sufficient (Dias and Maynard-Moody, 2007). A big question that remains is how public managers balance their need to demonstrate accountability and results in the short-term against their need to pursue broader, long-term organizational or program purposes.

Perhaps however, the biggest question related to performance management is how to measure the performance of collaborative service arrangements. The same managerial reform initiatives that demanded improved government performance also called for a shift toward more market-based governance (Osborne and Gaebler, 1993; Donahue and Nye, 2002). As a result, government agencies face the challenging and somewhat ironic mandate of providing citizens with high-performing programs and services while at the same time outsourcing at least some of their functions to private providers, and other governments, or working collaboratively through networks to fulfill their service obligations. Although performance measurement systems appear to offer a simple and value-neutral way of monitoring and improving government (Radin, 2006; Moynihan, 2008), scholars have recently argued that such simplicity is at odds with the complexity of contemporary governance (Frederickson and Frederickson, 2006; Moynihan et al., 2011).

Although performance of hierarchically structured contract arrangements is somewhat easier to measure, it is much more challenging to assess in collaborative service arrangements in which no single entity is "in charge." This type of loosely structured network participation is commonplace among local bureaucratic actors, creating scenarios in which participants are accountable to multiple principals and are often confronted with unclear goals. Performance management becomes increasingly complicated as the number of actors in a multi-organizational network increases. Even though network participants are united by a common policy objective, the diverse and sometimes conflicting motives of actors can lead to collective action problems. As group size increases, goal heterogeneity and preference divergence become increasingly likely, generating high transaction costs for all participants (Post, 2004). In addition to their collective goals, networks actors "face the challenge of reconciling the needs of multiple stakeholders, diverse expectations, and varying organizational missions and roles, while delivering a complex public service" (Romzek, 2008, 6). The need for network actors to be responsive to multiple principals often leads to role ambiguities, and uncertainty on the part of actors about how to prioritize performance goals. Moreover, the interdependence of network participants makes it difficult for network administrators to hold any one actor accountable for unsatisfactory performance.

Collaborative governance arrangements also lead to uncertainties about how performance should be measured. In large part, performance metrics are driven by normative valuations of what is important in any given situation. Increased effectiveness is often the rationale for creating collaborative governance arrangements, such as regional emergency management networks in which the collective resources and response of multiple jurisdictions to a disaster would be more effective in dealing with the problem than the response of any single local government. Yet placing a premium on effectiveness may require a tradeoff on other bureaucratic values such as efficiency and it also fragments accountability. Since public managers cannot satisfy all of these objectives at once, they must prioritize goals in each service delivery decision, and establish performance measures accordingly.

Given the complexity of measuring network performance, public management network scholars have called for measuring network effectiveness at multiple levels, even though performance at one level may conflict with another. Provan and Milward (2001) for example, have argued the need to assess network effectiveness at the community, network, and participant levels, while Mandell and Keast (2008) offer criteria for measuring performance at the environmental, organizational, and operational levels of the network. While these criteria offer a starting point, network scholars have yet to apply them in studies of network effectiveness. Thus, a central challenge for both network theorists and scholars of performance management is to test how well these conceptual criteria work at each level and the extent to which they can be integrated, so as to produce a refined framework for measuring network performance. Process goals are also an important but often overlooked dimension of network performance. Mandell and Keast (2008) have argued that conventional performance indicators such as cost and client outcomes by themselves offer an insufficient assessment of network effectiveness because they fail to acknowledge the relational dimensions that are so important to network performance. Another key challenge for measuring network performance then lies in specifying process measures, and identifying how they contribute to network outcomes at each level.

While public management research over the last decade has yielded some important insights about networks, many questions remain about how best to measure the performance of these ubiquitous multi-actor arrangements. One thing that is clear is that network behavior is defined by its policy context (Isett et al., 2011). Institutional rules, service markets, public values, and constellations of actors will vary across policy domains, limiting the extent to which we can apply public management network performance findings from one policy context to the next. We are also limited in our knowledge of how networks perform over time. Despite the availability of methodological tools to study networks at multiple time points, public management scholars have been slow to employ these methods. Research that directly addresses these limitations would help to improve our understanding of how local bureaucracies seek to measure and manage performance of their collaborative governance arrangements.

Public Service Motivation

Organizational effectiveness is directly affected by the behavior of individual employees whose performance is driven in large part, by their level of motivation. Administrative leaders of local bureaucracies must ensure that the local public workforce is highly motivated, because to a great extent, organizational performance and effectiveness are dependent upon it. However, local bureaucratic leaders face the challenge of maintaining morale and a high-performing workforce in the context of severe budget constraints and in an environment where public sector jobs are being increasingly contracted out to third parties. How do public managers motivate public employees to perform at their best? A vast literature on public service motivation or "PSM" suggests that this task is made somewhat easier for public managers because public employees tend to be intrinsically motivated, deriving rewards from the work itself rather than the promise of material rewards.

Perry and Wise (1990) are credited with being the intellectual pioneers of this concept, defining public service motivation as "an individual's predisposition to respond to motives grounded primarily or uniquely in public institutions and organizations." Examining the link between public service motivation and job performance among several thousand public employees, Alonso and Lewis (2001) found some evidence that higher public service motivation leads to better job performance, while Brewer and Selden (2000) found that both public service motivation and individual performance were linked to greater employee perceptions of organizational effectiveness. Since Perry and Wise's original formulation of the concept, PSM has become one of the most widely studied phenomena in public management research, with scholars seeking to understand its causes (Brewer, 2003; Bright, 2005; Moynihan and Pandey, 2007), consequences (Brewer and Selden, 2000; Alonso and Lewis, 2001), correlates (Crewson, 1997; Houston, 2000; Wright, 2004), and construct measurement (Perry, 1996; Coursey and Pandey, 1997). The discussion offered here does not attempt to review this voluminous literature (for a thorough review, see Perry and Hondeghem, 2008). Instead, this section considers the question of how public service motivation is affected by the contemporary governance trends of increased reliance on third party actors to carry out the business of government.

Although some studies have compared PSM levels amongst public, nonprofit, and for-profit employees (Houston, 2000), we know little about the relationship between PSM and the reliance of local bureaucracies on third party actors. The key question for local bureaucracy research is whether and to what extent public organizational transaction with third party actors affects public service motivation. This question is rich with research opportunities, as the existing PSM literature is largely silent on this issue. Extant literature showing that task environment has an effect on PSM (Wright, 2004) suggests that the type of collaborative governance arrangement may influence PSM, which may in turn influence organizational or program performance. Does PSM decrease in jurisdictions where levels of contracting and privatization are greater? If PSM levels are lower under these conditions, how is organizational or program performance affected? It is reasonable to conceive that levels of PSM might decline in local bureaucracies that currently outsource some local services, or are planning to outsource services, as public employees become threatened by reduced job security. On the other hand, it is possible that some types of collaborative governance arrangements may lead to higher levels of PSM. Because the PSM construct typically captures elements of altruism and reciprocity, some types of participation in collaborative governance arrangements may positively correlate with PSM levels. For example, public managers that choose to participate in voluntary, regional problem-solving networks may endorse greater levels of commitment to serving the public, based on a belief that their investment of time and energy contribute to the "common good," reinforcing their sense of public service motivation (Moynihan and Pandey, 2007).

For those who study public service motivation, the big questions going forward seem to revolve around how PSM is affected by contracting, privatization, and the need to devote an increasing share of one's day to network participation. The relationship between job performance, PSM, and material rewards also takes on a new dimension in the contemporary environment of resource scarcity and growing emphasis on efficiency gains. As Alonso and Lewis (2001) have shown, public employees perform better when they expect to receive a material reward for good performance, regardless of their level of public service motivation. For city managers and municipal department heads whose performance may be judged by their efficiency gains, high levels of public service motivation are likely to create role conflicts as managers will feel pulled between the need to protect their employees, and the need to outsource functions in order to capture efficiencies. Our understanding of the link between PSM and public organizational performance would be significantly enhanced through empirical research that takes into account how PSM affects, and is affected by, decisions to outsource public services.

Red Tape

Bureaucratic rules and routines may substantially influence organizational effectiveness, particularly when such rules have little significance to program goals or create excessive delays in implementing or accessing a program or service. A robust and growing literature has developed around the impact of bureaucratic rules or "red tape" on public organizational effectiveness. Building on the assumption of red tape as bureaucratic pathology, Bozeman (1993) defined red tape as "Organizational rules, regulations, and procedures that remain in force and entail a compliance burden for the organization but have no efficacy for the rules' functional object" (283). Alternatively stated, red tape involves excessive bureaucratic rules with "no redeeming value" for an organization's stakeholders, broadly defined (Bozeman, 1993).

Empirical research has demonstrated the adverse effects of red tape on the effectiveness of public organizations. Scott and Pandey (2000) found that level of red tape in an organization is linked to reduced levels of services to clients, and DeHart-Davis and Pandey (2005) have shown red tape to produce higher levels of managerial alienation. However, the presence of red tape may not necessarily doom an organization to poor performance. Pandey, Coursey, and Moynihan (2007) found that aspects of organizational culture can moderate the negative effects of red tape. Using qualitative data from in-depth interviews and quantitative data from surveys of more than 500 public managers in the U.S., these authors found that red tape in human resource systems and information systems had a negative effect on organizational effectiveness, but organizations that had a culture oriented toward growth, entrepreneurship, and commitment to innovation were more likely to overcome the burdens of red tape to demonstrate greater effectiveness (Pandey, Coursey, and Moynihan, 2007).

Even though red tape both creates obvious challenges for efficiency and hampers organizational performance, bureaucratic rules help to further other public goals such as safeguarding due process rights. Rules indeed serve an important function in public institutions, and some scholars have expressed dismay at the negative connotation of red tape. Goodsell (2000) for example, has argued that scholars must find a way to talk about bureaucratic rules that are effective. Dehart-Davis' (2009) theory of green tape offers a promising new direction for the study of bureaucratic effectiveness. Green tape refers to effective organizational rules that have the combined elements of "written requirements, with valid means-ends relationships, which employ optimal control, are consistently applied, and that have purposes understood by stakeholders" (Dehart-Davis, 2009, 362). Combining qualitative and quantitative data on worker perceptions from 645 municipal employees, Dehart-Davis confirms the construct validity of the elements of green tape theory, and articulates their causal mechanisms and expected effects on organizational outcomes. A set of testable propositions could be easily generated from this description. The theory of green tape opens a new door in the intellectual debate over bureaucratic effectiveness. The next step for research on bureaucratic effectiveness is to empirically test this theory to determine whether the elements of green tape indeed produce the hypothesized outcomes related to organizational effectiveness.

One general limitation of the existing research on bureaucratic performance is that most studies tend to rely on self-reported ratings as a measure of organizational effectiveness. The reliability of these study results could be enhanced through additional research that employs more objective measures of performance, such as actual client or constituent outcomes.

CONCLUSIONS

Efficiency, effectiveness, and responsiveness are key objectives of local bureaucracies and represent the core values of the professionals who manage and lead them. Moreover, concerns of efficiency, effectiveness, and responsiveness lie at the heart of many, if not most, of the questions driving local bureaucracy research. Under the contemporary conditions of resource scarcity and increased demands for performance, local governments must strive to accomplish all of these objectives, even though they are often at odds with one another. Local bureaucratic actors cannot simultaneously maximize objectives of efficiency, effectiveness, and responsiveness, and therefore must decide which objectives are most important in any given decision, taking into account the preferences of their elected political principals as well as those of citizens. Thus, the enduring question for local bureaucracy is how to balance the pursuit of these objectives, along with other public goals such as equity and accountability. In the context of a rapidly changing local electorate, and an increasing reliance upon third party actors and institutions, this task is made all the more challenging, ensuring an abundance of new questions for local bureaucracy research.

REFERENCES

Alonso P. and Lewis Gregory B. 2001. Public Service Motivation and Job Performance: Evidence from the Federal Sector. *The American Review of Public Administration*, 31: 363–380.

Askim, Jostein, Åge Johnsen, and Knut-Andreas Christophersen. 2008. Factors behind Organizational Learning from Benchmarking: Experiences from Norwegian Municipal Benchmarking Networks. *Journal of Public Administration Research and Theory*, 18 (2): 297–320.

Benton, J.E. and Gamble, D. 1984. City/county Consolidation and Economies of Scale: Evidence from a Time Series Analysis in Jacksonville, Florida. *Social Science Quarterly*, 65: 190–198.

Berenyi, E. and B. Stevens. 1988. Does Privatization Work? A Study of the Delivery of Eight Local Services. *State and Local Government Review*, 20: 11–21.

Bickers, Kenneth and Bob Stein. 1998. The Microfoundations of the Tiebout Model. *Urban Affairs Review*, 34(1): 76–93.

Bimber, Bruce. 2003. *Information and American Democracy: Technology in the Evolution of Political Power*. New York, NY: Cambridge University Press.

Blomgren-Bingham, Lisa, Tina Nabatchi, and Rosemary O'Leary. 2005. The New Governance: Practices and Processes for Citizen Participation in the Work of Government. *Public Administration Review*, 65(5): 547–558.

Bourdeaux, Carolyn and Grace Chikoto. 2008. Legislative Influences on Performance Management Reform. *Public Administration Review*, 68 (2): 253–265.

Boyne, George. 1998. Bureaucratic Theory Meets Reality: Public Choice and Service Contracting in U.S. Local Government. *Public Administration Review*, 58(6): 474–484.

Bozeman, Barry. 1993. A Theory of Government Red Tape. *Journal of Public Administration Research and Theory*, 3: 273–303.

Bradbury, Mark D. and J. Edward Kellough. 2008. Representative Bureaucracy: Exploring the Potential for Active Representation in Local Government. *Journal of Public Administration Research and Theory*, 18: 697–714.

Brewer, Gene A. 2003. Building Social Capital: Civic Attitudes and Behavior of Public Servants. *Journal of Public Administration Research and Theory*, 13(1): 5–26.

Brewer, Gene A. and Sally Coleman Selden. 2000. Why Elephants Gallop: Assessing and Predicting Organizational Performance in Federal Agencies. *Journal of Public Administration Research and Theory*, 10(4): 685–711.

Bright, L. 2005. Public Employees with High Levels of Public Service Motivation: Who are They, Where are They, and What do They Want? *Review of Public Personnel Administration*, 25(2): 138–154.

Brown, Trevor and Matthew Potoski. 2003a. Transaction Costs and Institutional Explanations for Government Service Production Decisions. *Journal of Public Administration Research and Theory*, 13 (4): 441–468.

Brown, Trevor and Matthew Potoski. 2003b. Managing contract performance: A transaction costs approach. *Journal of Policy Analysis and Management*, 22(2): 275–297.

Brown, Trevor and Matthew Potoski. 2003c. Contract Management Capacity in Municipal and County Governments. *Public Administration Review*, 63(2): 153–164.

Brown, Trevor and Matthew Potoski. 2004a. Assessing the Management Costs of Delivering Services Under Alternative Institutional Arrangements. *Journal of Public Procurement*, 4(3): 375–396.

Brown, Trevor and Matthew Potoski. 2004b. Managing the Public Service Market. *Public Administration Review*, 64(6): 656–668.

Brueckner, Jan K. and Luz Amparo Saavedra. 2001. Do Local Governments Engage in Strategic Property-Tax Competition? *National Tax Journal*, 54(3): 231–253.

Carty, Victoria. 2011. *Wired and Mobilizing: Social Movements, New Technology, and Electoral Politics*. New York, NY: Routledge Press.

Condrey, S.E. 1994. Organizational and Personnel Impacts of City-county Consolidation. *Journal of Urban Affairs*, 16: 371–383.

Coursey, David and Sanjay K. Pandey. 1997. Public Service Motivation Measurement: Testing an Abridged Version of Perry's Proposed Scale. *Administration and Society*, 39(5): 547–568.

Crewson, P.E. 1997. Public Service Motivation: Building Empirical Evidence of Incidence and Effect. *Journal of Public Administration Research and Theory*, 7(4): 499–518.

de Lancer Julnes, Patria and Marc Holzer. 2001. Promoting the Utilization of Performance Measures in Public Organizations: An Empirical Study of Factors Affecting Adoption and Implementation. *Public Administration Review* 61 (6): 693–708.

Dehart-Davis, Leisha. 2009. Green Tape: A Theory of Effective Organizational Rules. *Journal of Public Administration Research and Theory*, 19: 361–384.

DeHart-Davis, Leisha, and S. K. Pandey. 2005. Red Tape and Public Employees: Does Perceived Rule Dysfunction Alienate Managers? *Journal of Public Administration Research and Theory*, 15: 133–148.

Dias, Janice Johnson and Steven Maynard-Moody. 2007. For-profit Welfare: Contracts, Conflicts, and the Performance Paradox. *Journal of Public Administration Research and Theory* 17: 189–211.

Donahue, J. D. and Nye, J. S. 2002. *Market-Based Governance: Supply Side, Demand Side, Upside and Downside*. Washington, DC: Brookings Institution Press.

Downs, Anthony. 1994. *New Visions for Metropolitan America*. Washington, DC: The Brookings Institution.

Feiock, Richard C. 2004. *Metropolitan Governance: Conflict, Competition, and Cooperation*. Washington, DC: Georgetown University Press.

Feiock, Richard C. 2007. Rational Choice and Regional Governance. *Journal of Urban Affairs*, 29(1): 47–63.

Feiock, Richard C. and Jered B. Carr. 2001. Incentives, Entrepreneurs, and Boundary Change: A Collective Action Framework. *Urban Affairs Review*, 36: 382–405.

Feiock, Richard C., Jered B. Carr, and Linda Johnson. 2006. Structuring the Debate on Consolidation: A Response to Leland and Thurmaier. *Public Administration Review*, 66(2): 274–278.

Ferris, James M. and Elizabeth Graddy. 1986. Contracting Out: For What, with Whom? *Public Administration Review*, 46: 332–344.

Frederickson, David G. and H. George Frederickson. 2006. *Measuring the Performance of the Hollow State*. Washington DC: Georgetown University Press.

Frederickson, H. George. 1999. The Repositioning of American Public Administration. *PS: Political Science & Politics*, 32: 701–711.

Frederickson, H. George and Kevin B. Smith. 2003. *The Public Administration Theory Primer*. Boulder, CO: Westview Press.

Frey, William H., Alan Berube, Audrey Singer, and Jill H. Wilson. 2009. *Getting Current: Recent Demographic Trends in Metropolitan America*. The Brookings Institution. <www.brookings.edu>. Date accessed: September 24, 2010.

Goodsell, Charles T. 2000. Red Tape and a Theory of Bureaucratic Rules. *Public Administration Review*, 60(4): 373–375.

Hawkins, B. W., Ward, K. J., and Becker, M. P. (1991, Summer). Governmental Consolidation as a Strategy for Metropolitan Development. *Public Administration Quarterly*, 253–267.

Hefetz, Amir and Mildred Warner. 2004. Privatization and its Reverse: Explaining the Dynamics of the Government Contracting Process. *Journal of Public Administration Research and Theory*, 14(2): 171–190.

Houston, D. J. 2000. Public Service Motivation: A Multivariate Test. *Journal of Public Administration Research and Theory*, 10(4): 713–727.

Isett, Kimberly, Ines Mergel, Kelly LeRoux, Pamela Michen, and Karl Rathemeyer. 2011. Networks in Public Administration Scholarship: Understanding Where we are and Where we Need to Go. *Journal of Public Administration Theory and Research*, 21: 157–173.

Keiser, Lael R., Vicky M. Wilkins, Kenneth J. Meier, and Catherine A. Holland. 2002. Lipstick and Logarithms: Gender, Institutional Context, and Representative Bureaucracy. *American Political Science Review*, 96: 553–564.

Kelly, Janet. 2003. Citizen Satisfaction and Administrative Performance Measures: Is there Really a Link? *Urban Affairs Review*, 38: 863–868.

Kelly, Janet and David Swindell. 2002. Service Quality Variation Across Urban Space: First Steps Toward a Model of Citizen Satisfaction. *Journal of Urban Affairs*, 24(3): 271–288.

Kiewiet, D. 1991. Bureaucrats and Budgeting Outcomes: Quantitative Analyses. In A. Blais and S. Dion, eds, *The Budget-Maximizing Bureaucrat*. Pittsburgh, PA: University of Pittsburgh Press.

Leland, Suzanne and Gary Johnson. 2004. Consolidation as a Local Government Reform. In Jered B. Carr and Richard C. Feiock, eds, *City-County Consolidation and Its Alternatives: Shaping the Local Government Landscape*. Armonk, NY: M.E. Sharpe.

Leland, Suzanne M. and Kurt Thumainer, eds. 2004. *Case Studies of City-County Consolidation: Reshaping the Local Government Landscape*. Armonk, NY: M.E. Sharpe.

Leland, Suzanne M. and Kurt Thurmaier. 2010. *City-County Consolidation: Promises Made, Promises Kept?* Washingon, DC: Georgetown University Press.

LeRoux, Kelly and Jered B. Carr. 2010. Prospects for Centralizing Services in an Urban County: Evidence from Self-Organized Networks of Eight Local Public Services, *Journal of Urban Affairs*, 32(4): 449–470.

LeRoux, Kelly, Paul Brandenburger and Sanjay Pandey. 2009. Interlocal Service Cooperation in U.S. *Cities: A Social Network Explanation. Public Administration Review, 70*(2): 268–278.

LeRoux, Kelly and Sanjay Pandey. 2011. City Managers, Career Incentives and Municipal Service Decisions: The Effects of Managerial Ambition on Interlocal Service Delivery, *Public Administration Review, 71*(4): 627–636.

Lim, Hong-Hai. 2006. Representative Bureaucracy: Rethinking Substantive Effects and Active Representation. *Public Administration Review, 66*: 193–204.

Lineberry, Robert L. 1977. *Equality and Urban Policy: The Distribution of Municipal Public Services*. Beverly Hills, CA: Sage Publications.

Lowery, David and William E. Lyons, 1989. The Impact of Jurisdictional Boundaries: An Individual-Level Test of the Tiebout Model. *The Journal of Politics, 51*: 73–97.

Mandell, Myrna P. and Robin Keast. 2008. Evaluating the effectiveness of interorganizational relations through networks. *Public Management Review 10*: 716–731.

Marvel, Mary K. and Howard P. Marvel. 2007. Outsourcing Oversight: A Comparison of Monitoring for In-House and Contracted Services. *Public Administration Review, 67*(3): 521–530.

Meier, Kenneth J. 1993. Latinos and Representative Bureaucracy: Testing the Thompson and Henderson Hypotheses, *Journal of Public Administration Research and Theory, 3*(4): 393–414.

Meier, Kenneth J. and John Bohte. 2001. Structure and Discretion: Missing Links in Representative Bureaucracy. *Journal of Public Administration Research Theory, 11*: 455–470.

Meier, Kenneth J., and Jill Nicholson-Crotty. 2006. Gender, Representative Bureaucracy, and Law Enforcement: The Case of Sexual Assault. *Public Administration Review, 66*: 850–860.

Meier, Kenneth J., and Joseph J. Stewart, Jr. 1992. The Impact of Representative Bureaucracies: Educational Systems and Public Policies. *American Review of Public Administration, 22*: 157–171.

Melkers, Julia and John Clayton Thomas. 1998. What do Administrators Think Citizens Think? Administrator Predictions as an Adjunct to Citizen Surveys. *Public Administration Review, 58*(4): 327–334.

Melkers, Julia and Katherine Willoughby. 2005. Models of Performance-measurement Use in Local Governments: Understanding Budgeting, Communication, and Lasting Effects. *Public Administration Review 65* (2): 180–190.

Miller, Gary. 1992. *Managerial Dilemmas: The Political Economy of Hierarchy*. New York: Cambridge University Press.

Miller, Thomas I. and Michelle Miller Kobayashi. 2000. *Citizen Surveys: How to do Them, How to use Them, and What They Mean*. Washington, DC: ICMA, 2000.

Mladenka, Kenneth R. 1981. Citizen Demands and Urban Services: The Distribution of Bureaucratic Response in Chicago and Houston. *American Journal of Political Science, 25*: 708.

Moon. M. J. and P. DeLeon, 2001. Municipal Reinvention: Managerial Values and Diffusion Among Municipalities. *Journal of Public Administration Research and Theory, 11*(3): 327–351.

Morgan, David R. Robert England, and John Pelissero. 2007. *Managing Urban America*, 6th edn. Washington, DC: CQ Press.

Morgan, David R. and Hirlinger, M. 1991. Intergovernmental Service Contracts: A Multivariate Explanation. *Urban Affairs Quarterly, 27*(1): 128–144.

Mossberger, Karen, Caroline Tolbert and Ramona NcNeal. 2008. *Digital Citizenship: The Internet, Society, and Participation*. Cambridge, MA: The MIT Press.

Moynihan, Donald P. 2005. Goal-Based Learning and the Future of Performance Management. *Public Administration Review*, 65(2): 203–216.

Moynihan, Donald P. 2008. *The Dynamics of Performance Management: Constructing Information and Reform*. Washington DC: Georgetown University Press.

Moynihan, Donald P., Sergio Fernandez, Soonhee Kim, Kelly LeRoux, Suzanne J. Piotrowski, Bradley E. Wright, and Kaifeng Yang. 2011. Performance Regimes Amidst Governance Complexity. *Journal of Public Administration Research and Theory*, 21: 141–155.

Moynihan, Donald P. and Patricia W. Ingraham. 2004. Integrative Leadership in the Public Sector: A Model of Performance Information Use. *Administration & Society* 36: 427–453.

Moynihan, Donald P. and Noel Landuyt. 2009. How Do Public Organizations Learn? Bridging Structural and Cultural Divides. *Public Administration Review*, 69(6): 1097–1105.

Moynihan, Donald P. and Sanjay K. Pandey. 2007. Finding Workable Levers over Motivation: Comparing Job Satisfaction, Job Involvement, and Organizational Commitment. *Administration and Society*, 39(7): 803–832.

Nalbandian, John and J. Terry Edwards. 1983. The Values of Public Administrators: A Comparison With Lawyers, Social Workers, and Business Administrators. *Review of Public Personnel Administration*, 4(1): 114–127.

Osborne, David and Ted Gaebler. 1993. *Reinventing Government: How the Entrepreneurial Spirit is Transforming the Public Sector*. Penguin Books.

Pandey, Sanjay K., David H. Coursey, and Donald P. Moynihan. 2007. Organizational Effectiveness and Bureaucratic Red Tape: A Multimethod Study. *Public Performance and Management Review*, 30(3): 398–425.

Perry, James L. 1996. Measuring Public Service Motivation: An Assessment of Construct Reliability and Validity. *Journal of Public Administration Research and Theory*, 6(1): 5–22.

Perry, James L. and Anne Hondeghem. 2008. *Motivation in Public Management: The Call of Public Service*. Oxford University Press: New York, NY.

Perry, James L. and Lois Wise. 1990. The Motivational Bases of Public Service. *Public Administration Review*, 50: 367–373.

Peterson, Paul E. 1981. *City Limits*. Chicago, IL: University of Chicago Press.

Post, Stephanie S. 2004. Metropolitan Area Governance and Institutional Collective Action, in *Metropolitan Governance: Conflict, Competition, and Cooperation*, ed. Richard C. Feiock. Georgetown University Press.

Provan, Keith G. and H. Brinton Milward. 2001. Do Networks Really Work? A Framework for Evaluating Public Sector Organizational Networks. *Public Administration Review*, 61(4): 414–423.

Romzek, Barbara. 2008. The Tangled Web of Accountability in Contracting Networks: The Case of Welfare Reform. Paper presented at the Kettering Foundation Symposium on Accountability, May 22–23, 2008 Dayton, Ohio.

Savas, E.S. 2005. *Privatization in the City: Successes, Failures, Lessons*. Washington, DC: CQ Press.

Schneider, Mark. 1989. *The Competitive City. The Political Economy of Suburbia*. Pittsburgh: University of Pittsburgh Press.

Schneider, Mark, Melissa Marschall, Christine Roch, and Paul Teske. 1999. Heuristics, Low Information Rationality, and Choosing Public Goods: Broken Windows as Shortcuts to Information about School Performance. *Urban Affairs Review*, 34(5): 729–741.

Schneider, Mark, Paul Teske, Melissa Marschall, Christine Roch. 1998. Shopping for Schools: In the Land of the Blind, the One-Eyed Parent May be Enough. *American Journal of Political Science*, 42(3): 769–783.

Scott, P. G., and Sanjay K. Pandey. 2000. The Influence of Red Tape on Bureaucratic Behavior: An Experimental Simulation. *Journal of Policy Analysis and Management*, 19: 615–633.

Sowa, Jessica E. and Sally Coleman Selden. 2003. Administrative Discretion and Active Representation: An Expansion of the Theory of Representative Bureaucracy. *Public Administration Review*, 63: 700–710.

Teske, Paul, Mark Schneider, Michael Mintrom, Samuel Best. 1993. Establishing the Micro Foundations of a Macro Theory: Information, Movers, and the Competitive Local Market for Public Goods. *American Political Science Review*, 87(3): 702–713.

Theobald, Nick, and Donald P. Haider-Markel. 2009. Race, Bureaucracy, and Symbolic Representation: Interactions between Citizens and Police. *Journal of Public Administration Research and Theory*, 19: 409–426.

Thurmaier, Kurt and Curtis H. Wood. 2002. Interlocal Agreements as Overlapping Social Networks: Picket-Fence Regionalism in Metropolitan Kansas City. *Public Administration Review*, 62(5): 585–596.

Tiebout, Charles M. 1956. A Pure Theory of Local Expenditure. *The Journal of Political Economy*, 64(5): 416–424.

Van Slyke, David M. 2007. Agents or Stewards: Using Stewardship Theory to Understand the Government-Nonprofit Social Service Contracting Relationship. *Journal of Public Administration Research and Theory*, 17: 157–187.

Van Thiel, Sandra and Frans Leeuw. 2002. The Performance Paradox in the Public Sector. *Public Performance and Management Review*, 25(3): 267–281.

Warner Mildred and Amir Hefetz. 2008. Managing Markets for Public Service: The Role of Mixed Public-Private Delivery of Public Services. *Public Administration Review*, 68(1): 155–166.

Wholey, Joseph S. 1999. Peformance-Based Management: Responding to the Challenges. *Public Performance and Management Review*, 22(3): 288–307.

Williamson, Oliver E. 1981. The Economics of Organization: The Transaction Cost Approach. *The American Journal of Sociology* 87 (3): 548–577.

Wilkins, Vicky M. and Lael R. Keiser. 2006. Linking Passive and Active Representation for Gender: The Case of Child Support Agencies. *Journal of Public Administration Research and Theory*, 16: 87–102.

Wood, Curtis. 2006. Scope and Patterns of Metropolitan Governance in Urban America: Probing the Complexities in the Kansas City Region. *The American Review of Public Administration*, 36(3): 337–353.

Wright, Bradley E. 2004. The Role of Work Context in Work Motivation: A Public Sector Application of Goal and Social Cognitive Theories. *Journal of Public Administration Research and Theory*, 14(1): 59–78.

PART V

SUB-NATIONAL PUBLIC POLICY PROCESSES

CHAPTER 22

THE CONTEXT OF LOCAL POLICYMAKING

Who or What Governs?

ZOLTAN L. HAJNAL

THE core question driving the study of local politics is—who or what governs? From C. Wright Mills' "The Power Elite" to Robert Dahl's "Who Governs?" and on to Paul Peterson's "City Limits" there has been a long standing debate about the factors that most heavily influence local policy decisions. This is no idle or esoteric academic debate. Understanding who or what governs the local political arena is important. Although presidential and Congressional elections get much of our attention, urban politics represents a key component of American democracy. Policy decisions at the local level affect citizens profoundly and immediately. Local governments control basic services like public safety, education, and water and make critical decisions about land-use and development. Indeed, more than a quarter of all government expenditures—over one trillion dollars annually—are distributed at the local level. It is, therefore, not too much of a stretch to argue that "the functions of government that have most impact on citizen's daily lives" are within the purview of local governments (Oliver, 2001, 15). In short, it matters who wins and who loses in a political arena that touches regularly on the lives of residents.

In this chapter I offer a critical account of the strengths and weaknesses of the literature on local policy making. I proceed by detailing the different theoretical perspectives offered in the literature, outlining the empirical trajectory of the research, and then providing some assessments of where the literature stands today. That assessment highlights a number of critical concerns with the research including a tendency to focus on narrow outcomes, an inability to provide comprehensive tests that pit each of the different theories against each other, and a lack of attention to uncovering basic interests and divisions across the public. I close with some suggestions for future research that follow directly from gaps in the literature or from new demographic or technological imperatives.

THEORIES OF LOCAL GOVERNANCE

How do local governments make decisions about policy? What constrains those decisions? Whose voices are heard? A good portion of all of the research on urban politics has been devoted to answering these questions. All of this effort has spawned at least six different and often contrasting accounts of whom or what matters in local politics (see Stein, 1990, Judd and Swanstrom, 1994, and Pelissero, 2003, for overviews of this literature).

Early scholars of the local political arena concluded that a small set of elite actors who controlled major local financial resources dominated local decision-making (Hunter, 1953; Mills, 1956). Based largely on surveys of local residents that pointed to a small set of influential business men, elite theorists contend that local outcomes are more contingent on the desires of local business interests than on the preferences of the broader public or the wishes of local public officials

A related but distinct perspective is the economic imperatives model developed by Peterson (1981) and others (Buchanan, 1971; Dye, 1987). According to this view, local government decision making is largely a function of economic considerations. The central driving force in local politics in this model is economic competition across cities (Tiebout, 1956; Peterson, 1981). In order to avoid economic and social decline, cities must compete for mobile capital. This severely constrains local governments. Cities cannot tax mobile capital too heavily or redistribute too many resources to less advantaged segments of the population for fear that their actions will motivate businesses and wealthy residents to relocate. Instead they must seriously consider reducing taxes and providing a mix of services that is most likely to attract and/or retain more privileged economic interests. This should, according to most of these authors, result in a pro-growth focus and a range of spending policies that encourage economic development (Logan and Molotch, 1987; Elkin, 1987). If this theory is accurate we would expect to see generally limited redistributive spending. Moreover, if we do see expanded redistributive spending, it is likely to occur in cases where cities have an economic surplus and can afford to expend resources on what should be viewed as costly and unproductive programs.

The alternative most directly in competition with this economic imperatives model is a pluralist account of urban policy making. Rather than seeing local government decisions as fundamentally driven by economic constraints, pluralists see local policy as fundamentally driven by political considerations (Dahl, 1961; Meier et al., 1991; Donovan and Neiman, 1992; Goetz, 1994). The key to understanding local decision-making, according to pluralists, is to recognize that elected officials need public support in order to govern and win reelection. Since any official who does not heed this public pressure risks losing office, local governments should incorporate the preferences of a range of different citizens when enacting policy. Especially for important decisions that are highly contested by participants from diverse socioeconomic backgrounds, governmental policy should closely mirror public preferences. If, for example, most residents in a given locality favor greater redistribution of public resources, we should expect political actors in that locality to enact measures to increase redistribution. In this way, government should be open to influence from a wide range of groups, even those who do not formally participate in the process (Dahl, 1961).[1]

One alternative, regime theory, combines elements of each of the preceding accounts of local policy-making (Stone, 1989). According to regime theory, the extent to which elite power brokers, political decision makers, and economic imperatives dominate local outcomes can vary widely across contexts. Since neither public actors nor the private sector has the resources to unilaterally enact policy, each city's governing regime will be the result of a collaborative arrangement between public and private sectors. Just who governs will be dependent on the make-up of the local governing regime that comes out of that bargaining process. If, for example, minority politicians are able to join that governing coalition, then local policy is much more likely to favor the interests of the minority population (Browning et al., 1984). Two of the most well-known archetype governing regimes are machine cities (Gosnell, 1968; Royko, 1971) and reform cities (Finegold, 1995), although there is some dispute as to whom exactly machine and reform cities serve (Erie, 1988, Bridges, 1997; Trounstine, 2008)

According to another group of observers, local policy is less a function of economic competition or political preferences and more a function of local needs (Lineberry, 1977; Lipsky, 1980; Mladenka, 1980; Boyle and Jacobs, 1982; Feiock and West, 1993; but see Koehler and Wrightson, 1987). From this perspective, city governments operate in a technically efficient manner and distribute resources and services to those who need them. This is a view of city governments that sees local policy-making as an essentially apolitical process, driven by the services cities must provide and the bureaucrats who provide those services.

Institutional structure is yet another factor that according to many helps to constrain local government decisions (Sharp, 1991; Pelissero and Krebs, 1997; Sass, 2000). Institutionalists do not deny the existence of any of the other factors already mentioned. They do, however, contend that governing structures can also change the nature of the local political game and shape the incentives that local political actors face. This Institutionalist perspective comes in two variants: one that focuses on local institutions, and another that highlights the degree to which cities are subject to constraints from higher levels of government.

Although almost any institutional lever at the local level could conceivably help to determine government behavior, Institutionalist scholars have tended to focus on a handful of key structures. In particular, nonpartisan elections, the city manager form of government (as opposed to the mayor/council form), weaker mayoral powers, at-large elections, and the absence of term limits are all viewed by at least some urban scholars as reducing the responsiveness of local government to minority or lower-class interests (Banfield and Wilson, 1967; Lineberry and Fowler, 1967; Mladenka, 1989; Welch, 1990;

Bridges, 1997; Clingermayer and Feiock, 2001; but see Morgan and Pelissero, 1980). Although evidence for many of these relationships is limited, there is a widespread belief that reform institutions have been instrumental in maintaining middle-class white control in a number of urban centers by depoliticizing the governing process and shaping who wins elections (Judd and Swanstrom, 1994; Bridges, 1997).

Other Institutionalists point to the placement of local governments at the bottom of the hierarchy of the federal system as a critical factor in local policy-making (Browning et al., 1984; Saltzstein, 1986; Erie, 1988). Local governments are subjected to a range of laws and mandates that require spending in some areas and limit spending in others. Since a quarter of local government revenues are provided by state and federal governments and since much of this federal and state funding is earmarked toward specific functions, local governments may have little power to control the direction of their own spending. As Sharp and Maynard-Moody conclude, municipalities are "distinctly junior partners in a complex, intergovernmental system" (1991, 934). Thus, rather than reflect the preferences of local actors, local government spending may be more likely to reflect functional responsibilities imposed by others.

The Empirical Study of Local Policymaking

Along with these diverse theoretical accounts has come a parallel methodological narrative that has helped move us closer to a definitive account of the local policy-making context. The first attempts to answer the question of who governs relied largely on a reputation approach (Hunter, 1953; Mills, 1956) Scholars simply asked local actors to provide the names of individuals who were influential in local decision-making. That approach led inexorably to a small set of elite business leaders who, at least by the bulk of local perceptions, dominated the local political arena.

Dahl (1961) and other pluralists provided very different evidence to counter this elite perspective and to help support their own pluralist account. Rather than relying on the opinions of local actors, Dahl scrutinized a range of active local decisions in the city of New Haven. In each case, he determined which actors were involved, what the outcome of the process was, and then most importantly, whose preferences were aligned with that outcome. The striking finding from this kind of active decision-making approach was that in most cities winners shifted from one policy arena to the next (Sayre and Kaufman, 1960; Dahl, 1961). No single interest dominated. Rather, local policy appeared to be open to a range of divergent actors and interests. This decisional approach–modified in myriad ways–became the backbone for some of the most important analytical studies of major cities throughout the United States. These single city studies offered keen insight into the workings of a particular locale and helped to delineate the nature, dynamics, and consequences of machine leadership (Bridges, 1984; Royko, 1971), growth politics (Swanstrom, 1985; Davis, 1992), and other hybrid regimes (Stone, 1989).

An important early methodological critique of the pluralist approach that is still valid today and that could be directed at any of the different approaches is that urban scholars have tended to limit their attention to active decisions and ignored other potentially more important conflicts that are kept off the local agenda. True power, according to Bachrach and Baratz (1962), resided in the ability to prevent key reforms from even being considered. While research into the "two faces of power" provided an important corrective to pluralist accounts, researchers have, unfortunately, seldom been able to effectively identify or empirically assess areas of non-decision making.

The next important methodological step for scholars was to expand their empirical scope beyond the confines of a single city and to begin to engage in larger cross-city comparisons. Research to that point had greatly advanced our understanding of how different cities worked but it was hard to offer meaningful generalizations about urban politics based an analysis that rarely incorporated patterns from more than one or two cities. At the forefront of these comparative case study analyses were compelling accounts that highlighted the distinct nature of different subsets of cities (Browning et al., 1984; Welch and Bledsoe, 1988; Erie, 1988; Bridges, 1997).

The final logical step in this line of reasoning was to expand the scope of the research even further by trying to offer analyses of a representative set of cities that could speak to general tendencies across the entire nation. Using this large N approach, early seminal pieces by Peterson (1981), Morgan and Pelissero (1980), and Kerr and Mladenka (1994) analyzed key aspects of local government decision-making. With ever increasing data availability and an ever broadening set of empirical tools to analyze that data, the bulk of the published work on local government policymaking now consists mainly of different types of large N empirical tests. Although these kinds of studies have tended to offer little in the way of theoretical innovation, they have provided informative tests of specific policy areas.

WHO IS RIGHT? MYRIAD FINDINGS ON LOCAL GOVERNANCE

Ultimately then, which of these different theoretical perspectives about local government policy-making is right? Unfortunately, despite decades of research and a wide range of studies, researchers have been unable to offer a clear answer to this question. Instead, different empirical approaches examining different aspects of local government policy-making have often led to contrasting conclusions about local democracy.

Those who study economic influences, generally find that they matter. For example, Sharp and Maynard-Moody (1991) determined that the overall fiscal capacity of a municipality was critical in explaining local welfare spending. As predicted by Peterson (1981), cities with more money could afford to spend more on welfare. In another sign that competition for mobile capital restrains government spending, Schneider (1989) likewise found that cities that faced more competition from neighboring localities were apt to reduce overall spending. Likewise, Green and Fleischmann (1991) found that cities that had greater poverty tended to not to spend more on poverty alleviation but instead channeled their limited resources to development policy.

But research that seeks to understand the impact of different political factors also generally concludes that politics is of vital importance in the local political arena. Donovan and Neiman (1992) show quite clearly that the balance of local partisanship affects the adoption of local growth control ordinances. Mayoral partisanship has also been linked to local spending (Gerber and Hopkins, 2011; but see Ferreira and Gyourko, 2009). Partisanship also seems to be influential at different stages of service provision (Jones, 1981 but see Mladenka, 1980). Moreover, the impact of politics appears to extend beyond partisanship. Among other findings, several scholars have demonstrated a range of significant, if relatively small, impacts of minority representation on social welfare spending (Karnig and Welch, 1980), minority civil service employment (Eisinger,1982; Kerr and Mladenka, 1994), police practices (Browning, Marshall and Tabb, 1984), and educational policy (Meier and England, 1984; Meier et al., 1991). And others have linked voter turnout to government spending priorities (Hajnal, 2010). Surprisingly little, however, has been done to tie outcomes to citizen ideology or residents' issue preferences. One exception is in the area of policy implementation. Using surveys of police chiefs as well as contextual data, Haider-Markel (2002) found evidence of a link between (surrogates of) citizen preferences, local hate-crime policy, and law enforcement actions on hate-crime.

At the same time, studies that focus on institutional structure more often than not find it is the driving force behind local government policy. Sharp and Maynard-Moody (1991), in particular, conclude that social welfare spending is dominated by mandates from above. Other support for a top-down federalist view of municipal politics comes from Saltzstein (1989). Moreover, support for the power of institutions is not limited to a focus on federal structure. Although formal tests of local institutions have not all pointed in the same direction, there seems fairly strong evidence that at-large elections and other reform institutions can be used to limit participation which enables the local governing coalition to target amenities to their core supporters—often middle-class white residents (Bridges, 1997; Trounstine, 2008). Clingermayer and Feiock (2001) have also linked a variety of formal local institutions with different kinds of development policy. And Sharp (2002) has found a relationship between more open local institutions and more democratic outcomes on moral issues like gay rights and abortion. Finally, there is some suggestion that metropolitan areas with a more fragmented institutional structure are more likely to experience sprawl and to suffer from greater inequities (Lewis, 1996). Still other tests show limited institutional effects. Reformed structures matter little for gender representation (Bullock and MacManus, 1991) and, at least in one study, for the types of expenditures that municipalities choose (Morgan and Pellissero, 1980).[2]

Finally, there is also ample evidence that local policy decisions are based largely on the needs of the population and are thus more about technical efficiency than political, economic, or institutional imperatives. Boyle and Jacobs (1982), for example, find that the least advantaged neighborhoods in New York City received the most money for social services like welfare, education, and health services. Likewise, Mladenka (1980, 1981) showed that the distribution of services in Chicago was, with few exceptions, a function of population shifts, technological changes, and other professional criteria. In the same vein, Feiock and West (1993) find a clear link between actual needs and the adoption of solid waste recycling programs. Finally, Lewis and Ramakrishnan (2007) show that police practices toward immigrants are driven more by a range of pragmatic needs than by political sentiment and leadership.

Although each of these studies adds to our understanding of local policy-making, the sum of their parts is not as great as one might hope. In many ways, the end result of all of this research is confusion about what really matters in local democracy. There is little doubt that each of these different theoretical perspectives accurately reflects the local governing process in at least some domains and contexts. But because of the sheer variety of the findings, we get little sense of the overall picture. What is the dominant factor shaping local politics? What are the relative contributions of economic constraints, political imperatives, institutional structures, and bureaucratic needs?

Ongoing Concerns

In short, despite enormous attention to this question, developing and testing a model that definitively identifies the real power players in local democracy has proven to be a difficult task. The barriers have been both empirical and conceptual.[3] On the empirical side, two critical barriers stand out. First, one of the main problems with existing studies is that they have generally failed to offer tests that place each of these different accounts of urban policy making against each other in a single empirical model. Two of the most seminal studies of local democracy provide two of the clearest examples of this phenomenon. In trying to show that economic considerations dominate decision-making, Peterson (1981) includes no measures of political inputs in his analysis of local government behavior. Similarly, Dahl (1961) argues that political considerations are central but fails to incorporate potentially critical economic factors into his analysis. Subsequent research has done a better job of integrating a broader set of perspectives in their empirical models (e.g. Schneider, 1989; Sharp and Maynard-Moody, 1991; Donovan and Neiman, 1992; Feiock and West, 1993; Goetz, 1994) but few of these studies manage to incorporate the entire range of potential factors. Practically speaking, until we have a test that puts all of the different alternatives in one model, we cannot know who is right.

An equally important concern is that the few studies that have been able to incorporate each of the different theoretical accounts in one model are generally forced to limit their analysis to a narrow subset of policy questions. Feiock and West (1993), for example, are able to include a comprehensive set of independent variables but focus solely on the adoption of recycling programs. Similarly, Wald et al. (1996) provide a systematic analysis that is limited to understanding the adoption of sexual orientation anti-discrimination ordinances. We also now have a better idea of which factors govern decisions relating to gay rights (Sharp, 2002) and same-sex partner domestic partner policies (Haider-Markel et al., 2000). The problem is that we cannot assume that the variables that matter in one subset of the policy arena matter in others. We are, in short, missing the bigger picture. How does all of this add up to shape the overall pattern of local government priorities?[4]

Finally, even if these two empirical problems can be overcome, one conceptual problem remains. How do we define the players in the game of local politics and once identified, how do we assess and incorporate the interests of the various different players into our empirical models. In order to determine how well local democracy represents different local actors, we first need to know who the potential players are and what the preferences of the different players are. Put even more simply, we need to know who is competing, what they fighting over, and what each side wants.

And on these kinds of questions, urban politics research has been relatively quiet. We have plenty of national public opinion surveys and exit polls that can—at the national level—tell us not only what the main issues of the day are but also reveal which subsets of the population are most divided on those issues. But we cannot assume that the core issues and the key players at the national level are paralleled at the local level. Thus, we need to do similar leg work at the local level. However, in large part because of the costs involved and the disparate nature and timing of local elections, we have precious few surveys that go out to a representative sample of cities and respondents that also focus on local politics.

This is not to say that surveys, exit polls, and other in-depth analyses of issues and divisions at the local level do not exist. They do. And they can be compelling. In particular, there is fairly clear evidence that race can be a significant source of division in local politics. Of the many studies that focus on voting patterns by race, most find that racial divisions strongly structure vote choice in the cities and elections that they include in their studies (Lieske and Hillard, 1984; Henig, 1993; Collet, 2005; Barreto, 2007). But the evidence is not entirely consistent. Others find that the nature and size of racial divisions can vary considerably across cities and elections (Hajnal, 2006, Deleon and Naff, 2004, Kaufmann, 2004). And while we know something about the vote by race in a number of cities, we know considerably less about how much race or racial considerations shape policy preferences on the range of urban issues facing local governments (but see Lovrich, 1974; Alozie and McNamara, 2008).

Evidence on the relevance of class, partisanship, and ideology in local democracy is even sparser. Abrajano and Alvarez (2005) have identified ideology as a primary determinant of vote choice in one set of elections in Los Angeles and Oliver and Ha (2007) found that partisanship played an important role in suburban contests. In similar work, Krebs (1998) and Deleon (1992) found evidence of ideological divisions in Chicago and San Francisco. By contrast, in Bridges' (1997) analysis of several southwestern cities, class emerged as the primary electoral dividing line (but see Schneider, 1987;

Logan and Molotch, 1987; Clark, 1996). There has also been important work on sexuality and urban voting behavior (Wald et al., 1996; Bailey, 1999).

But in the end these studies are often limited to one election in one city or at most a number of respondents in handful of cities.[5] And they often reach contradictory conclusions about the players and divisions shaping local democracy. Surveys at particular times in particular locales and in-depth analysis of the politics of a single city can and do help to inform us about what residents care about in one context but it is dangerous to offer generalizations from these limited cases (Lovrich, 1974; Sonenshein, 1993; Mollenkopf, 1994; Alozie and McNamara, 2008).[6]

The result is that we lack sufficient understanding of just what urban politics is about. What are the core issues of the day in local politics? Do residents care most about local taxes, local race relations, local development policy, local services, or any number of other issues?[7] Or is local politics largely issueless as some maintain (Raymond, 1992)? Just as importantly, what are the dividing lines amongst the public on these core issues? Is local politics largely an ideological battle between liberals and conservatives, principally a class-based conflict between haves and have-nots, or primarily a racial contest between racial and ethnic groups?[8] Or are the contenders defined more by geography with different neighborhoods seeking to reallocate resources to within their own boundaries? In short, we need to know much more about the underlying distribution of interests at the local level and the dividing lines that are common across cities.

DIRECTIONS FOR FUTURE RESEARCH

How then do we move forward? In this next section, I highlight three different research paths that are derived directly from the three issues that I have identified. I then proceed to highlight three other research topics that flow less from past research and are instead areas where dramatic demographic changes provide a particularly strong motivation for study or where new technologies allow for potentially insightful new research.

Given the limited focus on broad outcomes that might provide insight into the overall winners and losers of local democracy, the first task is to come up with measures of important outcomes. There are myriad ways to think about and measure outcomes in the political arena. One obvious outcome that has been analyzed in depth is the kinds of candidates who win office. Studies of descriptive representation, in fact, abound in the urban politics literature (Bullock and MacManus, 1987, 1991; Alozie and Manganaro, 1993; Hajnal and Trounstine, 2005). We now know, for example, that while local institutional structure plays little role in the election of women to office at the local level (Bullock and MacManus, 1991), it can be critical in fostering the representation of blacks, Latinos, and Asian Americans in elected office (Bowler et al., 2003; Hajnal and Trounstine, 2005).

Another alternative is to assess which kinds of voters end up on the winning and losing side of elections. Do voters from a particular racial group, for example, consistently fail to get their candidates elected? Or similarly, is one political party better able to translate votes into seats than another? The number of articles addressing this latter topic is equally large (Stein and Kohfeld, 1991; Lieske, 1989; McCrary, 1990; Krebs, 1998; Hajnal, 2009).

These are, however, only interim outcomes. It matters which voters win and then who is elected to office but once in office elected officials still need to act. They have to choose which direction to take their city, district, or state. It is certainly important to uncover the factors that lead to greater openness to minority influence on the vote but counts of the number of female, black, Latino, or gay elected officials tell us little about how effective those representatives are once in office.[9] The end result could be widespread descriptive representation that fails to deliver real policy benefits. Ultimately what matters is not who is in government but rather what that government does. To determine who wins and who loses, we need to home in on the end products of local government— policies themselves.

Scholars have spent considerable effort assessing what local government does. But, as already noted, the bulk of these studies end with consideration of a particular policy decision or with an analysis of a small subset of policy areas; if we want to understand the big picture of who wins and why, we need to provide a measure that delineates the basic priorities of local government.

One relatively straightforward way to gauge this kind of overarching agenda is to look at how governments spend their money. At the local level, municipalities spend a lot of money—almost $1.5 trillion in 2007 (U.S. Census, 2007). Where that money goes and where it does not go obviously can have real consequences for large segments of the population. Given that cities and other localities have limited budgets and often limited means of raising extra resources, where they choose to spend their money is arguably one of the most important indications of their priorities. Money may also be one of the better markers of a program's reach or impact. Unless a local government actually commits substantial economic resources to a policy, the policy will often have a marginal impact.[10] A relatively brief assessment of local government budgets can thus provide us with a preliminary look at local government winners and losers. If we can break down spending into a reasonable set of categories, we can get a rough, first cut at the local policymaking environment.

Local governments can spend money on any number of different functions or programs.[11] Scholars of urban politics have, however, tended to classify spending into three basic categories (Peterson, 1981; Stein, 1990). According to this traditional accounting, local governments can choose to devote their resources to redistributive, developmental, or allocational spending. Redistributive policies are those that tend to target and benefit less advantaged residents. They include functions like welfare, public housing, health care, and education. Development policy, by contrast, tends to focus on programs which seek to encourage economic growth and the ongoing economic vitality of a city. Developmental spending includes outlays for highways, streets, transportation, and airports. Finally, allocational policy is defined as spending on a range of basic city services that can be considered housekeeping services. This includes services like police and fire protection, and sanitation.[12]

Using this categorization Figure 22.1 illustrates the spending patterns of local governments over the past 15 years.[13]

Probably, the most notable pattern that emerges is the limited nature of redistributive spending. Of all the money local governments spend, on average only 3.8 percent is directed toward redistributive functions. Particular redistributive programs like welfare (0.3 percent), public housing (1.7 percent), and public health (0.7 percent) each represent tiny fractions of government spending.[14] In short, the poor and the disadvantaged are not the main target of local government spending. This pattern seems to fit well with the economic imperatives story outlined by Peterson (1981). Cities are generally avoiding spending on redistributive programs that could be viewed as costly and unproductive—at least if one's main priority is attracting mobile capital.

At the same time, developmental spending far from dominates local government expenditures—spending on highways, streets, transportation, airports, and other general construction projects amounts on average to 20 percent of local budgets. This may outweigh redistributive spending, but it suggests that cities may not see development and the attraction of capital as their number one priority.

In fact, allocational spending accounts for the bulk of spending across these three core categories. On average, localities spend 31 percent of their budgets on police and fire protection, parks and recreation, sewage and waste. We cannot tell from these basic statistics whether localities spend money on these services to attract and retain middle- and upper-class residents and businesses, because they are pressured to do so by voters, or because higher levels of government force them to do so, or simply to meet the needs of their residents. Nevertheless, judging by these numbers, it is clear is that a big part of the job of local government is simply to provide basic services to their residents.

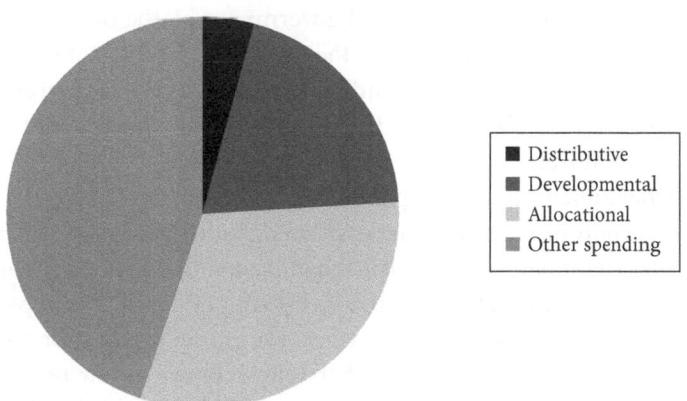

FIGURE 22.1 Local government spending

Note: Developed by the author based on data from the U.S. Census of Governments (2007).

Overall, these basic spending patterns suggest that the big losers in the arena of local democracy are those who favor more redistribution. Judging by the limited local survey data we have, that tends to be the poor, minorities, and other disadvantaged groups. These spending figures also suggest that the main winners are those who demand more basic services (often the white middle class). Substantial resources are also spent on development and in that sense business also comes out on top.

A quick examination of basic spending patterns is, however, far from the last word on local government policymaking. Critically, by looking at the overall distribution, it is difficult to infer the motivations of local policymakers. For example, since the direction of local government spending is in part mandated by state and federal grants, laws, and agencies, these patterns, in some ways, reflect the priorities of state and national government as much as they do local government priorities. Preexisting institutions and spending patterns may further constrain the current policymakers in any given city and help to shape the overall spending patterns we see. If we really want to understand local democracy, we have to understand the factors driving these local spending patterns.

To get at what is driving spending patterns, we need to focus on and analyze variation in local spending across municipalities or at changes in local spending over time in the same localities (e.g. Schneider, 1987; Hajnal, 2005). Fortunately, another quick examination of the spending data makes it clear that there is enormous variation in the pattern of expenditure across different localities. While the average municipality spends only 3.8 percent on redistribution, the standard deviation in redistributive spending across localities is 9.0 percent. At one extreme, over 10 percent of all municipalities spend a third or more of their expenditures on distributive functions. At the other, 10 percent spend next to nothing on policies like welfare, health, and housing. And although variation across cities is, in many ways, most remarkable for distributive spending, there is also considerable deviation in spending patterns for developmental and allocational expenditures. Across the nation, the standard deviation for developmental spending is 16.4 percent and for allocational spending 14.4 percent. Cities do not spend all of their money on the same things. Moreover, this variation in spending is not due solely to the different mandates that are placed on local government by the different state legislatures. There is still considerable variation in the allocation of funds for different cities in the same state. Standard deviation in spending within states is only marginally smaller than the nationwide figures. What all of this suggests is that there is a lot to explain in terms of local expenditures.

Even after we have uncovered basic spending patterns and the factors that drive them, urban scholars will only be partway to understanding local democracy. The distribution of spending is important but in the end it is the impact of that spending that really matters. For that, we need to look at the relative well-being of different groups across both time and context. Is the black-white income gap, for example, narrowing more rapidly in some cities than it is in others and if so, what policies or leaders are responsible for it? Similarly, by examining changes in the well-being of the bottom third of the income distribution vs. the top third, we can begin to get at the relative impact of local democracy on different classes. Measuring changes in the well-being of different groups at different times in different localities will not be easy, but outcomes like education, income, and employment are fundamental to understanding who is really losing, who is really gaining, and whether cities and local policy-making actually make a difference in the lives of residents.

A second equally important way forward concerns the production of data on basic preferences and the priorities of individual residents. As already noted, one of the most glaring absences in the study of local democracy is a thorough understanding of underlying divisions and policy preferences. Put simply, we have limited knowledge about what different groups in society want out of local government. What are their priorities? What are their policy positions on areas they are concerned about? And which sets of groups are most in conflict over those priorities and policy positions? Is local politics largely about class, race, ideology, party, neighborhood, or any number of other potentially relevant dimensions? The reason for this limited knowledge is clear—we do not have enough large-scale cross-city survey data on local public opinion. Given the problem, the way forward is clear—if expensive and time consuming. Researchers need to produce broad, nationwide surveys that focus on local issues.[15] These kinds of surveys are beginning to emerge and work by Oliver and Ha (2007) and others should be highlighted. But much more needs to be done. We already have a reasonably good understanding of divisions in the vote but in terms of divisions in policy, we are sorely lacking. Thus, new data accumulation should focus on the policy arena more than anything else. This will be hard work. The diversity of municipalities and institutional structures at the local level make it difficult to know what to ask and even harder to develop standard questions that apply across contexts. The monetary costs are also high. Surveys with sizeable samples and a representative set of cities are expensive. One potential solution—and perhaps even requirement—is collaborative research. Despite the costs, this kind of work is essential. Without good data on the players and issues that are the core of urban democracy, we have little hope of understanding the dynamics of local policy-making and even less hope of identifying winners and losers in local democracy.

A third research imperative is to combine the first two areas of study into comprehensive empirical tests. Once we have the right outcomes and the right inputs, we need to put it all together. We need to undertake more large N studies that are simultaneously able to examine major outcomes and include a comprehensive list of independent factors that could explain those outcomes. Only then will we be able to offer more authoritative statements about the factors that govern winning and losing in local democracy. In this vein, one method that could be particularly effective is time-series analysis. Given that local policy at any one point in time is strongly constrained by the outcomes of years or even decades of past policymaking, it may be more informative to look at marginal changes in policy rather than at overall policy. Change may isolate the factors that matter today, while absolute levels may incorporate influences from a diverse range of times and factors.

In addition to these three basic tasks, I would also call for more study of three areas of local democracy that have either become particularly important in light of demographic developments or that have become particularly feasible in light of technological developments.

The increase in large scale immigration and the transformation of America's racial and ethnic landscape raises a number of core questions about racial dynamics that beg for analysis at the local level. As we shift from a black-white dichotomy in which whites largely dominated to today's multi-racial complexity, it becomes more important and more difficult to understand American race relations and the nature of America's racial hierarchy. With a larger minority population and a more diverse set of racial groups, the imperatives for inter-racial cooperation grow and the sheer number of possible combinations of inter-racial coalitions multiplies. At the same time, an influx of a large number of "outsiders" raises concerns that natives will respond to this racial threat in any number of negative ways. In short, as the nation diversifies, questions about racial identity, inter-racial coalition building, and inter-racial conflict will all become more and more central.

Fortunately, local politics is the perfect venue to begin to answer these increasingly important questions. A large number of municipalities and wide variation in the racial makeup of those different localities means that scholars of local politics have more than enough cases and more than enough variation to get at core questions related to inter-racial dynamics. By looking at a representative range of localities, we can acquire a basic sense of which groups tend to work with which other groups, which groups are regularly in conflict with which other groups, and more generally assess how strained or cooperative race relations really are. Similarly, by looking at different cities, we can uncover the city-level characteristics that are associated with cooperation between say whites and Asian Americans and the factors that lead to conflict between—for example—blacks and Latinos. Through these investigations we can learn how different economic, demographic institutional features exacerbate tensions or encourage cooperation. And perhaps most importantly, by looking at different municipalities we can garner insight about the future of race relations in America. The racial makeup of many cities today mirrors the likely demographics of the nation in the decades to come. By focusing on and understanding how race "works" in these cities, we can predict how race will work in America and, if we are lucky, we can begin to try to mitigate some of the more problematic aspects of race. These questions are just as important at the national level as they are at the local level but there is little doubt that we can get more purchase on them at the local level.

The transformation from a primarily urban nation to a primarily suburban nation also suggests an arena for greater research. There have certainly been a number of important studies about geography and the importance of context in understanding local democracy. Oliver and Ha's (2007) analysis of the suburban vote comes to mind. Similarly, Burns (1994) has offered keen insight into the motivations behind the formation of different municipalities. And Jackson (1985) and Dreier et al. (2005) have in different ways underscored the importance of geography. But all too often, the study of local politics still means the study of urban politics. The suburbanization of American and the increasing number and diversity of municipal structures (e.g. local service districts and gated communities) mean that to understand how local democracy works, we need more than ever to understand how different kinds of places are different from each other. How does the politics of suburbia differ from the politics of central cities? Are the issues, divisions, and players the same or different? How does decision-making in "old-style" city governments differ from decision-making in local service districts or within the confines of gated communities. And critically, how are relations between these different governmental entities structured? Increasingly, if we want to do our jobs well, we need to consider context more seriously and be aware of the different kinds of places that individual Americans live in.

I would also call for the renewed study of elite politics. Decades ago, the study of the local policymaking began with a single-minded focus on local leaders (e.g. Hunter, 1953; Caro, 1974). That singular focus was not warranted. As many studies have shown, beyond a small cadre of leaders there are other actors and institutions that matter in local democracy. Since those early days we have perhaps moved too far away from the study of local elites. With a few important exceptions (e.g. Pelissero and Krebs, 1997; Trounstine, 2008), studies of local politics have not gone into depth in seeking to understand government leaders and the issues and motivations that govern their behavior. My guess is that this lack of attention is largely due to empirical barriers—it is often hard to assess the actions of a small number of leaders in a systematic way.[16] But new empirical techniques in other fields can now be applied to local elites to help answer core questions about local democracy. Specifically, new empirical tools, like Keith Poole's Nominate, that have revolutionized the study of Congress in the United States and legislatures in other countries could be harnessed to help researchers categorize roll-call voting in city councils and other local decision-making bodies. The result could be answers to questions like: what are the basic dimensions governing city council voting? What is the nature of the governing coalition in most cities? What are the district level factors that govern individual city council behavior?

Finally, in all of the endeavors that I am suggesting, I believe it is critical that scholars of local politics speak to the larger literature in American politics and beyond. If urban politics is to be as central in the field of political science as it once was, we have to ask questions that others beyond our field believe are important. And we have to answer those questions in unique and insightful ways. Fortuitously, with an extremely large number of cases and substantial variation across those cases, we have the basic empirical tools to answer almost any question political scientists can dream up. Urban politics once led the study of political science. It can lead again.

NOTES

1. While not entirely dismissing the notion that cities have to compete for people and capital, pluralists argue that there is ample room for politics to matter. Either because the constraints of the local economic marketplace are not totally binding or because a wider range of policies can be considered productive, there is considerable space within which city officials can move policy.

2. One concern with these institutional analyses is that they tend to assume that institutions are static or exogenous. But new evidence suggests that local institutions are often altered by local power players for their own advantage (Aghion et al., 2004; Trounstine, 2008). Thus it becomes difficult to know if institutions themselves independently shape outcomes or if local power players are the primary determinant of outcomes.

3. Beyond the three core concerns noted below are ongoing questions about sample size and measurement. Some of the more intriguing research is hurt by the limited number of cases it includes. We can, for example, follow the process of social services spending in New York City (Boyle and Jacobs, 1982) but will that inform us about decisions on the distribution of parks and other services in Chicago (Mladenka, 1980; Kochler and Wrightson, 1987) and will either case study give us a clear picture of what matters in cities around the nation? Case studies are important and insightful but broader studies are also needed, particularly ones that include smaller cities and suburbs in which the majority of the American public lives.

4. When research does attempt to get at these broader outcomes, it often has to revert to the use of subjective evaluations to determine who is responding to whom (Donovan and Neiman, 1992; Goetz, 1994; Hajnal and Clark, 1995). Asking elected officials which actors they respond to, as Hajnal and Clark (1995) do may say more about how the officials want to be perceived than about how they govern (also see Haider-Markel, 2004 on perception and misperception by local officials). To get at a better assessment of responsiveness, we need more concrete and objective measures of responses.

5. Broader data is, fortunately, beginning to emerge. The Knight Foundation's Community Indicators Surveys of 2000 and 2002 interviewed large numbers of respondents in 26 cities, Oliver and Ha (2009) undertook a fairly extensive survey of politics in 30 suburban communities, and Thomas Holbrook recently surveyed 40 cities across the country. Nevertheless, none of these projects allows for a wide-ranging assessment of political divisions and issues across a representative sample of municipalities.

6. In the absence of the systematic surveying of issue concerns and preferences across a wide, representative sample of municipalities, a number of studies have tried to assess winners and losers using demographics as a shortcut for different political interests (e.g. Banfield and Wilson, 1967; Clark and Ferguson, 1983, Koehler and Wrightson, 1987). But without knowing whether these demographic measures correspond to significant divisions within the community, analyzing variables like percent black or percent homeowner won't provide a definitive assessment of local policymaking.

7. Of course, it is possible and even likely that the issues that residents care about vary considerably from one resident to the next. That makes the task of determining the core issues and the winners and losers on those issues more difficult but no less necessary.

8. And if it is racial contest, then which racial and ethnic groups are pitted against each other?

9. A focus on descriptive representation also makes problematic assumptions about who can and who cannot represent minorities or other disadvantaged groups. Do white elected officials, in particular, never represent minority interests (Hajnal, 2009)? One study that does explore representation by members of a group versus sympathetic non-members is Haider-Markel et al. (2001), where the authors examine the relative influence of gay officials versus straight sympathetic officials in the adoption of local domestic partner policies.

10. Money is, of course, not a perfect measure of priorities or even of impact. It is clear that by focusing on spending one overlooks a range of critical decisions that are undetectable in budgets.

11. Local governments can also affect policy through more fundamental fiscal decisions like raising money via higher taxes or incurring greater debt. In other words, they can change the size of the existing revenue stream (see Schneider, 1988, 1989, and Krebs, 1997, for analysis of total government size and spending).

12. In the analysis that follows, spending on these three categories accounts on average for 55.5 percent of total government spending. Other government functions like debt repayment, insurance costs, and government administration are more difficult to categorize and do not fit neatly into this scheme.

13. Specifically, this is average spending for all cities surveyed by the International City Managers Association between 1991 and 2006. There is no stark pattern of change between the different years of the survey.

14. Another 4.6 percent is directed toward education, which, although generally redistributive in nature, can also regularly serve more advantaged segments of the community.

15. Conventional public opinion surveys are not the only option. Detailed data on priorities, preferences, and divisions can also be acquired by looking at campaign coverage, by analyzing public protests and other types of political gatherings, by examining public comments to politicians (both public and private), and other instances where public sentiments about policy are expressed. But collecting this data in a systematic and representative manner is by no means a small task.

16. A focus on voters rather than elites may also be because many believe that elites must respond to the imperatives of the electoral process. Yet, recent research suggests that local elites can and do manipulate institutions and other variables to mold their electoral coalitions (Trounstine, 2008). Moreover, even if elites are driven by voters rather than vice-versa, by studying elite behavior we may still be able to uncover what voters want.

REFERENCES

Abrajano, Marisa, and R. Michael Alvarez. 2005. A Natural Experiment of Race-Based and Issue Voting: The 2001 City of Los Angeles Elections. *American Politics Quarterly 58* (2): 203–218.

Aghion, Phillippe, Alberto Alesina, and Francesco Trebbi. 2004. Endogenous Political Institutions. *Quarterly Journal of Economics 119* (May): 565–612.

Alozie, Nicholas O., and Lynne L. Manganaro. 1993. Black and Hispanic Council Representation: Does Council Size Matter? *Urban Affairs Quarterly 29*: 276–298.

Alozie, Nicholas O., and Catherine McNamara. 2008. Anglo and Latino Differences in Willingness to Pay for Urban Public Services. *Social Science Quarterly 89*(2): 406–427.

Bachrach, Peter, and Morton S. Baratz. 1962. "The Two Faces of Power." *American Political Science Review 56* (4 (December)):947–52.

Bailey, Robert W. 1999. *Gay Politics, Urban Politics: Identity and Economics in the Urban Setting.* New York: Columbia University Press.

Banfield, Edward C., and James Q. Wilson. 1967. *City Politics.* Cambridge: Harvard University Press.

Barreto, Matt. 2007. Si Se Puede! Latino Candidates and the Mobilization of Latino Voters. *American Political Science Review 101* (3 (August)): 425–441.

Bowler, Shaun, Todd Donovan, and David Brockington. 2003. *Electoral Reform and Minority Representation: Local Experiments with Alternative Elections.* Columbus: Ohio State University Press.

Boyle, John, and David Jacobs. 1982. The Intracity Distribution of Services: A Multivariate Analysis. *The American Political Science Review 76* (2 (June)): 371–379.

Bridges, Amy. 1984. *A City in the Republic: Antebellum New York and the Origins of machine politics*. Cambridge: Cambridge University Press.

Bridges, Amy. 1997. *Morning Glories: Municipal Reform in the Southwest*. Princeton: Princeton University Press.

Browning, Rufus R., Dale Rogers Marshall, and David H. Tabb. 1984. *Protest is Not Enough*. Berkeley: University of California Press.

Buchanan, James. 1971. Principles of Urban Fiscal Strategy. *Public Choice 11*: 1–14.

Bullock, Charles, and Susan MacManus. 1987. Staggered Terms and Black Representation. *The Journal of Politics 49* (2 (May)): 543–552.

Bullock, Charles S., and Susan A. MacManus. 1991. Municipal Electoral Structure and the Election of Councilwomen. *Journal of Politics 53* (1 (February)): 75–89.

Burns, Nancy. 1994. *The Formation of American Local Governments*. New York: Oxford University Press.

Caro, Robert. 1974. *The Power Broker: Robert Moses and the Fall of New York*. New York: Knopf.

Clark, Terry N. 1996. Structural Realignments in American City Politics: Less Class, More Race and a New Political Culture. *Urban Affairs Review 31*(3): 367–403.

Clark, Terry N., and Lorna C. Ferguson. 1983. *City Money*. New York: Columbia University Press.

Clingermayer, James C., and Richard C. Feiock. 2001. *Institutional Constraints and Policy Choice: An Exploration of Local Governance*. Albany: State University of New York.

Collet, Christian. 2005. Bloc Voting, Polarization and the Panethnic Hypothesis: The Case of Little Saigon. *The Journal of Politics 67*(3): 907–933.

Dahl, Robert A. 1961. *Who Governs? Democracy and Power in the American City*. New Haven: Yale University Press.

Davis, Mike. 1992. *City of Quartz*. New York: Vintage Books.

Deleon, Richard. 1992. *Left Coast City*: Left Coast City: Progressive Politics in San Francisco, 1975–1991. Lawrence, KA: University of Kansas Press.

DeLeon, Richard, and Katherine C. Naff. 2004. Identity Politics and Local Political Culture. *Urban Affairs Review 39* (6 (July)): 689–719.

Donovan, Todd, and Max Neiman. 1992. Citizen Mobilization and the Adoption of Local Growth Control. *Western Political Quarterly 45* (3 (September)): 651–675.

Dreier, Mollenkopf, and Swanstrom. 2005. *Place Matters*. Kansas University Press.

Dye, Thomas. 1987. *Understanding Public Policy*. Englewood Cliffs, NJ: Prentice-Hall.

Eisenger, Peter K. 1982. "Black Employment in Municipal Jobs: The Impact of Black Political Power." *American Political Science Review 76*:380–92.

Elkin, Stephen L. 1987. *City and Regime in the American Republic*. Chicago: University of Chicago Press.

Erie, Steven. 1988. *Rainbow's End: Irish-Americans and the Dilemmas of Urban Machine Politics, 1840–1985*. Berkeley: University of California Press.

Feiock, Richard C., and Johathan P. West. 1993. Testing Competing Explanations for Policy Adoption: Municipal Solid Waste Recycling Programs. *Political Research Quarterly 46* (2 (June)): 399–419.

Ferreira, Fernando, and Joseph Gyourko. 2009. Do Political Parities Matter? Evidence from U. S. Cities. *The Quarterly Journal of Economics 124* (1): 399–422.

Finegold, Robert. 1995. *Experts and Politicians: Reform Challenges to Machine Politics in New York, Cleveland, and Chicago*. Princeton, NJ: Princeton University Press.

Gerber, Elisabether, and Daniel Hopkins. 2011. When Mayors Matter: Estimating the Impact of Mayoral Partisanship on City Policy. *American Journal of Political Science* 55 (2):326–339.

Goetz, Edward G. 1994. Expanding Possibilities in Local Development Policy: An Examination of U. S. Cities. *Political Research Quarterly 47* (1 (March)): 85–109.

Gosnell, Harold F. 1968. *Machine Politics: Chicago Model.* Chicago: University of Chicago.

Green, Gary P., and Arnold Fleischmann. 1991. Promoting Economic Development: A Comparison of Central Cities, Suburbs, and Nonmetropolitican Communities. *Urban Affairs Quarterly 27* (1(September)): 145–154.

Haider-Markel, Donald P. 2002. "Regulating Hate: State and Local Influences on Law Enforcement Actions Related to Hate Crime." *State Politics and Policy Quarterly 2* (2):126–160.

Haider-Markel, Donald P. 2004. "Perception and Misperception in Urban Criminal Justice Policy: The Case of Hate Crime." *Urban Affairs Review 39* (4):491–512.

Haider-Markel, Donald P, Mark R. Joslyn, and Chad J. Kniss. 2000. "Minority Group Interests and Political Representation: Gay Elected Officials in the Policy Process." *The Journal of Politics 62* (2): 568–577.

Hajnal, Zoltan, and Jessica Trounstine. 2005. Where Turnout Matters: The Consequences of Uneven Turnout in City Politics. *Journal of Politics 67* (2 (May)): 515–535.

Hajnal, Zoltan L. 2006. *Changing White Attitudes toward Black Political Leadership.* New York: Cambridge University Press.

Hajnal, Zoltan L. 2010. *America's Uneven Democracy: Turnout, Race, and Representation in City Politics.* Cambridge: Cambridge University Press.

Hajnal, Zoltan L. 2009. Who Loses in American Democracy? A Count of Votes Demonstrates the Limited Representation of African Americans. *American Political Science Review 103* (1 (February)): 37–57.

Hajnal, Zoltan L., and Terry N. Clark. 1998. The Local Interest Group System: Who Governs and Why? *Social Science Quarterly 79* (1): 227–241.

Henig, Jeffrey R. 1993. Race and Voting: Continuity and Change in the District of Columbia. *Urban Affairs Quarterly 28* (4): 544–573.

Hunter, Floyd. 1953. *Community Power Structure.* Chapel Hill, NC: University of North Carolina Press.

Jackson, Kenneth T. 1985. *Crabgrass Frontier: The Suburbanization of the United States.* New York: Oxford University Press.

Jones, Bryan D. 1981. Party and Bureaucracy: The Influence of Intermediary Groups on Urban Politics Public Service Delivery. *The American Political Science Review 75* (2): 689–700.

Judd, Dennis R., and Todd Swanstrom. 1994. *City Politics: Private Power and Public Policy.* New York: Harper Collins.

Karnig, Albert K., and Susan Welch. 1980. *Black Representation and Urban Policy.* Chicago: The University of Chicago Press.

Kaufmann, Karen. 2004. *The Urban Voter: Group Conflict and Mayoral Voting in American Cities.* Ann Arbor: University of Michigan Press.

Kerr, Brinck, and Kenneth R. Mladenka. 1994. Does Politics Matter? A Time-Series Analysis of Minority Employment Patters. *American Journal of Political Science 38* (4 (November)): 918–943.

Koehler, David H., and Margaret T. Wrightson. 1987. Inequality in the Delivery of Urban Services: A Reconsideration of the Chicago Parks. *The Journal of Politics 49* (1 (February)): 80–99.

Krebs, Timothy B. 1998. The Determinants of Candidates' Vote Share and Advantages of Incumbency in City Council Elections. *American Journal of Political Science 42* (July): 921–935.

Lewis, Paul G. 1996. *Shaping Surburbia: How Political Institutions Organize Urban Development*. Pittsburgh: University of Pittsburgh Press.

Lewis, Paul G., and S. Karthick Ramakrishnan. 2007. Police Practices in Immigrant-Destination Cities Political Control or Bureaucratic Professionalism? *Urban Affairs Review 42*(6): 874–900.

Lieske, Joel. 1989. The Political Dynamics of Urban Voting Behavior. *American Journal of Political Science 33*: 150–174.

Lieske, Joel, and Jan William Hillard. 1984. The Racial Factor in Urban Elections. *Western Political Quarterly 37*: 545–563.

Lineberry, Robert L. 1977. *Equality and Urban Politics: The Distribution of Municipal Public Services*. Beverly Hills: Sage.

Lineberry, Robert L., and Edmund P. Fowler. 1967. Reformism and Public Policies in American Cities. *The American Political Science Review 61* (September): 701–716.

Lipsky, MIchael. 1980. Street-Level Bureaucracy: Dillemas of the Individual In *Public Services*. New York: Russel Sage.

Logan, John R., and Harvey L. Molotch. 1987. *Urban Fortunes: The Political Economy of Place*. Berkeley: University of California Press.

Lovrich, Nicholas. 1974. Differing Priorities in an Urban Electorate: Service Priorities Among Anglo, Black, and Mexican-American Voters. *Social Science Quarterly 55* (2): 704–717.

McCrary, Peyton. 1990. Racially Polarized Voting in the South: Quantitative Evidence from the Courtroom. *Social Science History 14* (4): 507–531.

Meier, Kenneth J., and Robert E. England. 1984. "Black Representation and Educational Policy: Are They Related?" *American Political Science Review 78*: 392–403.

Meier, Kenneth J., Joseph Stewart Jr, and Robert E. England. 1991. The Politics of Bureaucratic Discretion: Educational Access and Urban Service. *American Journal of Political Science 35* (1 (February)): 155–177.

Mills, C. Wright. 1956. *The Power Elite*. New York: Oxford University Press.

Mladenka, Kenneth R. 1980. The Urban Bureaucracy and the Chicago Political Machine: Who Gets What and the Limits of Political Control. *The American Political Science Review 74* (2): 991–998.

Mladenka, Kenneth R. 1981. Citizen Demands and Urban Services: The Distribution of Bureaucratic Response in Chicago and Houston. *American Journal of Political Science 25* (4 (November)): 693–714.

Mladenka, Kenneth R. 1989. Blacks and Hispanics in Urban Politics. *American Political Science Review 83* (1): 165–191.

Mollenkopf, John H. 1994. *A Phoenix in the Ashes: The Rise and Fall of the Koch Coalition in New York City Politics*. Princeton: Princeton University Press.

Morgan, David R., and John P. Pelissero. 1980. Urban Policy: Does Political Structure Matter? *American Political Science Review 74* (4): 405–437.

Oliver, J. Eric. 2001. *Democracy in Suburbia*. Princeton, NJ: Princeton University Press.

Oliver, J. Eric, and Shang E. Ha. 2007. Vote Choice in Suburban Elections. *American Political Science Review 101* (3 (August)): 393–408.

Pelissero, John P., ed. 2003. *Cities, Politics, and Policy*. Washington: Congressional Quarterly Press.

Pelissero, John P., and Timothy B. Krebs. 1997. City Council Legislative Committees and Policy-Making in Large United States Cities. *American Journal of Political Science 41* (2 (April)): 499–518.

Peterson, Paul E. 1981. *City Limits*. Chicago: University of Chicago Press.

Raymond, Paul. 1992. The American Voter in a Nonpartisan, Urban Election. *American Politics Quarterly 20* (April): 247–260.

Royko, Mike. 1971. *Boss: Richard J. Daley of Chicago*. New York: Plume.

Saltzstein, Grace Hall. 1989. Black Mayors and Police Policies. *Journal of Politics 51* (3): 525–544.

Sass, Tim R. 2000. The Determinants of Hispanic Representation in Municipal Government. *Southern Economic Journal 66* (3): 609–630.

Sayre, Wallace S., and Herbert Kaufman. 1960. *Governing New York City*. New York: Russell Sage Foundation.

Schneider, Mark. 1987. Income Homogeneity and the Size of Suburban Government. *Journal of Politics 49*: 36–53.

Schneider, Mark. 1988. The Demand for the Suburban Public Work Force: Residents, Workers, and Politicians. *Journal of Politics 50*: 89–107.

Schneider, Mark. 1989. Intermunicipal Competition, Budget-Maximizing Bureaucrats, and the Level of Suburban Competition. *American Journal of Political Science 33* (3(August)): 612–628.

Sharp, Elaine B. 1991. Institutional Manifestations of Accessibility and Urban Economic Development Policy. *Western Political Quarterly 44* (1 (March)): 129–147.

Sharp, Elaine B. 2002. Culture, Institutions, and Urban Officials' Responses to Morality Issues. *Political Research Quarterly 55* (4 (December)): 861–883.

Sharp, Elaine B., and Steven Maynard-Moody. 1991. Theories of the Local Welfare Role. *American Journal of Political Science 35* (4 (November)): 934–950.

Sonenshein, Raphael J. 1993. *Politics in Black and White: Race and Power in Los Angeles*. Princeton, NJ: Princeton University Press.

Stein, Lana, and Carol W. Kohfeld. 1991. *St.* Louis's Black-White Elections: Products of Machine Factionalism and Polarization. *Urban Affairs Quarterly 27* (2): 227–248.

Stein, Robert M. 1990. *Urban Alternatives: Public and Private Markets in the Provision of Local Services*. Pittsburgh: University of Pittsburgh Press.

Stone, Clarence. 1989. *Regime Politics: Governing Atlanta, 1946–1988*. Lawrence: University Press of Kansas.

Swanstrom, Todd. 1985. *The Crisis of Growth Politics: Cleveland, Kucinich, and the Challenge of Urban Populism*. Philadelphia: Temple University Press.

Tiebout, Charles. 1956. A Pure Theory of Local Expenditures. *Journal of Political Economy 64*: 416–424.

Trounstine, Jessica. 2008. *Political Monopolies In American Cities: The Rise and Fall of Bosses and Reformers*. Chicago: University of Chicago Press.

U.S. Census Bureau. *U.S. Census of State and Local Governments—2007* [cited. Available from <http://www.census.gov//govs/local/historical_data_2007.html>.

Wald, Kenneth D., James W. Button, and Barbara A. Rienzo. 1996. The Politics of Gay Rights in American Communities: Explaining Antidiscrimination Ordinances and Policies. *American Journal of Political Science 40* (November): 1152–1178.

Welch, Susan. 1990. The Impact of At-Large Elections on the Representation of Blacks and Hispanics. *Journal of Politics 52*: 1050–1076.

Welch, Susan, and Timothy Bledsoe. 1988. *Urban Reform and Its Consequences*. Chicago: University of Chicago Press.

CHAPTER 23

THE CONTEXT OF STATE
POLICY POLICYMAKING

ROBERT C. LOWRY

It is one of the happy incidents of the federal system that a single courageous State may, if its citizens choose, serve as a laboratory; and try novel
social and economic experiments without risk to the rest of the country. *New State Ice Co. v. Liebmann* 285 U.S. 262, 311 (1932) (Brandeis, J.,
dissenting)

IN any study of state public policymaking the most obvious questions may be, "how
much variation exists across states in their public policies, and what explains this variation or the lack thereof?" Althoughthe reference to states as the laboratories of the federal system by Justice Brandeis suggests there will be large differences in policies across
the 50 states, there are many reasons to expect that the context in which state policymaking occurs will produce broadly similar policy outputs everywhere. Much attention
in recent years has been focused on the forces of globalization and how they limit the
ability of nation-states to adopt distinct domestic policies in a world where information, capital and (to a lesser extent) labor can move across national borders (e.g. Rodrik,
1997). These same arguments should apply at least as strongly to state policymaking,
given that states cannot regulate interstate commerce or limit the free flow of individuals across their borders with other states. Nonetheless, large differences across the states
persist in many areas of public policy, as detailed in chapters 28–40 of this *Handbook*.

This chapter examines the forces tending to produce convergence or divergence in
public policies adopted by the states. I first outline a framework for analysis that focuses
on four types of contextual factors: external constraints, resources, preferences, and
institutions. Although some evidence indicates that resources, preferences, and at
least one type of policy output—the scale of state government spending—did converge
during the 1960s and 1970s, little or no further convergence has occurred since about
1980. I then discuss each set of factors in turn, seeking to identify reasons for continued
diversity in state policy outputs. The final section identifies areas where further research
might be particularly useful and interesting.

FRAMEWORK FOR ANALYSIS

Plott's Fundamental Equation

Experimental economist Charles Plott (1979, 138) once formulated the following "fundamental equation:"

$$\text{Preferences} \times \text{Institutions} \times \text{Physical Possibilities} = \text{Outcomes}$$

where $\times$ is a generic operator that might best be described as "interacts with." The process represented by this equation involves combining individuals' preferences in the context of some institutional arrangements and the constraints imposed by the laws of physics and other objective realities in order to arrive at a collective decision. The key implication of Plott's equation is that a change in any of these three types of independent variables can lead to a change in outcomes, holding the other two types constant.

We can use a modified version of this equation to describe state public policymaking at a given point in time as:

$$\text{External Constraints} \times \text{Resources} \times \text{Preferences} \times \text{Institutions} = \text{Policy Outputs}$$

In this equation, "external constraints" refers to factors outside of the state that limit the options available to state policymakers, or influence their decisions. These include the U.S. Constitution, federal mandates and grant programs, and comparisons with other states.

"Resources" is another constraining factor. No matter how strong the demand for free public university education, for example, free public university education will not happen unless adequate resources can be found to pay for it. Resources can be divided into "own-source" resources—basically, the potential for state tax and fee revenues—and resources obtained from the federal government through intergovernmental transfers.

"Preferences" refers to the rankings assigned by individuals to different policy alternatives, or to the rankings assigned by voters to different candidates for elected office (Riker, 1982). Preferences are derived from demands for action to address a given issue or problem, beliefs about the underlying causes of problems and the likely consequences of choosing different alternatives, and normative ideas about the overall purpose of government and the relative merits of the public and private sectors. In the case of elections, they may also depend on retrospective evaluations of how incumbents have performed relative to some benchmark.

"Institutions" can be thought of as "the rules of the game in a society," or "the humanly devised constraints that shape human interaction" (North, 1990, 3). They include formal laws and regulations about who has authority to make different kinds of decisions and the processes to be used, as well as the unwritten norms that structure behavior in a society. I will focus primarily on the formal institutions that structure state policy making. A common question when analyzing state institutions is whether they are truly exogenous explanatory variables, or whether they are endogenous reflections of preferences.

Patterns of Convergence or Divergence

Neither external constraints, nor resources, preferences, institutions, nor policy outputs are readily captured by a single measure. Nonetheless, we can examine some measures of some of these concepts to see whether the states have become more or less alike in recent decades.

External constraints apply to all states, although changes in external constraints may affect different states very differently. There have been significant changes during the post- World War II period, most notably the Supreme Court decisions and federal legislation that ended the Jim Crow era in the South and contributed to the end of southern exceptionalism.

Own-source resources might be the easiest variable to measure in a way that is consistent and meaningful across states and time. Figure 23.1 shows the coefficient of variation (standard deviation divided by the mean) for real[1] personal income per capita for 1948–2006. Data for Alaska and Hawaii are omitted prior to 1959. Although state governments rely on many sources of revenue besides personal income taxes and some states have no income tax (Lowry, 2008), per capita personal income is still a reasonable measure of the overall tax base in most states. The data show that per capita personal

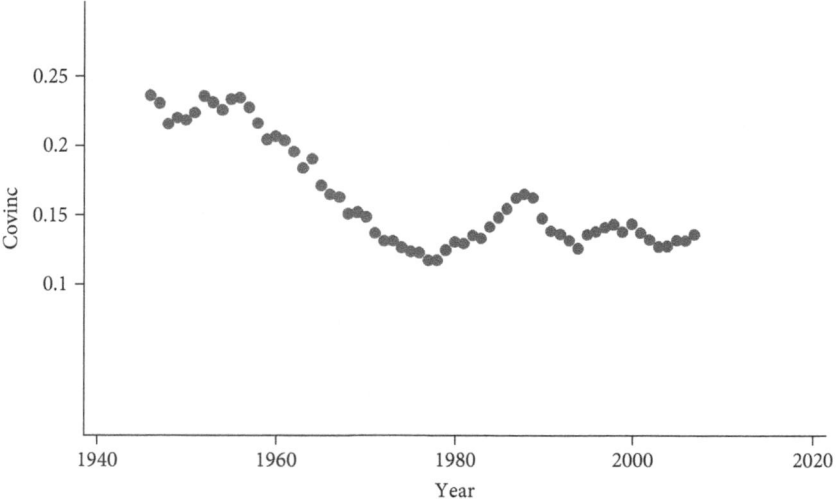

FIGURE 23.1 Coefficient of variation, real per capita personal income, 1948–2006

Notes: Data compiled by the author from the U.S. Census.

Alaska and Hawaii are excluded for 1948–58.

incomes converged from 1948 until about 1980. This was followed by divergence during the 1980s, a slight convergence during the early 1990s, and relatively stable variation thereafter.

Preferences over policy alternatives or candidates are often summarized in U.S. politics by measures of "ideology," measured on a scale from liberal to conservative. Berry, et al. (1998) devised a measure of citizen ideology in each state for 1960–98 that is based on ratings assigned to members of the state's congressional delegation by liberal or conservative interest groups.[2] This is not a direct measure of ideology, but it rests on the assumption that the voting behavior of members of Congress is an unbiased reflection of their constituents' preferences. It has the advantage of being readily computable for every state and every year. It has subsequently been widely used, defended in later publications (Berry et al., 2010), and updated.

Figure 23.2 shows the coefficient of variation by year for Berry et al.'s (1998) measure of citizen ideology from 1960 through 2006. The data are somewhat noisy, but indicate that there was a gradual convergence from the mid-1960s until the mid-1980s. This was followed by divergence in the early 1990s and no clear pattern thereafter.

Another way to summarize preferences is by looking at partisan choices in elections. Figure 23.3 shows the coefficient of variation for the Democrats' share of seats won by major party candidates in the lower chamber of the state legislature for 1949–2008. Nebraska is omitted throughout and Minnesota omitted prior to 1973 due to nonpartisan legislatures; Alaska and Hawaii are omitted before achieving statehood. The pattern shows strong convergence from 1949 until the mid-1970s and then no clear trend for the next 30 years. Data on partisan choices provide a distorted view of voters' preferences during the days of the one-party South. If we omit the 11 states of the Confederacy

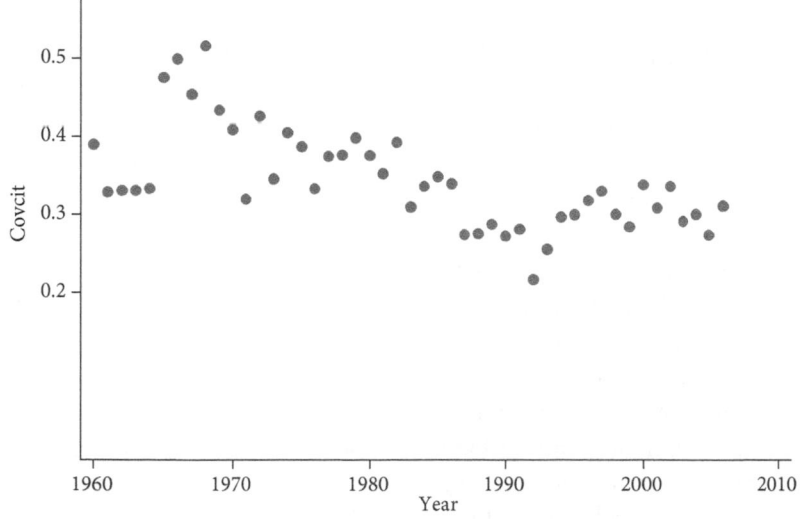

FIGURE 23.2 Coefficient of variation, citizen ideology, 1960–2006

Note: Compiled by the author based on Berry et al. (2010).

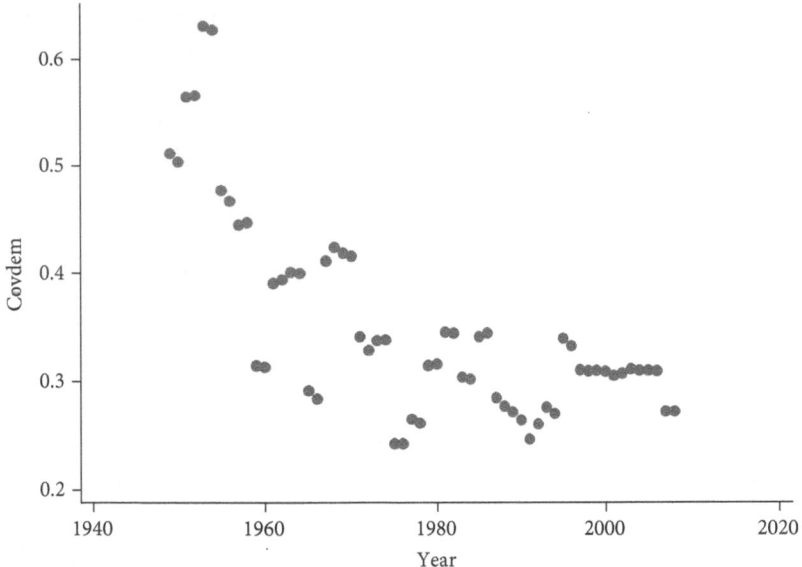

FIGURE 23.3 Coefficient of variation, percent democrats in the lower chamber of the state legislature, 1949–2008

Note: Compiled by the author; Nebraska omitted throughout; Minnesota omitted 1949–72; Alaska and Hawaii omitted 1949–58.

plus the border states of Maryland, West Virginia, Kentucky and Oklahoma, the coefficients of variation are slightly lower during the 1950s, but still decline slightly until the mid-1960s and show no clear pattern afterward. Consistent with this, Ansolabahere, Rodden and Snyder (2006, 115) show that one-party dominance of voting for President and statewide offices declined from about 1940 until the mid-1960s, then was slightly higher in the 1980s and 1990s but still well below its pre-World War II levels.

Although a great deal of research has been done on differences in state institutions, no research attempts to measure differences in institutions along a single dimension so that we might say whether they are becoming more or less similar across states. It seems highly unlikely that any such index would be very credible. With the exception of Jim Crow laws and practices, most differences in state institutions seem to be persisting, and some significant new differences have been created in recent years.

Policy outputs, like institutions, cannot readily be summarized by a single index. Although some scholars have calculated state policy liberalism scores (Erickson, Wright and McIver, 1993; Gray, 2008), these are ordinal measures that have not been calculated repeatedly over time. One output measure that is interesting, albeit incomplete, is the scale of state government spending. Figure 23.4 plots the coefficient of variation for real, per capita state government general expenditures from 1948 through 2006.[3] Hawaii is omitted prior to 1959 and Alaska throughout due to some extreme values caused by swings in severance tax revenues (Barrett et al., 2003). The pattern over time is a little noisier than the pattern for per capita personal income, but otherwise shows a pretty

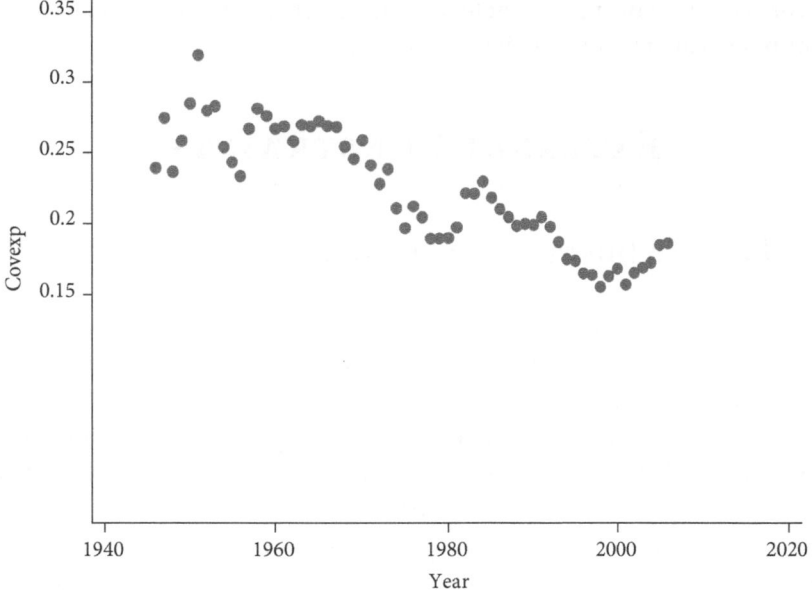

FIGURE 23.4 Coefficient of variation, real per capita state government general expenditures, 1948–2006

Notes: Compiled by the author; Hawaii is excluded for 1948–58; Alaska is excluded throughout.

close resemblance. Per capita spending converged from about 1960 until the late 1970s and from the late 1980s until the late 1990s, but diverged during most of the 1980s and the 2000s. Note also that in every year the coefficient of variation is greater for per capita government spending than for per capita personal income; coefficients for income range from about 0.1 to 0.25, while coefficients for government spending are mostly between 0.15 and 0.3. Thus, even without a sophisticated multivariate analysis, we can infer that differences across states in the scale of state government expenditure are due to more than differences in own-source resources.

The data in Figures 23.1–4 are incomplete and imperfect, but they nonetheless tell an interesting story. By various measures, states became more similar during the period from about 1960 until about 1980. They have not continued to converge since, and in some ways have become less similar during the 1990s and 2000s. Moreover, the absolute differences across states remain large. Consider the range of values for each of my measures in 2006. Per capita personal income in the wealthiest state (Connecticut) was more than 70 percent greater than in the poorest state (Mississippi). The most conservative state was Nebraska with a citizen ideology score of 22.6 on a scale of 0 to 100 (with lower values being more conservative), while the most liberal state was Vermont with a score of 93.9. Democrats' share of the lower chamber in the state legislature ranged from 18.6 percent in Idaho to 87.3 percent in Massachusetts. Finally, per capita general spending by state government was more than twice as high in Delaware as in Texas, although the highest figure was actually in Alaska. The remainder of this chapter discusses the various contextual factors that might tend to drive state policy outputs to be similar, or that contribute to maintaining significant differences.

External Constraints

Federal Law and Intergovernmental Relations

Federal law and federal-state intergovernmental relations set limits on what states can do, or establish incentives that affect state policymakers' decisions. One change in these constraints that helps to explain the convergence in the 1960s and 1970s is the elimination of Jim Crow laws and practices due to the Civil Rights Act of 1964 and the Voting Rights Act of 1965. Before this, the states making up the former Confederacy as well as some border states had a single-party system run by conservative white Democrats (Key, 1949; Aldrich, 2000). By the 1990s, southern states had two-party competition with the reconfigured Democrats being more closely aligned with their co-partisans elsewhere (Aldrich, 2000; Shafer and Johnston, 2006). While important political differences between the South and other parts of the country remain (Hayes and McKee, 2008), elimination of Jim Crow removed a major structural reason for Southern exceptionalism, such that differences are now more a matter of degree than kind.

Another change in external constraints comes from the Supreme Court's one-person one-vote jurisprudence beginning with *Baker v. Carr* (1962). Prior to these decisions, urban and suburban voters were underrepresented in many states. Ansolabehere, Gerber and Snyder (2002) analyze the consequences of the reforms that followed and find a significant redistribution of intergovernmental grants from state to local governments. They do not, however, report significant differences across states or regions in the extent of this redistribution.

Numerous specific areas of state policymaking have been influenced by the use of federal intergovernmental grants, mandates and preemption. This so-called "coercive federalism" (Posner, 2007) has been increasing in recent decades with periodic retrenchment after protests by state governors and sometimes congressional delegations (see chapter 2). Average real, per capita federal intergovernmental transfers to states quadrupled between 1960 and 2006, and with these extra transfers came extra leverage. Federal policymakers have used strings attached to federal funds to create uniformity in everything from highway speed limits (though this has since been repealed) to minimum drinking ages to mandatory testing of elementary and secondary school students. Other federal laws adopted under the authority of the interstate commerce and general welfare clauses mandate state programs that are often unfunded, or at best underfunded. Perhaps the most significant recent example is the "individual mandate" to purchase health insurance contained in the recent health care reform bill. This mandate has been challenged in court by 20 states claiming it exceeds Congress' power to regulate interstate commerce (Sack, 2010). Finally, the Supremacy clause of the Constitution forbids state or local laws that conflict with federal statutes in areas where the federal government has exercised its authority to act. Preemption also has been relatively common in recent decades, although its effect is not always to impose uniformity. For example, the 1970 Clean Air Act and its amendments preempted state air quality standards, but states are allowed to adopt standards stricter than the federal minimum (Potoski, 2001).

Interstate Comparisons

State policymaking may also be constrained by comparisons with other states. Besley and Case (1995) develop and provide evidence for a theory of "yardstick competition" that assumes voters compare tax changes in their state to tax changes in neighboring states when evaluating incumbent governors running for re-election. They argue this is one way for voters to get around the principal-agent problem where incumbents have superior information about whether a given tax increase is really necessary, given the cost of providing public services. While their evidence is limited to tax increases, the logic of using policy outputs in neighboring states as benchmarks to overcome asymmetric information problems applies much more generally.

A related phenomenon is interstate competition leading to a "race to the bottom" (RTB). Here, instead of voters looking to other states to evaluate incumbents, incumbents seek to avoid being at a competitive disadvantage with respect to other states. Empirical tests of this hypothesis have mostly focused on state welfare and environmental policies. In the former instance, it is argued that states do not want to become "welfare magnates" for the poor by offering benefits that are significantly more attractive than benefits offered by neighboring states (Bailey and Rom, 2004).[4] In the latter instance, the claim is that states will be driven by competition for industry to have lax environmental regulations or enforcement (Potoski, 2001; Konisky, 2007). The logic of interstate competition could be extended to other policies affecting means-tested benefit programs or regulation of business. In both cases, states have disincentives to differ from their neighbors in ways that make them more attractive to individuals who consume public resources or less attractive to business.

Although most studies of welfare policy simply test for a positive correlation between a state's welfare benefits and the benefits offered by its neighbors, Bailey and Rom (2004) note that the effect should be asymmetric; states that currently offer more generous benefits than their neighbors should tend to reduce benefits, but states that offer less generous benefits will not necessarily raise theirs. Moreover, since many social welfare programs are funded in part by federal intergovernmental grants, the RTB effect should be greatest for those programs where states have the most freedom to set eligibility criteria and benefits levels. They test these hypotheses using data on both eligibility criteria and benefits for Aid to Families with Dependent Children, Medicare, and Supplemental Security Income and find evidence that is generally supportive of their hypotheses. In fact, Bailey and Rom (2004), as well as most other studies focus on the relationship between welfare policies in all neighboring states. Berry and Baybeck (2005) use

Geographic Information Systems technology to take account of the distance between population centers in neighboring states. They do not find evidence that a concern for potential migration drives welfare policy.

Evidence for a race to the bottom in environmental policy is considerably weaker. Potoski (2001) finds that many states adopt air quality standards that are stricter than the federal minimum, and the probability each state does so is primarily a function of the strength of pro-environment interest groups and public opinion. Konisky (2007) applies Bailey and Rom's analysis to enforcement of environmental regulations. He finds that state enforcement is positively correlated with enforcement in competing states, but does not find any asymmetries. Thus, a given group of states will tend to have similar levels of enforcement, but this could result from either a race to the bottom *or* a race to the top. The latter has been labeled the "California effect" in the environmental literature (Konisky, 2007). States may want to provide an attractive environment where individuals—particularly well educated, highly productive employees—want to live, even at the cost of losing out on certain kinds of industry.

Taken together, the research on welfare and environmental policy suggest that interstate competition is frequently a factor, but it does not always lead to a race to the bottom and it is not always the most important factor. One weakness of this research is that most studies consider only competition between contiguous states. Konisky (2007) is an exception who looks at alternative definitions of groups of competing states.

Resources

Resources available to a state serve primarily as a constraint on the scale of state government, and in particular on certain kinds of expenditures such as entitlement programs and transfers to local governments. The data in Figure 23.1 indicated that state per capita incomes converged between the mid 1950s and the late 1970s, but have not continued to do so. Much of the convergence comes from the southern states catching up to the rest of the country as they made the conversion from a largely agricultural economy to a modern economy based on manufacturing and, increasingly, services and information.[5] Shafter and Johnston (2006) argue that economic development was more important to the transformation of party politics in the South than legal desegregation. Other scholars claim that, while the economic modernization of the South started prior to the civil rights movement, the two are not entirely separate. Wright (1999, 283) argues that during the Jim Crow era, the South suffered from a general inability "to join and take advantage of national and international networks of knowledge and culture." Many southern businessmen gradually realized it was in their interest to support desegregation so as to increase their ability to compete for outside capital (Jacoway and Colburn, 1982). Ultimately, federal civil rights legislation took the matter out of their hands (Wright, 1999).

The other main source of resources to support state government programs is transfers from the federal government. Federal transfers were equal to an average of 2.3 percent of state personal income in 1960, but 4.3 percent in 2006, and one of the classic justifications for federal intergovernmental grants is to redistribute resources across states (Rosen, 1992). The extent to which federal intergovernmental transfers equalize resources across states has been limited, however, by shifts in the types of grants used. During the 1960s and 1970s, a large share of federal transfers were in the form of block grants, some of which were specifically designated as revenue-sharing grants designed to redistribute resources to poorer state and local governments. Beginning in the 1980s, however, the trend has been to use more narrowly defined categorical or matching grants (Hanson, 2008). Matching grants could actually exacerbate disparities in resources, since wealthier states can generate more of their own tax revenues to spend on programs receiving a federal match.

The convergence in real, per capita personal income stopped around 1980, and there remain large differences across states in the resources available to support public programs. One obvious reason is that states differ in their natural advantages: their proximity to oceans and major rivers, the quality of the land for growing crops, the presence of timber, coal, and oil, and so on. This affects the overall level of economic activity, but also the kinds of taxes that might be imposed and the stability of revenue sources. The most extreme case is Alaska. Alaska has no state personal income tax and no general sales tax, yet in 2006 its per capita state general expenditures ranked first, almost 50 percent greater than second-place Delaware. In part this is due to its disproportionate share of federal intergovernmental transfers, but the main reason is that Alaska generates most of its own-source general revenue from severance taxes and other fees for mineral leases for oil. While this revenue source is a tremendous benefit to the citizens of Alaska, revenues can fluctuate widely with world oil prices (Barrett, et al., 2003). Other states with significant revenue from severance taxes include Texas, Louisiana, Oklahoma, and Wyoming (Lowry, 2008).

Another reason for differences in state resources is human capital, which may be approximated by education attainment. In 2007, the percentage of adults age 25 or above with high school degrees ranged from 78.5 (Mississippi) to 91.2 (Wyoming); the percentage with bachelor's degrees ranged from 17.3 (West Virginia) to 37.9 (Massachusetts) and, perhaps most important for economic growth in a post-industrial age, the percentage with advanced degrees ranged from 6.4 (Mississippi and North Dakota) to 16.0 (Massachusetts) (U.S. Census Bureau, 2010). Bivariate correlations between education attainment and real per capita personal income in 2007 are .345 for high school graduates, .676 for bachelor's degrees, and .682 for advanced degrees.

Education attainment illustrates the potential for migration to promote divergence rather than convergence. In 2008, just 58.9 percent of United States residents lived in the state where they were born; 27.3 percent had migrated from another state, 1.3 percent were U.S. natives born out of the country, and 12.5 percent were foreign born. The percentage of residents living in the state of their birth ranged from 79.6 in Louisiana to just 23.9 in Nevada, and was less than 50 percent in 12 states (U.S. Census Bureau, 2010). Although movement across state borders is substantial, this will not necessarily lead to greater homogeneity; it may also lead to more effective sorting by various characteristics. People with bachelor's and advanced degrees tend to congregate near one another in areas that have local economies that rely on information and advanced skills (Glaeser and Gottleib, 2009; Shapiro, 2006). Thus, the correlation between percent high school diplomas and percent bachelor's degrees is .525, and the correlation between high school diplomas and advanced degrees is just.311. This pattern in turn affects the incentives for states to invest in education. States that are sources of interstate migration have limited incentives to invest in public universities, since many of the students will leave after graduating (Lowry, 2001). This tends to create a pattern of path dependence separating states that are destinations for well-educated migrants and that invest in higher education for their own residents from states that are sources and have limited incentives to invest.

PREFERENCES

Although "preferences" may be taken as fundamental for purposes of running a laboratory experiment, in the real world they are derived from demands for action, beliefs and expectations about the consequences of different choices, and normative ideas about the role of government and the nature of the collective good. Differences in preferences may be due to differences in the physical environment, the attributes of individuals, or patterns of social interaction and normative values. Preferences with regard to policy alternatives may tend to converge when information and beliefs are spread through networks of policy entrepreneurs or professional policymakers and government employees.

The Physical Environment

The nature of demands on state government may vary with the raw number of people relative to land area, or the percentage of the population living in urban areas. Large cities have long been associated with high crime rates, poor public schools, and congested traffic, but also high incomes and vibrant arts and cultural communities. Although issues like crime control, elementary and secondary education, and public transportation may be regarded as primarily local government issues, more than a quarter of state government general expenditures consist of intergovernmental transfers to local governments (U.S. Census Bureau, 2010). The scale and composition of these transfers should depend on the types of communities where voters live. In 2000 the percentage of state residents living in "urban" areas ranged from 38.2 in Vermont to 94.4 in California.

Recent scholarship has focused increased attention on suburbs as entities having distinct political characteristics (e.g. Oliver, 2001; Oliver and Ha, 2007; Gainsborough, 2001; Williamson, 2008). Controlling for differences in socioeconomic status, people in the suburbs tend to be more conservative than those in central cities. A major question for this literature is whether there is something about living in the suburbs that produces different preferences, or whether people with certain political preferences also prefer to live in suburbs. Williamson (2008) finds that the likelihood of survey respondents reporting voting for Republicans or being conservative increases with the percentage of metropolitan residents who drive alone to work and decreases with the median age of the housing stock. He argues that "...recently built, car-oriented suburbs are constructed according to the proposition that the best sort of community is one that emphasizes the private enjoyment of space while maintaining public order..." (Williamson, 2008, 923). Williamson argues further that, although the selection effect does exist, the experience of living in these communities tends to strengthen preferences for Republican candidates and conservative policies.

Unfortunately, satisfactory measures of differences in living environments across states do not currently exist. There are no readily available statistics that measure the percentage of people living in suburbs, as opposed to central cities, across states. Population density is an even less satisfactory measure: some states, such as Texas, have lots of land and a relatively low population density, yet most of the residents are concentrated in large metropolitan areas.

Individual Attributes

Demands also differ across states due to differences in the attributes of the state's residents. One key dimension is the age composition of the population. States with many residents under the age of 18 have greater demand for public schools and a variety of social services such as foster care, adoption and day care. States with many residents over the age of 65 have more demands for health care and a different set of social services. Age composition is particularly important given that education and public welfare (which includes Medicaid) are the two largest areas of state government spending (U.S. Census Bureau, 2010). Moreover, the amount of income that a person makes and his/her expenditures on taxable goods vary significantly with age. In July 2008, the percentage of state residents under 18 years old varied from 20.8 in Vermont to 31.0 in Utah, while the percentage 65 and older varied from 7.3 in Alaska to 17.4 in Florida. If we combine these two categories, then the percentage of people who are particularly likely to demand public services but do not pay much in the way of taxes ranges from 33.5 percent in Alaska to 40.1 in Utah.

Although per capita personal income is a measure of the resources available to support public programs, the proportion of the population with low levels of income is a measure of the demand for means-tested public welfare programs. In 2007 the percentage of individuals with incomes below the official federal poverty line ranged from 7.1 in New Hampshire to 20.6 in Mississippi, while the percentage of families below the line ranged from 4.6 in New Hampshire to 16.3 in Mississippi. Of course, the poverty rate is inversely correlated with per capita income ($r = -.270$ for the individual poverty rate in

2007), so states with the greatest demands for means-tested public health and welfare programs tend to have the fewest resources to pay for these programs.

More generally, Meltzer and Richard (1981) argue that in a majoritarian political system, income distribution should determine both the progressivity of the tax structure and the size of government. The key variable in their model is the ratio of the median voter's income to the mean income. This ratio should be inversely related to both a progressive tax structure and government spending on redistributive programs. Empirical tests of their hypothesis using national data have produced mixed results (Mueller, 2003, 516–519). At the state level, income distribution might help to explain the extent to which states rely on personal income taxes, which are at least mildly progressive, versus general sales taxes, which are regressive, versus other kinds of taxes and fees.

Another source of differences in demand is the presence of foreign-born residents. Recent decades have seen historically high levels of immigration into the United States from other countries. While many new immigrants have settled in the traditional entry states such as California, Arizona, Texas and New York, others have moved to states in the interior. In 2008, the percentage of the resident population that was foreign born varied widely, from 1.3 in West Virginia to 26.8 in California (U.S. Census Bureau, 2010). However, the percentage of foreign born residents who entered the United States in 2000 or later was highest in Mississippi, followed by Kentucky, Alabama, Tennessee, the two Carolinas, Indiana and Iowa—all states where the percentage of foreign born residents was well below the national average. Thus, the numbers of foreign born residents are growing at the fastest rates in states where they have historically been low.

The presence of large or rapidly increasing numbers of foreign born residents generates demands for at least two kinds of policies. One is policies directed at residents with low English skills. A particularly controversial example of these is bilingual education, which can impose significant costs on state and local government. Many residents oppose bilingual education programs, both due to their cost and because these residents feel that immigrants should be encouraged to assimilate into the American "mainstream" as quickly as possible. Voters in California, Arizona and Massachusetts have adopted propositions that ended bilingual instruction in public schools in favor of intense "immersion" programs. Thirty states have enacted laws making English the official language, mostly since the mid-1980s (U.S. English, Inc., 2010). A second kind of demand is related specifically to illegal immigration. Concern over illegal immigrants has been high in recent years and proposals to increase border security and address the problem of illegal immigrants already in the United States have periodically made it onto the agenda of Congress, but no action has been taken (Greenblat, 2008). Frustrated by this lack of federal action, state officials have taken action to limit the access of illegal immigrants to public services and increase enforcement of existing laws (Hero and Preuhs, 2007; Markon and McCrummen, 2010).

Finally, there are large differences across states in the proportion of residents who are adherents[6] to different religious traditions and denominations (Association of Religion Data Archives, 2010). In 2000, the percentage of state residents who were adherents to mainline Protestant denominations ranged from 1.6 in Utah to 34.7 in North Dakota; for evangelical Protestants, the range was from 1.8 percent in Rhode Island to 43.7 percent in Arkansas; for Catholics, it was from 3.2 percent in Tennessee to 51.7 percent in Rhode Island. Glaeser and Ward (2006) argue that there is an enduring connection between religion and politics throughout American history, perhaps because "many people take their religious views far more seriously than views on other topics...It may [therefore] be easier for politicians to motivate voters by appealing to core religious values than to topics like tax policy" (142). Different religious beliefs translate into different demands for public policies on issues like abortion, gay rights, teaching about evolution, and even the environment (Haider-Markel and Meier, 1996; Lowry, 1998; Glaeser and Ward, 2006; Wilcox and Larson, 2006). Beginning in the 1980s, conservative Christian groups became well organized and active, particularly at the state level, as they sought to have their beliefs incorporated into state policy (Wilcox and Larson, 2006).

Religious practices also have indirect effects on the manner in which preferences are aggregated and transmitted to policymakers through nonreligious interest groups. Lowry (2005) finds that the number of civic organizations and citizen interest groups in a state increases with the proportion of residents who are mainline Protestants, but decreases with the proportion who are evangelical Protestants or Mormons.

Normative Beliefs and Social Interaction

We saw above that liberal-conservative ideology, as measured by Berry et al.'s (1998, 2010) index, continues to vary significantly across states. Erikson, Wright and McIver (1993), constructed another measure of state ideology by aggregating the responses from many CBS/New York Times opinion polls and calculating the number of respondents in each state and year who identified themselves as liberal, conservative or moderate. This would seem to give a more intuitive measure of ideology than Berry, et al., but it has some disadvantages. First, although Erickson, Wright, and McIver also updated their original data, it only runs from 1977 through 1999. Second, even after combining the data from all surveys conducted in a given year the number of respondents for some states can be quite small, such that the confidence interval about whatever ratio we calculate is large.

Erickson, Wright and McIver (1993) show that their measure of state citizen ideology based on survey data is correlated with an ordinal index of policy liberalism. However, while political ideology along a liberal-conservative scale is a handy way to summarize positions on a number of issues, it is not something that exists separate and apart from these positions. Rather, it is a device for mapping positions in a multidimensional policy space onto a single dimension (Hinich and Munger, 1994). It therefore has limited utility for explaining *why* the residents of different states tend to have different policy preferences.

A more fundamental concept that explains differences across states may be political culture, defined by Almond (1956, 396) as "a particular pattern of orientations to political action." This definition seems rather vague—Almond himself said that "the usefulness of the concept of political culture and its meaning may perhaps be conveyed more effectively through illustration." (1956, 394)—and political scientists have struggled to give it a more precise meaning (Lieske, 1993; Formisano, 2001). Nonetheless, the notion that the typical resident of Mississippi is just different from the typical resident of Maine in ways that cannot easily be measured but that have real consequences for state politics and policymaking has a lot of intuitive appeal.

The most famous use of political culture to explain differences among American states is that of Daniel Elazar (1972, 93–102), who argued that there are three main political subcultures within the United States: Individualistic, Moralistic and Traditionalistic. Each of these subcultures is characterized by a distinct set of attitudes toward government, bureaucracy and politics. Elazar summarized the individualistic subculture as "the conception of the democratic order as a marketplace. In its view, government is instituted for strictly utilitarian reasons...(94). The moralistic subculture "emphasizes the commonwealth conception as the basis for democratic government. Politics....is considered one of the great activities of man in his search for the good society...(96)."Finally, the traditionalistic subculture "reflects an older, pre-commercial attitude that accepts a substantially hierarchical society as part of the ordered nature of things....(99). Elazar argued that these three subcultures were brought to the United States by immigrants having different ethnic and religious backgrounds and spread unevenly as the settlers moved west. In general, strongly individualistic states tend to be in the Middle Atlantic region, the moralistic subculture tends to dominate in some New England states and the upper Midwest, the traditionalistic subculture dominates in the Southeast, and the Western states have a variety of classifications.

Although Elazar's classification scheme may seem intuitively appealing and has been cited numerous times, it has several limitations. First, the classification is based on his subjective assessment of each state and is not derived from objective data. Lieske (1993) argues that the classifications are circuitous to the extent that Elazar relies on past political behavior to define a concept for predicting future political behavior. Second, if political culture is determined by the origins of immigrants and their patterns of migration within the United States, then Elazar's map needs updating to account for the millions of immigrants in recent decades, particularly those from Latin America and Asia. Third, the causal mechanism whereby political culture affects policy outputs remains vague.

Other scholars have proposed alternative ways of defining the culture of American states. Lieske (1993) conducts factor analysis of "nonpolitical" variables including race, religion, ethnicity, occupation, and other demographics, and arrives at a scheme with ten regional subcultures. Hero and Tolbert (1996) and Hero (1998) argue that Elazar's groupings of states may be reasonable, but that he is mistaken in his analysis of the origins of subcultures. Rather, "the political culture conceptualization masks and may even be a surrogate for state racial/ethnic diversity" (Hero and Tolbert, 1996, 853). They argue that states can be classified according to whether they are racially and ethnically homogeneous, heterogeneous, or bifurcated, and that these classifications parallel what Elazar calls the moralistic, individualistic and traditionalistic subcultures, respectively.

Hero and Tolbert argue that categories based on racial and ethnic diversity are superior to Elazar's subcultures because they are "more clear, more precise, and dynamic" (1996, 854).

Another related concept that has received much attention in recent years is social capital. This literature was kick-started by Putnam's work on regional government in Italy (Putnam with Leonardi and Nanetti, 1993). Social capital is defined as "features of social organization, such as trust, norms, and networks that can improve the efficiency of society by facilitating coordinated actions." (1993, 167) Putnam (2000) later applied this concept to the United States. He first developed a state-level index of social capital from data on participation in voluntary and civic organizations, voter turnout, informal sociability and social trust (291). He then demonstrated that this index is correlated with a wide range of data measuring different aspects of well-being. Hero (2007) explicitly contrasts the racial diversity explanation for differences across states to the social capital explanation and concludes that when both are considered as independent variables, "diversity usually appears to be more important than social capital (17)."

The concepts of political culture, racial and ethnic diversity and social capital seem to be empirically related. States that Elazar classifies as moralistic and Hero and Tolbert classify as homogeneous tend to have high social capital; those that are classified as traditionalistic or racially and ethnically bifurcated tend to have low social capital; those that are classified as individualistic or racially and ethnically heterogeneous tend to be in the middle.

Regardless of whether we focus on political culture or social capital or racial and ethnic diversity, research indicates that social norms and patterns of interaction between individuals can have effects on government and policy outputs. King (1994) shows that Sharkansky's (1969) unidimensional index of political culture can in fact predict voter registration laws and voter turnout—it's simply conditional on laws based on that culture. Hero (2007) shows that voter turnout is lower in states with greater racial diversity, whereas the impact of social capital is conditional on racial diversity. Knack (2002) provides evidence that state governments are more effective in states with higher levels of social capital. Hero and Tolbert (1996) use separate measures of racial and white ethnic diversity to predict state Medicaid expenditures and adoption of English-only laws. Percival (2009) finds that prisoners are less likely to receive rehabilitation services in states with greater racial diversity. Alesina, Baqir and Easterly (1999) show that more ethnically fragmented cities and counties in the United States devote smaller shares of public spending to redistribution and productive public goods, and larger shares to crime prevention and patronage. To add another term to the discussion, they argue that racial and ethnic diversity leads to a lack of "social cohesion."

In sum, much research, starting with Elazar, focuses on the effects of individuals' attitudes toward and patterns of interaction with each other as an important independent variable explaining political behavior, the performance of public institutions, and policy outputs. However, debates continue over the underlying causes of these differences and the specific mechanisms whereby they affect politics and policy.

Policy Networks

Differences in the physical environment, individuals' attributes, and normative beliefs and social interactions all help to explain why individuals in different states tend to have different preferences over policy alternatives. However, unless policymakers are hyper-rational and perfectly informed, they cannot always identify the policy that maximizes some well-defined objective function (Simon, 1985). Rather, they will cast about for possible solutions that might be offered for the problem at hand. The literature on horizontal policy diffusion argues that policy innovations spread from state to state, and the probability that a given state adopts an innovation depends on the number of neighboring states that have adopted it (e.g. Berry and Berry, 1990, 1992). This result tells us little about the actual causal mechanism, nor does it predict which innovations will be adopted quickly and universally and which will spread only gradually. Mintrom (1997) argues that the causal mechanism involves policy entrepreneurs who seize on an innovation adopted elsewhere and press for passage in their own state. Schneider and Teske with Mintrom (1995) argue that the emergence of public sector entrepreneurs can be explained systematically, but relatively little is known about why policy entrepreneurs emerge when and where they do. Teodoro (2009) focuses on labor markets, and argues that local government managers hired from outside the jurisdiction are more likely to bring innovative ideas with them than those promoted from within. Nicholson-Crotty (2009) asks why some innovations spread so much faster than others. He argues innovations that offer simple solutions to highly salient issues tend to spread quickly. Those that are complex and address less salient issues spread more slowly, as policymakers in states that have not yet adopted them prefer to see how they play out over time before doing so.

Another venue for the generation and diffusion of policy ideas that has received relatively little attention in the political science literature is professional associations of state government officials. State governments in general have become much more professionalized in the past half century (see Chapters 14, 15, and 17), and this is reflected in the growth of organizations such as the National Governors Association, and National Conference of State Legislatures, the National Association of State Budget Officers, and many others. All of these organizations have professional staffs, collect data, publish reports on issues of concern to their members, and organize meetings where their members can interact. This creates a series of national networks where state government policymakers and administrators can exchange information and ideas with their peers elsewhere. This interaction should facilitate the spread of ideas and innovations, leading eventually to common approaches to similar problems. While it is unlikely that all 50 states will converge to a single approach in any given policy area, the exchange of ideas about good policies should tend to focus attention on a handful of approaches with different pros and cons.

This is not to say that all examples of policy diffusion result from networks of state-level actors or regional contagion effects. Haider-Markel (2001) finds that consideration of state laws banning same-sex marriage in the 1990s was primarily the result of a campaign organized by national interest groups. Similarly, Mooney (2009) reports that the spread of state legislative term limits in the 1990s was largely the work of a single national advocacy group.

State Institutions

Given a set of preferences, and contingent on external constraints and the resources available to support public programs, the policy outputs that emerge depend on how the preferences are combined to arrive at a collective decision: Whose preferences matter when, how much weight is given to the preferences of different individuals, and what decision rule is used to determine a final choice?

But are institutions really part of the context of state policymaking or are they, like policy outputs, products of that context? One key feature of institutions is that, once established, they are typically costly to change. Thus, North (1990) argues that an institution does not need to be optimal or efficient from the standpoint of any individual or group of individuals in order for it to be stable. So long as there is no group of individuals willing and able to bear the cost of change given the uncertainty about what might happen next, the institution will remain. In general, the more costly it is to change an institution and the longer it has been in place the more reasonable it is to treat it as an exogenous variable.

Rules written into state constitutions are the most obvious candidates for exogenous institutions. The general structure of state governments is quite uniform: bicameral legislatures (except for Nebraska) with members chosen by popular vote, and a separately elected executive. States differ in the number and identity of executive branch officers other than the governor who are chosen by popular election. While it seems reasonable that this would lead to differences in policy outputs, little research has been done. One exception is Provost's (2006) work on state attorneys general. Another difference that has received considerably more attention lately is the method for selecting state court judges (see Chapter 16). State judges can be appointed, elected in partisan elections, elected in nonpartisan elections, or appointed and then required to stand in a retention election. Research suggests that judicial elections and partisanship may affect outcomes on highly salient issues like abortion and the death penalty (Brace and Boyea, 2008; Calderone, Canes-Wrone and Clark, 2009), but little is known about whether and how methods for selecting judges affect outcomes in other areas of litigation.

One example of convergence in state institutions is the shift toward single-member districts for state legislatures. Although multi-member districts *per se* do not violate the United States Constitution, they do tend to suppress representation of minority groups that are geographically concentrated. Multi-member districts are therefore subject to challenge on the grounds that they are created with the intent to discriminate against minority groups (*Whitcomb v. Chavis* 1971). In state elections held in 1970–1, 31 states used multi-member districts to elect at least some members of the state legislature; by 2002–3, only ten states did so (Carsey et al., 2007). Adams (1996) finds that legislatures elected by single-member districts tend to have less ideological diversity than legislatures elected by multi-member districts, but no research shows a direct connection between the demise of multi-member districts and changes in policy outputs.

Perhaps the most fundamental differences in state institutions in terms of consequences for public policy are provisions for direct democracy (see Chapter 13). The 20 states that allow citizen-sponsored ballot initiatives have a channel for determining policy outputs that simply does not exist in other states. Research indicates that this results in systematic differences in fiscal policy (Matsusaka, 2004), abortion policy and campaign finance policy (Bowler and Donovan, 2004), and there was almost a one-to-one relationship between states that have the ballot initiative and states that adopted some form of legislative term limits in the 1990s (Mooney, 2009).[7] However, Monogan, Gray and Lowery (2009) find that the relationship between state citizen ideology and an ordinal index of policy liberalism is not affected by the presence or absence of the ballot initiative.

There are also many differences in institutions that affect specific policy areas, but many of these may themselves be endogenous reflections of preferences. Thus, Alt and Lowry (1994) treat state constitutional and statutory balanced budget requirements as exogenous, but Alt and Lowry (2010) treat procedural rules that affect the transparency of the budgeting process as endogenous.

Still other institutions regulate the formation and behavior of interest groups and wealthy individuals. States have widely differing laws regulating campaign contributions and spending; while some states allow unlimited spending and contributions to candidates by interest groups, corporations and labor unions, others tightly regulate contributions to candidates and provide public funding for at least some races (National Conference of State Legislatures, 2010).[8] So far there is little research that directly connects state campaign finance laws to policy outputs; most research has focused on dependent variables such as incumbent re-election rates and electoral competitiveness (e.g. Stratman and Aparicio-Castillo, 2006). If the ultimate purpose of campaign finance laws is to prevent wealthy interests from having undue influence over policy decisions, then there ought to be measurable differences in policy outputs between states with strict campaign finance regulations and those with lax regulations. States also have different laws on who must register as a lobbyist and what information they must provide. Lowery and Gray (1994) do not find a connection between the strictness of these laws and the number of organizations that register as lobbyists.

Finally, one institution that may not seem political but that has a significant effect on the composition of organized interests is state right-to-work laws. Right-to-work laws forbid collective bargaining agreements that make union membership or payment of fees in lieu of membership a condition of employment. As of 2009, 22 states had such laws, and ten had them written into the state constitution. In addition, Indiana has a right-to-work law that applies to education only (U.S. Department of Labor, 2010). Unions face much stiffer collective action problems in these states, and in 2006 average union membership relative to voting-age population was less than half as high in states with right-to-work laws as in states without them (including Indiana). The reduced importance of organized labor as a political force affects the politics surrounding a host of policy issues. In addition, Leighly and Nagler (2007) find that individuals are more likely to vote in states with greater union density, and the effects are concentrated among low- and middle-income voters.

DISCUSSION AND CONCLUSION

The context in which state policymaking occurs includes many different forces and constraints, some of which tend to push the states in the direction of uniformity of policy outputs, and others that push in the direction of diversity. The relative strength of these forces varies over time. While there appears to have been substantial convergence during the 1960s and 1970s according to various measures, this tendency has halted in recent decades and there has been some movement in the direction of greater diversity.

Much of the convergence was due to one-time events surrounding the elimination of Southern exceptionalism: the transition of the states formerly in the confederacy from a largely agricultural economy to a post-industrial economy, and the elimination of legal segregation and discrimination based on race. Other forces for convergence include federal revenue sharing grants and mandates, the growth of national networks of policy entrepreneurs and professional associations for state government officials, and the gradual elimination of multi-member districts in state legislatures.

Arrayed against these are the forces of divergence. Although there are no legal barriers to interstate migration and the costs of transportation are lower than ever, this has not resulted in a random reshuffling of the population so that states become more homogeneous. Rather, the opposite appears to be occurring as individuals with the means to move seek opportunities to live and work with others like themselves. Variations in per capita personal income and citizen ideology have fluctuated within narrow ranges since about 1980. Differences in the physical environment where people live translate into differences in demands for government action and perhaps normative beliefs. Other sources of differences in demands include the age composition of the population, the percentage of foreign-born residents, income distribution, and religion.

There are also clear differences across states in the way that individuals interact with others and their normative views on the proper functions of government. Some research refers to this as differences in political culture; other research focuses on the concept of social capital; and other research argues that it all stems from the racial and ethnic composition of the population. Whatever the appropriate term, there is mounting evidence that these patterns of social interaction matter.

Finally, there are many differences in state political and government institutions, although it is often a legitimate question whether these are part of the context of policymaking or some of the consequences of that context. One difference that is both exogenous to modern preferences and consequential is the ballot initiative, and much of the variation in certain other institutions such as legislative term limits and campaign finance laws follows from the use of the initiative.

What areas seem particularly promising for future research? I have noted a number of specific issues above, but will focus in this conclusion on two broad areas. One area that has received little attention until recently is the politics of suburbs and the effects of suburbia on political behavior and state policy. Although this may be considered by some a topic for local rather than state politics, it is highly relevant to state politics and policy for at least two reasons. First, if the act of living in the suburbs affects people's normative beliefs about the kind of community that is "best" (Gainsborough, 2001; Williamson, 2008), then the share of voters living in suburban areas will have an impact on state politics in general. Second, suburban areas have policy concerns that are distinct from the concerns of central cities and rural communities (Oliver 2003). This implies that elected representatives from suburban areas can be expected to have a different agenda in the legislature, and the demands of suburban local governments for intergovernmental transfers from state governments will be different from the demands of central city governments or local governments in rural areas.

The scarcity of research on the consequences of suburbanization is at least partly due to issues of data collection and availability. The only variables collected by standard sources of state-level data are population density and "urbanization" (e.g. U.S. Census Bureau, 2010), neither of which is an adequate measure of the different types of spatial environments where people live. It may be possible to develop more useful measures for future years using geographic information systems (GIS) technology. In the meantime, scholars will not be able to use a 50-state research design, but will need to concentrate on a few states or metropolitan areas where adequate data can be found.

Another area concerns what I have called patterns of social interaction and normative ideas about the proper role of government and the common good. Whatever label one uses, the quantity and quality of social interaction seems to depend on the mixture of races, ethnicities and religions present in the state's population. More work is needed to identify the most important sources of differences and the causal mechanisms that link those differences to policy outputs, particularly in light of recent waves of immigration from Latin America and Asia and increased numbers of non-Christian religious adherents.

Related to this is the question of whether there is anything that state policymakers can do to affect these patterns of social interaction in a positive way. Research so far is not sanguine on this point. Putnam's analysis of social capital in Italy traces the roots of contemporary patterns back hundreds of years and emphasizes their path dependent nature. He relates how one government reformer in a region with low social capital and low government performance remarked that Putnam's analysis was a "counsel of despair," as it suggests that contemporary reforms are likely to be ineffective in the face of centuries-old patterns of behavior (1993, 182). Neither Knack (2002) nor Lowry (2005) find evidence that there is much state policymakers can do to affect social capital or civil society, beyond the long–run effects of investing in education.

This path dependence, along with a variety of other factors such as resource constraints, federal mandates, and interstate competition, severely limit the extent to which state policymakers can truly engage in "novel social and economic experiments" of the type Justice Brandeis envisioned. Moreover, certain states repeatedly score low on a whole variety of measures of resources, education, social capital/civic engagement, and government performance, as well as various measures of outcomes related to quality of life. As North (1990) remarked, the fact that a set of social institutions and practices is stable does not necessarily mean that it is desirable. Further research on strategies for shifting from a "bad" equilibrium to a "good" one might lead to insights that would be highly beneficial for practitioners and scholars alike.

Notes

1. Current dollars were adjusted using regional CPI-U indices, with 1982–1984 = 100.
2. Interest group ratings are the percentage of votes on selected issues that each member casts agreeing with the liberal or conservative position. State ideology scores are derived by weighting the scores for different members of Congress or imputed scores for challengers and combining them. See Berry, et al. (1998) and Berry et al. (2010) for further explanation and validation.
3. General expenditures equal total expenditures less spending on liquor stores, public utilities, and insurance trusts.
4. The RTB effect can occur regardless whether individuals actually migrate across state lines to obtain better welfare benefits, so long as policymakers believe that they would. Bailey (2005) analyzes the migration choices of poor single mothers between 1985 and 1990. He concludes that family ties are the most important factor explaining migration choices, but differences in welfare benefits do have real effects. "Such effects are modest relative to state populations and budgets; whether they are modest with regard to the politics of state policymaking is an open question" (Bailey, 2005, 134).
5. If I redo Figure 23.1 showing variation in real per capita personal income after omitting 15 southern and border states there is a slight increase in variation during the 1950s, followed by a long, slow convergence until about 1980 and then a similar pattern thereafter. Overall the coefficients of variation stay within a narrower range, with the maximum value less than 0.2.
6. "Adherents" includes formal members of the church, as well as their children and other individuals who attend regularly. Some denominations do not recognize a distinction between members and adherents.
7. Some of these term limits have since been repealed or struck down by state supreme courts.
8. Some of these laws may be invalid in the wake of the U.S. Supreme Court's decision in Citizens United v. Federal Election Commission (2010) (Barber, 2010).

References

Adams, Greg. 1996. "Legislative Effects of Single-Member vs. Multi-Member Districts." *American Journal of Political Science 40*(February): 129–144.

Aldrich, John H. 2000. "Southern Parties in State and Nation." *The Journal of Politics 62*(August): 643–670.

Alesina, Alberto, Reza Baqir and William Easterly. 1999. "Public Goods and Ethnic Divisions." *Quarterly Journal of Economics* 114(November): 1243–1284.

Alt, James E. and Robert C. Lowry. 1994. "Divided Government, Fiscal Institutions and Budget Deficits: Evidence from the States." *American Political Science Review* 88(December): 811–828.

Alt, James E. and Robert C. Lowry. 2010. "Transparency and Accountability: Empirical Results for U.S. States." *Journal of Theoretical Politics* 22(October): 379–406.

Almond, Gabriel. 1956. "Comparative Political Systems." *The Journal of Politics* 18(August): 391–409.

Ansolabehere, Stephen, Alan Gerber and James M. Snyder, Jr. 2002. "Equal Votes, Equal Money: Court-Ordered Redistricting and Public Expenditures in the American States." *American Political Science Review* 96(December): 767–777.

Ansolabehere, Stephen, Johnathan Rodden and James M. Snyder Jr. 2006. "Purple America." *Journal of Economic Perspectives* 20(Spring): 97–118.

Association of Religion Data Archives. 2010. "U.S. Church Membership Data." <http://www.thearda.com/Archive/ChState.asp>. Last accessed May 22.

Bailey, Michael A. 2005. "Welfare and the Multifaceted Decision to Move." *American Political Science Review* 99(February): 125–135.

Bailey, Michael A. and Mark Carl Rom. 2004. "A Wider Race? Interstate Competition Across Health and Welfare Programs." *The Journal of Politics* 66(May): 326–347.

Baker v. Carr, 369 U.S. 182 (1962)

Barber, Denise Roth. 2010. "Citizens United v. Federal Election Commission: The Impacts— and Lack Thereof—on State Campaign Finance Law." National Institute on Money in State Politics. <http://www.followthemoney.org/press/PrintReportView.phtml?r=414> (accessed July 24)

Barrett, Katherin, Richard Greene, Michele Mariani, and Any Sostek. 2003. "The Way we Tax: A 50-State Report." *Governing*, February, 20–23.

Berry, Frances S. and William D. Berry. 1990. "State Lottery Adoptions as Policy Innovations: An Event History Analysis." *American Political Science Review* 84(June): 395–415.

Berry, Frances S. and William D. Berry. 1992. "Tax Innovation in the States: Capitalizing on Political Opportunity." *American Journal of Political Science* 36 (August): 715–742.

Berry, William D. and Brady Baybeck. 2005. "Using Geographic Information Systems to Study Interstate Competition." *American Political Science Review* 99(November): 505–519.

Berry, Wililam D., Richard C. Fording, Evan J. Ringquist, and Russell L. Hanson. 1998. "Measuring Citizen and Government Ideology in the States, 1960–1993." *American Journal of Political Science* 42(January): 327–348.

Berry, William D., Richard C. Fording, Evan J. Ringquist, Russell L. Hanson, and Carl E. Klarner. 2010. "Measuring Citizen and Government Ideology in the U. S. States: A Re-appraisal." *State Politics and Policy Quarterly* 10(Summer): 117–135.

Besley, Timothy and Anne Case. 1995. "Incumbent Behavior: Vote-Seeking, Tax-Setting and Yardstick Competition." *American Economic Review* 85(March): 25–45.

Bowler, Shaun and Todd Donovan. 2004. "Measuring the Effect of Direct Democracy on State Policy: Not All Initiatives are Created Equal." *State Politics and Policy Quarterly* 4(Fall): 345–363.

Brace, Paul and Brent D. Boyea. 2008. "State Public Opinion, the Death Penalty, and the Practice of Electing Judges." *American Political Science Review* 52(April): 360–372.

Calderone, Richard P., Brandice Canes-Wrone and Tom S. Clark. 2009. "Partisan Labels and Democratic Accountability: An Analysis of State Supreme Court Abortion Decisions." *The Journal of Politics* 71(April): 560–573.

Carsey, Thomas M., William D. Berry, Richard G. Niemi, Lynda W. Powell and James M. Snyder. STATE LEGISLATIVE ELECTION RETURNS, 1967–2003 [Computer file]. ICPSR21480-v1. Chapel Hill, North Carolina: University of North Carolina [producer], 2007. Ann Arbor, MI: Inter-university Consortium for Political and Social Research [distributor], April 22, 2008. doi:10.3886/ICPSR21480

Citizens United v. Federal Election Commission 558 U.S. 50 (2010).

Elazar, Daniel J. 1972. "The States and the Political Setting," in American Federalism: A View from the States 84–127. 2nd ed. New York: Thomas Y. Crowell Company.

Erikson, Robert S., Gerald C. Wright, and John P. McIver. 1993. Statehouse Democracy: Public Opinion and Policy in the American States. Cambridge: Cambridge University Press.

Formisano, Ronald P. 2001. "The Concept of Political Culture." Journal of Interdisciplinary History 31(Winter): 393–426.

Gainsborough, Janet. 2001. Fenced Off: The Suburbanization of American Politics. Washington, DC: Georgetown University Press.

Glaeser, Edward L. and Joshua D. Gottleib. 2009. "The Wealth of Cities: Agglomeration Effects and Spatial Equilibrium in the United States." Journal of Economic Literature 47(December): 983–1028.

Glaeser, Edward L. and Bryce A. Ward. 2006. "Myths and Realities of American Political Geography." Journal of Economic Perspectives 20(Spring): 119–144.

Gray, Virginia. 2008. "The Socioeconomic and Political Context of States." In Virginia Gray and Russell L. Hanson (eds.) Politics in the American States: A Comparative Analysis 1–29. 9th ed. Washington, DC: CQ Press.

Greenblat, Alan. 2008. "Immigration Debate: Can Politicians Find a Way to Curb Illegal Immigrants?" CQ Researcher 18:97–120, February 1.

Haider-Markel, Donald P. 2001. "Policy Diffusion as a Geographical Expansion of the Scope of Political Conflict: Same-Sex Marriage Bans in the 1990s." State Politics and Policy Quarterly 1(Spring): 5–26.

Haider-Markel, Donald P. and Kenneth J. Meier. 1996. "The Politics of Gay and Lesbian Rights: Expanding the Scope of the Conflict." The Journal of Politics 58(May): 332–349.

Hanson, Russell L. 2008. "Intergovernmental Relations." In Virginia Gray and Russell L. Hanson (eds.) Politics in the American States: A Comparative Analysis 30–60. 9th ed. Washington, DC: CQ Press.

Hayes, Danney and Seth C. McKee. 2008. "Toward a One-Party South?" American Politics Research 36(January): 3–32.

Hero, Rodney E. 1998. Faces of Inequality: Social Diversity in American Politics. New York: Oxford University Press.

Hero, Rodney E. 2007. Racial Diversity and Social Capital: Equality and Community in America. New York: Cambridge University Press.

Hero, Rodney E. and Robert R. Preuhs. 2007. "Immigration and the Evolving American Welfare State: Examining Policies in the U. S. States." American Journal of Political Science 51(July): 498–517.

Hero, Rodney E. and Caroline J. Tolbert. 1996. "A Racial\Ethnic Diversity Interpretation of Politics and Policy in the States of the U. S." American Journal of Political Science 40: 851–871.

Hinich, Melvin J. and Michael C. Munger. 1994. Ideology and the Theory of Political Choice. Ann Arbor, MI: The University of Michigan Press.

Jackoway, Elizabeth and David R. Colburn. 1982. Southern Businessmen and Desegregation. Baton Rouge, LA: Louisiana State University Press.

Key, V.O., Jr. 1949. *Southern Politics in State and Nation*. New York: Random House.

King, James D. 1994. "Political Culture, Registration Laws, and Voter Turnout Among the American States." *Publius: The Journal of Federalism* 24(Autumn): 115–127.

Knack, Stephen. 2002. "Social Capital and the Quality of Government: Evidence from the States." *American Journal of Political Science* 46(October): 772–785.

Konisky, David M. 2007. "Regulatory Competition and Environmental Enforcement: Is there a Race to the Bottom?" *American Journal of Political Science* 51(October): 853–872.

Leighley, Jan E. and Jonathan Nagler. 2007. "Unions, Voter Turnout and Class Bias in the U.S. Electorate, 1964–2004. *The Journal of Politics* 69(May): 430–441.

Lieske, Joel. 1993. "Regional Subcultures of the United States." *The Journal of Politics* 55(November): 888–913.

Lowery, David and Virginia Gray. 1994. "Do Lobbying Regulations Influence Lobbying Registrations?" *Social Science Quarterly* 75(2): 382–384.

Lowry, Robert C. 1998. "Religion and the Demand for Membership in Environmental Citizen Groups". *Public Choice* 94(March): 223–240.

Lowry, Robert C. 2001. "The Effects of State Political Interests and Campus Outputs on Public University Revenues." *Economics of Education Review* 20(April): 105–119.

Lowry, Robert C. 2005. "Explaining the Variation in Organized Civil Society Across States and Time." *The Journal of Politics* 67(May): 574–594.

Lowry, Robert C. 2008. "Fiscal Policy in the American States." In Virginia Gray and Russell L. Hanson (eds.) *Politics in the American States: A Comparative Analysis* 287–315. 9th ed. Washington, DC: CQ Press.

Markon, Jerry and Stephanie McCrummen. 2010. "Judge Blocks Some Sections of Arizona Law." *The Washington Post*, July 29, p. A01.

Matsusaka, John G. 2004. *For the Many or the Few: The Initiative, Public Policy and American Democracy*. Chicago, IL: University of Chicago Press.

Meltzer, Alan H. and Scott F. Richard. 1981. "A Rational Theory of the Size of Government." *Journal of Political Economy* 89(October): 914–927.

Mintrom, Michael. 1997. "Policy Entrepreneurs and the Diffusion of Innovation." *American Journal of Political Science* 41(July): 738–770.

Monogan, James, Virginia Gray and David Lowery. 2009. "Public Opinion, Organized Interests and Policy Congruence in Initiative and Noninitiative U. S. States." *State Politics and Policy Quarterly* 9(Fall): 304–324.

Mooney, Christopher Z. 2009. "Term Limits as a Boon to Legislative Scholarship: A Review." *State Politics and Policy Quarterly* 9(Summer): 204–228.

Mueller, Dennis C. 2003. *Public Choice III*. New York: Cambridge University Press.

National Conference of State Legislatures. 2010. "Elections and Campaigns." <http://www.ncsl.org/Default.aspx?TabID=746&tabs=1116,114,800#800> (accessed July 30).

Nicholson-Crotty, Sean. 2009. "The Politics of Diffusion: Public Policy in the American States." *The Journal of Politics* 71(January): 192–205.

North, Douglass C. 1990. *Institutions, Institutional Change and Economic Performance*. New York, NY: Cambridge University Press.

Oliver, J. Eric. 2001. *Democracy in Surburbia*. Princeton, NJ: Princeton University Press.

Oliver, J. Eric. 2003. "Suburban and Metropolitan Politics." In John P. Pelissero (ed.) *Cities, Politics and Policy: A Comparative Analysis* 312–335. Washington, DC: CQ Press.

Oliver, J. Eric and Shang E. Ha. 2007. "Vote Choice in Suburban Elections." *American Political Science Review* 101(July): 393–408.

Percival, Garrick L. 2009. "Testing the Impact of Racial Attitudes and Racial Diversity on Prisoner Re-entry Policies in the U. S. States." *State Politics and Policy Quarterly* 9(Summer): 176–203.

Plott, Charles R. 1979. "The Application of Laboratory Experimental Methods to Public Choice." In Clifford S. Russell (ed.) *Collective Decision Making: Applications from Public Choice Theory* 137–160. Baltimore, MD: Johns Hopkins University Press.

Posner, Paul. 2007. "The Politics of Coercive Federalism in the Bush Era." *Publius: The Journal of Federalism* 37(May): 390–412.

Potoski, Matthew. 2001. "Clean Air Federalism: Do States Race to the Bottom?" *Public Administration Review* 61(May/June): 335–342.

Provost, Colin. 2006. "The Politics of Consumer Protection: Explaining State Attorney General Participation in Multi-State Lawsuits." *Political Research Quarterly* 59(December): 609–618.

Putnam, Robert D. 2000. *Bowling Alone: The Collapse and Revival of American Community*. New York: Simon and Schuster.

Putnam, Robert D. with Robert Leonardi and Raffaella Y. Nanetti. 1993. *Making Democracy Work: Civic Traditions in Modern Italy*. Princeton, NJ: Princeton University Press.

Riker, William H. 1982. *Liberalism Against Populism: A Confrontation Between the Theory of Democracy and the Theory of Social Choice*. Prospect Heights, IL: Waveland Press, Inc.

Rodrik, Dani. 1997. *Has Globalization Gone Too Far?* Washington, DC: Institute for International Economics.

Rosen, Harvey S. 1992. *Public Finance*. Boston, MA: Irwin.

Sack, Kevin. 2010. "Florida Suit Poses a Challenge to Health Care Law." *The New York Times*. May 10.

Schneider, Mark and Paul Teske with Michael Mintrom. 1995. *Public Entrepreneurs: Agents for Change in American Government*. Princeton, NJ: Princeton University Press.

Shafter, Byron E. and Richard Johnston. 2006. *The End of Southern Exceptionalism: Class, Race, and Partisan Change in the Postwar South*. Cambridge, MA: Harvard University Press.

Shapiro, Jesse M. 2006. "Smart Cities: Quality of Life, Productivity, and the Growth Effects of Human Capital." *Review of Economics and Statistics* 88(May): 324–335.

Sharkansky, Ira. 1969. "The Utility of Elazar's Political Culture: A Research Note." *Polity* 2(Fall): 78–82.

Simon, Herbert. 1985. "Human Nature in Politics: The Dialogue of Psychology with Rational Choice." *American Political Science Review* 79(June): 293–304.

Stratman, Thomas and Francisco J. Aparicio-Castillo. 2006. "Competition Policy for Elections: Do Campaign Contribution Limits Matter?" *Public Choice* 127: 177–206.

Teodoro, Manuel P. 2009. "Bureaucratic Job Mobility and the Diffusion of Innovations." *American Journal of Political Science* 53(January): 175–189.

U.S. Census Bureau. Various. Statistical Abstract of the United States. 1950–2010. <http://www.census.gov/compendia/statab/> (last accessed July 9, 2010).

U.S. Department of Labor. 2010. "State Right-to-work Laws and Constitutional Amendments in Effect as of January 1, 2009 With Year of Passage" <http://www.dol.gov/whd/state/right-towork.htm> (accessed July 24).

U.S. English, Inc. 2010. "States with Official English Laws." <http://www.us-english.org/view/13> (accessed July 26).

Whitcomb v. Chavis, 403 U.S. 124 (1971).

Wilcox, Clyde and Carin Larson. 2006. *Onward Christian Soldiers: The Religious Right in American Politics*. Boulder, CO: Westview Press.

Williamson, Thad. 2008. "Sprawl, Spatial Location, and Politics: How Ideological Identification Tracks the Built Environment." *American Politics Research* 36(November): 903–933.

Wright, Gavin. 1999. "The Civil Rights Revolution as Economic History." *Journal of Economic History* 59(June): 267–289.

CHAPTER 24

STATE POLICY AND DEMOCRATIC REPRESENTATION

SAUNDRA K. SCHNEIDER AND
WILLIAM G. JACOBY

THE American states are often called "laboratories of democracy." This term originally referred to the flexibility that the states possess to try out different policy solutions to pressing social problems. But the term is also an apt description of the variability that exists across the states with respect to democratic representation of public interests. In this chapter, we will focus primarily on the second sense of this term by examining the relationship between citizen preferences and governmental policy. We regard the former as manifested most clearly in public opinion and the latter in the overt actions of public officials and institutions. So, the question to be addressed empirically is: what is the connection between the two?

Answering this question requires us to operationalize "public opinion" and "state policy." This is especially critical since the specific measures employed in previous research have affected the findings in very important ways. We begin the essay by considering the various approaches that have been employed in the scholarly literature to measure public opinion in the states. Next, we examine the ways that researchers have captured state-level public policy in empirical indicators. After that, we move on to discuss strategies for representing the relationship between state opinion and policy, as well as various factors that may mediate the connection between the two. Our objective is not only to provide broad coverage of the work that has already been carried out in this important subfield, but also to point to unresolved issues and potential future directions for scholarly research.

MEASURING CITIZEN PREFERENCES IN THE STATES

It would be impossible to investigate representation empirically without some overt measure of citizen preferences within the states. This is not a particularly new insight. Over the years, scholars of state politics have devoted a great deal of attention toward precisely this objective. The basic problem can be stated as follows. We would like to have accurate readings within the states of citizen preferences that are comparable across states and available over time. The various approaches to this problem can be divided into four categories: political culture; survey-based measures; indirect indicators; and simulation-based strategies. Let us consider each of these, in turn.

Political Culture

Political culture has been defined in many different ways. Generally, the term refers to a set of shared values which comprise a society's fundamental orientations toward politics and government. Political culture is not, in itself, synonymous with public opinion. But, it does serve as the basic underlying source of political preferences. Therefore, if it is possible to identify meaningful variability between state cultures, those same differences should be closely related to variations in state opinion. And that, in turn, should help explain why state governments pursue different policies.

As in so many areas of American political science, V. O. Key was really the first researcher to direct scholarly attention toward systematic differences in the interplay between social settings and political processes. His seminal work, *Southern Politics in State and Nation* (1949), builds upon a central theme that context matters for human behavior. And his detailed accounts of southern states in the 1940s provide convincing evidence that societal arrangements and practices shape the demands which are funneled to public officials. The drawback of Key's approach is that it requires direct observation of the sociopolitical system under investigation. Essentially, researchers have to immerse themselves in the culture to understand it. This raises questions about subjectivity in the findings, and also makes it very impractical for researchers who have more limited time and resources for field work.

Daniel J. Elazar (1966) continued the tradition of participant observation to elicit cultural characteristics of the states. But he also built upon his personal insights through careful analysis of historical records, focusing primarily on the ethnic and religious characteristics of state populations. Elazar's basic argument was that the nature of each state's initial settlers imposed a particular "stamp" on subsequent sociopolitical developments. As a result of this general process, state populations exhibit systematic differences in their understandings of legitimate political activity.

Elazar divided the states into three broad categories based upon the predominant ethnic and religious values of their populations. In moralist states, government is expected to play an active role in promoting societal welfare. Individualist states are those that favor the private marketplace for allocating resources, leaving government in a more subdued role as an umpire to guarantee orderly transactions. And, traditionalist states are characterized by elitist orientations that promote existing power structures and oppose any form of government intervention in society. Elazar believed that day-to-day public opinion within the states would flow from the type of political culture that characterized the respective populations.

Elazar's typology results in a relatively crude breakdown of the states that is, once again, open to criticism for its subjectivity. Ira Sharkansky (1969) attempted to address these concerns and develop a more systematic measure of cultural variation based upon specific state characteristics. He related Elazar's categories to specific measures of state political participation rates, state bureaucratic characteristics, and the scope of state policy programs. Sharkansky combined this information to produce a continuous bipolar scale ranging from moralist to traditionalist orientations, with individualist states falling in between those two extremes.

Although the work by Key, Elazar, and Sharkansky set the stage, a number of subsequent researchers have developed other taxonomies of state culture based upon socioeconomic and demographic characteristics (e.g., Luttbeg, 1971; Zelinsky, 1973; Gastil, 1975; Garreau, 1981). The general conclusion to be drawn from this line of work is that cultural differences break down along broad geographic lines, producing distinct regional subcultures across the United States. Still another approach begins with similar premises, but concludes that the states themselves are too crude a categorization to provide meaningful information about societal orientations. For example, Lieske (1993) identified "subcultural differences down to the county level . . . based entirely on 'nonpolitical' measures of American culture" (890).

Hero and Tolbert's (1996) approach is similar in spirit, but focuses more directly on racial and ethnic diversity within the states (also see Hero, 1996). All of these latter authors argue that within-state heterogeneity is sufficient to generate systematic effects on state policies.

There has been an enormous amount of research devoted to state political culture and its connection to state policy (e.g., Patterson, 1968; Luttbeg, 1971; Johnson, 1976; Joslyn, 1982; Savage, 1982; Fitzpatrick and Hero, 1988; Nardulli, 1990; Schlitz and Rainey, 1978; Elazar, 1994). Much of this work is based upon the assumption that state political culture is closely related, if not equivalent, to citizen preferences within the state. However, a number of authors have pointed out that this is a very troublesome assumption. There is a great deal of subjectivity in the research on state political culture (i.e., which specific characteristics are taken into consideration), and this raises serious questions about the accuracy with which empirical measures of culture really reflect public opinion (e.g., Hero and Tolbert, 1996). Studies that have tried to measure directly the connection between the indicators of state culture and citizens' political attitudes within the respective states have produced weak results at best (Lowery and Sigelman, 1982). So we believe there is good reason for skepticism about the degree to which existing measures of political culture are useful for studying democratic representation within the states.

Survey-Based Measures

It would be hard to find much disagreement with the assertion that citizen preferences are manifested directly in public opinion. And, if that is the case, it is "simply" a matter of finding appropriate state-level public opinion surveys to produce empirical summaries of citizens' orientations within each state. Unfortunately, however, this is not a straightforward endeavor. Surveys are not conducted uniformly across the states. Therefore, we generally do not have reliable readings of public opinion on common questions, at periodic time intervals within the respective states.

Of course, when such information is available, political scientists are happy to use it. This was precisely the objective of the Comparative State Elections Project (CSEP), an ambitious public opinion study carried out during the 1968 election period. CSEP relied upon a very large number of respondents to which differential weights could be applied in order to produce either one nationally-representative sample or separate representative samples of the electorates within 13 different states. Published work from CSEP includes a data book giving distributions of opinion on a fairly wide variety of policy issues (Black, Kovenock, Reynolds, 1974), and another volume containing chapters devoted to each of the 13 states written by political scientists who had expertise in each of those states (Kovenock, Prothro, and Associates, 1973). Although it was highly innovative in content and somewhat provocative in terms of its approaches to measuring public opinion, CSEP had very little influence on subsequent research in the field.

Another early effort was Robert Erikson's (1976) analysis of some nearly-forgotten state-level public opinion data from the 1930's. Erikson reminded the discipline that the pioneers of public opinion research (Gallup, Gosnell, Crossley, and others) had collected, analyzed, and reported substantial information about state-level opinion distribution on a number of political issues back in the 1930s. And, he showed that state opinion was correlated to state policy activity during that period.

Efforts like these capitalize on unusual datasets. Therefore, they represent exceptions rather than the standard practice in the study of state public opinion. Most researchers have relied instead on innovative approaches that leverage information about the states from national-level surveys.

By far, the most prominent effort along these lines has been the work carried out by Gerald Wright, Robert Erikson, and John McIver. For more than 25 years, their ongoing project has measured the party identification and liberal-conservative ideology of state electorates using data from *CBS News/New York Times* polls. The latter surveys are conducted at frequent intervals and they include standard questions about partisanship and ideology. Therefore, they can be pooled across time intervals, producing enough respondents to enable disaggregation across the individual states. After doing so, a score can be calculated to show the proportion of self-identified Democrats (or liberals) minus the proportion of self-identified Republicans (or conservatives) within each state.

These researchers report yearly partisanship and ideology scores for state electorates. However, they caution that their yearly values are probably unreliable, and that it is more appropriate to aggregate the state scores across longer time intervals, such as four-year presidential terms. Recently, the Gallup organization has also produced yearly state ideology and partisanship scores (Jones, 2009; Saad, 2009; Jones, 2010a; 2010b; Newport, 2010). These measures are taken from tracking polls which interview sizable numbers of respondents (at least 400) within each state. Apparently these measures were first produced in 2009. If they continue on into the future, the Gallup scores may well provide more reliable yearly measurement of the political orientations of state electorates.

One possible concern about the Erikson, Wright, and McIver measures is that they only capture "general" aspects of public opinion. Some scholars believe it is desirable to obtain empirical indicators of citizen preferences on specific issues. For example, Jones and Norrander (1996; also see Norrander, 2001) focus on the CPS Senate National Election Studies (SNES) conducted in 1988, 1990, and 1992. Unlike most of the biennial National Election Studies (NES), the SNES surveyed respondents by state, making it a very simple matter to calculate state-level mean scores on the issue-specific items included in the interview schedules. Paul Brace and his colleagues (Brace, Sims-Butler, Arceneaux, and Johnson, 2002) effectively combine the two preceding approaches by pooling a number of academic surveys from the NES and the General Social Surveys (GSS), and then disaggregating by state in a manner analogous to Erikson, Wright, and McIver. Once again, this enables the calculation of state-level means on survey items pertaining to specific public policy issues.

Carsey and Harden (2010) take advantage of several recent national surveys that have had enormous sample sizes: The 2000 and 2004 National Annenberg Election Surveys (n = 58,373 and n = 81,422, respectively) and the 2006 Cooperative Congressional Election Study (n = 36,420). With so many respondents, it is possible to break down each of these datasets by state and still have relatively reliable readings of within-state opinion. Doing so, they report measures of state partisanship, ideology, and public mood for each of the three years in which the surveys were conducted.

One potential limitation in all of the preceding measures is that each state is represented by a single score; there is no allowance for heterogeneity in state opinion. This is not especially problematic if the latter represents random variability. In that case, within-state variance simply reduces the reliability of measurement in the respective state scores. But if there are systematic elements to the within-state variation, then state scores could potentially miss important elements of public opinion. Norrander and Manzano (2010) argue that it is important to differentiate the opinions of various ethnic groups within state populations (also see Griffin and Newman, 2008). While this introduces considerable complexity into the measurement process, they maintain that it is important to differentiate these groups in order to understand democratic representation within the states.

An enormous amount of work has gone into the creation of these survey-based measures of state public opinion and all of the scholars who created them have done a tremendous service to the research community. The resultant variables are relatively easy to interpret, and their technical characteristics (e.g. reliabilities) are well-understood. Therefore, these variables have been widely used in analyses of state politics and policy.

Indirect Indicators of Citizen Preferences

Given the difficulties involved in finding and using state-level public opinion data, many scholars have turned instead to variables that function as indirect measures of citizen preferences. For example, all of the pioneering empirical studies of the determinants of state policies used exactly this strategy. Researchers like Dawson and Robinson (1963), Dye (1966), Hofferbert (1966), Sharkansky (1968), Sharkansky and Hofferbert (1969) and Jennings (1979) used a variety of variables to measure state "environments" (to use a term employed by Sharkansky and Hofferbert). The indicators included measures of interparty competition, legislative malapportionment, partisan composition of state legislatures, class support for parties, demographic characteristics and economic conditions. Although such variables were never explicitly identified as proxies for the sentiments of state citizens, it is clear that the analysts who used them believed that they were reasonable gauges of what the public wants. For example, Peterson (1995) says, "One should not ignore the political meaning hidden in demographic and economic variables. For example, the taxable resources of a state are not simply an economic factor...the variable also measures the public's demand for public services" (90).

Another well-established practice in the research community is to assume that mass preferences are reflected in the ideologies of elected public officials from the respective states. If that is the case, then the latter can "stand in" for the former in empirical models. Officeholders' ideologies can be measured using the rating scales that are produced on a regular basis by a variety of ideological interest groups. The mean ratings for a state's congressional delegation can be used to represent the ideology of the state's electorate. A number of researchers have used this strategy over the years, including Rabinowitz, Gurian, and MacDonald (1984), Holbrook-Provow and Poe (1987), and Barrilleaux and Miller (1988). Berry, Ringquist, Fording, and Hanson (1998) argue that officeholders' ideologies are a biased representation of citizen preferences because they are the winners of their respective elections and so their views do not correspond to the political orientations of the citizens who voted for the losing candidates. In order to correct for this problem, Berry et al. estimate the ideology of the losing candidate in each congressional district across the U. S. They then calculate district ideology scores as the sum of the ideologies of the winning and losing candidates in the most recent congressional election, each weighted by the amount of electoral support that the candidate received. The citizen ideology score for the state is calculated by taking the mean of its district ideology scores. Berry et al. argue that their citizen ideology variable "measures the average location of the active electorate in each state on a liberal-conservative continuum"

(Berry, Fording, Ringquist, Hanson, Klarner, 2010, 8, 117). This variable has received an enormous amount of attention and it has been employed for a variety of purposes in recent research on state politics and policy-making.

Indirect measures of state citizen preferences have definite practical advantages. They are constructed from information that is readily available; researchers who want to employ them in their own work need not have access to special datasets, and, the indirect measures can usually be calculated at regular time intervals. For example, the Berry et al. citizen ideology measure assigns a yearly score to each of the states. The problem, of course, is that indirect measures are dependent upon assumptions about the ways that the information they employ (e.g. interest group scores of incumbent officials) is related to citizen preferences. Recently, there has been a vigorous debate on this topic, with some scholars suggesting that the validity of these assumptions is tenuous at best (Brace, Arceneaux, Johnson, Ulbig, 2007; Erikson, Wright, McIver, 2007), and others ardently defending the use of indirect indicators (Berry, Ringquist, Fording, Hanson, 2007a; 2007b). While the jury is still out on this point, the sheer convenience of the Berry et al. citizen ideology variable probably guarantees that it will continue to be used by other scholars.

Simulation-Based Strategies

Many interesting characteristics of public opinion, for example, attitudes on specific political issues, are measured with some regularity at the national level. The challenge is to use the resultant national-level data to generate estimates of state-level public opinion. Simulation-based approaches attempt to do precisely this by combining information about (1) the relationship between individual attitudes and background characteristics, as measured in national sample surveys, and (2) the distributions of the background characteristics within the states.

The general approach is straightforward, and has been around for a long time. The first such simulation study was aimed at estimating the voting preferences of state electorates in the 1960 and 1964 presidential elections (Pool, Abelson, Popkin, 1965). The same approach was then used to estimate state public opinion by Weber, Hopkins, Mezey, and Munger (1972).

The method proceeds in three steps. First, a national survey is used to estimate preferences on a specified policy issue. The preferences are measured separately within each of several sociodemographic subgroups. Second, the sizes of the respective sociodemographic subgroups within each state are obtained from the U.S. Census and other reference sources. Third, within each state, the subgroup preferences (as measured in the national-level survey) are weighted by the within-state subgroup sizes and the weighted preferences are summed to produce a single preference score for each state.

More recent efforts have followed a similar approach, but have employed more sophisticated measurement procedures. Current approaches estimate individual opinions from demographic and geographic characteristics using multilevel regression models and Bayesian estimation procedures, followed by poststratification, or weights that reflect the composition of each state's electorate (Park, Gelman, Bafumi, 2004, 2006; Lax and Phillips, 2009b). Hence, the approach is now called "MRP" for multilevel regression and poststratification. This approach seems to provide more efficient use of the national-level survey data and more reliable estimates of the subgroup opinion distributions. But, at its core, the MRP approach still conceptualizes and operationalizes state public opinion as a weighted sum of subgroup opinion distributions.

Simulation-based approaches are an innovative strategy for using data that are available in order to estimate the desired, but nonexistent, information about citizen preferences within the states. As critics have pointed out (e.g., Seidman, 1975), the weakness of simulated public opinion is the stringency of the assumptions that are required to produce the estimates. For example, does the simulation model include the "right" background characteristics? Are their effects specified correctly? And, are the effects uniform across the states? Nevertheless, the proponents of simulation approaches make a strong case for the validity and reliability of their estimates.

Measuring Public Policy in the States

Overall, measurement issues regarding state-level public policy have not received a great deal of attention in the scholarly literature. We believe that the paucity of systematic research is due, at least in part, to an embarrassment of riches. There is a wide variety of possible variables that can be used as empirical reflections of governmental activity. Scholars typically select an indicator that is convenient for their immediate purposes. And, there is often little consideration given to the validity of the measures that are used (Burstein, 2003). Empirical indicators of policy activity in the states can be divided into two broad categories. First, there are measures that focus on specific aspects of single policies. Second, there are composite measures which combine information within or across policy areas. Let us consider each of these types of variables, in turn.

Policy-Specific Measures

Policy-specific indicators can be further subdivided into three sets: Program expenditures, program adoptions, and a residual category. By far, the most frequently-used type of measure involves the first of these, policy spending. Typically, a study will employ yearly expenditures for a specific policy area within each state. The "raw" spending figures are usually adjusted to take into account state population or the size of a program's constituent base; for example, education spending is often reported in units of dollars per student. The general idea behind the use of such indicators is that program spending is a tangible reflection of the degree to which a state government is willing to commit resources toward a particular societal concern.

Policy spending figures have a number of practical advantages for researchers. First, they are readily available from standard source material. For example, the U. S. Census publication *State Government Finances* reports state spending each year across a clearly defined set of categories. Second, they have desirable measurement properties; there is no debate about the fact that expenditure values can be interpreted as continuous, interval-level information. This makes them easy to use in standard statistical modeling procedures. Third, spending levels have a common and easily-understood unit of measurement, so they are immediately comparable across states and time. Again, adjustments can be made as necessary to account for such factors as geographic size and economic conditions. Given these characteristics, it is no surprise that program spending is such a popular approach for measuring state public policy (for examples, see Gray, 1974; Garand, 1985, 1988; Ringquist and Garand, 1999; Barrilleaux, Holbrook, Langer, 2002).

The next type of policy-specific indicator involves program enactment. Here the researcher identifies a particular action that states can take to address a social problem or achieve a policy objective. The measurement, itself, is a straightforward dichotomy: each state has either carried out the specified action or not. For example, Weber and Shaffer's (1972) early study of policy representation used measures indicating whether or not states had adopted right-to-work laws, statutes permitting teachers to unionize, and handgun permit requirements. More recently, Berry and Berry's (1990) seminal work on policy innovation used a dichotomous indicator showing whether each state had adopted a lottery in a given year.

The possibilities for policy enactment measures are virtually endless: Within each substantive policy area, there are many identifiable actions that state public officials might take, and each one of these could be used as the basis for a different empirical indicator. Regardless of the specific content, the defining characteristic of this type of policy variable is the focus on discrete actions by state governments. This approach does not make any attempt to incorporate information about the degree of commitment to a particular policy objective. But, just like the justification for spending data, policy enactments provide a clear standard for comparisons across states. And, while enactments presumably occur at a specific point in time, they can be regarded as a sort of "switch" that is in the "off" position prior to state adoptions, but "turned on" when the specified program step is enacted, and left in that position thereafter. In this manner, dichotomous policy enactments can be used to study temporal patterns in state policy-making. Again, the sheer flexibility of these measures undoubtedly accounts for their frequent appearance in the state policy literature (for some examples, see Gray, 1973; Eyestone, 1977; Allen, Pettus, and Haider-Markel, 2004; Preuhs, 2005; Lax and Phillips, 2010).

Because of its very nature, our residual category of policy-specific measures is difficult to summarize. We can only say that researchers sometimes focus on particular elements of governmental programs that are supposed to operationalize key characteristics of a given policy area. For example, Meier, Stewart, and England (1989) use graduation ratios, defined as the percentage of a state's African-American students graduating from high school, relative to the overall percentage of graduates within the state to measure student educational outcomes (also see Hero and Tolbert, 1996). And studies of social policies often employ the percentage of the population enrolled within a given program to indicate policy activity (e.g., Rom, 2008), or are covered by a specific policy (Haider-Markel and Meier, 1996). The implicit assumption behind such measures is that each policy is unique in terms of its sociopolitical objectives. Therefore, valid representations of policy activity must "reach into" the specifics of each program's content and outcomes.

Composite Measures of State Policy

The general idea behind composite measures is that public policy is a complex phenomenon which cannot be captured adequately by any single empirical indicator. Instead, policy-specific variables should be regarded as fundamental, but incomplete, components that need to be combined together in order to produce a more comprehensive representation of policy activity. The multiple-indicator approach is relevant both within and across substantive policy areas. This perspective underlies an ongoing research tradition that has led to several composite measures of governmental activity within the states.

The pioneer in this approach is Richard I. Hofferbert, who argues that state public policies have an underlying, common structure which transcends specific program areas. For example, he emphasizes the existence of "common policy orientations" (Hofferbert, 1966, 74) and suggests that "state political systems leave a distinctive imprint on *patterns* of public policies" (Sharkansky and Hofferbert, 1969, 867, emphasis added). The basic point is straightforward: State public policy is a general orientation on the part of each state government; it goes beyond the individual, specific actions that a state may undertake to address pressing social problems and issues (Crew, 1969). Although first articulated more than 40 years ago, this perspective still holds a prominent position among scholars of American state politics (Plotnick and Winters, 1985; Barrilleaux and Miller, 1988; Berry and Berry, 1990; Garand and Hendrick, 1991; Erikson, Wright, McIver, 1993; Gray, Lowery, Fellowes, McAtee, 2004; Monogan, Gray, Lowery, 2009).

Part of the early research agenda in this area was sensitive to the possibility of multiple components within general policy efforts. So, for example, Sharkansky and Hofferbert searched for the "*dimensions* of policy" within the states (1969, 867, emphasis in the original). Their factor analysis of a large set of specific policy variables produced two separate and orthogonal dimensions: A "welfare-education" factor and a "highways-natural resources" factor. In a similar vein, Gray (1974) ranked the states according to their expenditures on, and degrees of progressiveness with respect to, education, welfare, and civil rights policy-making. She reports that the rankings were largely uncorrelated and, therefore, concludes that state policy is an inherently multidimensional phenomenon (also see Eyestone, 1977).

More recent research has been less attentive to questions of multidimensionality and has focused instead on the measurement of a general ideological component in state policymaking. The two major works in this vein are Klingman and Lammers (1984) and Wright, Erikson, McIver (1987). Both of these sets of authors did the same basic thing, although the details differ somewhat across the two analyses. In each case, they use a data reduction methodology (principal components analysis in Klingman and Lammers and factor analysis in Wright et al.) to exploit the correlational structure of multiple policy indicators. The objective is to produce a broad measure of each state's "policy liberalism," defined loosely as a manifestation of the general liberal-conservative continuum. The argument is that this is the basic dimension along which all major polit-ical conflict in the United States takes place.

The Wright et al. variable has been used by many other researchers (e.g., Hill, Leighley, Hinton-Andersson, 1995; Lascher, Hagen, Rochlin, 1996; Hero, 1998) and it has been updated recently by Gray, 2008; Monogan, Gray, Lowery, 2009).

One potential problem with all of the preceding composite variables is that they combine diverse aspects of public policy-making in a non-differentiated fashion. And they pool information over time, sometimes spanning fairly long periods. In order to address these kinds of problems, a variant of the composite-measure approach attempts to isolate specific components of the more general policy process. For example, Walker's (1969) measure of state policy innovativeness combined information about program adoptions in 88 distinct areas in order to develop state-level scores showing each state's propensity to initiate new programs (also see Gray, 1973; Eyestone, 1977). More recently, Jacoby and Schneider (2001, 2009) develop a measure of yearly state spending priorities which gauges the degree to which each state commits resources to policy objectives that provide collective goods to the general population, versus policies that provide particu-larized benefits to specific subgroups. One important advantage of these more focused composite measures is that they can be related to other elements of the policy process. For example, how does innovativeness affect spending? And how do policy priorities influence specific program efforts? Questions like these address important aspects of governmental activity in the American states. But, it is impossible to examine such ques-tions with the undifferentiated composite measures which combine almost all aspects of the policy process.

The composite measures discussed so far incorporate information across multiple substantive program areas. It is important to emphasize that the composite approach has also been used within areas as well. Here, researchers usually develop a scale or index that summarizes the amount of effort that each state devotes to a particular policy objective. For example, Schneider, Jacoby, and Coggburn (1997) analyze state Medicaid efforts by fitting a nonparametric item response theory model to data on optional ser-vice adoptions. And, Arceneaux (2002) measures state abortion policy using an index based upon the number of restrictive provisions passed by the respective state legisla-tures. Policy-specific composite measures have also been used in many other substan-tive areas, including welfare policy (Hanson, 1983; Fellowes and Rowe, 2004), gay rights (Haider-Markel and Kaufman, 2006), environmental regulation (Koninsky, 2009), and child welfare (Gainsborough, 2009). Even though the focus is on a specific substantive policy in each of these works, the assumption remains that individual actions by public officials and institutions cannot tell the whole story. Instead, it is the structure or pattern of activity across a broad front that differentiates the states and reveals their relative positions with respect to a particular policy area.

Measuring the Relationship between Preferences and Policy

There is an extensive literature covering the relationship between citizen preferences and public policy in the American states; it would be impossible to provide a comprehensive listing of the studies that deal with this topic. In fact, much of the research cited so far in this chapter anticipates the current discussion, since most of the scholars interested in measuring state preferences and state policy are also interested in assessing the linkage between the two.

Virtually all studies of state policy representation take the following form: A policy variable is modeled as a function of some measure of citizen preferences, along with appropriate control variables. The specific methods used to estimate these models vary. Several of the early studies used simple and partial correlations (e.g. Dawson and Robinson, 1963; Weber and Shaffer, 1972). By far, the largest amount of work has employed multiple regression models (e.g. Sharkansky and Hofferbert, 1969; Lascher, Hagen, Rochlin, 1996; Haider-Markel and Meier, 1996; Hero, 1998; Jacoby and Schneider, 2001; Arceneaux, 2002; Monogan, Gray, Lowery, 2009). And, more recent studies have used regression variants such as logit and probit models (e.g. Gerber, 1996; Soss, Schram, Vartanian, O'Brien, 2001), simultaneous equation models (e.g. Hill and Hinton-Andersson, 1995; Koninsky, 2009), event history models (e.g. Berry and Berry, 1990), cross-sectional time-series models (Barrilleaux, Holbrook, Langer, 2002; Wood and Theobald, 2003), latent variable (i.e. "LISREL") models (Wright, Erikson, McIver, 1987), and multi-level models (Lax and Phillips, 2009b; 2010).

The results obtained from the empirical analyses vary widely. But the major factor generating these differences seems to be the type of variables used to measure the concepts, especially public opinion, rather than the precise model specifications or estimation procedures. In fact, that is exactly why we have devoted such attention in this chapter to the measurement of citizen preferences and public policy within the states.

A number of early, but very influential, studies found little relationship between the political elements of state environments and the content of policy outputs (Dawson and Robinson, 1963; Dye, 1966; Hofferbert, 1966). Specifically, socioeconomic factors dominated the influences on public policy, almost to the exclusion of more directly "political" variables. This was often interpreted as a sort of economic determinism. For example, Dye (1966) says "... *on the whole*, economic resources were more influential in shaping state policies than any of the political variables previously thought to be important in policy determination" (p. 29, emphasis in the original). But, other researchers (including some of the scholars that originally discovered these relationships) stressed that socioeconomic variables could also act as proxies for the content of political demands within the states (e.g. Hofferbert, 1974; Godwin and Shepard, 1976; Hayes and Stonecash, 1981).

In any case, these studies relied on highly indirect indicators of citizen preferences, such as the variables that tapped Elazar's political culture distinctions (Sharkansky, 1969) or "constructed" measures of political characteristics like malapportionment, party competition, and the partisan composition of state legislatures. The use of such variables to assess representation requires strong assumptions about the relationships between the indicators and citizens' actual preferences, and also about the ways that these indicators should impinge upon policy outcomes. For example, Hofferbert (1966) hypothesized that the degree of malapportionment in state legislatures should have a positive influence on adoption of progressive policies. In hindsight, this connection seems to be rather tenuous.

Other research paints a very different picture of the relationship between public opinion and state policy. The current scholarly consensus is that citizen preferences exert a strong influence on governmental activity within the states. Wright, Erikson, and McIver (1987) are probably most responsible for changing the prevailing view. And they certainly present some of the most forceful and persuasive arguments that it really is public opinion and not other elements of the political environment that is driving policy-making (also see Erikson, Wright, McIver, 1993). But there were a number of studies prior to this work that made the same point (e.g. Weber et al., 1972; Weber and Shaffer, 1972; Erikson, 1976; Nice, 1983; Plotnick and Winters, 1985).

It is important to emphasize that the impact of public opinion holds up even after other socioeconomic and political characteristics of the states are taken into account. And this influence does not operate solely through the electoral process; again, there is a direct connection between opinion and policy, even after the partisan and ideological orientations of state public officials are taken into account (Erikson, Wright, McIver, 1993). The evidence suggests that an opinion-sharing model is more appropriate than one in which legislators fear retribution in the form of electoral defeat (e.g. Hill and Hinton-Andersson, 1995; Soss et al., 2001; Wood and Theobald, 2003).

The impact of citizen preferences is apparent, regardless of whether the analytic models use composite measures of policy (e.g. Wright et al., 1987; Jacoby and Schneider, 2001; Schneider and Jacoby, 2006; Monogan et al., 2009) or program-specific indicators (e.g. Soss et al., 2001; Wood and Theobald, 2003). Public influence also occurs across models that look at program adoptions (e.g. Allen et al., 2004; Fellowes and Rowe, 2004; Lax and Phillips, 2009a) and those that predict policy expenditures and resource allocations (e.g. Barrilleaux et al., 2002; Berry, Fording, Hanson, 2003). Taken together, there is a large body of work which provides convincing evidence that public opinion permeates all aspects of the state policy-making process.

Although public opinion is certainly correlated with policy outputs, there are some important limits to the connection between the two. A number of policy-specific studies have shown that there are non-trivial "gaps" between some policy responses and majority opinions within the states. Much of this research has examined gay rights and other "morality" policies (e.g. Mooney and Lee, 1995; Haider-Markel and Kaufman, 2006; Lax and Phillips, 2009a), demonstrating that strong citizen support is sometimes not reflected very clearly in the passage of specific legislation. Lax and Phillips (2010) show that the degree of opinion-policy congruence differs quite a bit across issue areas. For example, they show that gay rights and gambling policies are particularly responsive to opinion distributions within the states, while certain aspects of education and immigration policy seem to be particularly insulated from citizen preferences. The level of congruence varies with specific policies and programs; it appears to be difficult to make any broad generalizations across policy areas (Burnstein, 2003).

Of course, there are several factors that mediate the representation process in important ways. Erikson, Wright, and McIver (1993) point out that any effects of public preferences must pass through the governmental institutions that are formally responsible for policymaking. So, it is reasonable to assume that characteristics of these institutions will affect representation. And that does seem to be the case. Characteristics of state political systems, including electoral competition (Barrilleaux, 1997; Barrilleaux et al., 2002), the composition and practices of state legislatures (Maestas, 2000; Burden, 2005), the ideology of state governors (Yates and Fording, 2005) and of judges in state courts (Brace, Langer, Hall, 2000) all affect the linkage between public opinion and policy.

Representation should also be facilitated when there are mechanisms that clarify the content of public demands. For example, mobilization of class interests seems to have a pronounced effect on the degree to which state policy provides welfare benefits to needy segments of the population (Hill and Leighley, 1992; Hill, Leighley, Hinton-Andersson, 1995). Similarly, mechanisms for direct democracy should facilitate the translation from citizen preferences to public policy. However, there is a lively and ongoing debate on this point, with some scholars saying that ballot initiatives do promote popular representation (e.g. Zax, 1989; Gerber, 1996; Arceneaux, 2002; Lupia and Matsusaka, 2004; Matsusaka, 2004; Bowler and Donovan, 2010; Lewis, 2011) and other researchers asserting that there is no discernible impact (Farnham, 1990; Lascher et al., 1996; Camobreco, 1998; Monogan et al., 2009). At least part of the source of this disagreement lies in the fact that the impact of direct democracy seems to depend heavily on which aspect of public policy is under investigation. Burden (2005) shows that ballot initiatives affect specific policy steps within the states, but not general state policy orientations. And basic questions have been raised about our ability to measure the mediating effects of initiatives on representation in the first place (Matsusaka, 2001; Hagen, Lascher, Camobreco, 2001).

Another factor that may affect the quality of representation is the interest group environment within a state (Gray and Lowery, 1996). Here again, the findings vary. Gray, Lowery and colleagues report that interest group density and diversity have very little impact on policy, either directly or by modifying the impact of public opinion and direct democracy mechanisms (Gray et al., 2004; Monogan et al., 2009). However, Jacoby and Schneider (2001) show that the direct impact of interest groups on state spending priorities is much stronger than that of state public opinion. They do point out that organized interests may actually contribute to representation by providing an indirect path for channeling citizens' preferences into governmental action (Schneider and Jacoby, 2006; also see Burstein, 2003).

Conclusions: Where Should We Go From Here?

Although its roots lay in earlier work, modern political science research on policy representation in the American states can be traced back to the 1960s. We believe there has been an enormous amount of progress in the ensuing years. Refinements in measures, model specification, and estimation procedures have generated a cumulating body of knowledge showing clearly that citizen preferences affect what states do. A number of prominent scholars blazed trails within this field, including V. O. Key Jr., Daniel Elazar, Richard Hofferbert, Ira Sharkansky, Thomas Dye, and Ronald Weber. But we believe it is critical to emphasize the pivotal contributions made by the team of Robert Erikson, Gerald Wright, and John McIver. Their work has both revitalized and changed the course of research on the linkages between state public opinion and state policy. All "modern" teams of research, such as William Berry and his colleagues, Paul Brace and his colleagues, Virginia Gray and David Lowery, and many others, have been working within the paradigm that Erikson, Wright, and McIver established.

Of course we believe there is much more work that needs to be done. For example, the search for valid and reliable measures of citizen preferences within the states remains ongoing. The difficulties will remain because of the problems involved in obtaining comparable readings of mass opinion across the states at regular time intervals. Given the high costs of public opinion surveys, it is unlikely that this situation will be resolved in the foreseeable future. Therefore, researchers in the field of state policy representation will continue to employ the indicators of public opinion that are already available.

Is this a bad state of affairs? We think not. Like Norrander (2007), we believe that these "... different measures of state public opinion reflect different components of public sentiment" (152). Rather than choosing one or the other variable as the operationalization of public opinion, it is better to recognize that mass political orientations are multifaceted, and that several dimensions of citizen attitudes have potential relevance to policy-making. Therefore, unless there are specific theoretical reasons to do otherwise, the respective variables should probably be used together in models of citizen influence on state policy. We find it interesting that few researchers so far have taken this perspective; so we believe it is an obvious direction to pursue in the future.

We think the area that needs the most attention is the measurement of public policy in the states. Researchers must keep in mind the reality that state-level decisions in any specific policy area generally will be affected by decisions in other policy areas, as well.

Therefore, it is critical to incorporate the relationships between policies into any work that investigates the determinants of state policy. This can be done by incorporating multiple policy indicators as endogenous variables in a statistical model (e.g. Garand, 1985, 1988; Garand and Hendrick, 1991). Or it can be accomplished by building the inter-relationships directly into the measurement process (Jacoby and Schneider, 2009). But if the latter approach is used, we argue that it is important to be explicit and specific about precisely what is being measured. Despite their common usage, we are very skeptical about the theoretical utility of general policy liberalism measures. For one thing, such variables are an amalgam of different things, usually spanning fairly long time intervals. So, in the end it is not at all clear which aspects of the policy process they are measuring (Burstein, 2003).

At the same time, there is some danger of tautology in the construction and use of these measures. Policy liberalism indicators seem to show that state policy-making varies along an ideological dimension. However, the composite variables themselves are constructed by combining indicators that are believed to reflect the liberal-conservative continuum. Therefore it hardly seems surprising (or interesting) that these composite variables exhibit ideological patterns of variability. We contend that a more productive approach is to seek out the dimensions upon which policies and policy-making actually do vary. Only through doing so will we be able to produce more realistic representations of what state governments do.

Finally, we believe there are additional factors that should be incorporated into models of democratic representation within the states. One area that could use attention is the measurement of interest group activity (Gray and Lowery, 1996). Variables that gauge the presence of organized groups and their efforts to affect policy within specific substantive areas would be particularly welcome. And, it is also important to recognize that, in themselves, individual states are not fully autonomous actors. States compete with each other to optimize their resource allocations. And they copy each other, emulating program steps that seem to work and avoiding those that do not. At the same time, all states rely on resources from the federal government and sometimes from local jurisdictions. These features are universally recognized and acknowledged in the state politics literature for their effects on policy outcomes (e.g. Peterson and Rom, 1989, 1990; Volden, 2002, 2006; Berry, Fording, Hanson, 2003; Hero and Preuhs, 2007). But, there has not been much (if any) work devoted to understanding whether these factors affect the translation from public opinion to public policy.

In conclusion, research on state policy and democratic representation comprises a very healthy area of scholarship. There is a consensus within the field that public opinion does have an important impact on state public policy-making. The remaining issues are matters of refining our understanding of this process, rather than breaking out in entirely new directions. But this leaves plenty of opportunity for additional research. The states are "laboratories of democracy," but we still need to determine the proper "formula" for translating citizen preferences into governmental activity.

REFERENCES

Allen, Mahalley D., Carrie Pettus, and Donald P. Haider-Markel. (2004). "Making the National Local: Specifying the Conditions for National Government Influence on State Policymaking." *State Politics and Policy Quarterly* 4(3):318–344.

Arceneaux, Kevin. (2002) "Direct Democracy and the Link Between Public Opinion and State Abortion Policy." *State Politics and Policy Quarterly* 2: 372–387.

Barrilleaux, Charles. (1997) "A Test of the Independent Influences of Electoral Competition and Party Strength in a Model of State Policy-Making." *American Journal of Political Science* 41: 1462–1466.

Barrilleaux, Charles; Thomas Holbrook; and Laura Langer. (2002) "Electoral Competition, Legislative Balance, and American State Welfare Policy." *American Journal of Political Science* 46: 215–227.

Barrilleaux, Charles and Mark Miller. (1988) "The Political Economy of State Medicaid Policy." *American Political Science Review* 82: 1089–1107.

Berry, Frances Stokes and William D. Berry. (1990) "State Lottery Adoptions as Policy Innovations: An Event History Analysis." *American Political Science Review* 84: 395–416.

Berry, William D.; Richard C. Fording; Russell L. Hanson. (2003) "Reassessing the 'Race to the Bottom' in State Welfare Policy." *Journal of Politics* 65: 327–349.

Berry, William D.; Richard C. Fording; Evan J. Ringquist; Russell L. Hanson; and Carl E. Klarner. (2010) "Measuring Citizen and Government Ideology in the U. S. States: A Re-appraisal." *State Politics and Policy Quarterly* 10: 117–135.

Berry, William D.; Evan J. Ringquist; Richard C. Fording; and Russell L. Hanson. (1998) "Measuring Citizen and Government Ideology in the American States, 1960–93." *American Journal of Political Science* 42: 327–348.

Berry, William D.; Evan J. Ringquist; Richard C. Fording; and Russell L. Hanson. (2007a) "The Measurement and Stability of State Citizen Ideology." *State Politics and Policy Quarterly* 7: 111–132.

Berry, William D.; Evan J. Ringquist; Richard C. Fording; and Russell L. Hanson. (2007b) "A Rejoinder: The Measurement and Stability of State Citizen Ideology." *State Politics and Policy Quarterly* 7: 160–166.

Black, Merle; David M. Kovenock; and William C. Reynolds. (1974) *Political Attitudes in the Nation and the States*. Chapel Hill, NC: Institute for Research in Social Science, University of North Carolina at Chapel Hill.

Bowler, Shaun and Todd Donovan. (2010) "Public Opinion, Direct Democracy and Fiscal Policy." Paper presented at the 2010 Annual Meeting of the Midwest Political Science Association.

Brace, Paul; Kevin Arceneaux; Martin Johnson; Stacy G. Ulbig. (2007) "Reply to 'The Measurement and Stability of State Citizen Ideology.'" *State Politics and Policy Quarterly* 7: 133–140.

Brace, Paul; Laura Langer Melinda Gann Hall. (2000) "Measuring the Preferences of State Supreme Court Judges." *Journal of Politics* 62: 387–413.

Brace, Paul; Kellie Sims-Butler; Kevin Arceneaux; Martin Johnson. (2002) "Public Opinion in the American States: New Perspectives Using National Survey Data." *American Journal of Political Science* 46: 173–189.

Burden, Barry C. (2005) "Institutions and Policy Representation in the States." *State Politics and Policy Quarterly* 5: 373–393.

Burstein, Paul. (2003) "The Impact of Public Opinion on Public Policy: A Review and an Agenda." *Political Research Quarterly* 56: 29–40.

Camobreco, John F. (1998) "Preferences, Fiscal Policy, and the Initiative Process." *Journal of Politics* 60: 819–829.

Carsey, Thomas M. and Jeffrey J. Harden. (2010) "New Measures of Partisanship, Ideology, and Policy Mood in the American States." *State Politics and Policy Quarterly* 10: 136–156.

Crew, Robert E. Jr. (1969) "Dimensions of Public Policy: A Factor Analysis of State Expenditures." *Social Science Quarterly* 50: 381–388.

Dawson, Richard E. and James A. Robinson. (1963) "Inter-Party Competition, Economic Variables, and Welfare Policies in the American States." *Journal of Politics* 25: 265–289.

Dye, Thomas. (1966) *Politics, Economics, and the Public: Policy Outcomes in the American States.* Chicago, IL: Rand-McNally.

Elazar, Daniel. (1966) *American Federalism: A View from the States.* New York, NY: Crowell.

Elazar, Daniel. (1994) *The American Mosaic: The Impact of Space, Time, and Culture on American Politics.* Boulder, CO: Westview Press.

Erikson, Robert S. (1976) "The Relationship Between Public Opinion and State Policy: A New Look Based on Some Forgotten Data." *American Journal of Political Science* 20: 25–36.

Erikson, Robert S., Gerald C. Wright, and John P. McIver. (1993) *Statehouse Democracy.* Cambridge, UK: Cambridge University Press.

Erikson, Robert S., Gerald C. Wright, and John P. McIver. (2007) "Measuring the Public's Ideological Preferences in the 50 States: Survey Responses Versus Roll Call Data." *State Politics and Policy Quarterly* 7: 141–151.

Eyestone, Robert. (1977) "Confusion, Diffusion, and Innovation." *American Political Science Review* 71: 441–447.

Farnham, Paul G. (1990) "The Impact of Citizen Influence on Local Government Expenditures." *Public Choice* 64: 201–211.

Fellowes, Matthew C. and Gretchen Rowe. (2004) "Politics of the New American Welfare States." *American Journal of Political Science* 48: 362–373.

Fitzpatrick, Jody L. and Rodney E. Hero. (1988) "Political Cultures and Political Characteristics of the American States." *Western Political Quarterly* 41: 145–153.

Gainsborough, Juliet F. (2009) "Scandals, Law Suits, and Politics: Child Welfare Policy in the U. S. States." *State Politics and Policy Quarterly* 9: 325–355.

Garand, James C. (1985) "Partisan Change and Shifting Expenditure Priorities in the American States, 1945–1978." *American Politics Quarterly* 13: 355–391.

Garand, James C. (1988) "Explaining Government Growth in the U. S. States." *American Political Science Review* 82: 837–849.

Garand, James C. and Rebecca M. Hendrick. (1991) "Expenditure Tradeoffs in the American States: A Longitudinal Test, 1948–1984." *Western Political Quarterly* 44: 915–940.

Garreau, Joel, (1981) *The Nine Nations of North America.* Boston, MA: Houghton-Mifflin.

Gastil, Raymond D. (1975) *Cultural Regions of the United States.* Seattle: University of Washington Press.

Gerber, Elisabeth R. (1996) "Legislatures, Initiatives, and Representation: The Effects of State Legislative Institutions on Policy." *Political Research Quarterly* 49: 263–286.

Godwin, Kenneth R. and W. Bruce Shepard. (1976) "Political Process and Public Expenditures: A Re-examination Based on Theories of Representative Government." *American Political Science Review* 70: 1127–1135.

Gray, Virginia. (1973) "Innovation in the States: A Diffusion Study." *American Political Science Review 68*: 1174–1185.

Gray, Virginia. (1974) "Expenditures and Innovation as Dimensions of 'Progressivism': A Note on the American States." *American Journal of Political Science 18*: 693–699.

Gray, Virginia (2008) "The Socioeconomic and Political Context of States." In Virginia Gray and Russell L. Hanson (Editors), *Politics in the American States, 9th Edition*, Washington, DC: CQ Press, pp. 1–29.

Gray, Virginia and David Lowery. (1996) *The Population Ecology of Interest Representation: Lobbying Communities in the American States*. Ann Arbor, MI: University of Michigan Press.

Gray, Virginia; David Lowery; Matthew Fellowes; Andrea McAtee. (2004) "Public Opinion, Public Policy, and Organized Interests in the American States." *Political Research Quarterly 57*: 411–420.

Griffin, John d. and Brian Newman. (2008) *Minority Report: Evaluating Political Equality in America*. Chicago, IL: University of Chicago Press.

Hagen, Michael G., Edward L. Lascher, Jr., and John F. Camobreco. (2001) "Response to Matsusaka: Estimating the Effect of Ballot Initiatives on Policy Responsiveness." *Journal of Politics 63*: 1257–1263.

Haider-Markel, Donald P., and Matthew S. Kaufman. (2006) "Public Opinion and Policy Making in the Culture Wars: Is There a Connection Between Opinion and State Policy on Gay and Lesbian Issues?" In Jeffrey E. Cohen (Editor), *Public Opinion in State Politics*. Stanford, CA: Stanford University Press, pp. 142–162.

Haider-Markel, Donald P., and Kenneth J. Meier. 1996. "The Politics of Gay and Lesbian Rights: Expanding the Scope of the Conflict." *Journal of Politics 58*(2): 332–349.

Hanson, Russell L. (1983) "The 'Content' of Welfare Policy: The States and Aid to Families with Dependent Children." *Journal of Politics 45*: 771–785.

Hayes, Susan W. and J. Stonecash. (1981) "The Source of Public Policy: Welfare Policy in the American States." *Policy Studies Journal 9*: 681–698.

Hero, Rodney E. (1998) *Faces of Inequality: Social Diversity in American Politics*. Oxford, UK: Oxford University Press.

Hero, Rodney E. and Robert R. Preuhs. (2007) "Immigration and the Evolving American Welfare State: Examining Policies in the U.S. States." *American Journal of Political Science 51*: 498–517.

Hero, Rodney E. and Caroline J. Tolbert (1996) "A Racial/Ethnic Diversity Interpretation of Politics and Policy in the States of the U. S." *American Journal of Political Science 40*: 851–871.

Hill, Kim Quaile and Angela Hinton-Andersson. (1995) "Pathways of Representation: A Causal Analysis of Public Opinion-Policy Linkages." *American Journal of Political Science 39*: 924–935.

Hill, Kim Quaile and Jan E. Leighley. (1992) "The Policy Consequences of Class Bias in State Electorates." *American Journal of Political Science 36*: 351–365.

Hill, Kim Quaile, Jan E. Leighley, and Angela Hinton-Andersson. (1995) "Lower Class Mobilization and Policy Linkage in the U. S. States." *American Journal of Political Science 39*: 75–86.

Hofferbert, Richard I. (1966) "Relationship Between Public Policy and Some Structural and Environmental Variables." *American Political Science Review 60*: 73–82.

Hofferbert, Richard I. (1974) *The Study of Public Policy*. Indianapolis, IN: Bobbs-Merrill.

Holbrook-Provow, Thomas and Steven Poe. (1987) "Measuring State Political Ideology." *American Politics Quarterly* 15: 399–416.

Jacoby, William G. and Saundra K. Schneider. (2001) "Variability in State Policy Priorities: An Empirical Analysis." *Journal of Politics* 63: 544–568.

Jacoby, William G. and Saundra K. Schneider. (2009) "A New Measure of Policy Spending Priorities in the American States." *Political Analysis* 17: 1–24.

Jennings, Edward T., Jr. (1979) "Competition, Constituencies, and Welfare Policies in American States." *American Political Science Review* 73: 414–429.

Johnson, Charles A. (1976) "Political Culture in American States: Elazar's Formulation Examined." *American Journal of Political Science* 20: 491–509.

Jones, Jeffrey M. (2009) "Political Party Affiliation: 30 States Blue, 4 Red in '09 So Far." Gallup.com's State of the State Series. <http://www.gallup.com/poll/122003/Political-Party-A_liation-States-Blue-Red-Far.aspx> last accessed February 5, 2011.

Jones, Jeffrey M. (2010a) "Party ID: Despite GOP Gains, Most States Remain Blue." Gallup.com's State of the State Series. <http://www.gallup.com/poll/125450/Party-Affliation-Despite-GOP-Gains-States-Remain-Blue.aspx> last accessed February 5, 2011.

Jones, Jeffrey M. (2010b) "Wyoming, Mississippi, Utah Rank as Most Conservative States." Gallup.com's State of the State Series. <http://www.gallup.com/poll/141677/Wyoming-Mississippi-Utah-Rank-Conservative-States.aspx> last accessed February 5, 2011.

Jones, Bradford S. and Barbara Norrander. (1996) "The Reliability of Aggregated Public Opinion Measures." *American Journal of Political Science* 40: 295–309.

Joslyn, Richard A. (1982) "Manifestations of Elazar's Political Subcultures: State Public Opinion and the Content of Political Campaign Advertising." In John Kincaid (Ed.), *Political Culture, Public Policy, and the American States*. Philadelphia: Institute for the Study of Human Issues.

Key, V. O., Jr. (1949) *Southern Politics in the State and Nation*. New York, NY: Knopf.

Klingman, David and William W. Lammers. (1984) "The 'General Policy Liberalism' Factor in American State Politics." *American Journal of Political Science* 28: 598–610.

Koninsky, David M. (2009) "Assessing U. S. State Susceptibility to Environmental Regulatory Competition." *State Politics and Policy Quarterly* 9: 404–428.

Kovenock, David M., James W. Prothro, and Associates. (1973) *Explaining the Vote: Presidential Choices in the Nation and the States, 1968 (Part II)*. Chapel Hill, NC: Institute for Research in Social Science, University of North Carolina at Chapel Hill.

Lascher, Edward L., Jr., Michael G. Hagen, and Steven A. Rochlin. (1996) "Gun Behind the Door? Ballot Initiatives, State Policies, and Public Opinion." *Journal of Politics* 58: 760–775.

Lax, Jeffrey R. and Justin H. Phillips. (2009a) "Gay Rights in the States: Public Opinion and Policy Responsiveness." *American Political Science Review* 103: 367–386.

Lax, Jeffrey R. and Justin H. Phillips. (2009b) "How Should We Estimate Public Opinion in The States?" *American Journal of Political Science* 53: 107–121.

Lax, Jeffrey R. and Justin H. Phillips. (2010) "The Democratic Deficit in the States." Unpublished manuscript.

Lewis, Daniel C. (2011) "Bypassing the Representational Filter? Minority Rights Policies under Direct Democracy Institutions." *State Politics and Policy Quarterly* (Forthcoming).

Lieske, Joel. (1993) "Regional Subcultures of the United States." *Journal of Politics* 55: 888–913.

Lowery, David and Lee Sigelman. (1982) "Political Culture and State Public Policy: The Missing Link." *Western Political Quarterly* 35: 376–384.

Lupia, Arthur and John G. Matsusaka. (2004) "Direct Democracy: New Approaches to Old Questions." *Annual Review of Political Science* 7: 463–482.

Luttbeg, Norman R. (1971) "Classifying the American States: An Empirical Attempt to Identify Internal Variations." *Midwest Journal of Political Science* 15: 703–721.

Maestas, Cherie. (2000) "Professional Legislators and Ambitious Politicians: Policy Responsiveness of State Institutions." *Legislative Studies Quarterly* 25: 663–690.

Matsusaka, John G. (2001) "Problems with a Methodology Used to Evaluate the Voter Initiative." *Journal of Politics* 63: 1250–1256.

Matsusaka, John G. (2004) *For the Many or the Few: The Initiative, Public Policy, and American Democracy*. Chicago, IL: University of Chicago Press.

Meier, Kenneth J., Joseph Stewart, Jr., and Robert England. (1989) *Race, Class, and Education: The Politics of Second Generation Discrimination*. Madison, WI: University of Wisconsin Press.

Monogan, James, and Virginia Gray David Lowery. (2009) "Public Opinion, Organized Interests, and Policy Congruence in Initiative and Noninitiative U. S. States." *State Politics and Policy Quarterly* 9: 304–324.

Mooney, Christopher Z. and Mei-Hsien Lee. (1995) "Legislative Morality in the American States: The Case of Pre-Roe Abortion Regulation Reform." *American Journal of Political Science* 39: 599–627.

Nardulli, Peter. (1990) "Political Subcultures in the American States: An Empirical Examination of Elazar's Formulation." *American Politics Quarterly* 18: 287–315.

Newport, Frank. (2010) "More States 'Competitive' in Terms of Party Identification." Gallup. com's State of the State Series. <http://www.gallup.com/poll/141548/States-Competitive-Te rms-Party-Identi_cation.aspx> last accessed February 5, 2011.

Nice, David C. (1983) "Representation in the States: Policymaking and Ideology." *Social Science Quarterly* 64: 404–411.

Norrander, Barbara. (2001) "Measuring State Public Opinion with the Senate National Election Study." *State Politics and Policy Quarterly* 1: 111–125.

Norrander, Barbara. (2007) "Comment: Choosing Among Indicators of State Public Opinion." *State Politics and Policy Quarterly* 7: 152–159.

Norrander, Barbara and Sylvia Manzano. (2010) "Minority Group Opinion in the U. S. States." *State Politics and Policy Quarterly* 10: 446–483.

Park, David K.; Andrew Gelman; Joseph Bafumi. (2004) "Bayesian Multilevel Estimation with Poststratification: State-Level Estimates from National Polls." *Political Analysis* 12: 375–385, pp. 209–228.

Park, David K.; Andrew Gelman; Joseph Bafumi. (2006) "State-Level Opinions from National Surveys: Poststratification Using Multilevel Logistic Regression." In Jeffrey E. Cohen (Editor), *Public Opinion in State Politics*. Stanford, CA: Stanford University Press.

Patterson, Samuel C. (1968) "The Political Cultures of the American States." *Journal of Politics* 30: 187–209.

Peterson, Paul E. (1995) *The Price of Federalism*. Washington, DC: The Brookings Institution.

Peterson, Paul E. and Mark Rom. (1989) "American Federalism, Welfare Policy, and Residential Choices." *American Political Science Review* 83: 711–728.

Peterson, Paul E. and Mark C. Rom (1990) *Welfare Magnets: A New Case for a National Standard*. Washington, DC: The Brookings Institution.

Pool, Ithiel de Sola; Robert Abelson; Samuel L. Popkin. (1965) *Candidates, Issues, and Strategies*. Cambridge, MA: MIT Press.

Plotnick, Robert D. and Richard F. Winters. (1985) "A Politico-Economic Theory of Income Redistribution." *American Political Science Review* 79: 458–473.

Preuhs, Robert R. (2005) "Descriptive Representation, Legislative Leadership, and Direct Democracy: Latino Influence on English Only Laws in the States, 1984–2002." *State Politics and Policy Quarterly 5*: 203–224.

Rabinowitz, George; Paul H. Gurian, Stuart E. MacDonald. (1984) "The Structure of Presidential Elections and the Process of Realignment, 1944 to 1980." *American Journal of Political Science 27*: 611–635.

Ringquist, Evan J. and James C. Garand. (1999) "Policy Change in the American States." In Ronald E. Weber and Paul Brace (Editors), *American State and Local Politics: Directions for the 21st Century*. New York, NY: Chatham House.

Rom, Mark Carl. (2008) "State Health and Welfare Programs." In Virginia Gray and Russell L. Hanson (Editors), *Politics in the American States: A Comparative Analysis, 9th Edition*. Washington, DC: CQ Press, 316–349.

Saad, Lydia. (2009) "Political Ideology: 'Conservative' Label Prevails in the South." Gallup.com's State of the State Series. <http://www.gallup.com/poll/122333/Political-Ideology-Conservative-Label-Prevails-South.aspx> last accessed February 5, 2011.

Savage, Robert L. (1982) "Looking for Political Subcultures: A Rummage Sale Approach." *Western Political Quarterly 34*: 331–336.

Schiltz, Timothy D. and R. Lee Rainey. (1978) "The Geographic Distribution of Elazar's Political Subcultures Among the American Public: A Research Note." *Western Political Quarterly 35*: 410–415.

Schneider, Saundra K. and William G. Jacoby. (2006) "Citizen Influences on State Policy Priorities: The Interplay of Public Opinion and Interest Groups." In Jeffrey E. Cohen (Ed.), *Public Opinion in State Politics*. Stanford, CA: Stanford University Press.

Schneider, Saundra K.; William G. Jacoby; Jerrell D. Coggburn. (1997) "The Structure of Bureaucratic Decisions in the American States." *Public Administration Review 57*: 240–249.

Seidman, David. (1975) "Simulation of Public Opinion: A Caveat." *Public Opinion Quarterly 39*: 331–342.

Sharkansky, Ira. (1968) "Economic Development, Regionalism, and State Political Systems." *Midwest Journal of Political Science 12*: 41–61.

Sharkansky, Ira. (1969) "The Utility of Elazar's Political Culture: A Research Note." *Polity 2*: 66–83.

Sharkansky, Ira and Richard I. Hofferbert. (1969) "Dimensions of State Politics, Economics, and Public Policy." *American Political Science Review 63*: 867–879.

Soss, Joe; Sanford F. Schram; Thomas P. Vartanian; Erin O'Brien. (2001) "Setting the Terms of Relief: Explaining State Policy Choices in the Devolution Revolution." *American Journal of Political Science 45*: 378–395.

Volden, Craig. (2002) "The Politics of Competitive Federalism: A Race to the Bottom in Welfare Benefits?" *American Journal of Political Science 46*: 352–363.

Volden, Craig. (2006) "States as Policy Laboratories: Emulating Success in the Children's Health Insurance Program." *American Journal of Political Science 50*: 294–312.

Walker, Jack L. (1969) "The Diffusion of Innovations Among the American States." *American Political Science Review 63*: 880–899.

Weber, Ronald E., Anne H. Hopkins, Michael L. Mezey, and Frank Munger. (1972) "Computer Simulation of State Electorates." *Public Opinion Quarterly 36*: 49–65.

Weber, Ronald E. and William R. Shaffer. (1972) "Public Opinion in American State Policy Making." *Midwest Journal of Political Science 16*: 633–649.

Wood, B. Dan and Nick Theobald. (2003) "Political Responsiveness and Equity in Public Education Finance." *Journal of Politics* 65: 718–738.

Wright, Gerald C., Robert S. Erikson, and John P. McIver. (1985) "Measuring State Partisanship with Survey Data." *Journal of Politics* 47: 469–489.

Wright, Gerald C., Robert S. Erikson, and John P. McIver. (1987) "Public Opinion and Policy Liberalism in the American States." *American Journal of Political Science* 31: 980–1001.

Yates, Jeff and Richard Fording. (2005) "Politics and State Punitiveness in Black and White." *Journal of Politics* 67: 1099–1121.

Zax, Jeffrey S. (1989) "Initiatives and Government Expenditures." *Public Choice* 63: 267–277.

Zelinsky, Wilbur. (1973) *The Cultural Geography of the United States*. Englewood Cliffs, NJ: Prentice-Hall.

CHAPTER 25

LOCAL POLICY AND DEMOCRATIC REPRESENTATION

CHRISTINE KELLEHER PALUS

SCHOLARS have long deliberated the manifestation of democracy within local governments.[1] Broadly speaking, the central question both motivating and unifying studies of democratic representation has been the following: How does government action reflect citizen preferences? As Burstein wrote, "No one believes that public opinion always determines public policy; few believe it never does" (2003, 29). Practically, however, and specifically in the study of local politics, the actual lines of research addressing this topic have become quite compartmentalized; rich bodies of work focus on one part of the system in isolation—such as elections or political institutions—instead of engaging how the various moving parts connect with one another to directly investigate whether, and if so how, the preferences of citizens are reflected in the policies of government. Although there are obviously exceptions to this generalization (for example, the classic works of Lineberry and Sharkansky, 1971; and Berry, Portney, and Thomson, 1993) as will be evidenced in this chapter I argue that a future agenda for the study of local policy and representation would benefit greatly from applying our knowledge within each of these areas towards broader system-level questions. At many junctures, however, debates over the appropriate unit of analysis, theoretical perspective, and methodological approach have divided those working on the topic of local policy and democratic representation.

First, what even constitutes "local"? City or suburb? Urban or rural? Town, township, village, borough, or county? While many of these words are used interchangeably (or even incorrectly), a focus on the central city has obviously been at the forefront of the literature, thanks to the foundational and groundbreaking work of scholars such as Dahl (1961), Banfield (1961), Bachrach and Baratz (1970), Peterson (1981), Stone (1989), and others. However, as Danielson and Lewis (1996) argued, "individual jurisdictions and political actors cannot be understood fully without an appreciation of how those places and people are situated within the wider urban community" (1996, 212). Additionally, Marando and Reeves (1991) in an aptly named piece, "Counties as Local Governments" posited that theories about cities are not always applicable for counties, and so scholars need to consider "their relationship to state government and their unique role as localities" (1991). Similarly, Benton et al. (2008) identified many challenges facing counties—in particular the increasing demand for services and new policy challenges in the presence of shrinking revenues.

Second, serious debates have ensued concerning the value of the theoretical contributions made by scholars of local politics. For example, some have specifically lamented the general state of urban politics scholarship (Peterson, 1981; Jones, 1989; Judd, 2005), contending that the field is plagued by theoretical stagnation, assuming a place "at the periphery of political science" (Sapotichne, Jones, and Wolfe, 2007). Sapotichne, et al. wrote (98): "the study of urban politics is collapsing into the academic equivalent of a black hole: The light it generates within cannot escape; furthermore, no light from outside can penetrate the event horizon." There are a variety of possible causes for this isolation and stagnation—for example, the dominance of regime theory as an explanatory framework and its isolation from mainstream political science, a pull towards ideological and advocacy research, and the inherently interdisciplinary nature of urban studies (Judd, 2005). Sharp (2007) attributed some of the struggles to a lack of attention on cultural issues (55). However, John (2009, 22) offers a very pragmatic perspective related to critiques of urban politics: "Rather than be downhearted at the lowly status of urban politics or over-inflated by a sense of its virtues, the urban researcher should be glad that the topic offers many natural advantages as well as offering interesting places like cities to study."

Third, from a methodological standpoint, despite the trend of "mainstream" political science towards the quantitative, many studies in local politics are primarily qualitative in nature. In recent years, however, the trend has switched much more in favor of large-n work. For example, Denters and Mossberger (2006) discuss the relevance and potential contributions of comparative research, while Marschall, Shah, and Ruhil (2011) advocate attention to local elections as fruitful avenues to examine questions related to participation, institutions, and race. This tendency does not however mean that case studies are a thing of the past, or should they have a lesser place in the study of local politics and democratic representation; rather, there appears instead to be great variation in terms of the methodology employed on these questions.

Despite these quarrels and debates, I emphasize concurrence on one point: the critical importance of local governments—broadly defined—within the system of democratic governance. "The bedrock of American local democratic theory is that the role of the local government is to reflect the will of the people and that direct individual participation in local government is the best means of achieving this end" (Wolman, 1995, 136). By design, local governments are positioned to be more aware of and in tune to the citizenry's political preferences. Officials are in close proximity to the people they serve and local governments offer a myriad of opportunities for individuals to become engaged in the political process. And, as demonstrated by Delli Carpini and Keeter (1996, 283), knowledge of local politics is highly correlated with knowledge of state and national politics. Citizens who become engaged at the most decentralized levels are most likely to get involved in other spheres of government. Local governments are therefore the arenas in which the idealistic tenets of representative democracy might be most effectively realized and expanded. "Local politics may be the door through which citizens of all economic and social backgrounds are brought into the political arena more generally" (Delli Carpini and Keeter, 284).

Local governments thus provide an ideal setting in which to investigate democratic representation and policy. "Town government is…the most primary unit of American democracy: it defines political membership, the agenda of local politics, and the way people interact. Municipal policies determine who lives in a community, what activities take place, what public issues its residents face, and even what types of public space it contains" (Oliver, 2001, 11). With nearly 90,000 units of local government varying in size, composition, and institutional structure, the local level provides a natural experiment to examine variation in the representational process that is not as obviously present anywhere else in our federal system. Additionally, recent events such as 9/11 and Hurricane Katrina have forced serious reconsiderations about local policy priorities and the nature of responsiveness from an intergovernmental framework (see Savitch, 2003 and Drier 2006).

The existing body of research to be highlighted in this chapter in many ways reflects this diversity. The question of "Who governs?" first posed by Robert Dahl in 1961, has not only served as a notable guidepost for many scholars, but it has also laid the foundation for a subsequent question of the utmost importance: "To what ends?" It is this line of inquiry that serves as a driving force underlying much of the scholarship on local democracy.

In this chapter, I outline the existing bodies of literature addressing the broad topic of local policy and democratic representation. I begin with foundational works, lingering controversies, and those explicitly focused on the question of the link between citizen opinion and public policies. I then move to discussions of the varied components of the political system, and how each serves as a mechanism for policymaking and democracy. I first explore citizenship and political participation—in particular, how varied forms of political expression influence the processes of democracy. Next, I overview the literature addressing how institutions of governance shape responsiveness—in other words, how aggregated preferences are communicated to elected and appointed officials via the variety of institutional mechanisms adopted by local domains. I conclude with critiques, future questions, and a call to utilize the great variation of local governments to further our knowledge about the manifestation of democracy and governance. I call upon scholars to think broadly and creatively about how they might most effectively study local policy and democratic representation.

A Brief History: Citizens, Policies, and Representation

The puzzles surrounding local policy and democratic representation are ones that scholars have wrestled with for decades. We already know a great deal about the operation of democracy in local government from many different angles, using multiple theoretical and methodological approaches, within and across various units of local government and public policy areas. Fueling the diversity of this body of work, however, are the obvious difficulties of studying the linkages between citizens and their governments.

First, whether the disposition of public opinion explicitly affects public policy has been a major theme within this body of work. The classic as well as more recent works conceptualize and measure representation via elite opinions, albeit in varying ways, and often as tied to political participation. Specifically, Prewitt and Eulau (1969; 1973), via interviews with council members, observed three types of representation in San Francisco Bay Area communities, explained by factors such as social pluralism, recruitment procedures, and elections. Verba and Nie (1972) and Hansen (1975) moved the inquiry further to a focus on "concurrence" by adding measures of citizen opinion to compare with the observations of elites. Verba and Nie observed heightened participation in light of greater concurrence, while Hansen's (1975) results affirmed the importance of political structures and institutions to political participation and responsiveness. Morgan (1973) observes congruence between citizens and elected officials, although argues that elections are not necessarily the only means by which it is produced. Hill and Matsubayashi's work continues the theme of concurrence, with their findings pointing to the role of social capital and civic engagement on responsiveness (2005). In their 2008 work, they find that church engagement explicitly enhances representation, as do more liberal religious values.

Later work has shifted more specifically to linking citizen opinions and ideology more broadly to the policy process and outcomes. For example, Marcal and Svorny (2000) focused on Los Angeles voters' opinions on the detachment of the San Fernando Valley; Sullivan (2007) examined citizens' opinions towards gentrification in Portland, and Wassmer and Lascher (2006) explained individual preferences for county growth and regional coordination. DeLeon (1992) offers a notable example of a "process" orientation through his rich case study of San Francisco. He identified three distinct ideologies in the city (liberalism, environmentalism, and populism) and traced how they were able to mobilize and ultimately establish a progressive urban regime.

Other work focused more on specific policy areas in a variety of local settings. In the 1990s, for example, topics included land use (Donovan and Neiman, 1992; Fleischmann and Pierannunzi, 1990), growth control (Donovan and Neiman, 1992), recycling programs (Feiock and West, 1993), economic development (Fleischmann, Green, and Kwong, 1992; Goetz, 1994; Pagano and Bowman, 1995; Goetz and Sidney, 1997), and welfare (Sharp and Maynard-Moody, 1991). In the 2000s, new focal points have emerged in response to critical junctures in our history—for example, the effect of 9/11 and terrorism policy (for example, West and Orr, 2005), Hurricane Katrina's legacy (Burns and Thomas, 2006), and the politics and policies of sustainable cities (Portney, 2003, 2005; Saha, 2009)—to name a few.

Finally, another whole body of work investigates the "policy possibilities" of local government; in other words, what are the options for policy and motivations for government at the local level? This line of scholarship became a dominant and controversial one. Paul Peterson contends that politics in local governments is unlike politics on the national and state levels (1981). Although the national and state governments can actively pursue a redistributive policy agenda, local entities are constrained. Instead, their primary focus is developmental policies—policies that will strengthen their relative "economic position, social prestige, or political power" (20). Peterson argues that local governments are motivated by land, labor, and capital and that Tiebout (1956, 29) sorting effects ultimately drive local policy; because an appealing match of services and taxes can make a locality a more attractive place to settle, "[c]ities…like private firms, compete with one another so as to maximize their economic position."

Schneider (1989) also uses a market paradigm to explain the actions and reactions of local governments to citizen demands. Like Peterson, he contends that local governments are motivated by the interests of the above-average taxpayer and the "local benefit/cost ratio" (201). On the supply side, he observes the activities of bureaucrats—in particular, their focus on budget maximization and their monopolistic control of information—as determinants of the bundle of services provided to citizens. Ultimately, the crux of his argument is that tax base maximization is the core pursuit in the local government market. Similarly, Tiebout sorting effects drive citizen choices and reactions. Molotch's growth machine hypothesis, contending that elite business interests determine policy (1976), is also relevant to this perspective.

These theoretical frameworks, however, may be less applicable for understanding local politics today (Henig, 1992). For example, in the area of development, politics, history, vision, and leadership are emphasized as determining the fate of cities—not just purely market forces (Pagano and Bowman, 1995). Lewis and Neiman (2009), in a very recent book, pointed to local government behaving as a trustee of citizens in the area of residential growth and development, rather than "captured" by economic interests and motivations. They contend that cities maneuver between "constituency demands, fiscal challenges, and constraints on their capacity to affect economic and demographic trends" (4). Their perspective, in other words, is "government-centered" (5). "[L]ocal officials, when government circumstances allow, are prepared to act as custodians or stewards of the community, entrusted by the public with the long-term viability of the local society and economy" (6).

Additionally, in recent years local governments have jumped to the forefront of ideological debates that used to fall exclusively under the jurisdiction of the national government. For example, they now find themselves engaged on a regular basis in "culture wars" (Sharp, 1999) and address controversial and clearly ideological topics such as gay marriage, affordable housing, and the environment (Sharp, 2002). Craw

(2004, 2006) also notes the increased role of local governments in the domain of redistributive policymaking, and specifically explores whether vertical or horizontal relationships within the federal system best explain the varied levels of welfare spending in local domains. If the federal government continues to devolve more and more authority to state and local domains as has been recently discussed (Kelleher and Yackee, 2004), we should expect continued attention by local governments to ideological issues.

More recently, Percival, Johnson, and Neiman (2009) and Palus (2010) directly challenged the assumptions of the Peterson school, looking at counties and cities, respectively. In their particular articles, they each demonstrated a link between the ideological dispositions of the public and the policies of government. As Percival, et al. noted: "[U]nder the right political and structural conditions, there is still room for local politics to influence policy choices at the local level of government" (175). Palus (2010, 144) wrote: "Clearly, cities concern themselves, to varying degrees, with more than just developmental policies and their relative economic position in a particular region, and when they do so they are responding to the desires of their publics."

Hajnal and Trounstine (2010) offer another recent example in this vein. Their focus, however, was on simultaneously testing political, economic, and bureaucratic explanations for spending in local governments. They generally followed the classification scheme used by Peterson (1981) and others. Ultimately, they find a "multifaceted" selection of influences for local policy—much more so than often presented in the literature. They note: "Local government budgets are a complex interplay of politics, economics, institutions, and basic needs…If we want to improve local policy outcomes or even if we just want to understand how certain outcomes are reached in our cities, we need to consider the interplay of all these factors" (1154).

In sum, the scholarship explicitly investigating the relationship between local policy and democratic representation still leaves many unanswered questions. And within this subset of work, there is very often notable and divisive compartmentalization. Moving forward, we will benefit greatly from efforts to transcend the silos we have created and instead work to more broadly investigate the complexities of local democracy.

CITIZENSHIP AND POLITICAL PARTICIPATION AS A MECHANISM FOR DEMOCRATIC REPRESENTATION

A second stream of literature dealing with local government policy and democratic representation is concerned with broad questions of citizenship and democracy within the polity. For example, do citizens participate in politics at the local level? Are citizens satisfied with the provision of services at the local level? How do institutional arrangements influence the degree of citizen participation? The central puzzle driving this research, whether implicitly or explicitly, is how political participation in all its many forms promotes governance of the highest quality; in other words, how does political participation serve as a mechanism for policymaking and democratic representation? As Lowndes (1995, 169) eloquently writes, "While participation may form an important basis for citizenship, it is perhaps most valuable in the context of a strong and vibrant representative democracy—where accountable representatives have the authority to evaluate needs, balance demands, establish priorities, and monitor the outcomes of the political system." Does participation beget policy? And how does policy encourage or discourage participation?

The problem with much of this work, however, is that it has generated a wide range of contradictory and conflicting conclusions (Kelleher and Lowery, 2004). Additionally, we also know that at the local level, the most traditional forum for participation— the electoral arena—is plagued by low turnout (Alford and Lee, 1968; Bridges, 1997; Trounstine, 2008). An obvious potential consequence of this is bias—governments may ultimately form policies that only address the needs of a small proportion of the city's residents. For example, Hajnal and Trounstine (2005) found negative consequences for Blacks and Hispanics as a result of low turnout in local elections. In this section, I outline the scholarship discussing local level political participation. I focus on individual, institutional, and organizational discussions most relevant to broader questions about local policy and representation.

The Who, Why, and How of Local Participation

Perhaps the most central and formative questions to understanding local democracy are the following: who participates at the local level, why, and how? Surprisingly, while volumes upon volumes have addressed this question in the realm of national politics and, to a lesser extent, in the states, at the local level it has been quite underexplored (Oliver, 2001; Sharp, 2003). And, when it has been investigated, large urban centers such as Chicago (Pelissero, Krebs, and Jenkins, 2000) and New York (Kaufmann, 2004) have again been a primary focus. Hajnal's recent book on local turnout and representation offers another example of attention to the big city, with his consideration of the twenty largest cities in the U.S. This work is quite novel in that it examines not only turnout but also the connections between turnout and the functioning of government, and in particular, with respect to race and representation.

There have been some notable studies focused on more "middle-sized" cities in addition to smaller units of local government. For example, Berry, Portney, and Thomson's (1993 classic work, *The Rebirth of Urban Democracy*, investigated five smaller cities— San Antonio, Birmingham, Dayton, Portland, and St. Paul—in addition to ten matched cities with similar population demographics (but differing participation patterns). Bryan (2003) documented the New England Town Meeting in Vermont, offering an unprecedented window into citizen participation in this system of direct democracy. Finally, Oliver's (2001) work investigated suburbs specifically—merging individual-level survey responses with Census data. He strongly advocates the importance of this unit of analysis as well, writing: "Suburbanization has been one of the biggest changes in American society over the past fifty years... Yet, despite the enormity of this suburban transformation, its implications for American democracy are largely unknown" (1).

To understand the link between participation, policy, and representation, it is necessary to begin with the following foundational question: *who* participates in local politics? Initial discussions often provided an answer to this question via a discussion of power structures for governance and participation in that regard rather than on individual patterns of involvement and the consequences of such for governance and representation (Oliver, 2001). Over the years, however, a body of knowledge more explicitly focused on individual-level patterns and trends of involvement has emerged. Some key findings in this regard follow. First, turnout at the local level is, for the most part, notably less than in national elections (Verba and Nie, 1972; Verba, Schlozman, and Brady, 1995; Hajnal, 2010). Second, "there is a severe demographic skew to the local electorate" (Hajnal, 2010, 38) towards wealthier, highly-educated whites. Finally, race has a complex influence on voting trends and participation (Kaufmann, 2004). In some cases, lower turnout has been reported among minorities (Pelissero, Krebs, and Jenkins, 2000) whereas in other cases, mobilization efforts in key elections have led to greater participation (for example, in New Haven as documented by Sumners and Klinker, 1991).

In addition to the "who" question, a subsequent area of inquiry moved to the following: *why* do people participate (or not) in local politics, and if so how? Here, the answers have investigated traditional individual-level explanations, institutional and/or spatial theories, or a combination of the two (for example, Oliver and Ha, 2007). In other words, context facilitates participation in local politics: the way in which we organize our neighborhoods, municipalities, and institutions has clear consequences for the manner and extent to which citizens are engaged in the political process and then, subsequently, for the nature of policies and the quality of representation.

Another common angle of analysis examines whether smaller or larger institutional settings promote political participation. Kelleher and Lowery (2004) offer a useful organizational scheme focused on two competing frameworks for understanding the consequences of metropolitan institutional structure—pro-fragmentation "small is beautiful" and pro-consolidation "large is lively."

On the "small is beautiful" side, a common conclusion is that participation is fostered in smaller or more homogeneous places—arguments central to the development of suburban America (Ross and Levine, 2001). Oliver's recent work (2001) is one very prominent example here—although his findings are slightly more nuanced. While he observes that citizens in smaller communities are more active in local politics and therefore more engaged in the political process, he also finds that economic segregation discourages participation. He writes: "Many suburban governments are constituted solely by people of one class, one race, or one type of land tenure. When municipal borders separate citizens in such ways, social conflicts that once existed among citizens are transformed into conflicts between local governments. This transformation of conflict...deters citizen involvement" (2001, 5–6). His 2007 article (with Ha) points to the importance of traditional drivers such as salience and partisanship, yet also acknowledges the varying impacts of both size and diversity. In a literature review dealing with diversity and participation by Costa and Kahn (2002), they note that participation is often higher in homogenous communities. Alesina and La Ferrara (2000) make a similar argument grounded in citizen preferences toward interacting with people who are most similar to them.

On the "large is lively" side, a number of opposing arguments are relevant—in particular, work by Feiock (2004) and others about the tension between conflict and cooperation with respect to interjurisdictional arrangements, as well as the new regionalism school, which offers sharp critiques of the currently fragmented state of metropolitan politics and policy. For example, Rusk (1995) and Massey and Denton (1993), argue about the connections between city and suburb and the necessity of new approaches to metropolitan solutions to common urban policy problems. Drier, Mollenkopf, and Swanstrom (2001) take a similar position, in a point linking participation, policy, and responsiveness: "The flight to the suburban fringe does not just sever social relations; it also severs political relations...The result is a bland politics at the local level that short-circuits the normal processes of political conflict and compromise and undermines civic participation in both cities and suburbs. The revival of American democracy requires new political institutions at the metropolitan level" (260).

Finally, how do people participate? At the individual level, scholars have pitted two theoretical traditions against one another to investigate this question. On the one hand, the public choice perspective proposes the vision of citizens as consumers (Tiebout, 1956; see also Ostrom, Tiebout, and Warren, 1961). Because they "vote with their feet" by moving to the jurisdiction that most closely matches their preferences, there is little need for traditional forms of participation. Instead, citizens are motivated by purely economic considerations. "Indeed, the public choice approach has, at best, a limited appreciation for the value of political participation as traditionally understood within political science" (Kelleher and Lowery, 2004, 724).

Hirschman's "Exit Voice Loyalty" model (1970) has been put forth, in various forms and iterations, as an alternative framework for understanding the "how" of local participation. Specifically, it expands upon the notion of "exit" as proposed by Tiebout and seeks to explain the manner in which citizens respond to dissatisfaction. Sharp (1984) was among the first to bring this model to studies of political science and, in particular, urban government. Her findings indicated that more highly educated citizens will exit only after they have attempted to voice their dissatisfaction (and in fact, as a last resort), whereas less educated citizens will opt for exit first. Her 1986 work similarly focuses on the individual and contextual factors mobilizing citizens to demand certain services from their localities. She ultimately asserts the importance of communication between individuals and their government officials as a critical link in the policy process. Lyons, Lowery, and DeHoog (1992) explored and expanded Hirschman's model, including the dimension of "neglect" through a study of Lexington and Louisville in Kentucky. They also investigated how jurisdiction-level arrangements influence participation. More recently, scholars such as Dowding, et al. (2000) have criticized this research trajectory, calling for greater clarification of Hirschman's original conceptions and more rigorous specifications in empirical investigations.

The work of Berry, Portney, and Thomson (1993) offers another critical framework for understanding how people participate in local politics—especially in ways beyond the voting box. Their work serves as a bridge to other work that links participation with the quality of representation and outcomes of governance. They focus on five cities that have excelled with respect to citizen participation. They selected these cities because "Birmingham, Dayton, Portland, San Antonio, and St. Paul stand in sharp contrast to the failures of participation, past and present... [E]ach developed neighborhood-based participation efforts that have transformed the political life of their communities" (47).

They note that standard explanations for participation such as demographics and political reform do not explain the success in these places; rather, it can be attributed to a number of other factors. For example, motivation—from citizen groups, government leaders, and federal policy—was key. Design elements such as small neighborhood groups and systematic communication systems also proved critical, as did "a rather sophisticated political balance" (50). The final reason they offer is that these places were able to achieve success before encountering serious financial or political roadblocks.

Other more recent works have explored the "how" of participation as well, with a pointed focus on the role and influence of organizations external to government as promoting engagement. For example, LeRoux (2007), building on the work of Hula and Jackson-Elmore (2001) and others, noted that while the tendency in the literature has been to emphasize the "advocacy roles" (411) of nonprofits, they also can serve as proponents for participation—and in particular, voting and contacting officials. Sidney (2009) offers insight into scholarship specifically focused on the poor in urban settings, noting "the importance of non-profit and community-based organizations in representing the interests of the poor, in responding to their needs through policy development and delivery, and in acting to build more egalitarian and democratic cities" (178).

A final area of scholarship related to the "how" question of participation, and similarly serving as a bridge to linking participation with representation more broadly, is the literature focused on trust, social capital and local government. While much of this work has again tended towards an "urban" focus, nonetheless it offers important insights into citizen views about and engagement with their communities, and how that has the potential to improve or hinder the quality of democratic governance. As Sullivan writes, "the adoption of social capital as a key policy instrument in urban governance raises some important questions for policymakers and scholars. These concern the roles of the local state and civil society organizations in contributing to or constraining social capital, the interaction of social capital with "race"/ethnicity, gender and class, and the influence of wider contextual factors on its development" (2009, 221).

In this area, some notable findings include the following. Rahn and Rudolph (2005) developed a multi-level model exploring various hypotheses about local trust. They observed both individual and city-level influences on trust, as well as cross-level interactions. As they note: "Trust in local government matters because it has important implications for local representation and governance" (552). For example, in the presence of scarce resources, elected officials "are increasingly likely to need the leeway that political trust affords (553)." Marschall and Shah (2007) focused their study on racial dimensions of trust with respect to local government and police, unpacking the relationships between individual opinions, descriptive representation patterns, and substantive policy changes. Goldfinger and Ferguson (2009), following in the lines of Cusack (1999) and Rice (2001), examined the relationship between social capital and government performance, ultimately finding a positive link. Although their study had a limited sample size, this observation has implications for the operation of democracy and the give-and-take between the civic life of citizens and the outputs of government.

To What Ends? How Participation Influences Policy and Representation

As the above sections illustrate, there is a notable body of work addressing varied dimensions of political participation, as the "who," "why," and "how" of citizen engagement are certainly central to the functioning of American democracy. I now turn to the consequences of this participation. How do these participation trends influence the policies that local governments debate and implement? As will become evident, there are many outcomes attributed to participation in our political system—some positive, some negative, and probably most often, a little of both. And so while not as vast as other bodies of work, this line of inquiry has certainly expanded and gained notable momentum in recent years—especially with respect to linking participation via electoral outcomes with subsequent policy decisions in local domains.

Berry, et al. (1995) offer one of the most notable findings related to the link between participation and government action. Citizens influenced the agenda and outcomes of government because of the strength of their neighborhood-based efforts. Of course, there was variation in terms of the degree of success. For example, while it was more difficult to actually get new items on the political agenda, these groups were successful in "creating boundaries" (133) for the already existing agenda as well as in influencing their individual council members.

Others have focused specifically on minorities, and how their mobilization leads to more responsive government and policies. For example, Browning, Marshall, and Tabb (1990) note that increased minority incorporation leads to more responsive government. They write: "The legacy of decades of minority mobilization is the realization of their right to participate in the governance of cities. It is also the institutionalization of their interests and more responsive policy than would otherwise be the case, under much tougher revenue constraints (28)." Marschall and Ruhil (2007) specifically look at whether increases in Black representation leads to greater satisfaction among Black residents, and then whether or not these perceptions are actually grounded in reality.

They find that in fact, "evaluations are rooted in tangible changes in policy and service outputs" (18).

Hajnal's (2010) recent work directly engages the question: "Does turnout matter?" However, he notes the dominance of national and state-level perspectives on this question. His shift to a local-level investigation is motivated by theoretical concern—namely, that "turnout will matter more in local contests than in national politics" because it is so low and unevenly distributed across different ethnic and racial minorities (24). In addition to exploring how turnout shapes mayoral and council elections, he then investigates its influence on government spending priorities. "The ultimate test of turnout is how it affects what a government does in office" (101). What he finds is that electoral participation does in fact influence governmental outcomes—and that the findings are skewed based on patterns of turnout linked with varying racial and economic characteristics. He concludes: "Turnout matters more when turnout is exceptionally low...where disadvantaged, minority groups represent large shares of the electorate...and where electoral competition is higher" (139). Trounstine (2008) had a related finding—that when elections are noncompetitive and regimes become dominant, "the distribution of government benefits changes" (879) to the detriment of many in the broader community.

Thus, although our knowledge on political participation is vast, it is also often disjointed. Additionally, it is perhaps most scarce on the topic that arguably has the greatest consequences for the operation of democracy—whether or not political participation in fact matters with respect to the policies formed by elected officials. This under-emphasis offers much fertile ground for the next generation of scholars to delve into, although requiring great creativity and perseverance with respect to data collection efforts. Nonetheless, the pursuit is most certainly one that has the potential to make great contributions to the entire discipline of political science.

Political Institutions, Local Policy, and Democracy

An extensive literature addressing institutions and policy exists at the local level. As Morgan, England, and Pelissero (2007) write, "The choice of political structure has certainly been the key decision for municipalities throughout the past century" (61). We know there is great variation that exists with respect to the institutional design choices that local governments make. Scholars have taken particular interest in how these choices translate public preferences into government action. In this section, I highlight how the research trajectories investigating local political institutions are relevant to the broader topic of local policy and democratic representation.

Most studies of local government and its institutions, especially in the 1950s and 1960s, focused specifically on urban governance and examined questions related to "community power" and "who governs" from two theoretical perspectives—elitist and pluralist (e.g. Hunter, 1953; Dahl, 1961). Bachrach and Baratz (1962, 1963) criticized both of these theories under the argument that they neglect an essential reality—non-decisions are as important as decisions. In a later attempt to reconcile the competing explanations of pluralists v. elitists, Stone (1989) and others pursued a new angle—regime theory—which has been perhaps the most dominant theoretical perspective to guide studies of local governance since.

One of the primary contributions of regime theory to our understanding of local institutions is its attention to both formal and informal influences on local government. It points to coordination issues between public and private entities (Stoker, 1995) and argues that governance occurs via the creation of these regimes bringing together both governmental and non-governmental actors. In other words, the purpose of the regime's existence is to "make and carry out governing decisions" (Stone, 1989, 6). In a recent work that reflects on the contributions of regime theory to studies of urban politics over the years, Stone offers some insightful reflections. He writes: "[P]olitical structure has an understructure that must be reckoned with . . . Governing, market processes, and civil society are woven together in intricate ways" (2008, 269).

There also has been a significant body of work focused very pointedly on specific institutional structures, and in particular, the implications of the Reform Movement in American politics; in fact, Wolman (1995) notes that most of the debates dealing with local government in the United States are driven by issues related to this movement. There is little consistency, however, among the findings of these countless studies. The Reform Movement of urban politics led to the following general changes in local government: council-manager rule, nonpartisan ballots, and at-large elections. The problem with this body of work is that because it offers multiple contradictory conclusions, especially in the earlier work, there is uncertainty regarding the role that institutional structures play in the policymaking process. For example, Lineberry and Fowler (1967), in one of the most cited works, investigated the effect of non-reformed versus reformed structures on policy outputs and concluded that nonpartisan elections and at-large constituencies (reformed governments) lead to less responsive government. However, Dutton and Northrop (1978) observed a positive association between reformed institutions and the influence of business and elite groups in government. In the domain of electoral politics, a large body of work contends that reformed institutions severely depress voter turnout (Alford and Lee, 1968; Karnig and Walter, 1983; Wood, 2002). Additionally, Welch and Bledsoe (1988) examined similar issues related to symbolic representation and electoral systems and concluded that, "when nonpartisan and at-large structures are combined, both lower income and educational groups and Democrats are strongly disadvantaged" (52–53).

Despite some earlier inconsistencies, I would argue in recent years that some clarity has emerged with respect to political institutions and their influence on the processes of democracy. This might be attributed to scholars fine-tuning the debates about institutional structure to focus more on specific policy issues. Or, perhaps it is the complementary perspectives of political science and public administration literatures, each offering valuable insights. Nonetheless there certainly is a significant collection of work investigating mayors, professional managers, and local councils. It is to this collection of findings that I now turn.

With respect to executives, a relevant literature for this chapter addresses the following question from a variety of angles: What role do executives play in the policymaking and implementation process? Here, I mean "executives" as most broadly defined, inclusive of both mayors (and their varying powers) and professional managers. Although some have explored the two simultaneously, a common line of inquiry, at least in their respective research trajectories, has often been to keep separate the "political" [mayor] from the "administrator" [manager]. As Fredrickson et al. (2004) document, however, "the structural differences between political and administrative cities have diminished and..., over time, the two types of city have come to resemble each other" (100).

At the mayoral end, Pressman's (1972) classic piece discusses how both individual and institutional characteristics influence a mayor's ability to achieve policy goals and respond to crises. Since then, the literature has been a mix of biographies, case studies, and more recently, empirical investigations. In many of these latter works, a focal point has been on how electoral victory influences governing activities. For example, McNitt (2010) looks specifically at tenure in office for mayors, ultimately finding that electoral success is driven by performance in office on policies such as development, law enforcement, and social services. Gerber and Hopkins (2011) examine mayoral partisanship as a predictor of spending patterns, and ultimately discover that Democrat mayors spend less on public safety.

Scholars have also investigated how race influences governance, and in particular, whether descriptive representation is associated with substantive representation. Some recent highlights from this line of work include the following. Marschall and Shah (2007), as discussed previously, looked specifically at issues related to trust in government and service satisfaction, although they investigated both mayoral and council trends. Pelissero, Holian, and Tomaka (2000) examined the consequences on fiscal policies, ultimately finding that the election of a minority mayor did not lead to significant changes in revenues or spending. Hopkins and McCabe (2010) build on this work with a much more expansive sample of 108 cities and ultimately have a similar finding–that the election of a black mayor leads to a majority of policies that are indistinguishable from places where a black mayor loses.

There is also a substantial literature dealing with professional local government management, as well as the interactions between mayors and managers. On the exclusively administrative side, while the ideal stemming from the Reform Movement was that "city government would be divorced from policy and policymaking" (Morgan, England, and Pelissero, 2007, 97), research has indicated a very different reality. As Nalbandian argues (1990, 654), "contemporary managers are involved in community political leadership even though they avoid formal involvement in electoral processes." Thus, there has been much research attempting to unpack the nature of a local government manager's involvement in the governing of a municipality. Svara (1985) re-conceptualized prior frameworks for understanding local manager behavior and ultimately proposed a four-level model focused on mission, policy, administration, and management.

On the relationship between the mayors and managers, discussions have constantly been framed and reframed in light of the classic "politics-administration dichotomy," with common themes including tension, cooperation, and complementarity. However, as Zhang and Feiock note (2009, 462), "the dichotomy model may have obscured our vision in evaluating city managers' role in policy decisions." As a result, perhaps the most insightful studies are ones that consider the interplay between the varying forms of political and administrative institutions in local government—the current reality referred to as the "adapted city."

For example, building on Clingermayer and Feiock's study of local institutions (2001) as well as Schneider and Teske's work on public entrepreneurs (1995), Krebs and Pelissero (2010) examined when urban administrators propose policy. They found that it is more likely in less conflictual settings; when a strong mayor is in place, and in the presence of partisan elections, the environment is such as to discourage policymaking by administrators. Zhang and Feiock (2009) seek to explain varying levels of manager influence in a locality. What they discover is that first, the vast majority are involved, at least minimally, in policymaking. Additionally, they find that mayors and managers work together more as partners, although still within "a hierarchical relationship." Finally, personal characteristics such as the mayor's prior experience and the levels of managerial professionalism are very important in explaining a manager's propensity towards a strong policy role.

Local legislative bodies are also important to our understanding of how institutions aid or abet the formation of local policy and resulting democratic responsiveness. The extant body of work here, however, is not nearly as extensive as the work on executives. Common angles of analysis with respect to city councils include who runs for office, why people choose to run, and who gets elected via at-large versus ward structures. Interestingly, with respect to motivation and interests, Svara (1990) found that councilors are actually not the strongest policymakers and instead are more concerned with constituent service. One could certainly interpret this as responsiveness—albeit not through the traditional institutional channels. Clingermayer and Feiock (1995) similarly focused on councilmember perceptions. They found that while there is general support among council members for targeted policies and benefits, it is stronger for minority legislators. Additionally, it is contingent upon partisanship and selection method. And so, while they do not pointedly investigate actual policy outcomes, this work offers important insights into policy priorities which may ultimately shape the agenda an elected official decides to pursue. Meier and England (1984) looked at the connection between descriptive and substantive representation on school boards specifically, and found that Black membership does in fact lead to more equitable policies.

There has also been attention directed to the policy processes at work in councils. Some prominent recent examples follow. How councils work was the focus of both Pelissero and Krebs (1997) and Johnson (2007); in particular, the committee structure. The former observed limited influence of committees on policy outputs, whereas the latter reformulated and reinterpreted the results and ultimately found that committees do in fact help in achieving "collective goods" such as aid from state governments. Adams (2004) documented the contributions of city council meetings to the quality of public discourse. He argued that: "Even though public meetings themselves are not deliberative, they can facilitate citizen participation and the development of good policy by assisting citizens in achieving their political goals" (43).

An additionally relevant line of inquiry has been in investigating how the mayor and/ or manager interact with the council to form policy. For example, Zeemering (2008) focused on how councils influence interlocal cooperation agreements, and compared it to the behavior of managers. He found that while these sorts of conversations are often thought to be more of a managerial activity, in fact, councilors are also interested in network development and assessment. As a result, he notes the following: "City managers must consider elected officials to be potentially interested participants in dialogue and negotiation about interlocal cooperation" (737).

In conclusion, the literature falling under the broad category of local political institutions is certainly a diverse one, extending well beyond what has been discussed here. Scholars have investigated the delivery of public policy from a variety of perspectives. The variation afforded by local governments offers scholars interested in understanding the effects of institutional design an embarrassment of riches. Moving forward, I encourage continued exploration of the consequences of a municipality's choice with respect to how its institutions are set up. A helpful line of inquiry would be a more deliberate attempt to link institutional designs and operations with actual, measurable, policy outcomes. A nice example in this regard is a recent work by Mullin (2008), who looked at special districts and the consequences they have for public policy and decision-making, ultimately finding that the effect varies based on the severity of the policy problem. Moving forward, additionally critical is a consideration of how informal institutions enter the scene, especially in light of passionate calls supporting an increased role for market forces combined with a decreasing role of government to deliver goods and services.

CRITIQUES, FUTURE QUESTIONS, AND CONCLUSIONS

The topic of local policy and democratic representation is one that has motivated generations of scholars. Although often the focal point for much investigation has been "the big city," there has been increasing attention to smaller municipalities as well. These collections have contributed a great deal both theoretically and empirically to our broader understanding of local governments.

In writing this chapter, however, I could not help but note the wide variety of angles from which the topic of local policy and representation has been addressed—for example, through the lenses of political economy, political participation, and institutional structure. While the extant body of work has no doubt been enriched by these multiple and varied perspectives, a consequence of scholars from countless subfields (and even from disciplines beyond political science) chiming-in on the topic is that at times the study of local politics sometimes feels disjointed and over-compartmentalized. Additionally complicating this are clear methodological biases and controversies that have prevented more productive exchanges between scholars working in this area.

This chapter began with two central propositions: 1) the centrality of local politics to understanding American democracy and 2) the necessity of a broader, system-level approach to understanding policymaking and responsiveness in local domains. Moving forward, I also argue that our understanding of local policy and representation must take a more prominent role in political science because, as Katznelson (2009) so eloquently wrote in a recent collection of essays on the city in American Political Development, "Cities present a privileged vantage point from which to ask fundamental questions, and deploy systematic historical and social science research and evidence to answer them" (246).

I would go so far as to broaden this statement—replacing "cities" with "localities"—and subsequently encourage scholars to do the same. Do not limit the inquiry on local policy and democratic representation to an exclusive focus on cities. Stop focusing on what divides the study of cities from smaller units of government and instead, embrace the variety of all local governments. Ask the big, tough, system-level questions that have the greatest relevance for the functioning of democracy. As Trounstine (2009, 612) wrote: "Studying local politics ought to be integral to the study of political science both because local politics is, in and of itself, important and because local context shapes state and national politics."

Similarly, moving forward, scholars should more directly engage established theories about policymaking at the national and state levels to inform our knowledge of local policy processes. This statement is not meant to discourage theory-building at the local level in and of itself as a useful enterprise. Fertile areas of scholarship at the local level could include more direct investigations of agenda-setting, the influence of organized interests, and policy implementation processes, all of which have been quite well-developed with respect to national and state trends. As Aiken, Newton, Friedland, and Martinotti (1987, 341) wrote, "Urban research, as its practitioners habitually complain, tends to suffer either from being fragmented, parochial and descriptive or from being highly theoretical yet abstract and removed from both practical political questions and empirical research." A potential remedy for this might be more deliberate efforts by scholars to harness the variation of local governments with greater effectiveness so as to inform most broadly questions and theories of interest to the American policy process.

It is a very exciting time to study local politics and policy. Local populations are rapidly changing, municipalities have a renewed focus and drive towards regional issues and metro concerns, and data to study municipalities is becoming more and more readily available. The challenge for us is to approach the study of local policy and democratic representation with renewed enthusiasm and creativity. We certainly have a rich foundation of scholarship to build upon.

Practitioners with their "boots on the ground" are constantly encouraged to build relationships, encourage cooperation, and achieve efficiency, equality, and effectiveness in the provision of public services. We, as scholars, must hold ourselves to a similarly high standard. We must build relationships across subfields, theoretical backgrounds, and methodological proclivities. We must work together to collect the richest data possible so that we fully utilize the inherent variation of local governments. And finally, we must strive for knowledge that investigates whether our system of democracy is truly providing the best possible public policies.

NOTE

1. The author wishes to thank Don Haider-Markel for his helpful suggestions as well as his patience. Additionally, my graduate students (now alumni) in the MPA Program at Villanova University—in particular, Marcelle Klahr and Andrew Todd—deserve my sincere appreciation for their research assistance.

REFERENCES

Adams, Brian. 2004. "Public Meetings and the Democratic Process." *Public Administration Review 64* (1): 43–54

Aiken, Michael, Kenneth Newton, Roger Friedland, and Guido Martinotti. 1987. "Urban Systems Theory and Urban Policy: A Four Nation Comparison." *British Journal of Political Science 17* (3): 341–358.

Alesina, Alberto, and Eliana La Ferrara. 2000. Participation in Heterogeneous Communities. *Quarterly Journal of Economics 115* (3): 847–904.

Alford, Robert and Eugene C. Lee. 1968. "Voting Turnout in American Cities." *American Political Science Review 62*(3): 796–813.

Bachrach, Peter, and Morton S. Baratz. 1962. "Two Faces of Power." *American Political Science Review 56*(4): 947–952.

Bachrach, Peter, and Morton S. Baratz. 1963. "Decisions and Nondecisions: An Analytical Framework." *American Political Science Review 57* (3): 632–642.

Bachrach, Peter, and Morton S. Baratz. 1970. *Power and Poverty: Theory and Practice.* New York: Oxford University Press.

Banfield, Edward. 1961. *Political Influence.* New York: Free Press.

Benton, J. Edwin, Jacqueline Byers, Beverly A. Cigler, Kenneth A. Klase, Donald C. Menzel, Tanis J. Salant, Gregory Streib, James H. Svara and William L. Waugh, Jr. 2008. "Service Challenges and Governance Issues Confronting American Counties in the 21st Century: An Overview". *State & Local Government Review 40* (1): 54–68.

Berry, Jeffrey, Kent Portney, and Ken Thomson. 1993. *The Rebirth of Urban Democracy.* Washington, DC: Brookings.

Bridges, Amy. 1997. *Morning Glories: Municipal Reform in the Southwest.* Princeton, NJ: Princeton University Press.

Browning, Rufus, Dale Rodgers Marshall, and David H. Tabb, eds. 1990. *Racial Politics in American Cities.* New York: Longman.

Bryan, Frank M. 2003. *Real democracy: The New England town meeting and how it works.* Chicago: University of Chicago Press.

Burstein, Paul. 2003. "The Impact of Public Opinion on Policy: A Review and an Agenda." *Political Research Quarterly 56* (1): 29–40.

Burns, Peter, and Matthew Thomas. 2006. "The Failure of the Nonregime: How Katrina Exposed New Orleans as a Regimeless City." *Urban Affairs Review 41* (4): 517–527.

Clingermayer, J. and R. Feiock. 1995. "Council Views Toward the Targeting of Development Policy. Benefits." *Journal of Politics 57*(1): 508–520.

Clingermayer, J. C., and R.C. Feiock. 2001. *Institutional constraints and policy choice.* Albany: State University of New York Press.

Costa, Dora L. and Matthew E. Kahn. 2003. "Civic Engagement and Community Heterogeneity: An Economist's Perspective." *Perspectives on Politics 1* (1): 103–112.

Craw, Michael. 2004. Bringing the City Back In: Municipal Government in U.S. Redistributive Policy. Doctoral Dissertation, Indiana University.

Craw, Michael. 2006. "Overcoming City Limits: Vertical and Horizontal Models of Local Redistributive Policymaking." *Social Sciences Quarterly 87* (2): 361–379.

Cusack, Thomas R. 1999. "Social capital, institutional structures, and democratic performance: A comparative study of German local governments." *European Journal of Political Research 35* (1): 1–34.

Dahl, Robert. 1961. *Who Governs?* New Haven: Yale University Press.

Danielson, Michael N. and Paul G. Lewis. 1996. "City Bound: Political Science and the American Metropolis." *Political Research Quarterly 49* (1): 203–220.

DeLeon, Richard. 1992. *Left Coast City: Progressive Politics in San Francisco, 1975–1991.* Kansas: University Press of Kansas.

Delli Carpini, Michael X., and Scott Keeter. 1996. *What Americans Know About Politics and Why It Matters.* New Haven, CT: Yale University Press.

Denters, Bas, and Karen Mossberger. 2006. "Building Blocks for a Methodology for Comparative Urban Political Research." *Urban Affairs Review 41* (4): 550–571.

Donovan, Todd, and Max Neiman. 1992. "Citizen Mobilization and the Adoption of Local Growth Control." *The Western Political Quarterly 45* (3): 651–675.

Dowding, Keith, Peter John, Thanos Mergoupis, and Mark Van Vugt. 2000. "Exit, voice and loyalty: Analytic and empirical developments." *European Journal of Political Research 37* (4): 469–495.

Drier, Peter. 2006. "Katrina and Power in America." *Urban Affairs Review 41* (1): 1–21.

Drier, Peter, John H. Mollenkopf, and Todd Swanstrom. 2001. *Place Matters.* Lawrence, KS: University of Kansas Press.

Dutton, William H., and Northrop Alana. 1978. "Municipal Reform and Group Influence." *American Journal of Political Science 22* (3): 691–711.

Eulau, Heinz, and Kenneth Prewitt. 1973. *Labyrinths of Democracy: Adaptations, Linkages, Representation, and Policies in Urban Politics.* Indianapolis: Bobbs-Merrill.

Feiock, Richard. 2004. *Metropolitan Governance: Conflict, Competition and Cooperation.* Washington, DC: Georgetown University Press.

Feiock, Richard, and Jonathan West. 1993. "Testing Competing Explanations for Policy Adoption: Municipal Solid Waste Recycling Programs." *Political Research Quarterly 46* (2): 399–419.

Fleischmann, Arnold, Gary Green, and Tsz Man Kwong. 1992. "What's a City to Do? Explaining Differences in Local Economic Development Policies." *Western Political Quarterly 45* (3): 677–700.

Fleischmann, Arnold, and Carol A. Pierannunzi. 1990. "Citizens, Development Interests, and Land-Use Regulation." *The Journal of Politics 52* (3): 838–853.

Fredrickson, H. George, Gary A. Johnson, Curtis H. Wood. 2004. *The Adapted City: Institutional Dynamics and Structural Change.* New York: M.E. Sharp.

Gerber, Elisabeth R., and Daniel J. Hopkins. 2011. "When Mayors Matter: Estimating the Impact of Mayoral Partisanship on City Policy." *American Journal of Political Science 55* (2): 326–339.

Goetz, Edward G. 1994. "Expanding Possibilities in Local Development Policy: An Examination of U. S. *Cities.*" *Political Research Quarterly 47* (1): 85–109.

Goetz, Edward G., and Mara S. Sidney. 1997. "Local Policy Subsystems: An Analysis of Community Development Policy Change." *Urban Affairs Review 32* (4): 490–512.

Goldfinger, Johnny, and Margaret R. Ferguson. 2009. "Social Capital and Governmental Performance in Large American Cities." *State and Local Government Review 41* (1): 25–36.

Hajnal, Zoltan. 2010. *America's Uneven Democracy: Race, Turnout, and Representation in City Politics.* New York: Cambridge University Press.

Hajnal, Zoltan, and Jessica Trounstine. 2005. "Where Turnout Matters: The Consequences of Uneven Turnout in City Politics." *Journal of Politics 67* (2): 515–535.

Hajnal, Zoltan, and Jessica Trounstine. 2010. "Who or What Governs? The Effects of Economics, Politics, Institutions, and Needs on Local Spending." *American Politics Research 38* (6): 1130–1163.

Hansen, Susan. 1975. "Participation, Political Structure, and Concurrence." *American Political Science Review 69* (4): 1181–1199.

Henig, Jeffrey. 1992. "Defining City Limits." *Urban Affairs Review 27* (3): 375–395.

Hill, Kim Quaile, and Tetsuya Matsubayashi. 2005. "Civic Engagement and Mass-Elite Policy Agenda Agreement in American Communities." *American Political Science Review 99* (2): 215–224.

Hill, Kim Quaile, and Tetsuya Matsubayashi. 2008. "Church Engagement, Religious Values, and Mass-Elite Policy Agenda Agreement in Local Communities." *American Journal of Political Science 52* (3): 570–584.

Hirschman, Albert. 1970. *Exit, Voice, and Loyalty.* Cambridge: Harvard University Press.

Hopkins, Daniel and McCabe, Katherine T., After it's Too Late: Estimating the Policy Impacts of Black Mayors Using Regression Discontinuity Design (June 11, 2010). Available at SSRN: <http://ssrn.com/abstract=1632390>.

Hula, Richard, and Cynthia Jackson-Elmore. 2001. "Nonprofit Organizations as Political Actors: Avenues for Minority Political Incorporation." *Policy Studies Review 18* (4): 27–47.

Hunter, Floyd. 1953. *Community Power Structure: A Study of Decision Makers.* Chapel Hill: University of North Carolina Press.

John, Peter. 2009. "Why Study Urban Politics?" In *Theories of Urban Politics, 2nd Edition,* ed. Jonathan Davies and David Imbroscio, 17–24. Washington, DC: Sage.

Johnson, Bertram. 2007. "Collective Action, City Council Committees, and State Aid to Cities." *Urban Affairs Review 42* (4): 457–478.

Jones, Bryan. 1989. "Why Weakness is a Strength: Some Thoughts on the Current State of Urban Analysis." *Urban Affairs Quarterly 25* (1): 30–40.

Judd, Dennis. 2005. "Everything is Always Going to Hell." *Urban Affairs Review 41* (2): 119–131.

Karnig, Albert, and B. Oliver Walter. 1983. "Decline in Municipal Voter Turnout: A Function of Changing Structure?" *American Politics Quarterly 11* (4): 491–506.

Katznelson, Ira. 2009. "Conclusion: On Diversity and the Accommodation of Injustice: A Code on Cities, Liberalism, and American Political Development." In *The City in American Political Development, Richard Dilworth, ed.* New York: Routledge. 246–257.

Kaufmann, Karen M. 2004. *The Urban Voter: Group Conflict and Mayoral Voting Behavior in American Cities.* Ann Arbor: The University of Michigan Press.

Kelleher, Christine and David Lowery. 2004. "Political Participation and Metropolitan Institutional Contexts." *Urban Affairs Review 39* (6): 720–757.

Kelleher, Christine A., and Susan Webb Yackee. 2004. "An Empirical Assessment of Devolution's Policy Impact." *Policy Studies Journal* 32 (2): 253–270.

Krebs, Timothy B., and John P. Pelissero. 2010. "Urban Managers and Public Policy: Do Institutional Arrangements Influence Decisions to Initiate Policy?" *Urban Affairs Review* 45 (3): 391–411.

Lewis, Paul, and Max Neiman. 2009. *Custodians of Place: Governing the Growth and Development of Cities*. Washington, DC: Georgetown University Press.

LeRoux, Kelly. 2007. "Nonprofits as Civic Intermediaries: The Role of Community-Based Organizations in Promoting Political Participation." *Urban Affairs Review* 42 (3): 410–422.

Lineberry, Robert, and Edmund Fowler. 1967. "Reforms and Public Policies in American Cities." *American Political Science Review* 61 (3): 701–716.

Lineberry, Robert, and Ira Sharkansky. 1971. *Urban Politics and Public Policy*. New York: Harper and Row.

Lowndes, Vivian. 1995. "Citizenship and Urban Politics." In *Theories of Urban Politics*. David Judge, Gerry Stoker, and Harold Wolman, eds. London: Sage. 160–180.

Lyons, W.E., David Lowery, and Ruth DeHoog. 1992. *The Politics of Dissatisfaction*. New York: M. E. Sharp, Inc.

Marando, Vincent, and Mavis Mann Reeves. 1991. "Counties as Local Governments: Research Issues and Questions." *Journal of Urban Affairs* 13 (1): 45–53.

Marcal, Leah, and Shirley Svorny. 2000. "Support for Municipal Detachment: Evidence from a Recent Survey of Los Angeles Voters." *Urban Affairs Review* 36 (1): 93–103.

Marschall, Melissa, and Anirudh Ruhil. 2007. "Substantive Symbols: The Attitudinal Dimension of Black Political Incorporation in Local Government." *American Journal of Political Science* 51 (1): 17–33.

Marschall, Melissa, and Paru Shah. 2007. "The Attitudinal Effects of Minority Incorporation: Examining the Racial Dimensions of Trust in Urban America. *Urban Affairs Review* 42 (5): 629–658.

Marschall, Melissa, Paru Shah, and Anirudh Ruhil. 2011. "The Study of Local Elections (Symposium): Editor's Introduction: A Looking Glass Into the Future." *PS: Political Science and Politics* 44 (1): 97–100.

Massey, Douglas S. and Nancy A. Denton. 1993. *American Apartheid*. Cambridge: Harvard University Press.

McNitt, Andrew. 2010. "Tenure in Office of Big City Mayors." *State and Local Government Review* 42 (1): 36–47.

Meier, Kenneth, and Robert England. 1984. "Black Representation and Educational Policy: Are They Related?" *The American Political Science Review* 78 (2): 392–403.

Molotch, Henry. 1976. "The City as Grown Machine: Toward a Political Economy of Place." *American Journal of Sociology* 82 (2): 309–332.

Morgan, David. 1973. "Political Linkage and Public Policy: Attitudinal Congruence between Citizens and Officials." *The Western Political Quarterly* 26 (2): 209–223.

Morgan, David, Robert England, and John Pelissero. 2007. *Managing Urban America*. 6th Edition. Washington, DC: CQ Press.

Mullin, Megan. 2008. "The Conditional Effect of Specialized Governance on Public Policy." *American Journal of Political Science* 52 (1): 124–140.

Nalbandian, John. 1990. "Tenets of Contemporary Professionalism in Local Government. *Public Administration Review* 50 (6):654–662.

Oliver, J. Eric. 2001. *Democracy in Suburbia*. New Jersey: Princeton University Press.

Oliver, J. Eric, and Shang Ha. 2007. "Vote Choice in Suburban Elections". *American Political Science Review 101* (3): 393–408.

Ostrom, Vincent, Charles Tiebout, and Robert Warren. 1961. "The Organization of Government in Metropolitan Areas: A Theoretical Inquiry." *American Political Science Review 55* (4): 831–842.

Pagano, Michael, and Ann O'M. Bowman. 1995. *Cityscapes and Capital: The Politics of Urban Development*. Baltimore: Johns Hopkins Press.

Palus, Christine Kelleher. 2010. "Responsiveness in American Local Governments." *State and Local Government Review 42* (2): 133–150.

Pelissero, John, David B. Holian, and Laura A. Tomaka. 2000. "Does Political Incorporation Matter? The Impact of Minority Mayors Over Time." *Urban Affairs Review 36* (1): 84–92.

Pelissero, John, and Timothy Krebs. 1997. "City Council Legislative Committees and Policymaking in Large United States Cities." *American Journal of Political Science 41* (2): 499–518.

Pelissero, John P., Timothy Krebs, and Shannon Jenkins. 2000. "Asian-Americans, Political Organizations, and Participation in Chicago's Electoral Precincts." *Urban Affairs Review 35* (6): 750–769.

Percival, Garrick, Martin Johnson, and Max Neiman. 2009. "Representation and Local Policy: Relating Ideology to County-Level Policy Adoption." *Political Research Quarterly*, 61(1): 164–177.

Peterson, Paul. 1981. *City Limits*. Chicago: The University of Chicago Press.

Portney, Kent. 2003. *Taking Sustainable Cities Seriously: Economic Development, the Environment, and Quality of Life in American Cities*. Cambridge, MA: MIT Press.

Portney, Kent. 2005. "Civic Engagement and Sustainable Cities in the U.S." *Public Administration Review 65* (5): 579–591.

Pressman, Jeffrey L. 1972. "Preconditions of Mayoral Leadership." *American Political Science Review 66* (1): 11–24.

Prewitt, Kenneth, and Heinz Eulau. 1969. "Political Matrix and Political Representation: Prolegomenon to a New Departure from an Old Problem." *American Political Science Review 63* (2): 427–441.

Rahn, Wendy, and Thomas J. Rudolph. 2005. "A Tale of Trust in American Cities." *Public Opinion Quarterly 69* (4): 530–560.

Rice, Tom W. 2001. "Social capital and government performance in Iowa communities." *Journal of Urban Affairs 23* (3–4): 375–389.

Ross, Bernhard H. and Myron A. Levine. 2001. *Urban Politics*. Itasca, Illinois: F. E. Peacock Publishers.

Rusk, David. 1995. *Cities Without Suburbs*. Baltimore, Maryland: Woodrow Wilson Center Press.

Saha, Devashree. 2009. "Factors Influencing Local Government Sustainability Efforts." *State and Local Government Review 41* (1): 39–48.

Sapotichne, Joshnua, Bryan D. Jones, and Michelle Wolfe. 2007. "Is Urban Politics a Black Hole? Analyzing the Boundary Between Political Science and Urban Politics." *Urban Affairs Review 43* (1): 76–106.

Savitch, Hank. 2003. "Does 9–11 Portend A New Paradigm For Cities?" *Urban Affairs Review 39* (1): 103–127.

Schneider, Mark, and Paul. Teske. 1995. *Public Entrepreneurs: Agents of Change in American Government*. Princeton, NJ: Princeton Univ. Press.

Schneider, Mark. 1989. *The Competitive City: The Political Economy of Suburbia*. Pittsburgh: University of Pittsburgh Press.

Sharp, Elaine. 1984. "Exit, Voice, and Loyalty in the Context of Local Government Problems." *Western Political Quarterly* 37 (1): 67–83.

Sharp, Elaine B. 1986. *Citizen Demand Making in the Urban Context.* University, Alabama: University of Alabama Press.

Sharp, Elaine B., *Ed.* 1999. Culture Wars and Local Politics. Kansas: University of Kansas Press.

Sharp, Elaine B. 2002. "Culture, Institutions, and Urban Officials' Responses to Morality Issues." *Political Research Quarterly* 55 (4): 861–883.

Sharp, Elaine. 2003. "Political Participation in Cities." In *Cities, Politics, and Policy: A Comparative Analysis.* Ed. John Pelissero. Washington, DC: CQ Press. 68–96.

Sharp, Elaine B. 2007. "Revitalizing Urban Research." *Urban Affairs Review* 43(1): 55–75.

Sharp, Elaine B., and Steven Maynard-Moody. 1991. "Theories of the Local Welfare Role." *American Journal of Political Science* 35 (4): 934–950.

Sidney, Mara. 2009. "Poverty, Inequality, and Social Exclusion." In *Theories of Urban Politics, Second Edition.* Washington, DC: Sage. Ed. Jonathan Davies and David L. Limbroscio. 171–187.

Stoker, Gerry. "Regime Theory and Urban Politics." 1995. In *Theories of Urban Politics.* David Judge, Gerry Stoker, and Harold Wolman, eds. London: Sage. 54–71.

Stone, Clarence. 1989. *Governing Atlanta: 1946–1988.* Kansas: University Press of Kansas.

Stone, Clarence. 2008. "Urban Politics Then and Now." In *Power in the City: Clarence Stone and the Politics of Inequality.* Marion Orr and Valerie Johnson, Eds. Kansas: University of Kansas Press. 265–316.

Sullivan, Daniel. 2007. Reassessing Gentrification: Measuring Residents' Opinions Using Survey Data." *Urban Affairs Review* 42 (4): 583–592.

Sullivan, Helen. 2009. "Social Capital." In *Theories of Urban Politics, 2nd Edition.* David Judge, Gerry Stoker, and Harold Wolman, eds. London: Sage. Washington, DC: Sage. 221–238.

Sumners, Mary, and Philip Klinker. 1991. "The Daniels Election in New Haven and the Failure of the Deracialization Hypothesis." *Urban Affairs Quarterly* 27 (2): 202–215.

Svara, James. 1985. "Dichotomy and Duality: Reconceptualizing the Relationship between Policy and Administration in Council-Manager Cities." *Public Administration Review* 45 (1): 221–232.

Svara, James. 1990. *Official Leadership in the City: Patterns of Conflict and Cooperation.* New York: Oxford University Press.

Tiebout, Charles. 1956. "A Pure Theory of Local Expenditures." *The Journal of Political Economy* 64 (5): 416–424.

Trounstine, Jessica. 2008. "Dominant Regimes and the Demise of Urban Democracy." *The Journal of Politics* 68 (4): 879–893.

Trounstine, Jessica. 2009 "All Politics is Local: The Re-emergence of the Study of City Politics." *Perspectives on Politics* 7 (3): 611–618.

Verba, Sidney, and Norman H. Nie. 1972. *Participation in America.* Chicago: University of Chicago Press.

Verba, Sidney, Kay Schlozman, and Henry Brady. 1995. *Voice and Equality.* Cambridge: Harvard University Press.

Wassmer, Robert W., and Edward Lascher. 2006. "Who Supports Local Growth and Regional Planning to Deal with its Consequences?" *Urban Affairs Review* 41 (5): 621–645.

Welch, Susan, and Bledsoe, Timothy. 1988. *Urban Reform and Its Consequences.* Chicago: University of Chicago Press.

West, Darrell, and Marion Orr. 2005. "Managing Citizen Fears: Public Attitudes Toward Urban Terrorism." *Urban Affairs Review 41* (1): 93–105.

Wolman, Harold. 1995. "Local Government Institutions and Democratic Governance." In *Theories of Urban Politics.* David Judge, Gerry Stoker, and Harold Wolman, eds. London: Sage. 135–159.

Wood, Curtis. 2002. "Voter Turnout in City Elections." *Urban Affairs Review 38* (2): 209–231.

Zeemering, E. (2008). "Governing Interlocal Cooperation: City Council Interests and the Implications for Public Management". *Public Administration Review 68* (4), 731–741.

Zhang, Yahon, and Richard C. Feiock. 2010. "City Managers' Policy Leadership in Council-Manager Cities." *Journal of Public Administration Research and Theory 20* (2): 461–476.

PART VI

SUB-NATIONAL PUBLIC POLICIES

CHAPTER 26

FISCAL POLICY IN THE AMERICAN STATES

JAMES C. GARAND, JUSTIN ULRICH, AND PING XU

ONE of the sharpest divisions in contemporary politics is based on disputes over spending and taxation issues. In the United States, citizens differ considerably in their views toward the proper size of the public sector, the relative mix of spending and taxation, and who will receive the benefits (and be responsible for the costs) of government programs. Americans differ over what spending priorities should be and which classes of individuals should receive the relative benefits of government spending and bear the relative burdens of taxation. The suggestion that politics is about "who gets what, when, and how" (Lasswell, 1936) or "the authoritative allocation of values" (Easton, 1953) rings true.

Of course, such disputes are not limited to the U.S. federal level. On the contrary, similar divisions about spending and taxation preferences arise in the American states (cf. Beck and Dye, 1982; Sears and Citrin, 1982; Beck, Rainey, and Traut, 1990; Garand and Blais, 2004). Within some constraints arising from the nature of the U.S. federal system and from state constitutional and statutory provisions, each state government is responsible for deciding the size of its public sector, its levels of spending and taxation, and the size of its budget deficits and surpluses. Given the schisms within state electorates relating to the proper role of government and the appropriate levels of government spending and taxation, it is no surprise that issues relating to government spending and tax policy are often highly contentious.

Public policies relating to the budget, taxation, and spending fall within the realm of *fiscal policy*, which is commonly defined as *the use of government spending, taxation, and budget deficits and surpluses to influence economic performance in a political system*. At the U.S. federal level, the national government has wide latitude to adopt spending and tax policies as a means of achieving macroeconomic outcomes—i.e., manipulating aggregate demand, lowering unemployment, and fostering steady economic growth. There is little doubt that national fiscal policy has an effect on economic performance, though there is some variation in (and debate about) how fiscal policy instruments are translated into specific economic outcomes. Of course, not all federal fiscal policies are intended solely to achieve the public good of favorable macroeconomic outcomes; rather, the federal government often uses the federal budget to reward individuals or geographic units through "pork-barrel" (localized spending) projects, to achieve other specific policy goals, or to redistribute wealth from one income group to another.

State governments also use fiscal policy, though the effects of state fiscal policy on state economic performance are less clear. The role of state governments in generating macroeconomic outcomes is in some dispute; indeed, some scholars suggest that state economies are driven largely by how the economy performs at the national level, with state governments having little sway over state economic conditions (Brace, 1991, 1993; Hendrick and Garand, 1991a) Other scholars find that state governments have fiscal policy tools at their disposal that can affect economic performance (Jones, 1990; Brace, 1993). In addition to the possible direct economic effects of state fiscal policy, state governments can also use their budgetary authority to distribute resources to specific subgroups or geographic areas, achieve other specific policy goals, or redistribute wealth from one income group to another. In essence, fiscal policy in the American states plays a multifaceted role in shaping economic, policy, redistributive, and political goals and outcomes.

In this article we explore the scholarly literature on American state fiscal policy. We begin by discussing what is known about the overall size of the public sector in the American states. We focus here on competing explanations of state government size and the empirical support for these explanations. Second, we consider separately the literatures on state spending policy and state revenue policy. In particular, we note that the theoretical frameworks that explain demand for spending and willingness to pay are quite distinct from each other, and this has implications for our understanding of variation in state spending and revenue levels. Third, we consider explicitly the scholarly literature on budgetary deficits and surpluses in the American states. In discussions of national fiscal policy, deficits and surpluses play a prominent role, yet it is unclear if deficits and surpluses in the American states play a similar role. Finally, we explore the effects of state fiscal policy as an independent variable. What are the economic, political, policy, and social effects of state fiscal policy?

One of the themes of this article is that there remains a substantial research agenda left in studying state fiscal policy. During the second half of the twentieth century, state-level data on expenditures, taxation, government size, intergovernmental grants, and economic performance became readily available, and during the 1970s, 1980s, and 1990s there was a veritable explosion of research on state fiscal policy. The pace of scholarly research by political scientists on state fiscal policy has slowed considerably during the first decade of the 2000s, and the result is that scientific progress in understanding state fiscal policy has leveled off. It would be only a slight exaggeration to suggest that the study of state fiscal policy has become somewhat of a "forgotten" area of study. There is a great deal that we still do not know about the size of the public sector, state spending and revenue policy, state deficits and surpluses, and the effects of state fiscal policy. In this article we point out many of these unanswered questions as a means of building a research agenda for future research on state fiscal policy.

THE SIZE OF THE PUBLIC SECTOR IN THE AMERICAN STATES

One of the critical questions about the role of state governments in shaping policy outcomes—including macroeconomic outcomes—is the overall size of the public sector. The size of government is one indicator of the level of policy activism by state governments, since a small public sector is unlikely to have the resources to play as active a role in achieving policy objectives. Moreover, the size of the public sector is a key indicator of state fiscal policy and the use of the state budget to achieve a wide range of policy goals.

Measuring the Size of the Public Sector

Before we can consider competing explanations of the size of the public sector, it is important to discuss how government size is measured in the extant literature. Most studies of public sector size use an indicator of state spending, usually divided by a variable that indicates the size of the state population (i.e., per capita spending) or the size of the total state economy, such as total personal income or Gross State Product (GSP). It is important to standardize raw spending by population or the size of the state economy, since a state such as California (with a large population and a large state economy) will naturally spend more than Wyoming (with a small population and a small state economy). There are other studies that measure the size of the public sector in the American states in terms of government employment (Weiher and Lorrence, 1991), though such measures are somewhat less relevant to studies of state fiscal policy.

The conventional measure of state government size is calculated by taking total state expenditures and dividing by the size of the total state economy. If one explores the trend in government size over time, one gets a good idea of how much the state political system is drawing from the private economy to fund government programs. However, scholars have noted that the inflation rates are different for the public and private sectors (Lowery and Berry, 1983; Berry and Lowery, 1984a, 1984b). Garand (1989) finds that the inflation rate for the private sector—as measured using the Gross National Product (GNP) price deflator—averages 4.6 percent per year from 1945 to 1985, and this compares to an inflation rate for state and local government purchases sector of 6.0 percent. Extending the time frame from 1945 to 1998, Garand and Baudoin (2003) find that the mean inflation rate for GNP is 4.0 percent, while the mean inflation rate for the state and local government purchases sector is 5.0 percent. Clearly, the inflation rate is higher in the state and local government sector than in the private sector. What explains the difference in the state and local government purchases and GNP price deflators has not been considered in the scholarly literature, though Lowery and Berry (1983) explore the determinants of the gap in inflation rates for the public and private sectors at the national level; understanding the inflation gap for the public and private sectors in the American states is certainly an important question, which warrants the attention of state politics scholars.

Why does this matter? First, if the price of state government goods and services rises at a faster rate than the overall economy, the purchasing power of state government will decline over time relative to that of the private sector. This means that to keep real government spending at a constant share of the real economy, it must increase at a faster rate than the private economy. This suggests that there will be constant pressure for state policy makers to increase the size of government over time in order to provide the same level of state government services. Second, increases in the size of the public sector over time does not necessarily mean that government is doing more; rather, increases in the size of the public sector can reflect both a government growth component (i.e., government is doing more) and an inflation component (i.e., the price of government rises at a faster rate than the price of the private sector). Indeed, Garand (1988b, 1991) develops a technique for decomposing increases in the size of state government into these two components, and he finds that from 1945 to 1984 almost 47 percent of government growth was due to differences in the inflation rates for the state government and private sectors. Finally, following the work by Berry and Lowery (1984b) at the national level, Garand (1989) explores the degree to which using nominal or real measures of government size has an effect on parameter estimates from models of state government size. He finds that there are moderate differences in the effects of key independent variables on government size, depending on whether a nominal or real measure of government size is used. These findings suggest that the measurement of government size has nontrivial implications for the inferences that scholars generate from their work on state government size.

Explaining State Government Size

Most studies show that the size of the public sector in the American states has increased in the post-WWII period (Garand 1988a, 1988b; Kapeluck, 2001; Garand and Baudoin, 2003). For instance, Kapeluck finds that the mean size of government has grown fairly steadily from 1945 to 1976, after which the rate of growth continued but at a slightly lower rate and reached a high of over 14 percent of total state personal income throughout the 1990s. Scholars have not continued to follow these trends into the 2000s, so more work is needed on patterns of government size over the past decade.

What explains variation across states and over time in the size of the public sector in the American states? Scholars have divided competing explanations of government size and government growth into two main categories (Lowery and Berry, 1983; Berry and Lowery, 1987; Garand, 1988a, 1989; Kapeluck, 2001). *Responsive government explanations* suggest that the size of the public sector reflects citizen demands for government goods and services in a state political system; simply, government growth or contraction is a function of citizen demands for more or less government. On the other hand, *excessive government explanations* suggest that the public sector itself is a player in determining the size of government; in this view, government grows in response to pressures from government actors for an expanded public sector.

Responsive government explanations: What are the responsive government explanations that are applicable to the size of government in the American states? First, Wagner's Law (Wagner, 1877) suggests that government grows as societies become more industrialized and (hence) urbanized, personal incomes grow, and the externalities associated with industrialization and urbanization create the need for government action. Despite its theoretical plausibility, at the state level there is relatively little support for Wagner's Law; indeed, Garand (1988a, 1993) finds little evidence to support Wagner's Law, though more recently Kapeluck (2001) finds that government size is larger in highly urbanized states.

Second, some responsive government explanations point to the importance of political parties in shaping the size of the public sector. The *party control explanation* suggests that government size is a function of control of state government by the Democratic (or more liberal) or Republican (or more conservative) parties. When state government institutions, such as the governorship and state legislature, are controlled by the more liberal party, one would expect that the size of the public sector will increase, with all else equal; on the other hand, when state government is controlled by the more conservative party, the size of government will either shrink, remain the same, or grow at a slower rate, with all else equal. Although this explanation seems very plausible, in the American states there is only mixed evidence for a systematic relationship between party control and state government size. Garand (1988a) finds that there is a relationship between party control of state government and growth in the public sector in only two states; on the other hand, Kapeluck (2001) uses pooled data from the American states for the time period from 1946 to 1997 and finds that Democratic control of state government has a significant positive effect on government size.

Another explanation relating to the role of political parties in shaping government size is the *interparty competition explanation*, which suggests that the public sector grows in response to higher levels of party competition in a given state. The reasoning is that the two political parties compete with one another for the affection of voters during periods of high competition, and the result is higher spending as the competing parties try to outbid each other for voter support. Thus far there is little empirical evidence to support this hypothesis as a general explanation of state government size (Kapeluck, 2001; Rogers and Rogers, 2000). It is unclear, however, how this explanation would fare in the current climate of enhanced political polarization at the state level (Garand, 2010).

Third, some scholars point to the effects of *political culture* as an explanation of variation in state government size. Some states are comprised of citizenries that are ideologically high demanders of government provision of goods and services, while other states have citizenries that demand less government. Most of the studies that consider the effects of political culture focus on the political ideology of state electorates; simply, states with relatively liberal electorates are expected to have larger state governments than states with relatively conservative electorates. Kapeluck (2001) finds some weak support for the political culture explanation, though more work is needed that takes advantage of improved measures of state ideology. Moreover, with increases in mass political polarization at the state level in the past 20 years, it is possible that the effects of state ideology on government size may be stronger; however, the effect of state mass polarization on the relationship between state ideology and government size has not been fully explored.

Fourth, the *political needs explanation* suggests that variation in state population characteristics helps to shape demand for the size of the state public sector. In particular, states with populations comprised of high demanders of government goods and services are likely to have larger public sectors than other states. High-demand groups include the young (those under 18), the elderly (those over 65), members of racial and ethnic minority groups (e.g., blacks, Latinos), the unemployed, public-sector employees, and members of labor unions. The results from previous research are somewhat mixed. For instance, Kapeluck (2001) finds that the under-18 population and state unemployment rate are associated with increased size of the public sector, but the black and over-65 populations are not.

Finally, there has been a considerable amount of scholarly work on the role of government institutions in shaping the size of the public sector in the American states. In particular, scholars have studied the effects of *fiscal constraints* that arise from efforts by state electorates to place institutional limits on state spending, state revenue, or the overall size of the state governmental sector. Krol (2007) summarizes the literature on fiscal constraints, which includes institutions such as the line-item veto (Nice, 1988; Alm and Evers, 1991), tax and/or expenditure limitations (Bails 1990; Cox and Lowery, 1990; New, 2010), and borrowing constraints (Kiewiet and Szakaly, 1996). Other institutional arrangements can have an effect on the size of the public sector as well. For instance, Gilligan and Matsusaka (2001) show convincingly that the number of seats in the upper chamber of state legislatures during the first half of the twentieth century is strongly and positively related to state expenditures and revenues. On the other hand, Kapeluck (2001) finds that the size of the upper house has a null effect and the size of the lower house a negative effect on state government size during the post-WWII era.

Excessive government explanations: There are numerous mechanisms through which processes associated with excessive government explanations work to increase the size of the public sector. First, perhaps the most widely cited excessive government explanation is the *fiscal illusion theory*, which suggests that governmental actors (1) seek increases in the size of the public sector for their own self-interest; and (2) manipulate demand for government goods and services by concealing the costs of government programs so that citizens demand more government than they would normally be willing to support with higher taxes. There are a number of illusory revenue mechanisms cited in the literature, such as withholding provisions and deficit spending, all of which are seen as preventing taxpayers from accurately estimating their tax burden. However, the fiscal illusion theory draws only mixed empirical support. Garand (1988a) finds evidence to support the fiscal illusion theory in only a small number of states. In his pooled analysis of data from the post-WWII period, Kapeluck (2001) finds that income taxes (which have withholding provisions) are unrelated to the size of the public sector, but state deficits have a strong positive effect on government size.

Second, the direct role of government employees in shaping the size of government has drawn considerable scholarly attention. The *bureau information monopoly* theory, most closely associated with Niskanen (1971), suggests that government bureaucrats use their advantage over information about the workings of their agencies to influence legislators charged with policymaking. Faced with these information asymmetries, legislators are poorly positioned to question agency requests for larger budgets. In the literature on state government growth, there have been no direct tests of this provocative theory. Unfortunately, there has been little research done to test Niskanen's theory at the state level, in no small part due to the difficulty in collecting the data necessary to test the theory in the American states. Alternatively, the *bureau voting theory* suggests that government employees use their voting strength in the electorate to shape the size of the public sector. This theory assumes that government employees are self-interested actors who have stronger preferences for an expanded governmental sector than other voters, are more likely to turn out to vote, and are more likely to vote for candidates who support an expanded public sector. Hence liberal candidates are advantaged by the electoral participation of a group of citizens who support greater government spending and who vote in sufficient numbers that they are likely to be overrepresented in the typical electorate (Garand, Parkhurst, and Seoud, 1991a, 1991b). Applied to the American states, the bureau voting theory has found strong empirical support in aggregate data (Garand, 1988a; Kapeluck, 2001), though there has been relatively little empirical evidence for the micro-level foundations of the theory (but see Garand and Blais, 2004; Garand et al., 1991b).

Third, the *intergovernmental grant explanation*, often described as the *flypaper effect*, emphasizes the role of the federal system in shaping the size of state government. The core idea here is that as intergovernmental grants flow to the states, policy makers in the states are faced with a choice. They can use federal funds as a substitute for state funds, essentially keeping the total size of the state public sector constant over time and adjusting the revenue burden on state citizens downward in response to the influx of federal funds. Alternatively, state policy makers can view intergovernmental funds as a source of additional revenue that can be added to the current level of state revenue; hence federal funds "stick" with the recipient state government and generate an overall increase in the size of the state public sector. The real question here is the degree to which a dollar of federal grants results in less than a dollar of increased state spending (i.e., a replacement effect) or more than a dollar of increased spending (i.e., the flypaper effect). The empirical results from studies of state government size have been mixed, with some scholars producing evidence that is more consistent with the replacement effect (Borcherding,

1977; Garand, 1988a, 1993), while others find evidence to support the flypaper effect (Kapeluck, 2001).

STATE SPENDING POLICY

The size of the public sector in each of the American states is a function of both spending and revenue levels. Because most states require or encourage a balanced budget, state spending is linked explicitly to the levels of revenue available to support such spending. However, the process that drives spending levels is somewhat different to that which drives revenue levels. Specifically, models of state government spending are largely driven by policy choices, with state officials deciding explicitly how much will be spent in total and for various categories of spending. State policy makers must account for public demands that are often relatively insensitive to the costs of the public sector, as well as the incentives built into the structure of democratic political systems that typically lead political elites to support spending levels that are high relative to the revenues required to cover the costs of that spending. In other words, the mass public often demands more government spending than it is willing to pay for, and political elites facilitate higher levels of spending because it is in their interests to do so.

On the other hand, the generation of revenue is hard work. For one thing, support for taxes necessary to fund state spending is usually far below support for spending, prompting some scholars to refer to a "something for nothing" mentality (Sears and Citrin, 1982). Indeed, scholars find that support for government spending usually exceeds support for taxes by a considerable amount (Welch, 1985; Garand and Blais, 2004), and state policy makers find it much more difficult to generate coalitions in favor of increased revenue than coalitions in favor of increased spending. Moreover, state revenue generation is dictated in part by policy choices, since state policy makers establish the types of taxes to be used, as well as setting tax rates. However, state revenue is also dictated in part by factors that are beyond the direct control of state policy makers, such as state economic performance. Ultimately, this means that state expenditure is typically more predictable than state revenue, and the uncertainty surrounding revenue generation can wreak havoc with state budgets, particularly during economic downturns.

In the United States, state government spending constitutes a substantial share of total government spending. In 2008, federal expenditures were $2655.4 billion, which represents 20.7 percent of Gross Domestic Product (GDP); on the other hand, state direct expenditure (i.e., without intergovernmental grants) was $1256.8 billion, or 8.7 percent of GDP, while local direct expenditure was 1577.3 billion, or 10.1 percent of GDP (U.S. Census Bureau 2010). Hence total state direct expenditure represents 21.6 percent of total federal, state, and local expenditure, compared to 51.3 percent for federal government expenditure and 27.1 percent of local direct government expenditure. However, the pattern of state spending differs from federal spending in many ways. First, state governments have different spending priorities than federal government. The U.S. federal government spends a substantial proportion of expenditure on national defense, but state governments do not need to spend on national defense at all. Moreover, the federal government focuses its spending on redistributive areas like welfare and entitlements such as Social Security and Medicaid, while state governments focus their spending on developmental areas like education, infrastructure, and public safety (Peterson 1995). Furthermore, state governments are better positioned to engage in explicit expenditure tradeoffs as a tool to shift spending priorities between different spending areas, since most states have constitutional or statutory restrictions on deficit spending (Garand and Hendrick 1991; Alt and Lowry, 1994; Poterba and Rueben 2001; Nicholson-Crotty, Theobald, and Wood 2006).

Second, the determinants of cross-state variations of state spending are quite different from over-time variations of federal spending. The unique social, economic, political, and demographic conditions of the American states result in spending policies that are quite distinct from one another (Dawson and Robinson 1963; Cnudde and McCrone, 1969; Tompkins 1975; Abrams and Dougan, 1986; Cox and McCubbins, 1991; Alt and Lowry 1994, 2000; Peterson, 1995; Bohn and Inman, 1996; Merrifield 2000). Unlike the case for the federal government, residents of states have higher levels of mobility to choose a state of residence that satisfies their preferences of public goods the best to move to (Tiebout, 1956; Lowery and Lyons, 1989; Lyons and Lowery, 1989; DeHoog, Lower, and Lyons, 1990; Peterson and Rom, 1990; Hawkins, 1992; Lyons, Lowery, and deHoog, 1992; Percy and Hawkins, 1992; Schram, Nitz, and Krueger, 1998; Allard and Danziger, 2000; Bailey, 2005). Given the market-like conditions created by the U.S. federal system, it is likely that public preferences exert a stronger influence on state spending policy. State expenditure policy can also be influenced by federal government spending such as federal aid (Osman 1966; Pogue and Sgontz 1968; Chubb, 1985; Abrams and Dougan, 1986; Bae and Feiock, 2004) or by spending in neighboring states (Baicker, 2005).

Areas of Spending and Expenditure Tradeoffs

Unlike the federal government, state governments do not expend resources on national defense. Instead, state governments focus their spending in areas such as education, public welfare, highways, health and hospitals, police and fire protection, and governmental administration, among others. In 2008, the first four of these spending categories—education, public welfare, highways, health and hospitals—comprised 78.5 percent of state general expenditure. During the same year, in which state government spending comprised 8.7 percent of GDP, on average the American states spent 3.8 percent of GDP on education, 2.9 percent of GDP on welfare programs, 0.8 percent of GDP on health and hospitals, and 0.7 percent on highways. On average, American states spent 36.4 percent of total spending on education, 27.4 percent on welfare, 7.5 percent on health and hospitals, and 7.1 percent on highways (U.S. Census Bureau, 2010).

Developmental vs. redistributive spending areas: Peterson (1995) finds that although both federal and state spending increased in the second half of the twentieth century, the patterns of change are different. According to Peterson, state governments focus their spending on developmental areas such as education, transportation, safety, natural resources, and utilities. Spending in developmental areas is not only greater than in redistributive areas, but developmental spending also grows at a faster rate. From 1962 to 1990, state spending in developmental areas increased from 3.55 percent of GNP to 5.08 percent in 1990. Instead, spending in redistributive areas like welfare, pension and medical insurance, health and hospitals, and housing only took up 1.44 percent of GNP in 1962 and 2.52 percent in 1990. In contrast, the federal government spends more money in redistributive areas, and federal spending in those areas grows much faster. Whether these patterns remain in force today should certainly be explored by state politics scholars.

Expenditure tradeoffs: When resources are limited, policy makers are often required to support increases in one expenditure category by taking resources from other expenditure categories. The result is what scholars have referred to as *tradeoffs* in spending across expenditure categories. Garand and Hendrick (1991, 917) define tradeoffs as "a systematic pattern of direct shifts in spending priorities from one spending category to another," while Berry and Lowery (1990, 671) describe tradeoffs as circumstances in which "the choice of an expenditure level for one category must affect the amount of money allocated to the other category, such that spending in one comes at the expense of the other."

At the federal level, the concept of expenditure tradeoffs was first used by scholars to describe the interrelationship of "guns vs. butter"—that is, the tradeoff between defense and domestic spending (Russet, 1982; Domke, Eichenberg, and Kelleher, 1983; Mintz, 1989; Mintz and Huang, 1990). There has been some consideration of spending tradeoffs at the American state level (Garand and Hendrick, 1991; Nicholson-Crotty, Theobold, and Wood, 2006), though the scholarly literature is less well developed. In one sense, the possibilities of tradeoff effects would seem to be greater at the state level than at the federal level. The reason for this is that most states have constitutional or statutory provisions that mandate a balanced budget, and the result is an environment of scarce resources that facilitates tradeoff behavior. On the other hand, at the federal level there is no balanced budget requirement, and the federal government can respond to resource scarcity by borrowing money and running deficits; hence in theory expenditure tradeoffs should be less likely to occur at the federal level than in the American states.

What do we know about tradeoffs at the state level? Garand and Hendrick (1991) capture expenditure tradeoffs among education, welfare, highways, and health spending categories by modeling changes in spending in each category as a function of changes in spending in other categories, as well as a series of control variables. If the coefficients of spending in other categories are negative, Garand and Hendrick suggest that there is a systematic pattern of tradeoffs. Their results provide evidence that priority changes in one spending category often come at the expense of priority changes for at least another spending area, and tradeoffs are also observed to take place in every state. However, the magnitude of tradeoff effects varies across the states and expenditure categories, and systematic tradeoffs do not occur with equal probability across states or all spending areas. Hendrick and Garand (1991b) explore the degree to which tradeoff effects are determined by political-strategic, organizational, and economic characteristics of the American states, and their findings point to the effects of these variables in shaping the relationships among spending priorities for the various expenditure categories. Finally, Nicholson-Crotty et al. (2006) adopt Berry and Lowery's (1990) admonition against the practice of regressing spending priorities in one area against spending priorities for other areas, and they adopt an approach in which tradeoffs between two expenditure categories are captured explicitly in the dependent variable.

Determinants of state spending priorities

States vary distinctly from one another in their spending policies. Not only is there considerable variation in the amount that states spend, their relative spending priorities are quite different as well. The study of the "nationalization" of state spending priorities—i.e., the degree to which the variance in state spending priorities has decreased over time—was once an important research question for American politics scholars (cf., Hofferbert, 1966; Hofferbert and Sharkansky, 1971; Kemp, 1978; Tucker, 1984), but this question has not been explored in some time. For instance, Peterson (1995) uses coefficients of variation for different spending areas to measure the extent to which the 50 states differ from one another in their spending priorities and whether state spending policies have become more divergent or uniform over time. He finds that states vary substantially in their spending policies, and the variation has not declined from 1962 to 1990. The question of how much state spending priorities are nationalized in recent years is worthy of scholarly attention, as is the question of what explains patterns of nationalization or divergence in spending priorities over time.

As noted, state government size is determined by responsive government explanations and excessive government explanations, and these can be applied to explain variations in federal and state spending over time. Determinants of cross-state variation in spending priorities can be different to the determinants of federal spending priorities over time for several reasons. First, unlike the federal government, which is only one unit, states differ from one another in terms of their various institutional settings, demographic attributes, and political and economic conditions, all of which can influence policy choices and processes in one way or another. Second, American citizens have a high level of mobility with which they can change their state of residence, based on their preferences for public goods; hence there are market-based incentives that motivate both citizens and governments such that public opinion of residents in each of the states can have a strong influence over state spending priorities. Finally, state spending can be influenced by the behavior of other governments. For instance, grants-in-aid from the federal government or the spending priorities of neighboring states can influence state spending priorities in individual states.

Unique state characteristics: States differ from one another in their institutional, political, economic, and social settings, and these settings can influence state spending priorities and processes. In terms of institutional variables, for instance, all states except for Vermont have *balanced-budget provisions* to some degree, which prevent state governments from carrying over deficits from one year to the next. Balanced-budget provisions restrain states' flexibility to increase spending by increasing state deficits (Alt and Lowry 1994; Bohn and Inman, 1996; Garand and Hendrick 1991; Poterba, 1994). By the same token, *divided government* makes expenditure and revenue decisions much more difficult (Alt and Lowry, 2000). Other institutional settings, such as *spending or revenue limits* and *restrictions on general obligation debt*, also restrain state spending (Poterba, 1994; Reuben, 1996; Bails and Tieslau, 2000; but see Cox and Lowery 1990).

State economic conditions influence spending priorities as well. States differ in the magnitude of their tax and revenue pools from which the resources to support state spending are drawn. Hence when the *tax capacity* or the level of *taxable income* of a state increases, there is often public or elite demand for greater public consumption, which leads to a higher level of state spending (Abrams and Dougan, 1986). Economic growth increases the revenue pool but decreases the need for greater spending, while economic contraction and high unemployment can result in decreased or stagnant revenue levels but increased demand for public expenditure.

Social and demographic attributes of the state also determine state spending levels and priorities. Simply, demand for government goods and services (and, hence, higher spending) is likely to be higher in states with certain population configurations. For instance, higher *poverty rates* may increase overall welfare spending, though high poverty rates may tend to depress welfare spending per recipient because states with higher poverty rates may try to "keep more poor people from migrating in by lowering redistributive expenditure" (Peterson, 1995, 93). States with higher *population density* tend to spend more on transportation and other developmental areas because denser populations are associated with higher social interdependence levels and induce high demands for spending in those areas (Peterson, 1995). States with higher percentages of *central city population* tend to spend more in both welfare and developmental areas (Peterson, 1995). The proportion of residents in the state population from disadvantaged racial and ethnic groups also directly influences the level of welfare expenditures (Tompkins, 1975).

Finally, state spending priorities are a function of political variables. States with Democratic governors and Democratic-majority legislatures are expected to allocate higher levels of resources to welfare and education (Garand, 1985). There is also speculation in the literature that high levels of interparty competition has a positive effect on state welfare spending; simply, when interparty competition is high, the two political parties are seen as competing for the votes of low-income voters, who are usually characterized by lower turnout rates. This hypothesis is usually attributed to Key (1949), though the evidence on this point is mixed (Dawson and Robinson, 1963; Dye, 1966; Hofferbert, 1966). However, what is most likely is that interparty competition acts as a mediating variable that translates other variables (such as party control of state government) into higher (or lower) welfare spending levels. For instance, Barrilleaux, Holbrook, and Langer (2002) find that Democratic control of the state legislature is positively related to state welfare spending only in states characterized by high levels of interparty competition.

Mass preferences toward state fiscal policy: State residents are mobile and can select the state or local community that best satisfies their preference for public goods (Tiebout, 1956). If residents are fully aware of the revenue and expenditure patterns of various states, they are able to react to the differences and move to the states that can best satisfy their spending and taxation preferences. For instance, parents with children in school can choose to move to states or communities that spend more on education, while elderly people can choose to move to states or communities that spend more on senior care. Given this, the preferences of state residents can exert an influence on state policy making (Tiebout, 1956; Erikson, Wright, and McIver, 1993).

One problem in this literature is that there is very little data available on the state spending and taxation preferences of state citizens. The work of Sears and Citrin (1982) is a classic exception, insofar as the authors focus on the attitudes toward spending and taxation among Californian citizens in the wake of the tax revolt associated with Proposition 13 in the late 1970s. There are occasional studies of spending and taxation preferences among citizens in individual states (e.g., Beck and Dye, 1982; Garand and Blais, 2004), but there are no data sources that capture systematically the attitudes of the mass public towards state spending and taxation across states and over a long period of time. Hence, scholars rely on general measures of state mass ideology (Erikson, Wright, and McIver, 1993; Berry, Ringquist, Fording and Hanson, 1998; Berry, Fording, Ringquist, Hanson, and Klarner, 2010). What this means is that there is relatively little research done on public preferences toward state fiscal policy, and this is a major shortcoming in the scholarly literature.

STATE REVENUE POLICY

The U.S. federal government has a wide array of options available when adopting revenue policies. However, state governments are constrained by constitutions, demographics, in-state actors, and even the federal government itself. Revenue policies at the state and local levels are extremely important; funds collected finance state agencies and social programs, as well as the numerous public-sector jobs at the state level required to administer those agencies and programs. During difficult economic times, most states are required either to reduce spending to match projected revenue or to increase revenue through new taxation. One need only look to the financial difficulties faced by state governments—especially for large states such as California, New York, and Illinois—during the period from 2008 to 2010 to understand the potentially devastating effect of revenue shortfalls on the public goods and services provided by state governments.

Determinants of Taxation

Attempts to explain the taxation policies of the American states have a long history in this literature (Bingham, Hawkins, and Hebert 1978). In an effort to test empirically some of the more common theories, Berry and Berry (1992) use pooled cross-sectional time-series data and events history analysis to test five explanations of state adoption of income taxes, gasoline taxes, or any taxes. They find particularly strong support for the role of politics in state tax adoption. Specifically, they find that state governments are more likely to institute taxes when there is a long time period before the next election cycle. State legislators may well believe that an increase in taxes is the fiscally appropriate thing to do, but taxes are unlikely to be popular with their electoral constituencies. Adopting new taxes would make the most sense during the time period in which elected officials do not face an imminent threat of electoral defeat as a result of having taken a stance in favor of tax adoption. Legislators are likely to reason that political behavior is also heavily shaped by more recent events, and if an election cycle is far in the future there is a strong likelihood that the voters will forget an increase in taxes that occurred months or even years ago in favor of more recent political actions.

Berry and Berry also find that political opportunities to increase taxes can arise during fiscal crises. When fiscal crises occur, policy makers must increase tax revenue if they want to maintain present levels of state services, given state constitutional or statutory mandates to balance the state budget. In addition, Berry and Berry speculate that states are more likely to adopt new tax policies when neighboring states have adopted new tax policies as well. The adoption of new taxes by other states may help to shield state legislators from the political costs of such policies. Berry and Berry (1992) find that their empirical evidence is consistent across tax instruments and different periods of analysis throughout the twentieth century and are able to justify the fiscal health explanation, the election cycle explanation, and the regional diffusion explanation as being valid explanations of state tax innovation.

Berry and Berry (1992) also consider the effects of economic development on state tax adoption. The economic development theory suggests that an increase in the private resource base—i.e., as reflected in increases in population, businesses in a state, or income—should also result in an increased probability of state tax adoption. However, they find little support for this theory. The authors also test for the effect of party control of state government on state tax adoption, but they find little evidence of a partisan control effect.

Berry and Berry (1994) extend their analysis of state tax adoption to cover increases in state tax rates, and their findings are hauntingly similar to those for state tax adoption. Simply, tax rate increases are more likely to occur during fiscal crises, when neighboring states have adopted tax rate increases, and early in elected officials' terms of office.

The Role of the Public

There has been some scholarly attention paid to the effect of public opinion on taxation policies. When examining the relationship between the mass public and state tax policy, it is important first to ascertain whether or not the public is able to link state government taxes to state government performance. Bowler and Donovan (1995) use survey data collected in five years—1983, 1985, 1987, 1989, and 1991—in which opinions about state tax rates and perception of government performance are measured. The authors find that citizens' hostility toward taxes is strongly related to the actual tax level, suggesting that the mass public has at least some knowledge about objective tax levels and is able to translate that knowledge into assessments of the tax system. Further, Bowler and Donovan find that the public is able to accurately attribute unpopular taxation policies to the state-elected officials who enacted the policies, although little is said about the role of the media and this connection. These findings may point towards an important relationship between public opinion and revenue policies. It would appear that the American mass public has a clear and consistent interpretation regarding state tax provisions. Voters would also seem able to hold elected officials responsible for unpopular taxes, especially when state taxes are already relatively high (Bowler and Donovan, 1995).

The findings by Bowler and Donovan are consistent with those of Attiyeh and Engle (1979) and Lowery and Sigelman (1981). These findings may be attributed to the fact that at the local level individuals have first-hand experience with the outcome of tax dollars being collected and then spent (Hawthorne and Jackson, 1987). However, there is still some debate regarding the public's level of economic knowledge.

State Tax Sources

Unlike the federal government, state governments do not have the constitutional authority to impose tariffs or other taxes on trade goods, and as a result the individual state governments have a relatively small number of options available when they consider raising revenue. The federal government does make contributions to the states through various intergovernmental grant and joint federal–state programs, but the amount available has varied considerably over time (Alt and Lowry, 1994). On the other hand, the U.S. federal system can also impose costs on the states. State governments are often required by the federal government to provide funds for unfunded mandates, which usually involve laws or regulations by the federal government that impose costs on state governments (Posner, 1998). States can generate their own revenues and benefit from intergovernmental grants from the federal government, but they also must bear the costs of federal legislation.

According to Campbell (2009), over the past 90 years the sources of state revenue have changed. In the 1920s, most state revenues came from property taxes. During this time period state governments were able to support their programs with this tax, but this began to change significantly in the 1930s. The Great Depression reduced the amount of property tax that the states had been receiving, and federal funds to the states also decreased. In response, most states began to adopt income and sales taxes and left most property taxes to the local governments, which were having an increasingly difficult time funding their own services (Campbell, 2008). Changes in the federal tax code also paved the way for state and local tax codes. In 1939, only 4 million households paid the federal income tax, but by 1945 that figure had jumped to 45 million households (Campbell, 2008). Income taxes had become part of American life.

Political pressure in the 1950s once again forced a change in state and local fiscal policy. Many in power had felt that the upper-class bore too much of the tax burden, and laws were rewritten so that the middle-class were made to pay a larger percentage of tax on their property and income. In an effort to keep programs fully funded and pay the balance of underfunded federal programs, state and local governments slowly raised income and property taxes. In some states, property taxes increased at a higher rate than home values. Citizens became increasingly frustrated with this state of affairs, and eventually this frustration was manifested at the polls. In California, rapidly increasing property values (and, more importantly, assessments of those property values) resulted in large increases in property taxes, and in 1978 voters passed Proposition 13, a ballot initiative that limited property tax increases. Similar measures were passed in other states, and a strong anti-tax sentiment extended to the national level (Martin, 2008). In response to a decrease in revenues, states began to turn to sales taxes. This consumption tax is easier to predict than a property tax, which may fluctuate rapidly based on the will of those in power at the state level. Sales taxes may also vary, but the consumer does not need to worry about paying sales tax on items that have already been purchased.

Where do state governments obtain their revenue? Across all states in 2008, 51.6 percent of revenue comes from taxation, while another 29.5 percent comes to states in the form of intergovernmental grants. Among the various tax categories, the largest two revenue sources are individual income taxes (representing 35.6 percent of all taxes collected) and general sales taxes (30.8 percent), followed by selective sales taxes (15.0 percent), corporate income taxes (6.5 percent), and license taxes (6.3 percent). However, the distribution of state revenue sources varies significantly across states. For instance, in 2008 six states did not report any revenue from the individual income tax, and another five states did not have revenue from the general sales tax (U.S. Census, 2010). Other states are highly reliant on these taxes for the lion's share of their revenue, so it is clear that states vary in their approaches to raising revenue. One unexplored issue in the literature on state revenue policy is what explains variation in states' reliance on different mixes of taxes in generating revenues. In other words, why do some states rely on sales taxes, while others rely on income taxes or other taxes?

DEFICITS AND SURPLUSES IN THE AMERICAN STATES

The use of deficits and surpluses at the national level to achieve macroeconomic goals has long been the subject of considerable debate. The federal government is legally permitted to generate deficits and, except for 1999 and 2000, has done so each year since

1960. The American states, however, are much more constrained in their legal authority to run deficits. As of 2010, 49 or 50 states—Vermont is the sole exception—have some kind of constitutional or statutory requirement designed to result in a balanced budget or budgetary surplus. According to the National Council of State Legislatures (2010): (1) in 44 states, the governor is required either by constitutional provision or by statute (or both) to submit a balanced budget to the legislature: (2) in 41 states, the legislature is required by constitutional provision or statute (or both) to pass a balanced budget; and (3) in 38 states, a budget deficit cannot be carried over from one fiscal year to the next. Clearly, the American states face an array of legal constraints relating to deficits and surpluses, and in most states budget deficits are prohibited by law.

That does not mean that there is no pressure on state governments to spend more than they take in. To the contrary, state governments face many of the same pressures that lead the federal government to spend in the red during the vast majority of fiscal years. For instance, state governments have an interest in facilitating favorable macroeconomic outcomes, and Keynesian economic theory places a great deal of emphasis on the role of deficits in stimulating the federal economy. If states are unable to generate deficit spending, the argument goes, an important macroeconomic policy tool has been taken from states' proverbial macroeconomic tool kits. Moreover, state governments face greater demand for spending from their constituents than demand for increased taxes. How states deal with the multitude of pressures for deficit spending varies considerably across the states, and this is the topic of this section.

Patterns of Deficits and Surpluses in the American States

Given the constitutional and legal incentives for balanced budgets in the states, it is no surprise that most states balance their budgets most of the time. In their study of budget deficits and surpluses in the American states from 1961 to 1997, Garand and Kapeluck (2004) find that in 82 percent of cases states had budget surpluses or balanced budgets. Moreover, there is a strong trend over time towards balanced budgets or budget surpluses. According to Garand and Kapeluck, in the first few years of the 1960s fewer than 50 percent of states balanced their budgets; after 1982, at least 90 percent of states balanced their budgets, and in some years (1985, 1986, and 1997) all states had a balanced budget or a budget surplus. There is, however, quite a bit of variation in the size of state deficits and surpluses; Garand and Kapeluck find that the mean budget surplus has increased over time, reaching almost 16 percent of state expenditures in 1997; however, the standard deviation of the gap between revenues and surpluses has also increased over time, meaning that states vary considerably in their deficit and surplus behavior.

What explains patterns of deficits and surpluses in the American states? First, economic variables have a strong effect on the size of state deficits and surpluses. On one hand, strong state economic performance is positively associated with revenue increases, so there is less pressure for states to have deficits or smaller surpluses when economic growth is high and unemployment is low. When the economy is weak, revenues are likely to decline, and this increases pressure for deficit spending or smaller surpluses. On the other hand, weak economic performance in a given state also creates pressure for state government officials to take action to improve state economic performance, and this means greater pressure for states to stimulate the economy through increased government spending. Garand and Kapeluck (2004) find considerable support for the role of economics in shaping state deficits and surpluses; they find that state economic growth has a positive effect on budget surpluses, while unemployment and inflation depress state surplus levels.

Second, constituency demand for government spending should have a strong negative effect on the magnitude of state budget surpluses. Some segments of state populations are typically high demanders of public goods and services due to need borne out of economic disadvantage, economic self-interest, or ideological considerations. Garand and Kapeluck find that states are more prone to budget deficits (or smaller surpluses) as a function of the size of the African-American, young (under 18), and elderly (over 65) populations. Moreover, states that are characterized by high levels of ideological liberalism among the mass public are also more likely to run smaller surpluses or increase debt (Clingermayer and Wood, 1995; Garand and Kapeluck, 2004).

Third, the role of partisan politics in shaping budget deficits and surpluses has had a prominent place in the scholarly literature on state deficits and surpluses. Scholars have focused considerable attention on the effects of party control of the legislature or governorship, particularly in terms of (1) whether the Democrats or Republicans hold unified control of state government; or (2) whether there is divided government between the two major parties. Regarding control of state government by the two major political parties, scholars have hypothesized that Democratic control is related to budget deficits or smaller surpluses, though the evidence underlying this hypothesis is weak (Alt and Lowry 1994; Garand and Kapeluck, 2004; see also Seitz, 2000). Even more intriguing is the suggestion that divided government increases the probability that state governments will experience budget deficits. The argument is that divided government creates gridlock between the two political parties that slows state responses to fiscal crises. Garand and Kapeluck (2004) do not find that budget deficits are significantly different under unified Democratic, unified Republican, or divided governments, though Poterba (1994) and Alt and Lowry (1994) find that unified governments are better able than divided governments to respond to fiscal crises and avoid deficits.

Finally, the role of institutions in shaping state deficits and surpluses has been a major feature of the scholarly literature on state fiscal policy. Perhaps the most notable institutional characteristic is state constitutional and statutory provisions that are intended to proscribe (or, at least, discourage) state deficits. The states vary in the stringency of these provisions, so while deficits are not permitted in some states, in other states deficits are permitted under certain circumstances. One institution that has drawn a great deal of attention is state carryover provisions, which prohibit states from carrying deficits over from one fiscal year to the next. Scholars have found that carryover provisions have a strong positive effect on budget surpluses, indicating that deficits are significantly less likely in those states with these provisions (Alt and Lowry, 1994; Poterba, 1994; Garand

and Kapeluck, 2004). In addition, election proximity can have a significant effect on state deficits and surpluses. During election years there is considerable pressure on elected officials to increase spending, and this makes surpluses much more difficult to achieve (Garand and Kapeluck, 2004). Moreover, Cummins (2008) contends that term limits reduce the size of state surpluses by reducing the level of policy experience held by elected officials, which is subsequently translated into weaker capacity of state government to avoid deficits. His findings are consistent with expectations insofar as term limits have a significant negative effect on the size of state surpluses.

The Role of the Federal Government

Funding provided by the federal government can also play a large role in state fiscal policy. During the time period from 1968 to 1987, 20–25 percent of all state spending was funded by the federal government (Alt and Lowry, 1994), and more recently that figure has approached 30 percent (U.S. Census Bureau, 2010). Clearly, these figures reveal the level to which state governments depend on federal funds when making budgetary decisions. Alt and Lowry (1994) also point out that state legislatures must often attempt to anticipate changes in federal aid due to changes in the national business cycle. An economic downturn in the steel belt can lead to a decrease in federal revenue, which can in turn lead to a decrease in funds available to the states—even those states that are geographically far removed from the economically suffering area.

State governments are often forced to fund federally mandated programs that are not fully funded by the federal government thereby (Chubb, 1985). These unfunded (or underfunded) mandates can be seen as reducing the autonomy of state governments and can play a crucial role in states' fiscal policymaking. Individual states may not approve of a mandated program but are forced to fund it, and during difficult economic times this can have the effect of forcing states to make a choice among diverting funds from other programs, raising additional revenue or, when possible, running deficits. National monetary policy can also affect interest rates on state bonds, and this in turn can have an impact on the amount states can borrow.

Deficit Constraints

As noted, with the exception of Vermont all states have a balanced budget rule in one form or another. Wagner (1999) differentiates the types of deficit constraints states can have into five categories: (1) the governor is required to submit a balanced budget; (2) the state legislature is required to adopt a balanced budget; (3) the state may carry forward a budget deficit to be corrected in the next fiscal year; (4) the state may not carry forward a budget deficit into the next budget cycle (which is 2 years for the 20 states operating on a biennial cycle); and (5) the state may not carry forward a budget deficit into the next fiscal year. Wagner's categories illustrate the widely different levels of constraint with which state legislatures and governors may have to deal. A lower level of restrictions may give more autonomy to state policy makers, but a hidden cost is that those who govern must make more intricate economic decisions that are not only based on local economics but also on national economic conditions.

However, state Supreme Courts have a long history of circumventing balanced budget laws by ruling that revenue bonds are not included in the calculation of constitutional debt limits (Quirk and Wein, 1971; Gelfand, 1979). In addition, Gramlich (1991) discusses how most states with balanced budget rules are permitted to run deficits so long as they are able to pay off the difference with cash in reserve. This creates an incentive for states to run a surplus whenever possible. Political institutions in general will often assist the state legislature in finding legal ways around any balanced budget requirements (Bunch, 1991). A state's credit history may also act as a constraint. In cases in which a state is willing and able to run a deficit, it must find investors who are willing to take the financial risk of investment. If individuals do not trust a state to pay back the full value of a bond, investment will not occur; regardless of the state's desires, deficit spending cannot occur. Moreover, states with poor credit histories or low bond ratings may face increased deficits or smaller surpluses based on the increased cost of borrowing that they face.

The level of constraint placed upon states has been shown to have an effect on a legislature's economic decisions (Alt and Lowry, 1994; Bohn and Inman, 1996; Levinson, 1998). States that are constitutionally required to have a balanced budget are more likely than other states to anticipate negative economic shocks, and as a result are more likely to save money to pay off any shortfall (Bohn and Inman, 1996). In turn, these anticipations can drive state macroeconomic outcomes. Saving money for an economic downturn may be beneficial, but as a result, any surplus funds (that may be used to prevent an economic downturn) cannot be immediately reinvested in the state economy.

State Fiscal Policy as an Independent Variable

State fiscal policy is the most important policy made by state governments. Good fiscal policy not only promotes macroeconomic stability and growth, it is also a powerful tool to reduce poverty and inequality. In this section, we discuss possible economic, political, policy, and social effects of state fiscal policy.

Economic Effects

Macroeconomic performance: In his *The General Theory of Employment, Interest and Money*, Keynes (1936) contends that governments can use fiscal policy to effectively manage the economy. In particular, governments can stimulate the economy and fight against unemployment rate by increasing deficit spending during recessions, and government can suppress inflation by cutting government outlays or increasing taxes during boom times. The theory, as heatedly debated as it could be, has been tested in empirical studies and has also been adopted in practice by many governments. Scholars have demonstrated in one way or another that fiscal policy can change economic outcomes in a short run, though arguably the market is primarily responsible for the long-run business cycle (Keynes, 1936; Tufte, 1975, 1978; Hibbs, 1977; Brace, 1989; Jones, 1990; Hendrick and Garand, 1991a; Poterba and Rueben, 2001). Although state governments typically lack the authority to create deficits, they can certainly use taxation and spending policy to manipulate economic growth, unemployment, and inflation rates by cooling down or stimulating the state economy.

To what extent can states adopt fiscal policies that affect state economic performance? There is actually a considerable amount of debate over this question. One primary bone of contention is the degree to which the performance of state economies is dependent on the performance of the national economy. Do state economies march in lockstep with the national economy, or is there sufficient variation in state economic performance to suggest that state governments can have an independent effect on their economies? Hendrick and Garand (1991a) show that more than half of the variation in economic performance is explained by the unique economic performance of state economies, though the state effect has taken a decidedly downward shift during the early 1960s, but has stabilized through 1985. On the other hand, Brace (1989, 1991) shows that the national influence on state economies has been on the decline; he finds that state variables did not have significant effects on state economic performance prior to 1980, but during the period from 1980 to 1985 finds that several state-level variables had strong effects on state per capita income. Moreover, Jones (1990) explores explicitly the effects of state policies on state economic performance, and he demonstrates that expenditures on education, highways, and policy and fire services promote business development and employment, while welfare expenditures depress business development and employment.

Stock and bonds market: State fiscal policy not only influences macroeconomic performance, but it also influences consumers' perception of economy and further yields of state bonds. Poterba and Rueben (2001) find that unexpected deficits are correlated with higher state bond yields, though the relationship is mediated by state fiscal institutions.

Political Effects

Economic voting: Since state fiscal policy affects macroeconomic performance and voters base their voting decisions (at least in part) on economic performance, state fiscal policy indirectly influences voting behavior. Economic voting theory argues that voters base their voting choices on retrospective (or sometimes prospective) evaluations of their own economic situations or the national economy (Downs, 1957; Fair, 1978; Tufte, 1978; Kramer, 1983; Markus, 1988; Campbell, 1992; Mackuen, Erikson, and Stimson, 1992;

Hetherington 1996; Holbrook and Garand, 1996; Lewis-Beck and Stegmaier, 2000; Nadeau and Lewis-Beck, 2001; Garand and Ulrich, 2008). Given that "pocketbook" voters (i.e., voters who base their voting choices on their own economic situation) and "sociotropic" voters (i.e., voters who base their voting choices on national economic performance) both exist, one could speculate that voters could base their vote choices on state economic performance. Actually, Cohen and King (2004) have found that voters are able to differentiate unemployment rates on the state and national level, and they reward governors if state unemployment rate is lower than the national unemployment rate and hold governors accountable if it is higher. Garand and Ulrich (2008) demonstrate that individuals' sociotropic evaluations of the national economy are shaped, at least in part, by state economic performance. Economic performance also influences popularity of governments and politicians (Mackuen, 1983; Conover and Feldman, 1986; Nadeau et al., 1999; Cohen and King, 2004; Garand and Ulrich, 2008).

One aspect of the political effects of state fiscal policy involves the electoral implications of tax increases. Scholars and political observers speculate that governors who support increases in state taxes will have a day of reckoning at the polls, and the implication is that there should be electoral retribution directed against state politicians who advocate tax increases. Kone and Winters (1993) explore the effects of increases in state income taxes, sales taxes, and any taxes on electoral support for gubernatorial candidates of the incumbent party from 1957 to 1985. They find that increases in state sales taxes have a negative effect on the electoral prospects of incumbent-party gubernatorial candidates, though the effect is asymmetrical—i.e., tax decreases do not have a positive effect commensurate with the negative effect of tax increases. Tax increases for other taxes have a weak or null effect on gubernatorial election outcomes.

Social Effects

Income inequality and poverty: The two components of state fiscal policy—taxation and spending—both have the potential to play a redistributive function in the American states. Progressive income taxes take a higher share of resources from those with higher incomes, and this provides a pool of resources that can (theoretically) be reallocated to the have-nots through a variety of redistributive programs. At the national level, Piketty and Saez (2003) find that steep, progressive income taxes and estate taxes prevent the wealthy from becoming wealthier. Peterson (1995) finds that greater spending on redistribution programs (such as welfare, pensions, and medical insurance) reduces the gap between the rich and poor. Scholars also find that Democratic presidents and policy liberalism both tend to suppress income inequality because they are both associated with more redistributive spending or pro-redistributive policies (Kelly, 2005; Bartels, 2008). Yet there has not been much research done to explore the degree to which state fiscal policy directly leads to lower levels of poverty and income inequality (cf., Xu and Garand, 2010). This shortcoming should be rectified in future research.

Welfare magnets: States differ in their welfare spending levels, and this variation can have important implications for the residential choices of those living in poverty. For example, in July 2006 the maximum monthly TANF case welfare benefits for a family of four was $1025 in Alaska and $194 in Mississippi (U.S. House Committee on Ways and Means, 2008). The large variation of welfare benefits potentially leads to a welfare magnetic effect. States with more generous welfare benefits would keep current poor people from leaving the state and attract additional poor people or immigrants to move into the state (Peterson and Rom, 1990; Peterson, 1995; Frey, Liaw, Xie, and Carlson, 1996; Borjas, 1999; Levine and Zimmerman, 1999; Bailey, 2005). Therefore states with generous welfare provisions like California and New Jersey attracted many immigrants in the past several decades. This is also why states with a higher poverty rate tend to spend less on welfare, because they do not want to attract more poor people.

In sum, if Keynes (1936) and his intellectual progeny are correct, state fiscal policy potentially can be used to manage macroeconomic performance. Deficit spending can stimulate the economy and reduce unemployment rate during recessions, while higher taxation and reductions in government expenditures can cool down the economy and reduce inflation in boom times. Not only can state fiscal policy be used to create the public good of strong state economic performance, it can also be used by politicians to manipulate economic performance for personal ends, such as for re-election. By influencing macroeconomic performance, fiscal policy also indirectly influences voting choices. It has been demonstrated that political business cycles exists in the United States, though further research is necessary to ascertain the degree to which political business cycles exist at the state level. Finally, the social effects of state fiscal policy are potentially nontrivial. Spending in redistributive areas can reduce poverty and inequality, but at the same time, it is possible that it creates a welfare magnetic effect. Compared to national-level studies, more studies need to be done on how state fiscal policy influences economics, politics, and society at the state level.

AN AGENDA FOR FUTURE RESEARCH

As noted at the outset of this chapter, the unfinished research agenda on state fiscal policy is very extensive. During the past four decades of the twentieth century, scholars devoted considerable attention to the study of state fiscal policy. In contract, over the past decade there has been a relative dearth of empirical studies of state fiscal policy, and this has left many unanswered questions relating to the topic. It is important for state politics scholars to redirect some of their energies to a resurgence of the study of state fiscal policy.

We suggest that there are some broad themes that may prove fruitful in rebuilding the state of scientific knowledge about state fiscal policy. First, given the relative inattention paid to state fiscal policy over the past decade, it is important for scholars to replicate, extend, and update research conducted in the latter half of the twentieth century. Many of the findings relating to the study of government size, spending, and tax policy, and deficits and surpluses are based on research conducted during the 1980s and 1990s, and extending these studies to cover data from more recent years is crucial. For instance, much of what we know about the determinants of government size is based on research findings from the 1980s and early 1990s, yet there have been considerable changes in the roles and responsibilities of state governments since that time. Moreover, the excellent works on state tax adoption (Berry and Berry, 1992, 1994) and the electoral implications of state tax changes (Kone and Winters, 1993) were conducted during the early 1990s, and it is important for scholars to extend this research stream to cover more recent data and political circumstances.

Second, although state fiscal policy has not drawn much scholarly attention over the past decade, the study of fiscal policy at the national and cross-national levels has continued unabated. State politics scholars have always taken advantage of theoretical perspectives, methodological approaches, and the research findings generated in national-level research, and it is important for state politics scholars interested in fiscal policy to continue to adapt research conducted at the national level to the state level. To take one example, Cameron (1978) has suggested that the growth of the public sectors in Western democracies is a function of globalization and economic interdependence among countries. Is this theoretical argument applicable to the American states? Are states that are heavily dependent on international trade more likely to increase the size of their public sectors than states that are less dependent? This is the kind of research question that has been generated in comparative cross-national research, but could be explored in research on the American states.

Third, it is important for state politics scholars to combine both macro- and micro-approaches in studying state fiscal policy. Most of the research in this research program has been conducted using aggregate data (e.g., state government size, spending and tax levels, budget deficits and surpluses). This is important and useful, but relatively little is known about the micro-level foundations of state fiscal policy. For one thing, most of the research on the fiscal policy preferences of Americans has been focused on the national level; with a few exceptions, little is known about Americans' knowledge of state economic conditions, their perceptions of the effectiveness of state fiscal policies, and the preferences and attitudes of Americans relating to state fiscal policy (Sears and Citrin, 1982; Garand and Blais, 2004). Moreover, there has been little micro-level research conducted on state political elites who are involved in the making of fiscal policy; for instance, what motivates state legislators and governors as they develop state fiscal policies? We suggest that an increase in the attention paid to the micro-level has the potential to generate important insights about state fiscal policy.

In specific terms, what are some of the unanswered research questions confronting state politics scholars studying state fiscal policy? Regarding state government size, first, it is important for scholars to explore the degree to which and why the inflation rates are different for the public and private sectors. There has been some research done at the federal level (Berry and Lowery, 1984a, 1984b), but this question has not been addressed at the state level. Second, the effects of party control of state government, mass political ideology, and interparty competition on government size has been studied in previous research, but not during the more recent time period characterized by such intense polarization at the mass level (Garand, 2010). What is the effect of political variables during the current period of high mass and elite polarization? Third, political scientists know woefully little about mass preferences relating to the size of the public sector. There has been a bit of resurgence in the study of state public opinion as new data and techniques have become available (cf., Cohen, 2006) and state politics scholars would find a fruitful research program in studying Americans' preferences toward the size of their state governments. Fourth, more research needs to be done on the effects of politically relevant groups on the size of state public sectors; for example, what is the role of public-sector unions in shaping increases in the size of state governments? Finally, most of the American states have faced a recent major fiscal crisis. It is important for scholars to categorize and study the determinants of how states respond to severe fiscal crises, particularly in terms of how they maintain or reduce the size of their public sectors in response to revenue shortfalls.

Regarding spending, revenues, and deficits and surpluses, there are several unanswered research questions. First, the research on expenditure tradeoffs needs to be updated. In particular, scholars should assess the degree to which there are expenditure tradeoffs among the various spending categories at the state level. But more importantly, scholars should focus attention on how and why tradeoff patterns vary across states and over time. What conditions facilitate and obstruct expenditure tradeoffs? Second, scholars have studied the degree to which state expenditure and revenue patterns have become nationalized, but this is an area of research that needs renewed attention, particularly in light of shifts over time in the relationship between the federal and state governments. Third, how do states respond to the expenditure and tax policies of their neighboring states? What, specifically, are the processes that result in the neighbor effect? Fourth, many states have constitutional or statutory requirements requiring a balanced budget or are unable to carry debt over to the next fiscal year. Bowler and Donovan (2004) look at these constraints and the ways in which local and state governments use existing laws to circumvent requirements. They find that during difficult economic times states with tax and expenditure limitations often seek to change their institutional structures in order to get around fiscal restrictions. To what extent do state governments change institutions during periods of fiscal crisis? Finally, we suggest the need for scholars to study public opinion relating to state taxes, expenditures, and deficits. For instance, scholars should consider the joint preferences that individuals have towards government spending and revenues (cf., Garand and Blais, 2004). Do individuals link their support for state spending with their willingness to pay (Green, 1992)? Do individuals shift their support for spending as a function of the need to generate additional revenue to support increased spending?

Finally, it is important for scholars to explore the effects of state fiscal policy on the workings of state political systems. First, state politics scholars have paid insufficient attention to the question of the effects of state spending, taxes, and deficits and surpluses on state economic performance. When states make investments in education or highways infrastructure, is there an economic development payoff at some point in the future? There are some hints of such effects in the work of Brace (1989, 1991), Hendrick and Garand (1991a), and Jones (1990), but political scientists should move beyond these efforts by updating the research program on the linkage between state fiscal policy and state economic performance. For instance, in those few cases where states generate deficits, does this have the effect of stimulating state economic performance, as suggested by Keynes? Second, what is the effect of state spending, taxation, and deficits and surpluses on individuals' trust in and support for state government? If state governments are doing good things with state expenditure, one would expect state citizens to develop positive evaluations of state government and state officials. On the other hand, do high taxes diminish individuals' support for state governments?

REFERENCES

Abrams, Burton andWilliam Dougan. 1986. "The Effects of Constitutional Restraints on Governmental Spending." *Public Choice 49*: 101–116.

Allard, Scott and Sheldon Danziger. 2000. "Welfare Magnets: Myth or Reality?" *Journal of Politics 62*: 350–368.

Alm, James and Mark Evers. 1991. "The Item Veto and State Government Expenditures" *Public Choice 68*: 1–15.

Alt, James and Robert Lowry. 1994. "Divided Government, Fiscal Institutions, and Budget Deficits: Evidence from the States." *American Political Science Review 88*: 811–828.

Alt, James and Robert Lowry. 2000. "A Dynamic Model of State Budget Outcomes Under Divided Partisan Government." *Journal of Politics 62*: 1035–1069.

Attiyeh, Richard and Engle, Robert F. (1979). "Testing some prepositions about proposition 13." *National Tax Journal 32*: 97–119.

Bae, San-Seok and Richard Feiock. 2004. "The Flypaper Effect Revisited: Intergovernmental Grants and Local Governance." *International Journal of Public Administration 27*: 577–596.

Baicker, Katherine. 2005. "The Spillover Effects of State Spending." *Journal of Public Economics 89*: 529–544.

Bailey, Michael A. 2005. "Welfare Migration and the Multifaceted Decision to Move." *American Political Science Review 99*: 125–135.

Bails, Dale 1990. "The Effectiveness of Tax–Expenditure Limitations: A Reevaluation." *American Journal of Economics and Sociology 49*: 223–238.

Bails, Dale and Margie A. Tieslau. 2000. "The Impact of Fiscal Constitutions on State and Local Expenditures." *Cato Journal 20*: 255–277.

Barrilleaux, Charles, Thomas Holbrook, and Laura Langer. 2002. "Electoral Competition, Legislative Balance, and American State Welfare Policy." *American Journal of Political Science 46*: 415–427.

Bartels, Larry. 2008. *Unequal Democracy: The Political Economy of the New Gilded Age*. New Jersey: Princeton University Press.

Beck, Paul Allen and Thomas Dye. 1982. "Sources of Public Opinion on Taxes: The Florida Case." *Journal of Politics 44*: 172–182.

Beck, Paul Allen, Hal Rainey, and Carol Traut. 1990. "Disadvantage, Disaffection, and Race as Divergent Bases for Citizen Fiscal Policy Preferences." *Journal of Politics 52*: 71–93.

Berry, Francis Stokes and William D. Berry. 1992. "Tax Innovation in the States: Capitalizing on Political Opportunity." *American Journal of Political Science 36*: 715–742.

Berry, Francis Stokes and William D. Berry. 1994. "The Politics of Tax Increases in the States." *American Journal of Political Science 38*: 855–859.

Berry, William and David Lowery. 1984a. "The Growing Cost of Government: A Test of Two Explanations." *Social Science Quarterly 65*: 735–749.

Berry, William and David Lowery. 1984b. "The Measurement of Government Size: Implications for the Study of Government Growth." *Journal of Politics 46*: 1193–1206

Berry, William and David Lowery. 1987. *Understanding United States Government Growth: An Empirical Analysis of the Post-War Era*. New York: Praeger.

Berry, William and David Lowery. 1990. "An Alternative Approach to Understanding Budgetary Trade-Offs." *American Journal of Political Science 34*: 671–705.

Berry, William D., Evan J. Ringquist, Richard C. Fording, and Russell L. Hanson. 1998. "Measuring Citizen and Government Ideology in the American States, 1960–93." *American Journal of Political Science 42*: 327–348.

Berry, William D., Richard C. Fording, Evan J. Ringquist, Russell L. Hanson, and Carl Klarner. 2010. "Measuring Citizen and Government Ideology in the American States: A Re-appraisal." *State Politics and Policy Quarterly 10*: 117–135.

Bingham, Richard, Brett Hawkins, and F. Ted Hebert. 1978. *The Politics of Raising State and Local Revenue*. New York: Praeger.

Bohn, Henning and Inman, Robert P. 1996. "Balanced-Budget Rules and Public Deficits: Evidence from the U.S. States." *Carnegie-Rochester Conference Series on Public Policy 45*: 13–76.

Borcherding, Thomas. 1977. "The Sources of Growth in Public Expenditures in the United States, 1902–1970." In Thomas Borcherding (ed.), *Budgets and Bureaucrats: The Sources of Government Growth*. Durham, NC: Duke University Press: 45–70.

Borjas, George J. 1999. "Immigration and Welfare Magnets." *Journal of Labor Economics 17*: 607–637.

Bowler, Shaun and Todd Donovan. 1995. "Popular Responsiveness to Taxation." *Political Research Quarterly 48*: 79–99.

Bowler, Shaun and Todd Donovan. 2004. "Evolution in State Governance Structures: Unintended Consequences of State Tax and Expenditure Limitations." *Political Research Quarterly 59*: 189–196.

Brace, Paul. 1989. "Isolating the Economies of States." *American Politics Quarterly 17*: 256–276.

Brace, Paul. 1991. "The Changing Context of State Political Economy." *Journal of Politics 53*: 297–317.

Brace, Paul. 1993. *State Government and Economic Performance*. Baltimore, Maryland: Johns Hopkins University Press.

Bunch, Beverly. 1991. "The Effects of Constitutional Debt Limits on State Government's Use of Public Authorities." *Public Choice 68*: 57–69.

Cameron, David. 1978. "The Expansion of the Public Economy: A Comparative Analysis." *American Political Science Review 72*: 1243–1261.

Campbell, Andrea. 2009. "What Americans Think of Taxes." In Isaac William Martin, Ajay K. Mehrotra, and Monica Presad (eds), The New Fiscal Sociology: Taxation in Comparative and Historical Perspective. New York: Cambridge University Press: 48–67.

Campbell, James. 1992. "Forecasting the Presidential Vote in the States." *American Journal of Political Science 36*: 386–407.

Chubb, John. 1985. "Federalism and the Bias for Centralization." In John Chubb and Paul E. Peterson (eds), *The New Direction in American Politics*. Washington, DC: Brookings Institution: 273–306.

Clingermayer, James and B. Dan Wood. 1995. "Disentangling Patterns of State Debt Financing." *American Political Science Review 89*: 108–120.

Cnudde, Charles F. and McCrone, Donald J. 1969. "Party Competition and Welfare Policies in the American States." *American Political Science Review 63*: 858–866.

Cohen, Jeffrey (ed.). 2006. *Public Opinion in State Politics*. Palo Alto, CA: Stanford University Press.

Cohen, Jeffrey and James King. 2004. "Relative Unemployment and Gubernatorial Popularity." *Journal of Politics 66*: 1267–1282).

Conover, Pamela and Stanley Feldman. 1986. "Emotional Reactions to the Economy: I'm Mad as Hell and I'm Not Going to Take It Anymore." *American Journal of Political Science 30*: 50–78.

Cox, James and David Lowery. 1990. "The Impact of the Tax Revolt Era State Fiscal Caps." *Social Science Quarterly 71*: 492–509.

Cox, Gary W. and Mathew D. McCubbins. 1991. "Divided Control of Fiscal Policy." In Gary W. Cox and Samuel Kernell (eds), *The Politics of Divided Government*. Boulder, CO: Westview Press: 155–78.

Cummins, Jeff. 2008. "Term Limits, Electoral Competition, and the Impact on State Fiscal Conditions." Paper presented at the 2008 annual meeting of the Western Political Science Association.

Dawson, Richard E. and James A. Robinson. 1963. "Inter-party Competition, Economic Variables, and Welfare Politics in American States." *Journal of Politics 25*: 265–289.

DeHoog, Ruth, David Lowery, and William Lyons. 1990. "Citizen Satisfaction with Local Governance: A Test of Individual, Jurisdictional, and City-specific Explanations." *Journal of Politics 52*: 807–837.

Domke, William, Richard Eichenberg, and Cathernine Kelleher. 1983. "The Illusion of Choice: Defense and Welfare in Advanced Industrial Democracies, 1948–1978." *American Political Science Review 77*: 19–35.

Downs, Anthony. 1957. *An Economic Theory of Democracy*. Ann Arbor, MI: University of Michigan Press.

Dye, Thomas. 1966. *Politics, Economics, and the Public: Policy Outcomes in the American States*. New York: Rand McNally.

Easton, David. 1953. *The Political System: An Inquiry into the State of Political Science*. New York: Alfred A. Knopf.

Erikson, Robert S., Gerald C. Wright, and John P. McIver. 1993. *Statehouse Democracy: Public Opinion and Policy in the American States*. Cambridge and New York: Cambridge University Press.

Erikson. Robert S., Michael B. Mackuen, and James A. Stimson. 2002. *The Macro Polity*. New York: Cambridge University Press.

Fair, Ray. 1978. "The Effect of Economic Events on Votes for President." *Review of Economics and Statistics 60*: 159–173.

Frey, William H., Kao-Lee Liaw, Yu Xie, and Marcia J. Carlson. 1996. "Interstate Migration of the U.S. Poverty Population: Immigration 'Pushes' and Welfare Magnet 'Pulls.'" *Population and Environment: A Journal of Interdisciplinary Studies 17*: 491–536.

Garand, James C. 1985. "Partisan Change and Shifting Expenditure Priorities in the American States, 1945–1978." *American Politics Quarterly 13*: 355–391.

Garand, James C. 1988a. "Explaining Government Growth in the U.S. States." *American Political Science Review* 82: 837–849.

Garand, James C. 1988b. "Measuring Government Growth in the American States: Decomposing Real Growth and Deflator Effects." *American Politics Quarterly* 16: 405–424.

Garand, James C. 1989. "Measuring Government Size in the American States: Implications for the Study of Government Growth." *Social Science Quarterly* 70: 487–496.

Garand, James C. 1991. "Decomposing Real and Deflator-based Government Growth: An Application to the American States." *Quality and Quantity* 25: 221–233.

Garand, James C. 1993. "New Perspectives on the Size of Government in the American States: A Pooled Analysis." Paper presented at the conference on The Politics of State Economic Development: Prospects and Problems in State Economic Intervention. Chicago, IL.

Garand, James C. 2010. "Income Inequality, Party Polarization, and Roll-Call Voting in the U.S. Senate." *Journal of Politics* 72: 1109–1128.

Garand, James C. and Kyle Baudoin. 2003. "Spending, Taxes, and Deficits: Fiscal Policy in the American States." In Virginia Gray and Russell Hanson (eds), *Politics in the American States (8th edition)*. Washington, DC: CQ Press: 290–317.

Garand, James C. and Andre Blais. 2004. "Understanding Joint Support for Government Spending and Taxes: Linking Benefits and Costs in the Mass Public." Paper presented at the 2004 annual meeting of the American Political Science Association, Chicago, IL.

Garand, James C. and Rebecca M. Hendrick. 1991. "Expenditure Tradeoffs in the American States: A Longitudinal Test, 1948–1984." *Western Political Quarterly* 44: 915–940.

Garand, James C. and Branwell Dubose Kapeluck. 2004. "Understanding Surpluses, Deficits, and Debt in the American States, 1961–1997." In Louis Imbeau and Francois Petry (eds), *Politics, Institutions, and Fiscal Policy: Public Deficits and Surpluses in Federated States*. Lexington, Massachusetts: Lexington Books: 49–87.

Garand, James C. and Justin Ulrich. 2008. "The Economy, Subjective Economic Evaluations, and the Presidential Vote." Paper presented at the 2008 annual meeting of the Midwest Political Science Association, Chicago, IL.

Garand, James C., Catherine Parkhurst, and Rusanne Seoud. 1991a. "Bureaucrats, Policy Attitudes, and Political Behavior: An Extension of the Bureau Voting Model of Government Growth." Journal of Public Administration Research and Theory 1: 177–212.

Garand, James C., Catherine Parkhurst, and Rusanne Jourdan Seoud. 1991b. "Testing the Bureau Voting Model: A Research Note on Federal and State-Local Employees." *Journal of Public Administration Research and Theory* 1: 229–233.

Gelfand, M. David. 1979. "Seeking Local Government Financial Integrity Through Debt Ceilings, Tax Limitations, and Expenditure Limits: The New York City Fiscal Crisis, the Taxpayer's Revolt, and Beyond." *Minnesota Law Review* 63: 545–608.

Gilligan, Thomas and John G. Matsusaka. 2001. "Fiscal Policy, Legislative Size, and Political Parties: Evidence from State and Local Governments in the First Half of the 20th Century." *National Tax Journal* 54: 57–82.

Gramlich, E. 1991. "The 1991 State and Local Fiscal Crisis." *Brookings Papers on Economic Activity* 2: 249–287.

Green, Donald. 1992. "The Price Elasticity of Mass Preferences." *American Political Science Review* 86: 128–148.

Hawthorne, Michael R. and John E. Jackson. 1987. "The Individual Political Economy of Federal Tax Policy." *American Political Science Review* 81: 757–774.

Hendrick, Rebecca M. and James C. Garand. 1991a. "Variation in State Economic Growth: Decomposing State, Regional, and National Effects." *Journal of Politics* 53: 1093–1110.

Hendrick, Rebecca M. and James C. Garand. 1991b. "Expenditure Tradeoffs in the U.S. States: A Pooled Analysis." *Journal of Public Administration Research and Theory* 1: 295–318.

Hetherington, Mark. 1996. "The Media's Role in Forming Voters' National Economic Evaluations in 1992." *American Journal of Political Science* 40: 372–395.

Hibbs, Douglas. 1977. "Political Parties and Macroeconomic Policy." *American Political Science Review* 71: 1467–1487.

Hofferbert, Richard I. 1966. "The Relation Between Public Policy and Some Structural and Environmental Variables in the American States." *American Political Science Review* 60: 83–92.

Hofferbert, Richard and Ira Sharkansky. 1971. "The Nationalization of State Politics." In Hofferbert, Richard I., and Ira Sharkansky (eds), *State and Urban Politics*. Boston, MA: Little, Brown: 463–74.

Holbrook, Thomas and James C. Garand. 1996. "Homo Economus? Economic Information and Economic Voting." *Political Research Quarterly* 49: 351–375.

Jones, Bryan. 1990. "Public Policies and Economic Growth in the American States." *Journal of Politics* 52: 219–233.

Kapeluck, Branwell Dubose. 2001. Government Growth in the Fifty States: A Test of Thirteen Models. Ph.D. dissertation, Louisiana State University.

Kelly, Nathan. 2005. "Political Choice, Public Policy, and Distributional Outcomes." *American Journal of Political Science* 49: 865–880.

Kemp, Kathleen. 1978. "Nationalization of the American States: A Text of the Thesis." *American Politics Quarterly* 6: 237–247.

Key, V.O. 1949. *Southern Politics in State and Nation*. New York: Alfred A. Knopf.

Keynes, John Maynard. 1936. *The General Theory of Employment, Interest and Money*. London: Macmillan.

Kiewiet, D. Roderick and Kristen Szakaly. 1996. "Constitutional Limitations on Borrowing: An Analysis of State Bond Indebtedness." *Journal of Law, Economics, and Organization* 12: 62–97.

Kone, Susan L. and Richard F. Winters. 1993. "Taxes and Voting: Electoral Retribution in the American States." *Journal of Politics* 55: 22–40.

Kramer, Gerald. 1983. "The Ecological Fallacy Revisited: Aggregate- versus Individual-level Findings on Economics and Elections, and Sociotropic Voting." *American Political Science Review* 77: 92–111.

Krol, Robert. 2007. "The Role of Fiscal and Political Institutions in Limiting the Size of State Government." *Cato Journal* 27: 431–445.

Lasswell, Harold. 1936. *Politics: Who Gets What, Where, When, and How?* New York: McGraw-Hill.

Levine, Phillip B. and David J. Zimmerman. 1999. "An Empirican Analysis of the Welfare Magnet Debate using the NLSY." *Journal of Population Economics* 12: 391–409.

Levinson, Arik. 1998. "Balanced Budgets and Business Cycles: Evidence from U.S. States." *National Tax Journal* 51: 715–732.

Lewis-Beck, Michael and Mary Stegmaier. 2000. "Economic Determinants of Electoral Outcomes." *Annual Review of Political Science* 3: 183–219.

Lowery, David and William Berry. 1983. "The Growth of Government in the United States: An Empirical Assessment of Competing Explanations." *American Journal of Political Science* 27: 665–694.

Lowery, David and William Lyons. 1989. "The Impact of Jurisdictional Boundaries: An Individual-Level Test of the Tiebout Model." *Journal of Politics 51*: 73–97.

Lowery, David and Lee Sigelman. 1981. "Understanding the Tax Revolt: Eight Explanations." *American Political Science Review 75*: 963–974.

Lyons, William and David Lowery. 1989. "Citizen Responses to Dissatisfaction in Urban Communities: A Partial Test of a General Model." *Journal of Politics 51*: 841–868.

Lyons, William, David Lowery, and Ruth DeHoog. 1992. *The Politics of Dissatisfaction: Citizens, Services, and Urban Institutions*. Armonk, NY: M.E. Sharpe.

MacKuen, Michael. 1983. "Political Drama, Economic Conditions, and the Dynamics of Presidential Popularity." *American Journal of Political Science 27*: 165–192.

MacKuen, Michael, Robert Erikson, and James Stimson. 1992. "Peasants or Bankers? The American Electorate and the U.S. Economy." *American Political Science Review 77*: 597–611.

Markus, Gregory. 1988. "The Impact of Personal and National Economic Conditions on the Presidential Vote: A Pooled Cross-Sectional Analysis." *American Journal of Political Science 32*: 137–154.

Martin, Isaac. 2008. *The Permanent Tax Revolt: How the Property Tax Transformed American Politics*. Palo Alto, CA: Stanford University Press.

Merrifield, John. 2000. "State Government Expenditure Determinants and Tax Revenue Determinants Revisited." *Public Choice 13*: 25–50.

Mintz, Alex. 1989. "Guns vs. Butter: A Disaggregated Analysis." *American Political Science Review 83*: 1285–1293.

Mintz, Alex and Chi Huang. 1990. "Defense Expenditures, Economic Growth, and the Peace Dividend." *American Political Science Review 85*: 1283–1293.

Nadeau, Richard and Michael Lewis-Beck. 2001. "National Economic Voting in U.S. Presidential Elections." *Journal of Politics 63*: 159–181.

Nadeau, Richard, Richard Niemi, David Fan, and Timothy Amato. 1999. "Elite Economic Forecasts, Economic News, Mass Economic Judgments, and Presidential Approval." *Journal of Politics 61*: 109–135.

National Council of State Legislatures. 2010. "NCSL Fiscal Brief: State Balanced Budget Provisions." Downloaded from <http://www.ncsl.org/documents/fiscal/StateBalancedBudgetProvisions2010.pdf> (accessed June 12, 2013).

New, Michael. 2010. "U.S. Tax and Expenditure Limitations: A Comparative Political Analysis." *State Politics and Policy Quarterly 10*: 25–50.

Nice, David. 1988. "The Line-Item Veto and Expenditure Restraint." *Journal of Politics 50*: 485–498.

Nicholson-Crotty, Sean, Nick A. Theobald, and B. Dan Wood. 2006. "Fiscal Federalism and Budgetary Tradeoffs in the American States." *Political Research Quarterly 59*: 313–321.

Niskanen, William. 1971. *Bureaucracy and Representative Government*. Chicago, IL: Aldine.

Osman, J.W. 1966. "The Dual Impact of Federal Aid on State and Local Government Expenditures." *National Tax Journal 19*: 362–372.

Percy, Stephen and Brett Hawkins. 1992. "Further Tests of Individual-level Propositions from the Tiebout Model." *Journal of Politics 54*: 1149–1157.

Peterson, Paul E. 1995. *The Price of Federalism*. Washington, DC: The Brookings Institutions.

Peterson, Paul E. and Mark C. Rom. 1990. *Welfare Magnets: A New Case for a National Standard*. Washington DC: Brooking Institution.

Piketty, Thomas and Emmanuel Saez. 2003. "Income Inequality in the United States, 1913–1998." *Quarterly Journal of Economics 118*: 1–39.

Pogue, Thomas F. and L. G. Sgontz. 1968. "The Effects of Grants-in-Aid on State-Local Spending." *National Tax Journal* 22: 190–199.

Posner, Paul L. 1998. *The Politics of Unfunded Mandates: Whither Federalism*. Washington, DC: Georgetown University Press.

Poterba, James M. 1994. "State Responses to Fiscal Crises: The Effects of Budgetary Institutions and Politics." *Journal of Political Economy* 102: 799–821.

Poterba, James M. and Kim S. Rueben. 2001. "Fiscal News, State Budget Rules, and Tax-exempt Bond Yields." *Journal of Urban Economics* 50: 537–562.

Quirk, William J. and Leon E. Wein. 1971. "A Short Constitutional History of Entities Commonly Known as Authorities." *Cornell Law Review* 57: 521–597.

Reuben, Kim S. 1996. Tax Limitations and Government Growth: The Effects of State Tax and Expenditure Limits on State and Local Governments. Unpublished paper. San Francisco: Public Policy Institute of California.

Rogers, Diane Lim and John H. Rogers. 2000. "Political Competition and State Government Size: Do Tighter Elections Produce Looser Budgets?" *Public Choice* 105: 1–21.

Russett, Bruce. 1982. "Defense Expenditures and National Well-being." *American Political Science Review* 76: 767–777.

Schram, Sanford, Lawrence Nitz, and Gary Krueger. 1998. "Without Cause or Effect: Reconsidering Welfare Migration as a Policy Problem." *American Journal of Political Science* 42: 210–230.

Sears, David and Jack Citrin. 1982. *Tax Revolt: Something for Nothing in California*. Berkeley, CA: University of California Press.

Seitz, Helmut. 2000. "Fiscal Policy, Deficits and Politics of Subnational Governments: The Case of the German Laender." *Public Choice* 63: 183–218.

Tiebout, Charles M. 1956. "A Pure Theory of Local Expenditures." *Journal of Political Economy* 64: 416–424.

Tompkins, Gary L. 1975. "A Causal Model of State Welfare Expenditures." *Journal of Politics*. 37: 392–416.

Tucker, Harvey. 1984. "The Nationalization of State Politics Revisited." *Western Political Quarterly* 37: 435–442.

Tufte, Edward 1975. "Determinants of the Outcomes of Midterm Congressional Elections." *American Political Science Review* 69: 812–826.

Tufte, Edward. 1978. *Political Control of the Economy*. Princeton, NJ: Princeton University Press.

U.S. Bureau of the Census. 2010. *Statistical Abstract of 2010*. Washington, DC: U.S. Census Bureau.

U.S. Census Bureau. 2010. Annual Surveys of State and Local Government Finances (various years). <http://www.census.gov/govs/state/historical_data.html>. Last accessed: July 12, 2013.

U.S. House Committee on Ways and Means. 2008. The Green Book 2008: Section 7. <http://democrats.waysandmeans.house.gov/2008-green-book>. Last accessed: July 12, 2013.

Wagner, Adolf. 1877. *Finanzwissenschaft*. Leipzig: C.F. Winter.

Wagner, Gary. 1999. Essays on the Political Economy of State Government Saving and the Role of Budget Stabilization Funds. Doctoral dissertation, West Virginia University.

Weiher, Gregory R. and Jon Lorence. 1991. "Growth in State Government Employment: A Time Series Analysis." *Western Political Quarterly* 44: 373–88.

Welch, Susan. 1985. "The 'More for Less' Paradox: Public Attitudes on Taxing and Spending." *Public Opinion Quarterly* 49: 310–316.

Xu, Ping and James C. Garand. 2010. "Economic Context and Americans' Perceptions of Income Inequality. *Social Science Quarterly* 91: 1220–1241.

CHAPTER 27

....

STATE ECONOMIC DEVELOPMENT

....

PAUL BRACE

In over two centuries, the American states have adopted policies to a stunning variety of issues. They have enslaved, segregated, and sterilized some of their citizens, and promoted various moral objectives. To contemporary eyes many of these efforts are sometimes terrifying, and at others comical. They came and went with ebbs and flows in American political development but from our inception as a nation, to the most recent legislative sessions, states consistently enacted policies to attract capital, jobs, or both, with the goal of facilitating prosperity. The persistence of this issue across time and space begs explanation: why have economic development issues been a pervasive feature of state political agendas across three centuries? This persistence across time is matched by prevalence across states, and suggests fundamental forces have operated on states old and new, and far and wide, that channel state political effort toward economic issues.

Before exploring the particulars of what has been done in the states, it is useful to first consider what they have not done and ponder why. At the extreme, political processes can seize the means of production or, less drastically, enact onerous taxes and pernicious regulations that undermine market economics. Alternatively, in a world of imperfect information, the operations of private markets can produce monopolies, exploit labor, and concentrate wealth in the hands of a few. Clearly, politics can create economic problems just as markets can cause political problems. The rules, stakes, and players of the game structure the precise balance of problems and solutions. In the American states this has contributed to a particular mixture of public and private endeavor. Many policy options are kept off the table: as semi-sovereign units with open economies where labor and capital may move freely between jurisdictions, states are disinclined to drive productive resources away through onerous taxes or regulations because these productive resources could and likely would seek more favorable locations.

What is it states do? States use the powers available to them to compete with other states to attract and nurture productive capacities. Most notably, states have continuously sought to attract capital to create infrastructure and other conditions conducive to private enterprise. Law and voters discipline this quest for capital: voter and business aversion to taxes, and legal restraints on state indebtedness, have given state economic development efforts a "fishes and loaves" character over time. Benefits become highlighted or exaggerated, while costs and risks are muddled or discounted. States are also induced to mimic politically successful economic development policies adopted in other states. In sum, the operating environments of states provide substantial motivation for economic development efforts, but the precise nature of their actions are shaped by political contingencies. Consequently, the intersection of the politically viable with what is economically sound has been irregular throughout American history.

As we will see below, states mobilized investment and productive resources that were decisive in hastening vital innovation that advanced state and national prosperity. Canals were built, steamboats were invented, railroads were constructed, and industries were nurtured. History also reveals, however, that states were capable of incurring crushing debts, encouraging ill-advised transportation projects, and conferring monopolies and special privileges in the guise of economic development. This persists in the contemporary era where many question whether states give away more then they can expect in return when they confer lavish business incentives, with burdens falling on taxpayers if they don't. Others question if these incentives harm rather than help state competitiveness by preserving less competitive firms.

THEORETICAL PERSPECTIVES OF STATE ECONOMIC DEVELOPMENT

The Good

At the most fundamental level, federalism places states in economic and political competition with one another. Charles Tiebout (1956) considered the theoretical implications of competing political jurisdictions that offer different combinations of taxes and services to potential residents and concluded that the opportunity for residents to "vote with their feet" could, in theory, induce efficiency in the provision of public goods. Governments that over tax will lose residents to those that tax less. More recently, Weingast (e.g., Montinola, Gabriella, Qian, and Weingast, 1995) elaborates the effects of this competition: by endowing control upon, and encouraging competition between, decentralized governments, federalism avoids the adverse consequences of centralized government's interference with otherwise competitive markets. Oates and Schwab (1991) argue that interjurisdictional fiscal competition is efficiency enhancing by bringing business tax payments closer in alignment with services received from the public sector. Similarly, Peterson (1995) contrasts the effects of what he describes as the Congressional (national) model of federalism with the functional (state) model of federalism, noting that the latter is more adept at promoting economic development due to the incentives and constraints federalism creates for subnational policy.

Ideally, interstate competition places brakes on intrusion in the market. When state taxes are higher capital investment will be undersupplied. State governments pitted in interstate competition for investment should reduce tax burdens on capital until the resultant tax revenues are in balance with the social costs the investments impose on the state. From this perspective, interstate competition for capital should produce socially optimal levels of government expenditure and private investment with the consequence of maximizing economic output. The arrangement encourages state governments to be innovative, small, and efficient.

The Bad

To achieve the ostensible benefits of interstate competition in economic development assumes state political actors in this process are economically rational and have the necessary information to make suitable calculations in devising policy. In practice, some benefits of state economic development efforts are direct and vivid, while the costs of additional stresses on state finances, infrastructure, labormarkets, and other businesses are obscure and distant. Moreover, economic development policy is more political than economic. The relevant decision makers are accountable to voters and weigh how voters weigh their development policy choices more heavily than if the complex costs of winning new investments outweigh their economic benefits. Moreover, constituents who stand to directly benefit or be injured by economic development policy are more likely to mobilize than the citizens who bear diffuse costs: political feasibility can countermand economic prudence. Economic development policies that produce short-term and visible political benefits with obscure and distant economic costs will be emphasized over those offering distant benefits or more obvious costs.

The Net

Interstate competition decisively shapes the agendas of state governments, isolating a domain of feasible alternatives to pursue state economic development. States can ill-afford bloated public bureaucracies, onerous taxes, or regulations because of the mobility of citizens and capital. Moreover, if they are to retain or attract productive resources, they must endeavor to promote economically favorable conditions through innovations in infrastructure and business conditions. Alternatively, the preoccupation with economic development can produce significant inequities, socializing economic risk and benefits while concentrating economic benefits. Competition for mobile capital can produce a public sector that is too small (Inman and Rubinfeld 1996), creating deficiencies in vital public services. It may make businesses less efficient because efforts at political influence to socialize their costs may yield more dividends than investment to improve their productive practices. It may cause structural imbalances in state economies. Footloose industries may gain leverage to secure tax incentives and subsidies while immobile industries that must locate near markets or natural resources enjoy no such leverage. This can produce financial and productive imbalances in states as the former become more profitable and attractive for private investment, while the latter enjoy lower profits and less private investment. State incentives may also promote concentration in industries that are particularly cost-sensitive, limiting state economic diversification while heightening state economic vulnerability.

EARLY STATE ECONOMIC DEVELOPMENT

Even as colonies, interjurisdictional economic competition was present. The American colonies were formed under mercantalist polices to achieve economic benefits for England. Owing to administrative realities, England conferred limited self-government on the colonies. Self-government created internal, vertical, and lateral political and economic relationships that placed pressures on the colonies that 1) promoted resistance to restrictions imposed vertically by England, 2) encouraged economic competition with other colonies for capital, and 3) made them responsive to the economic interests of their citizens. These vertical, lateral, and internal pressures are an enduring feature of American political and economic development. American federalism was the product of compromise flowing from intense political conflicts about the distribution of power between states and the newly created national government at the time of our Constitution. To resolve these conflicts sovereign powers were divided between states and the national government. Federalism established a structure that was stable in general but fluid in many details, creating both persistent and changing constraints and opportunities for state economic intervention. Economic effort and competition among the states have been its persistent feature. As noted by Alexander Hamilton (1961) "[c]ompetitions of commerce have become a fruitful source of contention" among the states. A contemporary observer notes "positive [economic] intervention by states has been present continuously" (Scheiber, 1987, 418).

In the historical survey that follows, five identifiable eras in state economic development efforts are identified. Across all eras, states labored to nurture their economic development, while each is distinguished by differing legal constraints shaping federal–state relations, the nature of the players involved, and the targets of state development efforts. While the general objectives remained constant, so too were vexing features of the development process: economic development policies produce uneven distributions of benefits and burdens fuelling both support and opposition. Clearly, if there were a panacea in state economic development policy it seems likely it would have been discovered in over 200 years of trying. Instead it has been, and remains, a topic of intense debate. This will not change.

STATE ENTREPRENEURISM IN THE ANTEBELLUM ERA

One of the most pressing domestic issues facing the new nation concerned infrastructure. To nurture economic endeavor, improved transportation was deemed essential. Alexander Hamilton, Washington's Secretary of the Treasury was a strong proponent of national intervention to promote internal improvements to stimulate the early American economy. In his 1791 Report on Manufactures he wrote, "the public purse must supply the deficiency of private resource. In what can it be so useful, as in prompting and improving the efforts of industry?" (Lind, 1997). Albert Gallatin, Jefferson's Secretary of the Treasury, also sought to promote internal improvements in the 1806 Report on Roads and Canals he presented to Congress. John Quincy Adams and later Henry Clay would similarly promote federal government intervention to subsidize transportation infrastructure to nurture economic development.

National effort to support internal improvements in this period was limited by state and sectional rivalries fearing growth in national power (Shaw, 1990). The opponents of federal intervention were prominent, powerful, and ultimately successful. In 1818 James Madison vetoed the Bonus Bill that would have used funds from the Second Bank of the United States to aid internal improvements. James Monroe initially vetoed the Cumberland Road Bill to create a road for westward expansion in 1822 but finally signed in his last day in office in 1825. Andrew Jackson vetoed the Maysville Road Bill in 1830 that would have expanded connections to the Cumberland Road. In 1846 James Polk vetoed the Rivers and Harbors Bill intended to provide federal funds to improve small harbors.

Federal economic intervention was limited in range and type; tariff policy, land disposal, management of the public domain, banking, monetary policies, and the awarding of patents for invention. Although influential they were limited in their effects on the economy's private sector. These restrained national efforts mirrored the limited capacity of the national government: none of these policies required extensive cash expenditures or costly administrative functions. Owing to federal limitations, it fell to states to develop policies for many internal improvements. As noted by Wallis and Weingast (2005, 1) "[i]n the antebellum era, American states rather than the national government actively promoted economic development, pouring huge resources into both financial institutions and large-scale internal improvements, such as canals and, later, railroads" with the states spending $450 million to the federal government's $54 million in the 1800 to 1860 period. The dispersal of power among the states allowed gentry leadership to overcome many obstacles "through a policy of mercantilism [that] made canals into instruments of economic development" (Shaw, 1990, 203). As noted by Mulcare (2008, 683) "[t]he failed [national] road and canal system, the devolution of national construction powers, the rejection of federal toll authority, and the reduction of federal appropriations options underscored states" rights legislators' efforts to maintain state authority and limit nationalists' efforts to expand federal [development] institutions." States "stimulated economic development by subsidizing agriculture and industry, investing in private enterprise, constructing internal improvements at public expense or lending the public credit for such purposes, and granting special privileges to private companies" (Gunn, 1979, 273). By 1836 states had chartered over 600 banks, with authorized capital of $480 million, paid in capital of almost $250 million, and state investment of at least $80 million (Wallis 2005). Their investment in transportation projects in roads, canals, railroads, and steamboats led to an economic revolution (Goodrich (1960). In this early era "the state was the most important arena for the formulation of social and economic policy" (Gunn, 1979, 276).

States were innovative and aggressive in using public authority to secure investment and mobilize private resources to promote economic objectives deemed to be in the "public interest." With few legal restrictions and public aversion to taxation, states were drawn to support projects that attracted domestic and foreign investment by incurring unsecured state debt. American bankers and wealthy individuals were an important source of funds, providing access to foreign capital that provided a majority of funding, particularly for canals. British investors earned higher interest on loans to American states than they could at home (Shaw, 1990, 206). Debts for proposed canal projects would be repaid through tolls and dividends upon their completion. If successful, these projects could pay off investors, earn money for the state, and stimulate state economies, all without raising taxes. Like water into wine, revenue-starved states used public authority to coordinate private enterprise and attract investment to develop ostensibly self-financing and supporting projects. The initial success of some projects encouraged additional investment, making capital abundant, and fuelled frenzied but often ill-conceived state efforts to compete for these funds through additional if less viable projects.

Good and Bad: Canals

New York's Erie Canal was a revolution in transportation and a revelation in state economic development policies other states would soon mimic. It established the New York Canal Fund to raise funds for construction. Using the credit of the state of New York, they sold bonds for 56 percent, with interest to be paid to investors from duties and a tax on land within 25 miles of the canal once constructed. This attracted eastern and foreign investors. Even before the canal was completed, tolls more than paid the interest, inspiring confidence in British money markets, and encouraging further investment in other American canals (Shaw, 1990, 207); it was political cold fusion.

Success in New York stimulated frenzied investment, inviting imitation in effort but not result. Caught up in the optimism canal investment funds could bring to his state, in 1836 Indiana Governor Noah Noble encouraged his legislature to follow the successful example. The legislature passed the aptly named Mammoth Internal Improvement Act to begin a variety of transportation construction projects, *all at the same time*, with an estimated cost of $10 million to be funded by investors.

In 1832 Indiana established a Canal Commission to sell bonds. One member was Samuel Hanna, a land speculator with property and stores who stood to profit from the canals. Dr Isaac Coe, another commissioner, secured loans from the Morris Canal and Banking Company that marketed the bonds in ways that bordered on "fraudulent" (Shaw, 1994, 139). Coe became a stockholder in the company and pocketed some of the funds before the company failed in 1839, jointly costing the state $3.5 million (Shaw, 1994). Indiana was particularly vulnerable in that year when a national financial panic resulted from mounting debts in many states financing similar projects. By 1841 the state was insolvent. Work on Indiana's canal construction would stop, only to be partly completed using scrip instead of cash to pay canal workers.

Indiana was like other states caught up in the frenzied state debt-driven economy of the 1830s. Illinois, Michigan, and Massachusetts started new canals and railroads, while New York, Ohio, and Pennsylvania continued to expand their systems. In the South, Alabama, Georgia, Florida, Mississippi, and Arkansas invested heavily in banks. To compete for investment, new state projects had riskier prospects for repayment with growing debt. Interstate competition also led states to adopt more lax and irresponsible policies for distribution of largesse or privilege to engage private enterprise. For example, in return for giving a substantial block of stock to the state, the Camden and Amboy railroad obtained a monopoly of the rail route in New Jersey connecting New York and Philadelphia; New York's Albany Regency, headed by future president Martin Van Buren, granted bank charters only to its political allies; Arkansas chartered a bank and capitalized it by issuing state bonds only to allow the bank to be controlled by two powerful families (Gunn, 1979).

Overall, the lure of "taxless" finance drove the pursuit of private investor dollars and conjoined political opportunities for public projects with private gain, promoting both progress but also irresponsible policies that caused state indebtedness to grow rapidly. Capital for these development efforts was commonly acquired through issuance of state bonds, but many of these bonds failed to yield anything close to expected returns, and many proceeds were lost to rampant speculation and corruption (Kiewet and Szakaly, 1996, 64). Maryland, Illinois, Michigan, Indiana, Mississippi, Louisiana, Arkansas, and Pennsylvania would default on their bonds, causing foreign investment in both public and private ventures to dry up across all states in the 1840s (Kiewet and Szakaly, 1996, 65). The boom in state canal, railroad, and bank investment all came to a crashing halt with the economic depression that began in 1839, created in large measure by state debt-driven economic development efforts. In the end, state competition for capital to promote economic development produced notable progress in the development of the nation's transportation infrastructure, filling a void left by the federal government's failure to act. Unfortunately, many of these efforts also were characterized by financial and political irresponsibility that imperiled state as well as national access to vital capital.

A Changed Legal Framework

The massive financial downturn and attendant state fiscal crises and defaults destroyed investor confidence, and corruption surrounding many of the privileges conferred by state legislatures threatened the political legitimacy of state governments. Important reforms emerged to regain investor and citizen confidence in state governments. Two reforms are most notable in terms of the trajectory state economic development efforts would take in the future. First, virtually all state constitutions adopted limitations on full faith and credit debt, requiring unconditional pledges by state governments to levy necessary taxes to meet interest and principal payments (Kiewet and Szakaly, 1996, 65). These hard budget constraints restricted state government latitude for active economic intervention: they could only finance what they could get voters to support. Second, to reduce opportunities for their governments to bestow corrupt privileges on favored interests, states adopted open incorporation laws offering the legal advantages of the corporate form to most lines of business. Taken together, these reforms ensured that the window for state action narrowed while the power of the non-governmental players in state economic development would grow. These changes would have monumental effects on state economic development in the future.

A series of very important Supreme Court cases in this period set additional boundaries for state economic intervention. The first concerned limitations on state actions concerning contracts. Starved for revenues in 1795 the Georgia legislature sold 35 million acres of what is now Alabama and Mississippi to pay its militia in what was known as the Yazoo Land Fraud. All but one legislator supporting the deal was bribed, and initial purchasers earned 650 percent profits (Powe, 2009, 59). After an electoral route, a new legislature rescinded the sale, but in *Fletcher* vs. *Peck* (1810) the US Supreme Court declared the Contract Clause of the Constitution protected private parties from state action without just compensation (further elaborated in *Martin* vs. *Hunter's Lessee* (1916), and *Dartmouth College* vs. *Woodward* (1819). This also marked the first time a state statute was declared unconstitutional, establishing that state action was subject to federal judicial review. Federal power would be further elaborated by *McCulloch* vs. *Maryland* (1819), which famously established the "Necessary and Proper" powers of Congress, and that states could not tax (or destroy) instrumentalities of the federal government within their boundaries.

The Supreme Court would further check state economic development policies using the Commerce Clause of the Constitution to establish notable ground rules for interstate competition. Consistent with the economic development practices of the time, the New York state legislature had granted Robert Livingston and Robert Fulton (both of whom also served on the Erie Canal Commission) a monopoly to its waterways for 30 years on the promise that they could invent, develop and operate a steamboat. Livingston and Fulton granted their rights to operate this monopoly steamship line between New York City and New Jersey to Aaron Ogden. Thomas Gibbons operated a ferry service unauthorized by the New York legislature, claiming he had been licensed by a 1793 act of Congress enrolling vessels trading along the seaboard. Gibbons challenged Ogden, eventually in the United States Supreme Court, where the Court declared Ogden's New York monopoly unconstitutional because the Commerce Clause of the U.S. Constitution grants Congress the power to regulate commerce among the several states (*Gibbons* vs. *Ogden*, 1824). The impact of this decision cannot be overestimated. The "secret" of American economic growth, English legal scholar Sir Henry Maine wrote in 1886, lay in "the [constitutional] Prohibition against levying duties on commodities passing from State to State... It secures to the producer the command of a free market over an enormous territory of vast natural wealth..." (Maine, 1886, 247).

Auditing Early State Economic Development

The agricultural and small business foundations of economic activity in this period were primitive by future standards, but features of state economic development from this era transcend time. State action was stimulated by federal inaction, driven by competition with other states in pursuit of capital, formulated to avoid taxation, and commonly dominated by prominent political and economic players that stood to make private gains or avoid costs from public projects. These are evergreen features of state economic development.

Legal innovations from this era also left a permanent imprint on the ground rules for future state economic efforts. They correspond remarkably well to theories highlighting important features of market-protecting federalism where governance structure affects the security and predictability of markets.(Williamson, 1985). First, a thriving economy requires a political foundation that limits the states ability to confiscate wealth (Weingast, 1995) and the Supreme Court provided such a limit in *Fletcher* vs. *Peck* and related cases. Second, it is important that there is a common market: states may not enact trade barriers (Weingast, 1995). This was accomplished in *Gibbons* vs. *Ogden*. Third, there must be a hierarchy with delineated lines of authority (Riker, 1964). This was made clear in *McCulloch* vs. *Maryland* and *Fletcher* vs. *Peck*. Fourth, subnational governments must face hard budget constraints that prohibit access to unlimited credit (Weingast, 1995). These constraints were enacted through state constitutional reform in the aftermath of the economic collapse of the late 1830s.

Although ushering in vitally important constraints on public authority, reforms in this era would also unleash new forms of private power. State reform of incorporation laws would create new players within the emergent framework of federalism. Private corporations with organizational, economic, and political power could not only respond to economic opportunities, they would engineer them as well. In so doing, private corporations would confound many of the positive benefits of the new legal and financial constraints.

Industrialization and the Rise of the Private Sector

Antebellum politics and reform reduced government authority at both the national and state levels (Wiebe, 1967; Skowronek, 1982). During the Civil War, however, the federal government became a Yankee Leviathan, creating the modern centralized bond market to finance the War (Bensel, 1990). Open incorporation reforms from before the War triggered the growth of private corporations with unprecedented advantages in information and organization, resulting in the "incorporation of America" (Trachtenberg, 1982) and a "managerial revolution" (Chandler, 1979). Private firms would use their organizational advantages and growing political and economic power in the new financial markets and political arenas to influence policy at both national and state levels.

Good and Bad: Railroads

A new ethos dawned after the Civil War. In the antebellum era, state intervention harnessed private endeavors to construct railroads under the assumption that these new highways would serve the common good rather than particular interests. Private firms would grow in number, size and power after the Civil War and would displace the public ethos with the drive for private profit.

As noted above, to secure public benefits, the nation's first train line was created with a monopoly charter to the Camden and Amboy Railroad Transportation Company. The monopoly was used to secure sales of stocks to finance construction, and the line was completed in 1833. The success of the project bred imitators so by 1840 only Arkansas, Missouri and Tennessee, and Vermont had not yet laid rail (Stover, 1997). In the new era of state debt constraints and open incorporation, past connections of actions to notions of "public interest" were supplanted by the private ethos of growing corporate power laying tracks wherever they could influence government largesse and private investment to their advantage. This fuelled explosive growth in railroad lines but the overheated politics and economics of finance and construction could lay tracks beyond the point of profitability in operations (Frank, 1989).

There were obvious benefits to this arrangement. In Washington, railroad interests secured lavish federal land grants to finance railroad construction. The states were similarly generous providing land grants and often conferring the power of eminent domain to railroads to attract them. Provided land or the power to seize land private firms facilitated rapid growth in the nation's railroads without direct taxation. This facilitated national expansion and economic integration. Railroads sold their lands to raise capital, promoting migration to their land grants, and drawing settlers to farm formerly uninhabited expanses. To make railroad operations profitable, these settlers would use them to ship and receive commodities and goods. There were also problems. The corporate drive for profit dictated the settlement of new territories, attracting migrants but creating new economic dependencies. Many new migrants became "vassals" (Frank, 1989) that were heavily dependent on the economic power of the railroads controlling the rates to transport production and goods.

A New Legal Environment

The economics of railroad construction would ultimately clash with those of railroad operation. Transcontinental and main line construction was commonly driven by more generous land grants. Many of these lines would suffer from underused capacity in operations that would drive transport rates low. To compensate, railroads would raise rates on feeder lines with the result that transportation costs to shippers were often much higher for short than for long hauls. This also meant that many costs of railroad mistakes in construction were effectively distributed to innocent bystanders. Corporate power also came to wield a chokehold on storage and handling of agricultural production. What is more, in increasingly centralized national financial markets, the value of money was shaped by financial manipulations of ever more powerful private corporations (Beckert 2001).

Publics once drawn to the benefits of infrastructure expansion came to be replaced by political movements reacting to new economic burdens created by private enterprise and finance. These movements sought state government action to re-establish "public interest" to combat the ills of private provision. Notably, the Granger Movement, founded in 1867, it grew to 850,000 members by 1875 as it came to advance policies to combat disadvantages farmers experienced in the new economic order (Nordin, 1974). This and parallel movements produced victories in state elections that led to the passage of so-called Granger laws to regulate railroads and warehouses in grain producing states heavily dependent on rail transport. These laws used the power of the state to set maximum rates for railroads and grain elevators, and imposed steep fines for corporations that failed to comply (e.g., Buck, 1913; Warren, 1926; Miller, 1971).

Ultimately, these new state regulatory efforts were challenged by the railroads in the U.S. Supreme Court. *Munn* vs. *Illinois* (1876) sustained the Granger contention that businesses of a public nature could, in accord with the federal Constitution, be subjected to state regulation—a precedent with far-reaching consequence. Unfortunately, the Munn decision created its own problems: the Commerce Clause meant states were allowed to regulate railroad transport only within their own boundaries, creating unsatisfactory conditions for shippers as well as the railroads. A mere 10 years later, the Supreme Court reversed the Munn decision (*Wabash* vs. *Illinois*, 1886) holding that states could not constitutionally regulate even the intrastate segment of interstate transportation. This would begin a new era that would last until the 1930s in which the Supreme Court would strike down many state laws regulating private businesses.

Auditing State Economic Development During Industrialization

In this era large corporate organizations with regional, national, or international economic interests could capitalize on their power of lateral mobility between states to gain political and economic advantages, and this was not limited to railroads. For example, in the 1880s and 90s the New England cotton textiles firms moved or opened branch plants in the South, attracted by the low taxes, low wage scales, the hostility to unions, and a legal climate that permitted child labor (which constituted 25 percent of the southeastern mill force, compared to a scant 6 percent in New England). In 1877 a mill in Huntsville, Alabama, allegedly employed children as young as 6, paying them only 8 cents a day. That year the state would pass legislation to restrict child labor to an eight-hour work day but this statute was repealed in 1895 in response to the demands of a mill owner that had moved his plant to the state from New England (Cobb, 2004, 72).

Large corporate organizations were also capable of playing their cards vertically to improve profitability, securing favorable laws and largess in Washington. They were also successful in securing legislation from Congress to supplant state authority. Moreover, private firms had the resources to mount successful legal challenges to unfavorable state legislation in the U.S. Supreme Court. Overall, while states continued to pursue economic development, the economic development process had changed. New players, possessing formidable political and economic clout, game the system. They not only responded to favorable state business conditions, they were increasingly capable of engineering them.

Reform and a New Order

The antebellum debt crisis provoked introspection about the scope and legitimacy of state government economic intervention and produced reforms that dramatically altered the balance between public and private economic intervention. At the close of the nineteenth century, growing corporate power, mounting social and economic challenges, and limits to state-level efforts to act provoked a "search for order" (Burnham, 1982, 47; Wiebe, 1967) culminating in the transformation of governmental authority (Buenker, 1977, 57; Skowronek, 1982; Amenta et al., 1987; Orloff, 1988; Skocpol, 1992). In this process, governmental forms and procedures necessary for securing order in industrial America emerged through "a labored exercise in creative destruction... [and] by an extended assault on the previously established governmental order [i.e., decentralized state]" (Skowronek, 1982, 9). Previously decentralized state governmental capacities located in dispersed "island communities" became increasingly unified and centralized in the national government (Wiebe, 1967, xiii), hastened by the adoption of the Sixteenth Amendment to the Constitution authorizing a federal income tax in 1913. Continuing state commitments and growing federal capacity produced a transitional period of "dual federalism" (Beer, 1973, 69).

States remained active in economic development in this period of dual federalism. Historians such as Morton Keller (1977), Ballard Campbell (1996), and William Brock (1984) emphasize the importance of state-level social and economic policymaking in the late nineteenth and early twentieth centuries. Before the 1930s, states remained the most important level of American government. State government in particular functioned as an agent of economic development (Holt, 1977, 8) and innovative public policies were widely diffused across states prior to the adoption of similar policies at the national level (Gray, 1973; Skocpol, 1992).

The federal government's power would grow in this era, increasing its administrative capacity, centralization, and resources as it took on expanding regulatory responsibilities in the modernizing economy. The transformation was accelerated by the economic crisis of the Great Depression that brought Franklin Roosevelt to the Presidency, and prompted New Deal legislation advancing the federal role in the economy through regulation, mandates, social insurance programs, and unprecedented new federal spending.

The New Deal programs were not without controversy and faced routine reversals by the U.S. Supreme Court propounding *laissez faire* principles to strike down programs enacted during Roosevelt's first 100 days. It would take the famous showdown between Franklin Roosevelt and the Supreme Court to reverse many of the policy limitations imposed by these decisions, and the Supreme Court's retreat from the judicial activism that restricted state and national economic intervention since the last century (*West Coast Hotel Co.* vs. *Parrish*, 1937).

After 1933 Washington assumed primary responsibility for economic stabilization (Redford, 1965; Hughes, 1977) and played a growing role in the economic development decisions of state governments and businesses. The Public Works Administration (PWA) handed out grants to build civil infrastructure, while the Federal Emergency Relief Administration (FERA), the Civil Works Administration (CWA), and the Works Progress Administration (WPA) granted state and local governments funds to provide relief and to build and maintain infrastructure. The Federal Housing Administration (FHA) sought to prop up the housing sector by insuring home improvement and mortgage loans. Other federal programs loaned funds to state and local governments, banks, homeowners, farmers, and industry to provide needed liquidity. These programs were attractive to states because they did not require state taxation or expenditure while creating political opportunities in Washington: Congressmen could deliver things like rural electrification, irrigation and roads to voters, jobs to workers and contracts to businesses.

GOOD AND BAD: STATE INDUSTRIAL RECRUITMENT

Modern state economic development programs are commonly traced to this era, and illustrate emerging as well as familiar themes. Mississippi was poorest state in the poorest region in the nation (Cobb, 2004). State employment had not expanded as rapidly as its population, creating a surplus labor supply exacerbated by the Depression and the growing mechanization of agriculture. Federal New Deal policies put money into the Mississippi economy through a variety of agencies and programs. The Agricultural Adjustment Agency (AAA) promised to raise farm prices through crop reduction; the Civilian Conservation Corps (CCC) hired young men to reforest badly eroded land; the WPA built piers, highways, schools, airports, and National Guard armories. The Tennessee Valley Authority and Rural Electrification Administration brought modernity to rural families where few families had access to electricity. Although Mississippians traditionally resisted federal programs, they supported the New Deal "stronger than horseradish" (Sullens, 1936).

As mayor of Columbia, Mississippi, Hugh Lawson White developed a plan in 1929 that recruited a Chicago shirt manufacturer by raising funds to construct a factory the firm would own after 10 years if they continued to employ local workers in sufficient numbers. Using this strategy, the town quickly recruited two more employers, and White would become governor by advocating a program to "Balance Agriculture with Industry" (BAWI) using public subsidies to construct factories to recruit employers willing to commit to employment and payroll targets. By the end of the 1950s firms attracted through BAWI bond subsidy programs employed roughly 36,000 workers with $100,000,000 in payrolls (Cobb, 2004, 39). The idea of bond-financed industrial subsidy quickly spread to Alabama, Kentucky, and Tennessee, and by 1962 nine additional southern states were using these subsidies, commonly augmented with tax exemptions, free or low-cost land or buildings, and low or no interest loans (Cobb, 2004, 39).

To secure New Deal funding during the Depression southern states joined a national movement toward planned economic growth by establishing state planning commissions. After World War II (WWII) these commissions in the south shifted their focus to industrial recruitment. By the end of WWII, their state development agencies would employ advertising, phone calls and visits by state representatives to recruit firms. Southern governors would become "supersalesmen" touting anti-union policies and pro-business incentives in their states (Cobb, 2004). The south initiated a new war between the states: by 1962 12 non-southern states would mimic these southern economic development programs.

Despite their proliferation, problems with these efforts were evident from the beginning (Cobb, 2004). Unsubsidized industries were left at a disadvantage. The expansion of these industrial bonds reduced the market for "public purpose" municipal securities to finance schools, streets, and hospitals. Fierce state competition produced heated bidding wars. Traditional southern industries such as textiles, apparel, footwear, hosiery, and furniture, where intense competition made all costs significant, would proliferate, tightening rather than loosening their grip on the region, and narrowing rather than diversifying their state economies. Finally, tax exemptions granted to recruit industries commonly depleted state revenues needed to provide public services to keep pace with new demands created by industrial growth (Cobb, 2004).

Early and fundamental problems notwithstanding, the attractions of this emergent strategy were powerful. Many areas using them had little to offer but a subsidized facility and unskilled labor. Proponents argued that they were necessary for economic survival. They were commonly advocated as state investments in payrolls presumed to induce a "multiplier effect" when increased spending by employers and employees would generate employment growth in other businesses. There were notable successes: in Lawton, Oklahoma, a new Goodyear plant brought 1,400 jobs and $7 million in bank deposits (Cobb, 2004, 42). Prospects like these were tantalizing but so is a flame to a moth. The record of state industrial recruitment is replete with examples that were at best questionable and at worst detrimental to the overall economic health of states, as closer examination reveals.

Auditing State Economic Development in the Reform Era

During the twentieth century the federal government grew to be a major player in state economic development and created new economic and political opportunities for states and businesses. Without raising taxes states could secure federal funds that improved infrastructure, funded contractors, and employed workers, all with seductive political benefits for state and national politicians. Federal programs and funds mitigated many traditional state economic development pressures. Most notably, important infrastructure improvements could be undertaken without local taxes so states rich and poor could build roads, dams and other capital improvements. As this leveled some of the playing field in interstate economic competition, state industrial recruitment strategies emerged as first southern and then other states sought competitive advantage in the environment made more equal by federal programs.

The economic results of federal and state efforts in this period were mixed. Large and small federal projects that produced obvious benefits for state economies: roads, bridges, damns, and water projects unarguably enhanced state infrastructure. At the same time, state industrial recruitment efforts benefited recruited industries, some newly employed workers, and the merchants and professionals gaining from "multiplier effects" or spillover business. On the bad side, political and economic incentives produced federal efforts not always suited to many state-level needs, over-supporting some activities while under-supporting others. Industrial recruitment commonly increased taxes for the bonds used for its finance or for the public services to support the growth. Public services like schools and law enforcement could face mounting demands without commensurate increases in the tax base supporting them. These strategies could also create new dependencies on corporations that became dominant employers and wielded power to keep out industries that would compete in the labor market, retarding economic expansion and diversification needed for long-term growth. Moreover, these efforts commonly attracted employers most sensitive to lower labor costs and anti-union policies, reinforcing low wages. In sum, state "beggar thy neighbor" competition for industry, while enriching some, could also "beggar thy (or many) citizens" with low paying jobs in economically vulnerable industries enjoying diminished public services.

Dueling Federalism

Federal expansion in this period blurred separate spheres of jurisdiction between nation and state (Wright, 1978; Kettl, 1988; Walker, 1981). Paul Peterson reasons that two different models of federalism were in operation during the latter half of the twentieth century (1995). The Congressional model of federalism was first driven by the Depression and sustained by electoral needs of Congresses drawn to electoral advantages from increased spending. After the Depression, federal spending was bolstered as inflation shifted federal taxpayers into ever-higher tax brackets, providing Congress with a growing source of finance and little fiscal discipline. At the same time a functional model of federalism was in operation at the subnational level. States, disciplined by market forces reflecting the mobility of residents and capital, and constrained in their indebtedness, actively pursued economic development.

From 1957 to 1977 intergovernmental grants to state and local governments for development rose from $9 billion to $75 billion (Peterson, 1995, 75). Federal grants-in-aid to states were directed at ending poverty, financing welfare reform, educating disadvantaged children, subsidizing low-income housing, encouraging mass transit, as well as economic development. These funds uniformly came with federal stipulations and regulations. Despite this growth in federal operations, developmental expenditures among the combined states and localities were more than two times those of the national government through the 1950s (Peterson, 1995, 69). In this period, federally tax-exempt state industrial development bonds became an increasingly popular tool among the states because the federal government bore most of their actual costs (Bridges, 1965).

While the influence of federal policies was felt everywhere, its effects in the south were most pronounced. It is estimated that federal defense expenditures during WWII increased the region's industrial capacity by 40 percent, increasing its share of federal payroll recipients from 19 to 27 percent, with its per capita income tripling during the 1940s (Cobb, 2004, 52). After the war powerful southern congressmen on Appropriations and Armed Services committees in the House and Senate were able to maintain the flow of military expenditures to their states. Expanding military installations were augmented with aerospace facilities like those in Huntsville, Alabama, and Houston, Texas. The Tennessee Valley Authority initiated during the New Deal provided a large injection of capital, created low-cost electricity, and stimulated improvements and services that facilitated additional industrial growth. Without federal expenditures, it is hard to imagine the dramatic transformation of the post-war southern economy would have occurred.

Despite the benefits of federal funds and the South's economic transformation, conservative, rural, and agrarian traditions of federal resistance persisted. This was particularly evident when it came to race relations and provoked a backlash against the federal government following the Supreme Court's ruling in *Brown* vs. *Board of Education* (1954) to integrate pubic schools. Here and elsewhere state and local officials, facing different economic and electoral forces, would grow to oppose stipulations placed on federal grants-in-aid. Southern states, piqued by civil rights reforms, would be drawn in by the "southern strategy" of the Republican party that opposed Congressional categorical grants that bolstered Democratic party power. Moreover, northern Congressmen, convinced the South's development was financed by the outflow of federal funds from their region, restricted federal tax exemptions for state industrial development bonds in 1968, leaving states and businesses everywhere to look for alternative channels for economic development assistance (Livingston, 1989).

With the 1968 election of Richard Nixon a "New Federalism" was initiated. Nixon produced a limited shift away from the categorical grants to states that allowed Democratic congresses to funnel money to their constituents and regulate how it was used for local purposes (and get themselves re-elected). These were replaced by federal block grants that distributed funds according to locally defined purposes. Ronald Reagan introduced his own "New Federalism," securing federal tax cuts that produced deficit politics in Congress, and curtailed federal spending on intergovernmental programs, particularly in the area of economic development. During Reagan's first term, appropriations for Small Business Administration programs, Economic Development Administration assistance, Community Development Block Grants, and Urban Development Action Grants were reduced by 35 percent (Eisinger, 1988). Owing to the federal government's financial retreat, and in the midst of a severe economic downturn, states were placed under increasing economic and political pressures.

Good and Bad: A Failed Experiment in the Laboratories of Democracy

The late 1970s and early 1980s resulted in a "perfect storm" for change in state economic development policymaking. As federal dominance of social and economic policy began to decline the states experienced a renaissance Rivlin (1992). National economic setbacks reverberated in the states. Weak economic growth and diminishing economic opportunities for many workers placed additional economic development pressures on the states, and heightened the state priorities to create and retain of good jobs for their citizens (Brace, 1993). Many states became skeptical of "smokestack chasing" industrial recruitment efforts because these policies rarely influenced business investment decisions and had few tangible effects on generating jobs (Eisinger, 1995). Beginning in the 1970s new state economic development efforts emerged to foster indigenous industries and promote state private entrepreneurial activity in growing industries (Eisinger, 1988;

Brace and Mucciaroni, 1991; Brace, 1993). States developed strategic plans to identify and develop market opportunities for state businesses and identify new industries with growth potential. Many states adopted policies to provide export assistance to exploit new markets, and venture capital to nurture new business. The new "entrepreneurial state" placed heightened emphasis on promoting the productive capacity and quality of the workforce through education and training, and the sophistication of state businesses to make them more competitive (Eisinger, 1988). Many of these new state efforts were lauded as a sign of a new and more sophisticated era in state economic development (Osborne, 1988).

Unfortunately, the new state entrepreneurialism could not counteract the national recession of the late 1980s and early 1990s. Caught in recurring booms and busts, costly entrepreneurial-based programs lacked sufficiency and could not be sustained (Brace, 1991; 1993, 1997). As Eisinger notes, "[h]allmark programs of the entrepreneurial state, such as state venture capital initiatives and high-tech research partnerships, whose development benefits lie in the uncertain future, lost much of their attraction" (Eisinger, 1995, 155). Forced to cut their budgets for these economic development programs, states retreated from commitments to science and technology partnerships, state venture capital funds, and closed or reduced overseas trade offices.

AUDITING STATE ECONOMIC DEVELOPMENT IN THE ERA OF DUELING FEDERALISM

Federal retreat signaled devolution of authority to the states first given increased authority over federal funds, but later given increased responsibility for raising revenues as federal expenditures declined. Without the cushion of federal dollars, and facing national economic set backs, states heightened their economic development efforts, developing new strategies as well as doubling down on their traditional efforts, triggering a "second war between the states" (*Newsweek*, 1988). In this battle, new economic development strategies with extended governmental commitment to programs seeking growth that was more comprehensive and long term were tried but largely abandoned in the face limited short-run returns during mounting economic challenges. What remained were state policies to attract business using favorable arrangements, and a growing expectation among businesses that they would receive them (Burnier, 1992; Lyne, 1992). This included expanded use of tax incentives to lure businesses; state investment tax credits allowing businesses to reduce their state income tax liability by a specified percentage of their new in-state investment in depreciable plant and equipment, and job-creation credits, measured as a multiple of a company's incremental in-state employment or payroll (Barrett, 1985; Mathesian, 1994). States also adopted non-tax incentives for businesses including state loans, subsidies and services (Spindler, 1992; Burstein and Rollick, 1994). These efforts spread across most states (Brace, 2002). One state survey found that only Wyoming had not adopted location incentives between 1991 and 1993 (Meyer and Hassig, 1993). By 1988, 32 states provided investment tax credits and 35 offered job creation credits (Chi, 1989). As of 1992 44 states offered some form of job creation credit (Spindler, 1994).

States sought competitive advantages in this new "war between the states" but these advantages eroded as interstate competition fuelled convergence in many economic development policies (Brace, 2002). Businesses could find attractive incentives almost everywhere but the proliferation of these programs created growing costs with diminished prospects. These costs may produce a "race to the bottom" as inducements to business reduce state resources for vital public services in police, education, and health. Incentive competition was a significant factor in the reduction of business tax revenues from one-half of state tax revenues in the 1950s to only one-quarter by 1990 (Greasser and Maury, 1994). They also fuelled a rapid escalation in the per job costs of recruitment. In 1980, Tennessee attracted a Nissan automobile plant offering 1,900 jobs at a cost of $33 million in incentives. Five years later, the cost for Tennessee to attract GM's Saturn with 6,000 jobs had risen to $150 million in state and local incentives (Milward and Newman, 1989). In 1993, Alabama assembled incentives costing over $300 million to attract a Mercedes-Benz plant employing 500 workers (Eisinger, 1995; Brace, 1997).

THE CURRENT MILIEU

Current state economic development takes place at the confluence of both familiar and new political and economic forces. States remain under pressure to develop their economies to secure jobs and stabilize their revenues. This pressure has been exacerbated by devolution of greater fiscal and legal authority to the states. Federal dollars continued to decline as a portion of state revenues, requiring states to rethink their policy commitments in the face of economic challenges and widespread anti-tax sentiment (Brace, 1997). It is too early to tell how federal TARP funds and other initiatives will alter this trend.

Legally, decisions by a conservative Supreme Court have limited national powers and protected state options (e.g., *United States* vs. *Lopez*, 1995; *Printz* vs. *United States*, 1997); the Court has also limited state economic development actions, repeatedly invalidating state tax provisions if they provide an in-state business or activity with protections or benefits that are not similarly available to its out-of-state competition or otherwise create inappropriate distinctions favoring local business activity (see, for example, *Bacchus Imports, Ltd.* vs. *Dias*, 1984; *Westinghouse Elec. Corp.* vs. *Tully*, 1984; *West Lynn Creamery Inc.* vs. *Healy*, 1994). In the emerging constitutional framework, state governments are more shielded from federal power but more constrained in their finances and economic development options.

In the new environment, incentives and other inducements have spread, adopted enthusiastically in some states while reluctantly in others because of mounting doubts about their effectiveness and growing concerns about their costs(e.g., Fox and Murray, 2004; Peters and Fisherm, 2004). This should not be surprising. The market economy operating through the lattice of federalism creates economic and policy opportunities that produce positive and negative outcomes. These outcomes shape constellations of interests seeking opportunity, protection or advantage which in turn shape political rewards and risks for state policymakers. These pressures are exacerbated by the growing sophistication of employers who can capitalize on the leverage afforded through lateral mobility. Clear-headed thinking about the limited efficacy of tax incentives and subsidies is often trumped by the attraction of taking visible steps to encourage economic growth that allow policymakers to take credit, and avoid blame for jobs moving out of state.

Good and Bad: Alabama

In many ways a thread runs through Alabama's political and economic development that embodies features of the main events and processes discussed to this point. The state was carved from lands involved in the Yazoo Land Scandal. In the early nineteenth century the state went into the banking business by issuing bonds on its own credit, lending the proceeds to businesses and individuals to promote economic development. Many borrowers defaulted on these loans, creating a financial crisis. By the time of their 1901 Constitutional Convention, 70 years later, these debts had still not been paid (Clark, 2002) and the Alabama Constitution explicitly proscribes many state economic development options. During the nineteenth century many Alabama counties and cities competed to attract railroads to their communities, with the hope that having a railroad would facilitate commerce and travel, improved job opportunities, and general economic well-being. These governments issued public debt and invested the proceeds in railroad and related enterprises as an incentive to locate in their jurisdictions. The state also issued bonds to support the railroads. When the railroads failed, or the expected benefits did not materialize, their governments were left with unmanageable debt loads, pushing some into default and insolvency (Clark, 2002).

Alabama was an early and enthusiastic adopter of the industrial recruitment strategies developed in the south. Capitalizing on its unskilled and cheap labor, the state recruited industry by marketing its poverty and extolling the benefits of cheap land, labor, and low taxes. The strategy worked to attract companies that benefited from low-cost land and raw materials, operating with low-skilled or non-skilled workers earning lower wages than their unionized counterparts in the northeast. The low cost factors that attracted them, however, hindered economic diversification and retarded improvements in education and general infrastructure. In the later half of the twentieth century It created dependence on low-wage, low-skill industries that that began to close their operations and move to even cheaper locales in foreign countries (Flynt, 2004).

Facing decline, and realizing their traditional economic development strategies were no longer viable, political and business leaders in the 1980s and 1990s formulated plans to attract large, sophisticated employers with targeted, large-sum inducements. In 1993 it offered Mercedes-Benz over $300 million in subsidies and other incentives to build a plant that would employ 1,500 workers. They would produce similar efforts to successfully recruit Honda, Toyota, and Hyundai. These firms have created relatively well-paid jobs and are expected to boost the overall technical capacity of the state. Notably, while there was not a single car produced in Alabama in 1995, the state produced over 800,000 automobiles in 2007 (Gross, 2008).

It is difficult to assess the overall effects of Alabama's contemporary efforts on its economy but after roughly 15 years it is reasonable to examine how the state compares to other states on important indicators. Alabama's poverty has traditionally been among the highest in the nation and despite recent efforts to grow its economy it remains among the nation's poorest states. By its own estimates, in 2007 the state ranked tenth in overall poverty and seventh among those 65 and over (*Tuscaloosa News*, 2007; Alabama Poverty Task Force, 2008). One study ranked Alabama's cost of business as 19 while education (47), technology and innovation (39), transportation (43), and quality of life (45) placed it among the lowest states on these indicators. An analysis of the overall effects of Alabama's fiscal structure on its growth rate using 2004 data found it to rank dead last among the states (Bania and Stone, 2008). The performance of Alabama's economy during the nation's 2008 recession provides another crude indicator of the relative success of its economic development efforts. In September of 2009 the state ranked tenth in unemployment and was particularly hard hit when the recession struck relatively high paying manufacturing and professional jobs (Associated Press, 2009). Exacerbating this, Alabama ranked dead last in the average weekly benefits paid to unemployed workers (*Propublica*, 2010).

It is important not to exaggerate the implications of these rankings. Alabama could have faired worse without the effects of its economic development programs. Despite this, some conclusions seem warranted. Alabama was poor and serious poverty remains. The state also remains among the bottom in many other socio-economic rankings. While securing coveted large employers with obvious attractions, Alabama's economic development programs have not produced a broad transformation of the state in this period. Alabama is a cheaper place to build cars for multinational automotive firms, with jobs and business for some, but there is little evidence that this has elevated the overall economic well-being of the state as it continues to score low on many indicators.

CONCLUSIONS

Much of the literature on state economic development is preoccupied with contemporary policies and events, largely focusing on post-WWII state industrial recruitment and related policies. This emphasis is not surprising because it addresses modern development issues, but it is also unfortunate because it fails to place these issues in a broader context. The survey of American political development presented here, while admittedly brief, reveals that state economic development has always been a dominant feature of our politics and economics. Interstate economic competition is older than the nation. Colonies organized for economic purposes were competitive organizations with limited self-government from the outset. It is older than our Constitution: interstate rivalries were a major reason for the Constitutional convention, and these rivalries dominated the politics that produced that document. Throughout history states have pursued opportunities to use their powers to secure public and private economic advantage. The framework for this pursuit has been shaped by federal action or inaction, legal reforms that altered options for state action, and the power of interests seeking to influence state economic development. At each stage, emerging constraints imparted stable elements, but also created new benefits and costs with new winners and losers, resulting in persistent instability as well.

Current issues in state economic development are nested within stable and unstable features of American federalism. Given formal state constitutional limits on debt and taxation, and informal limits borne of voter antipathy and fierce interstate competition, there remain limited opportunities for direct state investment. What remains are abundant opportunities to adopt policies to limit firm and investor tax exposure to attract or nurture coveted economic enterprises. The long-term economic costs of these policies are commonly vague as are their broad-based benefits. The political advantages, however, remain seductive. They afford opportunities to connect electorally popular symbolic and visible action to desirable public objectives. They also attract the demands of powerful and well-organized economic interests seeking private benefit where costs can be socialized.

Throughout this discussion, the good and bad features of economic development through history have been contrasted and this seems an apt way to conclude. In principle, state economic development efforts have promised broad benefits but in practice they have produced unbalanced rewards and costs. Federalism provides constant impetus for state intervention with notable constraints, but the politics of mobilization for state economic development intersect imperfectly with the economics of sound action. The state drive for development, both perpetuated and constrained by the federal structure attracts powerful economic interests seeking advantage through the socialization of burdens. At best these forces hasten critical innovations and at worst they promote gross economic irresponsibility. Moreover, interstate competition between states can compound unbalanced political processes within states to produce state strategies that are strikingly uniform in design yet collectively irresponsible. An Erie Canal, a railroad, or a new firm produced notable benefits initially but these successes were not uniformly replicated in other states as their efforts converged to produce similar projects with declining benefits, heightened costs, and greater risks. Hence, although state efforts seem forever likely, it is only incidentally viable in the long run because of the endemic imbalances it embodies. Successful strategies in some states become failed strategies in others as the marginal returns from these efforts are depleted through policy convergence among the states. In the end, the competitive environment of states ordains constraints and opportunities for economic action, while the politics between and within states limit the economic effectiveness of those actions.

REFERENCES

Supreme Court Cases

Bacchus Imports, Ltd. vs. *Dias,* 468 U.S. 263, 1984.
   Brown vs. *Board of Education,* 347 U.S. 483, 1954.
   Dartmouth College vs. *Woodward,* 7 U. S. 518, 1819.
   Fletcher vs. *Peck,* 10 U.S. 87, 1810
   Gibbons vs. *Ogden,* 22 U.S. 1, 1824.
   Martin vs. *Hunter's Lessee,* 14 U.S. 304, 1816.
   McCulloch vs. *Maryland,* 17 U.S. 316, 1819.
   Munn vs. *Illinois,* 94 U.S. 113, 1877.
   Printz vs. *United States,* 521 U.S. 898, 1997.
   United States vs.*Lopez,* 514 U.S. 549, 1995.
   Wabash, St. Louis & Pacific Railway Company vs. *Illinois,* 118 U.S. 557, 1886.
   West Coast Hotel Co. vs. *Parrish,* 300 U.S. 379, 1937.
   West Lynn Creamery Inc. vs. *Healy,* II4 S. Ct. 2205, 1994.
   Westinghouse Elec. Corp. vs. *Tully,* 466 U.S. 388, 1984.

Additional Works Cited

Alabama Poverty Task Force. 2008. *Final Report.* February.

Amenta, Edwin, Elisabeth S. Clemens, Jefren Olsen, Sunita Parikh, and Theda Skocpol. 1987. "The Political Origins of Unemployment Insurance in Five American States." *Studies in American Political Development* 2: 137–182.

Barrett, William J. 1985. "Note, Problems With State Aid to New or Expanding Businesses." *Southern California Law Review 58*: 1025–1026.

Beckert, Sven. 2001. *The Monied Metropolis: New York City and the Consolidation of the American Bourgeoisie, 1850-1896.* New York, NY: Cambridge University Press.

Bensel, Richard Franklin. 1990. *Yankee Leviathan: The Origins of Central State Authority in America, 1859-1877.* New York, NY: Cambridge University Press.

Brace, Paul. 1988. "The Political Economy of Collective Action: The Case of the American States." *Polity 20* (summer): 648–664.

Brace, Paul. 1989. "Isolating the Economies of States." *American Politics Quarterly 17* (August): 256–276.

Brace, Paul. 1991. "The Changing Context of State Political Economy." *Journal of Politics 53* (2): 297–317.

Brace, Paul. 1993. *State Government and Economic Performance.* Baltimore, MD: Johns Hopkins University Press.

Brace, Paul. 1997. "Do Local Taxes Break the Back of Development?" In Richard D. Bingham and Robert Mier (eds), *Dilemmas of Urban Economic Development.* Thousand Oaks, CA: Sage Publications.

Brace, Paul. 1999. "States and Localities Transformed." In Ronald Weber and Paul Brace (eds), *Change and Continuity in American State and Local Government.* New York, NY: Chatham House.

Brace, Paul. 2002. "Economic Development Policy in the American States: Back to an Inglorious Future?" In Cal Clark and Robert S. Montjoy (eds), *Globilization's Impact on State-Local Economic Development Policy.* Huntington, NY: Nova Science Publishers.

Brace, Paul. 2009. "Cooperation Between the States." In Donald P. Markel, et al. (eds), *Political Encyclopedia of U.S. States and Regions.* Washington, DC: Congressional Quarterly Press.

Brace, Paul. and Gary Mucciaroni. 1991. "The American States and the Shifting Locus of Positive Economic Intervention." *Policy Studies Review 10* (spring): 151–173.

Bridges, Benjamin Jr. 1965. "State and Local Inducements for Industry: Part I." *National Tax Journal 18*: 6–8.

Buck, Solon J. 1913. *The Granger Movement.* Cambridge, MA: Harvard University Press.

Buenker, John D. 1977. "Progressivism Essay." In John D. Buenker, John C. Burnham, and Robert M. Crunden (eds), *Progressivism.* Cambridge, MA: Schenkman.

Burnham, Walter Dean. 1982. *The Current Crisis in American Politics.* Oxford: Oxford University Press.

Burnier, De Lysa, 1992. "Becoming Competitive: How Policymakers View Incentive-Based Development Policy." *Economic Development Quarterly 6*: 14–21.

Burstein Melvin L. and Arthur J. Rolnick. 1995. "Congress Should End the Economic War Among the States." *Federal Reserve Bank of Minneapolis 1994 Annual Report.* Region 3.

Business Week. 1976. "The Second War Between the States." May 17: 92.

Chandler, Alfred D., Jr. 1977. *The Visible Hand: The Managerial Revolution in American Business.* New York, NY: Cambridge University Press.

Chi, Keon. 1989. *The States and Business Incentives: An Inventory of Tax and Financial Incentive Programs.* Lexington, KY: Council of State Governments.

Chief Executive. 2008. "Alabama Economic Statistics 2008." (<http://www.chiefexecutive.net/media/usbestandworststates/2009/USBestWorstState.aspx?state=Alabama>).

Cobb, James C. 1993. *The Selling of the South: The Southern Crusade for Industrial Development, 1936-90.* Urbana, IL: University of Illinois Press.

Cobb, James C. 2004. *Industrialization and Southern Society, 1877-1984.* Lexington, KY: University of Kentucky Press.

Courant, Paul N. 1994. "How Would You Know a Good Economic Development Policy If You Tripped Over One? Hint: Don't Just Count Jobs." *National Tax Journal 47*: 875–876.

Eisinger, Peter. *The Rise of the Entrepreneurial State: State and Local Development Policies in the United States.* Madison, WI: University of Wisconsin Press.

Eisinger, Peter. 1995. "State Economic Development in the 1990s: Politics and Policy Learning." *Economic Development Quarterly 9* (2): 146–158.

Fallon, Richard H. 2002. "The 'Conservative' Paths of the Rehnquist Court's Federalism Decisions." *The University of Chicago Law Review 69* (2): 429–494.

Frank, Thomas. 1989. "The Leviathan with Tentacles of Steel: Railroads in the Minds of Kansas Populists." *The Western Historical Quarterly 20* (1): 37–54

Gillman, Howard. 1993. *The Constitution Besieged: The Rise and Demise of the Lochner Era Police Power Jurisprudence.* Durham, NC: Duke University Press.

Goodrich, Carter. 1960. *Government Promotion of American Canals and Railroads, 1800–1890.* New York, NY: Columbia University Press.

Graeser, Laird and Al Maury. 1944. "Business Taxes—Quo Vadimus?" *State Tax Notes 7*: 917–918.

Hamilton, Alexander. 1997. "The Report on Manufactures." reprinted in Michael Lind, editor, *Hamilton's Republic.* New York, NY: Free Press.

Hamilton, Alexander. 1961. "The Federalist No. 7." In Clinton Rossiter (ed.) *Federalist Papers*. New York: New American Library.

Inman, Robert P., and Daniel L. Rubinfeld. 1996. "Designing Tax Policy in Federalist Economics: An Overview." *Journal of Public Economics 60*: 307–334.

Kettl, Donald F. 1988. *The Regulation of American Federalism*. Baltimore, MD: Johns Hopkins University Press.

Kiewet, D. Roderick, and Kristin Szakaly. 1996. "Constitutional Limits on Borrowing: An Analysis of State Bonded Indebtedness." *Journal of Law, Economics and Organization 12*(1): 62–97.

Livingston Michael. 1989. "Reform or Revolution? Tax-Exempt Bonds, the Legislative Process, and the Meaning of Tax Reform." *UC Davis Law Review 22*: 1165–1212.

Lyne, Jack. 1992. "Incentives Are Important Executives Say, but Business Concerns Drive the Location Process." *Site Location 37*: 282–283.

Mahtesian, Charles. 1994. "Romancing the Smokestack." *Governing 8* (November): 36–38.

Maine, Sir Henry. 1886. *Popular Government*. Indianapolis, IN: Liberty Fund, 1976.

Meyer, Georgina and John Hassig. 1993. "Economic Development Policy." *State Tax Notes 5*: 1229–1236.

Miller, George H. 1971. Railroads and the Granger Laws. Madison, WI: University of Wisconsin Press.

Milward, H. Brinton and Heidi Hosbach Newman. 1989. "State Incentive Packages and the Industrial Location Decision." *Economic Development Quarterly 3*: 179–187.

Montinola, Gabriella, Yingyi Qian and Barry R. Weingast. 1995. "Federalism, Chinese Style: The Political Basis for Economic Success in China." *World Politics 48* (1): 50–81.

Murray Matthew N. 1994. "Using State Policies to Promote Economic Development." *National Tax Association, Proceedings of Eight Sixth Annual Conference*: pp. 158–160.

Newsweek. 1988. "War Between the States." March 30: 45.

Nordin, Dennis S. 1974. *Rich Harvest: A History of the Grange, 1867–1900*. Jackson, MI: University Press of Mississippi.

Orloff, Ann Shola. 1988. "The Political Origins of America's Belated Welfare State." In Margaret Weir, Ann Shola Orloff, and Theda Skocpol (eds), *The Politics of Social Policy in the United States*. Princeton, NJ: Princeton University Press.

Osborne, David. 1988. *Laboratories of Democracy*. Cambridge, MA: Harvard Business Press.

Propublica, 2010. (<http://projects.propublica.org/unemployment/states/AL>), April 15.

Riker, William H. 1964. *Federalism: Origin, Operation and Significance*. Boston, MA: Little Brown.

Rivlin, Alice M. 1992. *Reviving the American Dream: The Economy, the States and the Federal Government*. Washington, DC: Brookings.

Schieber, Harry N. 1975. "Federalism and the American Economic Order, 1789-1910." Essays in Honor of J. Willard Hurst: Part One (Autumn). *Law & Society Review 10* (1): 57–118.

Shaw, Ronald E. 1990. *Canals for a Nation: The Canal Era in the United States, 1790-1860*. Lexington, KY: University of Kentucky Press.

Skocpol, Theda. 1992. *Protecting Soldiers and Mothers: The Politics of Social Provision in the United States, 1870s-1920s*. Cambridge, MA: Harvard University Press.

Skowronek, Stephen. 1982. *Building a New American State: The Expansion of National Administrative Capacities, 1877-1920*. Cambridge, MA: Cambridge University Press.

Spindler, Charles. 1994. "Winners and Losers in Industrial Recruitment: Mercedes-Benz and Alabama." *State and Local Government Review 26*: 192–201.

Stover, John F. 1997. *American Railroads*. Sec. Ed. Chicago, IL: University of Chicago Press.

Sullens, Frederick. 1936. "The South is Still Solid: Six Editors Render a Report," *Review of Reviews* January: 39.

Tiebout, Charles M. 1956. "A Pure Theory of Local Expenditures." *Journal of Political Economy* 64: 416–424.

Trachtenberg, Alan. 1982. *The Incorporation of America: Culture and Society in the Gilded Age.* New York, NY: Hill and Wang.

Tuscaloosa News. 2007. "Alabama Still One of 10 Poorest States." August 29.

Walker, David B. 1982. *Toward a Functioning Federalism.* Cambridge, MA: Winthrop.

Wall Street Journal. 2002. "How Big Incentives Won Alabama a Piece of the Auto Industry." April 3: 1.

Wallis, John Joseph. 2005. "Constitutions, Corporations, and Corruption: American States and Constitutional Change, 1842 to 1852." *The Journal of Economic History 65* (March): 211–256.

Wallis, John Joseph and Barry Weingast. 2005. "The Financing of 19th Century Internal Improvements." UC Berkeley: Department of Economics. Retrieved from: <http://escholarship.org/uc/item/7nh1c6df>.

Warren, Charles. 1926. *The Supreme Court in United States History,* Vol. 2: *1836-1918.* Boston, MA: Little, Brown.

Weingast, Barry R. 1993. "Constitution as Governance Structures: The Political Foundation of Secure Markets." *Journal of Institutional and Theoretical Economics 149*: 286–311.

Weingast Barry R. 1995. "The Economic Role of Political Institutions: Market-Preserving Federalism and Economic Development." *Journal of Law, Economics and Organizations 11*: 1

Wiebe, Robert H. 1967. *The Search for Order, 1877-1920.* New York, NY: Hill & Wang.

Williamson, Oliver. 1985. *The Economic Institutions of Capitalism.* New York: Free Press.

Wright, Deil S. 1978. *Understanding Intergovernmental Relations.* North Scituate, MA: Duxbury Press.

CHAPTER 28

··

EDUCATION POLICY

··

PAUL MANNA

THOSE hoping to better understand subnational governments would be well served to develop some expertise in education policy.[1] Clearly, all scholars of state and local settings need not make education their primary focus. Still, education has a major influence on the contexts in which subnational governments operate. The provision of education is a key area outlined in state constitutions. The nation's schools and universities consume large fractions of state and local budgets. Leaders at all levels of government and across time have touted the crucial role that education plays in sustaining the nation's economy and democracy. Recognizing education's importance in subnational settings, scholars working across various subfields of political science and public administration have found this policy area valuable for theory development and empirical study.[2]

Scholars of political institutions frequently note that states and localities provide useful variation to test theories originally developed in national venues. In education, multiple institutions have some hand in governing the production and implementation of policies that influence the nation's schools and universities (Masters, Salisbury, and Eliot, 1964; Campbell and Mazzoni, 1976; Lowry, 2001; Hicklin and Meier, 2008; Wirt and Kirst, 2009). They include state boards that oversee different aspects of elementary and secondary schooling, higher education, and in some cases vocational learning. Further, state education agencies, whose leaders can be elected or appointed, are the administrative workhorses that dispense federal and state funds, provide technical assistance, and direct implementation of state and federal policy.

Local institutions that govern education also vary. Today, the United States contains approximately 14,000 school districts (Berkman and Plutzer, 2005; Howell, 2005). In addition, a small but growing number of urban areas have empowered city mayors to choose the local superintendent, a function traditionally possessed by elected school boards (Henig and Rich, 2004; Wong et al., 2007). The emergence of public charter schools since the early 1990s, which are relieved of many regulatory requirements that apply to traditional public schools, have created new governing and oversight challenges (Shober, Manna, and Witte, 2006; Schneider and Buckley, 2007; Henig, 2008).

Additionally, state and local education policy provides openings for research on the political behavior of individuals and groups. These include opportunities for testing claims about the impact of different methods for choosing leaders, how those leaders represent their constituents, decision making among policy elites, and how citizens' choices affect educational and other outcomes (Schneider, Teske, and Marschall, 2000; Meier, O'Toole, and Nicholson-Crotty, 2004; Henig, 2009; Marschall, Ruhil, and Shah, 2010). Interest groups and extragovernmental organizations can have much influence on education through policy advocacy, lobbying, and campaign work or contributions. Atop the list of influencers are the nation's two major teacher unions—the National Education Association and the American Federation of Teachers—and various business groups. Other extragovernmental organizations wield power as philanthropic grant givers or service providers. For example, states and localities spend hundreds of millions of dollars annually in contracts with companies that develop and score standardized tests, produce textbooks, teacher guides, and computer technology, or provide tutoring services.

Finally, subnational education policy and politics present research opportunities for scholars of public management, administration, and bureaucracy (Chubb and Moe, 1990 Meier, Polinard, and Wrinkle, 2000; Meier et al., 2005; Manna, 2010). At the street level, teachers and other school staff confront ambiguous and sometimes conflicting laws or regulations, all the while teaching students from diverse backgrounds. As such, they wield much power to define the content of policy through their actions (Lipsky, 1980). Staff in district offices, state agencies, and the federal education department confront their own challenges as they administer dozens of programs that frequently exist in tension. Overall, during the past two decades the stakes for educational administration have increased as the states and federal government have embraced policies to promote accountability for educational performance.

This chapter's remaining discussion is designed to illustrate, not comprehensively describe, major streams of scholarship on state and local education policy from the past few decades. It focuses on three broad areas: markets, governance, and representation. That categorization provides a simple heuristic, rather than a clear delineation between major research programs. As readers will see, several works discussed below cut across these categories.

Education and Markets

Policies that promote school choice represent robust expressions of local control. Studies of local educational markets have addressed several specific research questions. Does school choice influence school operations and student outcomes? How do parents make decisions when they choose their children's schools? To what extent do local markets for education create positive or negative externalities that may influence the quality of education and democracy? These questions have important implications for how local markets for education are likely to function in practice. Answering them can also provide broader theoretical insights about institutional design and political behavior.

Markets versus Democratic Control

Energetic scholarly debates have focused on the potential educational outcomes that public institutions and markets might produce. Two of the most important scholars in this debate have been Chubb and Moe (1988, 1990), who helped influence numerous research agendas with their 1990 book, *Politics, Markets, and America's Schools.* In that work, the authors argue that public schools are destined to underperform because they are creatures of democratic control. Chubb and Moe (1990) note that policy makers in democracies must forge compromises to broker competing demands from various constituents; as a result, public schools must fulfill the desires of sometimes disparate groups, which attenuates school performance. Chubb and Moe (1990) argue that market systems work much differently. Those systems set free school-level leaders, teachers, and parents to organize school operations and select staff and curriculum based on criteria that the school itself deems important. That insulation from external interests, the authors argue, results in schools that better serve parents and their children, the most important consumers of education.

Chubb and Moe's (1990) provocative findings and recommendations for adopting school vouchers to improve educational performance prompted responses from other scholars. Henig (1994, 241) cautioned that "sharp and periodic reform efforts may accomplish less, in the long run, than sustained efforts that take time to nurture a supportive constituency and to solidify and institutionalize gains as they occur." The attractiveness of the market metaphor, Henig argues, is particularly appealing amidst perceptions—and in some communities the reality—that traditional public schools have struggled. Henig (1994, 146) summarizes the mixed track record of choice and other market-based reforms and notes the irony that "the study [Chubb and Moe, 1990] that has lent the greatest credence to the claim that 'choice works' does not include any direct indicators of choice at all." The upshot of Henig's (1994) work is that choice may indeed be a useful arrow in the quiver of education reformers, but broad improvements will require a reinvigorated sense of collective purpose, which narrow, market-based reforms are likely to undercut.

In a separate response, Smith and Meier (1994, 1995-) challenged the premise that bureaucracy necessarily promotes poor educational outcomes. Instead, they argue that increased bureaucratization (e.g., employing more staff and creating new programs) is a response to community needs. In other words, poor performance promotes a search for solutions and therefore increases bureaucracy, rather than bureaucracy undermining performance. Looking at data across state and local levels (and offering some international comparisons), they find that many of the education reforms of the 1980s that emerged after Chubb and Moe's (1990) data were collected, such as increasing course-taking requirements for students and adding requirements for prospective teachers, were positively associated with student outcomes. Further, direct measures of democratic control, such as whether local school districts elected their superintendent, had no effect. Elected superintendents were also associated with less bureaucracy, as measured by the number of school officials per student.

In a subsequent study, Meier, Polinard, and Wrinkle (2000) used eight years of data from over 1,000 school districts in Texas to show that poor school performance produces larger bureaucracies as districts attempt to respond to perceived needs. In so doing, the authors make a larger theoretical point, while crediting Chubb and Moe (1990) for offering a framework that invited careful thinking about institutions. Meier, Polinard, and Wrinkle (2000, 590) note that the issues at stake "are relevant not only to public policy debates but are also testable propositions that promise theoretical insight into how institutions respond to and influence their environments."

Outcomes in Local Markets

The emergence of public and privately funded school voucher programs during the 1990s further sharpened debates about educational markets and student achievement (Witte, 1998; Witte, 2000; Howell and Peterson, 2002; Howell, 2004). Those programs and the systematic evaluations accompanying them allowed political scientists (and other scholars) to more directly examine whether choice improved educational outcomes. A lively empirical debate about vouchers' effectiveness ensued, which frequently turned on methodological questions about how to account for selection bias and whether the policy experiments that seemed to provide great analytical leverage actually held up in practice. Although the arguments were sometimes intense and the published work voluminous, two key findings emerged. First, authors uniformly found that parents who chose their children's schools were more satisfied than parents who did not choose. Second, some achievement gains were apparent for voucher recipients, but they tended to be limited to certain student groups, or confined to particular subjects or grade levels. No evidence suggested that students using school vouchers did systematically worse than their peers.

Markets for education depend upon schools supplying educational services, but they also need parents who are willing and prepared to choose their children's schools. That requirement places parents in a challenging position for two reasons: schools are multidimensional institutions that can be difficult to evaluate, and choice presents parents with unfamiliar duties, given that most students attend schools based on their residency within an attendance boundary. Do these demands on parents suggest that educational markets may cease to function well?

In a research program focussing on consumer decision making in local markets for education, Schneider and several colleagues have examined that question in detail (Teske et al., 1993; Schneider et al., 1997a; Schneider et al., 1997b; Schneider et al., 1998; Schneider et al., 2000). These authors suggest that markets can promote beneficial outcomes even if all parents lack good information. That result is conditional upon the presence of at least some parents who serve as "marginal consumers," those who become knowledgeable about local school characteristics. Integrating scholarship on political behavior, networks, political psychology, and economics, Schneider, Teske, and Marschall (2000, 270) conclude their award-winning book, *Choosing Schools: Consumer Choice and the Quality of American Schools*, by observing that "Competitive markets do not need all consumers to be informed—competitive pressures can result even if a relatively small subset of consumers engage in informed, self-interested search."

The authors reach these conclusions using a creative research design involving four public school districts: Community districts 1 and 4 in New York City and in neighboring New Jersey, the Montclair Public Schools and the Morris School District. District 4 and Montclair incorporated public school choice, while the other two districts did not. Overall, the authors are not as optimistic as Chubb and Moe (1990, 217) that choice is a "panacea" that will eliminate the nation's educational ills. Nevertheless, Schneider, Teske, and Marschall (2000) note that on balance, choice tends to benefit the families that choose, although modestly, while not disadvantaging those who do not. Still, the authors caution that the discussion networks in which some parents participate are likely to provide better access to knowledgeable marginal consumers than others (Schneider et al., 1997b; Schneider, Teske, and Marschall, 2000). And further, the quality of those discussion networks are often driven by class or race, with more advantaged parents having access to more and better information.

Future Research

Political scientists and public administration scholars have contributed to a robust literature on school choice that has tested theories about market behavior and bureaucratic organizations, the academic performance of choice schools, and the ability of parents to meet the demands required for educational markets to function well. Despite these advances, several dimensions of school choice remain relatively unexplored. Consider three areas in particular.

First, research on the effects of school choice has tended to focus on student test score outcomes as the measure of program success. Although some have considered implications of choice on tolerance and adherence to democratic norms (Wolf, 2005) and recent (unpublished) evaluations of choice programs in Milwaukee and Washington, DC have studied additional outcomes, generally the best research designs and data have focused on student achievement in reading and math. Other outcomes deserve deeper examination, given that parents consider several ideas, beyond student achievement, when they choose schools (Howell, 2004; Schneider and Buckley, 2007).

Second, debates about whether choice influences certain outcomes are also somewhat limited, given that researchers have tended to leave schools' daily operations in unopened black boxes. Thus, in a multiple regression context, an independent variable tapping participation in a choice program (e.g., a student received a voucher or not; a student chose a charter school or not) may suggest achievement gains for students who choose, but what remains unknown are the practices the choice schools are pursuing that produce those results. Scholars should be more willing to engage schools on the ground level to study these practices.[3]

Finally, the literature has hardly considered the behavior of educational suppliers in markets for school choice. One premise of market-based reforms is that schools will adapt to compete for students. Yet just like parents, school leaders themselves face information problems when they interpret the signals that parents send when they leave or enter a particular school. Sometimes parents leave schools, although they appear quite satisfied with the quality of the academic program, teachers, school leadership, and safety. How schools and districts respond to competitive pressures is one area ripe with opportunity (Teske et al., 2001; Hess, 2002; Manna, 2002; Witte Schlomer, and Shober, 2007).

EDUCATION AND GOVERNANCE

Unlike the concept of "government," which suggests a relatively narrow focus on public institutions, the more multidimensional "governance" invites scholars to consider how those institutions can influence public and private actors as they manage a diverse menu of programs and policy tools.[4] Scholars have considered several ways that governance might influence public officials as they develop and implement education policy. How do local school system leaders define their agendas and manage policy given their political, financial, and institutional constraints? How do intergovernmental relationships influence these same local leaders, as well as administrators or elected officials at the state and federal level? What unique issues must state leaders confront as they oversee local systems, while simultaneously serving as conduits for federal policies and resources directed to influence local schooling? This section considers those questions by examining local leadership, local management and administration, and state politics and policy.

Local Leadership

Discussions about school board leadership have received increasing attention from political scientists and other scholars (Howell, 2005; Berry and West, 2010). In the current policy environment, people are beginning to question whether elected local boards themselves are viable entities for overseeing the nation's nearly 100,000 schools. The rise of the state standards movement and efforts to hold localities accountable for student learning has attenuated local control over curriculum, for example. Answering challenging technical questions, such as how to educate children with disabilities or those who are still learning English, often seem beyond the scope of what local boards, with their citizen leaders who often lack expertise in teaching or assessment, can manage.

Beyond board leadership, researchers have also examined local chief executives, either district superintendents or mayors who lead their city public schools. Studies of superintendents and mayors have identified a complicated web of constraints that challenge these individuals to produce policy agendas that simultaneously satisfy their constituents and improve student learning (Hess, 1999; Henig and Rich, 2004; Wong et al., 2007). Theoretically, scholars have identified models relating leadership to local outcomes. This work sometimes even suggests implications for leadership in other contexts and at other levels of government (Henig, 2009).

Hess's (1999) study of superintendents considers the incentives facing these district leaders as they build their policy agendas. Superintendents work under several constraints that limit their effectiveness. Urban school systems have tended to be "organizations with little accountability, difficult-to-control technical cores, and intense public scrutiny" (Hess, 1999, 31). Those factors and personal incentives that drive leaders to improve their own personal reputations lead them frequently to advance new initiatives, rather than seeing through potentially promising reforms of their predecessors. The ironic result, Hess (1999) notes, is that urban districts commonly experience too much, not too little, reform. The tendency of new leaders to overhaul existing approaches inevitably produces disappointment when improvements do not occur in the narrow timeframes that superintendents have promised.

School boards and superintendents have led nearly all American school systems for most of the country's history. Within the past decade or so mayoral control has emerged as an alternative in some urban districts. In these systems, mayors have captured traditional board functions: they choose school superintendents, set instructional agendas for schools, hire and fire central office and school personnel, open and close schools, and manage district funds. The theoretical arguments favoring mayoral control suggest that centralizing power over schools in city hall will eliminate the perverse incentives that Hess (1999) discusses, which drive districts to focus on symbolic, rather than substantive, reforms.

Although mayoral control is relatively rare, high-profile cases in New York City and the District of Columbia (among other places) have received much attention. Scholars have begun to examine the theoretical arguments for this approach and to develop empirical studies to test them. One example is the edited collection from Henig and Rich (2004), which presents case studies in six large, urban districts with mayoral control. In synthesizing the findings of these diverse cases, the editors conclude with a sense of "wary skepticism" about the potential for mayoral control to deliver on its promises (Henig and Rich, 2004, 251). The reason, the authors argue, is that improving urban education ultimately requires a strong collective commitment to address several factors that can undermine positive change. Given the right intersection of circumstances and a politically talented mayor, mayoral control may indeed foster improvements. But the editors and some contributors are not sanguine, given that there are many ways that the tight logic behind mayor-led systems may break down in practice (Meier, 2004).

In another major study, Wong and co-authors (2007) use a large-N statistical analysis to examine policy change in finance and staffing, student outcomes, and dynamics of local politics in cities with mayoral control. The authors note that mayoral control of schools is not randomly distributed across the country. Thus, they use a careful research design that generates a purposeful sample of 104 districts without mayoral control, which they compare to the 10 districts they identified with mayoral control. The authors' overall findings show that mayoral leadership is associated with higher reading and math achievement among elementary school students, more financial resources for instruction and less for administration, and higher placement of education on local political agendas. Those findings, they argue, "suggests that the first wave of mayoral control has been a success" (Wong et al., 2007, 198). The book's larger theoretical point shows how institutions can create enabling conditions that leaders may then leverage to improve organizational performance.

Local Management and Administration

In addition to studies examining how superintendents and mayors define reform agendas, other work has probed more detailed behaviors of leaders and managers as they administer regular school district functions. Most prominent among such work is the research program of Kenneth Meier and multiple collaborators, who have studied Texas school districts to develop more general insights about public management and administration.[5] A breezy overview of those studies (Meier, 2009) reveals that they have illuminated numerous factors influencing district operations, while simultaneously offering insights on larger theoretical questions. Consider two specific examples.

First is the matter of political control of the bureaucracy, a major focus of political scientists who study institutions. Much of this work in the discipline proceeds using principal–agent models, which presume asymmetries of goals and resources between political overseers of the bureaucracy (elected officials) and workers in government agencies (bureaucrats). A problematic assumption in that literature, argue Meier and O'Toole (2006), is that agency bureaucrats' preferences are assumed, rather than measured empirically and incorporated into models examining political control. In their work, these authors have shown "bureaucratic values to be far more influential in explaining bureaucratic outputs and outcomes than political factors" (Meier and O'Toole, 2006, 177). The theoretical upshot of these findings is potentially huge, especially if parallel results emerge in other settings with different data. Empirically, the authors urge subsequent researchers to "bring the bureaucracy back into the study of bureaucratic control," while noting how "apparent theoretical and practical insights" about control of the bureaucracy "should be critically reexamined" (Meier and O'Toole, 2006, 187).

A second issue concerns the development and operation of policy networks in public education. Networked actors are often considered superior to traditional hierarchical organizational forms, given the former's ability to react swiftly to changing circumstances, adapt to client needs, and invite participation from groups inside and outside government that possess specialized expertise. Meier and O'Toole have also used the

Texas case to examine administrative behavior in policy networks (Meier and O'Toole, 2001; Meier and O'/Toole, 2003; Meier and O'/Toole, 2004; O'Toole and Meier, 2004).

Conceptually, they agree that scholars have identified several ways that networks influence policy implementation, yet they highlight that the literature has struggled to show the impact of network management on policy outputs and outcomes. In one study, Meier and O'Toole (2003) examine the degree to which district superintendents built ties to key network actors: school board members, local business elites, other superintendents, state agency leaders and staff, and state legislators. The authors find that superintendents with more network connections tend to report greater district support from their local school boards, parents, and the overall community, suggesting that managers who build network ties see dividends from their actions. Further, the authors show that the impact of networking differs depending on local performance and context. Overall, the findings suggest that network management can be "an important tool for administrative success" (Meier and O'Toole, 2003, 697). Still, network outcomes are not uniformly positive. In a separate article, O'Toole and Meier (2004) examine the politics of network management. They show how networks can have "dark sides," which bias network outcomes toward more advantaged participants. In more general terms, the findings show how public administration and management can influence distributional politics.

State Politics and Policy

In addition to work on ground-level conditions that affect local school leaders and administrators, scholars have examined the broader intergovernmental forces influencing educational governance and management. The federal government's increasing levels of interest and involvement in education have energized scholarly studies of educational federalism. Although this overall volume is about state and local government, researchers examining state and local education policy must still engage the federal role. The main reason is that essentially all major federal education policies are administered by states and local school districts. Subnational policy choices themselves have tremendous influence on how federal policy operates.

Because federal policy implementation is dependent on subnational capacities and political contexts, researchers have focused much energy on the tension between the interests of federal program designers (in Congress and the federal bureaucracy) and state and local implementers. Chubb's (1985a, 1985b) analyses of federal education initiatives, while providing insights about implementation of the Elementary and Secondary Education Act and federal vocational education programs, helped contribute to broader debates about the nature of federal influence over state policy. Theoretically, Chubb's articles use education to address questions about regulation ("When is it likely to be excessive?"), oversight ("Under what conditions does monitoring reveal its impact?"), and program design ("When are grant recipients responsive to incentives?"). One broad implication of these studies is the need to develop research that simultaneously examines the economic relationships that federal grants establish and the political interests that motivate the givers and receivers of grant funds.

During the past decade, passage of the No Child Left Behind Act of 2001 (NCLB) has renewed interest in the relationship between local, state, and federal governments in education. Empirically, scholars have debated the extent to which NCLB has fundamentally reshaped educational federalism or whether persistent patterns of state and local dominance have persisted (McDermott and Jensen, 2005; McDonnell, 2005; McGuinn, 2005, 2006; Manna, 2006a; Wong and Sunderman 2007; Lowry, 2009; Manna, 2010). Theoretically, work on state-federal relations in education has, like Chubb's (1985a, 1985b) earlier contributions, prompted discussions about how federalism influences agenda setting (Manna, 2006b), and whether different models may be required, depending on the arena of education (pre-school, elementary and secondary, or higher education) under consideration (Lowry, 2009).

As this chapter's other sections show, the most developed research agendas on education in subnational governments have tended to focus on localities. Still, valuable work on the states themselves has emerged. Notably, Mintrom's studies (sometimes in collaboration with Vergari) have helped to bridge theoretical gaps between research on policy entrepreneurship, agenda setting, policy networks, and the diffusion of state policy innovations (Mintrom, 1997a; Mintrom, 1997b; Mintrom and Vergari, 1998; Mintrom, 2000). In his work, Mintrom uses original survey data of state policy entrepreneurs interested in school choice to examine how these advocates develop and promote their ideas. Although he focusses on the choice debate, Mintrom's theoretical propositions, research design, and results show how diffusion studies could be greatly enhanced by taking more direct account of entrepreneurs' actions. One interesting connection that such studies commonly miss, he notes, is the degree to which advocates working at the state level frequently draw upon and promote successes of local reforms. Thus, his work calls our attention to a "state-local nexus" (Mintrom, 1997b), which suggests diffusion processes operating simultaneously in horizontal (state to state) and vertical (state and local) ways.

Other state-level work has examined policy diffusion and the ways leaders manage ideas and institutions amidst challenges from other state actors, competing levels of government, and interest groups. Shober's (2010) book uses qualitative and advanced quantitative methods to study how state leaders in Georgia, Ohio, and Wisconsin developed and administered reform during the 1980s and 1990s. In so doing, he identifies two key variables—scope and autonomy—that influence agency success and have broad theoretical applicability for studies beyond education. State-centered studies on pre-school education have explored related ideas. Such work has helped to examine the efficacy of state approaches versus federal ones (Gormley and Phillips, 2005), the dynamics of interest group behavior and the diffusion of ideas (Karch, 2010), and the factors associated with pre-school investments (Rigby, 2007).

Studies of state higher education policy have exploited institutional variation to examine how structures and politics affect policy and student opportunities. Lowry (2001, 845) shows how different state governing arrangements influence the costs borne by students in tuition and fees and how universities spend funds across several functional areas. Theoretically, the results have implications for hierarchical control of bureaucratic agencies, the influence of politics on management, and the degree to which different institutional designs might produce similar outcomes. Other work exploiting variation in post-secondary education includes Knott and Payne (2004), who develop a classification scheme of higher education governance structures to investigate how structure influences revenue streams and scholarly productivity, and Nicholson-Crotty and Meier (2003) who show that structural choices can condition the influence of politics on state education finance. Finally, Hicklin and Meier (2008) focus on student outcomes and show that variation in higher education governance influences minority enrollments.

Future Research

While the literature in this section contains suggestions for pushing forward specific lines of inquiry, two additional areas seem ripe for future study. An initial area concerns administrative capacity. In my own experience, discussing education with policy makers and government administrators, everyone seems to agree that the capacity to implement policy is a hugely important variable influencing why policies succeed or fail. While that claim has some intuitive appeal, empirically the discussions are somewhat murky because "capacity" remains an elusive concept. Political scientists who are interested in educational governance could make important theoretical and empirical contributions by fleshing out this idea in more nuanced ways than is common in social science research, which frequently operationalizes capacity by counting up agency personnel, considering agency budget size, and sometimes enumerating the number of external constraints the agency confronts. Those measures are certainly good first cuts at the concept of capacity, but they omit other elements, such as the skill and knowledge of agency staff, the quality of their interactions, and the technical capabilities of their administrative systems, among other things.

Also, the literature on educational governance would benefit from more comparative research designs. Three potential comparisons seem especially promising. First, comparisons of policies addressing different levels of education, as Lowry (2009) has explored, can illustrate whether the institutional and political dynamics of education governance are common across pre-school, elementary and secondary, and higher education. Second, comparing education with other policy areas could reveal even broader theoretical concepts or relationships between institutions, policy, and outcomes, something that Marschall and Ruhil (2007) begin to examine. Finally, comparisons between leaders situated in similar administrative positions across levels of government (e.g., agency executives or managers) can reveal other empirical regularities relevant to institutions and politics. Henig's (2009) work on presidents, governors, and mayors—what he terms the "new education executives"—is one example.

REPRESENTATION

Scholars frequently have used subnational education policy to study the representation of group interests. Research on state and local education policy has addressed several questions that examine institutions, political behavior, interest groups, and race and politics. What factors influence the representation of minorities on local school boards? Does descriptive representation of different racial groups translate into substantive representation by influencing school policies, practices, and overall reform agendas? To what extent do racial minorities collaborate or compete in campaigns for local school offices? What powers do teacher unions wield in board elections? Do senior citizens pose a threat to school funding in local communities as often is assumed?

Race, Local Politics, and Policy

Consider first the role of race in local school board elections. One strand of this literature has focused on how different electoral systems might influence the descriptive representation of minority groups. A second major strand has examined what happens when members of minority groups serve on local school boards and as administrators and teachers. Rather than only considering electoral outcomes in which race is a dependent variable, these latter studies consider race as an independent variable to study its influence on substantive policy outputs and minority student outcomes. Some work has considered descriptive and substantive representation simultaneously.

Findings regarding descriptive representation have shown that board elections based on at-large representation tend to under-represent minority populations compared to ward-based systems, but the effects are inconsistent. In a study of urban school districts across the United States, Stewart, England, and Meier (1989) reported that blacks tended to be slightly over-represented in ward-based systems, under-represented in systems where board members are appointed, and much more under-represented in districts with at-large elections. In contrast, Meier and colleagues (2005) conducted a similar study and found that ward-based systems tended to attenuate Latino representation on the school board, a finding consistent with Leal, Martinez-Ebers, and Meier (2004), but had no statistically discernible effect on black representation.

More recent work from Marschall, Ruhil, and Shah (2010) has pushed the boundaries of research on descriptive representation and local school boards. These authors have identified two important limitations of prior work. Studies have nearly always focused on proportional representation at a particular moment in time. Further, they have tended to focus on a relatively limited set of independent variables, primarily the rules governing board selection (e.g., at-large, ward-based, or other systems) and the presence of minority groups in a local school district. Focusing on black representation on school boards and using a sample of 345 school districts from 1980 to 2000, Marschall, Ruhil, and Shah (2010) conceive of minority representation as following a two-step process. First is the initial step of breaking the color barrier on a local school board. The authors argue that going from none to some black representation represents an important substantive step. Second is the amount of black representation that emerges once the color barrier has been broken.

Marschall, Ruhil, and Shah (2010) report several interesting findings that have implications for prior studies and future work. First, they find that the presence of large black populations is most important for overcoming the representation hurdle, although their findings suggest that the probability of black representation is higher in districts with ward-based rather than at-large systems. Second, once blacks have made it over the representation hurdle, they find that an important and hitherto understudied variable— the number of seats on a school board—has a positive effect on black representation. That result holds for both at-large and ward-based systems. The authors conclude by underscoring the importance of board size: "legislative size may be an underappreciated mechanism by which to increase representation, particularly in AL [at-large] systems" (Marschall, Ruhil, and Shah 2010, 122–123).

Identifying the factors that may influence minority representation on local school boards begs an important follow-up question. Does descriptive representation translate into substantive representation that benefits minority groups? The empirical findings here tend to indicate that indeed, when members of racial minorities win seats on local school boards, specific practices and policies tend to benefit minority students. Marschall and Ruhil (2007) find evidence that descriptive representation matters at the broadest level of substantive representation, the amount of satisfaction that constituents express in their elected leaders. Using a survey of 3,000 black respondents across 53 school districts, the authors find that blacks were more likely to report higher levels of satisfaction with public schools when blacks served on the local school board or when the city had a black mayor. In addition to reporting these findings, the authors underscore the methodological advantages of studying representation using local governments, especially those overseeing schools. They explain that slightly more than 100 blacks have been elected to Congress since 1869, while there were nearly 1,900 elected to local school boards in the year 2000 alone.

Meier and his colleagues have studied more specific policy outputs to probe connections between descriptive and substantive representation (Fraga, Meier, and England, 1986; Leal, Martinez-Ebers, and Meier, 2004; Meier et al., 2005). Focusing on black and Hispanic students, they find direct and indirect links. Board representation of racial minorities is associated with greater numbers of that same minority group being hired into school administrative positions. In contrast, board representation is not directly related to the staffing patterns in a district's schools. However, the authors find indirect effects in that districts with more minority administrators are likely to have more minority teachers. That is perhaps understandable, given that boards commonly play some role in the hiring of district administrators and perhaps even school principals. Yet they delegate to these same administrators the power to hire teachers.

Linking these findings to some of their prior work on the subject, Meier and co-authors (2005, 767) note the importance of these personnel decisions, given that "both African American and Latino teachers positively influence the educational experience of minority students." In one of those studies, for example, Meier and England (1984) found that schools with more black teachers were less likely to practice "second generation discrimination" against black students. In other words, these schools were less likely to embrace low expectations for black students, such as assigning them to special education classes, suspending them at higher rates, and discouraging them from enrolling in classes providing academic enrichment.

These findings about descriptive and substantive representation also suggest an important theoretical point. Thinking about the relationships between actors at different levels—from elected positions to agency management to front-line employees—is fundamental to understanding how representation unfolds. As the work discussed in this section and other studies have shown, school districts and schools are valuable institutions for examining these issues (Meier, 1984; Stewart, England, and Meier, 1989; Meier, O'Toole, and Nicholson-Crotty, 2004).

Limits of Descriptive Representation

Interestingly, when considering local reform and educational performance more generally, the link between descriptive and substantive representation seems less sanguine in large urban districts. In their award-winning book, *The Color of School Reform: Race, Politics, and the Challenge of Urban Education*, Henig and colleagues (1999) find that the promise of black leadership in urban school districts is complicated by the myriad ways in which race interacts with local constituencies, persistent challenges, and reform agendas. One important variable that separates this work from that of Meier and his colleagues is that Henig's group focuses on school reform in minority-led cities—the District of Columbia, Baltimore, Detroit, and Atlanta—whereas Meier's team examines localities where racial minorities are in the numerical minority.

The optimism that Meier's studies of minority representation suggest are the launching point for Henig and his team's work. As an Urban League director from Atlanta noted in the early pages of the book, "I have always believed that if you could ever achieve equity in the administration of the school system, then it would improve the chances of black kids getting a better education" (Henig et al., 1999, 4). The authors find, however, that such optimism about minority leadership in urban districts has not translated into widespread gains in minority achievement. "Indeed," the authors note, "by most accounts the situation is bleaker than ever" (Henig et al., 1999, 6).

Conceptually, Henig et al. (1999) attempt to explain these educational outcomes in urban areas; they consider how race interacts with local conditions and influences the emergence of crucial civic capacity that can sustain educational reforms and improve educational outcomes for minority students. Their theoretical model posits that reform outcomes depend on the interaction of two key variables: the degree to which a city's politics is "racialized" and the amount of "fragmentation" among local groups, both inside and outside government, who can influence a city's education agenda. Henig et al.'s (1999) primary conclusions are that race remains a salient variable in local educational politics and, given that salience, it is incredibly difficult to maintain the local coalitions needed to sustain successful school reform agendas.

Other Group Interests

Beyond matters of race and representation, political scientists and public administration scholars have considered group interests in other contexts. Consider these two relatively recent illustrative examples. The initial one focuses on teacher unions, a powerful group in contemporary education policymaking. Given unions' strength, Moe (2006, 2009) has noted the empirical need for researchers to examine their substantive influence on politics and student outcomes, which he has studied by examining how unions affect school board elections and student achievement. Moe's theoretical insight is that teacher unions complicate traditional assumptions about principal–agent relationships between management and labor.

As Moe (2006) shows, teachers acting in local settings, often via union mobilization, have powerful impacts on the individuals who serve in school management positions. The reason is because teachers can strongly influence school board elections (where turnout typically is low) and therefore have a strong hand in choosing their overseers. Theoretically, this fact suggests that typical assumptions about principals and their ability to hold agents accountable for performance require rethinking and additional empirical study.

Another example is Berkman and Plutzer's (2005) study of policymaking in school districts. Their work attempts to study connections between local interests and school finance by considering a fundamental question about American democracy: Are local school districts responsive to the policy preferences of their constituents? Methodologically, the authors develop an innovative approach, called small polity inference, in which they leverage national and state-level public opinion data to infer citizen preferences in local districts. As a result, the authors become the first to "compare preferences for spending with actual spending in nearly all American school districts" (Berkman and Plutzer, 2005, xvi). Their findings have implications for the design of local rules for choosing school board members.

Further, Berkman and Plutzer (2005) examine teacher unions and another group, elderly citizens, to consider how these groups influence school finance decisions. Their findings regarding the elderly are particularly interesting. The authors show that the majority of elderly citizens are more likely to support school spending than others. That finding is contingent upon the elderly living in communities where "local property taxes generate a meaningful proportion of their total operating revenue" (Berkman and Plutzer, 2005, 142). That conclusion highlights how institutional design—here, the allocation of responsibility for funding schools—is associated with concrete policy results.

Future Research

Scholars studying state and local education policy through the lens of representation have produced numerous theoretical and empirical insights. Two additional areas could build on this foundation. First, although prior research has examined how the rules for selecting school board members can influence board composition, local campaigns for school board office have received much less attention. Some work has examined the potential for coalition building across racial minority groups in such elections. But those studies focus on group characteristics of local communities and the institutions that govern member selection, and not on the political behavior of elites on the campaign trail (Meier and Stewart, 1991; Rocha 2007). The rise of the accountability movement in education has produced much data on student achievement, which in theory was designed to promote transparency and public interest in school performance. It would be interesting to know whether such information has informed campaigns for local board positions.

Second, the same sorts of issues that scholars of local education politics have explored are also ripe for consideration at the state level. Beyond the studies of higher education noted in the prior section and other work that has examined state education policy in the context of American federalism, few scholars have taken up the call of pioneers in this area, who encouraged more rigorous state-level studies to understand how state institutions, activist groups, and political campaigns all intersect to represent competing interests (Masters, Salisbury, and Eliot, 1964). The diversity of state-level institutions responsible for governing education, coupled with the state-level influence of teacher unions and business, provides a great setting for such work (Campbell and Mazzoni, 1976; Wirt and Kirst, 2009).

ADDITIONAL DIRECTIONS AND CONCLUSIONS

Prior sections of this chapter have described key theoretical and empirical findings and suggested how researchers might push forward future studies on educational markets, governance, and representation. This concluding section describes five broader areas that present promising opportunities for scholars interested in these and other topics.

First, although research on subnational education policy has tended to favor local-level over state-level settings, many reasons exist to study the states more carefully (Masters, Salisbury, and Eliot, 1964; Campbell and Mazzoni, 1976; Shober, Manna, and Witte, 2006; Hicklin and Meier, 2008; Karch, 2010; Shober, 2010). The current menu of policies promoting standards-based reform and accountability for educational performance means that state policy choices will become even more consequential in the future. That continued state role and the emergence of more readily accessible data on state policy and performance, coupled with the states' institutional and political diversity, means that state education politics and policy will remain a highly relevant and theoretically promising arena for study.

Second, education policy debates frequently defy simplistic left–right conceptualizations common in the research literature and punditry on American politics. School choice, usually framed as conservative policy, has enjoyed support from an eclectic coalition of groups across the ideological spectrum, including civil rights advocates, business leaders, minority groups, and libertarians. Similarly, Democrats and Republicans, especially governors, have found common ground on standards-based reform. Political views in other education policy areas have tended to fall along more traditional lines, as with sex education, for example. Focusing on state and local settings, researchers could explore the different partisan and ideological coalitions that form around various education policies. That research would help build on prior state-policy work in these general areas (Wong and Shen, 2002; McDermott, 2003) and potentially produce new understandings of what it means for citizens to espouse particular ideological or partisan identifications.

Third, studies of state and local education policy could help revive what was once a burgeoning literature on political socialization. Thist prior work tended to find that families, not schools, were the most powerful force influencing children's beliefs about politics. But much has changed since then in family structures, how schools operate, the programs schools offer, and the students they serve. Schools are also more diverse places now than they were during the heyday of political socialization research. Do different institutional forms socialize students differently? Can state or local policy choices about curricular content influence subsequent political behavior or attitudes? Some critics have claimed that the current focus on accountability for reading and math instruction has caused schools to short-change history and citizenship studies. All of these factors have potential implications for how youth are socialized into the political system and, ultimately, for the health of American democracy.

Fourth, scholars of state and local education policy should consider engaging in more comparative work. One approach would be to compare education with other policy areas to identify more general propositions about behaviors and practices. In this spirit, prior research from Jacoby and Schneider (2001) has helped to situate education among a variety of other issues facing state policy makers, as Marschall and Ruhil's (2007) work has done in local settings. Seeing how education compares to other policy areas, as well as understanding how it interacts with them as states and localities develop their policy agendas, merits additional attention (Rigby, 2007). Comparing state and local education policy cross-nationally is another approach. One especially promising line of inquiry, as Wallner's (2010) work illustrates, would be to consider the emergence of federal and state policies promoting standards and accountability. Such policies have become more ubiquitous in the United States and abroad. Comparative work could help to reveal general insights about subnational institutions, performance, and the practice of accountability.

Fifth, more collaborative and systematic data collection efforts among scholars of state and local education policy could benefit the broader research community by sparking additional work in the diverse areas this chapter discusses. As scholars of state and local policy frequently note (Marschall, Ruhil, and Shah 2010), there are immense research challenges in education and other substantive areas, given the difficulty of developing comparable and complete data sets across subnational units and time. Local school board elections, for example, are particularly difficult to study, given that they require on-the-ground work to track campaign behavior and gather election returns, which typically are not maintained by public authorities in comprehensive or relatively easy-to-access data sets. Fortunately, a new collaboration of scholars, the recently formed Local Elections in America Project, is beginning to address these issues systematically (Marschall, Shah, and Ruhil 2011).

Other future research opportunities will emerge, given that education likely will remain high on state and local government agendas. That continuing presence means that researchers will have many opportunities to secure funding and contribute to relevant policy discussions. As the studies surveyed in this chapter illustrate, participating in such practical discussions need not undermine one's scholarly productivity. An overall virtue of studying subnational education policy is that researchers can help enrich popular debates while simultaneously advancing theoretical understandings of politics that appeal to political scientists and public administration scholars working across numerous subfields. Such work has the potential to bring out the best in what scholars can offer, both within and beyond the walls of academia.

Notes

1. I am grateful to Donald Haider-Markel, Jeffrey Henig, Andrew Karch, and Arnold Shober for providing superb feedback on earlier drafts.
2. Although researchers across the social sciences have studied subnational education policy and politics, this chapter delimits the discussion by focusing on work from political scientists and public administration scholars.
3. Witte's (2000) work on Milwaukee, which includes quantitative analyses and school case-studies, is an exception to the norm.
4. Research on educational markets, discussed in the previous section, is a subset of this larger area.
5. Although, this research program on Texas school districts and public management is one of the most notable and productive, other work has contributed to this discussion. Two recent books highlight the value of focusing on the actions of teachers and principals, classic examples of street level bureaucrats (Lipsky, 1980). The first is Abernathy's (2007) work on the No Child Left Behind Act, which includes analysis of school principals' behavior during implementation. The second is Berkman and Plutzer's (2010) work on the teaching of evolution in the public schools.

References

Abernathy, Scott F. 2007. *No Child Left Behind and the Public Schools*. Ann Arbor, MI: University of Michigan Press.

Berkman, Michael B. and Eric Plutzer. 2005. *Ten Thousand Democracies: Politics and Public Opinion in America's School Districts*. Washington, DC: Georgetown University Press.

Berkman, Michael and Eric Plutzer. 2010. *Evolution, Creationism, and the Battle to Control America's Classrooms*. New York: Cambridge University Press.

Berry, Christopher R. and Martin R. West. 2010. "The School Consolidation Movement and Student Outcomes." *Journal of Law, Economics, and Organization* 26 (1): 1–29.

Campbell, Roald F. and Tim L. Mazzoni Jr. 1976. *State Policy Making for the Public Schools: A Comparative Analysis of Policy Making for the Public Schools in Twelve States and a Treatment of State Governance Models.* Berkeley, CA: McCutchan Publishing Corporation.

Chubb, John E. 1985a. "Excessive Regulation: The Case of Federal Aid to Education." *Political Science Quarterly* 100 (2): 287–311.

Chubb, John E. 1985b. "The Political Economy of Federalism." *American Political Science Review* 79 (4): 994–1015.

Chubb, John E. and Terry M. Moe. 1988. "Politics, Markets, and the Organization of Schools." *American Political Science Review* 82 (4): 1065–1087.

Chubb, John E. and Terry M. Moe. 1990. *Politics, Markets, and America's Schools.* Washington, DC: Brookings Institution.

Fraga, Luis Ricardo, Kenneth J. Meier, and Robert E. England. 1986. "Hispanic Americans and Educational Policy: Limits to Equal Access." *Journal of Politics* 48(4): 850–876.

Gormley, William T. and Deborah Phillips. 2005. "The Effects of Universal Pre-K in Oklahoma: Research Highlights and Policy Implications." *Policy Studies Journal* 33 (1): 65–82.

Henig, Jeffrey R. 1994. *Rethinking School Choice: Limits of the Market Metaphor.* Princeton, NJ: Princeton University Press.

Henig, Jeffrey R. 2008. *Spin Cycle: How Research is Used in Policy Debates, the Case of Charter Schools.* New York: Russell Sage Foundation/Century Foundation.

Henig, Jeffrey R. 2009. "Mayors, Governors, and Presidents: The New Education Executives and the Rise of Educational Exceptionalism." *Peabody Journal of Education* 84 (3): 283–299.

Henig, Jeffrey R. and Wilbur C. Rich (eds). 2004. *Mayors in the Middle: Politics, Race, and Mayoral Control of Urban Schools.* Princeton, NJ: Princeton University Press.

Henig, Jeffrey R., Richard C. Hula, Marion Orr, and Desiree S. Pedescleaux. 1999. *The Color of School Reform: Race, Politics, and the Challenge of Urban Education.* Princeton, NJ: Princeton University Press.

Hess, Frederick M. 1999. *Spinning Wheels: The Politics of Urban School Reform.* Washington, DC: Brookings Institution.

Hess, Frederick M. 2002. *Revolution at the Margins: The Impact of Competition on Urban School Systems.* Washington, DC: Brookings Institution.

Hicklin, Alisa and Kenneth J. Meier. 2008. "Race, Structure, and State Governments: The Politics of Higher Education Diversity." *Journal of Politics* 70 (3): 851–860.

Howell, William G. 2004. "Dynamic Selection Effects in Means-tested, Urban School Voucher Programs." *Journal of Policy Analysis and Management* 23 (2): 225–250.

Howell, William G. 2005. *Besieged: School Boards and the Future of Education Politics.* Washington, DC: Brookings Institution.

Howell, William G. and Paul E. Peterson. 2002. *The Education Gap: Vouchers and Urban Schools.* Washington, DC: Brookings Institution.

Jacoby, William G. and Saundra K. Schneider. 2001. "Variability in State Policy Priorities: An Empirical Analysis." *Journal of Politics* 62 (2): 544–568.

Karch, Andrew. 2010. "Policy Feedback and Preschool Funding in the American States." *Policy Studies Journal* 38 (2): 217–234.

Knott, Jack H. and A. Abigail Payne. 2004. "The Impact of State Governance Structures on Management and Performance of Public Organizations: A Study of Higher Education Institutions." *Journal of Policy Analysis and Management* 23 (1): 13–30.

Leal, David L., Valerie Martinez-Ebers, and Kenneth J. Meier. 2004. "The Politics of Latino Education: The Biases of At-large Elections." *Journal of Politics 66* (4): 1224–1244.

Lipsky, Michael. 1980. *Street-level Bureaucracy: Dilemmas of the Individual in Public Services.* New York: Russell Sage Foundation.

Lowry, Robert C. 2001. "Governmental Structure, Trustee Selection, and Public University Prices and Spending: Multiple Means to Similar Ends." *American Journal of Political Science 45* (4): 845–861.

Lowry, Robert C. 2009. "Reauthorization of the Federal Higher Education Act and Accountability for Student Learning: The Dog that Didn't Bark." *Publius 39* (3): 506–526.

Manna, Paul F. 2002. "The Signals Parents Send When they Choose their Children's Schools." *Educational Policy 16* (3): 425–447.

Manna, Paul. 2006a. "Control, Persuasion and Educational Accountability: Implementing the No Child Left Behind Act." *Educational Policy 20* (3): 471–494.

Manna, Paul. 2006b. *School's In: Federalism and the National Education Agenda.* Washington, DC: Georgetown University Press.

Manna, Paul. 2010. *Collision Course: Federal Education Policy Meets State and Local Realities.* Washington, DC: CQ Press.

Marschall, Melissa J. and Anirudh V. S. Ruhil. 2007. "The Attitudinal Dimension of Black Political Incorporation in Local Government." *American Journal of Political Science 51* (1): 17–33.

Marschall, Melissa J., Anirudh V. S. Ruhil, and Paru R. Shah. 2010. "The New Racial Calculus: Electoral Institutions and Black Representation in Local Legislatures." *American Journal of Political Science 54* (1): 107–124.

Marschall, Melissa J., Paru Shah, and Anirudh Ruhil. 2011. "Symposium on the Study of Local Elections." *Editors' Introduction: A Looking Glass into the Future. PS: Political Science and Politics 44* (1): 97–100.

Masters, Nicholas A., Robert H. Salisbury, and Thomas H. Eliot. 1964. *State Politics and the Public Schools: An Exploratory Analysis.* New York: Alfred A. Knopf.

McDermott, Kathryn A. 2003. "What Causes Variation in States' Accountability Policies?" *Peabody Journal of Education 78* (4): 153–176.

McDermott, Kathryn A. and Laura S. Jensen. 2005. "Dubious Sovereignty: Federal Conditions of Aid and the No Child Left Behind Act." *Peabody Journal of Education 80* (2): 39–56.

McDonnell, Lorraine M. 2005. No Child Left Behind and the Federal Role in Education: Evolution or Revolution?." *Peabody Journal of Education 80* (2): 19–38.

McGuinn, Patrick. 2005. "The National Schoolmarm: No Child Left Behind and the New Educational Federalism." *Publius 35* (1): 41–68.

McGuinn, Patrick J. 2006. *No Child Left Behind and the Transformation of Federal Education Policy, 1965–2005.* Lawrence, KS: University of Kansas Press.

Meier, Kenneth J. 1984. "Teachers, Students, and Discrimination: The Policy Impact of Black Representation." *Journal of Politics 46* (1): 252–263.

Meier, Kenneth J. 2004. "Structure, Politics, and Policy: The Logic of Mayoral Control." In Jeffrey R. Henig and Wilbur C. Rich (eds), *Mayors in the Middle: Politics, Race, and Mayoral Control of Urban Schools..* Princeton, NJ: Princeton University Press, pp. 221–231.

Meier, Kenneth J. 2009. "Policy Theory, Policy Theory Everywhere: Ravings of a Deranged Policy Scholar." *Policy Studies Journal 37* (1): 5–11.

Meier, Kenneth J. and Robert E. England. 1984. "Black Representation and Educational Policy: Are They Related?" *American Political Science Review 78* (2): 392–403.

Meier, Kenneth J. and Laurence J. O'Toole Jr. 2001. "Managerial Strategies and Behavior in Networks: A Model with Evidence from U.S. Public Education." *Journal of Public Administration, Research, and Theory 11* (3): 271–293.

Meier, Kenneth J. and Laurence J. O'Toole Jr. 2003. "Public Management and Educational Performance: The Impact of Managerial Networking." *Public Administration Review 63* (6): 689–699.

Meier, Kenneth J. and Laurence J. O'Toole Jr. 2004. "Parkinson's Law and the New Public Management? Contracting Determinants and Service–Quality Consequences in Public Education." *Public Administration Review 64* (3): 342–352.

Meier, Kenneth J. and Laurence J. O'Toole Jr. 2006. "Political Control Versus Bureaucratic Values: Reframing the Debate." *Public Administration Review 66* (2): 177–192.

Meier, Kenneth J. and Joseph Stewart Jr. 1991. "Cooperation and Conflict in Multiracial School dDistricts." *Journal of Politics 53* (4): 1123–1133.

Meier, Kenneth J., J. L. Polinard, and Robert D. Wrinkle. 2000. "Bureaucracy and Organizational Performance: Causality Arguments about Public Schools." *American Journal of Political Science 44* (3): 590–602.

Meier, Kenneth J., Laurence J. O'Toole Jr, and Sean Nicholson-Crotty. 2004. "Multilevel Governance and Organizational Performance: Investigating the Political–Bureaucratic Labyrinth." *Journal of Policy Analysis and Management 23* (1): 31–48.

Meier, Kenneth J., Eric Gonzalez Juenke, Robert D. Wrinkle, and J. L. Polinard. 2005. "Structural Choices and Representational Biases: The Post-election Color of Representation." *American Journal of Political Science 49* (4): 758–768.

Mintrom, Michael. 1997a. "Policy Entrepreneurs and the Diffusion of Innovation." *American Journal of Political Science 41* (3): 738–770.

Mintrom, Michael. 1997b. "The State–Local Nexus in Policy Innovation Diffusion: The Case of School Choice." *Publius 27* (3): 41–59.

Mintrom, Michael. 2000. *Policy Entrepreneurs and School Choice*. Washington, DC: Georgetown University Press.

Mintrom, Michael and Sandra Vergari. 1998. "Policy Networks and Innovation Diffusion: The Case of State Education Reforms." *Journal of Politics 60* (1): 126–148.

Moe, Terry M. 2006. "Political Control and the Power of the Agent." *Journal of Law, Economics, & Organization 22* (1): 1–29.

Moe, Terry M. 2009. "Collective Bargaining and the Performance of the Public Schools." *American Journal of Political Science 53* (1): 156–174.

Nicholson-Crotty, Jill and Kenneth J. Meier. 2003. "Politics, Structure, and Public Policy: The Case of Higher Education." *Educational Policy 17* (1): 80–97.

O'Toole, Laurence J., Jr and Kenneth J. Meier. 2004. "Desperately Seeking Selznik: Cooptation and the Dark Side of Public Management in Networks." *Public Administration Review 64* (6): 681–693.

Rigby, Elizabeth. 2007. "Same Policy Area, Different Politics: How Characteristics of Policy Tools Alter the Determinants of Early Childhood Education Policy." *Policy Studies Journal 35* (4): 653–669.

Rocha, Rene R. 2007. "Black–Brown Coalitions in Local School Board Elections." *Political Research Quarterly 60* (2): 315–327.

Schneider, Mark and Jack Buckley. 2007. *Charter Schools: Hope or Hype?* Princeton, NJ: Princeton University Press.

Schneider, Mark, Paul Teske, Melissa Marschall, Michael Mintrom, and Christine Roch. 1997a. "Institutional Arrangements and the Creation of Social Capital: The Effects of Public School Choice." *American Political Science Review 91* (1): 82–93.

Schneider, Mark, Paul Teske, Christine Roch, and Melissa Marschall. 1997b. "Networks to Nowhere: Segregation and Stratification in Networks of Information About Schools." *American Journal of Political Science 41* (4): 1201–1223.

Schneider, Mark, Paul Teske, Melissa Marshall, and Christine Roch. 1998. "Shopping for Schools: In the Land of the Blind, the One-eyed Parent May Be Enough." *American Journal of Political Science 42* (3): 769–793.

Schneider, Mark, Paul Teske, and Melissa Marschall. 2000. *Choosing Schools: Consumer Choice and the Quality of American Schools.* Princeton, NJ: Princeton University Press.

Shober, Arnold F. 2010. *Splintered Accountability: State Governance and Education Reform.* Albany, NY: SUNY Press.

Shober, Arnold F., Paul Manna, and John F. Witte. 2006. "Flexibility Meets Accountability: State Charter School Laws and their Influence on the Formation of Charter Schools in the United States." *Policy Studies Journal 34* (4): 563–587.

Smith, Kevin B. and Kenneth J. Meier. 1994. "Politics, Bureaucrats, and Schools." *Public Administration Review 54* (4): 551–558.

Smith, Kevin B. and Kenneth J. Meier. 1995. *The Case Against School Choice: Politics, Markets, and Fools.* Armonk, NY: M. E. Sharpe.

Stewart, Joseph, Jr, Robert E. England, and Kenneth J. Meier. 1989. "Black Representation in Urban School Districts: From School Board to Office to Classroom." *Western Political Quarterly 42* (2): 287–305.

Teske, Paul, Mark Schneider, Michael Mintrom, and Samuel Best. 1993. "Establishing the Micro Foundations of a Macro Theory: Information, Movers, and the Competitive Local Market for Public Goods." *American Political Science Review 87* (3): 702–713.

Teske, Paul, Mark Schneider, Jack Buckley, and Sarah Clark. 2001. Can Charter Schools Change Traditional Public Schools?" In Paul E. Peterson and David E. Campbell (eds), *Charters, Vouchers, and Public Education.* Washington, DC: Brookings Institution.

Wallner, Jennifer. 2010. "Beyond National Standards: Reconciling Tension Between Federalism and the Welfare State." *Publius 40* (4): 646–671.

Wirt, Frederick M. and Michael W. Kirst. 2009. *The Political Dynamics of American Education,* 4th edition. Berkeley, CA: McCutchan Publishing Corporation.

Witte, John F.1998. "The Milwaukee Voucher Experiment." *Educational Evaluation and Policy Analysis 20* (4): 229–251.

Witte, John F. 2000. *The Market Approach to Education: An Analysis of America's First Voucher Program.* Princeton, NJ: Princeton University Press.

Witte, John F., Paul Schlomer, and Arnold F. Shober. 2007. "Going Charter? A Study of School District Competition in Wisconsin." *Peabody Journal of Education 82* (2): 410–439.

Wolf, Patrick J. 2005. "School Choice and Civic Values." In Julian Betts and Tom Loveless (eds), *Getting Choice Right: Ensuring Equity and Efficiency in Education Policy.* Washington, DC: Brookings Institution.

Wong, Kenneth K. and Francis X. Shen. 2002. "Politics of State-led Reform in Education: Market Competition and Electoral Dynamics." *Educational Policy 16* (1): 161–192.

Wong, Kenneth and Gail Sunderman. 2007. "Education Accountability as a Presidential Priority: No Child Left Behind and the Bush Presidency." *Publius 37* (3): 333–350.

Wong, Kenneth K., Francis X. Shen, Dorothea Anagnostopoulos, and Stacey Rutledge. 2007. *The Education Mayor: Improving America's Schools.* Washington, DC: Georgetown University Press.

CHAPTER 29

....

SOCIAL WELFARE POLICY

....

MARK CARL ROM

STATE social welfare policy is a big and meaty topic for political science research, but it is hardly an extraordinary one. It is important because the social welfare policies of states affect millions of lives, often providing a crucial safety net that cushions the needy from the hard floor of poverty. Yet is not an exceptional topic, as the principles that guide political action—and systematic research—are common across a wide range of policy areas. The complex politics of social welfare are not unlike those discernible elsewhere, especially those concerning redistributive policies (for general depictions of the policy process see, for example, Hill, 2009, and Birkland, 2010; for redistributive policies, see especially Lowi, 1972, and Wilson, 1980). There is no special reason to believe that the behavior of the various political actors—executives, legislators, judges, bureaucrats, journalists, activists, citizens—involved in the states' social welfare policies will differ in any substantial way from the behavior of those involved in policy at the national level, or within different policy domains at the state level. Political actors, acting upon incentives and goals within institutional frameworks, determine state social welfare policy.

Understanding the politics of social welfare policy at the national level can provide key insights into state-level politics and vice versa: the most important difference between the two levels of government, in terms of scholarly study, is that the 50 state governments create a much larger set of observations, making state social policy far more amenable than national social policy to quantitative research. Imagine, for example, that one could create a set of models to explain some set of social welfare policy outcomes, and that these models would be applied to national and state policies. We might reasonably expect that the same, or nearly the same, models would be suitable for studying both levels of government, although one might naturally anticipate that the models would produce somewhat different results regarding the magnitude and significance of particular relationships. The main advantage of state-level research, of course, is the vastly larger sample sizes that can be used to estimate the relationships.[1] The disadvantage of state-level research, however, can be the temptation to rely on quantitative models, which by their very nature require the researcher to (over)simplify complex concepts into data that can be measured consistently over time.

Scholarly writings on state social welfare policy would fill a very large bookshelf. This chapter focuses primarily on the section that contains the quantitative models, assessing common themes, strengths, and weaknesses. Before doing so, it first provides substantive background on social welfare programs, describes their politically relevant dimensions, and outlines the political arenas where policy choices are made.

SOCIAL WELFARE PROGRAMS

Social welfare programs either transfer income or provide services to individuals to improve the quality of their lives. The vast majority of social welfare spending is not aimed specifically at those in poverty, however, nor is it the product of state policy choices. For context, the largest national programs are Social Security, which spent about $700 billion dollars to provide pensions to the elderly, their dependents, survivors, and the disabled in 2011 (Office of Management and Budget, 2011, 229). Medicare, a program that provides medical benefits to the elderly, cost the federal government approximately $575 billion that same year in (Office of Management and Budget, 2011, 228). Public K-12 education, the largest social welfare program funded primarily by state and local governments, cost these governments over $600 billion in 2009 (U.S. Bureau of the Census, 2011, 143). Many additional billions of dollars are invisibly transferred towards social welfare functions through tax breaks for housing, education, medical care, and pensions (Howard, 1997).

Yet these social expenditures are not what is commonly known as welfare, which is the main focus of this chapter: welfare refers to those programs that provide public assistance only to the poor.[2] Federal, state and local governments administer a broad variety of welfare programs involving, for example, medical care, cash assistance, food, energy, housing, job training, and education, among other services. Much, but not all, welfare assistance is considered an entitlement. In an "entitlement program," any person eligible for benefits can obtain them; the government is obligated to provide the benefits necessary to fill all claims. In 2008, state and federal governments spent about $610 billion on means-tested, primarily entitlement, programs (U.S. Bureau of the Census, 2011, 350). State and local governments together spent over $400 billion on "public welfare" in 2008 (U.S. Bureau of the Census, 2008, Table 1), surely a substantial sum, but one dwarfed by federal spending on pensions and medical care for the elderly and state spending on public education.[3]

Medical programs are by far the largest federal (i.e., joint national and state) welfare programs, consuming more than half of the nation's welfare spending. Medicaid, which provides medical care to the poor, cost federal and state government spending some $350 billion in 2009, with state governments paying almost 40 percent of this amount (National Association of State Budget Officers (NASBO), 2010, 45). In 2009, fully

85 percent of state spending on welfare was devoted to medical care, primarily through the Medicaid program (NASBO, 2010, 30, 45).

Cash assistance programs now comprise only a modest share of state welfare spending, with the largest programs being Temporary Assistance for Needy Families (TANF), Supplemental Security Income (SSI), and General Assistance (GA). The states play a minor role in all other welfare programs (for example, nutritional assistance, job training, or educational aid to the poor), as almost all state welfare spending provides either medical or cash assistance. In 2009, state governments spent $17 billion on TANF and another $10 billion on SSI and GA (NASBO, 2010, 30, 32). Less than 50 percent of state spending on TANF was devoted to cash assistance, however, with the remainder devoted to other services such as child care, transportation, work-related activities, and administration. Most states provided little income support to the poor outside of TANF, as California alone accounted for 50 percent of the non-TANF cash assistance (NASBO, 2010, 32).

In order to understand the politics surrounding state welfare programs—especially Medicaid and TANF—this section provides a brief summary of those programs' key elements.

Medicaid

Medicaid provides medical care to low-income persons who are aged, blind, disabled; to poor families with children; to certain other pregnant women and children (for a summary of Medicaid eligibility, services, and funding, see Klees, Wolfe, and Curtis, 2010). Created during the Great Society efforts of the mid-1960s, Medicaid is an entitlement program, with the federal government and state governments sharing responsibility. The federal government establishes program guidelines concerning eligibility, services, and financing, and the state governments design and administer the program. The state and federal governments split the cost of the program based on the federally established matching rate that requires the more affluent states to pay a higher share of the cost.

If they are to receive federal funds, the federal government requires states to provide a broad list of medical services within Medicaid, including inpatient and outpatient hospital services as well as physicians' services, to the categorically needy. States are allowed to offer additional services such as the provision of drugs, eyeglasses, or psychiatric care, and they are also permitted to establish limits on recipients' use of the services (for example, on the number of hospital days reimbursed).

Until 2014, when the Affordable Care Act is scheduled to expand Medicaid eligibility, the program does not provide medical assistance to all those in poverty.[4] Until then, all states must provide Medicaid to individuals in "categorically needy" groups; for example, those eligible for SSI, although the states have broad discretion to determine who is eligible to receive Medicaid services.[5] States can also, at their option, provide coverage to those in "medically needy" groups—for example, those individuals who have extensive health needs but who do not quite fall within the administrative definition of poor. As of 2008, 34 states (and the District of Columbia) offered at least some services to the medically needy (Klees, Wolfe, and Curtis, 2010, 24). States are required to provide more extensive services to the categorically needy than to the medically needy.

Different categories of Medicaid have different needs and impose different demands on the program. Children comprise a majority of all recipients, but account for about 20 percent of the costs; for example, while benefits for the disabled account for some 45 percent of all benefits, less than 10 percent of all enrollees have disabilities.[6]

Medicaid does not have its own team of doctors. Instead, states reimburse private health-care providers, who deliver services to Medicaid recipients either through "fee for service" or "prepayment" (known variously as "managed care" or "HMO") plans. Within federal guidelines, the states set the reimbursement rates, although they are required to set them high enough so that Medicaid services will actually be available to recipients, at least to the extent that they are available to other residents in the state. Health-care providers cannot charge Medicaid patients additional fees above these amounts.

Medicaid eligibility historically has been linked to participation in other welfare programs, in particular Aid to Families with Dependent Children (AFDC, which was abolished in 1996 and replaced by TANF) and SSI. The federal government began gradually expanding coverage for other low-income pregnant women and children beginning in the mid-1980s. More recently, the Children's Health Insurance Program (CHIP), created by Congress in 1997, further expanded eligibility for medical services to uninsured children in families with incomes above the federal poverty level. Eligibility for and enrollment in Medicaid has been broadest for children in poverty: in the 2000s, about two-thirds of poor children under age six received benefits, compared with less than one-third of poor adults.

All individuals who are eligible for Medicaid are entitled to receive benefits, although many, in fact, do not claim these benefits. Federal and state governments are obligated to pay for the medical services obtained by eligible recipients. These governments can neither budget precisely how much they will spend on Medicaid each year nor limit expenses to a fixed amount. As a result, this open-ended entitlement program has become the biggest challenge for state budgets, accounting for 21 cents of every dollar the states spend (National Association of State Budget Officers, 2011, 43). Medicaid is the gorilla of state welfare programs: in 2010, it served over 60 million individuals, at a cost to the states of some $150 billion.

Temporary Assistance for Needy Families

Temporary Assistance for Needy Families (TANF) aspires to improve poor families' economic conditions and reduce their dependence on government by promoting work, encouraging marriage, and reducing out-of-wedlock pregnancies (for a summary, see Office of Family Assistance n.d.). Created in 1996, TANF replaced the AFDC program, which had been characterized in political debates as creating a culture of poverty or dependency. Although established by the federal government, TANF gives substantial authority to the states to determine who is eligible, what obligations they face, and what benefits they receive, as well as how the programs will be designed, implemented, and evaluated. Unlike Medicaid, TANF is not an entitlement program: states can deny benefits to any family or category of poor family. The federal government awards each state a block grant to pay for the program each year, with a state's grant based on a federal formula. The states are required to spend at least 80 percent as much as they had for AFDC in 1994; if they impose effective work requirements, they need spend only 75 percent as much. The states can—and do—use a substantial portion of their TANF funds for purposes other than providing cash benefits.

TANF is more concerned with changing recipient behavior than providing cash assistance. As a main goal of TANF is to promote work, states are required to enroll substantial shares of their caseloads in job-related activities; by 2006, each state was required to have 50 percent of the single parents and 90 percent of the two-parent families in the TANF caseload working or face financial penalties. To discourage dependency, the federal government will not allow its funds to provide benefits to families for more than five years, although a small portion of the recipients can be exempted from these time-limits. The states are allowed to terminate benefits earlier if they wish. To discourage childbearing, states may deny benefits to unmarried teenagers and their children or to children born while their mothers were receiving benefits. States may require school attendance by the parents if they have not completed high school, as well as numerous other behavioral requirements.

TANF enrollment, which had peaked at almost 13 million under its predecessor program (AFDC), had declined by about two-thirds to 4.3 million by 2010. TANF was scheduled for reauthorization in 2010, but the Congress enacted a one-year extension of the $16.5 billion block grant that funded it, an amount that has not changed since the program was established in 1996.

THE POLITICAL DIMENSIONS OF SOCIAL WELFARE POLICIES

These features of TANF and Medicaid suggest multiple politically relevant dimensions for social welfare scholars to analyze. First, TANF and Medicaid offer various kinds of *benefits*. Policymakers must therefore determine which kinds of benefits—and obligations—to provide within each program. While some benefits and obligations are determined by the federal governments, others are under the jurisdiction of state governments. This implies that state governments will seek to create the bundle of benefits and obligations that are consistent with the political preferences of the individual states. This topic has received the most scholarly attention, with most quantitative studies estimating the determinants of eligibility, benefits, and costs. Given the quantity of these studies, and their diversity in the dependent variables, I focus on them below in terms of their "generosity" (i.e., more generous programs have lower eligibility standards, greater benefits, and higher costs).

Second, TANF and Medicaid provide different kinds of benefits to different categories of *people*. TANF provides cash and other services to the *poor*. Medicaid offers care to the *sick* (who also happen to be poor). Although the recipients in both programs are poor, the sick are more often seen as worthy of sympathy ("we all can be sick, through no fault of our own") while the financially needy are more likely the subjects of scorn ("they have earned their poverty").[7] Although both programs yield benefits, they differ in the *moral hazard* they create: no reasonable person will seek to become ill in order to obtain medical care, although suspicion exists that some will indeed seek to receive TANF's benefits in order to improve their material condition. As a result, Medicaid has been less politically controversial than TANF and its predecessor AFDC. Medicaid's recipients may be seen as an object of sympathy, while TANF's beneficiaries are the object of suspicion. This implies that state policymakers will be more concerned with restricting the generosity of TANF, while perhaps more interested in expanding that of Medicaid.

Given how politically controversial it is, TANF has received much more attention from political scientists than has Medicaid. Even though TANF has contracted substantially while Medicaid has grown enormously during the past decade, no researchers apparently have systematically compared the two programs based on the idea that they provide benefits to different kinds of populations (but see Bailey and Rom, 2004). With few exceptions, researchers have studied the programs in isolation (for a counterexample, see Stuber and Kronebusch, 2004).

Third, TANF and Medicaid are both joint federal–state programs. This implies that the states will seek to influence the distribution of resources offered to them and requirements imposed on them. This topic has not been the focus of sustained scholarly inquiry and has received very little general scholarly attention, with the exception of the annual "the state of federalism" articles in *Publius* and some articles concentrating on Medicaid waivers (see, for example, Schneider, 1997, and Thompson and Burke, 2009).

Fourth, TANF and Medicaid both require the provision of goods and services to the poor. State governments have substantial discretion to determine how these resources are to be provided. For Medicaid, the services have always been delivered by nongovernmental medical providers, so the question has been how to use these providers most efficiently, with the options focusing on how the providers are to be reimbursed (for example, through fee-for-service or lump-sum plans) and organized (e.g., in some sort of health maintenance organization (HMO) or traditional individual offices) (see Schneider, 1997; Satterthwaite, 2002; Lockhart, Sims, and Klopfenstein, 2008). In contrast, AFDC's benefits were customarily distributed through governmental welfare offices, while TANF's benefits have at times been administered through public bureaucracies, nonprofit organizations, or for-profit firms, with the states determining which blend to adopt (Nathan and Gais, 1998; Gainsborough, 2003; Riccucci, 2005; Dias and Maynard-Moody, 2007).

Fifth, TANF and Medicaid vary dramatically in size. Medicaid accounts for 90 percent of combined TANF–Medicaid spending, and over 20 percent of total state spending. Medicaid thus puts far more financial pressure on the states than does TANF, and so the politics of Medicaid are much more likely to involve purely fiscal concerns. This fact has been the foundation of numerous analyses, most often in advocacy group publications or health policy journals such as *Health Affairs,* rather than political science journals.

The Political Arenas

Social welfare policy is contested in three different, but partially overlapping, arenas. A first arena is *within* the states. Here, the states' internal political dynamics are expected to determine policy choice, implementation, and consequences.[8] To understand these internal dynamics, the standard lists of political actors and forces involved in the public policy process have been examined. This list includes the governors, the legislature, political parties, interest groups, public opinion and ideology, social and demographic factors, economic conditions, and prior policy choices. Intrastate research has dominated political inquiry, and so will comprise the bulk the analysis. The key questions posed by intrastate research are: "What actors and conditions influence state policy choices?" and "What directions do these influences take?"

A second area is *between* the states. Here, the critical concern is whether the social welfare policies of other states influence the policy choices of a given state. Two main possibilities exist: emulation or competition. In emulation, a state imitates the policies of another state. It has long been established that policies diffuse among the states: in other words, states are likely to adopt policies that have been adopted by other states (beginning with Walker, 1969, and Gray 1973; for a recent review, see Karch, 2007). But diffusion is not necessarily the product of emulation. It is possible that some states sequentially adopt a particular policy not because they are imitating other states, but because a particular policy idea is sufficiently attractive that multiple states independently select it to address some policy problem (Boehmke, 2009).

The central questions thus are: "Do states actually emulate the social welfare policies of other states? and if so, what determines whether emulation occurs?", "Which states are emulated?", "Does it have to do with the internal political features of the emulating state?", and "Does it have to do with the features of the policy that is being emulated?"

Alternately, states strategically anticipate or react to the policies of other states to gain a competitive advantage or to avoid disadvantage. For redistributive policies such as welfare, this competition potentially leads to a "race-to-the-bottom."[9] The logic is straightforward. Welfare programs transfer resources from the affluent to the poor, which requires that the affluent are taxed to provide the resources. Redistributive programs provide incentives for the poor to relocate to areas with more generous welfare benefits, while at the same time inducing the wealthy to move to areas with lower tax burdens. To the extent that the affluent are politically desirable constituents, and the poor undesirable ones, states risk becoming "welfare magnets", which attract those in poverty while repelling the prosperous. This prospect—whether based on reality or fear—leads states to reduce the generosity of their welfare programs below the level they would choose absent such competition. The key questions concerning competition include: "Do welfare magnets exist?" and "Do the states engage in race to the bottom competition?"

A third area is *among* the states. Here, the states potentially work collectively (or in smaller groups) to shape the nature of the federal–state relationship, presumably to gain greater resources and/or more autonomy. The key questions are: "Under what circumstances do the states work collaboratively to influence social welfare policy?" and "In what circumstances are they successful in obtaining their policy goals?" Political scientists by and large have ignored these questions regarding state social welfare policies.

Political Focus

The political activities concerning social welfare policy occur at conceptually distinct stages.[10] The first is problem definition: what are the social problems that are to be addressed? The second is policy formulation: what are the tools that might be useful to remedy the policy problem, and how do they get on the policy agenda? This stage often involves policy entrepreneurs—those who advocate for specific solutions. The third is policy choice (alternatively called legitimation): in this stage, the social welfare policies are actually adopted by the legislature (or perhaps the bureaucracy). In the fourth stage, the policies are put into practice. Finally, the policies are evaluated to determine their effectiveness. Virtually all research conducted by political scientists has focused on the policy choice stage, although many policy researchers have concentrated on implementation and evaluation. The initial and final stages have, by and large, been ignored by political scientists.

The dimensions, arenas, and focus of state social welfare policies have all received at least some scholarly attention. Some topics, such as TANF benefits, interstate competition, and policy choice, have been extensively covered; others have earned scant scrutiny. The following sections survey the extant research, indicating areas where consensus has been reached, and where disputes and gaps remain.

Research on The Political Arenas

Substantial attention has been paid to the internal determinants of state TANF policies, lesser attention has been given to Medicaid policies, and yet less has been focused on comparing the policies across the two programs.

Legislatures: the quantitative research on state legislatures and social welfare policy is somewhat perplexing. Legislative variables have been defined inconsistently, and no clear trajectory towards improvement is noticeable. The impact of legislative variables on social welfare policy outcomes has been inconsistent, in part because of the differing dependent variables examined and in part because of the various control variables included in the models, but also because of the multiple ways that the legislative variables themselves have been defined. The cumulative understanding of the relationship between state legislatures and social welfare choices thus has been modest, and the results often seem contradictory.

The main problem has been in defining legislative variables that are theoretically important, analytically interesting, and actually measurable in ways that are consistent across place and time. Four legislative concepts seem important; each has been included in one study or another, but no study apparently includes all four concepts.

Partisan control is based on the assumption that control matters: the party with a legislative majority is able to obtain the policies it seeks, with unified control more powerful than divided control. The standard hypothesis is that Democratic-controlled legislatures will have more generous social welfare policies than those controlled by Republicans, with divided legislatures somewhere in the middle.[11] Partisan control can be defined either as an index or a series of dummy variables indicating whether both houses of the legislature are controlled by Republicans or Democrats, or whether the legislature is divided. The weakness of such a measure is that it ignores the margin of control: it treats a 51/49 partisan split the same as a 90/10 split.

Partisan strength instead focuses on the relative proportions of the two parties in the legislature, with the variable defined as (for example) the average of the percentage of the lower and upper house that is Democratic.[12] The assumption is that each unit increase in the size of a party will lead to some constant increase in the favored policy (or chance that the policy is adopted). Under the assumption that Democrats are more generous than Republicans, the implication is that increasing Democratic strength will lead to increasing welfare generosity.[13] This approach has two main flaws. One flaw is that it treats an increase in partisan strength from some trivial level (say, from 15 to 25 percent, which means in either case that the party is distinctly in the minority, presumably having little legislative power) the same as one that should be more politically relevant (say, from 45 to 55 percent, where control of the chamber actually switches).[14] A second flaw is that, if the scores from the two legislative chambers are combined, as they generally are, politically relevant aspects of strength will be misstated: a legislature with 70 percent Democrats in the lower body and 30 percent in the upper body will have the same strength score as a legislature evenly split in both houses. Early evidence of the impact of partisan strength accordingly was mixed: Barrilleaux (1997, 1462) says that "Longitudinal evidence consistently shows Democratic party strength to be associated with more liberal policy and Republican strength with more conservative policy [see, for example, Alt and Lowry, 1994], but... cross-sectional results associate Democratic party legislative strength with less liberal state policies" (Erikson, Wright, and McIver, 1989, 1993).

Partisan competition considers how closely divided the state's electoral institutions are along party lines, with the conventional view that increased competition leads to more liberal, and hence more generous, social welfare policies (Robertson, 1976). One common early measure of partisan competition was the "folded Ranney index" (for a description and critique, see Holbrook and Van Dunk, 1993, 955–956), which includes measures of partisan strength in the legislature, party control over the governor's office, the popular vote for the governor, among others). One weakness with this measure is that it measures partisan competition within the legislature, rather than competition at the polls. For example, compare a legislature with a 51–49 Republican majority—where all legislators of each party are elected unanimously to a legislature—with a 60–40 Republican edge—where every member of both parties was elected by a 51–49 margin. As partisan competition was defined by Ranney, the former legislature is much more "competitive" (2 percent difference) than the latter (20 percent difference), even though every member of the former legislature has a completely safe seat—that is, faces no competition—while every member of the latter faces highly competitive elections. Surely partisan competition is more intense in the latter case, although the Ranney variable does not recognize this (Barrilleaux, 1997).

A superior measure was consequently proposed by Holbrook and Van Dunk, who take into account the level of interparty competition at the district level (1993, 956), and the distinctiveness and importance of this measure was validated by Barrilleaux, who found that Democratic strength does not increase liberalism after controlling for partisan competition (Barrilleaux, 1997). Prior to Barrilleaux, Holbrook, and Langer (2002, 418) "nearly all of the research on competitiveness and policy in the American states has employed measures of competition that rely on the margin of seats." They argue that electoral competition should lead policies toward the median voter, not necessarily make them more liberal. To test this, they use a model including party strength, district-level interparty competition, and an interaction term to estimate per capita welfare spending. They find that party strength and competition had no independent impact on welfare expenditures, while the interaction of the two is small and marginally significant (Barrilleaux, Holbrook, and Langer 2002, 423): the states with the highest welfare generosity are those where Democratic strength *and* interparty competition are highest.

Partisan control, strength, and competition are analytically distinct concepts, but using all three in a single model can make it difficult to obtain precise estimates of their influence on social welfare policy, as strength and control will be closely correlated. The researcher, in choosing whether to use strength and control, thus faces the question: "Is party strength in the legislature or party control theoretically more important?" It is tempting to answer this empirically (e.g., by running one model with strength, and one with control, and selecting the model that produces better "fit"), but the answer then depends on the particular characteristics of the sample.[15] Still, it is difficult to understand why quantitative analyses of the determinants of state social welfare policies do not routinely use all three measures of legislative partisanship.

One final legislative concept bears mention. *Legislative professionalism* can be thought of as how closely state legislatures resemble the US Congress (e.g., full time, well paid, ample staff, research capacity, etc.), as compared to "citizen" legislatures (part time, low pay, little staff, etc.). The assumption is that highly professional legislatures will select policies that systematically differ from citizen legislatures and, in general, that professional legislatures will tend more towards policy activism and more generous social welfare policies.

Unfortunately, the quantitative models used to predict social welfare policies have not generally used a variety of the best available legislative indicators, so the results of these models do not produce as much consistent, coherent information as could be possible. For example, in the ten welfare policy models assessed, only two used indicators of partisan control, three incorporated legislative professionalism, six used measures of partisan strength, and six included partisan competition (and only four of the six used the variable constructed by Holbrook and Van Dunk, 1993). The typical study used only two legislative indicators. Of the eight health policy studies, four used a measure of partisan control, two used partisan strength, two used partisan competition, and one included legislative professionalism.

The findings of these studies are decidedly mixed. In some studies, partisan (Democratic) control led to more generous policies (Grogan, 1994; Boehmer et al., 2008; Lockhart, Giles-Sims, and Klopfenstein, 2008; Gray et al., 2009), while in other studies no such impact was found (Satterthwaite, 2002; Volden, 2002). Democratic party strength was linked to more generous policies on some dimensions in some studies (Bailey and Rom, 2004; Fellowes and Rowe, 2004; Barrilleaux and Brace, 2007; Preuhs, 2007) but not to other dimensions (Schneider and Jacoby, 1996; Bailey and Rom, 2004; Fellowes and Rowe, 2004; Preuhs, 2007). The impact of partisan competition was similarly mixed (Soss et al., 2001; Barrilleaux and Brace, 2007; Lockhart, Giles-Sims, and Klopfenstein, 2008). In short: the past decade of research has produced no clear statement about the relationship between legislative variables and social welfare policy choices. Given the importance of this issue, and the attention paid to it, that is a pity.

Governors: In 2000, one scholar claimed that:

> A striking feature of [welfare reform] has been the salient and often dominant role played by governors and top state executives and the contrasting political weakness of state legislatures. The recent history of devolution has largely been a history of executive action. Governors ... were very active in fashioning the new welfare policies, while state legislatures usually made only marginal changes before the legislation was finalized. If anything, the role of state legislatures has declined even further since the [1996 welfare] reforms were enacted. (Gais, 2000, cited in Caraley, 2001–2002, 542; see also Mead, 2004)

If it is true that governors often took the lead in reforming welfare, it is also true that gubernatorial variables are almost entirely missing in the quantitative analyses of welfare policy. In the ten quantitative studies on TANF policy choice conducted between 2000 and 2010 that were surveyed, only one (Preuhs, 2007) included a separate measure of gubernatorial control, while two other studies (Volden, 2002; Bailey and Rom, 2004) included gubernatorial control as one indicator in a broader measure of Democratic strength in state-elected offices. The Preuhs study included gubernatorial control as a dummy variable, and found that Democratic governors, on average, increased state welfare "effort" compared to Republican governors, while decreasing welfare "generosity" and having no impact on a welfare benefit index (2007, 285).

State governors have also been recognized as being centrally important to health policy reform, especially regarding Medicaid waivers (Gais and Fossett, 2005; Thompson and Burke, 2009). Only a couple of quantitative studies have included gubernatorial variables as independent indicators, however. Schneider and Jacoby (1996, 509) found that the governor's partisanship had no influence on the adoption of optional services in Medicaid. Gray et al. (2009, 102) found that Democratic gubernatorial control had a strong, positive impact on state efforts to provide universal health care. Grogan (1994), Satterthwaite (2002) and Volden (2006) combined the party of the governor in a broader measure of partisan strength, so it is not possible for the authors to identify the separate impact of the governor's party on Medicaid outcomes.

It is clearly a weakness, and it seems to be an unjustified one, to omit the state's key political leader from empirical models seeking to estimate political outcomes: at the very least, it seems reasonable to include an indicator of partisan gubernatorial control in such analyses. Simply including partisan control over the governor's office would be a substantial step forward, but it is probably an insufficient one. The states vary substantially in the powers they accord to their governors, and the governors have differed considerably in their willingness to use these powers. Future research might benefit by seeking to develop measures of gubernatorial strength and effort (see, for example, Dometrius, Burke, and Wright, 2008) to incorporate in welfare policy models.

Yet doing so might be a high-effort, low-yield endeavor. One of the central challenges of presidential scholarship has been the "small-N" problem: given how few Presidents the US has had, it has been difficult to make solid generalizations about their attributes that can be linked to policy choices. Even though there are thousands of "governor-years" to incorporate in social welfare policy models, it is perhaps the case that the governors lack the attributes necessary for variable creation: politically relevant features that can be consistently measured across place and time.

Bureaucracy: states vary in their administrative capacities. States with more competent bureaucracies are generally thought to use them: "stronger state institutions are linked to more innovative public policy making generally" (Barrilleaux and Brace, 2007, 668; see also Brace, 1993; Hedge, 1998). Bureaucracies are clearly important for social welfare policy: "Only a government that is competent, in both political and administrative ways, can carry out the complex measures that today's poverty seems to require. To overcome poverty, therefore, we must worry about governmental quality as much as the substance of the policy" (Mead, 2004, 261).

The choices administrative officials make—whether to influence or to determine policy—are fundamentally important for social welfare, but they have generally be ignored in quantitative models (Francis, 1998). Of the ten welfare studies assessed, only two contained administrative variables. Volden (2002, 358) found, contrary to his expectations, that states with "empowered welfare boards" actually had a lower probability of legislatively increased welfare benefits than states lacking such boards. Rodgers, Beamer, and Payne (2008, 534) conclude that states with more "governmental professionalism" (i.e., higher per capita legislative and bureaucratic spending) exert greater welfare effort. The few extant health policy studies indicate that states with greater administrative capacity have greater Medicaid expenditures per capita (Barrilleaux and Miller, 1988, 1098) and are more likely to enact state-based (redistributive) health-care policies and less likely to adopt market-based (developmental) reforms (Barrilleaux and Brace, 2007, 672). Schneider and Jacoby (1996, 509) find that states with local administration of Medicaid adopt more optional services than states with centralized administration.

It seems improbable that political scientists are blind to the influence that bureaucracy can have on social welfare policies. More likely, the quantitative researcher has virtually no administrative variables that can be consistently measured across the states and over time. As a result, the few studies that include administrative capacity rely on fairly crude measures, for example, average administrative salaries. It is probably too much to ask of the scholars investigating social welfare policies to construct more sophisticated indicators themselves, although it would be a valuable service to state policy researchers across a variety of policy domains if better measures were developed.

Interest groups: interest groups have a privileged position in American politics, but studies of social welfare policy have generally ignored their role. This is perhaps appropriate in studies of cash assistance programs, as there are few organized groups seeking to expand or contract this program. As Cook puts it, one "interest group" that is unlikely to have any influence over welfare policy is the poor themselves (see, for example, Cook et al., 1988). No quantitative study of AFDC/TANF examines interest group influence. Interest groups have featured more prominently in studies of health policy, although the measures of interest group activity are fairly crude and, as some scholars have put it, "It should also be clear.... that the influence of organized interests on public policy is, at least in the aggregate, quite small" (Gray et al., 2004, 419). Still, Gray et al. (2009, 102–103) found that interest group activity had a strong and predictable impacts on legislative activity on health-care reform, with increased support for reform, while Barrilleaux and Miller (1988, 1098) found that Medicaid effort increases with interest group density.

Ideology and public opinion: although paying scant attention to interest groups, social welfare policy scholars almost always include measures of state ideology or public opinion in their models. State ideology is most commonly measured by the techniques (or data) developed by Erikson, Wright, and McIver (1993) and Berry et al. (1998). Perhaps surprisingly (or perhaps not), the impacts of ideology and opinion have been mixed, with more liberal states generally, but not always, producing more generous social welfare policies. Studies finding evidence of liberal publics producing liberal policies include Barrilleaux and Miller (1988), Grogan (1994), Barrilleaux (1997), Fellowes and Rowe (2004), Avery and Peffley (2005), Hero and Preuhs (2007), and Rodgers, Beamer, and Payne (2008). Studies finding no impact of ideology on policy include Schneider and Jacoby (1996); Barrilleaux, Holbrook, and Langer (2002); Preuhs (2007); Lockhart, Giles-Sims, and Klopfenstein (2008); and Gray et al. (2009). Bailey and Rom (2004) show mixed results of ideology on AFDC, Medicaid, and SSI policy.

Race: the strongest and most consistent finding of the social welfare policy literature is that race matters, and not in a way that should be celebrated. Numerous studies have linked the racial characteristics of the states to welfare policy choices: specifically, that states with higher proportions of ethnic minorities, especially African Americans, have less generous welfare programs (Grogan, 1994; Soss et al., 2001; Rodgers, Beamer, and Payne, 2003; Bailey and Rom, 2004; Fellowes and Rowe, 2004; Avery and Peffley, 2005; Hero and Preuhs, 2007; Preuhs, 2007). Soss, Fording, and Schram (2008, 551–2) find that states pursue second-order devolution based on the prevalence and dispersion of African Americans on their TANF caseloads consistent with the view that "over the past century, welfare localism has consistently facilitated racialized practices of social control." More broadly, Schram (2005) contends that welfare programs perpetuate racial inequalities, not least because of the differential treatments of minority groups, especially blacks.

Although less commonly studied, a few studies have reported a negative reaction to Latinos in welfare policy (Soss et al., 2001; Fellowes and Rowe, 2004). Pruehs (2007, 285) found that Latino incorporation (i.e., extent of Latinos participating in the legislature) increased welfare effort, generosity, and benefits, whereas higher proportions of Latinos in the population decreased effort and benefits (while having no impact on generosity).

Not all scholars have found that larger minority populations are associated with less generous welfare programs. Volden (2002, 356) anticipated that states with higher proportions of minority (i.e., non-white) residents would be more likely to increase welfare benefits, under the somewhat odd assumption that welfare is "more strongly espoused" by minority groups. He finds support for this, with the probability of benefits strongly and positively associated with increases in minority populations. Barrilleaux and Bernick (2003) found that higher proportions of African Americans in the population lead to higher spending effort for general assistance programs.

Between the states: questions concerning policy emulation, welfare magnets and a potential race-to-the-bottom have drawn substantial scholarly attention. It has been clearly established that states "emulate" each other, at least if by emulate we mean adopt similar policies (e.g., Barrilleaux, Holbrook, and Langer, 2002; Satterthwaite, 2002; Fellowes and Rowe, 2004; Volden, 2002, 2006, and 2010; Barrilleaux and Brace, 2007; Hero and Preuhs, 2007; Gray et al., 2009; although see Boehmke, 2009). With the exception of Volden's work, these studies typically show that the states imitate each other, but not *why* or in *what* ways: Volden's research provides evidence that states with similar political dynamics tend to adopt similar policies. Further research along these lines is warranted.

Whether or not welfare magnets actually exist is worth knowing, but their existence is not essential for a race-to-the-bottom: the potential or the perception of the potential is. Early research on this topic produced mixed results, with some scholars arguing that state welfare policies affected migration (Peterson and Rom, 1990, and Rom, Peterson, and Scheve, 1998, while others came to the opposite conclusion (Schram and Soss, 1998; Schram, Nitz, and Krueger, 1998; Levine and Zimmerman, 1999; Allard and Danziger,

2000). More recently, Bailey (2005) provides compelling evidence that, at the margins, the poor do tend to locate in states offering more generous welfare benefits, and this finding has been supported by other research (Fiva, 2009). At the very least, it is understandable that state policymakers will be concerned about the prospect that offering generous welfare benefits *could* turn their state into a welfare magnet.

Does such a prospect lead to a raceto-the-bottom? Early research was generally supportive of the concept (Peterson and Rom, 1990; Schram and Krueger, 1994; Tweedie, 1994; Rom, Peterson, and Scheve, 1998; Figlio, Kolpin, and Reid, 1999; but see Dye, 1990). More recent research has continued to show evidence of welfare competition, but in more sophisticated and nuanced ways. Volden (2002) finds that states do not seek to undercut each other, but that they are reluctant to provide more generous programs unless their neighbors do so. In the most explicit test, Bailey and Rom (2004, but see also Berry and Baybeck, 2005) find strong evidence of a slow and variable race-to-the-bottom across the states regarding AFDC, Medicaid, and SSI-S. They test explicitly to determine whether states merely imitate each other, or whether states are differentially influenced by their neighboring states having less generous welfare programs. They find that the less generous states influence their neighbors on the most salient aspects—AFDC and Medicaid (benefits and access for AFDC, costs for Medicaid)—and across benefits, access, and costs for the SSI program. The estimated impacts of the less generous states are statistically significant and substantively important, if not large. The bottom-line finding of the race-to-the-bottom research is that interstate competition does serve to repress welfare generosity mildly, but the states are not exactly racing, and the competition does not push them to "the bottom."

Success and failure: one important line of research deserving more attention considers whether *good* policies tend to spread and whether *bad* policies fade away.[16] If the states are seen as "laboratories of democracy," it would be worth knowing how well the laboratories actually work. Unfortunately, scant attention has been paid to these questions (Rom, 2006). The noteworthy exception has been the research of Volden (2006, 2010). Examining the Children's Health Insurance Program (CHIP), Volden finds that states "tend to emulate those policies that have been shown to be successful at lowering the uninsurance rate of poor children in other states" (Volden, 2006, 299). The states also tend to emulate politically similar states, rather than just neighboring states, so that (for example) states with unified Republican governments tended to model themselves after other Republican states, or states with similar public ideologies generally moved towards each other. Volden (2010) also found that, under certain circumstances, states are more likely to abandon TANF policies that have proven to be unsuccessful elsewhere. In general, liberal states tend to learn from liberal states, and conservative ones also from their peers. States having more professional legislatures (i.e., better paid ones) also tend to learn more in the sense that they are more likely to abandon unsuccessful policies. The party of the governor had no impact on policy learning. Thompson and Burke (2009) show that, at least regarding Medicaid, the federal government also can learn from state experiments.

A Word on SSI/General Assistance

Cash assistance programs other than TANF have received virtually no attention from political scientists: the only articles examining the state-level determinants of the Supplemental Security Income (SSI) or General Assistance (GA) programs are Barrilleaux and Bernick (2003) and Bailey and Rom (2004). Using models similar to those common in AFDC/TANF research, they found similarly mixed results: the impacts of electoral competition, Democratic strength, public ideology, and race were not consistent in direction and significance.

Conclusions

This chapter has outlined the dimensions, arenas, and focus on state social welfare policies. This conclusion will summarize the state of political science research on these elements and offer some suggestions for further research.

The most heavily studied questions have involved the intrastate determinants of social welfare benefits. This research continues to be plagued by inconsistent research: the quantitative models routinely omit variables found important in other studies, or they include variables others omit. Other than asserting that race matters, and not in a way that reflects well on our body politic, it is challenging to find progress towards agreement on the factors that influence policy choice. This is perhaps inevitable, given the difficulties in defining politically relevant variables that are theoretically important, analytically compelling, and consistent over place and time. My hope is that this review at least highlights the main pitfalls of the existing research, so that a clever new cohort of scholars can build on it in a way that generates a more favorable review in the next *Handbook*.

Several clear research opportunities exist regarding the dimensions, arenas, and foci of social welfare policy. Scholars should more carefully examine the intrastate factors that favor certain kinds of social welfare policies (e.g., health care) over others (income support). Scholars might also usefully pay greater attention to interstate efforts to shape social welfare policy in terms of the benefits and burdens that the states themselves bear. Given Medicaid's enormity in importance and cost—and its certain future growth— much more political research should be conducted regarding benefit types, populations served, benefit provision, federal–state responsibilities, and program administration. If the health-care reforms of 2010 are implemented, rich new areas of research will be opened up.

As TANF has been fading away in size, cost, and controversy, it has also been declining as a subject of scholarly study. Much of the decline in academic interest is no doubt due to its diminished political importance, but another reason is that TANF is difficult to study quantitatively as the complexity of state programs has increased (yielding fewer dimensions that are consistent across the states) without growth data centralization. AFDC was easy to study: the federal government collected uniform data on recipients, benefits, and costs. Studying TANF is a challenge, as these data are less meaningful (in terms of understanding program dynamics) and less available through centralized repositories. Although TANF has not been in the spotlight in recent years, questions concerning how the states treat their most vulnerable populations will be central to the politics of the second decade of the twenty-firstst century. The ongoing economic problems, the growing economic inequalities, and the continuing fiscal stresses on the states dictate that political research is warranted.

NOTES

1. A 20-ear panel of the 50 states, for example, would yield 1,000 cases.
2. These programs are also called means-tested programs.
3. The data in the two preceding sentences are from different sources and are not directly comparable. Historically, state and local governments have accounted for about one-third of the total share of welfare expenditures.
4. Beginning in 2014, all individuals under age 65 living in families with incomes below 138 percent of the "family poverty line" become eligible for Medicaid if the ACA is fully implemented (Klees, Wolfe, and Curtis 2010, 25). The ACA was challenged in federal courts in 2010, and by early 2011 two federal district courts had struck down parts or all of the ACA, while two other courts have upheld the law. These challenges will certainly end up at the Supreme Court, where the outcome is uncertain.
5. This does not hold in Arizona, which since 1982 has been running a medical program for low-income residents as a demonstration project.
6. Author's calculations from data in Klees, Wolfe, and Curtis (2010, 29).
7. Numerous scholars have made this distinction between the "deserving" and "undeserving" poor (see, for example, Schneider and Ingram, 1993; Quadagno, 1994; Gilens, 1999; Soss et al., 2001; Barrilleaux and Bernick, 2003).
8. Research has suggested that state-only welfare policies are the products of a different kind of politics than those for joint federal programs (Barrilleaux and Bernick, 2000; Barrilleaux and Brace, 2007).
9. The origins of the phrase "race-to-the-bottom" are unclear, although the concept was used to discuss policy choices as early as the 1930s.
10. In reality, these stages often overlap.
11. Some studies acknowledge that until recent years Southern legislatures were uniformly Democratic *and* conservative, and so were not expected to show much generosity towards welfare programs.
12. Because state lower and upper houses are different sizes, an accurate measure would not simply be the total number of Democratic legislators divided by the total number of legislators. Some analyses simply use the proportion of the Democrats in the lower chamber (Barrilleaux and Brace, 2007).
13. Some scholars have combined partisan strength in the legislature with gubernatorial control, so, for example, the "total" strength of the Democratic party is the Democratic strength in the legislature (in percent) plus 100 if the governor is also a Democrat (Bailey

and Rom, 2004) or 3 if both chambers plus the governor are controlled by the Democrats, 2 if the Democrats have control of two of the three institutions, 1 if 1, and 0 if the Republicans control each institution (Satterthwaite, 2002).

14. The exception to this is when the dependent variable is binary and logistic regression is used. When this is the case, the impact of changes in the independent variable is lowest at the extremes and heightened over some narrower part of the range.

15. For example, Bailey and Rom (2004, 336) use a modified measure of party strength (percentage of legislature that is Democratic, but 100 if the Governor is also Democratic) while noting that "other partisanship variables were examined, with none causing substantial changes in the results."

16. Defining whether a policy is good or bad has both empirical and normative dimensions, of course. One way to assess whether a policy is good or bad concerns whether it makes progress towards its ostensible goal (e.g., do "work first" welfare programs increase gainful employment among TANF recipients?). Another way is to examine whether policies "work" to serve the political goals of their advocates (for example, a "work first" welfare program may bring political advantages to its sponsors, independent of whether it increases employment).

References

Allard, Scott and Sheldon Danziger. 2000. "Welfare Myth or Reality?" *Journal of Politics* 62: 350–368.

Alt, James E. and Robert C. Lowry. 1994. "Divided Government, Fiscal Institutions, and Budget Deficits: Evidence from the States." *American Political Science Review 88* (4): 811–828.

Avery, James M. and Mark Peffley. 2005. "Voter Registration Requirements, Voter Turnout, and Welfare Eligibility Policy: Class Bias Matters." *State Politics and Policy Quarterly 5* (1): 47–67.

Bailey, Michael A. 2005. "Welfare and the Multifaceted Decision to Move." *American Political Science Review 99*: 125–135.

Bailey, Michael A. and Mark Carl Rom. 2004. "A Wider Race? Interstate Competition Across Health and Welfare Programs." *The Journal of Politics 66* (2): 326–347.

Barrilleaux, Charles. 1997. "A Test of the Independent Influences of Electoral Competition and Party Strength in a Model of State Policy-Making." *American Journal of Political Science 41* (4): 1462–1466.

Barrilleaux, Charles and Ethan Bernick. 2003. "Deservingness, Discretion, and the State Politics of Welfare Spending, 1990–1996." *State Politics and Policy Quarterly 3* (1): 1–18.

Barrilleaux, Charles and Paul Brace. 2007. "Notes from the Laboratories of Democracy: State Government Enactments of Market- and State-Based Health Insurance Reforms in the 1990s." *Journal of Health Politics, Policy and Law 32* (4): 655–683.

Barrilleaux, Charles J. and Mark E. Miller. 1988. "The Political Economy of State Medicaid Policy." *American Political Science Review 82* (4): 1089–1107.

Barrilleaux, Charles, Thomas Holbrook, and Laura Langer. 2002. "Electoral Competition, Legislative Balance, and American State Welfare Policy." *American Journal of Political Science 46* (2): 415–427.

Berry, William D. and Brady Baybeck. 2005. "Using Geographic Information Systems to Study Interstate Competition." *American Political Science Review 99* (4): 505–519.

Berry, William D., Richard C. Fording and Russell L. Hanson. 2003. "Reassessing the 'Race to the Bottom' in State Welfare Policy." *Journal of Politics 65*: 327–349.

Birkland, Thomas A. 2010. *An Introduction to the Policy Process: Theories, Concepts, and Models of Public Policy Making*. New York: M. E. Sharpe.

Boehmer, Tegan K., Douglas A. Luke, Debra L. Haire-Joshu, Hannalori S. Bates, and Ross C. Brownson. 2008. "Preventing Childhood Obesity Through State Policy Predictors of Bill Enactment." *American Journal of Preventive Medicine 34* (4): 333–340.

Boehmke, Frederick J. 2009. "Ambiguities in the Dyadic Event History Approach to State Policy Emulation." *The Journal of Politics 71* (3): 1125–1140.

Brace, Paul. 1993. *State Governments and Economic Development*. (Baltimore: Johns Hopkins).

Caraley, Demetrio James. 2001–2002. "Ending Welfare as We Know It: A Reform Still in Progress." *Political Science Quarterly 116* (4); 525–560.

Cook, Fay Lomax, Edith J. Barrett, Susan J. Popkin, Emesto A. Constantino, and E. Kaufnan. 1988. *Convergent Perspectives on Social Welfare Policy: The Views from the General Public, Members of Congress, and AFDC Recipients*. Evanston, IL: Center for Urban Affairs and Policy Research.

Dias, Janice Johnson and Steven Maynard-Moody. 2007. "For-Profit Welfare: Contracts, Conflicts, and the Performance Paradox." *Journal of Public Administration Research and Theory 17* (2): 189–211.

Dometrius, Nelson C., Brendan F. Burke, and Deil S. Wright. 2008. "Strategies for Measuring Influence over State Agencies." *State Politics and Policy Quarterly 8* (1):88–100.

Dye, Thomas. R. 1990. "The Policy Consequences of Intergovernmental Competition." *Cato Journal 10*: 59–73.

Erikson, Robert S., Gerald C. Wright, and John P. McIver. 1989. "Political Parties, Public Opinion, and State Policy in the United States." *American Political Science Review 83* (September): 729–750.

Erikson, Robert S., Gerald C. Wright, and John P. McIver. 1993. *Statehouse Democracy: Public Opinion and Policy in the American States*. New York: Cambridge University Press.

Fellowes, Matthew C. and Gretchen Rowe. 2004, "Politics and the New American Welfare States." *American Journal of Political Science, 48* (2): 362–373.

Figlio, David N., Van W. Kolpin, and William E. Reid. 1999. "Do States Play Welfare Games?" *Journal of Urban Economics 46*: 437–454.

Fiva, Jon H. 2009. "Does Welfare Policy Affect Residential Choices? An Empirical Investigation Accounting for Policy Endogeneity." *Journal of Public Economics 93*: 529–540.

Francis, Richard M. 1998. "Predictions, Patterns, and Policymaking: A Regional Study of Devolution." *Publius 28* (3): 143–160.

Gainsborough, Juliet F. 2003. "To Devolve or Not to Devolve? Welfare Reform in the States." *Policy Studies Journal 31* (4): 603–623.

Gais, Thomas L. 2000. "Concluding Comments: Welfare Reform and Governance." In Carol S. Weissert, (ed.), *Learning from Leaders: Welfare Reform Politics and Policy in Five Midwestern States*. Albany, NY: Rockefeller Institute Press, pp. 173–189.

Gais, Thomas and James Fossett. 2005. "Federalism and the Executive Branch." In Joel D. Aberbach and Mark A. Peterson (eds), *The Executive Branch*. New York: Oxford University Press, pp. 486–524.

Gilens, Martin. 1999. *Why Americans Hate Welfare: Race, Media, and the Politics of Antipoverty Policy*. Chicago, IL: University of Chicago Press.

Gray, Virginia. 1973. "Innovation in the States: A Diffusion Study." *The American Political Science Review 67* (4): 1174–1185.

Gray, Virginia, David Lowery, James Monogan, and Erik K. Godwin. 2009. "Incrementing Toward Nowhere: Universal Health Care Coverage in the States." *Publius 40* (1): 82–113.

Gray, Virginia, David Lowery, Matthew Fellowes, and Andrea McAtee. 2004. "Public Opinion, Public Policy, and Organized Interests in the American States" *Political Research Quarterly 57* (3):411–20

Grogan, Colleen. 1994. "Political-Economic Factors Influencing State Medicaid Policy." *Political Research Quarterly 47* (3): 589–622.

Hedge, David. 1998. *Governance and the Changing American States.* Boulder, CO: Westview.

Hero, Rodney E. and Robert R. Preuhs. 2007. "Immigration and the Evolving American Welfare State: Examining Policies in the U.S. States." *American Journal of Political Science 51* (3): 498–517.

Hill, Michael. 2009. *The Public Policy Process,* 5th edn. New York: Pearson Education Limited.

Holbrook, Thomas and Emily Van Dunk. 1993. "Electoral Competition in the American States." *American Political Science Review 87* (4): 955–962.

Howard, Christopher. 1997. *The Hidden Welfare State: Tax Expenditures and Social Policy in the United States.* Princeton, New Jersey: Princeton University Press.

Karch, Andrew. 2007. "Emerging Issues and Future Directions in State Policy Diffusion Research." *State Politics and Policy Quarterly 7* (1): 54–80.

Klees, Barbara S., Christian J. Wolfe, and Catherine A. Curtis. 2010. Brief Summaries of Medicare and Medicaid. Centers for Medicare and Medicaid Services. U.S. Department of Health and Human Services. Website available at <https://www.cms.gov/MedicareProgramRatesStats/Downloads/MedicareMedicaidSummaries2010.pdf> (accessed February 2 2011).

Levine, Phillip and David Zimmerman. 1999. "An Empirical Analysis of the Welfare Magnet Debate Using the NLSY." *Journal of Population Economics 12:* 391–409.

Lockhart, Charles, Jean Giles-Sims, and Kristin Klopfenstein. 2008. "Cross-State Variation in Medicaid Support for Older Citizens in Long-Term Care Nursing Facilities." *State & Local Government Review 40* (3): 173–185.

Lowi, Theodore J. 1972. "Four Systems of Policy, Politics, and Choice." *Public Administration Review 32* (4): 298–310.

Mead, Lawrence M. 2004. *Government Matters: Welfare Reform in Wisconsin.* Princeton, NJ: Princeton University Press.

Nathan, Richard P. and Thomas L. Gais. 1998. "Early Findings About the Newest New Federalism for Welfare." *Publius 28* (3): 95–103.

National Association of State Budget Officers. 2010. *State Expenditure Report 2009.* Washington, DC: National Association of State Budget Officers. <http://www.nasbo.org/publications-data/state-expenditure-report/state-expenditure-report-2009-fiscal-2008-2010-data> (accessed July 20, 2013).

National Association of State Budget Officers. *2011. Fiscal Survey of States, Fall* 2011. Washington, DC: National Association of State Budget Officers. <http://www.nasbo.org/publications-data/fiscal-survey-states/fiscal-survey-states-fall-2011> (accessed July 20, 2013).

Office of Family Assistance. N.d. "Temporary Assistance for Needy Families: Eighth Annual Report to Congress." U.S. Department of Health and Human Services. Administration for Children and Families. Website available at <http://www.acf.hhs.gov/programs/ofa/data-reports/annualreport8/chapter00/chap00.htm> (accessed July 20, 2013)

Office of Management and Budget. 2011. *Historical Tables: Budget of the U.S., Fiscal 2011.* Washington, DC: Government Printing Office.

Peterson, Paul E., and Mark C. Rom. 1990. *Welfare Magnets: A New Case for a National Standard.* Washington, DC: The Brookings Institute.

Preuhs, Robert R. 2007. "Descriptive Representation as a Mechanism to Mitigate Policy Backlash: Latino Incorporation and Welfare Policy in the American States." *Political Research Quarterly* 60 (2): 277–292.

Quadagno, Jill. 1994. *The Color of Welfare: How Racism Undermined the War on Poverty.* New York: Oxford University Press.

Riccucci, Norma M. 2005. "Street-Level Bureaucrats and Intrastate Variation in the Implementation of Temporary Assistance for Needy Families Policies." *Journal of Public Administration Research and Theory* 15 (1): 89–111.

Rodgers, Harrell R. Jr, Glenn Beamer, and Lee Payne. 2008. "No Race in Any Direction: State Welfare and Income Regimes." *Policy Studies Journal* 36 (4): 525–542.

Rom, Mark Carl. 2006. "Taking the Brandeis Metaphor Seriously: Policy Experimentation within a Federal System." In Eric Patashnik and Alan Gerber (eds), *Promoting the General Welfare: New Perspectives on Government Performance.* Washington, DC: Brookings Institution, 256–281.

Rom, Mark C., Paul E. Peterson, and Kenneth F. Scheve, Jr. 1998. "Interstate Competition and Welfare Policy." *Publius* 28: 17–37.

Satterthwaite, Shad B. 2002. "Innovation and Diffusion of Managed Care in Medicaid Programs." *State & Local Government Review* 34 (2): 116–126.

Schneider, Anne and Helen Ingram. 1993. "Social Construction of Target Populations: Implications for Politics and Policy." *American Political Science Review* 87: 334–348.

Schneider, Saundra K. 1997. "Medicaid Section 1115 Waivers: Shifting Health Care Reform to the States." *Publius* 27 (2): 89–109.

Schneider, Saundra K., amd William G. Jacoby. 1996. "Influences on bureaucratic policy initiatives in the American states." *Journal of Public Administration Research and Theory,* 6 (4): 495–522.

Schram, Sanford F. 2005. "Contextualizing Racial Disparities in American Welfare Reform: Toward a New Poverty Research." *Perspectives on Politics* 3 (2): 253–268.

Schram, Sanford F. and Gary Krueger. 1994. "Welfare Magnets and Benefit Decline: Symbolic Problems and Substantive Consequences." *Publius* 24 (4): 61–82.

Schram, Sanford F. and Joe Soss. 1998. "Making Something out of Nothing: Welfare Reform and a New Race to the Bottom." *Publius* 28 (3): 67–88.

Schram, Sanford, Lawrence Nitz, and Gary Krueger. 1998. "Without Cause or Effect: Reconsidering Welfare Migration as a Policy Problem." *American Journal of Political Science* 42: 210–230.

Soss, Joe, Richard C. Fording and Sanford F. Schram. 2008. "The Color of Devolution: Race, Federalism, and the Politics of Social Control." *American Journal of Political Science* 52 (3): 536–553.

Soss, Joe, Sanford F. Schram, Thomas P. Vartanian, and Erin O'Brien. 2001. "Setting the Terms of Relief: Explaining State Policy Choices in the Devolution Revolution." *American Journal of Political Science* 45 (2): 378–395.

Stuber, Jennifer and Karl Kronebusch. 2004. "Stigma and Other Determinants of Participation in TANF and Medicaid." *Journal of Policy Analysis and Management* 23: 509–530.

Thompson, Frank J. and Courtney Burke. 2009. "Federalism by Waiver: Medicaid and the Transformation of Long-term Care." *Publius* 39 (1): 22–46.

Tweedie, Jack. 1994. "Resources Rather Than Needs: A State-Centered Model of Welfare Policymaking." *American Journal of Political Science* 38 (3): 651–672.

U.S. Bureau of the Census. 2008. State & Local Government Finance. <http://www.census.gov/prod/2011pubs/go8-alfin.pdf> (accessed July 20, 2013).

U.S. Bureau of the Census. 2011. *Statistical Abstract of the United States*. Washington, DC: Government Printing Office.

Volden, Craig. 2002. "The Politics of Competitive Federalism: A Race to the Bottom in Welfare Benefits?" *American Journal of Political Science* 46 (2): 352–363.

Volden, Craig. 2006. "States as Policy Laboratories: Emulating Success in the Children's Health Insurance Program." *American Journal of Political Science* 50 (2): 294–312.

Volden, Craig. 2010. "Failures: Diffusion, Learning, and Policy Abandonment." Paper prepared for the American Political Science Association Annual Research Conference. Washington, DC.

Walker, Jack L. 1969. "The Diffusion of Innovations Among the American States." *American Political Science Review* 63 (3): 880–899.

Wilson, James Q. 1980. *The Politics of Regulation*. New York: Basic Books.

CHAPTER 30

HEALTH CARE POLITICS
AND POLICY

CHARLES BARRILLEAUX

THE national government's March 2010[1] mandate that calls for expansion of health care coverage for US citizens creates a number of research possibilities in the area of state health politics and policymaking. Historically, there has been no overarching US health care policy, and state governments have long been influential in governing health care within their borders. Changes that may occur as a result of the 2010 reforms have broad repercussions for state politics and policy. The Obama plan calls for some sweeping changes, the effects of which remain to be seen; many of those changes cannot occur without the participation of state governments. Because of this, and because of the presence of fierce opposition to some pieces of the Obama plan, state health politics will be a venue for working out the implications of the 2010 national reforms. Outcomes at the state level will help determine the ultimate success or failure of that legislation. Thus the states are, and have been, the locations of a number of health policy battles over the years. The bill's opponents have taken some of the fight against its provisions to the states in the hopes of receiving favorable judicial decisions that allow them to avoid some of its mandates. In short, the substance of state health politics has been redefined at least partly by the enactment of a major piece of federal legislation, which will result in practical political problems in the states for the near future.

But even with the newly wrought political issues that emerge from the 2010 reform legislation, there are continuities in state health politics and policy. Thus we can think of state health politics as we do partisan realignment: it contains elements of secular change that are borne of ongoing political interests and policy choices, and of rapid change that is borne of major pieces of legislation. This is to be expected; health politics and policy in the US states are complex and dynamic. Their complexity is a function of the large number of interests involved, the variety of substantive problems that must be addressed, the size of state-specific health economies, the effects of federal government mandates on state behavior, and the need for health services among state citizens. The stakes of health politics are high; they determine who gets access to care, who pays for care, who provides care, what must be paid for, how much is to be paid, and more. These are long-lived concerns that give rise to longstanding political and policy interests. The result is an enduring health politics within each state, one that is attentive to ongoing internal issues and is also responsive to external shocks like changes in Medicaid or new mandates from the national government. Because of this, state health politics and policy represents an extraordinarily fertile area for research. In this essay, we focus on a handful of themes that illustrate what we believe to be among the areas most in need of research attention. This essay is intended to provoke other ideas for research and therefore does not include an exhaustive set of recommendations. Edward Miller (2005) provides an exhaustive meta-analysis of US-based studies of state health policy completed between 1975 and 2002. We recommend his paper as a guide to general expectations about health policy relationships among state governments and focus this paper on issues related to current policy issues.

The chapter is organized in five major sections following this introduction. The first of those (section 2) includes a discussion of research designs used and data applied to studying state-level health politics and policy. This is largely descriptive, rather than prescriptive, although we suggest ways to leverage some microdata that are seldom exploited by political scientists in ways that might allow better causal statements about the causes and effects of state health policies. Following that, in section 3, we discuss state and federal relationships in health policy-making, focusing in particular upon the two-way flow of information and ideas between the levels of government. Next, in section 4, we discuss research on the organization of state health governance organizations, the organization of state-level health interests, and on other manifestations of political activity in health care. As we will develop in that section, this constitutes an important and largely ignored area for research on health care issues in the states. Also under this umbrella we discuss the equity of health services delivery and access across the states. This, too, represents what we view as an important area, which remains largely unexplored by political scientists. We know, for example, that a large number of US citizens are without health insurance, but one thing that's lost in much of that discussion is that health coverage is not distributed uniformly amongst racial and ethnic groups, which we believe has political and policy relevance. In the fifth section, we turn our attention to research on health care outcomes in the states; that is, to research that models the effects of health rules and/or spending on the quality of care received. Some of this certainly is covered in the discussion of variations in access to care across states and among groups within states, but it is likewise important as an emerging research venue because of the political and policy issues it introduces. For example, some states have adopted school diet rules to combat what is viewed as an obesity epidemic in schools, something that is especially prevalent among poor children and has long-term consequences for health care spending. And some evidence suggests that urban sprawl contributes to this problem, as increasingly sedentary citizens are less apt to walk anywhere since their living circumstances dictate that they drive for groceries, to work, and so on (Leyden, 2003). The sixth, and final, section includes discussion of some areas for additional research and conclusions.

APPROACHES TO STATE HEALTH POLICY RESEARCH

Research on state-level health policy and politics, at its best, contributes both to theories of politics and policy and to understandings of the specifics of health politics. More often research does either one or the other; it is more difficult to achieve both ends. Research on health politics and policy is typically conducted as either large-N or case-studies of one or several states. Thus it suffers the usual problem of either being strong on generalizability or strong on internal validity, but seldom has both strengths. This is not unique to research on state health politics and policy but is endemic to the study of comparative and state and local politics generally.

We believe it possible to advance health politics and policy research by employing research designs that address the generalizability/internal validity tradeoff in a manner that allows statements about each. To explain, some recent papers that focus on state health politics and policy and seek to explain whether those policies matter (e.g., Barrilleaux et al., 2010; Bernick and Myers, 2008) use aggregate state-level data to assess policy impacts. Bernick and Myers determine whether relatively more liberal or more conservative state policies affect the percentage of people in a state uninsured, finding that only SCHIP (State Children's Health Insurance Program) is associated with increased insurance coverage for the poor. Barrilleaux and his colleagues, also using aggregate data, report different policy effects according to race and ethnicity; that is, some policies affect white citizens' insurance coverage but do not have an effect on coverage for Hispanic and African American citizens, and so on. (Each of these studies will be discussed in more length in a later section of this essay.) We believe better estimates of the effects of state-level policy decisions on insurance coverage, access to care, and other measures of policy impact could be gained by shifting to an analysis in which the individual is the unit of analysis in a multilevel research design in which a variety of factors hypothesized to influence health outcomes, including crucial individual demographic and, ideally, health status indicators may be controlled. Although there are examples of this sort of design in the health services research area, only a handful of such papers exist, most were completed before a number of important developments in hierarchical modeling, and as such are questionable empirically (e.g., Barrilleaux and Miller, 1992).

One valuable source of state-specific individual-level data is the Urban Institute's National Survey of America's Families (NSAF), a survey of over 100,000 families conducted in 1997, 1999, and 2002, with oversamples in 13 states (<http://www.urban.org/center/anf/nsaf.cfm>, now available through the ICPSR, study 4582). Those oversample states enable researchers to conduct microdata analyses that include state-specific information about health reforms. Another source for research using this design is the Basic Risk Factor Surveillance Surveys (BRFSS), which is collected at the state level by the Centers for Disease Control and has been collected monthly in each state since 1984 (<http://www.cdc.gov/BRFSS/>). BRFSS data are focused on health status and behavior, but include questions about insurance coverage and the like. With some work, state-level policy characteristics could be added to the dataset to enable researchers to address questions about policy impact. Of course, individual-level legislative votes could be analyzed similarly to determine why states adopt the policies they do, but problems of external validity arise because the wording of legislation is seldom identical across states, and many legislative votes fall along party lines.

STATE HEALTH CARE REFORM IN THE FEDERAL SETTING

Most developed nations have some form of planned health policy. The United States is different in that it has long had a system that contains a mixture of national, state, and at times even local responsibility for health care. This, of course, complicates things and makes it necessary to sort out the roles of governments in health care. At times, these responsibilities are borne by a single government, as with Medicare, which is the sole responsibility of the national government, or with some portions of Medicaid, which are strictly state government responsibility. For example, federal funds may not be used to pay for abortions under Medicaid; that is a state responsibility. States are also responsible for regulating insurance, financing health education programs, for licensing health providers, including physicians, and in some cases states are responsible for supporting county public health programs (Tallon and Nathan, 1992, 8). But what is most clear is that the management of health care is shared among states and the national government. Describing the national government as the "single most important force" in health policy making, Altman and Morgan (1983) describe the full range of state government responsibilities in health care:

> Broadly speaking, the health-related activities of state and local government are: traditional public health, including health monitoring, sanitation, and disease control; the financing and delivery of personal health services including Medicaid, mental health, and direct delivery through public hospitals and health departments; environmental protection, including protection against man-made environmental and occupational hazards; and the regulation of the providers of medical care through certificate-of-need and state rate setting as well as licensing and other functions.
>
> (Altman and Morgan, 1983)

Reflecting this argument, Mark Peterson (2001, 1218) noted that health care politics and policymaking in the United States is inseparable from issues of federalism. Drawing on Paul Peterson's (1995) functional theory, he notes that the interests of state

governments in the system make them unlikely to pursue redistributive health policies, as they will almost certainly defer to the national government in that area, but state
cooperation is crucial to any successful state health policymaking, given the fragmented
organization of care in the United States. It is important to recognize that state governments have been contentious in their relationship with the national government despite
the national government's control of finances. Some state governments have been
aggressive in their pursuit of more generous federal payments in Medicaid, some states
seek more freedom to organize programs while retaining national government contributions, and so on. In short, the relationship between states and the national government is one of shared responsibility, even though Washington clearly has more money
to spend. Greer and Jacobson (2010) review this relationship and, following the logic
of Peterson (1995), argue that the national government should take a stronger role in
the management of health policymaking because state governments are ill-equipped
to do so.

State Governments as Innovators

One theme that has been prominent in research in the period following the Clinton
administration's failed 1993 attempt to reform health care in the United States is that
states can act as policy innovators in health care policy. This is especially true since the
national government has heretofore been incapable of mustering votes to effect change.
Henry Aaron and Stuart Butler (2008) make a strong case for the states as the nexus
of health reform efforts: states can launch multiple aggressive reforms simultaneously,
thereby providing outlets to test several possibly contentious approaches simultaneously; it allows the "limited successive comparisons" (Lindblom, 1959) approach to policy change, thus limiting risk; and it accommodates variations among the states, thereby
increasing the probability that something works. Their argument, which preceded
the 2008 election, was skeptical about the possibility of national government legislation being passed by an incoming administration. These authors—writing from different policy and ideological perspectives—express a preference for national government
action, if only to provide more coordination over state efforts than has been the case in
past reform events, but are skeptical about the possibility of a president gaining passage
of a bill. (In fact, the political capital spent on health reform may prove to have been
extremely costly to the Obama administration.) Nonetheless, the enactment of legislation by the national government changes state roles considerably inasmuch as there now
is a clearer set of goals than existed before.

The states' role in health policymaking is changed dramatically in the wake of the
Obama administration's extraordinary success in passing legislation and contentious
partisan politics its passage provoked. The national government continues to lead in the
as it seeks to help clarify the 2010 legislation and to alter portions of that bill as needs
arise. But the collision of out-of-control costs and dwindling budgets creates an environment in which state governments are desperate for cost savings and skeptical of the

benefits of change. States continue performing as the "laboratories of democracy" suggested by Justice Brandeis in 1932, even if it is not for the progressive ends the Justice argued for in his dissent in *New State Ice Co. v. Liebmann* (1932). There, Justice Brandeis contested prevailing interpretations of the Fourteenth Amendment that disallowed state governments to regulate competition in free markets (there, the ice market), claiming that states were better equipped to understand the needs of their citizens and thus could declare public interest where it might not exist. Given that this was a dissent, the Court disagreed. In contemporary usage, the idea is removed from Justice Brandeis's progressive notions and suggests only that state governments are positioned to try things that the national government is either incapable or unwilling to do. In current context, some state governments might innovate to thwart some of the tenets of the Obama plan, or they might go in the opposite direction and require more stringent legislation.

This is to say that states are almost certain to be innovators, but that some of that innovation may serve the cause of limiting government roles in health care, rather than expanding them. Also, it is almost certain that the states will be used as venues to test the ability of the national government to enforce its health policy. Attorneys general from 13 states joined a suit against the federal government as of May 2010, claiming that the national government had over-reached in its health mandate. All but one of the states joining the suit is controlled by Republicans, giving the complaints a partisan aspect. As of summer 2010, six states had enacted laws that opposed the federal mandates. Five (Georgia, Idaho, Louisiana, Utah, and Virginia) were passed by legislatures and Missouri passed its law via referendum. There, 71 percent of Missouri voters supported the state's Proposition C, which forbids the state from forcing people to pay a penalty for failing to carry health insurance. The Missouri law is strong in its rejection of central tenets of the Obama plan—it rejects even some of the plan's features and it remains to be seen whether similar actions will follow in its wake. A handful of additional states are planning referendums. By April, 2011 and additional 13 states joined as petitioners in the suit, in which they claimed that the 2010 Patient Protection and Affordable Care (PPACA) to violate the Tenth Amendment of the United States' Constitution on the grounds that it violates states' rights by requiring citizens to enroll in an insurance program or pay a tax levied by the national government. A second complaint was that the national governments required state governments to expand their Medicaid programs to provide health insurance to persons with incomes at or below 138 percent of the federal poverty level (National Federation of Independent Business (NFIB), et al. vs. Sebelius, et al. 2011). In short, declining the national government mandate was a significant policy innovation for the states.

The Supreme Court's decision in NFIB v. Sebelius on June 28, 2012, provided partial wins for the petitioners and the Obama administration. The Court, in a 5–4 decision, sides-tepped the Tenth Amendment question by ruling that the PPACA was a tax and within the national government's legitimate powers. That constituted a win by the PPA-CA's supporters. The Court provided a win to the petitioners by ruling that the states cannot be forced to accept the Medicaid expansion that PPACA proscribes. As of mid-2013, the conflict is shifted to the Medicaid expansion question, with some states adopting the expansion, others not adopting, and others deciding what to do (Barrilleaux, 2013).

But it is also likely that states that have been health policy innovators during the past 50-odd years will continue to be so. For example, a number of states attempted to address the problem of uninsurance in the wake of the Clinton administration's failed attempt in 1993. Kansas legislators enacted a law to provide funding for primary-care services for the medically underserved (Carrasquillo, Himmelstein, Woolhandler, and Bor, 1999). Florida reorganized its health system during the 1990s and was aggressive in moving Medicaid enrollees to various forms of managed care (Fox, 1995). Both Florida and Kansas are now undoing earlier reforms and moving toward less active approaches. Hawaii and Vermont mandated universal coverage for their citizens (Fox 1995). Other states adopted a mixture of public- and private-sector reforms with the goal of expanding access to services (Sparer, 1999; Stream, 1999; Barrilleaux and Brace, 2007; Stream and Myers, 2010). This policy adoption and innovation history warrants further research as state governments begin to respond to a new set of federal incentives.

Variations in Health Status and Health Outcomes

One of the areas of research that has received relatively little attention among political scientists has to do with the effects of health spending and policy delivery on health outcomes. One of the most remarkable things about US health services is just how poor a return Americans receive on their enormous investment. The United States spends more than any other nation on health care but gets mediocre results. It ranks 51st in life expectancy among nations of the world: A person in the United States can expect to live 78.6 years, while a typical Canadian has a life expectancy of 81.6 years, ranking 13th in the world United States Central Intelligence Agency, 2013). Of course, some US citizens live longer because there are considerable variations by income, race, and ethnicity, but the fact remains that the United States spends a lot of money for not very impressive outcomes. The states also vary considerably in their health outcomes. Life expectancy in Mississippi is about 73.9 years; it is over 80 years in Connecticut, Minnesota, and Hawaii (Kaiser Family Foundation, 2010). About 62 percent of children in Idaho had access to medical and dental care in 2006 compared to 85 percent of Rhode Island children in that year. In short, there are tremendous variations in health access and health status among US citizens, and some of those variations are driven by something that occurs at the state level. Some of that is certainly health policy, as some states—like Rhode Island in the case of services for children—provide better services than others. But some of the differences are also driven by behavior and environment, as in poor nutrition, poor diet, and the like. Looking at data on hospital discharges in the 1990s, it was striking to see that the most common discharges in Utah were for broken legs and healthy births.

In Louisiana at the same time, the most common discharge was for stomach cancer. This suggests something about the effects of lifestyle and behavior. Research that focuses on how policy and behavior affect outcomes is an important component of new work on health politics and policy.

Although the relationships between health outcomes and health behavior are complex, some basic propositions are evident. Social and income inequality and poor allocation of services are key problems that affect health outcomes in the United States. Morone and Jacobs (2005) contend that health inequality is as severe a problem as income inequality because it determines whether and what types of health services people will receive. In the United States, where the assurance of care is questionable even with the passage of the Obama plan, health inequality may play a large role in health outcomes. Some of this inequality is due to poor finances, as well as poor access to care because of shortage of facilities and providers. But other causes are also evident. One is simply poor funding in some cases, as some state governments do not have the funds to provide as generously as they might like. In Medicaid, for example, it has long been noted that states may make strong policy efforts but, because of funding shortfalls, still fall short of providing particularly good services (e.g., Hanson, 1984). This is even more pronounced in areas other than Medicaid, where state governments do not receive federal reimbursements for their contributions, so may be even less able to provide adequately.

It is clear that costs of care contribute to the problem of poor health among large numbers of people. Certainly, people without insurance are strained to pay for care, and even people with insurance may not feel entirely able to use all the services they need. One useful stream of research would be to seek citizen preferences for types of services. This introduces a number of problems, most notably that there is some evidence that people do not have very good information about the quality of services (Bowers et al., 1994). State policy research might contribute through data collection and analysis. One possibility is that variations in demand for services vary by population cluster, possibly by race and ethnicity, and the like. Citizens in Oregon have found ways to manage the costs of care by making decisions to fund, for example, services for people that will result in reduced costs, longer life expectancies, and generally better outcomes, than to fund services that are more risky. In this vein, it is useful to think about ways to assess willingness to assume the risk of health care, which may vary by individual and may in fact vary by state according to norms of health treatment.

The other problem, noted above, is that individual behavior also affects health status, regardless of treatments. A number of risky behaviors are clearly linked to poor health outcomes. We know, for example, that smoking is bad for health, yet over 18 percent of adults continue to engage in that behavior. Indianans smoke at a higher rate than citizens of any other state—26 percent—while Utahans smoke at the nation's lowest rate—9.3 percent (Kaiser Family Foundation, 2010). There are also troubling incidences of diabetes, heart disease, and other avoidable/controllable diseases. Some of those are associated with income inequality and poverty, but some are also just poor behavior. One research program that might prove to be of great interest and value would address the extent to which people are willing to be responsible for their own health. Some evidence suggests not very, as the United States is in the midst of a chronic obesity epidemic, which is bad for health outcomes and is driven at least partly by poor diet. It would be interesting to learn, for example, whether citizens of states vary systematically in their dietary choices and whether those variations affect health outcomes. It seems clear, for example, that some individuals and populations are more inclined than others to eat foods that are unhealthy. It would also be useful to learn the relationship between those behaviors and policy. It is widely held in popular media, for example, that subsidized, high-calorie products lead to obesity. Testing relationships between that and policy would be of great interest.

Related to this is research on the effects of activity on health outcomes. As might be expected, more active individuals tend to be healthier, a result that has been extended to broader populations (see, e.g. Leyden, 2003). These questions might also be applied at the state level. For example, does reliance on cars result in more obesity? Does state-level development policy lend itself to the creation of more car-dependent neighborhoods and, in time, increase rates of obesity? Can state governments provide incentives for citizens to engage in more active lifestyles? These are all related to health care but in a form not typically addressed, inasmuch as most of our consideration has to do with medical aspects of health care, rather than with behaviors that might lend themselves to healthier lifestyles.

The Organization of Health

States are readily compared, and these comparisons can be especially valuable in research. We focus on three arenas in which a heightened focus on health on governance would be especially beneficial. The first is actual health care administration, i.e., the organization of agencies that are involved in health policymaking, which is a largely unexamined but important element of state policymaking. The second area is in the exchange between branches of government, including the courts, as well as executives and legislatures, and the third is the broader organization of interests and in particular racial and ethnic minorities, whose use of health services varies from those of whites and whose access to services may be affected as a result.

State Government Health Organization

Health services are complicated in a number of ways. At the state level, they are complicated by the existence of multiple governing organizations. Medicaid, for example, is governed by the national government and states, which introduces one level of conflict. Beyond that, some states have requirements for contributions by counties or other levels of government. States vary in the extent to which they provide administrative support for programs, and so on. And some states are generous with some blocs of recipients, yet are not generous with others, and so on. In short, just understanding Medicaid administration opens a number of interesting research avenues. For example, how does the cost of administration affect the administrative efficiency of state programs? Certainly, more administratively efficient programs are, as the name implies, more efficient, and as a result are less costly to run. However, it may be the case that some managerial in-efficiency is beneficial in some cases. Nursing home services, for example, may be managed most efficiently by one form of program, while services for inpatient care may be more effectively managed by something entirely different. The point is that assumptions about what constitutes the best way to run things may vary, and systematic evaluation of what works where and when would be well advised.

Although we know relatively little about how states vary in their administration of health care data, there is some evidence that it matters. For example, fairly early evidence suggests that state administration of Medicaid programs influences state program spending and policy design (Barrilleaux and Miller, 1988; Schneider, 1988, 1989; Schneider, Jacoby and Coggburn, 1997). Likewise, state health insurance organization affects the enactment of state health reform policies (Stream, 1999). There is also evidence that how states manage health information matters in decision making and policy formation (Overman and Cahill, 1994). Although administrative data are fairly difficult to collect, some fairly detailed information on basic state health records and on organization are available (National Association of Health Data Organizations (NAHDO)). Existing measures tend to be fairly crude, as in measures of administrative quality, which are not specific to health care. It would be useful, for example, to be able to determine whether a state's health administration is more or less competent or politically controlled than some other form of administration, as it would be useful to compare those measures across states.

Legislatures, Executives and Courts

It would also be useful to develop more nuanced understandings of how legislative and executive branch agencies behave towards one another and towards themselves. In the first case, standard examinations of interbranch behavior suggest, for example, that partisanship has fairly predictable effects on how health politics will be played out in the states. Democratic governors who face Republican legislators in all likelihood moderate their behaviors, while Republican governors do the same when faced with Democratic legislators, and so on (Kousser, 2002). It would also be interesting to develop better understanding of circumstances that might make Democrats and Republicans less likely to moderate their behavior; that is, in some cases we might learn that parties are more willing to engage in conflict at certain times than at others.

For example, until recently it appeared that neither party desired to be involved in much conflict surrounding Medicaid (Holahan and Headen, 2010), with each party agreeing to let the national government accept most additional costs of Medicaid from the 2010 health care reforms. By contrast, interparty conflicts over the broader reforms are wide, with significant disagreement between the two parties over outcomes. Esterling (2008) shows the behavior of Congress and state legislatures to work together on Medicaid to the extent that their interests coincide. Most recently, conservatives in the states are rejecting the PPACA Medicaid expansion that seemed to be among the least controversial elements of the bill prior to the 2012 Supreme Court decision. Thus there is evidence of mounting partisan conflict within state legislatures and between legislators and executives in regard to Medicaid expansion.

Moving beyond legislatures and executives, relatively little systematic research has been done to address issues facing state courts in health care discussions. This will in all likelihood change as state courts become involved in attempts to reduce the effects of the 2010 health reforms. In the recent past, several states have issued rulings or have begun the process of making decisions on health reform in the states, and in particular they are beginning to make choices regarding whether the 2010 reforms are legal. As the cases develop, it will be of obvious policy interest to analyze them with an eye to their legitimacy. It will also be useful to seek information on the politics of the court decisions, which can be expected to vary.

Interest Groups

Building upon their longstanding work on organized interests in the states, Virginia Gray and David Lowery (see, e.g., Gray and Lowery, 1996), along with some coauthors, have attempted what are in all likelihood the most systematic assessments of state-level health care interests on state health policy. Gray and Lowery have been persistent advocates of a particular method of measuring state-level interest group existence, which consists of collecting numbers of organized interests registrations over a now limited time period (for discussion, see Gray and Lowery, 1996). Even with this data limitation, their results in a handful of papers suggest that there are some influences of organized interests—including physician groups, pharmacists, and others—on health policymaking (Gray, Lowery, and Godwin, 2007a, 2007b). Their research returns mixed results on the effects of interests on state pharmacists, although they argue that wider health reform should be affected more strongly by interest groups (Gray et al., 2010). Specifically, they identify groups who are long expected to affect health care—physician organizations, business organizations, insurers, and possibly a mixture of civil rights, women's rights, and other advocacy organizations—as being especially interested in universal health adoptions in the states (Gray, et al., 2010, 94). The problem with their measure, which they acknowledge, is that it consists of a measure of the strength of state interest groups averaged in 1990 and 1997.

Given that the Gray and Lowery data are useful only as cross-sections, it would be useful if they were updated, although it isn't clear that this would really expand much of what we know about state interest groups, since the cross-sectional measures tend to dominate the longitudinal ones. However there are other approaches to measurement that might be useful. One that offers some promise but that is fairly cost-intensive involves measuring networks of interest contacts in the states. Kile (2005) accomplishes this with a survey of participants in state reforms of pharmaceutical policy. Using this approach, he demonstrates that groups have strong effects in that specific policy area. Presumably, similar measures would have similar results if the data were available for collection across a larger number of areas. Gray and Lowery have been persistent in their argument that the best way to measure interests is through counting them. In any event, having updated data, and possibly some that better capture the elements of state health policy that are of interest would be desirable.

Related to the study of state-level interests, Andrew Karch (2007, 162–163) shows state-level health interests to be largely focused only on a single state, rather than on multiple states. There is variation among organizations and states, however. Karch's work reinforces the long-held idea that state interests work both independently and in multi-state networks.

Health and Health Inequality

The relationship between health care and inequality can be better developed within the study of state politics (Morone and Jacobs, 2005). The effect of income inequality is researched broadly (Kelly, 2009) but the joint effects of health and income inequality are less often considered. Understanding this joint relationship is crucial for understanding social policy, as health and welfare are bound tightly, as are housing and other policies that combine to establish the extent to which people are well sustained. And the relationship is meaningful for policy because large numbers of people who appear to be doing fairly well financially are simultaneously uninsured, which at the best places them at risk of large financial loss and at worst drops them into poverty as a result of that loss. Thus there are measurement issues that arise concerning real economic well-being and policy issues from the possible income losses that arise as health costs enter the picture.

The big problem with disentangling the relationship between income and health has to do with determining whether income declines are caused by health declines or whether they are independent. One way to approach this problem that in some ways avoids the big question about economics is to focus on Medicaid, where there is some variation in earnings but it is fairly constrained among the states. Here, the question has to do with directions Medicaid may be expected to go. As has been noted in the past, the big question has long been whether Medicaid will become a more broadly generous program or whether it will retrench towards a "welfare medicine" model (Holahan and Cohen, 1986; Grogan and Patashnik, 2003). One argument favoring a broader form of policy inclusion, especially by businesses, is that the rise of low-wage, low-income jobs depends in part on the presence of some form of health insurance. Kazee (2006) describes this as "Wal-Mart welfare" and suggests that it may have the unexpected effect of increasing demand for care among some companies. Of course, this speculation is affected greatly by the 2010 health reform, but those reforms may have that sort of effect. There are clearly wide disparities among groups who receive health care, and those distinctions are likewise broad amongst recipients of Medicaid, where some beneficiaries receive greater service coverage than others, sometimes within the same state. For example, some states provide more generously for people who are among the program's basic service recipients and are less generous to others.

Another approach to studying inequality could come in viewing racial and ethnic variations in coverage among state populations. Although aggregate state-level data are limited, with only cross-sectional results available and data missing for some groups, it is clear that whites generally get better access to care than African American or Hispanic citizens (Barrilleaux et al., 2010). There is now a well-established literature on state-level health reforms designed to expand insurance coverage, which suggests that reforms have been generally weak and had minimal effect on policy outcomes (Barrilleaux and Brace, 2007; Bernick and Myers, 2008; Kail, Quadagno, and Dixon, 2009). Thus the evidence on state policies designed to increase health coverage seems to be that they offer little benefit, but what benefit does exist seems to be in areas that involve the states assuming risk; policies that involve businesses assuming risk have no discernible effects. However, these results differ when health care enrollees are broken down by race. As noted above, we then learn that whites have much better access to care and use of services than Hispanic or African American citizens. However, we also learn that minorities are able to affect the quality of care they get through their votes in legislative institutions and the like. Thus there is some evidence that political action has meaningful effects on state-level health coverage.

These results could be improved by expanding the pool of observations so that we can make inferences with more confidence. As noted above, the data for these analyses are limited to cross-sections, and in some cases those cross-sections have small Ns due to missing data problems. At present, the best source for data is from the Kaiser Family Foundation's web source (<http://kff.org/health-reform/>). These data are limited in that they are reported only as cross-sections, although it is likely that they can be expanded. Kail et al. (2009) create a set of longitudinal data on state health reform, but they do not contain measures of race and ethnicity.

WHERE TO GO FROM HERE? FINAL THOUGHTS AND CONCLUSIONS

New research on state health politics and policy can take a variety of approaches, many of which will be informed by the 2010 health reform and by past state policy reform enactments. Given the large number of possibilities, we suggest a few that we think are especially promising and apologize for no doubt ignoring some that are important.

Organizational Capacity

Corrigan and McNeill (2009) make a strong case for improving the quality of health care organization as a method for improving the quality of care. They focus on the hands-on side of health services, noting that the failure to integrate services across providers, including physicians, clinics, hospitals, and the like, constitutes a major failing in health services in the United States. In addition, they argue that failure to integrate information technology very successfully into these systems represents a failure to rationalize a complex system of care.

Research on state politics can contribute to this effort in a number of ways. The first is to seek to explain why care is so poorly integrated and to determine whether there are meaningful variations in its integration across the states or within states. The failure to integrate providers seems particularly strange, especially since provider networks are so important to ensuring continuity of care. But in a less applied view, it is interesting to determine what explains differences in the organization of services. Differences may be borne of political differences, information problems, disputes over how best to provide particular services, and other factors. Understanding variations in health organization is inherently interesting and may have a payoff for actual policy outputs.

Also, additional research on health interests would be useful. Research by Gray, Lowery and colleagues points to the importance of different groups in the health policymaking process; that is, some groups of physician providers may be more effective in gaining their preferences than others, and similar differences likely exist. Gray et al. (2007a) report strong effects of pharmaceutical interests in state policymaking in that area. In the past, health interests were viewed more monolithically, e.g., physician groups were thought to represent general health interests. Certainly, health interests compete amongst themselves for advantage. More extensive data collection would be a great aid in this area, and would likely have the payoff of providing better information about who gets what in health care. In addition, it would be useful to track the rise and fall of some interests, and more detailed data collection would be useful in this area.

Research on health governance institutions is also in order. Considerable research on small numbers of states and on single state cases exists in this area, but more broadly comparative information would be a great addition. Robert Hackey (1998), in a study of state health regulation, provides excellent in-depth analyses of legislative, executive, and interest-group politics in four northeastern states. His work, and state-level work by others some of whose work relies on cases or limited comparisons (e.g., Brown and Sparer, 2003; Grogan and Patashnik, 2005) provides a much more comprehensive assessment of the causes of policies and politics and typically emerges from research that is more broadly empirical in its approach. We think that this represents a challenge for people doing research which uses more data; that is, includes more cases. Although it requires hard work, it should be possible to collect better data, even if they do not cover the entire state, although careful sampling is desirable if comparisons are to be meaningful.

It would be useful, for example, to know whether the organization of health committees in legislatures matters in any way. Some states, for example, have relatively more centrally organized health committees, while others are more fragmented. That organization should matter, but it is not clear how. Similarly, it would be useful to know something about the organization of governors' offices in health care. For example, does the governor have a person in his or her cabinet that is responsible for health care, and if so, what are his or her educational characteristics? Is it a health person, or a legislative person, etc.? A number of questions like this are answerable and doing so would help bridge the large n—small n problem in state politics research. Better data collection will result in better analysis.

Race and Ethnicity in Health Care Research

We contend that racial and ethnic differences in access to care are extremely important, but not particularly thoroughly researched. As noted above, there are data collection problems in this area, but they are not insurmountable and clarifying differences helps address key questions about politics, as well as having the added advantage of providing useful information about public policy. Analyzing differences in access to care, types of care provided (e.g., variations in access to some procedures), and the like will require collection of more detailed data. Some of these data are available in microdata collections, such as the various health insurance surveys that have existed for years. Individual-level data can, of course, be analyzed and state-level characteristics can be ascribed to those individuals. Analyzing state-level data may require pooling data across states to provide aggregated state-years along the lines of Erikson, Wright, and McIver (1993) with their measure of state-level ideology. Expanding data available to study race and ethnicity in health services could also be used to develop better understanding of how health organizations operate. For example, collecting data on the racial and ethnic makeup of legislative committees would help determine whether representation affects access to health care services. Further, if suitable data are available across racial and ethnic groups, it would be possible to assess how different out-groups fare according to their representation. For example, does better representation for African American citizens change their access to health services, and if it does, does it also help, for example, Hispanic citizens, or does each population minority have to secure their own representation to gain full access to coverage?

Challenges to Federal Supremacy in Health Care

The attempts by some Republican attorneys general to challenge national government rights to enact legislation that increases health coverage via increased Medicaid coverage presents an opportunity for additional policy diffusion-style research. This is interesting in a way, because it constitutes an attempt to reduce state government policy activity versus other attempts to broaden policy.

The theoretical question of most interest in this has to do with rights in a federal system. However, it is complicated by largely party-driven differences. Democrats, supporters of the health bill, argued for the case being thrown out on the grounds that there is no harm done to the states by the bill. The opponents—mainly Republicans and some small business interests—claim that the bill requires that they purchase something they may not want, in this case health care. With the Roberts Court's decision in *NFIB v. Sebelius* (2012) the issue remains, as states and the national government continue to spar over their roles in determining which will prevail in determining the scope of insurance coverage among the public.

Can Medicaid and Other Existing Programs be Expanded to Improve Coverage?

This is again a practical question, but it is one that may prove important, especially if the national health policy is somehow weakened. Some states favor expanded coverage as promised by the federal legislation, others oppose it. Although there is a long history of research on Medicaid, this can be extended to assess what does and does not work with an eye to health policy design in the states. In addition, room remains for more theoretical work on Medicaid, studying various effects of organization, service delivery systems, and the like.

One area that deserves exploration in a nation contemplating serious health care reform has to do with the possibility of federalizing Medicaid. Sparer (2009) argues that Medicaid represents the logical program to extend to gain universal coverage across the nation. Medicaid programs vary markedly across the states, as is well developed in existing research (e.g., Hanson, 1984; Barrilleaux and Miller, 1988; Schneider, 1988; Grogan, 1993), and states have strong preferences about program design. However, as the battle over state rights to engage in health reform makes clear, states are likewise reluctant to pay for Medicaid. One line of research might focus on the possibility of state acceptance of federal government adoption of Medicaid. This could proceed in a few ways, none ideal. One approach is through surveys of citizens and elites, which would prove costly.

To conclude, health care is an interesting area for study for a number of reasons. At present, the short-term interest generated by the 2010 health reform act promises a good bit of work on issues of state versus federal government power, on specific health reform issues like whether a particular treatment is more or less effective than another, whether state variations in particular services matter financially or in health outcomes, and the like. Also, the emerging interest in diet and nutrition, and the beginnings of understanding of how those are linked to income, location, and behavior present fertile ground for additional research. Further research on state-level organizations, including health care governance institutions, is also needed to improve the quality of research on state health politics and policy. Also it seems reasonable to expect that existing political and policy solutions—like the health reform bill, current levels of service for particular groups, and the like—will continue to be dynamic and provide fertile ground for research.

Notes

1. Officially, the Patient Protection and Affordable Health Care Act (PPACA) and related Health Care and Education Reconciliation Act of 2010, also known as "Obamacare."

References

Aaron, Henry and S. M. Butler. 2008. "A Federalist Approach to Health Reform: The Worst Way, Except for All the Others." *Health Affairs 27* (3, Summer): 725–735.

Altman, D. E. and D. H. Morgan. 1983. "The Role of State and Local Government in Health." *Health Affairs 3* (Winter): 7–31.

Barrilleaux, C. and P. R. Brace. 2007. "Notes from the Laboratories of Democracy: State Government Enactments of Market- and State-Based Health Insurance Reforms in the 1990s." *Journal of Health Politics, Policy and Law 32* (4): 655–683.

Barrilleaux, C. and M. E. Miller. 1988. "The Political Economy of Medicaid." *American Political Science Review 82*(4): 1089–1107.

Barrilleaux, C. and M. E. Miller. 1992. "Decisions Without Consequences: Cost Control and Access in State Medicaid Programs." *Journal of Health Politics, Policy and Law 17* (1): 97–118.

Barrilleaux, C., G. Sanchez, R. Preuhs and R. Block. 2010. "Race, Ethnicity and Access to State Health Services." Presented at the 2010 meetings of the Southern Political Science Association, New Orleans, LA, January 8.

Barrilleaux, C. 2013. "A Little Bit of Need, a Lot of Politics: Governors' Medicaid Expansion Decisions." Presented at the 13th State Politics and Policy Meeting, Iowa City, IA, June1.

Basic Risk Factor Surveillance System (BRFSS). 2010. Centers for Disease Control, National Center for Chronic Disease Prevention and Health Promotion. <http://www.cdc.gov/BRFSS/> (accessed June 17, 2013).

Bernick, E. M. and N. Myers. 2008. "Treatment or Placebo: Are State Programs Decreasing the Proportion of Uninsured?" *Policy Studies Journal 36* (3): 367–384.

Bowers, M. R., J. E. Swan, and W. F. Koehler. 1994. "What Attributes Determine Quality and Satisfaction with Health Care Delivery?" *Health Care Management Review 19*: 44–55.

Brown, L. and M. Sparer. 2003. "Poor Program's Progress: The Unanticipated Politics of Medicaid Policy." *Health Affairs 22* (1): 31–44.

Carrasquillo, D., U. Himmelstein, S. Woolhandler and D. Bor. 1999. "Going Bare: Trends in Health Insurance Coverage, 1989 through 1996." *American Journal of Public Health 89* (1): 36–42.

Corrigan, J. and D. McNeill. 2009. "Building Organizational Capacity: A Cornerstone of Health System Reform." *Health Affairs 27* (2): w205–w215 <http://content.healthaffairs.org/cgi/content/full/28/2/w205> (accessed June 17, 2013).

Erikson, R., G. Wright, Jr, and J. McIver. 1993. *Statehouse Democracy*.New York: Cambridge University Press.

Esterling, K. 2008. "Does the Federal Government Learn from the States? Medicaid and the Limits of Expertise in the Intergovernmental Lobby." *Publius 39 (1)*: 1–31.

Fox, J. and J. Iglehart (eds). 1994. *Five States that Could Not Wait: Lessons for Health Reform from Florida, Hawaii, Minnesota, Oregon and Vermont*. Cambridge, MA: Blackwell.

Gray, Virginia and David Lowery. 1996. *The Population Ecology of Interest Representation: Lobbying Communities in the American States*. Ann Arbor, MI: University of Michigan Press.

Gray, Virginia, David Lowery, and Erik K. Godwin. 2007a. "Public Preferences and Organized Interests in Health Policy: State Pharmacy Assistance Programs as Innovations." *Journal of Health Politics, Policy and Law* 32 (1): 89–129.

Gray, Virginia, David Lowery, and Erik K. Godwin. 2007b. "The Political Management of Managed Care: Explaining Variations in State Health Maintenance Organization Regulations." *Journal of Health Politics, Policy and Law* 32 (3):457–495.

Gray, V., D. Lowery, J. Monogan, and E. K. Godwin. 2010. "Incrementing Toward Nowhere: Universal Health Care Coverage in the States." *Publius 40* (1): 82–113.

Greer, S. and P. D. Jacobson. 2010. "Health Reform and Federalism." *Journal of Health Politics, Policy and Law 35* (2):203–226.

Grogan, C. 1993. "Political?Economic Factors Influencing State Medicaid Policy." *Political Research Quarterly 46* (1): 5–25.

Grogan, C. and E. M. Patashnik. 2003. "Between Welfare Medicine and Mainstream Entitlement: Medicaid at the Political Crossroads." *Journal of Health Politics, Policy and Law 28* (5): 821–858.

Hackey, R. 1998. *Rethinking Health Care Policy: The New Politics of State Regulation.* Washington: Georgetown.

Hanson, R. L. 1984. "Medicaid and the Politics of Redistribution." *American Journal of Political Science 28*: 313–339.

Holahan, J. and J. W. Cohen. 1986. *Medicaid: The Trade-Off Between Cost Containment and Access to Care.* Washington, DC: Urban Institute.

Holahan, J. and I. Headen. 2010. *Medicaid Coverage and Spending in Health Reform: National and State-by-State Results for Adults at or Below 133 percent Poverty.* Washington, DC: Urban Institute.

Kail, Ben, Jill Quadagno, and Marc Dixon. 2009. "Can States Lead the Way to Universal Coverage? The Effect of Health Care Reform on the Uninsured." *Social Science Quarterly 90* (5): 1–20.

Kaiser Family Foundation. 2010. State Health Facts. <http://www.kff.org/statepolicy/index.cfm> (accessed June 17, 2013).

Kile. B. 2005. "Networks, Interest Groups, and the Diffusion of State Policy." Doctoral Dissertation, Florida State University, March 29.

Karch, A. 2007. *Democratic Laboratories: Policy Diffusion among the American States.* Ann Arbor, MI.

Kazee, Nicole. 2006. "Wal-Mart Welfare: Low Wage Firms and American Anti-Poverty Policy." Paper presented at the annual meeting of the The Midwest Political Science Association, Palmer House Hilton, Chicago, IL, April 20.

Kelly, N. J. 2009. *The Politics of Income Inequality in the United States.* New York: Cambridge University Press.

Kousser, T. 2002. "The Politics of Discretionary Medicaid Spending, 1980–1993." *Journal of Health Politics, Policy and Law 27*(4): 639–671.

Leyden, K. 2003. "The Importance of Walkable Neighborhoods." *American Journal of Public Health 93* (9): 1546–1551.

Lindblom, C. 1959. "The Science of 'Muddling Through.'" *Public Administration Review 19* (2, Spring): 79–88.

Miller, Edward A. 2005. "State Health Policy Making Determinants, Theory and Methods: A Synthesis." *Social Science and Medicine 61*: 2636–2657.

Morone, J. and L. Jacobs (eds). 2005. *Healthy, Wealthy, and Fair: Health Care and the Good Society*. New York: Oxford University Press.

National Association of Health Data Organizations. 2010. <http://www.nahdo.org/Home/tabid/36/Default.aspx>.

National Survey of America's Families (NSAF). 1997, 1999, 2002. Urban Institute. Available free online at the Inter-University Consortium for Political and Social Research <http://www.icpsr.umich.edu/icpsrweb/ICPSR/series/00216#summary> (accessed June 17, 2013), study 4582.

New State Ice Company v. Liebman. 1932. 285 US 262 vol. 285.

Overman, E. S. and A. G. Cahill. 1994. "Information, Market Government, and Health Policy: A Study of Health Data Organizations in the States." *Journal of Policy Analysis and Management 13* (4): 435–453.

Peterson, M. 2001. "Health Politics in a Federal System." *Journal of Health Politics, Policy and Law 26* (6): 1217–1222.

Peterson, P. 1995. *The Price of Federalism*. Washington, DC: Brookings.

Schneider, S. 1988. "Intergovernmental Influences on State Medicaid Programs." *Public Administration Review 48* (July/August): 756–763.

Schneider, S. 1989. "Governors and Health Care Policy." *Policy Studies Journal 17* (4, Summer): 809–826.

Schneider, S., W. Jacoby, and J. D. Coggburn. 1997. "The Structure of Bureaucratic Decisions in the American States." *Public Administration Review 57* (May/June): 240–249.

Sparer, M. 1999. "Myths and Misunderstandings: Health Policy, the Devolution Revolution, and the Push for Privatization." *American Behavioral Scientist 43*: 138–154.

Sparer, M. 2009. "Medicaid and the U.S. Path to National Health Insurance." *New England Journal of Medicine 360*: 323–325.

Stream, C. C. 1999. "Health Reform in the States: A Model of Small-Group Health Insurance Market Reforms." *Political Research Quarterly 52* (3): 499–525.

Stream, C. C. and N. Myers. 2010. "Risky Business: Effectiveness of State Market-Based Health Insurance Programs." *Journal of Health Politics, Policy and Law 35* (1): 29–48.

Supreme Court of the United States. 2012. "*National Federation of Independent Business, et al. v. Sebelius, Secretary of Health and Human Services of the United States, et al.*" No. 11–393.

Tallon, Jr J. R. and R. P. Nathan. 1992. "A Federal/State Partnership for Health System Reform." *Health Affairs 11* (1, Winter): 8–15.

US Central Intelligence Agency (CIA). 2013. World Factbook. Washington, DC: US Government Printing Office, <https://www.cia.gov/library/publications/the-world-factbook/rankorder/ 2102rank.html> (accessed July 8, 2013).

CHAPTER 31

....

CRIMINAL JUSTICE POLICY

....

GARRICK L. PERCIVAL

OVER the past three decades criminal justice policy has become one of the most salient issues in American domestic politics. This chapter reviews the emerging body of knowledge in criminal justice policy in the American states and outlines a research agenda that will guide state researchers working to advance our understanding of this vitally important policy domain.

In recent years, scholars have documented two clear trends in contemporary U.S. criminal justice policy. The first is that the criminal justice system has become at once more punitive and expansive in nature, reaching deep into American life. The second is that punishment emanating from the criminal justice system is not randomly distributed; rather, it is racially biased, disproportionately targeting racial and ethnic minorities and the urban poor. With these trends in mind, this chapter is organized around two broad questions about the politics of criminal justice policy in the American states. The first is what political forces cause governments to use more punitive forms of crime control? The second is how do political forces contribute to the disproportionate level of punishment imposed on racial and ethnic minority groups? In devoting attention to these questions, state and local government researchers have the opportunity to make significant and lasting contributions by moving the field to a more synthesized and theoretically shaped understanding of criminal justice policy in the U.S. states.

The government's capacity to take away one's liberty through imprisonment represents the height of state power. It is not surprising then that the first question organizing this chapter—what causes governments to use more coercive forms of crime control—has motivated a long line of inquiry across the social sciences (Chambliss, 1994; Tonry, 1995, 2009; Beckett, 1997; Beckett and Western, 2001; Garland, 2001; Gest, 2001; Greenberg and West, 2001; Jacobs and Carmichael, 2001; Wacquant, 2002; Yates and Fording, 2005; Simon, 2007). Research published over the past 20 years has increasingly found that political forces serve as powerful explanatory variables behind the country's reliance on more coercive criminal justice instruments. The extant literature on the politics of criminal justice can be divided into two strands separated most centrally by researchers' choices over how to conceptualize the American criminal justice system. The first strand includes many polemic studies that treat the U.S. criminal justice system as a comprehensive whole (Beckett, 1997; Garland, 2001; Gottschalk, 2006; Simon, 2007). These studies have been instrumental in advancing our understanding of the nature of political forces behind the overall rise in American punishment. However, in treating the American penal system as a comprehensive unit, this work overlooks the fact that the bulk of U.S. criminal justice policy results from the practices and processes of 50 different criminal justice systems at the sub-national level. This research often fails to adequately address reasons behind the significant variation in punishment practices found across the states and why some state governments use more coercive instruments of social control than others.

The second strand of research does just the opposite, conceptualizing criminal justice policy as a product of the decisions and processes connected to unique criminal justice systems at the sub-national level. Much of this work has been quantitative in nature using the 50 states in cross-sectional or time-series analyses, focused most intently on explaining variation in states' propensities to use more punitive forms of crime control (particularly states' use of imprisonment). However, this work seems to have run into a bit of an intellectual cul-de-sac. As will be discussed, what is needed are efforts that draw on both strands of literature to build a more synthesized theoretically shaped understanding of state criminal justice policy-making, asking what drives governments to punish, and how these choices contribute (or don't contribute) to the overall growth in punishment. This should involve investigating the *political forces and processes* that contribute to criminal justice actors' different understandings of crime and criminal activity and how variation in the meaning of crime within each state affects states' choices about the design and enforcement of punitive crime control policies. As part of this effort, future research also needs to include an expanded conceptualization of punishment than has been used thus far, investigate how punishment accumulates as an individual moves through different stages of the criminal justice system, and consider more carefully how national and state contextual forces operating across both space and time shape criminal justice outputs.

The unequal distribution of punishment imposed on racial and ethnic minorities is one of the most underreported and understudied social problems in post-civil-rights America. As will be discussed here, future research efforts should be focused on explaining a great paradox associated with race and the contemporary criminal justice system: in the post-civil-rights era the criminal justice system is ostensibly "colorblind," yet the rate at which African Americans and Latinos are under custodial control (relative to whites) continues to dramatically increase. Through theoretically grounded, research scholars need to investigate the casual mechanisms behind this largely silent civil rights crisis, as well as its social and political consequences.

What Causes Governments to use Punitive Mechanisms of Crime Control?

When viewing the U.S. criminal justice system as a whole, the past generation is a period best marked by the decline in offender rehabilitation efforts and the unprecedented rise in the use of punishment as the primary policy instrument used to combat crime (Chambliss, 1994; Tonry, 1995, 2009; Beckett, 1997; Garland, 2001; Gest, 2001; Wacquant, 2002; Simon, 2007). For much of the twentieth century the rate at which U.S. citizens were confined in federal, state, and local prisons and jails remained remarkably stable, varying slightly around a rate of about one hundred persons incarcerated per 100,000 population from the 1920s through the mid-to-late 1970s (Western, 2006). Yet over the next 30 years the U.S. penal population exploded, increasing nearly sevenfold from a total prison population of approximately 300,000 in 1970, to nearly 2.5 million in 2008. If the United States would hope to return the rate of incarceration in 1970, approximately *four out of five* people currently behind bars would have to be released today (Alexander, 2010). The U.S. now incarcerates its citizens at a rate higher than any other country in the world. The growth in the prison population has understandably received the bulk of attention, but research has also shown that the entire U.S. criminal justice apparatus has expanded and got harsher. Between 1980 and 2008 the total number of people under criminal justice supervision, which includes not only those incarcerated but those on probation and parole, increased from two to seven million. On any given day, one in 31 Americans are in prison, on probation, or parole (Pew Center on the States, 2009).

Over the years, an accumulating body of evidence has improved our ability to understand what has transpired. Shifts towards order-maintenance police strategies (Fagan and Davies, 2000), along with federal drug laws and free-flowing federal dollars sent to state and local law enforcement agencies helped propel the drug war and dramatically increased one's probability of entering the criminal justice system as a result of drug possession or other vagrancy violations. Drug offenses account for two-thirds of the rise in federal prison population and more than half of the rise in state prison population between 1985 and 2000 (Mauer, 2006). Dramatic shifts in criminal sentencing have also taken place. Laws that allow more juveniles to be tried as adults, laws that expand the number of offenses qualifying for the death penalty, and laws that replaced indeterminant sentencing structures with harsher determinant sentencing laws that impose 5-, 10-, 20-, or 30-year sentences (or lifetime sentences without the possibility of parole) for drug possession and firearms offenses have all been adopted.

Changes at the "back end" of the criminal justice system have also made it much more difficult for people with criminal records to exit the system. For example, the parole system has largely shifted from its original goal of aiding offenders' transitions back into community life, to a system based almost exclusively on surveillance (Petersilia, 2003). This has contributed to a high rate of recidivism as parolees get returned to prison in large numbers because of technical violations (Petersilia, 2003). Parole practices have been altered so dramatically in many jurisdictions that nationally parole violators comprise 35 percent of the prison admissions, up from only 1 percent in 1980 (Travis, 2005). Collectively these policies have not only increased an individual's chance of being imprisoned upon arrest, but once a person becomes ensnared in the system, it is more difficult than ever to leave (Mauer, 1999; Zimring, Hawkins, and Kamin 2001; Travis, 2005).

As Michael Tonry explains in his 2004 book *Thinking about Crime: Sense and Sensibility in American Penal Culture*, "governments decide how much punishment they want and these decisions arc in no simple way related to crime rates" (2004, 14). It is the premise that criminal justice governance and decisions about whether to use more or less coercive tools of crime control have little direct connection with actual crime rates that serves as a central component to the study of criminal justice politics and policy.

We know this in part because of empirical work coming out of criminology and sociology, which indicates that the reliance on coercive crime policies has been mostly independent of the actual crime rates and the use of coercive tools persists despite little evidence they have substantially reduced crime (Blumstein and Beck, 1999). Running counter to the public's opinion on crime, which almost always believes crime is on the rise (Gilliam and Iyengar, 2000; Roberts et al. 2002), crime rates in every state and just about every city in the U.S. have been on the decline since the early 1990s (Tonry, 2004). And with the veracity with which supporters of "get-tough" policy solutions advocated their policy positions through much of the hyper-punitive era of the 1980s and 1990s (see Wilson, 1983, 1990, 1994), it is natural to surmise that the long and precipitous drop in crime resulted from a greater reliance on imprisonment, with its espoused deterrence and incapacitation effects, zero-tolerance policing strategies, or more stringent parole practices. Nationally however, crime rates continued upward in the late 1980s even as the rate of imprisonment increased at one of its steepest rates in the "get-tough" era (Alexander, 2010). At the sub-national level, states and localities that largely avoided steep increases in imprisonment rates, zero-tolerance policing strategies, and stringent mandatory sentencing structures like "three strikes and you're out" laws witnessed similar reductions in crime as those states that *did* adopt such policies (Tonry, 2004).

Studies of stringent sentencing policies show little evidence that they serve as a deterrent to criminal activity (Carlson, 1982; Loftin, Heumann, and McDowall, 1983; Stolzenberg and D'Alessio, 1997). Alfred Blumstein, one of the leading researchers on crime control in the United States has noted that for many people, especially those in decimated urban ghettos with few viable legitimate economic opportunities, deterrence-based policies have little logic afforded them. Blumstein (1994) notes:

> However hard it is for rational folks to conceive it, there are some people who simply do not respond when a threat is presented to them.... For people who see no attractive option in the legitimate economy, and who are doubtful that they will live another ten years in any event, the threat of extended stay is likely to be far less threatening than it would be to a well-employed person with a family.

Other research has examined the effects of incapacitation on crime. Methodological approaches have differed, but the overall picture is that the effect of mass incarceration on the decline in crime is quite small. Bruce Western, in a methodologically rigorous examination of incarceration's effect on crime rates, estimated that "roughly nine-tenths of the decline in serious crime through the 1990s would have happened even without the prison boom" (2006, 185). At the back end of the system, studies indicate that more stringent parole supervision has no real impact on whether parolees are more likely to commit new crimes (Solomon, Kachnowski, and Bhati, 2005), suggesting that heightened parole surveillance has had no discernable impact on crime rates. Any argument that the adoption of harsh and coercive policy instruments is explained by their proven effectiveness in the evaluative research literature is misplaced.

The development of politically driven theoretical rationales of punishment have often run on two parallel tracks as researchers have come to focus on different research questions and different units, reflecting the different ways the U.S. criminal justice system has been conceptualized in the literature. Researchers who treat the American penal system as a comprehensive whole have focused on how political forces explain broad trends and changes in American criminal justice policy over time (Tonry, 1995, 2004; Beckett, 1997; Garland, 2001; Simon, 2007). But running on a parallel track has been another excellent body of research focused not so much on the rise in American punishment but on explaining variation in punishment practices (primarily measured through state imprisonment rates) at the sub-national level (Taggert and Winn, 1993; Chambliss, 1994; Meier, 1994; Marvell and Moody, 1996; Ouiment and Tremblay, 1996; Arvanites and Asher, 1998; Beckett and Western, 2001; Greenberg and West, 2001; Jacobs and Carmichael, 2001; Yates and Fording, 2005). Scholarship dating back to Stuart Scheingold's *Politics of Street Crime* (1984), in addition to more recent work by Vanessa Barker (2009), Lisa Miller (2008), and a host of quantitative 50-state studies published over the past decade, illustrate that if we examine criminal justice policy using a sub-national unit of analysis, the United States has neither a single nor coherent punishment policy. State governments tackle the crime problem quite differently from one another, with some contributing significantly to the rapid rise in imprisonment, while others have quietly confounded the overall trend by placing emphasis on community corrections and other alternatives to incarceration. Even within states, the use of punitive sanctions has been shown to vary as the local-level governments respond to local political forces (Percival, 2010).

For scholars taking a comprehensive view, theories used to explain the reliance on punitive approaches have proven to be wide-ranging. Katherine Beckett (1997) views the rise in American punishment as a function of partisan politics and changes in the political construction of crime. She documents how Republican-fueled partisan politics in the civil rights era framed criminal deviancy as a problem resulting from bad choices among an inherently dangerous (largely black) criminal class, which provided the causal logic and rationale for policies designed to strengthen government's control over criminal deviancy and its authority to punish (also see Davey, 1998; Weaver, 2007; Murakawa, 2008).

For others like Loic Wacquant (2002), Michelle Alexander (2010), and Douglas Massey (2007), the rise in punitive sanctions is largely based on social conflict and racial power. Wacquant (2002), for example, places the rise in mass imprisonment as only the most recent in a long line of "peculiar" institutions—including slavery, Jim Crow, and urban ghettoization—all designed to target poor blacks and maintain a racial caste system and white privilege. As each institution became weakened under its own weight, it was replaced by the next institution of racial control but refined to fit that day's political context and sensibilities. As slavery collapsed, it was replaced by Jim Crow segregation. With millions of blacks moving north to escape Jim Crow in the 1920s as part of the Great Migration, urban ghettos and housing discrimination kept blacks in a subordinate position. Following the end of Jim Crow, and as deindustrialization in the 1960s and 1970s made black labor less useful, the wars on crime and drugs began filling American prisons with poor black Americans, serving the very same function—only in different form—these previous institutions of racial power had in the past (Wacquant, 2002).

For David Garland (2001) problems associated with "late modernity" are viewed as the primary causal mechanism. For Garland, punitive sanctions serve as an "expressive" function for government, allowing lawmakers to show the public that something is being done about crime. Punitive crime policies are more about winning elections and rebuilding trust between citizens and their government than actually solving crime. In a similar vein, Jonathan Simon (2007) traces decades of American history and views modern crime policy as a function of the failures of the New Deal era. Crime serves as a totemic political symbol such that governments metaphorically "govern through crime."

Maria Gottschalk's (2006) *Prison and the Gallows* employs an American political development approach. In tracing over two centuries of American penal policy, Gottschalk argues in part that the structures and ideologies behind harsh contemporary penal policies have deep historical roots. Public anxieties connected to prostitution, alcohol, bootleggers, pornography, and gangsters have all ebbed and flowed over time, but these short-lived periods of heightened anxiety left behind a public more willing to accept morality-driven politics and ever- stronger law enforcement institutions.

Political theories of state-level punishment have been placed under a variety of different rubrics, but here they are divided into five broad categories. The first considered is conflict (or underclass) theory, which is derived from neo-Marxist and labeling theories of social control. Conflict theory directs our attention to the social ordering in society and political elites' attempts at maintaining social, political, and economic control. The central argument is that as the proportion of disfavored groups—typically racial minorities and the poor—grows in a given context, or as the gap between the haves and have-nots increases, political and economic elites see this as a threat and subsequently target the underclass for criminal sanctions as a way to control social unrest (Rusche and Kirchheimer, 1968). As Richard Quinney (1970, 17) noted long ago:By formulating criminal law (including legislative statutes, administrative rulings, and judicial decisions, some segments of society protect and perpetuate their own interests... It follows that the greater the conflict in interests between segments of society, the greater the probability that the power segments will formulate criminal definitions.

Empirical support for conflict theory is found in a variety of state-level studies. Greenberg and West (2001) find evidence that the percentage of blacks in a state (but not Latinos) is associated with higher state imprisonment rates. Similar evidence is found by Smith (2004). Other measures of social conflict, such as a state's unemployment or poverty rate, have only mixed support in the literature. Taggert and Winn (1993) show a link between poverty and state imprisonment rates, but more comprehensive political models using time-series analysis find state poverty rates have little or no impact on incarceration (Smith, 2004). Among variables used to test conflict/ underclass theory in the state politics literature, it is race (specifically the presence of African Americans within a state) that appears to have the most robust effects.

Public opinion, partisan, and electoral cycle effects provide a second, third, and fourth set of theoretical predictors of state-level punitiveness. The public opinion–crime policy linkage paints a "democracy-at-work" thesis, which posits that if voters send clear signals about wanting to deal harshly with criminals, more punitive policy will ensue as state lawmakers seek to be responsive to public demands, increasing their chances at reelection (Roberts and Stalans, 1997; Zimring and Johnson, 2006). It is helpful to differentiate between citizens' fear of crime and citizens' broader ideological orientations that structure attitudes about crime and punishment more generally (Brace et al., 2002). With the former, it is argued that growth in real crime rates (see LaFree, 2002), coupled with violence-led media imagery (Gilliam and Iyengar, 2000), has led to a greater sense of vulnerability, a greater fear of crime, and more punitive attitudes (Gest, 2001). The latter places an emphasis on state citizens' broad ideological orientations. It is hypothesized that citizens with conservative ideological orientations—those more likely to place blame for crime on the individual—will be more supportive of punitive crime policy responses.

The partisan thesis is largely generated from research documenting the Republican Party's Southern Strategy and its crime policy progeny after the 1960s. The expectation is that Republican-controlled governments will be more likely to pursue retributive and deterrence-based law-and-order positions in order to appeal to working-class white voters that would not otherwise benefit from Republican economic policies. In fact, some argue that getting "tough-on-crime" policies serves as an expressive act (much of it coded language for overt racial animus) that maximizes Republicans' electoral appeal among working-class white voters (see Beckett and Sasson, 2004).

With electoral cycle effects, the primary argument is that lawmakers, irrespective of their political party, will receive electoral benefits from tough-on-crime rhetoric and punitive policy stances (Kaminer, 1995; Windlesham, 1998; Gest, 2001). The theory posits that lawmakers, and in particular executives, will reap benefits from taking clear (and more punitive) crime positions during an election season. These incentives are hypothesized to generate a perpetual cycle of punitive crime policies as lawmakers adopt more stringent sentencing policies as an election becomes nearer.

State-level empirical tests of public opinion, partisan, and electoral cycle effects have been wide and varied. A number of studies find a relationship between broad measures of public opinion (political ideology) and imprisonment rates, with more conservative ideological orientations linked to higher state incarceration rates (Greenberg and West, 2001; Jacobs and Carmichael, 2001; Yates and Fording, 2005). In a 50-state pooled analysis using data from three Census years, Greenberg and West (2001) found no evidence that the partisan control of the executive affects state imprisonment patterns; however, other studies did show a link between greater Republican strength and higher imprisonment rates (Jacobs and Helms, 1996; Beckett and Western, 2001; Smith, 2004; Yates and Fording, 2005). Jacobs and Carmichael (2001) found that both Republican and state conservative ideology are positively associated with imprisonment rates, lending evidence that the effect of Republican strength on imprisonment is not just an underlying function of state conservatism. Independent of partisanship and public opinion, Smith (2004) finds evidence that state imprisonment patterns are influenced by electoral cycles. All else being equal, state imprisonment rates increase in those years where gubernatorial contests draw closer in time.

A last category of research has examined states' levels of punitiveness as a function of criminal sentencing policies. Many analysts view the rise in imprisonment as being directly tied to states' decisions to shift from indeterminant to determinant sentencing structures. Indeterminant sentencing structures, widely used until the late 1970s, gave judges and parole boards significant power to determine an offender's length of sentence. Judges had wide discretion to decide who went to prison and to set maximum and sometimes minimum terms. Decisions (and hence the final determinant of the actual amount of time an offender served) about prison release were placed in the hands of a parole board (Tonry, 1997). However judges and parole boards were commonly accused of being too lenient on criminals or racially biased in their decision making, and thus determinant sentencing laws (DSLs) were designed to take away judge and parole board discretion by instituting rigid sentencing guidelines using a two-axis grid system. With DSLs, individual sentencing decisions are based on the severity of the offense committed and a person's prior criminal record.

Some have argued that DSLs were never intended to increase a state's prison populations, but merely to act as a deterrent. But, if the motivation behind DSLs was incapacitation and opposition to "lenient" sentences, as some have argued (see Bennett, DiIulio, and Walters, 1996), we might expect them to have significant consequences on state imprisonment rates. A number of studies in recent years have tested the effects of state sentencing laws on prison admission and incarceration rates. Some of this work has been hampered by the use of single-point cross-sectional designs that make it difficult to make causal inferences about the dynamics of change in imprisonment rates (see Hewitt and Clear, 1983; Casper and Brereton, 1984; Bowers and Waltman, 1993; Sorensen and Stemen, 2002). To overcome this, Marvall and Moody (1996) employed a longitudinal design and found that DSLs had little impact on prison admission rates in those states adopting them. Using data from 1975 to 1998, Nicholson-Crotty (2004) found that mandatory sentencing policies do impact state imprisonment levels but the direction and magnitude of the effect is dependent on whether sentencing guidelines are tied to state corrections resources. States with mandatory sentencing laws that link sentencing decisions to state corrections resources actually saw their admissions decline between 1975 and 1998, while those that did not saw their prison rates increase. Nicholson-Crotty's research illustrates powerfully that not all mandatory sentencing regimes are the same and that nuanced differences in state sentencing structures can have important effects on imprisonment patterns at the sub-national level.

WHAT POLITICAL FORCES CAUSE GOVERNMENTS TO PUNISH? A RESEARCH AGENDA

As can be seen from the review above, researchers have made significant strides in our knowledge of the politics of punishment. Yet important shortcomings remain. The first is that the literature on the topic remains disjointed as researchers undertake analysis using different units of analysis and different conceptualizations of the U.S. criminal justice system. Taken as a whole, the U.S. has become more punitive, but state governments, that level of government where the bulk of criminal justice policymaking is carried out, are not equally punitive. State punishment choices vary as a function of a variety of political and policy found within each state.

What we need then is to integrate, synthesize, and expand on these research efforts. This can be done in a couple of ways. The first step is for state researchers to investigate the *political processes* by which state lawmakers, administrators, and criminal justice professionals construct the meaning of crime. That is, researchers should be focusing on extending our knowledge about how criminal justice policy actors come to understand what causes crime and factors that contribute to how they draw the line between criminal and noncriminal behavior. These political meanings should influence states' choices over what principles (retribution, incapacitation, rehabilitation) and policy instruments (incarceration or community corrections) to adopt in order to cope with crime. Significantly, if we draw on the findings of the existing literature, these choices should be shaped by state and national contextual forces over time. And as previous efforts have acknowledged, these choices are likely to be irrespective of what criminologists believe are the causes and solutions to crime (Scheingold, 1998; Tonry, 2004). For state politics researchers, focusing on the meaning of crime and how different meanings guide state punishment choices not only provides a rich theoretical basis from which to work, but also moves the field past this artificial state/national division. A synthesized approach *encourages* scholars to focus on how politics affects criminal justice processes and to examine how punishment decisions are shaped by state and national-level forces.

Thus a significant part of this effort toward integration and synthesis will require scholars to investigate the changing nature of federal–state relationships within the criminal justice domain and take stock of how national-level decisions and national-level thinking about crime (both past and present) influences state punishment choices. As Lisa Miller documents in her 2008 book, *The Perils of Federalism*, criminal justice policy, like many other policy domains, has become increasingly federalized over the past generation, as the national government has encroached on criminal justice policy matters traditionally reserved to the states and localities. Previous scholarship has documented a multitude of ways in which the national government can diffuse preferred policies down through the states (Stone, 1997; Allen, Pettus, and Haider-Markel, 2004). But not nearly enough attention has been devoted to how policy decisions, court rulings, and political discourse found at the national level influence punishment decisions at the sub-national level and how this shapes the broader punishment trends in the criminal justice system.

An often-lodged criticism of the criminological study of the politics of crime is that it views criminal justice policy in isolation, with little thought about how criminal justice policy might be explained by existing theories of public policymaking or how criminal justice policy fits within the context of governance with other social issues (Zimring and Johnson, 2006). Here too, having an eye toward the politics of the larger federalist system and how broader political forces shape state punishment choices should help in this regard. Soss, Fording, and Schram (2008) document how broad national political debate in the neoliberal era about what it means to be a "good citizen" and whether or not the poor are best served by more aid or more discipline, shaped contemporary welfare policy and how welfare services are delivered in the federalist system. Previous research shows evidence of strong correlations between punitive state welfare policies and more punitive criminal justice outcomes (Western and Pettit, 2000; Soss, Fording, and Schram, 2008) and thus we cannot fully understand states' punitiveness without taking into account how larger political forces politics help shape it.

When examining state-level contextual effects, future research efforts must look beyond ideology and partisanship. This will likely require researchers to place a renewed emphasis on comparative case studies or ethnographic criminal justice research such as Zimring, Hawkin, and Kamin's (2001) excellent account of California's "three strikes" law. Political scientists are especially well trained to contribute to our understanding about how and why different crime policy alternatives reach the governing agenda and the role that policy entrepreneurs and interest groups play in framing public problems and devising alternative policy solutions. As the criminal justice system has expanded, a key contextual variable that needs further attention is the growing number of groups whose instrumental (and power) interests are tied to the adoption of more punitive punishment policies (for example, see Haider-Markel, 1998). These include local police forces who have seen a cash windfall from the federal government's war on drugs, to private prison firms who profit from housing more prisoners, to rural (largely white) communities who disproportionately staff prisons, to corrections unions who gain job security and higher benefits packages with growing prison populations, to telephone companies who charge exorbitant fees and reap major profits from prisoners calling home. The modern U.S. penal system is a big business that ties a variety of groups' instrumental benefits to its existence and persistence. It may be that the mix of policy actors and entrepreneurs found at the state level, with their different experiences and beliefs about the anticipated consequences of various alternatives, plays a crucial role in how lawmakers and the broader public think about crime and the extent to which more punitive policy solutions are adopted to cope with it; yet this is something we know comparatively little about (although see Miller, 2008).

A second major shortcoming of the existing literature is the narrowly tailored conception of punishment. Future efforts will require researchers to build a more comprehensive conceptualization of punishment—moving beyond imprisonment and viewing punishment as a compounding product. Once a person is in the system, punishment can beget punishment, lending to an "accumulation of punishment" imposed on individuals as they enter and move through different stages of the criminal justice system. A more synthesized and expanded account of punishment asks researchers to place greater value on the political forces and mechanisms that shape punishment decisions at the front, middle, and back ends of the criminal justice system, and examine whether there is a certain "stickiness" to how political forces shape punishment choices at different stages of the criminal justice system.

This would certainly require more attention to the political forces shaping the adoption of maintenance order policing strategies (i.e. "broken windows") and the factors that contribute to local police officials' decisions to arrest and sweep into the system those individuals deemed to contribute to neighborhood "disorder" (Fagan and Davies, 2000; Harcourt, 2001). Despite challenges to the theory of crime that underlies "broken-windows" policing (Eck and Mcguire, 2000; Taylor, 2000; Harcourt and Ludwig, 2006), it has become used by many local police departments across the U.S. (Herbert and Brown, 2006). At the back end, we need a better understanding of the politics of parole and what causes parole officials in some states to return so many prisoners to prison on minor technical violations. To what extent are these decisions influenced by parole officials' different views about retribution, individual responsibility, or perceptions about offenders' likelihood of rehabilitation or future criminal activity? To what extent are revocation decisions influenced by the degree to which a state's politics are defined by group competition? Also at the back end of the system, researchers have largely overlooked states' decisions to adopt "collateral sanctions" or "invisible punishments"—unique forms of punishment adopted by state legislatures and state bureaucratic agencies that strip ex-offenders of particular rights, privileges, and social supports of full citizenship (Travis, 2005). Sanctions that strip ex-offenders of their rights to welfare services, food stamps, public housing, educational assistance, and drivers' licenses (among others) are applied at the time of conviction and continue to create significant barriers to an ex-offender's successful transition into mainstream society long after their criminal sentence has been completed (see Clear et al., 2001; Mauer and Chesney-Lind, 2002).

DISPROPORTIONATE LEVEL OF PUNISHMENT: RACIAL AND ETHNIC MINORITY GROUPS

In the "tough-on-crime" era, the U.S. criminal justice system has produced a great paradox that directly challenges the notion of fairness and equality in a democratic system. In the post-civil-rights era there is a widespread belief in a "post-racial" or "colorblind" American political and criminal justice system (Bobo, 2001), yet on the other hand, the criminal justice system continues to disproportionately ensnare blacks and Latinos (Pettit and Western, 2004). Black and Latino Americans comprise roughly 15 percent of the U.S. population, but today, people of color comprise half the prison population in many states' correctional systems (Pew Center on the States, 2008). Whites' (particularly poor whites') rate of incarceration has increased by about 6 percent between 1980 and 2000, but the rate of incarceration for African American men has increased 26-fold over this same period (Muwakkil, 2005). African American men, incarcerated at a rate 3,161 per 100,000 in 2008, and Latino men, incarcerated at a rate of 1,200 per 100,000, are respectively six times and two times more likely be incarcerated than white men (Cooper et al., 2009). Racial inequality in punishment can be found at multiple points in the criminal justice system, as minorities are overrepresented not only among prison inmates, but arrestees, probationers, and parolees (Pew Center on the States, 2008).

It is with this paradox in mind that I turn to the second question organizing this chapter: how do political forces contribute to the disproportionate level of punishment imposed on racial and ethnic minority groups? Early research devoted to this question found that the disproportionate rate of minority incarceration resulted from higher rates of criminality among minority groups in recent decades (Blumstein, 1982, 1993; Casper and Brereton, 1984). While blacks have greater involvement in violent crimes (Tonry, 1995), studies examining trends over a longer time horizon show that this is not the primary factor at work (Western, 2006). Black criminal offenses, including black drug-use rates, have remained roughly the same (or in fact declined slightly) over the past 30 years (Pettit and Western 2004), indicating that a spike in minority criminality is not the primary cause behind the growing level of racial and inequality in the criminal justice system.

Thus, scholars turned to developing political explanations. As discussed previously, a number of studies have documented Republican efforts to attract white working-class voters using racially coded "law and order" rhetoric (Beckett, 1997; Beckett and Sasson, 2004; Murakawa, 2008). The Republicans' success in building support for punitive policy solutions, in part by priming negative racial attitudes among whites, has motivated researchers to conduct more systematic tests of the interconnections between racial attitudes and crime.

Evidence from a growing body of public opinion research has shown that race shapes a variety of attitudes and preferences that have important implications for criminal justice policy. White racism traditionally consisted of a belief in the supposed genetic inferiority of blacks to whites; however, in contemporary times it is the "black-as-criminal" negative stereotype that has become pervasive (Gilliam and Iyengar, 2000). Primed in political discourse and television news, this stereotype involves the perception that blacks are a violent underclass more prone to criminal activity (Devine and Baker, 1991; Edsall and Edsall, 1992; Peffley and Hurwitz, 2002). Significantly, studies indicate that whites who view blacks as lazy and dangerous also express higher levels of support for tough crime policies such as the death penalty and longer prison sentences, in addition to showing higher levels of opposition to preventative policies (Kinder and Mendelberg, 1995; Kinder and Sanders, 1996; Roberts and Stalans, 1997; Gilliam and Iyengar, 2000; Gilliam et al., 2002; Peffley and Hurwitz, 2002; Green, Staerkle, and Sears, 2006; Zimring and Johnson, 2006). Race has also been linked to perceptions of criminality and disorder at the neighborhood level. Quillian and Pager (2001) found that a greater presence of black men living in a neighborhood increases residents' perceptions of the seriousness of the crime problem, even after controlling for real crime rates and other factors. Others have found that the racial, ethnic, and class composition of a neighborhood is positively associated with perceptions of disorder and dangerousness in that neighborhood (Sampson and Raudenbush, 2004).

A number of important studies have sought to explain how race-centered stereotypes in public opinion research shape crime policy choices and enforcement decisions at specific stages of the criminal justice system, namely policing, criminal sentencing, and imprisonment. At the front end of the criminal justice system, racial stereotypes are shown to affect police decisions about how to concentrate their patrol efforts and who to stop, search, and arrest. Racial profiling in motorist stops has received a lot of attention in the policing literature (Davis, 1997; Harris, 1999; Barlow and Barlow, 2002; Weitzer and Tuch, 2002; Petrocelli, Piquero, and Smith, 2003), yet the greatest influence racial stereotyping has on policing comes in the context of drug enforcement efforts, in particular, through the use of traffic stops to pursue drug trafficking (see Epp, Maynard-Moody, and Haider-Markel, 2013).

In 1982, the federal government officially declared the modern War on Drugs (Alexander, 2010). Since then, federal dollars sent down to the states and localities to wage it has meant that for local police forces anti-drug enforcement efforts have taken on a much greater importance. Racial minorities have overwhelmingly become the targets of such efforts. Black drug arrest rates quadrupled between 1980 and 2000, a rate far beyond that predicted by blacks' real rate of drug use, which has remained steady over time and is comparable to whites' rate of use (Tonry, 1995; Alexander, 2010). Indeed, Mauer and King (2007) report that nearly 80 percent of state prisoners serving time for drug offenses are black or Latino.

Contrary to popular perceptions, arrests for violent crime account for only a small fraction of all arrests, and thus the bulk of police activity involves policing minor crimes, including drug crimes. Police discretion about where to patrol and how to target their resources is at its maximum in this context (Duster, 1997), leaving plenty of room for race and racial stereotypes to shape police decisions about whom to stop, search, and arrest in connection with drugs (Tonry, 1995; Riley, 1997; D'Allesio, Stewart, and Stolzenberg, 2003; Beckett, Nyrop, Pfingst, and Bowen, 2005; Provine, 2007).

Data measuring individuals' involuntary contact with law enforcement are limited, but the evidence that is available indicates that contact is very common in minority communities (Gelman, Fagan, and Kiss, 2007; Goffman, 2009). In one study of Chicago, 70 percent of black men reported being stopped by the police in the previous year (Skogan, 2006). The findings from a set of influential studies on policing of illicit drugs in Seattle indicate that negative black stereotypes affect police decisions about what type of drug to target, what neighborhoods to patrol, and who to arrest (Beckett, Nyrop, Pfingst, and Bowen, 2005; Beckett, Nyrop, and Pfingst 2006). Although researchers documented hundreds of drug transactions in certain white neighborhoods, the Seattle police were found to focus their drug enforcement efforts almost exclusively on one downtown market that had a lower incidence of drug transactions, and overwhelmingly targeted crack cocaine—that drug in Seattle most often sold by blacks.

Studies of stereotypes linking minorities to illicit drug use show how this can happen. A historical review of drug enforcement patterns indicates that as a drug (or drug use) becomes more widely associated with racial and ethnic minorities, it has the effect of driving up public perceptions of that drug's dangerousness, and builds support for racially targeted drug sweeps and punitive drug laws (Duster, 1997; Reinarman and Levine, 1997). In the modern War on Drugs, this is best exemplified by stereotypes of "crack heads," "crack whores," and "crack babies", which connect poor urban blacks to crack cocaine. It is the stereotype of crack cocaine as the drug of choice for poor urban blacks that is credited for the adoption of crack cocaine penalties that are significantly harsher than those for powder cocaine—a drug that is popularly seen as less dangerous and more likely to be used by whites (Mauer and King, 2007). Beckett, Nyrop, Pfingst, and Bowen (2005) argue that the decision to concentrate policy drug enforcement efforts in open markets and on racial minorities reflects a "racialized" view of the drug problem. Policing strategies become predicated on the idea that the drug problem is largely a problem with blacks and that crack cocaine—the drug believed to be used by blacks—is that which is most dangerous (Tonry, 1995; Reinarnman and Levine, 1997; Beckett, Nyrop, Pfingst, and Bowen, 2005).

In addition to racially shaped policing and drug enforcement, other research has examined race and racial bias in another stage of the criminal justice process—criminal sentencing. In this literature, researchers often investigate whether among otherwise like-situated offenders, minority defendants are more likely to receive a prison term or a longer prison sentence than whites (Albonetti, 1997; Steffensmeier, Ulmer, and Kramer, 1998; Bushway and Piehl, 2001). Even with the widespread adoption of sentencing guidelines, which have reduced the level of racial bias in criminal sentencing (Tonry, 1997), a significant degree of research indicates that a defendant's race and ethnicity influences sentencing outcomes (Ulmer and Kramer, 1996; Bushway and Piehl, 2001; Bontrager, Bales, and Chiricos, 2005; Johnson, 2006).

How racial stereotypes lead to racially disparate sentencing decisions has not been adequately addressed in the sentencing literature, but we do know that the likelihood of finding racial disparities in individual sentencing decisions is partly shaped by contextual factors. Modern sentencing theories posit that sentencing decisions are not only based on "legal" factors—that is, individual case or offender characteristics—but also "extra-legal" factors, which operate in subtle yet important ways (Johnson, 2006). In statistical models of state-level sentencing, extra-legal factors have included measures of judge characteristics (such as race or sex of the judge), and broader contextual characteristics such as a court's size and resources, county crime rates, public opinion, or county racial characteristics (Dixon, 1995; Britt, 2000; Helms and Jacobs, 2002; Ulmer and Johnson, 2004; Bontrager, Bales, and Chiricos, 2005).

Female judges and black judges are found to impose less stringent sentences on minority defendants, controlling for other factors (Steffensmeier, Ulmer, and Kramer, 1998; Steffensmeier and Britt, 2001). The effect of communities' racial and ethnic minority composition on individual sentencing decisions is mixed. In the racial threat tradition, it is argued that a greater proportion of minorities living in a geographic locale triggers anti-minority fear and hostility among the majority white population, who then target racial minorities in the policy process for harsh treatment (Key, 1949; Blalock, 1967). Within the context of criminal sentencing, it follows that in more racially diverse contextual environments, racial minorities will be targeted for harsher sentences. In a study of sentencing in Pennsylvania, Britt (2000) finds little evidence that the minority composition at the county level affects the minority sentencing. However Johnson (2006) found that courts' willingness to circumvent sentencing guidelines varied in part by the percentage of minorities in courts' districts. Helms and Jacobs (2002), in an analysis of 337 jurisdictions in seven states, point to the importance of localized public opinion on sentencing decisions. They found that blacks are more likely to receive longer prison sentences in more conservative political environments (as measured by the percentage vote for George H. W. Bush).

A limited body of research has also sought to explain racial disparities in state prison admissions or state incarceration rates. Using state-level data from a single year, Bridges and Crutchfield (1988) find evidence that blacks' and whites' rates of imprisonment are a function of their relative involvement in crime. Yates (1997) uses a measure of black–white incarceration disparity as his central dependent variable and comes to a similar conclusion. Testing a more explicit political model of racial imprisonment disparities, Yates and Fording (2005) find that blacks are imprisoned at higher rates in more conservative states, but this relationship is weakened as black electoral strength increases. Percival (2010) examined blacks' and Latinos' rate of prison admissions, but uses the county as the primary unit of analysis. He finds that the rate at which racial and ethnic minorities are sent to state prison is a function of racial politics and ideological politics found at the local (county) level.

A Research Agenda and Conclusions

A review of the research conducted in recent years shows a number of important advancements in our knowledge of race and criminal justice policy. First, a wide body of important research has accumulated, which documents the scope and severity of racial inequality in multiple parts of the criminal justice system. Second, with advancements in public opinion research we have a greater base of knowledge about the nexus between racial attitudes and crime policy attitudes. Third, scholars have begun to explain how race shapes criminal justice processes and outcomes at single stages of the criminal justice process.

The next logical step is to continue to advance a broader, more systematic understanding of how racial politics produces racial inequalities in the criminal justice system in an era where overt expressions of racial animus are socially unacceptable. Future research efforts need to consider how racial forces contribute to racial inequality in the criminal justice system by shaping social stratifications over time and how often implicit racial beliefs held among policy actors in different contexts interact with the expansion of the penal system and discretionary authority of criminal justice actors to produce an inequality that compounds *across* different stages of the criminal justice system.

A pursuit of a broader, more systemic understanding of racial bias in the criminal justice system can guard against what Murakawa and Beckett (2010) suggest is a too narrowly tailored view of racial discrimination in criminal justice research. As these scholars cogently argue, social science researchers' search for causal mechanisms has been limited in scope, often mimicking the development of antidiscrimination law in the post-civil-rights era. As a result of Supreme Court decisions in high profile cases like *McCleskey v. Kemp* (1987), evidence of racial inequality in the criminal justice system must go beyond merely showing racial disparities in outcomes—racial discrimination requires evidence of overt racial bias or a single actor's (such as a judge or police officer) clear intent to discriminate (Murakawa and Beckett, 2010). In both antidiscrimination law and social science research, there is too often a presumption that a racially biased action or decision needs to be somehow disaggregated from larger criminal justice processes and identified at a single point in time (Murakawa and Beckett, 2010).

In future research efforts, what is required is a prominent position and appreciation for work showing that racial forces in the context of crime manifest themselves in systemic, complex, subtle, and long-term ways. For example, in state-level research investigating racial disparities in imprisonment, a broader systemic approach to race might involve studying how racial forces have contributed to social conditions that promote criminogenic behaviors among the urban poor, rather than merely modeling the (more theoretically limited) differential black/white offending patterns, as has been done previously (see Bridges and Crutchfield, 1988). Such an account of how racial politics causes racial inequality in the criminal justice system might include a systematic examination of how institutionalized racially discriminatory policies in housing, employment, and education have contributed to a set of social conditions that trap many blacks in poor urban ghettos suffering from a confluence of social disorders that generate violence and a clear pathway for more racial minorities to enter a criminal justice system that is difficult to exit (see Massey and Denton, 1993).

In a similar vein, studies of racial bias in criminal sentencing commonly control for a defendant's prior criminal history. A defendant's priors are commonly treated as a "non-racial" variable where it is predicted that following rigid determinant sentencing guidelines, those with prior records will receive longer prison sentences. However, this practice too minimizes potentially powerful racial effects, especially if we again consider the historical nexus between minorities' lack of economic opportunity (caused by institutionalized racism) and criminal activity, or research which shows police decisions about whom to arrest is shaped by race-laden stereotypes that shape beliefs about what drugs are most dangerous (crack cocaine), or what groups (blacks) are most likely to use drugs. Researchers can show that longer criminal records on average lead to longer prison sentences, but if they do this without taking into consideration the racial antecedents that produce lengthier criminal records among racial minorities, researchers are overlooking the complex ways racial political forces generate inequalities in the system.

Finally, a judge's "focal" concerns and whether a defendant is considered by the judge to be dangerous, culpable, or amenable to treatment, is commonly viewed in the sentencing literature as a contributing factor to whether an individual receives a more or less stringent sentence (Johnson, 2006). Yet here too, if a judge's focal perceptions of a defendant's characteristics are viewed the through the prism of public opinion research on race and crime, such focal concerns are not race-neutral, but influenced by implicit racial stereotypes of blacks and ethnic minorities within the context of crime (Murakawa and Beckett, 2010).

One of the chief challenges facing researchers in this area is to continue to build theoretically sound models of how racial beliefs shape policy choice and the mechanisms by which racial forces lead to the disproportionate level of punishment placed on racial and ethnic minorities. As the emerging body of public opinion research indicates, racial forces can work in subtle, often implicit ways. It is very possible to have someone espouse principals of racial equality and racial justice in public, yet have more negative racial beliefs unconsciously and unintentionally guide their decision making (Eberhardt and Goff, 2005; Massey, 2007; Provine, 2007). Importantly, overt racial bigotry is not necessary to produce policy choices that lead to racial inequalities in the criminal justice system.

State politics scholars have already begun to make important advancements about how race can affect policy choices in a "colorblind" society. For example, Soss, Fording, and Schram's (2008) Racial Classification Model (RCM) shows that when race becomes salient in a given policy context, racial stereotypes of the target group can be used by lawmakers and implementers as a social classification tool to guide their policy choices. When race is salient in a policy domain, the extent to which racial stereotypes affect lawmakers' constructions of target groups is determined by the degree to which a racial group's reputation produces meaningful differences in characteristics relevant to the achievement of policy goals, and the prevalence of a racial group in the target population. Soss, Fording, and Schram (2008, 540) note, "when the perceived difference between [racial] groups is negligible, racial categories should provide little traction for making policy choices. As the perceived contrast grows we should expect the utility of racial information to rise and racial patterned policy choices become more likely." Significantly, race becomes a more powerful organizational and conceptual tool as the prevalence of a racial group in the target population increases (Soss, Fording, and Schram, 2008). In the context of crime, as the proportion of blacks in the target group increases, it should cue more negative black crime-related stereotypes (i.e. viewing the target group as more dangerous, less amenable to treatment, more likely to use drugs, etc.) and produce more punitive policy choices. Much more research is needed, but the RCM may well explain how police make decisions on who to arrest, how prosecutors and judges come to make decisions related to sentencing, or the propensity of parole officials to send more parolees back to prison on minor technical violations. Punitive policy choices shaped by race can compound across each of the stage of the criminal justice system, but an important feature of the RCM is that discriminatory intent and racist antipathy among public officials are not required for racial characteristics and stereotypes to guide policy choices.

As we know from the discussion above, punishment in the criminal justice system is not randomly distributed, but is concentrated both racially and spatially. In some urban (mostly black) communities there are so many residents behind bars that researchers have coined them "million dollar blocks" in reference to the high cost of imprisonment. As the size of the minority custodial population continues to grow, future research efforts also need to focus on the social and political *consequences* for racial minorities and urban communities whose primary contact with government is disciplinary in nature, mostly defined by involuntary contact with law enforcement institutions such as police station, courtroom, prison cell, or parole office (Weaver and Lerman, 2010).

In recent years, research has documented that for black high school dropouts, contact with penal institutions is far more common than joining the military or getting married (Western, 2006). The social and economic effects of entering prison have proven to be astounding—leading to lower wages and employment, poorer health outcomes, decline in marriage rates, family destabilization, and diminishing social capital (Rose and Clear, 1998; Clear, Rose, and Ryder, 2001; Geller, Garfinkel, and Western, 2006).

Researchers have just begun to document how the carceral state influences democratic citizens' relationship to government and the quality of political representation for those tied to the penal system. Most of the research in this area has been on felon disenfranchisement (McLeod, White, and Gavin, 2003; Manza and Uggen, 2006). Manza and Uggen (2006) have estimated that about 8 percent of the black voting-age population is disenfranchised today, dramatically reshaping the electorate but also elections themselves.

Weaver and Lerman (2010) examined the effects of carceral contact on individual patterns of political mobilization and civic attachment. Controlling for a multitude of factors, the authors find individuals who have come into contact with carceral institutions are less likely to participate in civic groups and elections and are less trusting of government. As noted earlier, data on involuntary contact law enforcement institutions are in short supply, but future research efforts need to continue to measure how contact with penal and law enforcement institutions shape democratic citizenship. Because states have significantly different penal regimes, the states and localities offer an excellent venue to test the effects of law enforcement contact on various aspects of democratic citizenship and civic life.

The effect of the prison boom on the quality of minority representation is also an area of research ripe for study. For statistical purposes, the U.S. Census counts prisoners in the Census block that contains the prison, rather than the neighborhood in which prisoners lived prior to their incarceration. The process of counting prisoners where they are incarcerated, coupled with the fact that a disproportionate number of state prisoners are racial and ethnic minorities, produces a twenty-first-century version of the infamous 3/5 clause (Alexander, 2010). Minorities (prisoners) with no voting rights and no political power are counted in prison for representational purposes only. The benefits that accrue from this are mostly likely to be received by rural white communities (say in the form of additional seats in the state legislature or added monetary resources) where many state prisons are located. To date there have been few systematic examinations of mass imprisonment's effects on the nature and quality of minorities' political representation along these lines.

References

Albonetti, Celesta. 1997. "Sentencing under the Federal Sentencing Guidelines: Effects of Defendant Characteristics, Guilty Pleas, Departures on Sentencing Outcomes for Drug Offenses, 1991–1992." *Law and Society Review 31*: 789–822.

Alexander, Michelle. 2010. *The New Jim Crow: Mass Incarceration in the Age of Colorblindness*. New York: The New Press.

Allen, Mahally D., Carrie Pettus, and Donald P. Haider-Markel. 2004. "Making the National Local: Specifying the Conditions of National Government Influence on State Policymaking." *State Politics and Policy Quarterly 4*: 318–344.

Arvanites, Thomas M. and Martin A. Asher. 1998. "State and County Incarceration Rates: The Direct and Indirect Effects of Race and Inequality." *American Journal of Economics and Sociology 57*: 207–222.

Barker, Vanessa. 2009. *The Politics of Punishment: How the Democratic Process Shapes How America Punishes Offenders*. New York: Oxford University Press.

Barlow, David E. and Melissa Hickman Barlow. 2002. "Racial Profiling: A Survey of African American Police Officers." *Police Quarterly 5*: 334–358.

Beckett, Katherine. 1997. *Making Crime Pay: Law and Order in Contemporary American Politics*. New York: Oxford University Press.

Beckett, Katherine and Theodore Sasson. 2004. 2nd ed. *The Politics of Injustice: Crime and Punishment in America*. Thousand Oaks, CA: Sage.

Beckett, Katherine and Bruce Western. 2001. "Governing Social Marginality: Welfare, Incarceration and the Transformation of State Policy." *Punishment and Society 3*: 43–59.

Beckett, Katherine, Kris Nyrop, and Lori Pfingst. 2006. "Race, Drugs, and Policing: Understanding Disparities in Drug Delivery Arrests." *Criminology 44*: 105–137.

Beckett, Katherine, Kris Nyrop, Lori Pfingst, and Melissa Bowen. 2005. "Drug Use, Drug Arrests, and the Question of Race: Lessons from Seattle." *Social Problems 52*: 419–441.

Bennett, W., John DiIulio, and John P. Walters. 1996. *Body Count... Moral Poverty and How to Win America's War on Crime and Drugs.* New York: Simon & Schuster.

Blalock, Hubert M. Jr. 1967. *Toward a Theory of Minority-Group Relations.* New York: John Wiley and Sons.

Blumstein, Alfred. 1982. "On Racial Disproportionality of the United States' Prison Populations." *Journal of Criminal Law and Criminology, 73*: 1259–81.

Blumstein, Alfred. 1993. "Racial Disproportionality in the U.S. Prison Population Revisited." *University of Colorado Law Review, 64*: 743–60.

Blumstein, Alfred. 1994. "Prison." In James Q. Wilson and Joan Petersilia (eds), *Crime 387–419.* San Francisco: ICS.

Blumstein, Alfred and Allen J. Beck 1999. "Population Growth in U.S. Prisons, 1980–1996." *Crime and Justice 26*: 17–61.

Bobo, Lawrence D. 2001. "Racial Attitudes and Relations at the Close of the 21st Century." In Neil J. Smelser, William J. Wilson, and Faith Mitchell (eds), *America Becoming: Racial Trends and their Consequences Vol 1.*, 264–301. Washington, DC: National Academy Press.

Bowers, David A. and Jerold L. Waltman. 1993. "Do More Conservative States Impose Harsher Felony Sentences? An Exploratory Analysis of 32 States." *Criminal Justice Review 18*: 67–70.

Bontrager, Stephanie, William Bales, and Ted Chiricos. 2005. "Race, Ethnicity, Threat and the Labeling of Convicted Felons." *Criminology 43*: 589–622.

Brace, Paul, Kellie N. Butler, Kevin Arceneaux, and Martin Johnson. 2002. "Measuring Public Opinion in the American States: An Expanded Range of Aggregated Measures, 1974–1998." *American Journal of Political Science 46*: 173–189.

Bridges, George S. and Robert Crutchfield. 1988. "Law, Social Standing and Racial Disparities in Imprisonment." *Social Forces 66*: 699–724.

Britt, Chester. 2000. "Social Context and Racial Disparities in Punishment Decisions." *Justice Quarterly 17*: 707–732.

Bushway, Shawn and Anne Piehl. 2001. "Judging Judicial Discretion: Legal Factors and Racial Discrimination in Sentencing." *Law and Society Review 35*: 733–764.

Carlson, Kenneth. 1982. *Mandatory Sentencing: The Experience of Two States.* National Institute of Justice, U.S. Department of Justice: Washington, DC: U.S. Government Printing Office.

Casper, Jonathan D. and David Brereton. 1984. "Evaluating Criminal Justice Reforms." *Law and Society Review 18*: 121–144.

Chambliss, William J. 1994. "Policing the Ghetto Underclass: The Politics of Law and Law Enforcement." *Social Forces 41*: 177–194.

Clear, Todd R., Dina R. Rose, and Judith R. Ryder. 2001. "Incarceration and the Community: The Problem of Removing and Returning Offenders." *Crime and Delinquency 47*: 335–351.

Cooper, Matthew, William J. Sabol, and Heather C. West. 2009. *Prisoners in 2008.* Washington, DC: Bureau of Justice Statistics.

D'Alessio, Stewart J. and Lisa Stolzenberg. 2003. "Race and the Probability of Arrest." *Social Forces 81*: 1381–1397.

Davey, Joseph Dillon. 1998. *The Politics of Prison Expansion: Winning Elections by Waging on Crime.* Westport, CT: Greenwood Publishing Group.

Davis, Angela J. 1997. "Race, Cops, and Traffic Stops." *University of Miami Law Review 51*: 425–443.

Devine, Patricia G. and Sara Baker. 1991. "Measurement of Racial Stereotype Subtyping." *Personality and Social Psychology Bulletin 17*: 44–50.

Dixon, Jo. 1995. "The Organizational Context of Criminal Sentencing." *American Journal of Sociology 100*: 1157–1998.

Duster, Troy. 1997. "Pattern, Purpose and Race in the Drug War." In Craig Reinararman and Harry G. Levine (eds), *Crack in America: Demon Drugs and Social Justice* 260–87. Berkeley, CA: University of California Press.

Eberhardt, Jennifer L. and Phillip A. Goff. 2005. "Seeing Race." In Christian S. Crandall and March Schaller (eds), *Social Psychology of Prejudice: Historical and Contemporary Issues* 163–83. Lawrence, KS: Lewinian Press.

Eck, John E. and Edward R. Maguire. 2000. "Have Changes in Policing Reduced Violent Crime? An Assessment of the Evidence." In Alfred Bulmstein and J. Wallman (eds), *The Crime Drop in America*207-28. Cambridge: Cambridge University Press.

Edsall, Thomas B. and Mary D. Edsall. 1992. *Chain Reaction: The Impact of Race, Rights, and Taxes on American Politics*. New York: W.W. Nortan and Company.

Epp, Charles, Steven Maynard-Moody, and Donald P. Haider-Markel. 2013. *Pulled Over: Racial Framing of Police Stops*. Chicago, IL: University of Chicago Press (forthcoming).

Fagan, Jeffrey and Garth Davies. 2000. "Street Stops and Broken Windows: Terry, Race, and Disorder in New York City." *Fordham Urban Law Journal 28*: 457–504.

Garland, David. 2001. *The Culture of Control: Crime and Social Order in Contemporary Society*. Chicago, IL: University of Chicago Press.

Geller, Amanda, Irwin Garfinkel, and Bruce Western. 2006. "The Effects of Incarceration on Employment and Wages: An Analysis of the Fragile Families Survey." Princeton, NJ: Center for Research on Child Wellbeing.

Gelman, Andrew, Jeffrey Fagan, and Alex Kiss. 2007. "An Analysis of the New York City Police Department's 'Stop-and-Frisk' Policy in the Context of Claims of Racial Bias." *Journal of the American Statistical Association 102*: 813–823.

Gest, Ted. 2001. *Crime and Politics: Big Government's Erratic Campaign for Law and Order*. New York: Oxford University Press.

Gilliam, Franklin D. Jr and Shanto Iyengar. 2000. "Prime Suspects: The Influence of Local Television News on the Viewing Public." *American Journal of Political Science 44*: 560–573.

Gilliam, Franklin D. Jr, Nicholas A. Valentino, and Matthew M. Beckman. 2002. "Where You Live and What You Watch: The Impact of Racial Proximity and Local Television News on Attitudes About Race and Crime." *Political Research Quarterly 55*: 755–787.

Goffman, Alice. 2009. "On the Run: Wanted Black Men in a Philadelphia Ghetto." *American Sociological Review 74*: 339–357.

Gottschalk, Maria. 2006. *The Prison and the Gallows: The Politics of Mass Incarceration in America*. Cambridge, MA: Cambridge University Press.

Green, Eva G.T., Christian Staerkle, and David O. Sears. 2006. "Symbolic Racism and Whites' Attitudes towards Punitive and Preventive Crime Policies." *Law and Human Behavior 30*: 435–454.

Greenberg, David F. and Valerie West. 2001. "State Prison Populations and their Growth, 1971–1991." *Criminology 39*: 615–653.

Haider-Markel, Donald P. 1998. "The Politics of Social Regulatory Policy: State and Federal Hate Crime Policy and Implementation Effort." *Political Research Quarterly 51* (1): 69–88.

Harcourt, Bernard E. 2001. *Illusion of Order: The False Promise of Broken Windows Policing*. Cambridge, MA: Harvard University Press.

Harcourt, Bernard E. and Jens Ludwig. 2006. "Broken Windows: New Evidence from New York City and a Five-City Social Experiment." *University of Chicago Law Review* 73: 271–323.

Harris, David. 1999. *Driving While Black: Racial Profiling on America's Highways*. New York: American Civil Liberties Union.

Helms, Ronald and David Jacobs. 2002. "The Political Context of Sentencing: An Analysis of Community and Individual Determinants." *Social Forces* 81: 577–604.

Herbert, Steve and Elizabeth Brown. 2006. "Conceptions of Space and Crime in the Punitive Neoliberal City." *Antipode* 38: 755–777.

Hewitt, J. and Todd Clear. 1983. *Determinate Sentencing in California*. Lexington, KY: Council of State Governments.

Jacobs, David and Jason T. Carmichael. 2001. "The Politics of Punishment Across Time and Space: A Pooled Time-Series Analysis of Imprisonment Rates." *Social Forces* 80: 61–91.

Jacobs, David and Ronald E. Helms. 1996. "Toward a Political Model of Incarceration: A Time-Series Examination of Multiple Explanations for Prison Admission Rates." *American Journal of Sociology* 102: 323–357.

Johnson, Brian. 2006. "The Multilevel Context of Criminal Sentencing: Integrating Judge-and County-Level Influences." *Criminology* 44: 259–298.

Kaminer, Wendy. 19955. *It's All the Rage: Crime and Culture*. Reading, MA: Addison-Wesley.

Key, V. O. 1949. *Southern politics in state and nation*. New York: Alfred A. Knopf

Kinder, Donald R. and Tali Mendelberg. 1995. "Cracks in American Apartheid: The Political Impact of Prejudice among Desegregated Whites." *Journal of Politics* 57: 402–425.

Kinder, Donald R. and Lynn M. Sanders. 1996. *Divided by Color: Racial Politics and Democratic Ideals*. Chicago, IL: University of Chicago Press.

LaFree, Gary. 2002. "Too Much Democracy or Too Much Crime? Lessons from California's Three Strikes Law." *Law and Social Inquiry* 27: 875–902.

Loftin, Colin. Milton Heumann, and David McDowall. 1983. "Mandatory Sentencing and Firearms Violence: Evaluating an Alternative to Gun Control." *Law and Society Review* 17: 287–318.

Manza, Jeff and Christopher Uggen. 2006. *Locked Out: Felon Disenfranchisement and American Democracy*. New York: Oxford University Press.

Marvell, Thomas B., and Carlisle E. Moody. 1996. "Determinate Sentencing and Abolishing Parole: The Long-Term Impacts on Prisons and Crime." *Criminology* 34: 107–128.

Massey, Douglas S. 2007. *Categorically Unequal*. New York: Russell Sage Foundation.

Massey, Douglas S. and Nancy Denton. 1993. *American Apartheid: Segregation and the Making of the Underclass*. Cambridge: Harvard University Press.

Mauer, Marc. 1999. *The Race to Incarcerate*. New York: The New Press.

Mauer, Marc. 2006. *The Race to Incarcerate*, ev. edn. New York: The New Press.

Mauer, Marc and Meda Chesney-Lind. 2002. *Invisible Punishment: The Collateral Consequences of Mass Imprisonment*. New York: The New Press.

Mauer, Marc and Ryan King. 2007. *A 25-Year Quagmire: The "War on Drugs" and its Impact on American Society*. Washington, DC: The Sentencing Project.

McCloud, Aman, Ismail K. White, and Amelia R. Gavin. 2003. "The Locked Ballot Box: The Impact of State Criminal Disenfranchisement Laws on African American Voting Behavior and Implications for Reform." *Virginia Journal of Social Policy and Law* 11: 66–88.

Meier, Kenneth J. 1994. *The Politics of Sin: Drugs, Alcohol, and Public Policy*. Armonk, NY: M. E. Sharpe.

Miller, Lisa L. 2008. *The Perils of Federalism: Race, Poverty, and the Politics of Crime Control*. Oxford: Oxford University Press.

Murakawa, Naomi. 2008. "The Origins of the Carceral Crisis: Racial Order as Office 'Law and Order' in Postwar American Politics." In Joseph Lowndes, Julie Novkov, and Dorian Warren (eds), *Race and American Political Development* 234–54. New York: Routledge.

Murakawa, Naomi and Katherine Beckett. 2010. "The Penology of Racial Innocence: The Erasure of Racism in the Study and Practice of Punishment." *Law and Society Review* 44: 695–730.

Muwakkil, S. (2005) *Black Men: Missing*, <http://alternet.org/rights/22283/>.

Nicholson-Crotty, Sean. 2004. "The Impact of Sentencing Guidelines on State Level Sanctions: An Analysis over Time." *Crime and Delinquency* 50: 395–411.

Ouimet, Marc and Pierre Tremblay. 1996. "A Normative Theory of the Relationship Between Crime Rates and Imprisonment Rates: An Analysis of Penal Behavior of the U.S. *States from 1972* to 1992." *Journal of Research in Crime and Delinquency* 33: 109–112.

Peffley, Mark and Jon Hurwitz. 2002. "The Racial Components of 'Race-Neutral' Crime Policy Attitudes." *Political Psychology* 23: 59–75.

Pettit, Becky and Bruce Western. 2004. "Mass Imprisonment and the Life Course: Race and Class Inequality in U.S. Incarceration." *American Sociological Review* 69: 151–169.

Pew Center on the States. 2008. *One in 100: Behind Bars in American in 2008*. Washington, DC: Pew Charitable Trusts.

Pew Center on the States. 2009. *One in 31: The Long Reach of American Corrections*. Washington, DC: Pew Charitable Trusts.

Percival, Garrick L. 2010. "Ideology, Diversity, and Imprisonment: Considering the Influence of Local Politics on Racial and Ethnic Minority Incarceration Rates." *Social Science Quarterly* 91: 1063–1082.

Petersilia, Joan. 2003. *When Prisoners Come Home: Parole and Prisoner Reentry*. New York: Oxford University Press.

Petrocelli, Matthew, Alex R. Piquero, and Michael R. Smith. 2003. "Conflict Theory and Racial Profiling: An Empirical Analysis of Police Stop Data." *Journal of Criminal Justice* 31: 1–11.

Pettit, B. and Western B. (2004). "Mass imprisonment and the life course: race and class inequality in U.S. incarceration." *American Sociological Review* 69, 151–169.

Provine, Doris Marie. 2007. *Unequal under Law: Race in the War on Drugs*. Chicago: University Chicago Press.

Quillian, Lincoln and Devah Pager. 2001. "Black Neighbors, Higher Crime? The Role of Racial Stereotypes in Evaluations of Neighborhood Crime." *American Journal of Sociology* 107: 717–767.

Quinney, Richard. 1970. *The Social Reality of Crime*. Boston, MA: Little, Brown.

Reinarman, Craig and Harry G. Levine. 1997. *Crack in America: Demon Drugs and Social Justice*. Berkeley, CA: University of California Press.

Riley, Jack K. 1997. *Crack, Powder Cocaine, and Heroin: Drug Purchase and Use Patterns in Six Cities*. Washington, DC: National Institute of Justice and Office of National Drug Control Policy.

Roberts, Julian V. and Loretta J. Stalans. 1997. *Public Opinion, Crime, and Criminal Justice*. Boulder, CO: Westview.

Roberts, Julian V., Loretta J. Stalans, David Indermaur, and Mike Hough. 2002. *Penal Populism and Popular Opinion*. New York: Oxford University Press.

Rose, Dina R. and Todd R. Clear. 1998. "Incarceration, Social Capital, and Crime: Implications for Social Disorganization Theory." *Criminology* 36: 441–480.

Rusche, George and Otto Kirchheimer. 1968. *Punishment and Social Structure*. New York: Russell and Russell.

Sampson, Robert J. and Stephen W. Raudenbush. 2004. "Seeing Disorder: Neighborhood Stigma and the Social Construction of 'Broken Windows.'" *Social Psychology Quarterly* 67: 319–342.

Scheingold, Stuart. 1984. *The Politics of Law and Order: Street Crime and Public Policy*. New York: Longman.

Scheingold, Stuart. 1998. "Constructing the New Political Criminology: Power, Authority, and the Post-Liberal State." *Law and Social Inquiry* 23: 857–895.

Simon, Jonathan. 2007. *Governing Through Crime: How the War on Crime Transformed American Democracy and Created a Culture of Fear*. New York: Oxford University Press.

Skogan, Wesley. 2006. "Asymmetry in the Impact of Encounters with Police." *Policing and Society* 16: 99–126.

Smith, Kevin B. 2004. "The Politics of Punishment: Evaluating Political Explanations of Incarceration Rates." *The Journal of Politics* 66: 925–938.

Solomon, Amy, Vera Kachnowski, and Avi Bhati. 2005. "*Does Parole Work? Analyzing the Impact of Postprison Supervision on Rearrest Outcomes*." Washington, DC: The Urban Institute.

Sorensen, J., and D. Stemen. 2002. "The Effect of State Sentencing Policies on Incarceration Rates." *Crime and Delinquency* 48: 456–475.

Soss, Joe, Richard C. Fording, and Sanford F. Schram. 2008. "The Color of Devolution: Race, Federalism, and the Politics of Social Control." *American Journal of Political Science* 52: 536–553.

Steffensmeier, Darrell and Chester Britt. 2001. "Judges' Race and Judicial Decision Making: Do Black Judges Sentence Differently?" *Social Science Quarterly* 82: 749–764.

Steffensmeier, Darrell, Jeffery Ulmer, and John Kramer. 1998. "The Interaction of Race, Gender, and Age in Criminal Sentencing: The Punishment Cost of Being Young, Black, and Male." *Criminology* 36: 763–798.

Stolzenberg, Lisa and Stewart J. D'Alessio. 1997. "Three Strikes and You're Out: The Impact of California's Mandatory Sentencing Law on Serious Crime Rates." *Crime and Delinquency* 43: 457–469.

Stone, Deborah A. 1997. "State Innovation in Health Policy." In Alan A. Altshuler and Robert D. Behn (eds), *Innovation in American Government: Challenges, Opportunities and Dilemmas* 219–45. Washington, DC: Brookings Institution.

Taggart, William and Russell G. Winn. 1993. "Imprisonment in the American States." *Social Science Quarterly* 74: 736–749.

Taylor, Ralph. 2000. *Breaking Away From Broken Windows: Baltimore Neighborhoods and the Nationwide Fight Against Crime, Grime, Fear and Decline*. Boulder, CO: Westview Press.

Tonry, Michael. 1995. *Malign Neglect: Race, Crime, and Punishment in America*. New York: Oxford University Press.

Tonry. Michael. 1997. *Sentencing Matters*. New York: Oxford University Press.

Tonry, Michael. 2004. *Thinking About Crime: Sense and Sensibility in American Penal Culture*. New York: Oxford University Press.

Tonry, Michael. 2009. "Explanations of American Punishment Policies: A National History." *Punishment and Society* 11: 377–394.

Travis, Jeremy. 2005. *But They All Come Back: Facing the Challenges of Prisoner Reentry*. Washington, DC: The Urban Institute Press.

Ulmer, Jeffery T. and Brian Johnson. 2004. "Sentencing in Context: A Multi-Level Analysis." *Criminology* 42: 137–178.

Ulmer, Jeffery T. and John Kramer. 1996. "Court Communities Under Sentencing Guidelines: Dilemmas of Formal Rationality and Sentencing Disparity." *Criminology* 3: 306–332.

Wacquant, Loïc. 2002. "From Slavery to Mass Incarceration." *New Left Review* 13: 41–60.

Weaver, Vesla. 2007. "Frontlash: Race and the Development of Punitive Crime Policy." *Studies in American Political Development* 21: 230–265.

Weaver, Vesla and Amy E. Lerman. 2010. "The Political Consequences of the Carceral State." *American Political Science Review* 104: 817–834.

Weitzer, Ronald and Steven A. Tuch. 2002. "Perceptions of Racial Profiling: Race, Class, and Personal Experience." *Criminology* 40: 435–456.

Western, Bruce. 2006. *Punishment and Inequality in America*. New York: Russell Sage Foundation.

Western, Bruce and Becky Pettit. 2000. "Incarceration and Racial Inequality in Men's Employment." *Industrial and Labor Relations Review* 54 (1):3–16.

Wilson, James Q. 1983. *Thinking About Crime*, rev. edn. New York: Basic Books.

Wilson, James Q. 1990. "Drugs and Crime." In Michael Tonry and James Q. Wilson (eds), *Drugs and Crime* 521–45. Chicago, IL: Chicago University Press.

Wilson, James Q. 1994. "Crime and Public Policy." In James Q. Wilson and Joan Petersilia (eds), *Crime* 619–30. San Francisco: ICS.

Windlesham, Lord. 1998. *Politics, Punishment, and Populism*. New York: Oxford University Press.

Yates, Jeff. 1997. "Racial Incarceration Disparity among the States." *Social Science Quarterly* 78: 1001–1011.

Yates, Jeff and Richard Fording. 2005. "Politics and State Punitiveness in Black and White." *Journal of Politics* 67: 1099–1121.

Zimring, Franklin E. and David T. Johnson. 2006. "Public Opinion and the Governance of Punishment in Democratic Political Systems." *Annals of the Academy of Political and Social Science* 60: 266–280.

Zimring, Franklin E., Gordon Hawkins, and Sam Kamin. 2001. *Punishment and Democracy: Three Strikes and You're Out in California*. New York: Oxford University Press.

CHAPTER 32

··

MORALITY POLITICS

··

ALESHA E. DOAN

DURING the Great Awakenings in the eighteenth and nineteenth centuries, religious leaders invited Americans to discover or reconnect with their faith. Clergymen urged people to rely on emotion rather than reason to guide them in decision making. These heart versus head fights have resulted in recurring conflict over values, identity, and culture that routinely spill into the political domain.

Contemporary times are not different; several of the most enduring and contentious political debates over issues such as reproductive, civil rights, and criminal policy are undergirded by these familiar tenets. The impact of morality conflicts on the political landscape is widespread. These debates have involved political institutions at every level of government, impacted electoral outcomes, shaped agendas, and occupied significant space in citizen discourses. However, despite the historical and modern regularity of these debates, scholars have been slow to consider belief-laden conflicts within the purview of political science research.

Studies of morality politics emerged to fill this void and have grown into an identifiable body of work. This chapter explores the development and future direction of the morality politics literature. Attention will be given to the initial research in this field, which grew out of the policy typology literature that attempts to group disparate policies into robust categories based on commonly shared characteristics. A period of refinement and theory development followed the earlier works, and this research continues to fuel questions about the utility of this literature, specifically whether morality politics research has added descriptive knowledge or theoretical knowledge to the field. As the morality politics field has evolved, scholars have turned towards testing the impact it has had on the policymaking process.

The Development of Morality Politics
as a Field of Study

American history is replete with periods "of political insanity", where deep conflict has erupted, but the root cause involved a fight over the preeminence of values, not the allocation of material resources (Hunter, 1991, 33). Many attempts have been made over the years by elites and citizens to establish and regulate moral positions on issues. Towards the end of the twentieth century, some of the most intense moral conflicts were beginning to take shape in the political arena, even as Americans' attitudes about traditionally taboo social issues relating to premarital sex, gay and lesbian relationships, and childbearing practices were liberalizing (Pew Research Center for the People and the Press, 2007; Saad, 2010).

Although many issues were gaining political traction and becoming salient to the electorate, they were visibly absent in policy scholarship. Morality politics scholarship began in this context. Researchers started examining the role that values, identity, and culture had in shaping policy disputes (Tatalovich and Daynes, 1988; Tatalovich, Smith, and Bobic, 1994; Haider-Markel and Meier, 1996). The importance of ideological rather than economic cleavages were being investigated, leading one scholar to speculate that "the basis of political conflict in this country may be becoming, therefore, not who *gets* what but who *believes* what [emphasis in original]" (Mooney, 2001, 5; Weisberg, 2005).

Integrating morality policies into existing theories of public policy proved to be challenging and limited because dominant theories and models focused on the distribution, redistribution, and regulation of wealth. While Lowi's (1972) policy typology hypothesized that the nature of a policy shapes the political activity surrounding the policy, morality policies did not fit neatly into the existing categories. Some scholars posited that morality policies were regulatory in nature because they sought out "the exercise of legal authority to modify or replace community values, moral practices, and norms of interpersonal conduct with new standards of behavior" (Tatalovich and Daynes, 1988, 1). Yet others argued these policies approximated redistributive policies because "one segment of society attempts by government fiat to impose its values on the rest of society", thereby reallocating values among citizens (Meier, 1994, 4; Haider-Markel and Meier, 1996; Haider-Markel, 1998, 1999). Smith (2001) attempted to reconcile these two positions, claiming that rather than being at odds with each other, they were complimentary. Regardless of whether morality policies are classified as regulatory or redistributive, Smith argued, they are linked by a fundamental purpose—leveraging the government to legitimate a particular set of values.

Despite the different classifications assigned to morality policies, scholars saw utility in developing a typology. Research on morality policies grew out of this tradition, seeking to define the policy area and identify the type of politics that surround this unique subset of public policies. Many of the initial studies focused on determining whether or not morality policies were truly different to nonmorality policies, and positing theoretical generalizations that could be tested in subsequent research.

DEFINING MORALITY POLICY

Most morality policies are designed to instigate behavioral change that is regulated through laws (Tatalovich and Daynes, 1998, 1988). Policies governing activities such as the consumption of pornography, the legality of same-sex marriage, or the outcome to an unwanted pregnancy are aimed at shaping individual morality (Tatalovich and Daynes, 1998). However, some of these policies are directed at challenging the morality or immorality of the government's actions, such as its decision to implement capital punishment (Mooney, 2000, 2001). While disagreement exists over the precise definition of morality policy, most scholars use the term to refer to a unique category of public policies, where "at least one advocacy coalition involved has portrayed the issue as one of morality or sin and used moral arguments in its policy advocacy" (Haider-Markel and Meier, 1996, 333).

This definition precludes certain types of dispute from falling within the purview of morality policies and has led researchers to demarcate between contentious and consensus issue (Meier, 1999; Sharp, 1999, 2002; Mooney and Lee, 2000). Consensus issues include those that comprise only one legitimate moral perspective. Citizens commonly understand these as sin issues and very little variation exists among their attitudes toward the particular issue. Contentious issues, however, fall within the definition of morality policy because the conflict includes opposing sides, where at least one side roots its opposition in its respective sense of moral supremacy on the issue.

Conceptual ambiguity: since a strict definition of morality policy has not been agreed upon by scholars, several questions have surfaced regarding conceptual ambiguity. The range of issues falling within a loose definition of morality policy is potentially expansive, and they may change in accordance with time and geography. Mirroring a common critique of Lowi's policy typology, scholars pointed out that if the time frame of a particular policy under investigation is expanded or truncated the policy may no longer fit within the definition of a morality policy.

Meier's (1994) book, *The Politics of Sin*, profiles two cases in point—drug and alcohol consumption. Using a mixed-method approach, he documents the visibility and availability of opiates, cocaine, marijuana, and hallucinogenic drugs for medicinal and recreational purposes in the nineteenth century. Drug use evolved into a morality issue during the twentieth century. Alcohol use followed a similar trajectory, but was decriminalized following the repeal of prohibition in 1933, whereas drugs were increasingly criminalized and perceived as a morality issue during the twentieth century (Meier, 1994). Both of these cases elucidate how an issue may evolve into or out of a definition of morality policy, depending on what time period is being studied.

Because many issues oscillate over time between consensus and contentious politics, Mooney and Lee (2000) contend that morality issues should be conceptualized as a continuum between contentious and consensus politics, rather than conceptualizing them as isolated categories. While a continuum provides some needed flexibility for accommodating the fluctuation of policies over time, it falls short in resolving a key ambiguity. If morality policies vacillate between morality and nonmorality policies over time, it is conceivable that they are not fundamentally different from nonmorality policies, which can also exhibit a similar fluctuation when studied longitudinally.

Adding to the lack of specificity surrounding an appropriate time frame was a related question concerning whether morality issues were bound by geographical location. Several issues that researchers identified as morality issues were often classified as such on an ad hoc basis. Scant attention had been given to issues in countries outside of the United States or Britain and much of this research lacked a systematic analysis. Addressing this gap in research, Studlar (2001) undertook an examination of morality issues across 22 western democracies.

His analysis produced two main findings. First, despite the diverse institutional and cultural differences present in the countries, many issues were shared across national boarders. Abortion, gambling, alcohol/drugs, homosexuality, euthanasia, gun control, and ethnic/racial issues had been treated as morality policy issues in most (and in some cases all) of the countries. Abortion was the most prevalent morality policy concern, and all countries had dealt with it. The regulation of alcohol/drugs and the rights of gay and lesbian citizens were two other common issues. Over half of the countries had treated these issues as morality-based policies. Second, despite a few shared policy topics, the analysis determined that many issues were bound by geography. While citizens in the United States have sparred over the morality of capital punishment, it was a nonissue in the 21 other countries. Other issues, including women's rights, divorce, and animal rights exhibited more variation, being characterized as a morality issue in some countries but not others.

Based on these two findings, Studlar (2001) concludes that scholars should not hasten in making generalizations to other countries based on the morality policy conflicts in the United States. He also suggests that morality policies should be divided between "broadly shared" issues and culturally specific issues. Finally, Studlar encouraged future research to investigate "how the definition of morality policy changes over time, as with divorce in the United States, gambling in some jurisdictions, and even abortion in several countries" (Studlar, 2001, 50).

However, Smith and Tatalovich (2003) critique Studlar's research on two counts. First, they believe that the variation of issue salience found in the analysis is likely a function of time constraint. Some of the issues are dated and no longer salient, whereas other issues are too new to be salient in many of the countries included in his analysis. Second, Smith and Tatalovich contend that Studlar overemphasizes the importance of basic identities in morality disputes. "[W]e heartily agree that identity lies at the core of moral conflict, but no list can include all possible examples, nor can a summary of their policy attributes provide enough theoretical power to explain the emergence of morality politics or to account for their future manifestations" (Smith and Tatalovich, 2003, 240).

> Smith and Tatalovich argue that culture, rather than identity, provides a more robust theoretical explanation. Culture theory does not depend upon "basic identities" like race, gender, or language...The logic of culture theory is that moral conflicts are struggles between the forces of status-differentiation and the forces of status-egalitarianism. The first reflects the hierarchical bias that looks fondly upon traditional societies in which individuals and groups know their place. The latter includes other elites of many stripes on the Left who believe in universal principles of human dignity and human rights. (Smith and Tatalovich, 2003, 240)

Based on their in-depth case-studies of three morality issues (capital punishment, homosexuality, and abortion) in five democracies (Canada, United States, United Kingdom, France, and Germany), the authors draw two provocative conclusions. They claim that most morality policies are largely anti-majoritarianism and represent little parity between constituents' preferences and enacted policies. Smith and Tatalovich also contend that politicians frequently use institutional tools to avoid taking positions on controversial issues. In this regard, they find political accountability to be lacking when it comes to issues of morality. These findings are somewhat supported by the research that has emerged from studies focusing on the United States. However, their more universal generalizations have been tempered by research which suggests that political responsiveness and accountability are conditional in nature. When politically expedient, representatives are more likely to be both.

Smith and Tatalovich raise an important conceptual flag for morality scholars regarding identity. However, the findings of their research have been refined by other studies and their use of culture can be problematic. Neither culture nor identity is a theoretical panacea that explains morality policies. The importance of various attributes of identity changes over time. While some aspects of identity are permanent, values and culture are permeable. Morality conflicts unfold in political systems and these issues interact with established institutional arrangements. Excluding the interaction between these produces a deficient definition and, ultimately, a deficient explanation of morality policies.

Formalization: attempting to clarify some of the conceptual slippage in the definition of morality politics, Meier (1999, 2001) formalized several aspects of it in an effort to create a more generalizable theory that can accommodate the time and spatial concerns noted by other scholars. He combines morality, which he dubs "sin," with institutional factors to demonstrate how morality policies generate a unique brand of politics, how they can be transformed to more inclusive policies, and finally, to demonstrate why morality policies are likely to be unsuccessful.

Meier begins with a demand curve illustrating that individuals possess different tolerances for sinful behavior. The populous is divided along a spectrum, with willing participants and staunch abstainers marking the extremes. Willingness to participate is inversely linked to costs (legal, social, or otherwise) of participation. Regardless of where individuals fall under the preference curve, none of them will publicly advocate for sinful activity. As Meier points out, "Legislators do not rise and recite the joys of drunk driving, the pleasures of prostitution, or the thrill they get from serial killings" (Meier, 2001, 23). The end result is that a disjuncture exists between individuals' preferences for sinful activity versus the public perception of their preferences. Consequently, the inaccurate perceptions drive the formulation of morality policies. These policies are created in a vacuum that is devoid of balanced debate, leading to policies that are extreme.

The final factor in Meier's sin model is the role of institutions, particularly the law enforcement bureaucracies charged with implementing morality policies. He contends that these agencies tend to lack the capacity to engage in policy analysis, they rely on a lot of personnel, and they are rewarded by their output, namely, the number of arrests made for citizens violating the policy. Law enforcement bureaucracies routinely overestimate the degree of sin being committed in society because they exclusively encounter violators, prompting them to continually request a greater amount of resources.

The miscalculation of preferences, which is reinforced by public silence, combined with the mission of an enforcement bureaucracy, leads Meier to argue that morality policies are poorly conceived and destined to be unsuccessful. "This suggests that policy failures will be expensive failures because the moderating influences of incrementalism will be absent in policy design" (1999, 686).

However, Meier leaves open the possibility of an alternative scenario. He submits that a morality policy can be changed if the framing, and in turn the understanding of the issue, begins to shift. Once alternative viewpoints are exploited and the issue becomes more heterogeneous than simply one of sin, the policy may transform from a sin policy to a redistributive policy (Meier, 1999, 2001). Under these conditions, incremental policy changes in policy designs may become a more viable possibility.

Meier's formalized model of morality policy presented a large step forward in legitimizing it as a policy area worthy of study and corrected two issues. The curve is not bound by a set time frame or by a particular location, making it theoretically generalizable to any morality issue, spanning any time frame and occurring at any place. It also produced several testable propositions.

However, the formalized model left the door open for theoretical refinement. By Meier's own admission, the theory only tends to the demand side of sin issues, and largely ignores the supply side. Additionally, the relationship between information and demand as well as between framing and demand remains undetermined. Causality remains unspecified in terms of whether a new, nonmorality framing of a morality issue indicates that advocates are willing to vocalize latent preferences for the particular sin, or whether the new framing creates more demand for the sin. Of course, the possibility exists that in practice it is a combination of both information and changes in the issue framing that creates a new demand curve, which is an area that is in need of further development in this research.

CHARACTERISTICS OF MORALITY POLITICS

Complimenting the effort to formalize several aspects of a morality policy theory, researchers also turned their attention to identifying the politics surrounding these policies in order to enhance the generality and usefulness of a morality policy framework. Although morality policies are constrained by similar political and environmental factors that influence other types of policies, scholars have identified a set of characteristics thought to uniquely pertain to policies focusing on an absolute right or wrong. Intractability, simplicity, and salience have consistently been associated with morality policies. Scholars have attributed these key characteristics to the origin of the debates.

Intractability: at its core, morality policies involve conflict over individual belief systems that ascribe to opposing views of what is morally acceptable and unacceptable. Belief systems often stem from primary forms of individual identity, including factors such as a person's race, gender, sexual identity, nationality, or ethnicity, but belief systems are not exclusively bound to these. More permeable aspects of identity, such as religious beliefs, also factor heavily into these conflicts, providing morality policies with a peculiar intractability that is absent in other political disputes.

Studies have implied that the inherent inflexibility of morality conflicts relegates several lynchpins of the policy process, namely, compromise, negotiation, and diversified coalition building, to minor roles in the policymaking process (Mooney and Lee, 1995, 1999; Meier, 1999; Mooney, 2000, 2001). The rigid nature of these disputes is fueled by activists' perceptions that political compromise simply cheapens the very values being disputed. Research has found rigidity to be especially acute in conflicts related to issues of sex and sexuality, such as the fight over abortion rights, gay rights (particularly same-sex marriage), unmarried childbearing, and sexual education (Haider-Markel and Meier, 1996; Haider-Markel, 1999, 2001; Doan, 2007; Doan and Williams, 2008; Donovan, Tolbert, and Smith, 2008), but also on issues such as gun control and environmental protection (Lindaman and Haider-Markel, 2002).

Simplicity: many studies have found evidence indicating that the discourse pertaining to morality politics departs from that typically found in other policies. Elementary and nontechnical language is relied upon in morality disputes, and professional expertise is often negatively constructed (Lewis and Brooks, 2005). At times, policy experts are portrayed as the problem in morality contests and even pointed to as barriers that obstruct the crafting of a solution to the problem. Active participants rely on simplistic language to construct and frame the terms of the conflict.

Research has also documented that causal complexity is notably absent in morality policies. Simplistic rhetoric is used to discuss the conflict, even if the issue is complex or intertwined with macro socio-economic structure issues like systemic poverty and persistent racial inequality (Doan and Williams, 2008; Berkman and Plutzer, 2009). This rhetorical strategy reduces participation costs for people because knowledge-based prerequisites do not exist. Only the possession of a belief system is required, making these "easy issues" for the electorate (Carmines and Stimson, 1980; Lindaman and

Haider-Markel, 2002). In this regard, morality conflicts are accessible for general debate because most citizens ascribe to a set of values. Unlike other types of policies, people feel qualified to hold informed opinions and offer political evaluations about moral policies (Hunter, 1991; Meier, 1994, 1999; Tatalovich and Daynes, 1998; Mooney and Lee, 1999; Mooney, 2000, 2001). Thus, values and common sense, rather than expertise, generally drive policymaking in morality politics.

The information introduced by legislators mirrors the generally simplistic, nontechnical discourse that characterizes the politics surrounding morality issues. Goggin and Mooney (2001) examined two pieces of legislation that were being considered by Congress in 1988; one was a morality policy and the other a nonmorality policy. Title X of the Public Health Service Act was up for reauthorization. This piece of legislation became ensconced in the abortion conflict when antiabortion activists lobbied to have any government money that could potentially aid in funding abortions removed from the policy. President Reagan championed this cause, and consequently Title X became a source of significant deliberation in Congress. The Clean Air Act was also being considered for a redesign by Congress. The same members of Congress, who sat on the Health and Environment Subcommittee of the House Energy and Commerce Committee, were involved with both pieces of legislation.

Using dozens of interviews with people who were identified by congresspersons and their aids as information sources, the authors found that information was used differently in these two pieces of legislation. For the Clean Air Act, formal policy analysis governed the process. Expertise was solicited and technical information was far more likely to be invoked in the process, compared to Title X. Personal experiences that were purposefully selected by committee members were the primary information source used in deliberations over Title X. Outside expertise and technical information were far less likely to be used.

This study lends support to one of the hypotheses stemming from Meier's (1999, 2001) formalized morality politics theory; expertise will have little place in the policy process for morality policies. Based on their findings, Goggin and Mooney (2001) conclude that the selective use of information and the absence of expertise structuring morality policy deliberations have implications for policy design. Policy complications and unanticipated consequences are likely to be generated, while the underlying conflict is unlikely to be resolved in a manner that is palatable to most of the sides involved in the issue. Their findings track with other research.

However, other research has challenged the assumption that expertise has no role in morality politics. Several studies have documented a more recent and nuanced pattern concerning the role of expertise and information in protracted morality disputes. While values and common sense continue to occupy a central place in the politics surrounding these issues, active participants may also cultivate more sophisticated rhetoric and "scientific" information to bolster political support in these conflicts. As conflicts persist over a longer time frame, advocates who relied almost exclusively on morality arguments may amass and marshal new nonmorality evidence intended to support their cause.

For example, both prochoice and prolife organizations have enlisted help from national survey research firms to uncover issue frames that resonate the most with the public (Jelen and Wilcox, 2003). Moving into the twenty-first century, anti-abortion advocates increasingly began to promote arguments about the physical and psychological harm women experienced after receiving an abortion. Relying on professionals operating in their networks, abortion foes began collecting data to support these nonmorality arguments and bolster their position with more "scientific" evidence. This opened the door to pursuing incremental changes to morality policies (Doan, 2007).

But in both cases, injecting expertise from sources outside of active political participants—even if it was biased—provided political capital for these morality causes. More technical expert information served the purpose of increasing the legitimacy of the causes and lent credence to groups' attempts at expanding the issue framing in nonmorality terms. Using evidence-based arguments to diversify the framing of each issue opened up new institutional venues for advocates to lobby for their respective cause.

These two studies underscore a vexing problem in this literature, which formed the basis of some of the earlier critiques waged by scholars—time frame. The longevity of a morality conflict may directly influence whether the politics surrounding these policies are truly unusual. Given enough time, these studies imply that several of the phases of the morality politics process—issue framing, venue shopping, and conflict expansion—eventually mirror similar agenda-setting tactics and patterns found in nonmorality policy areas (Baumgartner and Jones, 1993; True et al., 2007).

Moreover, the assumption that nonincremental changes are usually pursued by groups in morality conflicts is largely dispelled by this research. While the catalyst for change may occur in a nonincremental way via a focusing event, this research suggests that the cultivation of outside "expert" information can be used by groups to pursue incremental rather than nonincremental strategies, even in the most contentious conflicts.

A similar ambiguity surfaced in research as scholars began investigating the final characteristic that had been identified as unique to morality policies—that of issue salience (Haider-Markel and Meier, 1996; Haider-Markel, 1999).

Salience: compared to "politics as usual," morality policies are thought to be highly salient. In some cases, studies have found that morality disputes are far more prone to result in conflict escalation, and, in some cases, even violence (Nice, 1988; Hunter, 1994; Meier, 1994; Mooney, 2001; Doan, 2007). The salience inherent in value-laden policy clashes, combined with the intractability and simplicity of these issues, led scholars to contend that morality policies tend to stimulate higher levels of citizen participation (Meier, 1994, 2001; Mooney, 2001). In turn, political responsiveness is expected to be heightened because constituents can easily become involved in morality disputes (Mooney and Lee, 1995; Haider-Markel and Meier, 1996).

However, Mooney and Schuldt's (2008) research contradicts and casts doubt on this key assumption. The results of their survey, which was administered to 700 respondents, indicated that morality disputes were no more salient, and on some issues even less, to individuals than several nonmorality issues. The authors consider the possibility that this finding may be related to the question wording used on the survey, which asked respondents about the personal *importance*, not the *salience*, of each issue, but they reject this possibility. Rather than measurement error, they take the survey results at face value and conclude that many morality issues are simply not personally relevant and therefore not salient to citizens. This finding presented a significant challenge to the prevailing assumption that morality politics are innately salient (see also Lindaman and Haider-Markel, 2002).

Conflict expansion around morality issues, and in turn political responsiveness to them, are more nuanced than scholars initially expected. As research progressed, scholars refined the conditions associated with political responsiveness and salience. The specific type of morality issues influences both. Sharp (2002, 2005) examined five different morality policy issues, including drug use, abortion, adult entertainment, gambling, and gay rights. She investigated local political responses to these disparate morality issues in ten regionally dispersed cities across the United States. Sharp found evidence that cities responded differently to these issues based on whether economic stakeholders were active participants in the conflict.

Variation was found in cities' responses to drug use, abortion, and gay rights, which could largely be accounted for by the differences in local subculture. However, adult entertainment and gambling were treated more uniformly across cities. This pattern held up despite the variation in local institutional arrangements and subculture. "Economic considerations supplant the subcultural explanations only when industry forces have clear-cut material stakes in the issue or when an issue has strong implications for the community's economic development" (Sharp, 2005, 197). Sharp concluded that a distinction exists between pure morality issues and material morality issues. Pure morality issues rarely have economic stakeholders involved in the conflict, whereas material morality issues generally can be characterized as conflicts involving economic stakeholders.

Consonant with these findings at the local level, Stabile (2007) found a similar pattern at the state level concerning cloning laws. Both morality and political economy determinants were related to a state's policy. The presence of a strong biotechnology industry resulted in more permissive cloning policies, whereas states that had stricter anti-abortion laws and more Evangelical Protestants had more restrictive cloning laws. Stabile's findings, in conjunction with other studies, provide evidence suggesting that organized economic interests generally displace morality interests in the policymaking process.

Political Responsiveness

Distinguishing between different types of morality policies has generated more than a descriptive refinement in categorization. It has motivated scholars to investigate the politics surrounding different types of morality policies. As this body of literature evolved, scholars started to mold their studies around questions that have a more global appeal to the broader field of American politics. Responsiveness and representation are two significant issues that this literature began to address.

Studies examining political responsiveness produced several interesting findings about the factors that structure the degree of responsiveness to morality issues. Politicians are more inclined to follow the contours of public opinion in response to *pure* morality issues as compared to *material* morality issues. Responsiveness is heightened further when public opinion is divided around a pure morality issue that is contentious. Mooney and Lee (2000) examine the abolishment and reenactment of the death penalty across the states in the U.S. They find that policymakers are influenced by mass opinion, particularly when the public's opinions are divided around an issue. However, public opinion does not exert a similar degree of influence when there is consensus about the issue (Mooney and Lee, 2000).

Norrander and Wilcox's (2001) research on abortion policy and public opinion echo these findings. They examine the influence of the electorate's opinion on states' passage of restrictive abortion policies in the post-1989 *Webster v. Reproductive Health Services* (492 U.S., 490) era. Most, but not all, of the abortion policies they examined were affected by constituency opinion as well as interest group support. Additionally, the results of the analyses indicated that democratic legislators were more supportive of liberalized policy measures, including support for public funding of abortions. Female legislators were also more favorable to liberal abortion policy and less inclined to support policy restricting minors' access to abortion services, even though public sentiment favored these policies. Norrander and Wilcox conclude that while public opinion matters, elite opinion is another important predictor in morality policy adoption.

However, Camobreco and Barnello (2008) contend that the influence of elites' opinions about abortion has lost importance over time and has been eclipsed by the electorate's abortion opinions, which have become the primary determinant in abortion policy. Calfano (2010) adds corroborating evidence in his study of political branding and state abortion policy. White evangelicals and Catholics are two groups that have a solid pro-life reputation, which he refers to as political branding. He argues that a group's branding is used by state representatives as a proxy measure of a constituent's opinion about abortion policy. Political brand can be leveraged as an asset that wields influence on representatives' abortion policy positions. The effect of branding depends on the religious cohesion of a district. Calfano concludes that branding helps translate constituency preferences into policy preferences and that representation—at least on abortion policy—is being achieved in state politics.

Other studies have compiled additional evidence documenting the conditional influence of public opinion on morality policies (Haider-Markel, 2001; Haider-Markel and Meier, 1996). Although public opinion on culture war issues has been popularly depicted as conflicts characterized by extreme ideological positions on the left and the right, research has indicated that individual opinion, and its effect, on many morality policies is contextual (Mooney and Lee, 2001; Lindaman and Haider-Markel, 2002; Haider-Markel and Kaufman, 2006). The electorate often holds ambivalent attitudes toward controversial topics, depending on which specific issue is being contemplated (Craig et al., 2005).

Several scholars argue that issue evolution, which polarizes political elites and induces mass opinion to follow suit, has been occurring in the political landscape and has led to long-term changes in party coalitions (Carmines and Stimson, 1980, 1989). Adams (1997) finds evidence of issue evolution around the abortion conflict. Based on his findings, he purports that morality policies are particularly ripe for issue evolution because they are "easy" issues (Carmines and Stimson, 1980), which lend themselves to conflict expansion and ultimately polarization among elites and the electorate.

Lindaman and Haider-Markel (2002) systematically investigated Adam's proposition regarding morality policies and issue evolution. They examined mass and elite opinions across four morality issues: lesbian and gay civil rights, pornography, gun control, and protection of the environment. Using congressional roll call votes to capture elites' opinions and the General Social Surveys to measure mass opinion, they tracked these issues from 1970 through 1999. The findings from their analyses produced mixed results. Polarization occurred among elites across all four issues; however, it did not occur for the masses. Evidence of issue evolution was uncovered for two issues—gun control and environmental protection—but not for lesbian and gay civil rights or pornography. Lindaman and Haider-Markel suggest that issue salience is the key to accounting for these differences. But the authors caution that their results may be capturing the beginning of issue evolution over lesbian and gay civil rights and pornography, particularly if these morality issues become salient to the public.

Issue salience has also surfaced as an important factor in subsequent research investigating the link between electoral opinion and political responsiveness to morality issues. Salience surrounding gay and lesbian rights has ramped up considerably in the United States. Several policies that are directly relevant to gay and lesbian citizens have been introduced in the states, creating an ideal comparative context for examining opinion-policy congruence across related issues.

Lax and Phillips' (2009) took advantage of this variation by investigating mass opinion on eight specific policy measures directly relevant to gay and lesbian citizens. The authors' evidence indicates that an opinion-policy linkage exists, but it is conditioned upon the relative salience of the particular policy being considered. When a policy is highly salient to the electorate, political responsiveness and congruence with mass opinion is also high. Lower salience translates into less responsiveness and incongruence. Their findings also flag a potentially troubling implication for morality conflicts. "Our results show that representative institutions do a poor job protecting minority rights even when the public *supports* the prominority position [emphasis in original]" (Lax and Phillips, 2009, 383). Powerful interest groups' preferences, in this case conservative religious interest groups, are overrepresented in the policy process and disrupt opinion?policy congruence (Lax and Phillips, 2009).

Salience created by morality policies at the state level can also influence politics at the national level. Research has found that the electorate tends to pay more attention to state ballot measures that pertain to morality issues (Nicholson, 2003). Donovan,

Tolbert, and Smith (2008) build on and extend this research by investigating the impact of state-level initiatives and referendums on presidential elections. The ban against same-sex marriage, which was proposed and passed in 13 states in 2004, coincided with a presidential election. The authors use these co-occurring events to determine whether media attention to the issue of same-sex marriage in these states increased the salience of this issue to voters and whether in turn, voters were more likely to evaluate presidential candidates based on their respective stances toward gay marriage. Donovan, Tolbert, and Smith find evidence that state-level initiatives banning same-sex marriage increased the salience of the issue and had a priming effect on voters in those states. Citizens in these states were more likely to cite gay marriage as an important issue that influenced their presidential candidate choice. Moreover, the findings from the authors' analysis indicate that this morality issue galvanized voters who were previously inattentive to the issue of same-sex marriage and who were not particularly interested in the presidential campaign.

These studies persuasively demonstrate the importance of salience, while also providing conclusive evidence that salience is not an inevitable feature of morality policies. Culture wars are not created equally; some resonate with the electorate, whereas others fail to generate an equivalent level of interest. Issue evolution, political responsiveness, and opinion—policy congruence are affected by the degree of salience surrounding an issue; findings that comport with the expectations and empirical findings that were laid out by several morality politics scholars (Meier, 1994, 2001; Haider-Markel and Meier, 1996; Haider-Markel, 1999; Mooney, 2001; Mooney and Lee, 2001, 2000; Mooney and Schuldt, 2008).

Moral Entrepreneurs

Many factors can affect whether a morality issue will gain traction with the electorate. Similar to the policy process governing other forms of policy, morality issues may arrive on the political agenda following an exogenous disruption or focusing event (Baumgartner and Jones, 1993; True et al., 2007). In cases involving material morality issues, studies have shown that elites, not the electorate, structure the terms and outcomes of the debate (Sharp, 2002, 2005). Elites may also dominate the policy process when there is a lower level of salience associated with a particular issue, even if the specific measure is related to a larger conflict, such as sexual violence, gay and lesbian civil rights, or the death penalty, which are generally topics salient to the public (Haider-Markel and Meier, 1996; Haider-Markel, 1998; Mooney and Lee, 2000; Cocca, 2002). Other studies suggest that under conditions of low salience or public opinion consensus, elites' ideology drives the policymaking process (Haider-Markel, 1999, 2001; Haider-Markel, Joslyn and Kniss, 2000; Mooney and Lee, 2000).

However, as research continued to become more rigorous, scholars started to sharpen their investigation into the role of political elites in morality policy disputes. Studies were pointing out that political elites were not simply passive actors in the morality policy process. Elites do more than respond to the electorate's opinion or substitute their own ideology when mass opinion provides little direction and the issue is not salient (Haider-Markel, 1999; Haider-Markel, Joslyn and Kniss, 2000).

Similar to nonmorality policies, elites are often crucial entrepreneurs in morality policymaking (Mintrom, 1997; Mintrom and Norman, 2009). Nicholson-Crotty and Meier (2005) argue that valence issues are suited to moral entrepreneurs, who function in a similar way to policy entrepreneurs, but they use different tools (i.e., moral suasion and deviant social constructions) to enact policy change. Their argument has been supported by studies indicating that the actions of political elites can essentially create new morality issues or stimulate issue salience through a variety of mechanisms.

Moral entrepreneurs can exploit an issue when no viable opposition exists. Consensus morality issues can become a fast track for the politically ambitious, who view these types of issues as "a painless way to make a political reputation" (Meier, 1994, 222; Meier, 2001). Criminal activity such as drinking and driving or drug use are two uncontested issues that can be parlayed into political capital for entrepreneurs (Meier, 1994; Houston and Richardson, 2004). Policy entrepreneurs, rather than state determinants, were also found to be the catalyst for other "get tough against crime" legislation introduced and enacted in the states (Williams, 2003).

In a related vein, entrepreneurs can also exploit the miscalculation of the populace's consensus on a morality issue and re-cast it as a nonmorality issue. For example, Brisbin (2001) traced the elimination of censorship in movies to the swift actions of policy entrepreneurs. They seized on the public's growing tolerance of sexual expression and ushered in a rating system to replace the practice of censorship.

Exploitation of social construction: however, much research has indicated that moral entrepreneurs are more likely to capitalize on a different form of exploitation, which is predicated on negative social constructions of a group. "Entrepreneurs are more likely to define deviance successfully when they can identify an entire group with a particular behavior and create fear that the behavior represents a danger not only to that group but also to the rest of society" (Nicholson-Crotty and Meier, 2005, 227). Political actors' perceptions and portrayal of a particular group's identity help shape the types of policies (either beneficial or punitive) which are designed for that group.

Ingram and Schneider describe the process of fusing social constructions and policy together as degenerative politics, "which is characterized by its exploitation of derogatory social constructions, manipulations of symbols or logic, and deceptive communications that masks the true purpose of policy" (Ingram and Schneider, 2005, 11). Many groups, from African Americans to immigrants to Japanese Americans, have been castigated and constructed as an undeserving constituency at various times in American history. Elites have used these negative social constructions to foster policies that aim to eliminate or significantly curtail the rights of these groups (Bensonsmith, 2005; DiAlto, 2005; Newton, 2005). Given the origin of these policies, they are frequently illogically designed, punitive, and ineffective (Schneider and Ingram, 1993; Meier, 1994, 2001; Ingram and Schneider, 2005; Nicholson-Crotty and Meier, 2005).

This dynamic makes morality policies ripe for political actors' gain at the expense of the policy's recipients. Social construction, similar to political branding, can be leveraged as an intangible yet effective resource in the policymaking process. Doan and Williams' (2008) research elucidates how political elites can build on prevailing social constructions to enact significant policy change.

Wedding the literatures of morality politics and social construction to investigate policies has helped bridge some previously unanswered questions. Research has strongly indicated that the level of salience is causally related to several measurable outcomes, ranging from political responsiveness to electoral outcomes. However, how and why these issues, relative to nonmorality issues, present opportunities that can more handily be manipulated and exploited for political gain has been less clear. Studies suggest that the absence of opposition on consensus issues or the strategic actions of entrepreneurs explain this, but they do not indicate why this expectation should uniquely apply to morality issues.

Social construction provides a large link. Issue salience can rapidly escalate, and these issues can be leveraged by elites because many of these morality issues are firmly linked to widespread social constructions of disadvantaged, marginalized, and vulnerable populations. These constructions are rooted deep in the collective history and psyche of society, and therefore it does not take nearly as much effort to capitalize on these as compared to the resources needed to refute, counter, and reformulate them.

Another look at institutions: morality politics scholars have long noted that federalism is an ideal setting for morality politics because it provides multiple institutional venues for these highly rancorous conflicts. Most morality disputes are fought at the state level, where states can accommodate the more homogenous preferences of their citizens on morality issues, instead of contending with the heterogeneous preferences of citizens that are expressed at the national level (Mooney, 2000). When morality policies are determined in states, policymakers can expedite the process of achieving parity between preferences and policy. Morality policies can then typically be moved from the active and contentious stage of policymaking into a dormant phase where stability has been achieved (Mooney, 2000).

However, studies have rivaled the notion that the state is the only arena where these disputes originate. The federal government can also generate instability by creating policy shocks, which can lead to conflicts that are difficult to reconcile. Abstinence-only education, instigated by Congress, is one instance of this disruption. Faced with implementing a morality policy that was at odds with many states' preferences, some states opted to mold the implementation of the policy around a looser interpretation of its guidelines (Arsneault, 2001; Vergari, 2001). But rather than hasten consensus and stability, bureaucratic discretion at the state level generated more conflict, which eventually resulted in the federal government tightening the requirements of the original law (Arseneault, 2001; Doan and Williams, 2008).[1]

The enactment of this policy underscores the capacity of political elites to initiate significant morality policy change at the national level. The actions of national policymakers have implications for morality politics, particularly in terms of disrupting the congruency between local culture and policy. Patton's (2007) research on the Supreme Court's influence on states' adoption of abortion policies provides additional empirical evidence, documenting the impact intergovernmental activity can have on morality policymaking in the states.

These, as well as other studies, indicate that there are a variety of institutional mechanisms that can be used to initiate morality conflict and socialize it among the electorate. For instance, some astute scholars have observed that contemporary American political parties are growing increasingly polarized around social issues. Examining party activists, Layman et al. (2010) yield evidence suggesting that changes in political elites' behavior, opposed to changes in the electorate, are responsible for the more pronounced ideological divide between the two major parties. Their research indicates that the interplay between institutional arrangements (the open nomination process) and the strategic election-seeking behavior of political hopefuls has created the opportunity for party activists to push their respective political parties away from centrist positions on a broad range of issues. "For many individuals, party support is a goal in its own right, motivating political involvement, shaping policy preferences, and serving as a potent force in structuring political change" (Layman et al., 2010, 344).

Although the research investigating the import of institutions is not as developed in this literature, it is a promising avenue for future research. While Meier's (1999, 2001) formalized model of morality politics explicitly included elements of behavior and institutions, the demand-creating role of the latter has not been given due attention by morality scholars. Yet political elites and institutions are central to the politics surrounding morality issues. These issues provide several strategic opportunities for the politically ambitious. Elites can use institutional decisions, arrangement, or rules to capitalize on new or existing morality issues.

CONCLUSIONS AND FUTURE PURSUITS

Morality policies tend to exhibit a remarkable resilience that beckons the electorate and elites to take up these issues and over time revisit many of them. This pattern has persisted throughout American history, regardless of whether scholars found it worthy of researching. Consequently, one of the most significant collective contributions of the morality politics research is the production of scientific evidence documenting the impact that values, identities, and culture may have on political life.

Scholars embarked on studies of morality policies modeled in the tradition of creating a typology. Similar to all typologies, a morality policy category represents an ideal classification that is rarely emulated in the real world. Scholars have spent considerable time defining morality politics and identifying the characteristics associated with these policies. A reasonable degree of consensus has been reached over a definition and the key characteristics, which has produced a solid foundation for locating factors that may be relevant in subsequent investigations.

However, while many of the characteristics have been supported by research, studies have also revealed many exceptions that run counter to the expectations stemming from the typology. Depending on the specific issue, the time period under investigation, and the operationalization of the outcome, the analyses produce different conclusions about the uniqueness and import of morality issues on politics. One of the more surprising findings may also be the most insightful: morality issues are not ranked as more salient than nonmorality issues (Mooney and Schuldt, 2008). Mooney and Schuldt (2008) speculate that morality policies are salient to those who are interested in the issue, and these loud voices have been mistakenly interpreted as widespread salience. In light of much of the research demonstrating the conditional nature of salience, their speculation seems more plausible. Elites play a crucial role in creating, fostering, and stabilizing salient morality issues. Rather than morality issues possessing an inherent saliency, the definition of these disputes (involving belief systems) lends them to being rapidly deployed among the electorate as a salient issue, but only when framed as such by elites.

Since its inception, the research on morality politics has expanded, and aspects of this literature have become incorporated into studies spanning well beyond the field of public policy. This growth also suggests a compass for the future direction of morality politics research. Using a typology approach to study, morality policy fostered research in an area that was largely overlooked in the public policy field. However, the literature needs to move beyond defining characteristics and finding exceptions to the general characteristics.

Morality issues generate much more attention than they appear to warrant in terms of their contribution to the maintenance and stability of democracy when measured against other policy issue areas such as economics, national security, or foreign policy. Moreover, out of the policy universe, morality policies comprise a very small sample of the policies that are attended to by government. Yet, these policies draw elites and masses alike to them, as well as stimulating public discourse.

The literature's implications for larger theoretical questions concerning democracy are of paramount importance. Many morality policy studies suggest that unlike any other group of issues, the ideals of representative democracy, particularly responsiveness and elite?mass opinion congruence, may best be reflected in the process of making morality policies. Conversely, other studies simultaneously unmask the limitations and even harm of representative and direct democracy on vulnerable groups of citizens. It is through this seeming contradiction in the findings that the clearest direction and the most significant future contribution of this literate rest: the morality policy process and the politics generated by it provide an important testing ground for democratic theory because they involve political behavior as well as political institutions.

Perhaps more than any other policy area, studies of morality politics have the potential to provide a location for testing the interplay of the tangible (i.e., institutions and behavior) and intangible (i.e., the manipulation of group attributes) causal mechanisms that produce political change. Morality politics are rationally and strategically used to influence the rules, arrangements, and outcomes in politics. The morality politics scholarship has drawn attention to a unique class of issues that are theoretically important to, and influential on, elite and mass political behavior, institutions, and the policymaking process. As this body of literature and real-world politics indicate, these polarizing conflicts are becoming even more important in the twenty-first century.

NOTE

1. See Haider-Markel (1998) for a similar pattern on hate crimes.

REFERENCES

Adams, Greg D. 1997. "Abortion: Evidence of an Issue Evolution." *American Journal of Political Science 41* (3): 718–737.

Arsneault, Shelly. 2001. "Values and Virtue: The Politics of Abstinence-Only Sex Education." *The American Review of Public Administration 31* (4): 436–454.

Baumgartner, Frank R. and Bryan D. Jones. 1993. *Agendas and Instability in American Politics.* Chicago, IL: University of Chicago Press.

Bensonsmith, Dionne. 2005. "Jezebels, Matriarchs, and Welfare Queens: The Moynihan Report of 1965 and the Social Construction of African-American Women in Welfare Policy." In Anne L. Schneider and Helen M. Ingram (eds), *Deserving and Entitled: Social Construction and Public Policy.* New York: State University of New York Press, pp. 243–259.

Berkman, Michael and Eric Plutzer. 2009. "Scientific Expertise and the Culture War: Public Opinion and the Teaching of Evolution in the American States." *Perspectives on Politics. 7* (3): 485–499.

Brisbin, Richard A. Jr. 2001. "From Censorship to Ratings: Substantive Rationality, Political Entrepreneurship, and Sex in the Movies." In Christopher Z. Mooney (ed.), *The Public Clash of Private Values.* New York: Chatham House Publishers, pp. 91–112.

Calfano, Brian Robert. 2010. "The Power of Brand: Beyond Interest Group Influence in U.S. State Abortion Politics." *State Politics & Policy Quarterly 10* (3): 227–247.

Camobreco, John and Michelle A. Barnello. 2008. "Democratic Responsiveness and Policy Shock: The Case of State Abortion Policy." *State Politics & Policy Quarterly 8* (1): 48–65.

Carmines, Edward G. and James A. Stimson. 1980. "The Two Faces of Issue Voting." *American Political Science Review 74* (1): 78–91.

Carmines, Edward G. and James A. Stimson. 1989. *Issue Evolution: Race and the Transformation of American Politics.* Princeton, NJ: Princeton University Press.

Cocca, Carolyn E. 2002. "The Politics of Statutory Rape Laws: Adoption and Reinventions of Morality Policy in the States, 1971–1999." *Polity 35* (1): 51–72.

Craig, Stephen C., Michael D. Martinez, James G. Kane, and Jason Gainous. 2005. "Core Values, Value Conflict, and Citizens' Ambivalence about Gay Rights." *Political Research Quarterly 58* (1): 5–17.

DiAlto, Stephanie J. 2005. "From 'Problem Minority' to 'Model Minority': The Changing Social Construction of Japanese Americans." In Anne L. Schneider and Helen M. Ingram (eds), *Deserving and Entitled: Social Construction and Public Policy.* New York: State University of New York Press, pp. 81–103.

Doan, Alesha E. 2007. *Opposition and Intimidation: The Abortion Wars and Strategies of Political Harassment.* Ann Arbor, MI: University of Michigan Press.

Doan, Alesha E. and Jean C. Williams. 2008. *Politics of Virginity: Abstinence in Sex Education.* Westport, CT: Praeger Publisher.

Donovan, Todd, Caroline J. Tolbert, and Daniel A. Smith. 2008. "Priming Presidential Votes by Direct Democracy." *The Journal of Politics 70* (4): 1217–1231.

Goggin, Malcolm L. and Christopher Z. Mooney. 2001. "Congressional Use of Policy Information on Fact and Value Issues." In Christopher Z. Mooney (ed.), *The Public Clash of Private Values.* New York: Chatham House Publishers, pp. 130–139.

Haider-Markel, Donald P. 1998. "The Politics of Social Regulatory Policy: State and Federal Hate Crime Policy and Implementation Effort." *Political Research Quarterly 51:* 69–88.

Haider-Markel, Donald P. 1999. "Morality Policy and Individual-level Political Behavior: The Case of Legislative Voting on Lesbian and Gay Issues." *Policy Studies Journal 27* (4): 735–749.

Haider-Markel, Donald P. 2001. "Morality in Congress? Legislative Voting on Gay Issues." In Christopher Z. Mooney (ed.), *The Public Clash of Private Values.* New York: Chatham House Publishers, pp. 115–129.

Haider-Markel, Donald P., and Matthew S. Kaufman. 2006. "Public Opinion and Policy Making in the Culture Wars: Is There a Connection between Opinion and Sate Policy on Gay and Lesbian Issues?" In Jeffrey E. Cohen (ed.), *Public Opinion in State Politics.* Stanford, CA: Stanford University, pp. 163–182.

Haider-Markel, Donald P. and Kenneth J. Meier. 1996. "The Politics of Gay and Lesbian Rights: Expanding the Scope of Conflict." *Journal of Politics 58* (May): 332–349.

Haider-Markel, Donald P, Mark R. Joslyn, and Chad J. Kniss. 2000. "Minority Group Interests and Political Representation: Gay Elected Officials in the Policy Process." *The Journal of Politics 62* (2): 568–577.

Houston, David J. and Lilliard E. Richardson Jr. 2004. "Drinking-and-Driving in America: A Test of Behavioral Assumptions Underlying Public Policy." *Political Research Quarterly 57* (1): 53–64.

Hunter, James Davidson. 1991. *Culture Wars: The Struggle to Define America.* New York: Basic Books.

Hunter, James Davidson. 1994. *Before the Shooting Begins: Searching for Democracy in America's Culture War.* New York: Free Press.

Ingram, Helen M. and Anne L. Schneider (eds), 2005. "Introduction: Public Policy and the Social Construction of Deservedness." In *Deserving and Entitled: Social Construction and Public Policy.* New York: State University of New York Press, pp. 1–28.

Jelen, Ted G. and Clyde Wilcox. 2003. "Causes and Consequences of Public Attitudes Toward Abortion: A Review and Research Agenda." *Political Research Quarterly 56* (4): 489–500.

Lax, Jeffrey R. and Justin H. Phillips. 2009. "Gay Rights in the States: Public Opinion and Policy Responsiveness." *American Political Science Review 103* (3): 367–386.

Layman, Geoffrey, Thomas M. Carsey, John C. Green, Richard Herrera, and Rosalyn Cooperman. 2010. "Activists and Conflict Extension in American Party Politics." *American Political Science Review 104* (2): 324–346.

Lewis, Gregory B. and Arthur, C. Brooks. 2005. "A Question of Morality: Artists' Values and Public Funding for the Arts." *Public Administration Review 65:* 8–17.

Lindaman, Kara and Donald P. Haider-Markel. 2002. "Issue Evolution, Political Parties, and the Culture Wars." *Political Research Quarterly 55* (1): 91–110.

Lowi, Theodore. 1972. "Four Systems of Politics, Policy, and Choice." *Public Administration Review 32:* 298–310.

Meier, Kenneth J. 1994. *The Politics of Sin: Drugs, Alcohol, and Public Policy*. New York: M. E. Sharpe.

Meier, Kenneth J. 1999. "Drugs, Sex, Rock, and Roll: A Theory of Morality Politics." *Policy Studies Journal 27* (4): 681–695.

Meier, Kenneth J. 2001. "Drugs, Sex, Rock, and Roll: A Theory of Morality Politics." In Christopher Z. Mooney (ed.), *The Public Clash of Private Values*. New York: Chatham House Publishers, pp. 21–36.

Mintrom, Michael. 1997. "Policy Entrepreneurs and the Diffusion of Innovation." *American Journal of Political Science 41* (3): 738–770.

Mintrom, Michael and Norman, P. 2009. "Policy Entrepreneurship and Policy Change." *Policy Studies Journal 37*: 649–667.

Mooney, Christopher. 2000. "The Decline of Federalism and the Rise of Morality-Policy Conflict in the United States." *Publius 30* (1/2): 171–189.

Mooney, Christopher Z. 2001. "The Public Clash of Private Values: The Politics of Morality Policy." In Christopher Z. Mooney (ed.), *The Public Clash of Private Values*. New York: Chatham House Publishers, pp. 3–20.

Mooney, Christopher and Mei-Hsien Lee. 1995. "Legislating Morality in the American States: The Case of Pre-Roe Abortion Regulation Reform." *American Journal of Political Science 39*: 599–627.

Mooney, Christopher and Mei-Hsien Lee. 1999. "The Temporal Diffusion of Morality Policy: The Case of Death Penalty Legislation in the American States." *Policy Studies Journal 27* (4): 766–780.

Mooney, Christopher and Mei-Hsien Lee. 2000. "The Influence of Values on Consensus and Contentious Morality Policy: U.S. Death Penalty Reform, 1965–82." *The Journal of Politics 62* (1): 223–239.

Mooney, Christopher Z. and Mei-Hsien Lee. 2001. "The Temporal Diffusion of Morality Policy: The Case of Death Penalty Legislation in the American States." In Christopher Z. Mooney (ed.), *The Public Clash of Private Values*. New York: Chatham House Publishers, pp. 170–183.

Mooney, Christopher Z. and Richard G. Schuldt. 2008. "Does Morality Policy Exist? Testing a Basic Assumption." *Policy Studies Journal 36* (2): 199–218.

Newton, Lina. 2005. "It is Not a Questions of Being Anti-Immigration: Categories of Deservedness in Immigration." In Anne L. Schneider and Helen M. Ingram (eds), *Deserving and Entitled: Social Construction and Public Policy*. New York: State University of New York Press, pp. 139–167.

Nice, David C. 1988. "Abortion Clinic Bombings as Political Violence." *American Journal of Political Science 32* (1): 178–195.

Nicholson, Stephen P. 2003. "The Political Environment and Ballot Proposition Awareness." *American Journal of Political Science 47* (3): 403–410.

Nicholson-Crotty, Sean and Kenneth J. Meier. 2005. "From Perception to Public Policy: Translating Social Constructions into Policy Designs." In Anne L. Schneider and Helen M. Ingram (eds), *Deserving and Entitled: Social Construction and Public Policy*. New York: State University of New York Press, pp. 223–242.

Norrander, Barbara and Clyde Wilcox. 2001. "Public Opinion and Policymaking in the States: The Case of Post-Roe Abortion Policy." In Christopher Z. Mooney (ed.), *The Public Clash of Private Values*. New York: Chatham House Publishers, pp. 143–159.

Patton, Dana. 2007. "The Supreme Court and Morality Policy Adoption in the American States." *Political Research Quarterly 60* (3): 468–488.

Pew Research Center for the People and the Press. 2007. "As Marriage and Parenthood Drift Apart, Public is Concerned about Social Impact." *Survey Reports* (July 1). Available at: <http://people-press.org/reports> (accessed June 18, 2013).

Saad, Lydia. 2010. "Four Moral Issues Sharply Divide Americans." Gallop (May 26, 2010). Available at: <http://www.gallup.com/poll/137357/four-moral-issues-sharply-divide-americans.aspx> (accessed June 18, 2013).

Schneider, Anne L. and Helen M. Ingram. 1993. "The Social Construction of Target Populations: Implications for Politics and Policy." *American Political Science Review 87* (2): 334–347.

Sharp, Elaine B. 1999. *Culture Wars and Local Politics*. Lawrence: University Press of Kansas.

Sharp, Elaine B. 2002. "Culture, Institutions, and Urban Officials' Responses to Morality Issues." *Political Research Quarterly 55* (4): 861–883.

Sharp, Elaine B. 2005. *Morality Politics in American Cities*. Lawrence: University Press of Kansas.

Smith, Kevin B. 2001. "Clean Thoughts and Dirty Minds: The Politics of Porn." In Christopher Z. Mooney (ed.), *The Public Clash of Private Values*. New York: Chatham House Publishers, pp. 187–200.

Smith, T. Alexander and Raymond Tatalovich. 2003. *Cultures at War: Moral Conflicts in Western Democracies*. Toronto, Canada: University of Toronto Press.

Stabile, Bonnie. 2007. "Demographic Profile of States with Human Cloning Laws." *Politics and the Life Sciences 26* (1): 43–50.

Studlar, Donley T. 2001. "What Constitutes Morality Policy? A Cross-National Analysis." In Christopher Z. Mooney (ed.), *The Public Clash of Private Values*. New York: Chatham House Publishers, pp. 37–51.

Tatalovich, Raymond and Byron W. Daynes. 1998. "Conclusion: Social Regulatory Policy Process." In Raymond Tatalovich and Byron Daynes (eds), *Moral Controversies in American Politics: Cases in Social Regulatory Policy*. New York: M. E. Sharpe, pp. 258–270.

Tatalovich, Raymond, and Byron W. Daynes. 1988. *Social Regulatory Policy: Moral Controversies in American Politics*. Boulder, CO: Westview Press.

Tatalovich, Ramond, T. Alexander Smith, and Michael P. Bobic. 1994. "Moral Conflict and the Policy Process." *Policy Currents 4*: 1–7.

True, James L., Bryan D. Jones, and Frank R. Baumgartner. 2007. "Punctuated-equilibrium Theory: Explaining Stability and Change in American Policymaking." In Paul A. Sabatier (ed.), *Theories of the Policy Process.*. Boulder, CO: Westview, pp. 155–188.

Vergari, 2001. "Morality Politics and the Implementation of Abstinence-Only Sex Education: A Case of Policy Compromise." In Christopher Z. Mooney (ed.), *The Public Clash of Private Values*. New York: Chatham House Publishers, pp. 201–210.

Webster v, *Reproductive Health Services*. 492 U.S., 490.

Weisberg, Herbert F. 2005. "The Structure of Moral Predispositions in Contemporary American Politics." *The Journal of Politics 67*: 646–668.

Williams, Jackson. 2003. "Criminal Justice Policy Innovation in the States." *Criminal Justice Policy Review 14* (3): 401–422.

CHAPTER 33

....

ENVIRONMENTAL POLICY

....

MICHAEL D. JONES, ELIZABETH A. SHANAHAN,
AND LISA J. HAMMER

IN 1973, renowned policy process scholar Paul A. Sabatier observed a trend in environmental policy that, in his estimation, provided fertile ground to observe and map the unique characteristics of the American federalist system (Sabatier, 1973, 217). Sabatier noted that the interactions between state and federal levels of government were critical in environmental policy, with overlapping and contested jurisdictions interacting with the unique characteristics of environmental policy that likely produced meaningful variations in policy outcomes and processes. Sabatier wanted to better understand those variations, and in 1973 he praised research for offering some insight into state and local environmental policy implementation and formulation.[1] However, concurrent with this praise, he also simultaneously maligned research in state and local environmental policy for being mostly descriptive, failing to build upon theory, and squandering a rather unique opportunity. That unique opportunity, of course, was the distinctly comparative essence of state and local environmental policy whereby scholars could, in theory, explain variation across states and—perhaps, should diligence and a bit of luck meet—speak to both better policy processes and better policy outcomes. That call was made nearly 40 years ago. This chapter describes where we are today, and makes an effort to assess how far we have come.

Our approach is not one that tries to catalogue everything that has been written and researched related to state and local environmental policy. Such a task approaches the impossible, or at least would require a career or two to accomplish. That is not to say we make no attempt to show the state of aggregate research. We do. However, we take a representative approach, selecting works that we view as seminal in emphasizing what we identify to be important themes and trends.

We approach our task by first offering a brief historical but policy-centered background, in which the reader can situate the development of state and local environmental policy. We pay considerable attention to the role of federalism in shaping that context, focusing on the dichotomy of centralist positions that advocate a strong role for the federal government, and decentralization, which posits a stronger role for states and local governments. No doubt the actual—and evolving—allocation of authority, responsibility, and power to federal, state, and local jurisdictions has helped form the unique characteristics of environmental policy in the United States. We conclude that the debate about the proper allocation of power continues, but that certain developments such as the proliferation of climate change mitigation policies strongly suggest a continued importance of state and local governments for policy innovation, adoption, and implementation.

The next section of the chapter attempts to summarize the state of academic and scientific research on state and local environmental policy. We find that comparative research seeking to explain environmental policy process and outcome variation across states has made considerable progress, rising to meet Sabatier's 1973 challenge. However, we also note that there is still considerable work to do. The next two sections try to give the reader an aggregate sense of what substantive environmental policy areas are being studied. We do this by reporting the aggregated peer-reviewed publications reported in three databases between 1980 and 2011. We also report the attention given to state and local environmental policy by political science.

Having provided a big-picture context, our next two sections attempt to drill a bit deeper by focusing on two areas that seemed especially important in our review. First, we offer a detailed account of the centrality of public participation to state and local environmental policy. We find that scholars are increasingly studying public participation and its role in state and local environmental policy, but more often than not sing its praises, while comparatively little attention has been given to the possible negatives.

Second, we offer an independent section on climate change policy, given its currency globally and its rapid success locally. Climate change policy, in our estimation, is a new generation of environmental policy that incorporates elements of participation, interlaces levels of government, but is predominantly emerging at the state and local level. More importantly, we argue, the proliferation of climate change mitigation and adaptation policies challenges the explanatory power of political science theories, with current explanations needing considerable buttressing.

Finally, we provide a brief discussion summarizing where we believe the study of state and local environmental policy is today. We find the research to be prolific, but we also find that research is diffuse, spanning many academic disciplines, subfields, and disciplines. We also find that where there are concentrations of research and scholarly attention, such as the areas of participation and climate change, we have produced considerable knowledge about state and local environmental policy. But therein is the rub; that is, in our estimation where scholarship has narrowed and focused its attention on state and local environmental policy, it has focused more so on the environmental part of the equation and less so on the state and local component. We conclude that the state and local dimension—the role of state and local institutions and their occupants—of environmental policy would benefit from further study, especially in more concentrated academic venues specializing in the study of state and local governance.

BACKGROUND

It has long been the case, even before the environmental decade of the 1970s, that environmental policy has been the province of state and local governments. A product of their practical concerns, states and local governments were some of the first to take steps regarding pollution measures, such as garbage removal (Melosi, 2008) and local smoke control ordinances (Glicksman, 2006). Although environmental responsibility has largely been assumed by state and local governments, the role of state and local governments in environmental policy has varied over time.

With the growing understanding that many environmental issues do not adhere to local or state political and jurisdictional boundaries, the flurry of 1970 federal regulation of pollution was widely supported. The seminal 1963 Clean Air Act pushed states to adhere to pollution abatement standards and to create implementation plans based on national guidelines (Vig and Kraft, 2009). Other federal control from this era came in the form of the revised Clean Air Act in 1970, the Clean Water Act in 1972, and a host of policies regarding pesticides, safe drinking water, resource conservation, hazardous waste (superfund), and importantly, the creation of the Environmental Protection Agency.

Although the federal government took originating control with the myriad of legislation in this environmental decade, Congress was clear that states were to remain in a primary role safeguarding public health and safety (Glicksman, 2006). As such, much of the new environmental legislation was implemented by state and local governments. For example, the 1972 Clean Water Act specifically notes that the federal government will recognize and preserve states' rights to prevent and reduce pollution and protect land and water resources. The responsibility of determining water quality standards under the Clean Water Act was also left to the states, although states' plans needed approval by the EPA. Furthermore, most of the federal pollution control legislation gives states the opportunity to request control of permit procedures, or other administrative control (Glicksman, 2006). Much of the early legislation also integrates jurisdictional responsibilities, creating federal–state partnerships. For example, the 1976 Resource Conservation and Recovery Act explicitly calls for a federal–state relationship to carry out its purpose. Most of the early federal environmental legislation also includes a significant role of the states regarding implementation. Importantly, the federal pollution control statute includes a savings clause, which reserves the right of any state to adopt more stringent pollution control measures (Glicksman, 2006).

The early 1970s, along with the implementation of major federal policies, was a time of optimism for federal and state environmental cooperation, as well as for future environmental quality. William Ruckelshaus, the first EPA administrator, wrote that it was time to address the "serious creakings" in the federal–state relationship and start on a foundation of mutual trust (Ruckelshaus, 1973, 1). He suggested a division of labor and commissioned a working group of state representatives to collaborate on policy ideas. His objectives included the strengthening of state environmental programs, continued and increasing financial support to states, as well as quickly determining the best federal levels of control. Finally, with close cooperation and heavy state and local responsibility, Ruckelshaus (1973) concluded that the United States was set to become a bright and clean nation.

The Decentralization Debate

Although national control was initially assumed, the vast majority of federal environmental policy relied on state and local implementation. Deemed decentralization, cooperative/fiscal federalism, or civic environmentalism, the basic justification for local policy responsibility is that the responsibility for providing a service should be placed with the smallest jurisdiction whose boundaries encompass the various benefits and costs associated with the provision of service (Oates and Portney, 2003). In 1973, Paul Sabatier described the structure of federal and state control as a rather distinct division of labor, with the federal government assuming primary responsibility for at least minimum standards, with the states and localities retaining primary responsibility for implementation "subject to as much oversight as Federal man power can provide" (Sabatier, 1973, 219). This command-and-control structure has resulted in a debate surrounding federalism and decentralization issues that has lasted for over three decades.

Richard Stewart's 1977 article is seen as a pivotal moment for local environmental policy. While stating that increased state and local environmental policy responsibility compromises federal programs, Stewart, an ardent advocate of centralization, concludes that Congress has a moral justification for power to mandate state controls on public pollution sources. Notable, however, is Stewart's discussion of centralization and his predictions of future state policy involvement. The benefits to decentralization, as Stewart saw them, are responsiveness, experimentation, self-determination, and diversity, while benefits to centralization include the ability to control or mediate the tragedy of the commons, transaction costs, disparities in effective representation, negative externalities, and costly bargaining and conflict. The inter-jurisdictional conflict and competition issue, or the race-to-the-bottom theory, became the major justification for centralized control. The claim is that local officials will set excessively lax standards to hold down costs for existing firms and in an effort to encourage business and economic growth (Oates and Portney, 2003).These issues have been repeatedly discussed and debated in the three decades since Stewart's article, and remain unresolved.

Scholars who take a position on the centralization/decentralization debate in environmental policy are often referred to as "first-generation" and "second-generation" thinkers. Etsy (1996) defines first-generation thinking. Epitomized by scholars like Richard Stewart (1977), first-generation scholarship advocates for centralization, relies heavily on common law nuisance principles and the potential ill-effects to state control after the original Clean Air Act, and draws our attention to the potential negatives of decentralization, such as the race to the bottom. The race to the bottom refers to a situation where competing states will systematically dismantle regulatory agencies and restraints in the pursuit of state interests, such as attracting businesses by offering lower taxes and oversight (see, for example, Rom, 2006). In short, first-generation theorizing indicated states would have trouble safeguarding the environment.

Second-generation thinking relied on five arguments for decentralization, including: the promotion of diversity, a states-as-laboratories argument, advocating that intergovernmental competition promotes efficiency and effectiveness, public choice claims regarding representation, rejection of morality-based arguments for federal regulation, and an assumption that pollution spillovers are insignificant (Etsy, 1996). Research emerged supporting this line of thinking. For example, List and Gerking (2000) present evidence that decentralization during Reagan's time did not produce a decline in environmental quality, indicating that there is more to states' quality measures than federal policy. Others (e.g. Frederickson and Millimet, 2002; Millimet, 2003; Rabe, 2003) conclude that a race to the bottom did not materialize during the 1980s; rather, there may have been a race to the top instead.

Along with questions regarding the theory behind state competition, the relationship between the federal government and the states has also been questioned. For example, rather than being a form of cooperativism, Welborne (1988) deems the joint responsibility of states and the federal government as conjoint in most cases. Conjoint federalism involves the intent to force state action with regulatory incentives, federal policy approval, with national standards as a fallback in the event of state participation. Conjoint authority involves a form of *de jure* implementation authority by the states, as opposed to any actual independent authority (Welborne, 1988). At the time of Welborne's article, the EPA had given states authority of over 700 federal programs, "including 82 percent of all programs related to the Clean Air Act" (Rabe, 2003). In any event, the evidence and arguments produced by first- and second-generation adherents have not been definitive in any real way, and the conversation continues.

At a Crossroads

The decentralization debate has lasted for the entire effective history of U.S. environmental policy. Our feel of the literature is of a consensus that state and local environmental policy and its relationship to federal regulation is at a crossroads, with scholars offering diverse and frequently innovative perspectives on the correct path forward. Some are quite pessimistic. For example, Fiorino (2000) argues that while states take independent action when implementing federal programs, and pass legislation on their own, most observers find that the current relationship between states and the federal government, as it relates to environmental policy, is highly centralized, unresponsive, and inefficient. Fiorino posits that such principles and capacities, if correct, pose significant obstacles to U.S. environmental policy agendas. Counter to Fiorino others, such as Huque and Watton (2010), suggest that the United States will continue along the path of devolution and decentralization as command-and-control measures give way to privatization.

Some scholars have suggested a hybrid solution to the decentralization debate. For example, Etsy (1996) offers a hybrid strategy, emphasizing centralization with concern for local knowledge—dependent upon the problem at hand and what sorts of regulatory failures are most significant. Similarly, Lemos and Agrawal (2006) promote emerging hybrid modes of governance and partnerships based on general trends of globalization, decentralization, market- and incentive-based governance, and cross-scale governance. Optimistically, these scholars emphasize the importance of collaboration among sub-national, national, and international governmental entities.

Other scholarship has offered innovative models of administration and interaction to resolve the decentralization debate. For example, recent literature (Osofsky, 2010) has stressed the importance of diagonal environmental mechanisms, which involve simultaneous vertical and horizontal interactions between groups. Hypothetically, such an arrangement might create a vertical relationship between the EPA and states, while also creating a horizontal relationship with stakeholders at the same level, which, some have argued, more closely matches the "cross-cutting" nature of the environmental problem itself (e.g., Osofsky, 2010). However, such changes may not come easily. Barry Rabe (2011) observes that it has proved difficult for any presidential administration to make any major shifts in the federal and state relationship in environmental policy; however, he also concedes that recent developments with the Obama administration may be changing that dynamic. In 2009, President Obama released a statement regarding the importance of state and local control of environmental policy, stating that preemption of state law should not be taken lightly. Osofsky (2010) notes that this presidential position, along with the Supreme Court's treatment of *Massachusetts v. EPA*, has put pressure on Congress to act. Perhaps with this recent confluence of political forces, we are seeing a new period of optimistic federalism, but that remains to be determined. Indeed, and as we discuss later in the chapter, we believe the issue of climate change is playing an important role in reshaping the relationship of state and local governments with the federal government.

The Study of State and Local Environmental Policy

Although the debate regarding the merits of decentralization has not been resolved, the number of state and local environmental policies and the range of issues they address have continued to swell behind the banter. These next sections attempt to provide a crude roadmap to the development of the research that has attempted to explain and, in some cases, predict environmental policy processes and outcomes. First we address the comparative research that has aspired to explain environmental policy variation across state and local jurisdictions. We then follow this section with a discussion of the substantive environmental policy areas studied at the state and local level that have been published in peer-reviewed journals between 1980 and 2011. We conclude this section by reporting how state and local environmental policy has fared in political science.

State Comparative Research

Sabatier (1973) indicated that because states had assumed significant autonomy in environmental policy implementation, comparative studies provided an invaluable opportunity to increase knowledge of the policy process. However, Sabatier also observed that much of the existing research at that time was "of little explanatory import, being either largely descriptive in nature or failing to depart from and build upon knowledge" (Sabatier, 1973, 223). In short, Sabatier called for more rigorous, theoretically driven research, and lots of it (Sabatier, 1973). How far have we come since 1973? In our estimation, in the past decades scholars have responded admirably, although there is still much work to do.

Several works do well to document and illustrate the progress that has been made in comparative state and local environmental policy scholarship. For example, Lester (1994) finds that Sabatier's call for further research had been answered in the form of descriptive, qualitative, and emerging quantitative studies, but there was still a need for a more comprehensive comparative theory that more carefully considers intergovernmental variables. He suggests two exemplar works in Ringquist (1993) and Lowry (1992) that future scholarship should emulate. Seemingly answering the call, Hays, Esler and Hays (1996), realizing that prior comparative studies focused on a variety of individual environmental policies, embarked on a study to assess a state's general commitment to the environment. They found that traditional variables explained little and that much of the variation in state environmental commitment could be explained by having liberal public opinion and organized interests. A few years later, Frederickson and Millimet (2002), found a positive association between nearby states' environmental policies occurring within a two-to-five-year window, although this relationship was not uniform across all U.S. regions and was conditioned by abatement costs.

In 2011, Rebecca Bromley-Trujillo, a doctoral student at Michigan State, completed a dissertation on state environmental policy that aimed to fill the substantial gaps in comparative state environmental policy research. Acknowledging the dearth of research, Bromley-Trujillo created a scale of environmental policy activity that was used to analyze state trends in 18 program types, including energy issues, climate change, brownfields, sustainable development, and air pollution. Her results specified the conditions under which environmental action was most likely to take place in a state. States that are democratically controlled, more ideologically liberal, had strong environmental interest group presences, and possessed sufficient wealth and administrative capacity were more likely to take environmental action. She found significant variation among states with regard to number and types of policies passed, policy areas, and implementation. However, Bromley-Trujillo indicates that generally, states tend to adopt policies when other governmental bodies fail to do so. Also, her scale demonstrates that states with higher activity levels are more likely to pursue additional policies, but which policy is chosen next is unpredictable. While Bromley-Trujillo notes that policy implementation is not analogous with positive outcomes, and that change in the political and economic climate for states has been in flux, overall, her research gives us a good idea of the current position of state environmental policy, and the field would benefit tremendously from more studies like it.

This section shows that since 1973 comparative environmental policy studies have emerged that have aspired to explain variation across states. We have cited some of these studies, and our representative sampling of that literature shows that remarkable progress has been made. We clearly have a better understanding of some of the variables that vary across states. However, those models are far from complete. No doubt future scholarship will build upon these studies, but as our next sections will show, environmental policy at the state and local level could benefit from both a more frequent and more concentrated presence in academic research.

Environmental Issue Foci in State and Local Environmental Policy

In this section, we address the substantive state and local environmental policy areas that have received attention in academic journals. To be sure, what can be categorized as environmental policy is frequently debated and somewhat of a moving target. For example, "environmentalists were once slow to embrace environmental justice (EJ)" as a legitimate part of environmental policy (Layzer, 2012, 104–105), but the EJ movement is now recognized by most scholars and activists as a critical aspect of environmental policy. With the malleability of the concept of environmental policy in mind, we initially approached the process of categorization inductively, reading journal abstracts, and getting a sense which environmental issues at the state and local level were receiving the most attention. After careful evaluation, we settled on 11 environmental policy areas we identified to be most relevant to the study of state and local policy: clean air, clean water, climate change, environmental justice, hazardous waste, land management, nuclear energy, solar power, waste management, wildlife management, and wind power.

In order to compute the number of publications in academic journals in each of the aforementioned categories, we conducted key word searches using three well-regarded scientific databases: Academic Search Complete, Info Trac, and Web of Science. We limited our search to peer-reviewed journal articles in the United States.[2] To add a temporal element to our analysis, which might help us spot trends in research topics, we further divided citations by decade, going back to the 1980s. For each substantive category, demarcated by decade, we averaged the three counts produced by each of the three databases to produce a mean score for each decade. Figure 33.1 illustrates our findings and Table 33.1 lists the journals identified in our search.

Although environmental policy clearly became a focus of scholars, pundits, and activists, beginning in the 1970s, Figure 33.1 illustrates that the trend did not immediately take in the study of state and local environmental policy. There are remarkably few studies focusing on environmental policy at the state and local levels in the 1980s and 1990s. The studies that do exist focus on clean air and water and waste management. Such a trend likely falls in line with the issue environment of the times as the 1967 Air Quality

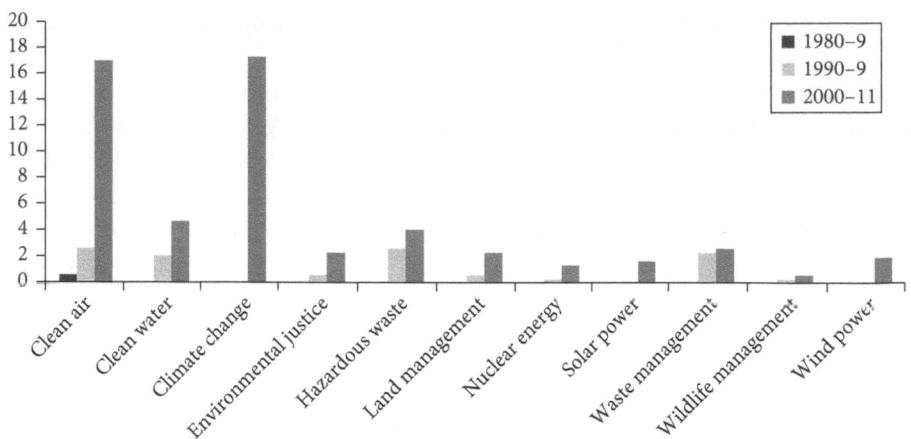

FIGURE 33.1 State and local environmental policy publications, by decade (1980–2011)

Note: Compiled by the authors.

Act and the 1965 Water Quality Act inched these issues to the forefront of people's concerns. Belatedly, researchers were responding to growing concerns and awareness.

Beginning at the turn of the century, however, we see tremendous growth across the board in the mean number of studies in our identified categories. All categories show mean research articles of at least a one, and two categories show incredible spikes in interest. Both climate change and clean air produced slightly over 15 research articles in the past decade. It is fair to say that the importance of state and local environmental policy, as indicated by the increased scholarly attention, has grown over the past decade. We surmise that a good portion of this increased attention is related, in particular, to the increased visibility of issues like climate change. Given the likely importance of climate change, we devote more attention to this critical subject later in the chapter.

Political Science and State and Local Environmental Policy

Previous sections demonstrate that state and local environmental policy is a far-ranging field of study, spanning disciplines, journals, and topical areas. In this section, we briefly examine to what extent the discipline of political science has paid attention to environmental policy at the state and local level. Our focus is on political science because we are political scientists by training. Aside from our obvious bias, as a discipline, political science has formal organizational sections and publication venues that would seem natural to the substance of state and local environmental policy. By our estimate, there are four formally designated sections of the American Political Science Association (APSA) directly relevant to state and local environmental policy: 1) *Federalism and Intergovernmental Relations;* 2) *Public Policy;* 3) *Science,*

Table 33.1 Academic Peer-reviewed Journals Publishing State and Local Environmental Policy Research, 1980–2011

The Policy Studies Journal

Review of Policy Research

The Urban Lawyer

Publius: The Journal of Federalism

Journal of Environmental Planning and Management

Natural Resources Journal

Journal of the American Institute of Planners

State Politics and Policy Quarterly

Environmental Politics

Public Administration Review

The Yale Law Journal

The American Review of Public Administration

Political Research Quarterly

American Journal of Community Psychology

Journal of the Water Pollution Control Federation

Annual Review Environmental Resources

Environmental and Resource Economics

Journal of Environmental Economics and Management

Public Administration Quarterly

Local Environment

Management of Environmental Quality: An International Journal

Policy Sciences

Journal of Urban Economics

Journal of Regional Science

Michigan Law Review

Wake Forest Law Review

Public Organization Review

Northwestern University Law Review

Washington University Journal of Law and Policy

Note: Table compiled by the authors.

Technology and Environmental Policy; and 4) *State Politics and Policy.* To assess the attention given to state and local environmental policy, we examine research publications in each of the official journals of each of the previously mentioned sections. These journals include *Publius, Policy Studies Journal* (PSJ), *Review of Policy Research* (RPR), and *State Politics and Policy Quarterly* (SPPQ). For good measure, we also include the official journal of the APSA—*the American Political Science Review* (APSR)—and the flagship journal of public administration—*Public Administration Review* (PAR).

A simple count of research articles addressing state and local environmental policy published in the journals mentioned in the previous paragraph was obtained by the authors. Excluding supplemental issues, book reviews, editor's notes, but including symposia, we examined all normal journal publications occurring in or between the years of 2001 and 2010. We limited our sample to only those articles dealing with issues in the United States. All articles directly addressing state and local environmental policy within the United States between the years 2001 and 2010 were coded as a one, otherwise they were coded zero. However, determining what actually counts as state and local environmental policy required a few choices.

We placed no limitations on the theoretical focus of the research, but of primary concern was that the substance of the research findings in some way be easily identified as of relevance to a state and/or local political jurisdictions dealing with environmental policy. Of course, this would not preclude federal involvement, as federalism necessarily permeates this literature; however, the study must in some obvious way make clear its relevance to state and local environmental policy. Typically, this meant the authors identified it as such (e.g., Potoski 2002). Other cases, where researchers did not directly identify the research as relevant to state and local jurisdictions, were less obvious; for example, Anderson et al. (2004) examine organizational interest and persistence at the state level. Their focus is clearly not on environmental policy, but does mention and present results related to environmental groups and their lobbying effectiveness (Anderson et al. 2004: 149). In such cases as the Anderson et al. (2004) example, we do not include such articles as clearly falling within the realm of state and local environmental policy. Substantively, we included all research where the authors clearly identified environmentally related policy. Figure 33.2 illustrates our findings.

Figure 33.2 illustrates that the bulk of attention to state and local policy issues is being given by the *Policy Studies Journal,* the generalist journal for public policy scholars. *Review of Policy Research* is a distant second, yielding 18 peer-reviewed articles over the 10-year span examined, followed by *Publius* (15), and *Public Administration Review* (13). In our view, these summative research measures indicate that state and local environmental policy is a salient issue to public administration, public policy scholars, and scholars studying federalism issues more generally. However, the presence of state and local environmental scholarship in the discipline more generally is understated and the lack of a sizeable presence of scholarship in *State Politics and Policy Quarterly* is surprising.

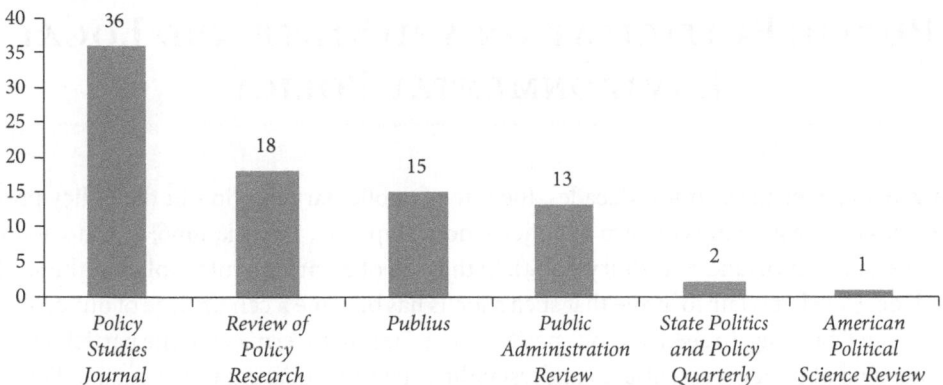

FIGURE 33.2 State and local environmental policy research, by *Political Science Journal* (2001–10).

Note: Compiled by the authors.

In the period from 2001 to 2010, the *American Political Science Review* (APSR) sports one research article dealing explicitly with state and local environmental policy. Fittingly, the article was co-authored by Paul Sabatier (Leach and Sabatier, 2005), introduced to our readers in the opening remarks of this chapter. Sabatier's goal was to improve the visibility and methodological rigor of studies in this area. He has made important strides on both fronts. However, the low number of research articles in the APSR does suggest scholars in political science have more work to do. On the other hand, *State Politics and Policy Quarterly*, the flagship journal of the state and local section of the American Political Science Association only published two articles in the same time period. *State Politics and Policy Quarterly* devoted its attention to other state-related policies, including redistricting, welfare policy, direct democracy, abortion, and elections, to name a few. This is telling, given the title and focus of the journal and, all things considered, *State Politics and Policy Quarterly* is a prime venue for research of the sort we are addressing in this chapter.

To this point, we have provided a background of the historical development of state and local environmental policy. We have framed that discussion within the context of federalism, focusing on the debate regarding the benefits and detriments of centralization and decentralization. We have also focused on the scholarly trends that have brought this literature to a perceived crossroads, paying particular attention to the contribution of comparative research. While these previous sections have taken a wide-angle, holistic picture of state and local environmental policy, our next sections focus the camera lens in, drilling down into what we believe are two substantive areas that having an understanding of is, in our view, absolutely essential to understanding this literature—public participation and climate change policy.

PUBLIC PARTICIPATION AND STATE AND LOCAL ENVIRONMENTAL POLICY

In general, over the past few decades, the role of public participation in the policy process has been a growing concern of policy scholarship (e.g., Dryzek, 1990; Fiorino, 1990; Fischer, 1993; Irvin and Stansbury, 2004). In the case of environmental policy at the state and local level, it is fair to argue that such a focus has become a centerpiece of our collective understanding. Indeed, it is our position that coming to terms with the participatory dimension of policy is essential to understanding state and local environmental policy.

Beginning in the 1970s, there was a pronounced effort by the public and government agencies alike to expand the role of rank-and-file citizens in environmental policy. Such efforts initially manifested themselves as critical facets of national policies such as the National Environmental Policy Act (NEPA) and the National Forest Management Act of 1976 (NFMA), both of which facilitated public participation in environmental policymaking. Perhaps unavoidably, the national trend personified by the aforementioned acts and those like them migrated to state and local jurisdictions, manifesting in a multitude of incarnations, ranging from stakeholder partnerships to public hearings (see Leach et al., 2002, 647). Researchers have devoted considerable efforts to explaining these participatory processes and what effect, if any, they have on state and local environmental policies. While what we have learned is significant, there are still considerable gaps in our knowledge.

Given the incredible amount of research that has been done in this area, we recognize that cataloging the body of work that has examined the role of participation in state and local environmental policy is beyond what one section in one chapter can accomplish (but see, for example, Beierle and Cayford, 2002; Chess and Purcell, 1999). Previous scholarship also points out that even providing a representative sample of such work can be prohibitively difficult (e.g., Newig and Fritsch, 2009, 198–199). What we can do, however, is synthesize relevant themes emergent in the literature and draw attention to what we believe are the important next steps for future scholarship. In brief, what follows does just this by first laying out the theoretical foundation. Next, we discuss a few representative studies of the substantive environmental issues that have been the focus of the work on participation at the state and local level. In particular, we focus on one study that we find especially illustrative in terms of both findings typically produced in this research and demonstrative of what gaps are present. Finally, we close by suggesting how we might best move forward.

Theoretical Underpinnings of Public Participation

A consensus on what, exactly, constitutes participation in state and local environmental policy does not exist (see Steelman and Ascher, 1997 for a salient discussion of public participation in policymaking), with definitions of participation ranging from "mere tokenism to collaborative partnerships" (Chess, 2000, 770). However, that is not to say that attempts have not been made to effectively categorize types of participation. For example, Leach et al. (2002) categorize participation into four categories: stakeholder partnerships, advisory committees, public hearings, and negotiated rule making, where each type of participation engages a different range of issues, involves differing numbers and types of participants, and occurs at differing points in the policy process (Leach et al., 2002, 647). Other scholarship has referred to participatory trends under the umbrella of *New Governance*, where there are quasi-legislative and quasi-judicial activities covering an array of practices including "deliberative democracy, e-democracy, public conversations, participatory budgeting, citizen juries, study circles, collaborative policy making, alternate dispute resolution, mediation, facilitation, early neutral assessment, and arbitration" (Bingham et al., 2005, 547). While the various categorizations certainly serve the functions of the scholarship that employ them, we find a particular characterization useful for the review presented here.

In evaluating the pros and cons of citizen participation in policy, Irvin and Stansbury (2004) demarcate participation in terms of the decision process and outcomes, and in terms of both the effect on citizens and government agencies. Table 33.2 is based on the framework in Irvin and Stansbury (2004, 56–58).

Table 33.2 Advantages and Disadvantages of Citizen Participation in State and Local Environmental Policy

	Citizens		Government	
	Advantages	Disadvantages	Advantages	Disadvantages
Decision Process	1. Education (learn from and inform government) 2. Persuade and enlighten government 3. Gain skills for activist citizenship	1. Time-consuming (even dull) 2. Pointless if decision is ignored.	1. Education (learn from and inform citizens) 2. Persuade citizens; build trust, and allow anxiety or hostility 3. Build strategic alliances 4. Gain legitimacy of decision	1. Time-consuming 2. Costly 3. May backfire, creating more hostility to government
Outcomes	1. Break gridlock; achieve outcomes 2. Gain some control over the policy process	1. Worse policy decision if influenced by opposing interest groups	1. Break gridlock; achieve outcomes 2. Avoid litigation costs 3. Better policy and implementation decisions	1. Loss of decision-making control 2. Possibility of bad decision that is politically impossible to ignore 3. Less budget for implementation of actual projects

Source: Compiled by the authors, based on Irvin and Stansbury (2004).

As Table 33.1 illustrates, Irvin and Stansbury (2004) conceive of participatory processes as having both beneficial and deleterious effects on policy. In terms of benefits, a more participatory-orientated process can both educate citizens about frequently complex issues, while also educating the government about citizen positions and concerns. Increased participation is also found to be a successful means to break gridlock and improve the quality of policy implementation, and create better policy more generally. In terms of potential negatives, Table 33.1 draws attention to the increased costs and loss of efficiency associated with increased citizen participation, while also illuminating that the policy decision making and implementation can be made worse, if the wrong interests establish control, or if government agencies lose control of the process. Using this scheme as a guide, we next briefly address the substantive foci of participation-orientated studies of environmental policy at the state and local level. Our reading of the literature suggests that research has tended toward focusing on illuminating the benefits of participation for citizens.

Public Participation, Environmental Issues, and Policy Outputs

Much like environmental policy at the state and local level in general, studies examining participation and state and local environmental policy have traversed many substantive issue areas. These areas include air quality (O'Rourke and Macey, 2003), environmental justice (e.g., Layzer, 2012) estuary policy (e.g., Koontz et al, 2004), open space (e.g., Layzer, 2002), water quality (e.g., Burroughs, 1999; Landre and Knuth, 1993), water shed management (Irvin and Stansbury, 2004; Leach et al., 2002), wildlife management (e.g., Todd, 2002), and hazardous waste cleanup (e.g., Daley, 2007), to name but a few.[3] In many of these studies, and others like them, the benefits from increased public involvement are clear. For example, Daley (2007) finds that states with more liberal citizens are more likely to develop formalized participation provisions in their hazardous waste programs. A later study by Daley (2008) finds that formalized participation (i.e., CAGs and TAGs) makes it more likely that hazardous waste cleanup efforts will be geared toward neutralizing waste, as opposed to containing it. Todd (2002), studying the controversial topic of wolf management, finds that it was a team of ordinary citizens that were able to form a consensus on a wolf management plan and that it was overwhelming public support for this plan that forced relevant agencies to "enforce the plan as written" (655). Neuman (1996), in a case study of the Umatilla Basin Project (a water rights dispute case), finds that mediation helped facilitate cooperation amongst interested groups, educated them about each other's positions, and that all parties "were generally pleased with the process and outcomes" (Neuman, 1996, 333). What these studies evidence is a more general trend in the literature where state and local environmental research has done an admirable job helping us understand the benefits of participation for citizens.

A particularly illustrative example of the more general trends in this vein of research is found in a thoughtfully written and rigorously implemented study by Dara O'Rourke and Gregg P. Macey (2003). Their study analyzes five different cases occurring in the states of Louisiana and California where the public participated directly in the implementation of environmental policy. In each of the cases, citizens were recruited to participate in monitoring air quality in select areas where polluters were believed to be violating established (but largely unpoliced) environmental standards. Orchestrated and directed by interested nongovernmental groups, citizens voluntarily served on "bucket brigades" that were directly involved in monitoring potential pollution sites. Members of the brigades used low-cost and low-tech air samplers to monitor the air quality near oil refineries, chemical factories, and power plants (O'Rourke and Macey, 2002, 385). The results of these efforts are telling.

Participation in the brigades was found to educate citizens about air quality in their communities, raise general levels of awareness, and gave communities a sense of empowerment. The bucket brigades also served as monitoring systems for the reactions of government agencies, pointing out gaps and inefficiencies. Agency responses to the monitoring, however, were mixed, with some viewing the brigades as a unique citizen complaint and others altering monitoring strategies (O'Rourke and Macey, 2002, 397).

Interpreted through the lens of Irvin and Stansbury (2004) (Table 33.1), two trends in the state and local environmental policy literature more generally are brought to the forefront by our exemplar case. First, the focus of O'Rourke and Macey's (2003) findings is clearly on the effect of participation on citizens, with a secondary focus on agencies and governments. Daley (2008), in her thorough review of the environmental policy literature, observes that such findings are a trend as "...we know comparatively less about the forces that shape agency decision making regarding the specific nature of public participation" (Daley, 2008, 22). Our reading of this literature concurs with Daley's assessment.

Table 33.1 also suggests that there are potential disadvantages to increased public participation. O'Rourke and Macey's (2003) study, however, does not emphasize these elements. Rather, their findings point to the benefits citizens incur through participation. While there is some commentary on the negatives of citizen involvement more generally (e.g., Irvin and Stansbury, 2004; Steelman and Ascher, 1997), there is a genuine trend in this line of research that either assumes or focuses on the positive elements of citizen involvement.[4]

While increased citizen participation in environmental policy is generally viewed and found to be a normatively "good" thing, there are also potential downsides, which could benefit from more thorough explanation. Providing an appropriate point of departure for future research, Steelman and Ascher (1997, 73) summarize these negatives. The public may not be sufficiently knowledgeable or competent to assess the information and risks associated with a policy. Increased public involvement has a tendency to make the process less efficient and more time-consuming. Finally, due in part to the aforementioned factors, preferences expressed by the public may be inconsistent, with the variation confusing policymakers as to what the public wants. In moving from the federal to local level of government, these problems may be exacerbated by a lack of experience on the part of local officials (Rosenbaum, 1978). This is a gap in our understanding that will most certainly need to be addressed.

It is clear that scholarship examining environmental policy at the state and local level has unearthed considerable knowledge regarding the role of participation. This knowledge has been especially helpful in informing us about the positive effect it has on citizens. Moving forward, scholarship will need to focus on the potential deleterious effects of this relationship, and more research is necessary regarding how this arrangement affects administrators and agencies. Our next section examines how climate change is altering the terrain of state and local environmental scholarship.

State and Local Climate Change Policy

The frequency and success of recent state and local policy development in taking measures to address climate change has surprised many scholars (e.g., Biermann and Pattberg, 2008; Lutsey and Sperling, 2008). This burgeoning of local-level climate change policy has been unexpected, given the global scale of this environmental issue, the assumption for the need for a multinational response, and the difficulties of the development of international policy (Cook, 2010; Hoffman, 2011). Some scholars posit that climate change policy has developed a special prosperous niche at the state and local level, in part, because of the unwillingness of the U.S. Senate to ratify the Kyoto Protocol in 1998. Coupled with the 2001 decision by George W. Bush to formally withdraw from the treaty, the resultant vacuum produced by a lack of federal involvement in the face of visible and actionable support within smaller governmental jurisdictions has produced remarkable and distinctive climate change policy innovations (Rabe, 2011; Urpelainen, 2009). Given this fairly recent and innovative trend, understanding the development of climate change policy within state and local jurisdictions is necessary when thinking about the future of state and local environmental policy more generally.

The range of what we refer to as state and local climate change policies (e.g., GHG mitigation, sustainable energy sources) occurs at three levels: regional, state, and local. Regional climate change policies include multiple states (and in some cases, Canadian provinces) implementing policies such as carbon cap-and-trade programs via inter-state agreements. Many of these collaborations have attracted considerable state support. For example, across three major regional subnational collaborations,[5] a total of 23 states and four Canadian provinces are participating in regional collaboration related to cap-and-trade.

Climate change policies are also occurring within particular states, with over half having adopted a "renewable portfolio standard", or a commitment to increase renewable energy sources and decrease fossil-based electricity (Rabe, 2011). In many cases, there is a sort of diffusion taking place, where one state adopts a policy and others quickly follow suit. For example, in 2002 California implemented stringent standards for emissions of carbon dioxide that were, in turn, adopted by 14 other states and finally by President Obama in 2009 (Rabe, 2011). Other state-level policies include varying GHG emission controls and carbon sequestration.

Finally, counties, cities, and towns have also been laboratories for the development of climate change policies (e.g., Bulkeley, 2010; Kousky and Schneider, 2003). One original factor in the success of climate change policies at the local level is the use of transnational municipal networks (Toly, 2008). For example, the International Council for Local Environmental Initiatives (ICLEI; <http://www.iclei.org>) has 1,200 members worldwide, with 545 members being U.S. cities. Other regional and municipal networks have also been quite effective. The U.S. Mayors Climate Protection Agreement (<http://www.usmayors.org/climateprotection/revised/>) has a growing membership of 1,500. At the county level, King County Washington has developed an award-winning protocol for counties and municipalities seeking both mitigation and adaptation policy initiatives (<http://your.kingcounty.gov/exec/news/2007/pdf/climateplan.pdf>). In all of these cases, localities are able to draw upon larger organizations for support. No doubt such efforts provide state and local governments with additional resources that improve the odds of policy success.

Overall, local policies, like that at the state level, tend to be focused on mitigation, but recent efforts such as the King County Washington plan are taking up adaptation as part of strategic planning. Adaptation is likely to become more common, but currently such responses are underdeveloped. In any case, the sheer proliferation of climate change policies, coupled with increasing collaboration and cooperation across governmental jurisdictions seriously challenges any notion that there has been a "race to the bottom" by state and local governments as centralists such as Stewart (1977) feared. In fact, there may very well be a "race to the top" taking place, but why?

Explaining the increasingly enigmatic development of climate change policy at the state and local level can sometimes be difficult using existing theories. Take, for example, one approach in rational choice theory. Rational choice expects that actors will free-ride when it comes to reducing carbon emissions. As the IPCC 2007 states, damage caused in one location is independent from the location of the polluting source, and yet the costs of reduction are incurred by the entity that reduces emissions. In other words, actors can reap the benefits of producing carbon, while others shoulder the burden of reducing carbon emissions. Thus, rational communities *should* continue to produce GHGs at the expense of others. The problem (for rational choice, anyway) is that communities and states are adopting policies that mediate and reduce GHGs despite what this theory would suggest is rational. Thus, a usually reliable rational choice model fails to adequately explain the emergence of local climate change policy. Alternative explanations have been proposed.

One explanation for the surge in climate change policy adoption is local "informational advantage" on the benefits of local climate change policy (Urpelainen, 2009, 83). A second explanation suggests that many state Governors have successfully framed climate change policies as opportunities for economic development, circumventing the problematic divergence of public opinion that frequently characterizes this issue (Rabe, 2008, but also see Nisbet and Myers, 2007). A third explanation (Teodoro, 2009) suggests that state leaders serve as policy entrepreneurs, who are also seeking to build a political reputation of innovation and prominence. However, there does not appear to be a consensus explanation, and there is fertile ground to be sowed for future research seeking to explain the proliferation and success of state and local climate change policy.

Although much of the scholarship regarding state and local climate change policy adoption treat this as an intriguing, puzzling, but generally positive event, there are some words of warning that deserve attention. Rabe (2011) identifies that a critical Supreme Court decision, *Massachusetts v. EPA* (2007), which resulted in carbon dioxide being defined as a pollutant to be regulated under the 1990 Clean Air Act Amendments, now creates an uncertain and perhaps more tense intergovernmental context for GHG reduction policies. Portney (2009) indicates that attention to why states and cities choose *not* to adopt climate change policies is as critical to understand as those that do. Sharp, Daley, and Lynch (2011) point out that climate change adoption is not the same as implementation, and need for understanding barriers to implementation such as institutional capacity and factors of political economy must be better understood. Finally, Bulkeley (2010) identifies that evaluation of the success of climate change policies that have been adopted is a challenge, given the relatively short time-scale involved and the fragmented nature of the data available. Given the general present-day context of bitter partisan divisions over environmental issues, it is perhaps too easy to fall into a false sense of relief over the emergence of what appears to be a growing unified front at the state and local level on climate change policy. However, and despite these words of caution, climate change policy at the state and local level is adorned with characteristics and traits that make it almost irresistible as an object of study. Bound within the overlapping jurisdictions of state, regional, and municipal governments, and usually neglected at the federal level, the proliferation of climate change mediation and adaptation policies are no doubt salient, controversial, and—at the moment, anyway—lacking sufficient explanation.

CONCLUSION

While it was 1973 when Sabatier identified unique opportunities for research in state and local environmental policy, nearly four decades later we have the opportunity to do the same. With a keen eye towards environmental policies, our reading of the literature allows us to identify four future directions for scholars and scholarship of state and local environmental policy. First, we concur with Rabe's (2011) work that draws a new descriptive model of the evolution of American federalism. Institutional demands such as the recent Supreme Court decision in *Massachusetts v. EPA* and overtures by the executive branch emphasizing the importance of state and local control are changing the landscape once again for state and local governments. This emerging relationship will need to be studied, as some of the characteristics are unlike those we have seen in the past. Second, comparative studies, especially in the fertile area of climate change policies, are still needed in order to better understand and articulate variables related to variation in participation rates, adoption rates, implementation successes, outcomes, and other policy consequential dependent variables of interest. Third, in the area of climate change policies, a concentration on the newly emerging adaptation strategies is a must, as are better explanations as to why climate change policies are so prolific. This area of study is both salient and controversial, but it does seem that public support is following policy adoption. As such, public participation in this policy area will add to the depth of the literature on the paradox of proximity of local participation in times of national apathy. Fourth, we suggest that scholars think about their work in the realm of state and local governance studies, and not only environmental policy studies at the local scale. To that end, editors of flagship journals can assist in the foci of state and local scholarship by having high-quality symposium editions that point the laser on issues such as evolving federalism and comparative studies. In sum, the area of state and local environmental policy studies is ripe with opportunities to advance the science behind state and local governance and environmental policymaking.

Notes

1. Importantly, Jenkins-Smith and Sabatier (1993) later successfully militated against the policy stages heuristic, which included the stages of formulation and implementation invoked here.

2. Terms were searched for in the "abstracts" or "topic" sections and kept as similar as possible across databases. Terms included in the search were environment* AND policy AND (state gov* or local gov* or county gov*) AND (policy area or policy area synonym or policy area synonym). Synonyms were used for policy areas. For example, "clean air" was searched for as a policy area, along with "air pollution" and "emissions" and "air quality" as synonyms.

3. See Ecopag at <http://www.edge-project.eu/ecopag/cases/table-of-cases/> (accessed June 14, 2013) for a representative listing of international participatory cases related to environmental policy.

4. For example, Eden (1996, 163) argues that "environmental policy depends for its success on public participation" (Eden, 1996, 163); Wesselink et al., 2011 observe that such assumptions have become the "mantra in environmental governance" (Wesselink et al., 2011, 2688).

5. Regional Greenhouse Gas Initiative in the Northeast <http://www.rggi.org/> (accessed June 14, 2013);
   Western Climate Initiative in the West <http://www.westernclimateinitiative.org/> (accessed June 14, 2013);
   Midwest Greenhouse Gas Reduction Accord <http://www.c2es.org/what_s_being_done/in_the_states/mggra> (accessed June 14, 2013).

REFERENCES

Anderson, Jennifer, Adam Newmark, Virginia Gray, and David Lowery. 2004. "Mayflies and Old Bulls: Organization Persistence in State Interest Communities." *State Politics and Policy Quarterly 4* (2): 140–160.

Biermann, Frank and Phillip Pattberg. 2008. "Global Environmental Governance: Taking Stock, Moving Forward." *Annual Review of Environment and Resources 33*: 277–294.

Bulkeley, Harriet. 2010. "Cities and the Governing of Climate Change." *Annual Review of Environment and Resources 35*: 229–253.

Burroughs, Richard. 1999. "When Stakeholders Choose: Process, Knowledge, and Motivation in Water Quality Decisions." *Society and Natural Resources 12* (8): 797–809.

Beierle, Thomas C. and Jerry Cayford. 2002. *Democracy in Practice: Public Participation in Environmental Decisions*. Washington, DC: Resources for the Future.

Bingham, Lisa Blomgren, Tina Nabatchi, and Rosemary O'Leary. 2005. "The New Governance: Practices and Processes for Stakeholder and Citizen Participation in the Work of Government." *Public Administration Review 65* (5): 547–558.

Bromley-Trujillo, Rebecca. 2011. Environmental Policy Support in the American States. (doctoral dissertation). Michigan State University, Retrieved from ProQuest.UMI 3468750.

Chess, Caron. 2000. "Evaluating Environmental Public Participation: Methodological Questions." *Journal of Environmental Planning and Management 43* (6): 769–784.

Chess, Caron and Kristen Purcell. 1999. "Public Participation and the Environment: Do We Know What Works?" *Environmental Science and Technology 33* (16): 2685–2692.

Cook, Brian J. 2010. "Arena of Power in Climate Change Policymaking." *Policy Studies Journal 38* (3): 465–486.

Daley, Dorothy. 2007. "Citizen Groups and Scientific Decision Making: Does Public Participation Influence Environmental Outcomes?" *Journal of Policy Analysis and Management 26* (2): 349–368.

Daley, Dorothy. 2008. "Public Participation and Environmental Policy: What Factors Shape State Agency's Public Participation Provisions?" *Review of Policy Research 25* (1): 21–35.

Dryzek, John S. 1990. *Discursive Democracy: Politics, Policy and Political Science*. Cambridge: Cambridge University Press.

Eden, Sally. 1996. "Public Participation in Environmental Policy: Considering Scientific, Counter-Scientific and Non-Scientific Contributions." *Public Understanding of Science*, 5: 183–240.

Etsy, Daniel C. 1996. "Revitalizing Environmental Federalism." *Michigan Law Review, 95* (3): 570–653.

Fiorino, Daniel J. 1990. "Citizen Participation and Environmental Risk: A Survey of Institutional Mechanisms." *Science, Technology, and Human \Values 15* (2): 226–243.

Fiorino, Daniel J. 2000. "Innovation in U.S. Environmental Policy: Is the Future Here?" *American Behavioral Scientist 44* (4): 538–547.

Fischer, Frank. 1993. "Citizen Participation and the Democratization of Policy Expertise: From Theoretical Inquiry to Practical Cases." *Policy Sciences 26*: 165–187.

Fredrikkson, Per G. and Daniel L. Millimet 2002. "Strategic Interaction and the Determination of Environmental Policy Across U.S. States." *Journal of Urban Economics 51*: 101–122.

Glicksman, Robert L. 2006. "From Cooperative to Inoperative Federalism: The Perverse Mutation of Environmental Law and Policy." *Wake Forest Law Review 41*: 720–803.

Hays, Scott, Michael Esler, and Carol E. Hays. 1996. "Environmental Commitment Among the States: Integrating Alternative Approaches to State Environmental Policy." *Publius 26* (2): 41–58.

Hoffman, Matthew. 2011. *Climate Governance at a Crossroads*. New York: Oxford University Press.

Huque, Ahmed Shafiqul and Nathan Watton. 2010. "Federalism and the Implementation of Environmental Policy: Changing Trends in Canada and the United States." *Public Organization Review 10*: 71–88.

International Council for Local Environmental Initiatives <http://www.iclei.org> (accessed June 14, 2013).

IPCC. 2007. *Climate Change 2007: Synthesis Report*. Geneva: Intergovernmental Panel on Climate Change.

Irvin, Renee A. and John Stansbury. 2004. "Citizen Participation in Decision Making: Is it Worth the Effort?" *Public Administration Review 64* (1): 55–65.

Jenkins-Smith, Hank and Paul A. Sabatier. 1993. "The Study of Public Policy Processes." In Paul A. Sabatier and Hank C. Jenkins-Smith (eds), *Policy Change and Learning: An Advocacy Coalition Approach*. Boulder, CO: Westview Press, pp. 1–9.

Koontz, Thomas M., Toddi A. Steelman, JoAnn Carmin, Katrina Smith Korfmacher, Cassandra Mosely, and Craig W. Thomas. 2004. *Collaborative Environmental Management: What Roles for Government?* Washington, DC: Resources for the Future.

Kousky, Carolyn and Stephen H. Schneider 2003. "Global Climate Change Policy: Will Cities Lead the Way?" *Climate Policy 3*: 359–372.

Landre, Betsey Kiernan and Barbara A. Knuth. 1993. "The Role of Agency Goals and Local Context in Great Lakes Water Resources Public Involvement Programs." *Environmental Management 17* (2): 153–165.

Layzer, Judith A. 2002. "Citizen Participation and Government Choice in Local Controversies." *Policy Studies Journal 30* (2): 193–207.

Layzer, Judith A. 2012. "Community Activism and Environmental Justice: The Dudley Street Neighborhood Initiative." In *The Environmental Case: Translating Values into Policy, Third Edition*. Washington, DC: CQ Press.

Leach, William D. and Paul A. Sabatier. 2005. "To Trust an Adversary: Integrating Rational and Psychological Models of Collaborative Policymaking." *American Political Science Review 99* (4): 491–503.

Leach, William D., Neil W. Pelkey, and Paul A. Sabatier. 2002. "Stakeholder Partnerships as Collaborative Policymaking: Evaluation Applied to Watershed Management in California and Washington." *Journal of Policy Analysis and Management 21* (4): 645–670.

Lester, James. 1994. "Comparative State Environmental Politics and Policy: The Evolution of a Literature." *Policy Studies Journal 22* (4): 696–700.

Lemos, Maria and Agrawal, Arun. 2006. "Environmental Governance." *Annual Review of Environmental Resources 31*: 297–325.

List, John A. and Shelby Gerking. 2000. "Regulatory Federalism and Environmental Protection in the United States." *Journal of Regional Science 40* (3): 453.

Lowry, William R. 1992. *The Dimensions of Federalism: State Governments and Pollution Control Policies*. Durham, NC: Duke University Press.

Lutsey, Nic and Daniel Sperling 2008."America's Bottom-up Climate Change Mitigation Policy." *Energy Policy 36*: 673–685.

Massachusetts v. EPA. 2007. 549 U.S., 497.

Melosi, Martin V. 2008. The Sanitary City: Environmental Services in Urban America from Colonial Times to the Present. Pittsburgh, PA: University of Pittsburgh Press.

Millimet, Daniel L. 2003. "Assessing the Empirical Impact of Environmental Federalism." Journal of Regional Science 43 (4): 711–733.

Neuman, Janet C. 1996. "Run, River, Run: Mediation of a Water-Rights Dispute Keeps Fish and Farmers Happy—For a Time." University of Colorado Law Review 67: 259–340.

Newig, Jens and Oliver Fritsch. 2009. "Environmental Governance: Participatory, Multi-Level— and Effective?." Environmental Policy and Governance 19: 197–214.

Nisbet, Matthew C. and Teresa Myers. 2007. "Trends: Twenty Years of Public Opinion about Global Warming." Public Opinion Quarterly 71 (3): 444–470.

Oates, Wallace E. and Portney, Paul R. 2003. "The Political Economy of Environmental Policy." In Karl-Göran. Maler and Jeffrey R. Vincent (eds), Handbook of Environmental Economics. Vol. 1. Boston: Elsevier Science B.V.: 325–354.

O'Rourke, Dara, and Gregg Macey. 2003. "Community Environmental Policing: Assessing New Strategies of Public Participation in Environmental Regulation." Journal of Policy Analysis and Management 22 (3): 383–414.

Osofsky, Hari, M. 2010. "The Future of Environmental Law and Complexities of Scale: Federalism Experiments with Climate Change Under the Clean Air Act." Washington University Journal of Law and Policy 32: 79.

Portney. Kent E. 2009. "Sustainability in American Cities: A Comprehensive Look at What Cities are Doing and Why." In Danial A. Mazmanian and Michael E. Kraft (eds), Topwar Sustainable Communities. Cambridge, MA: MIT Press, pp. 227–254.

Potoski, Matthew. 2002. "Designing Bureaucratic Responsiveness: Administrative Procedures and Agency Choice in State Environmental Policy." State Politics and Policy Quarterly 2 (1): 1–23.

Rabe, Barry G. 2003. "Power to the States: The Promise and Pitfalls of Decentralization." In Michael E. Kraft and Norman J. Vig (eds), Environmental Policy: New Directions for the Twenty-first Century. Washington, DC: CQ Press: 33–56.

Rabe, Barry. 2008. "States on Steroids: The Intergovernmental Odyssey of America Climate Change Policy." Review of Policy Research 25 (2): 105–128.

Rabe, Barry. 2011. "Contested Federalism and American Climate Policy." Publius 41 (3): 494–521.

Ringquist, Evan J. 1993. Environmental Protection at the State Level: Politics and Progress in Controlling Pollution. Armonk, NY: M. E. Sharpe.

Rom, Mark Varl. 2006. "Policy Races in the American States." In Kathryn Harrison (ed.), Racing to the Bottom? Vancouver: University of British Columbia Press, pp. 229–256.

Rosenbaum, Walter A. 1978. "Public Involvement as Reform and Ritual: The Development of Federal Participation Programs." In S. Langton (ed.), Citizen Participation in America. Lexington: Lexington Books: 81–96.

Ruckelshaus, William D. 1973. "Local Initiative in Pollution Control." Journal of the Water Pollution Control Federation 45 (1): 1–3.

Sabatier, Paul A. 1973. "State and Local Environmental Policy." Policy Studies Journal 1: 217–226.

Sharp, Elaine B., Dorothy M. Daley, and Michael S. Lynch. 2011. "Understanding Local Adoption and Implementation of Climate Change Mitigation Policy." Urban Affairs Review 47 (3): 433–457.

Steelman, Toddi A. and William Ascher. 1997. "Public Involvement Methods in Natural Resource Policy Making: Advantages, Disadvantages, and Trade-Offs." Policy Sciences 30: 71–90.

Stewart, Richard B. 1977. "Pyramids of Sacrifice? Problems of Federalism in Mandating State Implementation of National Environmental Policy." *The Yale Law Journal* 86 (6): 1196–1272.

Teodoro, Manuel 2009. "Contingent Professionalism: Bureaucratic Mobility and the Adoption of Water Conservation Rates." *Journal of Public Administration Research and Theory 20* (2): 437–459.

Todd, Susan. 2002. "Building Consensus on Divisive Issues: A Case Study of the Wolf Management Team." *Environmental Impact Assessment Review 22*: 655–684.

Toly, Noah. 2008. "Transnational Municipal Networks in Climate Politics: From Global Governance to Global Politics." *Globalizations 5* (3): 341–356.

Urpelainen, Johannes. 2009. "Explaining the Schwarzenegger Phenomenon: Local Frontrunners in Climate Policy." *Global Environmental Politics 9* (3): 82–105.

U.S. Mayors Climate Protection Agreement. 2009. <http://www.usmayors.org/climateprotection/revised/> (accessed June 14, 2013).

Welborne, David M. 1988. "Conjoint Federalism and Environmental Regulation in the United States." *Publius 18* (1): 27–43.

Wesselink, Anna, Jouni Paavola, Oliver Fritsch, and Ortwin Renn. 2011. "Rationales for Public Participation in Environmental Policy and Governance: Practitioner's Perspective." *Environmental Planning 43*: 2688–2704.

CHAPTER 34

....

STATE REGULATORY POLICY

....

PAUL TESKE AND COLIN PROVOST

To the layperson, state regulatory policy may seem fairly obscure. Citizens may believe that it doesn't impact their lives very directly, and they might therefore be largely "rationally ignorant" about the topic. In fact, however, like many areas of state and local policy, state regulations do impact people's lives a great deal—and probably daily—whether it is related to electricity pricing, telecommunications competition, occupational oversight over their barber, masseuse, or dentist, or state regulations of similar activities.

And, while the academic literature on state regulatory policy probably lags the parallel literature on regulation at the federal level, there is nevertheless a reasonably sized cottage industry around this topic from which we have learned a considerable amount in the past two decades. Here, we assess that knowledge. Still, many important and unanswered questions remain, which we also pose here.

Our goal is to highlight the findings from this literature, to show how it connects to broader topics in state and local public policy research, and to suggest some promising new avenues for research and enhanced understanding of state regulatory policy.

WHAT DO THE STATES REGULATE?

....

To start off, it is worth examining what areas state regulate, and why. States regulate several sectors of the economy in which there are demonstrable market failures, and where much of the impacts accrue relatively locally, in a geographic sense. These include: (1) monopolies or industries in which there is significant concern about competition, (2) asymmetric information, where producers usually know more about product quality than do consumers, an important justification for consumer-type regulation, and (3) externalities, where third parties are affected by a two-party transaction, such as environmental pollution.

Historically, the first area in which the states regulated was the monopoly domain. The earliest activity, actually starting in the colonial era, was around regulating insurance. Later, in the 1860s, well before the federal government regulated the interstate commerce aspects of transportation, states started to regulate the railroads (McCraw, 1984).

In the early 20th century, after the federal government had put into place antitrust legislation (which also followed earlier state antitrust efforts), states expanded their regulatory domains, often now institutionalized under public service or public utility commissions (PSC/PUCs), to cover the then-new technologies of telephones, electricity, and automotive transportation. Each of these industries started in a more localized context, in which state regulation made sense, before they expanded geographically, and became fully national (and now international) infrastructure systems. Even after federal regulation started, the states retained the intrastate dimensions of regulation, while the federal government focused upon interstate regulation (Teske, 1990).

As the technology changed in these industries, especially after World War II, each of these areas of competitive/monopoly regulation has been partly deregulated. In some cases either the state or the federal regulator presence has gone away (as with trucking regulations, see Teske et al., 1995), but in telecommunications and electricity regulation significant elements of both federal and state regulation remain in place, though in changed form.

Asymmetric information is a market failure that occurs when one party to a transaction knows significantly more than the other—raising the potential for unfair transactions. When this is more than trivial, a good argument can be made for regulation. While much of this type of regulation is national in scope, following true interstate commerce markets for most goods and services, some elements remain at the state level—most significantly housing regulations, some mortgage regulations, insurance regulation, occupational regulation, and some health regulation. Just as states were early regulators in monopoly regulation, many states sought to reduce the costs of acquiring information for consumers by enacting pure food laws in the early 20th century (Law 2003). More recently, in the past 30 years, state attorneys general have played an increasingly important role in enforcing consumer protection and antitrust laws, both within and across states.

Externalities are unpriced costs or benefits to third parties in a transaction—pollution is the classic negative externality. States began to regulate environmental pollution prior to the federal government (Moe, 1989), but the federal government took a leading role with the National Environmental Policy Act of 1970 in this largely interstate problem. States are largely responsible for implementing federal environmental regulations, but they typically have the discretion to implement even stronger regulations if they choose.

In addition to these economic, market-failure-justified sets of regulations, states also regulate in areas of social policy, such as alcohol consumption and abortion (e.g., Meier and Johnson, 1990; Mooney and Lee, 1995), whether the regulations, such as those on abortion, are effective or not (Meier et al., 1996). Those issues are discussed elsewhere in this handbook—specifically, in the chapter on morality politics—but we will mention them as they relate to our topics here.

Thus, theoretically, if there is a justification to regulate, and if the activity regulated is mostly localized, and/or at least fits under some historical or court-defined notion of intrastate commerce, then states will have authority to regulate it. In reality, that theoretical approach, modified by a path-dependent and highly political history, yields the actual state regulatory activities we see today.

PATTERNS OF FEDERAL-STATE INTERACTIONS

The history of state regulation is very much a function of the interaction patterns with the federal government role, which have vacillated over time. Historically, states were the first regulators, as economic changes and impacts were fairly localized in the pre-industrial and pre-corporate eras. Federal regulatory activities began most notably with the Interstate Commerce Act of 1887, the Sherman Antitrust Act of 1890 and the Clayton Antitrust Act of 1914. The Industrial Revolution spawned large corporations, such as Standard Oil, whose business activities stretched across state lines, thereby making the regulations by individual states increasingly difficult to maintain. Thus, while these laws were created at least partly at the behest of progressives, farmers, and urban reformers to create fairness in markets, they were also created to reduce the transaction and coordination costs of regulating such markets.

By the 1970s, many of the states' significant regulatory roles had been pre-empted by federal regulations, which had grown in leaps and bounds in the 1930s and 1960s. By 1980, President Reagan and conservatives in Congress were eager to return power to the states to beat back what they perceived as an overly active federal government, but this redistribution of power was uneven across regulatory domains. First, years of evidence compiled by professional economists had shown that federal agencies responsible for price and entry regulation of airlines, trucking, and telecommunications served to entrench the interests of large, existing market participants, while excluding access to industry newcomers (Stigler, 1971; Derthick and Quirk, 1985). Federal deregulation of these industries gave more power back to the states, but after observing some of the same economically inefficient practices occurring at the state level (Teske et al., 1995), Congress moved to pre-empt state regulation in transport sectors where it had not already done so. Thus, the states were left virtually powerless to regulate price or market entry in transportation. However, in telecommunications and electricity, each state had its choice of how it would re-regulate these markets and whether they would be opened up to competition.

President Reagan also sought to significantly diminish the role of federal antitrust and advertising regulations, but the states were less easily pre-empted in this case. State attorneys general (AGs), who are elected in 43 states, noticed the weakening of enforcement in consumer protection and antitrust law at the federal level, and seized the opportunity to band together and bring lawsuits against companies that violated unfair and deceptive advertising laws (Meier, 1987; Clayton, 1994; Provost, 2006). Many AGs realized that one state office often did not have the resources to legally outduel major, national corporations, but if offices teamed up to share information and resources, they essentially had the power to regulate at the national level (Lynch, 2001; Provost, 2006). While advertising and fraud lawsuits were the province of creative AGs looking to implement de facto national regulation, the state AGs did actually have authority in the area of antitrust. The passage of the Hart-Scott-Rodino Antitrust Improvements Act of 1976 enabled the states to prosecute abuses of market power and collect monetary damages for the states and the states' consumers, unlike the federal government, which could only obtain injunctive relief.

States have maintained a major role in environmental regulation, as most of the major federal environmental laws passed in the 1970s instituted minimum standards, which the states were allowed to exceed (Lowry, 1992). However, even where state autonomy is legally prescribed, presidential politics often leads to battles over pre-emption, as was frequently the case during the George W. Bush administration. After the Bush EPA decided not to federally regulate carbon dioxide emissions in early 2001, some states, such as California, sought to create programs that would. However, arguing that businesses needed consistent regulation across the U.S. and that the Clean Air Act did not give the EPA the authority to regulate such emissions, the Bush administration claimed primacy and refused to let the states adopt more stringent regulations. Ultimately, the Supreme Court ruled in favor of the states in 2007, in *Massachusetts vs. EPA*, stating that the Clean Air Act gave the EPA the necessary authority, which in turn would allow the states to create their own standards.

Through the 1980s and 1990s, states also found themselves gradually pre-empted out of banking regulation, as increasingly large banks lobbied Congress to lift restrictions and allow more interstate banking activities. States, through the power of their AGs, have still been allowed to prosecute for deceptive advertising (which mostly appears in the form of predatory lending, in banking), and in 2002 nearly all 50 states participated in a $484 million settlement against Household Finance. However, in 2004 the Office of Comptroller Currency issued regulations pre-empting the states from enforcing their own predatory lending laws against any federal OCC-chartered banks. Again, the rationale was to provide consistent regulations for banks and protect them from discrepancies in state regulations, but many AGs claimed that their inability to prosecute predatory lending cases exacerbated the global financial crisis.

In summary, the balance of authority between the states and the federal government is a complex one that is governed by many factors. On one hand, transaction cost economics dictates that some regulatory issues will require coordination across state lines and will be managed more effectively at the federal level (Beales and Muris, 1993; Viscusi, 1993). Additionally, gross discrepancies in regulatory quality at the state level may justify federal intervention, just as sizable differences in rates charged for intrastate railroad transport partly justified the creation of the Interstate Commerce Commission. Industry capture of state regulatory agencies also may justify pre-emption by federal authorities. On the other hand, regulation in a federalist system is also about power and ideology (Hedge and Scicchitano, 1994). Where pre-emption does not rule by congressional statute, Democratic presidents have typically cooperated with the states and allowed them to exceed federal standards. However, Republican presidents have done more to pre-empt state authority, in order to secure more relaxed overall standards, and to bring about consistent standards for business across states.

POLITICS OF STATE-LEVEL DECISION MAKING

When the states do have, and do utilize, regulatory authority, their actions are formulated through a complicated interaction of political and bureaucratic forces. What determines how these forces interact to produce regulatory policy? In studies of federal regulation, theories of regulatory capture dominated the literature for some time, advocating the idea that regulation was beneficial for regulated interests (Bernstein, 1955; Stigler, 1971; Peltzman, 1976; Becker, 1983). Wilson (1980) sought to modify this line of thinking by arguing that the influence of organized interests depended on the concentration of the costs and benefits of regulation. Thus, capture was really only likely when benefits were narrowly concentrated on business, but costs were scattered across diffuse and poorly organized consumers or taxpayers.

More recently, political science and public administration scholars have emphasized the point that political institutions have a significant impact on the creation and implementation of regulatory policy. Among these scholars, William Gormley (1986) has argued that the nature of a particular regulatory issue—particularly its salience and complexity—can help to determine which political institutions and organized interests will seek to influence the regulatory process.

The salience/complexity framework has been employed extensively at the state level in order to determine who participates in the creation and enforcement of regulatory policy. Gormley (1986) has argued that elected officials have greater control over policy implementation in issues that are in high in salience, but low in complexity, such as consumer protection. The high salience of the issue gives politicians incentives to exert their control, while the low degree of technical complexity enables them to do so. Additionally, the lack of technical complexity lowers barriers to understanding the issue, enabling citizen and consumer groups to lobby elected officials more confidently. In their meta-analysis of state regulation, Gerber and Teske (2000) find that elected officials and citizen interest groups are indeed influential in high salience/low complexity regulatory policies.

The role of state attorneys general (AGs) in consumer protection regulation is a prime example of the participation of elected officials in high salience/low complexity issues. While a multitude of political and economic factors determine how multi-state lawsuits are initiated, enforcement ultimately boils down to whether the AG thinks there has been a significant violation of state law. Thus, as public prosecutors, state AGs are equipped to handle the issue of consumer protection without further delegation of authority. As elected regulators, the decision making of state AGs is influenced by a combination of policymaking and electoral factors. On the policymaking side, Provost finds that AGs are more likely to join multi-state lawsuits, the more consumers are harmed by the regulatory violation in question (2010). Similarly, Spill et al. find that the more a state spent on Medicaid for tobacco-related diseases, the more eager were AGs to join the tobacco litigation (2001). On the electoral side, Provost (2010) also finds that AGs are responsive to the electorate in multi-state litigation, but only for cases involving Fortune 500 companies, while Spill et al. (2001) find that AGs representing tobacco-farming states were hesitant to join the tobacco litigation, whether they were Democrats or Republicans.

Regulatory policies that are both salient and complex yield a more nuanced picture. Because of an issue's technical complexity, politicians must delegate authority to bureaucrats with greater expertise, but because the issue is also salient, the politicians must ensure that such authority is not exploited to pursue different goals and must keep a watchful eye on bureaucratic behavior. To create a system of agency oversight, McCubbins, Noll, and Weingast (1987, 1989) argue that Congress attempts to "hard-wire" regulatory agencies according to its preferences, by mandating that agencies follow particular procedures, such as cost-benefit analysis or group consultation, a process also known as "stacking the deck" in favor of the enacting political coalition. McCubbins and Schwartz (1984) also argue that Congress can steer bureaucratic behavior through the use of "fire-alarm oversight" that enables affected constituents to voice their concerns if they believe agencies have deviated from their missions. Kathleen Bawn (1995) expands upon this deck-stacking theory by demonstrating that legislators are as concerned with the uncertainty of policymaking consequences (technical uncertainty), as they are with the uncertainty of bureaucratic behavior (procedural uncertainty). Indeed, this is the trade-off legislators face in salient and complex policies. Technical uncertainty, which represents policymaking complexity, spurs legislators to delegate more authority to regulators, while procedural uncertainty gives legislators the incentive to create procedural constraints that facilitate the monitoring of regulatory agency behavior. Legislators must figure out how to strike the right balance in delegating authority.

Although these delegation issues have been studied more using federal-level examples, there is some state-level literature. The most frequently cited example of policy issues that are high in salience and complexity is environmental regulation (Ringquist, 1993). The complexity of such regulation generally means that bureaucrats wield a greater degree of influence over policy implementation (Gerber and Teske, 2000; Potoski and Woods 2001), and the more challenging the pollution problem with which a state must contend, the more autonomy is generally given to the responsible agency (Potoski, 1999, 2002). However, state legislators also balance this autonomy with a degree of political control in order to prevent bureaucratic drift or capture by organized interests. Many legislatures exert influence by exercising review power over agency rule making (Gerber et al., 2005), and Woods (2005) finds that both legislative and executive review of rule making checks organized interest influence. Highly professional state legislatures—those with reasonably high salaries and staff resources—also attempt to "hard-wire" agency processes by instituting policy analysis procedures (Potoski, 1999; Potoski and Woods, 2001), procedures that Potoski (1999) argues help legislators to cope with the uncertainty of frequent political turnover. However, in order to institute some level of accountability, highly professional state legislatures employ fire-alarm oversight by requiring clean-air agencies to consult with both environmental and industry groups (Potoski, 1999). Reenock and Gerber (2008) find that hard-wiring procedures insulate bureaucrats, but also limit information exchanges with all but the most well-organized and well-resourced interests, thus reducing the scope of fire-alarm oversight. Thus, the body of evidence suggests that delegation of bureaucratic authority at the state level is not that different from delegation at the federal level, as we see hard-wiring of agency processes, as well as use of fire-alarm oversight at both levels.

Regulatory policy that may or may not be complex, but lacks salience, is often considered to be the most prone to capture by business interests. An absence of issue salience means that governors and legislatures can delegate authority to agencies more completely without instituting the administrative procedures that will ensure effective oversight. In some cases, policies will lack salience because they affect only a narrowly concentrated group of interests, thus allowing them to shape policy implementation, while poorly organized consumers take little action (Olson, 1965; Wilson, 1980). For example, the justification for occupational licensing regulations is that they alleviate information asymmetries by letting consumers know that a given doctor or lawyer is a qualified professional, not a fraud. On the other hand, such regulations can also serve as barriers to entry in the profession, thereby limiting supply and raising fees for those within the profession (Friedman, 1962; Stigler, 1971). To illustrate, Teske and Howard (2004) find that states with high average incomes for attorneys and high percentages of law degrees also have higher barriers to professional entry. Broscheid and Teske (2003) discover that state medical boards with more members of the public (representing consumers) enact fewer barriers to the medical profession.

Similar patterns have typically been found in the price and entry regulation of transport. Prior to federal deregulation of airlines and trucking in 1978 and 1980, respectively, federal regulation of those industries erected barriers to market and entry and kept rents high for existing companies (Stigler, 1971; Derthick and Quirk, 1985). In 1980, Congress passed the Motor Carrier Act, which deregulated trucking at the federal level, but did not pre-empt regulation at the state level until 1994. Thus, until 1994, strong state-level trucking representation has resulted in captured state-level trucking regulation that virtually mirrored pre-1980 federal regulation (Teske et al., 1995).

Although the regulation of natural monopolies, such as telecommunications and electricity, is typically considered complex, but not salient (Gormley, 1986; Gerber and Teske, 2000), its wide effect on citizens who rely on phones, electricity, the Internet, and television arguably raises its level of salience. This salience effect has been observed through the actions of elected public utility commissioners, as they seek to keep rates lower for residential electricity customers (Gormley, 1983; Berry, 1984; Ka and Teske, 2002), as well as for local telecommunications customers (Teske, Kim, and Buckley, 2004). The salience here is also demonstrated by the fact that elected legislators typically have clear preferences about utility regulation; for example, Democrats have been more likely to favor telecommunications competition (Teske, 1990).

Antitrust enforcement has also been typically labeled a low salience/high complexity issue. Thus, it surprises some observers that state AGs are involved in such enforcement, bringing lawsuits for vertical and horizontal price-fixing, monopolies, and mergers. The passage of Hart-Scott-Rodino and the ability to give money back to the states and to the consumers has raised the level of salience of antitrust cases in the eyes of the state AGs, who have brought cases against shoe manufacturers (Keds, Nine West, Reebok), contact-lens manufacturers (Ciba Vision, Johnson and Johnson), and pharmaceuticals (Merck, Mylan Laboratories), among other industries. However, antitrust law involves detailed economic analysis and many lawyers and economists believe that state AGs are ill-equipped to perform such analyses or that they enforce antitrust law using political and legal criteria rather than those of economic efficiency (see e.g. Zimmerman, 1999; Posner, 2004; Meyer, 2007). Thus, while state AGs do participate in complex policy issues, such as antitrust regulation, their participation is not without controversy.

ECONOMIC OUTCOMES AND DIFFUSION OF STATE REGULATORY DECISION MAKING

In this section, we move away from examining how state regulations are shaped and implemented to asking what the specific effects of regulation are and the impacts they have. There are multiple methods by which we can examine the effect of regulation. First, we can ask broadly whether regulations achieve their stated aim. Second, we can refine this metric to be more specific and ask what are the specific costs and benefits of regulations. Finally, we can ask whether state regulations cause other states to create similar regulations. In other words, is there a diffusion of particular types of regulation?

A very large literature has developed upon state diffusion of policies, including regulation but also examining other areas (Ringquist and Garand, 1999). This originated with seminal work by Walker (1969), Gray (1973), and Berry and Berry (1990, 1992) and now covers a wide range of topic areas (Andrews, 2000). Within the context of regulatory policy, diffusion of policies can happen because states learn from each other, but it can also happen because of economic competition. Critics of free international trade have frequently argued that discrepancies in regulatory standards between developed and developing nations cause firms to relocate to developing nations, due to the lower cost of regulatory compliance in those countries. While the differences in standards are not as stark, the same debate exists regarding interstate regulation in the U.S. Business interests will argue that state regulations stymie their investments, thereby causing them to relocate to other states. If states respond by steadily ratcheting down their regulations in order to keep or attract businesses, then we can see a "race-to-the-bottom" in regulatory standards or what has been called the "Delaware Effect." Delaware has provided very lax regulations for corporate charters, and for financial and credit-card firms, attracting a large number of firms, which have established headquarters there, and enhanced Delaware's economy and tax base.

At the same time, some have argued that large states can drive a "race-to-the-top" in regulation. Specifically, Vogel (1995) highlights the "California effect" in environmental regulation. Vogel argues that if one of the states/countries has strong environmental or consumer groups, and a large economy to which exporting states/countries want access, then that state/country can strengthen standards overall, rather than weaken them. For example, even prior to the creation of the EPA in 1970, California began regulating environmental pollution in a rigorous way, to protect the lifestyle (and air quality) of its citizens. It pushed automobile emission regulations beyond federal standards. Because California represents nearly 13 percent of the American market, rather than producing two different types of cars, auto makers met the tougher California standards with all of their cars. Thus, all states benefited from California's stronger regulatory policies.

Since Vogel's seminal work, further studies have asked whether races to the bottom exist in areas of state regulation, and markets and organized interests again appear to play a critical role (Swire, 1996; Romano, 1997). There are two potential dependent variables to employ in such studies: the behavior of the regulated firms or the behavior of the regulators. Some studies have examined whether firms move across state lines in order to obtain more lenient regulation, while other studies have analyzed whether regulations become weaker, in response to the threat of such movements. In the former case, Woods (2006) states that the literature demonstrates that regulatory costs are generally not high enough to justify the movement of firms across state lines, despite exceptions, such as the chemical industry (Feiock and Rowland, 1990), and small start-up firms (Bartik, 1989).

Despite this evidence, Engel's (1997) survey found that most state environmental regulators do believe that regulatory compliance costs play a large role in industry location. Moreover, even more regulators believed that these concerns had significant impacts on the creation and enforcement of state-level regulations. This is consistent with the fact that in many states now, the governor has a high-level office that advises him/her on the relationship between regulation and economic development (Teske, 2004).

However, the beliefs of regulators do not necessarily constitute evidence and some of the evidence is contrary to what regulators believe. Similar to Vogel's findings regarding mobile-source pollution regulation, Potoski (2001) finds that there is no race-to-the-bottom in stationary-source pollution regulation, partly because many states have strong environmental movements that push for regulations that are stronger than federal standards. Conversely, Woods (2006). examines surface-mining regulation and finds that if State X has stronger regulations than State Y, State X will respond by weakening the strength of its regulations Woods suggests that the inconsistent results between his work and that of Potoski (2001) may be due to the fact that standards do not race to the bottom, as Potoski finds, but that enforcement effort may, as Woods finds. Finally, Konisky (2007), in an examination of enforcement in air, water, and hazardous waste, finds that state enforcement levels will decrease in response to competing states that have also reduced their enforcement. However, states will also respond to increases in competing states' enforcement levels, by increasing their own levels of enforcement. Konisky suggests that increasing levels of enforcement may still reflect economic competition, but a different kind of competition—for service industries or for citizens who value environmental protection. Thus, overall, the body of research suggests that economic competition does significantly affect state regulatory standards and enforcement, but potentially in different directions, depending on citizen and firm preferences.

Although economic competition is clearly a concern for regulatory policymakers, there is also the question of whether states learn from each other's policies, thus enabling policies to diffuse throughout the states. Volden, Ting, and Carpenter (2008) challenge much of the existing research on this subject and theorize that ideologically moderate states are the ones more likely to adopt policies if there is evidence of success, while ideologically extreme states will be more immune to the evidence. And although most studies of state policy diffusion examine the issue "horizontally," that is, across the states, Shipan and Volden (2006) ask whether there are bottom-up diffusion effects. In other words, does local government adoption of particular regulations influence states to act similarly? The authors find that states with professional legislatures are likely to adopt statewide restrictions on smoking when local governments have already started to do so, thus producing what they call a "snowball effect." However, when legislatures are not professional, inaction follows at the state level, producing what the authors call a "pressure-valve effect." The authors also find that the snowball effect prevails when there are strong health interests in the state.

We have learned a great deal about the diffusion of state regulatory action in the past 20 years. Technical, policy, and political learning are important, but other factors also influence state politicians and regulators, and those factors may vary by type of industry regulated. While politics matters, so too do regulatory outcomes, such as prices, environmental quality, and innovation.

INTERNATIONAL DIMENSIONS AND COMPARISONS (E.U.)

Some natural comparisons have emerged about how state regulation works in the American context, compared to how regulation in Europe now operates, at both the national levels and the European level (Teske, 2004). At first glance, two crucial differences are apparent between the E.U. and U.S.

First, E.U. members are sovereign nations, unlike the American states, and hence may shy away from ceding authority to supranational institutions. Second, looking within the E.U., differences between governance structures and administrative traditions may be considerably larger than they appear within the U.S. Some nations, such as those in Scandinavia, have always had well-resourced, professional agencies, whereas others,

such as Romania and Bulgaria, are still very young democratic states that are still bat-
tling significant levels of corruption within their administrative structures.

Ultimately, the biggest similarity between the two systems is that they represent large
markets with numerous member states/countries. Each system has varying incentives
to harmonize its regulations across borders, which brings different levels of vertical
pressure in each system as well.

With regards to sovereignty, just as in the U.S., there is a complex exchange of authority between member states and the European Commission, European Council and
Parliament, and European Court of Justice. Member states jealously guard their right
to make policy as they see fit, but the E.U. single market also requires that member
states coordinate and harmonize legislation dealing with trade, competition law, and
monetary policy, among other areas. This balancing act has produced a research debate
between "intergovernmentalists," who see member states as the primary actors that
explicitly set and limit the E.U. supranational authority, and "supranationalists," who
see more of an entrepreneurial, policy-setting role for E.U. institutions (for more on this
debate, see Garrett (1995), Pollack (1997), and Stone Sweet and Brunell (1998)).

Competition law, trade, and monetary policy are all policy issues that, by their very
nature, cross national boundaries and require the coordinating hands of E.U. institutions; but what about issues that do not necessarily cross boundaries? In his analysis of
delegation in the E.U., Franchino (2004) finds that regulatory policies that are highly
complex or that can only go to the Commission with strict voting procedures are more
likely to stay in national government hands. This is demonstrated through policy areas,
such as environmental regulation, staying within the arena of national governments,
but other equally complex policy areas, such as competition law, being relegated to
the Commission because of their cross-boundary nature. While Franchino's findings
largely ring true, the ability of member states to use environmental laws, for example, as
non-tariff barriers increasingly requires the involvement of the Commission to produce
greater harmonization.

While harmonization may be the ideal in the E.U., this is not necessarily the case
among the American states. Where Congress does not explicitly assert authority or
pre-empt state authority, states are under no obligation to harmonize their regulations.
However, as shown in the previous section, they may be driven by economic competition to make their regulatory policies more similar. Additionally, harmonization may
occur because some states learn and imitate other states' policy adoptions.

Patterns of diffusion have also been observed in the E.U. For example, the emergence
of the single market and strict trade rules meant that member states were prohibited
from favoring national industries with non-tariff barriers, such as subsidies or overly
stringent regulations. This required a certain level of credible commitment by member
states, one more likely to be attained by independent regulatory agencies, which spread
throughout the E.U. in the 1980s and 1990s (Gilardi, 2005).

The roles of the highest courts in the U.S. and E.U. also provide an interesting contrast between the two federalist systems. In the E.U. policy debate, intergovernmentalists claim that member states set limits on the European Court of Justice's power by

strategically not complying with rulings that will be costly to home industries (Garrett, 1995). Supranationalists, on the other hand, see the court's autonomy as having grown over time, through a rising caseload (Stone Sweet and Brunell, 1998). Additionally, other scholars argue that member states do not strategically evade rulings, but rather they do not have the administrative capacity to comply with them (Tallberg, 2002).

Thus, the European Commission employs strategies of management and enforcement, where Commission officials work with member states to bring them into compliance with regulations, and they only bring enforcement actions to the ECJ as a last resort. In the U.S., agencies monitor levels of compliance throughout the nation, but there tends to be more emphasis on enforcement, rather than management of state activities.

Future Studies: What is the Literature Missing?

As with a number of fields of political science and public policy, researchers have generated a lot of new knowledge about state regulatory policy in the past two decades, but we have a great deal more to learn (see Teske, 1994). As we improve knowledge in this subfield, there are a few topics that are particularly worth the focused attention of researchers.

In particular, we have made great headway in understanding the diffusion of policies across states, how races to the bottom and to the top might work, with some real examples, and a little bit about how state institutions—legislatures, governors, bureaucracies, and courts—interact, though not nearly as much as we know at the federal level.

These knowledge gaps exist in part because comparative data are so hard to come by at the state level. A few non-academic organizations have begun to gather data across the 50 states for their own purposes, and researchers can sometimes "piggyback" on this to help better understand quantitative phenomena. But, if a researcher has to develop his/her own data on a specific state regulatory issues from the ground up, that remains quite challenging, and it certainly limits what we can study quantitatively across all 50 states.

Thus, as in a number of areas of state politics, there is much to be gained by providing support or funding for new databases. Projects that better assess state political culture (Berry et al., 1998) and the ideology of state-level institutional actors (Erikson et al., 1993) will give researchers better tools to understand the theoretical predictions of models that require quantitative assessment.

Challenges also remain because the states themselves do vary a great deal. Legislatures, in particular, vary from highly paid, highly professional, well-resourced organizations that meet often, in a few states, to those at the opposite extreme, with low pay, short meeting times, and few staff (e.g., Mooney, 1994). Obviously, rather than being able to make simple generalizations, the legislative role in regulatory policy may truly vary a lot at the state level.

Still, there are a number of political-institutional studies that could shed more light on the development and implementation of state regulatory policy. At the federal level, scholars have done some careful "micro" level studies of committee decisions, around the design of regulatory institutions, their funding, and the impacts of their delegated authority. Few similar studies have been done at the state level, where more legislators are part-time, and arguably might be less strategic, so these could be very revealing. Gerber et al. (2005) and Daley et al. (2007) are good first steps in this direction, but we need more state-level studies to thoroughly examine theories that are now mainly assessed at the federal level.

Governors are another set of state institutional actors who are also under-studied in their role in state regulation.. Some recent work is developing better quantitative measures of the ideologies of governors, and others are examining how governors' use of oversight cost-benefit analysis is influencing state regulation (Shapiro and Borie-Holtz, 2011). Currently, there is no question that they are key players in state regulatory policy, yet quantitative studies are limited in showing their impact (Teske, 2004). This could be a very fruitful area of study, especially for governors who see it as critical to balance their economic development and regulatory roles with the interests of businesses (Brace, 1993).

Outside of government, we need to develop and utilize better measures of the input and impact of interest groups on regulatory processes. We know that they are important—we have measured proxies of their input, but increasingly we have access to real lobbying and campaign contribution expenditures, which may have impacts upon outcomes. Proxy measures such as size of an industry or its reputed power in surveys seem inadequate, or at a minimum these need to be tested further and cross-correlated with more direct measures of inputs into state regulatory processes. Again, this is more of a data-availability issue than a gap in researchers' creativity.

There is also surprisingly little literature on the relationship of state regulation and the courts. At the federal level, a lot of interesting work has focused upon the fact that most major regulatory rule-makings get challenged in the courts, and are sometimes overturned. There is additional, nuanced theoretical work on how legislative design can shape the likely future bureaucratic and judicial interactions. All of this should be applicable at the state level, as well, and the variation in institutional form across the 50 states could again provide richer empirical tests of these theoretical interaction concepts. But, as in the other areas, this requires better data on the ideology of state supreme courts. And, while these newer measures will be helpful, we still need much more basic data about how often bureaucrats are overturned, for example (Graves and Teske, 2003).

On the economic side of state regulation, there is a lack of careful studies of many topics—cost/benefit studies and economic impacts of state regulation, and how those influence business locations. Industry location is a complicated subject—firms certainly incorporate the influence of taxes, market access, and transportation, but the role of regulation is not trivial. We have seen in this chapter how regulatory and/or economic competition between states and between the states and federal government can play a role in influencing business location. Given the integrated nature of the global economy, in the future, states may find themselves in competition with other countries as well.

The most enduring question in state regulatory policy has been and will continue to be, how will the American federal government balance its own regulatory policy autonomy against that of the states? Business interests that traditionally championed state regulation due to its lighter touch of regulation have found themselves running back to the federal government and away from state AGs in the name of more consistent and relaxed standards. While not all states are uniformly active in enforcing their regulations, state AGs feel that they play a vital role in the federal system and are not likely to relinquish their power easily. Given the penchant of Republican presidents to pre-empt strong state regulation, business groups will continue to lobby for favorable regulations at the federal level, but particularly when Republicans occupy the White House. In the meantime, they will also pay close attention to state-level electoral races, such as AG races. Such dynamics will ensure that we continue to see a somewhat volatile balance of power between the states and the federal government for years to come.

References

Andrews, Clinton. 2000. "Diffusion Pathways for Electricity Deregulation." *Publius: The Journal of Federalism 30* (3): 17–34.

Bartik, Timothy. 1989. "Small Business Start-Ups in the United States: Estimates of the Effects of the Characteristics of the States." *Southern Economic Journal 55*: 1004–1018.

Bawn, Kathleen. 1995. "Political Control vs. Expertise: Congressional Choices about Administrative Procedures." *American Political Science Review, 89* (March): 62–73.

Beales, J. Howard and Timothy Muris. 1993. *State and Federal Regulation of National Advertising.* Washington, DC: American Enterprise Institute for Public Policy Research.

Becker, Gary. 1983. "A Theory of Competition Among Pressure Groups for Political Influence." *Quarterly Journal of Economics 96*: 371–400.

Bernstein, Marver. 1955. *Regulating Business by Independent Commission.* Princeton: Princeton University Press.

Berry, Frances Stokes and William Berry. 1990. "State Lottery Adoption as Policy Innovation: An Event History Analysis." *American Political Science Review 84*: 395–415.

Berry, Frances Stokes and William Berry. 1992. "Tax Innovation in the States: Capitalizing on Political Opportunity." *American Journal of Political Science 36*: 715–742.

Berry, William. 1984. "An Alternative to the Capture Theory of Regulation: The Case of State Public Utility Commissions." *American Journal of Political Science 28*: 524–558.

Berry, William D., Evan J. Ringquist, Richard C. Fording, and Russell L. Hanson. 1998. "Measuring Citizens and Government Ideology in the American States, 1960-93." *American Journal of Political Science 42*: 327–348.

Brace, Paul. 1993. *State Government and Economic Performance.* Baltimore: Johns Hopkins University Press.

Broscheid, Andreas and Paul Teske. 2003. "Public Members on Medical Licensing Boards and the Choice of Entry Barriers." *Public Choice 114* (3–4): 445–459.

Clayton, Cornell W. 1994. "Law, Politics, and the New Federalism: State Attorneys General as National Policymakers." *Review of Politics 56*: 525–553.

Daley, Dorothy, Donald P. Haider-Markel, and Andrew Whitford. 2007. "Checks, Balances and the Costs of Regulation: Evidence from the American States." *Political Research Quarterly* 60 (4): 696–706.

Derthick, Marthaand Paul Quirk. 1985. *The Politics of Deregulation*. Washington DC: Brookings Institution Press.

Engel, Kirsten H. 1997. "State Environmental Standard Setting: Is There a Race and Is It to the Bottom?" *Hastings Law Journal 48*: 271–398.

Erikson, Robert, Gerald Wright, and John McIver. 1993. *Statehouse Democracy: Public Opinion and Policy in the American States*. New York: Cambridge University Press.

Feiock, Richard and C.K. Rowland. 1990. "Environmental Regulation and Economic Development: The Movement of Chemical Production Among States." *Western Political Quarterly 43*: 561–576.

Franchino, Fabio. 2004. "Delegating Powers in the European Community." *British Journal of Political Science 34*: 269–293.

Friedman, Milton. 1962. *Capitalism and Freedom*. Chicago: University of Chicago Press.

Garrett, Geoffrey. 1995. "The Politics of Legal Integration in the European Union." *International Organization 49*: 171–181.

Gerber, Brian, Cherie Maestas, and Nelson Dometrius. 2005. "State Influence over Agency Rulemaking: The Utility of Ex Ante Review." *State Politics and Policy Quarterly 5* (1): 24–46.

Gerber, Brian and Paul Teske. 2000. "Field Essay: Regulatory Policy-making in the American States: A Review of Theories and Evidence." *Political Research Quarterly 53* (4): 849–886.

Gilardi, Fabrizio. 2005. "The Institutional Foundations of Regulatory Capitalism: The Diffusion of Independent Regulatory Agencies in Western Europe." *Annals of the American Academy of Political and Social Science 598*: 84–101.

Gormley, William. 1983. *The Politics of Public Utility Regulation*. Pittsburgh: Pittsburgh University Press.

Gormley, William. 1986. "Regulatory Issue Networks in a Federal System." *Polity 18* (4): 595–620.

Graves, Scott and Paul Teske. 2003. "State Supreme Courts and Judicial Review of Regulation." *Albany Law Review 66*: 857–865.

Gray, Virginia. 1973. "Innovation in the States: A Diffusion Study." *American Political Science Review 67*:1174–1185.

Hedge, David M. and Michael J. Scicchitano. 1994. "Regulating in Space and Time: The Case of Regulatory Federalism." *Journal of Politics 56* (1): 134–153.

Ka, Sangjoon, and Paul Teske. 2002. "Ideology and Professionalism: Electricity Regulation over Time in the American States." *American Politics Research 30*: 323–343.

Konisky, David M. 2007. "Regulatory Competition and Environmental Enforcement: Is There a Race to the Bottom?" *American Journal of Political Science 51* (4): 853–872.

Law, Marc T. 2003. "The Origins of State Pure Food Regulation." *Journal of Economic History* 63 (4): 1103–1130.

Lowry, William R. 1992. *The Dimensions of Federalism: State Governments and Pollution Control Policies*. Durham, N.C.: Duke University Press.

Lynch, Jason. 2001. "Federalism, Separation of Powers and the Role of State Attorneys General in Multistate Litigation." *Columbia Law Review 101*: 1998–2032.

McCraw, Thomas K. 1984. *Prophets of Regulation*. Cambridge: Harvard University Press.

McCubbins, Matthew, Roger G. Noll, and Barry R. Weingast. 1987. "Administrative Procedures as Instruments of Political Control." *Journal of Law, Economics and Organization 3* (2): 243–277.

McCubbins, Matthew, Roger G. Noll and Barry R. Weingast. 1989. "Structure and Process, Politics and Policy: Administrative Arrangements and Political Control," *Virginia Law Review* 75: 431–482.

McCubbins, Matthew and Thomas Schwartz. 1984. "Congressional Oversight Overlooked: Police Patrols versus Fire Alarms." *American Journal of Political Science* 28 (1): 165–179.

Meier, Kenneth J. 1987. "The Political Economic of Consumer Protection: An Examination of State Legislation." *Western Political Quarterly* 30 (June): 343–359.

Meier, Kenneth J. and Cathy Johnson. 1990. "The Politics of Demon Rum: Regulating Alcohol and Its Deleterious Consequences." *American Politics Quarterly* 18: 404–429.

Meier, Kenneth J., Donald P. Haider-Markel, Anthony J. Stanislawski, and Deborah R. McFarlane. 1996. "The Impact of Post-Webster Restrictions on Abortion." *Demography* 33 (3): 307–312.

Meyer, Timothy. 2007. "Federalism and Accountability: State Attorneys General, Regulatory Litigation, and the New Federalism." *California Law Review* 885: 1–23.

Moe, Terry. 1989. "The Politics of Bureaucratic Structure." In John Chubb and Paul Peterson (eds), *Can the Government Govern?* Washington DC: Brookings Institutions.

Mooney, Chris. 1994. "Measuring U.S. State Legislative Professionalism: An Evaluation of Five Indices." *State and Local Government Review* 26: 70–78.

Mooney, Chris and Lee, M-H. 1995. "Legislative Morality in the American States: The Case of Pre-Roe Abortion Regulation Reform." *American Journal of Political Science* 39: 599–627.

Olson, Mancur. 1965. *The Logic of Collective Action*. Cambridge: Harvard University Press.

Peltzman, Sam. 1976. "Toward a More General Theory of Regulation." *Journal of Law and Economics* 19: 211–240.

Pollack, Mark. 1997. "Delegation, Agency and Agenda Setting in the European Community." *International Organization* 51: 99–134.

Posner, Richard. 2004. "Federalism and the Enforcement of Antitrust Laws by State Attorneys General." In Richard Epstein and Michael Greve (eds), *Competition Laws in Conflict: Antitrust Jurisdiction in the Global Economy*. Washington DC: American Enterprise Institute Press.

Potoski, Matthew. 1999. "Managing Uncertainty through Bureaucratic Design: Administrative Procedures and State Air Pollution Agencies." *Journal of Public Administration Research and Theory* 9 (4): 623–639.

Potoski, Matthew. 2001. "Clean Air Federalism: Do States Race to the Bottom?" *Public Administration Review* 61: 335–342.

Potoski, Matthew. 2002. "Designing Bureaucratic Responsiveness: Administrative Procedures and Agency Choice in State Environmental Policy." *State Politics and Policy Quarterly* 2: 1–23.

Potoski, Matthew and Neal D. Woods. 2001. "Designing State Clean Air Agencies: Administrative Procedures and Bureaucratic Autonomy." *Journal of Public Administration Research and Theory* 11 (2): 203–221.

Provost, Colin. 2006. "The Politics of Consumer Protection: Explaining State Attorney General Participation in Multi-State Lawsuits." *Political Research Quarterly* 59 (4): 609–618.

Provost, Colin. 2010. "An Integrated Model of U.S. State Attorney General Behavior in Multi-State Litigation." *State Politics and Policy Quarterly* 24 (1): 1–24.

Reenock, Christopher M. and Brian J. Gerber. 2008. "Political Insulation, Information Exchange, and Interest Group Access to the Bureaucracy." *Journal of Public Administration Research and Theory* 18 (3): 415–440.

Ringquist, Evan J. 1993. *Environmental Protection at the State Level: Politics and Progress in Controlling Pollution*. Armonk, NY: M.E. Sharpe.

Ringquist, Evan and James Garand. 1999. "Policy Change in the American States." In R. Weber and P. Brace (eds.), *American State and Local Politics*. New York: Chatham House.

Romano, Roberta. 1997. "State Competition for Corporate Charters." In John Ferejohn and Barry R. Weingast (eds.), *The New Federalism*. Stanford, CA: Hoover Institute Press, pp. 129–156.

Shapiro, Stuart and Debrah Borie-Holtz. 2011. "Lessons from New Jersey: What are the Effects of 'Administrative Procedures' Regulatory Reforms," *Regulation* 34 (1): 14–19.

Shipan, Charles R. and Craig Volden. 2006. "Bottom-Up Federalism: The Diffusion of Antismoking Policies from U.S. Cities to States." *American Journal of Political Science* 50 (4): 825–843.

Spill, Rorie, Michael Licari, and Leonard Ray. 2001. "Taking on Tobacco: Entrepreneurship and the Tobacco Litigation." *Political Research Quarterly* 54 (3): 605–622.

Stigler, George. 1971. "The Theory of Economic Regulation." *Bell Journal of Economics and Management Science* 2: 3–21.

Stone Sweet, Alec and Thomas Brunell. 1998. "Constructing a Supranational Constitution: Dispute Resolution and Governance in the European Community." *American Political Science Review* 92: 63–81.

Swire, Peter. 1996. "The Race to Laxity and the Race to Undesirability: Explaining Failures in Competition Among Jurisdictions in Environmental Law." *Yale Law and Policy Review/Yale Journal on Regulation* 14 (2): 67–110.

Tallberg, Jonas. 2002. "Paths to Compliance: Enforcement, Management and the European Union." *International Organization* 56: 609–643.

Teske, Paul. 1990. *After Divestiture: The Political Economy of State Telecommunications Regulation*. Albany, NY: State University of New York Press.

Teske, Paul. 1994. "The State of State Regulation." In David Rosenbloom and Richard Schwartz (eds), *Handbook of Regulation and Administrative Law* 37–82. New York: Marcel Dekker.

Teske, Paul. 2004. *Regulation in the States*. Washington, DC: Brookings Institution.

Teske, Paul, Samuel Best, and Michael Mintrom. 1995. *Deregulating Freight Transportation: Delivering the Goods*. Washington DC: American Enterprise Institute for Public Policy Research Press.

Teske, Paul and Robert Howard. 2004. "Occupational Regulation: Attorneys." In Paul Teske (ed.), *Regulation in the States*. Washington DC: Brookings Institution.

Teske, Paul, Junseok Kim, and Jack Buckley. 2004. "Monopoly Regulation: Telecommunicati ons." In Paul Teske (ed.), *Regulation in the States*. Washington DC: Brookings Institution.

Viscusi, W. Kip. 1993. *Product-Risk Labeling: A Federal Responsibility*. Washington, DC: American Enterprise Institute for Public Policy Research.

Vogel, David. 1995. *Trading Up: Consumer and Environmental Regulation and International Trade*. New York: Basic Books.

Volden, Craig, Michael Ting, and Daniel Carpenter. 2008. "A Formal Model of Learning and Policy Diffusion." *American Political Science Review* 102: 319–332.

Walker, Jack. 1969. "The Diffusion of Innovations among the American States." *American Political Science Review* 63: 880–899.

Wilson, James. 1980. *The Politics of Regulation*. New York: Basic Books.

Woods, Neal D. 2005. "Interest Group Influence on State Administrative Rule Making: The Impact of Rule Review." *American Review of Public Administration* 35 (4): 402–413.

Woods, Neal D. 2006. "Interstate Competition and Environmental Regulation: A Test of the Race-to-the-Bottom Thesis." *Social Science Quarterly* 87 (1): 174–189.

Zimmerman, David. 1999. "Why State Attorneys General Should Have a Limited Role in Enforcing the Federal Antitrust Law of Mergers." *Emory Law Journal* 48: 337–366.

CHAPTER 35

POLICIES TOWARDS MINORITY POPULATIONS

RICHARD C. FORDING AND JOHN POE

On July 2, 1964, President Lyndon Johnson signed the Civil Rights Act, which represented the most important civil rights victory for African Americans since emancipation. Only 13 months later, in 1965, Johnson signed the Voting Rights Act, ending decades of political disenfranchisement for African Americans in the South. The primary catalyst for these policies was the civil rights movement. For nearly a decade preceding the passage of these landmark bills, civil rights activists brought national attention to the various forms of discrimination in the South through mass marches and civil disobedience, eventually pressuring federal policymakers into acting.

The impact of the civil rights movement was felt far beyond the African American community, as it undoubtedly helped fuel political consciousness within many other minority groups in the United States. These groups organized in a similar fashion to fight for social, economic, and political equality, often relying on the same strategies used so effectively by blacks during the civil rights movement. The list of movements that followed reflected a broad range of groups in society, and included such important campaigns as the women's liberation movement, the Chicano movement, the American Indian movement, the disability rights movement, and the gay rights movement, among others.

Over the last four decades, these political struggles for social and political inclusion have resulted in a broad range of policy proposals that have been met with varying levels of success. Many minority groups have succeeded in winning important victories in national-level venues such as the U.S. Supreme Court and Congress. Yet, the federalist nature of the U.S. political system has often served to limit the success of minority groups due to the fact that significant policymaking authority over many issues relevant to minority rights continues to reside in state (and sometimes local) governments. In some cases, states have worked to gradually weaken the strength of rights-enhancing policies that were initially granted by the federal government. This is the case for abortion rights, where the Supreme Court's landmark decision (*Roe vs. Wade*, 1972) has been gradually weakened over the last four decades by state restrictions (Patton, 2007). For other issues, policymaking authority has remained exclusively at the state and local level, nearly assuring that universal rights-enhancing reforms will be difficult, if not impossible to achieve. Perhaps the most salient example of such a policy area is gay rights, where a majority of states have been effective in blocking such policies as gay marriage and adoption by gay couples.

In this chapter we review two decades of research on the policies that have evolved from these struggles for minority-group inclusion. Consistent with the focus of this series, we restrict our attention to minority-targeted policies that are most relevant to state or local governments. Although there have been several reviews of political science literature relevant to specific minority groups, we are not aware of any essays that have tried to examine research across such a broad range of minority groups as we consider in this chapter. Therefore, our first task is to identify the relevant literature and describe some broad trends in this research over the last 20 years. To accomplish this goal, we report the results of a content analysis of nine major political science and public policy journals. We present trends in the volume of scholarship on minority-targeted policies, as well as various trends in the content of these studies. Based on this analysis we find that the volume of research on minority-targeted policies has remained steady over time, but there have been significant changes in the content of these studies. In the second section we take a closer look at this research to examine the major questions that have been studied in the literature, as well as what we have learned about the politics and the impact of minority-targeted policies. Finally, we conclude by highlighting some recent trends in this literature that seem promising, as well as suggesting avenues for future research.

RECENT TRENDS IN THE VOLUME AND CONTENT OF RESEARCH ON MINORITY-TARGETED POLICIES

To begin our review, we must first define what we mean by a "minority group." Our definition is drawn from the literature on minority group relations in sociology and is based on two important criteria (Yetman, 1999). First, minority groups are "subordinate" to other groups in society in the sense that they possess less political power or control over their lives, compared to a "majority" or "dominant" group. Second, a minority group member is defined by some relatively fixed, ascriptive trait. In other words, membership in a minority group is not voluntary. An important feature of this definition is that a minority group may actually comprise a majority of the population. For example, women in the United States and (historically) blacks in South Africa are important examples of minority groups within their respective countries, yet both groups represent a majority of their country's population. In the United States, this led us to consider the following types of minority groups in our content analysis of the literature: racial minorities (blacks, Asians, Native Americans), ethnic minorities (Latinos), women, sexual minorities (gays and lesbians), and the disabled.

For the purposes of this chapter, we define a "minority-targeted policy" as any policy over which state or local governments have significant authority, and which is *explicitly* intended to affect a minority group(s). There are two features of this definition that require some elaboration. First, the anticipated effect on the minority group(s) may be positive or negative, and thus we consider policies that are either favored or opposed by the targeted minority group(s). Second, we restrict our attention to policies that *explicitly* target one or more minority groups. This leads us to exclude research on policies that might disproportionately *impact* a particular minority group if this is not the *explicit* intention of policymakers. Thus, we exclude welfare policies and criminal justice policies due to the fact that these policies are universal in intent, despite the fact that blacks and Latinos are disproportionately impacted by these policies.[1] We also exclude a small number of policies related to AIDS treatment, despite the fact that gay men have historically been more likely to contract AIDS. For this reason, it is important to recognize that our review does not encompass the entire range of policies that are important to the wellbeing of minority groups, nor does our definition capture the full set of policy demands made by minority groups in the United States.

Our sample of articles is based on the contents of nine political science journals, from 1990 through 2010. Among the nine journals, we include the top five journals in the United States that publish research across the entire range of subfields within American politics (including public policy). These five journals include the *American Political Science Review* (APSR), the *American Journal of Political Science* (AJPS), the *Journal of Politics* (JOP), *Political Research Quarterly* (PRQ, formerly *Western Political Quarterly*), and *American Politics Research* (APR, formerly *American Politics Quarterly*). In addition to these more general journals, we also include what many people would consider the top four outlets for public policy research by political scientists. These include the *Journal of Policy Analysis and Management* (JPAM), *Policy Studies Journal* (PSJ), *Social Science Quarterly* (SSQ), and *State Politics and Policy Quarterly* (SPPQ). Obviously, these nine journals do not represent the universe of public policy research outlets in political science. In addition, we do not examine books (although we do cite some books in our more detailed discussions). Yet, we feel that the contents of these journals will yield a highly representative sample for the purposes of our review.[2]

Trends Across Time and (Journal) Space

Based on our definitions, we identified 203 articles that focused either wholly or in part on one or more minority-targeted policies relevant to state or local governments. This equates to an average of ten articles per year across our nine journals. Figure 35.1 presents the total article count across the entire period of our analysis, 1990–2010. As can be seen, there is no discernible trend in the volume of research on minority-targeted policies during this 20-year period. This was somewhat surprising, given the apparent increase in interest among political scientists in recent years in the politics of race and ethnicity, as well as other forms of identity politics. Yet, this may merely suggest that the growth of research in this area has centered around questions that do not directly address minority-targeted *policies*, and instead focus on other (related) aspects of minority-group politics. At the very least, it does not appear that interest in this specific research area is declining.

Although the volume of articles has remained relatively constant over time, this is not the case for the distribution of articles across journals. This is clearly evident in Table 35.1, which presents the percentage distribution of articles on minority-targeted policies across the nine journals in our sample. As can be seen, approximately two-thirds of all the articles published on this topic during the 21-year period were published in just three journals—SSQ (37 percent), JOP (17 percent), and PRQ (16 percent). This pattern cannot be explained by journal prestige as these three journals are not unusual in that regard. Neither can the pattern be explained by the journal's willingness to publish policy research, since the two journals that exclusively publish policy research accounted for a mere 8 percent of articles (combined). Rather, the concentration of articles in these three journals can probably be attributed to two factors. First, these journals (SSQ, JOP, and PRQ) are affiliated with professional associations located in geographic regions that are heavily populated with minority (black and Latino) populations. Second, the relatively high rate of

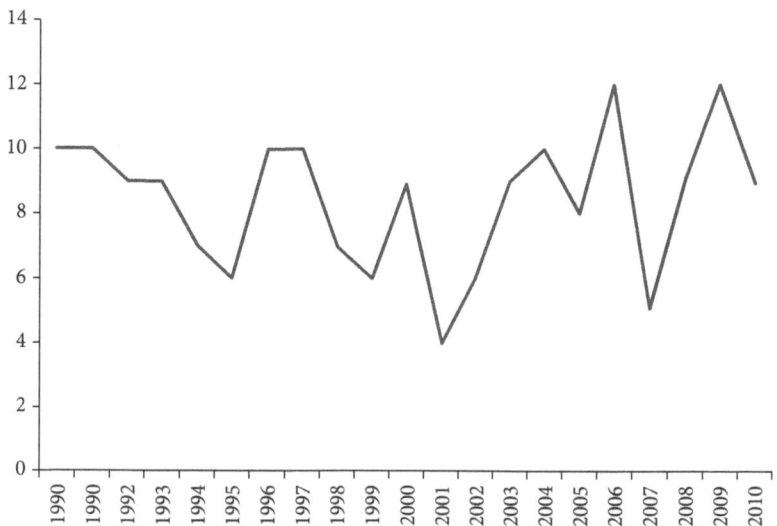

FIGURE 35.1 Yearly count of articles focusing on minority-targeted policies, 1990–2010

Note: The vertical axis represents the total number of articles on minority-targeted policies appearing in the following journals: *APSR, AJPS, JOP, APQ/APR, WPQ/PRQ, JPAM, PSJ,* and *SSQ. SPPQ* is omitted from this analysis since the journal did not exist prior to 2001.

Source: Compiled by the authors.

Table 35.1   Distribution of articles on minority-targeted policies, by journal

Journal	Percentage of articles
American Political Science Review	2.6
American Journal of Political Science	6.7
American Politics Research	3.6
Journal of Politics	16.1
Journal of Policy Analysis and Management	2.6
Political Research Quarterly	17.1
Policy Studies Journal	5.7
Social Science Quarterly	37.3
State Politics and Policy Quarterly	8.3
TOTAL	100

Note: State Politics and Policy Quarterly did not begin publishing until 2001.
Source: Compiled by the authors.

publication in SSQ undoubtedly reflects the interdisciplinary mission of the journal, and especially its large readership in sociology.

Trends in Content

Which minority groups have received the most attention in the literature? Overall, the answer is clear. Across the 21-year period, policies affecting blacks were the subject of 34 percent of the articles in our sample. Policies affecting women and Latinos received significant attention as well, with each group represented in 26 percent of the articles in our sample. The only other minority group represented in more than 10 percent of the articles was gays and lesbians (at 14 percent). Policies affecting these four groups—blacks, women, Latinos, and gays and lesbians—were a significant focus of approximately 87 percent of all articles published in our two-decade sample. We classified the group focus of the remaining 13 percent of articles as "other." This category consisted of articles dealing with policies related to the disabled (2.1 percent), Native Americans (1.6 percent), Asians (1.6 percent), and a handful of articles that deal with minority-targeted policies across a broad range of groups, and which therefore have no specific focus.

In Figure 35.2, we extend our analysis of group focus to explore the stability of this distribution over time. As can be seen in the figure, there have been significant changes in distribution of attention paid to these groups over the last two decades. For simplicity, we divide our sample into two time periods—1990–9 and 2000–10. During the 1990s, 75 percent of the articles focused on policies that were relevant to blacks (38.1 percent)

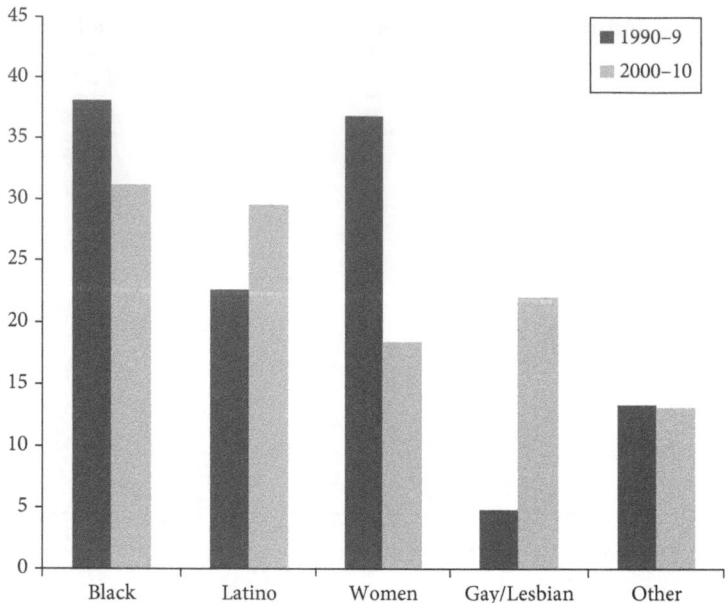

FIGURE 35.2 Number of articles on minority-targeted policies, by minority group and period

Note: The vertical axis represents the total number of articles on minority-targeted policies appearing in the following journals: *APSR, AJPS, JOP, APQ/APR, WPQ/PRQ, JPAM, PSJ,* and *SSQ. SPPQ* is omitted from this analysis since the journal did not exist prior to 2001.

Source: Compiled by the authors.

or women (37 percent). Latinos were the subject of 22 percent of articles, while policies affecting gays and lesbians were reflected in only 4 percent of the articles. During the 2000s, the picture changed considerably. The biggest increase was experienced for gays and lesbians, as the percentage of articles relevant to their interests increased to 22 percent. Research on policies related to Latinos also increased, but not as dramatically (from 22 percent to 29 percent). This increase in attention to policies affecting gays and lesbians and Latinos came at the expense of research on policies relevant to blacks and women. The decrease was especially pronounced for research on female-targeted policies, as the number of studies decreased by approximately 50 percent—from 37 to 18 percent. These trends are not too surprising and probably reflect a relatively higher level of policymaking activity during the 2000s in policy areas most relevant to gays and lesbians and, to a lesser extent, Latinos (and immigrants, more generally).

Trends in Policy Focus

In Table 35.2, we present the distribution of articles in our sample by their policy focus. For now, we present a broad overview of the policy content of this literature, leaving a detailed discussion of the findings of specific studies for the next section.

Table 35.2 Distribution of content of articles on minority-targeted policies, 1990–2010

General policy focus	Number of articles	Percentage of articles
Electoral system	52	26.3
Abortion	33	16.7
Affirmative action	23	11.6
Gay marriage/unions	19	9.6
Immigration	11	5.6
Multiple policies (across multiple groups)	9	4.5
Language policy	8	4.0
Racial symbols	5	2.5
Gay rights	5	2.5
Antidiscrimination laws	4	2.0
Native American	4	2.0
School segregation/desegregation	3	1.5
Rape/Domestic violence	3	1.5
Hate crime laws	3	1.5
Disability issues	3	1.5
AIDS policies	3	1.5
Sodomy laws	2	1.0
Women's suffrage	2	1.0
Title IX	2	1.0
Women's rights/issues (multiple)	1	0.5
Black rights/issues (multiple)	1	0.5
Minimum wage (women)	1	0.5
Racial profiling	1	0.5

Source: Compiled by the authors.

The table reveals that nearly two-thirds (64 percent) of the articles in our sample focused on one of only four types of policy. The policy area that received the most attention during the two-decade period, accounting for one-quarter (26 percent) of all the articles in our sample, was what we term "electoral system" policies. This is a rather broad category that includes studies on several different features of state and local election systems that have been explicitly linked to minority representation, often through court cases based on minority protections in the Voting Rights Act or the U.S. Constitution. At the local level, the majority of these studies have focused on the impact of single-member district (vs. at-large) election systems and the impact that this choice has on minority representation (Welch, 1990; Bullock and MacManus, 1991; Alozie, 1992; Trounstine and Valdini, 2008). A smaller number of studies have examined cumulative voting systems at the local level as an alternative strategy for maximizing minority representation (Cole and Taebel, 1992; Brockington, Donovan, et al., 1998). At the state level, there is an analogous, but smaller literature that examines the impact of single-member (vs. multi-member) district systems in state legislative elections (Moncrief and Thompson, 1992; Larimer, 2005). Yet, perhaps the most common area of focus within this category has been "racial gerrymandering" and its impact on both representational and policy outcomes (Cameron, Epstein, et al., 1996; LeVeaux and Garand, 2003; Grose, 2005). The minority groups of focus within this area have most often been racial and ethnic minorities (e.g., blacks and Latinos), but there has been some research on the impact of state and local election systems on the representation of women as well (Bullock and MacManus, 1991; Pritchard, 1992).

The second largest category of studies consists of articles on abortion policy (16.7 percent). A majority of these studies examine variation in state abortion policies and the adoption of restrictive abortion policies in the post-Roe era (Meier and McFarlane, 1993; Norrander and Wilcox, 1999; Roh and Haider–Markel, 2003; Patton, 2007). However, some studies have utilized data from the pre-Roe period to test theories of policymaking (Mooney and Lee, 1995; Nossiff, 1998). A second set of studies examines public opinion on abortion. These studies have examined a variety of factors, including gender (Berkman and O'Connor, 1993; Walzer, 1994) race and ethnicity (Dugger, 1991; Lynxwiler and Gay, 1994; Bolks, Evans, et al., 2000), and religion (O'Connor and Berkman, 1995; Welch, Leege, et al., 1995; Mulligan, 2006), among others. Finally, a handful of studies have examined the impact of abortion access and abortion policy stringency on a variety of outcomes (Haas-Wilson 1993; Korenman, Kaestner, et al., 2001).

Studies examining affirmative action policies and their consequences represent the third largest category in our sample. Many of these studies focus on the use of affirmative action in particular sectors of society, and include studies of the causes and consequences of minority employment in local government (Kerr and Mladenka, 1994; Button and Rienzo, 2003; Rocha and Hawes, 2009), the use of racial preferences in college admissions (Gruhl and Welch, 1990; Mumpower, Nath, et al., 2002; Niu, Sullivan, et al., 2008), and racial preferences in local government contracting (Klineberg and Kravitz, 2003). More recently, researchers have shifted their attention to efforts to use direct democracy to repeal or modify existing affirmative action laws (Tolbert and Grummel, 2003; Branton, 2004; Bowler, Nicholson, et al., 2006). Finally, a number of studies have examined the influence of racial and political attitudes on general support for affirmative action among whites (Tuch and Hughes, 1996; Kuklinski, Sniderman, et al., 1997; Feldman and Huddy, 2005).

The fourth largest category of studies, and the only other policy issue represented in ten percent or more of the studies in our sample was gay marriage and civil unions. Like abortion and affirmative action, research on this topic has examined general support for gay marriage among the mass public through an analysis of survey data (Olson,

Cadge, et al., 2006; Gaines and Garand, 2010; Sherkat, de Vries, et al., 2010). However, the vast majority of the studies in our sample examine policies surrounding gay marriage, and especially state and local policies that restrict or forbid gay marriage or civil unions. This research has examined policymaking through traditional legislative channels (Haider-Markel, 2001; Nicholson-Crotty, 2006), as well as the use of direct democracy to restrict gay rights (Barth, Overby, et al., 2009; Fleischmann and Moyer, 2009).

The remaining studies span a wide variety of policy issues, most of which are primarily relevant to one of the four minority groups that have received the majority of attention in the literature—blacks, Latinos, women, and gays and lesbians. A relatively small number of studies in our sample either focused on a different minority group, or they did not focus on a specific group at all, choosing instead to focus on a broad collection of minority-targeted policies.

MINORITY-TARGETED POLICIES: WHAT DO WE KNOW?

Having presented a detailed description of the research on minority-targeted policies over the last two decades, we now take a closer look at these studies to summarize the major findings that have emerged from this literature. We begin by summarizing the major theoretical frameworks that researchers have applied in their studies of minority-targeted policies, with a focus on the most important and widely used theories that have been applied to more than one group. We then discuss research on policies that target one or more of the four minority groups identified by our content analysis above.

Major Theoretical Frameworks

Over the last two decades, researchers have applied a wide range of theories and theoretical frameworks in their efforts to explain the incidence and impact of minority-targeted policies. One of the most important theoretical frameworks applied in this literature concerns the issue of minority representation, and in particular the extent to which minority elected officials are better than non-minorities at maximizing the substantive interests of minority-group members. Relying on the conceptual framework first introduced by Pitkin (1967), these studies ask: Does descriptive representation lead to better substantive representation? There is good reason to believe this might be the case. Minority elected officials share a common background and set of experiences with minority-group members that non-minorities cannot possibly match. Therefore, it seems reasonable that minority elected officials would be more sensitive to their group's needs and demands, and exert more effort in office to see that minority-group interests are maximized. However, others have challenged this claim for a variety of reasons, including racism and resistance within legislative bodies (Hedge, Button, et al., 1996; Hawkesworth, 2003), exclusion from dominant legislative coalitions (Browning, Marshall, et al., 1984), or electoral incentives that sufficiently motivate non-minority elected officials to be responsive to minority interests (Swain, 1995).

The relationship between descriptive and substantive representation has been thoroughly studied for black, Latino, and female elected officials. As we detail below, the findings for women are rather consistent in that female elected officials at all levels of government appear to be more supportive of policies that expand or protect women's rights (Reingold, 2000; Thomas and Welch, 2001; Swers, 2002). The findings for black and Latino elected officials are largely supportive of descriptive representation as well, especially for policymaking at the state and local level (Meier, Stewart, et al., 1989; Herring, 1990; Meier, Juenke, et al., 2005; Owens, 2005). Studies conducted at the congressional level are more mixed in their conclusions (Swain, 1995; Cameron, Epstein, et al., 1996; Lublin, 1997b).

Additionally, scholarship on gay and lesbian descriptive and substantive representation at the local and state level has shown a significant link between the election of gay officials and substantive representation in the policy process. Haider-Markel, Joslyn, and Kniss (2000) found that cities were more likely to adopt domestic-partner registries and domestic-partner benefits for government employees when the city council had gay or lesbian members. Likewise, Haider-Markel's (2007, 2010) analysis of state legislatures found that increased descriptive representation of gays and lesbians led to more pro-gay legislation being introduced and adopted. However, his analysis also reveals that increased descriptive representation can engender an anti-gay backlash in the states.

One of the earliest and most frequently applied theories is the "racial threat" hypothesis, which is most commonly associated with the early work of Key (1949) and Blalock (1967). Blalock maintained that majority group repression of a minority group is largely a function of two types of perceived threats—those originating from competition over economic resources, and those arising from competition for political power. An important corollary to this hypothesis is that the level of economic and political competition, and thus the level of perceived threat, is largely a function of minority-group size. More recently, Hero and Tolbert (1996) have offered an alternative framework that incorporates both racial and ethnic diversity. However, it is similar to the more traditional version of the racial threat thesis in that it posits a negative effect of group size on the expansion of minority rights. Studies testing the racial threat hypothesis have usually examined the relationship between black or Latino population size (variously defined) and white support for policies that restrict the rights of blacks and Latinos. Examples include studies of policies that restrict affirmative action (Tolbert and Hero, 2001; Tolbert and Grummel, 2003; Branton, 2004), policies that restrict the rights of immigrants (Hero and Tolbert, 1996; Hood and Morris, 2000; Tolbert and Hero, 2001; Rocha and Espino, 2009a), and policies that restrict "language rights" through such policies as "English-only" laws (Santoro, 1999; Tolbert and Hero, 2001; Preuhs, 2005; Rocha and Espino, 2009a).

A third major theoretical framework that has often been applied in the literature is the "morality policy" framework. Sometimes referred to as social regulatory policies or culture-war issues, morality policies include a broad range of policies that are characterized as a debate over first principles, where at least one group involved portrays an issue in terms of morality or sin and uses moral arguments to support a policy position (Meier, 1994; Mooney and Lee, 1995; Haider-Markel and Meier, 1996; Mooney, 2001). Several policies targeted at women and gays/lesbians fit this definition, with some of the most important examples including various types of abortion restrictions as well as gay and lesbian rights. Because morality policies are technically simple, highly salient, and have a relatively higher level of citizen participation, these policies are expected to engender a greater degree of democratic responsiveness from elected officials than non-morality policies. For the most part, this has been borne out by empirical studies of morality policy adoption, and show that morality policy adoptions seem to be related to factors that reflect the distribution of citizens' values (such as religious forces), public opinion, salience, and political variables such as the party affiliation of elected officials or electoral competition. This has certainly been found to be the case for state adoption of abortion policies (Meier and McFarlane, 1993; Mooney and Lee, 1995; Norrander and Wilcox, 1999; Arceneaux, 2002; Patton, 2007; Camobreco and Barnello, 2008). For reasons that are not clear, the morality policy framework has been less consistent in its ability to account for policy adoptions in the area of gay rights (Haider-Markel and Meier, 1996; Haider-Markel, 2001; Barclay and Fisher, 2003; Nicholson-Crotty, 2006).

Finally, a growing literature in the study of minority-targeted policies has applied or tested what we might term a "direct democracy" framework for understanding the adoption of minority-targeted policies, and especially those policies that restrict minority rights. While theories of the relationship between direct democracy and repression of minority rights (i.e. "majority tyranny") can be traced as far back as Madison's classic arguments presented in *The Federalist Papers*, scholarly interest in this possibility was sparked by the publication of Barbara Gamble's (1997) study which examined the use of direct democracy to consider various types of civil rights initiatives (housing and accommodations, school desegregation, gay rights, English language laws, and AIDS policies) between 1959 and 1993. Based on a simple cross-tabulation, she found that minority interests lost in 78 percent of these elections. The findings for gay civil rights cases were confirmed by Haider-Markel and Meier (2003), who extended the analysis through 1998.

Gamble's findings have sparked considerable debate and have led to several responses by scholars seeking to re-examine her conclusion that direct democracy inevitably leads to majority tyranny. Donovan and Bowler (1998) focused on gay civil rights and found that the negative effects of direct democracy were effectively negated in large, heterogeneous jurisdictions, where it is presumably more difficult for majority factions to form. This finding was confirmed to some degree by Nicholson-Crotty (2006) in his study of same-sex marriage bans, but disputed by Haider-Markel et al. (2007). Hajnal, Gerber, et al. (2002) examined a wide variety of direct democracy elections in California since 1978, comparing the outcomes to racial and ethnic group preferences as measured in state public-opinion polls. The authors found that the outcome of direct democracy elections were consistent with the preferences of racial and ethnic minorities (and especially blacks and Latinos) in a majority of cases, even on issues that were identified as being very important to them. Yet, they still found that blacks and Latinos regularly "lost" on issues that were directly targeted at racial and ethnic minorities (e.g., affirmative action, language policies, immigration). Combined with the results of subsequent studies that find a repressive effect of direct democracy on minority rights (Tolbert and Hero, 2001; Haider-Markel, Querze, et al., 2007), the debate would seem to be far from settled.

Minorities and State and Local Election Systems

As we have already documented, the most-studied minority-targeted policy area over the years has been electoral-system design. Since the passage of the Voting Rights Act in 1965, in combination with Supreme Court rulings (*Thornburg vs. Gingles*, 1986; see Kosterlitz, 1986), racial and ethnic minorities (mostly blacks and Latinos) have successfully pressured state and local governments into enacting a number of changes to their election systems to help enhance the election of minority-group members to office (Grofman, Handley, et al., 1994). More so than in any other social science discipline, political scientists have devoted considerable attention to the impact that these changes have had on the election of minorities and, in turn, how the election of minorities has impacted public policymaking.

The early literature focused primarily on the impact of electoral systems on black descriptive representation, and specifically the impact of single-member district systems. Most of these studies have examined local elections, and have generally found that compared to at-large election systems, single-member district systems do a much better job of ensuring that blacks are elected in proportion to their voting strength in the local population. This finding was especially robust among studies that examined data from the 1970s, in the immediate aftermath of the Voting Rights Act of 1965 (for reviews of this extensive research see Karnig and Welch, 1982; Engstrom and McDonald 1986; Grofman and Lijphart, 1986). However, studies that have relied on more recent data are not nearly as unanimous in their findings. Although blacks still seem to be better served by district systems (Bullock and MacManus, 1990; Arrington and Watts, 1991), several studies have found that the effect is not as great as it once was and appears to be limited to areas where the black population is relatively large and highly concentrated (Welch, 1990; Trounstine and Valdini, 2008). Far fewer studies have examined the effects of single-member district systems on black descriptive representation in state legislative elections, but the existing evidence suggests that single-member districts have at least as strong an effect on black descriptive representation (Moncrief and Thompson, 1992).

The evidence is not nearly as clear-cut concerning the effect of single-member districts on Latino representation. Some studies have indeed found that at-large systems depress Latino representation on city councils (Davidson and Korbel, 1981; Bezdek,

Billeaux, et al., 2000) and school boards (Davidson and Korbel, 1981; Meier and Stewart, 1991; Leal, Martinez-Ebers, et al., 2004). Yet, a significant number of studies have found the choice of electoral system to have little effect on Latino representation on city councils (Welch, 1990; Hajnal and Trounstine, 2005) or within state legislatures. Likewise Haider-Markel (2010) finds that district type has little influence on the electoral prospects of gays and lesbians running for state legislative office.

Further confusion over the democracy-enhancing benefits of single-member district election systems arises from the possibility that they serve to depress the election of women to office. This is the conclusion of the majority of studies that have examined this question at the state level (Welch, Ambrosius, et al., 1985; King, 2002). However, the evidence is less conclusive at the local level (Bullock and MacManus, 1991; Darcy, Welch, et al., 1994). Although the precise mechanism for such an effect is unclear, a number of possibilities have been offered, including bias among party elites in slating candidates and distributing resources (Clark, 1991; Carroll, 1994), or simply that (male) voters may be more willing to vote for a female when they have more than one vote to cast (Welch, Ambrosius, et al., 1985; Clark, 1991). Regardless of the reason, the possibility of this effect may result in a tradeoff between descriptive representation and substantive (policy) representation for blacks and Latinos due to the fact that women are much more likely to support a wide range of policies that are beneficial to blacks and Latinos (Thomas, 1994; Bratton and Haynie, 1999; Reingold, 2000).

The more recent literature on election-system design has focused on the consequences of electing blacks and Latinos to office. To answer this question, a significant literature has developed that examines the impact of the presence of black and Latino elected officials on a variety of political outcomes. Much of this literature has examined the impact of descriptive representation on political behavior. The vast majority of studies in this area have found that the presence of minority elected officials clearly has a positive impact on minority group attitudes toward the political system, leading to higher levels of political efficacy and political trust (Bobo and Gilliam, 1990; Pantoja and Segura, 2003), as well as increased interaction with elected officials (Gay, 2002). The evidence is not as clear concerning the effect of minority descriptive representation on voter turnout. Although a number of studies find a positive effect on turnout (Bobo and Gilliam, 1990; Vanderleeuw and Utter, 1993; Voss and Lublin, 2001; Herron and Sekhon, 2005; Whitby, 2007), a handful of studies are less optimistic, at least with respect to black voters (Gay, 2001; Griffin and Keane, 2006). Recently, scholars have extended research on the impact of black and Latino descriptive representation to its effects on white political attitudes and behavior. The findings of these studies are somewhat mixed, with some studies concluding that black representation often serves to enhance whites' views of blacks (Hajnal, 2001), while others conclude that minority empowerment leads to alienation and lower turnout among whites (Gay, 2001; Gay, 2002; Barreto, Segura, et al., 2004).

Perhaps the most controversial area of research on the impact of minority descriptive representation concerns its effects on policy outcomes, or what political scientists term substantive representation. Although the literature suggests that minority elected officials often face important obstacles that may limit their success (e.g., Browning,

Marshall, et al., 1984), empirical studies of state and local politics generally conclude that black and Latino representation in government promotes more favorable policy outcomes for minorities across a variety of policy areas. These include municipal services and programs (e.g., Browning, Marshall, et al., 1984), civil-service employment (Eisinger, 1982), police practices and oversight (Saltzstein, 1989), sentencing and incarceration (Welch, Combs, et al., 1988; Yates and Fording, 2005), education (Stewart Jr, England, et al., 1989; Meier, Juenke, et al., 2005), welfare (Fording, 2003), civil rights and civil liberties legislation (Herring, 1990), and state spending priorities (Owens, 2005), among others. While the causal mechanisms underlying the effect are generally unclear, at the very least the effect appears to be partly due to enhanced agenda-setting powers (Bratton and Haynie, 1999; Bratton, 2002).

Studies conducted at the congressional level are more controversial and raise important questions about the wisdom of using racially motivated redistricting as a strategy to maximize black substantive representation. With few exceptions (e.g., Swain, 1995), scholars on both sides of this debate generally agree that black representatives are more sensitive to the concerns of black constituents. Where scholars disagree is whether the maximization of black descriptive representation inherently leads to a tradeoff in substantive representation due to the "packing" of conservative, Republican, white voters in surrounding districts that naturally occurs when creating majority-black districts. According to critics, although substantive representation is enhanced in the (few) districts that are guaranteed to elect black representatives; this increase is more than offset by the decrease in substantive representation among the white representatives in surrounding districts. Several studies have indeed found such a tradeoff to exist (Cameron, Epstein, et al., 1996; Overby and Cosgrove, 1996; Lublin, 1997a, 1997b; Lublin and Voss, 2003). Others have argued that there is little evidence of such a tradeoff (Petrocik and Desposato, 1998; Shotts, 2003). The implications of this debate for the findings concerning the substantive impact of black representation at the state and local level are unclear. Nor has the research investigated the possibility of such a tradeoff with the creation of Latino-majority districts.

Black-Targeted Policies

In addition to the literature on electoral rules and direct democracy, the remaining literature on black-targeted policies has examined two types of policies—affirmative action (variously defined), and what we term "racially relevant symbolic policies." Although affirmative action policies also affect Latinos and women (to a lesser extent), the politics surrounding it has more often been cast as a "racial" (i.e. black–white) conflict, therefore we review these studies in this section.

Studies of affirmative action have pursued several different questions regarding the politics and impact of affirmative action. Many studies have examined white attitudes toward affirmative action to better understand the degree of white opposition and its sources. Much of this research has been motivated by the seemingly contradictory trends of increasing support for general principles of racial equality among whites, alongside deep and consistent opposition to specific policies, such as affirmative action, designed to promote racial equality. There has been considerable debate over the explanation for what has since become known as the "policy-implementation" gap. Some researchers have argued that opposition stems from adherence to ideological principles such as individualism, equal treatment, and other basic tenets of American culture that are perceived by many whites to be inconsistent with affirmative action. This perspective has been developed most forcefully by Sniderman and colleagues (Sniderman and Carmines, 1997; Sniderman, Crosby, et al., 2000).

A second group of researchers has argued that opposition to race-targeted policies such as affirmative action is deeply rooted in racial prejudice. These scholars have disagreed over the specific conceptualization of prejudice that is most important today. While some argue that traditional, overt prejudice is still important, many researchers maintain that a "new racism" is operating that is conveyed through white opposition to black demands and resentment over their special treatment (McConahay and Hough Jr, 1976; Kinder and Sanders, 1996; Bobo, Kluegel, et al., 1997; Henry and Sears, 2002). Many studies, utilizing different datasets and methodologies, have been conducted over the years in an attempt to determine which of these perspectives is most accurate. Although the debate is far from settled, there appears to be some degree of support for both explanations (Tuch and Hughes, 1996; Alvarez and Brehm, 1997; Feldman and Huddy, 2005).

Much of the remaining literature on affirmative action in political science has examined government policymaking or the impact of affirmative action. Santoro (1995) collected data on local government adoptions of affirmative action policies in employment and contracting. He found that city council diversity and black population size were the most significant correlates of local adoptions. As affirmative action has been gradually dismantled over the last two decades, several scholars have turned their attention to the politics of repeal, primarily through the mechanism of direct democracy. The findings from these studies indicate that election outcomes continue to be greatly affected by race, whether it is the race of the voter (Segura and Fraga, 2008), or the racial context in which voters reside (Tolbert and Hero, 2001; Tolbert and Grummel, 2003; Branton, 2004).

Several studies have examined the implementation and impact of affirmative action. Some scholars have studied these issues in a more indirect fashion, by examining the impact of one important consequence of affirmative action—minority representation in local and state bureaucracy. This literature has consistently found that a "representative bureaucracy" can have a significant impact on a variety of minority outcomes, including increased minority employment in local government (Kerr and Mladenka, 1994), as well as better performance by black students, both in absolute terms and relative to whites (Meier, Stewart, et al., 1989; Meier, Wrinkle, et al., 1999; Rocha and Hawes, 2009). More recently, scholars have turned their attention to the importance of affirmative action in university admissions in light of recent Supreme Court cases that have limited the use of racial preferences (Gruhl and Welch, 1990; Mumpower, Nath, et al., 2002; Hicklin and Meier, 2008).

A handful of studies have examined the politics of government adoption or repeal of racially relevant symbolic policies. Such policies include the designation of holidays or streets to honor Martin Luther King, Jr, the use of confederate symbols in state flags, and the removal of racist provisions from state constitutions. A primary question addressed in this research is the role of racial prejudice in explaining support for the anti-black position on these policies. The findings of these studies have been mixed, with some studies showing clear effects of prejudice (Orey, 2004; Hutchings, Walton, et al., 2010), and other studies suggesting that the role of prejudice is less clear (Sigelman and Walkosz, 1992; Voss and Miller, 2001).

Latino-Targeted Policies

Two additional types of policies that primarily affect Latinos have been the focus of significant attention in the literature—immigration policies and language policies. Studies of immigration policy and politics are the more numerous of the two and have increased in recent years, tracking the rise of immigration policy on the public agenda. Scholars have studied immigration policy from a variety of perspectives, but much of the literature examines state ballot initiatives intended to restrict the rights of immigrants. The major questions addressed in this literature revolve around the effects of race and ethnicity, and, in particular, whether the increase in support for restrictive immigration policies can be characterized as some form of racial backlash among whites. The literature clearly finds that white Anglos are most supportive of restrictive policies (Alvarez and Butterfield, 2000). Yet, most studies have been more interested in estimating the effects of the racial and ethnic context on white attitudes to test the racial threat hypothesis. Several studies have indeed found support for an effect of racial/ethnic context (Tolbert and Hero, 1996; Hood and Morris, 2000; Tolbert and Hero, 2001; Rocha and Espino, 2009b). However, the direction of the effect, and thus the existence of a white backlash, is disputed. Some studies find the effect of local diversity on support for restrictive immigration policy to be positive, and thus supportive of the backlash hypothesis (Tolbert and Hero, 1996; Tolbert and Hero, 2001). Other studies find a negative effect, which is consistent with the ameliorative effect of increased inter-racial contact (Hood and Morris, 2000; Rocha and Espino, 2009b). Extending the analysis to black voters, Hood and Morris (2000) found also found little support for an inter-group conflict effect, thus casting further doubt on backlash theory, at least as an explanation for the increasing popularity of policies designed to restrict immigrant rights.

Studies of language policy have either focused on the implementation of bilingual education mandated by the Bilingual Education Act of 1967, or the adoption of "English-only" laws, which emerged during the 1980s as a backlash against "language rights" policies calling for bilingual government services, including bilingual education (Citrin, Reingold, et al., 1990). A central question in all of these studies is how the presence of the Latino (or foreign-born) population affects the adoption of such laws, either indirectly through the Latino share of the state population, or more directly through

Latino descriptive representation. The existing evidence finds support for both types of effects. In one of the few local-level studies, Robinson (2002) studied bilingual education in Texas and found that implementation effort was significantly enhanced by the presence of Latino school board members. Most studies have examined the adoption of state English-only laws. This research has found that the relationship between Latino population and descriptive representation can be complex and may greatly depend on the presence or absence of the initiative process in a state (Santoro, 1999; Schildkraut, 2001; Tolbert and Hero, 2001; Preuhs, 2005; Casellas, 2009; Rocha and Espino, 2009b).

Female-Targeted Policies

By far, the most-studied policy relevant to women is abortion policy. Many studies of abortion policy have examined some aspect of abortion attitudes. This literature is quite large and has led to several interesting findings. Several studies have determined that public opinion on abortion is both highly salient and relatively stable across time (Wetstein, 1993; Sharp, 1999; Wilcox and Norrander, 2002). It is a source of political activism for many people (Verba, Schlozman, et al., 1995; Maxwell, 2002), and as a political issue abortion has been shown to influence voting decisions at every level of government, including elections for president (Smith, 1994; Abramowitz, 1996), Senate (Cook, et al., 1994a), governor (Cook, et al., 1994b), as well as other offices (Jelen, 1993). In fact, some evidence suggests that the abortion issue has influenced some voters to change parties (Adams, 1997; Killian and Wilcox, 2008).

Many studies have shown that abortion attitudes are related to several key demographic variables. This research finds that those who support the right to an abortion are generally more likely to be younger, as well as more educated (Cook, et al., 1992; Cook, et al., 1994a, 1994b; Wilcox and Norrander, 2002). There have been many studies of racial differences in support for abortion (Combs and Welch, 1982; Hall and Ferree, 1986; Wilcox, 1990; Cook, Jelen, et al., 1992). The findings from this literature have generally found that blacks and Latinos are less likely to support abortion rights, but these racial and ethnic differences disappear in some studies once the estimates are adjusted for differences in other correlates of abortion attitudes.

One of the most surprising findings in this literature has been the insignificance of gender in explaining mass abortion attitudes (Cook, Jelen, et al., 1992; Chaney, Alvarez, et al., 1998; Strickler and Danigelis, 2002). Yet, while this seems to be true among the mass public, this is less true among elites, and especially female policymakers. Indeed, several studies have found female policymakers to be more supportive of women's issues, including abortion rights (Berkman and O'Connor, 1993; Thomas and Welch, 2001).

Perhaps the most consistent finding in the literature is the influence of religion. Opposition is especially strong among Catholics (Welch, Leege, et al., 1995) as well as evangelical Protestants (Cook, Jelen, et al., 1992; Hoffmann and Miller, 1997). Interestingly, several studies have shown that frequent church attendance is related to greater opposition to abortion rights, even after controlling for religious affiliation (Cook, Jelen, et al., 1992; Emerson, 1996).

A second body of literature has examined abortion policymaking. Although some studies have focused on the politics of pre-Roe abortion policy (Mooney and Lee, 1995), most studies have focused on the adoption of abortion restrictions during the post-Roe period. The findings from this research are consistent with the morality policy framework, which cites the importance of public opinion, political/electoral competition, and religious values on public policymaking (Meier, 1994; Mooney, 2001). Specifically, this literature has found that the adoption of restrictive abortion policy is significantly related to public opinion (Norrander and Wilcox, 1999; Arceneaux, 2002; Camobreco and Barnello, 2008), the presence of Catholic and evangelical Protestant interest groups and churches (Meier and McFarlane, 1993; Roh and Haider-Markel, 2003; Calfano, 2010), the presence of female legislators and pro-choice interest groups (Berkman and O'Connor, 1993; Patton, 2007), and the presence of Republicans in the state legislature (Patton, 2007). Clearly, abortion policy is one policy area for which politics matters.

In contrast to the research on abortion, there has been relatively little research on other policies that target women, at least within the political science literature. Nevertheless, based on the few studies of the determinants of rape and domestic violence laws have been conducted, it appears that the politics surrounding such policies is much less ideologically charged and partisan-driven than abortion (Berger, Neuman, et al. 1991; Call, Nice, et al. 1991; Weldon 2006).

Gay-and-Lesbian-Targeted Policies

One of the fastest growing literatures on minority-targeted policies concerns issues affecting gays and lesbians. The most studied policy issue to date has been same-sex marriage and consists of two types of studies. First, several studies have examined individual attitudes toward same-sex marriage. As with abortion, there has been considerable attention devoted to the effects of religious beliefs, and especially evangelical beliefs on opposition to same-sex marriage (Wilcox and Norrander, 2002; Brewer and Wilcox, 2005; Haider-Markel and Joslyn, 2005, 2008; Whitehead, 2010). Independent of religious affiliation and beliefs, opposition has also been linked to church attendance (Brewer and Wilcox, 2005; Haider-Markel and Joslyn, 2008), as well as support for traditional moral values (Brewer, 2003; Rimmerman and Wilcox, 2007; Campbell and Monson, 2008).

Since the passage of Proposition 8 in California in 2008, there has been considerable interest in the effect of race on support for same-sex marriage due to the widely speculated effect of black and Latino support for the amendment. A recent study by Abrajano (2010) finds that blacks (but not Latinos) were indeed more likely to support California's gay marriage ban, and this effect held up even after controlling for religious and political variables. However, other research suggests that the effect may not be generalizable to the entire United States (Gaines and Garand, 2010), or to states in the South

(Barth, Overby, et al., 2009; Barth and Parry, 2009). Although blacks do generally display greater opposition to same-sex marriage in a bivariate relationship, the relationship appears to be almost entirely due to higher levels of religiosity among blacks (Sherkat, de Vries, et al., 2010).

A second set of studies examines the adoption of policies that restrict or ban same-sex marriage. Researchers have applied a variety of theoretical frameworks emphasizing different explanatory variables. One general finding that has emerged is that the politics of same-sex marriage seems to deviate in some ways from the politics of other morality policies. For example, several studies have found evidence that the partisanship of elected officials has little, if any impact on the adoption of gay marriage policies (Haider-Markel, 2001; Barclay and Fisher, 2003; Nicholson-Crotty, 2006). Nor have studies found particularly strong effects for indicators of public opinion (Barclay and Fisher, 2003) or party competition (Haider-Markel, 2001), although few studies have directly examined these effects. One possible reason for these findings is that such forces might only be expected to be operative under certain conditions (Haider-Markel and Meier, 1996). It is also likely that past indicators of public opinion have been too crude and are therefore plagued by measurement error. Indeed, when survey-based measures focusing on rather specific attitudes about gay rights/same-sex marriage are used, the relationship between public opinion and policy adoption appears quite strong (Lewis and Oh, 2008; Lax and Phillips, 2009).

Although the politics of same-sex marriage seems to have less to do with traditional partisan and ideological cleavages, scholars have offered some alternative explanations. The most consistent predictor of the restriction of gay marriage rights is the presence of Protestant fundamentalist and Catholic churches and interest groups (Haider-Markel, 2001; Nicholson-Crotty, 2006; Fleischmann and Moyer, 2009). Several studies have also found the presence of these religious groups to be an important predictor of gay rights laws more generally. This is true for studies conducted at the local level (Haider-Markel and Meier, 1996; Wald, Button, et al., 1996) as well as the state level (Lax and Phillips, 2009).

Several scholars have also turned their attention to how state government institutions, and in particular the presence of direct democracy might affect the adoption of gay rights laws. These studies are often motivated by the more general debate over the role of direct democracy in suppressing minority rights (Gamble, 1997; Haider-Markel et al., 2007), and have reached different conclusions. In their comprehensive study of the adoption of eight different restrictive gay rights laws, Lax and Phillips (2009) found that the presence of direct democracy in a state had no effect on adoption. This finding was consistent with Barclay and Fisher (2003), who examined the gay rights adoptions during the 1990s. Yet, at least three studies have reached the opposite conclusion. Nicholson-Crotty (2006) found that the presence of direct democracy was positively related to the adoption of same-sex marriage bans, but only among states that were relatively homogenous. Two other studies found a direct (positive) effect of direct democracy on gay marriage bans (Pappas, Mendez, et al., 2009; Lupia, Krupnikov, et al., 2010). While there is no obvious explanation for the divergent results, the latter two studies pay close attention to differences across states in access to the ballot in initiative states. This suggests that researchers should pay close attention to measurement issues in future research.

CONCLUSIONS AND FINAL THOUGHT ON WHAT WE NEED TO KNOW

As the previous sections have shown, we have learned a great deal from the last few decades of research on minority-targeted policies. Yet, there is still much to learn and there are important theoretical debates that remain to be resolved. We therefore conclude our review of research on minority-targeted policies by discussing some important gaps in the literature, offering some suggestions for the direction of future research. We begin with a discussion of some important limitations within existing debates, and then move to more general recommendations for new directions in research on minority-targeted policies.

Reexamining Old Questions

In recent years, there have been significant advances in social science methodology and data availability. Along with those advances have come appropriate increases in the threshold for what is considered acceptable evidence of causal relationships. Given these advances, it is important that we continue to re-examine "old" questions, even if these questions appear to have been settled by the weight of the published evidence, and especially if existing studies would benefit from recent advances.

One area where this strategy has been fruitfully employed has been the study of state and local electoral structure. Although there have been dozens of studies of the effects of single-member vs. at-large/multi-member district systems on the election of minorities, nearly all of these studies have been cross-sectional in nature. While cross-sectional research designs surely have value, they are relatively weak in internal validity. Trounstine and Valdini (2008) revisited this question, utilizing panel data to study the effect of electoral structure on city council diversity. In a similar fashion, King (2002) utilized state panel data to study the effect of electoral structure on the election of women to state legislatures. In the case of Trounstine and Valdini, the results indicated that at least some of the conclusions about the effects of electoral structure should be called into question. King's results, on the other hand, provided further confirmation of the previously published studies. Nevertheless, both types of knowledge are essential to our understanding of this very important question.

There are many more examples of research questions that could benefit from the application of new research designs. For example, the literature on descriptive representation has generally found that the presence of minority elected officials leads to better substantive representation. The most common research design for such studies is to regress a policy measure on a measure of descriptive representation, while controlling for constituency characteristics (as well as other possible variables). Yet, as we argued above, there is good reason to suspect that such a design suffers from endogeneity due to (1) our inability to precisely (or even adequately) measure constituent demand for the policy, and (2) the possibility that constituent demand for the policies is likely to be directly related to constituents' willingness to vote for a minority candidate. Thus, future research would benefit from additional research that utilizes a stronger identification strategy to estimate the causal effect of descriptive representation.

Research on the existence and impact of a "racial threat" suffers from similar, yet perhaps more intractable endogeneity issues. The most common approach to testing a "group threat effect" is to regress some measure of white support for a restrictive minority-targeted policy on the size of the minority population in some surrounding "context" that is identified by the researcher. The level of aggregation for the minority context variable has varied across studies, and has been measured at the state level down to the precinct level. The major endogeneity threat in this literature is fact that residential location is not entirely fixed. That is, white residents who do not like minorities can move to areas where there are few minorities. Similarly, minority-group members can choose to avoid residential areas that are populated by whites who are considered intolerant of their presence (albeit minority residential choices are probably more constrained). In either case, the endogeneity of residential choice presents an important challenge to the internal validity of nearly all of the past research on this question. Ironically, although we generally think of smaller units of analysis as being better than larger units, this particular problem is probably most severe for studies utilizing small levels of aggregation for their minority population variable, due to the fact that residential mobility is undoubtedly least constrained within cities and counties. This methodological problem is well-known in the literature, but has remained unsolved.

Broadening Our Focus

We conclude by suggesting that in the future, researchers broaden their analytical focus. Our content analysis, as well as our reading of this literature, suggests that we might think about doing this in several different ways. Our review of the literature revealed that the vast majority of studies of minority-targeted policies have focused on one minority group. Yet, to the extent that we wish to develop and test general theories of minority politics, single-group studies suffer from a lack of external validity. One research area in which scholars have often deviated from the norm of single-group studies is the literature on the relationship between minority rights and direct democracy. Several studies within this literature have studied policies affecting two or more minority groups (e.g., Gamble, 1997; Haider-Markel, 1998; Tolbert and Hero, 2001; Hajnal, Gerber, et al., 2002; Branton, 2004). To the extent that results diverge across groups, such studies provide potentially valuable insights concerning the conditions under which theories of direct democracy can be applied. Other recent examples of multi-group studies outside of the direct democracy literature include Trounstine and Valdini (2008, electoral structure), Rocha and Hawes (2009, education), and Bratton and Haynie (1999, descriptive representation), among others.

We do not mean to suggest that single-group studies should be avoided. Yet, within the set of single-group studies our content analysis also revealed that scholars have focused a highly disproportionate amount of attention to just a few specific policies. For example, studies of abortion and same-sex marriage comprised half or more of the all the studies of women and gays and lesbians, respectively. Just as expanding our focus to more than one group could provide greater leverage for answering important theoretical questions, the literature would benefit in much the same way by expanding our policy focus within studies of single groups. For women, this could mean comparing abortion policy outcomes to policies dealing with violence against women, or comparable worth policies. For gays and lesbians, this might mean more studies that explicitly compare the politics of same-sex marriage policies to the adoption of sodomy laws, as well as other policies affecting the rights of gays and lesbians (for example see Haider-Markel and Kaufman, 2006). And for Latinos, explicit comparative studies of the politics of immigration policies, language policies, and affirmative action, for example, could provide important insights concerning the relationship between minority-group mobilization, majority opposition, policy content, and policy outcomes.

Studies of minority-targeted policies would also benefit from incorporating a broader theoretical lens. There are at least three theoretical approaches that we feel could provide important insights into the politics of minority policymaking, yet which we feel have been underutilized within political science. First, despite its popularity in more qualitatively oriented studies of policymaking and courses on the policy process, Schneider and Ingram's theory of the social construction of target populations has been underutilized in studies of minority-targeted policies. While quantitative studies have frequently employed measures of public opinion in their models of policymaking, they generally use one of two types of measures—general measures of liberal-conservative ideology, or very specific measures of public attitudes toward a particular policy. Schneider and Ingram (1993) provide a more powerful framework for thinking about the impact of public opinion by suggesting that the social construction of a target group goes a long way toward explaining public opinion on a broad range of policies targeting that group. This conceptualization of public opinion would seem to be perfectly suited for explaining the politics of minority-targeted policies, since the target group is often very visible and majority (i.e. white or male) stereotypes of minority groups have been shown to play an important role in structuring policy attitudes. The social construction framework also incorporates the political power of the target group, and suggests that social construction and political power might work together in a non-additive fashion to influence policy outcomes.

A second theoretical framework that could be applied more frequently in the political science literature is referred to as "intersectionality," and is frequently applied in sociology and psychology. Intersectionality theory emphasizes that the meaning of one category of social identity can be altered when combined with another. The effect of overlapping identities has been most frequently studied with respect to minority groups, where researchers have studied the intersection of gender and race (Crenshaw, 1991; Hancock, 2004), as well as the intersection of sexual orientation and race (Gamson and Moon, 2004). The effect of multiple, overlapping identities can be exhibited in at least two ways that are relevant to the literature on the politics of minority-targeted policies. First, minority-group members with overlapping minority-group membership may have unique perspectives and ideologies that influence their political behavior, or if serving in public office, how they govern. Thus, theories of intersectionality would seem to be perfectly suited for studying the effects of descriptive representation. Individuals with overlapping minority group identities may also suffer from unique perceptions and stereotypes by other groups (e.g., stereotypes of black females, male Latinos, etc.). This could have important implications for how a minority target group is perceived, and drawing from social construction theory, could have an important impact on the policymaking process.

Finally, studies of minority-targeted policies would benefit from broadening the theoretical lens to include extra-institutional forces that might potentially contribute to minority group success or failure. In political science, it is natural that we focus on the characteristics of political institutions and the elites who occupy them in explaining policy outcomes. In addition, by definition, minority groups are subordinate groups and are often unable to exert significant political power. But we should not assume that minorities are powerless. Because of this power disparity, minorities must often rely on unconventional political strategies, either alone or in combination with conventional politics to achieve their goals. Two recent studies have recognized the potential importance of minority-group mobilization and have studied the effectiveness of social movement organizations (SMOs) on policymaking. Santoro and McGuire (1997) found that formal institutional power (descriptive representation) had little effect on the comprehensiveness of state affirmative action programs. Yet, this does not suggest that blacks were unable to exert any influence on state policymaking as the strength of civil rights SMOs had an important effect. In contrast, in their analysis of comparable worth policies for women, they found the opposite pattern of influence—SMOs had little impact while the presence of women in institutional positions of power was sufficient to exert influence on policymaking. In her study of state policy responsiveness to violence against women, Weldon (2006) found that the percentage of female state legislators was unrelated to state policy, while the mobilization of women's SMOs had a strong effect on state responsiveness. At the very least, since the strength of minority SMOs and the presence of minority elected officials are likely to be at least modestly correlated, these studies suggest that past studies of the impact of minority descriptive representation may have overstated the importance of institutional power. But most importantly, by broadening the analytical lens to include non-institutional channels, these studies have shown that minorities are not as powerless as we might otherwise think.

Notes

1. While one could reasonably argue that such policies should be included in any discussion of minority-targeted policies, these policy areas are covered elsewhere in this series.
2. We restricted our sample of articles to articles that report original research, rather than review articles, field essays, or articles in which the only purpose was to respond to another author or body of work.

References

Abrajano, M. 2010. "Are Blacks and Latinos Responsible for the Passage of Proposition 8? Analyzing Voter Attitudes on California's Proposal to Ban Same-Sex Marriage in 2008." *Political Research Quarterly* 63 (4): 922–932.

Abramowitz, A. I. 1996. "Bill and Al's Excellent Adventure." *American Politics Research* 24 (4): 434.

Adams, G. D. 1997. "Abortion: Evidence of an Issue Evolution." *American Journal of Political Science* 41 (3): 718–737.

Alozie, N. O. 1992. "The Election of Asians to City Councils." *Social Science Quarterly (University of Texas Press)* 73 (1): 90–100.

Alvarez, R. M. and J. Brehm. 1997. "Are Americans Ambivalent Towards Racial Policies?" *American Journal of Political Science* 41 (2): 345–374.

Alvarez, R. M. and T. L. Butterfield. 2000. "The Resurgence of Nativism in California? The Case of Proposition 187 and Illegal Immigration." *Social Science Quarterly (University of Texas Press)* 81 (1): 167–179.

Arceneaux, K. 2002. "Direct Democracy and the Link between Public Opinion and State Abortion Policy." *State Politics and Policy Quarterly*: 2 (4) 372–387.

Arrington, T. S. and T. G. Watts. 1991. "The Election of Blacks to School Boards in North Carolina." *The Western Political Quarterly* 44 (4): 1099–1105.

Barclay, S. and S. Fisher. 2003. "The States and the Differing Impetus for Divergent Paths on Same-Sex Marriage, 1990–2001." *Policy Studies Journal* 31 (3): 331–352.

Barreto, M. A., G. M. Segura, et al. 2004. "The Mobilizing Effect of Majority–Minority Districts on Latino Turnout." *The American Political Science Review* 98 (1): 65–75.

Barth, J., L. M. Overby, et al. 2009. "Community Context, Personal Contact, and Support for an Anti-Gay Rights Referendum." *Political Research Quarterly* 62 (2): 355–365.

Barth, J. and J. Parry. 2009. "2 > 1+1? The Impact of Contact with Gay and Lesbian Couples on Attitudes about Gays/Lesbians and Gay-Related Policies." *Politics and Policy* 37 (1): 31–50.

Berger, R. J., W. L. Neuman, et al. 1991. "The Social and Political Context of Rape Law Reform: An Aggregate Analysis." *Social Science Quarterly (University of Texas Press)* 72 (2): 221–238.

Berkman, M. B. and R. E. O'Connor. 1993. "Do Women Legislators Matter?: Female Legislators and State Abortion Policy." *American Politics Research* 21 (1): 102–124.

Bezdek, R. R., D. M. Billeaux, et al. 2000. "Latinos, At-Large Elections, and Political Change: Evidence from the 'Transition Zone.'" *Social Science Quarterly (University of Texas Press)* 81 (1): 207–225.

Blalock, H. M. 1967. *Toward a Theory of Minority-Group Relations*. New York, NY: Wiley.

Bobo, L. and F. D. Gilliam. 1990. "Race, Sociopolitical Participation, and Black Empowerment." *American Political Science Review* 84 (2): 377–393.

Bobo, L., J. R. Kluegel, et al. 1997. "Laissez-faire Racism: The Crystallization of a Kinder, Gentler, Antiblack Ideology." *Racial attitudes in the 1990s: Continuity and change Greenwood Publishing Group*: 15–42.

Bolks, S. M., D. Evans, et al. 2000. "Core Beliefs and Abortion Attitudes: A Look at Latinos." *Social Science Quarterly (University of Texas Press) 81* (1): 253–260.

Bowler, S., S. P. Nicholson, et al. 2006. "Earthquakes and Aftershocks: Race, Direct Democracy, and Partisan Change." *American Journal of Political Science 50* (1): 146–159.

Branton, R. P. 2004. "Voting in Initiative Elections: Does the Context of Racial and Ethnic Diversity Matter?" *State Politics and Policy Quarterly 4*(3): 294–317.

Bratton, K. A. 2002. "The Effect of Legislative Diversity on Agenda Setting: Evidence from Six State Legislatures." *American Politics Research 30* (2): 115–142.

Bratton, K. A. and K. L. Haynie. 1999. "Agenda Setting and Legislative Success in State Legislatures: The Effects of Gender and Race." *The Journal of Politics 61* (3): 658–679.

Brewer, P. 2003. "Values, Political Knowledge, and Public Opinion About Gay Rights." *Public Opinion Quarterly 67* (2): 173–201.

Brewer, P. and C. Wilcox. 2005. "Same-Sex Marriage and Civil Unions." *Public Opinion Quarterly 69* (4): 599–616.

Brockington, D., T. Donovan, et al. 1998. "Minority Representation under Cumulative and Limited Voting." *The Journal of Politics 60* (4): 1108–1125.

Browning, R. P., D. R. Marshall, et al. 1984. *Protest is Not Enough: The Struggle of Blacks and Hispanics for Equality in Urban Politics*. Berkeley, CA: University of California Press.

Bullock, C. S. and S. A. MacManus. 1990. "Structural Features of Municipalities and the Incidence of Hispanic Councilmembers." *Social Science Quarterly (University of Texas Press) 71* (4): 665–681.

Bullock, C. S. and S. A. MacManus. 1991. "Municipal Electoral Structure and the Election of Councilwomen." *The Journal of Politics 53* (1): 75–89.

Button, J. W. and B. A. Rienzo. 2003. "The Impact of Affirmative Action: Black Employment in Six Southern Cities." *Social Science Quarterly (Blackwell Publishing Limited) 84* (1): 1–14.

Calfano, B. R. 2010. "The Power of Brand: Beyond Interest Group Influence in US State Abortion Politics." *State Politics and Policy Quarterly 10* (3): 227–247.

Call, J. E., D. Nice, et al. 1991. "An Analysis of State Rape Shield Laws." *Social Science Quarterly (University of Texas Press) 72* (4): 774–788.

Cameron, C., D. Epstein, et al. 1996. "Do Majority–Minority Districts Maximize Substantive Black Representation in Congress?" *The American Political Science Review 90* (4): 794–812.

Camobreco, J. F. and M. A. Barnello. 2008. "Democratic Responsiveness and Policy Shock: The Case of State Abortion Policy." *State Politics and Policy Quarterly 8* (1): 48–65.

Campbell, D. E. and J. Q. Monson. 2008. "The Religion Card." *Public Opinion Quarterly 72* (3): 399–419.

Carroll, S. J. 1994. *Women as Candidates in American Politics*. Indiana University Press.

Casellas, J. 2009. "The Institutional and Demographic Determinants of Latino Representation in U.S. Legislatures." *Legislative Studies Quarterly 34* (3): 399–426.

Chaney, C. K., R. M. Alvarez, et al. 1998. "Explaining the Gender Gap in US Presidential Elections, 1980–1992." *Political Research Quarterly 51* (2): 311–339.

Citrin, J., B. Reingold, et al. 1990. "The 'Official English' Movement and the Symbolic Politics of Language in the United States." *The Western Political Quarterly 43* (3): 535–559.

Clark, J. 1991. "Getting There: Women in Political Office." *The ANNALS of the American Academy of Political and Social Science 515*: 63–76.

Cole, R. L. and D. A. Taebel. 1992. "Cumulative Voting in Local Elections: Lessons from the Alamogordo Experience." *Social Science Quarterly (University of Texas Press)* 73 (1): 194–201.

Combs, M. W. and S. Welch. 1982. "Blacks, Whites, and Attitudes Toward Abortion." *Public Opinion Quarterly* 46 (4): 510–520.

Cook, E. A., T. G. Jelen, et al. 1992. *Between Two Absolutes: Public Opinion and the Politics of Abortion*. Westview Press.

Cook, E. A., T. G. Jelen, et al. 1993. "State Political Cultures and Public Opinion about Abortion." *Political Research Quarterly* 46 (4): 771–781.

Cook, Elizabeth A., Ted G. Jelen, and Clyde Wilcox. 1994a. *Issue Voting in US Senate Elections: The Abortion Issue in 1990. Congress the Presidency* 21 (2): 99–111.

Cook, Elizabeth A., Ted G. Jelen, and Clyde Wilcox. 1994b. "Issue Voting in Gubernatorial Elections: Abortion and Post-Webster Politics." *The Journal of Politics* 56 (1): 187–199.

Crenshaw, K. 1991. "Mapping the Margins: Intersectionality, Identity Politics, and Violence against Women of Color." *Stanford Law Review* 43 (6): 1241–1299.

Darcy, R., S. Welch, et al. 1994. *Women, Elections, and Representation*. University of Nebraska Press.

Davidson, C. and G. Korbel. 1981. "At-Large Elections and Minority-Group Representation: A Re-examination of Historical and Contemporary Evidence." *The Journal of Politics* 43 (4): 982–1005.

Donovan, T. and S. Bowler. 1998. "Direct Democracy and Minority Rights: An Extension." *American Journal of Political Science* 42 (3): 1020–1024.

Dugger, K. 1991. "Race Differences in the Determinants of Support for Legalized Abortion." *Social Science Quarterly (University of Texas Press)* 72 (3): 570–587.

Eisinger, P. K. 1982. "Black Employment in Municipal Jobs: The Impact of Black Political Power." *The American Political Science Review* 76 (2): 380–392.

Emerson, M. O. 1996. "Through Tinted Glasses: Religion, Worldviews, and Abortion Attitudes." *Journal for the Scientific Study of Religion* 35 (1): 41–55.

Engstrom, R. and M. McDonald. 1986. "The Effect of At-Large versus District Elections on Racial Representation in US Municipalities." *Electoral Laws and their Political Consequences Algora Publishing*: 203–225.

Feldman, S. and L. Huddy. 2005. "Racial Resentment and White Opposition to Race-Conscious Programs: Principles or Prejudice?" *American Journal of Political Science* 49 (1): 168–183.

Fleischmann, A. and L. Moyer. 2009. "Competing Social Movements and Local Political Culture: Voting on Ballot Propositions to Ban Same-Sex Marriage in the U.S. States." *Social Science Quarterly (Blackwell Publishing Limited)* 90 (1): 134–149.

Fording, R. C. 2003. "'Laboratories of Democracy' or Symbolic Politics?" In *Race and the Politics of Welfare Reform*, University of Michigan Press. pp. 72–100.

Gaines, N. S. and J. C. Garand. 2010. "Morality, Equality, or Locality: Analyzing the Determinants of Support for Same-Sex Marriage." *Political Research Quarterly* 63 (3): 553–567.

Gamble, B. S. 1997. "Putting Civil Rights to a Popular Vote." *American Journal of Political Science* 41 (1): 245–269.

Gamson, J. and D. Moon. 2004. "The Sociology of Sexualities: Queer and Beyond." *Annual Review of Sociology* 30: 47–64.

Gay, C. 2001. "The Effect of Black Congressional Representation on Political Participation." *The American Political Science Review* 95 (3): 589–602.

Gay, C. 2002. "Spirals of Trust? The Effect of Descriptive Representation on the Relationship between Citizens and their Government." *American Journal of Political Science* 46 (4): 717–732.

Griffin, J. D. and M. Keane. 2006. "Descriptive Representation and the Composition of African American Turnout." *American Journal of Political Science 50* (4): 998–1012.

Grofman, B., L. Handley, et al. 1994. *Minority Representation and the Quest for Voting Equality*. Cambridge University Press.

Grofman, B. and A. Lijphart. 1986. *Electoral Laws and their Political Consequences*. Algora Publishing.

Grose, C. R. 2005. "Disentangling Constituency and Legislator Effects in Legislative Representation: Black Legislators or Black Districts?" *Social Science Quarterly 86* (2): 427–443.

Gruhl, J. and S. Welch. 1990. "The Impact of the 'Bakke' Decision on Black and Hispanic Enrollment in Medical and Law Schools." *Social Science Quarterly (University of Texas Press) 71* (3): 458–473.

Haas-Wilson, D. 1993. "The Economic Impact of State Restrictions on Abortion: Parental Consent and Notification Laws and Medicaid Funding Restrictions." *Journal of Policy Analysis and Management 12* (3): 498–511.

Haider-Markel, D. P. 1998. "The Politics of Social Regulatory Policy: State and Federal Hate Crime Policy and Implementation Effort." *Political Research Quarterly 51*: 69–88.

Haider-Markel, D. P. 1999. "Morality Policy and Individual-Level Political Behavior: The Case of Legislative Voting on Lesbian and Gay Issues." *Policy Studies Journal 27* (4): 735–749.

Haider-Markel, D. P. 2001. "Policy Diffusion as a Geographical Expansion of the Scope of Political Conflict: Same-Sex Marriage Bans in the 1990s." *State Politics and Policy Quarterly 1* (1): 5–26.

Haider-Markel, D. P. and M. R. Joslyn. 2005. "Attributions and the Regulation of Marriage: Considering the Parallels Between Race and Homosexuality." *Political Science 38* (02): 233–239.

Haider-Markel, D. P. and M. R. Joslyn. 2008. "Beliefs about the Origins of Homosexuality and Support for Gay Rights—An Empirical Test of Attribution Theory." *Public Opinion Quarterly 72* (2): 291–310.

Haider-Markel, D. P., M. R. Joslyn, and C. J. Kniss. 2000. "Minority Group Interests and Political Representation: Gay Elected Officials in the Policy Process." *The Journal of Politics 62* (2): 568–577.

Haider-Markel, D. P. and M. S. Kaufman. 2006. "Public Opinion and Policy Making in the Culture Wars: Is There a Connection between Opinion and Sate Policy on Gay and Lesbian Issues?" In J. E. Cohen (ed.), *Public Opinion in State Politics*. Stanford, CA: Stanford University.

Haider-Markel, D. P. and K. J. Meier. 1996. "The Politics of Gay and Lesbian Rights: Expanding the Scope of the Conflict." *Journal of Politics 58* (2): 332–349.

Haider-Markel, D. P. and K. J. Meier 2003. "Explaining Outcomes in the Battles over Lesbian and Gay Civil Rights." *Review of Policy Research 20* (4): 671–690.

Haider-Markel, D. P., A. Querze, et al. 2007. "Lose, Win, or Draw?: A Reexamination of Direct Democracy and Minority Rights." *Political Research Quarterly 60* (2): 304–314.

Haider-Markel, Donald P. 2007. "Representation and Backlash: The Positive and Negative Influence of Descriptive Representation." *Legislative Studies Quarterly 32* (1): 107–134.

Haider-Markel, D. P. 2010. *Out and Running: Gay and Lesbian Candidates, Elections, and Policy Representation*. Georgetown University Press.

Hajnal, Z. L. 2001. "White Residents, Black Incumbents, and a Declining Racial Divide." *American Political Science Review 95* (3): 603–617.

Hajnal, Z. L., E. R. Gerber, et al. 2002. "Minorities and Direct Legislation: Evidence from California Ballot Proposition Elections." *The Journal of Politics 64* (1): 154–177.

Hajnal, Z. L. and J. Trounstine. 2005. "Where Turnout Matters: The Consequences of Uneven Turnout in City Politics." *The Journal of Politics 67* (2): 515–535.

Hall, E. J. and M. M. Ferree. 1986. "Race Differences in Abortion Attitudes." *Public Opinion Quarterly 50* (2): 193–207.

Hancock, A. M. 2004. *The Politics of Disgust: The Public Identity of the Welfare Queen.* NYU Press.

Hawkesworth, M. 2003. "Congressional Enactments of Race–Gender: Toward a Theory of Raced–Gendered Institutions." *American Political Science Review 97* (4): 529–550.

Hedge, D., J. Button, et al. 1996. "Accounting for the Quality of Black Legislative Life: The View from the States." *American Journal of Political Science 40* (1): 82–98.

Henry, P. and D. O. Sears. 2002. "The Symbolic Racism 2000 Scale." *Political Psychology 23* (2): 253–283.

Hero, R. E. and C. J. Tolbert. 1996. "A Racial/Ethnic Diversity Interpretation of Politics and Policy in the States of the US." *American Journal of Political Science 40* (3): 851–871.

Herring, M. 1990. "Legislative Responsiveness to Black Constituents in Three Deep South States." *The Journal of Politics 52* (3): 740–758.

Herron, M. C. and J. S. Sekhon. 2005. "Black Candidates and Black Voters: Assessing the Impact of Candidate Race on Uncounted Vote Rates." *The Journal of Politics 67* (1): 154–177.

Hicklin, A. and K. J. Meier. 2008. "Race, Structure, and State Governments: The Politics of Higher Education Diversity." *The Journal of Politics 70* (3): 851–860.

Hoffmann, J. P. and A. S. Miller. 1997. "Social and Political Attitudes among Religious Groups: Convergence and Divergence over Time." *Journal for the Scientific Study of Religion 36* (1): 52–70.

Hood, M. V. and I. L. Morris. 2000. "Brother, Can You Spare a Dime? Racial/Ethnic Context and the Anglo Vote on Proposition 187." *Social Science Quarterly (University of Texas Press) 81* (1): 194–206.

Hutchings, V. L., H. Walton, et al. 2010. "The Impact of Explicit Racial Cues on Gender Differences in Support for Confederate Symbols and Partisanship." *The Journal of Politics 72* (4): 1175–1188.

Jelen, T. G. 1993. "The Political Consequences of Religious Group Attitudes." *The Journal of Politics 55* (1): 178–190.

Karnig, A. K. and S. Welch. 1982. "Electoral Structure and Black Representation on City Councils." *Social Science Quarterly 63* (1): 99–114.

Kerr, B. and K. R. Mladenka. 1994. "Does Politics Matter? A Time-Series Analysis of Minority Employment Patterns." *American Journal of Political Science 38* (4): 918–943.

Key, V. O. and A. Heard. 1949. *Southern Politics in State and Nation.* New York: Vintage Books.

Killian, M. and C. Wilcox. 2008. "Do Abortion Attitudes Lead to Party Switching?" *Political Research Quarterly 61* (4): 561–573.

Kinder, D. R. and L. M. Sanders. 1996. *Divided by Color: Racial Politics and Democratic Ideals.* University of Chicago Press.

King, J. D. 2002. "Single-Member Districts and the Representation of Women in American State Legislatures: The Effects of Electoral System Change." *State Politics and Policy Quarterly 2* (2): 161–175.

Klineberg, S. L. and D. A. Kravitz 2003. "Ethnic Differences in Predictors of Support for Municipal Affirmative Action Contracting." *Social Science Quarterly (Blackwell Publishing Limited) 84* (2): 425–440.

Korenman, Sanders, Robert Kaestner, and Theodore J. Joyce. 2001. "Unintended Pregnancy and the Consequences of Nonmarital Childbearing." In *Out of Wedlock: Causes and Consequences of Nonmarital Fertility*, pp. 259–286. New York: Russell Sage Foundation.

Kosterlitz, M. J. 1986. "Thornburg v. Gingles: The Supreme Court's New Test for Analyzing Minority Vote Dilution." *Catholic University Law Review 36*: 531–563.

Kuklinski, J. H., P. M. Sniderman, et al. 1997. "Racial Prejudice and Attitudes Toward Affirmative Action." *American Journal of Political Science 41* (2): 402–419.

Larimer, C. W. 2005. "The Impacts of Multimember State Legislative Districts on Welfare Policy." *State Politics and Policy Quarterly 5* (3): 265–282.

Lax, J. R. and J. H. Phillips. 2009. "Gay Rights in the States: Public Opinion and Policy Responsiveness." *American Political Science Review 103* (3): 367–385.

Leal, D. L., V. Martinez-Ebers, et al. 2004. "The Politics of Latino Education: The Biases of At-Large Elections." *The Journal of Politics 66* (4): 1224–1244.

LeVeaux, C. and J. C. Garand 2003. "Race–Based Redistricting, Core Constituencies, and Legislative Responsiveness to Constituency Change." *Social Science Quarterly (Blackwell Publishing Limited) 84* (1): 32–51.

Lewis, G. B. and S. S. Oh. 2008. "Public Opinion and State Action on Same-Sex Marriage." *State and Local Government Review 40* (1): 42–53.

Lublin, D. 1997a. *The Paradox of Representation*. Princeton, NJ: Princeton University Press.

Lublin, D. 1997b. "The Election of African Americans and Latinos to the U.S. House of Representatives, 1972–1994." *American Politics Research 25* (3): 269–286.

Lublin, D. and D. S. Voss 2003. "The Missing Middle: Why Median-Voter Theory Can't Save Democrats from Singing the Boll-Weevil Blues." *The Journal of Politics 65* (1): 227–237.

Lupia, A., Y. Krupnikov, et al. 2010. "Why State Constitutions Differ in their Treatment of Same-Sex Marriage." *The Journal of Politics 72* (4): 1222–1235.

Lynxwiler, J. and D. Gay. 1994. "Reconsidering Race Differences in Abortion Attitudes." *Social Science Quarterly (University of Texas Press) 75* (1): 67–84.

Maxwell, C. J. C. 2002. *Pro-Life Activists in America: Meaning, Motivation, and Direct Action.* Cambridge University Press.

McConahay, J. B. and J. C. Hough Jr. 1976. "Symbolic racism." *Journal of Social Issues 32* (2): 23–45.

Meier, K. J. 1994. *The Politics of Sin: Drugs, Alcohol, and Public Policy.* ME Sharpe Inc.

Meier, K. J., E. G. Juenke, et al. 2005. "Structural Choices and Representational Biases: The Post-Election Color of Representation." *American Journal of Political Science 49* (4): 758–768.

Meier, K. J. and D. R. McFarlane. 1993. "The Politics of Funding Abortion: State Responses to the Political Environment." *American Politics Research 21* (1): 81–101.

Meier, K. J. and J. Stewart. 1991. *The Politics of Hispanic Education: Un Paso Pa'lante y Dos Pa'tras.* State University of New York Press.

Meier, K. J., J. Stewart, et al. 1989. *Race, Class, and Education: The Politics of Second-Generation Discrimination.* University of Wisconsin Press.

Meier, K. J., R. D. Wrinkle, et al. 1999. "Representative Bureaucracy and Distributional Equity: Addressing the Hard Question." *The Journal of Politics 61* (4): 1025–1039.

Moncrief, G. F. and J. A. Thompson. 1992. "Electoral Structure and State Legislative Representation: A Research Note." *The Journal of Politics 54* (1): 246–256.

Mooney, C. Z. 2001. *The Public Clash of Private Values: The Politics of Morality Policy.* CQ Press.

Mooney, C. Z. and M. H. Lee. 1995. "Legislative Morality in the American States: The Case of Pre-Roe Abortion Regulation Reform." *American Journal of Political Science 39* (3): 599–627.

Mulligan, K. 2006. "Pope John Paul II and Catholic Opinion Toward the Death Penalty and Abortion." *Social Science Quarterly (Blackwell Publishing Limited)* 87 (3): 739–753.

Mumpower, J. L., R. Nath, et al. 2002. "Affirmative Action, Duality of Error, and the Consequences of Mispredicting the Academic Performance of African American College Applicants." *Journal of Policy Analysis and Management* 21 (1): 63–77.

Nicholson-Crotty, S. 2006. "Reassessing Madison's Diversity Hypothesis: The Case of Same-Sex Marriage." *The Journal of Politics* 68 (4): 922–930.

Niu, S. X., T. Sullivan, et al. 2008. "Minority Talent Loss and the Texas Top 10 Percent Law." *Social Science Quarterly (Blackwell Publishing Limited)* 89 (4): 831–845.

Norrander, B. and C. Wilcox. 1999. "Public Opinion and Policymaking in the States: The Case of Post-Roe Abortion Policy." *Policy Studies Journal* 27 (4): 707–722.

Nossiff, R. 1998. "Discourse, Party, and Policy: The Case of Abortion, 1965–1972." *Policy Studies Journal* 26 (2): 244–256.

O'Connor, R. E. and M. B. Berkman. 1995. "Religious Determinants of State Abortion Policy." *Social Science Quarterly (University of Texas Press)* 76 (2): 447–459.

Olson, L. R., W. Cadge, et al. 2006. "Religion and Public Opinion about Same-Sex Marriage." *Social Science Quarterly (Blackwell Publishing Limited)* 87 (2): 340–360.

Orey, B. D. A. 2004. "White Racial Attitudes and Support for the Mississippi State Flag." *American Politics Research* 32 (1): 102–116.

Overby, L. M. and K. M. Cosgrove. 1996. "Unintended Consequences? Racial Redistricting and the Representation of Minority Interests." *The Journal of Politics* 58 (2): 540–550.

Owens, C. T. 2005. "Black Substantive Representation in State Legislatures from 1971–1994." *Social Science Quarterly (Blackwell Publishing Limited)* 86 (4): 779–791.

Pantoja, A. D. and G. M. Segura 2003. "Does Ethnicity Matter? Descriptive Representation in Legislatures and Political Alienation Among Latinos." *Social Science Quarterly (Blackwell Publishing Limited)* 84 (2): 441–460.

Pappas, C., J. Mendez, et al. 2009. "The Negative Effects of Populism on Gay and Lesbian Rights." *Social Science Quarterly (Blackwell Publishing Limited)* 90 (1): 150–163.

Patton, D. 2007. "The Supreme Court and Morality Policy Adoption in the American States: The Impact of Constitutional Context." *Political Research Quarterly* 60 (3): 468–488.

Petrocik, J. R. and S. W. Desposato. 1998. "The Partisan Consequences of Majority–Minority Redistricting in the South, 1992 and 1994." *The Journal of Politics* 60 (3): 613–633.

Pitkin, H. F. (1967). *The Concept of Representation*. University of California Press.

Preuhs, R. R. 2005. "Descriptive Representation, Legislative Leadership, and Direct Democracy: Latino Influence on English Only Laws in the States, 1984–2002." *State Politics and Policy Quarterly* 5 (3): 203–224.

Pritchard, A. 1992. "Changes in Electoral Structures and the Success of Women Candidates: The Case of Florida." *Social Science Quarterly (University of Texas Press)* 73 (1): 62–70.

Reingold, B. 2000. *Representing Women: Sex, Gender, and Legislative Behavior in Arizona and California*. The University of North Carolina Press.

Rimmerman, C. A. and C. Wilcox. 2007. *The Politics of Same-Sex Marriage*. University of Chicago Press.

Robinson, S. E. 2002. "Rules, Roles, and Minority Representation: The Dynamics of Budgeting for Bilingual Education in Texas." *State Politics and Policy Quarterly* 2 (1): 52–65.

Rocha, R. R. and R. Espino. 2009a. "Racial Threat, Residential Segregation, and the Policy Attitudes of Anglos." *Political Research Quarterly* 62 (2): 415–426.

Rocha, R. R. and R. Espino. 2009b. "Segregation, Immigration, and Latino Participation in Ethnic Politics." *American Politics Research 38* (4): 614–635.

Rocha, R. R. and D. P. Hawes. 2009. "Racial Diversity, Representative Bureaucracy, and Equity in Multiracial School Districts." *Social Science Quarterly (Blackwell Publishing Limited) 90* (2): 326–344.

Roh, J. and D. P. Haider-Markel. 2003. "All Politics is Not Local: National Forces in State Abortion Initiatives." *Social Science Quarterly (Blackwell Publishing Limited) 84* (1): 15–31.

Saltzstein, G. H. 1989. "Black Mayors and Police Policies." *The Journal of Politics 51* (3): 525–544.

Santoro, W. A. 1995. "Black Politics and Employment Policies: The Determinants of Local Government Affirmative Action." *Social Science Quarterly (University of Texas Press) 76* (4): 794–806.

Santoro, W. A. 1999. "Conventional Politics Takes Center Stage: The Latino Struggle against English-Only Laws." *Social Forces 77* (3): 887–909.

Santoro, W. A. and G. M. McGuire. 1997. "Social Movement Insiders: The Impact of Institutional Activists on Affirmative Action and Comparable Worth Policies." *Social Problems 44* (4): 503–519.

Schildkraut, D. J. 2001. "Official-English and the States: Influences on Declaring English the Official Language in the United States." *Political Research Quarterly 54* (2): 445.

Schneider, A. and H. Ingram. 1993. "Social Construction of Target Populations: Implications for Politics and Policy." *American Political Science Review 87* (2): 334–347.

Segura, G. M. and L. R. Fraga. 2008. "Race and the Recall: Racial and Ethnic Polarization in the California Recall Election." *American Journal of Political Science 52* (2): 421–435.

Sharp, E. B. 1999. *The Sometime Connection: Public Opinion and Social Policy.* State University of New York Press.

Sherkat, D. E., K. M. de Vries, et al. 2010. "Race, Religion, and Opposition to Same-Sex Marriage." *Social Science Quarterly (Blackwell Publishing Limited) 91* (1): 80–98.

Shotts, K. W. 2003. "Does Racial Redistricting Cause Conservative Policy Outcomes? Policy Preferences of Southern Representatives in the 1980s and 1990s." *The Journal of Politics 65* (1): 216–226.

Sigelman, L. and B. J. Walkosz. 1992. "Letters to the Editor as a Public Opinion Thermometer: The Martin Luther King Holiday Vote in Arizona." *Social Science Quarterly (University of Texas Press) 73* (4): 938–946.

Smith, K. B. 1994. "Abortion Attitudes and Vote Choice in the 1984 and 1988 Presidential Elections." *American Politics Research 22* (3): 354–369.

Sniderman, P. M. and E. G. Carmines. 1997. *Reaching Beyond Race.* Harvard University Press.

Sniderman, P. M., G. C. Crosby, et al. 2000. "The Politics of Race." In Sears, D. O., et al. (Eds), *Racialized Politics: The Debate about Racism in America,* pp. 236–279. University of Chicago Press.

Stewart Jr, J., R. E. England, et al. 1989. "Black Representation in Urban School Districts: From School Board to Office to Classroom." *The Western Political Quarterly 42* (2): 287–305.

Strickler, J. and N. L. Danigelis. 2002. *Changing Frameworks in Attitudes toward Abortion.* Springer.

Swain, C. M. 1995. *Black Faces, Black Interests: The Representation of African Americans in Congress.* Harvard University Press.

Swers, M. L. 2002. *The Difference Women Make: The Policy Impact of Women in Congress.* University of Chicago Press.

Thomas, S. 1994. *How Women Legislate.* Oxford: Oxford University Press.

Thomas, S. and S. Welch. 2001. "The Impact of Women in State Legislatures." *The Impact of Women in Public Office*, pp. 146–184. Indiana University Press.

Tolbert, C. J. and J. A. Grummel. 2003. "Revisiting Racial Threat Hypothesis: White Voter Support for California's Proposition 209." *State Politics and Policy Quarterly 3* (2): 183–202.

Tolbert, C. J. and R. E. Hero. 1996. "Race/Ethnicity and Direct Democracy: An Analysis of California's Illegal Immigration Initiative." *The Journal of Politics 58* (3): 806–818.

Tolbert, C. J. and R. E. Hero. 2001. "Dealing with Diversity: Racial/Ethnic Context and Social Policy Change." *Political Research Quarterly 54* (3): 571–604.

Trounstine, J. and M. E. Valdini. 2008. "The Context Matters: The Effects of Single-Member versus At-Large Districts on City Council Diversity." *American Journal of Political Science 52* (3): 554–569.

Tuch, S. A. and M. Hughes. 1996. "Whites' Racial Policy Attitudes." *Social Science Quarterly (University of Texas Press) 77* (4): 723–745.

Vanderleeuw, J. M. and G. H. Utter. 1993. "Voter Roll-Off and the Electoral Context: A Test of Two Theses." *Social Science Quarterly (University of Texas Press) 74*: 664–664.

Verba, S., K. L. Schlozman, et al. 1995. *Voice and Equality: Civic Voluntarism in American Politics.* Harvard University Press.

Voss, D. S. and D. Lublin. 2001. "Black Incumbents, White Districts: An Appraisal of the 1996 Congressional Elections." *American Politics Research 29*: 141–182.

Voss, D. S. and P. Miller. 2001. "Following a False Trail: The Hunt for White Backlash in Kentucky's 1996 Desegregation Vote." *State Politics and Policy Quarterly 1* (1): 62–80.

Wald, K. D., J. W. Button, et al. 1996. "The Politics of Gay Rights in American Communities: Explaining Antidiscrimination Ordinances and Policies." *American Journal of Political Science 40* (4): 1152–1178.

Walzer, S. 1994. "The Role of Gender in Determining Abortion Attitudes." *Social Science Quarterly (University of Texas Press) 75* (3): 687–693.

Welch, M. R., D. C. Leege, et al. 1995. "Attitudes toward Abortion among U.S. Catholics: Another Case of Symbolic Politics?" *Social Science Quarterly (University of Texas Press) 76* (1): 142–157.

Welch, S. 1990. "The Impact of At-Large Elections on the Representation of Blacks and Hispanics." *The Journal of Politics 52* (4): 1050–1076.

Welch, S., M. M. Ambrosius, et al. 1985. "The Effect of Candidate Gender on Electoral Outcomes in State Legislative Races." *The Western Political Quarterly 38* (3): 464–475.

Welch, S., M. Combs, et al. 1988. "Do Black Judges Make a Difference?" *American Journal of Political Science 32* (1): 126–136.

Weldon, S. L. 2006. "Women's Movements, Identity Politics, and Policy Impacts: A Study of Policies on Violence against Women in the 50 United States." *Political Research Quarterly 59* (1): 111–122.

Wetstein, M. E. 1993. "A LISREL Model of Public Opinion on Abortion." *Understanding the New Politics of Abortion*, Sage Newbury Park, CA. pp. 57–70.

Whitby, K. J. 2007. "The Effect of Black Descriptive Representation on Black Electoral Turnout in the 2004 Elections." *Social Science Quarterly (Blackwell Publishing Limited) 88* (4): 1010–1023.

Whitehead, A. L. 2010. "Sacred Rites and Civil Rights: Religion's Effect on Attitudes Toward Same-Sex Unions and the Perceived Cause of Homosexuality." *Social Science Quarterly (Blackwell Publishing Limited) 91* (1): 63–79.

Wilcox, C. 1990. "Race Differences in Abortion Attitudes: Some Additional Evidence." *Public Opinion Quarterly 54* (2): 248–255.

Wilcox, C. and B. Norrander. 2002. "Of Moods and Morals: The Dynamics of Opinion on Abortion and Gay Rights." In *Understanding Public Opinion*. CQ Press Washington, DC, pp. 121–147.

Yates, J. and R. Fording. 2005. "Politics and State Punitiveness in Black and White." *The Journal of Politics 67* (4): 1099–1121.

Yetman, N. R. 1999. *Majority and Minority: The Dynamics of Race and Ethnicity in American Life*. Allyn & Bacon.

PART VII

CONCLUSION

CHAPTER 36

SUB-NATIONAL POLITICS

A Methodological Perspective

FREDERICK J. BOEHMKE AND
REGINA P. BRANTON

THE relationship between methods and state politics has grown over the years as the study of state politics has evolved. As a field, state politics has spent much of its history wrestling with the many challenges posed by studying up to 50 different political systems, systems that have exhibited (and still exhibit) varying degrees of openness and accessibility. On the one hand, we are offered the great experiment of state politics: no two states operate under the same political institutions, have the same residents, political cultures, or histories. The wealth of variation has offered researchers a wonderful opportunity to study the relationship between these different conditions and a variety of political outcomes and behaviors. Theories and relationships that can only be poorly tested at the national level with a handful of observations under generally consistent and slow-changing conditions can often be much more richly theorized and thoroughly vetted across the states.

Consider just a small sample of the great many questions that have been profitably studied at the state level: how characteristics of state legislatures such as professionalism (e.g., Squire, 1992) and term limits (e.g., Kousser, 2005) influence representation; how they influence policy implementation through oversight of the administrative branch (e.g., Huber and Shipan, 2002); how public opinion translates into policy outcomes (e.g., Erikson, Wright, and McIver, 1993); how new policies come about and diffuse across political units (e.g., Walker, 1969); or how political and economic circumstances affect whose voice is heard among organized interests (e.g., Gray and Lowery, 1996).

Of course, with these different political cultures and histories comes a great variety of challenges. The fundamental challenge of studying state politics involves striking the right balance between respecting the richness of each state's unique circumstances while still leveraging the commonalities in those circumstances to further our understanding of how institutions, behaviors, and cultures influence outcomes. As data availability, methodological tools, and measurement have evolved over time, the balance between these two goals has swung more and more towards large, cross-state and cross-time quantitative studies.

This evolution has followed and also dictated the use and development of political methodology for and by the field of state politics. There is no denying that the improved availability of data from state governments over the last two decades or so has accelerated this shift, with some states, such as Wisconsin, leading the way in open and accessible government. But with these newer and bigger datasets have come increasing methodological opportunities and challenges that scholars of state politics have begun to address, whether by importing and borrowing appropriate methodologies or, increasingly, by responding to the distinguishing features of state politics research by adapting existing methodologies or developing new methodologies.

This evolution of state politics methodology has moved through four general stages, though these shifts have not necessarily occurred at the same time within the different areas of study. The first stage involves the earliest work on a particular topic. These studies often raise new theoretical questions or study them for the first time in the American states. They may be based on a detailed analysis or case study of a single state or may involve a straightforward, cross-sectional analysis of interesting variation in a single variable across states, as with Everson's study of the effect of the initiative process on turnout (Everson, 1981) or Zeller's study of interest group registration laws (Zeller, 1958).

The second stage involves research designs that set out to provide a more systematic answer to the question posed in the original work, often by introducing larger, more comprehensive data or importing more advanced methodological techniques from other fields, such as Erikson, Wright, and McIver's (1993) construction of public and elite state-level ideology scores or Berry and Berry's (1990) introduction of event history analysis to the study of state policy adoption. In order to address questions more broadly, scholars often initially compile or borrow datasets, such as the American National Elections Study or the Current Population Survey, that afford the opportunity to do a 50, or nearly 50, state analysis. For example, Lowery and Gray (1993) use data on state interest group lobbying registrations to study the density of groups among the 50 states in 1980. At this point, the methods being used are generally straightforward applications of linear regression models for continuous or discrete outcomes.

In the third stage, individuals, or more often, teams of scholars embarked on large-scale data-gathering enterprises to develop comprehensive measures of a particular phenomenon, allowing multiple comparisons across states and over time. This shift largely began in the 1990s within state politics, covering the areas of legislative professionalism (Squire, 1992), interest-group representation (Gray and Lowery, 1996), public opinion (Erikson, Wright, and McIver, 1993; Berry, Ringquist, Fording, and Hanson, 1998), and state courts (Hall and Brace, 1999). And the creation of these datasets has continued into the past decade with large efforts covering, among other topics, state legislative election returns (Carsey, Niemi, Berry, Powell, and Snyder, 2008), listings of roll-call votes in state legislatures (Clark et al., 2009), the partisan composition of state legislatures (Klarner, 2003), and the use and content of ballot measures (Braunstein, 2004).

The creation of these large datasets has allowed scholars to study in more depth and breadth the interrelations between political outcomes and circumstances in the American states. Yet, in the fourth stage of the evolution of state politics methodology, they also begin to bring to the fore various methodological issues to address. For example, should we measure the potential effect of the initiative and referendum process on citizen behavior or policy outcomes through the number of initiatives on the ballot or through the difficulty of qualifying measures for the ballot (Bowler and Donovan, 2004)? How should we account for duration dependence in event history models of state policy adoption (Jones and Branton, 2005)? How can we account for the clustered nature of individuals or respondents when estimating and creating public opinion scores based on individual data (Lax and Phillips, 2009)?

Publications in *The Practical Researcher* series in *State Politics and Policy Quarterly* illustrate these patterns and demonstrate the great variety of challenges still facing state politics scholars interested in detailed single-state studies and multi-state studies. A quick review of the 36 articles published through the end of 2010 indicates that roughly one-third of them announce the release of a new dataset, about 20 percent present or discuss new and improved measures to consider, and a little over a quarter present methodological tools to improve statistical analysis.

In this chapter, we illustrate the evolution of methods in state politics in two specific areas of study—the study of state policy innovation and diffusion and the study and measure of state public opinion—by tracing out the history and major developments in each area. We then discuss a couple of ongoing debates and methodological discussions in which state politics scholars are making important contributions.

STATE POLICY INNOVATION

The study of the adoption and diffusion of public policy across the American states has been defined to a great extent by the varying methodological tools available to researchers at different points in time. Innovations have come in fits and starts that led to cycles of creative new research followed by a steady stream of refinements and new findings that gradually slowed before a new methodological innovation came along and redefined scholars' ability to ask and answer new questions; and perhaps more so than in the typical research area the study of state policy adoption and diffusion has been defined by the prevailing methodology.

The study of state policy innovation seeks to answer when and why states adopt, or innovate, new policies, building on Everett Rogers' work on the geographic diffusion of innovation, e.g., the spread of weed-spray technology among farmers (Rogers 1962). While some research focuses on the content of policies or on policy reinvention (how policies evolve among later adopters), most focus on the timing of initial policy innovation, arguing that whether a state has a given policy is a critical factor in its own right. Within the context of the study of state policy innovation, scholars are frequently interested in patterns of policy diffusion, which is the process through which one state's policy activity influences current or future activities among other states. The most common form of diffusion focuses on geographic contiguity.

In the field of political science, the study of policy innovation took shape with the seminal work of Jack Walker in 1969. In his article, "The Diffusion of Innovations among the American States," Walker assembled an impressive database of adoption dates for all 50 states for 88 different policies. This is clearly an early example of the compilation of large, 50-state datasets allowing state politics scholars to make broad comparisons across states, but also across policies. Using these different policy areas, Walker worked with the methodological tools available at the time to construct policy innovation scores for each state in order to determine whether states with various demographic and economic characteristics were more or less likely to innovate earlier or later than other states.

Walker's score normalizes policy innovativeness for each policy to lie between zero and one, and then averages the scores across all policies. For each policy then, the score is constructed by calculating the number of years it takes a state to adopt relative to the first adoption, then by normalizing this by dividing by the number of years it takes the last state to adopt, then subtracting this ratio from one so that larger scores correspond with more innovative states. Mathematically, the formula is as follows:

$$W_{ik} = 1 - \frac{Y_{ik} - Y_k^{First}}{Y_k^{Last} - Y_k^{First}},$$

where Y_{ik} indicates the year that state i adopts policy k and Y_k^{First} and Y_k^{Last} indicate the years of the first and last adoptions of the policy by any state. The process is repeated for all 88 different policies and the resulting scores are then averaged for each state. These scores, which are based on individual scores from policies that were adopted over periods of 40 to almost one hundred years, are then correlated and regressed on a handful of similarly averaged state demographic and economic characteristics in order to identify the correlates of policy innovation.

Although this score taps nicely into the tendency of states to adopt policies relatively sooner or later than other states, it has a number of methodological shortcomings in practice, some of which arise since it is rarely the case that all 50 states adopt a given policy. First, states that do not adopt a policy do not receive a corresponding score for that policy. Of course, we cannot know if a state will never adopt a specific policy, rather we just know whether it has adopted that policy at the point in time at which we conduct our study. This means that states that have not yet adopted when we collect our data can only be late adopters and must therefore have relatively low innovation scores. But we ignore this information when we construct innovation scores, leading to an upwardly biased average innovation score among states that tend to be laggards more often than not.

In addition to these criticisms, Gray (1973) raises some additional concerns about the way that Walker analyzes policy innovativeness. Based on her in-depth analysis of 12 different issues in three policy areas, she first notes that the patterns of policy innovation, as measured by the cumulative distribution of policy adoptions over time across the 50 states, vary across policy areas. Second, she notes that averaging scores and state characteristics over many decades will tend to obscure changes in innovativeness for individual states over time.[1] Third, she finds that the order of adoption varies greatly across her policy areas: states that are leaders in one policy area may be laggards in another. This leads her to "question the fundamental assumption of a 'composite innovation score'—namely, that 'innovativeness' exists as a single factor among states" (p. 1183).

Gray's methodological criticisms quickly shifted the growth of this novel line of inquiry and led it to stay somewhat disorganized for almost two decades. As Savage, one of a group of scholars who continued to research innovativeness as a general state trait (see, e.g., Savage, 1978), notes in his review of this literature that begins a special issue of *Publius* dedicated to the topic, there was a "failure to disseminate information about our research" (Savage, 1985: 5) among political scientists working in this field that hindered the emergence of a distinct research community and associated literature.

The articles that follow in that issue offer a variety of perspectives on policy diffusion, generally focusing on one specific aspect of the diffusion process. Further, many of them suggest an increased need for a focus on studying the changing conditions that influence policy adoption within a single policy area over time (e.g., Clark, 1985, Daniels and Darcy, 1985). Most, however, rely on correlation, graphical, or aggregate analysis of the total number of adopters over time, with the most common approach an aggregate model of the cumulative number of adopters depending on lagged adoptions and occasionally its square.[2] This heterogeneity in research methods can be viewed as a strength but also a weakness given the increased difficulty in comparing results across studies.

The field was therefore ripe for a methodological innovation to allow scholars to address the complexity of the hypotheses that were being developed, in particular to account for heterogeneity across states and across policies to understand the factors that lead to different rates and patterns of policy diffusion. In their 1990 article, Berry and Berry provided just such a methodology with the introduction and application of event history analysis (EHA) to the study of state policy diffusion. EHA, which had recently begun to see application in other disciplines (see, e.g., Allison, 1984), provided an opportunity to study the influence of both internal and external determinants of policy innovation, which had been modeled as distinct processes in the literature to that point. This is critical, since as Berry and Berry (1990) note, "[t]he separate treatment of the two models in the literature indicates a failure to recognize that regional diffusion is not a separate topic from innovation but, instead, one possible explanation for innovation" (396).

EHA analysis has the further benefit of allowing the researcher to account for how state characteristics and diffusion pressures vary over time, rather than just across states. This allowed researchers to overcome one of the primary limitations of cross-sectional analysis: independent variables could only be measured at one point in time (or calculated as an average over multiple years). This represents a major shortcoming in prior research since most policies diffuse over long periods of time, usually decades, leading to possibly great shifts in political circumstances in states. These shifts often represent the causes of policy innovation, making their incorporation into empirical models critical for better understanding the correlates of policy innovation. Even more obviously, external diffusion pressures, such as the number or percentage of innovators within a state's geographic region also change dramatically over time. EHA offered the insight that both adopting and failing to adopt is informative.

The introduction of EHA revitalized and unified the study of state policy innovation and diffusion and lead to a flurry of research in this area over the next decade. These studies employed a common methodological framework that allowed them to build upon each other by exploring the common characteristics of policy diffusion, such as regional diffusion pressures (see Mooney, 2001 for a review), the role of entrepreneurs (Mintrom and Vergari, 1998), interest groups and national forces (Haider-Markel, 2001), and differences in diffusion for different types of policies (Mooney and Lee, 1995). Over this decade, EHA came to dominate and even to define the study of state policy innovation.

Over time, though, scholars began to exhaust the great variety of questions that could now be studied or answered anew and progress in the field slowed as the methodological strictures of EHA both defined and limited the research design and approach to policy innovation. Scholars could introduce new variables and concepts into the analysis, but it became harder and harder to make novel contributions or address more complex theoretical issues over time as the possibilities were exhausted. Over the last decade, however, there has once again been a methodological push to advance the study of policy innovation, whether through new measures of key explanatory concepts, new measures of policy outcomes, or new methods for studying innovation.

Two studies focus on developing a richer measure of interstate policy diffusion pressures, illustrating the ability and willingness of state politics scholars to utilize different methodologies as appropriate to their questions. Focusing on economic competition pressures, Berry and Baybeck (2005) developed a much more precise measure of diffusion pressures by using geographic information systems (GIS). Rather than measuring diffusion pressures with the number of contiguous states who already have the policy innovation in question, they use GIS to measure the size of the population in neighboring states that might reasonably be expected to cross state borders to buy lottery tickets from a state that innovated by implementing a state lottery. This offers a much richer sense of the economic pressures to adopt a lottery and the results demonstrate that these pressures matter more than the simple number of contiguous adoptions.

In addition to also studying economic diffusion pressures, Boehmke and Witmer (2004) attempt to disentangle them from social learning as a motivation for cross-state diffusion in the context of the spread of Indian gaming across the American states. Rather than focus on a single indicator of policy innovation, they study the number of Indian gaming compacts agreed to by each state, utilizing an event count model rather than an event history model. Not only does this create a richer dependent variable, but it also creates a richer measure of policy in neighboring states. They find that social learning, measured by the number of neighboring states that have Indian gaming, matters more for initial innovation (i.e., the first compact signed in a state), but that economic competition, measured by the number of compacts signed in neighboring states, matters more for subsequent expansion in the number of compacts.

These methodological innovations were driven by the fact that scholars had largely mined the existing EHA approach and measures of policy innovation and diffusion for most of the information that it offered. In many cases, a straightforward discrete-outcome single-policy EHA was not sufficiently sophisticated to answer important questions. Scholars therefore continued to push the methodological boundaries in order to offer better answers.

Perhaps the most exciting of these new developments was Volden's (2006) dyadic EHA of policy emulation. Drawing on the intuition of dyadic models of international conflict, Volden suggested that we conceive of policy emulation as a dyadic event: one state emulates policy in another state.[3] This offers the opportunity to get closer to one of the original questions in the literature of whether some states are policy leaders and others policy laggards and whether laggard states merely act on their own or consciously emulate the innovations in leader states. By conceiving of diffusion and emulation as a dyadic concept, the dyadic EHA is able to model the characteristics of potential leader states in order to determine whether subsequent innovations by other states explicitly emulate innovations in some states rather than others and whether the pattern of emulation is determined by characteristics of leaders, laggards, or the interplay between the two. For example, do conservative states tend to emulate policy faster? Are they more likely to be emulated? Or do conservative states just emulate policy in other conservative states? The answer is that states tend to emulate policy choices in ideologically similar states rather than in any geographic neighbor.

The introduction of this method has led to a handful of methodological discussions and advances within the field of state politics, but also within the field of comparative politics, which has adapted this method for studying cross-national policy innovation and emulation (e.g., Gilardi, 2010). First, Boehmke (2009a) shows that a slight modification in the risk set is necessary to avoid the problem of false emulation: states can only emulate other states that have acted as policy leaders. If this is ignored, the dyadic approach has the potential to overstate policy emulation. Second, Gilardi (2010) discusses the appropriate approach for accounting for unobserved heterogeneity, whether by clustering on leader states, potential emulating states, or on each dyad or, alternatively, by estimating a multi-level model. Much work remains to be done in these and in other areas to fully understand and develop this innovative technique.

Finally, a related methodological issue to address in the area of policy innovation is how to use EHA (or some other method) to return to the study of commonalities and distinctiveness across policies. EHA has provided a great boost in understanding the diffusion of single policies and has created the opportunity to compare the influence of broad theoretically important categories of variables across policies, such as the influence of contiguous neighbors' adoptions, but it has proceeded one policy at a time (or by recycling one policy over and over, as with lottery adoptions). This limits the ability to make specific, statistically valid comparisons across policy areas in order to better understand the policy innovation process. It has also moved the field from the original question of policy innovativeness as a general characteristic of states to cataloguing a list of variables that matter for some policies and not for others.

A couple of methods have been utilized to look for such commonalities. Nicholson-Crotty (2009) moves away from the EHA approach to study which policies diffuse rapidly and which diffuse more slowly or stall out entirely. He is therefore able to account for policy-specific factors, such as issue salience and complexity, that influence the speed of diffusion (also see Boushey's (2010) book-length effort in this regard). However, the challenge remains: how to incorporate these types of policy-specific variables with the strengths of EHA, in particular its ability to incorporate internal and external features of states in the policy diffusion process.

The second method suggests a way to reunite internal, external, and policy-specific measures with the EHA framework. A handful of scholars have begun to pool analysis of multiple components within the same policy area. Policies often have many different parts and states may adopt none, some, or all of them, leading to very different policy profiles. As Boehmke (2009b) notes in his overview of these approaches, each policy may be analyzed separately in its own EHA, but one might also want to leverage commonalities across the components by modeling them together with possible allowances for differences across them in the baseline hazard or even in the effect of some of the independent variables. For example, Shipan and Volden (2006) study the diffusion of three different types of anti-smoking laws—bans in government buildings, in restaurants, and of out-of-package sales—separately as well as by pooling all three together into one analysis. By pooling analysis of multiple components or multiple policies, scholars can leverage the strength of EHA analysis of a single policy to look for commonalities in the sources of diffusion and innovation, while also incorporating the distinctiveness of each policy area through separate variables. While much of the research in this area uses the components of policies in the same fairly narrow issue area, the approach can easily be extended to pool the analysis of very distinct policies.

Overall, then, the study of state policy innovation has been largely defined by the prevailing methodological tools at the time, particularly the mostly correlational and aggregate analyses that took place through the 1970s and 1980s or the emergence and dominance of EHA in 1990 and after. This field demonstrates how state politics scholars have been in the forefront of methodological innovations across the field of political science, as evidenced by the introduction of EHA for studying policy innovation, the use of GIS to develop better measures of diffusion pressures, or the creation and development of the dyadic EHA model. Each introduction of a new methodology has allowed scholars to answer new questions about policy innovation and has broadened our understanding of this phenomenon.

ADVANCES IN STATE PUBLIC OPINION RESEARCH

As Cohen (2006a) aptly notes, the comparative study of state politics and policymaking spans several decades. Indeed, the 1960s and 1970s were marked by a steady stream of political science research dedicated to the comparative analysis of state politics (e.g., Dye, 1965; Hofferbert, 1966; Sharkansky, 1967). Yet, historically, the main issue facing the field was a lack of uniform state public opinion data across all 50 states. The lack of comparable state-level public opinion data made it difficult to explore the relationship between public opinion and state politics and policymaking. However, scholars within this field of study have worked to address this issue by developing and refining the methodological approaches used to estimate state public opinion.

As with the state policy and diffusion research, this line of research has periods of innovation followed by a series of works and then a new methodological innovation is introduced followed by another series of works. Generally speaking, the methodological innovations in this line of research involve simulating public opinion and estimating public opinion by disaggregation. From a substantive standpoint, the study of state public opinion has largely focused on determining if and how state-level public opinion influences elections and policy outcomes.

Early research on state public opinion employed simulation to estimate public opinion. Pool, Abelson, and Popkin (1965) offered one of the first, if not the first, examinations of state-level public opinion. Pool et al. (1965) utilized their simulated state public opinion to predict state-level presidential election outcomes. Pool and his colleagues developed 480 "voter types" based on factors such as sex, religion, party, race, income, regional residency, and population density. Next, they aggregated 64 national public opinion surveys conducted between 1952 and 1960. The national public opinion polls were then utilized to estimate the preferences of each "voter type." The authors then simulated state public opinion by constructing an index based on the average preference for each of the voter types weighted by the population size of each voter type in each state. The general approach introduced by Pool et al. (1965) is represented in the following formula:

$$StatePO_i = \sum_{j=1}^{n} \varphi_j \hat{y}_j,$$

where $StatePO_i$ represents the predicted public opinion for state i, φ_j is the proportion in state i of voter type j, and $\hat{Y}_j$ is the predicted public opinion for voter type j.

Weber, Hopkins, Mezey, and Munger (1972–3) utilized Pool et al.'s (1965) method to examine state-level public opinion on the death penalty and teacher unionization. Weber et al. extended the work of Pool et al. (1965) by expanding the number of "voter types" to 960 categories. Furthermore, Weber and Shaffer (1972) extend the work of Pool et al. (1965) by examining the relationship between state-level public opinion and policy outcomes. Their findings indicate that state public opinion plays an influential role in state policy outcomes.

Simulating public opinion appeared to be a plausible innovation that would advance the comparative study of state politics and policymaking; however, scholars quickly identified flaws with this technique. Notably Seidman (1975) outlined several methodological issues with simulation that he argued render it an unreliable approach to estimating public opinion. First, he argued the simulation approach utilized in this research assumed that the demographic categories utilized to develop the "voter types" were independent. He notes there may be interactive effects between the demographic categories that are associated with public opinion. Second, the simulation technique assumed that omitted demographic characteristics were not related to estimates of state public opinion. He argued there may be a host of demographic characteristics associated with the structure of public opinion beyond those used in the indices. Third, Seidman (1975) noted that simulation assumed, except for the differences in the demographic characteristics employed, that states were alike. Again, Seidman (1975) argues this assumption is extremely restrictive. These concerns halted the use of simulating state public opinion.

The second, and most dominant, methodological technique that uses national surveys to estimate state-level opinion is disaggregation, which was developed by Wright, Erikson, and McIver (1985, 1987) and Erikson, Wright, and McIver (1993). This approach pools large numbers of national public opinion polls and then disaggregates the data to calculate public opinion percentages by state. Specifically, Wright and his colleagues aggregated partisanship and ideology data from CBS News/*New York Times* polls conducted between 1976 and 1988. Using information supplied by over a 140,000 respondents, the authors generated measures of state-level partisanship and ideology. Erikson et al. (1993) evaluated the state-level ideology measures in relation to state-level policy outcomes and find a strong correlation between their measure and state policy outcomes. These measures of state-level partisanship and ideology have become the standard indicators utilized in the state politics literature (e.g., Hill and Leighley, 1992; Clingermayer and Wood, 1995; Hill, Leighley, and Hinton-Andersson, 1995; Liberman and Shaw, 2000).

Brace et al. (2002) offer an extension to the state public opinion research by estimating state-level public opinion on specific public policy items. Using Erikson et al.'s (1993) disaggregation technique they estimated state-level public opinion on numerous policy issues including abortion, environmentalism, welfare and capital punishment. Brace et al. (2002) used General Social Survey (GSS) data from 1974 to 1998 disaggregated at the state level to construct their measures of public opinion regarding the aforementioned policy areas. The authors argued this technique provides state politics researchers with the information necessary to examine if and how state public opinion on specific issues is associated with corresponding public policy outcomes at the state level.

Brace et al. (2004) follow up on the Brace et al. (2002) piece with an article that examines interstate versus intrastate variation in state-level public opinion over time.[4] The authors examine changes in state-level public opinion using two different sets of national survey data and state-level demographic indicators (Berry, Ringquist, Fording, and Hanson, 1998). The findings indicate for the observed time-period, public opinion within states is generally stable. Further, the majority of the variation in state-level public opinion occurs in cross-sectional differences across the states. Brace et al. (2004) assert the findings are important as it supports the idea that estimating public opinion using Erikson et al.'s (1993) technique is a viable option for scholars interested in the comparative study of state public opinion.

Although the disaggregation approach to estimating state-level public opinion is currently the standard method, there are methodological issues with this technique. First, in order to generate adequate sample sizes within each state it is necessary to pool survey data over a long span of time. Indeed, the typical study pools survey data for ten or more years. For example, Erikson et al. (1993) pooled data from surveys conducted between 1976 and 1988, while Brace et al. (2002) pooled data from 1974 to 1998. Given that survey houses tend to change the questions included on any given survey, this means that the number *and* type of issues for which state-level public opinion can be generated is often constrained. Second, and related to the first point, because it is often necessary to pool survey data conducted over a long time period, this calls into question the stability of public opinion over time. Consider, for instance, the issue of immigration. It is likely the case that changes in attitudes within some states changed dramatically as the distribution of immigrants migrated to non-traditional destination states such as North Carolina. This would make it difficult to construct a valid measure of public opinion toward immigration at least for a subset of states. Third, estimating state public opinion via the disaggregation approach does not obviate or overcome the sampling issue. National surveys tend not to use states as the primary sampling unit. Given that the primary sampling unit is not the state, it is possible that estimates of state public opinion may not accurately measure the true state public opinion.

Jones and Norrander (1996) address one of these critiques. They extend the literature by developing a way to address the sampling issue posed by estimating public opinion using data in which the state is not the primary sampling unit. Jones and Norrander (1996) use Erikson et al.'s (1993) technique to develop estimates of state-level public opinion on a range of policy issues using 1988–92 NES Senate election surveys. They argue these surveys are perfect for generating state-level public opinion measures because the primary sampling unit for the surveys is the state. Jones and Norrander (1996) pooled the data and calculated state-level measures of attitudes regarding abortion, ideology, and defense spending. Furthermore, they develop a method to test the reliability of aggregate-level—in this case state-level—measures of public opinion estimated based on individual-level data.

Jones and Norrander (1996) demonstrate that pooled national public opinion data can be used to estimate state-level public opinion and provide a technique that will allow researchers to assess the reliability of aggregate-level public opinion. Yet, as Cohen (2006b) indicates, even this approach is problematic for two logistical reasons. First, neither the NES nor any other survey house has conducted another survey of this type where the state is the primary sampling. Second, the questions asked on the existing surveys with states as the primary sampling unit focused on national issues as opposed to specific state-level issues. Of course, it is plausible that in the future the NES or another survey organization will conduct another state-level survey, but until then scholars are limited to this decades-old survey.

That said, Cohen (2003) cautions users and readers concerning a few issues this innovation presents. First, Cohen (2003) notes that the surveys included in the data are taken from a variety of survey organizations and that the quality of the surveys varied. Second, the questions across these surveys are not uniform. The wording format variation makes it difficult to make direct comparisons in approval ratings across the surveys (Cohen, 2003). Third, Cohen (2003) highlights the substantial amount of missing data. Not missing data from no response, but rather missing polls across the states. This potentially limits the types of research questions that can be addressed. Finally, Cohen (2003) raises questions regarding the samples drawn for the surveys. If the samples were not random then it is likely that the responses are not reflective of the state population. He cautions users of the data to consider the potential issues and try to address them empirically. That said, this is a new source for the study of state public opinion in that it encompasses attitudes on job approval at multiple levels, which serves as a rich resource for state politics scholars.

In recent years there have been two additional options for estimating state public opinion. The first option is a data source constructed by Beyle, Niemi, and Sigelman (2002). The team compiled data, the Official State Job Approval Rating Project, which include measures of state public opinion regarding the president, governor, and US senators. The team of researchers compiled the public opinion data using a variety of state-level public opinion surveys dating back to 1945. The data have been widely used in recent years (e.g., Bardwell, 2003; Cohen, 2003; Cohen and Powell, 2005; Hamman, 2006). Although not a methodological innovation, this dataset serves to advance the study of the impact of state public opinion by providing information regarding public approval of political leaders and governmental institutions.

The second option is a methodological innovation offered by Gelman and Little (1997) and Park, Gelman, and Bafumi (2006), which represents a new take on simulating public opinion forwarded by Pool et al. (1965) and Weber et al. (1972–3). Gelman and Little (1997) and Park et al. (2006) introduce a more methodologically sophisticated approach to simulating state public opinion. Specifically, these scholars utilize Bayesian statistics and multi-level modeling in the simulation technique. This approach offers an improvement over the earlier simulation approaches in that it generates more precise estimates of state public opinion. Lax and Phillips (2009) offer a detailed discussion of this approach noting the improvements. Further, their empirical evaluation of the method suggests this approach produces accurate and reliable estimates of state public opinion.

From a methodological standpoint, the work of Park et al. (2006) appears to be a fruitful path to pursue. This approach offers the opportunity to marry the finer qualities of both simulation and disaggregation. The multiple regression and post-stratification (MRP) approach incorporates the demographic data, yet is flexible enough to allow for non-demographic differences across states. Park et al. (2006) argue this renders improved state estimates, which is generally supported by the empirical evaluation offered by Lax and Phillips (2009). Further, this approach offers the opportunity to address some of the issues that face both the simulation and disaggregation techniques. As noted, this approach incorporates the demographic data, yet accounts for variation in public opinion across states not attributed to the demographic indicators. This addresses one of the key critiques of the simulation technique. Additionally, MRP is not limited by the sample size of respondents as it produces accurate estimates of state public opinion for not only large samples of respondents, but also small samples. This addresses one of the criticisms of the disaggregation approach. From a practical standpoint, this means the MRP approach provides scholars with the opportunity to address a broader range of issues. Given that scholars will not be tied to only those questions that are included on a decade or more of national surveys, the number of issues that can be addressed increases with MRP. This methodological innovation provides the opportunity to address more detailed questions of interest, such as how public opinion influences policy outcomes and how responsive is the government to state public opinion.

Additionally, the project initiated by Beyle et al. (2002) suggests that tapping into state-specific survey data may be a viable option for the future. Although developing a historic, comprehensive 50-state dataset composed of a variety of surveys is somewhat problematic (Cohen, 2003), it may be possible to cull together this sort of dataset moving forward. Given the decreased costs in conducting such polls and the increased interest in state-specific attitudes, compiling an annual or biannual dataset of state surveys may be plausible. Indeed, Cohen (2006b: 259) notes "[a]s news organizations and other commercial ventures have found a commercial use for state polls and as polls have become less costly... the volume of state polls has exploded." If this trend continues, it may be possible to maintain a pooled cross-sectional dataset of state polls. Yet, there are constraints to this approach in that the number of issues that researchers will be able to explore will be limited by the availability of consistent questions across surveys and over time. Additionally, this approach will likewise have to deal with many of the aforementioned issues that face the project led by Beyle et al. (2002).

CURRENT DEBATES AND FUTURE DIRECTIONS

With these histories in mind, in this section we discuss a number of additional areas of current debate in the context of state politics methodology. In particular, we focus on generating appropriate measures of uncertainty for data with repeated observations from states and on how to incorporate into and model geographic information in state politics research. These are not necessarily areas that have been ignored in the literature, but recent methodological developments and data availability have brought them to the fore. Further, both are still current debates, providing many opportunities to address unanswered questions and improve our understanding over the next few years and even decades.

Addressing State Heterogeneity

One of the fundamental goals of state politics scholars is to identify how differences across states lead to differences in political outcomes across states, whether in the context of state policies, spending, forms of political participation, interest-group populations, or representation in legislatures. Scholars have documented a host of institutional, cultural, demographic, legal, and historical factors that influence some or all of these outcomes. Yet one of the fundamental challenges confronting researchers is to distinguish between the influence of some set of observed features of state environments and the unique features of each state that may be much more difficult to observe. This challenge manifests itself in multiple ways. First, it may occur through the potential for interdependency among these different features: for example, do states with a particular institutional structure tend to have certain types of laws that might influence turnout? Do those laws depend on the political and demographic characteristics of the state's population or voters? And how does the legislature react to those various inputs considering the consequences of the potential laws for its constituents and its members' preferences? Second, how do we account for the structure of unobserved information? Are individuals—whether elected officials or voters or bureaucrats—in the same state similar in ways that we cannot observe? Do they face common unobserved characteristics based on a state's political or cultural context?

In the end, both of these concerns are about the difficulty and often the inability to observe heterogeneity within and across states and in the form that that heterogeneity takes. The first set of consequences falls broadly under the category of endogeneity or omitted variable bias, whereas the second requires distinguishing between unobserved state-level and individual-level randomness and properly addressing the structure of the two within and across states. Here we focus on some recent developments motivated and centered largely in the state politics literature for the former.

Researchers have become increasingly attuned to the possibility and consequences of structured patterns of unobservable factors across and within states and state politics researchers have increasingly led in the exploration and comparison of different methodologies for producing more accurate and appropriate measures of uncertainty. There are a couple of different settings that one might consider: cross-sectional time-series data (e.g., state-level outcomes observed over multiple time periods) and clustered or multi-level data (e.g., many states and multiple individuals within each state). Attention has focused in particular on the second structure in recent years.

Until recent years, state politics scholars (and political scientists in general) have largely ignored these issues. But as the availability of datasets with many individuals in each state has grown, and as the literature has progressed, scholars have become more attuned to concerns about the accuracy of our standard errors. In an article published just a few years ago, Primo, Jacobsmeier, and Milyo (2007) conducted a survey of articles published in *State Politics and Policy Quarterly* and find that the authors of most of them did not address the issue at all, whereas just a few made corrections for the clustered structure of their data.

Including the aforementioned article, however, the last few years have witnessed a veritable explosion of attention and research on this topic, much of it done by state politics methodologists. Further, the primary thrust of this research has been to compare different approaches to addressing the issue and to offer recommendations for applied researchers. In general, these possible solutions involve one of either estimating clustered/robust standard errors or some form of multi-level modeling. In the first approach, observations are grouped by state to account for possible heteroskedasticity and correlation in the error terms for individuals within state. If this structure is ignored, standard errors are commonly estimated to be smaller than they should be.

In the second approach, multi-level, also known as hierarchical, modeling offers a structure to incorporate observed and stochastic variables that operate at the individual level as well as those that occur at the aggregate, or state, level (see, e.g., Gelman and Hill, 2007). This approach offers a well-known structure for explicitly developing both the individual- and group-level components of the model. This is critical in much of state politics research as we are interested in understanding both how individual-level factors influence behavior and how state-level characteristics influence behavior either independently or by modifying the relationship between individual-level factors and outcomes. Multi-level modeling helps improve estimates of uncertainty by allowing users to allow for both individual-level errors and state-level errors. The latter are particularly important for accounting for features of state politics that we cannot measure or that we fail to include in our models. Acknowledging that these errors are common to all individuals in a given state recognizes that we have less information than the total number of observations, but (generally) more information than the number of groups. While the basic structure of multi-level modeling includes familiar models such as random and fixed effects as special cases, more advanced versions allow for more complicated patterns of state-level variation, such as random slopes, which allow the effect of an individual-level variable to vary across states.

State politics researchers have recently led the charge for understanding the conditions under which these various models produce more accurate estimates of standard errors, as well as introducing additional methods to further improve performance. As noted previously, we start with the acknowledgement by Primo, Jacobsmeier, and Milyo (2007) that state politics scholars were not doing a good job accounting for these different structures of uncertainty. After discussing the relative advantages and disadvantages of clustering and multi-level modeling, they recommend clustering given its ease of use and relatively fewer assumptions and provide an example to demonstrate the consequences for standard errors.

One of the problems with multi-level modeling that they note is the practical difficulty in obtaining estimates, which made the technique less practical. But, as computers have advanced, this has become less of a concern, making possible a full-blown comparison of the different techniques under different data structures, in particular the number of states, the number of individuals observed in each state, as well as the relative balance in the number of individuals observed across states. Indeed, Arceneaux and Nickerson (2009) note that under appropriate conditions there is little difference in the analytic results across these different models, in particular once the number of clusters is at least 20.

Yet, given the variety of configurations that state politics scholars might face in terms of the number of clusters and the number of individuals and how they are distributed across clusters, the preferred approach varies in different settings. Harden (2011) investigates this in a *State Politics and Policy Quarterly* article by performing a series of Monte Carlo experiments. In addition to comparing robust clustered standard errors to naïve OLS standard errors, Harden discusses the bootstrap clustered standard error, which re-samples entire clusters rather than single individuals. He finds that, as expected, unadjusted OLS standard errors are generally biased downwards and that while robust clustered standard errors perform better, they too understate uncertainty under various conditions, for example with small numbers of clusters (see also Cameron, Gelbach, and Miller, 2008). Of particular interest for state politics scholars, Harden finds that robust clustered standard errors suffer from downward bias more for state-level variables rather than for individual-level variables, even with 50 or more clusters. The bootstrap clustered standard error, however, performs much better across a wide variety of conditions.

Even with this recent research, additional work remains to be done to ensure that proper inferences are drawn with appropriate measures of uncertainty. The Monte Carlo approach taken by Harden is helpful for supplementing the analytic results of Arceneaux and Nickerson (2009) and highlights the importance of considering the kinds of data structures that state politics scholars might face. A comparison of robust clustered standard errors and bootstrap clustered standard errors to those resulting from multi-level modeling would be helpful. Further, many state politics datasets include an unbalanced number of observations, the consequences of which have not been explored in much detail. How do the various estimators perform when some clusters have large numbers of observations while others have fewer? Or when some have very small numbers of observations, e.g., less than the 15 or so often recommended for effective use of multi-level models? Further, what is the relative performance under more complicated multi-level structures or when we introduce multiple periods of observation?

Finally, rather than model the unobserved differences as random effects, one could also treat them as fixed effects. This approach has the advantage of making fewer assumptions (i.e., that the group-level differences do not correlate with any of the included covariates), but often proves problematic for researchers interested in the effect of state-level variables, which do not vary across individuals within states within a single time-period and generally change only very slowly over time. Inclusion of such variables with fixed effects is impossible given the perfect collinearity that results. The fixed-effects vector decomposition method developed in the context of comparative politics by Plümper and Troeger (2007), however, overcomes this problem, but has yet to be used in the context of state politics research, let alone compared to the various approaches discussed above.[5]

The Role of Geography

A second emerging area of opportunity in state politics research revolves around the growing attention to the role of geography for understanding political behavior and political outcomes in the context of state politics. State politics offers an excellent opportunity to more richly consider the role of geography because of its pre-existing attention to how geographic units interact and the variation across states in the construction and context of those environments. The opportunity to consider and model the role of such factors has increased greatly over the last decade or so with the availability and geographic information systems (GIS) software to construct exceedingly detailed information about the geographic structure of political entities and relational measures of such structures and individuals who live within them.

Simultaneously, there has been a growing interest in spatial regression techniques to account for possible non-independence across spatially related data (e.g., Beck, Gleditsch, and Beardsley, 2006; Franzese and Hays, 2007; Darmofal, 2009). These models allow scholars to account for spatial dependence across observations, following the idea that what happens in one place is linked to outcomes in other places. State politics scholars are, of course, familiar with this logic given our history of interest in processes such as policy diffusion and the potential for a race-to-the-bottom in state social services such as welfare (Peterson and Rom, 1990; Volden, 2002; Berry and Baybeck, 2005). In some cases, spatial dependence may reflect nuisance, but in state politics literature it also often represents substance. Do states learn from each other? Are their decisions strategically made in competition with each other? Are there unmodeled, common regional shocks that influence some groups of states differently than others? Spatial analysis allows researchers a way to attempt to address these types of question. Further, these models can be extended to simultaneously account for multiple forms of spatial dependence that do not even have to reflect geographic relationships, but could represent other relationships such as political culture, public opinion, or networks of interest groups, administrators, or elected officials.

A notable example of the use of GIS in the context of state policy innovation and diffusion is Berry and Baybeck's (2005) previously discussed study of lottery adoptions and welfare benefit levels. Since one of the theoretical arguments for how these policies or levels might diffuse is that individuals from one state might cross state borders to buy a lottery ticket or move across the border for better benefits, they use GIS to measure the size of the population in neighboring states that lives within a specific distance (e.g., 50 miles) of the state in question and use this as an explanatory variable in their model of policy adoption or outcomes. Their findings provide evidence that suggests economic competition is a mechanism for diffusion in both of these areas of public policy.

GIS and spatial analysis has also been used in the study of individual-level behavior. For example, scholars have used GIS to examine how geographic context influences voting and voter turnout in state elections (Branton et al., 2007; Dyck and Seabrook, 2010). Branton et al. (2007) use GIS to measure spatial proximity to the U.S.–Mexico border in order to predict Anglo voting on immigration related ballot initiatives. Dyck and Seabrook (2010) use GIS to identify the racial/ethnic and socioeconomic makeup of the areas in which voters reside. They then use this measure to examine mobilization effects of direct democracy in a variety of electoral contexts.

DISCUSSION AND CONCLUSION

The study of political methodology in state politics has already produced many important advances substantively, as well as methodologically, to the broader field of political science. And the timing seems right for that pace to continue and even accelerate as state politics researchers face ever-expanding opportunities and challenges. The continual generation of new, large datasets allowing for more comprehensive across-state and over-time comparisons both encourages and facilitates the introduction and exploration of existing methods from political science and from other disciplines as well as the generation of new approaches to address the intricate circumstances faced by researchers interested in state politics.

The growing attention to causality and matching in the discipline raises a host of interesting possibilities for researchers interested in untangling the complex web that is state politics. How can we address the possible endogeneity of political institutions when considering their effect on policy outcomes or individual behavior? Consider, for example, Matsusaka (2005) and Marschall and Ruhil's (2005a, 2005b) exchange on the possible endogeneity of the initiative process for state policy outcomes or Malhotra's (2008) use of matching to study the effect of legislative professionalism on state spending. Relatedly, how can we ensure that the comparisons that we make across states reflect the true mechanism of interest and not some correlated but theoretically unrelated factor?

Although these are all challenges that we (still) face as a field, the good news is that state politics scholars are ever vigilant in using current methodological tools to address these questions. The even better news is that they are increasingly the source of some of those tools as well. This can only improve the quality of our analyses as state politics researchers in the field are most attuned to the needs of state politics research. And while these can all be rightly viewed as challenges, we can also view them as state politics researchers always have: opportunities to leverage in new ways the great variation across states to better understand how circumstances influence outcomes and behavior.

Notes

1. See also Eyestone (1977) for a discussion of variation in innovativeness across policies and time.
2. Though see Puro, Bergerson, and Puro (1985) for a regression-based approach with the dependent variable a binary indicator for whether each state adopted the Missouri Plan by 1976.
3. See Gilardi and Fuglister (2008) for a nice exposition of this method.
4. This study led to a spirited debate regarding the measurement of state public opinion. Berry et al. (1998) develop a longitudinal measure of state ideology using election returns, roll-call votes, and partisan demographics on state government ideology. The crux of the debate centers on two issues: (1) what the two different measures are actually measuring; and (2) the stability of intrastate public opinion over time. See Norrander (2007) for a clear discussion of the debate and issues surrounding the different measures.
5. See also Breusch et al. (n.d.) and Greene (2011) for some criticisms and necessary adjustments to the FEVD standard errors.

References

Allison, Paul D. 1984. *Event History Analysis Data*. Beverly Hills. Sage.

Arceneaux, Kevin and David W. Nickerson. 2009. "Modeling Certainty with Clustered Data: A Comparison of Methods." *Political Analysis 17* (2): 177–190.

Bardwell, Kedron. 2003. "Not All Money Is Equal: The Differential Effect of Spending by Incumbents and Challengers in Gubernatorial Primaries." *State Politics and Policy Quarterly 3* (3): 294–308.

Beck, Nathaniel L., Kristian Skrede Gleditsch, and Kyle C. Beardsley. 2006. "Space is More than Geography: Using Spatial Econometrics in the Study of Political Economy." *International Studies Quarterly 50* (1): 27–44.

Berry, Francis Stokes and William D. Berry. 1990. State Lottery Adoptions as Policy Innovations: An Event History Analysis. *American Political Science Review 84* (2): 395–415.

Berry, William D. and Brady Baybeck. 2005. "Using Geographic Information Systems to Study Interstate Competition." *American Political Science Review 99* (4): 505–519.

Berry, William, Evan Ringquist, Richard Fording, and Russell Hanson. 1998. "Measuring Citizen and Government Ideology in the American States, 1960–1993." *American Journal of Political Science 42* (1): 327–348.

Beyle, Thad, Richard G. Niemi, and Lee Sigelman. 2002. "Gubernatorial, Senatorial, and State-level Presidential Job Approval: The U.S. Officials Job Approval Ratings (JAR) Collection." *State Politics and Policy Quarterly 2* (3): 215–231.

Boehmke, Frederick J. 2009a. "Policy Emulation or Policy Convergence? Potential Ambiguities in the Dyadic Event History Approach to State Policy Emulation." *Journal of Politics 71* (3): 1125–1140.

Boehmke, Frederick J. 2009b. "Approaches to Modeling the Adoption and Modification of Policies with Multiple Components." *State Politics and Policy Quarterly* 9 (2): 229–252.

Boehmke, Frederick J., and Richard Witmer. 2004. "Disentangling Diffusion: The Effects of Social Learning and Economic Competition on State Policy Innovation and Expansion." *Political Research Quarterly* 57 (1): 39–51.

Boushey, Graeme. 2010. *Policy Diffusion Dynamics in America*. New York: Cambridge University Press.

Bowler, Shaun and Todd Donovan. 2004. "Measuring the Effect of Direct Democracy on State Policy: Not All Initiatives Are Created Equal." *State Politics and Policy Quarterly* 4 (3): 345–363.

Brace, Paul, Kevin Arceneaux, Martin Johnson, and Stacy Ulbig. 2004. "Does State Political Ideology Change over Time?" *Political Research Quarterly* 57 (4): 529–540.

Brace, Paul, Kellie Sims-Butler, Kevin Arceneaux, and Martin Johnson. 2002. "Public Opinion in the American States: New Perspectives Using National Survey Data." *American Journal of Political Science* 46 (1): 173–189.

Branton, Regina P., Gavin Dillingham, Johanna Dunaway, and Beth Miller. 2007. "Anglo Voting on Nativist Ballot Initiatives The Impact of Spatial Proximity to the US–Mexico Border." *Social Science Quarterly* 88 (3): 882–897.

Braunstein, Richard. 2004. *Initiative and Referendum Voting: Governing Through Direct Democracy in the United States*. New York: LFB Scholarly Publishing.

Breusch, Trevor, Michael Ward, Hoa Nguyen, and Tom Kompas. n.d. "On the Fixed-Effect Vector Decomposition." *Political Analysis*.

Cameron, A. Colin, Jonah B. Gelbach, and Douglas L. Miller. 2008. "Bootstrap Based Improvements for Inference with Clustered Errors." *Review of Economics and Statistics* 90 (3): 414–427.

Carsey, Thomas M., Richard G. Niemi, William D. Berry, Lynda W. Powell, and James M. Snyder. 2008. "State Legislative Elections, 1967–2003: Announcing the Completion of a Cleaned and Updated Dataset." *State Politics and Policy Quarterly* 9 (3): 356–370.

Clark, Kim B. 1985. "The Interaction of Design Hierarchies and Market Concepts in Technological Evolution." *Research Policy* 14: 235–251.

Clark, Jennifer Hayes, Tracy Osborn, Jonathan Winburn, and Gerald C. Wright. 2009. "Representation in U.S. Legislatures: The Acquisition and Analysis of U.S. State Legislative Roll-Call Data." *State Politics and Policy Quarterly* 9 (3): 356–370.

Clingermayer, James and B. Dan Wood. 1995. "Disentangling Patterns of State Debt Financing." *American Political Science Review* 89 (1): 108–120.

Cohen, Jeffrey. 2003. "The Polls: State-level Presidential Approval: Results from the Job Approval Project." *Presidential Studies Quarterly* 33 (1): 211–220.

Cohen, Jeffrey. 2006a. "Introduction: Studying Public Opinion in the American States." In Jeffrey Cohen (ed.), *Public Opinion in State Politics*, 3–18. Stanford, CA: Stanford University Press.

Cohen, Jeffrey. 2006b. "Conclusions: Where Have We Been, Where Should We Go." In Jeffrey Cohen (ed.), *Public Opinion in State Politics*, 254–270. Stanford, CA: Stanford University Press.

Cohen, Jeffrey and Richard Powell. 2005. "Building Public Support from the Grassroots Up: The Impact of Presidential Travel on State-Level Approval." *Presidential Studies Quarterly* 35 (1): 11–27.

Daniels, Mark R., and Robert E. Darcy. 1985. "As Time Goes by: The Arrested Diffusion of the Equal Rights Amendment." *Publius* 15 (4): 51–60.

Darmofal, David. 2009. "Bayesian Spatial Survival Models for Political Event Processes." *American Journal of Political Science 53* (1): 241–257.

Dyck, Joshua and Nicholas Seabrook. 2010. "Mobilized by Direct Democracy: Short-Term Versus Long-Term Effects and the Geography of Turnout in Ballot Measure Elections." *Social Science Quarterly 91* (1): 188–208.

Dye, Thomas. 1965. "Malapportionment and Public Policy in the States." *Journal of Politics 27* (3): 586–601.

Erikson, Robert S., Gerald C. Wright, and John P. McIver. 1993. *Statehouse Democracy: Public Opinion and Policy in the American States*. Cambridge: Cambridge University Press.

Everson, David H. 1981. "The Effects of Initiatives on Voter Turnout: A Comparative State Analysis." *The Western Political Quarterly 34* (3): 415–425.

Eyestone, Robert. 1977. "Confusion, Diffusion, and Innovation." *American Political Science Review 71* (2): 441–447.

Franzese Jr, Robert J. and Jude C. Hays. 2007. "Spatial Econometric Models of Cross-Sectional Interdependence in Political Science Panel and Time-Series-Cross-Section Data." *Political Analysis 15* (2): 140–164.

Gelman, Andrew and Jennifer Hill. 2007. *Data Analysis Using Regression and Multilevel/ Hierarchical Models*. Cambridge: Cambridge University Press.

Gelman, Andrew and Thomas Little. 1997. "Poststratification into Many Categories Using Hierarchical Logistic Regression." *Survey Methodology 23* (2): 338–356.

Gilardi, Fabrizio. 2010. "Who Learns from What in Policy Diffusion Processes?" *American Journal of Political Science 54* (3): 650–666.

Gilardi, Fabrizio and Katharina Fuglister. 2008. "Empirical Modeling of Policy Diffusion in Federal States: The Dyadic Approach." *Swiss Political Science Review 14* (3): 413–450.

Gray, Virginia. 1973. "Innovation in the States: A Diffusion Study." *American Political Science Review 67* (4): 1174–1185.

Gray, Virginia and David Lowery. 1996. *The Population Ecology of Interest Representation*. Ann Arbor: The University of Michigan Press.

Greene, William H. 2011. "Fixed Effects Vector Decomposition: A Magical Solution to the Problem of Time Invariant Variables in Fixed Effects Models?" *19* (2): 135–146.

Haider-Markel, Donald P. 2001. "Policy Diffusion as a Geographical Expansion of the Scope of Political Conflict: Same-Sex Marriage Bans in the 1990s." *State Politics and Policy Quarterly 1* (1): 5–26.

Hall, Melinda Gann and Paul Brace. 1999. "The State Supreme Court Data Project." *Law and Courts 9*: 21–23.

Hamman, John. 2006. "Public Opinion in the States: Determinants of Legislative Job Performance." In Jeffrey Cohen (ed.), *Public Opinion in State Politics*, 79–101. Stanford, CA: Stanford University Press.

Harden, Jeffrey J. 2011. "A Bootstrap Method for Conducting Statistical Inference with Clustered Data." *State Politics and Policy Quarterly 11*(2): 223–246.

Hill, Kim and Jan Leighley. 1992. "The Policy Consequences of Class Bias in State Electorates." *American Journal of Political Science 36* (2): 351–365.

Hill, Kim Q., Jan Leighley, and Angela Hinton-Andersson. 1995. "Lower-Class Mobilization and Policy Linkage in the U.S. States." *American Journal of Political Science 39* (1): 75–86.

Hofferbert, Richard. 1966. "The Relation between Public Policy and Some Structural Environmental Variables in the American States." *American Political Science Review 60* (1): 73–82.

Huber, John D. and Charles R. Shipan. 2002. *Deliberate Discretion? The Institutional Foundations of Bureaucratic Autonomy*. New York: Cambridge University Press.

Jones, Bradford S. and Regina P. Branton. 2005. "Beyond Logit and Probit: Cox Duration Models of Single, Repeating, and Competing Events for State Policy Adoption." *State Politics and Policy Quarterly 5* (4): 420–443.

Jones, Bradford and Barbara Norrander. 1996. "The Reliability of Aggregated Public Opinion Measures." *American Journal of Political Science 40* (1): 295–309.

Klarner, Carl. 2003. "The Measurement of the Partisan Balance of State Government." *State Politics and Policy Quarterly 3* (3): 309–319.

Kousser, Thad. 2005. *Term Limits and the Dismantling of State Legislative Professionalism*. New York: Cambridge University Press.

Lax, Jeffrey and Justin Phillips. 2009. "How Should We Estimate Public Opinion in the States?" *American Journal of Political Science 53* (1): 107–121.

Lieberman, Robert and Greg Shaw. 2000. "Looking Inward, Looking Outward: The Politics of State Welfare Innovation under Devolution." *Political Research Quarterly 53* (2): 215–240.

Lowery, David and Virginia Gray. 1993. "The Density of State Interest Group Systems." *The Journal of Politics 55* (1): 191–206.

Malhotra, Neil. 2008. "Disentangling the Relationship between Legislative Professionalism and Government Spending," *Legislative Studies Quarterly 33, 3*(1): 1–28.

Marschall, Melissa J. and Amrudh V. S. Ruhil. 2005a. "Fiscal Effects of the Voter Initiative Reconsidered: Addressing Endogeneity." *State Politics and Policy Quarterly 5* (4): 327–355.

Marschall, Melissa J. and Amrudh V. S. Ruhil. 2005b. "Of Models and Methods: A Response to Matsusaka." *State Politics and Policy Quarterly 5* (4): 364–372.

Matsusaka, John G. 2005. "The Endogeneity of the Initiative: A Comment on Marschall and Ruhil." *State Politics and Policy Quarterly 5* (4): 356–363.

Mintrom, Michael, and Sandra Vergari. 1998. "Policy Networks and Innovation Diffusion: The Case of State Education Reforms." *Journal of Politics 60*(1): 126–148.

Mooney, Christopher Z. 2001. Modeling Regional Effects on State Policy Diffusion. *Political Research Quarterly 54* (1): 103–124.

Mooney, Christopher Z. and Mei-Hsien Lee. 1995. Legislative Morality in the American States: The Case of Pre-Roe Abortion Regulation Reform. *American Journal of Political Science 39* (3): 599–627.

Nicholson-Crotty, Sean. 2009. "The Politics of Diffusion: Public Policy in the American States." *The Journal of Politics 71* (1): 192–205.

Norrander, Barbara. 2007. "Comment: Choosing Among Indicators of State Public Opinion." *State Politics and Policy Quarterly 7* (2): 125–159.

Park, David, Joseph Bafumi, and Andrew Gelman. 2006. "State-Level Opinions from National Surveys: Poststratification Using Multilevel Logistic Regression." In Jeffrey Cohen (ed.), *Public Opinion in State Politics*, 209–228. Stanford, CA: Stanford University Press.

Peterson, Paul E. and Mark C. Rom. 1990. *Welfare Magnets: A New Case for a National Standard*. Washington, DC: The Brookings Institute.

Plümper, Thomas and Vera E. Troeger. 2007. "Efficient Estimation of Time-Invariant and Rarely Changing Variables in Panel Data Analysis with Unit Effects." *Political Analysis 15* (2): 124–139.

Pool, Ithiel de Sola, Robert Abelson, and Samuel Popkin. 1965. *Candidates, Issues and Strategies*. Cambridge, MA: MIT Press.

Primo, David M., Matthew L. Jacobsmeier, and Jeffrey Milyo. 2007. "Estimating the Impact of State Policies and Institutions with Mixed-Level Data." *State Politics and Policy Quarterly 7* (4): 446–459.

Puro, Marsha, Peter J. Bergerson, and Steven Puro. 1985. "An Analysis of Judicial Diffusion: Adoption of the Missouri Plan in the American States." *Publius 15* (4): 85–97.

Rogers, Everett. 1962. *Diffusion of Innovation* (1st ed.). New York, NY: Free Press.

Savage, Robert L. 1978. "Policy Innovativeness as a Trait of American States." *The Journal of Politics 40* (1): 212–224.

Savage, Robert L. 1985. Diffusion Research Traditions and the Spread of Policy Innovations in a Federal System. *Publius: The Journal of Federalism 15* (1): 1–27.

Seidman, David. 1975. "Simulation of Public Opinion: A Caveat." *Public Opinion Quarterly 39* (3): 331–342.

Sharkansky, Ira. 1967. "Government Expenditures and Public Policies in the American States." *American Political Science Review 61*: 1066–1077.

Shipan, Charles R. and Craig Volden. 2006. Bottom-up Federalism: The Diffusion of Antismoking Policies from U.S. Cities to States. *American Journal of Political Science 50* (4): 825–843.

Squire, Peverill. 1992. "Legislative Professionalization and Membership Diversity in State Legislatures." *Legislative Studies Quarterly 17*: 69–79.

Volden, Craig. 2002. "The Politics of Competitive Federalism: A Race to the Bottom in Welfare Benefits?" *American Journal of Political Science 46*(2): 352–363.

Volden, Craig. 2006. States as Policy Laboratories: Emulating Success in the Children's Health Insurance Program. *American Journal of Political Science 50* (2): 294–312.

Walker, Jack L. 1969. "The Diffusion of Innovations among the American States." *American Political Science Review 63* (3): 880–899.

Weber, Ronald, Anne Hopkins, Michael Mezey, and Frank Munger. 1972–1973. "Computer Simulation of State Electorates." *Public Opinion Quarterly 36*: 49–65.

Weber, Ronald and William Shaffer. 1972. "Public Opinion and American State Policy-Making." *Midwest Journal of Political Science 16* (4): 683–699.

Wright, Gerald, Robert Erikson, and John McIver. 1985. "Measuring State Partisanship and Ideology with Survey Data." *Journal of Politics 47* (2): 469–489.

Wright, Gerald, Robert Erikson, and John McIver. 1987. "Public Opinion and Policy Liberalism in the American States." *American Journal of Political Science 31* (3): 980–1007.

Zeller, Belle. 1958. "Regulation of Pressure Groups and Lobbyists." *Annals of the American Academy of Political and Social Science 319*: 94–103.

CHAPTER 37

....

SUB-NATIONAL POLITICS

A National Political Perspective

....

BERTRAM JOHNSON

JAMES Madison, arguing in 1788 against a political opposition suspicious of centralized power, explained that the "character" of the new U.S. system would be neither entirely "national" nor entirely "federal." In contrast with arguments elsewhere in *The Federalist Papers*, his perspective in *Federalist 39* is strikingly atheoretical. Other compromises at the convention, such as bicameralism, modes of representation, and the size of the House and Senate all prompted robust and principled defenses from Madison. But the most he could do in explaining the particular system of layered sovereignty between the states and the central government was to proclaim it as sort of a muddle: "The proposed Constitution ... is, in strictness, neither a national nor a federal Constitution, but a composition of both" (Hamilton, Madison, and Jay, 2003 [1788]: 242).

Modern political scientists have at times been more exasperated with federalism than Madison was. William Riker (1964) criticized federalism as privileging harmful and inefficient minority preferences; others consider the multiplicity of governments in the U.S. to be a curious historical accident and little more. Research on the relationship between lower levels of government and higher levels of government has produced many accounts of how layered governments work in particular cases; and many arguments about the legal and economic consequences of layering. However, political scientists are only beginning to develop a comprehensive view of how multi-tiered institutional structures interact with the political incentives of key actors to produce policy outcomes. Future research should focus on the political nature of these interactions. Our goal should be a more systematic understanding of federalism as a "supremely political institution" (Anton, 1989: 230).

THREE TRADITIONS IN RESEARCH ON SUB-NATIONAL POLITICS FROM A NATIONAL PERSPECTIVE

The U.S. federal system is fundamentally a system of layered governments. The Constitution outlines this layering only with respect to the divisions between states and the national government, but in practice, municipalities, counties, and an array of different types of special districts also play important roles, interacting with one another as they do so. In considering this complex system, most scholars have adopted one of three major approaches: first, a legal approach that emphasizes a lack of formal powers at lower levels; second, a fiscal federalism tradition that focuses on considerations of efficiency; and third, a literature on intergovernmental policy that focuses on public administration. Each has contributed insights and generated much valuable research, but each also presents key questions that political scientists ought to be able to answer.

Legal Approaches

Viewed in isolation, institutions usually appear powerful; viewed in the context of the surrounding environment, they often appear weak. Research on the presidency (Neustadt, 1990) and on the Supreme Court (Rosenberg, 2008), has confirmed this insight repeatedly. The shock in the urban politics subfield at arguments that emphasized the context within which cities operated (i.e., Peterson, 1981) was partly the result of such a change in perspective. In contrast with the presidency and the Court, however, states, and especially cities, lack well defined formal powers. In fact, the formal rules that have developed over the course of history usually exaggerate the susceptibility of sub-governments to interference from above.

Dillon's Rule is the fundamental legal stricture affecting cities. Coined by 19th-century Iowa judge John F. Dillon, and taught to generations of young lawyers who read his classic *Commentaries on the Law of Municipal Corporations*, this axiom declares that cities are "creatures of the states." At the very least, this is a truism: cities were created by the states, and as "municipal corporations" are legal entities of the state governments. In a broader sense, Dillon's Rule implies that cities are powerless to do anything in the absence of a state's permission. As Edward Banfield and James Q. Wilson memorably put it, "a city cannot operate a peanut stand at the city zoo without first getting the state legislature to pass an enabling law, unless, perchance, the city's charter or some previously enacted law unmistakably covers the sale of peanuts" (Banfield and Wilson, 1963: 65). Gerald Frug and David Barron agree: cities "only have power to the extent they are given it by statutes and constitutional provisions adopted by state government" (Frug and Barron, 2008: 231). Incidents such as New York City's virtual takeover by the state in the wake of its 1970s fiscal crisis and Detroit's 2013 bankruptcy under the governance of a state appointee provide bleak confirmation that each city has only as much freedom as its state allows it.

States would appear to be on much stronger legal footing in their relationship with the national government. The U.S. Constitution stipulates that they possess broad residual powers, that their boundaries cannot be changed without their permission, and that they will have equal representation in the Senate. (Madison himself pointed this out in his defense of the federal system.) Yet since 1937, when the Supreme Court expanded the scope of permissible commerce clause regulation, the national government has encroached on state powers with only brief respites. Congress has especially wide latitude in passing economic legislation. As recent state-level changes in marijuana policy show, the federal government allows states autonomy in certain economic areas because it chooses to do so—not because it must.

Studies that examine local interaction with higher levels over legal distinctions such as home rule (a carve-out of particular local powers in state constitutions) and the powers delegated to the states by the federal government tend to see lower levels of government as fighting defensive battles from positions of vulnerability. As Berman puts it, "the legislative task [of localities] is primarily a defensive one of trying to ward off threats to their authority" (Berman, 2003: 37). Joseph Zimmerman (2008) similarly sees recent state–national relations as a battle by states to stave off encroaching Congressional pre-emption of state authority.

But despite these areas of weakness, a focus on the legal relationship between levels of government understates the true power of actors at lower levels of government over policies enacted at higher levels. Apparent weakness in formal authority can obscure quite substantial political strengths. One need look no further than municipal history to find accounts of powerful "bosses" that had no official formal powers at all, yet exercised considerable influence over both local and state governments. More broadly, the defensive posture of cities bears some resemblance to that of interest groups that lobby Congress. In the case of interest groups, each sees itself as vulnerable, but collectively the interest-group system is an important political force. A renewed focus on the political—rather than legal—aspects of intergovernmental relations would take this possibility more seriously. It should move away from accounts of weakness and towards studies of the conditions affecting weakness and strength.

Specifically, political science research should better define the *circumstances under which local governments are weaker and the circumstances under which they are likely to be stronger in pressing claims at higher levels of government.*

Fiscal Federalism

Scholars of fiscal federalism treat a system of layered governments as a potential tool for the efficient design and implementation of policy. Fiscal federalism's roots can be found in arguments such as that of Charles Tiebout (1956) that a multiplicity of sub-national governments can reveal the demand functions of "consumer-voters" more effectively than a monolithic national system, resulting in aggregate levels of policy provision that better reflect preferences.

The "first generation" fiscal federalists broadened this economics-based approach by focusing not only on the multiplicity of governments, but also on their layered nature. A system of different governments with different size and scope allowed for a determination of the optimal governmental level for policy provision (Oates, 1972). First generation fiscal federalists saw the federal structure as a means by which resources could be efficiently allocated. Assigning the right policies to the right level of government could minimize externalities and maximize the congruence between policies and resident preferences. The result was Pareto superior relative to centralized policy enactment. Oates referred to this point as the "decentralization theorem" (Oates, 1972, 2008). Chief among the tools in the fiscal federalists' arsenal was the intergovernmental grant. Targeted in the right way, grants could make government cheaper and more effective.

So-called "second-generation" fiscal federalists have grown more skeptical of the possibility for optimal policy assignment. Influenced by the Chicago School of economics, these later theorists see policy makers as influential, rent-seeking actors with institutional resources at their disposal (Weingast, 2009). As rent-seekers out for themselves, political entrepreneurs cannot be trusted to assign resources optimally. Of particular relevance in the wake of the 2008 financial crisis and recession is the possibility that localities—and even states—may engage in fiscally irresponsible behavior, knowing that higher levels of government will inevitably bail them out.

Paul Peterson makes a similar argument about politicians' behavior (1981, 1995). Cities are good at development policy, argues Peterson, because this activity matches cities' need to attract mobile capital and skilled labor; state governments and especially the national government ought to be in charge of most social policy because of their broader revenue pools and their stronger position with respect to mobile capital. But higher-level politicians have incentives to engage in credit-claiming for development policy and blame avoidance for redistribution, so they enact policies that are the opposite of those that are optimal. The "price of federalism" is the resulting inefficiency.

This newer fiscal federalism research heads in a productive direction, paralleling developments both in economics and political science to take more seriously the preferences of government actors and the ways in which institutions shape these preferences. Jonathan Rodden (2006), in particular, makes impressive strides in linking the considerations of key political actors with consequences for efficient fiscal policy. Yet fiscal federalism's focus on efficiency is too narrow to admit of a comprehensive political interpretation of federalism. The key political concept of the representation of constituent preferences is not taken seriously enough. First-generation fiscal federalism takes the public's preferences as if they were clear and easily articulated. Second-generation fiscal federalism considers public preferences to be less important than the rent-seeking behavior of politicians. Political science studies can supplement this research by incorporating more realistic models of representation.

Specifically, political scientists should work towards a clearer understanding of *how local and state institutions determine which preferences are represented, how they are represented, and how differential representation affects various public policy areas—including, but not limited to, fiscal policy.*

Intergovernmental Policy

A third approach to the study of layered federal institutions has been to focus on the design and implementation of intergovernmental policy. This tradition extends from the discussion of dual versus cooperative federalism (Grodzins, 1966; Elazar, 1966) and continues into works that chronicle the development of federal policy through several generations of "new federalisms" (Conlan, 1998; Walker, 2000) to studies of particular policies and policy areas such as welfare, Medicaid, environmental policy, and transportation policy.

These studies typically characterize relationships between different levels of government as complex and contingent (Wright, 1978). Intergovernmental policy research often shows federal, state, and local policy formation and enactment to be mixed together like the proverbial "marble cake," or plagued by principal–agent problems that makes it difficult to say which level actually produces policy (Pressman and Wildavsky, 1984). Martha Derthick's study of the tobacco policy formulated by a concerted push from state attorneys general in the late 1990s shows how major national policy change can occur even when typical policymaking arenas (such as the passage of Congressional legislation) are bypassed (Derthick, 2004).

This literature often does a fine job of presenting intergovernmental interactions as political. Bargaining and negotiation is a central theme (Wright, 1978; Liebschutz, 1991), and the success and failure of political actors depends on a number of familiar political factors: institutional position, interest group allies, electoral success, and so on. According to Altshuler and Luberoff's excellent account of Boston's "Big Dig," for example, the shape of the project was determined by entrepreneurial bureaucrats, a constellation of interest groups on both sides, the preferences of local residents, key representatives in Washington, DC, and a succession of governors (Altshuler and Luberoff, 2003).

Studies of intergovernmental policy have been less successful in offering theories that might add some regularity and prediction to the complex intergovernmental environment. To be sure, it may be the case that public policymaking involves random and contingent factors that are inherently unpredictable (Baumgartner and Jones, 1993). But there are features of the intergovernmental framework that make intergovernmental policymaking at least somewhat systematic. Regular elections, elected officials, and substantial bureaucracies are a few of these. As respects these elements, at least, policymaking has predictable contours.

Political science research should specify *which political actors, constituencies, and processes are likely to characterize the intergovernmental public policymaking process and when certain actors, constituencies, and institutions are more or less likely to play central roles.*

In sum, many accounts of intergovernmental relations in the past 50 years conclude with a sense of exasperation, or of irreducible complexity, or both. U.S. history has produced similar puzzlement among policymakers. The Nixon, Reagan, and Gingrich "New Federalisms" each changed intergovernmental policy in lasting ways, but in each case these programs were eroded or superseded by later policies. Partnerships between the national, state, and local governments that the Department of Homeland Security has sought to build in the aftermath of 9–11 are at times tense, and at times subject to political maneuvering that frustrates national security experts. Hurricane Katrina exposed disturbing coordination problems between levels of government—problems that 2010's Deepwater Horizon oil spill revealed to be still unresolved. Fiscal crises in cities and states highlight issues of moral hazard, the potential for dependency on higher levels of government, and the extent to which local political impasses can have negative externalities.

Existing literature has provided many valuable insights about the above. The second-generation fiscal federalism literature would be a good fit to understand fiscal crises, for example. Students of policy implementation in the Great Society would not have been surprised by the Katrina episode. But political science could do more to provide a comprehensive political perspective that would make sense of many of these themes at the same time. Research within the last 15 years has begun to move in the right direction. In the last section, I suggest how the field might move forward, highlighting important themes and exemplary recent research.

A New Political Synthesis

A more comprehensive approach would view the various governments operating in the intergovernmental system as *institutional structures* that have claims on each other, occupied by *political entrepreneurs* motivated by their own career goals who succeed or fail largely because of how they respond to *constituent interests*. There are three important components to this perspective. First, each government entity is an institutional structure: a durable set of rules that guide behavior. Second, political entrepreneurs occupy these institutions. These entrepreneurs are self-interested actors, chiefly motivated by re-election or the equivalent in career advancement (a city manager may wish to jump to a bigger city, for example). They can be expected to act strategically to pursue their goals. Finally, constituents play a crucial role in defining the incentives of elite actors. But the relative role of constituencies—and their composition—can be altered by institutional structures. In the simplest terms, a city government could draw its boundaries to include some populations and/or exclude others. In more complex situations, rules may encourage or discourage certain people from participating (Burns, 1994).

There are at least three productive insights that flow from such a view of the intergovernmental system. First, the interest-group literature teaches us that political actors in most organizations that have claims on institutions must pay significant organizational and maintenance costs (Olson, 1965; Moe, 1980). But officials in local and state governments do not have this problem: because they have been granted institutional structures and taxation powers, this matter is essentially settled. Therefore, local and state governments might be seen as particularly stable (and therefore advantaged) "interest groups" in the federal system. They are more durable than other groups, and their durability subsidizes (and advantages) the interests of those who have access to these institutions.

In one line of research consistent with this perspective, Nancy Burns and Gerald Gamm have found that local governments have been historically quite effective in extracting desired resources from state governments in the form of special legislation (Burns and Gamm, 1997). Municipal governments have lobbied for their constituency interests at the state level, and state legislators have appeared eager to provide particularized benefits to these interests, as the legislative politics literature would predict. Burns and Gamm's meticulous study of local legislation across five decades shows that "the ordinary work of state politics was local affairs, and an ordinary branch of local politics was the state legislature" (Burns and Gamm, 1997: 90). Other studies have also found that local government structure appears to affect the success or failure with which cities can extract such benefits from higher levels (Johnson, 2007).

Second, because institutions at different levels of government are differently structured, with different combinations of constituents, political entrepreneurs should, on average, move to the level at which they are most advantaged. It is probably no accident, for example, that local officials are more likely to be business owners, and state legislators are more likely to be lawyers. Lisa Miller (2008) has found that groups, too, move to their area of greatest advantage, and makes the important observation that a system of layered institutions itself advantages the groups that can move with greatest ease from one level to another. Federalism, she argues "divides and conquers, isolating poorly resourced groups from one another and making it difficult for them to hold legislators accountable to their interests" (Miller, 2008: 175).

This point about accountability leads to a third significant insight that flows from a political perspective on federalism. A system of layered institutions can allow political actors to manipulate the extent to which they are held accountable by constituent groups. Jessica Trounstine (2008), in her clever study of Chicago and San Jose, argues that elites in both machine and reform cities have done their best to alter institutions to make themselves less accountable to constituencies that might oppose them. This phenomenon might be further multiplied when we expand our view to the system of layered governments that exists in the United States.

Indeed, Chris Berry's research provides a clear example of this phenomenon. In a study of layered special purpose governments, Berry concludes that such governance "in 3-D" allows political actors to respond to limited constituencies and externalize the costs of governance, turning local tax bases into common pool resources that are over exploited (Berry, 2009). "[R]ather than engaging with each other in a broad-ranging contest over collectively decided priorities and purposes, local interest groups are increasingly withdrawing into a collection of narrower, well-partitioned realms of influence that intersect only on the tax bill" (Berry, 2009: 195).

Preliminary answers to the questions posed above should follow from these illustrations of how a national political perspective on sub-national politics could work in practice:

1) *Under what circumstances are local governments weaker and under what circumstances are they likely to be stronger in pressing claims at higher levels of government?*

Local governments are stronger in the intergovernmental arena if their institutions effectively resolve their problems of internal organization and maintenance. They are also stronger to the extent that they represent and encompass constituencies that are relevant to political actors at other levels, and to the extent that they are compatible with the preferences of relevant elite actors (see Filippov, Ordeshook, and Shvetsova, 2004).

2) *How do local and state institutions determine which preferences are represented, how they are represented, and how differential representation affects various public policy areas—including, but not limited to, fiscal policy?*

Representation may be an effect of—as well as a cause of—elite actions. A layered system of institutions allows elites to shunt decision-making power to arenas in which they are most likely to win, which often means placing them outside the reach of at least some constituencies.

3) *Which political actors, constituencies, and processes are likely to characterize the intergovernmental public policymaking process, and when are certain actors, constituencies, and institutions more or less likely to play central roles?*

Voters and groups with interests consistent with those of the designers and leaders of institutions will be granted representation more often than those with interests inconsistent with those of these elites. Competition among elites for votes will tend to broaden representation; the lack of competition (which is often an effect of shifting decision-making power to another level of government) will tend to diminish it.

James Madison's view of the federal structure was essentially right. It is a complex system of multiple governments that no single principle can explain in its entirety. A political perspective on sub-national government does, however, promise to advance our understanding of the system by focusing on how key features of politics shape this complex environment.

REFERENCES

Altshuler, Alan and David Luberoff. 2003. *Mega-Projects: The Changing Politics of Public Investment*. Washington, DC: Brookings Institution Press.

Anton, Thomas J. 1989. *American Federalism and Public Policy: How the System Works.* New York: Random House.

Banfield, Edward C. and James Q. Wilson. 1963. *City Politics.* New York: Random House.

Baumgartner, Frank R. and Bryan D. Jones. 1993. *Agendas and Instability in American Politics.* Chicago: University of Chicago Press.

Berman, David R. 2003. *Local Government and the States: Autonomy, Politics, and Policy.* Armonk, NY: M.E. Sharpe.

Berry, Christopher R. 2009. *Imperfect Union: Representation and Taxation in Multilevel Governments.* New York: Cambridge University Press.

Burns, Nancy. 1994. *The Formation of American Local Governments: Private Values in Public Institutions.* New York: Oxford University Press.

Burns, Nancy and Gerald Gamm. 1997. "Creatures of the State: State Politics and Local Government 1871–1921." *Urban Affairs Review 33* (1): 59–96.

Conlan, Timothy J. 1998. *From New Federalism to Devolution: Twenty-Five Years of Intergovernmental Reform.* Washington, DC: Brookings Institution Press.

Derthick, Martha A. 2004. *Up in Smoke: From Legislation to Litigation in Tobacco Politics* (2nd edition). Washington, DC: CQ Press.

Elazar, Daniel. 1966. *American Federalism: A View from the States.* New York: Crowell.

Filippov, Mikhail, Peter C. Ordeshook, and Olga Shvetsova. 2004. *Designing Federalism: A Theory of Self-Sustainable Federal Institutions.* New York: Cambridge University Press.

Frug, Gerald E. and David J. Barron. 2008. *City Bound: How States Stifle Urban Innovation.* Ithaca, NY: Cornell University Press.

Grodzins, Morton. 1966. *The American System: A New View of Government in the United States.* Chicago: Rand McNally.

Hamilton, Alexander, James Madison, and John Jay. 2003 [1788]. *The Federalist Papers.* New York: Penguin.

Johnson, Bertram. 2007. "Collective Action, City Council Committees, and State Aid to Cities." *Urban Affairs Review 42* (4): 457–478.

Liebschutz, Sarah F. 1991. *Bargaining Under Federalism: Contemporary New York.* Albany, NY: State University of New York Press.

Miller, Lisa L. 2008. *The Perils of Federalism: Race, Poverty, and the Politics of Crime Control.* New York: Oxford University Press.

Moe, Terry M. 1980. *The Organization of Interests: Incentives and Internal Dynamics of Political Interest Groups.* Chicago: University of Chicago Press.

Neustadt, Richard E. 1990. *Presidential Power and the Modern Presidents.* New York: The Free Press.

Oates, Wallace. 1972. *Fiscal Federalism.* New York: Harcourt Brace Jovanovich.

Oates, Wallace. 2008. "On the Evolution of Fiscal Federalism: Theory and Institutions." *National Tax Journal 61* (2): 313–334.

Olson, Mancur. 1965. *The Logic of Collective Action: Public Goods and the Theory of Groups.* Cambridge, MA: Harvard University Press.

Peterson, Paul E. 1981. *City Limits.* Chicago: University of Chicago Press.

Peterson, Paul E. 1995. *The Price of Federalism.* Washington, DC: Brookings Institution Press.

Pressman, Jeffrey F. and Aaron Wildavsky. 1984. *Implementation* (3rd edition expanded). Berkeley: University of California Press.

Riker, William. 1964. *Federalism: Origin, Operation, Significance.* Boston: Little, Brown and Company.

Rodden, Jonathan A. 2006. *Hamilton's Paradox: The Promise and Peril of Fiscal Federalism*. New York: Cambridge University Press.

Rosenberg, Gerald N. 2008. *The Hollow Hope: Can Courts Bring About Social Change?* (2nd edition). Chicago: University of Chicago Press.

Tiebout, Charles. 1956. "A Pure Theory of Local Expenditures." *Journal of Political Economy 64* (5): 416–424.

Trounstine, Jessica. 2008. *Political Monopolies in American Cities: The Rise and Fall of Bosses and Reformers*. Chicago: University of Chicago Press.

Walker, David B. 2000. *The Rebirth of Federalism: Slouching Toward Washington*. Chappaqua, NY: Chatham House.

Weingast, Barry R. 2009. "Second Generation Fiscal Federalism: The Implications of Fiscal Incentives." *Journal of Urban Economics 65*: 279–293.

Wright, Deil S. 1978. *Understanding Intergovernmental Relations: Public Policy and Participants' Perspectives in Local, State, and National Governments*. North Scituate, MA: Duxbury Press.

Zimmerman, Joseph F. 2008. *Contemporary American Federalism: The Growth of National Power*. Albany, NY: State University of New York Press.

CHAPTER 38

....

SUB-NATIONAL POLITICS

A Comparative Perspective

....

NICOLE BOLLEYER

COMPARATIVE work on sub-national politics is characterized by a multitude of substantive focuses and methodological perspectives. To some extent, this is due to the fuzzy nature of the concept of the "sub-national" itself, which can include everything that is neither national, nor international, nor supra-national. And even this analytical boundary turns out to be artificial once considering sub-national activities that travel across national borders. Intergovernmental cooperation between 'neighboring' American governors and Canadian premiers is only one example. The "new" regionalism in the context of the European Union capturing inter-regional cooperation that often crosses national boundaries is another (e.g., Hocking, 1999; Scott, 1999; Blatter, 2001; Perkmann, 2003, 2007). Despite these complexities, this chapter argues that a systematic mapping of the existing work on sub-national politics along substantive and methodological lines allows us to identify dominant trends in the literature and—as the flip side of the same coin—to specify areas of research that have received only little attention so far.

Having touched upon the difficulty of demarcating *sub-national politics* as an *empirical phenomenon* and, with it, as a target for comparative research, a fundamental divide along the kind of sub-national unit researchers focus on in the first place deserves highlighting: namely, between the study of local government on the one hand and state and regional governments on the other.[1] Each dimension has been intensively analyzed and has developed into a separate field of research. Until today, the study of local government and the field of regional and federal studies have remained surprisingly separate. This contribution follows this tradition and deliberately focuses on *state and regional governments*[2] because these tend to be more powerful and possess a wider variety of competences than local governments, at least when it comes to legislative powers. As far as state and regional governments are analyzed in their interplay with the national government (which is one of three analytical perspectives we look at in detail later), the behavior of state and regional governments tends to have wider repercussions for the overall working of multi-level systems.

Talking about state and regional governments, research on both governments with and without constitutionally guaranteed legislative competences is considered here, i.e., work on governments operating in constitutionally federal systems and in decentralized systems, as long as the lower-level units have final say in at least one area of legislative competence (Watts, 1999a; Thorlakson, 2003). Only legislative authority allows both sets of governments to genuinely generate their own answers to policy problems. Whether the distinction between constitutionally federal systems such as the U.S. or Canada and "devolved" or "decentralized" systems[3] such as the U.K. or Spain generates systematic differences in the working of these multi-level systems, is subject to debate, though (on the U.K. see Laffin and Thomas (1999); on Spain see Moreno (1999, 2000); for a systemic overview see Swenden (2006)). It can be argued that relations between constituent governments and governmental levels are likely to be more diverse in terms of state units being ready to exploit their spaces of autonomy and to engage in conflicts in federal than in devolved or decentralized systems. When sub-national authority is constitutionally guaranteed, conflicts cannot be resolved by the unilateral withdrawal of competences or the threat thereof from one governmental level by the other. Leaving the decisions of constitutional courts aside, authority cannot be surrendered without the explicit consent of each tier, which assures the constitutional equality of the interacting governments. In this sense, federal systems—in contrast to decentralized unions—realize the strictest form of vertical power-dispersion, which should strengthen the position of state and regional governments in federal–state interaction (Elazar, 1993; Watts, 1998, 1999a; Thorlakson, 2003). At the same time, whether the unilateral withdrawal (or re-centralization) of Scottish competences by the U.K. government or of Catalan competences by the Spanish government is feasible in practice is very doubtful.[4] Although this issue is so far unresolved, the trend towards decentralization and regionalization of formally unitary systems observed over the last decades pushes us to move beyond constitutionally fully federalized regimes when putting the literature on American sub-national politics into comparative perspective.

What will become clear in the later analysis is that the constitutional status of sub-units in federal systems is often linked to a symmetrical competence distribution among them, which, in turn, creates a stronger tendency on behalf of scholars to perceive state governments as forming a part of one governmental level. This analytical perspective is much more prominent in the federalism literature—and with it in work on American sub-national politics—than in the literature on decentralizing or devolved unitary systems. In the latter settings, the various regional governments, depending on their respective (mainly cultural) distinctiveness, have been often treated differently by the central government, leading to a scholarly approach that naturally pays more attention to the distinctiveness of individual sub-units.

Having narrowed down the realm of the "sub-national" for the purpose of this chapter, a few remarks need to be made regarding the understanding of "politics", since its understanding defines the core actors we will look at in the following sections. This chapter takes an institutional perspective focusing on those state or regional actors—be they the whole government units or sub-units acting within them—that are formally involved in the making of collectively binding decisions within a state and regional government or across several levels of government. It concentrates on the working of processes ("politics") within state and regional governments but also within the multi-level system as a whole, which is inevitably shaped by the nature of the constitutional setting, the "polity." One final restriction needs mentioning: this chapter deliberately remains in the realm of fully consolidated (federal, decentralized or devolved) democracies. Sub-national politics is an increasingly important field of study in research on new democracies, transition systems, semi-democracies, or non-democratic regimes (e.g., Wibbels, 2005; Eaton, 2006; Landry, 2008; Falleti, 2010, 2011). Still, while being interested in the jurisdictional allocation of powers and its potential impact on multi-level dynamics and, more particularly, how the study of American sub-national dynamics (evidently embedded in a long-lived democratic setting) compares to dynamics in other systems, it is useful to focus on those contexts, in which adherence to constitutional norms can be reasonably assumed.

Based on these first demarcations, the following section presents two basic dimensions along which the literature on sub-national politics can be systematized, which will lead to a matrix allowing us to highlight existing caveats in the literature and, simultaneously, to put the work on American sub-national politics in a comparative context.

Distinguishing Perspectives on Sub-National Politics

Of the two dimensions that are used in the following to systematize the literature on sub-national politics, the first captures the *substantive focus* of the research capturing *the way in which the individual state or regional government is conceptualized or approached.* The second dimension specifies the research's *methodological focus*, either looking at *one particular case in depth or engaging in analyses comparing several cases* (which can be several state or regional governments, several arrangements of regional cooperation, or the horizontal dynamics in several federal systems, for instance). While - in principle - analytically independent from each other, these two dimensions are often intertwined, which is why the assessment of their interplay helps us to show how and why certain research themes tend to be more prominent, while others remain relatively neglected.

Conceptualizing Governments as Self-Contained or as Embedded Entities

A state or regional government can be conceptualized as *a self-contained polity* or conceptualized as *embedded units within a multi-layered polity*, i.e., a system composed of several governments each of which possesses its own legislative competences and can generate its own answers to some of the policy problems it faces. One might label the two outlooks as state and regional governments as "political systems" vs. state and regional governments as "constituent parts". Choosing the first perspective, we would perceive California as a political system in its own right and mainly focus on its internal working (e.g., the interaction between the governor and the state legislature) and how various processes changed over time (e.g., Turner and Vieg, 1967; Cluver and Syer, 1980; Field, 2010). We would be less concerned with California's position in the American federal system, its vertical relations to the federal government, or its horizontal relations to other state governments, issues becoming more relevant once choosing the second perspective: California as one state among several embedded in a multi-level structure. Clearly, state and regional governments are by definition *embedded entities within a composite polity* next to other state or regional units facing a central level of government. Yet depending on the analytical perspective scholars choose, this fact is stressed more strongly rather than left aside. A perspective focusing on the embeddedness of state and regional governments leads us to analyze its mode of interaction with other government units or levels and their consequences for the overall working of the system, which brings us to the sphere of intergovernmental relations (IGR). This field of study has been particularly prominent within federalism studies but is increasingly important for the study of decentralized and devolved systems as well, reflecting a trend towards regional empowerment across a range of Western democracies (Hooghe et al., 2010). In both literatures the working relations between governments embedded in an overall constitutional architecture are essential for the understanding of these systems' working and evolution.

Within the literature that approaches state and regional governments as embedded units, we can make a further distinction. Federalism research has tended to look at all state governments in a system and how they generally position themselves in a particular federal system *as one "governmental level"* that faces the federal or central government as a counter-player. The less prominent alternative—compared to the systemic perspective just mentioned—is to look at *regionally restricted forms of cooperation* involving different subsets of state or regional governments.

Perceiving state governments as part of one level brings us to the question of pressures towards (de)centralization and how they are handled in different multi-level polities, implying a focus on vertical dynamics. Research on American federalism is exemplary for this, with a large literature on the driving forces of competence centralization and decentralization across levels of governments. The perspective on state governments as part of one overall sub-governmental level can, in principle, be equally applied to the study of horizontal coordination of policies across sub-national boundaries directed towards collective problem-solving which not necessarily presupposes central-level involvement. Yet research on American federalism has paid comparatively little attention to these horizontal dynamics, which is representative of the wider literature on constitutionally federal systems. While having shown relatively little interest in horizontal coordination processes, it further tends to approach multi-level dynamics from the perspective of the "center", i.e., the federal government as opposed to the "lower level."

Moving to the analysis of regionally based cooperation, this perspective tends to be narrower in its empirical scope than the systemic perspective just introduced, as far as it looks at less inclusive forms of cooperation among a subset of state and regional governments (including bilateral and multilateral arrangements) that are often driven by socioeconomic or cultural similarities between subunits embedded in the same multi-level system. At the same time it can be broader since these forms of regional cooperation are not necessarily contained within the boundaries of nation states (e.g., Hocking, 1999; Scott, 1999; Blatter, 2001; Perkmann, 2003, 2007). Given similar challenges of border regions, for instance, they might be more likely cooperation partners than state or regional governments belonging to the same constitutional system which face very different challenges.

In analytical terms, both these perspectives consider the embeddedness of state and regional governments and start out from the similarities between several of these governments. Yet—depending on the perspective taken—the nature of these similarities is different, which makes it worthwhile to distinguish the two. The *systemic perspective* looks at similarities and shared problems resulting from a shared constitutional or formal-legal status in the same multi-level system (i.e., which determines units' belonging to the same governmental level), while the *regionalist perspective* looks at a broader range of more "substantive" similarities (e.g., social, socioeconomic, environmental, cultural, or linguistic) that can underlie cooperation. This difference, in turn, is one reason why works taking a systemic perspective have a stronger tendency to focus on vertical relations with the higher level. The regional cooperation perspective, in contrast, more naturally leads to a consideration of horizontal relations.

Consequently, we end up with three different strands of research, defined by their substantive focus. Naturally they overlap to some extent and are inevitably simplifications of varieties of research forming part of a large body of literature on sub-national politics. Nonetheless, they are helpful for capturing the different ways researchers have approached different aspects of sub-national politics, especially once we simultaneously consider the methodological perspectives with which they tend to go hand in hand. The first strand corresponds to what is commonly called the country or case-study literature in comparative politics consisting of in-depth analyses of particular polities, which might be labeled as *polity-centered perspective considering state and regional governments as self-contained entities*. As we can analyze France and Italy as political systems, so we can analyze Texas, Bavaria or Catalonia. Naturally, equivalence of national and sub-national polities is most pronounced when comparing national polities with state governments that have their own constitutions, constitutionally guaranteed powers (that cannot be withdrawn unilaterally by the center) and have their own national identities (e.g. Flanders). Furthermore, while the level of interdependence between the constitutive governments of federal or devolved systems seems particularly intense when compared to the interdependence between nation states in the international arena, this is only a difference in degree. In an age of globalization national democracies can hardly be considered as independent units (Börzel, 2001; Lazar et al., 2003), although comparative cross-national research tends to make this assumption implicitly or explicitly (Mair,

1996). At the same time, regional governments—especially in pluri-national federations – aspire to maintain their own diplomatic relations with foreign powers, traditionally considered as a prerogative of the 'national level' (e.g. Wyn Jones and Royles, 2012). While both the second and third strand perceive state and regional governments as embedded units, the *systemic perspective* on sub-national politics looks at governments as part of a governmental level, while a *regionalist perspective* puts more emphasis on the 'actorness' of individual governments shaping cooperation, cooperation that ranges from bilateral ad hoc agreements between regional governments within the same system to long-lasting interstate arrangements traveling across national borders.

Which Type of Comparison?

The second ordering dimension looks at whether research focuses on one particular case or engages in an analysis of several cases or settings. Mirroring the substantive dimension just introduced, these can be state or regional governments, arrangements of regional cooperation, or multi-level systems composed of state and regional governments. "Case" is understood here as the empirical unit of reference which is targeted by an analysis (which is not necessarily the same as the unit of analysis in terms of research design).[5] Depending on the substantive perspectives chosen, we will see that either *case-specific studies* or *comparisons across cases* tend to be more or less prominent.

Table 38.1 shows a six-field matrix defined by the distinctions introduced so far. Looking within each analytical category, we find most work located in categories A1, B1, and C1 respectively, works that focus on one particular case. In the single-case-study category A1, for instance, we find a wide range of work assessing the current working of a system in depth or assessing its internal changes over time. How intensely specific state

Table 38.1 Three Perspectives on Sub-national Politics

Substantive focus	Methodological perspective	
	Single case assessment or within-case comparisons	Comparisons across cases
Polity-centered perspective (governments as self-contained actor)	A1	A2
Systemic perspective (dynamics in systems composed of governments)	B1	B2
Regionalist perspective (relations between several governments)	C1	C2

Source: Developed by the author.

and regional governments are studied *as self-contained polities* (A1) tends to depend on their importance (size, formal power) and their distinctiveness (culturally or linguistically) within the setting in which they operate.

When conceptualizing state and regional governments as *embedded units*, we find work looking at bilateral or multilateral relations between (often neighboring) state or regional governments (C1 and C2), reflecting a regionalist perspective. So far, we find relatively little work comparing several arrangements of regional cooperation (C2). Being interested in how sub-national politics shape the macro dynamics of a polity, we look at the state or regional level of government—its internal dynamics (horizontal) or its relation to the federal government (vertical)—to capture a federal or decentralized polity's overall dynamics (B1 and B2). While we find numerous works taking a systemic perspective both with a focus on one or several federal, decentralized or devolved systems, there is less work on horizontal coordination (B1 and B2). This is because state and regional governments are analyzed as part of a sub-national 'level of government', with little scholarly attention to this level's 'internal life' (Benz, 2004), a tendency that is particularly pronounced in the literature on U.S. federalism and IGR, with its strong focus on vertical interaction (Trench, 2006).

THREE PERSPECTIVES ON SUB-NATIONAL POLITICS: VIRTUES AND CAVEATS

In the following section each of the three substantive perspectives is laid out in greater detail, contrasting case-oriented with cross-case comparisons, which will help us to highlight certain caveats the various literatures have produced and, more particularly, place the diverse literature on American sub-national politics in a comparative context.

The Polity-Centered Perspective

National democracies are considered as natural building blocks of comparative politics research (Mair, 1996). To each of them a considerable country literature is dedicated, irrespective of a country's relative distinctiveness.[6] Taking a polity-centered perspective on state and regional governments, in contrast, tends to be driven by the relative specificity of the case chosen, relative to the other sub-national governments in their respective system. It therefore lends itself less to comparisons across cases than the other two substantive strands, although we find some work in the area of multi-national federations, for instance on the recruitment patterns of regional elites in multi-national systems, that engages in comparisons of similarly specific and culturally distinct regional governments in their respective settings—e.g., Scotland and Catalonia (Stolz, 2010). While in the U.S. range of case-study literature on individual "state polities" tends to grow with the size and economic power of the state—think of Texas or California (e.g., Cluver and Syer, 1980; Field, 2010; Halter, 2010)—in pluri-national systems it is more strongly related to the cultural distinctiveness of the regional government, which is often reflected in constitutional arrangements that privilege these governments over other regional governments operating in the same system—think of Catalonia, Scotland, or Quebec (Agranoff, 1999; Swenden, 2006).

As insightful as this literature concentrating on one sub-national polity is, not the least because it provides an important building block for any wider comparative study, it is not unusual that such studies are inductive and do not put forward an explicit theoretical framework.[7] The use of distinct concepts and measures often prevents us from integrating findings of different studies and thereby arriving at more widely applicable conclusions. Starting out from an assumption of distinctiveness of an individual sub-national polity, the question of comparability to other cases seems to be less relevant from the start. In the U.S. literature, where the states are culturally relatively less distinct (compared to multilingual federations, for instance), we find few theory-driven small-N comparisons to explore states' internal dynamics in greater depth. Comparative (mostly quantitative) studies that include all states tend to focus on one specific institutional element instead, e.g., the composition (Sanbonmatsu, 2002) or professionalization of state legislatures (e.g., Moncrief, 1994; Moncrief et al., 1996, 2004) or the distinct nature of state parties (e.g., Jewell and Olson 1978; Jewell and Morehouse, 2000; for a cross-national comparison, see Thorlakson, 2009). An increasingly prominent strand in cross-national research engages in the study of regional parties and partisan dynamics at the sub-national level. This literature often takes a systemic point of view and looks at the implications of party-political incongruence within and across government levels for the working of the system as a whole, either focusing on one case (e.g., Lehmbruch, 1978; Swenden, 2002) or several federal systems (e.g., Scharpf, 1995; Downs 1998; Bolleyer and Bytzek 2009). Given the institutionally fragmented nature of the American system and the organizational weakness of political parties (Katz and Kolodny, 1994; Fiorina, 2002), government units are not internally integrated by political parties and therefore not predominantly divided by party-political conflict as in other federal systems (Bolleyer, 2011). As a consequence, party-political incongruence is less looked at from a systemic perspective, while polity-centered work is more prominent. Accordingly, we find insightful comparative studies on how the party-political orientation of governor and legislatures shapes the law-making process or the ideological leaning of state legislation (e.g., Berry et al., 1998; for an overview, see Moncrief et al., 1996).

More generally, taking a polity-centered perspective, while opting for an explicitly comparative approach (i.e., including wider range or all state or regional governments), can open up fascinating possibilities for combining methodological rigor with case-specific knowledge (for the systematic coverage of several American states, see Gray and Eisinger (1991), Dye (1985), and Jacob and Vines (1965); on other federal systems, see Vatter (2002) and Dyck (1986)). In more general terms, comparative work on sub-national politics can help us to cope with methodological problems, most notably of having a too small N and too many variables. The systematic examination of institutional differences across state or regional governments operating in the same system increases our capacity to control for alternative influences (Snyder, 2001).

The Systemic Perspective

State and regional governments, even though formally belonging to the same "governmental level," do not necessarily have identical competences, although in federal systems a rather symmetrical competence distribution across the various subunits is relatively common. In decentralized unions—that are often pluri-national (i.e., sub-national units are culturally diverse)—asymmetry occurs more frequently (Agranoff, 1999). Despite these differences, these two types of regime have in common that their allocation of competences is inherently dynamic (Benz and Broschek, 2013). Competences can be moved from one level to the other, if they cannot be handled efficiently at the level to which they are assigned. Accordingly, a considerable strand in federalism research deals with the question of how far federal systems have centralized or decentralized over time and why, be it against the opposition of or in agreement with sub-national governments, be it through formal federal reform or the reallocation of competences through judicial review (Filippov et al., 2004; Behnke and Benz, 2009; Benz and Broschek, 2013).

The literature that looks at federal dynamics in the U.S. setting is impressive, yet characterized by a variety of conceptualizations and measures of (de)centralization that makes a final judgement about the state of the system and its development over time difficult (e.g., Milton, 1984; Elazar, 1990, 1991; Conlan, 2006). This situation calls for more work that combines a variety of indicators to capture different dimensions of (de)centralization (e.g., fiscal and jurisdictional), separates measures of decentralization from those of interdependence and puts the U.S. in a cross-national perspective (Rodden, 2004; Bolleyer and Thorlakson, 2012). To understand the dynamics of multi-level systems more generally is particularly relevant since in a range of unitary systems, a reverse process has been observed, whereby regional governments were empowered as a response to regional-nationalist demands or attempts to make government more efficient to bring it closer to the people (Agranoff, 2004; Hooghe et al. 2010).

Both observations—centralizing tendencies in federal systems and the decentralization (or in some cases federalization) of unitary states—highlight that systems that allocate competences to several governments are by definition dynamic rather than static, or, in other words, inherently unstable. The conceptualization of the evolution of federal and multi-level systems in the context of a cross-nationally applicable framework still poses a major challenge and the question whether these dynamics are predominantly driven by constitutional, institutional, party-political, or cultural factors has remained a major debate for decades (e.g., Riker, 1964; Gunlicks, 1988; Watts, 1999b; Chhibber and Kollman, 2004; Thorlakson, 2003, 2007, 2009; Benz and Broschek, 2013).

Particularly, works with an exclusive focus on one system or setting risk producing certain biases. Just to mention one example in the study of U.S. federalism: Cammisa (1995) examined the influence of American intergovernmental arrangements such as the National Governors' Association on federal legislation. An opening statement of her study asserts that the implementation function assigned to the states has, as a consequence, led to a second function of state governments as constituents for federal programs, rather than making them autonomous legislators of their own (a role one might assign to the states looking at the constitutionally defined distribution of competences). This second function that is driven by the specificities of policies (not by the exercise (and protection) of state legislative power more generally) defines the nature of state governments in the American system and finds expression in an array of intergovernmental arrangements representing institutional roles (e.g., the governors, the legislators, all kinds of public officials) rather than the states as coherent governmental actors (Camissa, 1995: 1). Unlike premier and ministerial conferences in other federal systems such as in Canada, Switzerland, or Germany, which can speak for a group of states or regional governments and engage in negotiations with the federal government leading to political agreements on policies, the governors cannot speak or act on behalf of the states (Beyle and Muchmore, 1983). In fact, none of the governors could effectively bind his or her state legislature to an intergovernmental agreement as a Canadian premier could, which is why the National Governors' Association, as with most other intergovernmental bodies operating in the U.S., concentrates on lobbying. The fragmentation of the intergovernmental arena into numerous intergovernmental arrangements that operate like interest groups is perceived as "natural development," in no need of explanation. Following Cammisa, the federal system has become circular: since federal programs are implemented by state and local governments, the latter (in the form of multiple specialist associations) lobby federal legislation (Cammisa, 1995: 1; see also Haider, 1974; Arnold and Plant, 1994; Wolpe and Levine 1996).[8]

Although the metaphor of circularity might indeed capture dominant federal–state dynamics in the U.S., if one takes a comparative perspective, one recognizes that state and regional governments in many other federal countries have major—or nearly exclusive—responsibilities for policy implementation (Bolleyer and Thorlakson, 2012). Despite similar starting conditions in terms of the allocation of powers, intergovernmental bodies have still not developed along similar institutional or functional lines into interest groups as they did in U.S. federalism.[9] Accordingly, the nature of American IGR and, with it, the nature of U.S. sub-national politics as far as the role of the states in the federal arena is concerned, is far from representative for IGR in other federal systems, in which sub-national executives, individually and collectively, can negotiate with (not lobby) the federal government over issues of shared concern on behalf of their governments.

Sbragia (2006) has rightly emphasized that in order to understand U.S. federalism we need to consider state governments in their dual role as independent decision-makers and as implementors. Starting from here, we need to ask why U.S. state governments have set up—at least from a comparative viewpoint—intergovernmental structures with a very specific functional orientation that are untypical for most long-lived federal and decentralized democracies. In any case, we cannot consider this functional orientation as "natural" side-effect of their implementation responsibilities. Considered from a comparative perspective, the states' weakness—states which, according to Riker, never act as one unit against the center (1964: 103–4) but instead engage in lobby activities like any other interest group—turns into a puzzle, a puzzle easily overlooked from within the American politics literature.[10]

This is not to say that such empirical characterizations are "wrong," but that puzzles easily turn into "blind spots" that remain uncontested and thus unanalyzed when exclusively approached from "within" a country-specific literature. This also means that the micro dynamics underlying the "normal" or "typical" macro dynamics of a specific federal setting remain often under-explored, which sheds light on the need to assess the 'actorness' of state and regional governments (Hocking, 1999) or, as might be more appropriate in the U.S. case, the lacking actorness of state governments. The American states are characterized by their inability to act in a coherent manner and, unlike regional and state governments in other systems, best understood as internally fragmented units that do not speak with one coherent voice (either individually or collectively). Accordingly, they are represented by a multitude of institutionally and functionally defined associations that pursue partially overlapping but also contradictory interests.

One remarkable feature of American IGR is the separate organization of governors and legislatures, the National Governors Association and the National Council of State Legislatures. One source of the peculiar nature of American IGR as compared to other long-lived democracies lies indeed in the institutional divide between executives and legislatures. This divide remains un-bridged by party political ties, even if we find the same party dominating both branches, since parties as organizations are weak (Katz and Kolodny, 1994; Fiorina, 2002). There are natural limits to cooperation between executives and legislators. While both branches were originally organized in the Council of State Governments (which still exists as an umbrella organization today, but is mainly a support structure), first the governors and then the legislators split to form their own associations to pursue their particular interests.

Due to their different interest profiles, the NGA and the NCLS pursue different strategies. This discrepancy becomes particularly evident when central interference in state jurisdictions is concerned. Governors tend to be less concerned by federal pre-emption as far as the federal policy benefits the states and facilitates the delivery of services on the state level, while legislatures show more explicit opposition towards central interference into state jurisdictions. Both associations argue to defend state autonomy but their understanding of autonomy is shaped by their institutional outlooks. This is different from systems composed of parliamentary governments, where executives and legislative majorities form a unit of action, which inevitably shapes their operation in IGR. This implies less power for the legislatures "on their own" but means that executives identify with the interest of protecting legislative autonomy.[11] Governors and state legislatures are distanced further since legislators deal with a wide range of issues. Executives tend to specialize more, supported by a range of policy experts in their administrations, which also means the latter tend to be superior in expertise, making them the more interesting point of contact for federal officials.

These observations lead us back to the more general features of the "systemic perspective" on sub-national politics: its focus on the "vertical axis" and on cross-level interaction. The horizontal interaction between state and regional governments has been studied much less. This is partially rooted in how we approach multi-level systems conceptually. Hooghe and Marks, for instance, identify the "individual government" as the core unit in federal governance, while defining the latter as a governance system composed of "levels" (2003: 236–7). As a consequence, the internal dynamics of the levels themselves are rarely looked at as an explanatory factor (e.g., Kelemen, 2004). Arrangements for horizontal cooperation, however, crucially shape the capacity of sub-national governments to push for shared interests against the federal government and to engage in policy coordination. Since centralization is accelerated by the incapacity of state governments to fight off central interference collectively and to coordinate policy without central support, to understand the macro dynamics of a federal system in the longer term, we need to go beyond the study of vertical relations only.

This is particularly important with regard to the literature on U.S. federalism. Paradoxically, the evaluations of American federalism in the literature are extremely diverse and, at the same time, very uniform. While the model of dual federalism is considered inadequate to describe processes of federal interaction, it is still less clear what could reasonably replace this approach. Scholars like Elazar (1990, 1991) have argued that "cooperative federalism" is the framework that provides for the best account of the existing pattern of intense interaction; others have observed a shift towards a more "coercive cooperation" due to the growing dominance of central funding and federal pre-emption (Grodzins, 1966; Conlan, 2006; Kincaid, 1990, 2003). Since there is wide agreement that due to its heavy constitutional fragmentation American IGR is an inherently difficult phenomenon to study (Wright, 1982; O'Toole, 2000), debates circle around the specification of periods characterized by particular (predominantly vertical) interaction patterns instead of identifying enduring features of American IGR per se (for an exception, see Derthick, 2001).

Ironically, the perceived diversity and variability of IGR did not lead to a similarly broad variety of perspectives. Work on American IGR tends to focus overwhelmingly on federal grants and the implications of conditions attached to them and the study of fiscal federalism (Trench, 2006: 228; see, for instance, Nathan and Lago, 1990; Tannenwald and Cowan, 1997; Rodden, 2006). The latter is only one component of the vertical dimension of American federalism, however. Similar patterns appear in more specific analyses of state lobbying in the federal arena, already referred to, which distinguish phases of intergovernmental lobbying according to the dominant interplay between states' fiscal dependency and federal activism (Haider, 1974; Cammisa, 1995: 117). Work on the horizontal dimension, i.e., interstate relations, is relatively rare (Gray, 1973; Zimmerman, 1990, 2001, 2002; Bowman, 2002, 2004).

Although this tendency to neglect U.S. interstate relations, to some extent, reflects the vertical orientation of actors in this system, we find similar tendencies in the study of other federal systems. Sub-national politics, i.e., the behavior of state and regional governments, is predominantly studied with regard to the central government, while the internal life of the horizontal axis is explored comparatively little (but see Benz, 2004; Bolleyer, 2009).[12] This brings us back to the tendency in the U.S. literature to consider the states as a naturally inferior level of government that is further weakened due to its status as an intermediary tier facing not only a strong center but also powerful local governments (Wright, 1982). This tendency, however, is less pronounced in works taking a regionalist perspective on sub-national politics, to which we turn in the following section.

The Regionalist Perspective

Throughout the last decades, governments in federal systems such as the U.S. and international multi-level settings such as the European Union have been increasingly confronted with boundary-crossing problems. Accordingly, the interaction density between government units has steadily increased throughout the last decades (see, among others, Börzel, 2001, 2002; Lazar et al., 2003; Sbragia, 2006). Governments have responded to these growing interdependencies and the regionalist perspective on sub-national politics looks at how sub-national governments attempt to solve collective problems through non-hierarchical arrangements (i.e., thereby preventing the centralization of competences) (Bolleyer and Börzel, 2010). This literature is particularly interesting since it nicely links the comparative politics literature to work on international relations. This is especially the case because we find arrangements of regional cooperation across national borders. Attempts of sub-national governments to create shared horizontal institutions to solve problems that transcend their individual jurisdictions (without compromising their formal power) are equivalent to the problems nation states face when creating supra-national regimes and international organizations (Scharpf, 1997). In both constellations the involvement of an external enforcer of collective agreements is either not feasible or rejected by the coordination partners.

The extent to which governments in such situations try to act in an autonomous manner and protect their individual share of power (rather than engage in horizontal cooperation to solve a problem collectively) is an output of the interplay of constitutional, fiscal, political, and cultural aspects. It is not a constitutive element of the co-existence of multiple governments as is sometimes assumed in studies focusing on the pluri-national federations (e.g., Lecours, 2004). State and regional governments in some systems might prefer to set up strong intergovernmental structures that facilitate mutual exchange and thereby voluntarily reduce their degree of individual independence or autonomy; others might try to minimize any coordination with other units to maximize their leeway. Intergovernmental competition is not the natural outcome of a federal constitution (Chapman, 1993: 75–6; Heinmiller, 2002). This is noteworthy because the reference to "de facto independence" or "autonomy" in some definitions of federalism (see, for instance, Wheare 1951; for an overview of conceptions, see Thorlakson (2003); for an overview of measures, see Rodden (2004)) already implies an orientation towards autonomy protection, and hence competition across governments. What studies on regionally based cooperation show is that competition is only one end of the behavioral continuum that sub-national actors can engage in—cooperation is the other. To explain the dominant orientation of actors and to capture the relative conflict between actors' individual strategic interests and their orientation towards collective problem-solving is thus a major challenge in this strand of the literature.

Accordingly, the "regionalist strand" of the literature can be divided into theoretical work dealing with questions of coordination and cooperation within and across sub-national governments (Scharpf, 1997, 2001; Peters, 1998) and work assessing individual cooperation arrangements between sub-national governments in one or more political system in depth (e.g., Gage, 1992; Blatter, 2001; Grees, 1996; Trees, 2005; Scott, 1999; Savoie, 2003). The former has not been developed to assess regional cooperation in particular, yet belongs in this category due to its focus on the solution of shared problems the participants (in our case state and regional governments) are interested in solving collectively through voluntary cooperation. The scope of this non-hierarchical cooperation depends on the respective preference configuration and political orientations of interaction units, which gives cooperation arrangements an immense variety, ranging from competitive relations, unilateral adaptation, and ad-hoc coordination to the voluntary negotiation and ratification of mutually binding horizontal agreements (e.g., Peters, 1998; Peters and Pierre, 2001; Opeskin, 2001; Kenyon and Kincaid, 1991; Metcalfe, 1994, 1997; Scharpf, 2001). These works can be further divided into those assuming governments to behave in a problem-oriented and rationalist manner when engaging in coordination (e.g., Scharpf, 1997, 2001; Metcalfe, 1994, 1997) and those that stress the potential discrepancies between government capacity and political will, as well as short-term political and long-term policy benefits, which account for the choice of inefficient strategies in horizontal sub-national interaction in particular institutional settings (e.g., Benz, 2004; Peters, 1998; Skogstad, 2000; Bolleyer and Börzel, 2010). Another dividing line lies in the purpose of coordination: while the strand assuming governments to be driven by problem-solving focuses on policy coordination, the strand that more strongly considers the political constraints governments face also considers the arrangements for strategic position-taking or lobbying already alluded to when discussing the systemic perspective on sub-national politics.

Returning to particular cases, when approaching cooperation structures from a "systemic perspective," we focus on the National Governors Association (Haider, 1974), the Canadian Council of the Federation (Simmons, 2004; Simeon, 2005), or the Swiss Cantonal Conference of Executives (Vatter, 2002; Trees, 2005). In part, those bodies engage in horizontal policy coordination as well, yet unlike regional arrangements each is defined by the formal status of its members, who together constitute the regional level of government in the overall polity. Regional cooperation, in contrast, is more problem-specific and is often underpinned by cultural or socioeconomic similarities between the members, which implies a higher level of preference homogeneity as one precondition for non-hierarchical coordination. Unlike nationwide intergovernmental arrangements, regionalist arrangements are not defined in terms of formal-legal characteristics, giving them a greater striking variety, which is why comparative work across a range of settings or even within the same systemic context is relatively rare.[13]

The setting-up of regional arrangements can be triggered by the feeling that the interests of the particular region are not considered sufficiently in nationwide bodies to give regional interests an effective voice. Looking at multinational federations such as Switzerland, we find that the French-speaking cantons organized at the regional level because they perceived the Conference of Cantonal Executives (which includes representatives of all cantons and, in principle, is the collective voice of all of them) as "German-dominated." In a similar vein, the Maritime and the Western premiers in Canada set up their own council to prevent their regions being disadvantaged in nationwide negotiations.

Most of these bodies, however, also serve as a forum to address substantive problems concerning the regions and engage with different intensities in the coordination of policy. In fact, in most federal systems most horizontal policy coordination takes place on a regional scale, handled by regional bodies rather than by nationwide arrangements. Although transaction costs to coordinate this are lower, if fewer governments participate, the greater homogeneity of preferences due to regional similarities is likely to play a role as well. The reasons why governments operating in the same setting engage in these processes more or less often are wide-ranging, yet several studies point to the relevance of the size of state or regional units and their proximity, intensifying spillover effects from one jurisdiction to the other (e.g., Nice, 1987; Bowman, 2002, 2004; Bochsler, 2006). Naturally, coordination intensity differs across policy areas, one important aspect being how legislative power is assigned to the regional level, which differs from one policy area to the other. Yet while the allocation of exclusive competences to the state and regional governments is usually expected to minimize coordination pressure (Thorlakson, 2003), this is more convincing vertically—with regard to regional–central coordination—than horizontally, with regard to the coordination among state and regional governments. If whole blocks of competences are assigned to the state and regional level, horizontal spillover effects are likely to be much more intense, which shows, for instance, in the relative level of institutionalization of policy-specific intergovernmental bodies that facilitate coordination between ministers or administrators in charge of particular policy areas. Everything being equal, horizontal institutionalization of IGR is strengthened by a wide range of legislative competences rather than weakened (Bolleyer, 2009). Naturally the types of conflict dominating the policy field play a role as well, leading us back to Lowi's seminal work distinguishing redistributive, distributive, and regulative types of policy (1964). Naturally, if interstate coordination has heavy redistributive implications across the jurisdictions involved, voluntary coordination between the latter is easily undermined (Scharpf, 1997).

Returning to the U.S., we find numerous regional branches of the major state associations: the National Governors' Association (NGA), [14] the National Council of State Legislatures (NCSL),[15] and the umbrella organization the Council of State Governments (CSG).[16] Legislative and executive bodies that are active within the same region reproduce the national divide between the NGA and NCSL, characterized by the separate lobbying activities described earlier, but simply operating on a smaller scale. Again, unlike intergovernmental bodies in other countries, they focus on lobbying activities directed towards the federal government. Although they serve as platforms to exchange best practices that might support horizontal policy diffusion across state borders, what to adopt and what not, is not specified in any explicit agreements.

As far as the overall territorial dynamics are concerned, the interaction between nationwide and regionally based intergovernmental bodies tends to be more centrally dominated compared to processes in other federal systems in which state governments (in terms of formal competences and fiscal power) are similarly powerful, such as Canada or Switzerland. Regional associations in the U.S. remain in charge of an issue as long as the national association does not occupy it. Once this happens, they reorient their priorities, which is strikingly different from a division of labor between regionally based and national issues that exists in other systems. In the U.S., intergovernmental issues remain regional until a national body, such as the NGA, says they are national, which strikingly mirrors the interaction between Congress and the states as far as the definition of state competences is concerned (Crihfield and Reeves, 1974).

From a state perspective, intra-horizontal competition for influence on central decisions between an array of regional and national intergovernmental bodies naturally complicates efforts of horizontal policy coordination. Unlike lobbying, where each branch can engage separately, policy coordination across state boundaries regularly presupposes coordination between executive and legislature within each of the states, which often fails due to inter-branch rivalry. In this sense, the dominance of the federal government in IGR and the weakness of "horizontal federalism" are both generated by high levels of interstate and intrastate fragmentation and, on top of that, are mutually reinforcing: the disunity among the states in the coordination of state policy allows Congress to legitimize its own action within state jurisdiction, being able to justify such actions by highlighting the failure of the states 'to do the job by themselves' (Derthick, 2001: 38–39).

Yet while interstate relations tend to be difficult, this does not mean that policy coordination across the American states does not take place. If only due to capacity reasons, the federal government cannot handle any boundary-crossing problem that emerges on a regional basis. While the vertical dimension of American IGR is characterized by a focus on federal lobbying, interaction patterns and structures on the horizontal dimension are comparatively more diverse. Instruments for horizontal cooperation span a considerable continuum in terms of formalization, which brings us back to the variety of coordination modes specified by the theoretical literature. The most formal instrument of interstate agreement has constitutional status, requires ratification by state legislatures, and out-rules conflicting state legislation as long as in force. While being a reliable mechanism once in place (given the possibility of legal enforcement), executive–legislative divides (compulsory power-sharing) tend to undermine the cooperative interplay of the two branches. Their setting-up takes a long time and most of them are only joined by few states (Bowman, 2002, 2004). Furthermore, formal compact commissions that are set up to regulate certain policy rarely capture whole sectors (to keep concessions in terms of legislative authority limited) and are used infrequently since state legislatures are eager to protect their law-making power. Alternatives are mechanisms such as memoranda of understanding and ad hoc commissions that are set up by administrators that provide for more flexible pathways of interstate coordination (Zimmerman, 1990, 2001, 2002) up to a range of advisory bodies facilitating policy diffusion (e.g., by identifying model laws to encourage their adoption in other states, such as the CSG).

Stressing the importance of inter-branch divides, the less formal pathways are particularly attractive because they avoid legislative involvement ex ante, such as memoranda of understanding between governors, or, as in the case of diffusion, maintain individual legislative authority. Their reliability is, however, lower. Finally, despite this wide variety of mechanisms, we do not find political negotiations generating non-formal yet collectively binding agreements, as are often used in other multi-level systems, which gives American IGR an administrative rather than political character when compared to other federal systems.

CONCLUSION

American scholars have long argued that American state actors accepted the "realism of the administrative state" and cared less about competence distribution than about the "realities" of funding, implementation, and coalition-building around concrete programs (Arnold and Plant, 1994: 106; Wolpe and Levine, 1996). One crucial part of the "reality" which nourishes this acceptance is the unequal capacity of the two governmental levels to coordinate internally, a challenge that is much more pronounced for the American states than for parliamentary sub-national governments such as the Canadian provinces (Esman 1984). On the vertical dimension of American IGR, this coordination failure finds reflection in the states' division into various associations pursuing different institutional interests rather than unifying the states by articulating one shared state position. Similarly, horizontal interstate coordination is weakened by institutionally generated intrastate divides. The internal dynamics of state governments—that are more strongly shaped by institutional fragmentation than partisan cohesion—has been impressively projected outside state boundaries, fundamentally affecting the role of state governments can play in the American federal system. Taking a systemic perspective, American IGR is therefore less executive-dominated but more prone to centralization than systems in which state and regional governments are internally less divided and more capable of building a common front and assuring the horizontal coordination of policy without central support. It is an irony that, in U.S. federalism, where the state legislatures are most active as separate actors from their executives, state competences end up less protected than in a system such as Canada (Bolleyer, 2010). In Canada, provincial legislatures are, in effect, dominated by their executives. At the same time, provincial premiers, unlike U.S. governors, are closely tied to their legislative majorities and consider the protection of provincial powers as a core interest, while, as argued earlier, state governments and legislatures in the U.S. do not unite along these lines. While the U.S. stands out—particularly when compared to the mostly parliamentary federations among Western democracies—the source of the peculiarity of American sub-national politics can best be understood when approached from a cross-national perspective.

Naturally, the characterization of state legislatures as weak is more convincing from a systemic perspective than a polity-centered one. Looking at the role of legislatures *within* individual states and contrasting them with the power of provincial parliaments towards their executives, the latter are much more of a "rubber stamp" for executive initiatives than the former (Moncrief, 1994). This observation leads us back to the importance of being aware of the respective analytical perspectives on sub-national politics underlying existing work, work marked by a immense variety this chapter could only touch upon. The analytical perspective chosen inevitably shapes the findings we end up with, which is why future work on sub-national politics should attempt to bring the various traditions discussed in this chapter—each of which has its own advantages—closer together. By doing so, we can explore the specificities of American sub-national politics in a systematic manner and put them in a cross-national context, without taking them for idiosyncrasies.

Notes

1. Considering both the U.S. terminology as well as the terminology dominant in the comparative literature, state government and regional government are considered as equivalent terms referring to the governmental layer below the national and above the local.
2. To avoid ambiguity, throughout this chapter "government" refers to the whole governmental unit including executive, parliament or legislature, and judiciary, etc., and is not equivalent to the executive branch of government (as is quite frequently done in the literature).
3. "Decentralization" and "devolution" are used as equivalent terms.
4. With regard to the Spanish case, for instance, one might argue that the weakening or even the abolition of the Autonomous Communities (ACs) would be unacceptable from the point of view of citizens who strongly identify with their AC. Based on this line of reasoning, one can consider the Spanish system as "functionally equivalent" to a constitutionally federalized system because the co-existence of the federal government and the ACs-though not formally—is de facto constitutive of the Spanish polity (Moreno, 1999, 2000).
5. For instance, while the case referred to can be Scotland as a regional government, the unit of analysis might be the Scottish premier, whose position towards his legislature is comparatively assessed before and after U.K. devolution.
6. Although size and perceived importance on the world stage will lead to increased attention to particular nation states, we still find a large number of in-depth studies also of smaller, supposedly less important countries (especially in the language of the country).
7. Note that single case studies are not necessarily descriptive but can contribute to theory formation (Gerring, 2004).
8. In a similar vein, Krause and Bowman (2005: 364) start their analysis of the impact of partisan politics in U.S. federalism from the claim that a hierarchical perspective on policymaking in U.S. federalism is rooted in the Constitution. Therefore an examination of the

balance of intergovernmental policymaking power can be made looking at vertical relations only and can be exclusively based on the analysis of national-level decisions.

9. On Canadian IGR see Simeon (1972, 2001, 2005) and Lazar et al. (2003); on German IGR see Lehmbruch 1978; and Scharpf 1988; for comparative studies see Watts (1999), Braun (2000), and Bolleyer and Bytzek (2009).

10. Similar to the 'normality' of the states' deference to the center in the U.S., Swiss federalism tends to be labeled as "cooperative" (e.g., Braun, 2000; Vatter, 2002). As a regime, the Swiss system is regularly classified as the prototype of a consensus democracy. Research on consociational and consensus democracy has extensively analyzed polities whose basic logic is most fundamentally characterized by power-sharing and power-dispersion. The latter tendency is thought to apply to executive–legislative relations, corporatist structures, and IGR alike. Following Armingeon: "cooperative behaviour [in the federal arena] is stabilized by the surrounding fora of decision-making. Conflictual strategies in the federalist arena would be in sharp contrast to the style of decision-making in the remaining arenas" (2000: 124). Whilst the empirical characterization is convincing, this claim is not sufficiently specific: most fundamentally, it leaves implicit which mechanisms drive a positive spillover of internal power-sharing processes in the government units-often labeled as "consociationalism"—into the intergovernmental arena. In fact, the idea that different forms of power-sharing should reinforce each other is not self-evident, neither theoretically nor empirically. If this is so, we cannot conclude from the formation of oversized coalition governments (i.e., executive power-sharing) to cooperative inter-cantonal or cantonal-federal relations.

11. Accordingly, the nature of executive-legislative relations in state and regional governments helps us to account for levels of inter-parliamentary activism, i.e., attempts of legislatures to organize separately and counter executive dominance in IGR (Bolleyer, 2010).

12. This does not mean that we do not find a range of works on the American states. Those books, however, tend to take a polity-centered perspective. They are invaluable sources about the working of the states as political systems, but their internal dynamics and their horizontal interaction is rarely assessed with regard to the macro dynamics of American federalism or the American political system as a whole.

13. A fascinating area of study is the cooperation among border regions (Blatter 2001). Not only does this phenomenon cross-cut the subfields of comparative politics and international relations, it also presses us to bring together analytical perspectives developed in two relatively separate field to explore the same phenomenon.

14. These are Western Governors' Associations, the Midwest Governors' Conference, New England's Governors' Conference, Border Governors' Conference, Coalition of Northeastern Governors, Council of Great Lakes Governors, and Southern Governors' Association.

15. These are the NCSL Midwestern Region, Southern Region, Western Region, and Eastern Region.

16. These are the CSG-Midwest, CSG-South, CSG-East, and CSG-West. Note that, unlike the Council of the Federation in Canada (composed of the provincial premiers), the CSG cannot speak on behalf of the states as government units. Politically, the associations representing the branches are the more important actors in the intergovernmental arena, reflecting the institutional divisions shaping American IGR.

REFERENCES

Agranoff, Robert. 1999. *Accommodating Diversity: Asymmetry in Federal States*. Baden-Baden: Nomos.

Agranoff, Robert. 2004. "Autonomy, Devolution, and Intergovernmental Relations." *Regional and Federal Studies 14* (1): 26–65.

Armingeon, Klaus. 2000. "Swiss Federalism in Comparative Perspective." In U. Wachendorfer-Schmidt (ed.), *Federalism and Political Performance*. London: Routledge.

Arnold, David S. and Jeremy Plant. 1994. *Public Official Associations and State and Local Government*. Fairfax: George Mason University Press.

Behnke, Nathalie and Arthur Benz (eds.) 2009. The Politics of Constitutional Change between Reform and Evolution, Special Issue of *Publius: The Journal of Federalism* 39 (2).

Benz, Arthur (ed.). 2004. *Governance—Regieren in Komplexen Regelsystemen*. Wiesbaden: VS Verlag für Sozialwissenschaften.

Benz, Arthur and Jörg Broschek (eds.) 2013. *Federal Dynamics: Continuity, Change and the Varieties of Federalism*. Oxford: Oxford University Press

Berry, William D., Evan J. Ringquist, Richard C. Fording, and Russell L. Hanson. 1998. "Measuring Citizen and Government Ideology in the American States, 1960–93." *American Journal of Political Science 42* (1): 327–348.

Beyle, Thad L. and Lynn R. Muchmore (eds). 1983. *Being Governor: The View from the Office*. Durham: Duke Press Policy Studies.

Blatter, Joachim K. 2001. "Debordering the World of States: Towards a Multi-Level System in Europe and a Multi-Polity System in North America? Insights from Border Regions." *European Journal of International Relations 7* (2): 175–209.

Bochsler, Daniel. 2006. "Quantitative Analyse der Konkordate: Abkommen unter Nachbarn oder unter Freunden?" Working Paper. Geneva: Université de Genève.

Bolleyer, Nicole. 2009. *Intergovernmental Cooperation—Rational Choices in Federal Systems and Beyond*. Oxford: Oxford University Press.

Bolleyer, Nicole. 2010. "Why Legislatures Organise: Inter-Parliamentary Activism in Federal Systems and its Consequences." *Journal of Legislative Studies 16* (4): 411–437.

Bolleyer, Nicole. 2011. "Party Linkage and Policy Coordination." *Governance 24* (3): 467–492.

Bolleyer, Nicole and Tanja A. Börzel. 2010. "Non-Hierarchical Policy Coordination in Multi-level Systems." *European Political Science Review 2* (2): 157–185.

Bolleyer, Nicole and Evelyn Bytzek. 2009. "Conflict and Institutionalization in Intergovernmental Relations: A Comparative Assessment of Government Congruence in Six Countries." *Regional and Federal Studies 19* (3): 371–397.

Bolleyer, Nicole and Lori Thorlakson. 2012. "Beyond Decentralization: The Study of Interdependence in Federal Systems". *Publius: The Journal of Federalism 42* (4): 2012: 566–591.

Börzel, Tanja A. 2001. "Föderative Staaten in einer Entgrenzten Welt: Regionaler Standortwettbewerb oder Gemeinsames Regieren Jenseits des Nationalstaates." In A. Benz and G. Lehmbruch (eds), *Föderalismus. Analysen in Entwicklungsgeschichtlicher Perspektive, PVS Sonderheft 32*. Wiesbaden: Nomos.

Börzel, Tanja A. 2002. *States and Regions in the European Union: Institutional Adaptation in Germany and Spain*. Cambridge: Cambridge University Press.

Bowman, Ann O'M. 2002. "American Federalism on the Horizon." *Publius: The Journal of Federalism 32*: 3–22.

Bowman, Ann O'M. 2004. "Horizontal Federalism: Exploring Interstate Interaction." *Journal of Public Administration Research 14*: 535–546.

Braun, Dietmar. 2000. *Public Policy and Federalism*. Aldershot: Ashgate.

Cammisa, Anne M. 1995. *Governments as Interest Groups*. Westport: Praeger.

Chapman, Ralph J. K. 1993. "Structure, Process and the Federal Factor: Complexity and Entanglement in Federations." In M. Burgess and A.-G. Gagnon (eds), *Comparative Federalism and Federation: Competing Traditions and Future Directions*. New York: Harvester Wheatsheaf.

Chhibber, Pradeep K. and Ken Kollman. 2004. *The Formation of National Party Systems: Federalism and Party Competition in Canada, Great Britain, India, and the United States*. Princeton: Princeton University Press.

Cluver, John H. and John C. Syer. 1980. *Power and Politics in California*. New York: Wiley.

Conlan, Timothy J. 2006. "From Cooperative to Opportunistic Federalism: Reflections on the Half-Century Anniversary of the Commission on Intergovernmental Relations." *Public Administration Review 66* (5): 663–676.

Crihfield, Brevard and Clyde H. Reeves. 1974. "Intergovernmental Relations: A View from the States." *Annals of the American Academy of Political and Social Science 416*: 99–107.

Derthick, Martha. 2001. *Keeping the Compound Republic: Essays on Federalism*. Washington DC: Brookings.

Downs, William M. 1998. *Coalition Government Subnational Style: Multiparty Politics in Europe's Regional Parliaments*. Columbus: Ohio State University Press.

Dyck, Rand. 1986. *Provincial Politics in Canada*. Scarborough: Prentice Hall.

Dye, Thomas R. 1985. *Politics in States and Communities*. Englewood Cliffs: Prentice-Hall.

Eaton, Kent. 2006. "Decentralization's Nondemocratic Roots: Military Reforms of Subnational Governments in Latin America." *Latin American Politics and Society 48* (1): 1–26.

Elazar, Daniel S. 1990. "Opening the Third Century of American Federalism: Issues and Prospects." In J. Kincaid (ed.), *American Federalism: The Third Century*. Newbury Park: Sage.

Elazar, Daniel S. 1993. "International and Comparative Federalism". *PS: Political Science and Politics 26* (2): 190–195.

Elazar, Daniel S. 1991. "Cooperative Federalism." In D. A. Kenyon and K. Kincaid (eds.), *Competition Among States and Local Governments: Efficiency and Equity in American Federalism*. Washington DC: The Urban Institute Press.

Esman, Milton J. 1984. "Federalism and Modernization: Canada and the United States." *Publius: The Journal of Federalism 14* (1): 21–38.

Falleti, Tulia. 2010. *Decentralization and Subnational Politics in Latin America*. New York: Cambridge University Press.

Falleti, Tulia. 2011. "Varieties of Authoritarianism: The Organization of the Military State and its Effect on Federalism in Argentina and Brazil." *Studies in Comparative and International Development 46*: 137–142.

Field, Mona. 2010. *California Government and Politics Today*. New York: Longman.

Filippov, Mikhail, Peter C. Ordeshook, and Olga Shvetsova. 2004. *Designing Federalism, A Theory of Self-Sustainable Federal Institutions*. Cambridge: Cambridge University Press.

Fiorina, Morris P. 2002. "Parties and Partisanship: A 40-Years Retrospective." *Political Behavior 24* (2): 93–115.

Gage, Robert W. 1992. "Sector Alignments of Regional Councils: Implications for Intergovernmental Relations in the 1990s." *American Review of Public Administration 22* (3): 207–224.

Gerring, John. 2004. "What Is a Case Study and What Is it Good for?" *American Political Science Review* 98: 341–354.

Gray, Virginia. 1973. "Innovation in the States, A Diffusion Study." *American Political Science Review* 67: 1174–1185.

Gray, Virginia and Peter Eisinger. 1991. *American States and Cities*. New York: HarperCollins.

Grees, Franz. 1996. "Interstate Cooperation and Territorial Representation in Intermestic Politics." *Publius: The Journal of Federalism* 26 (1): 53–71.

Grodzins, Morton. 1966. *The American System: A New View of Government in the United States*. New Brunswick: Transaction Books.

Gunlicks, Arthur B. 1988. "Constitutional Law and the Protection of Subnational Governments in the United States and West Germany." *Publius: The Journal of Federalism* 18 (1): 141–158.

Haider, Donald H. 1974. *When Governments Go to Washington: Governors, Mayors and Intergovernmental Lobbying*. New York: The Free Press.

Halter, Gary M. 2010. *Government and Politics of Texas*. New York: McGraw-Hill.

Heinmiller, B. Timothy. 2002. "Finding a Way Forward in the Study of Intergovernmental Policy-Making." *Canadian Public Administration* 45 (3): 427–433.

Hocking, Brian. 1999. "Patrolling the 'Frontier': Globalization, Localization and the 'Actorness' of Non-Central Governments." In F. Aldecoa and M. Keating (eds), *Paradiplomacy in Action: The Foreign Relations of Subnational Governments*. London: Frank Cass.

Hooghe, Liesbet and Gary Marks. 2003. "Unraveling the Central State, but How?" *American Political Science Review* 97 (2): 233–243.

Hooghe, Liesbet, Gary Marks, and Arjan H. Schakel. 2010. *The Rise of Regional Authority: A Comparative Study of 42 Democracies (1950–2006)*. London: Routledge.

Jacob, H. and K. N. Vines. 1965. *Politics in the American States, A Comparative Analysis*. Boston and Toronto: Little, Brown and Company.

Jewell, Malcolm E. and Sarah M. Morehouse. 2000. *Political Parties and Elections in American States* (4th ed.). Washington DC: CQ Press.

Jewell, Malcolm E. and David M. Olson. 1978. *American State Political Parties and Elections*. Homewood, IL: The Dorsey Press.

Katz, Richard S. and Robin Kolodny. 1994. "Party Organizations as Empty Vessels: Parties in American Politics." In R. S. Katz and P. Mair (eds), *How Parties Organize: Change and Adaptation in Party Organizations in Western Democracies*. London: Sage.

Kelemen, R. Daniel. 2004. *The Rules of Federalism: Institutions and Regulatory Politics in Europe and Beyond*. Cambridge: Harvard University Press.

Kenyon, Daphne A. and John Kincaid (eds). 1991. *Competition among States and Local Governments: Efficiency and Equity in American Federalism*. Washington DC: The Urban Institute Press.

Kincaid, John. 1990. "From Cooperative to Coercive Federalism." In J. Kincaid (ed.), *American Federalism: The Third Century*. Newbury Park: Sage.

Kincaid, John. 2003. "Globalization and Federalism in the United States: Continuity in Adaptation." In H. Lazar, H. Telford, and R. L. Watts (eds), *The Impact of Global and Regional Integration on Federal Systems, A Comparative Analysis*. Montreal and Kingston: McGill-Queen's University Press.

Krause, George A. and Ann O'M. Bowman. 2005. "Adverse Selection, Political Parties, and Policy Delegation in the American Federal System." *The Journal of Law, Economics and Organization* 21 (2): 359–387.

Laffin, Martin and Alys Thomas. 1999. "The United Kingdom: Federalism in Denial?" *Publius: The Journal of Federalism* 29 (3): 89–107.

Landry, Pierre F. 2008. *Decentralized Authoritarianism in China: The Communist Party's Control of Local Elites in the Post-Mao Era*. New York: Cambridge University Press.

Lazar, Harvey, Hamish Telford, and Ronald L. Watts. 2003. "Divergent Trajectories: The Impact of Global and Regional Integration on Federal Systems." In H. Lazar, H. Telford, and R. L. Watts (eds.), *The Impact of Global and Regional Integration on Federal Systems, A Comparative Analysis*. Montreal and Kingston: McGill-Queen's University Press.

Lecours, André. 2004. "Moreno's Multiple Ethnoterritorial Concurrence Model: A Re-formulation." *Regional and Federal Studies* 14 (1): 66–88.

Lehmbruch, Gerhard. 1978. "Party and Federation in Germany: A Developmental Dilemma". *Government and Opposition* 13: 151–77.

Lowi, Theodore J. 1964. "American Business, Public Policy, Case-Studies, and Political Theory". *World Politics* 16 (4): 677–715.

Mair, Peter. 1996. "Comparative Politics: An Overview." In Robert E. Goodin and Hans-Dieter Klingemann (eds), *A New Handbook of Political Science*. Oxford: Oxford University Press.

Metcalfe, Les. 1994. "International Policy Co-ordination and Public Management Reform." *International Review of Administrative Sciences* 60: 271–290.

Metcalfe, Les. 1997. "Flexible Federalism." Paper presented at the conference on Civil Service Systems in Comparative Perspective, Indiana University, Bloomington, Indiana. April 1997.

Moncrief, Gary F. 1994. "Professionalization and Careerism in Canadian Provincial Assemblies: Comparison to U.S. State Legislatures." *Legislative Studies Quarterly* 19 (1): 33–48.

Moncrief, Gary F., Richard Niemi, and Lynda Powell. 2004. "Time, Term Limits and Turnover: Trends in Membership Turnover in U.S. State Legislatures." *Legislative Studies Quarterly* 29: 357–382.

Moncrief, Gary, F., J. Thompson, and W. Cassie. 1996. "Revisiting the State of U.S. State Legislative Research." *Legislative Studies Quarterly* 21: 301–336.

Moreno, Luis. 1999. "Asymmetry in Spain: Federalism in the Making?" In R. Agranoff (ed.), *Accomodating Diversity in Federal States*. Baden-Baden: Nomos.

Moreno, Luis. 2000. *The Federalization of Spain*. London and Durham NC: Frank Cass/Duke Press Policy Studies.

Nathan, Richard P. and John R. Lago. 1990. "Intergovernmental Fiscal Roles and Relations." *Annals of the American Academy of Political and Social Science* 509: 36–47.

Nice, David S. 1987. "State Participation in Interstate Compacts." *Publius: The Journal of Federalism* 17 (2): 69–83.

Opeskin, Brian R. 2001. "Mechanisms for Intergovernmental Relations in Federations." *International Science Journal* 52 (167): 129–138.

O'Toole, Laurence J. Jr (ed.). 2000. *American Intergovernmental Relations*. Washington DC: Congressional Quarterly Press.

Perkmann, Markus. 2003. "Cross-Border Regions in Europe: Significance and Drivers of Regional Cross-Border Co-operation." *European Urban and Regional Studies* 10 (2): 153–171.

Perkmann, Markus. 2007. "Policy Entrepreneurship and Multilevel Governance: A Comparative Study of European Cross-border Regions." *Environment and Planning C* 25 (6): 861–879.

Peters, B. Guy. 1998. "Managing Horizontal Government." Canadian Center for Management Development.

Peters, B. Guy and Jon Pierre. 2001. "Developments in Intergovernmental Relations: Towards Multi-level Governance." *Policy & Politics 29* (2): 131–135.

Riker, William. 1964. *Federalism, Origin, Operation, Significance.* Boston: Little Brown.

Rodden, Jonathan A. 2004. "Comparative Federalism and Decentralization: On Meaning and Measurement." *Comparative Politics 36*: 481–501.

Rodden, Jonathan A. 2006. *Hamilton's Paradox: The Promise and Perils of Fiscal Federalism.* Cambridge: Cambridge University Press.

Sanbonmatsu, Kira. 2002. "Political Parties and the Recruitment of Women to State Legislatures." *Journal of Politics 64*: 791–809.

Savoie, D. J. 2003. "Regional Development: A Policy for All Seasons." In F. Rocher and M. Smith (eds), *New Trends in Canadian Federalism.* Peterborough: Broadview Press.

Sbragia, Alberta M. 2006. "American Federalism and Intergovernmental Relations." In R. A. W. Rhodes, S. A. Binder, and B. Rockman (eds), *The Oxford Handbook of Political Institutions.* Oxford: Oxford University Press.

Scharpf, Fritz W. 1988. "The Joint-decision Trap: Lessons from German Federalism and European Integration". *Public Administration 66* (2): 239–78.

Scharpf, Fritz W. 1995. "Federal Arrangements and Multi-Party Systems". *Australian Journal of Political Science 30*: 27–39.

Scharpf, Fritz W. 1997. *Games Real Actors Play. Actor-centered Institutionalism in Policy Research.* Oxford: Oxford University Press.

Scharpf, Fritz W. 2001. "What Have We Learned? Problem-Solving Capacity of the Multilevel European Polity." MPIfG Working Paper 01/4: 1–49.

Scott, James Wesley. 1999. "European and North American Contexts for Cross-border Regionalism." *Regional Studies 33* (7): 605–617.

Simeon, Richard. 2005. "Plus ça change: Intergovernmental Relations Then and Now." *Policy Options* (March/April): 84–87.

Simmons, Julie. 2004. "Securing the Threads of Co-operation in the Tapestry of Intergovernmental Relations: Does the Institutionalization of Ministerial Conferences Matter?" In J. P. Meekison, H. Telfor,d, and H. Lazar (eds), *Reconsidering the Institutions of Canadian Federalism.* Montreal: McGill-Queen's University Press.

Skogstad, Grace. 2000. "Canada: Dual and Executive Federalism, Ineffective Problem-Solving." In D. Braun (ed.), *Public Policy and Federalism.* Aldershot: Athenaeum Press.

Snyder, Richard. 2001. "Scaling Down: The Subnational Comparative Method." *Studies in Comparative International Development 36* (1): 93–110.

Stolz, Klaus. 2010. *Towards a Regional Political Class? Professional Politicians and Regional Institutions in Catalonia and Scotland.* Manchester: Manchester University Press.

Swenden, Wilfried. 2002. "Asymmetric Federalism and Coalition-Making in Belgium." *Publius: The Journal of Federalism 32* (3): 67–87.

Swenden, Wilfried. 2006. *Federalism and Regionalism in Western Europe, A Comparative and Thematic Analysis.* Basingstoke: Palgrave Macmillan.

Tannenwald, Robert and Jonathan Cowan. 1997. "Fiscal Capacity, Fiscal Need, and Fiscal Comfort among U.S. States: New Evidence." *Publius: The Journal of Federalism 27* (5): 113–125.

Thorlakson, Lori. 2003. "Comparing Federal Institutions: Power and Representation in Six Federations." *West European Politics 2* (6): 1–22.

Thorlakson, Lori. 2007. "An Institutional Explanation of Party System Congruence: Evidence from Six Federations." *European Journal of Political Research 46*: 69–95.

Thorlakson, Lori. 2009. "Patterns of Party Integration, Influence and Autonomy in Seven Federations." *Party Politics 15* (2): 157–177.

Trees, Patrick. 2005a. *Zusammenarbeit der Direktorenkonferenzen mit den Regierungskonferenzen, Analyse Verschiedener Modelle.* Unpublished MA Thesis. University of Bern.

Trench, Alan. 2006. "Intergovernmental Relations: In Search of a Theory." In S. L. Greer (ed.), *Territory, Democracy and Justice: Regionalism and Federalism in Western Democracies.* Basingstoke: Macmillan.

Turner, Henry A. and John A. Vieg 1967. *The Government and Politics of California.* New York: McGraw-Hill.

Vatter, Adrian. 2002. *Kantonale Demokratien im Vergleich: Entstehungsgründe, Interaktionen und Wirkungen Politischer Institutionen in den Schweizer Kantonen.* Opladen: Leske und Budrich.

Watts, Ronald L. 1998. "Federalism, Federal Political Systems, and Federations". *Annual Review of Political Science 1*: 117–137.

Watts, Ronald L. 1999a. *Comparing Federal Systems.* Montreal: McGill-Queen's University Press.

Watts, Ronald L. 1999b. *The Spending Power in Federal Systems: A Comparative Study.* Kingston: Institute of Intergovernmental Relations.

Wheare, K. C. 1951. *Modern Constitutions.* London: Oxford University Press.

Wibbels, Erik. 2005. *Federalism and the Market: Intergovernmental Conflict and Economic Reform in the Developing World.* Cambridge: Cambridge University Press.

Wolpe, Bruce C. and Bertram J. Levine. 1996. *Lobbying Congress: How the System Works.* Washington DC: Congressional Quarterly Inc.

Wright, Deil S. 1982. *Understanding Intergovernmental Relations.* Monterey: Brooks/Cole.

Wyn Jones, Richard and Elin Royles. 2012. "Wales in the World, Intergovernmental Relations and Sub-state Diplomacy". *British Journal of Politics and International Relations 14* (2): 250–269

Zimmerman, Joseph F. 1990. "Regulating Intergovernmental Relations in the 1990s." In J. Kincaid (ed.), *American Federalism: The Third Century.* Newbury Park: Sage.

Zimmerman, Joseph F. 2001. *Interstate Cooperation, Compacts and Administrative Agreements.* Westport: Praeger.

Zimmerman, Joseph F. 2002. *Interstate Relations: The Neglected Dimension of Federalism.* Westport: Praeger.

CHAPTER 39

....

CONCLUSION

The Study of State and Local
Politics and Policy

....

DONALD P. HAIDER-MARKEL

As the chapters in this volume make clear, we have come a long way in the study of state and local politics and policy. The body of literature the authors have highlighted demonstrates that the 1960s and 70s case studies of state and local politics have been buttressed by large-scale empirical studies that, in some cases, have supported earlier claims, in others, pushed conventional wisdom to the exit door, but in still others, pointed to new and perhaps more interesting questions.

In these final few pages I take a moment to highlight a few items that I would like to focus on as well as what is missing in this volume. My emphasis to readers is to concentrate on the chapters in the volume versus the introduction and conclusion for the major insights into sub-national politics. That said there are a few nuggets I picked up along the way of editing this volume that I would like to pass along to readers.

First, I am hard pressed to find a more rewarding subfield to explore in political science or policy studies for the twenty-first century. The subfield truly allows for theory testing in a comparative context that has many benefits and few drawbacks. In addition, as the responsibilities of sub-national governments continue to grow, the potential for examinations of political behavior, institutions, and policy grow as well.

Second, areas that were little studied in the past have taken on a new relevance in the past few decades as their utility for examining a number of social science theories has become more apparent. Take for example direct democracy. Historically it has been viewed as an exception to the rule of how the political and policy process works in the U.S. But over the last 20 or so years the field has exploded with scholars making use of direct democracy contests to enhance our understanding of public opinion and voting behavior (Smith and Tolbert, 2010), the strategic efforts of political parties (Donovan et al., 2008), and the success and failure of social movements (see Chapter 12 for a review).

Third, although political science has often been known for its willingness to borrow theories from other disciplines, this is as apparent in the subfield of sub-national politics as it is in any subfield in the discipline. Researchers in this subfield routinely borrow from biology, epidemiology, economics, psychology, and sociology, among others. As evidenced by the chapters in this volume, our generous borrowing of theories strengthens the subfield and the discipline as a whole as scholars share ideas and concepts across disciplines to improve our understanding of many areas from the decisionmaking of executives, to the functioning of state courts, to the attitudes and behaviors of citizens.

Finally, the volume reflects some continuing gaps in the subfield while it highlights much of what we do know. Some readers will note the lack of a chapter focused specifically on the role of political communications or the news media. Although I had originally planned for such a chapter it failed to appear in any acceptable form. What is clear is that the public is woefully uninformed about state and local government (Moy and Hussain, 2011). In part this is because of the lack of news media attention (Rosenthal, 1998), but is also because few aspects of sub-national government grab the attention of citizens (Andrews and Caren, 2010), even though the actions of sub-national governments have a much greater impact on our everyday lives than do the decisions of actors in the national government (Mooney, 1998), and citizens trust state and local government far more than they do the national government (Jones, 2012). For the typical researcher this set of facts should invoke a variety of intriguing research questions; yet, we still know very little about local media and how citizens develop their views about sub-national government. A solid summary of what is known and unknown in this area is sorely needed.

And although homeland security and emergency management issues are touched on in a number of chapters, I would have preferred to have a chapter solely devoted to these issues since they so strongly reflect the nature of intergovernmental relations in the U.S. and the evolving nature of sub-national government responsibilities (see for example Eller and Gerber, 2010). Since the attacks on September 11, 2001, state governments have adopted new laws regarding terrorist acts, consolidated agencies charged with law enforcement and emergency response, and taken new steps to stem the flow undocumented immigrants. Each of these areas seems to be the preview of the national government but sub-national governments have chosen to act on the own, in part, because state and local governments have traditionally been responsible for most criminal justice policy and for maintaining the civil order. But as the national government has increasingly involved itself in criminal justice issues, whether they involve terrorism or not, the tension between governments as to who has policy jurisdiction has served to highlight the often vague language of the Constitution and dilemma of which level of government citizens tend to trust to act appropriately. These issues offer important insights into the American governmental system and federal governmental systems in general and are deserving of a more complete examination.

As a final word I thank all of the contributors to this volume for their hard and thoughtful work on these chapters. The incentive to participate in a project like this stems from the ability to influence the next generation of scholars and not from any financial or academic recognition. I am in your debt.

References

Andrews, Kenneth and Neil Caren. 2010. "Making the News: Movement Organizations, Media Attention, and the Public Agenda." *American Sociological Review 75* (6): 841–866.

Todd Donovan, Caroline J. Tolbert, and Daniel A. Smith. 2008. "Priming Presidential Votes by Direct Democracy." *Journal of Politics 70*: 1217–1231.

Eller, Warren S. and Brian J. Gerber. 2010. "Contemplating the Role of Precision and Range in Homeland Security Policy Analysis: A Response to Mueller." *Policy Studies Journal* 38 (1): 23–39.

Jones, Jeffrey M. 2012. "In U.S., Trust in State, Local Governments Up; Sixty-five percent trust their state government, 74% their local." *Gallup New Service*, 26 September 2012. <http://www.gallup.com/poll/157700/trust-state-local-governments.aspx>

Mooney, Christopher Z. 1998. "Why Do They Tax Dogs in West Virginia? Teaching Political Science through Comparative State Politics." *PS: Political Science & Politics 31*: 199–203.

Moy, Patricia and Muzammil M. Hussain. 2011. "Media influences on political trust and Engagement." In Robert Y. Shapiro and Lawrence R. Jacobs (eds), *The Oxford Handbook of American Public Opinion And The Media*. New York: Oxford University Press, pp. 220–235.

Rosenthal, Alan. 1998. *The Decline of Representative Democracy: Process, Participation, and Power in State Legislatures*. Washington, DC: Congressional Quarterly Press.

Smith, Daniel A. and Caroline J. Tolbert. 2010. "Direct Democracy, Public Opinion, and Candidate Choice." *Public Opinion Quarterly 74* (1): 85–108.

INDEX